*The Institutions of France under the
Absolute Monarchy: 1598–1789*

VOLUME II

The Organs of State and Society

Roland E. Mousnier

Translated by Arthur Goldhammer

The Institutions of France under the Absolute Monarchy 1598–1789

VOLUME II

The Organs of State and Society

The University of Chicago Press

Chicago and London

ROLAND E. MOUSNIER is professor emeritus of modern history
at the University of Paris–Sorbonne. Volume I of *The Institutions of France under the Absolute Monarchy, 1598–1789*, was
published by The University of Chicago Press in 1979.

This work originally appeared in French as *Les Institutions de
la France sous la monarchie absolue, 1598–1789*, volume 2:
Les Organes de l'Etat et la Société, © 1980 by Presses Univer-
sitaires de France.

Publication of this work was made possible in part by a grant
from the Publication Program of the National Endowment for
the Humanities, an independent federal agency.

The University of Chicago Press, Chicago 60637
The University of Chicago Press, Ltd., London
© 1984 by The University of Chicago
All rights reserved. Published 1984
Printed in the United States of America

91 90 89 88 87 86 85 84   5 4 3 2 1

Library of Congress Cataloging in Publication Data
(Revised for volume 2)

Mousnier, Roland E.
    The institutions of France under the absolute monarchy,
1598–1789.

    Vol. 2 translated by Arthur Goldhammer.
    Translation of: Les institutions de la France sous la
monarchie absolue, 1598–1789.
    Includes bibliographies and index.
    Contents: v. 1. Society and the state—v. 2. The
organs of state and society.
    1. France—Social conditions. 2. Social classes—
France—History. 3. France—Politics and government—
1598–1789. I. Title.

HN425.M6813   306'.0944   78-26857
ISBN 0-226-54327-7 (v. 1)
ISBN 0-226-54328-5 (v. 2)

To all the historians and scholars
—the salt of the earth—
without whose work this attempt at
synthesis and explanation would
have been impossible

Contents

3   *Government "par Grand Conseil"*

4   *The Sovereign and Lower Courts of Law and Administration*

5   *The United General Farms of the King's Domains and Rights*

6   *The King's* Commissaires

7 The Emergence of a Bureaucracy

8 The Battle between the Officeholders and the Commissaires: A Dispute That Lasted Three Hundred Years

Notes on the Guides to Further Reading

Because of the enormous amount of material and the limited space available, it has been necessary to make very rigid and sometimes painful choices.

The "Guides to Further Reading" are not bibliographies of the subjects treated and mention only a small portion of the sources and works examined. The works that have been singled out are mentioned only to allow the reader to carry his studies further.

Introduction

War and the State

During the period under study France remained a monarchy. It has been said many times that the seventeenth and eighteenth centuries were a period of unbroken tradition. The history of this period has been described as "static," because the pace of change in society and government was so slow in comparison with the rapid change to which we have become accustomed in the nineteenth and especially the twentieth century. Still, great changes were made in government—so great, in fact, that historians accustomed to weighing their words carefully have used the term "revolution" to describe the creation of provincial *intendants* in the years after 1635 and the reform of the king's Council in 1661.[1] On the surface things may have seemed the same, but profound changes had occurred. The battle between *officiers* and *commissaires* set the pace. Among the great strides taken were the shift from judicial to executive government and administration, the establishment of a genuine bureaucracy of appointed officials, and the creation of a corps of functionaries. These changes affected the stability of the social orders and the relations among them in many ways. They also gave rise to new social groups and possibly to new social strata.

More than anything else, war, both civil and foreign, seems to have been responsible for these innovations. Ever larger armies and fleets made imperious demands for more, better, and more costly armament. Taxes had to be raised beyond what the king's subjects deemed legitimate limits, and fairly often beyond what the taxpayers really could afford to pay. The difficulties of levying taxes, contributions, and forced loans of one sort or another, and the opposition to such levies, frequently involving armed conflict, forced the royal government, more often than not against its will, to accomplish its ends either by turning to new institutions or by changing the way in which old institutions functioned, and to circumvent freedoms, exemptions, and privileges of many kinds, whether of corps, provinces, fiefs, seigneuries, cities, or communities, even though these were well-established customs, consecrated by tradition. The taxpayers, pressed with demands for money, sought to procure it by whatever means were available, consequently increasing the volume of production and trade, and the government, concerned to increase the tax base, tried to help by taking an increasingly active role in the economic life of the nation. The war government fell into habits that in many cases endured in periods of peace. The despotic and tyrannical appearance of these practices provoked criticism of the monarchy and of the society and gave rise to projects for far-reaching reform of the society and state. Thus, directly or indirectly, war turns out once again to have been a powerful factor of change, perhaps the preponderant factor.

The Periods

We may say that war, civil or foreign, was constant throughout the period under consideration, though its intensity and extent varied. It was during the periods of the greatest wars that the greatest changes occurred in the government and organs of state. After the signing of the Edict of Nantes and the peace of Vervins in 1598, the kingdom enjoyed a period of relative peace, both internally and externally. But this peace was only relative, since Henri IV had to wage war against the duke of Savoy in 1600, from which he obtained, under the terms of the Treaty of Lyon of 17 January 1601, Bresse, Le Bugey, Valromey, and the Gex region in exchange for the trans-Alpine marquisate of Saluces. Beginning in 1604, Henri IV armed himself against Spain, against which he had offered to declare war in support of the Dutch; the king had always anticipated resumption of open hostility against the Spanish. He steadily subsidized the United Provinces with money and troops. In late 1609 and 1610 he amassed great quantities of weaponry preparatory to taking a hand in the conflict between Clèves and de Juliers on the one hand and the allies and protégés of the emperor on the other, and it was as he was making ready to assume command of his army in Germany that he was assassinated on 14 May 1610. After the murder of the king, the princes of the blood and the grandees became embroiled in dispute. In 1614 they took to arms, and the young king had to campaign in the west of France from July to September. After the Estates General of 1614–15, the princes seceded, and the king was forced to take to the field once again. Finally, a truce was declared at Loudun on 21 February 1616, and it was followed by the Treaty of Loudun on 3 May. Thus, both within the borders of France and outside them, peace was only relative. Accounts of the king's finances like the invaluable tables of Mallet show us, however, that the military effort during this period was still relatively slight. Receipts and expenditures begin to swell after 1616 in the wake of civil and foreign wars. The period 1598–1615 may be regarded as one of relative calm, a period of normalcy as far as the organization of the state was concerned.

By contrast, after 1617, the revolts of the grandees and even the queen mother and the armed Protestant uprisings forced Louis XIII to take to the field again. At the same time, the Thirty Years' War and the pretensions of the Habsburgs of Spain and Austria to universal domination obliged the king to increase his "covert" subsidies and troop shipments to the United Provinces, to the Protestant princes of Germany, to the Swiss and Grisons, in order to close the military routes between the Spanish possessions in Italy and those in the Low Countries. These routes, which traversed the Valtellina and other Alpine valleys and passes, were the great highways between the Europe of the Mediterranean and the Europe of the North and Baltic seas. In 1630 the king made the "great choice." He gave up all thought of establishing order within France in order to defend the independence of the kingdom and the liberties of Europe against the Habsburgs. He held on to Pignerol, which enabled him to strike beyond the Alps and to cut the Spanish supply line between Genoa and Milan. He entered into an alliance with Gustavus Adolphus, the king of Sweden. And he inched toward the Rhine, taking certain Alsatian cities under his protection. Finally, in 1635, after his Swedish allies were defeated at Nordlingen in 1634, he declared war on the king of Spain, thereby officially embarking on "open" warfare. The war was fought on all the frontiers of France. An inordinate effort was required of the kingdom, the more so because subsidies had to be sent to the Portuguese and Catalonians to aid them in their revolt against Spain. This effort gave rise to well-known internal uprisings, among others the revolt of the Nu-Pieds in Normandy in 1638 and 1639, of the Croquants in Périgord, and, finally, the general rising known as the Fronde, which lasted from 1648 to 1653.

Because of these rebellions, the war with Spain dragged on until the Treaty of the Pyrenees in 1659, even though the king had defeated the Austrian Habsburgs in a victory sanctioned by the Treaties of Westphalia (24 October 1648), which dismembered the Germanic Holy Roman Empire and insured European stability. The war government had to circumvent traditional laws, customs, privileges, and liberties and had to countenance innovations in the operation of the king's Council, the use of royal *commissaires*, including the notorious provincial *intendants*, and the excessive use of tax farmers—*fermiers, partisans*, and *traitants*—which led to conflicts with the princes and grandees, the king's ordinary officers, the provinces, the cities, and the communities, forcing them all into rebellion.

We may look upon the period 1659–72 as one during which the kingdom enjoyed a relative peace, the minor War of Devolution of 1667 being a short and relatively inexpensive interlude. Louis XIV took advantage of this respite to attempt a reorganization of his kingdom, seeking to reconcile tradition, the wishes of the Frondeurs, and the need for change. Beginning with the start of the Dutch War in 1672, however, the king was drawn into one long and ruinous war after another against a variety of European coalitions. France became like a "great castle under siege." Meanwhile, on the seas and in the colonies, the "second Hundred Years' War" began against England and its puppet, the United Provinces, for control of the high seas, access to the Spanish and Portuguese empires in America, commercial hegemony, and, through it, worldwide political hegemony. The war with Holland lasted from 1672 to 1679 and ended in the Treaty of Nijmegen. It was followed by a period of armed peace punctuated by annexations accomplished during the lull. There was a short war against Spain and the Truce of Regensburg (1684); the war of the League of Augsburg lasted from 1679 to 1688 and was concluded by the Treaty of Ryswick (1697), in which France lost ground for the first time; the War of the Spanish Succession began in 1702 and ended when the Treaties of Utrecht were signed with the maritime powers and their allies in 1713, and when the Treaty of Rastadt was signed with the emperor in 1714. Foreign war was everlasting, and internal insurrection persistent, with uprisings at Boulogne in 1662, a long rebellion led by Audijos in the Béarnaise region, revolts in the Cévennes, the so-called *révoltes du papier timbre* in Guyenne and Bretagne (where it would be more correct to call it the revolt of the Torreben), the long war against the Camisards, and other conflicts, veritable civil wars, which in some cases lasted many years and mobilized considerable numbers of troops. The government of Louis XIV was a war government, a despotism; during his reign, the *commissaires* got the upper hand over the *officiers*.

Compared with the age of Louis XIV, the eighteenth century looks like a period of peace. The impact of war was probably felt less by the French people, because a period of long-term economic growth began in the years 1726–30, with fluctuations around the long-term trend occurring in decennial and interdecennial cycles and, further, because the wars of this period were fought outside the territories ruled by the kings of France, whose subjects no longer suffered the ills or experienced the fear of invasion. Furthermore, the period 1715–40 may be considered a period of peace, because the War of the Polish Succession was neither long nor costly. After 1740, however, France was involved in major wars on land and sea. The War of the Austrian Succession lasted from 1740 to 1748 and ended with the peace of Aix-la-Chapelle—the "stupid treaty" *par excellence*, to hear the fishwives tell it, since it entailed a switch of allegiances, a shift from war against the House of Austria to alliance with Austria against Prussia. The Seven Years' War was fought from 1756 to 1763. During all this period the "second Hundred Years' War" with England raged on. With the Treaty of Paris in 1763 the colonial empire was lost. Choiseul was armed in preparation for revenge against England. Then came the American War for Independence, which was won by the French, culminating in the Treaty of Paris of 1783. All these wars were waged with ever larger armies and fleets, equipped with increasingly sophisticated and costly weaponry; in artillery, for example, the system of Vallières was replaced by the Gribeauval system, which was still in use in the time of Napoleon. All this drained the coffers of the state and moved the government to undertake reforms that intensified the struggle between *officiers* and *commissaires*. In the end, it was the deficit, enormously increased by the American War for Independence and Necker's speculations, that aroused and paved the way for the opposition of the *parlements* and the revolt of the aristocracy that began in 1787 and forced the king to convoke the Estates General of 1789.

War was the most potent factor in the transformations that occurred between 1598 and 1789.

Note

1. Michel Antoine, Roland Mousnier.

Guide to Further Reading

Les Archives nationales. Etat général des fonds. 1: L'Ancien Régime. Archives nationales, 1978.

Bibliographie annuelle de l'histoire de France du cinquième siècle à 1939, issued each year, beginning in 1953, by the Editions du Centre National de la Recherche Scientifique.

Braudel, Fernand, and Ernest Labrousse, eds. *Histoire économique et sociale de la France.* Paris: PUF. Vol. 1: *1450–1660,* by Fernand Braudel, Pierre Chaunu, and Richard Gascon, 1977; vol. 2: *1660–1789,* by Ernest Labrousse, Pierre Léon, Pierre Goubert, Jean Bouvier, Charles Carrière, and Paul Harsin, 1970.

Furetière, Antoine (abbé de Chalivoy and member of l'Académie française). *Dictionnaire universel.* 3 vols. The Hague and Rotterdam: Arnout & Reiniers Leers, 1690.

Guyot, J. N. *Répertoire universel et raisonné de jurisprudence civile, criminelle, canonique et bénéficiale.* 17 vols. Visse, 1784–85.

Isambert (Jourdan, Decrusy, Isambert). *Recueil général des anciennes lois françaises depuis l'an 420 jusqu'à la Révolution de 1789.* Librairie de Plon Frères, undated, vols. 15–29.

Isnard, Albert, and Mme S. Honoré, *"Actes royaux," jusqu' en 1789.* 6 vols. *Catalogue général des livres imprimés de la Bibliothèque Nationale.* Imprimerie Nationale, 1910–57.

Lavisse, Ernest. *Histoire de France depuis les origines jusqu' à la Revolution* (Hachette, 1911): vol. 6, part 2, *Henri IV et Louis XIII, 1598–1643,* by J.H. Mariéjol; vol. 7, parts 1 and 2, *Louis XIV, 1643–1685,* by E. Lavisse; vol. 8, part 1, *Louis XIV, 1685–1715,* by A.-R. de Saint Léger, A. Rébelliau, P. Sagnac, and E. Lavisse, and part 2, *Le règne de Louis XV, 1715–1774,* by H. Carré; vol. 9, part 1, *Le règne de Louis XVI, 1774–1789,* by H. Carré, P. Sagnac, and E. Lavisse.

The three volumes on Louis XIV were reissued in 1978 by Librairie Jules Tallandier, with a preface by Roland Mousnier.

Savary des Bruslons, Jacques (*Inspecteur général des Manufactures* for the king). *Dictionnaire universel de commerce, d'histoire naturelle et des arts et métiers.* 4 vols. New ed. Copenhagen: C. L. & Ant. Philibert, 1759.

1 The King

1   The Education of the King

Role and Qualities of the King

The king was the first organ of state. Embodying the sovereignty of the state, the king was supposed, in principle, to govern personally and to be providence and father to his subjects. More than that, the kings of France were supposed to assure the continuity of the kingdom and its vital order by respecting the fundamental laws of the realm and evincing the virtues that all kings were presumed to share. The royal office influenced all life in the kingdom. "The object of the history of a Kingdom or Nation is the Prince and the State: there lies the center, as it were, around which everything else must revolve."[1] Accordingly, histories of France in the seventeenth century, known as "*livres de vie*," were above all histories of dynasties, lineages, branches, and reigns. The passage from one line of kings to another, from the Merovingians to the Carolingians, or from the Carolingians to the Capetians, indicated a decay of the dynasty in power—witness the epithet "*rois fainéants*" [or "slothful kings," as the later Merovingians were known— trans.]—and the rise of a new stock imbued with power and virtue. A king demonstrated his fitness for office, his harmony with the vital order willed by God, by exhibiting certain virtues and avoiding certain vices. Such *Histoires de France* as those of Scipion Dupleix, published between 1621 and 1648, of F. E. de Mézeray, published between 1643 and 1651, of Bossuet, written for the Grand Dauphin between 1670 and 1680, of Cordemoy, published between 1685 and 1689, and of G. Daniel, published in its entirety in 1713, enumerated these virtues and vices. Before 1630 the primary virtue was piety, followed by justice, courage, and, further down the list, goodness, magnanimity, love of the people. After 1630, other qualities were added to these fundamental ones: the king should show himself to be an amateur of art and letters, should display generosity, and should know how to make himself loved. After 1680, he was supposed to involve himself in the affairs of state with courage, prudence, and application. The great vices at all times were lust, cruelty, "*ardeur téméraire*," and weakness. The king's education

3

was therefore primarily moral and secondarily professional. It was chiefly an apprenticeship during the first half of the seventeenth century and in some respects remained so until the Revolution, but, as times changed, the role of book learning grew steadily and took precedence over apprenticeship during the last third of the seventeenth century.

The Dauphin and the Children of France

The upbringing of the Children of France was conducted with an eye to their eventual assumption of royal office, a likelihood in the case of the dauphin and a possibility for the others. They saw their father and mother only rarely, at times set by protocol. They had their own "household" and a corps of officers responsible for turning out future kings and princes. The eldest son, heir to the throne, had been known as the "dauphin" ever since Humbert II ceded the Dauphiné to Philippe VI in 1349 on condition that the name dauphin (lord of the Dauphiné) always be borne by the eldest son of the king of France. The other children were, properly speaking, "Children of France," sons or daughters of France and grandsons and granddaughters of France, i.e., sons or daughters of the king or grandsons and granddaughters of the king or his predecessor. More distant offspring of the royal line were merely "princes of the blood." The grandsons of France sat before queens and rode in their carriages. Each had a "household," with a *premier écuyer, premier aumônier, premier maître d'hôtel*, bodyguards, Swiss guards, chaplains who responded at mass, and a priest who offered them the corporal to kiss at the end of the service. The princes of the blood did not have the benefit of all these services.

The Children of France were addressed as "royal highness," the princes of the blood as "most serene highness." At birth the sons of France received the blue ribbon, insignia of the Order of the Holy Spirit; the princes of the blood did not receive theirs until age fifteen.

After their first communion, the sons of France were received into the Orders of the Holy Spirit, Saint Michel, and Saint Louis. In the case of the princes of the blood this was not obligatory.

The dauphin was addressed as "Monseigneur"; the king's brother, wife, and daughter, respectively, as "Monsieur," "Madame," and "Mademoiselle." The unmarried daughters of the king were addressed by their first names, preceded by "Madame." The head of the House of Condé was known as "Monsieur le Prince," but in 1703, Louis III de Condé, no longer the first prince of the blood, became "Monsieur le Duc."

The Education of the Dauphin from Birth to Age Seven

When the dauphin was born, the captain of the guard left the king with the queen and, along with an escort of officers and bodyguards, took the child and delivered it into the custody of his governess and physician. Until the age of seven, the dauphin would live mainly with women.

The governess was responsible for keeping watch over the future sovereign's health and welfare. She was supposed to shape his predilections, give him his first lessons, and inculcate guiding principles. She swore an oath into the king's hands and, by custom, held her post for life. By tradition the dauphin called her "mama." Until the dauphin reached the age of seven, she represented him, giving orders to the *maréchal de France de service*, to the captain of the royal guard, and to the governor of the castle inhabited by the dauphin. She also responded to sermons.

The governess of the dauphin had the right to ride in the queen's carriage and enjoyed *grandes entrées* with the king. She lived in the palace in intimacy with the royal family. Her allowance was large, and she received a generous pension and jewels. She bequeathed her responsibilities to a member of her family. La maréchale de la Mothe, governess of the son, the grandsons, and the great-grandsons of Louis XIV, bequeathed her office to her daughter, Mme de Ventadour; the latter left hers to the wife of her grandson, the princesse de Soubise; when the princess died, her office passed to her granddaughter, Mme de Tallard; it then went to her mother, Mme de Marsan, then to the niece of Mme de Marsan, Mme de Rohan-Guéménée. Between 1664 and 1782, the office remained in the same family.

The governess was tied to her ward. She was not allowed to leave his vicinity, day or night. She slept in the same room. She could not wear mourning for members of her own family. Henri IV refused to allow Mme de Monglat the right to wear mourning for her husband or to cry after his death.

A single governess had charge of the early education of all the Children of France, legitimate and illegitimate.

From the time of Louis XIII, etiquette and drawing were taught by assistant governesses.

The dauphin had a nurse, with four or five others "in reserve." To be nurse to the dauphin was a "dignity" in the social hierarchy, which opened the way to social ascent for the family thus honored. Mme Ancelin, nurse of Louis XIV, was a simple peasant; but one of her sons became bishop of Tulle, and one of her grandsons became *gentilhomme ordinaire* of the king's household. Beginning with the Grand Dauphin, the son of Louis XIV, there grew up a custom that, after the dauphin's weaning, the nurse became first chambermaid of the little prince and later of his wife. The nurse's husband became *contrôleur général de la Chambre*. Both received handsome pensions. Mme Mercier, who nursed Louis XV, was the wife of a blacksmith. She had five children. The eldest became *maître d'hôtel* of the dauphine and *contrôleur général de la bouche* of the queen's household; the second, lieutenant general of the armies of the king; the third, squadron commander; the fourth, canon of the Sainte-Chapelle, with 50,000 écus annual income from his ecclesiastical benefices; the fifth, *directeur des fermes* at Toulouse.

Besides his nurses, the dauphin had eight chambermaids and valets at his service.

In theory, the dauphin was brought up by women until he reached the age of seven. But his first physician could exert great influence over him, as we see in the case of Héroard, first physician to Louis XIII, who lived with his patient, played the part of "a tender mother" toward him, and imposed on him a discipline that some have blamed for the oddities and failings of this great king.

From Seven to Fourteen Years of Age

At age seven the dauphin or prince moved to a new apartment and received officers. From age seven on, the sons of France lived with men. From the time of Henri IV's second son, Gaston d'Orléans, they enjoyed the services of a captain of the guard, a *maître de la garde-robe*, a *premier écuyer*, a *premier maître d'hôtel*, an *intendant* and a *contrôleur général* of the household, and an *aumônier ordinaire*, along with subordinates serving under each of these department heads, and, in addition, *gentilshommes de la manche* and *enfants d'honneur*. The household of the dauphin, the son of Louis XV, numbered seventy-seven persons. This figure does not include coachmen or stablekeepers, as the dauphin was identified with the king and enjoyed the same general services as his father.

All the sons of France, including the dauphin, fell under the tutelage of a single governor (*gouverneur*), a high-ranking personage but one whose charge of their education could be revoked *ad nutum*. However, the duc de Villeroi, Louis XIV's governor, and the duc de Châtillon, a Villeroi, Louis XV's governor, were responsible to a *surintendant de l'éducation*, respectively Mazarin and the duc de Maine. Upon leaving his position the governor retained his emoluments and lodging and became *premier gentilhomme de la Chambre* and *maître de la garde-robe*. Almost by law, his wife was entitled to the position of *dame d'honneur* to the dauphine. The governor enjoyed *grandes entrées* to the king, his family had the right to *entrées* in the train of the dauphin, and he could ride in the king's carriages. Serving under him were one or more assistant governors, who swore an oath into his hands.

The dauphin and the sons of France shared a common tutor. Beginning with Hardouin de Beaumont de Péréfixe, Louis XIV's tutor, the tutor was always a bishop or eligible for a bishopric, with the exception of Perigny. Each prince had, in addition, an assistant tutor and a reader. The tutor enjoyed only *entrées de la Chambre du Roi*. Fleury was the first to ride in the royal carriages. The tutor was always elected to l'Académie française.

The governor took an oath to form the prince's spirit—his courage, manners, and heart according to the virtues, and his mind according to precepts deemed useful for the conduct of life, knowledge of the world, and success in affairs of state. The tutor swore to bring the child up to love and fear

God, to correct his manners, and to train his mind through knowledge of letters and the sciences.

The king's confessor heard the confessions of the Children of France. From the time of Henri IV and Père Coton, this post was filled by Jesuits.

The dauphin's education was regarded as complete when he reached the age of royal majority fixed by the fundamental laws of the kingdom—in other words, at the beginning of his fourteenth year. For the other Children of France, education ended with the seventeenth year.

Note

1. P. G. Daniel, *Histoire de France* (Paris, 1713), vol. 1, p. xxiii.

2 The Education of Kings in the Seventeenth Century

The kings of the seventeenth century were educated mainly by apprenticeship. They were soldiers first and foremost. Their formal instruction was slight, as their entourage wished it to be. The education of kings consisted chiefly in instruction in morals, based on examples from the past, and in practical training in soldiery and statecraft.

Henri IV

The foregoing description fits the case of Henri IV. Born Henri de Bourbon in 1553, he had the good fortune not to have had at first any claim to the throne, since Henri II had several sons. The future king was himself the third son of Antoine de Bourbon and Jeanne d'Albret, but his two older brothers died while young. Henri was raised by his grandfather, Henri d'Albret, and his mother; from the age of seventeen months, he was raised by his mother on instructions from his grandfather. Suckled in a peasant cottage, he was returned after weaning to his governess, Suzanne de Bourbon-Busset in the *château de* Coarrazé. There he lived with peasant children, wore coarse clothing, and ate whole-wheat bread, cheese, and garlic. Barefooted and bareheaded, he ran and climbed like any young boy.

At the age of four, in 1557, he came to court for the first time. Henri II, we are told, wanted him to stay. Jeanne d'Albret refused. She took him back to Béarn, where he resumed his peasant's life. In 1562, at the age of nine, he was turned over to his governors, including two *gentilshommes*, Pontus de Pons and de Beauvoir, a tutor, de La Gaucherie, and an assistant tutor, Palma Cayet—all ardent Protestants—under the watchful eye of Jeanne d'Albret. Henri learned horsemanship, fencing, shooting, and hunting. As for Latin and Greek, he was content to memorize certain maxims, such as "Conquer or die," which became his motto. History was taught him in the form of biographies of illustrious men, taken from Plutarch; these inspired in him the desire to imitate Caesar and Scipio Africanus. He also practiced drawing and living languages—Spanish and Italian. He spent two years at the Collège de Navarre, chiefly in order to learn something about men. There he translated Caesar's *Commentaries* and learned practical mathematics, useful in the construction of fortifications. Above all, he visited hospitals, hospices, and printshops.

His education was brief. By 1567, at the age of fourteen, he was with the army; beginning in 1569, he served under Coligny and fought throughout France. From 1572 to 1576 he was a prisoner at the court of Catherine de Médicis, where he learned dissimulation, intrigue, and the art of negotiation.

Throughout his life he was a soldier who withstood fatigue and exposed himself to every danger. He never ceased to be an enthusiast for physical exercise, horsemanship, arms, swimming, dancing, tennis, ballplaying, pall-mall, billiards, and hunting, particularly of fox and boar.

This education was partly responsible for his vigorous character and body and his sure judgment of men and circumstances.

Louis XIII

Louis XIII was born on 27 September 1601. This made his sign Libra, or the scales of justice, which earned him the epithet Louis the Just. Godson of the pope, Louis was given into the charge of his governess, Mme de Montglat, the wife of the king's *premier maître d'hôtel*. She had previously been given responsibility for Henri IV's children by Gabrielle d'Estrées and later took charge of bastards born to three other royal favorites. During childhood and adolescence the most important person in the future king's life was his first physician, Jean Héroard, who for twenty-six years kept a diary on the physical and moral health of his patient. At the Château de Saint-Germain Louis XIII received a rough-and-ready education. Economy was the watchword. There was no luxury, no retinue, but perhaps too much strictness, too many rules, too harsh a discipline, particularly of the digestive tract, and too free a use of the whip and the rod. We may speculate whether it was not this treatment that turned a robust child into a stammering, melancholy, and taciturn hypochondriac. It was perhaps in reaction to this upbringing that the king became irascible, obstinate, and domineering, and yet he was a man who constantly sought in others a tenderness that he never found.

His governor was Gilles de Souvré, marquis of Courtenvaux, governor of Touraine and later Maréchal de France, a supporter of Henri III and one of the first to rally to Henri IV—a loyal retainer. He was assisted by de Préau, nephew of Souvré. There was a series of tutors: Vanquelin des Yveteaux, from 6 March 1609 to July 1611, followed by Nicolas Le Fèvre, and finally Davis de Rivault, sieur de Fleurance and theorist of the society of orders.

Louis XIII began to read and write at age five. His teachers were not overambitious, and the dauphin had little liking for studies. He preferred working with his hands. In his childhood he learned a few Latin words, some Bible stories, proverbs from Solomon, and, on Sundays, a little catechism composed by Père Coton. Des Yveteaux tried to teach him some Latin maxims, a bit of geography, and the deeds of illustrious men. His successors kept up lessons in Latin, but Louis XIII learned little of the language. He never studied Greek and disliked history. In geography, on the other hand, he was amused by drawing maps. He failed to master geometry and never learned to speak Spanish.

By contrast, he had a taste for such manual skills as masonry, carpentry, and locksmithing. Even in adulthood he remained a fine blacksmith, locksmith, and printer. He had a shop on the third floor of the Louvre. In any discipline or art that involved the use of the hands or the body he took an interest and was successful. He practiced drawing with Israël Henriet and painting with Simon Vouet. He was a good musician. He took up horsemanship on 6 July 1615, under the instruction of the celebrated Antoine de Pluvinel, and excelled at it from the first. He danced with dignity and grace.

As for the kingly craft, he learned what he needed to know from court intrigues, conspiracies, council sessions, and military expeditions. He was a good soldier, brave and well versed in the art of war, aware of the necessities of troop concentrations and logistics, and never reluctant to advance, sword in hand, under fire from enemy positions. He was a prince who sensed the needs of the state, the dignity and the grandeur required of a king of France. A secret mistrust of himself prevented him from commanding, however. His defects and his qualities alike obliged him to rely on a principal minister, and, once he found a man equal to the job, his own pride and obstinacy worked wonders.

Louis XIV

In 1638 Louis XIII named the marquise de Lansac, daughter of the maréchal de Souvré, governess of the dauphin. After 1640 she also became governess of the dauphin's younger brother. Following the death of Louis XIII, she was replaced by the marquise de Senecey, formerly *dame d'honneur* to Anne of Austria.

In March 1646, the queen mother named the marquis de Villeroy governor, but Mazarin became "*Surintendant au gouvernement et à la conduite de la personne du roi et de celle de M. le duc d'Anjou.*"

As tutor, Louis XIV had a doctor from the Sorbonne, the abbé Hardouin de Beaumont de Péréfixe, formerly chamberlain to Cardinal Richelieu. On 28 May 1644, he became bishop of Rodez and for a time, from 20 April 1649, until 1656, he relinquished his tutorship. During hs absence he was replaced by a former chaplain to Louis XIII, the abbé Laurent de Brisacier.

As confessor, Louis XIV was assigned, on 28 October 1649, Père Charles Paulin, superior of the professed house of Jesuits at Paris, who at times also played the role of "*assistant pour les belles-lettres.*"

A second tutor joined Péréfixe in May 1652: La Mothe Le Vayer. In 1647 Péréfixe had published the *Institutio principis*, and in 1640 La Mothe Le

Vayer had published *De l'instruction de Monseigneur le Dauphin*. Le Vayer also published *L'economique du prince* in 1653 and *La politique du prince* in 1654.

The work of the tutors probably ended in 1656.

In addition, Louis XIV took lessons in each of the following arts: mathematics, military exercises, shooting, writing, dancing, tennis, lute, drawing, Italian, and horsemanship.

Contemporary opinion had it that Louis XIV was not very well educated. He learned a little Latin from the Port-Royal grammar, *Nouvelle méthode pour apprendre facilement et en peu de temps la langue latine*. He wrote Latin compositions, and one notebook of these, corrected in the king's own hand, exists today as French manuscript 3858 in the Cabinet des Manuscrits of the Bibliothèque Nationale of Paris. He was made to write: "Meminero me esse infra Deum. Ludovicus." ("I shall remember that I am beneath God. Louis.") Thus these compositions were both exercises in translation and lessons in morality. At the age of thirteen, in 1651, he translated a portion of Caesar's *Commentaries*, the bedside reading of politicians and generals. He read the *Histoire de France*, drew maps, did mathematical exercises, but mainly danced, took walks, exercised his body, and played war, besieging and defending the earthen fort built for his games in the Tuileries gardens. La Porte, his *premier valet de chambre*, read to him from Mézeray's *Histoire de France* in the evenings. The young king himself read the *Mémoires* of Philippe de Commynes, the "breviary" of the emperor Charles V, *Don Quixote* (1646), Scarron's *Roman comique* (1651), and, later, at the time of his affair with Marie de Mancini, collections of poetry and comedies.

He seems, however, not to have taken his ideas from books but rather from observing his entourage and circumstances. Anne of Austria probably inspired his respect for things holy and for religious practice. She herself spent several hours each day in her private chapel, fasted, took communion every week, showed particular veneration for the Holy Virgin and the relics of the saints, made novenas, never missed the stations of Advent and Lent, and so on. She had a passion for authority and communicated it to the young king. The entire royal entourage, moreover, repeatedly told the king that he was the master. One of his writing models was "Homage is due to kings; they do as they please."

Nicolas de Neufville, marquis de Villeroy, told Louis about events in which he had taken part, as well as anecdotes of the old court.

Péréfixe constantly repeated that the king must himself discharge all his functions, take a hand in the labors of state, and know the kingdom inside and out. He should preside over the councils and always keep an eye on the state of finances by seeing to it that he was kept apprised of the latest accounts.

Probably the major influence on the king was that of Mazarin, who guided his apprenticeship. As early as 1649, when the king was eleven, the cardinal had him attend meetings of the *Conseil d'Etat*, and at these sessions he was soon all ears. After the Fronde, when Louis was fifteen, the cardinal presented him with a series of problems in politics, graduated in difficulty. Regular days were designated for council meetings to be held in the presence of the king. At these sessions, more and more difficult problems were discussed, and the members of the Council explained their opinions to the young king. Mazarin also spent an hour to an hour and a half each day closeted with the king in his study. A *secrétaire d'Etat* was called in to give reports. Mazarin explained to the king how the problems outlined were to be dealt with. Thus the king studied the affairs of state at firsthand. Mazarin had him attend formal audiences with various ambassadors. The king was present, for example, at an audience with the ambassador of the United Provinces on 12 April 1657, concerning the capture of two French vessels by the Dutch Admiral Ruyter, and showed severity toward the Dutch representative. Mazarin kept Louis apprised of all matters of consequence.

Mazarin constantly encouraged Louis XIV to take himself in hand and to think only of the good of the state, of becoming a great king, and of learning his kingly craft, everything else being regarded as subsidiary. In the last months of the cardinal's life, the king came to see him several times each day. The cardinal advised him "not to trust any individual in matters of great moment." On Monday, 7 March 1661, they held their last conversation. A few hours after Mazarin's death on 9 March at the Louvre, the king dictated to sieur Rose, his *secrétaire de cabinet*, a summary of this conversation, and throughout his reign he adhered faithfully to the maxims there laid down.[1]

Finally, the king was trained as a soldier. From 1653 on, when he was fifteen, the king was with the army constantly in the war against Spain. There he profited from the lessons of Turenne. He learned the military craft by practicing it, and he excelled at it. The Sun King may have become a bureaucrat-king, but he remained a soldier-king to the end.

Note

1. Pierre Clément, *Lettres, instructions et mémoires de Colbert* (Imprimerie Impériale, 1861), vol. 1, appendix 17, pp. 535–36.

3   The Education of Kings in the Eighteenth Century

Beginning with the second half of the seventeenth century and the descendants of Louis XIV, book learning began to take precedence over apprenticeship and the classroom over the open air. Confined to Versailles and familiar at firsthand with very little that went on outside, the future kings were educated from books and state papers and grew up more as bureaucrats than as soldiers. They had little contact with the realities of life and gradually lost touch with their kingdom.

Louis XV

Louis XV was born on 15 February 1710, of the marriage of the duc de Bourgogne to Marie-Adélaïde of Savoy. He was their third son. The duchesse de Ventadour was governess to the Children of France, having inherited the post from her mother, the maréchale de la Mothe, in actuality from 1704 and in title from 6 January 1709, when the maréchale died at age eighty-five. It was the duchess who saved Louis, then duc d'Anjou, from the measles, one of the epidemics that decimated the royal family, by the simple expedient of keeping him warm. In his will, Louis XIV named the maréchal de Villeroi governor on 2 August 1714, and in the codicil of 23 August 1715 he appointed Fleury, formerly bishop of Fréjus, tutor, and the Jesuit Père Le Tellier confessor. Villeroi had been raised with Louis XIV, his father having been the king's governor, and he adored the Great King. Fleury was the son of a simple tithe collector. Born in 1653, he had been bishop of Fréjus from 1699 to 1715.

On 9 September 1715, Louis XV went to live first at Vincennes and later at the Louvre, where he remained until May 1722. He was good-looking but frail, so that Mme de Ventadour gave in to him in everything and did not insist that he apply himself to even the lightest task. He learned nothing. On 15 February 1717, he was again entrusted to Villeroi, who taught him to think of himself as a man apart, having nothing in common with the rest of mankind. The people belonged to him. All rights were his. In particular, it

13

was up to him to distribute honors and privileges and to assign men by his grace to their place in the social hierarchy.

The schedule of lessons was strenuous: every day there was writing, Latin, history, and, three times a week, mathematics and dance. The lessons themselves, however, were less strenuous. Fleury cheered up his young charge, distracted him, played cards with him. Translations to and from Latin of texts taken from the Bible were of a sort that would not have taxed the ability of a rank beginner in a French *lycée* of some years back, when Latin was still taught seriously. The history of France was boiled down to names and dates, without reflection on events or consideration of the lessons to be drawn from them. Louis XV took lessons in astronomy, botany, and gardening. He made little progress in mathematics. Lieutenant général Puységur instructed him in the military art. The king commanded a regiment of young lords, participated in exercises on the terrace of the Tuileries, and laid siege to a fort at Montreuil. He practiced dancing, horsemanship, shooting, and hunting.

Villeroi was arrested and exiled on 10 August 1722 and replaced by the duc de Charost, Sully's grandnephew.

Louis XV was anointed at Reims on 25 October 1722. He was presented to the Council for the first time on 18 February 1720, at the age of ten. His attendance at council meetings was infrequent, and he appeared to take no interest in the proceedings. After the king's anointment, the regent attempted to instruct him in affairs of state, but the daily lessons lasted only half an hour. A text on politics was prepared by Ledran, *chef du dépôt des Affaires étrangères*, one on war by Briquet, *premier commis à la Guerre*, and another on finance by Fagon and d'Ormesson, *intendants des Finances*. A minister, Dubois, read these texts to the king, and the regent added explanations and commentaries. The course was interrupted by the regent's death. Fleury did not carry it on, nor did he attempt to educate Louis XV as Mazarin had educated Louis XIV.

The young king spent part of his time hunting, gardening, raising chickens and pigeons, printing, turning wood, and cooking. He had no opportunity to go to war. It was only later that he educated himself through the practice of his kingly craft and became a great king.

Louis XVI

Prior to his accession to the throne, Louis XVI was doubtless the least educated of all the kings we have discussed. Louis-Auguste, duc de Berry, was born on 23 August 1754, of the marriage of the dauphin, son of Louis XV, to his second wife, Marie-Josèphe of Saxony. His governess was the comtesse de Marsan, *née* Rohan-Soubise; his governor, comte de la Vauguyon, lieutenant general of the king's armies, and, as of September 1758, duke and peer; his tutor was Jean-Gilles de Coetloquet, doctor of the Sorbonne and bishop of Limoges. The dauphin and dauphine closely supervised the education of the duc de Berry, laying down the plan of study. Marie-Josèphe gave lessons in religion and history, and the dauphin lessons in languages along with moral guidance. But they died, in 1766 and 1767 respectively. La Vauguyon succumbed in 1772.

The duc de Berry was delicate. He was brought up in the country, at Bellevue, and had a predilection for working with his hands. His manners and habits were those of a workman. But he learned enough Latin to read Tacitus, Suetonius, and Seneca and enough English to translate the *History of Charles I* and Gibbon. He received the encyclopedic education then in vogue at the Collège de Sorèze and many other schools. Louis XVI studied mathematics, geography, some physics, astronomy, and chemistry. He did land surveying, mapping, and triangulation and drew maps of the area around Versailles. He took an interest in the navy, of which he had extensive knowledge, and personally reviewed and completed the instructions for La Pérouse. His misfortune was his predilection for Nicole and Fénelon. He read the latter's *Télémaque* assiduously and from it excerpted maxims and precepts. From these he compiled a treatise, *De la monarchie tempérée*, divided into chapters entitled "On the person of the prince," "On the authority of the corps within the State," "On the character of monarchy." Throughout his life he remained under the sway of the political ideas of Fénelon, who was, in the words of Louis XIV, "the most chimerical noble spirit in the realm" and who dreamed of nothing but the reestablishment of the political power of the high nobility and the *grands corps*.

The duc de Berry was never admitted to the Council. Unbeknown to Louis XV, he was instructed in the arts of war and administration by an officer, the marquis de Pezay. During the last four years of his life Louis XV personally instructed the future king. The duc de Berry was much given to drawing up plans of action. He tried to put various of these programs into effect during the course of his reign. For this he tried to enlist the help of the very ministries whose ministers were constantly being replaced. The king's actions were often hesitant, and he was plagued by second thoughts.

Louis XVI

Louix XVI was inadequately prepared when he became king at the age of nineteen. He had never seen the Invalides or the Ecole Militaire. He did not know Paris. His tastes ran not to affairs of state but to activities like gardening, tilling, locksmithing, and masonry. He made keys, locks, and tweezers. The sense of state that was developed to the full in Louis XIV and even in Louis XV was lacking in him. His uncertainty, hesitation, and wavering resolution had of course something to do with a weakness of character, but mistaken political conceptions also played a part, as did his attachment to the aristocratic views of Fénelon and the entourage of the duc de Bourgogne. Hence he was incapable of imposing the needed reforms on the orders and corps of the state, and he lost the monarchy.

4   The King's Work

In principle, the king himself governed the kingdom and made his own decisions. But he had to govern "through the *Grand Conseil*." It was his duty to inform himself, to inquire about the opinions of the various interested parties and weigh them before making up his mind, which, in theory, expressed the deepest desires of the French nation. Thus there were three aspects to the king's work. First, the life of the court, with its receptions and ceremonies, in which the king saw everyone who might play a role in governing, administering, or representing interests within the kingdom; he scrutinized these men, heard out what they had to say, and came to his own judgment. Second, the king presided over the royal councils of government. Finally, he worked in his study, together with people he thought it worthwhile to consult, such as *secrétaires d'Etat*, ministers, loyal supporters, and relatives, and in conjunction with them made decisions—as he was entitled to do, because, whenever the king discussed matters of state with anyone, it was the "king in his Council" at work. In particular, the king saw each of the four secretaries of state in turn. They brought him the "*liasse*," or packet of papers pertaining to matters requiring decision. The secretary of state would explain the substance of the affair, and the king would decide. The manner in which the king worked, and the proportion of his time devoted to each aspect of his job, varied according to the personality of the sovereign, the political circumstances, and the organization of the bureaucracy. Indeed, at the beginning of the seventeenth century, a ministry was no more than a secretary of state together with a few *commis* responsible for preparing and publishing the king's decisions. The wars, however, made it necessary to increase the number of *commis* and to introduce a hierarchical organization in the various ministries. By the end of the eighteenth century, a ministry of Versailles was a bureaucracy in which department heads could take decisions in the name of the king, based on precedent, normally without any direct intervention on the king's part. Monocracy had been transformed into bureaucracy.

A man of war, always on the move, Henri IV did little office work. He took his decisions in a sort of high council, attended by chancellor de Bellièvre, Rosny (who in 1604 became the duc de Sully), Sillery, Villeroi, and the *président* Jeannin. Henri IV held his council in the morning while walking in the gardens or in a gallery. He made resolutions and gave orders. Only one *secrétaire d'Etat*, Villeroi, who advised the king on policy, walked with him; the others were present but at a distance, and they approached the king only when called upon to provide information or to receive an order.

When the princes of the blood arrived, they waited. When the king saw them, however, he would beckon and do a turn around the garden or hall with them, to distinguish them from the common run of mortals. If need be, he discussed affairs of state with them and solicited their opinions.

Outside this council, Sully, the king's most loyal servant, who filled the role of *surintendant des Finances*, or one of the *secrétaires d'Etat* or a *conseiller d'Etat* responsible for a particular matter or a *commissaire extraordinaire* might see the king in his study or in a hallway or on his walk, report to him, and await his orders. Henri IV decided everything, even matters as seemingly unimportant as the sale of a couple of offices. He had a good memory and a sharp mind, and was quick to come to a decision. As a soldier, he took in a situation at a glance and then acted accordingly.

Melancholy, morose, and abrupt, the nervous Louis XIII was ill served by his physical makeup, which thwarted his dreams of authority and grandeur. A stutterer who suffered from enlarged adenoids and later from intestinal tuberculosis, he had a short attention span and found it difficult to express himself. He sometimes fell into periods of melancholy and depression, during which everything seemed black to him. Nevertheless, he had a sense of sovereignty, of the state he embodied, and of his own authority, as well as of the role that France was destined to play in Europe—an idea of the grandeur of France. What he needed was a prime minister. Even after he found Richelieu, he did not cease to govern. He had frequent interviews with his principal minister. He received him in his study and listened to his explanations. He read Richelieu's reports and notes, annotated them, and indicated his decisions in the margins. He corresponded frequently with his minister. Everything that Richelieu accomplished was accomplished on orders from the king, sometimes even on the king's initiative. Louis XIII effectively assumed his governmental responsibilities. This suffering and anguished individual was a leader and a great king.

With Louis XIV, the king became more and more a bureaucrat, obliged to spend long days at his worktable and to observe a schedule of monastic regularity. Saint-Simon's words are familiar: "With an almanach and a watch, one could be three hundred leagues away and still say what the king was doing." On one day at the beginning of his personal government, the young king presided over a meeting of the *Conseil des Finances* from ten in the morning until half past one in the afternoon; he had lunch and then presided over another council; in the evening he presided over a third council meeting that lasted until ten o'clock. In between, he received a number of persons and dispatched mail. His schedule on that particular day was only slightly more arduous than usual. In 1661 he created a high council, the *Conseil royal des Finances*, over which he presided twice a week. It had few members, and Colbert kept the minutes. The king himself played the role of *surintendant des Finances* at these meetings. "To his Majesty" alone was reserved "signature of all ordinances concerning budgetary and cash payments," all *états de distribution des finances, brevets de la taille*, and *rôles de l'Epargne*. "The king wrote more than a hired writer would have done."[1] He did everything that used to be done by a *surintendant des Finances*.

The *Conseil des Finances* was supposed to set the monarchy's fiscal and financial policies and in the early stages actually did so. Later, decisions were taken mainly by the king together with Colbert, who became *contrôleur général des Finances* in 1665. After Colbert, the king reached his decisions in conjunction with his successors in the post of *contrôleur général*. For the sake of form, they were then presented to the *Conseil* and approved without debate.

Besides working in council and in his office, Louis XIV gave many audiences, allowed himself to be approached freely, as was customary with the kings of France, and listened attentively to complaints. He held many private conversations with ministers and others whose opinions he valued. From the time he rose each day until the time of mass, the secretaries of state awaited opportunities to approach the king, to bring matters of state to his attention, and to receive his orders. The king lent his ear to courtiers and officers of his household, watched everything that went on, and missed nothing of importance wherever he went. He was as familiar with the private predilections of the ladies of the court as he was with the problems of European politics.

After the death of Louvois in 1691, the king was obliged to increase the amount of time he devoted to office work, owing to the growing specialization and size of the bureaucracy, which operated out of the two wings of the *château* of Versailles, on either side of the court. He dictated important letters to the *maréchaux* and other military commanders and even wrote some letters personally. He worked out the plans of military operations. He took a hand in administrative questions of every sort. From 1700 on, he actually governed two kingdoms, France and Spain, and had to devote eight or nine hours a day to office work. Frequently he met with one council in the morning and another in the afternoon. He even worked after supper. He followed the progress of military operations and sent advice and orders to the commanders in the field. He either read or had read to him all dispatches from abroad. He wrote or dictated a large number of letters. He held audiences in connection with matters of all sorts. Often he worked at night in Madame de Maintenon's apartment. On either side of the chimney were armchairs for the king and his wife, and nearby stood a stool for the minister and a table for his bag. On a typical day the king used to work with the minister he had summoned until ten at night and then take his supper.

Louis XIV worked in this way right up to his death in 1715. After the Treaties of Utrecht, signed in 1713, he personally revised French policy from top to bottom and, in his instructions to the nation's ambassadors, laid down the major lines of French foreign policy in the eighteenth century.

Louis XV

Louis XV returned to Versailles in 1722 and remained there until his death in 1774. He adopted Louis XIV's court ceremonial, based on a strict calendar and daily schedule. But this routine, which had sustained the Great King in his work, was a painful burden to his successor. In public, Louis XV was stiff and silent. He had a great need for exercise, without which he suffered from rheumatism and jaundice. Much of his time was taken up with hunting. Afterward, at his *petits soupers*, he ate much of what he had bagged.

The king relied on his prime minister until he was thirty-two, at which point he decided that he wanted to govern personally. He was intelligent and had a quick, sharp mind. Usually he was right, but the fear of being wrong gnawed at him. He did not dare press his opinion in council or guide and, if need be, reprimand his ministers. He liked to work alone, in his study, surrounded by notes, papers, and files. He meticulously filed his papers in cabinets made for the purpose, labeling each file with his own hand; there were files for statements, receipts, balances, letters, lists, plans, directories, and catalogs of every shape, kind, and importance. In January 1743, when Fleury died, the king announced that he would govern personally in the tradition of Louis XIV. He tried. In the morning he would deliberate with his ministers and then work an hour or two before supper with one of the secretaries of state. At around ten he would return to his office to read the opinions of certain individuals, such as the duc de Noailles. He consulted his files and came to a reasonable decision. But then he would be afraid to urge that decision on his ministers and generals. A timid man, the king acted only by fits and starts, explosively, when he was exasperated. This explains in part why he carried on a diplomacy of his own with foreign powers, using his own agents without the knowledge of his ministers—the so-called *secret du roi*.

Louis XV had faith in the monarchy and a sense of the state. He wrote to Noailles concerning "the late king, my great-grandfather, whom I want to imitate as much as I possibly can." But he lacked the Great King's inner resolve. He was also the victim of a considerable propaganda effort. He liked artists and scientists but was horrified by men of letters, particularly the *philosophes* and *encyclopédistes*, whom he regarded as idle visionaries. Unfortunately, these idle visionaries ruled public opinion, and they were aided by courtiers jealous of the king's ministers, mistresses, and favorites, who stirred up the crowd. Louis XV had public opinion against him, while his government, owing to his timidity, lacked unity and direction.

Louis XVI

Louis XVI worked regularly with his ministers. He was not without common sense and a sharp mind but found thinking distasteful, decision embarrassing, and expression difficult. He spent too much time hunting and working with his hands. Not much of a man for the court, he detested painting, disliked all the arts, and was bored at the theater, where he sometimes whistled at the actors. All of this cost him prestige. Torn between utopian political principles and circumstantial necessities, and of weak character to boot, he was incapable either of holding on to his ministers, who came and went constantly, or of laying down a policy to which he could make them adhere. Hence each minister went his own way, and there was no comprehensive direction to the government. The king continued to work but ceased to govern.

It bears repeating that the government meanwhile had become an enormous bureaucratic machine. The ideal of a king governing personally in conjunction with his councils was a thing of the past. The councils, which turned out political and administrative decrees in due form, were merely a sham, a fiction. The real government lay in the bureaus, filled with *commis*, who often made decisions personally on the basis of precedent and who implemented those decisions by executive fiat. The system escaped the king's control. Louis XIV was a better head of state than Louis XV and infinitely better than Louis XVI. Still, it is by no means certain that he would have been able to master the machine in the last third of the eighteenth century. A complete reorganization of the central organs of government would have been required; in particular, groups of ministers would have had to be transformed into ministries.

Note

1. Letter from Chancellor Ponchartrain to Desmaretz, 2 July, Archives nationales, G7–532.

Guide to Further Reading

Babelon, Jean. *Henri IV*. Fayard, 1982.
Broglie, Gabriel de. "Le sacre de Louis XVI, d'après des documents inédits." *Revue des deux mondes* 7 (1974): 41–56.
Carré, Henri. *L'enfance et la première jeunesse de Louis XIV*. 1944.
Chevallier, Pierre. *Louis XIII*. Paris: Arthème Fayard, 1979.

Druon, H. *Histoire de l'éducation des princes dans la Maison des Bourbons de France.* 2 vols. P. Lethielleux, 1897.

Girault de Coursac, Pierrette. *L'éducation d'un roi: Louis XVI.* Paris: Gallimard, 1972. Collection "La suite des temps," vol. 47.

Hardouin de Beaumont de Péréfixe. *Institutio Principis.* 1647.

Lacour-Gayet, G. *L'éducation politique de Louis XIV.* 1898. 2d ed., 1923.

La Mothe Le Vayer. *De l'instruction de Monseigneur le Dauphin.* 1640.

Levron, Jacques. *Louis le Bien-Aimé.* Perrin, 1965.

Louis XIV. *Mémoires pour l'éducation du Dauphin.* 2 vols. Editions Dreyss, 1860.

Marvick, Elisabeth Wirth. "The Character of Louis XIII: The Role of His Physician." *Journal of Interdisciplinary History* 4 (1974): 347–74.

Mousnier, Roland. *La monarchie absolue en Europe du Ve siècle à nos jours.* Paris: PUF, 1982.

Saint-René Taillandier (Mme). *La jeunesse du Grand Roi: Louis XIV et Anne d'Autriche.* Paris: Plon, 1945.

Tyvaert, Michel. "L'image du roi: Légitimité et moralité royales dans les histoires de France au XVIIe siècle." *Revue d'histoire moderne et contemporaine* 21 (1974): 521–47.

Vauyuelin des Yveteaux, Nicolas. *Institution du Prince.* 1643.

Wolf, John B. "Formation of a King," in *Louis XIV and the Craft of Kingship*, ed. John C. Rule. Columbus: Ohio State University Press, 1969, pp. 102–31.

2 Public Office

The king made and shaped his decisions in conjunction with the public officials who carried them out at his behest. Posts could be held in fief, including judicial posts and posts in "police" or administration. Since the fiefs had become patrimonial property, fief-holders served the public as lords of a fief. In the seventeenth and eighteenth centuries there were still enfeoffed *prévôts*, enfeoffed *sergents*, and enfeoffed mayors in certain places. These posts were held as fiefs and had all the characteristics of fiefs. Such cases were rare, however. Public posts were most commonly of four types, and there were four corresponding types of public agents: *officiers*, *commissaires*, *fermiers*, and *fonctionnaires*. The latter emerged only in the second half of the eighteenth century.

During the seventeenth and eighteenth centuries there occurred an acceleration of an evolution that had begun much earlier, namely, the transition of the monarchy from a judicial to an administrative system.

The king was, first of all, a judge. Right up to the eve of the Revolution, his power to command and make law derived from his position as supreme judge. Originally, then, the king made sure that justice and order would prevail by punishing crimes and offenses when accusations were brought or, again, in the civil realm, by pronouncing which of the parties to a dispute was in the right. To this end, he delegated his judicial powers to magistrates: his *officiers*, or officeholders. In addition, he took the view that lords, sitting in judgment, were carrying out his judicial function for him and in his name.[1]

Very early, though, the idea gained currency that it was better to prevent crimes and misdemeanors than to punish them. They could be prevented by satisfying the needs of the public for roads and provisions, by regulating prices and working conditions, and so on. Things of this sort were referred to by the men of the time as matters of "police." "Police" included much that would nowadays be called "administration." Until the middle of the eighteenth century, however, the word "administration" was never used without a complement. People spoke of the "administration of justice" and of "administering justice," just as we speak of "administering medication" to a person who is sick. Only after 1756 do we find the sovereign courts of the realm and the governors and commanders-in-chief of provinces using the words "administration" and "to administer" without a complement and in an absolute sense, referring to the satisfaction of the public's daily needs. At that time "administration" began to replace "police" in this broader sense. The word "police" did not lose its old meaning altogether, but it came to be used more often in a restricted sense, meaning "the maintenance of order through the pursuit and arrest of delinquents and criminals."

A new idea also became commonplace: namely, that in some cases the king ought not to confine his activities to mere regulation of production and trade among his subjects but rather should himself become a producer, manufacturer, and builder. Consider roads, for example. The king's duty was, first, to assure the security of those who traveled on the roads and, second, to supervise those responsible for building and maintaining them. Wherever he was not directly *seigneur* of the region through which a road passed, however, the king did not concern himself with roadbuilding or repair. As late as 1603, this was still the view taken by Charondas Le Caron (*Commentaires sur la somme rurale*, de Bouthillier): "The king is the chief surveyor [*grand voyer*] of the kingdom and conservator of the public ways, for the safety and tranquillity of his subjects and of foreigners visiting his kingdom. . . . It is asked, Who is responsible for the repair of public roads and ways? It is argued that the *seigneurs* who collect the tolls and fees and enjoy the right of *haute justice* and *seigneurie* over said roads and ways ought to maintain and repair them." Thus there was a division of labor: the king was responsible for security, the *seigneurs* for repair and maintenance. Even at this early date, however, Sully, who was in charge of finances, made known his conviction that the king ought to establish a program of public works and use his own technicians to carry it out, for otherwise the roads would be badly neglected. Drawing the consequences from Sully's report, Nicolas Berger, Grand Voyer of France, wrote in 1622 that "it is to the king and sovereign lord that primary responsibility for the Guard and superintendence of these [roads] must fall, not as things within their domain, but in that they are the legitimate guardians and conservators of the public good." The king was the guardian of roads not only within his domain but throughout the kingdom, and not only in matters of security but also in matters of maintenance, repair, and construction. This principle of guardianship would little by little be extended to other objects of concern. This tendency was inspired or reinforced by the theory of the *directe royale universelle* (see vol. 1, p. 542).

The changes that occurred in the relative importance of three of the four types of royal agents may be taken as hallmarks of the progressive extension of the role of the state, as it was conceived by men of the time: paramount initially were the *officiers*, followed by the *commissaires*, the best known of which are, of course, the notorious *"intendants des provinces,"* and, finally, the *fonctionnaires*. The latter emerged only toward the middle of the eighteenth century and came into their own only with the Revolution. But their advent was prefigured by a whole hierarchy of *commissaires* and *commis*, so that, by 1756, the administrative practices and administrative structure of the nineteenth century had already been laid down in outline and to some extent even fleshed out. Finally, kings in every period found it convenient to deal with private persons for the collection of taxes and dues, the sale of domains and offices, the management of operations that involved the receipt of cash, and the direction of public works, turning either to the highest bidder or to the lowest as the case required. These private persons or corporations included *"fermiers"* or "farmers" of one sort or another, who were called *partisans*, *traitants*, or, more generally, *financiers* in the case of taxes and loans, and who operated with the help and under the sole control of the king's *officiers* and *commissaires*.

Note

1. See vol. 1, chap. 11.

5 Officeholders

The king was the supreme judge of the realm, and all his other functions—
"police" or administration, defense, and security—derived from his role as
judge. Since the king did not, at least not until the Second Coming, enjoy
the gift of being everywhere at once, he could not personally carry out all
his functions everywhere in the kingdom. An office carried with it the power
to relieve the king of functions that were intimately associated with his
jurisdiction and administration. By virtue of the plenitude and universality
of his power, the king delegated some of the powers that were his to his
officeholders.[1] Their authority was the king's and not their own.

Office conferred with it "the honors, prerogatives, and preeminences belonging to it." With the office went a title, an honorific quality which the
officeholder could claim and attach to his name. Honor and reverence were
conferred along with office: to the officeholder went honor, rank, and *séance*,
or precedence in seating, as well as immunities and privileges. In a society
of orders, in which social status was conferred by the degree of dignity, the
office was a "*dignité ordinaire avec fonction publique*."[2] The precise rank
attaching to an office in the society of orders depended on its importance,
but, all other things being equal, the *estat* of an officeholder was always
higher than, the position in the social hierarchy always superior to, that of
a nonofficeholder.

The functions of the office were renumerated by *gages* or *traitement*, the
office itself being held in trust, so that if there were any profits, these belonged
to the king. As wages were always insufficient and reportedly remunerated
only certain posts, the king suffered the officeholder to pay himself in part
"*par ses mains*," in the form of either an *épice* (*douceur*) or *commission* for
a judicial officeholder or *droits et taxations* for a financial officeholder.

The office entailed residential obligations, periodically renewed in a series
of ordinances dating back to 1303 and never respected. The holding of more
than one office was prohibited, and magistrates were not allowed to participate in commerce while exercising the functions of their office.

The officeholder was secure in his post, despite the clause in the *lettre de provision* confirming his appointment which read, "so long as he shall please us." Sixteenth-century jurists lumped the office together with the ecclesiastical benefice, which was held for life and could be relinquished by the titulary, and contrasted it with the fief, domanial and hereditary, and the commission, which could be revoked at will. The officeholder's security of tenure grew up by custom. Historians have made much of Louis XI's declaration of 20 October 1467, in which the king forbade himself to transfer title to an office or to remove its titulary and stated that an office could be vacated only by the death or resignation of the officeholder or by judicially proved malfeasance. In fact, these principles had already been laid down before the time of Louis XI, and arbitrary removals of officeholders continued after Louis XI and right up to the end of the eighteenth century.

So much for the legal characteristics of the office.

The Sale of Offices

In the seventeenth and eighteenth centuries the office was seen as a public function that could be bought and sold and had certain of the characteristics of private property. To obtain an office, a private individual would in many cases be required to pay a sum of money to the king. When the *finance* was paid, the king would confer the office on the buyer by means of a *lettre de provision*. It was said in those days that he "provided" the buyer with the office. The officeholder then had to be received by the *compagnie* having jurisdiction over his office. If he could not win acceptance, the king was obliged to reimburse him and provide him with another office. The officeholder received into his post swore an oath, whereupon his office became irrevocable and inamovable, except in case of malfeasance and reimbursement by the king. He could sell his charge to a third party or bequeath it to an heir. In such cases he would remit his charge to the king, indicating the name of the person he desired as a successor. He was said to "resign" his charge in favor of someone else, whereupon he became known as the *résignant* and the person to whom he passed on his charge became the *résignataire*. Thus officeholders treated their offices as private property and looked upon them as part of their patrimony. In law, however, the officeholder was not the owner of the office, the title and function of which attached to authority vested in the officeholder by the king. Only the king could vest that authority in someone else, and it could not be transferred by inheritance, sale, or resignation. Only the *"finance"* of the office was the property of the officeholder, and this must not be confused with the *corps* of the office itself. The officeholder could always claim the *"finance,"* but by law the office was at the disposal of the king. The office's legal character was not affected by its sale.

The Categories of Offices

Contemporaries distinguished between ordinary and extraordinary offices. Ordinary offices included those of judges responsible for civil and criminal justice, such as the offices of magistrates of the *parlements, présidiaux, bailliages,* and *sénéchaussées,* and their subdivisions, *prévôtés, vicomtés,* and *vigueries.* Their functions also included the powers of "police" or general administration. Extraordinary offices were those in which magistrates were responsible essentially for specialized administrative functions and for administrative prosecutions. These were considered to be separate from the ordinary offices. Among them were the offices of finance—*trésoriers, élus,* and *grenetiers* or officials in charge of salt warehouses; the offices of the *Eaux et Forêts;* those of the Admiralty; and so on.

As the sale of offices was extended, contemporaries came to make further distinctions between casual, domanial, and hereditary offices.

Casual offices were those that could be vacated by death, malfeasance, or nonfeasance, or by incompatability [i.e., the holding of another office incompatible with the office in question—trans.], in which case they reverted to the king, who could dispose of them as he wished. Most offices, both in the courts and in finance, fell into this category. The offices of the king's and queen's household and the provinces, as well as military offices, were usually casual.

Domanial offices were presumed to be part of the Crown's domain and regular income. The king sold these offices but permanently reserved the right to buy them back if the needs of war required it, as was the case with the rest of the royal domain. The buyer became the king's proxy as *seigneur,* however. Thus in no case could the office be vacated: not for reasons of incompatibility, because a domanial office could be held along with any other office; not for malfeasance or nonfeasance, because the owner of a domanial office could give it out to be farmed, just as the king did; and not by death, because the domanial office passed to the heirs of the purchaser without formal proceedings. Domanial offices could be owned by women or minors, who might entrust execution of the office to a farmer, except for clerkships in the sovereign courts, which had to be executed personally. The king could reclaim these offices only by reimbursing their owners in a general resale or when a private individual auctioned one off to a third party. Both casual and domanial offices were sold at auction by the king. But domanial offices were actually sold at public "candle auctions" (at which bidding continued until a candle had burned down). Appointment to domanial offices was not by *lettre de provision,* but by a deed of title (*acte d'adjudication*) and a contract of sale drawn up by the Conseil des Finances and approved by the Conseil d'Etat. Domanial offices included notaryships, scribes (*tabellionages*), clerkships, sealkeepers, and "offices of police" such as wine brokers, fabric measurers, corn and coal carriers, wood measurers, and so on. The king could, however, classify an office as casual or domanial as he pleased.

Hereditary offices were a form of property. They could be sold, pledged, and conveyed to heirs without the king's consent. Thus they had the characteristics of fiefs. They could be transferred from one person to another without *lettres de provision*. In this respect they differed from casual offices, which entitled the holder only to the usufruct and could be transferred only with the express consent of the patron in a *lettre de provision*. The king did not, however, lose all of his power over hereditary offices. He sold them with a permanent option to buy them back. He could always regain control by reimbursing the owner. The king could make any office hereditary if he wished.

In practice, officeholders considered their offices to be part of their property. In 1637 Théophraste Renaudot published in *La semaine du bureau d'adresse* the following advertisement:

Offices for sale or exchange.
For sale: one office of Conseiller du Roy, *Receveur général des Finances à quatre journées de Paris*, with *gages et droits* of 6,700 livres, at a price of 90,000 livres; payment is flexible, and an exchange for another office, house, or otherwise may be acceptable.
For sale: an office of Lieutenant de Robecourte, *a grand Prévôt*, at an *honeste prix*.
For sale: seigneurial lands.
For sale or lease: houses and common land.[3]

Once the sale of offices had become commonplace, the king often resorted to the expedient of doubling or tripling the number of offices whenever his coffers were low. A given office might then be held by three men, referred to as the *ancien*, the *alternatif*, and the *triennal*. Each would execute the office in turn, in yearly rotation. Similarly, the king sometimes doubled the number of offices in an entire *corps*, each office being executed for six months by one nominee and for six months by another. The *anciens* could buy out the *alternatif* or the *triennal* or, under the second system, the nominee for the second semester.

Nomination to Offices

By law, the king was entitled to create offices at will and dispose of them as he pleased. Only he could create these positions: "The creation of offices is a royal right, belonging to none other than We Ourselves." The king created offices in his Council. It was up to the *surintendant* or *contrôleur général des Finances* to take the initiative when the treasury was short of funds. An *intendant des Finances* would then draft an edict of creation, which would be brought before the Conseil des Finances. If the Council approved, the edict would be sent to the Conseil d'Etat et des Finances, which had to be informed because it had administrative jurisdiction. Once approved by the latter, the edict would be sent to the *parlements*, and if a financial office was involved, also to the Chambres des Comptes and Cours des Aides, which would register it. If there was concern about difficulties with the sovereign courts, the king could make do with a declaration registered by the *grand chancellerie* and published for the audience of France.

Only the patron (*collateur*) could dispose of offices, and there was but a single patron, the sovereign prince. He could confer an office as a gift by brevet; generally, however, he sold it.

The *grands officiers* of the Crown—that is, the primary officeholders in the main state functions,[4] and the primary officeholders in the king's household, those who assisted the king personally and served him daily[5]—were chosen by the king himself from among the great families of France or from among his favorites. The king provided these offices by letters patent sealed with the great seal. The *grands officiers* of the Crown swore an oath into the king's hands; the principal officeholders in the king's household swore either into the king's hands or into the hands of the *grand officier* of the Crown to whom they were responsible; the latter inscribed them on the payroll (*état de gages*). Military offices, such as *lieutenant général de l'armée- maréchal de camp, colonel de régiment, capitaine de compagnie, maréchal de logis*, and certain others, were conferred by royal brevet, after receipt of which the officer was allowed to swear an oath.

The sale or transfer of a casual office in the judiciary or finance had to be carried out according to prescribed forms. Each week, the *contrôleur général des Finances* or one of the *intendants des Finances* acting on his orders drew up a list of newly created offices and of offices left vacant by death, resignation, or forfeiture. In 1638, it was decided that the *trésorier des parties casuelles* would draw up the list of resigned offices, which would merely be checked by the *intendant des Finances*. For each category, two lists were prepared, one for large offices, the other for small. These lists were presented to the Conseil des Finances, which assessed all new and resigned offices for tax purposes after receiving a report from an *intendant des Finances* concerning their market value.

The tax rolls, signed by the secretary of the Conseil, were presented by the *intendants des Finances* to the *contrôle général des Finances* for registration. A secretary gave an authenticated copy of the roll to the *trésorier des parties casuelles*, who made out the receipts. The original of the roll was then sent to the *chancellerie*, where *lettres de provision* for each office were prepared.

For offices resigned, the *trésorier des parties casuelles* and the *trésorier du marc d'or*[6] received the money, and a notary and secretary of the king attached to the *grande chancellerie* drafted the *lettres de provision* and attached the proxy, whereupon the seal could be affixed.

For offices left vacant by death and for newly created offices, however, a sale at auction was necessary. Bidders could consult the list of offices at the *contrôle général* or at the office of the *trésorier des parties casuelles*.

From 1613 on, auctions were advertised by announcements posted on the doors of the Conseils, the *chancellerie*, and the offices of the *surintendant des Finances*, specifying the offices for sale, the taxes, the day, and the hour. Bids were received by the *contrôleur général des Finances* and one of the *intendants des Finances*, and possibly by the *garde des rôles des offices de France*, on Tuesday, Thursday, and Saturday afternoons, in the offices of the *contrôleur général des Finances*. The *trésorier des parties casuelles* and the *garde des rôles des offices de France* attended the auctions, each with a copy of the tax rolls. Bidders stated their names and qualities and recorded their bids above the taxation in the register of the *contrôle général*. The highest bidder paid the sum due on the following day to the *trésorier des parties casuelles* and had a petition to the king drawn up by one of the king's notary-secretaries. The *contrôleur général* prepared a secret report on the highest bidder. If this report was favorable, the Conseil des Finances awarded the office and gave the *trésorier des parties casuelles* authorization to issue a receipt. The highest bidder also paid the *droit de marc d'or*. The *contrôleur général des Finances* verified the receipts, marked an approval on the back, and indicated the final sale in his register. The bidder had an authenticated copy of the original receipts prepared by a notary-secretary of the king and kept the copy. The notary-secretary attached the originals of the *lettres de provision* that he had previously drawn up and took all the documents to the *chancellerie* to receive the seal.

Provision of Offices

By law, all officeholders were provided their offices by the king—even the least important of them, such as *huissiers* and *sergents*. Louis XIII even went so far as to seal by his own hand the *lettres de provision* of the *garde des Sceaux* of Châteauneuf and the *premier président* of the *parlement* of Le Jay, as a special honor to Richelieu, whose men the nominees were. The king almost always delegated this power to the chancellor, however, or to his *garde des Sceaux*, if the chancellor no longer had possession of the seals.

After the auctions, the *garde des rôles des offices de France* would bring to the chancellery the original rolls of sales or resignation taxes that had been submitted to the Council along with the name of the highest bidder for offices on which bids were made. For a long period of time the *garde des rôles* was a mere *commis* of the chancellor. The first one was Gilbert de Combault, *premier secrétaire de l'Hôpital*, who held the post from 1560 to 1616. The job continued to be treated as a *commission* until March 1631. At that time the king created four offices bearing the appellation *garde des rôles des offices de France;* each of the four titularies served for a quarter as *audienciers*. The chancellor retained the right to nominate men to this post, and his nominees swore an oath to him. The *garde des rôles* received objections to the affixing of the seal raised by creditors or rival candidates and reported to the chancellor at the time the seal was to be applied. *Lettres de provision* were couched in invariable terms. The king's notary-secretary signed them on the crease, after the words: *Par Le Roy*. The *grand audiencier* sorted the *lettres de provision* and tied them in bundles along with the receipts. If several candidates disputed an office, they could submit a *requête* to the chancellor, who was obliged to hold an open hearing in the presence of two *maîtres des requêtes* following the *grand déjeuner*. The *maîtres des requêtes* took the *requêtes* of the parties to the case and presented them to the Conseil d'Etat et des Finances. On the day the seals were to be affixed, according to the usual procedure, the letters were sealed by the chancellor, taxed by the *grand audiencier*, and delivered to the secretaries who had drawn them up. The secretaries took care of the taxes and delivered the *lettres de provision* to their clients.

Reception into Offices

The man provided with an office was not yet an officeholder in the full sense of the word. The *lettre de provision* gave him title to, *seigneurie* over, the office. But he also had to acquire the order and character of officeholder through reception, and the possession and exercise of the office through installation. In theory the king himself received all officeholders. Louis XIII did so for chancellors and *gardes des Sceaux* and for the *premiers présidents* of the *parlements*. The king made the *Conseil privé* or one of the *maîtres des requêtes* of his *hôtel* responsible for the reception when those who were supposed to receive the new officeholders failed to do so out of malevolence or self-interest. As a general rule, he left the reception up to the sovereign courts.

The Grand Conseil received its presidents and councillors. The *parlements* received their officeholders, as well as all judicial officeholders who fell under their immediate jurisdiction: *baillis*, *sénéchaux*, *lieutenants généraux* and *particuliers*, *vicomtes*, *prévôts*, *conseillers des bailliages*, *des sénéchaussées*, and *des sièges présidiaux*, *juges des Eaux et Forêts*, etc. The Cours des Aides received their officeholders as well as officeholders with jurisdiction in financial matters who were also received by the Chambre des Comptes: *trésoriers généraux de France*, *élus*, *contrôleurs des aides* and *des tailles des élections*, etc.

The lesser officeholders, who held offices in the ministries or elsewhere, were received at the place where they were to exercise their functions: *huissiers audienciers* either at the *bailliage* or the *présidial* or the *élection* or the *grenier à sel* (salt warehouse) or the *maîtrise des Eaux et Forêts* or the *maréchaussée*—in general, at whatever department was mentioned in their *lettres de provision*. The *gardes* and *contrôleurs des grandes et petites mesures* at a salt warehouse were received at that warehouse. Certain domanial officeholders who had police powers, such as controllers, markers, and inspectors of fabrics or other products and foodstuffs had to be received by the *élus* of the *élection*. Registration of the contract of sale at the *élection*'s registry took the place of registration of the *lettre de provision*.

The man provided with an office was obliged to submit a request to be received by the *corps d'officiers* appropriate to his position. After deliberation, a clerk of the corps would mark the words "let it be shown to the *Procureur général du Roy*" on the request and send it to the *procureur*. The latter ordered an investigation into the life, morals, and relations of the candidate and verified that he adhered to the Catholic, Apostolic, and Roman faith and was loyal to the king. The investigation was carried out by the *procureur*'s proxy in the place where the candidate had resided for the past five years. The proxy would have the *lieutenant général* hear testimony from a priest and four former officeholders or *avocats* who were neither friends nor enemies of the candidate and who were, in addition, neither his relatives nor allies nor domestics. The proxy would personally verify the date of the candidate's baptism, before 1631 through witnesses, after 1631 by excerpting from the baptismal registers. He would also check the date of the candidate's father's marriage contract and compare the property of the candidate with the cost of his office. The *lieutenant général* signed a certificate indicating what relatives and allies the candidate might have in the place in which he wished to be received. The candidate had to submit to the *procureur général* a list of witnesses, from which the *procureur* chose some names to be heard by the proxy and by a councillor assigned to this task. When the investigation was complete, the procureur general prepared a summary listing all the documents collected.

The *procureur* could decide to reject the candidate's request. Possible reasons for rejection were spelled out in the Châteauneuf regulations of 1631 and in the Séguier regulations: conviction for debt or for a dishonorable crime, the presence of relatives such as a father, uncle, or brother, or want of maturity and experience. All offices in the sovereign courts required candidates to be over twenty-five and to have served at the court as *avocat* for four years; to be *président*, a candidate had to be forty and to have served for ten years as *conseiller* or *lieutenant général de bailliage* or *de sénéchaussée* or for a long time as an *avocat*. To be *lieutenant général* or *maître des requêtes* one had to be thirty-two or to have served six years in a sovereign court. To be *conseiller de siège présidial*, one had to be twenty-five and to have served three years as an *avocat*. For the offices of *receveur* or *contrôleur des Finances*, one also had to be twenty-five. The king sometimes issued letters of dispensation, and in some cases officeholders were received in Finance despite their youth, provided a larger security was posted.

The court then undertook to examine the candidate. No relative, friend, or ally of the candidate was supposed to be in attendance. For a Cour de Justice, the candidate was supposed to begin by making a speech in Latin: this was the test of "general culture." Next, he was questioned about a law selected at random three days earlier and studied by him in the meantime: this was the test of "legal culture." Finally, compendia of laws, customs, and decrees were supposed to be brought in, and three times, "*à la fortuite ouverture des livres*," the candidate was required to improvise an explanation of the passage upon which the examiner's hand fell by chance: this was the "practical text," ostensibly a stringent one. To be *conseiller* in a *présidial*, the candidate had to submit to a practical test on Roman law, canon law, customary law, and royal ordinances. If the candidate did not perform adequately, the court could allow him a period of time to prepare for a second examination. It could also give him a more practical and therefore easier test, requiring him to examine the papers pertaining to a case and give a report on it to the court.

If the candidate's answers were satisfactory, the court issued a decree declaring him received and the candidate swore an oath. For *présidents* and *conseillers de parlement*, *baillis*, *sénéchaux*, and their *lieutenants*, the clerk read the following oath and the candidate swore after him: "You swear that, in order to arrive at this *estat*, you have not given or caused to be given or promised to give, by your own hand or by that of another, gold, silver, or the equivalent thereof. You swear to execute this office faithfully and well, to administer justice to the poor as to the rich without regard to persons, to keep the ordinances, and to hold the deliberations of the court private and secret, and everywhere and in all things to behave as one good and notable [*un bon et notable*] ought to do in sovereign court." The candidate then swore allegiance to the Roman, Apostolic, and Catholic faith and loyalty to the king. In 1596 the Assemblée des Notables had asked that the clause about not having paid anything be suppressed. It became increasingly rare after the reign of Henri IV and finally fell into disuse.

Installation in Offices

The installation of the candidate received as an officeholder was carried out by the corps in which he was to execute his office. Not all the members of a tribunal belonged to the corps. In the *présidiaux*, for example, the *officiers comptables* and *officiers ministériels*, though received and registered by a *présidial*, were members only of the *présidial* and not of the *corps des présidiaux*. These included *receveurs des consignations*, *commissaires aux saisies réelles*, *greffiers*, *procureurs*, *notaires*, *huissiers*, and *sergents*. "The *corps des présidiaux* consisted only of *présidents*, *lieutenants généraux civils* and *criminels*, *lieutenants particuliers*, *conseillers*, *commissaires examinateurs*, *enquêteurs*, *procureurs du roi*, *avocats du roi*, *baillis d'épée*, and *chevaliers d'honneur*," that is, of all officeholders having the character of magistrate.[7] In a *bailliage* and *siège présidial*, the new officeholder, accompanied by an officeholder of the same rank, appeared in gown before the *lieutenant général président présidial*. A day was set for the installation. Then, wearing his gown, he visited his future colleagues. On the day of the installation, the *président* stated that he had a *lettre de provision* and an *acte de reception en parlement* pertaining to so-and-so who was asking to be presented. The court gave its assent. A *conseiller* was assigned to introduce the new member into the *Chambre du Conseil*. The newcomer requested certification of the presentation of his *lettre de provision* and *acte de reception*. The two documents were read and the *présidial* granted certification. The *lieutenant général* made a speech detailing the functions of the new member and emphasizing the need for unity among the members of the corps, and he then gave the brotherly kiss. All the officeholders went as a body to the audience, where the newcomer took his seat and formal possession of his office. Minutes of the installation ceremony were recorded in the *présidial*'s register, whereupon the newcomer became an officeholder in the full sense of the word. Installations in the other corps were similar.

To receive payment of his salary, the officeholder had only to submit his *lettres de provision* and *arrêt de reception* to the *trésoriers généraux de France*, who approved them and gave orders to the *receveur* and *payeur des gages* of the corps to which the new member belonged to pay his salary and dues. From that moment on, the new officeholder enjoyed the full rights of his office.

The Paulette, or Annual Dues

Prior to Paulet's edict of 1604, the king accepted resignations from any office. The *grands officiers*, *officiers de la Maison*, and military officers had to discuss their resignation directly with the king. In financial and judicial offices, the resigning officeholder was in theory supposed to appear in person before the chancellor, who represented the king. In practice, the *résignant* appeared before a royal or seigneurial notary and completed a procuration *ad resignandum* in order to resign. Full power was given to the *procureur* to remit and resign the office to the king so that it might be provided to the *résignataire* and no other. The procuration was usually sent, subsequent to the meeting of the Council, to one of the king's notary-secretaries. He would inscribe the name of one of his *commis*, who played the role of *procureur*. The latter would convey the document to the *contrôleur général des Finances*, who would record it on the roll of resigned offices to be assessed and assigned by the Council.

The king usually took nothing for resignations from the *grands offices* of the Crown, the offices of his household, or military offices. For the rest, he collected a tax known as the *quart denier*, equivalent to one-quarter of the value of the office as assessed by the Council. This tax was viewed as an equivalent of the *droits de mutation* in the case of a fief. Prior to payment of the tax, the king could demand that the resignation be cancelled and the office sold for the benefit of a creditor or given to a candidate of his own choosing. After payment, however, his acceptance of the resignation became final. The king also collected the *marc d'or* or *droit de serment*.

The chancellery attached a condition of validity to the *lettres de provision* issued subsequent to a resignation: "Provided that the *résignant* lives for a period of forty days after the date of the present letter." The letters were dated on the day the *quart denier* was received. The forty-day waiting period could be prolonged to as much as two or three months after resignation, because it was not until the office had been assessed that the *quart denier* could be paid, and the Council sometimes took three to four weeks to act. The forty-days clause had been intended to insure that offices would become vacant upon the death of the officeholder, so as to allow the king to hand them out to loyal supporters, either as gifts or at his own expense. The clause made it impossible for an officeholder to resign on his deathbed and thereby pass the office on to a man of his own choosing.

Officeholders were therefore inclined to grant themselves exemption from the forty-days clause. Sovereign courts ceased to pay heed to the clause in *lettres de provision* for judicial offices, particularly where resignations from father to son, brother to brother, or uncle to nephew were involved.

Furthermore, some officeholders had paid the king cash in exchange for the "reversion" of their office. The officeholder resigned in favor of his son, nephew, brother, or son-in-law. The *résignataire* was "provided" and "received" for the oath of office but did not immediately take up his functions. Instead, the *résignant* continued to execute the office. When the *résignant* was absent or sick, the *résignataire* filled in for him. The *résignataire* had actually been received into the office, however, and became its sole possessor upon the death or retirement of the *résignant*.

Many officeholders benefited from the "reversion edicts" issued in 1567, in January, June, and July of 1568, in 1576, and, finally, in July of 1586. In return for an obligatory loan of one-third of the office's assessed value, officeholders were collectively authorized to resign, and this authorization was coupled with guarantees for their heirs. Any officeholder who agreed to the payment of one-third of the assessed value of his office could resign whenever he chose, and if he submitted an affidavit sworn before a royal judge in the presence of two notables that he was in good health at the time he paid the *tiers denier*, he was granted dispensation from the forty-days clause and exemption from all resignation taxes. If the officeholder resigned in favor of a son or son-in-law, and if the *résignataire* happened to die before the *résignant*, the office would revert to the latter, who could dispose of it as specified in the edict. If the officeholder died without having resigned, his widow and heirs could name a candidate to the king. If the officeholder died without having resigned and left young children, the widow and tutors could send *lettres d'office* in the name of the minor child, and until he came of age they could appoint a *commis* to execute the office.

Offices tended to remain within a family or a small group of related families.

Henri IV began the struggle. By edict in January 1597 he ordered the sovereign courts to observe the forty-days clause in *lettres de provision* scrupulously, failing which the letters would become void. The chancellery thereafter applied the seal to *lettres de provision* only after the forty days had elapsed and continued to insert the clause in new letters. By edicts issued in December 1597 and on 30 June 1598, all reversions were revoked, except those of the king's notary-secretaries. Those who had obtained individual reversions in exchange for cash payments were allowed to resign within the year without payment of the *quart denier*, and those who had already named their successor and had him received had six months to make up their minds whether to keep the office themselves or pass it on to their designated successor. All other officeholders had to renounce, in writing, the rights conferred on them by the edict of July 1586. They received increased salaries as interest on the sum paid for the reversion. When they resigned, the resignation tax was deducted from what they had paid for the reversion.

The heritability of offices was threatened by the king's actions. Many heirs sought to circumvent the forty-days clause by nefarious means. Some drew up procurations of resignation after the death of the officeholder. Others concealed the death of the officeholder as long as they possibly could, preserving the body in salt if need be. In 1599, the family of a *président* in the *parlement* of Toulouse paid the resignation tax twelve days after the death of the *résignant*, and the family of a *conseiller* paid its tax five days after his death. These families therefore had to pretend that the dead man was actually sick in bed for periods of fifty-two and forty-five days, respectively. Such practices were said to be common in the jurisdiction of the Toulouse *parlement*. Many officeholders in remote provinces did not even bother to apply to the king for *lettres de provision*. They obtained offices by having other *officiers* enter their names into a register, thus depriving the sovereign of the right to nominate his own men and gain the proceeds from sale of the office.

In 1600 and 1601, the *parties casuelles* yielded scarcely more than 500,000 livres annual revenue, 150,000 of which came from judicial offices. The Biron conspiracy of 1602 revealed that discontent was rampant among officeholders and even among some nobles. Henri IV had been unable to keep his courtiers from obtaining offices for their protégés and clients. The king received many proposals that he grant exemption from the forty-days rule. An edict declaring offices to be fiefs had even been drawn up in connection with the suggestions submitted by Jacques Leschassier, probably in 1597, which some officeholders in the sovereign courts were still eager to see implemented. What they wanted was for offices to be made either fiefs or *censives* and thus patrimonial property held of the king. Inheritance would be accompanied by the payment of mutations, *droits de relief*, and *droits de rachat* in the case of fiefs and *lods et ventes* in the case of *censives*, which also called for the payment of an annual *cens*. Such a measure would have deprived the king of control over all his offices. A strong class of feudal officeholders would have been constituted.

In September 1602 Rosny submitted a counterproposal to the *Conseil d'Etat et des Finances*. As drafted, the edict contained two main points:

exemption from the forty-days clause was to be granted to officeholders, and the revenues of the *parties casuelles* were to be given out to farmers.

The plan for the farm had been submitted by one Charles Paulet, sieur de Coubéron and secretary of the king's Chamber. Contemporaries doubted that he was its true author. Indeed, the royal declaration establishing the annual dues asserted that the king had taken action in response to remonstrances from the most senior officers of his sovereign courts, who had been spurred on by fears that the value of their offices was plummeting. This suggests that the project was actually hatched by certain *présidents* and *conseillers*, who had chosen Paulet as the man to represent them. The plan aroused violent opposition on the part of the chancellor Bellièvre. He apparently intended to do away with a good many offices and perhaps even venality itself, on the grounds that it was becoming an unworkable system. He was afraid that the sale of offices made them accessible to men who were incapable or corrupt. Venality tended to lower standards of official conduct and to raise the price of offices, thus putting them out of the reach of *gentilshommes* and exclusively into the hands of sons of *financiers*. Selling offices also led to neglect of commerce and industry. The king, however, wished to encourage his officers to do their duty by offering them an important but revocable advantage, and he wanted to discourage the *Grands* from acquiring supporters by handing out offices as patronage. He therefore backed the plan, which within two years was put into effect.

The decree instituting annual dues and the contract with Paulet was issued on 7 December 1604. Parts of it were reiterated in an edict of 12 December. The new system was a kind of insurance policy. The king showed "favor" to all officeholders in the kingdom. He granted dispensation from the feared forty-days clause. In return, the officeholder, to obtain exemption from the clause if he should resign within any given year, had only to pay, between the first of January and the fifteenth of February, a sum equal to one-sixtieth of the value placed on his office by the Council. Officeholders who paid this sum would be required to pay a resignation tax of only one-eighth the value of the office, rather than one-quarter. If, moreover, the officeholder died without having resigned and the office was not *supprimable*, his widow and heirs could sell it for their own advantage provided they paid a tax of one-eighth of the selling price. If, on the other hand, the office was *supprimable*, that is, if it had been created since the death of Henri II, it was declared vacant upon the death of the officeholder and reverted to the farmer for resale. But officeholders were officially granted the right to resign on the point of death, thereby securing the office as a part of the patrimonial property, except in case of sudden death of the holder of a *supprimable* office. Still subject to the forty-days clause, unless special dispensation was granted by the king, were the offices of his major representatives: *premiers présidents* of the sovereign courts, *procureurs du roi* and *avocats du roi*, and *lieutenants généraux civils* of the bailliages and *sénéchaussées* in which there was a *présidial*.

The favor of the annual payment was granted at the king's pleasure. The declaration was published only in the *grande chancellerie*. To revoke the right of annual payment and of exemption from the forty-days clause, all that was necessary, therefore, was another *déclaration en chancellerie*, avoiding the need for verification in the sovereign courts.

The annual dues, along with all income accruing to the *parties casuelles* from offices vacated by death, forfeiture, or resignation, were farmed out to Charles Paulet for a period of six years in exchange for 900,000 livres per year, increased to 1,006,000 livres per year in 1605. Paulet was given the right to hire *commis* empowered to scour the kingdom for offices vacated by death, to enlist the support of royal judges, and to appoint collectors for the annual dues.

The major difference between the annual dues and the inheritance edicts was that the procedure associated with the former was more flexible and regular. No matter when he bought his charge, the officeholder could insure that his heirs would receive either the office or its value without having to wait for issuance of an inheritance edict or to curry favor with a courtier. The king, for his part, was assured of receiving a regular and steady income, on which he could count in preparing his budget, and against which he could borrow from *partisans* when his treasury was strapped for funds.

The first man to whom the annual dues and the income accruing to the *parties casuelles* were farmed out was Charles Paulet, sieur de Coubéron, *secrétaire de la Chambre du Roi*, who was born into a Languedocian family of financial officeholders. One relative had been named *contrôleur général des Finances* in Languedoc in 1562; another, Jacques, *secrétaire ordinaire de la Chambre du Roi*, was registrar at the Bureau des Finances in Paris in 1609; a third, Jean, was *contrôleur* of Queen Marguerite's household and of the salt warehouse at Brie-Comte-Robert in 1610. Charles Paulet was also involved in various joint farms (*parties*).

The decree of 7 December 1604 allowed Paulet to share the farming of the offices of France with noblemen, who did not, in so doing, derogate from nobility, as well as with officeholders who were not subject to the strict letter of the ordinances. If Paulet should die, it was understood that his associates would suggest to the king a candidate to succeed him in the farm, which would continue without interruption. Paulet was therefore not so much a *partisan* dealing with the king as the principal of a group of *financiers*. Among Paulet's associates and backers we find some of the king's notary-secretaries, who were discontent with merely drafting *actes de chancellerie* and eager to play the role of "financiers": Jean le Prévôt, sieur de Saint-Germain de Lassies, Nicolas Bigot, Jean Marteau. There were officeholders, such as Pierre Longuet, *général en la Cour des Monnaies;* and "*bourgeois de Paris*," such as Nicolas Carrel and Pierre Fougères, sieur de Fourcroy, many of them rentiers with an interest in the king's affairs. Paulet's group was thus a corporation of "financiers," of men who handled the king's money, who farmed the *parties casuelles;* Paulet was merely the chief executive of this corporation, whose authority was delegated by its "board of directors." It is his name, however, that has been preserved for posterity in the decrees of the Council.

Receipts for the annual dues signed by Paulet were commonly known as "Paulettes," and the words "j'ai Pauleté," "j'ai payé la Paulette," were commonly employed by the duespayers. The word "Paulette" thus passed into common parlance, even though the official designation was "*droit annuel*," or annual dues.

The *parties casuelles* remained. Much of the income was not farmed out. As in the past, the *trésorier des parties casuelles* received money for resignations, for offices vacated by death, and for forfeitures. He paid these sums into the farmer's account in the central treasury (*Epargne*); the farmer was also entitled to half the income from fines, forfeitures, or confiscations due in judgments against those who violated the articles of contract. When the sum in the farmer's account equaled what that farmer owed the king, the *trésorier des parties casuelles* paid the rest to the farmer.

The business was a poor one, and on 24 December 1605 Paulet gave up his farm to another "financier," Bénigne Saulnier. Paulet pursued his career as a *partisan*, however, and was reputed to be a very wealthy man. Assisted by his wife, a noted coquette, he received the leading courtiers, attracted by the beauty of his daughter Angélique, one of Henri IV's mistresses. Some say that the king was on his way to visit Angélique at the *hôtel* of the financier Zamet in the rue Saint-Antoine when he was assassinated on 14 May 1610, in the rue de la Ferronerie. Paulet and his daughter, who became one of the *précieuses*, were later honored under the names Straton and Elize in Mlle de Scudéry's *Grand Cyrus*. Genealogists used to try to link Paulet to two English families by the name of Pawlet, one of the marquis of Winchester, the other of the knight of Hinton.

Bénigne Saulnier was assigned rights to Paulet's contract as of 1 January 1606, for a period of six years, in exchange for 1,106,000 livres per year. An audacious spirit and the ambition of a "new man" drove him to the adventure. He belonged to a family that had risen rapidly from the world of culture and commerce to that of finance and its associated offices. During the second half of the sixteenth century, the Saulniers were Protestants who kept vineyards in the region of Paris and sold their wine in the city. They married their daughters to Parisian merchants, journeymen, truckfarmers, masons, racketmakers, and stonecutters. Eventually they moved to Paris. Bénigne Saulnier's elder brother became one of the king's notary-secretaries and married into a Parisian *bourgeois* family, the de Bourges. A younger brother of Bénigne became a notary at the Châtelet in Paris. In 1603 Bénigne acquired the offices of *receveur général des Finances* at Lyon and of *trésorier des Fortifications* in the Lyon region. While farming the offices of France, he entered into joint farms of many kinds. He helped some of his brothers get offices as *receveurs généraux des Finances*. His leading associate was Jean Palot, notary-secretary of the king and of the *collège des Cinquante-quatre*, established in 1570, and secretary of the king's Chamber, who had for some time been involved in all sorts of joint farms and who became, during the period of Saulnier's farm, *contrôleur général de l'extraordinaire des guerres*. He played an important role, attested by the fact that in Normandy the popular name for the annual dues was not Paulette but Palotte. Another of Saulnier's partners was the wealthy financier Jean de Moisset, who held the lease on the *cinq grosses fermes*, the farm on the *aides*, and partnerships in several other farms. Around these three partners was a group of financiers, royal notary-secretaries, *receveurs généraux des Finances*, *partisans*, and merchants with contacts in the leading financial centers, Paris and Lyon— some Protestant, the other on good terms with the Protestants.

Bénigne Saulnier held his contract until 31 December 1611. In the end it proved ruinous. The debt to the king was not liquidated until 1615. Bénigne Saulnier was able to buy an office as *receveur général des Finances* at Lyon in 1616. But there was a long hiatus in his career as a *partisan*. His family continued its ascent, however. One of his nephews, François, was a *conseiller* in the *parlement* of Paris in 1619.

On 20 September 1611, the Regency Council decided to extend the favor of exemption from the forty-days clause for six years beginning on 1 January 1612, and to farm out the collection of the annual dues and the income to the *parties casuelles*, with certain modifications of the rules. Henceforth, payment of the annual dues gained exemption from the forty-days clause only if the officeholder resigned in favor of his son or son-in-law. The annual payment no longer insured that the heirs would receive either the office or its value, but only a sum equal to twice the assessed value of the office, an amount less than the market price, which in many cases ran as high as three times the assessed value. The king himself reserved the right to dispose of offices on which annual dues had not been paid, whether they were resigned or not, so that he might recognize and compensate the services of meritorious individuals. In certain cases, when important offices, such as those of the *parlements*, the *premiers présidents* of the Chambres des Comptes and the Cours des Aides, the *lieutenants généraux* of the *sièges présidiaux*, and the *trésoriers de l'Epargne*, were vacated by death, the *partisan* would take only twice the assessed value, and the king would give the office to a person of his choosing, paying the beneficiary the difference between the market price and twice the assessed value. The king could thereby choose men of value to fill his offices and reward them for their devotion.

On 1 October 1611, the farm was awarded to Claude Marcel for 1,660,000 livres per year. The new farmer belonged to an old Parisian family with several branches that can be traced back to the end of the fourteenth century. His grandfather had been *intendant* and *contrôleur général des Finances* under Henri IV when the king reconquered his kingdom. His father, a notary-secretary of the king, and later *maître des Comptes*, died in 1596. His uncle, Mathieu Marcel, had been a member of the Grand Conseil and later of the Conseil d'Etat. Claude Marcel was a noble, sieur de Bouqeval and *avocat au parlement*, but he may not yet have been a member of the Grand Conseil when he took over the farming of the offices of France.

Among Claude Marcel's associates were royal notary-secretaries, including Jean le Prévôt, seigneur de Saint-Germain de Lassies, and Gabriel de Guénégaud; "financiers," such as the Barbin brothers—Claude Barbin, a *bourgeois* of Paris and *intendant particulier* to Marie de Médicis who became *contrôleur general des Finances* in 1616, and Dreux Barbin, seigneur and baron de Bruy in Champagne; financial officeholders, such as Henry le Mareschal, seigneur de Lassay and *trésorier de France* at Bourges; and Guillaume Le Gruer, seigneur de Morville. Claude Marcel, member of a family of loyal supporters of Henri IV, some of whose members held posts in the sovereign courts and the Conseil d'Etat, headed a group of *financiers* who actually performed the functions of the office. The receipts for the annual dues were signed by Le Gruer. They were controlled by the Barbin brothers, agents of the regent, who also controlled the receipts for the *marc d'or* and the *lettres de provision*.

Following protests by officeholders, the terms of the farm were changed back to those in force in the time of Paulet and Saulnier. This change was accomplished by *lettres de cachet* issued on 29 March 1612. The king lowered the price of the farm by 100,000 livres and turned over to the farmers any offices vacated by death. This farm proved as ruinous as the preceding one, and the farmers obtained release from their contract on 18 December 1613.

The reason these three successive farms proved failures was the very success of the annual dues. Officeholders rushed to pay the fee. The jurist Loyseau, author of the *Cinq livres du droit des offices*, was an eyewitness:

At the beginning of January of last year, 1608, during the freeze, I took it in mind, as I was in Paris, to go one night to the residence of the *partisan du droit annuel des Offices*, to talk over some questions concerning this chapter with him. I had chosen the time of my visit badly. Inside, I found a huge troop of officeholders, shoving and pushing to get near anyone who would lend them money: some of them, having just come in from outside, had not taken the time to remove their boots. I noticed that as soon as they were dispatched, they all went straightaway to a nearby Notary to draw up their procuration of resignation, and it seemed to me that they pretended to be walking on ice, for fear of taking a false step, so terrified were they of dying on the way. Finally, at night's end, when the *partisan* had closed his register, I heard a great murmur from those who remained to be dealt with, insisting that their money be accepted, since, as they said, there was no way of knowing that they would not die that very night.

The more the farmer took in in the form of annual dues, the less he got from the *quart denier* on resignations and the less he stood to make on offices vacated by death. The success of the annual dues ruined the farmers. The king was the great beneficiary. For eight years he enjoyed a regular income. The thorough investigations carried out by the farmers, the risk of being haled into court, and the advantages to be had from payment of the annual dues induced many officeholders to regularize their situations. The health of the *parties casuelles* was thus restored, much to the king's benefit.

The failure of the farmers did not spell an end to the annual dues. By decree of the Council on 28 November 1613, the *trésorier des parties casuelles* was made responsible for the levy of the tax, to be collected by *commis* employed by the *bureaux des Finances des généralités;* a regulation issued on 14 February 1614 laid down procedures for checking the collection of the tax.

Beginning in late 1614, however, the annual dues came under general attack. The charge made was that the dues had raised the price of offices so high that they were out of reach of many men of merit and particularly of *gentilshommes*. Furthermore, the dues were said to have made offices hereditary and to have confined them to specific families; to have prevented new men from rising in the social hierarchy, as *avocats* had been able to do in the past, thereby depreciating the profession of *avocat;* and to have forced officeholders to prevaricate so as to recoup the enormous sums expended in purchasing their offices—to mention a few of the charges that were made. Upon request of the nobility and clergy at the Estates General of 1614–15, and despite the opposition of the sovereign courts, the king announced that the annual dues would be eliminated as of 1 January 1618. In the midst of an ensuing war of pamphlets, and despite the dilatory responses of the Assemblée des Notables of Rouen in 1617, the Council issued a decree on 15 January 1618, revoking the exemption from the forty-days clause and eliminating the annual dues. The decree postponed prohibiting the sale of offices.

This left the king to grapple with the disadvantages he had faced earlier. The revolt of the queen mother, followed by that of the Protestants, forced him to win the allegiance of the *parlements* and other officeholders. Thus the annual dues were reinstated by decree of the Council on 31 July 1620, for a period of nine years beginning on 1 January 1621 and ending on 31 December 1629. The terms, however, were not to the liking of the sovereign courts, which took advantage of the situation to obtain a favorable ruling formalized by the declaration of 22 February 1621. In the end, the *maîtres des requêtes* and officers of the sovereign courts, along with the *trésoriers de France* falling under the jurisdiction of the courts (but not the *premiers présidents* and *procureurs généraux* of the *parlements* who had not been covered by the annual dues) were granted coverage under the terms of the original contract with Paulet. Other officeholders were treated more harshly, causing a rift to develop between them and the sovereign courts. The victimized officeholders wailed that they had been fleeced, skinned alive, and driven to despair. On 31 March 1621, the king drove an even deeper wedge into the ranks of his officeholders. All judicial officeholders outside the sovereign courts were required to lend the king one-thirtieth of the assessed value of their offices as a prerequisite to payment of the annual dues; all financial officeholders were obliged to make a loan of one-twentieth the value of the office. These loans were to be repaid in the form of a deduction from the tax on the first resignation. The king thereby imposed greater burdens on the holders of offices of lesser dignity. He appealed to their self-interest and self-esteem, on the grounds that they had a more direct influence on the preservation of law and order and were more directly responsible for the execution of the royal will. With these new rules established, collection of the annual dues could get under way.

At the end of 1629, a rumor spread that the annual dues would be discontinued. Richelieu was hostile to them. In 1625 he had written a memorandum to the king, stating that "Your Majesty . . . should not continue the annual dues and should end the sale of offices, sources of innumerable evils, injurious to Your Majesty's authority and to the pure administration of justice." After the fall of La Rochelle, he read to the king from his memoirs: "The Paulette should not be reestablished when it expires in one year; to abase and moderate those *compagnies* which, by laying claim to sovereignty, come every day into conflict with the good of the kingdom."[8] But the king's "great choice" of April 1630, the resumption of the war in Italy, the disgrace of the queen mother, the flight to foreign lands of the king's brother, the proliferation of rebellions within the kingdom, and the opposition of the Paris *parlement*, which the king was forced to order on 13 May 1631 to keep its fingers out of affairs of state, all obliged the king to reinstate the favor of the annual dues to officeholders. The royal government attempted to obtain substantial loans in return for this favor. This led to difficult negotiations that dragged on till February 1633. Thereafter, one by one, the favor of annual dues under the terms accorded to Paulet was obtained by the *parlement* of Paris (22 August 1631), the Chambre des Comptes of Paris (2 August 1631), nearly all the sovereign courts (25 November 1631), the Chambre des Comptes of Rouen (22 January 1632), and the *trésoriers de France* (5 February 1633). As of 21 December 1630, other officeholders were allowed to pay annual dues on condition that they lend the king twenty percent of the assessed value of their office. Their successors would not be obliged to pay this loan.

When France moved from covert to open warfare in the Thirty Years' War with Louis XIII's declaration of war against Spain on 29 May 1635, and the emperor's declaration of war against Louis XIII in 1636, the king used the annual dues to obtain a huge loan. On 28 October 1636, he extended his favor for a period of six years for all officeholders, from 1 January 1639 to 31 December 1644, without any loan, but on condition that the dues for 1637 and 1638 be paid all at once prior to 15 January 1637; dues for the three following years were to be paid prior to 31 April 1637; and dues for the next three years, prior to 30 July. The sums paid were to be deducted from the tax on the officeholder's first resignation. The four sovereign courts of Paris were exempt from the loan. Exemption was eventually obtained by the other sovereign courts and by the *trésoriers de France*.

The officeholders, however, refused to pay. In 1638, the king won control
of Alsace, cut the Spanish supply line between Milan and the Low Countries,
and in 1639 joined with the Swedes in a two-pronged offensive, the Swedish
forces attacking through Saxony and the French through upper Germany.
To meet the requirements of the war, the king again made use of the annual
dues. A royal declaration of October 1638 nullified the declaration of 28
October 1636. The favor of the annual dues was extended for nine years,
from January 1639 to 31 December 1647. Since the price of offices had
doubled or tripled since 1604, the king increased the 1604 assessments of
the value of offices by one-third: an office assessed at 3,000 livres would
now be assessed at 4,000. The members of the sovereign courts were obliged
to lend the king one-eighth of the value of their offices, the *trésoriers de
France* and officeholders in the *sièges présidiaux*, one-sixth; other officeholders had to lend one-fifth of the value of their offices.

This measure, which was accompanied by the creation of new offices, the
establishment of *gabelles*, regulations on the trades, and taxes of all sorts,
stirred up resistance everywhere, and even rebellion in some cases. The ·
usual negotiations were begun between the sovereign courts and the government. The *parlement* and the Chambre des Comptes of Paris were exempted from the loan on 12 May 1639, and little by little the other sovereign
courts and the *trésoriers de France* also obtained exemptions. The Chambre
des Comptes of Pau was exempted in October 1639, the *parlement* of Bordeaux on 25 February 1641. Once they were exempted from the loan, the
courts confirmed the government's fiscal edicts. Other officeholders were
exempted from the loan in return for the payment of taxes on salary increases: this exemption was obtained on 30 November 1639 by the *officiers
des élections*, the *receveurs* and *contrôleurs généraux des Finances*, and the
trésoriers and *contrôleurs des Ponts et Chaussées;* and on 3 July 1640 by
all other judicial and financial officeholders.

The officeholders put up a stiff resistance, however. They paid nothing.
Receipts of annual dues fell drastically after 1639, even though the king had
appointed, on 30 April 1640, two *huissiers collecteurs du droit annuel* in
each *élection*. As a matter of fact, the annual dues had become so heavy
and the conditions surrounding them so onerous that many officeholders
would no longer pay: they may have hoped that their heirs would be able
to buy exemption from the forty-days clause or even the office itself after
it was vacated by death on better terms.

The king had never stopped granting *survivances* to his loyal supporters,
governors, generals, and *présidents de parlement*. After 1630, however, and
especially after 1635, he frequently sold these survivor's rights or included
them in the privileges of the office in order to facilitate its sale. Many officeholders were granted *hérédités* in exchange for cash. On 6 December
1638, he confirmed all *hérédités* and *survivances* in exchange for payment
of various taxes. Then, in October 1641 he revoked them all, but reinstated
them on 25 January 1642; however, the holders of *hérédités* had to pay

permanent annual dues to the king of one-sixtieth the value of the office, and the holders of *survivances* dues of one-hundredth the value of the office; everyone had to pay dues of one-tenth the value for *mutations*. These offices took on the character of fiefs: "Hereditarily held in perpetuity, [they] shall be as property and heritage in the *mouvance* of our royal Seigneurie and heredity."

From 1604 until about 1640, most officeholders remained loyal to the king and kept the populace loyal in order to have the right to pay the annual dues. The sovereign courts wanted not only to have the right to pay the dues but to have it on better terms than the other officeholders, with whom they split, thus weakening the "fourth estate" of *gens de robe*, which aspired to govern the kingdom. The courts therefore bowed before the sovereign and registered his *édits bursaux* and even his *édits politiques*.

The enormous needs created by the series of wars led the government to change the character of the annual dues. Henri IV had used them as a regular income. After 1620, with the introduction of the system of loans required as prerequisites to the payment of dues, loans that were subsequently repaid by deductions from the tax on resignations, the whole arrangement was reduced to a mere expedient for raising revenues in the short run at the cost of reducing the future receipts of the *parties casuelles*. With the involvement of the kingdom in the Thirty Years' War, reliance on this expedient became more and more obvious. Fiscal demands on officeholders grew to the point where, by the end of Louis XIII's reign, the question of annual dues, coupled with that of the creation of new offices, gave rise to discontent, resistance, and rebellion throughout the kingdom. The issue of the annual dues became one of the many factors that contributed to the Fronde.

In October 1646 the king revoked all *survivances* and *hérédités* previously granted and required the former beneficiaries to pay annual dues. Offices that had not been assessed in 1605 for payment of annual dues were to be assessed now. *Survivances* were retained by all officeholders in the *petites* and *grandes chancelleries; greffiers* kept their *hérédités* along with the domanial character of their office, except for those in the Bureaux des Finances, the *élections*, the salt warehouses, and in cities and communities, whose offices were declared casual and subject to the annual dues.

Granted in 1638 for a period of nine years, the permission to pay the annual dues expired on 31 December 1647. As usual, the government delayed renewal of the grant as long as possible in order to oblige the *parlement* to confirm the *édits bursaux*, and *parlement* simulated strenuous opposition in order to obtain the annual dues on the best possible terms. The king again attempted to drive a wedge into the ranks of the officeholders. On 13 March 1648, he granted permission to pay the annual dues to all financial officeholders in exchange for a loan of one-sixth the value of the office according to the 1638 assessment for officers of the *présidiaux* and one-fifth for other officers. When it seemed that *parlement* would not come through, the king's Council granted permission to pay the annual dues in exchange for elimination of four years' salary payments in a declaration issued on 29 April 1648. Only the *parlement* of Paris was to receive the permission for free. Members of the *parlement* recalled how the king had gained control of the situation in 1621 and 1630 by dividing the officeholders, granting permission to pay the annual dues on different terms. *Parlement* responded with an *arrêt d'union* creating the *assemblée de la Chambre Saint-Louis* on 13 May. On 18 May, the Council eliminated the annual dues. In order to get them back, *parlement* put forth a series of increasingly exorbitant political demands as a way of forcing the court to act. Just as *parlement* was issuing its 31 July declaration prohibiting the sovereign courts from further meetings, the Council granted it permission to pay the annual dues on the same terms as in 1604, the most advantageous that could have been hoped for. But *parlement* had gone too far. It stuck by its resistance, and its example led to a general revolt, the Fronde.

After the Fronde, the allotted period for enjoyment of exemption from the forty-days clause through payment of the annual dues elapsed, on 31 December 1656. On 15 January 1657, in a declaration registered *en audience de France*, the king accorded officeholders the right to pay the annual dues until 31 December 1665. He exempted them from payment of any loan or advance, some in compensation for services rendered and taking their gratitude for granted, others because they had bought salary increases from the king. *Apanagés* and *engagistes* [see below for an explanation of these terms— trans.] were denied the right to collect annual dues, this being "one of the principal marks of sovereignty"; officeholders under them were to pay their annual dues to the king. Exceptions were made for the queen mother and the duc d'Orléans. The declaration of October 1646 revoking *hérédités* and *survivances* was reaffirmed. The regulation of 6 October 1638 was to be observed. Offices for receiving the annual dues would be established in cities under the jurisdiction of the *parlement* and Cour des Aides of Paris in which *généralités* were established. The declaration of 15 March 1657 reestablished the rights of the *apanagés* and *engagistes*, since it had proved impossible to reimburse them. Another declaration, issued on 16 August 1657, reestablished all *hérédités* and *survivances* and, in addition, the *survivance* of the *maréchaussée*. It was decided in March 1659 that the beneficiary would pay a tax of one-tenth the assessed value of the office at the time of *mutations* and resignations.

An edict of December 1656, along with regulations issued on 1 and 6 April 1658, dealt with the *marc d'or* that had to be paid by all officeholders upon receipt of their provisions and that had been granted in perpetuity to the Ordre du Saint-Esprit. The amount of this fee was doubled, ranging from 3,024 livres for the *premier président* of the *parlement* of Paris to 42 livres for the lowliest notaries, *sergents*, and *huissiers*. Four offices, designated *secrétaires du roi, gardes et dépositaires des quittances du marc d'or des offices de France*, were created on 19 March 1657 to receive these payments, each of the four secretaries filling the post for a quarter.

Louis XIV, in the first few years of his personal government, worked diligently to reduce the disadvantages associated with the sale of offices: namely, the excessively high price of offices, which put them out of reach of many *gentilshommes* and men of talent, and the de facto appropriation of offices, which deprived the king of the right to choose his own officers. In December 1665, all offices were freshly assessed, a maximum price was set for each, and the king reserved the right to choose the *premiers présidents*, the *procureurs*, and the *avocats généraux* of the sovereign courts. In a declaration issued on 27 November 1671, the king reserved the right to choose all officeholders; the men chosen by the king were supposed to pay the price of the office to the *trésorier des parties casuelles*, who would then remit the sum either to the heirs of the defunct officeholder or to the person to whom they had promised the office. The widows and heirs of deceased officeholders frequently got around these measures, however, by raising objections to the affixing of the seal to the new nominee's *lettres de provision*, thereby preventing "provision" of the office to the person chosen by the king for a period of some years. The price of offices was increased by one-sixth on 7 November 1676, in exchange for a forced loan in the form of a salary increase, but, with the advent of peace, the price was reduced in October 1678 to the 1665 level.

Every nine years, the king regularly renewed the exemption from the forty-days clause, provided the annual dues were paid each year. In order to be allowed to pay the dues, however, the members of the sovereign courts were forced, during periods of war, to pay for an increase in salary with each renewal, or in other words, to underwrite a series of forced loans. Other officers were also obliged at each renewal to make a loan to the king of either one-sixth or one-fifth of the official value of their offices.

In the hard times that accompanied the War of the Spanish Succession during the nine years' grant of permission to pay the annual dues accorded in the declaration of 27 August 1701, and expiring on 31 December 1710, an edict of December 1709, registered by the *parlement* of Paris on 14 December 1709, eliminated the loan and the annual dues, placed all the offices of the realm on the same footing, and accorded the *survivance* to all as of 31 December 1710, provided that an annual payment of one-sixteenth the value of the office was made. In return, the officeholders, their widows, children, heirs, or executors were allowed to dispose of the office "as of something belonging to them . . . and to secure . . . the property of the aforesaid." The prices fixed for offices were increased to allow the owners to sell them at whatever price they wished. Excepted from this ruling and obliged to pay annual dues as before were the offices and domains of the duc d'Orléans, the offices of pledged (*engagé*) domains, admiralty offices falling under the *revenus casuels* of the Grand Admiral, artillery offices, and offices to which nominations were made by the chancellor or *garde des Sceaux*, as well as offices that paid their *redevance annuelle* to the *receveur* of the Hôtel de Ville of Paris.[9]

Throughout his reign, the king also toyed with the *survivances* and *hé-rédités*, periodically eliminating them and then restoring them in exchange for payment to meet the necessities of war. The *hérédités* and *survivances* were revoked on 30 May 1661, excepting offices of the *grande* and *petite chancellerie* and court clerks (save those of the bureaux des Finances, elections, salt warehouses, cities and communities). *Procureurs* were deprived of *hérédité* by the edict of 1664. At the beginning of the Dutch War, the king reestablished the *survivance de la maréchaussée* by declaration of 16 March 1672 in exchange for a payment of two quarters' salary; this was renewed on 7 January 1690. On 23 March 1672, he reaffirmed the *hérédité* for the notaries and scribes, reestablished it for the *procureurs*, and reaffirmed it for *huissiers*, *sergents*, and *archers*, in exchange for payment. This *hérédité* was reaffirmed in July 1690 on the same terms. All *hérédités* and *survivances* previously granted, whether to categories of officeholders or to individuals or upon creation of specific offices, were reaffirmed in August 1701 in exchange for cash. Other *hérédités* or *survivances* were granted in 1706 and 1708 to various officeholders.[10] Finally, in 1709 came the *grande survivance*.

Louis XIV clearly saw the need to abolish the sale of offices, took measures to reduce the harm that it caused, but was overwhelmed by the needs of war.

The regency continued the *grande survivance générale* of 1709. It was not until 9 August 1722 that a declaration issued at Versailles and registered on 5 September by the *parlement* of Paris revoked this *survivance* and reestablished the annual dues. Members of the Council and of the sovereign courts were exempt and retained their *survivances*, but at each *mutation* were required to pay the *droit de survivance* plus a surcharge of one-third. All other officeholders had to pay one-third of the loan and annual dues in advance in each three-year period during the nine years of the grant. Their widows, children, or heirs had to pay a fee of one-eighth the value of the office within six months of the death of the titulary; the fee was doubled if not paid within two years, and tripled beyond that. Those "provided" with newly created offices were supposed to pay the first third of the annual dues during the two months of *provisions*. Any who did not pay the annual dues while the offices were next open would not be received during the nine-year period of the grant, "though they would be allowed the faculty of disposing of the office upon payment of twice the resignation fee and provided they lived for forty days from the date of approval of the receipt for the aforesaid double fee, pursuant to the regulation of 1638; in case of death within the said forty days, their offices shall be taxed vacant to our profit."[11]

Any offices created from this date forth, whether as hereditary offices or offices granted with rights of reversion, would require payment of one-eighth of one-third of their basic cost with a surcharge of 2 sols per livre plus an additional one-quarter. Officeholders under the jurisdiction of pledged domains subject to the loan would be required to pay this loan to the king before being granted permission to pay the annual dues by the *engagiste*, in addition to which they had to pay a one-tenth fee upon nomination. Exceptions were made for officeholders under the duc d'Orléans, the regent, the admiralty (for offices nominated by the Grand Admiral), the chancelleries, and the regions of Artois, Flanders, and Alsace controlled by France.

From this point on, the annual dues were renewed regularly for one nine-year period after another. Beginning in 1740, the declaration of renewal was registered in the Cour des Aides of Paris. This registration by the sovereign courts would seem to have established the annual dues on a more solid footing. A decree of the Council was still required each year to "open" the annual dues, however. Thus, even with registration, the king could halt collection of the annual dues if he was not satisfied with his officeholders.

The loan in exchange for which permission to pay the annual dues was granted was a heavy burden on the officeholders. There were frauds. Some officers feigned resignation and had receipts for payment of the *droit de mutation* issued under aliases. The supposed *résignataires* made no attempt to have themselves "provided" offices, and the would-be *résignants* continued to enjoy the benefits of office. When they died, their offices were not declared vacant, even though they had not made the loan to the king and had not paid the annual dues. On 12 January 1751, the Council issued a decree requiring all bearers of resignation receipts to apply for provision within six months.[12]

The royal administration was benevolent. *Lettres de provision* sometimes allowed *résignataires* to execute their office concurrently with the *résignant* or after his voluntary resignation or even his death. A council decree of 25 November 1755 stated that in these cases the *résignants* were to continue to pay the loan and annual dues until they had ceased to execute the office.[13]

Many widows, children, heirs, creditors, contractors, or owners of offices, held for them by virtue either of payment of the annual dues or of rights of *survivance* or *hérédité*, held on to their offices indefinitely without applying for provision, no doubt while waiting for a member of the family to reach the age required for the office in question. A Council decree of 12 September 1748 allowed them a period of thirty years from the death of the officeholder to name a living person, in order to allow the king to collect his *droits de mutation*. Beyond that period, the office was supposed to be declared vacant to the king's profit.

The Edict of Versailles of February 1771, which was registered in *audience de France* on 23 May and by the Chambre des Comptes of Paris on 21 June, while reaffirming the principle that the king is free to choose the successor of any officeholder since the officeholder and his heirs can lay claim only to the "*finance*" of the office but not to its "*corps*," set the terms of a new assessment of the offices of the realm by declaration of the "*propriétaires d'offices*,"[14] who were to determine the value of their own offices. This would become the price of the office in case of reimbursement by the king. The king announced his intention to eliminate a large number of offices. He got rid of all *survivances* and *hérédités* and made all the offices of the realm subject to the loan and payment of annual dues. The king expressly reserved the right to dispose of offices left vacant by death, resignation, or otherwise, by giving them to persons he deemed suitable (article 18).

As of November 1772, the loan and annual dues were replaced by a one percent tax on the new assessment, and the resignation and nomination dues were set at one twenty-fourth the value of the office plus two sols per livre, to be doubled or tripled in the cases set forth in the various edicts and declarations. With allusion to the "Paulette," the one percent tax was known as the "seurette."

The *présidents* and *conseillers* of the higher courts, the *présidents*, *maîtres*, *correcteurs*, and *auditeurs* of the Chambres des Comptes, the *avocats généraux du roi*, the *procureurs généraux du roi*, the *greffiers en chef* of these courts and chambers, the *intendants des Finances* and *du Commerce*, the *maîtres des requêtes*, the *gardes du Trésor royal*, and the *trésoriers des parties casuelles* held on to their *survivances*, according to the declaration of August 1722, with a *droit de mutation* of one-sixteenth plus 2 sols per livre, with double or triple payment required in certain cases.

The king reserved the right to nominate candidates for his offices and promised indemnity to the *apanagés* and *engagistes* who were stripped of the right of nomination. This did not apply to the duc d'Orléans, the first prince of the blood.

In letters patent dated 27 February 1780, and registered by the *parlement* of Paris on 29 February, whose purpose was "to meet the continuing needs of the war," the king offered his officeholders the possibility of buying back the right to pay annual dues for a period of eight years in exchange for payment of six years' dues prior to 1 October 1780. This was therefore a sort of loan at interest. There was a suggestion that this redemption would be renewed. Since the annual collection would be diminished, it would be possible to eliminate some of the provincial collectors of annual dues and other fees owing to the casual incomes treasury. The redemption was supposed to remain in effect through 31 December 1788. Officeholders who did not participate were to be subject to payment of twice the normal mutation fee and twice the normal annual dues for all years in arrears, and this obligation would apply to their widows and heirs in case of their death. If the widows and heirs did not pay all these debts, the king reserved the right to "provide" the office himself. Anyone who lent money to an officeholder for the purpose of making this redemption would be entitled to a special privilege and to preference over all other creditors against the price of the office involved. The appanages of the king's brothers and of his cousin, the duc d'Orléans, were excepted.

In actuality, not all officeholders made the redemption, and collection of the one percent tax was continued.

Offices at the Disposal of Subjects of the King

The king granted certain of his subjects the right to choose many officeholders. Officeholders so chosen remained officers of the king. But the king left the responsibility of nominating and "providing" these offices up to someone else. A subject nominated a person for an office when he designated a candidate to the king, who then had royal *lettres de provision* issued. A subject "provided" when he issued his own *lettres de provision* to his candidate.

Officeholders

Most of the *grands officiers* of the Crown, the *grands officiers* of the house-holds of queens, princes, and princesses, certain provincial governors, and some lesser officeholders were granted the right to nominate or provide offices.

The *grands officiers* of the Crown were regarded as sovereign chiefs in their departments under the king's authority, and as such they were allowed to recruit certain of their own subordinates. By the beginning of the seventeenth century, the chancellor no longer disposed of chancellery offices (*maîtres des requêtes, grands audienciers, contrôleurs de l'audience de France*). The constable and marshals of France no longer nominated the officers of the gendarmerie (*commissaires, contrôleurs, payeurs*). The *grand maître des Eaux et Forêts* no longer had rights over the *forestiers*. And the *grands officiers* of the king's household no longer controlled the major household posts, which the king reserved for himself.

However, each marshal of France still controlled one *commissaire des guerres* and a few other offices. The *grand colonel* of France or colonel general of the infantry, the duc d'Epernon, could nominate candidates for all standing regimental offices in both peacetime and wartime until 1605. After 1605, Henri IV reserved for himself the right to choose the *mestres de camp* of these regiments and alternated with the *grand colonel* in nominating candidates to the companies of the guard regiment. The *grand colonel* continued to nominate the captains of the other regiments of infantry. Admirals nominated candidates to all judicial offices under their jurisdiction: *lieutenants, avocats, procureurs*, and *greffiers*. The *grand maître de l'artillerie* nominated candidates to all offices under him.

The *grands officiers* of the king's household retained control of the "*menus offices.*" The grand chamberlain chose the *gentilshommes de la Chambre*. The *grand maître de France* controlled most of the officeholders in the "seven offices" *de bouche:* pantlers, cupbearers, and cooks "*de bouche*"; pantlers, cupbearers, and cooks "*du commun*"; and cooks. It may be that the *grand maître* satisfied himself in many cases with choosing the "chefs" and left the recruitment of their "aides" and "sommiers" to them. The *grand prévôt de l'Hôtel* could choose his own *lieutenants* and *procureurs*. He would name them to the king, but his *greffiers, huissiers*, and *archers* he provided himself. The Master of the Royal Hunt and the Master of the Wolf Hunt chose the huntmasters for the entire kingdom. Choice was limited by the rule that only nobles could occupy certain offices—*gentilshommes de la Chambre, gentilshommes* of the two companies of Cent-Gentils-hommes, *gentilshommes* of the hunt, squires of the stable, and archers of the guard—and by the rule that only commoners could be selected for certain others, such as the "seven offices *de bouche*."

The *grands officiers* presented their candidates to the king through letters of nomination. For provincial offices, the king then issued *lettres de provision*. For household offices, he would issue a letter of retainer drawn up by one of the four secretaries of state and sealed with the royal seal. In addition, the candidate's nomination was certified by inscription on the payroll at the behest of the *grand officier* with the approval of the king. Only the *grand maître de l'artillerie* had the power to approve his own payroll. *Grands officiers* personally received their nominees for the oath. They also accepted resignations before they were turned over to the king or chancellor.

The *grands officiers* exacted a high price for their nominations, provisions, and permission to resign.

The household offices of the queen, of Monsieur, the king's brother, and of the princes and princesses of the blood were accorded similar concessions and brought the same high prices.

As the king's *lieutenants*, the provincial governors often named the governors of the cities under them as well as the captains of fortified castles and citadels. Some provincial governors had rights over some or all of the offices in their provinces. The governor of Dauphiné himself provided practically all royal offices in the king's stead: captaincies of cities and castles as well as judicial and financial posts (excepting those in the *parlement* and Chambre des Comptes, the *trésoriers de France*, and the *receveur général des Finances*). The governor maintained his own *parties casuelles*, entrusted to the *receveur général des Finances*. These rights were reaffirmed on 14 July 1612 for the benefit of the comte de Soissons, then governor, who also gained the right to exempt officeholders from the forty-days clause and to levy the annual dues for his own benefit. The king's governor and *lieutenant général* for Burgundy and Bresse always enjoyed the right to nominate candidates for the offices of *prévôts généraux* and *particuliers* as well as to name their *lieutenants* in Burgundy and in the counties of Mâconnais, Auxerrois, Bar-sur-Seine, Bresse, Bugey, and Valromey. Certain officeholders had the power, inherent in their offices, to nominate candidates to subordinate positions. For example, the *maître particulier ancien des Eaux et Forêts* of Troyes nominated men to serve as sworn master woodmen and charcoalmen to the city.

The *Apanagés* and *Engagistes*

These subjects of the king could nominate candidates to and provide royal offices on lands and *seigneuries* belonging to the Crown's domain.

An appanage was a concession of a fief of the Crown to a child of France. Property in the domain was transferred to the child of France under the law of inheritance, as his share in his father's patrimony. In the absence of male heirs, the appanage reverted to the king. The king's Council and various jurists identified the appanages with the lands assigned to widowed queens as their dower and to the daughters of France as their dowry out of respect for the royal blood, since these lands were actually regarded as pledged as security for the *deniers dotaux*.

The *engagement* or pledge was a sale of part of the royal domain to a private individual. Since the Moulins ordinance of 1566, such sales were subject to a permanent option of repurchase, because the ordinance had declared the royal domain to be inalienable except for the needs of war.

Titularies of appanages were known as *apanagés*, and of pledged lands as *engagistes*. The extent of the rights of *apanagés* and *engagistes* depended entirely on the king's will or on the agreement struck with each individual.

In lands given as appanage or assimilated thereto, Queen Marguerite, the first wife of Henri IV, enjoyed from 1578 until her death in 1615 the right to provide ordinary offices and to nominate to extraordinary offices attaching to the granted territory: the duchy of Valois, the counties of Senlis, Agenais, Condomois, Rouergue, Lauraguais, the judgeships of Albigeois, Ryeux, Rivière-Verdun, the castellany of Esson, and the *seigneuries* of Laon and Château-Thierry.

The dowager queen Louise, widow of Henri III, had the right to provide all the offices of the duchy of Berry.

Marie de Médicis, widow of Henri IV, received as her dower fifteen *seigneuries* with the right of provision to all offices: the duchy of Bourbonnais, the county of la Marche, the duchy of Auvergne, the county of Auvergne and Clermont, the barony of La Tour, the county of Forez, the county of Nantes, and the castellany of Guérande, among others.

Gaston d'Orléans, the brother of Louis XIII, received as his appanage in 1626 on the occasion of his wedding the duchies of Orléans and Chartres and the county of Blois, with the right of provision to ordinary offices, except for the *prévôts des maréchaux* and their *lieutenants*, *greffiers*, and *archers*. His appanage was extended in 1627 with the addition of the county of Limours, in 1628 with the *seigneurie* of Montargis, and in 1630 with the duchy of Valois.

The rights of *engagistes* varied. Some had full rights of provision to all offices. In general these were the ones to whom lands had been pledged prior to the ordinance of 1566. These lands were engaged as fiefs, in perpetuity, with no repurchase option. During the reigns of Henri IV and Louis XIII such *engagistes* included the duc de Nemours, the duc de Nevers, peer of France, and the duc de Liancourt, *premier écuyer du roi*.

Most *engagistes* were entitled to provide ordinary offices and to nominate candidates for extraordinary offices. In this category during the same period were the duc de Guise and the duc de Mayenne, the sieur de Vitry, captain of the bodyguard, the Montpensiers, the Longuevilles, the duc de Wurtemberg, and, somewhat later, the queen, Marie de Médicis, etc.

Other *engagistes* enjoyed only the right to nominate candidates to both ordinary and extraordinary offices; still others had only the right to provide ordinary offices; and others only the right to nominate to ordinary offices. Finally, some individuals had control over offices without having any rights over the corresponding lands. For example, the family of the ducs d'Halluin, sieurs de Piennes, had been granted as a pledge control over the offices of *sénéchaux*, *alloués*, and *procureurs du roi* in nine jurisdictions of Brittany (Vannes, Brest, Dinan, etc.).

The possessors of the alienated portion of the domain organized their *parties casuelles* in the same way as the king, and after the Paulet edict sometimes farmed them out. They sold offices left vacant by death, traded in resignations, subjected their officeholders to the forty-days clause, exempted them from it in exchange for cash, and peddled *survivances*. When the Paulet edict was issued, the officeholders included within contracts for pledged lands belonging to the royal domain were excluded from its provisions. Upon request of the officeholders serving under several of these possessors, however, the king granted the latter permission to bestow upon their officers exemption from the forty-days clause and to collect the annual dues for their own benefit. Among those granted such permission in 1608 were the duc de Nevers, the prince de Joinville, and the queen, Marie de Médicis; in 1611, it was granted to Queen Marguerite. The fate of officeholders attached to the alienated portions of the royal domain matched that of other officeholders between 1614 and 1618 and, again, between 1618 and 1620.

The edict reestablishing the annual dues on 31 July 1620 included all officeholders under the control of *apanagés* and *engagistes*, whom the king allowed to appropriate the proceeds of the loan. He allowed their officeholders to pay the annual dues to the royal *parties casuelles* and authorized the *engagistes* to recover the amounts due them from the royal treasury. Offices were reassessed in 1621. In 1630 offices attached to the alienated domain were subject to the same fate as other offices. On 22 October 1638, however, a declaration was issued that accomplished a veritable *coup d'état* at the expense of the *engagistes*. The king reserved for himself the sums generated by the loans and annual dues from all extraordinary offices and from those ordinary offices that had been created since the concession or pledge of portions of the royal domain.

The *Seigneurs* and the Cities

Seigneurs having high, middle, or low powers of justice [see vol. 1, p. 507—trans.] also had serving under them judicial, financial, and ministerial officers. They chose men to fill their offices, sold offices left vacant by death, gave *lettres de provision*, accepted resignations with or without the forty-days clause, and gave or sold rights of survivorship. The sale of offices assured officeholders that they would not be summarily removed from their posts. In small *seigneuries* whose relatively unimportant offices were not sold, officeholders lived in fear of being removed. *Seigneurs* often farmed out their financial and ministerial offices: *receveurs*, *tabellions*, *greffiers*, and *sergents*.[15]

Cities, too, had officers, under the *corps de ville:* these included the *procureur syndic*, the *clerk de ville* or *greffier*, the treasurer, the captain of the watch, and the *commissaire de police*, as well as "domanial" or "police" officers, such as cloth measurers, leather inspectors, charcoal weighers and warehousemen, corn weighers, wine inspectors, etc. The *corps de ville*, made up of *échevins*, *consuls*, or *jurats*, depending on the place, either bestowed these offices and responsibilities itself or nominated a candidate to the king when the office was a royal one, such as that of the *procureur syndic* of Bordeaux.[16]

Consequences

In the opinion of contemporaries, this series of concessions made by the king to certain of his subjects created grave dangers for the king's power— from treason, first of all. The *parlement* of Paris and the Estates General were fearful lest kidnappers or assassins pay their way into the king's household service among his officers and lest the governors of frontier fortresses who had bought their posts be corrupted by foreign princes. The history of the wars of the time shows that certain of these officers, at any rate, were indeed subject to peculiar weaknesses.

There was another danger: the spread of rebellion. Anyone entitled to "provide" or even merely to nominate to offices at once became a power to be reckoned with. Anyone ambitious for a post and any officer eager to pass his position on to a son could easily become the devoted servant of such a person. Such sentiments could reinforce bonds of fealty or create bonds of clienteleship. These sentiments were not limited solely to the *noblesse d'épée* but gradually overtook the *noblesse de robe* and *de finance*, as well as the world of merchants and shippers and journeymen craftsmen. If the man in control of coveted offices happened to be a prince of the blood, he was all the more likely to attract followers, because a rebel of such august rank always made peace with the king in the end, with favorable terms for his *fidèles*, clients, and partisans.

Thus, from the king's entourage down to the most miserable of peasants, the system of offices helped strengthen chains of interest and influence. The king's brother, Monsieur, the queens, and the various princes and princesses all controlled household offices. The *grands offices* of the Crown almost always remained within certain lineages. Since many lesser offices were controlled by the men in these positions, they could acquire over the space of several generations a considerable clientele of wealthy and ambitious dependents.

The princes of the blood and *grands seigneurs* controlled many royal offices in the provinces. As military commanders, they had the right to name regimental and company officers. As provincial governors, they frequently enjoyed the right to nominate the governors of fortresses. They also controlled many judicial and financial offices. Among the holders of these offices they recruited many devoted supporters, even though these were ostensibly men responsible for executing the king's wishes and filling the royal coffers. In addition to these clients, great nobles always enjoyed support in their own provinces—the Longueville in Normandy, the Montmorency in Languedoc, the Guise in Provence, the d'Epernon in Guyenne, the Grammont in Béarn and Labord—from a host of families, noble and common, sword and gown, who, traditionally, generation after generation, remained "pledged," "obligated," or "devoted" to them and served them better than they served the king—or, rather, served the king through the agency of the great noble.

These allies, *fidèles*, and clients were in many cases themselves possessors of alienated portions of the royal domain and *seigneurs justiciers* with influence over other royal officeholders, over their seigneurial officers, over the *bourgeois* of small cities and towns, and even over the peasants themselves, who aspired to the offices of every rank that pullulated in the very depths of the countryside. These *seigneurs* dominated their vassals and *censitaires* and above all their peasants. Through their officers, they could make life tolerable or impossible. On occasion, the *seigneur* could exert a powerful economic influence as a great landowner able to offer employment and to provide certain products not produced in the region. Many took their seigneurial duties seriously. They protected their men, thereby insuring their own feudal and seigneurial dues and farm leases. They armed their tenants against the royal tax collectors, against bivouacking royal troops, and, during the civil wars, against all sorts of armed bands, and protected the harvests and livestock of their men. They represented their men before various judicial bodies and, if need be, before the king's Council itself. Nicolas Romé, baron of the barony and *haute justice* of Bec-Crespin in upper Normandy, exacted from the Rouen *parlement* in September 1610 exemption for all his tenants and vassals from all tolls and *corvées* throughout Normandy. In 1611 he took up the defense of residents of four of his parishes who had been designated by the *élus* of Montivilliers to participate in draining the ditches of Le Harve. To be sure, peasants may well have continued to feel hatred and envy to the bottoms of their hearts against men of superior "estate." But it was in their interest to follow their lord, even into rebellion, if only to be in a position to turn the tables when they had the upper hand. It was rarely in the interest of peasants to be for the king if their lord was against, given that royal troops pillaged as much as any other, so that the peasant without local protection was sure to be the victim.

At times unified fronts did form against the king: humiliated *gentils-hommes*, officeholders hurt by the creation of new offices and the obligation to pay forced loans, city-dwellers overwhelmed by taxes and ruined by monopolies, and peasants crushed by the burden of taxation were always ready for revolt. All that was needed was for a prince of the blood to give the signal and whole provinces would rise en masse, tied together by family links, fealties, clientele relationships, and by the bonds between orders and "estates" created by the system of offices. This is the best explanation of the ease with which princes found support, fortifications, troops, money from the royal coffers, supplies, and political theorists in all their undertakings against royal power not only in the time of the League but also during the minority of Louis XIII and the Fronde. This also explains in part why the king, too, had to have his own chains of *créatures*, *fidèles*, and clients, to stand up to the rebellions, and why he had to seek means such as the Paulette to secure the loyalty of the officers under his control.

Notes

1. Edict of 23 May 1771. Isambert, vol. 23, p. 515.
2. Loyseau, *Offices*, pp. 13–14.
3. In "La Prise de la ville de Bergerac et entière dissipation des Croquans par le duc de La Valette, avec la Semaine du Bureau d'adresse. Du Bureau d'Adresse, au grand Coq, rue de la Calandre, sortant au Marché-Neuf, à Paris. MDCXXXVII. Avec privilège."
4. For justice, the chancellor of France; for war, the constable of France, eliminated in 1627, the marshals of France, the admiral of France, the *grand colonel* of France, a post raised to the status of Crown office in 1584 for d'Epernon, and the *grand maître de l'Artillerie* of France.
5. The grand chamberlain of France, the *grand maître* of France, the *grand aumônier* of France, the *grand écuyer* of France, and the *grand veneur;* the *grand prévôt de l'Hôtel du Roi;* and the *grand maître des Eaux et Forêts*.
6. The *marc d'or* was a fee for swearing an oath that had to be paid before the *lettres de provision* could be sealed.
7. Archives Nationales, A.D. 9, 451: Instructions to the *commis* regarding collection of the loan and annual dues for the year 1724.
8. R. Mousnier, *La vénalité des offices sous Henri IV et Louis XIII*, 2d ed. (Paris: PUF, 1971), pp. 291–92.
9. Archives Nationales, A.D. 9, 449.
10. Ibid.
11. Bibliothèque National, F. 23622 (640), 8p.
12. Archives Nationales, A.D. 9, 452.
13. Ibid.
14. The Chambre des Comptes corrected: "The owners of the prices of offices."
15. Concerning the seignorial judges, see Mousnier, *Institutions*, vol. 1, pp. 527–28; and *Vénalité*, pp. 325–31.
16. See vol. 1, p. 570.

6   The *Commissaires*

The king could have certain functions performed by commission. The men designated to carry them out were then called *commissaires*, a category that included ambassadors, members of the State Council, sealkeepers (*gardes des Sceaux*), *surintendants des Finances, gouverneurs* and *lieutenants généraux des provinces*, and *intendants des provinces*.

The king could confer offices by commission. During the troubles with the League, some offices in the *parlement* of Paris—*conseillers* and *procureur général*—were not attributed as offices but rather exercised by royal commission. Under normal circumstances, the posts of *premier président* and *présidents des Chambres des Enquêtes* were exercised by commission.

Finally, the king could, at any time, commission one of his officers to do something not included under his normal responsibilities, or have him carry out one of his usual responsibilities outside his normal jurisdiction, or have him carry out one of his usual responsibilities within his normal jurisdiction but in preference to any of his colleagues. For example, it was part of the normal responsibility of *maîtres des requêtes* to make inspection tours or journeys every year. The king could take advantage of their travels and entrust to them the task of publishing or enforcing some provision of an edict or Council decree, opening a farm office, organizing a tax levy, taking action against criminals, etc. The *trésoriers de France* were allowed to apportion and levy the *tailles* only if they received an annual commission from the Council to do so. On 19 June 1635, the king sent a commission to the *lieutenant général* in the *sénéchaussée* and *siège présidial* of Lyon "to look into the books of all the merchants of the city in order to ascertain the property of Spaniards and other subjects of foreign princes," when he began "overt" warfare against Spain. On 21 June 1635, the *procureur du roi* of the jurisdiction of Mantes was named *commissaire du régalement des tailles* (i.e., for the apportionment of the *tailles*) at Péronne, because the king did not trust his financial officers there. On 6 December 1640, we find three *tresoriers généraux de France* at Moulins, as *commissaires généraux* sent by the king to oversee supplies for his troops in the *généralité* of Moulins. On 16 April 1643, we find that the king chose several *conseillers* of the *parlement* of Bordeaux as *commissaires* for the purpose of investigating who had altered and shaved the coin of the realm.

Jurists took great pains to distinguish between ordinary and extraordinary commissions. Ostensibly, ordinary commissions were commissions to execute the responsibilities of an officer. Thus members of the State Council, sealkeepers, and *surintendants des Finances* had ordinary commissions. Extraordinary commissions were commissions to execute a function not permanent in nature, such as an embassy or a captaincy, as well as functions pertaining to objects other than ordinary justice, such as the function of governor, governors being commissioned to use force.

Men who performed functions that had first been treated as commissions before being raised to the status of offices continued to be called *commissaires* even though they had ceased to be such according to the strict definition. Among these were the *commissaires aux requêtes* of the palace, the *commissaires des guerres*, and the *commissaires du Châtelet* of Paris, the ancestors of the present-day *commissaires de police*.

The *commissaire* was regarded as a sort of *procureur*. Thus he was required to receive letters of commission from the *grande chancellerie de France*, signed by a secretary of state and sealed with the Great Seal in yellow wax on parchment. The commission was supposed to list in detail all the powers and functions entrusted to him, in the same way as the *procureur*'s procuration.

The *commissaire* was then supposed to publish his letters of commission *en justice* at the place where he intended to exercise his powers, since no one was required to recognize or to obey a *commissaire* if he could claim to be unaware of that *commissaire*'s powers. The regular judge in a particular place could even prohibit the *commissaire* from exercising his commission and inform against any *commissaire* who might undertake to perform a public act without first having published the letters detailing his powers. Provincial governors, therefore, had their letters confirmed by the *parlement* having jurisdiction over their province, because publication by *parlement* served as public notification, making publication of their commission in the lower courts unnecessary. Governors even used to take an oath before *parlement*, but this was for the purpose of being seated and had nothing to do with their commission. The *intendants des provinces* were despised by the *parlements* and therefore had their commissions published instead by the *présidiaux* having jurisdiction over their *généralité*.

The letters of commission defined and narrowly circumscribed the powers of the *commissaire*. He was bound to abide scrupulously by the terms of his commission. Just as the *procureur* was constrained by his procuration, so the *commissaire* was not allowed to go beyond the limits spelled out in the letter, which he was bound to interpret in the narrowest possible sense, "for this reason, that commissions are specific, extraordinary and burdensome charges. By contrast, the charge of an officer is general, regular, and a boon, and he is allowed to extend his powers in the light of considerations of equity and justice, since the law or edict creating his office cannot have foreseen every particular occurrence." [1] A *commissaire* had no power beyond that specifically and expressly granted to him. In affairs of state, it was deemed undesirable for any *commissaire* to exceed the limits of his commission, even if his purpose was to serve the public good; even if successful, anyone who did so deserved to be repudiated.

A *commissaire*'s acts and orders had no intrinsic validity, unlike the acts and orders of a judge. They were valid only if his commission specifically granted him the powers required, except in the case of *grands commissaires* such as ambassadors or governors, whose commissions were a matter of public record.

Jurisdiction over cases in the courts was sometimes assigned by special commission. Such assignments were often at variance with common law and therefore required knowledge of the details of cases already in progress or else had to reflect the king's express will and personal orders. The king, being all-powerful, could overrule judges, take cases away from any court, and entrust them to any person he wished.

Commissions carried with them no definite rank. But *commissaires* did enjoy the privileges of rank while performing their commissions. They were then even more worthy of respect than officeholders, because they represented the king in a more direct and personal way. According to canon law, "omnis delegatus major est ordinario in re delegata." The owner of an office, of course, had precedence over a *commissaire* exercising an office of the same rank, even if he had less seniority. For example, a *commis* serving as a *conseiller* in the Paris *parlement* followed after *conseillers* who owned their offices. A *conseiller* in the Grande Chambre of the Paris *parlement* was in fact once commissioned to fill the office of *procureur général*, and two regular *avocats* were commissioned to fill the offices of *avocats généraux*. The *procureur général* then marched ahead of the two *avocats généraux*, even though ordinarily he would have marched between them.

Similarly, *commissaires* had rank if their commission included command or established rank in the places and over the persons covered by their command, not merely while carrying out their commission but throughout its duration. This rank was due to the force and authority of command, which made something in the nature of subjects of those over whom it extended. "Thus it is seen that Governors of Provinces and Cities, though mere *commissaires*, nevertheless hold the first rank in those places, specifically preceding even judges, inasmuch as the command of arms is more noble than the command of justice." [2]

In regard to the "title of dignity," another part of the honor of public service, *commissaires*, in particular those exercising permanent rather than temporary charges, usurped titles of dignity similar to those of officeholders. Ambassadors, members of the State Council, and governors of provinces and cities qualified themselves as "knights" and therefore insisted that their wives be addressed as "Madame." Since "titles of dignity" lasted a lifetime, they retained their titles after the expiration of their commissions.

Anyone provided an office by commission was supposed to receive all of its *gages et droits*. Other *commissaires* received no salary, but some benefited from pensions or annual allowances. Many profited from "taxations," that is, the right to appropriate a percentage of whatever sums they handled, or received other public emoluments.

The death of a *commissaire* nullified his commission. If it was later bestowed upon another individual, it was no longer the same commission, but a new one.

A commission could not be resigned in favor of another person. A *commissaire* could step down, however, if he had a legitimate excuse. The king was under no obligation to grant the commission to any other person.

A commission could be terminated by completion of the assigned mission, expiration of the term of the commission, or revocation. Revocation took effect as soon as the *commissaire* was notified. In equity, a *commissaire*'s acts were deemed valid as long as he had not been notified of revocation of his commission. Letters of revocation often included the clause, "effective on the day notification is made."

All commissions granted by a king expired when he died. Actions already under way that could not be halted were continued for the sake of the general interest, however. If a commission was essential to the general welfare, it remained in force even after the king who had granted it died. The crown itself did not die, and, since the commission represented the crown more than the person of the king, whatever the *commissaire* did retained its force and remained in effect. All general, regular, and essential commissions were to remain in force after the death of the king until revoked by his successor as a matter of public interest, this being preferable to strict adherence to form. Commissions that remained in force were not to be exercised, however, unless there was an urgent need to do so. The governors of provinces and cities, for example, continued to exercise their commission to "protect the peace and security of the country" after the death of the king who had appointed them, but they were bound to make no changes in the way things were done.

The king employed a host of *commissaires* to carry out all sorts of commonplace missions. It seems certain that without them the state apparatus would have functioned slowly and laboriously, because the system of officeholders was formalistic and rigid and the conflicting interests of the various corps, localities, and regions hampered its operation.

Notes

1. Loyseau, *Offices*, vol. 4, chap. 5 (p. 450 of the 1640 edition published by Pierre Lamy, Paris).

2. Ibid., p. 451.

7   The *Fermiers*

A considerable portion of the king's taxes and other revenues was levied by *fermiers*. The king farmed out the revenues of the Crown domain, the immovable or corporeal domain (*censives*, ground rents) as well as the movable or incorporeal domain (sales of cut wood, grasses, cheese, and acorns, the proceeds of fines and condemnations, fees for deliveries and postal services, for the manufacture of powder and saltpeter, for operating mines, forges, and quarries, *droit de marque* on metals and other products, seal fees for all documents sealed by the chancellery, dues from the tobacco monopoly, stamp fees on notarized documents, etc.).[1] In some provinces the king farmed the income from the *gabelle*, or monopoly on the sale of salt. The king farmed the *aides* or imposts on foodstuffs, commodities, and drinks. From 1643 until the end of the Fronde, the king even farmed the fundamental direct tax, the *tailles* and *crues*.

Private individuals who paid the king a fixed sum for the right to collect these revenues and claim the surplus as compensation for their trouble and costs were known as *fermiers*, or "farmers." For example, each of the royal domains was leased out. When ordered to do so by the Conseil des Finances, the *trésoriers de France* in a *généralité* posted signs detailing the nature of the domain and then held a "candle auction" for the lease. The lease was drawn up by either the Conseil d'Etat et des Finances or the Grande Direction des Finances. The award of the lease was supposed to be registered and publicized, but this was not always done. The *fermier général*, or general farmer, could enter into subcontracts with other farmers. The various farmers were allowed to send *procureurs* and *commis* to represent them in places throughout the area in which they were authorized to collect revenues. The names, guarantees, and residences of all farmers and subfarmers and lessees and sublessees were supposed to be sent to the *trésoriers de France* and to the *contrôleur général des Finances*, but this was seldom done.

The farms enabled the king to make do with fewer agents and left the petty detail of collecting revenues, as well as the bad reputation that went along with the task, to private individuals, while assuring the government of the receipt of definite sums of money which could be counted on in budget forecasts.

As soon as the threat of war, civil or foreign, made it necessary to arm, and even more when the king actually went to war, the ordinary revenues of the monarchy inevitably proved insufficient, however. The king had no state bank. It was necessary to resort to "extraordinary affairs," such as the sale of offices, *survivances*, *hérédités*, and salary increases, taxes on the rich, the creation of *rentes*, recasting or redenomination of coinage, and alienation of regular revenues. Private individuals took it upon themselves to collect taxes or obligatory loans from the taxpayers, advancing large sums of money to the king for the privilege of reimbursing themselves out of what they collected, any profit accruing to the collector. These were also *fermiers*, but following the constitutive act of the Chambre de Justice of 1607, they were called *traitants* and *partisans*, because the contracts and deeds stipulating the terms of their agreement with the king were known as *traités* or *partis*.

The king also had recourse to "lenders," who were distinguished from *traitants* and *partisans* by the fact that the lender did not personally recover the money he lent the king.

Finally, the king also used the services of *donneurs d'avis*. These were private individuals who proposed to the king that he levy a new tax and then asked for the right to collect it. To do this, they submitted an *avis* to the king's Council. The Council then issued a decree ordering the *donneur d'avis* to submit memoranda and instructions concerning the *avis* to a state councillor, a council secretary, or an *intendant des Finances*. If the appropriate official deemed the *avis* "just and reasonable" in his report, the Council issued a second decree granting the *donneur d'avis* a commission ranging from one-tenth to one-third of the presumed revenues for his "*droict d'advis*." The proposed tax might then be levied by a *traitant*. If the Council entrusted the levying of the special tax to the *donneur d'avis* himself, he then became a *traitant*.

The *donneurs d'avis* were always on the lookout for anything that might yield income for the royal treasury. In 1649, one of them proposed a tax on chimneys, which was not accepted. In 1652, the sieur Ferris submitted an *avis* concerning the elimination of two quarters of salaries, pensions, *rentes*, and other charges on the royal domains, a measure that would have yielded 96,805 livres, of which he asked one-fifth. *Donneurs d'avis* rummaged through the accounts of the *recettes générales* in the hope of finding either debit balances, accounts left in suspension because the receipts had not yet been entered by the accountants, or embezzlements, which they hastened to report. They went after *fermiers* and *traitants* in the same way.

Taken together, the *fermiers*, *traitants*, *partisans*, lenders, and *donneurs d'avis* constituted a group referred to by contemporaries as the "*financiers*." A *financier* was any person who handled the king's money. He is not to be confused with the banker, who did business with the money of private individuals. Of course, the same person could be both a *financier* and a banker.

Fermiers, *traitants*, and *partisans* did not usually operate alone, owing to the large sums of money that had to be advanced. Instead, they formed associations of from two to ten persons, sometimes more, the share of each partner in the profits being proportional to the amount he advanced. Partnership agreements were drawn up and notarized by the notaries at the Châtelet in Paris. Each partner lent his name to the association, which was stipulated in the agreement along with the purpose of the *traité* and the share of each partner. In order for the partnership to deliberate and take decisions, it was stated that a certain number of the partners had to be present. The original of the contract and the documents needed for its execution were returned to one of the partners, who took responsibility for verifying and holding the receipts, keeping the records, and paying each partner as the revenues came in. Subcontractors to the partners were not allowed to participate in the deliberations of the corporation or to demand any accounting from anyone except the partner to whom they subcontracted. If a partner died, his widow and heirs had no right to examine the affairs of the corporation but retained the share of the deceased. Places and times were fixed for partnership meetings, and provisions were made for the keeping of minutes. In case of dispute, the partners agreed to abide by the arbitration of a third party, a mutual friend, or the judgment of a sovereign court. In fact, however, they often had recourse to the king's Council.

The partnership, having entered into a contract with the king, then executed that contract by means of subcontracts. Contractors and subcontractors sent their agents into the field armed with the necessary papers.

The *traité* or *parti* between the partnership and the king was concluded, during the first half of the seventeenth century, with the Conseil d'Etat et des Finances, which formalized the agreement in the form of a decree known as the *résultat du Conseil:* typical preambles were "Articles et conditions accordées par le roy en son Conseil à" or "Traités et conditions." This was followed by the name and title of the *traitant* and a detailed account of the purpose of the *traité*. The king was supposed to take care of issuing edicts bearing on either the creation of offices, the constitution of new *rentes*, or the levying of special taxes, as well as of recording those edicts with the Chambre des Comptes, the Cour des Aides, the *parlement*, and the Bureau de Finance involved. This was to be done within six months. Where the creation of offices or the levy of dues was expected to arouse the opposition of the sovereign courts, the king was supposed to issue not an edict but *lettres de déclaration* sealed by the Grande Chancellerie and recorded in the Audience de France.

The *traité* listed the offices, *rentes*, and taxes created, and the dues, privileges, exemptions, and confirmations to be enjoyed by the newly appointed officeholder or individual.

The king agreed to set aside funds for the salaries, dues, and bonuses of the new officeholders, for the arrears of newly created rents, or for dues and increases that may have been acquired by certain individuals. For this purpose, he was supposed to have issued the papers necessary to relieve the *receveurs généraux* and *fermiers* of any obligation, assigning the funds to the *traitant*, who had the use of them until the offices were sold or the tax fully paid.

Subsequent costs of the *traité* were generally borne by the king or deducted from the last payments under the contract: such costs might include the construction of an office for new officeholders, reimbursement of old officeholders and of individuals injured by the creation or levy of taxes, bonuses to *commis* at the rate of three deniers per livre, *épices*, preparation and rendering of accounts to the Chambre des Comptes or Cour des Aides, and payments to the *trésorier des parties casuelles*.

The contract further indicated the resources placed at the disposal of the *traitant*. Within eight days, the tax rolls were supposed to be drawn up by the Council, based on information gathered in the field by the *traitant*. A draft of the roll remained at the Council's record office. Copies signed by the *greffier* and checked by a council secretary were issued. Sometimes the job of preparing the rolls and distribution lists based on the *traitant*'s memoranda fell to the *intendant de justice, police, et finance* of the *généralité*, who was given a commission by royal decree to proceed with the work.

Tax receipts were then issued by the *trésorier des parties casuelles* or the *trésorier des deniers extraordinaires*. The names and qualities and sometimes even the sums to be raised were almost always left blank. When offices were involved, the treasurer also issued the *partisan* receipts for the *marc d'or* and *lettres de provision*, already sealed but with the names left blank. The blank receipts were approved in advance by the *contrôleur général des Finances*. Payment was ordered by special decree, which then served as a receipt when it came time to render accounts.

By submitting receipts, the *traitant* promised to pay the treasurer the sums indicated in the receipts within the time prescribed, either in cash or in central treasury receipts drawn in his name, and to provide within two or three years *mandements* or *rescriptions* from the treasurer of the central treasury. The latter were orders to the treasurer to pay a certain sum into the central treasury and attested to the reality of the payment.

When the *traité* concerned newly created *rentes*, the *partisan* was supposed to submit copies of the contracts constituting the *rentes*.

The *trésorier des parties casuelles* had the right to pursue the *traitant* and compel payment of amounts due.

All decrees and other documents necessary to the recovery of the funds advanced to the king or to the sale were supposed to be sent by the king to the *traitant*, who was granted the right to take measures against those who refused to pay the taxes, including imprisonment. Coercion was normally exercised by imposing a series of fines whose amount increased with each new order of the *huissier*.

Most of the time *traitants* were obliged to make use of *exempts* and *archers*. After an insolvent individual received three summonses from the *huissier*, he would be held under guard by these troops.

The *traitant* could enter into partnership with anyone he wished, noble and commoner alike. He was exempted in advance from actions or taxes imposed by a Chambre de Justice, as were his guarantors and partners. He did not make accountings to the Chambre des Comptes but merely reported to the king's Council. The king reserved the right to have his Council judge any disputes or controversies arising out of the *traité*. The *traitant* could not be stripped of his *traité* without reimbursement in full for all monies advanced and payment of compensation.

The *traitant* received a remittance of a quarter, a third, and in some cases as much as a half of the amount of the *traité*, for which he received a cash payment order payable by the treasurer of the central treasury. He also enjoyed a remittance of two or three sols per livre for each livre that he took beyond the contract amount. Finally, he collected the difference between the sum paid to the king and the amount actually raised by cashing in the blank receipts. For this purpose, the Conseil des Finances issued a decree ordering the treasurer of the central treasury to pay a certain amount to a specific person out of the funds coming in from the treasurers named and for the reasons indicated. The decree stated that this amount "will be used for the first cash acquittance, to be sent by certification in favor of the person named herein." The decree served as an order for payment of cash. The person named then went to the central treasury and obtained payment. At the end of the quarter, the amounts of the various payment orders were added up and the treasurer of the central treasury received a certification from the Conseil des Finances justifying the total. The Conseil then sent the Chambre des Comptes an acquittance for this total amount. This document obliged the Chambre to allocate the total in its accounts to the treasurer of the central treasury, without further justification.

The provincial governors, *lieutenant généraux, maréchaux de camp, prévôts des maréchaux*, their *lieutenants* and *archers, intendants de justice, police, et finance*, and *trésoriers de France* were obliged to enforce execution of the *traité*.

The *traitant* made a rather large advance to the king upon issuance of the articles of his *traité*. He paid a part of the surplus eight days after the verification of the edict, and the rest in regular payments, the first of which was often made on the day he received his receipts from the treasurer. The *traitant* frequently took it upon himself to buy back *rentes* for the king's profit. He was reimbursed for this at the rate of 7 percent by cash payment order. The *traité* often figured in a series of assignments of debt by the king's creditors, and in some cases the *traitant* dealt solely with assignees, who received all payments accruing from the *traité*.

Financiers used to contract with the king in the form of a *parti* or *traité* for the issuance of *rentes* on the Hôtel de Ville of Paris, and thereby, in reality, on the royal domains, *tailles*, *aides*, *gabelles*, and *traites;* for the sale of newly created offices; for the recovery of indirect imposts, *aides*, *gabelles*, *traites*, and even, from 1643 to 1661, for the recovery of the fundamental direct tax, the *taille* and its associated levies; and, finally, for loans, preferably of short term.

A physical person was required to serve as the *traitant* responsible to the king. One partner represented the rest. The use of "fronts" or "dummy partners" was universal and enabled all sorts of people to enter into *partis* with the king. *Traitants* often used the name of one of their "domestics," a member of the *familia*.[2] *Donneurs d'avis* were often court nobles, who approached the king in behalf of a *bourgeois* of Paris, an *avocat* in the *parlement* or at the Châtelet, a squire, a merchant, or a minor officer, who actually did the research. Courtiers served as intermediaries with the king, the *surintendant des Finances*, one of the *intendants des Finances*, or the *contrôleur général des Finances*. The lesser figure served as the "front man," and the courtier collected a part of the regular *droit d'avis* or a special *droit* of his own. Thus, during the Fronde, Catherine Henriette de Joyeuse, duchesse de Guise, relayed an *avis* proposed by an *avocat* in the *parlement*. The *duchesse* received four-ninths of the resulting revenue, two-ninths for her *droit d'avis* and another two-ninths for debts the king owed her. The *avocat* received one-ninth for his labor, trouble, and expenses.

Important financial officeholders and men in the entourage of the king's Council played the role of *traitants* and *partisans* under the cover of "front men." During the Fronde, the *trésorier des parties casuelles*, Housset, engaged in a number of *partis*, all under the name of Jean Lenoz, a humble domestic. François Catelan, secretary of the Council, used the names of his *commis*, Meysonnier, and his nephew, Moisel. By means of such subterfuges, it often happened that the king's *traitants* and *partisans* were in fact important treasurers of the Crown or the royal household, royal secretary-notaries, council secretaries, or *receveurs généraux des finances* of the *généralités*. At the very least they participated in *traités* and *partis*. Courtiers and members of the sovereign courts also took part. Among these were La Vieuville, surintendant des Finances in 1623, who subsequently fell into disgrace and was later recalled at the time of the Fronde; Beaumarchais, treasurer of the central treasury, who was hanged in effigy; Bullion, son of a *maître des requêtes*, himself a *conseiller* in the *parlement*, and later *président aux Enquêtes*, a *fidèle* of Richelieu, and *surintendant des Finances*, an important *traitant* and friend of other *traitants;* Particelli d'Emery, *intendant* and later *surintendant des Finances*, whose son Thoré became a *conseiller* in *parlement* but continued as a partner in various *traités* and who was nearly killed by the mob in 1648; two *présidents du parlement*, Le Coigneux and Le Ragois de Bretonvilliers, who participated in many *partis;* and later the *procureur général* Fouquet, *surintendant des Finances*. Many moneylenders backed the *traitants*, who accepted deposits like bankers. In return for the funds advanced, the treasury issued royal securities to the *traitants*, who had exclusive rights to negotiate them. Court bankers and exchange brokers (who were made officers in 1572) accepted funds from private individuals for use in transactions with *traitants*. Secrecy was guaranteed to the contributors. In 1638 five brokers (Sabathier, Andréossy, Léony, La Chapelle, and Sebier) advanced Richelieu 38 million livres to aid Portugal in its revolt against Spain. The *traitants* had associates in all the major cities of the kingdom as well as abroad. Bankers, *bourgeois* of Paris, *gentils-hommes*, and *robins* all lent money to *traitants* and *partisans*. The procedure was to go to a notary and have a contract drawn up, specifying that the money must be lent to the king. *Financiers* also signed private contracts with individual partners, whose names were not mentioned, thus guaranteeing total anonymity.

Activity as a *traitant* often ran in families, and *traitants* were frequently blood relations. They were *fidèles*, or at any rate clients, of the king's principal minister, Richelieu or Mazarin, or of the *surintendant des Finances*—without a protector at court, there was no chance of success. Le Camus, Tubeuf, and Cornuel had family ties with the *surintendant* Particelli d'Emery. Le Camus became *contrôleur général des Finances* and left more than 400,000 *écus* to each of his nine children. Jacques Tubeuf, grandson of a butcher, who began his career as a *commis* of maréchal d'Effiat, the *surintendant des Finances*, became *intendant des Finances*, attached himself to Mazarin, became a *conseiller du roi*, and, later, *président* of the Chambre des Comptes. Cornuel, the "soul of Bullion," also became *intendant des Finances*. His brother had been *trésorier de l'Extraordinaire des guerres*. Cornuel had Ragoumois and Maury for *commis*, d'Alibert as confidant, and Betaut and Lefèvre as partners. Lefèvre, once a trader in oil, made his fortune by bringing in wine during the siege of Paris in 1649 as well as through a number of *traités* involving assessments on officeholders.

Bordier, son of a candlemaker in the place Maubert, gave his daughter a dowry of 800,000 livres, built a castle at Le Raincy for more than 400,000 écus, and bought his office as *intendant des Finances* for 800,000 livres before dying in 1660. His son bought a councillorship in the *parlement* and later became *président* of the Cour des Aides under the title M. de Raincys. His sons-in-law, Galland and Morain, both became *maîtres des requêtes*. Galland, son of a *président* of Château-Landon, had earlier borrowed money to buy himself a post as *receveur des tailles* at Crépy-en-Valois, thrived there, participated in a number of *partis*, and was able to buy a post as *maître des requêtes* of the Hôtel du Roi.

The best-known *partisans* from the Fronde were La Rallière; Tabouret, a partner of Catelan; Montauron, the commissary and friend of literature, Corneille's protector; the Monnerot brothers; and François Catelan. The elder Monnerot, Pierre, *receveur général des Finances* of Orléans, contracted for the *rentes* of the Hôtel de Ville of Paris assigned out of the *tailles*, from which he amassed a huge fortune through embezzlement, later becoming *trésorier des parties casuelles*. His two sons were the sieur de Fère-sur-Seine, *conseiller* at the Châtelet, and the marquis de Siberville in Normandy. His younger brother, Nicolas, *receveur général des Finances* of Lyon, was involved in the farm on the *gabelles* and became a royal secretary in 1654. He had in the meantime married Madeleine de Brouilly, widow of the seigneur de Vitermont, captain of the guard, who was immensely wealthy. The father of the Monnerots was a *huissier*.

François Catelan, a native of Dauphiné, served de Cornuel, who arranged his marriage. He began participating in *partis* as early as 1635 under the name of Moysel, his nephew, for whom he had obtained a legal change of name. In 1637 François Catelan bought a post as secretary of the Council for 33,000 livres; he was accused of having falsified certain rolls. His great specialty was the elimination of salaries, dues, and income of officeholders, which explains why his house was pillaged in 1648 by some of them. Catelan passed himself off as the scion of an old Breton noble family, the son of Jean Catelan, sieur du Bois, a squire and captain in the League. In 1668 *commissaires* in Brittany officially recognized his right to this title in a decision handed down in Rennes. His three daughters married the marquis de Jonsac, the comte d'Estaing, and Louis de Maupeou, governor of Ath. His son Théophile, sieur de Sablonnière, became *capitaine des chasses de La Varenne du Louvre*, and later, in 1706, governor of the Tuileries.

There is no doubt that a certain social mobility resulted from involvement with the king's finances. In general, the social origins of *traitants* and *partisans* were higher than what was generally attributed to them in pamphlets and broadsides, in which they figured as sons of lackeys and shopkeepers. But there is no question that they did rise in the social hierarchy, not only because of their wealth but also because service to the king, whatever its nature, invariably brought with it a certain dignity. If many financial officeholders were *traitants*, it is also true that many *traitants* came to hold offices in finance as *receveurs généraux*, *trésoriers* of one sort or another, Council secretaries, *intendants des Finances*, or royal secretary-notaries. Some even rose to positions in the sovereign courts concerned with financial matters, the Chambre des Comptes and Cours des Aides. Thus the holders of financial offices, particularly accountants, *receveurs*, and *trésoriers*, formed, along with the *traitants* and *partisans*, a distinct professional milieu, which tended through marriage to become a distinct level in the social hierarchy. It should be noted, however, that *traitants* and *partisans* generally married women of lower status, more often daughters of small retail merchants than of important wholesalers and businessmen.

The sons of *partisans* did not carry on in the same line of business as their fathers. They rose to offices in the sovereign courts and even the *parlements*, and in some cases to positions as *maîtres des requêtes* and other officers of the royal household. Some lived nobly on a *seigneurie* or *fief de dignité*. Most, however, married the daughters of merchants and wholesalers, and marriages with the daughters of high nobility were rare. The ranks of the high and ancient nobility remained closed to these recently ennobled men. Marriages between the daughters of *traitants* and great nobles were a special case of female hypergamy and do not indicate the existence of either a unified social group or relations between two social groups on a footing of equality.

Members of all orders of French society were involved in the business affairs of the *traitants* by way of partnership or investment in their activities.

Notes

1. For a nearly complete list, see Moreau de Beaumont, *Mémoires concernant les impositions et les droits en Europe* (Paris, 1787–89), vol. 4: *Le domaine*.
2. See vol. 1, chap. 2.

8   The Functionaries

The functionaries slowly came into their own during the eighteenth century. The year 1747 might be taken as a landmark date, for it was then that the first corps of functionaries was created with the founding of the Ecole des Ponts et Chaussées. But even before then, *commis* employed by the ministries, the *intendances*, the *subdélégations*, and, outside the official government structure, the *ferme générale* had gradually come to resemble more and more what we think of as functionaries or bureaucrats. By the beginning of the Seven Years' War in 1756, this group of public and semipublic officials had created a bureaucracy already similar in many respects to the administrations we associate with postrevolutionary governments of the early nineteenth centuries, staffed by corps of functionaries.

Recruitment for the bureaucracy was always competitive, relying sometimes on tests, sometimes on competition for diplomas and credentials, and often on both in combination. Competitive recruitment assured that functionaries would be competent and honorable men.

The status of the functionary was specified both by custom and by written regulation and was determined by the state. The functionary accepted his status along with his post. The state was free to modify that status at will. The functionary's status determined his obligations and his rewards.

In the first place, the functionary owed the state absolute obedience. He had to ignore his own feelings and act as though the orders he received were strictly consistent with the public good. He therefore had to be guarded in speaking about public matters of any kind and show discretion in regard to everything related to his official function. He was obliged to live in the place where he performed his function, alongside the people he served, so as not to lose any time or suffer any fatigue in traveling from his residence to his office—these were prerequisites for doing a good job. The dignity of his own life should be such as to win respect for the government he represented. Accordingly, functionaries in the eighteenth century needed the king's permission to marry, and they were allowed to marry only brides equipped with an appropriate dowry who had never worked with their hands—a crucial prerequisite. The functionary was also required to frequent the best society in keeping with his own status; an engineer of the Ponts et Chaussées who did not succeed in the social world was not retained by the king. Functionaries should be diligent, punctual, zealous, and efficient in their work. They received no leaves or vacations and were always on call, unless special authorization was received from the king.

Functionaries enjoyed certain advantages. They held permanent tenure in their posts. They received a *traitement* rather than a *salaire*, since payment was not for service or labor but rather the means to live in a dignified manner in keeping with their rank. The functionary was supposed to receive only a modest stipend for his services, his true reward being the honor of serving king and public to the best of his ability, a service that earned him a special dignity in the eyes of his fellow citizens. Zealous and successful functionaries might receive additional rewards from the king in the form of bonuses and pensions.

Functionaries could also look forward to promotion within the bureaucracy. In theory, any functionary who learned the necessary skills and showed unfailing obedience and unflagging zeal could win promotion in his post or move to a new post in a higher echelon of the bureaucracy. If he climbed to higher levels, his stipend rose accordingly, and he could count on receiving a decoration and possibly even a noble title.

Functionaries kept their posts for life, as long as they were able to carry out their duties. A man who wished to retire after long service was almost always given a pension and an honorific title with a rank corresponding to his position, however. A functionary who was survived by his wife could rest assured that she would continue to collect all or part of his pension.

As far as the king was concerned, functionaries were more tractable and efficient than officers who owned their offices. The prominence of the functionary increased apace with the growth of bureaucracies, budgets, taxes, correspondence, archives, and statistics and paralleled the routinization of the business of government.

Conclusion to Part 2
The Rivalry between the
Officeholders and the *Commissaires:*
The "Three-Hundred-Year Process"

The period we are studying saw the continuation and aggravation of a struggle that began at the end of the fifteenth century: the conflict between the king's officeholders and the royal *commissaires*.

In many respects, what had once been the officeholders' advantages became liabilities in different circumstances. Officeholders were obliged to take a legalistic approach to public affairs, using procedures that guaranteed respect for the laws of the country and for the reciprocal rights of the parties but worked very slowly. A *requête* had to be submitted to the *procureur du roi*, a meeting called, a presentation made by an *avocat du roi*, a series of opinions heard, a vote taken or consensus arrived at, a decree drawn up and registered by a *greffier*, notification made by a *huissier* for execution, and so on—and all of this had to be done according to rigid procedures that laid down the sequence of acts and the forms to be followed. Owing to this formalism, the corps of officeholders were machines that ground very slowly indeed.

It was difficult to get much work out of an officeholder. He could not be removed from his post unless malfeasance was proved in court, and collegiality tended to dilute responsibility. Many officeholders did little work, and, when they did work, worked slowly. Often, they did not reside in the place where they held their post and made only brief appearances—this was particularly true of the *trésoriers de France*. The most zealous of them had a tendency to get bogged down in routine, which was graced with the name of "tradition."

It was difficult to obtain quick obedience to orders among officeholders. They had a very exalted and very peculiar view of their functions, to which they gave vent time and time again in remonstrances of the *parlements* and other corps of magistrates such as the *corps des présidiaux* and of the bureaux des Finances. Listen, for example, to what the officeholders of the *présidial* of Montauban had to say to Chancellor Séguier on 4 May 1633:

The condition in which we find ourselves, honored by tokens of the royal authority, guardians of the sacred trust of justice, obliges us to govern our actions with the utmost care so that, in all our conduct, we remain constantly faithful and humbly obedient servants of the king, and, further, maintain an unsullied integrity in all our functions and charges and uphold the dignity of justice. In the one, we must passionately desire His Majesty's approval and the approval of those His Majesty has seen fit to set above us, to render a faithful account of all our deportment; in addition, we must satisfy our own consciences, and, lastly, we must maintain a correct balance among our duties, not only reciprocally as between ourselves, but also between ourselves and others.[1]

In other words, the officeholders took the view that they owed the king their loyalty. This implied, first of all, that they should do nothing that might injure the king, hence nothing that might cause the deterioration of his goods, his domain, his finance, his buildings, or the resources of the state. It implied, further, that they must not betray the king's trust. Loyalty also obliged officeholders to do whatever it was within their power to do to secure the king's good, embodying the common good of the kingdom; thus they must obey.

However, officeholders felt that their obedience to the king should not be unconditional or unlimited. They also had an obligation to respect the demands of justice: of commutative justice, which gave to each what was his, and of distributive justice, which set each man in the post and rank he ought to occupy in society. Implicit in the respect for justice was adherence to custom and law. If the king's orders infringed the law or broke with custom, the officeholder was bound not to obey.

Finally, officeholders believed that, as guardians of justice, they were called upon to see to it that justice was done to the king's subjects. They were therefore bound, they felt, to play the role of arbitrators between the king and his subjects and of protectors of the latter.

Implicit in these three views was the notion that the officeholders had the power to sit in judgment on the orders of the government and on new laws, the power to suspend execution of those orders and laws, the power to remonstrate with the king in order to point out to him the defects and drawbacks they contained, and the power to insist that orders and laws be reconsidered and reformulated.

These discretionary powers were reinforced by the constitutions of corps of officers authorized to give voice to the general will. By tradition and custom these corps enjoyed certain liberties and privileges. They were further strengthened by the fact that officers could not be removed and by the interests fostered by the sale of offices and their bequest from generation to generation within a small group of families, made possible by the annual dues, the *survivances*, and the *hérédités*. The corps of officers increasingly served to maintain the social standing and political power of the families that controlled them and consequently of other families in a similar social position, those that enjoyed noble titles and privileges, owned *seigneuries*, or possessed ecclesiastical benefices. Officeholders generally opposed any changes that might alter the social and political status quo.

Now, the seventeenth and eighteenth centuries were punctuated by major wars, so that equipping the army and navy was a primary concern. This required modernization of the tax system, which in turn affected the structure and equilibrium of society. Edicts imposing new or special taxes had to be registered and executed quickly. Traitors, spies, enemy propagandists, and people who failed to pay their taxes had to be dealt with through emergency measures. Officeholders generally opposed the measures that were most urgently required or at best moved too slowly and ineffectively.

The king was therefore forced to have recourse to extraordinary measures, which gradually came to seem routine. He thus shared in a general European movement brought on by the wars that raged on the Continent. In theory, the king was supposed to govern "par Grand Conseil." His will was supposed to be shaped in his Council. He had, moreover, won the right to choose more or less whom he wished to serve on his Council. Still, the Council routine proved too slow and too apt to allow opposition. The king became more and more accustomed to taking his decisions in the company of a "favorite," a "creature," a "principal minister" like Richelieu or Mazarin, or a secretary of state looked upon by the officeholders as a *commissaire*. Many decisions came to be presented to the Council only for the sake of form, so that they might be issued as Council decrees. After the "revolution" of 1661 and the beginning of Louis XIV's personal government, which transferred control of the government from the chancellor of France to the *contrôleur général des Finances*, there were even cases in which *arrêts du Conseil* were issued by the offices of the *contrôle général* or the secretaries of state even though they had never been considered in council; nevertheless, the chancellor signed them on the king's orders.

To execute his decisions in the provinces, the king made increasing use of *commissaires* of one sort or another, above all the notorious "intendants de justice, police et finance," "*commissaires* detached for execution of the king's orders." The intendants, together with their subdelegates and *commis*, eventually extended the royal power throughout the kingdom. A network of *commissaires* and *commis* supervised, stimulated, and guided the officeholders and in many cases simply took over their jobs: for example, in the assessment and collection of the new taxes—the *capitation*, the "tenth," the "twentieth"—and in matters of general "police." Little by little, the officeholders found that their social prestige and status were suffering as a result, and that their powers were diminished and their incomes reduced.

The officeholders, led by the sovereign courts, waged an unrelenting battle against the *commissaires* and others whom they regarded as such—the Council, the governors, and the provincial intendants in particular. This struggle helped set the tempo of life—private life as well as political life—during the last two centuries of the "absolute" monarchy. The struggle brought the sovereign courts into systematic opposition to the royal government and eventually into open revolt, leading ultimately to revolutionary concepts subversive of the customary constitution of the kingdom. This was the "three-hundred-year process" of which Chancellor Maupeou spoke.

Note

1. R. Mousnier, *Lettres et mémoires adressés au chancelier Séguier* (Paris: PUF, 1964), vol. 1, pp. 227–28.

Guide to Further Reading

Baxter, Douglas Clark. *Servants of the Sword: French Intendants of the Army, 1630–70.* Champaign: University of Illinois Press, 1976.

Bonney, Richard. *Political Change in France under Richelieu and Mazarin (1624–1661).* New York: Oxford University Press, 1978.

Dent, Julian. *Crisis in Finance: Crown, Financiers, and Society in Seventeenth Century France.* New York: St. Martin's Press, 1973.

Dessert, Daniel. "Le 'laquais-financier' au Grand Siècle: Mythe ou réalité?" *XVIIe siècle* 31 (1979): 21–36.

———— and Journet, J. L. "Le lobby Colbert: Un royaume ou une affaire de famille?" *Annales E.S.C.* 30 (1975): 1303–29.

Durand, Yves. *Les fermiers-généraux en France au XVIIIe siècle.* Paris: PUF, 1971.

Guyot and Merlin. *Traité des droits, fonctions, franchises, exemptions, prérogatives et privilèges annexés en France à chaque dignité, à chaque office, à chaque état.* 3 vols. Visse, 1786–88.

Jacquard, Andrée (Mme Chauleur). *Le rôle des traitants dans l'histoire et l'administration financière de la France de 1643 à 1653.* 3 vols., mimeographed. University of Paris—Sorbonne, Centre de Recherches sur la Civilisation de l'Europe Moderne.

Loyseau, Charles. "Cinq livres du droit des offices," *Œuvres.* Pierre Lamy, 1640.

Mousnier, Roland. *La vénalité des offices sous Henri IV et Louis XIII.* 1st ed., Rouen: Maugard, 1945; 2d ed., Paris: PUF, 1971.

Petot, Jean. *Histoire de l'administration des Ponts et Chaussées (1599–1815).* Marcel Rivière, 1958.

3 Government "par Grand Conseil"

The king was sovereign. In his person all powers were concentrated. He was supposed to exercise those powers personally. Personal government by the king, the king's presence, and the king's personal orders were constantly called for by the Estates General and the provincial Estates, the cities, the communities of inhabitants, the corps, the publicists, and the pamphleteers. The king was a judge. All his acts of government were the acts of a judge. He "judged" the affairs of state. When he went to war, what he was doing, legally speaking, was pronouncing a judgment against another state and causing that judgment to be executed by his armies. The king's justice was of two kinds: commutative, which insured that each man would keep what was his and which involved rights and property; and distributive, which involved the attribution of ranks, dignities, and advantages by grace or in return for services rendered to the body social. The king's justice subsumed the whole of government and administration. Thus the decisions of the king, whether laws, regulations, administrative rulings, or judgments in favor of one or another of two parties in dispute, were supposed to be issued in legal form. This was a further reason in favor of governing "par Conseils," through Councils.

The king of France was supposed to govern "par Grand Conseil," in Guillaume de Seyssel's celebrated phrase. He was supposed to shape his will, which was law, in the company of councillors, some of whom owed their position as councillors to birth, others to their office, and still others to their loyalty to the king, whose creatures they were. What happened over the course of the two centuries we are studying is that the king came less and less to govern in conjunction with councillors who owed their position to birth (such as the members of his own lineage) and less and less in conjunction with councillors who owed their position to their office (such as the chancellor, whose role and influence declined after the Fronde); by contrast, he governed more and more with the help of an ever smaller number of his own creatures, to the point where he was taking decisions alone after conferring with each of his ministers in turn, meetings of the Council being held in many cases only for the sake of form.

All those who saw the king daily and who lived with him, the Court of France, may be considered to be a sort of Council, within which the king assembled a smaller body, the "king's Council."

The court was made up of four groups: the *Grands Officiers de la Couronne*, in principle the heads of the major departments of state, such as the chancellor and the constable; the king's household, which included all the institutionalized services responsible for attending to the king's daily needs, to his religious life, his security, his lodging, his clothing, his meals, and his amusements; the households of the queens, the Children of France, and the princes and princesses of the blood; and, finally, private individuals, mainly nobles, who waited on the king and were ready to serve him as dictated by their fidelity as subjects and vassals, in particular in council or in the army.

Nobles who lived at court and saw the king were called courtiers, regardless of whether they were nobles of gown or sword, of ancient stock or recent title. But the various departments of the royal and princely households, the Councils, and the courts included a good many commoners drawn from various levels of the social hierarchy. The court epitomized all the orders of the kingdom.

Many social and political functions essential to the kingdom were performed by the court. In their behavior and way of life the members of the court were supposed to exemplify the ideal subject of the king to all the kingdom's social groups: in particular, this was the role of the dukes-and-peers. The court was the judge of the "point of honor," the prime regulator of the society of orders, and set the example for the kingdom in this regard: in particular, the *maréchaux de France* and their Cour de Connétablie were final arbiters in this area. The king could at any time ask advice of any member of the court, and most, though not all, of those commissioned by the king to represent him on special missions were chosen from among the persons residing at court.

The court was divided into "cabals," pressure groups that sought to obtain power, prestige, money, posts, offices, and commissions. These cabals recruited their members among the courtiers, in the households of the princes of the blood, among the dukes-and-peers, the high nobility, the *maréchaux de France*, and government circles. Their membership was constantly shifting, but some cabals lasted as long as twenty-five years in succession. They were constituted on the basis of ties of kinship, patronage, loyalty, and friendship and had connections with the army, the Church, financial circles, and the bureaucracy. We can identify three cabals around the king in 1709. One was led by Mme de Maintenon and included several marshals (Harcourt, Boufflers, Villeroi, Huxelles), the secretary of state for war, Voysin, two sons-in-law of Louvois (Villeroi and La Rocheguyon), and the Pontchartrains. Another was the cabal of the duc de Bourgogne, which included the sons-in-law of Jean-Baptiste Colbert (the duc de Beauvilliers and the duc de Chevreuse), both ministers, Desmaretz, the *directeur des Finances* and nephew of Colbert, Fénelon, the archbishop of Cambrai, the Sulpicians, and the Jesuits. Finally, there was the cabal of Monseigneur, the Grand Dauphin, father of the duc de Bourgogne, with the Cour de Meudon, the duc d'Antin, the prince de Vaudemont, Mlle Choin, Mlle de Lillebonne, and Mme d'Epinay.

We shall be looking at the various groups at court one by one.

9

The Royal Family: The Princes of the Blood, the Appanages, the Regencies

The Royal Family

The royal family included, in the first place, all males of Capetian blood eligible to accede to the throne. The customary statutes of the realm had bestowed kingship on the reigning branch, to be transmitted by primogeniture through the male line. Women and descendants through the female line were forever prohibited from claiming the crown. This custom was gradually supplanted by the fundamental law of France, according to which the crown devolved upon the respective branches of the Capetian family in order of their proximity to the reigning dynasty. Within each branch, the crown was to pass from the eldest son to the next eldest and so on. Males eligible to wear the crown were supposed to be ready to accede to the throne at any moment. Since the royal family was pledged to serve the public, they were not allowed to renounce this obligation. In theory, then, the king was supposed to consult with members of his family concerning important matters of state and use them on state missions. The members of the royal family (including the queen mother, even when there was no regency, and the queen, even though women were not allowed to accede to the throne) took part in the most important policy councils and had missions entrusted to them by the king. Their participation in the Council is stated explicitly in the preambles to many royal edicts. "Be it known that, in the opinion of our Council, at which were present our very dear companion and spouse, and several princes of our blood, and other princes and officers of our Crown and other great personages, and by our certain knowledge, full power, and royal authority . . ."[1] Similar or identical texts are commonplace. It was Louis XIV who, when he took charge of the government after the death of Mazarin in 1661, broke with custom and excluded from the highest Council the queens and all members of the royal family. This exclusion was not permanent, however. Because government was carried out "par Grand Conseil," it is therefore incumbent upon us to examine the royal family.

85

The Queen

During the period we are interested in, the kings and dauphins of France married foreign princesses for reasons of international politics. In addition, in the case of Henri IV there was the further need to pay off debts owed to the Médicis. In marrying Marie de Médicis, Henri IV married "la grosse banquière." The marriage contracts between French kings and dauphins and foreign princesses were thus received by secretaries of state in the other countries involved and sealed with the great seal of the appropriate country's crown. Sovereigns and their heirs were married by proxy, since "political prudence made it advisable not to risk their own lives outside their borders." The king commissioned whomever he pleased to serve as proxy—a minister, an ambassador, a provincial governor, a state councillor, a cardinal. The king's representative was provided with a power of attorney authorizing him to conclude a marriage contract just as the king himself would have done and to promise that the king "will ratify and agree to whatever is done, said, and agreed." To the power of attorney were attached instructions concerning the dowry, renunciation of the right of succession, etc. The power of attorney was in fact a commission in the form of letters patent signed by the king, countersigned by a secretary of state, sealed with the great seal on a plain bit of yellow wax, registered at the *parlement* of Paris, and signed by the *procureur général du roi*. It was customary, moreover, to send along one or two French secretaries of state, generally the secretary of state for foreign affairs and the secretary of state attached to the king's household. They took part in drawing up the contract and suggested clauses for inclusion. Nicolas Brûlart, vicomte de Puisieux, negotiated the marriage contract of Henri IV; Pierre Brûlart and Antoine Pothier took care of the Spanish marriages; Henri-Louis de Loménie and Hugues de Lionne, the marriage of Louis XIV; Colbert, that of the Grand Dauphin. The contract was signed at the court of the bride-to-be. The marriage contract was coupled with an international treaty, and this was made explicit in the case of the marriage of Louis XIV to Marie-Thérèse. Article 33 of the Treaty of the Pyrenees made this marriage contract a part of European public law: "Which separate treaty and marriage convention [*capitulation de mariage*] have the same force and validity as the present peace treaty, being the principal and most worthy part thereof, as well as the greatest and most precious guarantee of its duration."[2] The chancellor of France affixed the great seal to these marriage contracts before making them public and executory. He thereby gave notice that the king was calling for execution of the contract throughout the kingdom. These contracts had to be registered in all the *parlements* of France. On 27 July 1660, Louis XIV sent a commission to the *procureur général* of the Paris *parlement* in order to insure that his marriage contract would be registered at the same time as the Treaty of the Pyrenees and "in the same form used for the treaty signed at Vervins in the year 1598." Authenticated copies were sent to the *bailliages* and *sénéchausées* for registration there. Since the marriage contracts contained financial clauses, they were also registered in the Chambres des Comptes and Cours des Aides.

By the time we are concerned with here, the rite of anointment and coronation of the queen in the basilica of Saint-Denis had fallen into disuse. Marie de Médicis, the wife of Henri IV, was the last queen to be anointed, on 13 May 1610, in the church of Saint-Denis in France. The anointment was followed by a solemn entry into the capital, Paris. This ceremony survived. Louis XIII and Anne of Austria entered the city without fanfare on 16 May 1616. The entry of Louis XIV and Marie-Thérèse on 26 August 1660 was an apotheosis. For Marie Leczinska, the ceremony was one of the utmost simplicity, taking place on 4 October 1728. On 8 February 1779, for the entry of Marie-Antoinette, the sovereigns made a point of not indulging in the "pomp, more impressive than useful, of the old celebrations."

The title of queen did not grant sovereign authority or the right to govern the kingdom to its holder. "The kingdom cannot fall to the distaff side" (Loysel). The queen could, however, "take a very large share in the public administration."[3] Besides her role in the Council, she could receive missions even where no regency was involved. Louis XIII named Marie de Médicis governor of the province of Anjou as well as of Brouage, Oleron, and the isle of Ré, by letters of provision dated 18 June 1619 and 4 February 1627, registered at the *parlement* of Paris. Such missions became increasingly rare, however.

The queen did not share community property with the king, her husband, because whatever was acquired by kings went to the profit of the kingdom, "their mystical and most privileged spouse."[4] The king had the right only to make gifts of chattels, cash, and acquests not yet incorporated into the Crown's domain. For having married a man whose private person was absorbed by his public person, the queen stood at a disadvantage compared with other women. The sovereign had no property of his own. The community of property between spouses was incompatible with the notion of sovereignty and the principle of inalienability of the royal domain. The kingdom of France was neither the property nor the patrimony of the kings. It was their office. They were merely its administrators, the supreme magistrates. The crown domain was not their personal property. The "king is a man of the state." He was stripped of his juridical personhood. When Henri IV issued letters on 13 April 1590, declaring his private domain independent of the domain of the Crown, the Navarrist *parlement* of Paris, meeting at Tours, refused to register them. The *procureur général du roi*, La Guesle, opposed registration because "the king, by his accession to the throne, contracts with the Crown a mystical and perpetual marriage, and the personal goods of the king are the dowry of the royal *fiancée*." Ultimately, in an edict of July 1607, Henri IV declared that his private domain had been united with the crown domain at the moment of his accession to the throne. If the king made further acquisitions of property, they were immediately incorporated into the crown domain. The king was therefore unable to give the queen any rights over a mass of goods that he did not own.

Beyond that, the queen was not even allowed to share the enjoyment of the Crown's property, for that property was one of the attributes of sovereignty, and sovereignty could not be subdivided. "The king is monarch and has no companion in his royal majesty. External honors can be communicated to the wives of kings; but that which is of his majesty, representing his power and dignity, resides inextricably in his person alone."[5] Thus the king shared the royal honors with his spouse, but there was no community of property between them. By dint of the royal function, the king was devoted to the public. "The purse of the king is that of the people, not the private purse of kings and queens."[6] The crown jewels were entrusted to the queen's custody, on condition that she restore them to the woman who would succeed her as the wife of her son, and they remained distinct from her own jewels and precious items which she may have brought with her.

The marriage of the king and queen, like that of any of their subjects, was indissoluble, in keeping with the words of Jesus Christ and the law of the Roman Catholic church. The king could not divorce. The king did not divorce Queen Marguerite in 1599. Rather, the pope annulled the marriage, that is, declared that it never existed, because Marguerite de Valois and Henri IV were related in a degree that precluded marriage; because Henri IV had been compelled to enter into this marriage after Saint Bartholomew and his will was not free, nor, for that matter, was Marguerite's; and, finally, because there was between them a spiritual kinship that precluded marriage, since Marguerite's father, Henri II, had in 1554 served as godfather to the future Henri IV.

Widowed, the queen of France was entitled to no "nuptial gains" save the annuity on her dower in domanial lands or other state revenues. By virtue of the ordinance of Blois (articles 330 and 332), the dower was constituted of lands bearing the title of duchy or county up to the value of 3,333 écus income. The remainder was paid out of *aides*, *tailles*, and the like, as well as extraordinary levies. The dowager queen received her income from the royal *receveurs* and *fermiers*. A château was left to her as a residence.

The queen enjoyed the same honors as the king. When she made a solemn procession of entrance into a city, she was allowed to grant letters of remission to all prisoners held there. Like the king, she could plead through the *procureur général*. Like the dukes-and-peers, she had her days assigned in rotation in the *parlement*, and in general she enjoyed all the privileges of the dukes-and-peers. She was exempt from all chancellery dues. She had the same preferential rights for the recovery of monies due her as the king did. On her private domains she enjoyed all the privileges accorded the crown domain. Whether or not she had precedence over the queen mother remains in doubt. The queen was supposed to be served in dignity. She therefore had a household distinct from the king's, in that the queen's household was dissolved by her death, while the king's was permanent, since "the king never dies."

The king could contract a marriage in secret. This was the case with the marriage of Louis XIV after he was widowed to Madame de Maintenon. This secret marriage was not clandestine. It was celebrated according to the forms prescribed by the Council of Trent, with witnesses of the number and quality required. The bride was not entitled, however, to the title of queen with its attendant benefits. The king granted her matrimonial benefits by unilateral act rather than by contract. Madame de Maintenon thus received a pension and, later, was made head of Saint-Cyr, to which she retired after the king's death.

The Children of France[7]

The eldest son of France and heir apparent to the throne bore the title of "dauphin," which was also assumed by the king in all acts of sovereignty concerning the province of Dauphiné. The eldest son of France assumed no title other than the following: "by the grace of God, eldest son of France, Dauphin de Viennois." No other prince of the royal house had the right to use the formula, "by the grace of God." The Paris *parlement* granted the eldest son of France the exclusive title of "Monseigneur" when it was requested by Louis XIV upon the birth of the dauphin. It was customary when the heir apparent was born to celebrate a *Te Deum*, and for the king to create a certain number of *brevets de maîtrise* in each trade guild. This was done by edict in November 1601 by Henri IV, and later by Louis XIV "in favor of the birth of monseigneur le Dauphin, first son of France and heir to the throne." On 9 June 1782, instead of creating *brevets*, Louis XVI freed prisoners held in the prisons of Paris who had not been rendered unworthy of grace by the nature of their crimes.

When the dauphin entered a city for the first time, he had the right to set free the prisoners there. As long as the king was alive, the dauphin had only that share in the government of the state that his father was willing to grant him. If the king was prevented from governing by illness, madness, abduction, or other accident, the dauphin could assume the title of regent of the kingdom and as such exercise all the prerogatives of sovereignty. The dauphins of France had separate households, as did the dauphines, their wives.[8]

The "sons of France" were the male children and grandchildren of the kings. This title was also given to the great-grandchildren of kings when the reigning king was himself only the grandson of a king; in this case they had the additional advantage of being the king's nephew. The king's next eldest brother, born the second son of France, bore the title "Monsieur," "absolutely and without appendage." Similarly, his wife was called "Madame" and his daughter "Mademoiselle." During *lits de justice*, Monsieur, the king's brother, sat on the king's right and nearer to him than anyone else, and all the princes who were sons of France sat with the princes of the blood. In public ceremonies the sons of France other than the dauphin were entitled only to the title of Monsieur. From 1776 on, however, on express orders of the king, the Chambre des Comptes and the Cour des Aides were obliged to call them "Monseigneur." The sons of France assumed the title "royal highness" after 1641, when Louis XIII's brother, the duc d'Orléans, used it for the first time.

The sons of France had the right to remove any case in which they had an interest from the jurisdiction of the Paris *parlement*. In public opinion they were exempt from duels in purely civil matters, but not if they were accused of murder or treason. The king and magistrates held that they must respect the laws against duels, however. They each had their own household, as did their wives.[9]

The daughters, granddaughters, and even great-granddaughters of kings (when they were nieces of the reigning king) bore the title, "princess, daughter of France." The daughters of the king, his sisters, and the eldest daughter of the dauphin were called "Madame," followed by their Christian name. The other daughters of France were called "Mademoiselle," followed by their Christian name. They enjoyed honors similar to those enjoyed by the sons of France.

The Princes of the Blood

A prince of the blood, or prince of the Crown, was "a man who, by the most authentic and pure genealogies, is descended from male to male and by legitimate marriage from a king of France, and who, for that reason alone, is born and apt to succeed to the Crown, if he becomes eldest, of this august race."[10] This excellent definition needs to be completed. Filiation was not sufficient. Recognition by the king as a prince of the blood was also necessary. The sovereign proclaimed as princes of the blood only those descendants of the kings of France who were near-enough relatives and *grands seigneurs* and who had held high offices and dignities in the kingdom. The Courtenays, descendants of Pierre de France, the seventh son of Louis VI (the Fat), who took the name Courtenay in 1150 upon marrying Elizabeth, the daughter of Renaud de Courtenay, a descendant of Robert the Pious, were never able to gain recognition of their quality as princes of the blood, being rejected in 1620 and again in 1787. In effect, even though they had given four emperors to Constantinople, a queen to Hungary, and an empress to Trebizond, in France they remained no more than minor lords of the Paris region and rather distant relatives of the king. Other legitimate descendants through the male line of the kings of France were never recognized as princes of the blood: the Dreux, the Bourgognes, the Sambernons, the Montagus, the Carencys. Kings continued to exclude males of the Capetian family whose descendance began with Saint Louis and males of the cadet branches of great princely families. The kings were always concerned not to increase unreasonably the number of pretenders by birth to the government of provinces and fortresses and to fiefs, pensions, and Church property. The Houses of the princes of the blood were the Bourbons, the Orléans, the Anjou, and the Alençon.

Strictly speaking, a prince is "he who has sovereignty." But the kings of France bestowed the honorary title of prince on those of their relatives whose degree of succession made them or their progeny likely to accede to sovereignty. The succession to the Crown was based on a parentela system. Each parentela was called in succession; the call passed to the next parentela only when its predecessor was exhausted, no matter what the distance between the heir and the defunct king. If the eldest son died before acceding to the throne and had no legitimate sons, his next eldest brother succeeded his father. If the monarch died without leaving a legitimate male descendant, the call then went to his next eldest brother. If there was none, the next parentela was called. Thus Henri IV, descendant of Robert de Clermont, son of Saint Louis, succeeded Henri III, although they were related only in the twenty-first degree. According to Balde, the Crown of France could be transmitted down to the thousandth degree. The Declaration of 2 July 1717 concerning the succession of the Crown stipulated that it was devolved upon the "House of France," the Capetian line, until it was exhausted.

Designation of the eldest occurred within each parentela, so that a nephew might precede his uncle to the throne. The Crown was "awarded to the eldest son of the eldest son." Henri IV took the Crown ahead of his uncle Charles, cardinal de Bourbon, by the ordinary degrees of succession a nearer relative of Henri III, because Henri IV was the eldest son of Antoine de Bourbon, himself the elder brother of Charles de Bourbon, duc de Vendôme, and because his uncle Charles, cardinal de Bourbon, was only the younger brother of Antoine de Bourbon, as the third son of Charles de Bourbon. As the son of Charles de Bourbon, he was a nearer relative to Henri III than Henri IV was, but the latter was the eldest son of the eldest branch of sons of Charles de Bourbon. Upon the death of Louis XIV, his great-grandson Louis XV, son of Louis, dauphin, duc de Bourgogne, who was in turn the eldest son of Louis, the Grand Dauphin, in turn the son of Louis XIV, had no difficulty claiming the Crown ahead of his uncles, Philippe d'Anjou (Philip V, king of Spain) and Charles, duc de Berry, the younger brothers of the dauphin, Louis.

The masculinity principle also carried the day. Not only women but also their male descendants were precluded from acceding to the throne of France. The title "princess of the blood" was a matter of social consideration without dynastic consequence. Princesses of the blood who did not marry princes of the blood lost their honors after marriage, because a woman took on the condition of her husband; these honors could, however, be preserved by a brevet from the king, as in the case of Anne-Genevière de Bourbon, the eldest sister of the Grand Condé, born a princess of the blood, who married a duc de Longueville. It is true that her husband did have pretentions to the title of prince of the blood.

The bastards of the kings of France and of the princes of the blood were not princes of the blood and could not accede to the throne. Their father could and often did legitimate them, but only for civil purposes: legitimation allowed them to inherit private property, to receive donations, and to be provided with offices and dignities. These matters were set forth in letters patent issued by Henri IV in 1595, April 1599, January 1603, and January and March 1608, whereby he legitimated his natural children: César de Vendôme, Alexandre de Bourbon, Gaston de Foix, Antoine, comte de Moret, and Jeanne-Baptiste de Bourbon. Legitimated royal sons were usually abundantly provided with offices and dignities. César, the son of Gabrielle d'Estrées and Henri IV, was duc de Vendôme, duc d'Etampes, duc de Mercoeur, duc de Beaufort, duc de Penthièvre, peer of France, prince de Martigues, comte de Buzançais, seigneur d'Anet, gouverneur de Bretagne, and grand maître chef et surintendant général de la Navigation et Commerce de France. Louis XIII received him into the Ordre du Saint-Esprit.

There were attempts to win exceptions for the bastards. To begin with, efforts were made in behalf of the descendants of Dunois, bastard of Orléans. In a brevet issued on 5 April 1571 by Charles IX to Léonor d'Orléans, duc de Longueville, it was declared that the duke's predecessors had always been held to be princes of the blood and that recognition of this title would be extended henceforth to his descendants. Letters patent were drawn up for the purpose in September 1571, but the Paris *parlement* refused to register them. Louis XIV reaffirmed the declaration in letters patent of April 1653, but these were not registered either.

In an edict of July 1714 Louis XIV attempted to have his legitimated bastards authorized to succeed him after the princes of the blood.[11] Faced with the decimation of his family by disease, the king said that his desire was to prevent the misfortunes and uprisings that might result if no prince of his royal blood should be available to take the throne. In that case, the edict stipulated that the Crown would duly and legally devolve upon Louis-Auguste de Bourbon, duc de Maine, who had been legitimated in December 1673, and, if he should be unavailable, the Crown would pass to Louis-Alexandre de Bourbon, comte de Toulouse, legitimated in November 1681, and to their male children and descendants born or to be born in legitimate marriages in perpetuity, in the order of succession and always preferring the older to the cadet branch. Like the princes of the blood, these princes were granted *entrée* and *séance* at the Paris *parlement*, and they were not required to take the oath even if they had no peerage. They were to enjoy all the honors of princes of the blood in *parlement* and in all ceremonies, as were all their descendants in perpetuity. They ranked after the other princes of the blood and before all other princes of sovereign houses and all other *seigneurs* of any dignity whatsoever. The *parlement* of Paris registered this edict on 2 August 1714. A declaration of 23 May 1715 confirmed that there was to be no difference between the princes of the royal blood and the legitimated sons of Louis XIV.

After the death of the Great King, the princes of the blood who were cousins of Louis XV, the duc de Bourbon, the comte de Charolais, and the prince de Conti asked that the edict and declaration be revoked. In an edict of July 1717 concerning the succession to the throne, Louis XV argued that, owing to the fundamental laws of his kingdom, he was "fortunately powerless" to make any disposition of the Crown, which was his only for the good and safety of the state, and, further, that if the House of France should happen to vanish, it would be up to the state alone to determine the Crown's disposition, up to the French nation itself to repair the misfortune by the wisdom of its choice; in consequence, he declared that only descendants by legitimate filiation of the kings of France were recognized as princes of the blood and annulled the edict of July 1714 and the declaration of May 1715.[12]

Thus even legitimated bastards remained excluded from the succession to the Crown.

Also excluded were "foreign princes," that is, "those who, though born French and subjects of the king, are issued from sovereign houses outside the kingdom," such as the dukes of Nevers, descendants of the princes of Mantua. The king granted them only the honors and prerogatives of the princes of the blood. Political necessities compelled Louis XIV to attempt to get around this provision in behalf of the House of Lorraine. By the Treaty of Montmartre of 6 February 1662, Duke Charles IV or Lorraine ceded his states to Louis XIV in exchange for the rank of prince of the blood and authorization for the House of Lorraine to take its place in the line of succession to the Crown of France immediately after the House of Bourbon. But the chancellor warned Louis XIV that he could not make princes of the blood by declaration, that kings could make princes of the blood only with their wives, the queens. The *parlement* let it be known that it would not register the treaty, and Louis XIV had to enforce registration with a *lit de justice* on 27 February 1662. Fortunately, Charles IV did not execute the treaty, and Louis XIV was forced to take the duchy. The Treaty of Metz of 31 May 1663 based the acquisition of Lorraine on the rights of conquest. The situation of "foreign princes" with regard to the French Crown was not changed.

Princes of the blood could not cease to be princes of the blood. They were supposed to be prepared to accede to the throne of France at any time. They could not renounce their vocation. They did not relinquish it if they accepted another sovereignty. The renunciation of the French Crown by Philippe, duc d'Anjou, when he became Philip V, king of Spain, was *ipso jure* null and void, even though it was confirmed by the Treaties of Utrecht and registered by the *parlement* of Paris. If any of his descendants are alive today, they are duly entitled to accede to the throne of France in order of succession and always preferring the elder to the cadet branch.

The hierarchy of princes of the blood was ordered by proximity to the Crown, which established orders and ranks. In the first rank of the first order was the dauphin. In the second rank were the next eldest sons of France and other sons of France. In the third rank were the "grandsons of France" and their sisters, sons, and daughters—grandsons and granddaughters of the reigning king. In the second order, fourth and fifth rank, were the sons, daughters, grandsons, and granddaughters of the defunct king, that is, the brothers, sisters, nephews, and nieces of the reigning king. In the third order were all the other princes of the blood, the rank of each being determined by his proximity to the crown.

The edict of May 1711 concerning the duchies and peerages of France points out, in its first article, that the princes of the royal blood were to be honored everywhere according to the dignity of their rank and the elevation of their birth; that they represented the ancient peers of France at the anointment of kings; that they were entitled to *entrée*, *séance*, and *voix délibérative* in the courts of *parlement* at age fifteen, in both audiences and Council, without any formality, even if they possessed no peerage.

According to the regulation of 1688, the sons of France were entitled to the title of Royal Highness, and the princes of the blood to the title of Most Serene Highness. The dauphin had the right to precede his name with the honorific, "most high, most powerful and excellent prince"; Monsieur, "most high and most powerful prince"; the princes of the blood, "most high and powerful prince"; and the princes of foreign houses, "high and powerful prince."

All were exempt from the payment of tolls and *droits de greffe* and *signature*, verification of seal and registration, fees for verification of deeds and writs, and *droits d'insinuation* until 29 September 1722.

They were exempt from seigneurial dues in the *mouvance* of the king.

When the court traveled, they enjoyed the privilege known as "*avoir le pour*." When the royal harbingers went ahead to mark the lodgings with chalk, they indicated the rooms of persons who were not princes by writing merely their name and title, while the rooms of princes were marked "Pour Monseigneur le duc d'Orléans," "Pour Monseigneur le prince de Condé," etc.

The Appanages

The appanage of a prince of the blood and son or grandson of France was what was given to him so that he might live in a manner appropriate to his estate. The appanage consisted of property given by kings to their brothers or sons, and, in the absence of sons, to their grandsons, for their daily bread and subsistence. Princes of the blood who were neither sons nor brothers of the king were not entitled to an appanage; however, if they lacked sufficient means to live in a manner befitting their rank, they were entitled to an "establishment." The king made up appanages out of fiefs under the Crown's jurisdiction having at least the dignity of duchy or county. To do this he prepared constitutive letters for each appanage, and these had to be registered by the *parlement* of Paris. In letters patent of 7 December 1766, it was declared that this institution was "placed among the fundamental laws of our monarchy." The king's obligation to his sisters and daughters was not an appanage but marriage. The letters patent stipulated the renunciation of the beneficiary to all lands and *seigneuries*, whether joined or not to the Crown, and to all movable property and acquisitions in real property that would have devolved upon the beneficiary by the death of his father, the defunct king. Thus the appanage was constituted with inheritable title, to take the place of the beneficiary's share in the late king's bequest. It comprised the beneficiary's legitimate portion and represented the price of his renunciation of the succession in favor of his elder brother.

The prince with an appanage exercised regalian rights. Justice was done in his name and by his officers. As soon as the appanage was established, the *juges des exempts et cas royaux* were obliged to leave. If a vacancy occurred in one of the offices attached to the appanage, the prince nominated a new candidate and the king provided the office. The prince with appanage was entitled to nominate and present candidates to abbeys, priories, and all other consistorial benefices, excepting bishoprics. He had the right to strike coinage, even in gold. He had all rights of household, land, justice, and seigneury. He could set up tribunals equal in power and authority to the superior courts of the provinces, and these were allowed to judge even royal cases. He was allowed to set up judicial commissions or Grands-Jours in the cities of his appanage to hear cases as a court of last appeal; these had competence over all persons subject to the courts. He was allowed to levy *tailles* and other taxes on his subjects, a right confirmed by letters patent of October 1645. He granted letters of pardon, safe-conduct, and privilege. He had the enjoyment of frank fees, exchange, amortization, and new acquests. He could plead through a *procureur* in all the king's courts, including the *parlement* of Paris, and his *procureur* was treated in the same manner as the *procureur général du roi*, as confirmed by letters patent of 24 October 1680.

With royal authorization, the prince with appanage was allowed to have a chancellor and a chancellery with seals for the provision of the officeholders of the appanage and other offices for which he enjoyed rights of collation or nomination. Letters patent of January 1724 registered at the Cour des Aides on 8 February granted the duc d'Orléans the right to have in his appanage a chancellor and keeper of the seals, a *contrôleur*, a *chauffe-cire* (wax-melter), and two *huissiers*.

The *apanagé* was not allowed to issue laws, regulations, or statutes in the form of letters patent in his appanage according to the decree of the *parlement* of Paris of 20 March 1706. He could not even regulate hunting on his lands. But the king could always issue letters patent for the execution of a regulation or statute proposed by the *apanagé* prince.

The royal sovereignty was guaranteed by the fact that the king expressly reserved sovereignty to himself, along with rights of jurisdiction, liege homages and faith, the protection of churches, and cognizance of royal cases, and also because a reversion clause applied to the appanage. The appanage was transmissible to the male descendants of the *apanagé* prince under the same rules that applied to the French Crown. If, however, male progeny of the *apanagé* prince or his male descendants were lacking, so that not one remained, even if there were daughters or males descended from daughters, the appanage was voided, and the fiefs and *seigneuries* of which it was composed reverted to the crown.

One problem with political implications stirred debate: Was the appanagist a usufructuary or an owner? Dupuis in his *Traité du duché de Bourgogne*, the *avocat général* Omer Talon in his public charge of 1641, Grainville in his *Arrêts de la Quatrième Chambre des Enquêtes*, and Prost de Royer as late as 1786 all held that he was a simple usufructuary.

The letters patent constituting the appanages bestowed upon them all the characteristics of fiefs, however, with beneficial seigneury going to the *apanagé* prince, while the king retained direct seigneury. Consequently, the appanage was indeed property. This was clearly enunciated in the preamble to the letters patent of 16 September 1766: "The law of appanage constitutes the prince who possesses the appanage as its true *seigneur* and owner," and, farther on, "the duc d'Orléans, being the perpetual true owner and landlord of the appanage . . ." In 1769, Séguier, the *avocat général*, in the case of the duc d'Orléans against the churches of Chartres and Orléans, declared the prince the true owner of his appanage, despite the entailment in favor of his male descendants, because "an heir appointed under entailment is nonetheless owner of the thing he must transmit, despite the necessity of the bequest, which he cannot escape."[13]

Among the *apanagés* princes we find Gaston de France, brother of Louis XIII, for the duchies of Orléans and Chartres and the county of Blois (edict of July 1626); and Philippe de France, Louis XIV's only brother, and his male descendants, for the duchies of Orléans, Valois, and Chartres and the *seigneurie* of Montargis (edict of March 1661). This appanage was progressively enlarged to include the duchy of Nemours, the counties of Dourdan and Romorantin, the marquisates of Coucy and Folembray (24 April 1672), the Palais-Royal (February 1692), the *hôtel* du Grand-Ferrare at Fontainebleau (27 July 1740), the county of Soissons and the domains of Laon, Crépy-en-Laonnais, and Noyon (28 January 1751), the domains of Marle, La Fère, Ham, and Saint-Gobain, dependencies of the county of Vermandois, and, finally, the canal of l'Ourcq and the *hôtel* of Plessis-Châtillon, attached to the Palais-Royal, relinquished to the king by the duc d'Orléans and joined to the crown domain (16 September and 7 December 1766).

Along with their male descendants, the following were also *apanagés* princes: Charles de France, duc de Berry, grandson of Louis XIV and son of Louis, dauphin, the younger brother of the duc de Bourgogne, for the duchies of Alençon and Angoulême, the county of Ponthieu, and other fiefs (edict of June 1710); Louis-Stanislas-Xavier, grandson of Louis XV, for the duchy of Anjou, the county of Maine, the county of Perche, and other fiefs and *seigneuries* (edict of April 1771); and the comte d'Artois, for the duchy and county of Auvergne, the duchy of Angoulême, and other *seigneuries* (edict of October 1773). The latter appanage was expanded to include the duchy of Berry (letters patent of June 1776).

In 1786, the duc d'Orléans, Louis-Philippe-Joseph I, known after 12 September 1792 as Philippe-Egalité, set up a company to administer his domains. In that year the appanage produced a gross income of 4,347,760 livres out of 7,969,440 livres gross income for all the property of the House of Orléans, from which 1,674,775 livres must be deducted for expenses. Later, the income of the appanage increased by 500,000 livres.

An appanage had a council presided over by a chancellor whose nomination was ratified by the king and registered by the Cour des Aides. The council included a chancellor, a *surintendant des Finances*, two *secrétaires des Commandements*, two *intendants des Finances*, one *trésorier général*, fourteen *conseillers*, one business agent, one archivist, one secretary, four *maîtres des requêtes*, and two *huissiers*. Subordinate to the council were a finance committee, a secretariat, and, from 1786 to 1788, an administrative committee or company, all presided over by the chancellor. Between 1786 and 1790 the council met 125 times, and the minutes of the meetings cover 4,177 questions of various kinds.

The National Constituent Assembly issued a decree on 13 August 1790, approved by Louis XVI on 2 September, abolishing the appanages as of 1 January 1791. They thereupon became national property. The creation of new appanages in the future was forbidden.

The Regencies

Contemporaries used the term *régent* (or *régente*, in the case of a woman) to denote the person who, during the minority, absence, or illness of the king, governed the kingdom in His Majesty's name. Under an edict issued in 1374 by Charles V, the eldest son of the French king attained his majority upon completion of his thirteenth year. When the young king began his fourteenth year, he "assumed control of the government and administration of the kingdom, received homages and oaths of fealty from his subjects, and . . . might cause himself to be anointed and to receive all the insignia of royalty . . . as though an adult of twenty-five years of age."[14]

Despite this rule, the king's eldest son actually became king on the day his father died. The opinion that a king was not king if he had not been anointed was no longer held by anyone. "Our kings are kings by succession and not otherwise. . . . Death seizes the living and . . . we have a [new] king as soon as the [old] one is dead." Placing the natural order above the sacred and mysterious order, contemporaries believed that the safest bet was to follow the most natural order of succession.[15] Anointment no longer made the king king. Whenever *avocats généraux* and chancellors broached this subject, the phrase "the natural order" recurred constantly.

There was always a king, then. But if the king was a minor child, or if the sovereign was absent or incapacitated, it became necessary to organize a government in his stead. The obvious choice to head such a government, following "the natural order," was either the king's mother or wife or one of his uncles or brothers. Since the days of Blanche de Castille, the mother of Saint Louis, a customary practice had grown up, a practice that had been used nine times (according to a statement made by the *avocat général* Omer Talon on 21 April 1643): this was to designate the king's mother as regent and the brother of the defunct king, Monsieur, the uncle of the reigning king, as *lieutenant général du roi* in the provinces. If the king's mother was also dead, the eldest uncle of the king took the title of regent.

An invariable procedure had been established. A declaration of will by the defunct king was required, along with the accord of the French nation, represented by the *parlement* of Paris, assembled with the princes of the blood, the peers of France, the *grands officiers de la Couronne*, and representatives of the king's Council, failing a meeting of the Estates General. The dead king might make his will apparent by having the queen anointed and crowned during his lifetime, as Henri IV did for Marie de Médicis, or by having a royal declaration registered at the *parlement* of Paris, as Louis XIII did for Anne of Austria on 21 April 1643, or by conferring a particular distinction, as Louis XIV did with regard to the duc d'Orléans, first prince of the blood. The latter was not designated regent by the king's will of 2 August 1714, filed at the *parlement* of Paris, but was rather named head of the future Regency Council. In all cases, moreover, public statements of the dead king were required, as witnessed by the chancellor and *avocat général*. Even for the duc d'Orléans, the king's men invoked, on 2 September 1715, "the last words spoken to us by the king, that he had not prejudiced the rights of his birth in any way."[16]

The dead king's declaration of will was supposed to be approved by a decree of the Paris *parlement* meeting together with the princes of the blood, the peers of France, the *grands officiers de la Couronne*, and the members of the Conseil d'Etat, who together constituted a group that spoke on behalf of the kingdom. A day or two after this decree was issued, the king, who, though a minor, still exercised legislative power, was supposed to come to *parlement* and hold a *lit de justice* in the presence of the personages just named. At this time a second decree was issued, confirming the first, along with an edict establishing the regency and appointing the regent, who was to be responsible for educating the minor king and for administering the kingdom, as set forth in the original decree of the Paris *parlement*.

This procedure was followed on 14–15 May 1610, when Marie de Médicis became regent, on 20–21 April and 18 May 1643, when Anne of Austria became regent, and on 2–12 September 1715, when the duc d'Orléans became regent.

When the king's expressed wish violated the customary constitution of the kingdom in some respects, it was not followed in every detail. Thus

Louis XIII's declaration of 20 April, which subjected the future regent Anne of Austria to the decisions of a council whose members were chosen by the king and whose advice, decided by majority vote, she was bound to follow, was not fully respected. Nor was Louis XIV's decision to appoint a Regency Council, which was supposed to be ruled by majority vote, with the role of the duc d'Orléans reduced to that of chairman. Now, France was an absolute monarchy and there was supposed to be a single head of government, wielding absolute power. Thus the *parlement*, meeting as a plenary court, reestablished the right of Anne of Austria, as regent, to determine the membership of the Council at will and to reach her decisions on her own after hearing its advice; and in 1715 it reestablished the duc d'Orléans as the sole regent. These actions have improperly been called "*cassations*" by the *parlement* of Louis XIII's declaration and Louis XIV's will, respectively.

By law, the powers of the regent were the same as those of a king in his majority and in full possession of his faculties, who was present to govern his kingdom. Regents exercised all the powers of sovereignty under the same conditions as the king. In fact, however, many residents of the kingdom did not feel they owed the regent the same obedience as they owed a king in his majority.

The regency was terminated when the king made a formal declaration of his majority in *lit de justice* at the *parlement* of Paris. Louis XIII did so on 2 October 1614; Louis XIV, on 2 October 1651; and Louis XV, on 23 February 1723.

Documents inaugurating and terminating the regency were sent by the *parlement* of Paris to all *bailliages* and *sénéchaussées* in its jurisdiction and to all other *parlements* in the kingdom to be read, registered, and published.

Notes

1. Henri IV, "Edit sur la réunion à la Couronne de l'ancien patrimoine privé du roi," Paris, July 1607, in Isambert, vol. 15, p. 330.
2. Cited by Monique Valtat, *Les contrats de mariage dans la famille royale en France au XVIIe siècle* (A & J. Picard, 1933), p. 30, based on Archives Nationales K. 540, no. 34.
3. Guyot and Merlin, *Traité des droits* (Visse, 1787), vol. 2, p. 213.
4. Cardin Le Bret, *De la souveraineté*, book I, chap. 1, p. 47.
5. Guy Coquille, *Institution au droict des François*, vol. 1, p. 1; Loysel, *Institutes coutumières*, no. 22, cited by Valtat, *Les contrats*, p. 58.
6. Du Tillet, *Recueil des rois de France*, p. 147, Loysel, p. 60.
7. See this volume, chap. 1: "The Education of the King."
8. See the protocol concerning the dauphin in Guyot and Merlin, *Traité des droits*, vol. 2, pp. 303–4.
9. See details in Guyot and Merlin, ibid., pp. 331–49.
10. Saint-Simon, "Mémoire sur l'intérêt des princes du sang à empêcher tout agrandissement des enfants légitimes du roi," in *Ecrits inédits de Saint Simon*, P. Faugère (ed.), vol. 2, p. 78.
11. Isambert, vol. 21, pp. 144 ff.

12. Ibid., pp. 144–48.
13. Dupin, pp. 132–37.
14. Dupuy, *Traité de la majorité de nos rois et des régences du royaume* (1655), p. 7.
15. Ibid., pp. 12, 13.
16. Guyot and Merlin, *Traité des droits*, vol. 2, p. 16.

10

The Dukes-and-Peers, the High Crown Officers, the King's Household

The Dukes-and-Peers

At court, the dukes-and-peers stood near the summit of the social hierarchy, just below the princes of the blood. As individuals, they carried out various functions within the royal household; as a group, however, they had but one function, an important one: to embody the official social ideal, which was held out as a model to the entire kingdom. We may include within this group individuals who were not peers but bore the hereditary title of duke.

The king could confer peerage on a county or duchy. Duke-peers and count-peers possessed the highest dignity in the kingdom after the royal dignity. They were addressed in the following terms: "Très haut et très puissant seigneur," "Monseigneur," and "Votre Grandeur." They had the right to wear the ducal coronet and cloak with ermine collar representing the tunic worn by knights over their armor. They enjoyed the honors of the court. They were allowed to enter royal palaces on horseback or in carriages and could ride in the king's carriages. Their wives were entitled to be seated on a *tabouret* in the presence of the queen. In marriage ceremonies, baptisms, burials, banquets, and *Te Deums*, they immediately followed the Children of France and the princes of the blood. In marriage contracts, they signed after the princes of the blood. In the anointment of the king of France, the ecclesiastical peers—the archbishop-duke of Reims, the bishop-dukes of Laon and Langres, the bishop-counts of Beauvais, Châlons, and Noyon—and the lay peers representing the dukes of Burgundy, Guyenne, and Normandy and the counts of Toulouse, Flanders, and Champagne played the essential role. When a *lit de justice* was held in *parlement*, they sat, without unbuckling their swords, on high chairs above the gowned councillors. They did not kneel to speak to the king. In the presence of the sovereign they gave their opinion before the *présidents à mortier*. Besides their right to sit at *lits de justice*, they were entitled to speak and vote at all sessions of *parlement*. Their affairs and the affairs of their peerages were judged in

101

Grand-Chambre, with a sufficient number of peers in attendance. Their special courts fell directly under the jurisdiction of *parlement*.

As peers, however, they held no political power. Cases of treason were taken away from *parlement* and entrusted to special judicial commissions, as in the case of Biron in 1602 and Montmorency in 1633. They did not sit ex officio in the councils of government. From 1667 on, they did not even come to the *Conseil privé* or the *Conseil des parties* unless invited by the king.

The group in question was a small one. Between 1589 and 1723, 396 laymen belonging to 113 families and possessing 132 dignities bore the title of peer or just plain duke: 290 duke-peers, 21 count-peers, 5 peers with neither duchies nor counties, and 80 dukes without peerages. Among the ecclesiastics there were 5 peers in 1589. In 1643 this number rose to 6 and in 1674 to 7 with the creation of the duchy-peerage of Saint-Cloud for the archbishop of Paris; in 1715 it rose to 8. From 1643 on, ecclesiastics who left a see with peerage and were named to a see without peerage retained their privileges as peers of France, thanks to royal brevet. There were in all 45 ecclesiastical peers belonging to 38 families.

We can distinguish three categories of lay peers. The first included the "Capetian" princes, peers by birthright: 14 Children of France, 27 princes of the blood, 21 bastard princes, or 62 peers in all. The second included "foreign" princes in whose families a peerage was hereditary. There were eight such families in all: Clèves, Luxembourg, Lorraine, Savoy-Nemours, Gonzaga-Mantua, Grimaldi-Monaco, La Tour-d'Auvergne, and Rohan. This accounted for 69 dukes-and-peers. The third included *gentilshommes* from 72 families, accounting for 224 peers bearing 82 dignities. In 1589, 11 peers came from this group; in 1643, 28; in 1661, 38; in 1715, 48; in 1723, 52.

Dukes-and-peers were generally drawn from old families of the *noblesse d'épée*. Of the sixty-six families of *gentilshommes* that yielded dukes-and-peers in the seventeenth century, most can be traced back to the thirteenth and fourteenth centuries, two can be traced to the tenth century, and only a few were as recent as the fifteenth century. These families and individuals had long served France at war and had long been faithful to the king. The only exception was the family of Chancellor Séguier, duc de Villemort, in 1650. The others were *maréchaux de France* or generals. Half were married to the daughters of dukes-and-peers, 35 percent to the daughters of marquis, counts, and barons, and 15 percent to the daughters of noble *robins* and owners of *seigneuries*. The average age of men who became dukes-and-peers was forty-eight.

The dukes-and-peers formed a group of wealthy feudal and seigneurial rentiers who sought to acquire fiefs, particularly large *fiefs de dignité*. When they held office, they also received emoluments, bonuses, and pensions from the king. At the time of marriage, the fortunes of the Capetian princes ranged from 1,500,000 to 3,000,000 livres on the average; of the foreign prince-peers, from 1,350,000 to 1,700,000 livres; for the *gentilshommes*-peers and dukes, from 800,000 to 1,000,000 livres.

Fortunes at death were even larger. Henri II de Condé in 1651 left real estate worth 7,430,240 livres and bringing in 371,512 livres per year, along with *rentes* payable by the king bringing in 75,662 livres on a principal of 756,620 livres. The *hôtel* de Condé was estimated to be worth 450,000 livres. Eighteen hundred thousand livres cash were needed to liquidate his debts. At the time of death, many of these fortunes exceeded 2,000,000 livres.

All this wealth sustained a life-style in which, for the sake of prestige, large expenditures for pomp and dazzling luxury were obligatory.

The peers as a group were conscious of their preeminence and social role and stubbornly defended their privileges against the other orders. On these matters, one need only read the *Mémoires* and *Ecrits politiques* of Saint-Simon.

The High Crown Officers

The *"Etats de la France,"* which first appeared in 1648 but did not begin annual publication until 1661, included the following officers in the category of *grands officiers de la Couronne*, or high crown officers: the chancellor of France, whom we shall study in connection with the Royal Councils, the constable and marshals of France, the *grand amiral* and the *général des Galères*, and the *grand maître de l'Artillerie de France*, because the king's principal role was to secure justice by force of arms. Some high dignitaries of the king's household were also high crown officers.

The Constable and the Marshals of France

The constable was the head of the army. The high noble who filled this office was a constant threat. For this reason, the functions of the office were eliminated in 1627 upon the death of the duc de Lesdiguières. The title remained in the *Etats de la France* until the eighteenth century. The constable had the authority of command and the power to issue orders, and he could use coercion to see that his orders were carried out. His assistants, the marshals of France, inherited his powers as a body in 1627. As the leading crown officers and heads of the nobility, the marshals not only commanded the military but also contributed in two other ways to the government of the society of orders, to the enforcement of the laws, and to the preservation of domestic tranquillity. First, they decided questions of honor and thereby helped to maintain control over the society of orders. They had jurisdiction over disputes between *gentilshommes* or involving *gentilshommes*. Because of their estate, the marshals of France were responsible for supervising the behavior of the nobility. Second, they maintained discipline in the military. They judged crimes committed by soldiers and kept order in the field and in camps along the route of march where soldiers might be stationed.

Points of honor were raised whenever the distinctive qualities of the *gentil-homme* or soldier were in question: among these were gallantry, veracity, loyalty, largesse, and the duty to shun base or mechanical employments. Slurs on a man's honor were supposed to be punished by the judgment of God, rendered in the form of a duel. But dueling violated the tenets of Christianity, the official religion; "Thou shalt not kill" is the fifth com- mandment. Dueling also conflicted with *raison d'état:* the killing of large numbers of *gentilshommes* in duels deprived the state of its best soldiers.

Hence dueling was prohibited by edict and ordinance, and violators were punished. It was not up to the marshals of France to judge duels once they had taken place; this was within the jurisdiction of ordinary judges. The marshals of France were, however, qualified to prevent duels. They could have anyone they feared might become involved in a duel arrested and imprisoned, as well as any relatives and friends who might take part in the dispute. They were also empowered to arrest seconds and others informed of a prospective duel who failed to notify the marshals, even if the duel never actually took place.

The point of honor was a delicate matter. The royal government was forced to take great pains to diminish the frequency of dueling. A whole body of law was required, beginning with Charles IX's Moulins ordinance of 1566. This ordinance prohibited assembly of ten or more *gentilshommes* or other persons bearing arms and enjoined subjects not to settle disputes "by arms or combat" on the pretext of "insults" or wrongs suffered, particularly "contradictions." In such cases, the victim, if at court, was supposed to go to the constables and marshals of France or, if in the provinces, to the provincial governor. An attempt would be made to reconcile the two parties. If this failed, they would be sent back to the constables and marshals of France, who would take care of the question of honor. Subsequently, edict after edict was promulgated, each repeating the provisions of the previous one and attempting to close any loopholes by stiffening the penalties, in- creasing the satisfaction to be rendered to the offended party, and institu- tionalizing means of preventing duels. These include Henri IV's edicts of 1602 and of Fontainebleau, registered at *parlement* on 26 June 1609, making duelists guilty of the crime of *lèse-majesté;* the declarations of Louis XIII on 1 July 1611, 18 January and 4 March 1612, 1 October 1614, 14 July 1617, and 26 June 1624, together with the edicts of the same king issued in August 1623, February 1626, and on 29 May 1634; the edict of Louis XIV of June 1643 confirmed by declaration of 13 March 1646; the edicts of the same king issued in September 1641 and August 1679, supplemented by regulations issued by the marshals of France on 22 August 1653 and 22 August 1679; the edict of Versailles of December 1704; and the declaration of Versailles of 28 October 1711. Finally, Louis XV issued an edict in February 1723 and confirmed the new regulations of the marshals in a declaration on 12 April 1723.

Custom so favored dueling that, whenever a duel occurred, the king was overwhelmed by entreaties in behalf of the guilty parties and often issued pardons, nullifying the effect of his edicts and declarations. The only way to deal with the problem was to work on the custom that encouraged it. This was one aspect of the Catholic Renaissance. In July 1651, at the urging of the Compagnie du Saint-Sacrement, a large number of *gentilshommes* "declared publicly and on solemn oath to reject all appeals [to duel] and never to fight a duel for any reason, to bear witness in every possible way to their detestation of dueling as something entirely contrary to reason, goodness, and the laws of the state, and incompatible with salvation and the Christian religion." They submitted this document to the marshals of France, who stated that it was "in compliance with the Edicts of the King and the Laws of honor, as well as with the laws of the true religion." They exhorted all the *gentilshommes* of the realm to sign and asked the signers to confer among themselves concerning the satisfactions to be given in case of an offense to honor, so that these might be examined and a report made to His Majesty. This resulted in the laws and regulations of 1653. The king insisted on the duty of *gentilshommes* to "serve in our armies, there to maintain, by the justice of our arms against our enemies, the reputation of our Crown, and to share in this sole true glory, which is acquired by serving one's Prince and one's Fatherland in a legitimate war" (edict of June 1643). Finally, Louis XIV, after beginning his personal government, firmly applied all edicts and regulations concerning dueling. By the end of his reign, the number of duels had declined greatly. Under Louis XV, there was no further legislation after 1723 concerning points of honor and duels. Doubtless there were still duels. But the carnage and slaughter that had prevailed under Henri IV, Louis XIII, and right up to the beginning of Louis XIV's personal government had been stopped.

The Connétablie *and* Maréchaussée

To "police" the kingdom and secure domestic tranquillity, the marshals of France relied on the *Cour de la Connétablie et Maréchaussée de France à la Table de Marbre du Palais* in Paris. By the beginning of the period that interests us, the members of this court had become a corps of professional magistrates responsible for justice and administration. The court included a *lieutenant général des maréchaux de France*, a *lieutenant particulier*, "volunteer judges" chosen by the former members from among the men of law, a *procureur du roi*, a *greffier*, and *huissiers* who conveyed documents to the parties and saw to the execution of the court's decisions. The *lieutenants* were magistrates received by the *parlement* of Paris; they bought their offices.

The marshals of France also had control over the company of the *prévôt général de la Connétablie et Maréchaussée de France*, the judge in charge of the king's armies and camps, who was known as the *grand prévôt de la Connétablie*. The latter submitted to the king nominations of officeholders and guards in his company; *lettres de provision* were prepared by the chancellery. The *grand prévôt* had the right to speak and vote on issues relating to interrogations, receptions, and oaths involving the *prévôts* of the provincial marshals, *vis-baillis*, *vis-sénéchaux*, and *lieutenants criminels de robe courte et maréchaussée*, as well as the right of inspection over them. He commanded the *maréchaussées*, took cognizance of all *cas prévotaux*, and enforced military ordinances. He was judge of last resort in civil and criminal matters and matters of police pertaining to the camps and armies; he set rations and issued passports to merchants, commissaries, and artisans following the armies. Under him served three *lieutenants anciens*, one with long gown, two newly created *lieutenants*, one *procureur du roi*, one *greffier*, four *exempts*, forty-eight guards with one commissary and one watchmaker, one *premier assesseur*, and one *premier huissier exploitant* (process server).

When there was more than one army, the *prévôt de la Connétablie* accompanied the royal army, while his lieutenants served with the other armies. The *officiers d'épée* of this company served and guarded the *maréchal de France ancien*. They were detached to guard persons of quality who became involved in disputes with one another.

The marshals of France controlled a *prévôt général des Monnaies et Maréchaussées de France*, who had under him a number of *lieutenants* and *exempts*, a *greffier*, and forty *archers* empowered to serve writs throughout the kingdom.

Within each province or government, the marshals of France commanded a *prévôt général des Connétables et Maréchaux de France*, sometimes called *prévôt provincial des Maréchaux*. One such was the *prévôt général des Connétables et Maréchaux de France au gouvernement et généralité de Paris et Isle-de-France*, who had under him 4 *lieutenants*, 1 *guidon*, 8 *exempts*, 100 *archers*, 25 of them mounted, dispersed all around Paris in seven brigades responsible for the security of the countryside. At the beginning of Louis XVI's reign there were thirty-three *prévôts provinciaux des maréchaux*.

In many but not all *bailliages and sénéchaussées* there were *prévôts particuliers des maréchaux*, commanding a number of *exempts* and *archers* that varied from place to place.

Maréchaussée functions were also carried out in the *présidiaux* by *lieutenants criminels de robe courte*, and in the *bailliages* and *sénéchaussées* by *vis-baillis* and *vis-sénéchaux*.

All the *officiers d'épée* of the *maréchaussée* were members of the king's *gendarmerie*. They took precedence over all other troops, including the bourgeois militias and town watches and guards.

The *corps de maréchaussée* was reorganized and expanded on several occasions. In March 1720, thirty companies of the *maréchaussée* were created, including one in the duchy of Burgundy. This creation was confirmed by the edict of July 1721, which continued the right of the king's governor and *lieutenant général* to fill all offices and places in these companies in the provinces of Burgundy, Bresse, Bugey, Valromey, and Gex.

In October 1738, a company was created in the provinces of Lorraine and Barrois by edict of the king of Poland, duke of Lorraine. It was absorbed into the other companies of the kingdom by edict of July 1767.

A company was set up on the island of Corsica by ordinances of 27 December 1769, and 24 March 1772.

The ordinance of 28 April 1778 inaugurated a comprehensive reorganization. Article XVII of that ordinance ended the sale of the offices of *prévôts généraux* and their *lieutenants*, which henceforth were to be awarded by commission. All the companies of the *maréchaussée*, including that of the province and principality of Dombes, were to make up the corps of the *maréchaussée*, still to be headed by the *sieurs maréchaux de France*. The corps consisted of 6 inspectors general, 33 *prévôts généraux*, 108 *lieutenants*, 150 *sous-lieutenants* who replaced the *exempts*, 150 *maréchaux des logis*, 650 *brigadiers*, 2,400 *cavaliers* (a term that began to replace *archer*), and 33 trumpeters.

All the *prévôts*, *particuliers*, and *lieutenants* of the *maréchaussée* were eliminated in the provinces of Burgundy, Bresse, Bugey, and Valromey, because the prince de Condé relinquished his right to their services.

The inspectors general were granted the rank of *mestre de camps;* the *prévôts généraux*, the rank of lieutenant-colonel; the *lieutenants*, the rank of captain; the *sous-lieutenants*, the rank of lieutenant; the *maréchaux des logis*, the rank of *maréchal des logis chef*. The senior *maréchal* in each company was supposed to receive a commission as *sous-lieutenant* of cavalry after five years of service. Brigadiers received the rank of *maréchal des logis* and *cavaliers* that of brigadier of cavalry.

The posts of *prévôt général* and *lieutenant* continued to be awarded, upon presentation by the *sieurs maréchaux de France*, to senior officers in the *maréchaussée* of the rank immediately below, or to officers in cavalry and infantry regiments with ten years of service and four years in grade. The governor and lieutenant general of Burgundy, Bresse, Bugey, and Valromey was supposed to present candidates for these posts in these provinces.

The *cavalier* positions were supposed to be given to *cavaliers*, *dragons*, and *hussards*, 5 feet 4 inches in height, who ostensibly knew how to read and write and had sixteen years' service. They were supposed to be proposed to the secretary of state for war by the *prévôts généraux*. Of the *exempts*, those most distinguished by birth, service, and good conduct were supposed to be promoted to the rank of *sous-lieutenant*. The rest were to be retired from the service or allowed to continue as *maréchaux des logis* while awaiting a vacancy in the rank of *sous-lieutenant*.

The *maréchaussée* was to be divided into four-man *brigades*, each with a *brigadier*, evenly dispersed throughout the kingdom, with no distinction between provinces, *généralités*, and *jurisdictions*.

This organization anticipated that of the *gendarmerie* during the nineteenth and twentieth centuries.

Taking the pre-1778 *maréchaussée* as a whole, we may say that historians have generally underestimated its size and effectiveness. The marshals and *prévôts généraux* could indeed concentrate the *maréchaussée*'s forces, if need be, just as is done in the twentieth century, though of course more slowly. When the gravity of the situation called for it, moreover, they could also call up "*bourgeois*" and other inhabitants of cities, *bourgs*, and villages, have them assemble at the sound of the tocsin, put arms into their hands, and have them trained and led by the elite troops of the *maréchaussée*. Just such an action was expressly ordered by the edict of June 1643 for the purpose of searching the châteaux of princes and crown officers for duelists in hiding.

The competence of the *Connétablie et Maréchaussée de France* extended, first of all, to what were called *cas prévotaux:* questions of ransom and booty; disputes over the execution of contracts concerning soldiers, members of the *maréchaussée*, and commissaries; cases involving personal loans, purchases, and notes to innkeepers made by soldiers and military officers; theft and murder on the highways; rapes, kidnappings, and abductions; counterfeiting; dueling; sodomy, incest, bigamy, atheism, sacrilege, blasphemy, and witchcraft; deeds of war; rebellions and resistance to magistrates or military forces; and discipline within the *maréchaussée*.

Its competence extended to all civil trials of soldiers and to all crimes committed by or against soldiers; to all cases of military discipline, "police" of the highways, and public safety—including the tracking and arrest of wrongdoers and other enemies of the state; protection of travelers by keeping the highways free and secure; the maintenance of order during festivals and assemblies; and, in general, the maintenance of public safety and tranquillity.

According to the ordinance of 28 April 1778, an inspection was to be carried out each day of the highways and lesser roads and of all suspect places in the "district," in *bourgs*, villages, and hamlets, by two men from each brigade. They were to gather information about travelers, suspects, criminals, and delinquents and, when called for, to make arrests. The *brigadiers* were to prepare inspection reports and send them to the *lieutenants* of the district. They were responsible for obtaining lists of foreigners staying at inns in the area. They arrested low-ranking officers and soldiers who caused trouble or disturbed the peace or whose leaves had expired. They were to visit fairs and markets to keep order and to patrol the most highly traveled routes for a distance of two leagues around the market site to protect merchants and other individuals returning home. They kept the *intendants* informed of any events requiring prompt action to maintain order and keep the peace. They carried out orders from the king, the secretaries of state, the governors and commandants of provinces, general officers commanding divisions of royal troops, and orders from the *premiers présidents* and *procureurs généraux* in regard to matters of justice and general police, court receipts, processions, etc. They also took orders from the *intendants*, especially in regard to the assessment of taxes and the recruitment of provincial soldiers; and they provided troops to escort royal monies upon orders of the *receveurs* and *trésoriers*. Judges had to make written requisitions in which it was forbidden to use terms such as "order," "enjoin," "mandate." The *intendant* had to use the following formula: "The service of the king requires that [so and so] order . . . , do . . . , proceed to . . . , arrest . . . , and that he apprise us of the execution of that which is hereinabove prescribed by us in the name of His Majesty. Done at . . ." In case of insults or rebellions against the *maréchaussée*, the criminals were supposed to be arrested and the case submitted to the *procureur du roi de la Connétablie et Maréchaussée de France* at Paris to be decided there. In *cas prévotaux* the ordinance of 1670 was supposed to be applied.

The Admiral of France

The admiral of France was a high crown officer, but his authority extended over only a portion of the French coast. In Brittany the governors carried out the admiral's functions and the *sénéchaux* had judicial jurisdiction over acts committed at sea. There was an admiral of Guyenne, who covered the coastline from Brittany to Spain. On the Atlantic, the jurisdiction of the admiral of France scarcely extended beyond the special admiralties of La Rochelle and Sables-d'Olonne. There was an admiral for the "seas of the Levant" in charge of the defense, police, and surveillance of the ports and coasts of Provence and Languedoc; the fleets were commanded by the *général des galères*. The fact that jurisdiction over the French coast was divided among four admiralties made it difficult to arrive at a common policy for the development of maritime commerce and the navy. Attempts at unification were made from the beginning of the seventeenth century on.

In 1612, Henri, duc de Montmorency, became admiral of France. In 1614 he also assumed the post of admiral of Guyenne. In addition, he had the power to fill the office of admiral of Brittany. He received lavish honors: at sea and in the ports his person was surrounded by "guards of the Flag"; at night his ship was distinguished by a golden lantern at the stern; by day the royal banner waved from the top of his tallest mast; the king of France called him "My cousin." More than that, he enjoyed considerable powers. He was effectively in command of the Atlantic fleets. He nominated all officers and *commissaires* of the royal navy, the port authorities, and the coast guard. He ordered and directed the construction, refitting, equipment, and provisioning of all warships. He approved all expenditures made by the *trésoriers de la Marine*, and the navy's budget was not subject to audit by the *surintendant des Finances*. His jurisdictional powers were extensive.

Eventually, however, this independent power came to be seen as a threat to the power of the king. Richelieu was concerned about it. Beyond that, he wanted to respond in some way to the creation of the *Almirantazgo* in Spain in 1624. This was an admiralty that operated as an agency of the Spanish commercial monopoly, sent fleets of commercial ships to sea, provided them with an escort of men-of-war, investigated suspicious ships at sea, and forced merchants to post bond as guarantee that they would use the proceeds from the sale of imported articles to buy items for export. In October 1626, the cardinal-minister had himself named to the newly created post of *grand maître, chef et surintendant général de la Navigation et du Commerce de France*, and in January 1627 he had the office of admiral of France eliminated. He established his authority over the admiralties of Guyenne, Bordeaux, and Bayonne. In Brittany he had himself named governor on 16 September 1631 and henceforth performed the functions of the admiral of Brittany, though he failed to apply the edict of 1640 creating seven admiralty offices in the province. Since the last admiral of the "seas of the Levant," Charles, duc de Guise, had fled in the wake of accusations of rebellion in August 1631, his admiralty disappeared, and on 18 January 1633 the *lettres de provision* of the *grand maître* were registered at the admiralty of Marseilles. Thus both the eastern and western fleets came under the direction of one man. Royal letters dated 18 March 1627 gave Richelieu the power to set up maritime companies. Navigation, navy, and commerce were all placed in his hands. Richelieu made use of two new agents, who were destined to a bright future: the *commissaire inspecteur* and the *intendant de marine*. After 1631, however, the cardinal was increasingly absorbed by the Thirty Years' War.

After Richelieu's death on 4 December 1642, his nephew and heir, Jean-Armand de Maillé, marquis de Brézé, succeeded him, remaining in the post until he was killed on 4 June 1646 in the battle of Orbitello. The queen regent, Anne of Austria, then took the post of *grand maître* for herself, and a short while thereafter became governor of Brittany as well. On 12 May 1650, she resigned from the post of *grand maître* in favor of César, duc de Vendôme, the son of Henri IV and Gabrielle d'Estrées. He died on 22 October 1665. His son François, duc de Beaufort, was the last *grand maître*. He was killed on 16 June 1669, near Crete, then under siege by the Turks. Vendôme and Beaufort both took the title *chef des flottes* and assumed the power to nominate officers, who swore oaths of loyalty to them personally. The situation was once again what it had been before the abolition of the office of admiral of France.

In fact, it was even more threatening, since the admiral or *grand maître* was not merely the head of a hierarchy of military and judicial officers but the natural protector, as it were, of a world of coastal landowners and *seigneurs*, who stubbornly defended their privileges against the royal policy of unification. Along the coasts and the banks of navigable stretches of water, a chain of landowners enjoyed hereditary privileges ranging from specific rights under maritime law, such as ownership of seized goods and wrecks, to ordinary dockage fees. For example, no boat could land anywhere along the banks of the Garonne, the Dordogne, or the Adour without paying the landowner a landing or anchorage fee, toll, or other exaction. When the right of the *jurade* of Bordeaux to exercise powers of "police" over the quays of that city was confirmed in 1687, it immediately imposed duties on boats hauling stone, oranges, and wheat. Every landowner with coastal property did the same thing. Fishermen, who were organized in confraternities according to statutes that extended back to the Middle Ages, fiercely defended their exemptions.

All these interests were united by a tacit understanding opposed to any attempts to impose new orders or regulations that might diminish ancient privileges. These common interests had political consequences. Some *seigneurs* organized and attracted supporters. D'Epernon made trouble for the cardinal-admiral de Sourdi out of spite for having been stripped of his maritime rights on the coast of the Buch region. The maréchal d'Ornano and the amiral de Montmorency joined Gaston d'Orléans in his fight against Louis XIII and Richelieu. The prince de Condé moved closer to the Frondeurs in part because his claims to the admiralty were not met with success. Fouquet based his hopes while in Belle-Isle on the tradition of coastal exemptions, privileges, and liberties.

This explains why Colbert revived the old royal tradition of separation of dignity and authority. In February 1669 he was named *secrétaire d'Etat à la Marine.* Upon the death of Beaufort he had the office of *grand maître* eliminated. An edict of November 1669 reestablished the post of admiral of France; it still had a large income but no real power. This state of affairs was ratified by the ordinances of 1681 and 1689. The king reserved the right to nominate and provide the offices of vice-admiral, *lieutenant-général,* and *chef d'escadre;* captains, lieutenants, and ensigns of ships, frigates, and fire ships; captains and officers of the port authorities and coast guards; *intendants, commissaires,* and *contrôleurs généraux* and *particuliers* of naval stores—in short, all those empowered to take initiatives and execute decisions. The king also claimed all powers in regard to the construction and refitting of his ships, the purchase of supplies and armaments, and, in general, the creation and maintenance of war materiel, means of transport, and ancillary equipment. Finally, the king claimed the power to approve all expenditures made by the *trésoriers de la marine;* in other words, he assumed control over the budget of the royal navy.

The admiral retained the right to command the primary naval fleet, provided he accepted the king's orders. In other words, he was left mainly with a lucrative source of income and certain honorific formalities. Court decisions were handed down in the admiral's name in all admiralty courts. The admiral proposed to the king nominations for the offices of *lieutenants, conseillers, avocats* and *procureurs du roi, greffiers, huissiers,* and *sergents* in the *sièges généraux* and *particuliers* of the admiralty—that is, he nominated men to fill the posts of judicial magistrates and auxiliaries. The king gave them their *lettres de provision.*

The admiral granted leaves, passports, commissions, and safe-conduct passes to the captains and masters of men-of-war and cargo ships. He issued contracts for the ballasting and deballasting of oceangoing vessels, for the maintenance of fires, buoys, and beacons, and for the inspection of ports, coasts, and roads.

A tenth of the ransoms for seizures made on the high seas or coastal waters, all fines imposed by the *sièges particuliers*, half of those imposed at the Tables de Marbre, half the fees for anchorage, buoys, and beacons, and a third of the value of items washed ashore by the waves or taken from the sea-bottom went to the admiral.

The admiral of France was constantly involved in conflict with the governor of Brittany. By decree of the Council on 30 May 1701, only the port of Brest was left under the authority of the admiral. The only way the admiral could exercise authority in Brittany was to have himself named governor of the province, as the count of Toulouse did on 19 March 1695.

The establishment of the Council of Seizures in 1695 further diminished his powers.

The fact is that Louis XIV's bastard sons and their descendants who became admirals of France had no more than an honorific title to this high crown office—quite against their own wishes, of course—and could neither make themselves useful nor take any initiatives. These included Louis de Bourbon, comte de Vermandois (1669–19 November 1683), Louis-Alexandre de Bourbon, comte de Toulouse (23 November 1683–1737), and his son, Louis-Jean-Marie de Bourbon, duc de Penthièvre, who was named as heir to the office in January 1734 and who succeeded his father as admiral of France and governor of Brittany on 1 December 1737.

The real power was henceforth exercised by a royal minister, the *secrétaire d'Etat à la Marine*, and the clerks who served under him. The most minute administrative matters were brought to his attention. The Paris offices succeeded "in persuading the minister that he could not afford to lose control over a single detail."

The King's Household

The principal department heads within the king's household were generally regarded as high crown officers ex officio.

The Grand Aumônier de France

First among the departments of the king's household was that of the *grand aumônier de France*. This post was held in 1665 by Antoine Barberini, nephew of Pope Urban VIII, camerlengo of the Roman Catholic church, archbishop of Reims, first duke-and-peer of France, abbé de Saint-Evraul, etc., born commander of the Orders of the King and normally responsible for investigating the lives and morals of the knights of the Order and for receiving their professions of faith. He swore an oath of fealty directly into the hands of the king. Oaths of fealty were sworn to him by eight *aumôniers servants*, nine chaplains, eight clerics of the royal oratory and chapel, one *confesseur du commun*, etc. He certified the oath of fealty sworn on the

Gospel during mass to the king by all new archbishops, bishops, grand priors, and certain abbots. He was in charge of releasing prisoners on behalf of the king, as well as for the ceremonies associated with the king's accession, anointment, marriage, and first entry into a city, and for important annual festivals. He was bishop of the court. He baptized kings, princes, and god-children of kings and queens, gave their first communion, and administered the other sacraments. He officiated at the engagement and marriage cere-monies of princes and princesses. He appointed a vicar-general to serve under him. Under his authority were the leper-houses of France, the readers of the Royal College,[1] the college of Maître Gervais, the college of Navarre, the hospitals of the Quinze-Vingt, the Haduriettes, the Six-Vingt *aveugles* of Chartres, and other similar establishments.

The *premier aumônier* fulfilled all the functions of the *grand aumônier* in his absence. The king's eight *aumôniers* served quarterly terms and were required to attend the king's rising, mass, dinner, supper, and retirement and to administer the sacraments to the king and court. Eight chaplains and eight clerics, also serving quarterly terms, were available to replace the *aumôniers* during absences; there were also two chapel clerks, one master of the oratory and one chapel music master, both bishops, eight chaplains for grand masses, five clerics and four music masters serving quarterly terms, the king's confessor, always a Jesuit, five chaplains of Saint-Roch or *cha-pelains du commun*, the *confesseur du commun*, the chaplains of the guard companies, musketeers, etc. The king's ecclesiastical officers always sat on His Majesty's right in chapel, while bishops and abbots sat only on his left.

The Grand Maître

The post of *grand maître de la Maison du Roi*, which in 1665 was held by Monsieur le Prince, Louis de Bourbon, prince de Condé, and Monsieur le Duc, his son, as heir, was considered to have descended from the office of mayor of the palace under the first French royal dynasty. It was the *grand maître* who, when the king died, threw his staff on the king's casket before the assembled officers to indicate that their responsibilities were at an end; the king's heir then reinstated them by his grace. The *grand maître* filled the seven kitchen offices, whose holders swore an oath of fealty to him and were under his jurisdiction. Ever since the time of the comte de Soissons, *grand maître* under Henri IV, the *grands maîtres* had voluntarily relinquished their responsibility for the royal food and libation to the king himself. The *grand maître* also received an oath of fealty from the *écuyers* of the Petite Ecurie, the chaplains of Saint-Roch, etc. When he did ceremonial service and accompanied the king's meats, he marched at the head of all the *maîtres d'hôtel* and serving gentlemen and held his staff high, while all the other *maîtres d'hôtel* held theirs low in his presence. It was he who presented the king his napkin. The *bureau du roi* met under his authority.

In the absence of the *grand maître*, the *premier maître d'hôtel* replaced him; every morning he accompanied the king's bouillon and received the king's orders for food and drink. There were twelve *maîtres d'hôtel* serving quarterly terms and one ordinary *maître d'hôtel*.

The *bureau du roi* met on Tuesdays and Thursdays. Participants were supposed to include the *premier maître d'hôtel*, the *maîtres d'hôtel* for that quarter, the *maîtres de la Chambre aux deniers* (*ancien*, *alternatif*, and *triennal* serving in rotation), and their clerks, who received the funds for provisions for the royal household along with wages for the officers and liveried servants. Two *contrôleurs généraux* served for half a year each, and their *commis* had the status of officeholders. The expense accounts were kept by sixteen clerks serving quarterly terms.

The names of the seven offices were as follows: the *Gobelet* and *la Cuisine-bouche pour le service du roi; la Paneterie-commun; l'Echansonnerie-commun, la Cuisine-commun, la Fruiterie-commun*, and *la Fourière pour le bois*.

A large number of officers served in each of these offices. For example, the *Cuisine-bouche du roi* included eight squires, one ordinary squire, four master cooks, four *hâteurs* (meat chefs), four soup cooks, four pastry makers, three kitchen boys, four bearers, four keepers of the china—all serving quarterly terms—two ushers, two clerks of the pantry, two clerks of the spit, and two call boys—serving six-month terms—three dishwashers and six *serts d'eau*—serving two-month terms—and, finally, an ordinary clerk of the hunt.

For the king's dinner, there was one grand pantler, one grand cupbearer, one squire meatcutter, thirty-six serving gentlemen, and twelve ushers of the dining room, serving quarterly terms.

All officers in the seven offices were entitled to wear swords, even while serving.

In addition to the foregoing officers, there were four barber-surgeons, one regular captain of the convoy, caterers, and provisioning merchants including bakers, wine-sellers, linen dealers, and so on.

The Grand Chambellan

The *grand chambellan*, or grand chamberlain, served and did the honors in the king's Chamber, presented the king's nightshirt, and witnessed the oath of fealty sworn into the king's hands by the dukes and other vassals, the marshals of France, the governors of provinces and fortresses, and the high crown officers. When the king held a *lit de justice* or meeting of the Estates General, the grand chamberlain sat at his feet on a square of purple velvet covered with golden *fleurs de lys*. At audiences with ambassadors, he stood behind the king's chair. When the king died, it was the grand chamberlain who wrapped his body in the shroud, assisted by the *gentilshommes de la Chambre*.

Under the grand chamberlain were the four *premiers gentilshommes de la Chambre*, who served yearly terms. They performed the duties of the grand chamberlain in his absence; during their year's service, they received the oaths of the other officers of the Chamber and rode in the king's carriage.

Each had six pages of the Chamber, who received instruction in a variety of activities appropriate to gentlemen of their station.

The secretaries of the Chamber were. none other than the secretaries of state.

There were four *premiers valets de chambre*, sixteen *huissiers de la Chambre*, serving quarterly terms, two *huissiers ordinaires de l'anti-chambre*, two *huissiers de Cabinet*, serving six month terms, some forty *valets de chambre*, some serving quarterly terms and others serving in alternate years, twelve coat-holders, who served quarterly terms, and one coat-holder who was also responsible for handling the king's balls in the *jeu de paume*, two harquebus carriers, serving half-year terms, one ordinary armor carrier, one first barber-*valet de chambre*, eight barbers-*valets de chambre* serving quarterly terms, one ordinary barber, eight tapestry makers-*valets de chambre*, four watchmakers serving quarterly terms, three bone setters serving four-month terms, one *opérateur du roi pour la pierre*, six *garçons ordinaire de la Chambre*, nine bed and furniture movers, serving quarterly terms, the captain of the mules, and a number of painters, shoemakers, carpenters, glaziers, locksmiths, and sculptors, all of whom bore the title *valets de chambre*.

A similar retinue of officers served the wardrobe.

The king's Cabinet included the following departments: the Cabinet of Affairs and Dispatches, staffed by four secretaries, who took care of the king's private affairs and served quarterly terms, and several couriers; the Cabinet of Books, to which a copy of every book printed by privilege had to be submitted according to letters patent issued in August 1658; and, attached to the latter department, the king's public library, located in the university, to which two copies of books printed by privilege had to be submitted. The king's Cabinet included a reader of the chamber and of the cabinet, a reader in charge of celestial and terrestrial globes, an ecclesiastical reader, several interpreters, and a number of historiographers. Also included in the king's Cabinet were the Cabinet of Antiques and the Cabinet of Arms.

Four other corps belonged to the Chamber: the Birds of the Chamber, one flock for the fields and another *vol pour Pie*, independent of the great falconer; the small dogs of the Chamber; the trumpets and drums of the Chamber, under the orders of the Grande Ecurie; the furniture repository; and the musicians of the Chamber.

Many persons called themselves *gentilshommes de la Chambre* though they had neither rank nor salary.

The twenty-five *gentilshommes ordinaires* of the king's household, who served six-month terms, were at the king's beck and call, ready to receive his orders, to carry on negotiations abroad, to raise troops, to assume commands in the army, to set up winter quarters, to convey the king's wishes to the provinces, *parlements*, and sovereign courts, to serve as the king's *aides de camp* when he was with the army, and to escort prisoners of rank to the dungeons. Out of this group came several marshals of France and knights of the Order.

The king's household included medical personnel: one first physician, one ordinary physician, eight physicians serving quarterly terms, a similar roster of surgeons, four apothecaries and a like number of aides, serving quarterly terms, a number of apothecary-distillers, herbalists, and the like.

The Grand Ecuyer

The *Grand Ecuyer* of France, or Master of the Horse, swore an oath of fealty into the hands of the king. Almost all the other stable officers swore oaths of fealty to the Grand Ecuyer. He had the power to fill most vacant posts in the Grande and Petite Ecuries (Great and Small Stables), the royal stud farms, and associated organs; he also selected most of the merchants and craftsmen who supplied these operations. He approved and signed the personnel lists. No other equerry could school *gentilshommes* in military horsemanship and other maneuvers appropriate to the nobility without orders from the Master of the Horse. The king honored the Grand Ecuyer by making room for him in his carriage after the princes of the blood, and, when the king campaigned on horseback, the Master of the Horse stayed close to the person of His Majesty. All new horses entering Paris were sent to the Grand Ecurie to do homage to the king; the best were kept for His Majesty's service.

The staff of the Grande Ecurie included the first equerry and a number of other equerries, twenty-four pages well-versed in horsemanship, fencing, strategy, cartography, music, and other pursuits; the governors of the pages, masters, preceptors, forty-two footmen, eight quartermasters, ten coachmen, three postilions, eight blacksmiths, forty stable boys, fifty aides, and a number of riders, chaplains, physicians, surgeons, apothecaries, armorers, light infantrymen, cooks, sommeliers, washermen serving quarterly terms, guards, innumerable suppliers, and one hundred twenty horses.

The stud farm at Saint-Léger near Montfort-l'Amaury was headed by an equerry who had under him fourteen guards, two stable boys, two aides, and a number of marshals, surgeons, apothecaries, stud horses, mares, foals, and so on.

The twenty-seven heralds-at-arms each bore the name of a province, except the first, the king-at-arms, who was known as "Mont-joye Saint-Denis." In addition there were so-called "poursuivants-at-arms."

The Petite Ecurie, where the horses the king used regularly were kept, had a first equerry, who swore an oath of fealty into the hands of the king, an ordinary equerry, and twenty equerries serving quarterly terms, who swore oaths of fealty into the hands of the *grand maître* of the king's household. The equerry of the day had to attend the king's awakening and follow the king's horse or carriage at all times, dogging the king's steps and entering wherever he entered. The staff of the Petite Ecurie included twenty-one pages, a governor, a preceptor, a silversmith, a physician, four surgeons, one apothecary, one light infantryman, two dancing masters, two men-at-arms, a pacer, two oilskin carriers, several masters, four quartermasters, one *écuyer ordinaire de cuisine*, two *garçons ordinaires des pages*, one washerman, seventeen ordinary footmen, four blacksmiths, twelve stable-boys, several chair carriers, three master coachmen in charge of carriages, barouches, etc.

Liveried officers of the Grand Ecurie wore a distinctive braid around the wrist of their coatsleeves; those of the Petite Ecurie wore theirs on their trouser leg.

The Household Militia

There were two sorts of royal guards: those who served inside the palace and those who served outside. Inside there were four companies of body-guards, Scottish and French; the Hundred Swiss, the company of archers of the Grand Prévôt, and the Guards of the Gate. Outside guards included a company of men-at-arms and a company of light horse among the cavalry, and two regiments of French and Swiss guards among the infantry. There were also mounted musketeers, one company on white horses, and, from the time of Mazarin on, another on black horses.

There were also the Cent-Gentilshommes halberdiers, who actually numbered two hundred, a first company known as the *ancienne bande* and a second company in addition.

To be sure that the guards were above suspicion, the troops were mingled, so that the captain on duty served with the lieutenant of another captain and the ensign of yet another; in addition, the guards themselves were mixed.

The Scottish company consisted of twenty-five *gentilshommes, gardes de la Manche*. Two by two, wearing white smocks with frills of gold and silver, maces in front and back, with the motto, "Erit haec quoque cognita monstres," and holding silver-edged halberds with damascened blades, their swords at their sides, they flanked the king at mass, at dinner, and at supper. At night, it was the task of one *garde de la Manche* to close all the doors and guard the keys to the palace. Every third evening, this task was entrusted to one of the Scottish guards. Six *gardes de la Manche* escorted the king to special ceremonies, such as anointments, meetings of *parlement*, and funerals.

The bodyguards were always posted directly in front of the king's ante-chamber. A sentinel armed with a carbine stood guard night and day outside the guardroom. When a grandee arrived, the guards in the guardroom formed an honor guard in two ranks and led him through the guardroom to the door of the antechamber.

The king ordinarily gave the queen eighteen of his French guards, with one *exempt*, and six Swiss guards.

The guards were served by several boys, who made up their beds, brought them the wine of the watch, etc.

The following personages were allowed to enter the royal palaces in carriage or sedan chair: all princes and cardinals, ordinary and extraordinary ambassadors of crowned heads, all dukes-and-peers of France, all marshals of France and other crown officers, and the *premiers officiers* and *officières* of the queen. This right was also tendered to a few others.

The Grand Maréchal des Logis

The king's household also included the *grand maréchal des logis*, or chief quartermaster, who was responsible for marking out lodgings for the king's household; under him served twelve quartermaster-sergeants, four corps quartermasters, forty ordinary quartermasters recommended by the companies of men-at-arms, and the *capitaine général des guides* and his men.

The Prévôt de l'Hôtel

The *juge ordinaire* of the king's household was the *prévôt de l'Hôtel, grand prévôt de France*, and he was assisted by officers named by him but provided by the king: the *lieutenant général civil et criminel*, the *lieutenant particulier civil et criminel*, the *procureur du roi*, the *greffier en chef civil et criminel* with his clerks and *procureur* candidates, a *premier* and twelve other *huissiers*, two royal notaries, and one executor of criminal judgments. The *prévôté de l'Hôtel* was located at first in the Louvre but after the death of Louis XIII moved to Fort-L'Evêque and finally met in the chamber of the Grand Conseil, where it had its hearing room, council chamber, civil and criminal registry, and bailiffs' office. On 8 September 1658, the king ordered its headquarters moved back to the Louvre. Hearings were held on Tuesdays, Thursdays, and Saturdays. In civil matters appeals were made to the Grand Conseil. In criminal matters the *prévôt de l'Hôtel* was the sovereign judge along with the *maîtres des requêtes* and magistrates of the Grand Conseil. Officers of the king's household, court, and retinue had the right to plead their cases before this tribunal.

The Grand Maître des Cérémonies

The *grand maître des cérémonies* of France, who swore an oath into the hands of the *grand maître* of the king's household, supervised a *maître des cérémonies* and an *aide des cérémonies*. They arranged all royal ceremonies and were responsible, in particular, for establishing the order of precedence at baptisms, marriages, anointments, obsequies and funerals of kings and queens, inaugurations of Estates General, *lits de justice* and royal meetings of the sovereign courts, and receptions of ordinary and extraordinary ambassadors.

Two protocol officers, serving six-month terms, were responsible for receiving and introducing into the king's chamber all foreign princes and princesses, ambassadors, gentleman representatives, residents, agents, and deputies, as well as all other persons of public notoriety.

The Buildings

Work on the king's châteaux and houses was the responsibility of a *surintendant et ordonnateur general des bâtiments et maisons royales, jardins et tapisseries du roi* (i.e., the official in charge of the royal buildings, gardens, and tapestries), four *intendants des bâtiments*, four *contrôleurs des bâtiments*, and four *trésoriers des bâtiments*. Each royal castle had a captain, a lieutenant, a chaplain, a concierge, porters, guards and *mortes-payes*, and clock-tenders.

The Hunt

The pleasures of the king were the responsibility of the Grand Veneur, or Master of the Royal Hunt, four lieutenants of the hunt, and forty-two *gentilshommes* of the hunt, all serving quarterly terms, along with various dog handlers, quartermasters, pages, blacksmiths, surgeons, dog-gelders, rabies-healers, menders of hunting togs, supply-masters, convoyers, archers, and four treasurers of the hunt. Several captains of the hunt supervised the various forests and game preserves. The grand falconer swore an oath into the hands of the king and filled all posts connected with the various flocks— of kites, herons, rooks, for the fields, rivers, meadows, etc. The grand master of the wolf hunt was served by a lieutenant and sublieutenant. *Lieutenants particuliers* served in the provinces.

Privileged Merchants and Craftsmen

The privileged merchants and craftsmen who waited on the court were named by the *prévôt de l'Hôtel*, who was their judge, guardian, and protector. They had a chaplain and were exempt from all imposts, tolls, duties, *passages*, *issues*, *gabelles*, and various other fees. There were 364 of them in 52 different trades ranging from wine merchants to makers of farthingales and including tailors, poulterers, saddlers, greengrocers and fruiters, perfumed glovers, parchment dealers, engravers and gilders, etc.

All officers of the royal household were exempt from the *tailles* and from *aides* on wines made from grapes grown by them. As for precedence in rank, they marched after the *conseillers* of *bailliages*, *sénéchaussées*, and *sièges présidiaux*, and ahead of the officeholders of *élections*, salt warehouses, and nonroyal judges.

The Grande Venerie de France

In reality, all the departments of the royal household were complex organizations with branches throughout the kingdom. Consider, for example, the *grande venerie de France*. The Grand Veneur, or Master of the Hunt, a high crown officer and invariably a member of one of the leading families of the kingdom, organized the king's hunts, the role of which was to hone in peacetime the martial skills of the sovereign and his courtiers. The Master of the Hunt saw to it that deer and boar were not hunted by private individuals without special authorization, which they could grant (ordinance of 23 March 1635, reaffirmed in 1656). The Master of the Hunt had his headquarters at the *capitainerie royale des chasses de la Varenne* in the Louvre. Violations of hunting regulations in the provinces were reported to him by the *maîtrises des Eaux et Forêts* or local presidial courts; judgment in these cases was his.

The *capitaineries royales des chasses* were game preserves, regions administered by officers of the king's household in which the right to hunt was the king's alone; these regions came under the jurisdiction of a special tribunal. There were twenty-four of them under Henri IV and thirty-nine in 1689, not counting the *capitaineries des chasses* of the provincial governors and great lords. In 1699 Louis XIV eliminated ninety-two of these preserves and kept thirteen. In 1789 eleven remained, all in the Ile-de-France.

La Varenne du Louvre

For example, the *capitainerie des chasses de la Varenne du Louvre*, created by Henri IV on 25 March 1594, covered territory on both sides of the Seine from Saint-Denis to Villeneuve-le-Roi between the *capitainerie* of Saint-Germain-en-Laye and that of Livry. In 1676 the *capitaineries* of the Louvre and Livry were broken up by the creation of the *capitainerie* of Vincennes. In 1705, the *capitainerie* of the Louvre was limited by the creation of another *capitainerie*, that of the Varenne des Tuileries, to territory south of the Seine as far as Fresnes, Rungis, and Orly. In addition to forests, these territories included "game coverts," one-acre rectangular plots planted with birch, ash, and sycamore.

In 1597 the personnel consisted of one bailiff and captain of the hunt, one *lieutenant général*, one *procureur du roi*, one *greffier*, twelve regular guards, and eight mounted guards. In 1789, it consisted of a captain of the hunt, a *lieutenant général*, a *lieutenant de robe courte*, two *sous-lieutenants*, a *procureur du roi* and his two substitutes, a *greffier en chef*, a sealkeeper, an inspector general, an inspector, a *premier exempt* and ten other *exempts*, a receiver of fines, a surveyor, a fox catcher, two *huissiers*, and ten clerks serving under the captain.

These officials were responsible for preventing poaching, particularly by *seigneurs* and *laboureurs* from nearby villages. They were supposed to see to it that no houses were built, ditches dug, gardens or meadows laid out, or stone walls erected, and to fill in unused quarries. The Compiègne ordinance of June 1624 was reiterated many times. According to the ordinance of 1560, the officials of the hunt were supposed to prevent hunting in cultivated fields as soon as the stalks of wheat appeared. In 1709 another ordinance prohibited hunting once a field was seeded. The king circumvented these prohibitions but always compensated the farmers for the damage he caused.

The tribunal of the *capitainerie de la Varenne du Louvre* met in the hall of the Hundred Swiss at the Louvre from 20 January 1598 until 2 November

1789. On the average, hearings were held every two weeks. At each session fifteen or so cases would be decided. The procedure was the same as at the Châtelet or in the presidial courts in criminal and penal cases: the game warden would make a report, followed by a requisition from the *procureur du roi;* an informational order would then be issued and a further investigation conducted; this would be followed by a new requisition, an arrest, a final requisition, and sentencing or release of the accused. The fine for letting a dog run loose was ten livres; for exploring rabbit warrens in the absence of the game wardens, the fine was twenty livres.

In 1765, Beaumarchais reintroduced the Assises, or periodic courts held in the villages, at which the bailiff would settle disputes brought before him by the villagers. Beaumarchais's plan was to hold such courts three times a year. Successful at first, thanks to the curiosity of the villagers, these courts quickly ceased to interest the populace and disappeared in 1767.

Appeals from these courts went to the king's Council and, between 1618 and 1656, to the Grand Conseil. *Parlement* received the appeal. But the magistrates of the Grand Conseil as well as of *parlement* had extensive property holdings in the Varenne du Louvre, so that they systematically set aside all penalties imposed by the lower courts. The *parlement* continued to receive appeals and the Council continued to quash its decrees until the end of Louis XIV's reign. In 1715 the victory went to the Council.

The Social Composition of the King's Household

The staff of the king's household epitomized the social stratification of the kingdom. The highest posts were given to the princes of the blood, the peers of France, and members of the highest nobility; in many cases these posts were kept within the same family for long periods of time. In 1694 the *grand aumônier de France*, born commander of the king's Orders, was Emmanuel-Théodore de la Tour d'Auvergne, cardinal of Bouillon, bishop of Albano, doctor of the House and Society of the Sorbonne, and brother of the duc de Bouillon, *grand chambellan* of France. The cardinal had held this post since 1671. The *grand maître* of the king's household was always a Condé; since 25 July 1685 it had been M. le Prince, Henry-Jules de Bourbon, prince de Condé, prince of the blood, duc d'Enghien, and governor of Burgundy and Bresse, with M. le Duc, his son, holding rights of survivorship. The *grand chambellan* was always from the house of Bouillon. In 1694, it was Godefroy-Frédéric-Maurice de la Tour d'Auvergne, sovereign duke of Bouillon, duc d'Albret and de Château-Thierry, peer of France, and governor of upper and lower Auvergne. The Grand Ecuyer of France was from Lorraine. In 1694, it was M. le comte d'Armagnac, Louis de Lorraine, great hereditary seneschal of Burgundy, governor of Anjou, and peer of France. His son had been received as heir to his posts. The Master of the Hunt was François, duc de La Rochefoucauld, prince de Marsillac, peer of France, and *grand-maître de la garde-robe du roy*. His son held the rights of survivorship.

The next lower posts went to the high-ranking nobility. Just below the *grand aumônier*, the *premier aumônier* was Messire Pierre du Comboust de Coislin, bishop of Orléans, whose nephew held the rights of survivorship. Below the *grand maître*, the *premier maître d'hôtel* was Louis Sauguin, marquis de Livry, captain of the hunt for the forest of Livry and Bondis, the husband of Marie-Antoinette de Beauvillier, daughter of the duc de Saint-Aignan. Below the *grand chambellan*, the four *premiers gentilshommes de la Chambre* were the duc d'Aumont, peer of France, governor of the Boulonnais; Leon Potier, duc de Gesvres in Valois, peer of France and governor of Paris; the duc de la Trémoille, duc de Thouars, peer of France; the duc de Beauvillier-Saint-Aignan, peer of France and governor of the Children of France. The *premier écuyer* of the Grande Ecurie was the comte de Lyonne. Below the constable, among the thirteen marshals of France, we find the most illustrious names: the d'Humières, the d'Estrées, the Joyeuse, the Villeroy, the Choiseul, the Luxembourg, with one Montmorency, the Lorge, the Noailles—all dukes, marquis, counts, and frequently peers, as well as governors. There were only two exceptions: the marquis de Boufflers, and Nicolas Catinat, who was merely *seigneur* of Saint-Gratien.

The four companies of bodyguards were commanded by four marshals: the duc de Noailles, peer of France, the duc de Duras, the duc de Luxembourg, peer of France, and the duc de Lorge. The *capitaine-colonel* of the Hundred Swiss was Michel-François Le Tellier, marquis de Courtenvaux, comte de Beaumont. The king himself was captain of his men-at-arms, but the *capitaine-lieutenant* was the prince de Soubise, François de Rohan, comte de Rochefort, governor of Champagne and Brie, and *lieutenant général* of the king's armies. Again, the king was also captain of the light horse of the royal guard; his *capitaine-lieutenant* was Charles-Honoré d'Albert, duc de Chevreuse et de Lunes, peer of France. The captain of the first company of the king's musketeers was the king; the *capitaine-lieutenant* was M. de Melun de Maupertuis, *lieutenant-général* of the king's armies; the *sous-lieutenant* was M. d'Artagnan, brigadier. Colonel of the regiment of French guards was Louis-François, marquis de Boufflers, marshal of France. The thirty-two captains of the guard all held the rank of colonel.

Posts of middle rank went to ordinary *gentilshommes*, in some cases to men of high nobility, in others to *gentilshommes* of recent date and even to newly ennobled persons. The king's household was an agency of social mobility. Serving under the *grand maître* were the king's thirty-six serving gentlemen, pantlers, cupbearers, and meatcutters and the twelve *maîtres d'hôtel*, all bearing either the title of *chevalier*, which carried with it a place in the high nobility, or that of *écuyer*. Under the *grand chambellan* were the ordinary gentlemen of the king's Chamber, who numbered twenty-five under Henri IV and who were supposed to be always at the king's beck and call, ready to receive his commands, transmit orders to the provinces, *parlements*, and other sovereign courts, and represent him abroad. Many other *gentilshommes* served in other posts. Among the four *premiers valets de chambre ordinaires* were M. de Nyett, marquis de La Neuville and governor of Limoges, as well as an ordinary gentleman, M. Quentin, sieur de la Vienne, marquis de Chancenets.

In the lowest positions we find commoners of every rank. Serving under the *grand maître* in the departments of the Gobelet, Paneterie-bouche, and Echansonnerie-bouche were *bourgeois* wealthy enough to be *seigneurs* of a *seigneurie*. Among the aides, *sommiers*, wine servers, and the like were representatives of all the lower orders: from small merchants, journeymen masters, and *compagnons* without quality down to kitchen boys and other lackeys. Similarly, under the *grand chambellan* we find men of every rank, ranging from merchants and wholesalers down to stableboys and including artisans, glaziers, locksmiths, carpenters, cabinetmakers, painters, sculptors, furniture movers, etc. All these individuals obtained some measure of social advancement and consideration as a result of their work in the king's household.

The Role of Authority and Unification of the King's Household

The personnel of the king's household constituted chains bound together by ties of fealty, which strengthened the connection between the king and the kingdom. Department heads swore an oath to the king and in turn received the oath of loyalty to the king from their direct subordinates, and so on down the line. For example, the *grand aumônier* swore an oath into the hands of the king and then received the oaths of the bishops, which ran as follows: "I swear by the very holy and sacred name of God, Sire, and promise to Your Majesty that, as long as I shall live, I shall be a faithful subject and servant. That I shall work with all my power in your service and for the good of your State. That I shall not harm Your Majesty or your State by my participation in any council, design, or undertaking. And if anything of the kind comes to my attention, I shall make it known to Your Majesty. May God and these holy Gospels aid me in my purpose." The king distributed throughout the provinces commissions for officers of the royal household. These helped to create loyal supporters and representatives in the most remote provinces. Further work remains to be done to see whether these commissions always corresponded to actual services at court. Family and not merely personal loyalties were involved. *Survivances* made half the posts hereditary, not even counting those that were passed on to nephews or cousins.

Much of the household staff did not serve continuously. Some worked one year out of four, for example; others, three or six months out of twelve. The four *premiers gentilshommes de la Chambre* served one year in four; the two *grands maîtres de la garde-robe*, every other year. The *gentilshommes ordinaire de la Chambre du roi* served six months per year, twelve of them attending the king during one semester, and thirteen during the other. The bulk of the staff served for three months each year: the twelve *maîtres d'hotel*, all *gentilshommes*, the thirty-six serving gentlemen, the four *secré-*

taires de la Chambre, the secretaries of the Cabinet of Affairs and Dispatches, the four companies of the bodyguard, the four captains of the guard, the thirty-two *valets de chambre*, the twelve lieutenants of the guard, the *maîtres des requêtes de l'Hôtel*, etc.

The first consequence of this system was that the household officers were left free to serve the king in other ways, particularly as *commissaires*. A further consequence was that they were able to go back to their property in the provinces, bringing with them the style of life, the wit, and the maxims of the court. Thus the court was not only an effective agency of government but also a powerful unifying force in the kingdom, encouraging worship of the king, feelings of loyalty, and the notion of *raison d'état*. The court impressed on the minds of the French people the idea that the king was above humanity, as connoted by the decorative symbolism of the royal dwellings and the ceremonial symbolism of rites such as the king's rising, retiring, and dinner, which had an almost religious mystique.

When the king dined in public, his table was set up in his antechamber. When His Majesty called for the meat course, the *maître d'hôtel* on duty that day, the serving gentlemen, and the clerk supervisor on call all went to the "Bouche," or department of the kitchens in charge of preparing the king's food. The *écuyer-bouche* would then offer the *maître d'hôtel* two pieces of bread. With these the *maître d'hôtel* would touch the king's meat; he would then hand one piece to the *écuyer-bouche* and eat the other himself, to be sure that the food had not been poisoned. The serving gentlemen, the supervisor clerk, and the *officiers de la Bouche* would then each take a plate. The *maître d'hôtel*, who held the staff of command, marched at the head of the line, just behind the dining-room usher, who carried a smaller staff. Two bodyguards escorted the meat. At the king's table, the *maître d'hôtel* would bow to the royal place setting, even if the king had not yet arrived. The serving gentleman who was carrying the first plate would test it for poison and then have all the other plates tested by the person carrying each one.

The serving gentlemen who were acting as cupbearer and meatcarver were stationed at the king's table, facing the king. When the king asked for something to drink, the cupbearer would shout, "Drink for the king." Preceded by a guard, he would then go to the buffet. The chief cupbearer would hand him a saucer with a glass inverted on top of it, a cover, and an enamel sampling cup, and would then himself carry the two decanters, one of wine, the other of water, over to the king. The chief cupbearer then bowed to the king, rinsed the glass that the cupbearer was holding on the saucer, and filled it with wine and water. The chief and the cupbearer would then test the mix on themselves. Then the serving gentleman would carry the glass to the king, who drank, while the cupbearer held the saucer under the glass. The cupbearer then took the empty glass, bowed to the king, and returned the glass to the chief cupbearer.

The serving gentleman acting as meatcarver would test all the dishes, the bread, and even the napkins with a piece of bread, which he then gave to the officer of the Gobelet who had set the table. The meatcarver uncovered and displayed all the dishes, carved all the meats, and changed the king's plates and napkins with each course. At the end of the dinner he presented the king with a napkin to wash himself.

The napkins were brought to the table in a nef covered with a scented cushion. The king's *aumônier* would uncover the nef, the cupbearer would hold the cushion, and the meatcarver would remove the napkins.

The king was presented his napkin by the princes of the blood when they were present at dinner. In important ceremonies, the functions of the serving gentlemen were taken over by the grand pantler, cupbearer, and meatcarver.

All the departments of the king's household had another responsibility in addition to the role they played in assuring the king's well-being and amusement and in governing the kingdom: namely, to shape the minds and hearts of the French people and thereby contribute to the harmony of French society. Consider the king's music, for example. The Venetian ambassador wrote that Louis XIV spent 100 million a year on music. The court did in fact consume a great deal of music for liturgies, masses, *Te Deums*, Requiems, festivals, balls, operas, ballets, meals, promenades, and periods of relaxation. The court lived on a wealth of sound.

This was not merely because its members had a taste for and took pleasure in music. The people of this time were convinced that music was necessary to the morality of man and the tranquillity of the state. These ideas originated with Plato, inspired by the Pythagoreans. From Plato they were passed on to the Alexandrian Greeks, to Saint Augustine, to Boethius, to Marsilio Ficino and the Platonic Academy of Florence, to the circle of Marguerite de Navarre, to the poets of the Pléiade, to Marin Mersenne of the convent of the Minimes in the place Royale (*Quaestiones celeberrimae in Genesim*, 1632; *Harmonie universelle*, 1634), and to René Descartes (*Compendium musicae*). After 1660 a number of anonymous writers on musical subjects made these ideas commonplace. They were frequently invoked in *Le Mercure galant*, which printed court news and gossip. In the October 1680 issue, the poet Rault, from Rouen, explained that harmony was a divine creation, since everything in the world is essentially number, weight, and measure. Music, embodying all of these, reproduced the essence of the world. Through harmony it expressed the movement of the planets and the essence of nature. In creating musical harmony, the composer supplied mankind with the principle of its existence as well as the principle of its government, for music established harmony in the state by analogy with the harmony of the Universe; music established harmony in the soul of man by its numerical intervals in pitch and rhythm; the forms of good music reinforced the fundamental laws of the state. Music helped the king and the magistrates to maintain law and order. Louis XIV was aware of this—the pages of *Le Mercure galant* are full of essays of this sort on music and dance. Ballets and operas were a necessary part of good government, of a well-ordered, harmonious, and moral state and society.

These ideas gave rise to institutions. Under Louis XIV and Louis XV there were a hundred or so musician-officers; there were also "*ordinaires de la musique du roi,*" who were not officers but hired on retainer and provided with allowances, bonuses, and pensions. There were also "*extraordinaires,*" artists from the town, soloists, and visiting foreigners, as well as "musicians following the court," who received letters from the *grand prévôt de l'Hôtel* and were employed from time to time. It was common for many posts to be held by the same person, and posts were often passed on to heirs. After twenty-five consecutive years in the same post, a musician was eligible to be officially declared a veteran and receive a pension. Officially, musicians were grouped in various departments of the monarchy. Some served under the *grand aumônier* in the chapel, the chapel-oratory for liturgy, and the music-chapel. Others, such as Lully, Delalande, and Destouches, made themselves illustrious in the service of the *grand chambellan*, providing music for royal dinners, festivals, anointments, marriages, and funerals. Still others worked for the Grand Ecurie, which also employed dancing-masters to teach pages and down-at-heels provincial gentlemen between 15 and 16 years of age the arts of fencing, dance, etiquette, mathematics, drawing, writing, and mounted acrobatics. Other musicians were employed by the king's Cabinet, which organized the group of "little violins," and the household militia, all of whose companies had musicians, trumpeters, tympanists, fifers. The musketeers also used oboes in all their entertainments.

The households of the queens, princes, and princesses of the blood were similar to those of the king.

The Court Residences

Between the entry of Henri IV into Paris in 1594 and the death of Anne of Austria in 1666, the court usually resided in that city, the kingdom's capital. The king spent his winters at Paris, and visited Fontainebleau, Saint-Germain, Chantilly, and Versailles (where a first *pavillon* was built in 1622 and a second in 1627) during the summer. The king frequently returned to Paris during the summer, however, to receive ambassadors and provincial delegations and to hold council meetings. The king lived in the Louvre, the royal residence since the time of Catherine de Médicis. From 1643 to 1652, Anne of Austria and the young Louis XIV lived in the Palais-Cardinal.

The court was a large group. Civilians alone numbered 1,517 under Henri IV, and in 1648 the household militia nominally numbered 17,083 men, many of whom were with the army, however. The Louvre was too small. Neither members of civilian households nor of the household militia nor domestic servants lived there. They came to perform their various functions at different times of the day, from five in the morning until eleven at night. A crowd of pages, attendants, coachmen, serving boys, aides, and soldiers mingled there with people of all sorts, for the Louvre was open to all. Everywhere the colors of the Bourbons were in view: blue, white, and pink.

The French guards wore blue uniforms with collars and ornaments in red bordered with white. The Musketeers, created in 1622, wore red uniforms and blue hats with large crosses, and so on.

After 1666 Louis XIV began staying at Versailles for longer and longer periods. On 6 May 1682, he moved there with his court and remained until his death. The regent took the young Louis XV back to Paris. In 1723, however, Louis XV returned to Versailles, and the court remained there until 6 October 1789. Blue, white, and red continued to be the royal colors. Lodgings had to be found at Versailles for the members of the court, though some of them had a *hôtel*, house, or apartment in either Versailles or Paris (Paris and Versailles were thought of as being parts of one large city). Counting domestics, Versailles housed a population of 10,000 persons in 1744, or so we are told.

The court, then, was an essential instrument for preserving the social structure, making the society dependent on the king, and keeping the king's subjects obedient to his will.

The Decline of the Court and the Royal Household

As the ministers, the secretaries of state, the *côntroleur général des Finances*, and the various bureaus they controlled claimed broader and broader powers, the royal household came to be thought of as having responsibilities limited to the king's domestic service. This changed perception probably reflected an actual reduction in the household's powers. According to the *Almanach royal* of 1763, many services that were legally the responsibility of high crown officers and officers of the royal household were in fact distributed among various jurisdictions and bureaus, ranging from the councils and ministers to bureaus such as the *prévôté de l'Hôtel*, the admiralty of France, the artillery of France, etc. The sense of the unity and role of the court was lost, and the court became merely the king's immediate entourage, devoted to his well-being and amusement. The bulk of administrative and political power was now wielded by the ministerial bureaus and the bureaus of the councils. The proliferation of clerks laid the groundwork for the bureaucratic administration of the nineteenth century, diminishing the importance of the court.

The new administrative practices, coupled with the changed perception of the court's role, led Louis XVI to reduce the number of household officers as an economy measure.

The reorganization of the army between 1775 and 1777 led to the virtual disappearance of the household militia. The civilian household was gradually pruned back in a series of measures, principally in 1779–80 and 1787. Before 1779 there had been a large number of accountants and treasurers in the royal household: *maître de la Chambre aux Deniers, trésorier de l'Argenterie, trésorier des Menus-Plaisirs,* etc. One of Necker's advisers proposed the following three-point reform:

—strip the high crown officers of all power over expenditures;

—replace all the special treasurers by a single general treasurer of the royal household;

—eliminate all the *intendants* and *contrôleurs généraux*.

This reform was accomplished by the edicts of July 1779 and January and August 1780.

The edict of January 1780 created a "General Bureau of Royal Household Expenditures," consisting of five *commissaires généraux* to be named (and removed) by the secretary of state for the royal household (one *commissaire* for the kitchen, one for amusements and Chamber business, one for furniture, one for stables and the hunt, and one for various other departments), two *maîtres des comptes*, one first clerk of the royal household, one newly created *trésorier général* (edict of July 1779), one secretary, and one *intendant du Trésor royal*. The edict of March 1780 authorized the *commissaires généraux* to hold other posts in the royal household as well. If they were not noble, they were given the title of *écuyer* and required to post a bond of 500,000 livres. These were thus *bourgeois* living nobly and on the way to ennoblement. In fact, some first clerks of the royal household acquired the post of *commissaire général* in addition to their clerkships. The *commissaires généraux* signed contracts along with the minister, examined expenditure reports, and collectively signed payment orders. The secretary of state acting as minister of the royal household was in charge of the bureau. It was he who authorized or rejected expenditures. Directly under him was the *contrôleur général des Finances*.

In reality, it was not long before the secretary of state for the royal household began making decisions on his own in consultation with individual *commissaires généraux*, so that by 1789 the bureau was merely a formality. Despite the letters patent of 20 March 1782, which ostensibly mandated that accounts must be signed by the *grand maître* and *grand écuyer*, the minister of the royal household continued to have sole charge of the household finances.

Another edict, issued in August 1780, eliminated 406 posts in the departments of the *grand maître*, the *Bouche du roi*, and the *Commun*.

An edict of 9 August 1787 upset the traditional organization of service on a quarterly basis, even though "serving for a quarter" had been considered an honor. As of 12 January 1788, all services of the Chambre du Roi that had been carried out on a quarterly basis were now to be carried out on a half-yearly basis, and half of the posts were eliminated. Exceptions were made for the *premiers gentilshommes de la Chambre* and the *premiers valets de chambre*, four of whom were retained in each category. The same was true in the *garde-robe*, where, in addition, twenty-eight privileged offices in arts and crafts that had been casual offices responsible to the *grand maître de la garde-robe*, the duc de Liancourt, were eliminated.

As of 1 October 1787, the Grande and Petite *écuries* were combined. In fact, the Petite Ecurie was eliminated. A large number of pages, equerries, and bureaus disappeared. The number of royal equerries serving on a quarterly basis was cut in half, and the remaining equerries had to serve for six months at a time. The number of horses, carriages, and personnel attached to the Ecurie was cut to the bare minimum. Also eliminated on the same date were the whole of the grand falconry, the flock, the headquarters of the wolf hunt, and the dog pack used in hunting wild boar.

The household militia had already been cut drastically. The king reorganized the men-at-arms and the light horse, sent the officers back to the regular army, and reimbursed them what they had paid for their offices. The company of gate guards was also reorganized.

In the queen's household, the king ordered the elimination of all inessential posts in the Bouche, the Chambre, and the Ecurie. Despite the reimbursements and retirements that had to be paid, he anticipated a gain of 900,000 livres for the royal treasury.

The king ordered the demolition or sale of the châteaux of Choisy, La Muette, Madrid, Vincennes, and Blois, and the sale of all his houses in Paris.

Other posts were eliminated in March 1789.

On the eve of the Revolution, the royal household had almost disappeared. The court had lost all its political and social functions. Its only remaining function was to serve the king and his family personally. All governmental and administrative functions were handled by the ministries. The destruction of the royal household may have greatly facilitated the movements of 1789.

Note

1. Collège de France.

11   Chancellors, Councils, and Ministers from 1598 to 1661

In principle the king's Council was his court. The detached branches of the "Cour le Roi"—the *parlement*, the Chambre des Comptes, and the Cour des Aides—always laid claim to being the king's Council. In actuality, however, the king governed in conjunction with a council whose members he had gained the right to choose himself, more or less freely. To be sure, he accepted as council members people who claimed membership as their birthright—members of his family, the queen, his eldest son, the princes of the blood, and the peers. The king named some persons to his Council by virtue of their functions—the chancellor of France and the high crown officers, for example. The most stable and active element of the council membership, however, consisted of the king's *fidèles*, his devoted servants. Neither the Estates General nor the *parlement* could force the king to accept a specific individual as a councillor. This relative freedom to choose the members of his Council was all the more important since it was there that the king made up his mind. He made decisions in Council. His decisions were then issued as *arrêts du Conseil*, or council decrees, sometimes in the form of letters patent, sometimes not. Once issued as decrees, the king's decisions were ready to be put into effect.

In important governmental affairs, the king was always in attendance at meetings of his Council. Decrees bore the formula, "The king being in his Council." These decrees were orders. In routine judicial and police matters that could be settled in accordance with precedents, however, the king was not present, though it was assumed that he was. This fiction was necessary because, without it, council decrees would not have been binding. The Council by itself did not exist. Hence no power could be delegated to it. The king was supposed to make all decisions. In such cases, council decrees bore the formula, "The king in his Council." These were known as "decrees upon request."

In principle there was but one king's Council. In fact, this Council met in a variety of sessions, each of which was called a council of some sort. A distinction should be made, first of all, between Councils of Government and Councils of Justice and Police, the former dealing with administrative matters and the latter with disputes.

The Councils of Government were composed of the king's favorites and *fidèles*, along with cardinals, bishops, princes, dukes, marshals of France, chancellors, secretaries of state, and other persons chosen by the king and given his confidence. The membership changed with changes in royal favor and policy.

Under Henri IV and Louis XIII and during the first part of Louis XIV's reign, there was a Supreme Council consisting of the king and one or more other individuals, which came to a decision on the most delicate matters before they were submitted to the Council of Government. This was known as the "Secret Council" or "Conseil de Cabinet"; its membership was limited to Louis XIII and Richelieu and sometimes Séguier, for example.

The "Conseil des Affaires," known after 1643 as the "Conseil d'En Haut," always included the king, the ministers of state (the prime minister, the chancellor or keeper of the seals, the chief justice, the *surintendant des Finances*, the *chef des Finances*, and the secretary of state for foreign affairs), the *secrétaire d'état en mois*, a variety of people whose advice the king wished to solicit, members of the Conseil d'Etat, and the *maîtres des requêtes* from whom the king had requested a report. The competence of this Council extended "generally to affairs of the greatest importance such as it please His Majesty to ordain." In 1633, it consisted of Louis XIII, Richelieu, Séguier, the keeper of the seals, Bullion, the *surintendant*, Chavigny, and Sublet de Noyers.

The "Conseil des Dépêches," responsible for provincial matters and the internal administration of the kingdom, met from time to time after 1617. It was organized on a permanent basis between 1649 and 1652, during the Fronde.

The "Conseil des Finances" or "Conseil de la Direction," or "Grande Direction," gathered resources and approved expenditures. It was a higher council, consisting of the chancellor or keeper of the seals, the *surintendant des Finances*, the *contrôleurs généraux des Finances*, and the *trésorier de l'Epargne;* Council secretaries and secretaries of state were entitled to take part in its deliberations. The agenda of this Council was prepared by the "Petite Direction," made up of specialists: *surintendants des Finances, directeurs des Finances, contrôleurs généraux des Finances, intendants des Finances*, and various *trésoriers*.

There were two councils for routine administrative matters and private disputes: the Conseil d'Etat et des Finances and the Conseil privé or Conseil des Parties. Members were named to serve on both councils at the same time. A career as a state councillor began with these two councils. *Maîtres des requêtes* reported to the Conseil privé and offered their opinions. From 1624 on they also had access to the Conseil d'Etat et des Finances, and soon thereafter they were offering opinions there, too. Princes of the blood, cardinals, other princes, dukes-and-peers, high crown officers, secretaries of state, and *intendants des Finances* had access to these two councils and could take part in deliberations and vote.

At the beginning of the period we are studying, the Conseil d'Etat et des Finances was a political and administrative council. Little by little, it lost most of its responsibilities. From 1623 on, it was merely the section of the king's Council that heard litigation in matters of finance involving disputes between private individuals and *traitants*, the financial affairs of the clergy, disputes over the reimbursement of officeholders, the award of farms, contracts for public works, leases, and contracts for supplies and munitions. After 1644, it retained jurisdiction only over contract awards and cases between private individuals involving financial matters.

The Conseil privé or Conseil des Parties, on the other hand, increased in importance. It accepted most appeals of cases between private parties and took on an administrative and policymaking role. It had always had appellate jurisdiction over decrees of the sovereign courts. From 1630 on, it began examining remonstrances from the sovereign courts. After 1645, it assumed jurisdiction over rebellions against council decrees, ordinances of military and provincial intendants, *trésoriers de France*, and various royal *commissaires*. It became a key instrument of absolutism.

Other sections of the king's Council, long contemplated, began to be created in 1643.

A Conseil de Conscience, concerned with nominations to ecclesiastical benefices, was instituted by Anne of Austria upon the death of Louis XIII, whose idea it had been. It consisted of Mazarin, the bishops of Lisieux and Beauvais, and "M. Vincent, General of the Fathers of the Mission"—Saint Vincent de Paul. The two bishops later became estranged from the court and were not replaced.

A War Council was created on 2 September 1616, but it met only once. In 1617 the king proposed an identical council to the notables, but nothing was ever done about it. The duc d'Orléans, *lieutenant général des armées du roi*, established a War Council in 1643. This time it took root and flourished. According to the *Etats de la France*, it met in the king's Chamber and "ordinarily" included the king, the prime minister (always), the ministers of state, the marshals of France, the senior *lieutenants généraux* in the armies, and the secretaries of state.

Preparatory work for all the councils was done by a variety of committees. There were permanent committees attached to all the councils, in addition to the bureaus of the secretaries of state, the preliminary ministerial meetings, the Direction des Finances, and the Assemblée des Maîtres des Requêtes. Committees were generally composed of three or four councillors and an *intendant des Finances*. Each committee dealt with a number of provinces. Committee members reported on *cahiers*, articles, remonstrances, and requests sent to the council, and they prepared decrees. Every so often, after a year or two or three, councillors switched provinces. Some reports were turned over to *maîtres des requêtes*.

These committees were reorganized in accordance with regulations issued on 21 May 1615; further regulations, issued at Tours on 6 August 1619 improved the organization of the committees attached to the Conseil des Finances. Four committees were set up, each responsible for several tax farms dispersed all over France and for several *généralités*, located close to one another but constituting two or three separate groups. The farms did not coincide with the groups of *généralités:* the farm of the *comptablie* or tax district of Bordeaux was assigned to the committee responsible for the *généralités* of Bourges, Soissons, Limoges, Dauphiné, and Moulins. This organization does not seem to have changed prior to 1666.

The important Paris regulations of 16 June 1627 instituted ten other committees to serve all the councils, dealing with such matters as the clergy, tax farms, suits arising out of taxes, police, public assistance, inventions, arts and manufactures, war, justice, the *"religion prétendue réformée"* (Protestantism), shipping and commerce, foreigners, and complaints from the provinces (Languedoc, Normandy, Brittany, Burgundy, and Béarn). These committees were supposed to consist of five to seven councillors. The ministers Richelieu and Schomberg, the *surintendant des Finances*, d'Effiat, the twelve ordinary councillors, and the semestrial councillor Collemoulins from Rouen were supposed to sit on these committees, to which the chancellor could name other state councillors, *maîtres des requêtes*, prelates in matters concerning the clergy, guild masters, and other technicians. Richelieu was the sole member of the Committee on Shipping and Commerce, except at such times "as he shall be pleased to assemble the Council." Schomberg served only on the War Committee. D'Effiat belonged to two committees, the younger Châteauneuf to five, and Champigny to seven.

Besides these permanent committees, temporary committees were set up to study a specific matter, to put an edict into effect, or to sit in judgment. In the latter cases they were viewed as detached fragments of the Council, veritable temporary subcouncils with full powers to issue decrees, as, for example, in the case of the Chambre de Justice de l'Arsenal of 1631, or that of the committee that sat in judgment over the governors of La Capelle and the Châtelet after the capture of Corbie. The councils were so overburdened, however, that proposed decrees submitted by the permanent committees were turned into official decrees by the signature of the chancellor without ever being deliberated in any council.

Efforts were made to gather the minutes of council decrees that remained dispersed among the various council secretaries and their heirs in order to have them transcribed, assembled in one room at the Louvre, and entrusted to professional archivists.

The Personnel of the Royal Councils

The ministers of state had access to the king's Council. Ministers of state included all those who were called by the king to appear before the Conseil des Affaires or Conseil d'En-Haut. Some of these owed their access merely to a brevet. One minister of state might be given the title "Principal Minister," as Richelieu was in 1629 and Mazarin later on.

Sully, Richelieu, and Mazarin held a number of posts at the same time. Sully was *conseiller d'Etat, surintendant des Finances, grand voyer de France, grand maître de l'artillerie,* superintendent of buildings and fortifications, grand master of ports and harbors, and hereditary captain of streams and rivers. Richelieu, who abolished the posts of constable and admiral, was named "Principal Ministre de nostre Conseil d'Etat" on 21 November 1629 and was also grand master, chief, and general superintendent of shipping and commerce (1626), governor of La Rochelle and the Aunis region (1630), peer of France (1631), governor and lieutenant general of Brittany, governor of the city of Nantes (1632), colonel of a regiment of mounted French musketeers known as "dragoons" (1635), cardinal of the Holy Roman Church, abbot general of the Cluniac order, abbot of eighteen abbeys, prior of two priories, including Saint-Martin-des-Champs in Paris, and *proviseur* of the Sorbonne.

Mazarin was the general superintendent and comptroller of buildings, arts, and manufactures, superintendent in charge of the upbringing and education of the king and Monsieur (from 15 March 1646 until approximately 1658), minister and head of the Council, duke-and-peer of France with a duchy-peerage consisting of the Nivernais, the Donziois, and Mayenne, *bailli, gruyer, et maître des Eaux et Forêts* of La Fère, the county of Marle, Ham, and the forest of Saint-Gobain, captain and governor of the château of Fontainebleau, the château of Vincennes, and the park of Beauté, governor and lieutenant for the king in the governments of La Rochelle, Aunis, Brouage, the islands of Oléron and Ré, the city and government of Brisach and its dependent region, and upper and lower Auvergne, cardinal of the Holy Roman Church, bishop of Metz, abbot of nineteen abbeys including Saint-Denis-en-France, prior of Chastenay, and, in 1660, *proviseur* of the Sorbonne.

The time of Richelieu and Mazarin has been called the "Ministerial Age" by some historians, thus playing down the role of Louis XIII, who bore the true responsibility for French policy.

The Chancellor of France and His Assistants

The chancellor of France, *chef de la Justice,* was in this period always a minister and even a sort of viceroy.

The chancellery of France was a tribunal where laws, acts, dispatches, and letters expressing the unmediated will of the king received the seal. The chancellor of France was a magistrate, first among the high crown officers and head of the judicial system. He was named by the king for life and could not be removed from office; he swore an oath into the hands of the king. His *lettres de provision* were registered in all the sovereign courts, and he was entitled to sit on all of them. He could never be stripped of his functions except in case of legally established and sanctioned malfeasance. If he fell into disfavor, the king was obliged to leave him his title, with its concomitant dignities, privileges, and emoluments. In fact, however, the king could strip the chancellor of his functions, take back the seals of France, and name a Keeper of the Seals, a mere *commissaire*, to fill the post.

The chancellor received the faith and homage for fiefs of rank—duchies, marquisates, counties, and baronies—under the king's immediate jurisdiction.

He could be named to command military expeditions, as Séguier was appointed to put down the revolt of the Nu-Pieds in Normandy in 1638 and 1639 and to punish the rebels.

The king could delegate any of the royal powers to the chancellor by commission; the chancellor could preside over the Estates General and the Assemblies of Notables, as Sillery did in 1614, as Du Vair did at Rouen in 1617, and as Marillac did in Paris in 1626.

The chancellor presided over all the king's councils, except the Conseil des Affaires or Conseil d'En-Haut.

The chancellor prepared, drafted, and sent to the sovereign courts all edicts, declarations, and letters patent.

The chancellor served as intermediary between the king and the sovereign courts in *lits de justice* and in receiving remonstrances and deputations.

The chancellor was the "king's spokesman" and interpreted his will.

The chancellor supervised the sealing and dispatching by the chancellery of all letters of grace and justice that concerned the state or the status and honor of persons residing in France. The "graces" of the king included gifts, nominations, ennoblements, privileges, distinctions, abolitions, and amnesties. The chancellor applied the seal to laws and letters pertaining to public order and recruitment for public office. He did not, however, apply the seal mechanically. The *grand audiencier de France* reported on every document that was submitted for sealing. The chancellor consulted with the *maîtres des requêtes* and *conseillers d'Etat* who were attached to the department of the seals in the chancellery. He had the firm right to refuse to seal any edict, declaration, letter patent, or provision of office that he deemed contrary to the common good, even against the opinion of the majority of the Council and the decision of the king. He was obliged to give in only upon formal order from the king. As long as an act remained unsealed, it was null and void: the royal will could not be executed.

The chancellor headed all the tribunals of France. He controlled recruitment for seats on these tribunals, since it was he who applied the seal to all provisions of office. He also had disciplinary power over the tribunals. They consulted with him about the interpretation of the laws. He replied in the form of declarations and letters missive, which were registered and had the force of law. He could preside over the *parlement* and the Grand Conseil.

The chancellor was responsible for the "police" of *belles-lettres* and science. He was head of the universities, colleges, and academies and supervised all printers and booksellers.

A chancellor with character who pleased the king could play the leading role in the government and administration of the kingdom. Under Richelieu and Mazarin, Pierre Séguier played a commanding role from 1633 to 1649. He named the majority of military and provincial *intendants*—his *créatures*.

The chancellor filled all posts in the chancellery, assisted mainly by the *corps des notaires, secrétaires du roi, Maison et Couronne de France*, or royal secretaries, and by the *corps des maîtres des requêtes de l'Hôtel du roi*.

The Chancellery of France

"The Chancellery of France, or *Grande Chancellerie*, so named to distinguish it from the chancelleries serving the superior and presidial courts, is a tribunal which seals, either with the Great Seal or the seal of the dauphin, all laws, acts, dispatches, and letters that emanate from the immediate will of the king."[1]

The Great Seal was the seal kept by the chancellor or keeper of the seals for the purpose of sealing edicts, ordinances, declarations, letters patent, provisions of offices and other posts, letters of abolition, remission, naturalization, and, in general, all letters emanating directly from the royal power. The Great Seal depicts the king seated on his throne, holding the scepter and the hand of justice. The coat of arms of France was engraved on the counterseal.

The seal of the dauphin was used to seal all dispatches for the dauphine. The king was shown mounted and armed. On the counterseal were imprinted the coats of arms of France and the dauphine.

The Small Seal was affixed to letters sent to the chancelleries attached to the various royal courts.

The *scel du secret* was the king's own cachet, or private seal.

Almost all dispatches from the *grand chancellerie* were sealed with the Great Seal in yellow wax, except for edicts, letters of remission, and, generally, letters headed "A tous présens et à venir," which were sealed with the Great Seal in green wax over knotted cords of red and green silk.

In 1788 the chancellery of France comprised the following personnel: the chancellor or keeper of the seals, who headed the department; two *maîtres des requêtes;* two *grands rapporteurs* and correctors of letters; one *procureur général;* three hundred *notaires secrétaires du roi, Maison et Couronne de France et de ses Finances;* four *grands audienciers de France;* four *contrôleurs genéraux de l'audience;* four *gardes des rôles des offices de France;* four keepers of mrotgages and distraints on the king's finances; one *trésorier général* of the seal; four sealers; four *huissiers;* one wax-melter; two coffer bearers; one ordinary messenger of the *grande chancellerie* and attendant of the Grand Conseil; one *aumônier;* one quartermaster; one physician; one secretary of the seal; one tax and dues collector attached to the office of the chancellor and keeper of the seals.

The "audience of the seal" proceeded as follows. After the chancellor's entry into the Seal Chamber, the chancellery's coffer bearer would bring in the coffer in which the seals were kept. Bareheaded, the wax-melter would pay homage to the seals and then take the coffer and offer it to the chancellor. The chancellor would remove the keys from his pocket, open the coffer, and hand the seals to the wax-melter.

To affix the seal, the chancellor was supposed to be seated alone in a chair behind a table. Standing in front of him were the *grand audiencier de France*, the wax-melter, the *contrôleur*, and the *garde des rôles des offices de France;* seated next to the chancellor but at a separate table were the *maîtres des requêtes*. The secretaries of state assisted.

The *grand audiencier* would present the letters to the chancellor and summarize the contents. If required, as in cases of *lettres de provisions* for offices, the *garde des rôles des offices* or, in other cases, a *contrôleur* would examine the receipts and their copies, detach the original to be sent to the Chambre des Comptes, leaving the copy attached to letters of provision or ennoblement, and so on. If there were problems, the chancellor would consult with the *maîtres des requêtes* and secretaries of state. If he rejected the letters, they were returned to the *grand audiencier* who gave them back to the parties involved. If there was disagreement among the chancellor and the *maîtres des requêtes* or secretaries of state, the letters would be sent back to the appropriate session of the Council for further deliberation. If everything was in order, the secretaries of state would sign the letters and the wax-melter would affix the seal using the softened wax, which was formed into small rounds or slugs by an aide stationed nearby. Once sealed, the letters would be taken by the *contrôleur de l'audience* and placed in a large coffer at the end of the table.

When all the letters had been disposed of, the wax-melter was supposed to replace the seals in their coffer and hand the coffer to the chancellor. The chancellor would then close it and have it carried to a designated location by one of his domestics.

The large coffer holding the letters would then be carried to the office of the *grand audiencier* by the chancellery's coffer bearer. There, the letters would be checked by the *contrôleur* on duty during that quarter, in the presence of the *grand audiencier* and a number of *secrétaires de l'audience*. The *grand audiencier* and the *contrôleur* would read the letters out loud and state the tax due. During the audience, the clerk of the *grand audiencier* then delivered the letters to the *notaires et secrétaires du roi, Maison et Couronne de France* who had drawn them up, or to their clerks, and collect the taxes due. The notary-secretaries then delivered them to their clients.

As of 7 December 1618, the *audienciers, contrôleurs*, and notary-secretaries began farming the taxes on all letters sealed. In 1624 they paid the king 24,000 livres per annum for the privilege.

When there was neither a chancellor nor a Keeper of the Seals, the king could affix the seal himself, as Louis XIII did after the death of the constable de Luynes, between 15 and 24 December 1621; the king was assisted by his Council in applying the seal. After the death of Méric de Vic d'Armenonville, Louis XIII entrusted the seal to a committee of four state councillors and six *maîtres des requêtes* from 2 September to 23 September 1622.

After the death of Chancellor Séguier, Louis XIV decided to retain the seals himself and to have letters sealed in his presence one day a week, at nine o'clock in the morning, in a room of whatever royal house he happened to be occupying. This was the subject of the regulation of 4 February 1672. The king required the assistance of six ordinary state councillors and six *maîtres des requêtes* on duty for the quarter, plus the councillor of the Grand Conseil who was serving as *grand rapporteur* for the semester. The secretaries of state presented the judicial letters; reports were made by the *maîtres des requêtes* and the *grand rapporteur;* deliberation followed, and the decision was taken by the king. The king wielded the seal in this manner eleven times between 6 February and 11 April 1672. Louis XV did the same between 4 March 1757 and 14 October 1761.

At the *grande chancellerie*, the *conseillers du roi, notaires, secrétaires du roi, Maison et Couronne de France*[2] were commonly referred to as royal secretaries. The secretaries of state, the secretaries and *greffiers* of the king's councils, and the *greffiers en chef civils* or *criminels* of the *parlement*, Chambre des Comptes, Cour des Aides, Grand Conseil, and Cour des Monnaies of Paris were supposed to be provided an office as royal secretaries. Beginning in 1726, the secretaries of state received individual letters of dispensation.

The secretaries who served in the *petites chancelleries* had the right only to the title "*Secrétaires du roi, Maison et Couronne de France.*" *Greffiers* in the sovereign courts of the provinces were required only to obtain one of these *petite chancellerie* offices.

The number of secretaries in the *grande chancellerie* was increased considerably prior to 1661. In 1598 there were already three "colleges" of such secretaries. The senior college of Six-Vingt (120) was divided into two orders of sixty *boursiers* and sixty *gagers*. The king belonged to the first order and had a *bourse*. The money deposited in these *bourses* was taken from the taxes paid for use of the seal. The College of the Cinquante-Quarte (54), founded in September 1570, grew little by little under Charles IX. An edict of January 1583 granted it the same privileges as the Six-Vingt, with separate *bourses*. The Vingt-Six (26) was founded by Henri III (edict of September 1587).

In 1606 Henri IV added to these the offices of royal secretary that he and the duc de Mayenne had created during the period of unrest. With these he founded the College of the Soixante-Quatre (64), which on 27 June 1607 became the College of the Soixante-Cinq (65) and in December 1607 the College of the Soixante-Six (66). In October 1641, Louis XIII added forty-six more secretaryships, creating the new College of the Cent-Douze (112).

By edict of March 1605, Henri IV created twenty-six offices of royal secretaries, known as secretaries of finance, because only those who held commissions to sign financial documents could be named to fill these offices. On 11 March 1606, he made these offices into a corps and college on the model of the Six-Vingt. Ten new members were added by the edict of 10 December 1625, registered on 6 March 1626, creating the College of the Trente-Six (36), and eighty-four additional members were added in December 1635 to create the College of the Six-Vingt des Finances.

By edict of December 1607, Henri IV created twenty new offices for the benefit of persons who had held similar offices in his kingdom of Navarre before its annexation to the kingdom of France.

An edict of March 1655 created forty-six offices modeled on those of the College of the Cinquante-Quatre, into which they were included. In April 1657, however, thirty-four additional offices were created and combined with the previous forty-six to form the new College of the Quatre-Vingt (80).

As of 1657, then, there were 506 royal secretaryships.

After the Peace of the Pyrenees in April 1664, Louis XIV, taking the view that wealthy merchants had bought these offices to ennoble their families and had therefore abandoned their business and commerce, let only five of these colleges stand: the Six-Vingt (which was expanded by 1 to 121 members), the Cinquante-Quatre, the Soxiante-Six (reduced by 1 to 65), the Trente-Six des Finances, and the Vingt. Thus only 296 royal secretaryships remained.

In April 1672 an edict combined all the royal secretaries into a single college and reduced the number to 240 in all. After May 1691, a number of posts were created, for the most part redeemed from existing royal secretaries. Nevertheless, by December 1697, there were 340. An edict of October 1727 reduced the number to 300, and the Company of Royal Secretaries remained at this level until the Revolution.

In principle the royal secretaries were supposed to sign all dispatches from the king's Council, the chancelleries, and the sovereign courts. In practice, however, only those who were secretaries of finance signed dispatches from the Conseil des Finances. Only the secretaries of the chancellery of France could dispatch and sign letters of grace and justice issued there. They were known as *rapporteurs nés* of the letters of grace, which they presented for sealing.

Royal secretaries from the *grande chancellerie* could exercise their functions in the *petites chancelleries* attached to the sovereign courts and the presidial courts if they happened to find themselves there. As notaries they were allowed to authenticate all sorts of documents, but the decree of the *parlement* of Paris of 15 June 1602, which invalidated a will received by a royal secretary, thereby reaffirmed the regulations granting notaries the exclusive right to negotiate engagements and handle their disposition. An exception to the rule was the inventory made in 1666 of the furniture belonging to the late Anne of Austria, which was drawn up by a royal secretary. Article 13 of the edict of November 1582, confirmed by the edict of April 1664, made it obligatory for royal secretaries to live in the proximity of the king, the chancellor, and the councils, and to carry out their functions there. Many omitted to do so, however. The edict of April 1672, confirmed by the edicts of May 1691 and February 1694 designed to facilitate the sale of newly created offices, granted royal secretaries official dispensation from the residence and function requirements. Authentications of documents by royal secretaries were exempt from the control fees when they involved acts emanating from the Council, the *grande chancellerie*, and the sovereign courts, but subject to these fees in all other cases.

The *grands audienciers* were royal secretaries whose main function was to report on letters from their department prior to sealing and tax those that received the seal. There were four of them, serving quarterly terms. They held rights of survivorship to their offices. They administered the monies derived from use of the seal. Along with the four *contrôleurs généraux* they constituted a separate corps and enjoyed precedence over the royal secretaries, though this was a matter of constant dispute.

The four conservators of mortgages were created by edict of March 1673. The edict of March 1788 made them conservators of liens against the royal finances as well.

The four *gardes des rôles des offices de France* were created by edict of March 1631. The *trésoriers généraux du sceau* (*ancien, alternatif*, and *triennal*) were created by edict of December 1635. All these functions had previously been carried out by clerks of the chancellor. All these officeholders were *secrétaires du roi nés*.

The *Maîtres des Requêtes de l'Hôtel du Roi*

The *maîtres des requêtes de l'Hôtel du roi* were like the chancellor's assessors. They were considered to belong to the corps of the Paris *parlement* and sat in the *grand-chambre* after the *présidents à mortier* and before the councillors. Members of the royal household, they conducted a tribunal at the Palace on the Ile de la Cité, where their offices were located and where they took cognizance "of certain distinguished matters assigned to them by ordinance." On an extraordinary basis, they sat in sovereign and final judgment in a court of seven members over all sorts of cases referred to them by council decree or arising out of execution of decrees of the Conseil privé. They dealt with errors committed in the courts under the jurisdiction of the Council. They had jurisdiction over sealed letters according printing privileges or permission to print and over petitions alleging errors in decrees of the sovereign courts. On a regular basis, they had original jurisdiction over all actions that could be brought by virtue of the right of *committimus*. This was a right accorded by the king to certain persons to plead before certain judges and to take cases in which they had an interest away from other tribunals by virtue of the king's protection and safeguard. The right of *committimus*, the purpose of which was to make the work of officeholders and *commissaires* easier by relieving them of the need to undertake burdensome journeys in order to plead cases, played an important political role. Office-holders and notables who had worked in the king's behalf in their provinces and against the interests of the corps of officeholders and of privileged persons there, and who feared reprisals in the form of cases brought for dubious motives and judged with partiality, could take advantage of the right of *committimus* to petition the tribunal of the *Hôtel*, which would protect them. The right of *committimus* made it easier for the king to find devoted men in the provinces and to gain obedience to his will in remote places. Under the regulation of 26 January 1610, the *maîtres des requêtes* heard regular cases on Wednesdays and Saturdays and extraordinary cases on Mondays and Thursdays at ten o'clock in the morning.

In the king's Council, the *maîtres des requêtes* gave reports on judicial affairs to be settled by council decree and sometimes also on financial affairs, although the *intendants des Finances* claimed to have the exclusive right to report on financial matters. The importance of the *maîtres des requêtes* in the councils grew constantly, for the councils could not be held without them. They participated in more and more sections of the Council as time went by.

At the Audience of the Seal, the *maîtres des requêtes* assisted the chancellor. They reported on each document presented for sealing before handing it to the chancellor. The chancellor would make up his mind about whether or not to affix the seal on the basis of this report. In chancelleries attached to the sovereign and presidial courts, *maîtres des requêtes* were authorized to affix the seal as representatives of the chancellor. Royal secretaries accused of malfeasance were judged by a tribunal composed of *maîtres des requêtes* and presided over by the chancellor. The chancellor commissioned *maîtres des requêtes* to make judgments concerning errors in chancellery letters. A council decree of 2 December 1619 confirmed this power for the Bordeaux chancellery. Since Charles VIII's edict of 11 December 1493 provided that *lettres de provision* were to be sealed at the chancellery, the *maîtres des requêtes* had "jurisdiction over and full cognizance of all offices in our kingdom." As a result, they played an important role in recruiting men to fill public offices and in supervising the manner in which the duties of office were executed. They also enjoyed the privilege of presiding over the Grand Conseil.

The *maîtres des requêtes* had "regular jurisdiction throughout the kingdoms, *pays*, and *seigneuries*" of the king of France. They could serve as *présidents* in the courts of *baillis*, *sénéchaux*, and other officers with judicial powers, and had jurisdiction coextensive with that of a *bailli* or *sénéchal*. They were supposed to tour their assigned districts and receive complaints, grievances, and reports of wrongs and injustices committed against the king's subjects by local officeholders. They were then empowered either to take corrective measures themselves or to notify the king so that he could take the necessary steps (edict of 1493).

The *maître*'s power while on inspection tour was spelled out by Henri II's edict of August 1553, issued in the midst of a period of civil war and upheaval. *Maîtres* were supposed to inquire about heresies and about the zeal of judges in punishing them. They were to investigate the diligence of judicial officers, hear complaints, and punish wrongdoing. They were to aid in the collection of monies due the king and to find out how the people were being treated by tax collectors and farmers. They were also supposed to keep an eye out for speculation with royal treasury funds. They were to find out how royal troops were treating the civilian population and look into cases brought by the *prévôts des maréchaux* and presidial judges. Briefs for the constable of France were to be prepared if any wrongdoing was discovered. *Maîtres* were to consult with the syndics of the people concerning the assessment of taxes for way stations, fortifications, munitions, and trails, to ensure that the tax burden would be equally distributed. They were to audit the administration of municipal funds and *octrois* and accounts of receipts and expenditures. In general they were to report on all errors, abuses, peculations, harassment, and oppression. Sanctions, remedial measures, and reforms were in principle left up to the king's Council to decide. This edict was still in force in the seventeenth century. It contained some of the principal powers accorded to the provincial intendants and suggested several others.

In 1623, the *requêtes de l'Hôtel* included fifty-six *maîtres des requêtes*, one *avocat du roi*, one *greffier*, and eight *huissiers*. To judge by the series of edicts of creation, there should have been sixty-two *maîtres des requêtes*. Louis XIII created two in August 1631, two by edict of Paris on 20 December 1635, and eight by edict of Saint-Germain-en-Laye in December 1635, which was registered and would have made seventy-four in all. The *Etat de la France* of 1642 says that there were seventy; that of 1648 says there were sixty-two.

The *maîtres des requêtes* served one quarter with the *requêtes de l'Hôtel*, one quarter with the king's Council. During the remaining portion of the year they were available to make inspection tours and to undertake other commissions. They could also be placed on detached service for longer periods of time, determinate or indeterminate.

To become a *maître des requêtes*, according to the letters patent of 5 February 1598, one had to be thirty-two years of age; to have been *conseiller* in a sovereign court or *lieutenant général de bailliage* for six years, or to have executed another judicial post or to have been an *avocat* in a sovereign court for twelve years, with honor, experience, and merit. The registration decree issued by the Paris *parlement* on 9 March 1602, added an amendment: anyone received as *maître des requêtes* would be entitled to sit on the king's Council and to have access to *parlement* only if he had served ten years in a sovereign court or in the office of *maître des requêtes*.

Maîtres des requêtes could become ambassadors. In addition, they always claimed a monopoly over the commissions of *intendants d'armée* and *intendants des provinces*. The king always asserted his right to choose anyone he deemed worthy and capable of filling these posts. In fact, however, he named very few *intendants* from outside the corps of *maîtres des requêtes*.

The *maîtres des requêtes* formed part of a social group whose kernel was composed of officeholders in the royal court and household, of men serving the king's Council in some capacity, and of officeholders in the sovereign courts.[3]

The Secretaries of State

The four secretaries of state were chosen by the king from among the *notaires, secrétaires du roi, Maison et Couronne de France*. They had to belong to this corps and possess its brevet before receiving the brevet of secretary of state.[4] The secretaries of state in effect played the role of notaries, preparing documents that gave official status to the wishes of their clients. The secretaries of state took note of the decisions taken in the king's Council, prepared the necessary dispatches, had them signed by the king, and then countersigned them. Their countersignature was not a political check but a confirmation that the signature really was that of the king and that the act was in compliance with the decision taken by the king in his Council. The countersignature of the secretary of state served to authenticate the act.

The secretaries of state kept records of council decisions and prepared dossiers containing all material pertinent to a case for submission to the Council. They were therefore well informed about affairs of state, so that the king, ministers, and various councils often called upon them to give advice. They did so either orally or in writing. The Conseil d'Affaires or Conseil d'En-Haut sometimes called upon a secretary of state to act as a minister, but secretaries were not necessarily ministers.

Each secretary of state performed a variety of tasks. Each was responsible for a number of different provinces of France. Some had further responsibility for foreign relations connected with the provincial affairs for which they were responsible. Beyond these general responsibilities, they might be assigned specific duties. The secretaries of state began specializing quite early. A special secretariat developed to handle foreign affairs, and another to handle military affairs. The latter took on particular importance after the office of constable was eliminated. The responsibilities of the department headed by the sieur de Loménie and his son and designated heir, the sieur de La Ville-aux-Clercs, were fixed by the regulation of 11 March 1626 and included the royal household, Paris, the Ile-de-France, Orléans, Berry, Soissons, and the *parlement* of Navarre. The responsibilities of the department headed by Phélypeaux, sieur d'Herbault, included "all foreigners," Languedoc, Guyenne, Brouage, Aunis, La Rochelle, and general affairs involving Huguenots. The sieur d'Ocquerre had responsibility for Auvergne, the Bourbonnais, Nivernais, Burgundy, Champagne, Bresse, Picardy, Normandy, Brittany, the Trois Evêchés, Lorraine, and the western fleet. The sieur de Beauclerc had responsibility for war, the *taillon*, artillery, Poitou,

Marche, Limousin, Angoumois, Saintonge, Lyonnais, Dauphiné, Provence, and the eastern fleet. Each secretary was responsible for fortifications in his own department.

The secretaries of state attended the awakening of the king. They were always available to receive and transmit his orders. All bore responsibility for correspondence with their department, including governors, intendants, magistrates, treasurers, and so on. All possessed a brevet as *conseiller d'Etat* giving them access to the councils. Each served a one-month stint on the various councils. Standing, the secretary of state on duty for the month took note of all decisions and gave reports when asked to do so. In the Conseil des Dépêches the secretaries of state were *rapporteurs né*. In the Conseil d'Affaires or Conseil d'En-Haut, there were two secretaries of state: the secretary of state for foreign affairs, serving as minister, and the secretary of state on duty that month, serving as notary.

For three months of the year, each secretary of state was responsible for letters, gifts, bonuses, pensions, posts, archbishoprics, bishoprics, and other benefices awarded by the king.

The secretaries of state were responsible for drawing up edicts, ordinances, peace treaties, treaties of alliance, commercial treaties, and marriage contracts for the royal family. They issued authentic copies of minutes on file in their archives. The families of the secretaries of state conserved state papers as their own personal papers. When the son of a secretary of state became in turn a secretary of state in his own right, he thus had considerable documentation on which he might draw. This was the case in the sixteenth century with the L'Aubespine, Bochetel, and de Neuville families. Under Henri IV, Nicolas de Neuville, seigneur de Villeroy, was responsible for correspondence with foreign countries.

The secretaries of state were essential instruments of the royal power. Even when they were not officially ministers, they played a ministerial role. Apart from their council functions, the secretaries of state met with the king, one at a time, in long working sessions, and many decisions were reached by the king in conjunction with a secretary of state before being brought before the Conseil des Affaires or the Conseil d'En-Haut. This was already the case under Henri IV and Louis XIII. A form of executive government was thus taking shape under the guise of judicial government.

The secretaries of state carried out their functions with the aid of clerks, who constituted a sort of rudimentary bureaucracy. The clerks first enter the scene in 1567. In May 1588, a regulation allowed each secretary of state one *commis* and six clerks, to be named by the secretary of state and approved by the king. On 15 February 1599, Henri IV issued a regulation which gave the former *commis* the title "*premier commis*" or "*principal commis*"; the clerks were henceforth known as "*commis*." It was decided that the *premier commis* could draft and initial dispatches. Each secretary of state had one or two *premiers commis*. Villeroy, secretary of state for foreign affairs until 1616, had as his *premier commis* Paul Phélypeaux, seigneur de Pontchartrain. Phélypeaux in turn became secretary of state in 1610 and died in 1621. He was the brother of Raymond Phélypeaux, sieur d'Herbault, who became secretary of state for foreign affairs in 1624. His nephew, Paul Ardier, his sister's son, became *premier commis* for foreign affairs in 1624.

Villeroy was replaced in 1616 by Villarceaux, whose *premier commis* until 1624 was Barat. In 1623 and 1624, Villarceaux took on a second *premier commis* by the name of Foureau. In 1624, foreign affairs were divided up among four secretaries of state: Antoine Loménie de Brienne, Phélypeaux d'Herbault, Potier d'Ocquerre de Gesvres. The fourth secretary of state, Beauclerc, was responsible for war. As his third *premier commis*, Phélypeaux brought in Paul Ardier. In 1626 foreign affairs were consolidated under Phélypeaux d'Herbault. Paul Ardier stayed on as *premier commis*, successively serving under Herbault, Claude Bouthillier (1629–32), and Léon Bouthillier, sieur de Chavigny (1632–43). Henri-Auguste de Loménie de Brienne, seigneur de La Ville-aux-Clercs, succeeded them as secretary of state for foreign affairs until 1663; after 1651, his son, Henri-Louis de Loménie de Brienne assisted him as his heir. Brienne's *premier commis* was Parayre. A second *premier commis* was added in 1659, one Du Fresne, and, in 1661, a third, named Ariste. The clerks began to specialize: Du Fresne concerned himself with Germany and somewhat later with maritime issues; Parayre took care of the provinces of the Brienne.

The secretary of state employed a secretary to supervise his clerks. Brienne's secretary was Finet, who was succeeded by a clerk by the name of Barthe.

The clerks did the preliminary work for the secretaries of state. They prepared notes, instructions for ambassadors, and dispatches and submitted them to the secretary of state for signature. They gave their opinions, preserved the traditions and methods of the foreign service, and inspired foreign policy. Devoted to the interests of the kingdom as to a religion, they worked in obscurity to settle the politics of Europe and sacrificed themselves to the grandeur of France. All the *premiers commis* had access to the king. Paul Ardier was at Louis XIII's side at La Rochelle and Suse. They served in their posts for long periods, eight to ten years on the average.

> Hard-working, knowledgeable, discreet, familiar with the checkerboard of European states, then so complex, with the personnel of the courts, with public law, treaties, and the mechanics and organization of the Germanic Corps and the Empire, and familiar as well with the various sorts of international claims and *casus belli* with all the mysteries and arcana of the chancelleries, these men were asked to prepare memoirs on the thorniest questions, and did so overnight with exactness and clarity, and yet it never even occurred to anyone to attach their names to these endeavors.[5]

These words, which Sainte-Beuve meant to describe the clerks in foreign affairs, could equally well be applied to the other secretaries of state, *mutatis mutandis*.

Under Louis XVI, a minister of state could at any time involve himself in debate over any affair of general interest, but he was genuinely important only if he was at the same time a secretary of state.

The *Surintendant des Finances:* His Departments and Assistants

The *surintendant des Finances*, the *contrôleur général des Finances*, and the *intendants des Finances* belonged to the staff of the royal councils, but these technicians, so deeply involved in the world of finance, deserve a chapter in their own right.

The *Conseillers d'Etat*

The number of people bearing the title *"conseiller d'Etat"* was quite high. In effect, this was an honorific post that the king awarded as the needs of policy dictated: to reward his supporters and win over his opponents. Under the regencies, the ranks of the *conseillers d'Etat* swelled to the proportions of a mob.

Among the *conseillers d'Etat* we find princes of the blood, cardinals, other princes, dukes-and-peers, crown officers including the marshals of France, the governors and *lieutenants généraux* of provinces who had taken the oath as councillors, archbishops and bishops who attended at court when in the vicinity, and, finally, all sorts of people who held a brevet awarding the title *conseiller d'Etat*. Repeated efforts were made to reduce the number of dignitaries bearing this mark of distinction and to identify those among them who might actually attend council meetings and carry out functions (regulations of Compiègne of June 1624, of Chateaubriant, of La Rochelle of 3 January 1628, ordinance of Marillac of January 1629, regulations of May 1644, 1 April 1655, and 1 May 1657).

Of the *conseillers d'Etat* who actually served, a distinction was made between "ordinary councillors," those "whom his Majesty . . . ordinarily employs in the greatest and most important affairs of his state, both inside the kingdom and out," "semester councillors," who served six months per year, and "trimester" or "quadrimester councillors," who served three or four months per year. In all there were generally thirty-two to thirty-four *conseillers d'Etat* in actual service. Depending on the period, ten, twelve, or eighteen of these were ordinary councillors, three of them clergymen and three from the *noblesse d'épée*.

The *conseillers d'Etat* were chosen for the most part from among the *gens de robe longue*. By the time of Henri IV *robins* predominated in all the councils, whereas, under Henri III, the Council included fifteen *gentils-hommes*, six ecclesiastics, and only four *robins*. In the period we are interested in, the king governed with the aid not of men of the sword but rather of men of the pen—officeholders named to serve on the Conseil d'Etat, most of them ennobled.

Among these *robins*, about half were drawn from the corps of the *maîtres des requêtes*. The career of André d'Ormesson seems to have been typical. A *maître des requêtes*, he received a brevet as *conseiller d'Etat* in April 1615; this allowed him access to council meetings to give reports when asked, but it did not make him an active *conseiller d'Etat*. After serving as an *intendant* in Champagne, he obtained an actual Council seat (on the Conseil d'Etat et des Finances and the Conseil privé ou des Parties) as a quadri-mestrial councillor in January 1626. After serving as a *commissaire* at the Estates of Brittany, he was made a semestrial councillor in January 1633. He was then made a member of the Conseil des Finances. The chancellor had him seated as an ordinary councillor as of July 1634, and in April 1636 he received his *brevet d'ordinaire*.

Many *maîtres des requêtes* never became active *conseillers d'Etat*. The king was concerned to hold on to an adequate number of experienced *maîtres des requêtes* with time-ripened knowledge of their responsibilities.

The king deliberately maintained a balance between the active state councillors drawn from the corps of *maîtres des requêtes* and those drawn from the sovereign courts. The king seated on his Council *présidents* from the Paris *parlement*, members of the Grand Conseil and the Cour des Aides, and *présidents* of provincial *parlements* and Chambres des Comptes. He needed to establish personal bonds of loyalty with men having connections and influence in these corps, as well as to dampen the contentious spirit of the leaders of the sovereign courts by holding out the hope of higher honors and profits. In addition, the sovereign courts still had enormous "police," i.e., administrative, powers.

The Paris *parlement* was still tremendously prestigious. It often happened that the eldest son of a family of *conseillers d'Etat* drawn from the corps of *maîtres des requêtes* chose to pursue a career in the Paris *parlement* rather than the Conseil d'Etat. His own eldest son would do the same in turn, and the family would thereby consolidate its position among the "Fathers of the Country."

The *robins* belonging to the corps of *maîtres des requêtes*, and the king's Council constituted a different group, politically speaking, from the *robins* in the sovereign courts, with whom they frequently came into conflict; but the two groups formed part of a single social group. The reader will find the information he needs concerning the social position and mental outlook of the *maître des requêtes* and *conseillers d'Etat* in two of my other books.[6]

Council Officers

The king's Council was served by officers who bought their positions. There were four *secrétaires des Finances*, serving quarterly terms, to prepare rolls, draw up dispatches, and so on. These offices were often purchased by *traitants* and *partisans*. There were also four secretaries and *greffiers* of the Conseil privé, who served on a quarterly basis, and four *greffiers gardesacs* per quarter. All had clerks serving under them.

The *commissaires du Conseil* had *greffiers*. The *"huissiers ordinaires des Conseils d'Etat et privé du roi"* had the exclusive right to give notice of council proceedings and of the activities of *commissaires ordinaires* and *extraordinaires* and to execute decrees, judgments, and commissions of the Council throughout the kingdom. Along with the *huissiers* of the *grande chancellerie*, they also had the exclusive right to notify mortgagers and the treasury of opposition to the affixing of the seal and of opposition to the seal for all offices, as well as the lifting of such oppositions.

Some secretaries, *greffiers*, and *huissiers* wearied of the obligation to travel with the king's retinue in time of civil or foreign war. They would hire clerks to carry out their duties and content themselves with collecting their official compensation and other fees. On 14 June 1629, in the camp near Alès, the king issued a regulation depriving officials who were absent from their posts without authorization of the income from their offices.

A regulation of June 1597 had laid it down that litigants must file petitions through an *avocat*. A regulation of May 1643 required these *avocats* to be registered by the chancellor and to swear an oath into his hands. In September of 1643 an edict created 160 offices of *avocats au Conseil*. This number was increased to 200 in January of 1644. These *avocats* formed a company, which examined prospective new members before receiving them into its ranks. The syndics of this company monitored the private morals and professional ethics of its members and protected their monopoly.

From 1598 to 1661

Government by "Créatures"

The ministers and secretaries of state were the "creatures" or *"fidèles"* of the king or his principal minister, referred to as the "protector" or "master."[7] Richelieu was a creature of Louis XIII. The correspondence between the king and his minister shows mutual respect and affection, a concern of each for the health and interests of the other. The ministry was based on the personal relations between the king and his minister.

Richelieu placed a whole chain of creatures at the king's disposal. The chancellor, the *surintendant des Finances*, and the secretaries of state all referred to themselves as Richelieu's creatures in their letters to him. It was Richelieu's wish that all who came into contact with the king should be his creatures and should have sworn to obey him fully, without reservation. To begin with, Richelieu gave the king his family.[8] All the members of his family, the Du Plessis and the La Porte, rose along with the prime minister to positions of political or ecclesiastical power and social prestige. His brother became a cardinal; his niece, duchesse d'Aiguillon; his cousin La Meilleraye, marshal of France; his nephew du Pont de Courlay, *général des galères*. All his relatives were awarded numerous offices. Sometimes they showed themselves unworthy of the confidence of the head of the family by their incompetence or independence. But Richelieu never revoked a favor granted to a member of his family.

Richelieu further supplied the king with a large group of creatures including Leon Bouthillier, the sieur de Chavigny and secretary of state for foreign affairs, Sublet de Noyers, secretary of state for war, and Bouthillier and Bullion, who became *surintendants des Finances*.

The Bouthillier family was tied to the La Porte family over several generations. Denis Bouthillier, seigneur de Fouilletourte, had been the clerk of François de La Porte, Richelieu's maternal grandfather. When François de La Porte died, he left a number of lawyers beholden to him to Denis Bouthillier, to whose care he also entrusted his grandchildren, their father having died. One of Denis Bouthillier's sons, Claude, became a councillor in the Paris *parlement* in 1613. Richelieu recommended him to Marie de Médicis. Claude was thereupon named *secrétaire des Commandments* to the queen mother and, later, secretary of state. His brother Denis, seigneur de Rancé, succeeded him as *secrétaire des Commandments* to the queen mother and later became *conseiller d'Etat*. Both kept Richelieu apprised of the queen mother's doings and conveyed messages from Richelieu to Marie de Médicis.

There were two other Bouthillier brothers. Richelieu had Victor (d. 1670) named bishop of Boulogne and, later, coadjutor to the archbishop of Tours. Victor Bouthillier reported to Richelieu on religious and economic matters in the regions to which he was posted. In return Richelieu had him named *aumônier* to Gaston d'Orléans. The fourth Bouthillier brother, Sebastian, was bishop of Aire and prior of La Cochère. In 1619, he was the one who urged Marie de Médicis to revoke the orders exiling Richelieu to Avignon. Dispatched to Rome, he helped to expedite Richelieu's promotion to cardinal. Through such men, whose fortunes were bound up with his own, Richelieu was able to keep abreast of court intrigue and conspiracy. His *fidèles* occupied the key posts.

These *fidèles* in turn had their own creatures and families, which they placed at Richelieu's disposal. The Bouthilliers' third cousins and uncles by marriage received offices, pensions, priories, abbeys, and chaplainships thanks to their influence with Richelieu. In this way, chains of loyalty were created, enabling Richelieu and the king to enforce their will throughout the kingdom, transmitting orders down the line from creature to creature.

In September 1628, Nicolas Potier, sieur d'Ocquerre and secretary of state, died. Under the influence of Marie de Médicis and Richelieu, Louis XIII named Claude Bouthillier secretary of state. Claude paid 200,000 livres and Marie de Médicis 100,000 to the d'Ocquerre as compensation, for the post should have gone to a member of that family. Upon the death of Raymond Phélypeaux, sieur d'Herbault, in May 1629, Richelieu removed a Phélypeaux by the name of La Vrillière, a creature of de Marillac, the keeper of the seals and a *dévot* opposed to Richelieu's policies, from a post in foreign affairs and nominated Claude Bouthillier in his place. La Vrillière was named secretary of state and kept the rest of d'Herbault's department. In 1632, upon the death of d'Effiat, the *surintendant des Finances*, Claude Bouthillier became surintendant with Claude de Bullion.

Claude Bouthillier had married his only son, Léon, sieur de Chavigny, to the only daughter of the seigneur de Villesavin, a Phélypeaux. Chavigny became *conseiller* in the Paris *parlement* and then, in 1632, secretary of state for foreign affairs *en survivance*.

Claude de Bullion belonged to a wealthy family devoted to the service of the king. His father had held offices under Henri III, and his mother was a Lamoignon. Claude was *conseiller* in the Paris *parlement* and, later, *maître des requêtes* and *conseiller d'Etat* under Henri IV; he became *surintendant* of Navarre in 1612, and chancellor to the queen mother in 1615. He sat on the Conseil d'Etat et des Finances and the Conseil privé, was *commissaire* in Rouen in 1617 responsible for enforcing execution of the decrees of the king's Council, joined the Conseil des Finances in 1619, and in June 1624 was granted the privilege of serving on all the councils. During the difficult years between 1624 and 1630 he became one of Richelieu's *fidèles* and kept the prime minister informed of intrigues at court. In 1632 he was named *surintendant des Finances* conjointly with Claude Bouthillier, and he continued alone in the post after Bouthillier's death. He did not hesitate to violate Richelieu's orders in matters of finance, in Richelieu's own interest. He died in 1640.

François Sublet, *chevalier*, seigneur de Noyers, belonged to a family that had held royal offices for several generations. His father, Jean Sublet, was a *maître des comptes*. His mother, Magdeleine Bochart, belonged to a family of *conseillers* in the Paris *parlement*. His mother's brother Jean Bochart de Champigny became *surintendant des Finances* in 1624 and, later, *premier président* in the Paris *parlement*. He chose his nephew François as his clerk in finance, then had him buy a post as *intendant des Finances* in 1628. Sublet carried out numerous missions in the provinces, particularly Picardy, rebuilding fortresses and levying troops. He joined the circle of Richelieu's *fidèles* in 1628. Richelieu's maternal grandmother was a Bochart, from the same branch of the family as Sublet's mother. François was employed from 1630 on as *intendant des armées du Nord-Est et de Lorraine*. In 1636 he became secretary of state for war.

Chavigny and Sublet de Noyers had the special responsibility of choosing the opportune moment to submit Richelieu's letters and suggestions to the king and of keeping Richelieu informed as to the king's mood. Louis XIII spent some time each day working alone with Richelieu and with one or two secretaries of state, as well as with his own secretaries, chiefly Lucas. Many suggestions were made and decisions reached through letters sent to the king at all hours of the day or night. The king, his creature Richelieu, and

Richelieu's creatures made up the government, the group that formulated policy and made decisions.

The *premiers commis* and the other clerks of the secretaries of state were creatures of the latter. They took care not only of the king's business but also of the personal affairs of the secretaries of state, acting as confidants in family matters and in some cases as executors of their estates.

The same was true for the *surintendant des Finances*. He offered the king the services of his creatures: the *intendants des Finances*, finance clerks, *traitants*, and *partisans*. Some historians have failed to notice this. Struck by the rapid, excessive, dishonest, and scandalous acquisition of wealth by certain *traitants* and *partisans*, these historians have concluded that somehow the "financiers" had seized control of the state. They have not given sufficient weight to what the king obtained in return: the budgetary resources necessary to carry out his policies, resources which he could not otherwise have laid hold of. Nor have they paid sufficient attention to the fact that the nomination of a *surintendant* was made in exchange for that official's gift to the king of a chain of creatures, including a syndicate of *partisans* and *traitants* and a circle of *fidèles*, comprising financial officeholders and *financiers*, followers of the *surintendant* who offered their services to the king.

The system worked as follows. The king had his creature, the principal minister. The principal minister served the king with the aid of his own creatures: the chancellor, the secretaries of state, the *surintendant des Finances*. Each of these fulfilled his obligations with the help of creatures of his own, and so on right down to the bottom of the hierarchy and out to the most remote parts of the kingdom. Long chains of loyal creatures, further extended and enlarged by clientele relationships, were the means by which government and administration became possible.

In general, the ministers and their creatures were nobles by virtue of their office and were characterized as *bourgeois* by the old nobility of the sword. The *premiers commis* were themselves ennobled and awarded brevets as *conseillers d'Etat*.[9]

From 1661 to 1715

In certain respects, the same characteristics continue to apply to ministers, secretaries of state, and *conseillers d'Etat* during the period of Louis XIV's personal government. They were still members of loyal families and creatures, but now of the king rather than of his principal minister. They were still nobles by virtue of their office and still characterized as *bourgeois* by the old nobility of the sword and the high nobility of dukes-and-peers. These characteristics continue to apply until 1789, although the bonds of loyalty were weakened during the second half of the eighteenth century and increasingly supplanted by more straightforward ties of clientship. However, the king changed the way the government worked so profoundly that it was possible for M. Antoine to speak of a "revolution," the revolution of 1661.

King, Prime Minister, and Surintendant

On 9 March 1661, after the death of Mazarin, Louis XIV announced that he was going to govern by himself. For fifty-four years he remained true to his word. He put an end to the "ministeriate" and became his own Prime Minister, in response to the wishes of the French nation as a whole and, in particular, the Frondeurs. Like his predecessors, but in a more systematic manner, the king worked each day in collaboration with his creatures, the ministers and secretaries of state. He received them in the afternoon and evening, studied and discussed affairs of state in their company, and came to a decision. The packet of papers brought to the king during these sessions was referred to as the *liasse*, "the king's work." In 1705, "the king worked with M. de Chamillart in Mme de Maintenon's apartment on Sunday and Wednesday evenings; on Tuesdays he worked with M. de Pontchartrain on naval affairs; on Mondays with M. le Peletier de Souzy on fortifications and engineering matters. In addition, the king often worked on special matters."[10] He also worked with Torcy, but not in Mme de Maintenon's apartment.

Together with the ministers and secretaries of state, he did preliminary work in preparation for Council meetings, but only complex or important questions were submitted to the councils. The king usually reached decisions in tête-à-tête with individual ministers, even on matters that should normally have been presented to the Council. At the instigation of the king, the decisions were then couched in the form of fictitious council decrees to make them enforceable.

The Purge of the Councils

The king no longer wanted to have men serving on his councils who held their place as a permanent title by virtue of their birth or office, that is, by right. He rid the Conseil d'En-Haut of members of the royal family, princes of the blood, dukes-and-peers, marshals of France, and all who had been appointed by ministerial letter or brevet. Ministers of state were no longer named by letter or brevet. They were invited to each meeting by the king or by a *huissier*. When they stopped being invited, they ceased to be ministers. In this way Louis XIV got rid of the queen mother, his brother Monsieur, the cardinals, the prelates, the princes of the blood, the grandees, and even the chancellor of France. In March 1661, the ministers included the *surintendant*, Fouquet, the secretary of state for war, Le Tellier, and de Lionne, who was in charge of foreign affairs; they were referred to as "the Triad." In September, Colbert replaced Fouquet. Henceforth the ministers of state were merely low-born *commis*, though nobles ex officio: the creatures and instruments of the king.

The Degradation of the Chancellor of France

The king set out to humble the high crown officers. The offices of constable and admiral had already been eliminated. Louis XIV degraded the office of chancellor of France. This move was facilitated by the condition of Pierre Séguier. In 1661 Séguier was seventy-three, weak, and in poor health; he died almost senile on 28 January 1672. The king let him keep his honors, rights of precedence, and stately trappings but withdrew his powers and responsibilities. When Séguier died, the king kept the seals and held the *audience du sceau* himself. When he launched the Dutch War, he decided not to eliminate the office of chancellor. As keeper of the seals he nominated Etienne d'Aligre, dean of the council, to whom he accorded the title of chancellor on 8 January 1674. This was a way of continuing the same system by giving the office to an old man in the twilight of life and little inclined to stand out against the will of the king. When d'Aligre died, the king named the seventy-seven-year-old Le Tellier to replace him in October 1677. When he died in October 1685, he was replaced by Boucherat, at sixty-nine an ailing and apathetic old man. When Pontchartrain became chancellor in September 1699, he was only fifty-six and a man with a "sharp, quick mind . . . [and an] enterprising character." But by this time the routine of the office was too deeply rooted and venerable to overcome.

Signs of the degradation of the chancellor's office were numerous. To begin with, the chancellor, in theory head of the royal councils, no longer enjoyed ex officio access to the Conseil d'En-Haut. He was no longer a minister of state ex officio. Séguier was not a minister of state, nor were d'Aligre and Boucherat. Le Tellier and Pontchartrain did attend the Conseil d'En-Haut, but they had been ministers before becoming keepers of the seals.

The chancellor was not ex officio a member of the new Conseil des Finances. When he did attend meetings of this Council, he did not play the leading role. He no longer took part in administering the royal finances.

He lost the authority that he had had for centuries over waterways and forests.

He lost the right to nominate the provincial intendants.

He lost his power to approve letters patent in finance at the chancellery level. The secretaries of state were required to sign financial dispatches without examination, so long as they were submitted with the signature of the *contrôleur général* on the minutes. The chancellor was forced to seal these acts without debate. Affixing of the seal was a mere formality.

The chancellor lost his right to take part in the administration of military affairs.

Even though in outward appearance judicial, administrative, and legislative matters were not much changed, and the chancellor continued to preside over councils and committees, in fact he received orders from the king in regard to all matters. These were transmitted by a *commis* such as Colbert, who might even give orders himself in the king's name. The chancellor no longer had any initiative and lost his earlier authority.

Although he was the natural head of all tribunals, the chancellor was not allowed to concern himself with the new colonial courts of justice: these came under the jurisdiction of the secretary of state for the navy.

To a great extent the chancellor was reduced to a mere figurehead.

The Promotion of the Contrôleur Général des Finances; *the Government Councils*

All power was wielded by the king and concentrated in the area of finance. A royal *commis*, the *contrôleur général des Finances*, assumed responsibility for all financial matters and gained authority over all departments of the administration.

From time to time the king held meetings of the Conseil d'En-Haut or, as it came to be called at the end of the century, the Conseil d'Etat. This council consisted of only three to five ministers, joined on rare occasions by the king's possible successors. The grand dauphin attended in July 1691 and the duc de Bourgogne in December 1702. The king generally chose his ministers from among the secretaries of state, people who were, according to Saint-Simon, duke-and-peer, "utterly and completely common." As the grandees saw them, these were rank commoners, mere *commis* of the king. On this view of the matter, it did indeed seem that the king was governing alone. Some secretaries of state never became ministers (Guénégaud, Barbezieux Jérôme de Pontchartrain, the Châteauneuf, La Vrillière). Not even the secretary of state for foreign affairs was a minister ex officio. For three years Torcy was not a minister and was obliged to deposit his dossiers in the council chamber to be reported on by his father-in-law, Pomponne, who was a minister of state. This Council had unlimited jurisdiction. It concerned itself with all the most important affairs, both internal and external. Meetings took place on Wednesdays, Thursdays, and Sundays every week, and every other week on Monday mornings between mass and "dinner," that is, the *grand déjeûner*.

Although the Conseil des Dépêches was the second council of government, the most important, after the Conseil d'Etat, was the Conseil royal des Finances, commonly known as the "Conseil royal." Fouquet was arrested on 5 September 1661. The post of *surintendant des Finances* was eliminated on 15 September. The king became his own *surintendant des Finances* as well as his own prime minister. To help him in these posts he created the Conseil royal des Finances, whose jurisdiction extended to matters previously resolved and executed by the *surintendant des Finances* alone. The king always sat on this Council. With him was a figure known as the "Chef du Conseil royal des Finances" and three councillors, one of whom was an *intendant des Finances*. The king decided when to invite the chancellor. The chef du Conseil royal was usually a figurehead. The first one was the first maréchal de Villeroy, who died in 1685; he was succeeded by the duc de

Beauvillier, who had some influence; after him came the second maréchal de Villeroy, an incompetent.

The Conseil royal met three times per week; beginning in April 1665 it met first on Tuesdays and Thursdays, and, later, on Tuesdays and Saturdays. His Majesty reserved the right "to sign all ordinances concerning budgetary and cash expenditures" and all *états de distribution des finances*, *brevets de la taille*, and *rôles de l'Epargne*. He actually verified all the bookkeeping. In the Conseil royal, the king did with his own hand what the *surintendant* had done in his office. "The king writes more than a paid scribe would do."[11]

Apart from this accounting job, the Conseil royal also set financial and economic policy for the monarchy and resolved disputes. At one point it even moved into an area of responsibility beyond finance, when the king's Council regulation of 17 June 1687 was adopted in the Conseil royal des Finances.

The leading figure, after the king, was the *intendant des Finances*, who took the minutes. This post was filled by Colbert, who headed the department in charge of the "*états de distribution des finances*." At one time a creature of Le Tellier and, later, of Mazarin, Colbert became the king's creature. As head of the Conseil royal des Finances, the king allowed him to centralize control first over financial matters and then over most of the government; this made it easier for the king to assert his own leadership and control. In this way, Louis XIV created a tradition of government that lasted until the Revolution. In January 1664, Colbert, who was already *intendant des Finances*, *ministre d'Etat*, and *conseiller d'Etat*, became *surintendant des Bâtiments royaux*. In November 1665 he relinquished his post as *intendant*. The king took upon himself full responsibility for general supervision of finances. The *contrôleur général des Finances* was made responsible for all financial affairs throughout the kingdom. In February 1669, the king named Colbert *secrétaire d'Etat* to the royal household, and in March named him *secrétaire d'Etat* for the navy, which Colbert had been heading in a semi-official capacity since 1662; finally, in August 1670, Colbert was made *grand maître et surintendant des Mines et Minières de France*. Simultaneous possession of a commission as *contrôleur général* and of two secretaryships helped Colbert to initiate a tradition of concentration of powers, since the *contrôleur général* had authority in the areas of financial, fiscal, and economic policy, and the secretaries of state were responsible for issuing laws, promulgating council degrees, and dispatching letters patent, while the secretary of state for the royal household promulgated acts of general consequence pertaining to the entire kingdom.

Thus the king made the *contrôle général* the motor of the kingdom. The *contrôleur général* monopolized control over taxes, farms, coinage, the royal domain, bridges and highways, internal and foreign trade, and streams and forests. He had sole control over the nomination of provincial intendants, excepting those in border provinces. He initiated legislation and the codification of laws: among the measures taken were the civil ordinance of April

1667, the judicial reform of August 1669, the ordinance concerning streams and forests of August 1669, the criminal ordinance of August 1670, the commercial ordinance of March 1670, and the naval ordinance of August 1681. He was behind the holding of "Grands Jours," set up the colonial courts of justice, and reformed the Conseil privé in 1672 and 1673. The only areas not under the control of the *contrôleur général* were matters within the jurisdiction of the secretary of state for war, administration of the royal armies, designation of intendants to serve in border provinces, and matters within the competence of the secretary of state for foreign affairs and his department, in which, moreover, members of Colbert's family were serving. From this point until the end of the absolute monarchy the influence of the *contrôleur général* constantly extended far beyond the limits of financial and economic policy per se.

This influence extended beyond the limits of the Conseil royal. The Council itself was absorbed with keeping accounts and resolving disputes. There came a time, hard to pinpoint exactly, when it ceased to set the monarchy's financial and fiscal policies. After Colbert, the crucial decisions were made by the king, meeting privately with the *contrôleur général*. They were then presented to the Council and approved without real debate. This was the case for the *capitation* of 1695 and the *dixième* of 1710. The king, moreover, was bogged down in the work of accounting, and though he did indeed manage to avoid dealing with cases of fraud and misappropriation, he was obliged to leave the problems of increasing taxes and creating new sources of revenue up to the *contrôleur général*, assisted by an *intendant*. The *contrôleur·général* would draw up a bursal edict and have it approved by the king. He would then issue a council decree which had never been seen by any council and which was signed by a secretary of state and stamped by the chancellor without discussion. The *contrôleur général* was a despot. This was the beginning of the ministerial despotism so much criticized at the time of the Revolution.

A growing number of government orders were promulgated without being couched in the form of council decrees, as *lettres de cachet* or *lettres circulaires*. By this time the signature of the king and of a secretary of state, in the first case, or of the *contrôleur général* alone, in the king's name, in the second case, was enough to enforce obedience. In many matters even the legal forms were no longer observed. Orders were given by executive fiat. Speed and efficiency were enhanced. Guarantees vanished. The arbitrary exercise of power reinforced the despotic tendencies of the regime.

The membership of the Conseil des Dépêches, which read dispatches from the provinces and from *commissaires* and governers in the field and drafted replies, invariably included the king, the chancellor, the ministers of state, the head of the Conseil royal des Finances, and the secretaries of state. It was in this council that the princes of the blood began their political education. The Grand Dauphin had the right to participate in debate and to cast a vote in this council from 1688 on; the duc de Bourgogne from October

1699 on; and the duc de Berry from December 1712 on. Monsieur, the king's brother, never participated. The Council was supposed to come to decisions concerning current affairs in the provinces, but the king dealt with these matters along with his ministers. As a result, council meetings gradually became less frequent. In 1661 this council met twice a week. By 1700 or so, it was meeting every other Monday morning. By 1715 meetings had diminished to once a month.

The Conseil royal de Commerce was created on 3 August 1664. It included the king, the chancellor, the head of the Conseil royal des Finances, Colbert, Le Tellier, de Lionne, d'Aligre, and de Sève, a member of the Conseil royal des Finances. It met at first once every two weeks. Then the frequency of meetings diminished, because the king began making decisions in commercial matters in conjunction with Colbert. This Council vanished in 1676.

The Conseil de Conscience included, in 1661, the king; his confessor, Père Annat; the *grand aumônier de France*, de La Mothe-Houdancourt, bishop of Rennes; Marca, bishop of Toulouse; and Hardouin de Péréfixe, bishop of Rodez. This council decided on the distribution of benefices. One after another, its members died, until it was reduced in the end to the king and his confessor.

At the time the Edict of Nantes was revoked, there existed a Conseil pour la religion prétendue réformée, or Council for Protestantism. The king did not sit on this council. It was revived in July 1699.

Councils for administration and for the Settlement of Disputes

The importance of the councils for administration and for the settlement of disputes declined. Designated as a group by the expression "Conseil d'Etat privé, Finances et Direction," these included, first of all, the Conseil d'Etat privé and the Conseil d'Etat et des Finances, a single council made up of *conseillers d'Etat* and of *maîtres des requêtes*, which met one day as the Conseil privé, another day as the Conseil d'Etat et des Finances. At the beginning Louis XIV sometimes attended, but eventually he ceased to come altogether. His armchair remained at the head of the table, in the chairman's place, as a symbol of his presence.

The Conseil d'Etat privé or Conseil des Parties met twice a week. It accepted petitions on appeal, cases taken out of the jurisdiction of other courts, and cases involving conflicts of jurisdiction. It played a discreet but important role in maintaining the authority of the monarchy. It was not exempt from disorder. This centered on the designation of *rapporteurs*. The parties would bribe the *greffiers* to obtain a *rapporteur* favorable to their cause. Regulations issued on 3 January 1673 and 27 October 1674 attempted to remedy this situation. Then d'Aligre decided to assign cases himself. Le Tellier dealt with appeals. The regulations of 17 June 1687, the declaration of 29 July 1701, and the council decree of 3 February 1714 covered attempts by the parties to impugn *rapporteurs* and the introduction of appeals.

The Conseil d'Etat et des Finances had already been drastically curtailed in 1631. Its responsibility had been limited to dealing with disputes in connection with financial matters. Its decline continued. It was still meeting in April 1674. By 1697 it had disappeared; we do not know precisely when. With the decline of the chancellor of France, what happened, in effect, was that many financial matters were dealt with administratively rather than in the courts. They were either resolved or sent on by the *contrôleur général*, the *intendants des Finances*, and the *intendants de Commerce*. The Conseil d'Etat et des Finances was no longer necessary.

Another of these councils was the "Grande Direction" or "Conseil des Finances," which continued to exist and to play an active role, though somewhat curtailed by the existence of the Conseil royal des Finances. It was a council no longer of government but merely of administration. The chancellor presided over its meetings once every two weeks. An important role was played by the *intendants des Finances*, who enjoyed access, membership, and the right to vote and participate in debate from 1657 on. In 1660 their number was reduced to two. Always chosen from among the *maîtres des requêtes*, they were increased to three in January 1673 and were ex officio members of the Conseil d'Etat. In February 1690 the number of *intendants des Finances* was increased to six. In 1701 it was reduced to four, but two *directeurs des finances* were named to report to the Conseil royal. These posts were eliminated in 1708, but the king named seven *intendants des Finances* and six *intendants de Commerce*.

The work of the Grande Direction was always prepared by the "Petite Direction." The latter met once every two weeks in the offices of the head of the Conseil royal des Finances. It included the *contrôleur général* and certain *intendants des Finances*, *trésoriers*, and *receveurs*.

The work of the Grande and Petite Direction was always prepared by the "Petite Direction." The latter met once every two weeks in the offices of the head of the Conseil royal des Finances. It included the *contrôleur général* and certain *intendants des Finances, trésoriers*, and *receveurs*.

The work of the Grande and Petite Direction was prepared by various bureaus. *Rapporteurs* were given permanent tenure in each category of affairs, being nominated by council decree upon recommendation of the *contrôleur général*. Most were *maîtres des requêtes*, but there were also three or four *conseillers d'Etat* and one or two *intendants des Finances*. After Pussort's death in February 1697, there was a tendency to centralize these bureaus, one taking charge of the *gabelles*, another of the *cinq grosses fermes* along with associated entries and dues, another of *aides*, still another of *tailles*, and so on. Yet another office took charge of the royal domains, and in 1701 and 1702 this bureau was made responsible for the *aides* as well, replacing the department mentioned previously. Subsequently, there was no further change in these offices down to 1787.

From 1690 on, the head of the Conseil royal, the *contrôleur général*, the *conseillers d'Etat* who were members of the Conseil royal, and the *intendants des Finances* who were the sole *rapporteurs* in that council met informally in what was called the "assembly of *intendants de finance*."

As in the past, the effective chief of finance, the *contrôleur général*, who supplanted the *surintendant des Finances*, gave the king a whole string of "creatures," relatives, *fidèles*, and clients, many of whom were or became council secretaries, *receveurs généraux des Finances des généralités, trésoriers des Etats du Languedoc et du Dauphiné, fermiers généraux* (all of whom were also *traitants* and *partisans*), and *traitants* and *partisans*. Most of these men not only furthered the minister's financial policy but also supported his economic policy and participated in his trading companies, mines, industrial enterprises, canon foundries, arms factories, and so forth.

The "Revolution" of 1661

The formula according to which "the king governs through the Grand Conseil" persisted under Louis XIV. But it had become a myth, a fiction. Increasingly, it served as a mask to cover the reality, which was that decisions were being taking by one man—the king, the *contrôleur général*, one *commis* or another—or were the result of the deliberations of informal committees, where the decisive role was often played by the *rapporteur*. The councils became a magnificent façade. Officially, the government remained judicial in form. But the functions of government were now only partly carried out in the courts, less and less so as time went by. Quick and efficient, the executive form of government was well suited to the needs of warfare and so won out over the judicial. Executive government curtailed legal guarantees, however, and opened the way to arbitrariness and depotism, which, in the guise of parliamentarism, were to become the primary characteristics of French governments in the nineteenth and twentieth centuries.

This was a political revolution. It was also the beginning of a social revolution. The monarchy, and especially Louis XIV, eliminated some high crown officers, reduced the status of others, excluded from the councils all who were entitled to seats by virtue of their birth or position, diminished the role of the councils, and entrusted power to recently ennobled men rather than to the great families and their suites of vassals; they thereby broke the ties between the monarchy and the customary structure of French society. By changing, in fact, the political structure of the state, the traditional constitution of the kingdom, the monarchy also altered the distribution of power and, consequently, of influence and wealth within the social hierarchy, modifying the social hierarchy itself in the process. By giving precedence to fiscal concerns and to the fiscal spirit rather than to the ideas of dignity, honor (transmitted by birth more than acquired), and justice, the king undermined the society of orders. He thereby began the transition from a society of orders to a society of classes and from the absolute monarchy to the centralized bureaucratic state.

Polysynody, 1715, 1718, 1723

When Louis XIV died, his successor Louis XV was five years old. Because the new king was a minor child, a regency was necessary. According to the fundamental laws of the kingdom, the regency could fall only to the duc d'Orléans, a man of amoral, dissolute character. In his will of 2 August 1714, Louis XIV sought to limit the power of the regent by establishing the composition of the Regency Council, where all matters were supposed to be decided by plurality vote, and by separating the regency from the tutelage of the minor king, which Louis XIV entrusted to one of his bastards, the duc de Maine.

The duc d'Orléans was bent on keeping for himself the omnipotence that Louis XIV had achieved. He therefore approached the aristocrats who held fast to the ideas current in the entourage of the duc de Bourgogne and who wanted the principal posts in government for themselves, and he also approached the *parlement*. On 2 September 1715, he went to the Paris *parlement* for the opening of Louis XIV's will. He told the magistrates that he intended to govern "with the aid of your counsel and your wise remonstrances." He restored to *parlement* its political role. Furthermore, he announced that he would create, around the Regency Council, other councils to deal with important affairs. The *parlement* thereupon paid no further heed to the late king's will and declared the duc d'Orleáns "regent of France, empowered . . . to administer the affairs of the kingdom during the minority of the king," with the power to choose the members of the Regency Council and the other councils at his own discretion. On 15 September a royal declaration established a number of councils to manage the affairs of the kingdom. This system was known as "polysynody."

The regent was granted and exercised all the powers that the traditional constitution afforded the monarch. In particular, by virtue of the declaration of 23 September 1715, and the regulation of 14 November, the regent, like his uncle Louis XIV, assumed the post of *surintendant des Finances* in sole charge of all expenditures.

By the declaration of 15 September the Conseil privé, the Grande Direction, and the Petite Direction were retained; these continued to be the preserve of *conseillers d'Etat* and *maîtres des requêtes*. No changes were made in the councils for administration and resolution of disputes.

By all appearances, however, the government was completely revamped. All the councils of government were fused within the Regency Council, which, as of 18 September 1715 began meeting four times per week, on Sunday and Wednesday morning for foreign affairs (as the Conseil d'Etat), on Saturday afternoon for finance (as the Conseil royal des Finances), and on Tuesday afternoon for military, naval, and provincial affairs (as the Conseil des Dépêches). Seated on a stool, the regent presided over these meetings, with the king presumed to be present and his chair placed at the head of the table. Decisions were ratified by a plurality of votes. From the time he was ten, Louis XV attended these meetings regularly, for the first time on 18 February 1720. The Regency Council was in charge of the education of the minor king. The chancellor was therefore a member ex officio, as were the members of the royal family as soon as they reached the requisite age: in 1715 the duc de Bourbon became a member with the title "head of the Regency Council," along with the legitimized bastards of the former king, the duc du Maine and the comte de Toulouse; in 1717, the prince de Conti; in 1718, the duc de Chartres; in 1720, the comte de Charolais. The two *conseillers d'Etat* who had belonged to the Conseil royal des Finances sat on the Regency Council when it dealt with financial matters; they bore the title of "*conseillers au Conseil de Régence pour les finances.*"

All the responsibilities attributed to the secretaries of state, the *contrôleur général des Finances*, the *intendants des Finances*, and the *intendants de Commerce* were transferred to the Conseils de la Polysynodie. The secretaries of state were reduced to signing dispatches under orders. They were excluded from the Regency Council, with the exception of La Vrillière, who continued to be in charge of administration of the royal household and of the *pays d'Etats* but attended the Council only to take down the minutes of the meetings. There were now only three secretaries of state, the one responsible for military affairs having been eliminated by edict of January 1716. All were new men. The post of *contrôleur général* was kept but without an occupant. Seven positions with the rank of *intendant des Finances* and all six *intendants du Commerce* were eliminated by edict in October 1715.

The declaration of 15 September 1715 established six special councils for the discussion and settlement of affairs, decisions being left up to the Regency Council. These were the Councils of Conscience, Foreign Affairs, War, Finance, Navy, and Interior. Commercial matters were within the jurisdiction of two councils, Finance and Navy. Because of the disadvantages of this arrangement, a declaration of 14 December 1715 established a Council of Commerce. All these councils were chaired by great lords, cardinals, marshals, dukes-and-peers. They were surrounded by other great lords, dukes, marquis, and counts. Below them the regent appointed ecclesiastics, *conseillers d'Etat*, *maîtres des requêtes*, and members of *parlement*. The high nobility of court and sword attempted to take its revenge against the *noblesse de robe*. These councils were not part of the king's Council. They issued neither judgments nor decrees. They were rather collegial ministries whose purpose was to lay the groundwork for meetings of the Regency Council. Their chairmen reported to the regent on specified days.

Collegiality is by definition equivalent to impotence. The regent gave out posts with the title "councillor on the Regency Council," as was traditional under regency governments. These councillors numbered 12 in 1716, 14 in 1717, 29 in 1719, 33 in 1721, 35 in 1722. Some were incapable, others were troublemakers. By 1715 the regent was forced to resign himself to consulting with diplomats, prelates, and magistrates in informal meetings held in his office. Foreign policy was carried out secretly by the regent and the abbé

Dubois. Beginning in 1717, the regent frequently turned questions over to members of the Regency Council for examination in "committee." The regent disposed of many matters alone with the president of the Council of Finance or with a former *premier commis* from the time of Louis XIV, M. Le Couturier. The Regency Council met less and less frequently as time went by. By 1718 it was no more than a formality. All major decisions were issued from the regent's office.

The Councils of the Polysynody, which were intended to replace the ministries, wasted their time quarreling among themselves and, within each council, disputing questions of etiquette and precedence. Only the Council of Finance remained active and effective up to the beginning of 1718, under the energetic chairmanship of the duc de Noailles. It fell, however, into the same habits as the *contrôle général des Finances*, issuing with no legal right numerous financial decrees that were not discussed in the Regency Council but rather adopted in private work sessions between the chairman and the regent; a list of such decrees was then read out for form's sake at the meeting of the Regency Council devoted to financial matters. In the other councils, disorder, confusion, powerlessness, and anarchy reigned. On 7 September 1718, the regent suspended the Regency Council and all the other councils until 15 October. On 24 September he eliminated the Councils of Conscience, Foreign Affairs, Interior, and War. On the same day he commissioned M. Le Blanc as secretary of state for war and the abbé Dubois as secretary of state for foreign affairs, adding their names to three secretaries of state who were kept on. On 19 September he reestablished the secretaries of state in their functions, divided the various provinces and powers among them, and granted them access to, and the right to vote and take part in debate in, the Regency Council, to which they henceforth reported on matters of state.

From October 1718 on, the regent was omnipotent. Little by little, the old councils of government were reestablished. The Regency Council was reduced to one meeting a week, during which it did no more than approve, for the sake of form, decisions prepared in advance, discussed and adopted elsewhere. The regent, the keeper of the seals, and the five secretaries of state met at least once a month in a meeting that contemporaries called by its true name: the Conseil des Dépêches.

After Law's resignation from the *contrôle général des Finances* on 29 May 1720 (he had been appointed on 5 January), the Council of Finance was gradually expanded, up to 12 December, with the addition of the *contrôleur général* Le Pelletier de La Houssaye and a number of *maître des requêtes*, veritable *intendants des Finances*, who held the title "*commissaires des finances*." In March 1722, five posts as *intendants des Finances* were reestablished and bestowed upon the *commissaires des Finances* appointed in 1720 and 1721. The Council of Finance in fact operated like the earlier Conseil royal des Finances, supported by a large number of special commissions, leaving but a shadow of power to the Regency Council.

A Bureau of Health and a Council of Health were established in 1721.

A new Council of Conscience, a true government council, was established by the declaration of 4 August 1720.

In mid-June of 1722, the king moved back to Versailles. Dubois, nominated cardinal in July 1721, was named prime minister on 22 August 1722. The government councils, the Council of Conscience, the Conseil royal des Finances, the Conseil des Dépêches, and the Council of Health were openly and officially declared to exist. They were described as government councils by the *Almanach royal* of 1723. On 25 October 1722, Louis XV was anointed at Reims. The king began his fourteenth year on 16 February 1723, thereby entering adulthood. On 23 February he held a *lit du justice* at the *parlement* of Paris and proclaimed his majority. The regency was over.

The Councils, 1723 to 1789

In this period the importance of the councils continued to decline and that of the king's work with his ministers continued to increase. There was perhaps an even greater increase in the importance of the work done by the ministers in conjunction with bureaucrats serving under them in a whole hierarchy of assemblies, committees, commissions, and bureaus; the procedures adopted were quick and in many cases not officially recognized, but they accounted for the bulk of the work of the government. During a period when armaments became more and more costly, the increased importance of the bureaucracy seems to have been related to the increased role of finance and the relative decline of the magistracy.

The King's Work

Of central importance was the king's work with his ministers and various other functionaries, as well as the work done by the *contrôleur général des Finances* in conjunction with the *intendants des Finances* and the *premiers commis*.

In the Cabinet du Roi at Versailles, the sovereign, seated at his cylindrical desk, used to receive his visitors, each carrying a morocco leather portfolio. The king met in this way with the chancellor, the secretaries of state, the *contrôleur général des Finances*, the prelate responsible for the award of benefices, the chief bursar, the *surintendant des Bâtiments*, the first architect, the governor of the château of Versailles, the director of fortifications, and the captains of the household militia.

The prime minister, the duc d'Orléans, the duc de Bourbon, and Cardinal Fleury all helped the king with his work and noted down his decisions. When the king met with an official, that official's superior in the hierarchy also attended. Thus, when the king received the lieutenant of police for Paris, the secretary of state responsible for Paris was also present.

When the king agreed with the conclusions of a report or memorandum submitted for his consideration, he marked the document with the word "good" or "approved." He decided what questions were to be brought up before the Council. Many questions that should have been taken to the Council were decided by the king alone, especially in the areas of finance, the army, and the navy. These decisions were often couched in the form of council decrees, even though the Council had never seen them.

The Work of the Contrôleur Général

The *contrôleur général des Finances* met weekly with each *intendant des Finances* and each *intendant du Commerce*. They explained the gist of each case, and the *contrôleur* made his decision. Many of these decisions were couched in the form of council decrees. The *contrôleur* thus disposed of questions pertaining to streams and forests and tax farms and even settled disputes by issuing decrees which, though never seen by the Council, bore the formula, "By the king in his Council."

The *contrôleur general* also met with the *premiers commis* of the various bureaus. Together, they went over the documents and reached decisions which were then issued as council decrees. The same is true of the *intendants des Finances* in their work with the *premiers commis*.

Many decisions of this sort were couched in forms other than Council decrees. Some were issued in the form of written documents that were neither sealed nor registered but validated merely by signature. Among these were ordinances bearing neither an address nor a seal and introduced by the words, "*De par le Roi*," "*Il est ordonné que*," "*Le Roi veut et ordonne*." These were laws or regulations. They laid down the organization of the royal household, the academies, the colonies, the navy, and the army, and ordered military or naval reforms. They were validated by the king's signature, countersigned by a secretary of state. There was the "*Ordre du Roi*," *lettre de cachet* or cash order, signed by the king and countersigned by a secretary of state. There was also the "*Décision du Conseil*," a sort of executive order issued by the *contrôleur général* and approved by an *intendant des provinces* and dealing with *corvées*, *aides*, farms, or local finances. There were missives and ministerial dispatches pertaining to diplomatic and military decisions and to matters of internal administration, and "memoirs to be used as instructions" given to the king's representatives abroad, to captains in the army and cavalry, to *royal commissaires*, to the provincial Estates, and to the governors general and intendants in the colonies.

All of these various forms escaped the control of the seal and took the place of ministerial orders and proclamations that were always somewhat improper, because in theory the king had all the powers and could not delegate them. The disadvantage was that ministerial orders and proclamations were relatively easy to modify or revoke, far more so than council decrees; because Council decrees were used in trivial affairs, respect for them was lost and the authority of the government was weakened.

Informal agencies responsible for readying materials for the king's work, as well as that of the *contrôleur général* and the councils, proliferated. These agencies sometimes became decision-making bodies as well.

Ministerial Committees and Commissions

Ministerial committees met without formal invitation on Mondays from 1737 until 1744. Their purpose was debate and preparation of decisions. They coordinated the actions of the various ministers. From 1747, they were allowed to meet only on orders from the king, so as to prevent the formation of a Cabinet Council or Council of Ministers, which would have diminished the king's power. These committees laid the groundwork for meetings of the Conseil d'Etat and the Conseil des Dépêches but never of the Conseil des Finances.

Special commissions assisted the various councils. For the Conseil des Dépêches, these commissions were made up of members of the Council, magistrates from the courts and tribunals, bishops, curates, *avocats*, and experts of all professions. Their role was to look into certain matters and prepare reports. Sometimes they served as courts of appeal. They were political and administrative commissions. Some lasted for quite a while. The Commission des Secours, composed of prelates and *maîtres des requêtes*, was established in 1727 to examine requests for help submitted by religious establishments for young girls. The Commission des Réguliers was established in 1766 to reform abuses in the monasteries and orders of the kingdom. It included five archbishops, five *conseillers d'Etat*, four theologians, four *avocats*, and one secretary. The king approved its decisions. It eliminated 450 monasteries and 9 religious orders.

For the Conseil royal des Finances, the Bureau of Commerce was established on 22 June 1722 and included the *contrôleur général*, the secretary of state for the navy, several *conseillers d'Etat*, *maîtres des requêtes*, *intendants du commerce*, and *députés du commerce* elected by the Chambers of Commerce. This commission issued council decrees.

The Commission des Péages included *conseillers d'Etat* and *maîtres des requêtes*. It verified the authenticity of seigneurial and other titles to the right of levying tolls.

A commission was established in 1739 for the fees collected from docks, ports, harbors, roadsteads, shores, and riverbanks. The *conseillers d'Etat* and *maîtres des requêtes* who sat on this commission issued decisions in the form of Council decrees or acts under its charter.

During time of war a commission known as the Conseil des Prises, established on 23 September 1676, and another known as the Commission des Vivres et Etapes, which survived after the death of Louis XIV, were called into being.

Other special commissions subordinate to the council and known as "bureaus" also existed. To give a few examples: in 1763 a bureau for "the alienation of the combined domains" was established; there was a commission to judge disputes relating to the pensions of oblates or monks, legacies, real estate, and rights, privileges, immunities, and possessions attributed to the Hôtel royal des Invalides and the Ecole royale militaire, and to administer the calendar and appeals from the ordinances of the intendants with regard to such disputes; there was a bureau for the treasury and accounts of the *commis* administering the property of fugitive Calvinists; a bureau for disputes relating to payments in writing and bank accounts; a bureau for disputes concerning shares in the Compagnie des Indes and land concessions in Louisiana; a bureau for the liquidation of the *communautés, arts et métiers* of Paris and for the auditing and revision of their accounts since 1689; a bureau for matters pertaining to the union of benefices in the houses and colleges of the Jesuits, and a bureau for the liquidation of the debts of the navy and the colonies, to name a few.

The Assemblée des Intendants de Finance met from 1690 until October 1715, at which date the *intendants de Finance* were eliminated. They were reestablished in 1722 but began meeting again only after 1730. They held their meeting each week at the residence of their most senior member. The meeting sometimes cleared up a difficult point for an *intendant des Finances*. Sometimes it functioned as a special commission of the Conseil royal des Finances, even going so far as to issue judgments. Sometimes it took the place of the council itself. It worked quickly and reached decisions rapidly.

The Bureaus and the Commis

The chancellor, the secretaries of state, and the *contrôleur général* were served by bureaus of *commis* who received the mail, excerpted its contents, prepared reports, answered letters, and drew up the texts of laws and regulations.

The chancellor made do with a few secretaries, because he had the services of court personnel, who followed the procedures of the courts. Thus he employed 350 persons in connection with the seal: *maîtres des requêtes*, assessors, *grands rapporteurs, grands audienciers*, royal secretaries, and so on. In the councils there were *conseillers d'Etat, maîtres des requêtes, secrétaires-greffiers, huissiers*, and *avocats*.

The secretariats of state that dealt with more technical matters were more fully developed than the rest. The secretariat for war, for example, employed thirteen *premiers commis* or bureau chiefs in 1759; that for the navy employed eight *premiers commis* for the secretariat and seven bureaus; in 1775 there were ten *premiers commis* and twelve bureaus; foreign affairs had, besides the minister's secretariat, six *premiers commis* for six bureaus.

The largest number of bureaus was to be found in the *contrôle général des Finances*. The *premier commis des Finances*, keeper of the royal treasury and a division chief of sorts, supervised six or seven *premiers commis* or bureau chiefs. The *contrôleur général* and the *intendants des Finances* each had the services of *premiers commis*. The *contrôleur général* had five of them in 1762, eight in 1775. In all, there were thirty-two *premiers commis* in 1762, thirty-three in 1775.

Each *premier commis* supervised three or four *commis:* in 1718, for example, the staff consisted of one head *commis*, two *commis* scribes, and one scribe.

Over-all, foreign affairs employed 40 people in 1788; the navy employed 105 in 1775; the war department, 54 in 1735; finance, around 150 to 160 in 1775. Each bureau was responsible for affairs of a certain kind, its own particular specialty.

Some of these bureaus were located at Versailles in long, low buildings alongside the great entry court. Others were in Paris. In 1763, four of the five *premiers commis* of the *contrôleur général* had their offices in Paris: M. Parent was located in the rue Poissonière, near the Boulevard; M. Cromot du Bourg in the rue Cadet; M. de Villiers in the rue du Petit-Musc; M. Barbey in the rue des Juifs. Only M. Mesnard de Cornichard had his offices at Versailles. The *premiers commis* of the *intendants des Finances* were all located in offices dispersed throughout Paris.

The proliferation of the bureaucracy spelled the end of the councils. During the period in question, the Conseil royal des Finances became a fiction. The others seemed to fare well, even better than they had done under Louis XIV, but, to judge by the number and importance of the cases dealt with, it is certain that they suffered a decline.

In finance, the *contrôle général* was all-powerful. Meetings of the Conseil royal des Finances became less and less frequent. The Conseil royal de Commerce ceased to meet altogether soon after its creation. Hardly one financial decree in twenty was really considered by the Council. The Conseil royal des Finances became a myth. The only *rapporteur* in this council was the *contrôleur général des Finances*. He alone was familiar with the affairs to be considered. Of necessity the decisions of the Council conformed to his wishes. Bored and weary, the members of the Council finally left it up to the *contrôleur général* to make all decisions alone in his offices. The *contrôleur général* became the driving force behind the kingdom's tax system, economy, and general administration.

Precedents made his task in making decisions easier. Jurists collected, explained, and commented upon the texts of laws and regulations in various treatises and compendia in jurisprudence. Among these were Pecquet (*Les loix forestières*, 1753), La Poix de Freminville (*Traité général du gouvernement des biens et affaires des communautés d'habitants*, 1760), Lefebvre de La Planche (*Traité du Domaine*, 1764), Chailland (*Dictionnaire raisonné des eaux et forêts*, 1769), the *Code voiturin*, which dealt with postal and shipping services, to name a few.

The Omnipotence of the Contrôle Général

Decisions were made by the *contrôleur général*, the *intendants des Finances*, and the *premiers commis* whenever a case could be subsumed under a category treated by the law or legal commentary, provided it had been investigated locally by a competent authority, such as an *intendant*, a *sub-*

délégué, an engineer from the Ponts et Chaussées, or a *grand maître des Eaux et Forêts*. The documents were transmitted to a royal council only when the case was an extraordinary one of general interest.

The *contrôleur général* and the *intendants des Finances* gathered an abundance of detailed information in a multitude of inquiries. After 1772 a statistical department was set up in the *contrôle général*. An infinite number of figures were collected. This resulted in a belief in the infallibility of the bureaucracy and the futility of the councils. It was at this point that there grew up, under the influence first of Cartesianism and then of the philosophy of the Enlightenment, an ideological spirit, a taste for abstract constructions deduced from a few clear principles. The spread of mathematical instruction and technical schools such as those associated with Bridges and Highways, Mines, and Artillery fostered a faith in plans carefully worked out by specialists competent in their own area, and added to the contempt for the councils.

The *contrôleur général* and the *intendants des Finances* were located in Paris, as were the *fermiers généraux*, the *receveurs généraux*, and the *trésoriers généraux*. A committee of *receveurs généraux* met each week in Paris. This was one more reason to reduce the frequency of meetings of the Conseil royal des Finances. The situation was the reverse for the secretariats of the state for war and foreign affairs, which were located at Versailles.

The *contrôleur général* had full authority over matters of general police, finance, commerce, circulation of currency, banking, and, in general, anything that might be used to create taxable resources and credit. As the kingdom's minister of the interior, he intervened in everything. He created new taxes, had assessments made, arranged for them to be collected, and oversaw the accounting, which was done by the *intendants des Finances* who also sat in judgment over disputed cases. The *contrôleur général* made the finance ministry a collegial structure and obliged economic interest groups and *financiers* to accommodate to it. The *receveurs généraux des Finances* set up a common treasury under the regency. They met every week and transmitted the results of their meeting to the *intendant des Finances* in charge of general receipts; the latter official then reported, in their presence, to the *contrôleur général* on the following day. The *receveurs généraux* maintained a number of bureaus, which employed eighty-two people in 1726. In 1725 a bureau was set up to handle the *cinquantième*, employing thirty-six people. The *premier commis* for the *receveurs généraux* was M. Delpech, who was also *premier commis* for M. d'Ormesson, the *intendant des Finances* in charge of general receipts. In 1771 Terray established the committee of *receveurs généraux* for the domains and forests, which met every week in Paris.

The term "Finance" was applied to the whole range of organizations that included the *contrôleur général*, the *intendants des Finances* and *du Commerce*, the *receveurs généraux des Finances*, the various departments under them, the *financiers* with an interest in the various farms, administrations, and business deals pertaining to the royal revenue, as well as their correspondents, cashiers, bankers, auditors, guards, surveyors, resellers, *gabelous*, and "cellar rats."

The *contrôleur général* refused to allow any other department to involve itself in financial, fiscal, economic, or commercial matters. Instead, on the pretext of monitoring how the royal funds were being used, he intervened in the affairs of the other ministries. The *contrôleur général* claimed to be a secretary of state. Bear in mind that he nominated the *intendants* of non-border provinces and that all the secretaries of state were obliged to sign financial dispatches without debate and the chancellor was obliged to seal them without protest. Because of the absence of jurisdictional guarantees in regard to the investigation and judgment of disputed cases, it was possible for the courts to protest against the very principle of administrative justice and incite attacks on ministerial despotism.

The Decline of the Councils

The Conseil royal des Finances, reconstituted in 1722, was composed of the king, the dauphin, the prime minister, the chancellor, the head of the Conseil royal, and of *conseillers d'Etat* who had received a letter designating them "Conseiller au Conseil royal des Finances," of whom there were at first two and later, around 1769, five. The Conseil royal met on Tuesdays. From 1728 on, the meetings became less and less frequent. From fifty times a year at the beginning, the frequency of meetings declined to twenty-eight in 1736 and to seven or eight per year from 1759 on.

The Conseil royal de Commerce reemerged in 1730. It met every other Tuesday. Within a short time its meetings became infrequent and sporadic. Several years went by without a single meeting. By the end of Louis XV's reign, it had disappeared. Its work was carried out by the Bureau de Commerce.

Around 4,000 council decrees were issued each year. More than two-thirds of these were in finance. The rest were issued by other councils, where it seems they really were discussed.

To consider government councils first, the Conseil d'Etat, on which the king sat in person, met Sundays and Wednesdays from ten o'clock in the morning until one o'clock in the afternoon. In addition, special councils were held as mail dispatches came in. There were 120 to 130 meetings per year. The king always attended this council in person. The membership included the ministers of state but never the chancellor. From 1723 on, this council was supposed to concern itself with all foreign affairs and with important resolutions pertaining to the central areas of government: war, finance, navy, commerce, justice, general police. After a few years, the Council limited itself to foreign affairs and military and naval matters, owing to competition from the Conseil des Dépêches. The secretaries of state served as *rapporteurs*.

Beginning in 1730 the Conseil des Dépêches grew considerably in importance in the wake of religious and parliamentary disputes. It met on Tuesdays and whenever a political or religious crisis erupted, forty to fifty times in a calm year and sixty to seventy times in a year of crisis. Its competence extended to all internal affairs. The *contrôleur général* never attended. The chancellor was a member ex officio. The main *rapporteurs* were the chancellor and the secretaries of state.

The Conseil de Conscience, reestablished in 1720, consisted of ecclesiastics. It met on Thursdays, some forty times per year. The royal declaration of 24 March 1730 proclaiming the bull *Unigenitus* the law of the land, triggered opposition from *parlement*. The Conseil de Conscience was no longer adequate to its purpose. It met for the last time on 28 January 1732.

As for the councils dealing with administrative matters and the settlement of disputes, the Conseil d'Etat privé or Conseil des Parties was composed of the king (although Louis XV attended only twice, on 3 May 1762 and 22 December 1766), the chancellor, who presided, *conseillers d'Etat, maîtres des requêtes*, secretaries of state, the *contrôleur général*, and *intendants des Finances*. After 1760, the *intendants des Finances* no longer attended. Each session brought together fifty to sixty participants. From 1705, the Council began meeting on Mondays, once a week rather than twice. It did not meet during the weeks of Easter, Pentecost, or Assumption or during the vacation from October until Saint Martin's day in November. The *maîtres des requêtes* served as *rapporteurs*. The council worked with regularity and efficiency.

The Grande Direction met regularly in the chamber of the Conseil des Parties. Attending were, presumably, the chancellor, the head of the Conseil royal des Finances, the *contrôleur général*, the members of the financial bureaus of the councils on *Domaines et Aides* and *Gabelles et Tailles*. The *maîtres des requêtes* acted as *rapporteurs*. Formally, the Council was supposed to meet every two weeks. In actuality it held no more than six to twelve meetings per year, because the *contrôleur général* did not steer cases in its direction.

The Petite Direction gathered in the apartment of the head of the Conseil royal des Finances. It included the *contrôleur général*, the *intendants des Finances*, the *conseillers d'Etat* who were members of the bureaus of Domaines et Aides and Gabelles et Tailles. Intended to relieve the Grande Direction of part of its burden, it almost ceased to exist in the end. It did not meet from 1722, when Villeroy was exiled, until 1730. Reestablished in October 1730, it met only twice a quarter. It was actually replaced by the assembly of *intendants des Finances*.

The Council Commissions

The "bureaus" of the Council, which should not be confounded with the bureaus of the *commis* of the *contrôleur général* and secretaries of state, were commissions. When a commission met, it was said to be "holding bureau." These commissions were made up of eight to ten *conseillers d'Etat*, chosen by the chancellor at the beginning of each year to lay the groundwork for the sessions of the Conseil d'Etat privé and the Directions. Among these in 1763 were four "bureaus" of lawsuits and appeals, one "bureau" for ecclesiastical affairs, one "bureau" for petitions and entreaties pertaining to the Conservation of Lyon, one "bureau" for French colonial legislation and for the transmission of petitions, entreaties, and other matters in dispute concerning the inhabitants of the colonies or their property, one "bureau" concerned with appeals of judgments of jurisdiction handed down in favor of the *prévôts des maréchaux* or presidial judges, and a "bureau" to deal with chancellery affairs and matters related to printing and publication. On 31 July 1699, a Conseil de Chancellerie was established to deal with petitions concerning infractions of the rules by the royal chancelleries, with two *maîtres des requêtes*. Then, in 1703, its jurisdiction was extended to include contraventions of edicts, declarations, decrees, and regulations dealing with publication and printing, and two additional *maîtres des requêtes* were appointed. After 1723, this "bureau" included two *conseillers d'Etat* and four to six *maîtres des requêtes* chosen by the chancellor. It met on Mondays after the Conseil des Parties. The chancellor made the decisions, with no presentation to the Council. The "bureau" of Postes et Messageries had been in existence since 1676. Under Louis XVI it became, on 16 April 1777, an extraordinary commission, with four to five *conseillers d'Etat* and three to four *maîtres des requêtes*, named to their posts by *arrêts en finance* for life terms, unless they resigned; they received special emoluments. The "bureau" of legislation, created in 1727 by d'Aguesseau, was made up of four *conseillers d'Etat* along with one or two *maîtres des requêtes*, who served as *rapporteurs*. It prepared royal ordinances and sent questionnaires to the superior courts. Proposed articles were drafted by *avocats* and secretaries of state. The "bureau" then examined and amended them. It remained in operation right up to the Revolution. The "bureau" *des réunions* was intended to reduce the number of judicial seats and officeholders. It consisted of four to five *conseillers d'Etat* and of a *maître des requêtes*, who served as *rapporteur*. All of these were chosen by the chancellor from among the members of his family or his creatures, as were the members of the "bureau" of legislation or the "bureau" of the chancellery. In all these "bureaus," and in the temporary commissions that were set up from time to time, service was unpaid except in special cases.

Two "bureaus" had been attached since 1701 or 1702 to the Directions des Finances: the "bureau des Domaines," which met on Tuesday afternoons and dealt with the domains, *aides*, and *octrois;* and the "bureau des Gabelles" or "bureau des Finances" or "bureau des Fermes," which met on Friday mornings and dealt with *gabelles*, the *cinq grosses fermes*, and other financial matters. The members were named by council decree for life, unless they resigned. They included the *contrôleur général*, the councillors of the Conseil royal, the *intendants des Finances*, certain *conseillers d'Etat*, and three to five *maîtres des requêtes*. They were paid 2,000 livres per year for the bureau des Domaines and 3,000 livres per year for the bureau des Gabelles. These two "bureaus" were probably active. Sometimes they sat as extraordinary commissions to judge cases on appeal. They were probably empowered to scrutinize cases transmitted directly to them by the *contrôleur général*, with the *contrôleur* then making decisions on the basis of their recommendations without submitting the matters to the Directions.

Louis XVI's Reforms

Under Louis XVI, Joly de Fleury organized, on 26 February 1783, a Committee of Finance made up of the keeper of the seals, the head of the Conseil royal, and the *contrôleur général*, who served as *rapporteur* and secretary. The concern of this committee was supposed to be the reduction of debts and expenditures connected with the army and navy. It was a war machine aimed against the secretaries of state responsible for those departments. Calonne allowed it to die.

Loménie de Brienne established a Conseil royal des Finances et du Commerce on 5 June 1787. It was supposed to include Brienne, the *contrôleur général*, and two members of the Conseil royal des Finances. It was intended to lay the groundwork for the work of the council and to replace all the bureaus and commissions concerned with financial matters. The Petite Direction was eliminated on 27 October 1787. The Grande Direction remained—on paper at any rate.

On 25 March 1788, Brienne set up a consultative committee for the reform of the royal treasury. A committee "for administrative affairs" appeared for the first time in the *Almanach royal* for 1789, but it was said to have been in existence for several years. It consisted of the *contrôleur général* and five *intendants des Finances*.

The Minister of the Interior

With the rise of the ministerial bureaus, we see the gradual formation of a corps of state employees that came closer and closer to a corps of functionaries, though without yet having acquired the status characteristic of the latter. Take the ministry of foreign affairs, for example. The secretary of state for foreign affairs was himself a specialized bureaucrat. During the second half of the eighteenth century he was usually drawn from an old family of high nobility, however. After the marquis d'Argenson (1744–47), who came from a family of *conseillers d'Etat* issued from the old *noblesse d'épée*, the post went to Puzieulx (1747–51), who was only of the seventh degree of nobility but whose family had a ministerial tradition dating back more than a century. Bernis (1757–58), the duc de Choiseul (1758–61 and again in 1766–70), the comte de Choiseul, duc de Praslin (1761–66), and the duc d'Aiguillon (1771–74), to name a few, were all knights of ancient extraction.

As principal *rapporteur* to the Conseil d'Etat, the secretary of state read a portion of the dispatches and memoirs and suggested responses and decisions to be taken. In the time of the marquis d'Argenson, dispatches began to bear the notations, "read to the king," "seen by the Council," "reported on to the Council." The secretary of state himself read dispatches marked "for you alone" and studied their contents. He received foreign ambassadors every week. On incoming dispatches he noted his thoughts and decisions. He read the replies in draft and marked them "cleared for dispatch" or "approved." He himself drafted the most important dispatches, memoirs, plans, and agendas. D'Argenson rose at five o'clock in the morning.

The secretary of state made use of the bureaus. Two secretaries were responsible for liaison between him and the bureaus, and the three formed a sort of ministerial staff or cabinet. Under the marquis de Torcy, the comte de Ligny, who was first secretary, took dictation from the minister, issued ordinances and passports, kept a copy of the accounts, and dispatched the secret correspondence. The second secretary, Jean-Gabriel de La Porte du Theil, assisted his colleague and prepared extracts from dispatches and letters.

Furthermore, from 1747 to 1766 the minister enjoyed the services of a "secretary for foreign affairs," an ordinary *commis* responsible for taking note of the secretary of state's directives, for delivering letters to the bureaus to be deciphered, and so on.

In 1766, Choiseul, who was secretary of state for both foreign affairs and war, organized a secrétairerie of ten persons, common to both departments. It ceased to exist in 1770.

D'Aiguillon went back to the two-secretary system. The secretaries working under him opened all letters and dispatches except those marked "for you alone." On each they marked the date of arrival, the name of the sender, and the name of the *premier commis* to whom the document was to be sent, and then had it delivered by one of the three office boys.

Depending on the period, there were two or three political bureaus to handle diplomatic correspondence. Each bureau had a *premier commis* and several subordinate *commis*. In July 1768 there were five *commis* in the bureau of the abbé de La Ville, eight in the Gerard's bureau, and two in Bournonville's bureau; in 1773, there were six with de La Ville and ten with Gerard.

Each bureau was responsible for a geographical sector. In 1727, Du Theil handled Italy, Spain, Portugal, Lorraine, and Turkey; Le Dran handled the court of Vienna, the prince electors of the Rhine, Ratisbon, imperial Flanders, and Switzerland; the younger Antoine Pecquet handled England, Holland, a portion of the Empire, the countries of the north, Poland, and Muscovy.

Du Theil left in 1745 and Dran in 1749. This marked the end of the *premiers commis* who had been trained during the time of Louis XIV. The change of personnel roughly coincided with the end of the War of the Austrian Succession.

Commis in the political bureaus served for long periods. Hence, on occasion, *premiers commis* made decisions in the place of the secretary of state, particularly when he was not up to his job. This was the case with the marquis de Bussy, *premier commis* under the secretary of state Saint-Contest (1751–54), and with the abbé de La Ville under Rouillé (1754–57).

The bureaus were housed at Versailles in the left wing of the Cour des Ministres. On the ground floor were the apartments of the secretary of state, on the second floor those of the *premiers commis*, and on the third floor, the bureaus. Until mid-century officials were not obliged to be present. The *commis* worked at home and were absent from their offices for whole days at a time. In 1767 a regulation required them to be present from nine in the morning until one in the afternoon and from five until nine in the evening. One *commis* from each bureau had to be present at four o'clock. During busy periods there was always someone present.

The *premiers commis* worked with the secretary of state. They reported to him on the political correspondence that had arrived on the preceding day, received his orders concerning replies to be made, drafted the replies, and made copies, omitting the correspondence that the secretary of state reserved for himself. They prepared historical memoirs, negotiating positions, plans of conduct, and instructions for ambassadors. They translated letters into foreign languages. These men—Pecquet, Du Theil, Le Dran, Gerard, de La Ville—and others of their kind were diligent workers.

In each bureau, a principal *commis* worked under the *premier commis* and supervised the ordinary *commis*. All served as copyists, preparing fair copies from drafts, and sent dispatches. In 1749 they began numbering all dispatches in the order they were sent. They enciphered dispatches using some fifteen different ciphers, which were changed often. In 1767 they began to specialize, each taking responsibility for a certain number of European courts.

The political bureaus followed the court of France to Compiègne and Fontainebleau in summer and autumn. Several *commis* always stayed behind in the bureaus at Versailles. The bureaus followed the king on his campaigns into Lorraine, Alsace, Flanders, and Belgium during the War of the Austrian Succession.

Other bureaus also assisted in the work of the secretariat for foreign affairs: the archives, the *bureau des fonds*, the cipher bureau, which existed only from 1749 to 1755, and the interpreters' bureau, as well as the bureau of provinces (since the secretary of state for foreign affairs bore responsibility for the administration of various provinces from 1723 to 1747 and from 1754 to 1757).

The *dépôt des archives* was established by Torcy in 1711. It was first entrusted to Yves de Saint-Prest, formerly a councillor on the Grand Conseil and a historian. From 1712 until his death in 1720, Saint-Prest was also director of an Academy of Politics intended to train future diplomats.

Archival records of more recent date than 1680 had been kept at Versailles. In 1715 they were transported to Paris and combined with other records, the whole collection being entrusted to a *commis*, Nicolas-Louis Le Dran. This inaugurated a dual system of management of the archives. Le Dran became *premier commis politique*, was dismissed with thanks in 1730, recalled in 1740, and retired at the age of sixty-three in 1749; however, from

1715 until 1762, when he was seventy-four, he had charge of the archives. Other guardians of the records included the abbé de La Ville, Du Theil, Durand, and Semonin.

The records were first kept in the *pavillon des Petits-Pères* in the place de la Victoire near Torcy's garden, then under the roof of the Vieux-Louvre above the Royal Chapel, where they filled seven rooms. They were transferred to Versailles to the fifth floor of a *hôtel* that was completed in 1763 and housed offices of the ministry of foreign affairs on the second floor and the navy on the third and fourth. The archives occupied eight rooms, not counting the chief's apartment. Records from 1660 on were kept there. The bureaus sent over their papers when they became overloaded. The records were also augmented by acquisitions and gifts. In 1705, Torcy donated the Richelieu papers from the legacy of Madame d'Aiguillon. Law's papers were added in 1729. In 1732, 462 volumes from Mazarin's ministry were acquired, and in 1733 the papers of Bouthillier de Chavigny. In 1760 the duchesse de Valentinois donated the papers of her grandfather, the duc de Saint-Simon.

The *premier commis du dépôt*, assisted by three or four other *commis*, classified the documents, had them bound into volumes, and prepared inventories, tables, and catalogues. He looked up old affairs in the records when these had a bearing on present policy.

The *bureau des fonds* was established in 1725 to administer the budget allocated by the king to foreign affairs. At the end of each year, the secretary of state reported to the king on how the appropriated funds had been used and requested the king to approve the proposed budget for the following year. If the king approved, he ordered the *contrôleur général* to provide the funds and arrange for the necessary payments. If unforseen expenses were incurred during the year, the king issued a *"bon du roi,"* or royal note, to cover them.

The secretary of state was the person authorized to pass on expenditures. Each quarter he certified the statements of distribution of funds. In the case of a new item of expenditure, he had a special statement drawn up. He sent all these statements to the *contrôleur général* so that a source of funds could be assigned to cover each payment. The secretary of state had orders for each expenditure drawn up, signed them, and sent them to the *contrôleur général*, who then had the visa applied, signed the papers, presented them to the king for his signature, and then sent them back to the secretary of state. Until 1759, the *contrôleur general* sent the orders for transfer of funds (*assignations*) either to the *Trésor royal*, which paid them, or to a banker, who drew up letters of exchange for foreign payment: among the bankers called on were Samuel Bernard until 1737 and Paris de Monmartel from 1736 to 1759, to name two. After 1759, the *assignations* were sent to an accountant, "the court banker" (who was Laborde from 1759–67, Magon de La Balue from 1767–70, Beaujon from 1772–74, etc.).

In addition, the *bureau des fonds* took care of pensions, gifts, and *dignités;* passports; permissions to reside in France; permissions to French subjects to reside abroad; and *La Gazette de France*, whose contents it watched closely. Under Choiseul, this periodical was attached to the ministry of foreign officers and edited by its agents.

The bureau of interpreters was established in 1753 and entrusted to Edné-Jacques Genêt. It was established on a firm footing by Genêt's students in 1763. This bureau was responsible for all translations. From 1756 on, it examined the English with an eye to evaluating England's strength. Thorough familiarity with the law and institutions of foreign countries was required of its members.

The careers of *premiers commis*, principal *commis*, and ordinary *commis* were very much like the careers of functionaries. In theory, they served at the pleasure of the secretary of state, who appointed them and could remove them at will. Such posts were rarely bequeathed to heirs. The younger Pecquet and the younger Genêt (1781) are sometimes mentioned as exceptions to this rule. Recruitment relied on family support, such as the recommendation of an uncle. Social relations also helped: the abbé de La Ville became preceptor of the children of the marquis de Fénelon, who was ambassador to The Hague in 1730, and the ambassador launched his career. Nicolas-Louis Le Dran, while at seminary, occupied the cell next to that of Père Pouget, who later introduced him to Colbert de Croissy, bishop of Montpellier. The bishop recommended Le Dran to Torcy, his elder brother, and Le Dran was accepted as a *commis* in October 1711.

All the *commis* were educated in the *collèges* of the Jesuits, frequently at the *collège* Louis-le-Grand in Paris. Later, they studied law and gained a knowledge of foreign languages. *Commis* began their careers in the secretariat of state between the ages of twenty and forty. The average beginner's age was twenty-eight. Those who became *premiers commis* did so between the ages of twenty-five and fifty, thirty-nine on the average. From 1725 on, *premiers commis* were no longer recruited among the *commis* of the ministry of foreign affairs but rather among the agents of the *Contrôle général*, the navy, the war department, and especially among former embassy secretaries responsible for handling affairs in foreign countries.

Commis and *premiers commis* served for long periods of time, as long as 47, 48, or even, in the case of Le Dran, 51 years. Thus, in reality, they enjoyed a stable tenure of office. Normally, they could expect to enjoy retirement after 32, 34, or 36 years. Their salaries were graded by seniority, and they received annual bonuses as well as special bonuses when they established residence at Versailles, married, or married off their daughters or nieces—lifetime bonuses for their services, free of all taxes. Retirement pensions sometimes equaled the regular salary, in which cases they were characterized as "conserved emoluments." A portion of these benefits could revert to the man's widow and another portion to his children.

Even under Louis XVI (probably in 1783), the *premiers commis* acquired a sort of formal establishment (*titularization*) in their positions. A royal brevet granted them the title of "*Secrétaire au Conseil d'Etat*," and they were presented to the king when nominated. Now, this brevet was a formal document issued by a secretary of state, through which the king accorded a favor, a title and dignity, a rank in the army, or some such benefit: not only was it a solemn document producible in court, it was also a permanent award with no time limit. Thus the *premiers commis* came quite close to the status of functionaries.

The social status of *premiers commis* and *commis* was middling. During the course of the century, however, the gap between the *premiers commis* and the ordinary *commis* increased. Of the twenty-six *premiers commis* under Louis XV, only one, Du Theil, can be regarded as a noble of ancient extraction. Five were of recent nobility and owed their nobility to offices held by ancestors who served as *échevins*, *secrétaires du roi*, or *robins*. The rest were commoners of varying backgrounds: sons of soldiers, of minor magistrates, often of notaries or *payeurs des rentes sur l'Hôtel de Ville*. Many were born in Paris, but they were Parisians of recent date, from Alsatian families like the Gérards, or families of Lorraine, Franche-Comté, or Champagne. Prior to 1740, they made modest marriages. After that date they began marrying the daughters of magistrates in provincial sovereign courts, the Cours des Aides, the Cours des Monnaies, and of *fermiers généraux*. They therefore began to rate a higher esteem. They married late, at age thirty-eight on the average. Seven of them received letters of nobility in compensation for their services.

Ordinary *commis* were of still more modest origin, though a few petty *gentilshommes* sometimes slipped in among them. One does find a few sons of minor magistrates, officials of the royal household (*valets de pied*, *garçons de la Chambre*), and *commis* from the bureaus of the secretaries of state. Usually, they were sons of storekeepers, hatters, clothiers, upholsterers, tailors, apothecaries, and goldsmiths. They married the daughters of lower-ranking officials of the royal and princely households, of merchants, and, in a few cases, of *commis* of the secretaries of state. They received decorations. The *gentilshommes* among them were made knights of the Order of Notre-Dame du Mont-Carmel and Saint-Lazare of Jerusalem.

At the beginning of the eighteenth century, relations between the *premiers commis* and *commis* were benevolent on the part of the former, respectful on the part of the latter, and friendly on both sides. The *premiers commis* attended their subordinates' weddings and were godfathers to their children. After the middle of the century, the gap between the upper and lower echelons gradually widened as the *premiers commis* rose in the social hierarchy, as specialization of the *commis* made the nature of their work more routine, and as their number increased, as always decreasing the esteem in which they were held by society.

Relations among the *commis* working together in a particular bureau were good, even warm in many cases. *Commis* frequently served as godfathers and tutors to each other's children. They maintained cordial relations with the members of nearby bureaus. Early in the century they tended to have many children, but this became less and less common. Their family life continued to be dignified, however.

Generally speaking, *premiers commis* left disparate and not particularly impressive fortunes. Duché left 765,000 livres; Conrad-Alexandre Gérard, 561,000 livres but with 110,000 livres of debts; Le Dran, 160,000 livres; the abbé de La Ville, 28,000 livres; and Magnan, 20,000 livres. The large fortunes originated with advantageous marriages.

The *premiers commis* lived in Versailles, generally in rented quarters. Their apartments contained seven or eight main rooms, for which they paid 1,600 to 3,000 livres in rent. On the average there were six servants: a governess, a cook, a chambermaid, a valet, a kitchen boy, and a porter. Their libraries were well stocked. Works in history and law, particularly natural law and international law, predominated. Next most important were works in belles-lettres and philosophy (Seneca, Plato). Some collected paintings or took an interest in music.

The *commis* owned little. Dupuise left 1,589 livres, 3 sols, 2 deniers; Pierre Mignon, 1,390 livres; Joubain de Doisu, 14,075 livres. The only wealthy *commis* was Boullé, the son of a clothier, who left 232,697 livres. The *commis* lived in Versailles in rented quarters. Their apartments had three or four main rooms, a salon, a dining room, bedrooms, and a kitchen. They paid rents of 300 to 400 livres and employed a serving woman. *Commis* owned few books. In 1782, however, four of them were freemasons and belonged to the "Patriotism" lodge along with thirteen employees of the war department, seven of the navy department, four of the royal household, and two of the *Contrôle général*.

Thus the social level of *premiers commis* was quite different from that of ordinary *commis*. The social hierarchy corresponded to the professional hierarchy. Both *premiers commis* and ordinary *commis* were state employees of a particular kind, members of a category that was later to develop into a civil service. State service did not allow these men to amass great fortunes, but it did protect them from want and afford them a kind of dignity, or at least respectability. Their increasing numbers and growing role reflect the growth of the state apparatus and the real change in the constitution of the kingdom.

Conclusion: Ambivalence

When the king was anointed, he swore an oath to uphold the traditional constitution of the kingdom. He therefore believed he had an obligation to perpetuate the ancient judicial form of issuing decrees through a council. The adherence to this formalism hampered the operations of the government and disturbed the balance among its parts. What was needed, as becomes clear when we look at the changes that occurred spontaneously in response to the needs of the moment from the revolution of 1661 onward, was a cabinet council presided over by the king, coupled with a simplified system for issuing decrees and regulations through the ministries in addition to the more solemn acts, laws, and decrees issued by the council. What actually happened, however, was that the collective decision-making of the councils was gradually supplanted by independent decision-making by officials in the administrative hierarchy, who worked privately with their subordinates. The transition from judicial forms of administration to executive forms was not yet complete. After 1715, the government did not seriously consider the question of whether the revolution of 1661 could be undone and judicial forms reinstated. Nor did it carefully consider the changeover to executive forms and take conscious steps to carry the transition through, despite the work of Maupeou. The government's ambivalent approach further undermined its authority and prevented it from imposing the necessary reforms on the sovereign courts. This failure was one of the causes of the Revolution of 1789.

Notes

1. Guyot and Merlin, *Traité des droits*, vol. 4, p. 103.

2. See vol. 1, p. 437.

3. Concerning the social situation and mental attitudes of the *maîtres des requêtes*, see Roland Mousnier, *Lettres et mémoires adressés au chancelier Séguier*, vol. 1, especially pp. 53–59, 65–112, and 168–83.

4. It was only after 1727 and Chauvelin, secretary of state for foreign affairs, that they received individual dispensation from this brevet in the form of letters from the king authorizing them to sign orders without having been provided an office of *secrétaire du roi*.

5. Sainte-Beuve, *Nouveaux Lundis*, vol. 10, p. 23.

6. Mousnier, *Lettres et mémoires;* and *Le Conseil du Roi de Louis XII à la Révolution* (Paris: PUF, 1970).

7. See vol. 1, chap. 3.

8. See vol. 1, chap. 2.

9. See the case of Pierre Séguier, which seems typical: Mousnier, *Lettres et mémoires*, vol. 1, pp. 26–41.

10. Dangeau, *Journal*, vol. 10, p. 504.

11. Letter from chancellor de Pontchartrain to *contrôleur général* Desmaretz, 2 July, year unknown.

12

The *Surintendant des Finances*, the *Contrôleur Général des Finances*, and Their Departments

From 1598 to 1661

In theory, the king in his Council was supposed to be in charge of the state's finances, the creation of resources, and the auditing of expenditures. But finance was a specialty, a technical subject. Specialists were needed to prepare the Council's work and carry out the decisions taken. Such specialists were always employed, and it was in fact these men who were in charge of finance. Until 1661, however, there was continual oscillation between a more collegial approach and a more personal, individual approach, as the idea of the Council changed and extraordinary needs arose. In the end the more personal approach won out, owing to its greater efficiency.

From Collegiality to Individualism

Upon the death of François d'O, governor of Paris and, from 1578 to 1594, *surintendant des Finances*, Henri IV eliminated the office of *surintendant* in October 1594 and replaced it with an eight-member council. It did not function satisfactorily and was eliminated perhaps as early as 1596. The Conseil d'Etat et des Finances took control of finance. From 1599 on, however, a member of this council by the name of Rosny, *gentilhomme* and soldier, exercised the functions of *surintendant*. In 1601, the title reappeared in administrative correspondence. Rosny, however, had neither a brevet nor a commission as *surintendant*, and the post was not officially reestablished. When, in 1604, Rosny became the duc de Sully, he tried to get the king's Council to apply the seal without question to whatever documents he might send him. This seems to have become the standard practice sometime after 1650. Sully points ahead to the revolution of 1661. After the death of Henri IV, he was forced to retire on 5 February 1611.

The regent returned to a council of three directors playing the role of *surintendant:* these were Guillaume de Laubespine, sieur de Châteauneuf, and the *présidents* Thou and Jeannin. The latter, who held the title of *contrôleur général*, played the leading role. In 1616 he received a brevet as *surintendant*, and the post was thereby reestablished. After him, Schomberg was named *surintendant* by ordinary commission. In 1623 La Vieuville became *surintendant*, but this *homme d'épée* was assisted by a council of six directors.

Subsequently, financial administration was repeatedly entrusted to two *surintendants* serving jointly: this occurred between 1624 and 1626, 1632 and 1640 (Bullion and Bouthillier), 1643 and 1647 (Bailleul and d'Avaux), 1653 and 1659 (Servien and Fouquet). From July 1648 until April 1649, the maréchal de La Meilleraye was the sole *surintendant* assisted by two directors. Then, in 1649–50, these two directors, Aligre and Morangis, served alone. Subsequently, there were three directors who continued to serve under all *surintendants*. The last *commission* as *surintendant général* was given to Fouquet on 21 February 1659, after the death of Servien. Fouquet was arrested on 5 September 1661. The *surintendance* was abolished on 15 September 1661.

Fluctuating political currents and problems of public credit therefore created enormous difficulties in moving from a collegial system toward a personal system.

The Functions of the Surintendant

The functions of the *surintendant* were complex. To begin with, he played a role in the formulation of policy and in general administration. He was one of the leading *conseillers d'Etat*. A regulation of September 1624 made him personally a member of the Conseil d'En-Haut. The regulation of 18 January 1630 made him one of the ministers of state. After 1643, as soon as a man was named *surintendant* he immediately received letters appointing him minister of state. As such he could be made responsible for any state business whatsoever and could sign drafts originating with any section of the Council. He could correspond with governors, army generals, and ambassadors.

In finance, the *surintendant* was the principal auditor of all funds. He proposed a budget of receipts and expenditures to the Conseil des Finances. At the beginning of the year he submitted an "estimated list" of receipts based on information supplied by the *trésoriers généraux de France* or the farmers. At the end of the year he submitted a "true list" of monies actually received and spent. In fact both lists were only approximations, for want of a cadastral survey, a census, and statistical records—besides which a portion of the state's expenditures had to be kept secret.

For the Council he prepared all information concerning the yield of the royal domain, the amount of tax receipts including *tailles* and *crues*, *aides* and *gabelles*, the amounts needed for extraordinary expenditures, the distribution by *généralités*, the political consequences, and the dangers of rebellion.

He worked with the secretaries of state and attempted to reduce their expenditures. Bullion kept records for the war department indicating the number of troops of each type and listing the amounts due. He compared these with the reports of the secretary of state for war and investigated any discrepancies.

The *surintendant* decided how expenditures were to be assigned to receipts and whether payment would be made by transfer of obligation or in cash and whether transfers would be carried over against receipts from the following year. Through short-term assignations of expenditures to reliable receipts he was able to control all policy.

With regard to payments, the *surintendant* issued "payment orders" drawn on the *trésorier de l'Epargne*, who could resort to two methods of payment: *mandements* and *rescriptions*. The *mandement* was an order drawn up on parchment and sent to a *trésorier* or *receveur*, instructing him to pay cash to the bearer, whose name was indicated along with the sum to be paid out of funds deriving from some tax or extraordinary affair. When endorsed by the payee upon receipt of the cash, the *mandement* was held as a receipt by the *trésorier* or *receveur*. The total number of *mandements* was relatively small, because cash payments were rare. In many cases the *trésorier* or *receveur* no longer held cash from the source specified by the *mandement*.

The *rescription* was used more often. It was an order drawn up on paper and addressed to a *trésorier* or *receveur*, instructing him to pay the amount indicated some months later, or, if need be, in the following year or some other year, over the course of a specified period of time and using money from a specified source. The *rescription* thus gave rise to a payment on account. After payment, the *trésoriers* and *receveurs* gave the rescriptions to the *trésorier de l'Epargne*, who tore them up and remitted receipts as if the money had been paid in cash by the Epargne. In the accounts of the *trésoriers* and *receveurs*, the sums paid against rescriptions figured without distinction of any kind under the head of sums paid in cash at the Epargne against receipt. *Rescriptions* made it possible to anticipate future receipts. This encouraged loans. In 1632, for example, the king needed 100,000 livres "for urgent business." A lender agreed to advance this amount provided he received the *rescription* of the *trésorier de l'Epargne* drawn on Mathieu Garnier, *trésorier des parties casuelles* to be reimbursed out of funds to be derived from the offices of *contrôleur au régalement des tailles*; this condition was accepted. If the payee named in the *rescription* had need of liquid funds prior to the date of maturity, he could obtain an advance against the *rescription* from another individual. The *tresorier de l'Epargne* could use *rescriptions* backed by the funds to be collected in the future by *trésoriers*, *receveurs*, and *traitants* to obtain, within a very short period, loans from private sources for the full anticipated amount. The lender was of course given a rebate, which was disguised by the issuance of a cash receipt. The *surintendant* had coins struck. He also varied the value of the currency.

His main task, however, was to arrange for the public debt. During the period we are considering, the regular sources of state finance, i.e., the yield of the royal domain and of taxes (direct taxes, such as *tailles*, *taillons*, *crues*, *subsistances*, *étapes*, and other taxes paid to the *recettes générales*; indirect taxes, such as *aides*, *gabelles*, and *traites*; gratuitous gifts and other funds appropriated by the provincial Estates and the Assemblies of the Clergy) were always insufficient to meet the needs of war. It was increasingly necessary to have recourse to extraordinary measures (*rentes sur l'Hôtel de Ville*, sale of offices, increases in salaries and dues, forced loans, short-term borrowing). *Surintendants des Finances* were chosen for their contacts in the world of *financiers* and for their ability to find people willing to participate in these extraordinary measures, especially loans. This was the case with Particelli d'Emery, *intendant des Finances* from 1631 to 1643, *contrôleur général des Finances* from 1643 to 1647, and *surintendant des Finances* from 1647 to 1648. It was also the case with Nicolas Fouquet, *maître des requêtes*, *intendant d'armée* and later *de province*, *procureur général* of the Paris *parlement* in 1650, *surintendant des Finances adjoint* as of 3 February 1653, who was given special charge of public borrowing from December 1654 on.

The *surintendant* used his personal fortune to lend money to the king and to guarantee the loans made by *financiers*. He used his influence over his family and the family of his wife in the same way, as well as his relations with *conseillers d'Etat*, *maîtres des requêtes*, and members of the sovereign courts—circles in which he had established clients and *fidèles*, and he did also among the financial officeholders and *financiers*. Thus the principal function of the *surintendant* was to inspire confidence and to maintain the state's credit by giving assurances that money lent would be repaid and rewarded with high rates of interest. The *surintendant* negotiated contracts with *traitants* for the collection of taxes and for purchases of corn, bread, and munitions of all sorts. The *financiers* were often his creatures and clients and were obligated to him in a variety of ways. Public opinion, however, held him to be their tool: the crown, it was said, was "a vassal and tributary of the *financiers*."[1]

The *surintendant* made use of the services of a *premier commis* and several ordinary *commis*. The *premier commis*, in particular, was well acquainted with the *financiers*, inspired confidence in them, and had influence over them; he was not obliged to be especially scrupulous in his observance of the law. As the person who drafted administrative memoranda and issued payment orders, he practically controlled the rate of interest. He was free to take a wide range of personal initiatives.

The *surintendant* negotiated with the *parlements* and other sovereign courts and with the *procureurs généraux du roi* over the registration of bursal edicts, including edicts for the creation of offices.

The *surintendants* were either blooded nobles and men of the sword like Sully, La Vieuville, and La Meilleraye or, more commonly, members of the *grande robe*, the nobility of office, such as Claude de Bullion, Claude Bouthillier, Abel Servien, and Nicolas Fouquet, men drawn from the same social group as Chancellor Seguier, the secretaries of state, the *conseillers d'Etat*, and the *maîtres des requêtes*. A few were "new men" from the world of finance who wasted no time in merging with the nobles of rank. One such was Particelli d'Emery. All were creatures of the king or prime minister and as such members of an exclusive circle.

The Contrôleur Général des Finances

A similar problem of whether to choose a collegial administration or a personalized administration arose in connection with the position of *contrôleur général des Finances*. In this case, however, there was the further difficulty of freeing the post from its original responsibilities in the area of surveillance and monitoring. Monitoring was first carried out by members of the Chambre des Comptes. The *contrôleur général* never completely got away from this responsibility. He retained the quality of *magistrat des Comptes* with jurisdictional powers.

The ordinance of 5 May 1527 established two auditors of the Chambre des Comptes as *contrôleurs généraux de l'Epargne, des deniers extraordinaires et des parties casuelles.* The *contrôle général des Finances* was established and rules for its operation laid down by the ordinances of 12 April 1547, 25 October 1554, and October 1556. The ordinance of 1547, further provided that, if the *contrôleur général* was prevented from exercising his duties, he would be replaced by *greffiers* from the Chambre des Comptes. After 1554 there was supposed to be no more than one *contrôleur général* in office at any given time. From 1594 to 1596, however, eight *intendants des Finances* served collectively as *contrôleurs généraux*. The government subsequently returned to an individual regime. In 1596 the *contrôleur général* was Saldagnes; in 1599, Jean de Vienne, sieur d'Incarville; in 1603, Charles Duret. The regulation of 5 February 1611 made Pierre Jeannin, baron de Montjeu, *contrôleur général des Finances* with the powers of *surintendant*. When he was named *surintendant des Finances* in 1616, the post of *contrôleur général* passed to Claude Barbin, seigneur de Broges, who in fact exercised all financial powers. Subsequent *contrôleurs généraux* included Gilles de Maupeou, sieur d'Ableiges, in 1617; Pierre de Castille in 1619; then, under La Vieuville, in 1623, Bochart de Champigny, who remained *contrôleur général* when he was named *surintendant* on 27 August 1624; next, in 1626, Simon Marion, baron de Durye, *président au* Grand Conseil. Between 1629 and 1633 the office was dismembered. Five people were commissioned to exercise its duties over a portion of the year: Castille, Chevry, Sublet, Malier, Duhoussay. Then the government went back to a single *contrôleur général* from 1633 to 1636—first Chevry, followed in 1636 by Corbinelli. For a time during 1637, four people were given the job: Macré, Duhoussay, Cornuel, Particelli. In 1638, Particelli alone was commissioned, and in 1638 it was Duret. On 25 February 1641, the *intendant des Finances* Jacques Tuboeuf was charged with the functions of *contrôleur général des Finances*.

In November 1643, the *contrôle général* was again made a distinct entity for the benefit of Particelli d'Emery, who took the following oath:

You swear and promise God to serve the king faithfully and well in the estate and office of *contrôleur général* of his finances, which His Majesty has provided you; to follow and cause to be followed the regulations that have been made concerning the use of his money; to devote your full attention to preventing any abuse; to see to it that those who are and will be under your control are honest men who will faithfully discharge the responsibilities you may give them; to inform the king promptly of any malversations that may be committed; to accept no pension, bounty, or allowance from anyone but His Majesty; and, generally, to treat the responsibilities of your office as a good and faithful subject and servant should and is bound to do.[2]

Particelli sat on the Chambre des Comptes and had the right to vote and take part in debates within that body, where he enjoyed precedence over the *maîtres des comptes*. He was in fact in control of the state's finances. On 16 July 1647, he became *surintendant* while maintaining power over the *contrôle général des Finances*.

In 1649 the *contrôle général* was again placed under the direction of Antoine Le Camus. In 1655 there were two *contrôleurs généraux*, Antoine Le Camus and Claude Ménardeau, who was also *directeur des Finances*. In 1657 the *contrôle général* was entrusted to a triumvirate, Le Tellier, Barthélemy Hervart, and Louis Le Tonnelier de Breteuil. In 1659 it seems that Seraphin de Mauroy was added to this group.

The functions of the *contrôleur général* from 1598 to 1661 are obscure. This should be a fertile area for research.

Based on earlier laws, we can describe what he should have been doing. Two *contrôleurs généraux* were established by the ordinance of 12 April 1547. One of them was supposed to reside in Paris and record the receipts and expenditures of the central treasury in a register kept at the Louvre. He was supposed to endorse all receipts issued by the central treasurer to the tax collectors who remitted sums to the treasury, mainly the *receveurs généraux des Finances*. He was also supposed to endorse all receipts given to the central treasurer for payments made and to keep a register containing the names of those to whom the central treasury had made payments, the reasons for payments made in the form of *mandements patents*, the date of each receipt, the nature of the currency, the number of items and the price of each item; and, finally, he was to initial each article. The second *contrôleur général* was supposed to follow the court. He was also supposed to keep similar registers and sign receipts issued by the central treasurer for assignation of debts to particular sources of revenue. These receipts were admissible before the Chambres des Comptes as acquittances for the *receveurs généraux* only if they had been verified and signed.

The edict of 25 October 1554 established a single *contrôleur général*. His salary was supposed to be equal to that of the *surintendant*, 10,000 livres *tournois*. If he was ill or otherwise prevented from carrying out his duties, he could have himself replaced by a *commis* chosen from among the *secré-*

taires du roi. He was responsible for endorsing all receipts, *mandements* bearing discharge, and *rescriptions* to the *receveurs généraux* or other parties, and for comparing these with the *états*, *rôles*, and *cahiers* submitted to the *trésoriers.* He was supposed to keep two registers, one for the Council and one for himself. He was responsible for signing, at the beginning of each year, the estimates submitted by the *trésoriers généraux de France.* At the end of the year, he approved their true accounts of receipts and expenditures, as well as the true accounts submitted by all the various accountants. He was supposed to verify the sums and initial each page. Only when all this was done could the accounts be presented to the Council. Six months after the expiration of each fiscal year, the *contrôleur général* was supposed to send his register of verified receipts and other documents, duly signed, to the Chambre des Comptes. No unverified receipt was admissible before the Chambre des Comptes. A list of accounts in arrears was supposed to be transmitted to the *contrôleur général* by the *procureur général* of the Chambre des Comptes.

The ordinance of October 1556 allowed the *contrôleur général* to employ a *commis.* It stipulated that he must be neither an auditor nor an accountant. The ordinance established the procedures for verifying the treasury's receipts. Either the *contrôleur général* or his *commis* was supposed to oversee the remittance of funds to the treasurer of the central treasury; to keep records of the transport and carriage costs for bringing the funds to the treasury; to sign a certificate for monies placed in reserve in a treasury other than the central treasury at the king's behest; to notify the council if the *receveurs généraux* were late in submitting their quarterly accounts. The ordinance further stipulated how expenditures were to be audited. The *contrôleur général* was supposed to keep a record of *mandements patents* sent to the treasurer of the central treasury and verify the receipts issued by the central treasurer to the *receveurs généraux* who had remitted money in transit to the king. The *contrôleur général* was also supposed to send the council a quarterly statement of expenditures and receipts prepared by the treasurer of the central treasury at the Louvre.

The regulation of 7 October 1645 ordered the *contrôleur général* to sign all decrees issued by the Conseil des Finances and reaffirmed the provisions of the edict of 25 October 1554 concerning his signing of estimated and true statements of account.

During this period the *contrôle général des Finances* became a bureaucratic administration including *contrôleurs généraux*, *intendants des Finances*, and a bureau of scribes under the direction of the *commis* who kept records of all funds. It is difficult, however, to know whether or not the letter of the law was actually followed. In the time of Particelli d'Emery and Barthélemy Hervart, the *contrôleurs généraux* seem to have been employed mainly in securing short-term loans for the government; they apparently violated all the rules in seeking credit by making promises of high interest and certain repayment to *partisans* and *traitants.*

The Intendants des Finances

The *intendants des Finances* are not at all well-known as individuals. In theory they were direct subordinates of the *contrôleur général*. They were required by the ordinance of 1523 to prepare statements of taxes assessed and collected and to supervise the transfer of funds.

Initially, commissions seem to have been given to two *intendants*. Their number subsequently increased and the position seems to have been given the status of an office, but any office could be awarded by commission. Sully was assisted by four *intendants des Finances*, including the Protestants Arnauld and Maupéou. They met for discussion in a group known as the *Petite Direction des Finances* and made decisions that were subsequently taken before the councils. In addition, however, Sully worked alone with each *intendant des Finances*, one by one. Many decisions were reached by Sully together with an *intendant* and signed by Sully after a simple report had been made to the king, without consideration by the councils; the king ordered a secretary of state and the chancellor to sign, because a *surintendant des Finances* was not authorized to sign orders.

In principle the functions of the *intendants des Finances* were not very different from those of the *contrôleur général des Finances*. They could even be called upon to sign payment orders, to negotiate with *traitants* and *partisans*, and to conclude *traités* for *les affaires extraordinaires*.

In 1643 there were four *intendants des Finances*: Jacques Tubeuf, Séraphin de Mauroy, Claude Le Charon, and Pierre Mallier de Moncharville. In 1649 four new offices were created and sold to Jacques Le Tillier, Jacques Bordier, Guillaume de Bordeaux, and Etienne Foulle. In 1649 Le Charon died and was replaced by Hervart. In 1650 Tubeuf and Mallier resigned their offices and were replaced by Pierre Gargan and Denis Marin. In 1654 four new posts were created and sold to Jacques Paget, Claude de Boislève, Guillaume de Brisacier, and Claude Housset. In October 1658, the twelve offices were reduced to four, held by Mauroy, Le Tillier, Bordier, and Bordeaux. In 1661 only two remained, occupied by Jean-Baptiste Colbert and Marin.

Most of the *intendants des Finances* were themselves *financiers*, *traitants*, military suppliers, and lenders. Some were indeed quite important in the world of finance, especially Delorme, Boislève, and Hervart.

The Accountants

Receipts and expenditures were handled by accountants. The head accountant was the treasurer of the central treasury. It was at the central treasury that all funds "duly accruing" to the king arrived, while disbursements were made locally after authorization by *receveurs particuliers des élections*, *receveurs généraux des généralités*, and other local treasurers. In fact, many funds "duly accruing" to the king were also paid out locally on behalf of the central administration and against *rescription* from the treasurer of the central treasury. There were two of these *trésoriers de l'Epargne* at the beginning of the seventeenth century, one regular and one alternate, each serving in the post for a year at a time. A third treasurer was added under Louis XIII, and each served in rotation every third year. Each *trésorier de l'Epargne* was required to keep two registers, one of receipts, the other of expenditures. Each week the *trésorier de l'Epargne* on duty would report to the Council on what he had taken in and paid out during that week. He prepared statements of account for approval by the Council. Once approved, they were transcribed into the registers of the central treasury and then burned. Cash receipts and acquittances were compared with the registers on a monthly, quarterly, and yearly basis by the Chambre des Comptes, and the registers were certified. In reality, however, because the original statements were destroyed, a clever bookkeeper could easily circumvent the audit by the Chambre des Comptes.

The *trésoriers de l'Epargne* took part in all the deals between *financiers* and the state and made short-term loans to the government. Among the *trésoriers de l'Epargne* we find the two La Bazinières, the son succeeding the father in 1642; Bertrand de La Bazinière was a minor, however, and discharged his duties through a proxy until he reached his majority in 1653. Another was Henri de Guénégaud. When he became secretary of state in 1643, his brother succeeded him. Yet another was Nicolas Jeannin de Castille, a clever and unscrupulous man.

Each *trésorier de l'Epargne* employed a *premier commis*; for example, Jacques Rollot served under Claude de Guénégaud. The *premier commis* personally recruited his *commis*, who prepared the statements of account to be submitted to the Conseil des Finances. It sometimes happened that, after the Council had certified the accounts, the *commis* inserted fictitious transactions.

When the *trésorier de l'Epargne* was unable to pay a debt, he issued the creditor a *billet de l'Epargne* or treasury bill, acknowledging the debt and indicating what source of funds would be used to pay it. The treasury bill differed from the *mandement* and *rescription* in that it contained no order of payment to a *receveur*. The creditor who needed cash could negotiate the bill, but of course for less than its nominal value.

Working under the *trésorier de l'Epargne* were accountants of secondary rank. To begin with, there was the *trésorier des parties casuelles et inopinées*. He received the *revenus casuels* and paid the funds over to the *trésorier de l'Epargne*, who then issued him a receipt and made payments. To speed things up and reduce the transfer of cash, when *partisans* holding blank receipts from the *trésorier des parties casuelles* sold offices or collected taxes, they paid the money directly into the central treasury. But the receipts issued by the *trésorier des parties casuelles* were previously registered by the *contrôle général des Finances*. The Chambre des Comptes, equipped with duplicate records, called upon the treasurer to account for the use of the sums he was supposed to have received. In order to justify the payment, a fictitious order was established on paper. The *partisans*, upon receiving their receipts from the *trésorier des parties casuelles*, gave him written promises to deliver funds to his credit. After making their payment to the central treasury, they would give the *trésorier des parties casuelles* the receipts issued by the *trésorier de l'Epargne*. Thus, on paper, and as far as the people from the Chambre des Comptes were concerned, the money followed a normal route: the copies of the receipts from the *trésorier des parties casuelles* on the books of the *contrôle général des Finances* attested to the fact that the treasurer had received funds from certain individuals, and he could prove that he had made payments to the central treasury by exhibiting his receipts from the *trésorier de l'Epargne*.

The *trésorier des parties casuelles* then acted as cashier. He issued funds from his reserves to the officeholders or private individuals assigned to be paid from that source by the *trésorier de l'Epargne* on orders of the Council. The *trésorier des parties casuelles* paid out funds against a *mandement* or *rescription*. In order to avoid unnecessary costs and handling of the funds and to accelerate payment, the *trésorier des parties casuelles* frequently received orders to pay not in cash but rather in the form of receipts for offices or taxes; these would be given either directly to the king's creditors, who would then have to sell the offices or recover the taxes themselves, or would be remitted to a private individual especially instructed to make a specific payment. In order to do this, the *trésorier des parties casuelles* was issued a Council decree, *mandement*, or *rescription* from the *trésorier de l'Epargne* ordering him to pay the corresponding amount. Thus, on paper he had received the money and delivered it in payment, whereas in reality not a single écu had passed through his hands.

These paper manipulations accelerated the sale of offices and loan operations by allowing rebates. For example, the *trésorier des parties casuelles* would issue receipts for 6,000 livres for offices sold to private individuals who had actually paid only 5,000 but who would receive emoluments corresponding to the sum of 6,000 in virtue of the receipt from the *parties casuelles*; this made the offices more attractive and made them easier to resell. The documents, however, showed that the treasurer had received 6,000 livres. The auditors would want to know how this sum was used. To cover him, the *trésorier de l'Epargne*, to whom he paid 5,000 livres per office, would give him receipts for 6,000 livres. This, in turn, left the *trésorier de l'Epargne* short 1,000 livres. The king would then issue cash receipts for as many times 1,000 livres as there were offices sold, i.e., payment orders for this amount with no justification of use and no receipt from the recipients. The documents, then, showed that money had been paid into the *Trésor des parties casuelles*, that funds had been transferred from the *parties casuelles* to the *Epargne*, and that the *Epargne* had used these funds in a transaction that never actually took place. The same thing could be done for a loan to the king. These practices make it difficult to use the existing financial records.

The *trésorier des parties casuelles* was audited by both the Conseil des Finances and the Chambre des Comptes. Following the completion of his year of duty, he was required to submit a detailed accounting of his receipts and expenditures to the Council. The Council then verified this statement by comparison with the registers of the *contrôle général*, the registers of the chancellery for the provision of offices, and the registers of the Epargne. It then certified the statement. The *trésorier des parties casuelles* could then account to the Chambre des Comptes.

Was this auditing, so meticulous in theory, effective in practice? It may not always have been done carefully. In 1612 Claude de Montescot, *trésorier des parties casuelles*, had not yet submitted his statement for 1609 to the Council. The *trésoriers des parties casuelles* sold offices that had not been assessed by the Council, which knew nothing about the sale, and the *lettres de provision* were sealed surreptitiously. No trace of such sales is to be found in the records; such actions escaped all control. Finally, there was no guarantee that a *trésorier des parties casuelles* might not enter into an understanding with a *trésorier de l'Epargne:* all that was necessary for a large sum of money to disappear was a receipt from the *trésorier de l'Epargne* and a cash-payment order that the *trésorier* could have signed with the help of a conniving secretary of state, *surintendant*, or council member (since most cash orders were not signed by the king personally). In 1624 Richelieu issued an order for the arrest of Beaumarchais, *trésorier de l'Epargne*, and de Ligny, *trésorier des parties casuelles*. He thought there was sufficient evidence to issue a warrant for another *trésorier des parties casuelles*, Barentin. In 1625 he believed that the *trésoriers des parties casuelles* and *des Ponts et Chaussées* were robbing the king of a million livres a year.

Among the other accountants of the central administration, we find the *trésorier général* for offerings, alms, and devotions to the king, of which there were four posts, all held by a single individual; the three *trésoriers généraux* of the royal household, who served one after another on a yearly basis; four *contrôleurs*; four *trésoriers des Menus-Plaisirs du Roi*; four *trésoriers de l'Argenterie* for the king's clothing and furniture; and two *intendants* and *contrôleurs*. There were also three *maîtres de la Chambre aux deniers*, who alternated with two *contrôleurs généraux* in half-yearly terms and took care of expenditures for food and service by the royal household; four *trésoriers des Ecuries*, assisted by a *contrôleur*; four *trésoriers* for each company of the bodyguard, along with their *contrôleurs*; three *trésoriers* of the Cent-Suisses and their *contrôleurs*; four *trésoriers de la prévôté de l'Hôtel* and their *contrôleurs*; three *trésoriers* of the regiment of French guards and their *contrôleurs*; three *trésoriers* of the regiment of Swiss guards and their *contrôleurs*; the *trésoriers* of each of the other companies of the royal household and their *contrôleurs*; the four *trésoriers* for game preserves and hunting; the three *trésoriers* of buildings; the *trésoriers des Guerres* and *de l'Extraordinaire des Guerres* and their *contrôleurs*; and the *trésoriers des Ligues suisses*. These treasurers received their money from the central treasury on a monthly basis, except for the treasurers of the companies of bodyguards, who received theirs on a weekly basis. There may have been other treasurers whose offices existed only as circumstances dictated, such as the *trésorier général* for the sale and resale of the domain, a post that was filled in 1639.

Abuses of Trust

Like other administrative officials, all of these accountants had a hard time distinguishing between private and public affairs. *Surintendants* and *intendants des Finances*, members of the Council, and *trésoriers de l'Epargne* often used cash-payment orders to make gifts to their friends and diverted public funds for their personal use. It was also common for ministers and treasurers to advance the king money out of their personal fortunes or on their own credit, and in such cases they regarded it as natural that they should reap a profit. The *trésoriers de l'Epargne, des parties casuelles, de l'ordinaire* and *de l'extraordinaire des guerres*, among others, participated in all the *partis* and pretended that the *partisans* had actually made large advances. They issued receipts for loans without the knowledge of the Council and without decree or ordinance. These fictitious loans then had to be reimbursed along with interest and fees, and the beneficiaries shared their profits with the treasurers. All the treasurers and not just those connected to the central administration—including even *receveurs généraux* and *particuliers* of the *généralités* and *élections*—made expenditures other than those contained in the statements of account sent to them by the Council. They added fictitious expenses, fabricated bogus statements and false payment orders, acquired false receipts and acquittances, and settled supposed debts of the king that had never been authenticated. Since they served on a triennial rotation, they counted their fees and emoluments twice, one year and two years after their service. They pretended to have spent all the money available to them and even to have exceeded the amount received, asserting that the king owed them for the additional money they had laid out, along with interest on the sums advanced. They pretended that taxpayers had not paid, pretended to advance to the king out of their own funds what they had in fact already collected in taxes, and thus obtained heavy payments of interest. Thefts were especially significant in the army. Commissaries had troop commanders sign blank requisitions, marked missing soldiers down as present, revived the dead, inscribed imaginary names on bogus rosters, used dummies, counted days of labor for handling cannon balls that never actually occurred, and lined their pockets, in some cases with the connivence of officers in the military. Bread was ill-cooked so as to weigh more, and hay was sold wet. Flour was adulterated and deteriorated quickly, so that it had to be replaced. Officers took part in these fraudulent practices along with the merchants. Wagoneers stole and sold the contents of caissons. The signatures of naval treasurers and commissaries were falsified, and the writing was so unclear that it was impossible to check the accounts. According to Richelieu, the siege of Montauban, which had cost 15 million, should have cost only 2 million.[3] The money drained from the royal coffers owing to the thievery of the king's agents must be counted in the millions.

Among the suspects in this sort of business are some of the most illustrious names of the period: Sully, La Vieuville, Bullion, Richelieu himself. Mazarin, who upon his death in March 1661 left 38,000,000 to 39,000,000 livres with debts of 1,421,000 livres—the largest fortune of the Ancien Régime, surpassing that of Richelieu (22,400,000 livres with 6,498,907 livres of debt), Henri II de Condè (14,600,794 livres), and chancellor Séguier (around 4,000,000 livres)—was the most important commissary of his age, at times involved in dealings with the military amounting to as much as 2,000,000 livres. He was one of the largest contractors for royal dues, particularly salt duties; one of the largest buyers of treasury bills, of which he held some 5,140,000 livres worth, assigned to general tax receipts, the farm on the *gabelle*, and the 35 *sols de Brouage*; and one of the largest lenders to the king, who between 1657 and 1661 lent 1,100,000 livres to the government for naval expenditures, although it is difficult to decide how much of this was financial aid to the king by the first servant of the state and how much was speculation pure and simple.

Fraudulent practices multiplied all the disadvantages associated with inequality of taxation.

From 1661 to 1715

The study of the king's Council has already led us to single out the importance of the revolution of 1661 and the preponderant role in the government played subsequently by the *contrôleur général des Finances*. A few further details will suffice to complete this picture.

Louis XIV felt that he had been robbed by Fouquet, who was also becoming a political threat. He therefore had the *surintendant* arrested, established a Chambre de Justice to hit at the *financiers*, *fidèles*, and clients associated with the disgraced *surintendant*, and secured the services of a new *fidèle*, Jean-Baptiste Colbert (left free by the death of his protector, Mazarin), and his own retinue of *financiers*, *fidèles*, and clients. Louis XIV eliminated the post of *surintendant* on 15 September 1661, but not the functions that went with the job, which from this date he carried out personally. After Louis, these functions were in theory still exercised by the king but in practice by the *contrôleur général des Finances*. Between 1661 and 1665 a series of measures were enacted that tended to give responsibility for the must important functions—those of *contrôleur général* and *intendant des Finances*—either to ordinary *commissaires* directly dependent on the king and removable *ad nutum* or to officeholders in whom the king could place complete confidence.

Since the peace of the Pyrenees there had been two *contrôleurs généraux des Finances* who owned their offices, Breteuil and Hervart, and two *intendants des Finances*, one of them being Jean-Baptiste Colbert, who took office on 16 March 1661. Colbert began as *intendant des Finances* responsible for reports. In fact he made everything connected with finance his province—that is, virtually the entire government.

A second phase began in 1664 and 1665. In April 1664, an edict eliminated the offices of *trésorier de l'Epargne* and *trésorier des parties casuelles* along with their *premiers commis*. The king put this measure forward as a logical follow-up to the elimination of the post of *surintendant*, a way of reestab-lishing control over the major fiscal officials who relied on "the selection or rejection that we are able to make" in order to prevent "immense sums from being remitted by the central treasury to others through the acceptance of bills negotiated at low prices, through payment orders issued in settlement of nonexecuted contracts, through other payment orders issued in payment of interest on presumed loans, through orders for the alienation of rents, and through the renewal of old bills." Between 1651 and 1660 more than 80 million livres had been consumed in this way, despite ordinances prohibiting the *trésorier de l'Epargne* from issuing bills. In order to prevent a return to these practices, the king converted the office of *trésorier de l'Epargne* into a commission and renamed it the *garde du Trésor royal*; the same was done for the office of *trésorier des parties casuelles*, which became the *receveur des Revenus casuels*.

On 12 December 1665, the king decided to reimburse Breteuil and Hervart the money they had paid for their offices and to place the *contrôle général* under the sole control of Colbert. Until fully reimbursed, however, Breteil and Hervart were commissioned to fill the post jointly with Colbert. Colbert, however, was supposed to have first signature of all documents issued by the *contrôle* and enjoyed precedence in everything. Breteuil and Hervart alternately added their signatures, each serving for a quarter. Whichever one was on duty in a particular quarter was to sit on Colbert's left in the Conseil des Finances, in the place of the most senior *intendant des Finances*, who would sit on the other side of the king's chair.

Colbert's commission gave him *entrée* to all the councils of state and financial organs, in which he was entitled to vote and to take part in debate; he was empowered to audit all receipts, *mandements*, and *rescriptions* issued by the *garde du Trésor royal* and the *trésorier des revenus casuels*, as well as all tax receipts, both ordinary and extraordinary; he checked all com-missions issued for the levy of taxes; all *octrois*, gifts, *acquits patents*, reimbursements, and rolls of validation and reestablishment; he had the power to report to the Council on all matters, whether concerning the king's service or not; he had the option of naming a *commis* to fill in for him if he was absent, sick, or legitimately hindered from performing his duties; he had permission to hold a commission as *contrôleur general des Finances* concurrently with his office of *intendant des Finances*. The commission was registered by the Chambre des Comptes. Chancellor Séguier accepted the oath of the new *contrôleur général* and handed him his commission.

The *contrôleur général*'s "department," that is to say, the affairs with which he was directly concerned, included all matters within the purview of the *Trésor royal* and the *parties casuelles*; tax farmers; the clergy; internal and foreign commerce; the Compagnie des Indes; special military affairs and logistics for the infantry and artillery; rents and currency; the *pays d'Etats*, the *parlements*, and the sovereign courts; bridges and highways; embankments, dams, and roadways in Paris; manufacturing; *octrois* of the cities and community debts; the *Ligues suisses*; and the *caisse générale des amortissements*. Each *intendant des Finances* had his own department under Colbert's over-all authority.

Colbert remained *contrôleur général* until his death in 1683. On 6 September 1683, he was succeeded by Claude Le Peletier, *seigneur* of Villeneuve-le-Roi, *président* in the *parlement* of Paris, and *prévôt des marchands* of that city. He was succeeded on 20 September 1689 by Louis Phélypeaux, comte de Pontchartrain and *intendant des Finances*. Then, on 5 September 1699, the post went to Michel de Chamillart, marquis de Cany and comte de La Suze, who was also an *intendant des Finances* and who served as *contrôleur général* until 15 September 1715. After Colbert, then, the average term of office of a *contrôleur general* was eight years.

The commission of the *contrôleur général* was accepted by the chancellor of France, to whom the *contrôleur*-designate swore an oath before a meeting of the Chambre des Comptes. The *contrôleur général* held a seat on this sovereign court and enjoyed precedence over the *maîtres des comptes*; he had the right to vote and to take part in debate. The *premier président* made a welcoming speech. If the Chambre des Comptes was on vacation, the new *contrôleur* swore a provisional oath into the hands of the chancellor, and his actions were validated by royal letter until such time as he was able to swear an oath before the Chambre.

The *contrôleur général* became a member of the Conseil royal des Finances, where he served as *rapporteur*; his opinion always held sway.

He also became a member of the Conseil des Finances. There he reported on cases that had been studied in advance by the *intendants des Finances* or by his own *commis*. Desmaretz sometimes sent an *intendant des Finances* to report in his place. The sessions of the Council were held for the sake of form. Everything was worked out in advance by the *contrôleur général* in conjunction with an *intendant des Finances* and approved by the king prior to the council meeting. Many cases were not even discussed before the Council. Edicts, declarations, and regulations bore the phrase, "On the advice of our Council." This was merely a stylistic flourish.

The *contrôleur général* belonged to the Grande Direction, the Petite Direction, and the Conseil de Commerce, where he served as *rapporteur*. Whatever he asked for he got.

By virtue of the terms of his commission and the first article of the regulation of 1673, the *contrôleur général* sat on the Conseil des Parties. In soliciting his advice, the chancellor doffed his hat, as he did for the *doyen*.

When the case involved a financial dispute, the *contrôleur général* suggested to the chancellor the name of a person to act as *rapporteur*.

By courtesy and custom the *contrôleur général* had the title of "minister" but not "minister of state." He was not a member ex officio of the Conseil d'En-Haut. Pontchartrain became a member of that body only after a year as *contrôleur général*, Chamillart after fourteen months, Desmaretz after eight months, and Le Peletier upon quitting his post.

By the same token, the *contrôleur général*, unlike the *surintendant*, did not issue formal orders. Only the chancellor and the secretaries of state had the power to issue formal orders over their own signatures. For example, a secretary of state might write, "Garde me mon Trésor royal, Monseigneur . . . , pay in cash . . . ," while the *contrôleur général* would write, "It is ordered that the Garde du Trésor royal, Monseigneur . . . , shall pay cash . . . ." In practice, correspondence was prepared by the *contrôleur général*, signed by a secretary of state, and stamped and sealed by the chancellor. Louis XIV had wished to avoid giving too much power to the *contrôleurs généraux*, but in fact correspondence prepared by the *contrôleurs* was signed, stamped, and sealed without further ado.

In reality, the *contrôleur général* exercised considerable power. On Wednesday, 12 June 1697, at midnight, the *intendant* of Soissons requested general powers to sit in final judgment over rioters arrested at several locations within his *département*. His request arrived in Paris during the night of 13 June. On 15 June the *contrôleur général*, Pontchartrain, wrote in the margin of the letter, "Give full attention to this decree so that I can dispatch it to him today." The decree was issued and sent out the very same day, after having been seen by a secretary of state and someone at the chancellery; it was an order bearing the formula, "the king being in his Council." Cases of this type are common.

The *contrôleur général* submitted to the kings the names of persons to be nominated as *intendants des provinces*, except for the *pays d'Etats*, where the nomination of *intendants* continued to be left up to the secretary of state for war. The *intendants* referred to the *contrôleur* in all matters, even for the execution of orders that they received from other secretaries of state, and sent him proposed council decrees. The *contrôleur général* decided on all matters of finance, usually in his own apartments in conjunction only with an *intendant des Finances*, who served him as *commis*, or in some cases directly with the *traitant*. If the affair was a particularly important one, the *contrôleur général* would take it up directly with the king during one of their private meetings, and a council decree would be issued even though the matter had never been taken up by the Conseil des Finances, whose members would learn of it only after the printed decree had been published. Sometimes a presentation would be made to the Council for the sake of form. On 30 September 1710, Desmartez went before the Conseil des Finances with the edict of the Dixième in his pouch. He read it through from beginning to end. The king asked Daguesseau for his opinion; being the lowest ranking member of the Council, he was required to speak first. In view of the importance of the edict and the lack of time to consider the matter, Daguesseau asked to be excused from offering his opinion. The king said that Daguesseau was right, that Desmartez had explained the edict to him, that his feeling was that it ought to be adopted as it stood, and that further discussion would be a waste of time. The duc de Beauvillier said that the edict was preferable to seeing France laid waste by the enemy. The other councillors held their tongues, and the edict was adopted, signed, sealed, and registered. The presentation to the Conseil des Finances was merely ceremonial.

The power of the *contrôleur général* was enhanced by the organization of an increasingly elaborate apparatus for the collection of statistics, inspection, and regulation of the financial bureaucracy. Take the wool industry, for example. This was of great importance because every French peasant kept sheep and at the very least sold the fleece, and also because wool was the fundamental raw material in a putting-out industry that was an important source of employment in the countryside. Peasants, men and women alike, worked at the manufacture of wool cloth during the winter months in almost every part of the country. The women did spinning and the men weaving, even in poor and mountainous areas like the Cévennes and the Gévaudan where winters were long and hard. Some of this wool fabric was exported. The sale of fleece and fabric made it possible for the peasants to pay their taxes, improved the balance of trade, and brought precious metals into the country.

Colbert therefore undertook to investigate the wool industry with an eye to improving its operation. In April 1663 his brother, Charles Colbert de Croissy, began looking into these matters in Alsace, Lorraine, and the Trois-Evêchés. In 1664 Colbert issued orders to certain *maîtres des requêtes* to look into the wool industry throughout the country. Later on, *commis* were used for this purpose rather than *maîtres des requêtes* and provincial *intendants*. These *commis* were known from 1689 on as "inspectors of manufactories." In 1727 they began to take an interest in linen as well as wool. These investigations were carried out in 1664–65, from 1669 until 1682, and from 1697 until 1701. Related research was done in 1708 in connection with the major investigation undertaken by the *intendants* on behalf of the duc de Bourgogne. The inspectors visited manufactories two to four times per year, submitted semi-annual reports, and gathered statistics that within a short time were being presented in tabular form: these included such items as the number of pieces of fabric manufactured, the length and width of the pieces, the average price per aune (a measure of length somewhat longer than a yard) or per piece, the quality of raw material used, the price of the raw material, and the number of looms in use.

Colbert protected the wool industry against English and Dutch competition with the tariffs of 1664 and 1667. He upgraded quality with such measures as the manufacturing regulations of 8 April 1666, the general regulations of

1669 concerning the weaving of woolen fabrics, which were registered by the Paris *parlement* on 13 August 1669, and forty-two other regulations issued prior to his death. These regulations standardized the length and width of pieces, set the warp and woof, established standards of quality and origin for the raw wool employed, the dyes used, the dyeing procedures adopted, and so on.

These regulations were indispensable because of the state of mind that existed among French manufacturers and persisted as late as the second half of the eighteenth century. Reports from provincial *intendants* and inspectors of manufactories in Languedoc are in agreement. Manufacturers in Languedoc did not concern themselves with quality. They required their workers to work too fast, and the result was a product of poor quality. For their reputations they showed no concern. The Turks were therefore unhappy with the fabrics they were receiving from France and turned instead to the English and the Dutch. In effect, the aim of French manufacturers was to earn enough money quickly so they could rise to a higher status in society. Their purpose was to acquire the offices and posts that carried with them higher social esteem. Hence they were not worried about the future of the industry. By contrast, English merchants perfected their manufacturing techniques, because they intended to stay in business and therefore wished to establish a good reputation. Full freedom of manufacture was therefore suitable to England, whereas France required state intervention and regulation.

The results were good. In 1669 France produced 670,000 pieces of cloth; in 1692, 1,000,000 pieces; in 1708, 1,215,000. At the end of the seventeenth century Languedoc was exporting 2,000 pieces of cloth to the Levant each year; by 1700 this figure had risen to more than 6,000 pieces, and in 1713 the Marseille office counted 32,240 pieces.

Contrôleurs généraux after Colbert continued the same kinds of policies.

The *contrôleurs généraux des Finances* were recruited from families belonging to the *noblesse de robe*, including both families of long-standing nobility and families recently ennobled by virtue of holding office. They held *fiefs de dignité* such as marquisates, counties, and baronies and thereby came to occupy a place in the feudal and seigneurial hierarchy. Colbert owned five marquisates. Chamillart was marquis de Cany. The *contrôleur général* was served by an *écuyer*, hence by someone who was in principle a noble and perhaps even a *gentilhomme*. On New Year's Day he received a delegation of magistrates clad in their long gowns. The wives of Chamillart and subsequent *contrôleurs généraux* were presented at court. Colbert's daughters became duchesses of Beauvilliers, Chevreuse, and Mortemart; Chamillart's daughters became the marquise of Brézé and the duchesses of La Feuillade and Lorge. Desmaretz's son, a marquis, became maréchal de France.

Contrôleurs généraux were privileged individuals. They enjoyed the privileges of commensals and secretaries of the king. They were exempt from trusteeships, guardianships, municipal employments, churchwardenships, watch and guard duty, loans, reliefs, redemptions, *quints* and *requints*, *lods et ventes*, tolls and *barrages*, fees for sealing and registry, *insinuations*, *francs-fiefs*, *aides*, *gabelles*, *tailles*, special subsidies, *octrois*, *insinuations des villes et communautés*, *bans*, *arrière-bans*, billeting of soldiers, and *gîtes*, to name a few.

Contrôleurs généraux received a salary. In 1683 the compensation came to 36,000 livres, but there were bonuses besides. For ten months in 1708 Desmartez earned 88,333 livres, 6 sols, and 8 deniers. In addition, he received fees for stamping treasury receipts, free tickets to the theater, royal bonuses, gold tokens offered by the provincial estates, cities, companies, and guilds, and small gifts from the provincial *intendants* such as game, horses, wines, and regional specialties.

The Intendants des Finances

Between 1660 and 1690 commissions were held at all times by two *intendants des Finances*. In February 1690 the needs of war impelled the king to revoke these commissions and to create instead four offices with the title *intendant des Finances*. By 1708 the number had increased to eight, and in 1715 there were still seven.

The *intendants des Finances* held the title of *conseillers d'Etat*, with the accompanying rank and the privilege of sitting on the king's Council as of the day of their reception in office. They could rise to the post of *contrôleur général des Finances*. All the *contrôleurs généraux* under Louis XIV, except Claude Le Peletier, were initially *intendants des Finances*.

Each *intendant* worked at home and had his offices there, and each enjoyed the services of one or more *premiers commis*. Each *premier commis* worked at home and was assisted by a number of *commis*.

Intendants did not specialize. Each one had his own allotment of work but without division of labor. Each *intendant* took an interest in several areas of general affairs concerning the entire kingdom.

Intendants prepared council decrees, letters patent, and ordinances for the signature of the *contrôleur général*. *Directeurs des Finances*, at times when there were such, worked under the authority of the *intendants*.

The *intendants* met every week at the home of the head of the Conseil royal des Finances, who chaired the meeting. The *contrôleur général* attended, and the *intendants* served as *rapporteurs*.

In 1708 the king established four offices of *intendants de commerce*. Each of these was responsible for certain provinces as well as for certain industries dispersed throughout the kingdom. All were entitled to take part in debate and to vote in the Conseil du Commerce, which was under the direct authority of the *contrôleur général*.

The bureaus of the *contrôle général des Finances* seem to have been quite modest as late as the time of Colbert. Colbert employed a *premier commis*, La Houssaye, a principal *commis*, a secretary, and four ordinary *commis*. Later on, these bureaus grew in size and complexity.

Indeed, there was an institutional revolution in 1661. It was marked by the liberation of financial administration from the chancellor's judicial control and by the growth of the *contrôle général* as an autonomous body for the control of the state's financial affairs.

Polysynody and the Reign of Louis XV, 1715–74

The office of *contrôleur général des Finances* was abolished in September 1715, and the offices of *intendant des Finances* and *du Commerce* were abolished in October. The upper echelons of the financial administration were taken over by an *ordonnateur*, none other than the regent, the duc d'Orléans, and by a Conseil des Finances presided over by the duc de Noailles. This council laid the groundwork for decisions to be taken by the Regency Council. Auditing was done by two *gardes des registres du contrôle* under the authority of a Council member. This amounted to a return to the collegial system, and although the Conseil des Finances was, thanks to the duc de Noailles, the most orderly and active of the councils, the results were not good.

On 28 January 1718, the marquis d'Argenson became *directeur des Finances*. Finally, on 5 January 1720, John Law was named *contrôleur général des Finances*, a post he held until 29 May. At the same time the positions of *intendant des Finances* and *intendant du Commerce* were reestablished. John Law was succeeded by Le Peletier des Forts, who held the title of *commissaire général des Finances* from 7 June until December of 1720, whereupon the title of *contrôleur général* was reinstated.

The *contrôleur général*, the *intendants des Finances*, and the bureaus of the *contrôle général* under Louis XV were sufficiently discussed in the course of our treatment of the work of the Council under this king. It is probably enough to round out what has already been said with a discussion of the distribution of the work load in 1763.

The Distribution of the Work Load

In 1763 the *contrôleur général des Finances* was M. Bertin, minister of state and *conseiller ordinaire* on the king's Council. His offices were located in the rue Neuve-des-Petits-Champs. Included within his department were the *Trésor royal*, the *parties casuelles*, the *direction générale* for all royal farms, the clergy, trade within the kingdom and overland foreign commerce, the Compagnie des Indes, the *extraordinaire des guerres*, responsibility for military rations, supply lines, and artillery, all rents, the *pays d'Etats*, coinage, the *parlements* and superior courts, bridges and highways, dykes and levees, the toll gates and streets of Paris, factories, *octrois* of cities, community debts, the *Ligues suisses*, the two sols per livre of the *dixième*, the *vingtièmes*, and the *caisse générale des amortissements*.

M. Trudaine, *intendant des Finances*, rue des Vieilles-Audriettes, had in his department the *gabelles* of France, the Lyonnais, Provence, Dauphiné, and Languedoc, among others, the *cinq grosses fermes*, the *états des Fermes*, the *états des Finances* for Brittany and Provence, routine matters connected with bridges and highways, dykes and levees, and the streets of Paris, the royal nurseries, and commercial ports.

Monsieur d'Ormesson, *intendant des Finances*, rue du Pas-de-la-Mule, took care of the *tailles*, the *taillon*, the *capitation*, taxes on the provinces of Flanders, Franche-Comté, and Alsace, the *dixième de retenue*, way stations, accounts of the *pays d'élections*, the clergy, powder and saltpeter, the *extraordinaire des guerres*, Burgundy, and the audit of true accounts certified by the council.

M. de Courteille, *intendant des Finances*, rue de l'Université, was responsible for the domains and their accounts, the farm of the *greffes*, the *parlements*, the western domain, the *Ligues suisses*, the Grand Conseil, amortization, *francs-fiefs*, newly acquired property and usages, the *octrois* of the cities, community debts, the remains of the *régie de Bourrié* for the resale of offices of *receveurs* and *contrôleurs des octrois*, the *vingtièmes*, the two sols per livre of the *dixième*, and the accounts of the *généralités* of Toulouse and Montpellier.

M. Chauvelin, *intendant des Finances*, rue Portefoin, was in charge of *aides* and associated dues, fees for the stamping of notarized acts, *insinuations* and the *centième denier*, the *droits de petit sel*, the *contrôle des petits exploits*, the farm on the reinstated dues enjoyed by the farmers of the *Aides* and the *Domaine*, the farm on the *marque des fers*, the farm on the *marque d'or* and the *marque d'argent*, the farm on tallow, the farm on taxes and woodcutting in Brittany, the Chambres des Comptes, the Cours des Aides, routine matters connected with coinage, and the bureaux des Finances.

The department of M. Moreau de Beaumont, *intendant des Finances*, rue Saint-Honoré, attended to routine matters concerning the *Trésor royal* and its expenditures, to the *caisse des amortissements*, to rents, to retail sales, to supervision of the *contrôleur des restes* and the *contrôleur des bons d'états du Conseil*, to the accounts of hospitals and charity homes in all provinces of the kingdom, to the regulation of the *marc d'or*, and to the accounts of Navarre and Béarn.

As for trade within the kingdom and foreign trade overland, M. Boula de Quincy, *intendant du Commerce*, rue Neuve-Saint-François, was responsible for Normandy, Brittany, and the *généralités* of Orléans, Bourges, and Moulins, for stocking manufacture, and for other hosiery works. M. de Montaran, *intendant du Commerce*, rue du Grand-Chantier, was responsible for the *généralité de Paris*, excluding the city itself, for Roussillon, Languedoc, Provence, Dauphiné, Auvergne, the *généralités* of Montauban, Auch, and Béarn, and for the manufacture of linen and linen goods. M. Potier, *intendant du Commerce*, residing in the Saint-Merry cloister, dealt with the affairs of the *généralité* of Soissons, Picardy, Artois, Flanders, Hainault, Champagne, the Trois-Evêchés, and Alsace, and with paper mills and tanneries. Finally,

M. de Cotte, *intendant du Commerce* with offices in the Galeries du Louvre, took care of the Lyonnais, Forez, Beaujolais, the duchy and county of Burgundy, Bresse, the province of Maine, Poitou, the *généralités* of Limoges, Tours, La Rochelle, and Bordeaux, and silk manufacturing.

Maritime commerce was divided between M. le duc de Choiseul, peer of France, minister and secretary of state, rue Richelieu, and M. le duc de Praslin, minister and secretary of state, rue de Sevres. Choiseul concerned himself with the French islands in America and "with everything involving America," as well as with "fishing for cod, herring, whale, and other fishes." Praslin took care of trade in the Mediterranean (the ports of the Levant and all the states of the Great Sultan, Barbary, the coasts of Italy, and the Mediterranean coasts of Spain), as well as trade with Holland, England, Scotland, Ireland, Sweden, Denmark, Hamburg, Danzig, "other northern lands in the Baltic Sea," and Russia.

Thus the principles of organization had not changed. Specialization had not proceeded very far. Each *intendant* was responsible for certain geographical areas and for a few items of the state's business, with an imperfect division of labor and much overlap. The departments of the *contrôleur général* and of the *intendants des Finances* included items classified under the same headings. Most likely they dealt with these matters on different levels.

The End of the Reign of Louis XV and the Age of Louis XVI, 1771 to 1789

The age of Louis XVI was one of far-reaching reforms that helped to trigger the Revolution by upsetting not only the organization of the government bureaucracy but the very principles on which that organization was based, principles connected with the very foundations of French society. Two parallel trends are in evidence: first, venal officeholders were replaced by hired employees; and second, aristocratic magistrates were replaced by men chosen for their talents, who over the years formed a group that grew into something like our modern civil service. One manifestation of these trends was the replacement of financial officials who simultaneously held public office and made loans to the state, and who often failed to distinguish between their own funds and those of the state, by salaried public officials responsible for collecting taxes and floating loans. All these reforms, which were well advanced prior to 5 May 1789, were carried through by the Constituent Assembly.

The reforms were carried out in two stages. The first phase began when the abbé Terray came to office after the death of Louis XV and continued into the early years of Louis XVI's reign under Turgot and Necker, covering the years 1771 to 1781. Between 1781 and 1787 there was some backsliding under Joly de Fleury and Calonne. The second phase ran from 1787 until 1789 and is associated with the names of Loménie de Brienne and later Necker.

The Growth of the Power of the Head Financial Official

The power of the man in charge of royal finance grew to the point where he acted virtually as a prime minister. The head financial official was not always called the *contrôleur général*. In fact, Jacques Necker, a foreigner and a Protestant, held the titles of *directeur général des Finances* from 1777 to 1781 and minister of state from 1788 to 1790. Joly de Fleury was named minister of state and finance from 1781 to 1783 and was sometimes referred to as the *administrateur général*. Loménie de Brienne was *chef du Conseil royal des Finances* and then principal minister during 1787 and 1788.

The changing title is indicative of the increasing power of the top financial official. In the midst of financial and political difficulties the king ceased to act as his own prime minister and *surintendant des Finances*. The *chef des Finances*, even when he was only *contrôleur général des Finances*, was in law as well as in fact a minister of finance and almost a prime minister. Furthermore, Turgot, Joly de Fleury, Calonne, Loménie de Brienne, and Necker during his second ministry all sat on the Conseil d'Etat. Between 1777 and 1783 auditing was supervised by the two *gardes des registres du contrôle général des Finances*. Between 1787 and 1790 a *contrôleur général des Finances* was placed under the orders of the minister of finance.

Whatever the official title, *contrôleur général* or minister, the *chef des Finances* continued to work with the king. The Conseil royal des Finances did less and less work and lost its independence. By 1787, to all intents and purposes, the Council no longer existed. The names of its members still appeared in the *Almanach royal* and on the registers of the *Trésor royal*, which paid their salaries. But the Council was now meeting only seven or eight times a year rather than every Tuesday.

The fiction of Council decrees was maintained. The *contrôleur général* or minister took proposed decrees drawn up by *commis* in his bureaus or in the bureaus of the *intendants des Finances* to the king for his approval. The king wrote his decision at the bottom of these proposals. They were then returned to the *commis* so that they could prepare a final decree. If an individual or body wished to bring a case before the Council (in reality before the minister and the king), it was necessary to have an *avocat* draw up a petition to be brought to the king by the *contrôleur général* as part of the king's "paperwork."

The Fate of the Intendants des Finances *and the* Intendants du Commerce

The *contrôleur général* was assisted by six *intendants des Finances* and a number of *intendants du Commerce*, who were chosen from among the *maîtres des requêtes*. They owned their own offices and ranked as magistrates, inferior to the *contrôleur général* but autonomous in their own departments thanks to their status as officeholders. Each met privately with the *contrôleur général*, who submitted their proposals to the king. The *contrôleur général* called all of them together for a weekly meeting. In 1787 the schedule of these meetings was published in the *Almanach royal*, and they thereby acquired a sort of official status.

Much criticism was leveled at the *intendants des Finances* on account of their high-handedness in dealing with litigation. Accordingly, an edict of June 1777 eliminated their offices along with those of the *intendants du Commerce*. They were replaced by a *comité contentieux des Finances* consisting of three judges, increased to four in 1781. The judgments rendered by this body were issued in the form of council decrees. Many cases were referred to the Conseil privé, however, while others were sent to the Conseil royal des Finances. The *comité contentieux* was eliminated in 1791.

The *intendants des Finances* and *intendants du Commerce* were reinstated in 1781 after the fall of Necker. They were no longer offices, however, but merely commissions, limited to matters of financial administration.

The Conseil royal des Finances et du Commerce and the new committees have already been discussed in connection with the king's Council under Louis XVI.

The word "budget," originally an English parliamentary term, was first used in French sometime between 1780 and 1790, but there was as yet no budget as such.

The Bureaucracy

The actual work was done by a "bureaucracy" under the supervision of the *chef des Finances*. The term "bureaucracy" first appears around 1780. The *contrôle général des Finances* was composed of various bureaus. Some of these were located in the Hôtel du contrôle général in Paris, the former Hôtel de Pontchartrain. These bureaus were referred to as the "*contrôle général des Finances*" and also as the "*Département des Finances*" or "*Administration des Finances*." They were responsible for preparing tax rolls and accounts of payments, rents, and pensions for financial officials, *receveurs*, *trésoriers*, and *payeurs* and for keeping books recording all transactions based on receipts, authenticated statements, and other information.

In 1788 the financial bureaucracy consisted of 38 bureaus employing 265 *commis*. The *ferme générale* had 4 bureaus and 21 *commis*. The *régie générale* had 1 bureau employing 6 *commis*. One *intendant des Finances* supervised 5 bureaus. Another was in charge of 7 bureaus, employing 44 *commis*, which dealt with the royal domain. A third *intendant des Finances* supervised 12 bureaus employing 94 *commis* and dealing with the *receveurs généraux des Finances* (*taille*, *capitation*, and *vingtième*). In charge of day-to-day financial operations was a *premier commis des Finances* who ran 7 bureaus and employed 46 *commis* and who was associated with the *gardes du Trésor royal* and the *trésoriers*. For the *payeurs des rentes* there was 1 bureau with 3 *commis*. Another bureau, employing 5 *commis*, handled the sale of *rentes* and offices. One bureau with 5 *commis* serviced the *revenus casuels*.

Other matters were dealt with by 25 other bureaus. One department concerned itself with matters of economic importance, including public works, dikes, highways, bridges, the streets of Paris, and repairs on the royal domain. Another dealt with mines, ore deposits, and salt marshes. Another kept an eye on the balance of trade. Another supervised tariff and customs reform. Another dealt with streams and forests and fisheries. And finally there was a department in charge of industrial inspection.

There were bureaus responsible for public health and assistance: hospitals, the poor, prisons, poorhouses, and food and fuel for Paris.

Other bureaus dealt with questions of public order, municipalities, postal service, the provincial estates and assemblies, the Royal Veterinary School at Charenton, and so forth.

Finally, some bureaus were concerned with carrying out investigations to collect information and statistics. Bréquigny collected royal edicts and declarations. Dupont de Nemours headed a bureau that gathered information on foreign tariffs and commercial laws. Under the authority of J.-B. François de La Michodière, Le Quesne headed a bureau that kept population tables and a map showing the distribution of population and births. Isaac Potier was the head of a bureau concerned with the balance of trade with foreign countries, which in 1781 was detached from the *Ferme générale*. The abbé Peron was responsible for legislation concerning loans against salary. The *gardes* Bozetet des Bordes and Coquelay were charged with keeping records of minutes and special dispatches pertaining to finance. Jacob-Nicolas Moreau, historiographer to the king, kept papers pertaining to the financial administration. Laurent kept records of decrees issued by the Conseil privé. Villiers du Terrage, finally, filed papers pertaining to the *pays d'Etat*, the *Eaux et Forêts*, and so forth.

There was a Bureau of Dispatches staffed by a *premier commis*, a *chef*, and six or seven ordinary *commis*, who routed mail to the appropriate bureau. Villiers du Terrage, assisted by seven *commis*, was in charge of sending edicts, declarations, and Council decrees to the interested parties. Another bureau supervised the Royal Lottery, established in 1776.

In all, 360 employees worked for the *contrôle général*, 30 of whom were *premiers commis*, 30 more, working directly under them, *chefs de bureaux*, 205 *commis*, and 30 office boys. Each *premier commis* rented office space and furnished his offices himself and later obtained compensation from the minister. Employees were paid by the agencies for which they worked: the *régie générale*, the *Domaine royal*, the *parties casuelles*, etc. They received monthly or quarterly payments plus an annual bonus. The total paid out in salaries and bonuses each year came to 1,463,967 livres.

Financial Officials and Their Bureaus

Most of the financial officials owned their offices, whether a *trésorier*, *receveur*, or *payeur*. A few were *commissaires*. They swore an oath to the Chambre des Comptes to which they were responsible. Their profession was governed by statute, and they were obliged to obey a variety of edicts, regulations, council decrees, and royal letters. Still, their office afforded them a certain dignity and autonomy.

Offices remained the dynastic property of the families of their owners. More than ten financial officials during the reigns of Louis XV and Louis XVI came from the Random family. As for the Meulans, Charles-Louis-Jacques Meulan inherited the office of *receveur général des Finances* from his father. His uncle, Meulan de La Sourdière, was *payeur des rentes*. Another uncle, Guy Martin Terre du Petitval, was *receveur général du Domaine et Forêts*. Among the Taverniers, Guillaume Tavernier de Boulogne, paymaster for the Orléans finance bureau and secretary-comptroller attached to the chancellery of the Cour des Comptes, *fermier général* and agent for *aides et finances* in Franche-Comté, had two sons: the elder, Guillaume Pierre, born in 1710, was *trésorier général* for the American colonies and later *trésorier général* for *l'extraordinaire des guerres*; his younger brother, Philippe-Guillaume, born in 1712, was *receveur général* for Poitou in 1749 and *fermier général* in 1780 and again in 1786.

Not all financial officials received salaries sufficient to maintain themselves decently according to their rank and status, as the *commis* did; their wages amounted to about 5 percent of the official value of the office. They did receive certain other fees as well as a percentage of the funds they handled, bonuses, and pensions. Thus they were not paid anything like a salary, or compensation for the economic value of the work they did, but rather something in the nature of a rent based on the value of the office, a profit in the form of fees accruing to them by virtue of their position, or a commission based on the volume of money they handled.

Financial officials employed their own *commis*, whom they were free to choose, compensate, and dismiss without the king's intervention. In some cases, such as the *gardes du Trésor royal*, the crown gave a fixed sum to the official as a contribution toward the remuneration of his *commis*. Officials had complete control over their departments. They could organize them in any way they wished and promote employees as they liked.

The ambition of every *premier commis*, *chef de bureau*, and *commis* was to own an office. A few of them were allowed to buy an office that had been resigned or left vacant as compensation for their services. For example, René-Augustin Marigner, born in 1731, worked for eighteen years first as a *commis* and later as *premier commis* in the bureaus of a *garde du Trésor royal*. In 1764 he was able to purchase an office of *payeur des rentes*, which he held until 1785. He then became *trésorier général de la Maison de la comtesse de Provence*, the sister-in-law of Louis XVI. Then, on 30 September 1789, he was received as *receveur général des Finances* in Paris. He took in his son as a partner—a son who was no longer merely Marigner, but Marigner de La Crouzardière.

These new men generally followed similar career trajectories. They began as ordinary *commis* and then after a few years moved up to *premier commis*.

Until 1777, the next step was to acquire an office as *receveur général des Domaines et Forêts*, which was relatively inexpensive. Once they had acquired a sufficient number of contacts, influence, and money, they could move up to the more highly prized and more expensive offices, such as *receveur particulier* or *payeur des rentes*. Finally, after they had made contacts in high places, the way was open to offices costing several hundreds of thousands of livres, such as *receveur général, trésorier général,* or *fermier général*. For those who were not already noble there glimmered hopes of ennoblement for themselves or their children. Many acquired nobility by buying an office of *secrétaire du roi*. Others received letters of nobility from the king. They formed a rising *noblesse de finance*, reminiscent of the *noblesse de robe* that had formed two centuries earlier. Money was not enough, however. To consolidate their gains, they also needed to enter into clientele relationships with their social superiors and to win recognition as a group of their new social status.

The Receveurs *and* Payeurs

There were two major categories of accounting officials: first, the *receveur-payeurs*, who collected the funds coming in from the various taxes and loans and disbursed funds to cover certain expenditures; and, second, the plain *payeurs*, who received their funds from some *receveur-payeur*.

The highest-ranking *receveur-payeurs* were the two *gardes du Trésor royal*. According to the edict of June 1748 this office was worth 1,200,000 livres. They earned 5 percent of the official value of the office in salary plus 12,000 additional livres when they were actually on duty; they also received 1,500 livres in salary for their work on the council and 60,000 livres, increased by Necker to 85,000, to cover the wages and expenses of their *commis*. These offices were family property. In 1749 Charles-Pierre Savalette de Magnanville took the first of the two posts. In 1773 his son, Charles-Pierre-Paul Savalette de Langes became his assistant and designated heir. In November 1785 they switched positions, Langes becoming the titulary of the post and Magnanville his assistant and designated heir. Both men were *maîtres des requêtes* and *conseillers d'Etat*. The father was for a time *intendant* of Tours. The family could claim three degrees of nobility and thus came close, in principle, to the *gentilhommerie*.

As for the second *garde du Trésor royal*, Joseph Micault d'Harvelay succeeded his great-uncle, Jean Paris de Montmartel, in 1755. In January 1785 he passed his post on to his nephew, François-Louis-Joseph Laborde de Méréville, who had been his assistant and designated heir since 1777. Laborde named his father, Jean-Joseph de Laborde, former banker to the court, as his assistant and designated heir. Jean-Joseph and Micault had married the two daughters of Nettine, a Belgian banker to the court.

The *receveurs généraux des revenus casuels* replaced the three *trésoriers des parties casuelles* after the latter posts were eliminated by an edict of April 1664. At first two *receveurs* were named by commission, but an edict of February 1689 converted these positions to offices, and a third was added in December 1695. Edicts of December 1716 and June 1717 set the official value of the office at 1,000,000 livres, with a salary of 50,000 livres. Numerous *receveurs particuliers des revenus casuels* did their work in the provinces.

The *marc d'or*, a fee charged in addition to the seal fee for *lettres de provision* for offices, letters of ennoblement, exemptions from age requirements, and so on was collected by the *trésoriers du marc d'or*, who paid the *rentes sur l'Ordre du Saint-Esprit*. There were two such offices, each valued officially at 500,000 livres, and their titularies were assisted by two *contrôleurs*, whose offices were valued at 100,000 livres. They received salaries amounting to 5 percent of the value of their offices. In addition, the *trésoriers* collected an additional fee of 2.5 percent of the funds they handled.

The *receveurs généraux des Finances* collected all direct taxes: the *taille*, the *capitation*, and the *vingtièmes*. There were fifty of them, two in each of the twenty *généralités* of the *pays d'élections*, the rest in the *pays d'Etats*. They served in alternate years, half in even years, half in odd years. Each owned his office as individual property. The office for the *généralité* of Montauban, which was created in January 1635 and sold for 30,000 livres, was worth 770,000 livres under Louis XVI; that of Bourges was worth 250,000; that of Paris, 1,280,000. All told, these offices were worth 26,000,000 livres. Each posted a bond, received his tax lists from the king, kept his own personal accounts, and administered his *généralité* without accounting for his actions to any of the others. Nevertheless, as a group the *receveurs* formed a kind of *corps* in that they had a common treasury, the *Caisse commune des recettes générales des finances*, created by the declaration of 10 June 1716, into which they paid the balance of what they collected after deducting their own costs. For the king, this was a reserve of unspent funds out of the general receipts. The *caissier général* was Jean-Claude Geoffroy d'Assy. Four bureaus were attached to the *Caisse commune*: a bureau of bonds, a bookkeeping bureau, a disbursement bureau, and a bureau of accounts. The *caissier general* and the *commis* and *premiers commis* who worked in these bureaus were paid out of the *Caisse commune* at the discretion of the *contrôleur général*.

Prior to 1775, the *receveur général* dealt with *receveurs particuliers* in each *élection* of his *généralité*. Each *receveur particulier* relied in turn on tax collectors in every parish. For 209 *élections* there were 418 offices of *receveurs particuliers*, filled by 317 different individuals, 101 of them holding two offices. The average value of the office was 100,000 livres. All told, they represented a value of 28,000,000 to 29,000,000 livres in 1771. In 1780 these *receveurs* raised 139,000,000 livres in taxes. Remunerated at the rate of 10 percent of the value of the office (5 percent of their investment, 2 percent for expenses, 3 percent in net profits), they were paid about 10,000 livres each, or 350,000 livres in all. They cost the king about 0.25 percent of his tax revenues.

The *receveurs généraux* handled 148,000,000 livres of the king's revenues. Each was paid 50,000 livres on the average, or 10 percent of their investment in the office. They cost the king 0.166 percent of his taxes. These calculations do not include the profits they made on their loans to the king, however.

The *receveurs des domaines et bois* included 152 *receveurs particuliers*, 152 *receveurs des amendes* in the *maîtres des eaux et forêts*, 49 *gardes généraux* and *collecteurs des amendes*, 64 *receveurs généraux des domaines et bois*, and 64 *contrôleurs généraux*, members of the last two categories serving in alternate years. Many people held more than one of these posts: in 1774 there were 36 *receveurs généraux des domaines et bois*. All these offices were abolished by Necker in August 1777. Their functions were subsequently carried out by a royal administration, the *administration générale des domaines*.

Other *receveur-payeurs* handled different portions of the king's funds: the *receveur de la capitation de la Cour*, the *receveur général des "Boètes de Monnayes de France,"* the *régisseur des économats* for the revenues from vacant benefices and church property acquired by the king, the *receveur général du Clergé*, etc.

Among the *receveur-payeurs* we should include the *fermiers généraux* who were not officeholders but financiers involved in contracts with the king. The *Ferme générale* was of such great importance, however, that a separate portion of this volume will be devoted to it.

The regular *payeurs* obtained funds from one or more *receveur-payeurs*. Each was assisted by a *contrôleur*. Among them we find the *trésoriers payeurs des rentes sur l'Hôtel de Ville de Paris*. There were 50 of them from 1720 to 1758, 69 from 1758 to 1760, 73 from 1760 to 1768, and 79 from 1769 to 1772. The edict of May 1772 reduced the number to 30, each of whom held two offices, with 30 *contrôleurs*. Some paid a particular type of *rente* (three, for example, paid *rentes* on the clergy), others paid a particular category of *rentiers*. In the latter case, the *rentiers* were arranged in alphabetical order, and the letters of the alphabet were divided up among the *payeurs*. Each *payeur* was individually responsible to the Chambre des Comptes. Each opened his offices to the public one day a week. *Payeurs* employed two to five *commis*. They kept their own books, unlike other financial officials, whose books were kept by *procureurs* of the Chambre des Comptes.

The *payeurs* formed a "company" with a dean and a subdean. A syndic spoke for the group. They held meetings as a group for the service of the king and their own interests. On 3 January 1762, a committee was formed to prepare for these annual general meetings. Its membership included the dean and subdean of the company, four permanent members, and six members elected each year.

Each corps of officeholders had *payeurs* responsible for disbursing salary payments. The Paris *parlement* had three *receveur-payeurs* for its salaries (*ancien, alternatif*, and *triennal*), assisted by three *contrôleurs*. The same was true for all the *parlements*, Chambres des Comptes, and Cours des Aides, as well as for the officeholders of the Grande Chancellerie, the Châtelet de Paris, and so on.

There were *trésoriers des deniers royaux* working for thirty different organizations, including fifty *trésoriers generaux* and their *contrôleurs* and a large number of *trésoriers particuliers*. The royal household employed fifteen *trésoriers généraux* and their fifteen *contrôleurs généraux*. Attached to the secretariat for war were two *trésoriers généraux de l'ordinaire des guerres*, *de la gendarmerie*, and for the troops of the royal household; two *trésoriers généraux de l'extraordinaire des guerres*; one *trésorier général* for artillery and engineers; one *trésorier général* for military bonuses; one *trésorier général* for fortifications; two *trésorier généraux* and *payeurs* for the Invalides; three *trésoriers généraux* for the *Ligues suisses* and *grisons*; one *trésorier général* for the military school; and so on. The Ponts et Chaussées had their *trésoriers généraux* and 52 *trésoriers particuliers*. And so on.

Financial Officials and Public Borrowing

The king used his financial officials to float public loans. France had no central bank. The Bank of France was not founded until 1800. The Caisse d'Escompte established by Turgot in 1776 did not perform the functions of a bank. In order to obtain short-term credit the government turned to its own financial officials. Lending money to the king was part of their official responsibility and was not without risks; many went bankrupt.

The financial system stood in constant need of borrowed funds. Separate treasuries were continually receiving and disbursing funds. Sometimes there was a surplus of receipts, sometimes a deficit. In case of deficit the treasurer could not ask for the surplus from another treasury to be diverted into his coffers. He had to find his own source of funds, whether by digging into his personal fortune or by asking for loans from relatives, friends, and people in parts of the country where he was well-known. He then lent the money to the state and recovered what he and his creditors had advanced later on, when the tax revenues came in. He charged interest for the immobilization of his funds and for the risks run, a practice that was condoned by the Catholic church. When taxes were received before payment was due to the king, the money was considered to be "sterile and dead for service." The official was then allowed to lend it out at short term and for interest in the private sector.

For loans to the king financial officials frequently issued bearer bills at 4, 5 and 6 percent interest, and these circulated as legal tender. The two *gardes du Trésor royal* issued *rescriptions* and bills with the help of court bankers such as Samuel Bernard, Jean Paris de Montmartel, and others. The position of court banker was temporarily eliminated on 1 January 1767. In 1778 its services were limited to the financial department of the ministry of foreign affairs. The *receveurs généraux des Finances* issued *rescriptions*. Reimbursement and interest payments were effected by cash-payment orders for the "replacement of sums paid" or the "replacement of advances."

All this short-term borrowing was controlled by the *"faiseurs de service,"* who took care of "service to the royal treasury," a dozen "financiers" who each took responsibility for discounting bills and *rescriptions* one month out of the year. Among them were Nicolas Beaujon (1718–86), court banker until 1778 and then *receveur général* first of La Rochelle and later of Rouen, who in 1773 advanced 61,000,000 of a loan amounting to 201,000,000 in all; the two *gardes du Trésor*; five *trésoriers généraux*, including Baudard de Saint-James and Mégret de Sérilly; five *receveurs généraux*; one *caissier* of the Compagnie des Indes; Jacques Necker himself, while he was prime minister; and two financiers and bankers, Jacques Marquet de Bourgade (1718–84), who was a friend and adviser of the *contrôleur général*, Joly de Fleury, and Jean-Baptiste Magon de La Balue (1713–94), court banker in 1769.

Treasury bills were negotiated on the Paris Bourse. Thus it was possible for a *receveur général des Finances* to engage in the following transaction. Suppose that, on the 1st of the month, he received from his *receveurs particuliers* 200,000 livres that did not have to be paid to the king until the 30th. He could then go to the Bourse and buy 200,000 livres worth of treasury bills due on the 30th at a 6 percent discount. He could then use these bills to pay what he owed on the 30th at their face value. His profit on the exchange would be 12,000 livres.

All financial officials participated in this sort of game. All major offices in finance were held by wealthy men with good credit. They were all forced to borrow to buy their offices. Baudard de Saint-James borrowed 714,000 livres from nine friends, acquaintances, and colleagues in order to become *trésorier général de la Marine*; his creditors included a *conseiller* in *parlement*, a *conseiller d'Etat*, a *trésorier de France*, a master of ceremonies at court, army officers, and a number of "Bourgeois de Paris." Officials gave lenders bearer bills in exchange for their money. These bills were attractive to people with savings to invest. Small towns and people with ready cash wrote to the *receveurs généraux* offering to make loans.

Some financial officials invested money in commercial and industrial enterprises of public interest. This practice was traditional, but its scale now was certainly greater than it had been in the past. In 1778 Gabriel Prevost, *trésorier général des Ponts et Chaussées*, invested 12,000 livres in a spinning mill at Sers, 30,000 livres in a royal weaving works at Bourges, 30,000 in forges at Beaumont and La Belouze (Nièvre), 4,000 in a soda works, 50,000 in mines in Lower Brittany, 40,000 in the military hospital company, 60,000 in a Paris insurance company, and various other amounts in a Spanish gunpowder and saltpeter concern, in the Lisbon commercial firm of Pedegache & Co., and in a number of naval armaments manufacturers. Baudard de Saint-James, *trésorier de la Marine*, the *receveurs généraux* Marquet Desgrèves and the Meulans, and Millin Duperreaux, *receveur général* and administrator of the royal lottery, all invested in commercial and industrial concerns. The Compagnie des Eaux de Paris was financed by Magon de La Balue, Micault d'Harvelay, Mégret de Sérilly, and Baudard de Saint-James.

Similarly, some *receveurs particuliers* invested in land as well as in public and private firms.

Thus, under Louis XVI, some financial officials behaved like capitalist enterpreneurs in certain of their activities.

Officials in finance made huge profits but also ran great risks. They were personally responsible for the solvency of the treasury they administered. Bankruptcies were frequent, less so in the organized corps, which could but did not always guarantee *rescriptions* and bills issued by defaulting members, but more common among isolated individual financiers. In 1787 the Chambre des Comptes informed the king that fifty *caissiers* had gone bankrupt over the previous twenty years. There were some resounding failures even among the best known of the great tycoons, such as Baudard de Saint-James.

The Conflict between the Magistrates and the Commis

Magistrates and *commissaires* battled for control of this extensive bureaucracy. The minister and his private secretaries had little power over the "département des Finances," or, rather, as one said, over "les départements," because the minister himself directly controlled only a dozen bureaus. Most of the bureaus were under the control of officeholders who owned their posts, six *intendants des Finances* and four *intendants du Commerce* who were magistrates invested with personal power. Aristocratic in character and enjoying an elevated social position, they behaved in a somewhat contemptuous way toward the *premiers commis*, *chefs de bureaux*, and *commis* serving under them. According to Auget de Montyon, writing in June 1781, magistrates regarded their *commis* as "subalterns who have neither hereditary virtues to imitate nor public reputations to maintain," a fine definition *a contrario* of a social order.

Turgot, Joly de Fleury, Lefebvre d'Ormesson, and Calonne made no effort to reduce the magistrates' essentially aristocratic personal power, and Joly de Fleury and Calonne even restored some of the powers that had been taken from them by Necker.

Necker had two reasons for being hostile to the magistrates in 1777. Himself a mere *directeur général*, a *commis* rather than a *magistrate*, and a Protestant and foreigner to boot, he found it impossible to force the magistrates to obey his orders. The *intendants des Finances* refused to work with a minister who was not admitted to any of the councils. Trudaine de Montigny, who had the reputation of being an enlightened soul, nevertheless refused to head the Ponts et Chaussées under Necker. Necker therefore resolved to govern with the help of the *premiers commis*. In June 1777 he eliminated the *intendants des Finances* and *du Commerce*. He assumed direct control over the seven key bureaus: taxes, farms, Ponts et Chaussées, *Régie générale*, and so on, with no magistrate intervening between him and the *premiers commis* in each of these bureaus. He governed mainly with the aid of the *premier commis des Finances*. He had Bertrand Dufresne named *premier secrétaire du Trésor* and Nicolas Beaujon, a man with a logical mind, a character of strict honesty, skill in all areas of finance, and a capacity to work eighteen hours a day, named banker to the court and *receveur général des Finances* for La Rochelle. As the man in charge of the "département du trésor royal," Dufresne handled no money. His job was to keep constant tabs on all arrivals, shipments, and disbursements of funds, to monitor the work of financial officials and see to it that they followed the rules, to report on any irregularities and suggest sanctions and remedies to the minister. Every month he tabulated all disbursements, assigning a source of income to each item of expenditure. He kept a list of financiers and bankers from whom money could be borrowed in case of emergency. Seven bureaus worked under him, employing 33 *commis* and 4 office boys. Each had its own *chef*. The *chefs de bureau* were paid more than the *premiers commis* of the *contrôle général des Finances*, 24,000 to 30,000 livres annually compared with only 8,000 to 15,000 for the *premiers commis*. Necker aimed to control the kingdom's finances and reform the financial administration with the help of Dufresne and the *premiers commis des Finances*.

Necker also wanted to replace financial officeholders by salaried *commis*. He had against him a coalition of magistrates and officeholders. After Necker, Marquet de Bourgade, a close friend and confidant of the new *contrôleur général*, Joly de Fleury, had the mediocre Achille-Joseph Gojard named *premier commis des Finances*, a post in which he served from the end of 1781 until August 1788. Joly de Fleury favored the magistrates, replaced three *premiers commis* by three *maîtres des requêtes* to whom he offered commissions as *intendants des Finances* for the *Fermes générales*, *Mines et Minerais*, and *Ponts et Chaussées*. Calonne went even further. He chose nine *intendants* among the *maîtres des requêtes* to head the *départements des Finances* and offered commissions to seven other *maîtres des requêtes* for various bureaus. Every Wednesday, an Assembly of Magistrates from the departments of finance met under the chairmanship of the *conseiller d'Etat* Lenoir, at his residence.

Loménie de Brienne went back to Necker's policy. He reduced the number of departments of finance. He revoked the commissions of the *intendants des Finances* and the other *maîtres des requêtes*. He granted only four commissions to *maîtres des requêtes* for the major departments: Domaines; *rentes*, bridges, hospitals, and prisons; taxes; the *Ferme générale* and *Régie générale*. The four departments of the *intendants de commerce* were combined in one under the *intendant* Tolozan.

Necker kept this organization under his second ministry, which began in August of 1788. He combined the bureaus of the *premier commis des Finances* with those of the *Trésor*. He named Bertrand Dufresne *intendant du Trésor*, but Dufresne remained a *commis* and became neither a magistrate nor an officeholder. Serving under him was a *premier commis des Finances* by the name of Fontaine, who was given the title of *premier commis du Trésor royal*. Necker thus went back to the idea of using administrators who were *commis* and almost functionaries rather than royal officeholders who owned their offices. Necker brought about the victory of bureaucracy over aristocracy.

The victorious bureaucracy was still, however, staffed by clients devoted to patrons, by creatures dedicated to their protectors. Ministers and *contrôleurs généraux* were in any case dependent on public opinion. They were named by the king subject to pressure from friends and relatives at court. They cultivated popularity and sought to influence public opinion through books and pamphlets. In 1781 Necker published *Le Compte rendu au roi*, nothing less than an appeal to the people of France. He had pictures of himself circulated among the populace. His partisans said he deserved a place alongside Colbert and Sully. *Contrôleurs généraux* gained and lost power depending on the vagaries of petitions, remonstrances, and pressure from the sovereign courts, the provincial estates, the nobles, the bishops, the financiers, the cities, the corps, and above all the oligarchic pressure groups that lobbied the court and dominated the Paris Bourse.

Ministers and *contrôleurs généraux* named their own men to be *premiers commis* and got rid of men loyal to their predecessors. Turgot sacked the *premier commis des Finances*, Armand Le Clerc, and replaced him with his friend Jean de Vaine. Necker dismissed de Vaine and appointed Armand Dufresne, and so on. The same tale can be told of the other *premiers commis* and *chefs de bureau*. Turgot replaced Destouches and Dupuy, who were allies of Terray, with Le Seur and Charles de La Croix, the latter having been one of his secretaries when he was *intendant* at Limoges.

Many courtiers, magistrates, and *premiers commis* had relatives and friends named to posts as *chefs de bureau*. Charles Hersemalle de La Roche became *premier commis* in the bureau des Dépêches in 1778. Working in his bureau were his son-in-law, Etienne-Marie Denois, the son of a *premier commis* of the secretary of state for war; his nephew, Bouconvillier; a cousin by marriage, Pardon; a protégé of Louis XVI's aunt Mme Victoire by the name of Meslin; the son-in-law of another *premier commis*, who was a protégé of Mme Adélaïde, another of the king's aunts; the son of one of the queen's *valets de chambre*; and the nephew of a *premier commis* of the *Routes et Ponts*, to name a few.

What mattered most, however, were the ties among the bureaucrats. There grew up a nexus of families that had long traditions of bureaucratic service. The La Roche family, for example, had provided bureaucrats since 1712. Seven *premiers commis* from this family remained in office throughout the reign of Louis XVI as ministers came and went. Three generations of Villiers served as *premiers commis* in the same bureaus from 1726 until April 13, 1794. This case was not unusual.

The bureaucrats triumphed with the Revolution. Competent and hard-working, these *commis* benefitted from the change of regime, which brought with it the victory of the functionaries and "men of talent" over magistrate officeholders and even *commissaires*. Jean de Vaine, *premier commis des Finances* under Turgot from 1774 to 1777, became *commissaire du Trésor* under the Constituent Assembly; under the Consulate he was named *conseiller d'Etat* in the finance section and was elected a member of the Institute. He died on 16 March 1803.

Bertrand Dufresne became *directeur général du Trésor public* on 17 September 1790, after Necker's resignation, and continued in that post until the end of 1792. Under the Directory he was elected to the Assemblée des Cinq-Cents. During the Consulate he was appointed *conseiller d'Etat* and *chef du Trésor* on 25 December 1800. He died in 1801. Bonaparte had a bust of him placed in the Trésor on 19 February 1802.

Joseph-Alexandre Bergon served through the Revolution as *chef de bureau* in the administration of Eaux et Forêts until Napoleon made him *conseiller d'Etat*. Quite a few *premiers commis* and *chefs de bureau* remained on the job throughout the period of the Revolution and into the Empire, whereas magistrate officeholders were swept away in 1790 and 1791. The bureaucrats, now become functionaries, were among the beneficiaries of the Revolution.

Notes

1. Isaac Bourgoin, *La chasse aux larrons* (Paris, 1617).

2. Quoted in A. de Boislisle, *Correspondance des contrôleurs généraux avec les intendants des Finances*, vol. 1, p. 542.

3. *Mémoires*, vol. 3: *1620–1633*, p. 165.

13 Government by *Grand Conseil:* The Estates General

It will no doubt come as a surprise to the reader to find the Estates General classed among the central organs of government. They are usually viewed as popular representative bodies. Such a view ignores the fact that the Estates General consisted of men delegated by the subjects of the kingdom to give the king the benefit of their counsel, at his request. The members of the Estates were royal councillors. All three orders—clergy, nobility, and third estate—were represented. But these political and juridical orders did not correspond to the actual social orders within the kingdom. The actual social orders were constituted by a tacit consensus based on common value judgments and formed spontaneously within the society. During the fourteenth century, the king had chosen to group these natural social orders together in a particular way for political purposes, and it was this grouping that gave rise to the three familiar legal and political orders. The delegates representing the three orders did not act as deputies but rather as subjects and vassals of the king, who came to offer him their advice. Although they might thereby make the wishes of their electors known to the king, their role remained a purely consultative one.

The Estates General of 1614–15

The king was forced to undertake this consultation by an armed uprising of the princes of the blood, including Henri II de Condé, the first prince of the blood, the new duc de Mayenne, and the ducs de Nevers, de Bouillon, and de Longueville. The princes of the blood claimed that, during a period of royal minority and regency, they had the right to an actual share in government and complained of being excluded by the regent, Marie de Médicis, and her favorite, Concini, under the ministerial regime. The princes of the blood left the court, Condé issued his manifesto of 19 February 1614, and the princes began recruiting troops. The regent believed she had no choice but to sign the treaty of Sainte-Menehould with them on 15 May 1614, one condition of which was the calling of the Estates General. On 7 June the queen sent a letter convening a meeting at Sens on 10 September.

But the rebel princes had lost the contest in advance. The duc de Vendôme rebelled in his government of Brittany. The young king led an army there in July 1614. The sight of the boy king on horseback in the royal role of defender of the populace roused enthusiasm and fervor. Vendôme was forced to come to Nantes and surrender. The king returned to Paris on 16 September. On 2 October he went to *parlement* and there proclaimed his majority in his fourteenth year as laid down by the fundamental laws of the kingdom. The princes of the blood thereby lost one of their best arguments. What is more, a controversy over tyrannicide was then at its height, accompanied by a flurry of brochures and treatises. After the assassination of two French kings in twenty-one years, many Frenchmen wanted to place the king, the embodiment of the kingdom, high enough so that no one would think of making an attempt on his life or authority. They therefore wished to condemn any theory favorable to the deposition or murder of the king and to assert the inviolability of his person, his complete independence in the temporal realm, and his supreme sovereignty. Accordingly, the elections to the Estates General turned out favorable to the king. The meeting was transferred to Paris by letters patent of 4 October. On 27 October 1614, the formal opening session was held at the Hôtel de Bourbon.

Convocation and Elections

By letters patent the king had convoked notables from the three estates of the realm, nobility, clergy, and third estate, in order to hear their remonstrances,[1] complaints, and grievances, their opinions on political matters, on "the administration of justice, police, and finance," on the reform of abuses, on the good of the orders, on alleviation of the people's burden, and on the means for achieving these goals. Their role was supposed to be a purely consultative one, in which they offered the benefit of their counsel to the king, who expected that they would want to offer their opinion out of affection for him and devotion to his service for the sake of the kingdom and all its subjects. When the court judged that it had been adequately informed, the meeting of the Estates General was over. Before the members could return home, however, they had to await the king's leave. Though elected, the notables who sat on the Estates were not deputies in the modern sense. They were advisers of the king, not representatives of the nation.

Royal letters of convocation were sent to the *lieutenants généraux* of the *bailliages* and *sénéchaussées*. Upon request of the *procureur du roi*, the *lieutenant général* ordered that the letters be read and published before the courts of the *bailliage* or *sénéchaussée*. He set a date and place for the meeting of the three orders. Sergeants notified interested parties of the receipt of the royal letters. For the clergy, notification was made to the bishop for all ecclesiastics of the diocese and to the judges of castellanies or the corresponding divisions of *bailliages* and *sénéchaussées* for ecclesiastics under the jurisdiction of other dioceses. For the nobility, the judges of castellanies or of the corresponding divisions of *bailliages* or *sénéchaussées* were notified, and they passed the word on to each *gentilhomme* individually. For the third estate, the principal magistrates in the capital of the *bailliage* were notified, as well as the judges in each castellany or corresponding division of *bailliages* and *sénéchaussées*, who would then publicize the news at sittings of court and thereby spread the word around the countryside.

Elections for the third estate were carried out at two levels. For each castellany or corresponding division, villages and towns were supposed to elect one representative and combine their *cahiers de doléances*, or lists of grievances, into a single *cahier* for the district.

Those elected from the various castellanies or corresponding divisions would then meet together with the principal judge from each district and the *bourgeois* of the capital city of the *bailliage* or *sénéchaussée* in a general assembly. There they would elect the representative for the third estate from the *bailliage* or *sénéchaussée* and would combine the various *cahiers de doléances* into one *cahier* for the whole district.

This system was intended to insure that the cities and officeholders would dominate.

For the clergy and nobility elections took place in a single step. The ecclesiastics met in an assembly for the *bailliage* or *sénéchaussée* and elected a representative of the clergy, and the *gentilshommes* similarly elected a representative of the nobility.

Thus each *bailliage* or *sénéchaussée* was supposed to be represented in the Estates General by three persons, one for each order.

There were many exceptions to the pattern described above. In Dauphiné, Brittany, and Provence, for example, it was the provincial Estates that elected delegates to the Estates General. In Bordeaux the archbishopric took care of choosing the representative of the clergy. An electoral committee whose membership was limited to seven persons (two canons delegated by the chapter of the metropolitan church of Saint-André, two canons delegated by the Saint-Surin chapter, a canon of Saint-André, and two Bordeaux curates delegated by the curates and other benefice-holders in the diocese) unanimously elected cardinal de Sourdis, archbishop and primate of Aquitaine, on 24 July 1614, to be the delegate to the Estates General, and on 30 July Joachim Levenier, canon and grand vicar, announced the results of this election to the assembly of the three orders held in the archbishopric of Bordeaux.

All these practices insured that the composition of the Estates General would be highly aristocratic or oligarchic.

Composition

In the Estates General 103 *circonscriptions* were represented: 59 *bailliages*, 28 *sénéchaussées*, 3 *gouvernements particuliers* (Peronne, Montdidier, Roye), 1 duchy (Albert), 3 counties (Bigorre, Foix, Comminges), 4 "*pays*" (the "pays et jugerie de Rivière-Verdun," the "Haut Pays de Limosin," the "Bas-Pays de Limosin," and "la Ville de Calais et pays reconquis"), 2 cities (Arles, Marseille), and 3 *Pays d'Etats* (Brittany, Dauphiné, and Provence). Not all of these districts actually sent the three delegates allowed. The pays et jugerie de Rivière-Verdun, for example, had only two (Rivière-Verdun, a bishop whom the *pays* shared with the county of Comminges, and a judicial officeholder representing the third estate). Other districts had more than three, such as the "Bas-Pays de Limosin," with Tulle, Brive, and Uzerche, which had two delegates for the nobility, one for the clergy, and three for the third estate; and the city and *bailliage* of Rouen, which had one delegate for the nobility, two for the clergy (a bishop and an abbot), and two for the third estate, one of whom was a judicial officeholder.

The clerical order had 135 representatives, of whom 59 were archbishops or bishops, 39 canons, 33 monks, abbots, or priors, and 4 *aumôniers du roi*. Thirty-two of the archbishops and bishops actually sat on the king's Council. There were only 5 curates, 4 of them heading large cures like that of Saint-Paul in Paris and only 1 country curate, from Buncey in the *bailliage* of La Montagne in Burgundy. Thus the clerical order was represented, in the majority, by holders of benefices appointed by the king, a quarter of whom were in fact members of his Council.

The nobility had 137 delegates: 60 great nobles without office, 6 *baillis*, 40 officers of the royal army or governors, 13 of whom were *conseillers d'Etat*, 19 holders of court offices, such as *gentilshommes de la Chambre du roi*, 1 of whom was a *conseiller d'Etat*, and finally 12 more *conseillers d'Etat*. Thus 78 of the representatives of the nobility held royal offices and 26 were *conseillers d'Etat*, in connection with which it should be noted that 70 votes constituted an absolute majority of this order.

There were 169 representatives of the third estate: 58 *lieutenants généraux* of *bailliages* and *sénéchaussées*, 63 other court officers from the same districts, 30 *avocats*, and 18 municipal magistrates. Of the 169 delegates, 121 were royal officeholders, 114 of them court officers. The "fourth estate" spoken of by Montaigne was thus in the majority by a wide margin.

Some who were legally nobles sat in the third estate: 1 baron (*lieutenant général du haut Limousin*), 4 *messires*, knights, and 26 *ecuyers* (11 lieutenants généraux, 9 other officers, and 5 municipal magistrates). Legally, these men were nobles, but not socially: the *gentilshommes* did not, in general, recognize their "quality."

Forty representatives bore the title "noble homme." In all but a few provinces this title had been devalued and designated nothing more than a notable, usually an officeholder in the process of acquiring nobility.

Seventy-two men were distinguished as "sieur de" this or that, being owners of *seigneuries*, a form of property that carried with it a share in governmental power, social rank, and a title. The majority were commoners (31 *lieutenants généraux*, 22 other officeholders, 8 municipal magistrates, and 6 *avocats*).

We find 2 merchants (Poitiers, La Rochelle), 3 "bourgeois de" (Orléans, Limoges, Pays de Gex), 6 *syndics d'Etats provinciaux*, 1 *secrétaire d'Etats de Dauphiné*, 1 *greffier des Etats de Provence*, all important commoners, 5 of them distinguished as "sieur de." Constantin Housset of the parish of Flamanville in Normandy may have been a wealthy plowman. There is no trace of manual laborers.

Of the 187 representatives of the third estate 115 were therefore plain commoners; 156 out of 187 were in fact common despite their ownership of *seigneuries*, and all were considered to be commoners, or "bourgeois," by the *gentilshommes*. But this was a "bourgeoisie" of the pen. There were 121 royal officeholders out of 187 representatives: counting the municipal magistrates, 139 of the 187 representatives made their living with pen and ink; if we also count the employees of the provincial Estates, 147; and if we add the *avocats*, most of whom aspired to own offices, 177 out of 187. Occupations related to the production and distribution of material goods are virtually unrepresented.

According to the ideas of the time, however, there is no doubt that the delegates were seen as representative of the third estate. Indeed, they were the *sanior pars* of that estate. It should not be forgotten, moreover, that the judicial officeholders, who accounted for a majority of the delegates, thought of themselves as owing the king fidelity and hence obedience but owing a duty to their offices as well: to command respect for justice and hence to work for equity between the king and his subjects and for the protection of the latter.

Organization

Plenary sessions of the Estates General used to be held at the hôtel du Petit-Bourbon, between the Louvre and the church of Saint-Germain-l'Auxerrois. Each order met separately to deliberate in working groups. On 13 October 1614, the king decided that the clergy would meet in the convent of the Grands-Augustins on the quays of the Left Bank. The nobility was to meet in the convent of the Cordeliers near the present-day rue de l'Ecole de Médecine. The third estate was to meet at the Hôtel de Ville in the place de Grève on the Right Bank. However, the nobility and the third estate gained permission to meet alongside the clergy in order to profit from its wisdom, the nobility in a neighboring room and the third estate in the refectory of the Grands-Augustins.

Each order had its own president, secretary, and office staff. Presiding over the clergy was the cardinal de Joyeuse, archbishop of Rouen; president of the nobility was Henry de Bauffremont, baron de Sennecey, a captain with fifty troops in his command; the president of the third estate was Robert Miron, *président aux requêtes* in the Paris *parlement* and *prévôt des marchands*.

Only the clergy set up a timetable and an agenda. It met twice a day, from eight until eleven in the morning and from two to four in the afternoon. At the morning sessions questions of general interest were discussed. Work on the clergy's *cahier* proceeded in the afternoon. The clergy's timetable was passed on to the nobility and the third estate, over which the clergy exerted the influence of counselor and guide. Consultations were held among the clergy and the other two estates. In addition, the clergy designated a preacher to deliver the sermon at Sunday mass, which was attended every Sunday by all members of the Estates General. In theory the sermon was supposed to be a paraphrase and explanation of the Epistle and Gospel. In fact the preacher said only a few words about the holy texts and devoted most of his sermon to political matters. The clergy gave the orator his theme and a list of points to cover, as we see in the case of the speech Richelieu delivered on 23 February 1615, in his capacity as bishop of Luçon to close the meeting of the Estates: the ecclesiastical chamber had provided him with a thirteen-point outline of his speech. The clergy named a new preacher each Sunday. Camus, bishop of Belley, preached on three occasions, however.

Each order was seated by government and subdivision. There were twelve governments in each order, each with its own president. The problem of voting was never definitively resolved, however: Should voting be by government, with one vote for each, or by *bailliage,* or by head? Depending on what system was adopted, the results could be very different: the government of the Ile-de-France included 14 *bailliages;* the government of Burgundy, 12; the government of Normandy, 7; the government of Picardy, 5; the government of Guyenne, 16; and the government of Orléans, 19. The results of a vote could be reversed if the representatives voted by *bailliages* and *sénéchaussées* rather than by government.

The orders communicated with one another through ambassadors. An official orator set forth the proposals of his order. The ambassador then withdrew, and the order he had visited began its deliberations. Then it would dispatch an ambassador in turn to deliver its response, and so on. This procedure was quite slow and tended to accentuate divergences of opinion. The orders had great difficulty reaching agreement.

On 4 November 1614, the clergy proposed a common plan of action to the third estate. Under this proposal, the three orders would first reach agreement before presenting identical proposals to the king. They were then supposed to await the king's answer before submitting further proposals. In this way the Estates General would have been presenting its demands "in the name of all France." Such demands would have carried with them great moral authority. It would have been difficult for the king to refuse to grant the wishes of the entire nation. What is more, the Estates could have gone on meeting until satisfaction had been obtained, since the custom was not to dismiss the session until a complete *cahier* had been prepared by each order. The Estates could have gone on presenting new demands and could thus have remained in session continuously. This would have made a custom of their participation in the formulation of legislation and regulations. France would have been transformed from an absolute monarchy into a State of

Estates, a *Ständestaat*, a monarchy tempered by the influence of the Estates General. But the third estate feared that it would always be outvoted by the clergy and the nobility. Its exaggerated Gallicanism made it suspicious of the clergy. On 8 November it rejected this proposal. The king was subsequently able to forbid an innovation that would have made the Estates General into a sort of permanent national assembly. As a result the Estates remained powerless.

Conflicts between the Orders: Venality of Office and the Paulette

Political clashes between the orders forced them to turn to the king, who remained in control. The first conflict to erupt was between the nobility and the third estate. The nobility clung to the schematic old idea of a sort of social division of labor, according to which the clergy was supposed to be responsible for relations with God, the nobility for defense, security, law and order, military leadership, and police, and the third estate for the production of material wealth, agriculture, skilled crafts, and trade. Now, in the view of the nobility, the third estate was abandoning its own sphere of responsibility and encroaching on that of the *gentilshommes*. The third estate was taking over royal offices, military commands, the courts, and police matters, and officeholders were even claiming superiority over the "people," that is, over the three orders.

As a consequence, the *gentilshommes* demanded that they be given all the offices of *prévôts des maréchaux*, *vis-baillis*, and *vis-sénéchaux*, or, in other words, a near monopoly of police of the highways; all the *grandes maîtrises* and *maîtrises particulières des Eaux et Forêts*, because the high price of wood had driven *seigneurs* generally to reserve the forests of their domains for their own use and because water and wood were the basis of civilization; all first magistracies in the cities; all offices of *bailli* and *sénéchal;* half the offices of *trésoriers de France;* at least a third of the offices of the sovereign courts, *parlements*, Chambres des Comptes, and Cours des Aides; a third of the offices of all *corps de magistrats* in justice and finance; protection for their seigneurial courts against the officers of the *bailliages* and *sénéchaussées;* authorization to engage in commerce without derogation of nobility, which authorization might be taken as an encroachment on the third estate's territory; and a prohibition against members of the third estate wearing the same clothes as *gentilshommes* and *demoiselles*, so that it would be possible to distinguish a person's quality at a glance.

The *gentilshommes* took the offensive against the Paulette. On 12 November 1614, the marquis d'Urfé proposed asking the king to suspend the issuance of receipts for the annual dues in the provinces. This was a prelude to an abolition of the Paulette, which was requested in several *cahiers*. The nobility blamed the annual dues for the increase in the price of offices, which had climbed far more steeply than the price of grain or the value of ground rent, thus putting many offices out of reach of the nobility. On 13 November the nobility voted to adopt the marquis d'Urfé's proposal. The clergy followed suit the next day. The proposal was then communicated to the third estate, which agreed to go along. As a matter of fact, quite a few of the third estate's own *cahiers* in the *bailliages* and *sénéchaussées* asked for abolition of the sale of offices, elimination of the annual dues, and election of officeholders, or, if not election, then at least selection by the king from a list of elected candidates. The delegates of the third estate could not go against the wishes of their constituents, but, as officeholders, they found a way to ward off a danger to their own position. They also asked for elimination of the forty-days clause and suspension of issuance of receipts for the *tailles* for the purpose of diminishing them by 4,000,000 livres. Elimination of the annual dues and a decrease in the *tailles*, however, would have increased the deficit to 5,600,000 livres. The third estate therefore asked that that amount be taken out of the pensions of the nobility. It said that its demands were a package and could not be separated from one another.

The *gentilshommes* responded by declaring the third estate's proposals "ridiculous." They proposed treating the suspension of the annual dues as a separate issue. On 17 November 1614, the clergy and the nobility submitted their proposals to the king, and the third estate submitted its proposals separately. This day proved decisive. By separately submitting different sets of demands to the king, the estates gave the monarch a chance to act as arbiter between them. The king thought it wise to drag matters out as long as possible and to grant each order only a part of what it wanted. In this way he could keep them at odds and dependent on his arbitration. By leaving the orders divided and powerless, the king could await the moment when they would submit their *cahiers* and then disperse them without allowing them an opportunity to diminish his authority.

The strife between the orders grew increasingly bitter. On 17 November, President Savaron said that it was not the annual dues "that have deprived the nobility of judicial honors but rather [the nobility's] long-held opinion that study and learning make a man less courageous and make his generosity seem like cowardice and poltroonery." He also attacked pensions, saying that "it is neither proper nor just that the nobility serves the king for money given in the form of pensions, when loyalty and service were in fact the king's natural due." This was a pointed remark, because it was commonly held that a *gentilhomme* ought to live by his *rentes*. Rumor further amplified the point. Malevolent gossips accused Savaron of having said "that His Majesty had been obliged to buy their [the nobles'] loyalty with money and that these expenses had reduced the people to grazing and eating grass like animals." The *gentilshommes* sprang to the attack. Some hurled insults at Savaron and threatened his life. One expressed the opinion that M. Savaron ought to be turned over to the pages and lackeys. The nobility demanded that the third estate send a conciliatory delegation and a declaration that it had not intended to offend the *gentilshommes*. The clergy put itself forward as a mediator. The third estate sent a deputation with the *lieutenant civil* of

Paris, Henri de Mesmes, as speaker on 24 November 1614. Unfortunately, de Mesmes uttered in the Chamber of the Nobility the famous words,

> that the Three Orders were three brothers, children of their common mother, France. . . . That the Clergy was . . . the eldest, the Nobility the next eldest, and the Third Estate the youngest. That, for this reason, the Third Estate had always recognized that Messieurs of the Nobility were in some degree elevated above it . . . but also that the Nobility must recognize the Third Estate as its brother and not hold it in such contempt as to count it for nothing, since it was made up of a number of remarkable persons, who held responsibility and rank . . . and, furthermore, that in many private families it often came to pass that the elder brothers squandered house and home while the younger brothers restored them to health and glory.

These words caused a furor. The *gentilshommes* protested against new insults even more serious than the earlier ones. The nobility went to complain to the king on 26 November. Bauffremont, baron de Sennecey, protested the third estate's insult in the following terms: the third estate, he said, was an

> order made up of the populace of cities and fields, the latter being nearly all subjects and vassals, the former being bourgeois, merchants, artisans, and a few officeholders. These are the people who, ignoring their status and without the consent of those whom they represent, want to compare themselves to us. I am ashamed, Sire. . . . Render judgment, Sire, and by a most just declaration make them do their duty.

Sennecey had the unanimous approval of the nobility. The *gentilshommes* closed with the words:

> We do not want to be called brothers by cobblers and bootmakers. Between us and them there is as much difference as between the master and the valet.

The king forced the third estate to apologize. On 5 December, the *lieutenant général* of Angers and Florimond Rapine went to express their regrets to the nobility: the words of their delegate, they said, had been misinterpreted. This question continued to divide the nobility and the third estate to the end, however. More than that, the orders had once again been forced to turn to the king as arbiter, and the nobility had even called upon the king's absolute authority to keep each order in its place.

The Conflict between the Orders: The King's Sovereignty

This clash between the nobility and the third estate was followed by another between the latter and the clergy. In the important European question of the power of the popes over kings, the main objective of the Gallican officeholders of the third estate was to assert the total sovereignty of the king of

France against the pretentions of the pope. This they attempted to do in the first article of their *cahier général*, which was based on the *cahier* of the government of Paris and the Ile-de-France. The latter *cahier* was read in the presence of delegates from the eleven other governments. Each delegate followed along in the *cahier* of his own government. Article by article, additions and corrections were made to establish the *cahier général* of the third estate. On 15 December 1614, the first article was adopted by ten votes out of twelve: the king was asked to issue a proclamation through the Estates General declaring it to be the fundamental law of the land that the king of France holds his crown of God alone; that he is sovereign in his own state; and that, in consequence, no power, spiritual or temporal, pope or emperor, can deprive him of his kingdom or exempt his subjects from the ties of loyalty and duty of obedience they owe their king. All the king's subjects were supposed to recognize this fundamental law as in keeping with the word of God; all delegates to the Estates General, all holders of offices and benefices throughout the kingdom were supposed to swear their allegiance to the law and sign its text; and all preceptors, regents, doctors, and preachers were to be obliged to teach it.

At the same time, the Paris *parlement* in its decree of 2 January 1615 reiterated all the decrees against tyrannicide and the Jesuits that it had promulgated since the 1561 decree condemning the *bachelier* Tanquerel and requiring him to make amends for having argued that the pope has the power to depose the king.

The article drafted by the third estate was communicated in late December of 1614 to the clergy and the nobility. Emotions ran high. The clergy deemed the text unacceptable. Cardinal du Perron, archbishop of Sens, was sent as an ambassador to the nobility, which rallied to the clergy's side. On 2 January 1615, the clergy sent a delegation to the Chamber of the Third Estate in the wake of a sermon by Camus reproaching the third estate for taking an interest in problems beyond its capacity. Du Perron laid out the clergy's views for the third estate. He identified three points in the article drafted by his opponents.

First, there was the question of the king's physical safety. The clergy and nobility agreed that "in no case is it permissible to assassinate a king," even a tyrant. The clergy and the nobility supported the decree of the Council of Constance, session 15: whoever assassinated a king was anathematized, accursed, and damned as a matter of divine and theological certainty.

Second, as to the question of the dignity and temporal sovereignty of the kings of France, clergy and nobility were agreed: "Our kings are sovereigns in all temporal matters in their kingdom and are not vassals of the pope or any other prince, and in the administration of things temporal they depend immediately on God and recognize no other power than His above them." This, too, was a certainty, but of a human and historical nature: Pope Innocent III had recognized that the king of France had no superior in the temporal realm.

The third point, however, was open to dispute. If a prince who had sworn an oath to live and die in the Catholic religion became a heretic or an apostate and tried to force his subjects to do the same, could his subjects be released from their oath of loyalty, and, if so, who had the power to release them? The third estate had answered in the negative. The rest of the Catholic church, however, including the Gallican church, answered in the affirmative: the offending prince could be stripped of his rights as one guilty of a felony, and it was up to the pope or a Church council to release the king's subjects from their oath.

Both the negative and the affirmative were "problematic" opinions. The opinion of the third estate was not contrary to the faith, nor was the opinion of the majority of the Catholic church. Thus the third estate could not legitimately maintain that its article was "in keeping with the word of God," nor could it force others to swear an oath holding that it was so. To make such an oath obligatory would be "to compel souls and ensnare consciences." The third estate was usurping the spiritual powers to judge the faith and decide dogma. If laymen dared to take the judgment of the faith upon themselves, the door would be opened to heresies of every sort, and this would obviously and inevitably lead to schism, "because, inasmuch as all other Catholic peoples adhere to this doctrine, we cannot declare it contrary to the word of God, impious, and detestable" without renouncing "the communion of the head and the other parts of the Church" and without confessing "that the Church has for centuries been not the Church of God, but the synagogue of Satan, the bride not of Christ but of the Devil." The third estate was following in the footsteps of the English Protestants, James I, Buchanan, and so on. It would once again plunge France into the throes of civil war.

After Du Perron's speech the clergy decided, on 5 January 1615, to have the decree of the 15th session of the Council of Constance condemning tyrannicide republished. On the same day it submitted a petition to the king asking that *parlement*'s decree of 2 January be quashed and stricken from the court registers along with the indictment of *avocat général* Servin, that *parlement* be forbidden to make judgments concerning religion, Church doctrine, and matters of state, and that the *avocat général* be prohibited from taking cognizance of Church matters even on the pretext of an *appel comme d'abus*.

On 6 January, the king held a special meeting of the Conseil d'En-Haut. The prince de Condé demonstrated the logic that led from the doctrine of the pope's indirect power over kings, the position supported by the Jesuits and Cardinal du Perron, to regicide:

> Your Majesty, according to what they say, is committing a sin. The king is admonished for the third time. Your Majesty continues, he is excommunicated. He does not repent, and he is deposed. Your subjects are absolved of the loyalty that is their due. So long as Louis XIII was king,

no one was permitted to kill him. But once the king is no longer king, another legitimate king takes his place. If he then continues his battle against the spiritual authority of the pope and the temporal authority of the newly chosen monarch, who calls himself king, he is truly a usurper, guilty of *lèse-majesté* human and divine, and, as such, proscribed: anyone may kill him.

The clergy and the nobility were adamant. On 14 January 1615, the cardinals obtained a conference with the king's Council. It was decided that the king would have the article withdrawn from the *cahier* of the third estate. On 15 January the delegates of the third estate were called to the Louvre. The queen told them that her son was grateful for their intentions but that he had assumed personal jurisdiction in this matter and would make his own judgment: he therefore ordered them to bring him the article. They did so the very same evening. On the 19th, the queen said in their presence that her son thanked them with all his heart for the care they had shown for his well-being but that there was no further need to place the article in the *cahier*, since they had presented it to him and it would have to be left at that.

This ecclesiastical legerdemain caused a scandal in the Chamber of the Third Estate. For three days the delegates discussed whether it was best to keep the article at the top of their *cahier* and protest the way the king was being circumvented or to give in and submit remonstrances. The first course was favored by the majority of *bailliages* and *sénéchaussées*, but voting in the third estate was by governments and the second course won out. Savaron, de Mesmes, and 120 other delegates declared their opposition to this resolution on the grounds that it was carried by a minority. They won the concession that, even though the article would not be inserted into the *cahier général*, a place would be formally set aside for it. In the certified copies, following the first page and the title, "On the fundamental laws of the state," there was a blank space and a note that read as follows: "The first article, excerpted from the minutes of the Chamber of the Third Estate, was presented to the king in advance of the first *cahier* upon orders of His Majesty, who has promised to respond." The *avocat général* Servin had the first article printed and distributed under the title, "fundamental law of the kingdom." Louis XIV had it adopted by the assembly of the clergy in the Gallican declaration of 19 March 1682.

The Triumph of Royal Absolutism

Because the orders were divided, they were unable to resolve the fundamental parliamentary problems: how could the king be forced to abide by the measures proposed in the *cahiers*, how could their execution be followed up, and how could the Estates take part in drafting the kingdom's laws and regulations?

On 30 January 1615, the nobility and the clergy asked the king for permission to assemble as a body until he had responded to the *cahiers*, as well as for permission to name six persons to be appointed by the king to his Council for the purpose of participating in its deliberations over the responses to the *cahiers* and explaining the views of the Estates General to the Council while keeping the former informed of the work of the latter. The purpose of this proposal was to formalize collaboration between the Estates General and the royal government and to afford the Estates some measure of control and influence. But the third estate refused to join with the two other orders. The king merely allowed the delegates to remain in Paris as individuals until he had given his response and appointed delegates to explain the articles to royal *commissaires* outside the Council.

On 9 February the clergy and the nobility asked for authorization to assemble as a body in Estates General after the submission of the *cahiers*, to send twelve delegates to discussions with royal *commissaires*, and to reject those *commissaires* in whom they had no confidence. This time the third estate went along. Once at the Louvre, however, the bishop of Grenoble could not keep from adding to the other demands a call for revocation of the annual dues. The agreement among the orders broke down. The king was able to reject the petition.

On 23 February 1615, the *cahiers* of the clergy, the nobility, and the third estate were submitted to the king. The delegates who remained in Paris continued to meet as private individuals in unofficial sessions, delegates for each estate meeting at the residence of the president of their order. On 24 March they were called to the Louvre. The chancellor of France announced to them that the sale of offices had been suspended, that pensions would be reduced, and that a *chambre de justice* had been set up to look into the dealings of the financiers. "As for the rest of the demands, he [the king] will attend to them as soon as possible." The delegates were dismissed and went home. There was no further discussion of the second article submitted by the third estate: establishing regular intervals for meetings of the Estates General, to be held once every ten years. The clergy and nobility had not touched on this point. Meetings of the Estates General remained at the discretion of the king.

Thus the orders of the kingdom had placed all power in the hands of the king. They had turned to his absolute authority to settle their disputes and unanimously ratified that authority. The third estate had declared the king sovereign and stated that he had no superior in the temporal realm, that he held his powers immediately from God, and that those who rose up against him were "rebels, violators of the fundamental laws of the kingdom, and criminals guilty of *lèse-majesté* in the first degree." The clergy had gone even further, threatening rebels with eternal torture and begging the king to use his absolute authority against the first article submitted by the third estate and against the decree of *parlement*. The nobility had asked the king to use his absolute authority against the social pretentions of the third estate.

All three orders were unanimous in recognizing the omnipotence of the king, in calling upon his services, and in leaving the resolution of outstanding problems to his discretion. The delegates to the Estates General abandoned France to royal absolutism. Ultimately, this outcome can be traced in large measure back to Ravaillac's stabbing of Henri IV.

The inability of the three orders to agree proved fatal to the Estates General. The king henceforth governed without its advice. Not until an attempt at revolution had been made with the Fronde was the king compelled, on 23 January 1649, to convoke a meeting of the Estates General for the following 15 March at Orléans. By February deputies had been elected and *cahiers* drafted in various parts of the country. After the peace of Rueil of 11 March and the end of the so-called Fronde *parlementaire*, however, the king used the campaign against the Spanish as a pretext for postponing the meeting until 1 October and then, on 18 September for adjourning it until further notice. In the summer of 1650, the nobility, irritated by these delays, held meetings around the country in order to force the king to open the meeting of the Estates General. In Paris an assembly of the nobility inched toward rebellion. The queen resigned herself to convoking a meeting of the Estates set for 1 October 1651 in Tours. From July until September of 1651 assemblies of the three orders were held in the *bailliages* and *sénéchaussées* for the purpose of selecting delegates and drafting *cahiers*. Events took another course, however: the king solemnly declared his majority before *parlement*, Mazarin ended his flight and returned to France, the royal armies were victorious over the forces of the rebel princes, and the meeting of the Estates General was once again postponed until 1 November 1652, after which no more was heard about it.

Thus the monarchy's main source of advice disappeared at the very moment the king was moving farther and farther away from government "by Grand Conseil" and the courts and moving slowly toward executive forms of bureaucratic government.

The Estates General were to meet again in 1789, but in a quite different spirit, as representatives of the kingdom. The meeting quickly turned into a National Assembly. It seems best to delay consideration of this development until the end of the present work.

Note

1. A remonstrance was a humble supplication submitted to the king by one of his subjects, begging the monarch to consider the unfortunate drawbacks and consequences of some royal edict or order.

14 Government by *Grand Conseil:* The Assemblies of Notables

Here we shall treat only those assemblies of notables that took place prior to the pre-Revolutionary period: the assembly of Rouen and Paris (3 December 1617–29 January 1618), the assembly of Fontainebleau (1625), whose purpose was to support Richelieu's foreign policy, and the assembly of Paris (30 November 1626–24 February 1627). The assemblies of 1787 and 1788 are apparently of a different type, and it seems best to defer treatment of them until the end of the book.

An assembly of notables was an expanded version of the king's Council. Several times each year, whenever the king needed to cast a wider net in search of information for making decisions or preparing edicts and ordinances concerning matters of particular gravity, he would enlarge his Council with personalities chosen because of their social and professional standing or their competence to pronounce on the matters at hand. Even in 1626, the king's original intention was to expand his Council by inviting the *présidents* and *procureurs généraux* of the *parlements* to attend on 15 November. He then decided to invite other influential figures, and the Council grew to the proportions of an assembly of notables. Such an assembly was not, however, an abbreviated version of the Estates General. Its nature was different, as the king made clear in his *brevet* of 7 December 1617, and his letters patent of the same date.[1] The assembly was a "council."[2]

The Estates General were made up of persons elected by the subjects of the realm. An assembly of notables consisted of persons chosen by the king for their "zeal" and "devotion," their "fidelity" to the sovereign. The Estates General submitted "complaints" and could take the initiative in formulating them. An assembly of notables gave whatever "advice" the king asked for concerning ways of repairing the defects of which the Estates General complained, ways of dealing with other problems and of responding to proposals made to the king, and, in general, ways of helping to assure the well-being and permanence of the state.

The assembly of notables was not identical in composition to the Estates General. To begin with, there was no third estate. The king chose members

229

from among the clergy, the nobility, and the officeholders. Disputes between officeholders and nobles for seating in the assembly of 1617 are clear evidence that the royal officeholders did not represent the third estate, in that they were held to be noble by profession and most of them were in fact *gentils-hommes* from old families. Herein lies the point of the king's decision not to grant the magistrates of the sovereign courts precedence over the *noblesse d'épée*, despite which he seated the nobles around him (or the *présidents*, when the king was absent) and, after them, the clergy on his right and officeholders on his left. The king stipulated, however, that this decision should in no way prejudice the position of the nobility in the Estates General, where it ranked second, always after the clergy and before the third estate.

An assembly of notables was essentially a selection of nobles of various kinds and ranks, drawn from different parts of the kingdom. The opening ceremonies of the assembly of 1617, held on 4 December, were attended by fifteen *nobles d'épée*, including Hercules de Rohan, duc de Montbazon, peer and *grand veneur de France*, a marshal of France, Charles de Cossé, comte de Brissac, and three well-known Protestants, Odet de La Noue, Charles de Coligny, sieur d'Andelot, and Philippe de Mornay, sieur de Plessis; there were also twenty-six *nobles de robe*, including the *premiers présidets* of the *parlements* of Paris, Toulouse, Grenoble, Dijon, Rouen, Aix, and Rennes; the *procureurs généraux* of these *parlements;* the *premiers présidents* and *procureurs généraux* of the Chambres des Comptes and Cours des Aides of Paris and Rouen; the *lieutenant civil* of Paris; the *prévôt des marchands* of Paris; and members of the clergy, drawn chiefly from the *noblesse d'épée* but also from the *noblesse de robe* (from families such as the Harlays and Mirons), including two cardinals, Du Perron and La Rochefoucauld, five archbishops (from Auch, Narbonne, Arles, Rouen, and Tours), and six bishops (from Angers, Chalons, Paris, Grenoble, Poitiers, and Triguier). Counting the king's brother, there were supposed to be equal numbers of representatives of the sword and the gown.

Classed by districts of *parlement*, there were, from the Paris district, the archbishop of Tours, three bishops (Paris, Oitiers, and Angers), four *gentils-hommes*, and seven officeholders. From the district of each other *parlement*, the king had chosen one archbishop or bishop, one or two *gentilshommes*, and the *président* and *procureur général* of the *parlement* in question. Six officeholders had been invited from the district of the Rouen *parlement* on account of its three sovereign courts. Thus, out of 54 notables, the king had chosen only 15 persons from the district of the Paris *parlement*, to which we should perhaps add the presidents and vice-presidents of the assembly, bringing the total to 20 representatives for the largest district in the kingdom.

The *premier président* and the *procureur général* of the Bordeaux *parlement* did not attend for reasons of illness.

The composition of the assembly of notables of 1626–27, while largely similar from a social standpoint, was rather different from a political standpoint. Out of 55 notables there were only 10 *gentilshommes*, including the maréchal de La Force; 19 *premiers présidents, présidents,* and *procureurs généraux* from the *parlements,* 4 *premiers présidents* and *procureurs généraux* from the Chambres des Comptes of Paris and Rouen, 4 *premiers présidents* and *procureurs généraux* from the Cours des Aides of Paris and Rouen, the *lieutenant civil* of Paris, and the *prévôt des marchands* of Paris, for a total of 29 *robins,* and 13 prelates, including the cardinal de La Valette. Except for the *présidents* attached to the duc d'Orléans, the king excluded princes, peers, dukes, and most of the other grandees, who had been compromised in the recent political intrigues. The prince de Condé was banished from court, the comte de Soissons was out of the kingdom, and the duc de Vendôme was in prison. The king had invited the duc de Guise and the duc de Nemours but had sent word through the keeper of the seals that he wished them to abstain, whereupon the two dukes disqualified themselves, citing reasons of precedence. This time the assembly included only one Protestant, the maréchal de La Force, who was *président adjoint;* nine of the archbishops and bishops were from the north of the Loire, and six of them had *robin* backgrounds. In this case the *robins* were in the majority. But the assembly was still a selection of nobles loyal to the king.

Besides the individuals mentioned above, Louis XIII invited to Rouen a number of men who did not deliberate with the assembly but rather met with the king to hear the assembly's proposals and give their own opinion. This group consisted of princes, dukes-and-peers, and crown officers, along with fourteen members chosen from the king's Council, including, as chairman, Jeannin, the *surintendant des Finances,* Maupeou, *contrôleur général des Finances,* Castille and Déageant, both *intendants des Finances,* and de Chevry, *président des Comptes.*

Things were essentially the same in 1627, when, on 24 February, Louis XIII received the notables' proposals in an expanded council including the principal minister, Richelieu, the Keeper of the Seals, de Marillac, the maréchal de Schomberg, a few princes, crown officers, *seigneurs* and *gentilshommes,* and secretaries of state, as well as the *surintendant des Finances.*

Thus the assembly of notables was an enlargement of the king's Council, comprising a central core surrounded by two concentric circles. The core was the ordinary king's Council. The first concentric circle consisted of the king's ministers along with those princes, crown officers, and important financial officials whom the king wished to consult. And finally, the outer circle was the assembly of notables itself. The advice of the notables was examined in the inner circle and then in the regular Council, where decisions were finally taken and the suggestions of the assembly were turned into ordinances, edicts, and decrees or else rejected.

The king was represented in the assembly by a *président* and several *présidents adjoints,* whom he appointed himself. In 1617–18 and 1626–27 the *président* was the king's only brother, Gaston, duc d'Anjou and later duc d'Orléans. The *présidents adjoints* in 1617 were Messeigneurs les Illustrimes Jacques, cardinal Du Perron and François, cardinal de La Rochefoucault; Messire Hercules de Rohan, duc de Montbazon, peer and *grand veneur de France;* and Messire Charles de Cosse, comte de Brissac and *maréchal de France.* In 1626–27 they were Louis, cardinal de La Valette, *lieutenant général* of the king's armies; Jacques Nompar de Caumont, duc de La Force and *maréchal de France;* and François de Bassompierre, *maréchal de France* and ambassador to England.

In 1617 the king allowed the notables to choose their own *greffier.* They did not wish to choose one of their own for the post, because the *greffier* could not express an opinion and that was what they had been called by the king to do. They asked the king for permission to take his council secretary for the quarter, sieur Jean de Flécelles, as *greffier*, and the king complied.

In 1626 the king chose as *greffier* the *trésorier général de France*, Paul Arder, the chief *commis* of Phélypeaux d'Herbault, secretary of state for foreign affairs.

The *greffier* had his desk in the center of the square formed by the benches of the notables, facing the *présidents.*

The notables also enjoyed the services of a *huissier.* In 1617 the post was held by Georges Le Cirier, His Majesty's *premier huissier* in the Conseil d'Etat et privé.

Prior to the opening of the Assembly of Notables, the king and the attending notables took part in a high mass, where a prelate delivered a sermon appropriate to the occasion. On 30 April 1626, the bishop of Nantes preached on the day's Gospel, "Come unto me," and then urged the notables to offer their opinion to the king in "candor and truthfulness." He also exhorted the king to be just to his people and merciful to those who offended against his law.

The agenda and issues to be dealt with were left to the king's initiative. Every morning he gave the *procureur général* of the Paris *parlement* a list of proposals drawn up by a few members of his Council; in 1617 this work was done by the chancellor, Sillery, the keeper of the seals, Villeroy, and the *président*, Jeannin. The *procureur général* then took this list to the *président* of the notables and his assistants, who in turn presented them to the assembly. The assembly then discussed the proposals and in theory formulated its own position on the issues during the same day. In 1617 Richelieu observed that this procedure "was not apt to foster wise and mature deliberation."

In both 1617 and 1626, the king's intention was to have the clergy, *noblesse d'épée*, and officeholders vote separately by corps in three chambers. In 1617 the officeholders rebelled. They felt that this procedure would have diminished their status, since they were not there to represent the third estate. They argued that they ought to have the same rank as in those situations where they preceded the nobility by dint of their having jurisdiction over it. More than that, the *parlements* represented the Estates General and took the place of the clergy and the nobility. The officeholders threatened to boycott the assembly. The same thing happened in 1626. The officeholders had no desire to be separated from the clergy and the nobility "in order to be cast down into a third and lowest order." That anyone should wish to pass them off as a third estate was absurd, since the Paris *parlement* included princes of the blood and crown officers among its members. In 1626 this dispute became entangled with another between the Paris *parlement* and its provincial counterparts. The Paris *parlement* claimed certain prerogatives, for which the symbol was that it was known simply as *parlement*, without the name of the place in which it was located. The provincial *parlements* did not recognize these prerogatives and persisted in using the appellation *parlement de Paris*.

After much difficulty, the king ultimately recognized that the magistrates stood on a more or less equal footing with the clergy and the *noblesse d'épée*. Deliberations took place in an assembly of ecclesiastics, nobles, and office-holders. Voting was by head, and a plurality of votes carried the question. In 1617, when the issue involved church matters, the *présidents* were supposed to give the floor first to members of the clergy and subsequently to those deemed most likely to shed light on the question; when the issue involved the nobility, the floor was to be given first to the nobles and then to the most competent individuals among the rest of the body; if the issue concerned the courts, the floor was to be given first to members of the *parlements* and then to others in the same fashion; if finance was involved, members of the Chambres des Comptes and Cours des Aides were to speak first and then others competent to address such questions were to follow. In 1626–27, the duc d'Orléans generally called first upon the *premier président* of the Paris *parlement* to give his opinion and cast his vote and then upon the other members of the Paris *parlement*, followed by the other *parlements* in order of seniority, the *lieutenant civil*, the Chambre des Comptes, and the Cours des Aides; after these came the *nobles d'épée*, the *conseillers d'Etat* preceding the *chevaliers de l'Ordre;* after them came the clergy, starting with those of lowest rank; and, finally, the *présidents adjoints* were the last to give their opinions and cast their votes. The *greffier* recorded the vote of each member. The general opinion was decided by a plurality of the votes cast.

Meetings were supposed to be held every day from nine o'clock until noon. In actuality, however, the notables met thirty-five times between 7 December 1626, and 23 February 1627. The procedure was for the *greffier* to read the proposition under consideration. The notables then inquired about previous ordinances, opinions rendered by previous assemblies, and other relevant information, such as statements of tax receipts, debts, pensions, expenses, and reports from provincial *parlements* and governors concerning fortifications that were no longer serviceable. In 1626–27 certain issues received special attention. Committees were set up to deal with finances, "police" and the army, and fortifications. The *commissaires* reported to the assembly and were the first to offer their opinions.

The *greffier* noted down on slips of paper the key points of the discussion, the personal opinions of the members of the assembly, and the votes cast. Using these notes he then produced the minutes or "outcome" of the session. At the beginning of each meeting the *greffier* would read the "outcome" of the previous meeting that he had prepared and edited. The assembly then voted its approval before moving on to consider another royal proposition.

The outcomes for each session were then combined at the end of the assembly into a general "outcome," signed by the *président* and the *présidents adjoints*. The *greffier* then compiled the various "propositions" and "outcomes" in a *cahier* representing the opinion of the assembly, which was then submitted to the king by the *président* in the closing ceremonies. The *cahier* was then read to the enlarged king's Council, whose members were called upon to give their opinions at once.

The power of decision was still the king's. In 1617, the king issued an order on 28 December commanding the notables to come to Paris. On 29 January 1618, while the king was at the castle of Madrid, the notables assembled to receive his orders. The chancellor announced that the king had granted permission for them to return to their homes and posts. He was satisfied with their diligence, affection, and loyalty. He promised to send the *parlements* an edict concerning the *cahiers* submitted by the Estates General as well as their own propositions. An edict was drawn up in July 1618, but it was never submitted to the sovereign courts, no doubt because the king's favorite, Luynes, had had the notables convoked chiefly to approve the change of government, the execution of the maréchal d'Ancre, and the banishment of the queen mother.

After the assembly of 1626–27, Marillac, the keeper of the seals, made use of the *cahiers* of the Estates General of 1614–15, the proposed edict drawn up in the wake of the Rouen Assembly of 1617, and the *cahier* of the assembly of 1626–27 in preparing (in 1629) the "Royal Ordinance concerning the complaints and grievances made by the Estates of his kingdom convoked and assembled in the city of Paris in the years 1614 and 1615 and concerning the advice given His Majesty by the assemblies of notables held at Rouen in the year 1617 and at Paris in the year 1626."[3] But this Marillac Ordinance, commonly known as the Code Michaud, was not accepted by the Paris *parlement* and remained without effect, at least within its jurisdiction.

Notes

1. Mathieu Molé, *Mémoires* (Société historique de France, 1855), vol. 1, pp. 158–60.

2. Letters of convocation, 1626–27, in Jeanne Petit, *L'assemblée des Notables de 1626–1627* (Ecole Pratique des Hautes Etudes: Sciences historiques et philologiques, 1937).

3. Isambert, vol. 16, p. 223.

15   The Force of Royal Orders

All decisions of the government and central administration were couched in the form of royal orders. These orders were issued in various forms, such as laws, judgments, and royal commands. Some orders were uttered by the king himself. These were binding without further formalities, since no one could legitimately oppose the express wishes of the king. The order given by Louis XIII to Vitry, the captain of his guard, instructing him to kill Concini, the maréchal d'Ancre, was of this kind. Vitry carried it out because the order was tantamount to a judgment by the king in his capacity as chief justice of the realm and fountainhead of all law. Most royal orders were written, however. This was necessary because the affairs of state were so various and because governmental agents were dispersed over a wide area. Written orders were issued in a variety of forms. The form chosen in any particular case depended on the circumstances: whether the case fell within the jurisdiction of magistrates to whom the king had delegated judicial powers, whether it was necessary to give proof of the king's wishes, and whether political conditions demanded one form of order rather than another.

During the seventeenth and eighteenth centuries we see a gradual intensification of processes which began in the preceding centuries and led to the development of absolutism, or, rather, to increasing bureaucratic centralism, which was confused with absolutism. We witness a gradual shift from orders issued as personal letters to orders couched in the form of anonymous memoranda, from authenticated open letters to sealed letters not authenticated by any regular procedure, from validation by seal, representing presumptive witness of the king's wishes, to validation by signature, from the register of originals to bundles of "original minutes," from verification by the Grande Chancellerie to verification by specialized bureaus, and from decisions made in council, at least in principle, to more or less openly avowed individual decision-making.

Written Orders Cleared by the Chancellery

Written royal orders with binding force can be divided into two categories: those cleared by the chancellery and those sent directly by the king to his agents or subjects and from his agents to their subordinates or other subjects.

All legislative acts were cleared through the chancellery. So were *lettres de justice* or *mandements de rendre la justice*, which were issued by the king when an injured individual, rather than take his case to a local judge, turned directly to the sovereign. If the petitioner's case seemed well-founded, the king would have a *lettre de justice* issued in his behalf, ordering the competent judge to find in favor of the petitioner, provided the facts were indeed as presented in the petition. The judge's role was thus limited to one of fact-finding. *Lettres de justice* came in a variety of forms: *reliefs d'appel, compulsoires* (subpoenas), *commissions pour assigner*, letters *pareatis* (which made a judgment executory in another jurisdiction), annulments, civil petitions, and so on. The chancellery also cleared *lettres de grace* granted by the king, who used them not only to pardon those found guilty in criminal cases but also to award certain social privileges and ranks through the bestowal of gifts, pensions, lands, as well as *lettres de committimus*, naturalization, legitimation, nobility, rehabilitation, and the like. Finally, the chancellery approved orders and dispatches having to do with administration and finance.

All these various types of letters had to be drafted on parchment according to specific and immutable forms. They were supposed to be open letters sealed with the Great Seal and thus subject to authentication by the chancellor, assisted by the *grand audiencier* and a number of *maîtres des requêtes*.[1] These letters owed their authenticity and binding force to the respect of time-honored forms and formalities.

Grandes Lettres Patentes

Grandes lettres patentes opened with a heading, an address, and the formula "Henry [or Louis], par la grâce de Dieu, roi de France et de Navarre, à tous présens et à venir, salut." If the letter concerned the Dauphiné, the preamble included the words, "Roi de France, Dauphin de Viennois, Comte de Valentinois et de Diois." If it concerned Provence, it bore the inscription, "Roi de France, comte de Provence, Forcalquier et terres adjacentes." In the case of Brittany, however, there was no special formula, because the province was regarded as having been incorporated into the kingdom since 1532. The preamble was followed by an explanation of the situation that had given rise to the king's intervention, and then came the royal order, which in edicts was introduced by the formula, "Avons dit, statué et ordonné, statuons, ordonnons, voulons et nous plaist," followed by the substance of the order. The letter ended with the formula, "Si donnons en mandement par ces présentes," followed by a clause attesting to the permanence of the order and the manner of its corroboration: "Et afin que ce soit chose ferme et stable à toujours, nous avons fait mettre nostre scel à ces dites présentes." Assertion that the order reflected the express will of the king was contained in the words, "Car tel est notre plaisir." Then came the date, indicating the month and year (both the calendar year and the year of the king's reign), but normally not the day of the month.

At the bottom came the king's signature, frequently traced by a *secrétaire de la main*. A *secrétaire d'Etat* signed on the fold, together with the words "Par le roy, N." The countersignature of the secretary of state was not a political countersignature but merely a mark of notarization attesting to the authenticity of the royal signature.

The "perpetuity clause" was included in acts intended to remain in effect indefinitely, in which case the seal was set in green wax over green and red cord. It was understood, however, that an edict was perpetual and irrevocable only as long as the king was not compelled to modify it for the sake of the common good.

Ordinances and edicts were issued in the form of *grandes lettres patentes* by the chancellery. Ordinances were important laws of general interest to the entire kingdom. They were often promulgated in response to remonstrances. Edicts were laws issued by the king at his own instigation and concerned with a specific matter, applicable either to the entire kingdom or simply to one or more provinces.

Grandes lettres patentes had to be registered not only by the chancellery but also by the sovereign courts responsible for the execution of royal decisions and the enforcement of the laws of the state. This procedure provided for the promulgation, publication, execution, and conservation of royal acts. A *grande lettre patente* sent to a court was read in a public audience and transcribed by the *greffier* into a special register. This transcription became the original to which reference was to be made in the future. The *greffier* wrote an indication of the registration on the fold or back of the letter and signed it. The formula used was, "Lu et publié à la requête" or "du consentement" or "ouï le procureur général du roi, à . . . , en . . . ," depending on whether the *procureur du roi* approved the contents without reservation, approved with reservations, or disapproved, respectively. This was followed by the day, month, and year and the signature of the *greffier*. If registration was carried out under orders issued as jussive letters or in *lit de justice*, the words "de l'exprès commandement du roi" were added as a disclaimer and a reproach. Registration or "verification" was intended as a procedural measure. The sovereign courts did all they could to use it as a lever giving them some influence over the king's powers to make laws and regulations and have them enforced.

Registration was carried out in the provincial courts and special jurisdictions as well as in Paris. But the Paris *parlement* had the privilege of always being the first to register any order.

The officeholders responsible for executing an order attached their mark to the royal document sent them by means of a parchment ribbon. This was called their "attache," and it bore the signets or cachets in red wax of the officers present at the audience.

Petites Lettres Patentes

Petites lettres patentes were generally issued for some special purpose and had a temporary effect. For that reason they were sealed with yellow wax over a double tassel. The address and salutation were as follows: "A tous ceux qui ces présentes lettres verront, salut." The corroboration and seal were indicated by the formula, "En tesmoing de laquelle chose nous avons fait mettre notre scel à ces presentes." The date included the day of the month.

Petites lettres patentes were used for royal declarations and legislative acts intended to explain, interpret, or modify the provisions of ordinances and edicts.

Petites lettres patentes were ordinarily used for *lettres de justice* and *lettres de grâce*. A. Giry lists thirty-two different kinds.[2] It is worth citing a few examples. Among the items that took the form of *petites lettres patentes* were: *lettres d'abolition*, or documents whereby the king "annuls, pardons, suspends, effaces, and abolishes" a crime and eliminates the penalty imposed on the guilty party, which in many cases was a corps or city guilty of insurrection; letters of ennoblement; letters of commission for the exercise of a special temporary function, the prosecution of a criminal case, the levy of a tax, etc.; letters of *committimus*, which granted permission to plead a case before specific judges and which could also be issued as "lettres du petit sceau," with one or more *fleurs de lys*, by the *petites chancelleries* attached to the royal courts and jurisdictions as subordinate departments of the *chancellerie de France;* letters waiving the age requirement for the holding of an office, awarding an academic position, or declaring a blood kinship, etc.; jussive letters, whereby the king ordered a recalcitrant court to register some ordinance, edict, declaration, or other letters patent; *lettres de marque* or reprisal authorizing the seizure of the property of foreigners equivalent in value to that acquired by them when their own sovereign refused to see that justice was done; *lettres de naturalité*, whereby the king conferred upon a foreigner the same rights and privileges as if he had been born in the kingdom, without, however, making him a naturalized Frenchman; *lettres de provision*, whereby the king bestowed some office; *lettres de requête civile*, ordering judges of the sovereign courts to allow the petitioner to present arguments against a final judgment on the grounds of error or fraud by the other party to the case left unchallenged at the time; *lettres de terrier*, which could also be issued by the *petites chancelleries*, allowing a lord to force his vassals and tenants to produce their deeds for the purpose of preparing a *terrier*, or official record of the assignment of the domains of a *seigneurie*, based on the declarations of the individuals concerned and indicating in detail the dues, *cens*, *rentes*, *prestations*, *corvées*, and so on, connected with the land.

Petites lettres patentes were also used for issuing various instructions, in which case they bore a special salutation and the injunction, "Si vous mandons et ordonnons." Letters of instruction were sealed in yellow wax on a single tassel.

In theory, *petites lettres patentes* were supposed to undergo the formalities of registration and *attache*.

Mixed Documents: Council Decrees

Council decrees could be couched in the form of letters patent, in which case they would be subject to registration and *attache*. But they could also be sent directly to the parties concerned, whether agents of the king or private individuals, or else notification could be made through a *huissier*. Since the beginning of the seventeenth century no minutes or summary had been kept of council meetings. Each *rapporteur* drew up his decree in advance. The Council would then amend the proposal if necessary before granting its approval, whereupon the decree was sometimes transcribed onto a register. But since this copy was not signed, whereas the draft of the decree was signed by the *rapporteur*, the chancellor, and the secretary of state concerned with the matter, it was the common practice down to the end of the ancien régime to regard the "original draft" as the authentic copy. The collections of drafts replaced the council registers. Each secretary of state kept in his offices drafts of decrees involving his department. He had draft decrees he had presented to the Council bound under his coat of arms into volumes containing almost exclusively *arrêts en commandement*.

Drafts of decrees were in the form of notes rather than in epistolary form. Drafts often began with a statement of the facts introduced by the formula, "Sur ce qui a esté représenté au Roy en son Conseil" or "Sur le rapport fait au Roy estant en son Conseil" in the case of an *arrêt en commandement*. This might be followed by a list of documents, decrees, ordinances, notes, and other information shown to the king in the course of laying out the facts. Then came the king's decision, introduced by the formula "Le Roy en son Conseil" or "Sa Majesté estant en son Conseil" for an *arrêt en commandement*. The decree ended with the words, "Faict au Conseil d'Estat du Roy tenu à Paris le," followed by the day, month, and year, or with the words "Faict au Conseil d'Estat du Roy, Sa Majesté y séant" for an *arrêt en commandement*, with the date indicated in the same manner. In all cases, the signatures of the chancellor, the secretary of state, and the *rapporteur* were required; in judicial matters one or more *maîtres des requêtes* also had to sign, and in financial matters one or more *intendants des Finances*, or, at any rate, their signatures were necessary in principle.

When a decree rendered a judgment in a civil case or was issued upon petition, it began by stating the parties to the case and other parties involved: "Between attorney so-and-so and attorney so-and-so," etc. Then came the words "Veu par le roy en son Conseil," a list of petitions submitted by the parties and of documents used at various stages of the proceedings, such as writs, decrees, subpoenas, and the like, followed by the king's decision: "Le Roy en son Conseil." After this came the place, date, and signatures, just as for other kinds of decrees.

Council decrees were issued with the preamble "Extrait des registres du Conseil," even though this reference was usually fictitious and no council register contained the original but only a copy signed by the council secretary. The secretaries of state continued to assume responsibility for sending *arrêts en commandement*.

The "original draft" signed by the members of the Council was therefore the authentic version from which official certified copies could be made and sent over the signature of a secretary. The procedure was highly flexible.

Provincial *parlements*, attached to the notion of personal power, sometimes refused to register decrees issued by the Conseil d'Etat in the form of excerpts from the registers because these excerpts were not "addressed" to the *parlement* in question. In such cases the decrees would be reissued in the form of letters patent.

Direct Orders from the King

The king also issued orders directly to the members of his "cabinet" (the four cabinet secretaries, who served quarterly, and their *commis*) and to the secretaries of state with whom he met in succession. Since at least the time of Louis XI, certain of these secretaries were designated "secrétaires de la main," "able and authorized" to imitate the king's handwriting and signature. Under Louis XIV, for example, Toussaint Rose, marquis de Coye and secretary of the cabinet, imitated the king's style and hand perfectly and wrote all letters in the king's hand.

Under the King's Cachet

Some of these documents were sent under the king's secret seal—his "petit signet" or "petit cachet" in red wax, which had to be broken in order to open the letter—while others went out over a signature alone without a seal.

Also sent under the king's cachet were "letters missive," which included his private correspondence. In the case of private letters, sometimes written by the king himself, he alone signed. But he also used letters missive to give orders to his agents abroad and at home, including even military leaders, the chancellor, his principal advisers, and so on. In such cases the letters were signed by the king and a secretary of state. They would open with an apostrophe, sometimes followed by a name or epithet and then a salutation: "Monsieur le Maréchal." The form was quite free. The letter would end with a salutation in the form of a wish and the place, day, month, and year. The letter was folded. It was sealed with a strip of paper that was passed through little slits and usually bore the addressee's name and the secret seal.

Lettres Closes

Lettres closes were sent under the king's cachet and generally used whenever the king addressed himself directly not to a physical person but to a moral person such as a corps, a city, or a community. *Lettres closes* began with the formula, "De par le roy," followed by an apostrophe: "Nos amés et féaulx" or "Chers et bien amés." Then came an exposé of the facts followed by the king's decision: "Nous voulons et vous mandons." The final clauses were injunctive or comminatory: "sans y fère faulte ny difficulté" or "et à ce ne faites faulte." A common closing was, "Car tel est nostre plaisir." The place, day, month, and year would follow without mention of the seal. The letter would then be signed by the king and the secretary of state. The manner of closing and sealing was the same as for the letters missive.

The *lettre close* was often used as a circular letter, in which case it might be printed.

The central administration used the *lettre close* to communicate with the various corps of royal officeholders and even with individual officeholders on a wide variety of subjects.

Stamped Letters

For regulations and ordinances concerning police matters, orders for arrest or imprisonment, payment orders, letters of safeguard (by which the king placed a person or his property under royal protection), safe-conducts, passports, and *retenues* (i.e., posts in the royal household or the households of the princes of the blood to which the king reserved the right to make nominations using *lettres de retenue*), the king used "stamped letters" written on parchment and left open, sealed with the secret seal on a patch of red wax. The seal was "stamped" on a square piece of paper that covered the wax. This practice was beginning to give way to the use of the dry stamp as early as the beginning of the seventeenth century.

Stamped letters began with the formula, "De par le Roy." Next came an apostrophe, "to so-and-so," followed by the word "salut." After this came an exposé: "Savoir faison que." Next, the declaration of will: "Si voulons et vous mandons que." Then, the final clause, "Car tel est nostre plaisir," followed by the date and the notice of the secret seal: "Donné à . . . soubz le sceau de nostre secret." After this, the day, month, and year. The letter was signed not by the king but only by a secretary of state: "Par le roy."

Lettres de Cachet

Also sent under the secret seal were the so-called *lettres de cachet*, a term that first appeared in 1560 but did not become current until Richelieu's ministry, after which it remained in common usage down to the time of the

Revolution. *Lettres de cachet* have enjoyed a kind of notoriety owing to the Bastille. Their main use was not, however, for arrests, incarcerations, and exiles. Owing to the exigencies of war and the necessity to act quickly and forcefully, these letters became a key instrument in the king's exercise of personal power as well as essential to the efficiency of the central government and administration. They were used in all cases where the king (or his ministers, acting in his name) was obliged to give notice of the sovereign's express personal will: in order to convoke a political or judicial body of some sort or instruct it to deliberate on a particular matter and reach some sort of conclusion, to organize and supervise public ceremonies, to promote an officer to a higher rank, etc. Any urgent order could be issued in the form of a *lettre de cachet*.

The usual formula was the following: "M. N., I am sending you this letter to tell you that you must do such and such a thing at such and such a time. And this being the only purpose of the present letter, I pray to God, M. N., that he keep you under his holy protection." The place and date came next, followed by the king's signature. At the very bottom the letter was countersigned by one of the secretaries of state.

The document was folded and refolded several times. It was then slit along the free edges in such a way that the slit passed through all the folds of the paper. A strip of paper similar to a double tail was then passed through the slit. The royal cachet was affixed over this strip onto wax that was covered over with paper. The address was written on the back of the letter on one of the visible sides of the fold.

Use of *lettres de cachet* became so common that each secretary of state always had on hand several hundred blank *lettres de cachet* bearing the king's signature. The secretary of state had only to fill in the blank portion with an order and countersign. Needless to say, the king's signature had been affixed by a "secrétaire de la main." Malesherbes observed that there was not enough time in the day for the king to sign the hundreds of orders issued in the form of *lettres de cachet*. Of most of the orders issued over his signature, the king was either unaware or aware only in the most general way.

Unsealed Letters

More and more orders were issued without being sealed, over the signature of the king and the countersignature of a secretary of state. Nothing else was required to make these orders binding.

Payment Orders

Two kinds of payment orders were addressed to the *trésoriers royaux: acquits patents*, which mentioned the name of the bearer and the reason for the expenditure, and *acquits de comptant*, in which neither the name of the bearer nor the reason for the expenditure was mentioned. These orders began with the words, "De par le roy." Then came an apostrophe addressed to the recipient: "Trésorier de mon Epargne" or "Garde de mon trésor royal." Then came the order "to pay" or "nous voulons et vous mandons." The method of payment was next, followed by the clause, "car tel est nostre plaisir," the date in full, the signature of the king, and the signature of the secretary of state. After payment the signature was crossed out and the document was signed a second time by the king after verification of the accounts in council.

Ordinances without Address or Seal

"Ordinances without address or seal" were used mainly for the execution of decisions outside the competence of the courts, the army, the "police," and the general administration, and more especially in matters of public safety and colonization, but they could also be used in virtually any matter, including benefices for the clergy, ceremonial questions, court etiquette, calling Council meetings, etc. The term "regulation" gradually came to rival "ordinance" as the designation for such documents.

Ordinances began with the preamble, "De par le roy." Then came the formula, "Le Roy désirant" or "Ordre que le Roy veult estre dorénavant observé." This was followed by an explanation of the reasons. Then came a declaration of will: "a ordonné" or "veult et entend" or "et premièrement ledit seigneur veult." Finally, the gist of the decision was set forth, often divided into a number of articles. Next came the date in full followed by the signatures of the king and a secretary of state.

Ordinances and regulations completely escaped the chancellor's control. During the second half of the eighteenth century, these documents were made public at the Audience of the Seal, but they were not sealed and required neither a report nor registration. Responsibility for all matters treated by documents of this kind was thus transferred from the chancellor and the chancellery to specialized departments of the bureaucracy.

Brevets

Brevets were also issued without seals. They were used to keep a record of decisions whose effects were delayed, such as the award of an office not yet vacant or an authorization to inherit. They were also used to record decisions that were strictly reserved to the king himself, such as the nomination of a minister or a *conseiller d'Etat*, appointment of an officer to a specific rank in the military, appointment of a clergyman to a benefice under royal advowson, nomination to a post filled by *retenue*, award of a rank such as erection of a barony or duchy-peerage, award of gifts and pensions, authorizations to bear arms—in short, any favor that the king could award to an individual.

Brevets began by recounting the circumstances of time and place: "Aujourd'hui, 20e Jour de Janvier 1604, le Roy estant à Paris, désirant." Then came the gist of the matter and the certification that the king had given the order to draw up the brevet to the secretary of state, who speaks throughout in the first person: "Et de ce m'a Sadicte Majeste commandé expédier le présent brevet" or "En tesmoing de quoy Sadicte Majesté m'a commandé expedier le présent brevet qu'elle a pour ce signe de sa main et faict contresigner par moy son secrétaire d'Estat." Both the king and the secretary of state affixed their signatures.

Trends

It is common to distinguish at least some of the cases in which the king used specific types of documents. What has never, as far as I know, been done is to try in a methodical way to find out the legal and political reasons why one form was preferred to another and attempt to establish a classification.

To the very end the king continued to use the most ancient forms, such as letters of chancellery and council decrees. There were of course fiscal reasons for the persistent use of letters of chancellery, since a fee was charged for the issuance of such letters. In the case of both letters of chancellery and council decrees, the king was obliged to preserve the old forms by his role as a judge and by his oath of anointment. In many cases, as we have seen, council decrees were merely a fiction that disguised decisions made by the king personally. During the two centuries we are examining, however, the number of orders issued under the secret seal or over the king's signature alone continued to increase, as did the importance of the subjects treated in this way; the form of these orders shifted from that of a letter to that of an official report. In other words, the work of government and administration was increasingly done not by councils but by individuals working alone in offices, dealing individually with their subordinates and private individuals from whom they received information and to whom they issued orders. They examined the files and made decisions on their own. Relations in the hierarchy were less and less relations of man to man and more and more relations between anonymous and abstract entities, relations of the government to its subjects and of the administration to the administered. This was what the *parlements* characterized as "ministerial despotism." The evolution of the administration did not, of course, come to an end during these two centuries. The old and the new coexisted in inverse proportion. I have merely tried to indicate the tendency of the ongoing changes.

Guide to Further Reading

Sources for Chapter 9

Guyot and Merlin, *Traité des droits . . . annexés en France à chaque dignité*, vol. 2. Visse, 1787.

Anselm (Father), continued by M. du Fourny. *Histoire généalogique et chronologique de la Maison royale de France*. Revised, corrected, and expanded by Fathers Ange and Simplicien. 9 vols. Compagnie des Libraires, 1726–33.

Loyseau, Charles. "Des ordres et simples dignités," in *Oeuvres*, vol. 2. Pierre Lamy, 1640.
Le Bret, Cardin. *De la souveraineté*. 1632.
Dupuy, *Traité de la majorité de nos roys et des régences du royaume*. Mathurin du Puis & Edmé Martin, 1655.
Du Four de Longuerue. "Traité des apanages et partage des Enfants de France," in *Recueil des pièces intéressantes pour servir à l'histoire de France*, vol. 24. Geneva, 1769. (Bibliothèque Nationale 8°L 4613).

Works Pertaining to the Material in Chapter 9

Barry, Françoise. *La reine de France*. Editions du Scorpion, 1964.
Calmette, Joseph. *Les rois de France*. 1943.
Dupin, André-Marie J.-J. *Des apanages en général et en particulier de l'apanage d'Orléans*. 1827.
Funck-Brentano, Franz. *Ce qu'était un roi de France*. Hachette, 1940.
Hisler, Anne-Léa. *Rois et gouvernants de la France*. 1964.
Hyslop, Beatrice F. *L'apanage de Philippe-Egalité, duc d'Orléans (1785–1791)*. Société des Etudes robespierristes, 1965.
Le Roy, Yves. "La notion de prince du sang." Mimeographed thesis for Diplôme d'Etudes Supérieures in Public Law. Faculté de Droit et des Sciences économiques. Paris, undated.
Maffert, L. A. *Les apanages en France du XVIe au XIXe siècle*. Rousseau, 1900.
Perrière, H. de la. *Le roi légitime: La loi de dévolution du trône dans la Maison de France*. Daragon, 1910.
Valtat, Monique. *Les contrats de mariage dans la famille royale en France au XVIIe siècle*. A. & J. Picard, 1933.

Works Pertaining to the Material in Chapters 10, 11, and 12

Antoine, Michel. *Le Conseil du roi sous Louis XV*. Droz, 1970.
———. *Le gouvernement et l'administration sous Louis XV: Dictionnaire biographique*. Paris: Editions du Centre National de Recherche Scientifique, 1978.
Armstrong, John A. "Old Regime Administrative Elites." *Revue internationale des sciences administratives* 38 (1972): 21–40.
———. "Old Regime Governors: Bureaucratic and Patrimonial Attitudes." *Comparative Studies in Social History* 14 (1972): 2–29.
Barbiche, Bernard. *Sully*. Albin Michel, 1978.
Beaufort, de. *Recueil concernant le tribunal de Nosseigneurs les Maréchaux de France*. 2 vols. 1784.
Benoît, Marcelle. *Versailles et les musiciens du roi, 1661–1733. Etude institutionelle et sociale*. A. & J. Picard, 1971.
———. *Musique de cour, 1661–1733. Chapelle, chambre, écurie. Recueil de textes et documents*. A. & J. Picard, 1971.
Bérenger, Jean. "Pour une enquête européenne: Le problème du ministériat au XVIIe siècle." *Annales E.S.C.* 29 (1974): 166–92.
Boislisle, A. M. de. *Correspondance des contrôleurs généraux des Finances avec les intendants des provinces, 1683–1715*. 3 vols. Imprimerie Nationale, 1884–97.
Bosher, J. F. *French Finances, 1770–1795: From Business to Bureaucracy*. Cambridge, Eng.: Cambridge University Press, 1970.
Bourgeon, Jean-Louis. *Les Colbert avant Colbert*. Paris: PUF, 1971.
Clément, P. *Lettres, instructions et mémoires de Colbert*. 10 vols. Imprimerie Impériale (later Imprimerie Nationale), 1861–82.
Delpeuch, Emma. "Les marchands et artisans suivant la Cour." *Revue d'histoire du droit français et étranger* 52 (1974): 379–413.
Dent, Julian. *Crisis in Finance*.
Devismes, Roland. *La cour à Versailles: Versailles sous Louis XIV*. Pensée universelle, 1975.

Elias, Norbert. *La société de cour*. Calmann-Lévy, 1974.

Guichard, Georges. *La juridiction des prévôts de la Connétablie et des Maréchaux de France*. Lille: Imprimerie Duriez-Bataille, 1926.

Hardy, Sébastien. *Le guidon général des Finances*. 1631 ed.

Isherwood, Robert M. *Music in the Service of the King: France in the Seventeenth Century*. Ithaca, N.Y.: Cornell University Press, 1973.

Labatut, Jean-Pierre. *Les ducs et pairs de France au XVIIe siècle*. Paris: PUF, 1972.

Labourdette, Jean-François. "Conseils à un duc de La Trémoille à son entrée dans le monde." *Enquêtes et documents*. Vol. 2, pp. 73–184. Université de Nantes, 1972.

Le Barrois d'Orgeval, Gabriel. *Le tribunal de la Connétablie de France, du XIVe siècle à 1790*. De Boccard, 1917.

———. *Le maréchalat de France, des origines à nos jours*. 2 vols. Editions Occitania, 1932.

Lepointe, Gabriel, and Robert Villers. "Le régime monocratique dans les trois derniers siècles de l'ancienne France," in *La Monocratie*, part 2, pp. 276–697. Recueils de la Société Jean-Bodin, vol. 21. Brussels: Editions de la Librairie Encyclopédique, 1969.

Le Roy Ladurie, Emmanuel, "Système de la cour (Versailles vers 1709)," in *L'arc* 65 (1976).

Luçay, Hélion (comte de). *Les Secrétaires d'Etat depuis leur institution jusqu'à la mort de Louis XV*. 1881.

Markovitch, Tihomir J. "Le triple centenaire de Colbert: L'enquête, les règlements, les inspecteurs." *Revue d'histoire économique et sociale* 49 (1971): 305–24.

Mesnard, P. *Projets de gouvernement du duc de Bourgogne, Dauphin*. Hachette, 1860.

Meyer, Jean. *Colbert*. Paris: Hachette, 1981.

Michaud, Hélène. "Aux origines du secrétariat d'Etat à la Guerre: les règlements de 1617–1619." *Revue d'histoire moderne et contemporaine* 19 (1972): 389–413.

Mitchell, John Hewitt. *The Court of Connétablie: A Study of a French Administrative Tribunal during the Reign of Henry IV*. New Haven, Conn.: Yale University Press, 1947.

Mougel, François-Charles. "Les Princes de Conti, seigneurs de Pézenas (1651–1783)." *Etudes sur Pézenas* 2 (1971): 4–26.

Mousnier, Roland. *Le Conseil du roi, de la mort d'Henri IV au gouvernement personnel de Louis XIV*. Studies published by the Société d'Histoire moderne, vol. 1. Paris, 1947. Reprinted in *La plume, la faucille et le marteau*. Paris: PUF, 1970, pp. 141–78.

———. "Les règlements du Conseil du roi sous Louis XIII." *Annuaire-Bulletin de la Société de l'Histoire de France*, 1946.

———. "Comment les Français du XVIIe siècle voyaient la Constitution." *XVIIe siècle* 25–26 (1955). Reprinted in *La plume, la faucille et le marteau*.

———. "Paris, capitale politique, au Moyen Age et dans les temps modernes." *Cahiers de Civilisations*, 1962. Reprinted in *La plume, la faucille et le marteau*.

———. *Lettres et mémoires adressés au chancelier Séguier*. 2 vols. Paris: PUF, 1964.

———. "La participation des gouvernés à l'activité des gouvernants dans la France des XVIIe et XVIIIe siècles," in *Gouvernés et gouvernants*, part 3, pp. 235–98. Recueils de la Société Jean-Bodin, vol. 24 (with bibliography). Reprinted in *La plume, la faucille et le marteau*, pp. 231–64 (without bibliography).

———. "D'Aguesseau et le tournant des ordres aux classes sociales." *Revue d'histoire économique et sociale* 49 (1971): 449–64.

———. "Les concepts d'ordres, d'états, de fidélité et de monarchie absolue en France de la fin du XVe à la fin du XVIIIe siècle." *Revue historique*, April–June 1972, pp. 289–312.

———. "Les fidélités et les clientèles en France aux XVIe; XVIIe; et XVIIIe siècles." *Histoire sociale* 15 (May 1982), pp. 35–46.

Murat, Inès. *Colbert*. Fayard, 1980.

Parker, David. "The Social Foundation of French Absolutism (1610–1670)." *Past and Present* 53 (1971): 67–89.

Piccioni, Camille. *Les premiers commis des affaires étrangères au XVIIe et au XVIIIe siècle*. E. De Boccard, 1928.

Ranum, Orest. *Artisans of Glory: Historical Thought in Seventeenth Century France*. Chapel Hill: University of North Carolina Press, 1980.

Saint-Simon. *Ecrits inédits de Saint-Simon*, ed. P. Faugère. 8 vols. Hachette, 1880–93.

———. *Mémoires*, ed. A. de Boislisle. 41 vols. Hachette, 1923–28.

Samoyault, Jean-Pierre. *Les bureaux du secrétariat d'Etat des affaires etrangères sous Louis XV*. A. Pedone, 1971.

Shennan, G. H. *Government and Society in France (1461–1661)*. London: Allen, 1969.

Viollet, P. *Le roi et ses ministres pendant les trois derniers siècles de la monarchie*. Librairie de la Société du Recueil Sirey, 1912.

Works Pertaining to the Material in Chapters 13 and 14

Camus, Jean-Pierre. *Homélies des Etats généraux (1614–1615)*, ed. Jean Descrains. Geneva: Droz and Paris: Minard, 1970.

Chartier, Roger. "A propos des Etats généraux de 1614." *Revue d'histoire moderne et contemporaine* 23 (1976): 68–79.

——— and J. de Nagle. "Les cahiers de doléances de 1614." *Annales E.S.C.*, December 1973, pp. 1484–94.

——— and D. Richet. *Représentation et vouloir politiques: Autour des Etats Généraux de 1614*. Editions de l'Ecole des hautes études en sciences sociales, 1982.

Durrand, Yves. *Cahiers de paroisses du bailliage de Troyes pour les Etats généraux de 1614*. Paris: PUF, 1966.

Gutton, Jean-Pierre. "Le cahier de doléances de la noblesse du Beaujolais aux Etats généraux de 1614." *Revue historique* 253 (1975): 107–18.

Hayden, Michael. *France and the Estates General of 1614*. Cambridge, Eng.: Cambridge University Press, 1974.

Jouanna, Arlette. *L'idée de race en France au XVIᵉ siècle et au début du XVIIᵉ siècle, 1498–1614*. 3 vols. Paris: Librairie Honoré-Champion, 1976. Vol. 3, pp. 1273–1300.

Lublinskaja, Alexandra. "Les Etats généraux de 1614–1615 en France," in *Album Helen Cam*. Studies presented to the Commission internationale pour l'histoire des Assemblées d'Etats. Vol. 23. Louvain: Beatrice Nauwelaerts, 1960, pp. 231–45.

Mousnier, Roland. *L'assassinat d'Henri IV: Le problème de tyrannicide et l'affermissement de la monarchie absolue*: Les Etats généraux de 1614–1615, pp. 246–66. Paris: Gallimard, 1964.

———. *La vénalité des offices sous Henri IV and Louis XIII*: L'Assemblée des Notables de 1617–1618, pp. 631 ff. Paris: PUF, 1971.

Petit, Jeanne. *L'Assemblée des Notables de 1626–1627*. Ecole pratique des hautes études, sciences, historiques et philologiques, 1937.

Russell-Major, J. *The Deputies to the Estates General in Renaissance France*. Madison: University of Wisconsin Press, 1960.

———. *Representative Government in Early Modern France*. New Haven, Conn., and London: Yale University Press, 1980.

Soule, Claude. "Les Etats généraux de France (1302–1789)," in *Etude historique, comparative et doctrinale*. Studies presented to the Commission internationale pour l'histoire des Assemblées d'Etats, vol. 35. Heule (Belgium): U.G.A., 1968.

Works Pertaining to the material in Chapter 15

Bouard, Alain de. *Manuel de diplomatique française et pontificale*. 2 vols. Picard, 1929–52.

Giry, A. *Manuel de diplomatique*. Hachette, 1894.

Michaud, Hélène. *La Grande Chancellerie et les Ecritures royales au XVIᵉ siècle (1515–1589)*. Paris: PUF, 1967.

Tessier, Georges. *Diplomatique royale française*. Picard, 1962.

4 The Sovereign and Lower Courts of Law and and Administration

Below the organs of government came a hierarchy of tribunals responsible for dispensing justice and hence for administration. The king delegated to each tribunal the power to render judgments in his name. This power gave rise to further powers of "police" and hence of administration, similar to the powers of the king. Each tribunal had a civil jurisdiction. The courts sat in judgment over disputes between the king's subjects concerning their social status or their property. The court determined which of the contesting parties was in the right in such matters as conflicting claims to an inheritance or disputes about kinship. Thus the courts played a part in distributive justice, giving to each what was his, and in commutative justice, placing each man where he belonged in society. In addition, all courts also had criminal jurisdiction. They sat in judgment in cases of violation of both natural law and civil law, that is, of crimes, such as murder, theft, fraud, fornication, adultery, violation of religious vows, and so on. Since, however, prevention is better than cure and eliminating the opportunity to do wrong better than punishing misdeeds, every tribunal exercised powers of "police" or administration. Police, in the broad sense, embraced not only the totality of the laws but also the rules of order and conduct that had to be observed in order to insure the continued well-being of state and society. "Police" refers to whatever has to do with meeting the daily needs of the public: examples include seeing to the cleanliness of a city and the security of its inhabitants, price controls on foodstuffs, enforcement of statutes concerning merchants and artisans, and regulations concerning workers' wages.

In theory an ordinary tribunal had the power to judge in all these matters. However, some cases were so special and required such specific competence that the king removed them, at least in part, from the competence of ordinary tribunals and entrusted them instead either to extraordinary tribunals or assigned jurisdictions, such as the Eaux et Forêts, the Admiralty Courts, the Connétablie, the Cours des Monnaies, the Juges-Consuls des Marchands, and the like.

16   The Judicial Hierarchy and the Competence of the Courts

Distribution of Jurisdiction: By Geography or by Type of Case

The boundaries of the kingdom were uncertain. Some provinces were not part of the kingdom and belonged to the king as personal possessions:[1] these included Provence, where the king was count; Marseille, which was not part of Provence, but a "separate state"; Arles, "a state joined to another"; Béarn, which considered itself a sovereign state under the sworn protection of the king of France; and Navarre. The Estates of Navarre claimed to be Estates General and on 6 March 1789 asserted that "Navarre is not a province of France; it is a separate kingdom subject to the king of France, but distinct from and independent of the kingdom of France."[2] The king of France was also king of Navarre. Brittany, on the other hand, had been considered an integral part of the kingdom since 1532. France consisted of the whole group of kingdoms, provinces, and *pays* under the domination of the king of France.

The boundaries between these possessions and foreign countries remained in doubt despite continual efforts to make them more precise. In Merzig and Saargau, for example, the king of France and the Elector of Treves continued to exercise joint sovereignty and jurisdiction. A treaty of exchange was necessary to put an end, more or less, to this state of affairs, and one was signed on 1 July 1778.

Near the border with the Austrian-ruled Low Countries and the bishopric of Liège, certain villages were shared by France and the Empire: a portion of the village of Emmerin was under the Empire's jurisdiction, while another portion was governed by the French *subdélégation* of Lille.

The king possessed a number of foreign enclaves: the villages of Barbemon, Erpion, Reulies, and Bossu-lès-Walcourt near Maubeuge; the "pays des cinq villes" or "pays d'entre Sambre et Meuse," "pays outre Meuse," "pays Gallo-Liègeois," Marienbourg, Philippeville, Givet, Fumay, and Revin, which together laid claim to the status of a province. The borders of this province were disputed at several points by the prince-bishop of Liège, the duc de Bouillon, and the kings of France and Austria. The treaty of 24

May 1772 with the state of Liège did not succeed in establishing the precise boundaries. These examples are only a few among many.

Within France there were also foreign enclaves: the Comtat Venaissin, the papal state of Avignon, the principality of Orange, and the county of Montbéliard, whose prince and staatholder was the duke of Würtemberg; in the principality of Mandeure, which had long been under the sovereignty of the duke of Würtemberg, the village of Courcelles, a small, self-governing state under the high patronage of the archbishop of Besançon; the principality of Salm; the county of Saarverden including Saarbruck, the sovereignty of the princes of Nassau; Mulhouse, a sovereign state of the Swiss Confederation; the county of Sault, sovereignty of the duc de Villeroy, bordering the Comtat; and the sovereignty of Bidache in the Pyrenees, the property of the prince de Gramont.

Inside the kingdom the situation was no more clear. Provinces, *gouvernements généraux*, *généralites*, bishoprics, *bailliages*, and *sénéchaussées* overlapped one another, took in parts of some parishes, and even disputed possession of certain parishes or shared them with another jurisdiction in alternate years: a parish might belong to one *bailliage* one year and to a neighboring *bailliage* the next. In 1789, 1,800 parishes were in this situation.

The *généralité* of Bourges included parts of the provinces of Nivernais, Bourbonnais, Poitou, and other neighboring provinces. The *intendant* of Tours included within his *généralité* the three provinces of Touraine, Maine, and Anjou. The province of Angoumois was divided among the three *intendances* of Limoges, La Rochelle, and Poitiers. Auvergne was divided into two provinces, Haute Auvergne and Basse Auvergne. Walloon Flanders and maritime Flanders were considered by some to be two distinct provinces.

Certain cities were under the jurisdiction not of the nearby royal court but rather of some other court located a good distance away. Inhabitants of these cities were forced to pass through the jurisdiction of the first court in order to be judged by the second. The castellany of Béthisy-Verberie, today in the *département de l'Oise* in the *arrondissement* of Senlis, was once under the jurisdiction of the *siège présidial* of Crépy-en-Valois. In September 1703 the king established a *bailliage en chef* at Villers-Cotterêts, which was given jurisdiction over the castellany of Béthisy. Citizens were obliged to pass through Crépy in order to appear in court three leagues away.

At Saint-Paul-Trois-Châteaux in the Rhône valley there was a system known as the *biennes*: the episcopal magistrate and the royal magistrate took turns, each sitting in the seat of justice for two years at a time. The courts of Gévaudan were shared between the king and the bishop of Mende: one year the courts would be held at Marvejols under judges appointed by the king, the next year they would be at Mende under judges named by the bishop. At Puy-en-Velay justice was administered in alternate weeks by the *bailliage* and common court of the bishop and the judges of the royal *sénéchaussée*.

Sometimes entire regions were in dispute. The *bailliages* of Compiègne and Crépy-en-Valois both claimed jurisdiction over the *prévôté* of Pierrefonds. Crépy-en-Valois won out in 1758. For more than two centuries the *bailliage* of Auxerre pressed suit against the ducs de Nevers to detach the barony of Donzy from the *bailliage* of Nivernais. A decree of the Paris *parlement* in 1745 validated the claim of the *bailliage* of Auxerre to possession and jurisdiction over the Donziois. Different jurisdictions quarreled over particular parishes. In 1776 Prunay-sous-Ablis, located in the *bailliage* of Montfort-l'Amaury, was claimed by Chartres, Dourdan, and Etampes.

The competence of the various courts was no better delineated. In theory, *bailliages* and *sénéchaussées* had exclusive jurisdiction over royal cases, but the *prévôté* of Montmedy also heard such cases. In seigneurial jurisdictions, following the example of the royal *baillis* and *prévôts*, the judges exercised their powers only over a specific category of individuals. Thus the *premier président* Molé in the eighteenth century held as a fief "*tabellionnage, justice et juridiction* of cases involving nobles in the castellany of Luzarches."

Each court had to face problems of the territorial and jurisdictional extent of its competence. Conflicts were unending.

The Judicial Hierarchy and the Territorial Distribution of the Courts

To begin with, there were two echelons of ordinary and extraordinary tribunals: the "courts" and the "jurisdictions."[3] At the top of the hierarchy were the sovereign courts (known as "superior courts" after 1661 when Louis XIV began his personal government), so called because in theory there was no appeal from their decisions. They pronounced decrees (*arrêts*) rather than sentences. A "decree," according to Furetière's definition, was a "hard and fast judgment by a sovereign power." A sentence, on the other hand, was subject to appeal. Finally, a decision (*arrêté*) was a "resolution taken by a Company" after a deliberation on some subject. The highest of the ordinary courts were the *parlements;* after them came the Requêtes de l'Hôtel du Roi and the Requêtes du Palais attached to the various *parlements*. The extraordinary courts and courts of attribution were, to begin with the highest, the Grand Conseil, the Chambres des Comptes, and the Cours des Aides; then came the *trésoriers de France* of the bureaux de Finances (who, though ostensibly members of the Chambres des Comptes, had periodically to seek confirmation of this disputed membership), the Cours des Monnaies, and the Tables de Marbre for the Eaux et Forêts, the Admiralty, and the Connétablie and Maréchaussée de France.

Juridictions or lower courts pronounced sentences which were subject to appeal. Constituting a third echelon in the judicial hierarchy, the ordinary lower courts included the *présidiaux*, the *bailliages*, and the *sénéchaussées*. The jurisdictions of attribution included the courts of the *grands maîtres des Eaux et Forets*, the *connétablies* or courts of the *prévôts généraux des connétables et maréchaux de France*, the *sièges généraux d'amirauté*, and the *sièges des conservateurs des privilèges des universités*.

In the fourth echelon, depending on the region, we find castellanies, *prévôtés, vicomtés, bailies*, and *vigueries*. Among the jurisdictions of attribution were the *élections*, the salt warehouses, the *maîtrises particulières des Eaux et Forêts*, the *sièges particuliers d'amirautés*, the *connétablies* or *sièges des prévôts particuliers des maréchaux*, the *conversations des privilèges des foires*, and the *justices des "hôtels et maisons de ville."*

In the fifth echelon were the "seigneurial courts, equally for duchies and peerages as for others directly subject to our courts."

The sixth echelon comprised other seigneurial courts "not directly under the jurisdiction of *parlement*."

These various echelons of the judicial hierarchy were often gathered together in one place. Thus in Paris, the capital of France, we find between the rue de la Barillerie and the rue de Harlai on the Ile de la Cité courts whose jurisdiction extended over the entire kingdom or over a large portion of the kingdom: the Paris *parlement*, "the first in the kingdom," a Chambre des Comptes, a Cour des Monnaies, and, at the Table de Marbre du Palais, the Connétablie et Maréchaussée de France, the Eaux et Forêts, and the Admiralty.[4]

We also find lower tribunals with merely regional or local functions, including one court, composed of *trésoriers de France* and *trésoriers généraux des Finances de la généralité de Paris*, which was combined with a Chambre du Domaine or Chambre du Trésor, and a number of jurisdictions, such as the *élection de Paris*, the *maîtrise particulière des Eaux et Forêts de l'Ile-de-France*, and the *bailliage du Palais*, which had civil and criminal jurisdiction and police powers over the administrative and judicial complex on the Ile de la Cité, powers limited by the edict of February 1674 to the chambers and courtrooms of the Palais.

Not on the Ile de la Cité itself but quite nearby on the right bank of the Seine were the courts of the city of Paris, the *prévôté et vicomté de Paris*, the *bailliage* and *présidial*, and the Paris salt warehouse, all located at the Châtelet. Besides these tribunals, there were also the jurisdiction of the Hôtel de Ville, the *siège de justice des Juges et Consuls* for hearing commercial cases, the Chambre de l'Arsenal, and the jurisdiction of the Varenne du Louvre.

Finally, there were 25 seigneurial courts in Paris, 19 of which were either eliminated or reduced to jurisdiction over a tiny territory by the edict of February 1674.

The same was true in all provinces that had *parlements* of their own. Consider the example of Franche-Comté. The *parlement* of Franche-Comté began sitting in Besançon in 1676, along with the *prévôt général de la maréchaussée de Franche-Comté*, the Justice de la Monnaie, presided over by the *général provincial*, and the *bailliage* of Besançon, which was established and 1676 and later combined with a *présidial* established by an edict of

September 1696, whose jurisdiction extended to the *bailliages* of Besançon, Baume, and Ornans. There were also a *maîtrise des Eaux et Forêts* under the jurisdiction of the Chambre des Eaux et Forêts et Requêtes du Palais and a *lieutenance de la maréchaussée* for the *bailliages* of Besançon, Dôle, Pontarlier, Baume, Ornans, and Quingey. There were also an Officialité or bishop's court for the diocese; a Nouvelle Mairie or court for Besançon and its suburbs, with a mayor, a *lieutenant de police* and his *lieutenant de mairie;* the *bailliage* of the Abbaye de Saint-Paul, which heard cases from the rue Saint-Paul and a portion of the rue du Chateur; the Vicomté et Ancienne Mairie, a fief of the House of Orange, reestablished in 1698 as a result of the treaty of Ryswick and allowing appeal to the *bailliage* and from the *bailliage* to the *parlement;* the courts of the metropolitan chapter, which dealt with such church hirelings as canons, cantors, and musicians; and the university courts, which judged members and employees of the university.

Things were roughly similar in all judicial seats, though the scale of operations varied. A city with a *bailliage* might also be home to a *prévôté*, *élection*, salt warehouse, municipal courts, and seigneurial courts, at least until the edict of April 1749, which laid it down that, in cities with a *bailliage* or *sénéchaussée*, these tribunals would subsume the *prévôté* or *vicomté* or castellany or *bailie* or *viguerie* of the area and take over its functions. In some cases a *présidial* might be added to this list, or a *maîtrise particulière des Eaux et Forêts*, a *connétablie*, an *amirauté particulière*, or a *juge consul*.

Thus for the most part the courts were concentrated in the cities.

Ordinary Tribunals and Their Competence

Parlements

The *parlements* were the highest-ranking of the ordinary tribunals and were themselves ranked in order of their establishment. The first use of the word "parlement" was in 1239 to denote the king's court. At first the term was usually applied to a conference, but it quickly came to denote an assembly of royal councillors, independent of the Curia Regis and chiefly concerned with dispensing justice. The separation may have been complete as early as 1253. *Parlement* seems to have become established in a fixed location by the reign of Philip III (Philip the Bold), sometime before 1278. The *parlement* of Paris was considered the *parlement par excellence*. Its territorial jurisdiction, which at first extended over the entire kingdom, was whittled down as other *parlements* were established. In the seventeenth and eighteenth centuries the jurisdiction of the Paris *parlement* took in the Ile-de-France, Picardy, the Boulonnais, Calais, Dunkirk (from 1664 on), Brie, Champagne, Beauce, Sologne, Berry, Nivernais, Bourbonnais, Mâconnais, la Marche, Auvergne, Lyonnais, Forez, Beaujolais, Perche, Maine, Anjou, Touraine, Poitou, Aunis and Rochelais, and Angoumois.

Second among the *parlements* was the *parlement* of Toulouse, which grew out of a court of justice established by Philip the Bold on 18 January 1279. The Toulouse *parlement* itself was instituted in 1302 and installed on 23 December 1303, at the Palais Narbonais, once the palace of the Visigoth kings. After many vicissitudes it was reestablished by letters patent of 11 October 1443 and opened on 4 June 1444. Its jurisdiction at first extended over the entire southwestern portion of the kingdom, but by the period that concerns us it had been reduced considerably, covering upper and lower Languedoc, the Cévennes, a portion of Provence and the regions on the right bank of the Rhône up to the gates of Lyon, Rouergue up to the border of Auvergne, Vivarais, Gévaudan, Quercy, Armagnac, and, in the Pyrenees, the counties of Foix, Couserans, Comminges, Bigorre, Nebousan, and the Quatre-Vallées. The Toulouse *parlement* coexisted with provincial Estates (the Estates of Languedoc and of the Pyreneean regions) which accepted financial edicts at the same time it did.

Third place among the *parlements* was disputed between Grenoble and Bordeaux. The *parlement* of Grenoble claimed the honor on the grounds that it had been established in 1453 by Louis XI, who was then dauphin and who turned the dauphin's Grand Conseil of his appanage into a *parlement*. The Grenoble *parlement* objected that the Bordeaux *parlement* had not been established by Louis XI until 10 June 1462. But the Bordeaux *parlement* claimed to have been founded by Charles VII in 1451. In 1624 the two courts took their dispute to the king's Council. The Council determined that neither claim was definitive and ordered that the *premiers présidents* of the two *parlements* should alternate in precedence. Both parties protested. The case was once again brought before the king's Council in 1661. By letters patent of 30 December 1661, Louis XIV upheld the previous decision: alternating priority.

In the nineteenth century a scholar discovered that a "supreme court" that had the characteristics of a *parlement* had been at work in Bordeaux in 1452.[5]

Following alphabetical order, we shall place Bordeaux first. The jurisdiction of the *parlement* of Bordeaux included the Bordelais, Guyenne, Gascony, the Landes, Agenais, Bazadais, Périgord, Limousin, and Saintonge. This territory was largely broken up, being interspersed with areas under the jurisdiction of the *parlement* of Toulouse. The jurisdiction of the Grenoble *parlement* took in the whole of Dauphiné.

In fifth place was the *parlement* of Dijon, established by Louis XI with letters patent of March 1476, with jurisdiction at that time covering the duchy and county of Burgundy and the lands beyond the Saône. Foreign policy and the war against the Habsburgs cut its jurisdiction down, at first in fact and later officially, to the duchy alone. Then Henri IV expanded it, as a result of the Treaty of Lyon of 1601, to include Bresse, Bugey, and Valromey. *Parlement* sat in the palace of justice that had been completed under Henri II in the gardens of the Chambre des Comptes on the site of the house of the original dukes of Burgundy. Audiences were held in the great hall or "gilded hall."

Sixth place went to the *parlement* of Rouen, established by Louis XII, who in 1499 responded to the grievances and complaints of the people of the region and transformed the Echiquier de Normandie into a *parlement* in continuous session. It had jurisdiction over Normandy.

Seventh place was occupied by the *parlement* of Aix-en-Provence, established by Louis XII in July 1501 "for the lands and coasts of Provence, Forcalquier, and adjacent regions." It replaced the sovereign council.

In eighth place we find the *parlement* of Rennes, which succeeded the *Grands Jours* reorganized by Charles VIII in 1495. This body met too infrequently, however, and cases dragged on forever. Accordingly, Henri II, by edict of Fontainebleau dated March 1554, established a "court of *parlement*, ordinary seat of sovereign justice for the country and duchy of Brittany," which met in two three-month sessions each year, one at Rennes, the other at Nantes. Then, on 4 March 1561, Charles IX transferred it to Rennes, where the governor of the provincial Estates was located. In disgrace from 1675 to 1690 because of the stamped-paper rebellion, *parlement* moved to Vannes but later returned to Rennes. An edict of March 1724 made it annual. Its jurisdiction was Brittany.

The ninth rank was occupied by the *parlement* of Pau, established in 1620, whose jurisdiction included Béarn, Navarre, and Soule, all *pays d'Etats*.

In tenth place was the *parlement* of Metz, which had been established in 1633 presumably to deal with the Trois-Evêchés and other conquered territory: Toul, Verdun, Sarrelouis, Sedan, Thionville, Longwy, Mouzon, Mohon, Montmedy, Phillipsbourg, Sarrebourg, and Vic. Staffed by young magistrates recruited in many cases from Parisian families and faithful to the king, men just beginning their careers, this *parlement* in fact helped to extend French influence when the fortunes of war permitted. After 1714 its official jurisdiction was expanded to include the Metz region. The Metz *parlement* was eliminated by an edict of October 1771 and its jurisdiction joined to that of the *parlement* of Nancy. On 26 September 1775, however, the Metz *parlement* was reinstated.

In eleventh place, perhaps, was the *parlement* of Douai, which grew out of the Conseil supérieur of Tournai, set up in April 1688 to deal with conquered territory lying between France and the Low Countries. In February 1686 this council became the *parlement* of Tournai. When Tournai fell to the enemy in 1709, *parlement* was transferred by ordinance of 20 August 1709 to Cambrai and then in December 1713 to Douai. It was eliminated in connection with the reforms of Chancellor Maupeou, and its jurisdiction was joined to that of the Conseil supérieur of Arras. Then the edict of September 1771 established a Conseil supérieur at Douai to serve as court of last resort in the area that had been under the jurisdiction of the old *parlement*, but with no general power to certify laws. The edict of November 1774 reestablished the *parlement* of Douai so as not to prejudice the privileges of the

Flemings. The jurisdiction of the Douai *parlement* comprised the southern portion of maritime Flanders, Walloon Flanders, Cambrésis, the French Hainault, Philippeville, Marienbourg, Chimay, and a few enclaves in the Austrian-dominated portion of the Low Countries. This *parlement* coexisted with the provincial Estates of Walloon Flanders and of Cambrésis.

In 1664 Dunkirk, Bourbourg, and Garvelines, all cities of maritime Flanders, were incorporated into the jurisdiction of the Paris *parlement*. Appeals from tribunals in these three cities were taken first to the Conseil supérieur of Artois and then to the *parlement* of Paris. They were judged according to Flemish usages, however, these being based on Roman law, in contrast to the usages of Artois, which were based on customary law.

Twelfth in order of priority was the *parlement* of Besançon. It was the successor to the Habsburg *parlement* of Dôle, which had been suspended by the Spaniards after the precipitous capitulation of 1668, then reinstituted by Louis XIV on 17 June 1674, after the reconquest of Franche-Comté, and later transferred to Besançon by letters patent of 22 August 1676. It had jurisdiction over the province of Franche-Comté.

Thirteenth in rank was the *parlement* of Nancy. By an edict of September 1634, Louis XIII had closed the sovereign court in conquered Lorraine known as the *assises de l'Ancienne Chevalerie*. Its jurisdiction had been turned over to the sovereign council of Nancy, which was supposed to have responsibility for all Lorraine. In that part of the Barrois not held as a fief of the Crown of France and also captured from the duc de Lorraine, the king retained the Cour des Grands Jours de Saint-Mihiel and expanded its jurisdiction to include the "old Barrois," which was a fief of the Crown of France. The new court declared the treaty of Saint-Germain invalid. Louis XIII invaded Lorraine on 6 December 1641. The *parlement* of Metz recovered jurisdiction over the two duchies of Lorraine as well as the nonfief portion of the Barrois.

Under the terms of the treaty of Vincennes of 28 February 1661, Charles IV regained his states. By edict of 26 March 1661, he reestablished the sovereign court and divided it into two chambers, one for the duchy of Lorraine and the other for the nonfief portion of the Barrois.

On 26 August 1670, after Nancy had been taken by the maréchal de Créqui, Louis XIV transferred power over the sovereign court's jurisdiction to the Metz *parlement*.

On 30 October 1697, the Treaty of Ryswick ceded Lorraine to Duke Leopold. On 13 February 1698, the sovereign court was reestablished.

Under the terms of the Treaty of Vienna of 1736, King Stanislas of Poland, Louis XV's father-in-law, was granted possession of the duchies of Lorraine and Bar. Leopold's son Francis III received the grand-duchy of Tuscany as compensation. Upon the death of Stanislas on 23 February 1766, Lorraine was reunited to France. By edict of February 28, Louis XV confirmed the sovereign court by provision, despite the opposition of the Metz *parlement*, which invoked the decrees issued by the king's Council on 17 October 1718, and 19 September 1761, promising it control over the sovereign court's jurisdiction. On 26 September 1775, a royal edict bestowed upon this sovereign court the title of *parlement*. Its area of jurisdiction remained unchanged, covering the duchies of Lorraine and Bar.

Analogous to the *parlements*, the sovereign councils or superior councils were tribunals established by the king in conquered provinces. These might later be turned into *parlements*. The sovereign council of Dombes, established in 1523, became the parlement of Trévoux from 1661 to 1775. The sovereign council of Pignerol was in operation from 1631 to 1696. The sovereign council of Artois, established at Arras by the Emperor Charles V in 1540, was confirmed by Louis XIII in 1641. The sovereign council of Roussillon was established in Perpignan in 1640. The sovereign council of Alsace was established at Ensisheim in 1657, moved to Brisach, and finally located at Colmar in 1698. The sovereign council of Corsica was established in 1769.

All the *parlements* were modeled on the *parlement* of Paris and enjoyed the same powers, rights, honors, privileges, preeminences, and liberties. Thus, to illustrate the competence of *parlements* in general, we may regard the *parlement* of Paris as typical, even though there were some differences from one *parlement* to another.

The *parlement* of Paris was a "Company" and therefore a corps and a college with a voice and procedures for expressing a common will. The Paris *parlement* acted as a court of peers for the entire kingdom, both in judging cases and in giving advice in matters of government or administration. In this period the magistrates were sometimes joined by the king, who came to *parlement* whenever he saw fit to hold a *lit de justice* or to hear the "advice of his *parlement* concerning matters submitted to its consideration." The chancellor, the keeper of the seals, the princes of the blood, who were entitled to seats as soon as they reached fifteen years of age, the six ecclesiastical peers, six lay peers, and a number of *conseillers d'Etat* and *maîtres des requêtes* also took part at various times.

As the "sovereign consistory of the law," *parlement* registered edicts, ordinances, royal declarations, letters patent, and decrees issued in the form of letters patent. It frequently amended them through its registration decrees and even rejected some. The *parlement* had the duty to remonstrate with the king when it deemed royal decisions to be in contradiction with earlier laws and regulations or contrary to the public interest; it thus had the power to point out to the king the defects, disadvantages, and dangers in his decisions, thereby giving rise to further deliberations of the king in his Council and possibly to new orders. The registration by the Paris *parlement* of certain important ordinances, edicts, or regulations made them enforceable throughout the kingdom. This was true of matters of government; in most cases of laws or regulations of importance only for administrative or judicial purposes, however, registration by the Paris *parlement* made a measure enforceable only within its own jurisdiction.

The Paris *parlement* enjoyed sole competence throughout the kingdom in regard to the "regale," or right of the king to enjoy the temporal revenues from vacant episcopal sees (temporal regale) and to present to benefices other than cures (spiritual regale) while waiting for the see to be filled.

As a "sovereign court" of justice and later as a "superior court," *parlement* had jurisdiction over "important affairs" and "cases concerning the estate of the *Grands* of the kingdom," as well as primary jurisdiction over such matters as cases involving the king, the Crown, the royal domain, or persons, communities, churches, abbeys, and other establishments enjoying the king's protection.

The *parlement* of Paris decided whether "sentences brought before it on appeal were well- or ill-founded," including appeals from the *bailliages* and *sénéchaussées*, for example. It reviewed the decrees of the other sovereign courts.

The Paris *parlement* heard the oaths of *baillis*, *sénéchaux*, governors and captains of provinces and cities, admirals, and marshals prior to their reception into office.

It was responsible for important police matters in its district and in particular for the city in which it sat, Paris.

One historial has given a good description of the competence of a *parlement*, based on the decrees of the *parlement* of Besançon:

> *Parlement* had jurisdiction over everything having to do with fiefs, finance, important police matters, defense of cities, fortifications, the pay and levy of troops, billeting, transportation, and subsistence of soldiers, legal formalization of acquisitions made by religious communities, surveillance of church-connected colleges, hospitals, prisons, and factories, defense of the Catholic religion, punishment of abuses by the spiritual authorities, liberties of the Gallican church, alleviation of peasant suffering in case of crop failure, price controls on bread and other much-needed commodities, stocking of markets, observation and reform of local customs, interpretation of regulations, upkeep of the cities and public sanitation, surveillance of beggars and vagabonds, recruitment of the militia, award of public works contracts by competitive bidding or administrative decision, horse-breeding, cadastral surveys, the sol, and construction of roads and canals.[6]

To this list we may add the defense of local and provincial privileges and liberties and adaptation of French law to local and provincial customs and usages.

The competence of any *parlement* naturally included the competence of any officeholder under its control.

All of these functions were carried out according to judicial procedures. The foregoing discussion should give some idea how the apparently restrictive definition given by Jean-Claude-Joseph de Ferrière in his *Dictionnaire de droit* should be understood: "*Parlement* is a sovereign company established by the king to judge, as a court of last resort, disputes between private individuals and to render decisions on appeals of sentences issued by lower judges." This definition may well have been imposed by the royal government.

Présidiaux, Bailliages, *and* Sénéchaussées

The district over which each *parlement* or sovereign council had jurisdiction was further subdivided into smaller districts under the supervision of lower courts subsidiary to the *parlement* or sovereign council, namely, the royal *bailliages* and *sénéchaussées*. These tribunals were similar. *Bailliages* were located mainly in the northern half of the kingdom and *sénéchaussées* in the southern half, but there were numerous exceptions to this rule. Brittany and the Boulonnais, for example, were regions in which justice was administered by *sénéchaussées*, while Labourd was a *bailliage*. Broadly speaking, whatever can be said about *bailliages* also applies to *sénéchaussées*.

It is difficult to give a complete list of all the *bailliages* and *sénéchaussées*. The royal administration itself may well have been incapable of supplying such a list. The list given by Armand Brette in his *Atlas* was not a true list of *bailliages* and *sénéchaussées* but merely a list of electoral districts qualified as *bailliages* for the Estates General of 1789. For electoral purposes, the royal government had considered the district of any tribunal that heard *cas royaux* (see vol. 1, p. 505) to be a *bailliage*. Courts other than *bailliages* and *sénéchaussées* were in some instances empowered to hear *cas royaux*, however. The number of *bailliages* and *sénéchaussées* is said to have been 100 in 1614 and more than 400 in 1789.

A *bailliage* or *sénéchaussée* had jurisdiction over a district that was not a cohesive, compact, well-defined territorial unit such as a commune or other administrative subdivision. It was rather a composite of various spheres of influence, similar to the district of a lower royal court or seigneurial court. Within each sphere of influence the court's authority applied to a heterogeneous assortment of entities: lay and ecclesiastical fiefs and *arrière*-fiefs, ecclesiastical benefices, religious communities, urban communities, and rural communities. The administrative geography was influenced by the organizational structure of the administration, which was in turn influenced by the social structure.

As an example, consider the *bailliage* that was known as the *prévôté et vicomté de Paris*. Because of the importance of the capital city, this was often referred to simply as the *ville et prévôté* or *ville et vicomté*. It had jurisdiction over an area ostensibly determined by the feudal hierarchy, incorporating three realms of jurisdiction: a domanial realm, a feudal realm, and a realm over which the royal courts had cognizance.

The dominal realm included royal rights and property. Cases pertaining to these were judged by the *prévôtés* and associated royal courts. It also included royal castellanies, made up of one or more fiefs. In some *prévôtés*, like that of Saint-Germain-en-Laye, there was no castellany. The importance of this realm of jurisdiction declined during the seventeenth century.

Feudal jurisdiction covered all direct vassals of the king, both lay and ecclesiastic. Its scope was gradually curtailed by the creation of duchy-peerages.

Finally, there was the realm covered by the ordinary royal courts. This included both cases within the competence of *prévôtés* and other royal tribunals and cases that, after trial in the seigneurial courts, could be appealed directly to the Châtelet of Paris, the seat of the *prévôt de la ville, prévôté, et vicomté de Paris*. Not included was an assortment of properties and judicial districts under the direct jurisdiction of the Paris *parlement*: temporalities of the churches, duchy-peerages, and royal residences together with their assorted forests, mills, and game preserves (which in the eighteenth century included the royal residences of Versailles, Meudon, Choisy-le-Roi, and Vincennes plus their secondary royal *bailliages*). Also excluded were certain forests under the jurisdiction of the *maîtrise des Eaux et Forêts* of Paris.

Thanks to its power to hear *cas royaux* and cases involving taxes, the *prévôté et vicomté de Paris* also had sovereign jurisdiction over rear-vassals and their subjects in these matters.

The king's agents could intervene in any *seigneurie* in any case involving the king's person, authority, property, or money, owing to the power of jurisdiction over *cas royaux*. After the declaration of 9 April 1736 (and 17 August 1737, for parish priests under the supervision of the Châtelet), jurisdiction over royal cases was further construed as extending over all parishes and religious communities that had their baptismal, marriage, and burial records initialed by representatives of the Châtelet. This was the beginning of an attempt to define this type of jurisdiction in a uniform manner. Eventually, this led to the definition of the type of district known as a *circonscription*.

It was no doubt taxation, however, that played the largest role in establishing a uniform definition of royal jurisdiction. During the fourteenth century taxes were levied by both royal and seigneurial castellanies and, within each castellany, in the so-called communities of inhabitants, which were fiscal rather than parochial in nature. These communities were homogeneous entities for the purpose of collecting taxes, and ultimately they were grouped together to form *circonscriptions*.

Thus fiscal districts very early became true *circonscriptions*. The élection of Paris continued to be divided into castellanies until the beginning of the seventeenth century, and the list of its castellanies was quite different from the list of its judicial *prévôtés*. It was the fiscal districts that were used as the basis for electing representatives from the communities of inhabitants to the Estates General. The communities called together to elect representatives were the communities consisting of persons grouped together for tax purposes, whereas the communities included in the districts having jurisdiction over royal cases were parochial communities.

For seventeenth- and eighteenth-century magistrates, the jurisdiction of a *bailliage* consisted of a list of localities and fiefs over which various rights could be exercised; it was not a district marked out on a map. The *procureurs du roi* responsible for drawing up and preserving these lists left out changes and made omissions and errors. This led to competition between rival royal jurisdictions with claims over the same fiefs or communities.

The Présidiaux

As heirs of the ancient *praesides provinciarum*, certain *bailliages* and *sénéchaussées* were granted, in 1552, ultimate jurisdiction over certain cases.

On 15 February 1552 (old style 1551), an edict was registered establishing a presidial jurisdiction in each *bailliage* that could conveniently accommodate one. Thus new magistracies were created. Under the provisions of the edict's first article, the *présidial* had sovereign and final jurisdiction in all civil cases involving sums of 250 livres *tournois* or less in nonrepeated transactions and 10 livres *tournois* or less in rent. Cases involving up to 500 livres *tournois* in nonrepeated transactions and up to 20 livres *tournois* in rent could, according to the second article, be judged by the *présidial* on commission, but the parties could appeal to *parlement*. Appeal was for arbitration, however, and did not result in a stay of execution of the sentence. The party in whose favor sentence had been handed down could have the judgment executed by posting a sufficient bond or by making himself bailee of the disputed goods.

In either case at least seven councillors were needed before a judgment could be returned, failing which sentences were submitted to appeal and could not be executed; the property in dispute remained in bailment.

As for criminal cases, the *présidial* had jurisdiction over what were known as "prevotal" or "presidial" cases. Jurisdiction over certain cases was concurrent with the *prévôts des maréchaux*.

The purpose of the edict was to free the *parlements* of the burden of hearing minor cases, the *parlements* then being so inundated that some cases had to wait more than five years for final judgment. At the same time it saved the parties to a case the costs they would have incurred because of the distance between their location and the site of the nearest sovereign court.

Under the edict each *présidial* heard appeals from a number of *bailliages*. A *présidial* might therefore have jurisdiction over quite an extensive area. The *présidial* that was established in the *bailliage* of Montbrison in January 1637 had jurisdiction over 13 walled cities, 400 parishes, 26 royal castellanies, and 4 *sièges particuliers*. The *présidial* was joined to a *bailliage*, however. This *bailliage* had presidial jurisdiction only as set forth in the edict of 1551–52. In all other cases it covered its own jurisdiction, which was independent of the jurisdiction of the *présidial* and limited to the territory of its *bailliage*, with no authority over the other *bailliages* included within the jurisdiction of the *présidial*. In some cases it is difficult to distinguish between the decisions of the *présidial* and the decisions of the *bailliage* with which it was combined. The *présidial* and its associated *bailliage* formed a single body that rendered judgment sometimes as a *présidial* and sometimes as a *bailliage*.

The *parlements* remained bitter enemies of the *présidiaux* and would register edicts concerning them only "on express command of the king," thereby underscoring, as the members of *parlement* saw it, the temporary nature of these measures. Every day they continued to hear appeals of judgments rendered under the provisions of the first article of the edict.

The edict of 27 December 1574 established the competence of the *présidiaux*. The Grand Conseil adjudicated disputes between *parlements* and *présidiaux* and reviewed the decisions of judges. It was usually the Grand Conseil that authenticated edicts establishing *présidiaux*, and its members were commissioned to install new tribunals. The ordinances of 1669 and 1737 upheld the right of the Grand Conseil to adjudicate disputes between *parlements* and *présidiaux*.

A *présidial* was worth a fortune to a city because it attracted the parties to cases, lawyers, and other court officials; it was also an honor to have one. It was thus easy for the king to establish *présidiaux* in times of financial distress brought on by war. Initially there were some sixty *présidiaux*.[7] Between 1580 and 1710 the number almost doubled. Louis XIII alone created nearly 30 *présidiaux*: among these were Lectoure (1622–34), Nerac (1629), Montauban (1630), Bueret, Milhau, Rodez, Brioude, Le Puy-en-Velay (1635), and Valence (1636), to name a few. The trend resumed between the War of the League of Augsburg and the War of the Spanish Succession. The year 1696 saw the creation of the *présidiaux* of Burgundy and Franche-Comté, followed in 1704 by new establishments at Ypres and Valenciennes.

The king twice attempted to place the *présidiaux* on a semestrial basis in order to increase the number of officeholders attached to them; these attempts were made in 1627 and in January of 1648. *Parlement* refused to verify the first edict. On the second it was obliged to give in, but the Fronde prevented the edict's execution.

Like the *bailliages*, the *présidiaux* entered on a period of decline. The profits accruing to the offices associated with them began to fall. For one thing, each time a new *présidial* was established, the jurisdiction of one or more old ones would be curtailed and the number of cases heard and *épices* collected would decrease. For another, the value of the livre *tournoi* fell and prices rose, while the salaries of officeholders remained fixed. The threshold determining the competence of the *présidial* to hear a case remained fixed at 250 livres. During the sixteenth century this amount was equal to the inheritance of a wealthy peasant or the inventory of a small merchant. By 1764, however, it had lost four-fifths of its value. According to the *présidial* of Lons-le-Saulnier, the *marc d'argent* was worth 14 livres 5 sols *tournois* in 1552 but 48 livres in 1764. The *setier* of Paris (a measure of corn) was worth about 2 livres 5 sols *tournois* in 1550 but 17 to 18 livres in 1764. This devaluation greatly reduced the number of cases falling within the jurisdiction of the *présidiaux*. The recruitment of officers and their zeal in their duties suffered the consequences.

The king attempted to repair the damage by giving precise definitions of areas of jurisdiction and competence and by raising the threshold below which the *présidiaux* were empowered to hear cases. The royal declaration of 29 May 1702 defined the respective attributions of *bailliages* and *présidiaux*. From that date on, the *présidiaux* were to have final jurisdiction over personal cases and also over crimes committed in the *bailliage* in which the *présidial* was located. The *bailliages* within the territory of a *présidial* would have first jurisdiction over crimes committed in their districts, and appeals would go to the *présidial*. The *bailliages* would have jurisdiction over *cas royaux*. Other crimes were to be handled by local judges with appeal to *parlement*.

During the time when d'Aguesseau was chancellor the king closed down the *prévôtés royales* located in the same cities as *bailiages*. He closed them one at a time, first in Provins in May 1733, next in Le Mans in January 1734, next in Clermont-en-Beauvais in April 1734, and so on. Most such *prévôtés* were gone by the time all were eliminated in one fell swoop by the edict of June 1749. Under the provisions of the declaration of 10 July 1739, *cas prévôtaux* whose worth did not exceed the limits established by the edict were to be treated as presidial cases in places where the *bailliage* was also a *présidial*. All other cases were to be tried before the *bailliages*.

Finally, after many petitions by the *présidiaux* and a goodly number of investigations, the threshold determining the extent of their jurisdiction was increased. Even before this, at the time Lorraine was reunited to France, the *présidiaux* then established in Nancy, Diequze, Mirecourt, and Saint-Dié were given final jurisdiction in cases up to 1,200 livres in value under the terms of an edict of June 1772. Then in October 1774 another edict increased the threshold to 2,000 livres principal and 80 livres rent for cases of the first kind and 4,000 livres principal and 160 livres rent for cases of the second kind, so as to spare citizens the need to abandon their families and businesses and embark on costly journeys in order to obtain justice in cases involving modest sums of money.

The *parlements* and ordinary *bailliages* opposed this move. They maintained that twenty-four out of twenty-five cases appealed to *parlements* in the provinces involved values under 2,000 livres, and the new edict would have taken these cases out of *parlement*'s jurisdiction. The ordinary *bailliages* feared that three-quarters of their cases would now be tried before the *présidiaux*. The upshot was that a regulation was issued in August 1777 revoking the second article of the edict. As for the first article, the jurisdiction of the *présidiaux* was limited to cases involving cash amounts up to 2,000 livres; they were forbidden to visit real property or to estimate the value of movable property. *Présidial* and *bailliage* cases were to be heard in the same way, without distinction. In addition, the August 1777 edict accorded to the *parquet* of *parlement* the same role played previously by the Grand Conseil. Article 26 of title II of the ordinance of 1737 was revoked. The Grand Conseil was stripped of its prerogatives with regard to the *présidiaux*. The parties to a case were left to choose freely whether to seek trial before *parlement* or the *présidial*. In case one party appealed a sentence from a lower court to *parlement* and the other to the *présidial*, the *présidial* was to decide its own competence in the matter. An appeal of its decision would be judged in summary fashion by the *parquet* of *parlement*.

The *présidiaux* lost a portion of their jurisdiction and half of their cases. In 1778 the severity of these measures was somewhat alleviated.

But the idea spread of according the right of final judgment, the so-called *présidialité*, to the *bailliages*. An edict of 1769 had accorded to all *bailliages* under the direct jurisdiction of the Paris *parlement* the right to judgment without appeal in all purely personal cases whose value did not exceed 40 livres. The declaration of 18 August 1785 stipulated that such cases would be judged summarily without the participation of the *procureur*. The ordinance of May 1788 issued by Lamoignon, keeper of the seals, established two classes of *bailliages*. There were to be forty-seven *grands bailliages* with two chambers each. The first chamber would have final judgment in cases up to 20,000 livres brought before it on appeal from lower courts. The second chamber would hear cases subject to further appeal. All other *bailliages* not eliminated by the ordinance were made into *présidiaux*. They were to have final judgment in civil cases up to 4,000 livres in value. Appeals of sentences handed down by these tribunals in cases whose value ranged from 4,000 to 20,000 livres were to be heard by the first chambers of the *grands bailliages*. In cases whose value exceeded 20,000 livres, the appeal could be taken directly to the sovereign courts. The ordinance was never put into effect, however.

Although the *présidiaux* remained in existence, they were moribund when they were finally abolished by the decrees of 6, 7, and 11 September 1790.

Unlike the other *présidiaux*, the *présidiaux* in Franche-Comté had jurisdiction over tax matters. The edict of September 1696 gave them jurisdiction over allegations of overtaxation. The declaration of 18 May 1706 added the power to hear all cases pertaining to ordinary taxes (excluding the *capitation*, the *dixième*, and the *vingtièmes*), with final judgment in cases up to 20 livres and appeal to the Chambre des Comptes at Dôle above that amount. These *présidiaux* were supposed to employ a simplified procedure, hearing cases summarily in open session without *épices* or emoluments.

Bailliages and Sénéchaussées

The *bailli* (probably from the Latin *bajulus*, meaning "guard" or "protector") was a royal officer *d'épée* in whose name justice was dispensed within a certain district. The *bailliage* was a tribunal consisting of judges who were royal officeholders and who dispensed justice in the name of the *bailli*. The word *bailliage* was also used to refer to the geographical area over which this tribunal had jurisdiction.

Baillis and *sénéchaux* had to be *gentilshommes* with noble names and coats of arms and thus descended from a nobility traceable at least as far back as Philip the Fair and supposed to have originated in time immemorial. They were also supposed to have served as officers in the king's army according to article 21 of the ordinance of Moulins of 1560 and article 263 of the ordinance of Blois of 1579 confirmed by council decree of 16 December 1759, couched in the form of letters patent registered at the Chambre des Comptes of Paris on 12 January 1760.

Baillis and *sénéchaux* were supposed to be at least thirty years of age, but exceptions were often granted. They were received by the Grand-Chambre of *parlement*, where they swore an oath and were installed in the seat of their *bailliage* or *sénéchaussée*.

According to the ordinance of 3 May 1519, reaffirmed by the regulatory decree of 21 July 1759, all judgments handed down by the *bailliage*, all commissions addressed to it, and all documents prepared by notaries and scribes within its jurisdiction were required to mention the *bailli* in the heading. When a response to a petition was required, the *lieutenant général* of the *bailliage* or other magistrate used the words, "M. le Bailli declares and orders," except in the case of a presidial decree or judgment. Presidial judgments bore the heading, "The men holding the presidial seat of." The *bailli* or *sénéchal* was entitled to preside over any session of court or any audience, on which occasion he wore a black coat with collar and sword (edict of February 1705). He was also entitled to preside over presidial sessions but not to vote or to take part in debate, for he had no degree in the law. In Provence, however, the *sénéchaux* offered their opinions along with the other judges.

The real functions of the *baillis* and *sénéchaux* were mainly military and political. They mustered the *ban* and *arrière-ban* and commanded the troops, besides which they were responsible for guarding, defending, and fortifying cities. They assumed the leadership of the nobility whenever it was granted the privilege of assembling, although they did not call themselves "heads of the nobility," the only head of the nobility being the king (council decree of 30 October 1761). They received all letters issuing from the court, the governor of the province, or the *intendant* of the *généralité* and notified the *lieutenant général* of the *bailliage* of receipt. The *lieutenant général* would then assemble all the officeholders of the place so that the letters and packages could be opened in the Chambre du Conseil and their contents considered in the presence of the *bailli* or *sénéchal*.

In reality, though, since the *bailli* or *sénéchal* was usually away with the army, even these functions were performed by a magistrate, the *lieutenant général*, who was assisted by the "king's men," the *avocat* and the *procureur*, who normally gave the *bailli* the benefit of their counsel whenever he was present.

The competence of the magistrates of the *bailliage*, of course, included the competence of all lower judges, even for the first hearing of a case, just as the competence of the *parlements* included the competence of the *bailliages* and *sénéchaussées*.

In the civil domain *bailliages* and *sénéchaussées* were competent to hear any case involving the nobility, that is, all personal affairs of nobles, a term that included the king's secretaries, the *premiers officiers en chef* of the royal household, and the king's *gentilshommes ordinaires*, according to decrees of *parlement* of 27 July 1598, and 5 June 1659. If the case involved real property or a mortgage, however, the judge of the place where the property was located had the right to hear the case. The *baillis* could intervene to forestall action in some cases in which nobles were involved: wardships and trusteeships involving minor nobles; the division of bequests involving a noble, even if a portion of the bequest consisted of common property; actions involving notes of hand or promises made under private seal. They had jurisdiction over the seizure of common property from noble persons if such seizures were carried out as a result of judgments handed down by a lower court within their jurisdiction.

They also had jurisdiction over all matters pertaining to the nature, existence, or extent of fiefs or noble property. When it was a question of payment, the *prévôts* or seigneurial judges had competence to hear the case under the provisions of the regulation of 23 May 1626 and the civil ordinance of 1667.

Baillis were authorized to attend to all matters pertaining to the honorific rights of the Church, including *banc, chapelle, litre funèbre*, and *honneurs*.

Their next main area of competence included all *cas royaux* or cases involving the king, whether in regard to his person or domain or in regard to the police of his kingdom or the rights attaching to the sovereign power.

In the civil domain, the *cas royaux* included, first of all, any matter pertaining to a royal office, such as examination and acceptance of prospective officeholders, cases involving either officeholders or the rights attaching to their offices, seizure of offices and seals affixed to the minutes, papers, and effects of notaries, *receveurs des consignations*, and *commissaires aux saisies réelles*, and inspection and supervision of officeholders. Also included were the registration of edicts, ordinances, letters patent, and royal declarations.

Next came claims against the property or income of the king's domain (until 1627). In April of 1627 an edict gave responsibility in these cases to the *trésoriers de France*, except in Orléanais, an appanage, and later in Lorraine, where the *trésoriers de France* had no jurisdiction.

Next were the fiefs of the royal *mouvance* and the faith and homage of the king's vassals.

Then came the *droits d'aubaine, bâtardise, deshérence, confiscation, francs-fiefs, amortissements*, and new acquisitions.

Next were cases involving the public streets and highways, city fortifications, navigable rivers, islands and landings, unowned lands, and properties or domains attaching to royal cities, as set forth in the decree of the Paris *parlement* dated 11 December 1627.

Next were disputes over *tailles*, *aides*, *gabelles*, *contrôle*, *centième denier*, *capitation*, and all royal taxes and monies, although in fact between 1635 and 1648 and after 1656 the *intendants* and *commissaires* played an increasingly large role in affairs of this kind.

Next were cases pertaining to the constitution of duchies, peerages, marquisates, counties, baronies, and other *fiefs de dignité* and cases involving the concession of privileges to cities, communities, universities, academies, "or other private parties."

Then came all cases pertaining to the estate or rights of the nobility, privileges and rights of justice, the naturalization of foreigners, the legitimation of bastards, letters of grace, remission, abolition, or commutation of sentence, letters of rehabilitation, emancipation, and age benefit, change of name and armorial bearings, and all letters granting royal favor of any kind, including concessions of fairs and markets.

Next came matters involving the king's dignity and sovereignty in regard to his relations with the Church and the clergy and cases concerning royal establishment of churches, chapters, abbeys, priories, commanderies, hospitals, communities, and academies; the maintenance of Church discipline and police and the application of canon and ecclesiastical law so as to insure that there would be no conflict with temporal authority; jurisdiction over infringements of the liberties of the Gallican church by the Roman *curia;* prohibition of activities of the ecclesiastical authorities likely to be inimical to the royal authority or to disturb the peace and tranquillity of the state; all matters involving benefices; and administration of the property of people who had fled for reasons of religion, according to the edict of December 1688.

Next came cases involving the patrimonial funds of the cities, the *octroi*, and usurpation of city rights such as grazing and pasturage.

Next, the general police of the kingdom, civil status, marriages, baptisms, and burials.

Next, the general police of forests and rivers in matters of interest to the king and the general public. The bulk of such matters were entrusted to officeholders in the *maîtrises*.

Then came the execution of official and consular sentences as set forth in edicts of November 1563 and September 1610.

Next were all cases to which the *procureur du roi* for the *bailliage* was a party.

In the criminal domain, *cas royaux* included offenses against the majesty of the sovereign, the rights of his crown, the dignity of his officers, and the safety of the public.

Next came, first of all, crimes of *lèse-majesté* committed against the king's person or the state, and, second, leagues, associations, revolts, uprisings, seditious speeches or writings, plots, treason, and defeatism. The edict of August 1669 and the declaration of 14 July 1682 added to the list of crimes leaving the kingdom to live abroad and rebellion against orders and commands issued by the king or the secretaries of state. By tradition *parlement* had exclusive jurisdiction over crimes of *lèse-majesté* of the first order. But the criminal ordinance of 1670 granted jurisdiction over *lèse-majesté* of any sort to the *baillis* and *sénéchaux*.

Then came cases involving the carrying of weapons such as rifles, swords, pistols, or alpenstocks.

Next were cases of illegal assembly, sedition, inciting riot, and scandalous preaching.

Next were acts of violence or "public force."

Then came alteration of money and the use or manufacture of counterfeit money, which was also included in the list of *cas prévôtaux* by the declaration of 1731.

Next came malfeasance and other crimes committed by royal officeholders, according to the decree of 30 August 1606. Jurisdiction over these cases was denied to seigneurial officeholders. In any case, the principal officers of *bailliages* and *sénéchaussées* could be judged only by the *parlements*. Under the edict of March 1551, royal officeholders in extraordinary jurisdictions or jurisdictions of attribution could be judged only by their superiors. For example, the *élus*, the *receveurs des tailles*, the *juges des traites*, and the officers of salt warehouses could be judged only by the Cours des Aides. The judges of the Eaux et Forêts, the *juges des traites*, the *juges des élections*, the judges of the salt warehouses, and the admiralty judges had jurisdiction over malfeasance by their *huissiers* and *sergents* (ordinance of the Eaux et Forêts, August 1699, ordinances of the Fermes, 1681–87, ordinance of the Navy Department, 1688).

Next came disorders due to heresy and disruptions to divine worship.

Next came violations of safeguard, embezzlement, the levying of taxes without royal commission, falsification of the royal seal, arson of cities, churches, and other public places, escapes from royal prisons, the destruction of city walls or fortifications, the theft of patrimonial funds or the *octroi;* activities inimical to the safety of royal roads, oppressions and exactions by lords against their vassals, premeditated murder, dueling, crimes against nature, sodomy, etc.

Then came secular simony.

Besides *cas royaux* the *bailliages* and *sénéchausées* also had jurisdiction over all crimes and misdemeanors committed within their district, even in the forests or on streams and rivers, provided they had nothing to do with hunting or fishing. The murder of a traveler in a forest in order to steal his money would be an example of such a crime. In these cases, the *baillis* and *sénéchaux* had the power to claim jurisdiction and take the case away from seigneurial judges within twenty-four hours of the commission of the crime or misdemeanor and away from *prévôts* and similar officers within seventy-two hours.

The *baillis* and *sénéchaux* had exclusive jurisdiction over *cas royaux*. Lower judges had the power only to investigate the accused and issue a warrant for his arrest and then to send either the prisoner or the files in the case to the *bailli* or *sénéchal*.

Baillis and *sénéchaux* had jurisdiction over privileged cases involving ecclesiastics, including both crimes, or violations of natural or civil law with the intention to do wrong, and misdemeanors, or intentional injuries. There were purely ecclesiastical misdemeanors, which involved matters of ecclesiastical discipline, were subject to punishment under canon law, and were best left to the appropriate church authorities. Common misdemeanors such as ordinary larceny, unpremeditated homicide, insults, concubinage, and simony, all crimes deserving punishment more severe than the Church was able to inflict, could be prosecuted either by the *bailliage* or by the Church authorities, but judgment by the latter was preferred. Some crimes and misdemeanors committed by ecclesiastics entailed penalties involving death, personal restraint, or penal servitude, however, and these punishments, which went beyond the penalties set forth in canon law, could not be administered by Church judges. Such cases were referred to as "privileged" and included, for example, crimes and misdemeanors against the welfare and tranquillity of the public, highway robbery, carrying of prohibited weapons, and public violence. Judgment in such matters was reserved to the royal judge.

The *baillis* and *sénéchaux* also had jurisdiction over all crimes or misdemeanors in which the defendant was an ecclesiastic or *gentilhomme* and all crimes committed by officers of the judiciary.

The *ballis* and *sénéchaux* might also claim jurisdiction in certain cases in competition with the *prévôts des maréchaux* or *présidiaux*. *Cas prévôtaux*, some of which also figured in the list of *cas royaux*, were crimes that demanded prompt punishment or that were unworthy of the favor of appeal or else crimes that were committed by persons of low or contemptible status.

The nature of these cases was further specified by the criminal ordinance of 1670, which was amended and extended by the declaration of 5 February 1731.

A distinction was made between *cas prévôtaux* classed as such because of the quality of the persons involved and *cas prévôtaux* classed as such because of the nature of the crime. In the first category were crimes committed by vagabonds and vagrants, persons without any profession or trade, with no fixed abode, and no visible means of support. It was necessary to arrest such people, even if no charges or accusations had been made against them, because they represented a burden upon and a "threat to civil society." The same was true of able-bodied beggars without home or hearth. Repeat offenders also fell into this category; if they had violated parole, however, exclusive jurisdiction belonged to the judge granting parole. This class also included soldiers who extorted money, abused their authority, or committed other crimes, whether on campaign or in places of assembly or bivouac, as well as anyone—even civilians—who aided or abetted a deserter.

Cas prévôtaux classed as such because of the nature of the crime included highway robbery, but not robbery committed in the streets of cities; thefts involving breaking and entering, but only if weapons or violent acts were involved, or if walled enclosures, roofs, or outside doors or windows were penetrated. Sacrilegious acts involving breach of close were also included, under the same conditions just mentioned. So were cases involving sedition or public disturbance and illegal assembly or muster involving the bearing of arms.

Questions of competence gave rise to further distinctions. In cities in which *prévôts des maréchaux* resided, *cas prévôtaux* classed as such because of the quality of the accused fell within their competence. Presidial judges were denied jurisdiction in cases involving crimes committed by deserters and their accomplices, these crimes being purely military matters. Presidial judges competed with the *prévôts des maréchaux* for jurisdiction over crimes committed within the district of a *bailliage* or *sénéchaussée* to which the *présidial* was attached, and preference went to the presidial judges if they issued a warrant prior to or on the same day as the *prévôts des maréchaux*. If the crime was committed in the district of one of the other *bailliages* or *sénéchaussées* under the jurisdiction of the *présidial*, however, jurisdiction fell to the *baillis* or *sénéchaux* and the case could be appealed to *parlement*. This procedure was upheld by declaration of 29 May 1702. The *baillis* and *sénéchaux* had priority over the *maréchaux* if they issued a warrant first or on the same day.

The competence of ordinary judges was further extended in 1702 and again in 1731. In regard, first of all, to *cas prévôtaux* classed as such because of the quality of the accused, all royal judges (and even judges of *seigneurs* with powers of high justice, considered royal judges in such cases) were given jurisdiction subject to appeal. In such cases they competed with the *prévôts des maréchaux* but enjoyed priority if they investigated or issued a warrant first or on the same day. In 1731 all ordinary judges, including seigneurial judges, were accorded the power to investigate, interrogate, and issue warrants in all *cas prévôtaux* classed as such because of the nature of the crime, and not merely in cases of flagrant violation. The *prévôts des maréchaux*, on the other hand, were given permission to investigate, interrogate, and issue warrants in connection with ordinary crimes and misdemeanors.

Thus wrongdoers were prosecuted more forcefully than before. A judgment of competence was still needed, however, before the power to judge crimes and misdemeanors could be attributed.

The ordinary courts of the city, *prévôté*, and *vicomté* of Paris, or Châtelet of Paris,[8] in which the *prévôt* was a *noble d'épée*, was in fact a *bailliage* to which a *présidial* was attached.

The Châtelet was the seat of the *prévôté*, *bailliage*, and *présidial* of Paris, its suburbs, and the district under the jurisdiction of the *prévôté* of Paris. As a royal *bailli*, the *prévôt* of Paris was an appellate judge for lower royal and seigneurial courts located within his district. The competence of the Châtelet of Paris extended well beyond that district, however, because it enjoyed the "right of pursuit." In other words, officers of the Châtelet were empowered to continue, anywhere in the kingdom, cases begun at the Châtelet. Jurisdiction could be assigned under the seal of the Châtelet. The Châtelet therefore had jurisdiction over all cases involving documents prepared by its notaries. These notaries were entitled to perform their functions anywhere in the kingdom. These privileges were upheld by council decrees issued in opposition to the *parlement* of Normandy on 1 June 1672, 3 July 1673, and 12 May 1684. But the Châtelet was under the control of the Paris *parlement. Parlement* not only heard appeals of judgments handed down by the Châtelet but also it held audiences at the Châtelet five times each year, on Tuesday of Holy Week, on the Friday before Pentecost, on the eve of Assumption, on the eve of St. Simon's and St. Jude's day (27 October), and on the day before Christmas Eve. On each occasion the *lieutenant civil*, the *lieutenant criminel*, the *lieutenant criminel de robe courte*, the king's men, and, later, the *lieutenant de police* were present "so as to be ready to respond in case there is any complaint against them."

During the eighteenth century the Châtelet steadily expanded its competence at the expense of the *Bureau de la Ville*, the *prévôt des marchands*, and the aldermen of Paris. In theory the Châtelet was responsible, through its *commissaires*, for carrying out certain functions in the sixteen *quartiers* of the city, and the *Bureau de la Ville* was responsible, through its *quartiniers*, for carrying out certain other functions. Between 1663 and 1673, however, there came to be a distinction between the *quartiers* "of the city" and the *quartiers* "of the Châtelet." The council decree of 14 January 1702 once again unified the administrative geography of Paris, establishing 20 *quartiers* over which both sets of tribunals had jurisdiction. But another council decree, dated 3 February 1703, reestablished the 16 *quartiers* for the jurisdiction of the *Bureau de la Ville* while reserving the 20 *quartiers* of the 1702 partition for the jurisdiction of the Châtelet. During the *lieutenance* of Feydeau de Marville (1740–47), Parisians showed an increasing tendency to have recourse to the *commissaires* in preference to the *quartiniers*.

The Châtelet asserted its claims in 1697. The *prévôt des marchands* and the aldermen had no competence beyond certain affairs of navigation and commerce on the Seine. The remainder of the jurisdiction of the *Bureau de la Ville* was limited to "enterprises . . . within the ordinary royal jurisdiction." The Châtelet claimed exclusive jurisdiction in general police matters as well as the right to issue ordinances and to have them published and posted publicly. The Châtelet conceded to the *Bureau de la Ville* the right to participate in particular police matters and apply specific punishments to each offense, subject to concurring jurisdiction with the officers of the Châtelet, which claimed priority. The Châtelet accorded the *Bureau de la Ville* some role in consular jurisdiction, specifically, "the right to exclusive jurisdiction in disputes between merchants on the river, mariners, and others employed in the navigation, operation, or unloading of boats, as long as said disputes are limited to payment for merchandise, carriage, or other remuneration in connection with commerce."⁹ The Châtelet refused to accord the *Bureau de la Ville* any general competence in matters pertaining to the provisioning of Paris. Jurisdiction over cases involving corn, wine, and wood was conceded only when these commodities arrived in the city by water. On behalf of the *lieutenant général de police* the Châtelet claimed jurisdiction over the quays in all matters not related to navigation in the strict sense. And so on. In the end the actual functions of the *prévôt des marchands*, aldermen, and *quartiniers* were considerably curtailed.

Judges in the Ordinary Lower Courts

The territory under the jurisdiction of a *bailliage* or *sénéchaussée* was divided into districts served by lower courts. These were known by various names, depending on the place. In Normandy they were called *prévôtés* or *vicomtés*. In Languedoc and Provence they were called *vigueries* or *bailies*. In Ile-de-France, Champagne, and elsewhere they were known as castellanies and sometimes as *bailliages*. All these various units had similar if not identical competence, and what can be said about the *prévôtés* applies to the others, with minor differences.

The *baillis* and *sénéchaux* were the superiors of the *prévôts*, supervising their activities and hearing appeals of their decisions.

The *prévôts* and their counterparts in the other types of district had first jurisdiction over all cases involving commoners residing within their district, even if noble property was involved, provided the case involved personal possession and concerned contracts or payments. In cases involving ownership, quality, or share in feudal rights, faith and homage, *aveux* and census, receipt by sovereign hand or feudal redemption, competence belonged to the *bailliage* or *sénéchaussée*. The latter were also competent to hear cases in which one party was noble or where the ownership of an estate or city domain was involved. The division of competence between *baillis* and *sénéchaux* on the one hand and *prévôts* on the other was based largely on the principle that judgment should be rendered by peers of the parties to a case.

Under these conditions, the *prévôts* had jurisdiction over cases between commoners when fiefs and noble inheritances were at stake (decrees of the Paris *parlement* dated 27 September 1624 and 20 April 1660); over the nomination of tutors, executors, and administrators, even in cases in which the bequests were noble and subject to accounting procedures applicable to noble property (decrees of the Paris *parlement* dated 11 December 1627 and 20 April 1660); over any suit pertaining to real estate or mortgage associated with a commoner's bequest of property located within the *prévôté*, even if the parties were noble; over the division of property and entailed estates among commoners even if the estate consisted of fiefs or noble bequests; over writs on seized real property, if the bequests and the parties subject to seizure were commoners; over all cases involving ecclesiastical commoners (decree of the Paris *parlement* dated 17 January 1708) and over all commoners holding royal office in the *présidiaux* and *élections*, as long as the case did not concern their offices (decrees of the Paris *parlement* dated 5 June 1659, 30 July 1679, and 9 August 1654); over cases involving churches, chapels, religious communities, abbeys, priories, chapters, vestries, commanderies, hospitals, and infirmaries, unless custodial letters had been issued; over cases to which the mayor and aldermen of the *prévôt*'s place of residence were parties; over disputes involving the repair of walls, gates, towers, fortifications, quays, and roads and paths of cities and royal *prévôtés*; over simple, straightforward *cas royaux* such as the execution of letters of chancellery not specifically addressed to the *baillis* or cases involving royal offices and their subsidiary rights.

The *prévôts* competed with the *baillis* and *sénéchaux* for jurisdiction over certain cases; their jurisdiction might be overruled in some instances, but in any case they superseded the seigneurial judges in such matters. These included royal privileges and farms on the royal domain, when the case involved a question of payment only and the dues themselves were not contested or when the *procureur du roi* was not a party to the case, the *trésoriers de France* being competent in these two circumstances; cases involving stewardship; cases appealed directly or indirectly from a seigneurial court, as long as they were not claimed by the *seigneur* or his *procureur fiscal*, or cases originating in a contract between persons subject to seigneurial jurisdiction in which the contract was signed under royal seal and made subject to the *prévôt*'s jurisdiction; oppositions to marriages, clandestine marriages, or marriages between persons under seigneurial jurisdiction that violated the provisions of the relevant ordinances (decree of 16 July 1708); disputes relative to ordinances issued by bishops and archdeacons in the course of their visits concerning reduction of *bancs* or *sépultures*, the repair of churches, the accounts of church factories, and the like; actions or confinement resulting from decisions handed down by church judges; the execution of consular judgments; confirmation of arbitration settlements involving commoners under the *prévôt*'s jurisdiction.

The *prévôts* had *droit d'assises* over persons under their jurisdiction but were not allowed to invite judges whose decisions were subject to appeal to the *prévôt*. They executed decisions handed down by the assizes of the *baillis* and *sénéchaux* in cases originally heard by the *prévôtés* (the Crémieu edict and decrees of the Paris *parlement* dated 5 June 1659, 20 April 1660, and 9 August 1684).

The *bailli* was bound to refer to the *prévôt* any case within the competence of the latter that might be brought to him for first hearing.

In criminal matters, if the ordinary judge of the place where the crime was committed had not conducted an investigation and issued a warrant within three days thereafter, the superior judge could assume jurisdiction. According to the decree of 5 June 1569, however, the superior judge was bound to refer the case to the lower judge if the latter subsequently claimed jurisdiction and if negligence could not be proved.

The Extraordinary Tribunals and Tribunals of Attribution

The Sovereign Courts, the Grand Conseil, *the* Chambres des Comptes, *the* Cours des Aides, *and the* Cours des Monnaies

Grand Conseil. By a process analogous to the separation of such specialized components as *parlement* from the old Curia Regis, the Grand Conseil was first detached from the Grand Conseil du Roi during the reign of Charles VII and then made into a sovereign court by edict of Charles VIII on 2 August 1497, and by edict of Louis XII on 13 July 1498. By 1598 it had become a court of attribution that the king could use as a court of justice superior to all others. Although its territorial jurisdiction extended in principle to the entire kingdom, *unico universus* (though residents of such conquered or reconquered territories as Flanders, Hainault, Alsace, Franche-Comté, and Roussillon could not be required to appear in court outside their province and were therefore not bound to plead before it), the competence of the Grand Conseil varied with the needs of the kings, who never managed to learn how to utilize this court to full advantage and gradually allowed its importance to decline.

As an exceptional court, the Grand Conseil had civil and criminal competence as broad as that of the *parlements*. If need be, it could even replace them. In fact it did replace the *parlement* of Burgundy, which was prohibited from meeting in 1659. In 1753 it was put on notice to replace the *parlement* of Paris. The Grand Conseil had the power to publish and duly register ordinances, edicts, royal declarations, and letters patent for the entire kingdom and to supplant all the *parlements* in their political role.

But the king made use of the Grand Conseil as dictated by the needs of policy and high administration, awarding it jurisdiction, sometimes as a favor, sometimes by general summons (*évocation*), over all cases involving a corps, a community, or an individual, or, again, awarding it by special summons jurisdiction over some specific case. General summonses were issued in behalf of the merchants of La Rochelle in 1597, of Bordeaux in 1616, of Normandy in 1618, and of the Compagnie des Iles d'Amerique in March 1642. Other general summonses favored certain financiers along with their servants, agents, and clerks. Still others favored certain *grands seigneurs*, such as Cardinal Richelieu, the ducs de Richelieu, Cardinal Mazarin, the ducs de Mazarin, the ducs de Broglie, and so on. General summonses were also issued in behalf of certain monasteries such as the abbey of Val-de-Grâce, of religious orders such as Grandmont in 1627 and Prémontré in 1629, and of religious congregations such as the Oratoire on 7 January 1629, the Mission on 28 February 1684, the Jesuits on 30 June 1738, and the Benedictines of Saint-Maur on 19 April 1739. Still others favored such corps as the king's secretaries, the *trésoriers de France*, and so on. Summonses were also used to attribute jurisdiction to the Grand Conseil in cases where one party suspected the regular judge of partiality owing to his relations or alliances or to personal emity.

In its role as a conciliator of conflicts, the Grand Conseil had jurisdiction over contradictions between decrees issued by different *parlements*, over jurisdictional conflicts between the *parlements* and the *présidiaux*, in which it had the final say, and over jurisdictional conflicts between the *présidiaux* and the *prévôts des maréchaux*. It also adjudicated conflicts between judges responsible to different sovereign courts, as between ordinary royal judges, who were responsible to the *parlements*, and *élus*, who were responsible to the Cours des Aides.

In its role as an administrative tribunal, the Grand Conseil had jurisdiction over cases pertaining to possessions of archbishoprics, bishoprics, and abbeys that were at the king's disposal under the terms of the Concordat of Bologna of 1516. It also had jurisdiction over cases pertaining to benefices to which nominations could be made by the chancellor, the *maîtres des requêtes*, the *président* and members of the *parlement* of Paris, and the cardinals and other prelates of the kingdom under the terms of various papal indults. It had jurisdiction over expectative graces granted by the king upon his accession to the throne or upon receiving the oath of fidelity of some bishop, over stewards of archbishoprics, bishoprics, and abbeys and other benefices subject to royal patronage, over redemption of alienated Church property (20 December 1648), and over the execution of the declaration of 18 December 1634 concerning priestly emoluments. By Norman tradition, during periods when the patronage of a benefice was in dispute or left to one of the king's minor immediate vassals, nomination to the benefices of the province of Rouen then being up to the king, the Grand Conseil was empowered to act in his behalf. As guardian of the privileges and jurisdiction of the *grand aumônier*, the Grand Conseil was given general power to hear cases concerning positions in monasteries set aside for soldiers crippled in the line of duty (June 1606) and cases of interest to infirmaries and hospitals. The Grand Conseil heard appeals from the Chamber on General Hospital Reform (1606, 1612). The competence of the Paris *parlement* was reduced to the regale alone.

As part of the king's entourage, the Grand Conseil heard appeals from the *prévôt de l'Hôtel du Roi* in civil cases involving the king's commensals, the privileged merchants, and the ambassadors and other foreigners who followed the court. It heard appeals of judgments handed down in cases of hunting violations by the captain of the Varenne du Louvre. It heard cases concerning frank-fees and new acquisitions, searches of the royal domain (Guyenne, Languedoc, Aunis, 1609, 1625, 1664), bankrupts, stage coaches, toll gates, navigation on certain rivers, landings on rivers flowing through more than one jurisdiction, prohibition of certain merchandise in the kingdom (June 1738), and many other matters—in short, whatever cases the king wanted it to hear.

In regard to disputes between the king and the *parlements*, the Grand Conseil might have served the king as a useful tool, since it could stand in for any of the *parlements*, in particular in the registration of edicts. It was consequently the *bête noire* of the *parlements*, which went so far as to challenge its status as a sovereign court. The king did not make skillful use of the Grand Conseil, however, and in fact steadily curtailed its competence. As early as the sixteenth century it had lost to the Conseil d'Etat the power to quash decrees and to settle jurisdictional disputes between the sovereign courts. The edict of January 1768 eliminated the general summonses to which the Grand Conseil owed most of the cases brought before it. On the ecclesiastical side it retained jurisdiction only over disputes involving the status of orders, possessions attaching to benefices, building repair, and petitions involving monks, incumbent clergymen, and congregations. Eliminated on 13 April 1771, the Grand Conseil was reestablished on 12 November 1774 but in August 1777 lost its role as final arbiter and guardian of the jurisdiction of the *présidiaux*. By the end of the Ancien Régime it was hearing less than half the number of cases it had heard in an earlier period.

Chambres des Comptes. The Chambres des Comptes were sovereign courts responsible for accounting for the use of public funds, overseeing the upkeep of the royal domain and its subsidiary rights, and adjudicating any cases that might arise out of these responsibilities. There were independent Chambres des Comptes in Paris, Dijon (for Burgundy), Grenoble (for Dauphiné), Nantes (for Brittany), and Blois (for the appanage of the duc d'Orléans). The Cours des Aides were sovereign courts that served as final arbiter of cases involving *aides*, *tailles*, *gabelles*, *octrois*, *droits de marques* and other *droits de subsides* levied under royal authority. There were autonomous Cours des Aides in Paris, Montauban (first located in Cahors in 1642 and transferred to Montauban in 1661), Bordeaux (established in 1637), and Clermont in Auvergne. Several Chambres des Comptes were also Cours des Aides, including those in Aix-en-Provence, Montpellier (for Languedoc), Rouen (for Normandy), and Dôle (for Franche-Comté). Three *parlements* (Grenoble, Dijon, and Rennes) were also Cours des Aides. The *parlements* of Pau and Metz were at the same time also Chambres des Comptes and Cours des Aides.

The Chambres des Comptes ranked just below the *parlements* and the Cours des Aides just below the Chambres des Comptes.

The Chambre des Comptes of Paris had jurisdiction over the *généralités* of Paris, Soissons, Amiens, Chalons, Orléans, Bourges, Moulins, Poitiers, Limoges, Riom, Lyon, Bordeaux, Montauban, La Rochelle, and Tours. It registered the oaths of fidelity sworn by archbishops, bishops, abbots, and other persons granted benefices under royal patronage as well as heads of orders who were subject to regale. It received the faith and homage of the king's vassals for the lands, titles, principalities, peerages, duchies, marquisates, counties, and baronies in its possession. It kept the *aveux* and *dénombrements* and faith and homage of fiefs, lands, and *seigneuries* received by the *trésoriers de France*. It registered royal declarations impinging on royal domains, income, and finance, including declarations of war, peace treaties, marriage contracts involving the kings and Children of France, appanages, redemptions and alienations of parts of the domain, *lettres de naturalité* and *amortissement*, legitimations, gifts, pensions, bonuses, letters establishing peerages, duchies, marquisates, counties, baronies, castellanies, *hautes justices*, letters of ennoblement, and confirmations and rehabilitations of nobility. It certified the privileges of provinces and cities and letters granting permission to establish fairs and markets, letters of exemption, and so on. It examined and approved the accounts of the royal treasury, the royal household, the princely households, and all account officers, treasurers, and tax collectors within its purview. It adjudicated disputes arising out of any of these matters. In civil matters there was in principle no recourse against judgments and decrees handed down by the Chambre des Comptes except a review by the same chamber, as set forth in the Moulins ordinance of 1566. In criminal matters it had full investigatory powers up to but not including torture. The *parlement* and Chambre des Comptes met jointly to consider pleas by the *procureur général* and *avocats généraux* and then issued a common opinion. Cases were heard and reviewed in the Chambre du Conseil by one *président* and five or six *conseillers* from *parlement* and one *président* and five or six *maîtres des comptes*. The *président* of *parlement* presided. He was assisted by two *greffiers*, one from *parlement* and one from the Chambre des Comptes. Decrees were headed "la Chambre du Conseil et Chambre des Comptes."

Cours des Aides. The jurisdiction of the Cour des Aides of Paris was almost the same as that of the *parlement* of Paris. It did not include Auvergne, which was assigned to the Cour des Aides of Clermont-Ferrand in 1551, but did include Saintonge and the *élections* of Cognac, Saint-Jean-d'Angely, and Sables-d'Olonne, which were within the purview of the *parlement* of Bordeaux. It was final arbiter in both civil and criminal cases of appeals arising out of all trials and disputes involving *tailles* and *gabelles*, the *cinq grosses fermes*, entry and exit duties, *octrois*, and all other imposts. It adjudicated disputed nobility and even titles when privileges were in question. It gave its approval to letters restoring nobility after derogation. It had jurisdiction over all disputes among farmers of monies owed the king, their partners and backers, other associates, and clerks. It had jurisdiction over writs for the seizure of real property, that is, court orders stating that all formalities had been observed for a piece of property to be sold by the court and awarding free and clear title to the highest bidder in cases involving sale for payment of debts to the king. It was sole judge of its officers' privileges, to the exclusion of the Paris *parlement* and the provincial *parlements* and Cours des Aides. Its officers could obtain their *committimus* from the chancellor by submitting excerpts from the transcript kept by the *greffier* of the Cour des Aides.

Cours des Monnaies. The Cour des Monnaies was the heir of the Chambre des Monnaies established in 1358. It was made a sovereign court by the edict of January 1552 and ranked just below the Cour des Aides. Its jurisdiction was vast but did not include all the territory ruled by the king of France. An edict of June 1694 established a Cour des Monnaies in Lyon with jurisdiction over the provinces, *généralités*, and *départements* of Lyon, Dauphiné, Provence, Auvergne, Toulouse, Montpellier, Montauban, and Bayonne. In October 1705 the provinces and *pays* of Breese, Bugey, Valromey, and Gex were added. The edict of August 1771 did away with the Cour in Lyon in favor of the one in Paris. From January to March 1645 there existed two other Cours des Monnaies, one in Lyon, the other in Libourne. In addition, the Chambre des Comptes at Dôle and the *parlements* of Metz and Pau played the role of Cours des Monnaies in their districts until 1771 and 1775, respectively.

Until 1661 the Cour des Monnaies drew up all edicts involving currency. It registered not only these edicts but also all associated regulations. It drafted orders for the mints and supervised their operation. It checked samples of all coins after manufacture to see that they had the proper inscription, weight, and quality and issued a "visa of conformity" prior to circulation. It had jurisdiction over currency officials, mint personnel, gold and silver merchants, goldsmiths, jewelers, melters, molders, and other users of gold and silver, and, in general, anything having to do with the sale, purchase, use, or manufacture of gold and silver, including both civil and criminal charges resulting from abuses, embezzlements, and other offenses. It had charge of the national weight standards and samples of precious metals. Every year a *conseiller* from the court would have all the public measures stamped with a *fleur de lis* using the king's stamp. The Cour des Monnaies also issued permits to print books on currency matters.

After the Conseil royal des Finances was established in 1661, the Cour des Monnaies was forced to relinquish responsibility for preparing monetary edicts. After the establishment of the Régie des Monnaies in 1696, the mints were supervised by the bureaus of the finance ministry, with the Cour des Monnaies retaining the right to inspect the precious metals, stamps, machines, and weight standards.

Finance

Bureaux des Finances. For financial purposes at a level below that of the Chambres des Comptes and Cours des Aides the territory ruled by the kings of France was divided into districts known as *généralités*, in each of which was located a *bureau des Finances* staffed by *trésoriers de France* and *trésoriers généraux des Finances*. On the eve of the Fronde there were 22 *généralités*, distributed as follows: 14 in the jurisdiction of the Chambre des Comptes of Paris, including Amiens, Bordeaux, Bourges, Châlons, Limoges, Lyon, Montauban (established in January 1635), Moulins, Orléans, Paris,

Poitiers, Riom, Soissons, and Tours; 3 in the jurisdiction of the Chambre des Comptes of Rouen, at Alençon (established in May 1636), Caen, and Rouen; 2 in the jurisdiction of the Cour des Comptes of Montpellier, at Montpellier and Toulouse; 1 in the jurisdiction of the Cour des Comptes of Aix, at Aix; 1 in the jurisdiction of the Chambre des Comptes of Dijon, at Dijon; and 1 in the jurisdiction of the Chambre des Comptes of Grenoble, at Grenoble. In addition there were *trésoriers de France* with the Chambres des Comptes at Nantes and Blois.

By the eve of the Revolution the number of *généralités* had increased to 27, and each had its own *bureau des Finances*. In addition to the foregoing, there were *généralités* at Auch (established in 1716), Besançon,[10] La Rochelle, Lille (established in September 1691), and Metz. The exact number of *généralités* varies from author to author, and some of them confuse *généralités* with *intendances*. The king frequently changed the number of *généralités* and *intendances* and varied the limits of their jurisdiction. Between 1760 and 1789 the jurisdictions of the *intendances* of Auch, Pau, Bayonne, and Bordeaux were changed. In July 1787 an edict divided between the *intendances* of Bordeaux and Auch responsibility for "the *département* that today comprises the *intendance* of Pau and Bayonne." There was a *bureau de Finances* at Vannes from 1694 to 1700.

In principle the *trésoriers de France* and *trésoriers généraux des Finances* were regarded as members of the Chambres des Comptes and had jurisdiction over all royal finances, "all pecuniary impositions established by the sovereign or accorded by the people and falling on the property of his subjects or on their persons, which belong to him by virtue of his sovereignty, including, in particular, the *tailles*, *aides*, *gabelles*, *traites foraines*, *étapes*, *décimes*, and *octrois*."[11]

They received the oaths of officials of the *élections*, salt warehouses, and general and special tax bureaus. All these officials submitted their accounts to the treasurers for audit before taking them to the Chambre des Comptes.

The treasurers were responsible for the assessment and levying of taxes in the *pays d'élection* and annually received the brevet for the *taille* from the king's Council. In *pays d'élection* they made the circuit of *élections* in their *généralité*. During the month of August they advised the king's Council on how the tax burden should be distributed among the various *élections*. In September the Council decided on the distribution to be adopted and sent commissions for the collections of taxes to the *trésoriers de France*. When the commissions were received at the *bureau des Finances*, the treasurers would attach their seals before sending the commissions on to the *élus*. The *trésoriers de France* then supervised the distribution of the *tailles* assessed on each parish by the *élus*. Recruitment lists were sent to the *receveurs généraux* in the *généralité* and to the *receveurs particuliers* in the *élections*.

The treasurers began working under the authority of the *intendant* after the council decree of 8 September 1634 and definitively after the declaration of 16 April 1643, with an interruption of several years because of the Fronde.

The brevet of the *taille* was sent to the *intendants* as well as the treasurers. The *intendant* carried out his own investigations and sent the king's Council his personal opinion as to how the *taille* should be distributed. Commissions for collection of the tax were addressed to the *intendants* as well as the *trésoriers de France* and the *élus*. The *trésoriers de France* attached their seals to the document and then sent it to the *intendant*. The *intendant* obtained from the king's Council commissions for two *trésoriers de France* to work with him and the *élus* on the problem of dividing the *taille* among the different parishes.

Besides the *taille* there were other taxes, such as the *taillon*, the *crues*, "food and tools for troops in winter quarters," *étapes*, collection costs, *droits de quittance*, *port de commission*, etc. The edict of July 1717 took responsibility for the *étapes* away from the *bureaux des Finances* and gave it to the *intendants*.

In the *pays d'Etats*, all of which collected *taille réelle* except for Burgundy, which collected *taille personelle*, one of the *trésoriers de France* informed the Estates of the amount of the "free offering" requested by the king. The Estates then took charge of assessing each diocese and *viguerie* and of supervising collection. In Normandy, where there were both Estates and *élections*, the *trésoriers de France* took part in dividing the tax between *élections* and parishes.

The *trésoriers de France* contracted with tax farmers for the collection of *aides* or *droits* on traffic and the consumption of certain commodities in the auditory of each *élection* and in the presence of the *élus* and the *procureur du roi* for the *élection*. They then registered these contracts, particularly when the *aides* had been farmed out by the Council.

The *trésoriers de France* oversaw the *gabelle* or salt tax. The sale of salt was compulsory on the border of regions of *grande gabelle*. A *trésorier de France* guided salt-warehouse officials in assessing the *sel du devoir* that each parish was obligated to buy. Within the region purchase was voluntary as long as it exceeded an annual minimum of one *minot* (about 39 liters) for every fourteen persons, or a little less than 3 kilograms per person. The *trésoriers de France* organized, supervised, and controlled the salt operations.

The *trésoriers de France* registered the lease on the *traites foraines* or dues on goods entering or leaving the kingdom. After the edict of August 1594 this activity was administered by the *trésoriers généraux des traites*, who were assisted by harbormasters, lieutenants, guards, weighers, counters, measurers, inspectors, and scribes.

The *trésoriers de France* saw to it that laws concerning currency were published and enforced.

The *trésoriers de France* audited the tax collectors' true accounts of the urban *octrois* and received security bonds from the collectors.

The *trésoriers de France* were supposed to make the rounds in their districts and collect the grievances of the residences. They were supposed to investigate reports of extortion and embezzlement in connection with the levy of *tailles*, *aides*, and *gabelles*.

The *trésoriers de France* received royal instructions for the payment of officials' stipends, pensions, and "alms fiefs." Excerpts from these instructions were sent to the *receveurs généraux* and *particuliers*.

In the area of roads and highways, the post of *grand voyer* of France was created in 1599 for Sully. In August 1621 an edict gave the *trésoriers de France* jurisdiction over bridges and highways. Then, in February 1626 another edict eliminated the post of *grand voyer*. The *trésoriers de France* were made responsible for the Grande Voirie or highway department and were given jurisdiction over highways, public roads, and streets "in cities and suburbs" or *petite voirie*. In April 1627 they were given, in addition to the management or administrative responsibilities they already had, responsibility for initial hearing of disputes involving the roadways, a responsibility that had previously been exercised by regular judges. After the office of *grand voyer* of Paris (which had been filled by Sully's son, the comte d'Orval) was done away with in 1635, the treasurers of the Paris office were given jurisdiction over the roadways of Paris, including administration of streets and boulevards, duties on provisions, and questions of alignment of houses and buildings within the city, *prévôté*, and *vicomté* of Paris. The edict gave the same powers to all *bureaux de Finances* in the cities of their *généralités*.

But many *seigneurs hauts justiciers* claimed jurisdiction over major and minor roads within their purview. In 1661 and 1670, decrees of the Paris *parlement* upheld the claims of the archbishop of Paris and the abbots of Saint-Germain-des-Prés and Sainte-Geneviève to jurisdiction over *petite voirie*. But a judgment handed down by the Chambre du Trésor in 1674, which was approved by *parlement*, and a decree of the king's Council issued in 1699 bestowed full powers on the *bureau des Finances* of Paris and perhaps by the same reading of the law on all the other *bureaux des Finances*. Throughout the eighteenth century, debate continued between the school of Patas du Bourgneuf, which held that supervision of roadways had always been a royal prerogative, and the school of Daniel Jousse, a *conseiller* in the *bailliage et siège présidial* of Orléans, which maintained that *seigneurs hauts justiciers* retained their prior rights over roadways. The courts seem to have issued contradictory opinions on the matter.

The king's Council employed three *trésoriers de France* as *commissaires* in charge of the streets of Paris and the bridges and highways of the *généralité*.

As for the royal domain, the Crémieu edict (June 1536) accorded jurisdiction over disputes pertaining to the domain to the *baillis* and *sénéchaux*, with the right of appeal to the appropriate *parlement*. This jurisdiction was shared throughout the kingdom by the Chambre du Trésor, which until 1693 was presided over by a *trésorier de France*. The Chambre had exclusive jurisdiction in the *prévôté* and *vicomté* of Paris and the eight *bailliages* of Melun, Brie-Comte-Robert, Etampes, Dourdan, Mantes, Meulan, Beaumont-sur-Oise, and Crépy-en-Valois, with appeals being heard by the Paris *parlement* no matter where the property in litigation was located.

The edict of April 1627 transferred jurisdiction over domanial cases to the *bureaux des Finances*. For cases involving values of less than 250 livres capital and 10 livres rent there was no appeal. More significant cases required the payment of a deposit to the court of up to twice the amount at stake and could be appealed to the *parlement* in whose district the bureau was located. But the *bureaux des Finances* regarded themselves as sovereign courts, and some refused to allow appeals. In the *généralité* of Paris, the *baillis* retained jurisdiction over the portion of the district not subject to the Chambre de Trésor until 1693, when that portion was joined to the *bureau des Finances* of Paris. At that time the number of *trésoriers de France* was increased, and each worked six months for the *bureau des Finances* and six months for the Chambre du Trésor or Chambre du Domaine; one *avocat du roi* and one *procureur du roi* were assigned permanently to each Chambre. Jurisdiction over the domain in the three *généralités* of Normandy remained with the viscounts until 1694. In Moulins, jurisdiction over the domain remained with a Chambre du Domaine, a legacy of the ducs de Bourbon, which had competence for the Bourbonnais and the Marche, and with the Chambre des Comptes for the duchy of Nevers in Nivernais and the officers of the princesse de Carignan and the comtesse de Soissons at Château-Chinon. In the *généralité* of Orléans a high proportion of domanial cases were heard by a Chambre des Comptes that employed a *trésorier de France* and heard cases from the duchy-peerage of Vendôme and the appanage of the duc d'Orléans, the duchy of Orléans and the county of Blois. There was constant conflict with the *parlements* over the question of which bureau decisions were matters of litigation subject to appeal to *parlement* and which were administrative matters within the purview of the king's Council.

The *bureaux des Finances* were always responsible for the "management, organization, and administration" of the royal domain. Contracts of sale or exchange were signed by a *trésorier de France* with authorization from the king. The *trésoriers de France* made inquiries about all fiefs held of the king and prepared inventories of the associated lands, *seigneuries*, and dues for each *bailliage* and *sénéchaussée*. The edict of April 1627 made them responsible, in addition, for receiving faith and homage as well as for *avuex* and *dénombrements*, except for the *généralité* of Paris, where these duties continued to fall to the Chambre des Comptes. The decree of 19 January 1668 restored responsibility for homages pertaining to *fiefs de dignité* (duchies, marquisates, counties, baronies, and castellanies) to the Chambres des Comptes, while leaving responsibility for homages for other fiefs to the *bureaux des Finances*, unless an individual vassal preferred to do homage to one of the Chambre des Comptes. The edict of April 1627 gave the *bureaux des Finances* jurisdiction over *lettres de souffrance*, which allowed minor children to enjoy the revenues of a fief, and *lettres de confortmain*, which authorized *seigneurs* without judicial powers to seize their vassals' fiefs.

Letters of seisin were issued by the *trésoriers de France* to the purchasers of *censives*. *Trésoriers* were represented on the commissions responsible for revising the land registers as well as on the Sovereign Chamber for the Register of the Royal Domain, which was established in December 1652 and given jurisdiction over the entire kingdom on 26 March 1659.

The *trésoriers de France* supervised repairs to all buildings owned by the king, including palaces, castles, royal houses, *hôtels*, courts, prisons, and jails.

The *trésoriers de France* charged the *receveurs du domaine* with the task of collecting the immutable or enfeoffed domanial proceeds, under the supervision of *contrôleurs du domaine*; such income included the *cens, surcens*, rents, and other periodic dues of fixed amount.

The domain's variable proceeds were farmed out to the highest bidder. First, the so-called *petit domaine* was put out to farm. This consisted of "lands, meadows, and marshes of indefinite extent," the improvement of which the king hoped to encourage by farming out the product. Second, the *trésoriers de France* were also responsible for farming out inheritances, houses, mills, and banal ovens and presses; *champarts, terrages*, and tithes held in fief; the *dixième* on mines; dues on roadways, fairs and markets, toll gates and barricades, wagons, weighing, mining, measurement of wheat and other grains, assaying, scribes' fees and fees for notarization of documents and writs, fines and compensations. In Flanders the dues known as "*quatre membres*" were farmed out. And in Hainault there was farming of dues on "fires and chimneys" and libations.

The *trésoriers de France* oversaw the *domaine casuel*. They prepared inventories of property owned by foreigners residing in France who died childless and without *lettres de naturalité*; such property reverted to the king by virtue of the *droit d'aubaine*. They also inventoried the property of bastards who died childless, intestate, and without letters of legitimation; such property also reverted to the king unless claimed by a *seigneur haut justicier* under rights of escheat, confiscation, dereliction, or abandonment. Property reverting to the king was either joined to the royal domain or sold.

The *trésoriers de France* charged the *receveurs des domaines* to collect feudal dues such as *quint et requint, lods et ventes, relief* and *rachat*.

The *trésoriers de France* had jurisdiction over frank-fees due from commoners who had acquired noble fiefs and heritages. By edict of March 1655 these fees were transformed into an annual fee of one-twentieth of the revenue from the property, payable at the beginning of each year. The *trésoriers* also had jurisdiction over fees due on property newly acquired by ecclesiastical establishments and over amortization fees due on acquisitions by mortmain. These fees were assessed by a commission on which the *trésoriers de France* were represented; after the edict of December 1652 they were assessed by a Sovereign Chamber for Frank Fees, New Acquests, and Amortizations, which was made up of members of *parlement*, the Chambre des

Comptes, and the Chambre du Trésor, some *trésoriers de France*, and, later, the *intendants*.

The *trésoriers de France* prepared inventories of property in litigation when the patronage of a benefice was contested and of property in regale in case a vacancy occurred in an archbishopric, a bishopric, an abbey, a priory, or a consistorial benefice. The *trésoriers* administered such property and oversaw the collection of income by the *receveurs des domaines*. The edict of December 1691 instituted stewardships for the administration of vacant benefices, and the product of the regale was used for the upkeep of converted Protestants, for the repair of churches, and for the payment of pensions to needy ecclesiastics. The stewards were raised to the status of officials and placed under the control of royal judges, thus diminishing the power of the *trésoriers de France*.

Little by little the *intendants* enroached on the power of the *trésoriers de France* and *trésoriers généraux des Finances*, reducing them in the end to a merely formal role.

Elections. In the so-called *pays d'élections*, the *généralités* were divided into *élections*. There were 177 *élections* in 1648 and 179 in 1788.[12] *Elections* could be found in the *généralités* of Paris, Amiens, Bordeaux, Bourges, Châlons, Limoges, Lyon, Montauban, Moulins, Orléans, Poitiers, Riom, Soissons, Tours, Rouen, Caen, Alençon, Dijon, Grenoble, and Auch.

The distribution of *élections* varied widely. The *généralité* of Paris had 21, that of Lyon, 5.[13] The "administrative" jurisdiction of the *élus* extended to all taxes except for the *gabelle* and the *traites*. In particular, it included assessment of the *taille* to be paid by each parish of the *élection*. The *élus* had jurisdiction over all suits and disputes arising out of the *tailles*, *aides*, and other taxes within their administrative competence. For example, the *élus* had jurisdiction over suits charging overassessment, that is, suits brought by one parish or individual against another, the plaintiff charging that its assessment for the *taille* was too high and that the defendant's was too low and asking for relief at the expense of the defendant. Decisions of the *élus* could be appealed to the Cour des Aides. The *élus*, who were received by the Cour des Aides, objected to their subordination to the *trésoriers généraux de France*, officers subordinate to the Chambre des Comptes. Their wish was that the Chambre des Comptes merely register their *lettres de provision*, without requiring them to swear an oath for reception into office. In addition, they wanted to receive edicts and letters patent of a general nature only from the Cour des Aides, and they wanted freedom from the supervision and audit of the *trésoriers de France*. They did not like to be made to report (standing and bareheaded) to the *trésoriers* or to submit to the supervision of a *trésorier* in assessing parishes for the *taille*. Conflict was unending.

Salt Warehouses. Analogous to the situation of the *élus* was that of the official magistrates of the salt warehouses in regions where the *grande ga-*

belle was enforced, that is, in the *généralités* of Paris, Amiens, Bourges, Châlons, Moulins, Orléans, Soissons, Tours, Rouen, Caen, Alençon, Burgundy excluding the Mâconnais, and a portion of the *généralité* of Riom. The salt warehouses were places where salt was stored under the administration of salt officials and sold to users. As far as their "administrative" jurisdiction was concerned, the salt magistrates reported to the *trésoriers généraux de France*. They also had jurisdiction over suits and disputes arising out of their administration of the distribution and sale of salt and associated royal dues. Appeals of their decisions were heard by the Cour des Aides. Received by the Cour des Aides, they were required to swear an oath to the *trésoriers de France*, who had the power to inspect the salt warehouses and issue orders to the salt officials.

In 1648 there were 199 salt warehouses in France (105 of them selling salt on a voluntary basis and 94 making compulsory tax sales) and 30 *chambres à sel* (11 making voluntary sales, 19 making compulsory sales). The *généralité* of Tours had 27 salt warehouses, and there were 8 in the *généralité* of Bourges. There were no salt warehouses in the *généralités* of Bordeaux, Limoges, Montauban, Poitiers, and Riom.

In regions where the *petite gabelle* was enforced (Mâconnais, Beaujolais, Forez, Lyonnais, Bresse, Bugey, Valromey, upper Auvergne, Velay, Vivarais, Languedoc, Dauphiné, and Provence) there were 52 salt warehouses under Louis XIV. Jurisdiction over disputes was usually exercised initially by general inspectors of the *gabelle*. In Languedoc there were general inspectors in the seat of each *sénéchaussée* at Beaucaire, Carcassonne, and Toulouse, with lieutenants at Montpellier, Aigues-Mortes, and Pezenas. The situation in Provence was similar. After 1667 this was also true of the farm known as "the kingdom's share," which covered Lyonnais, Mâconnais, Beaujolais, Forez, Bresse, Bugey, and Valromey.

Les Eaux et Forêts

Among the special courts, the Eaux et Forêts had an organization of their own appropriate to a civilization that was based on water and wood. The forest played an important part in everyday life. Hunting formed part of the constant military training in which the king's *gentilshommes* took part; the king himself was the first *gentilhomme* of the kingdom and supreme commander of its troops. As the rural population rose and cities and towns expanded, there was an increasing need for wood for construction, fuel, and additional food for both humans and animals. In order to keep the forests from being destroyed, it thus became important to establish rights of usage. These included, first of all, rules governing the use of wood good only for burning, such as dead, fallen, or naturally uprooted trees and standing deadwood, and such other "deadwood" as thorns, alder, furze, juniper, willow, elder, bramble, and sometimes prickwood and holly. Better-grade woods were reserved for use in construction, plows, tools, ships, walls, and barrels.

Forest rights also covered the gathering of wild fruits, beechnuts, and acorns, the stripping of bark, and the use of trees uprooted by the wind.

There were also rights of pasturage, which included pannage, or the feeding of pigs on beechnuts and acorns, which was allowed from Saint Michael's day (29 September) or St. Remy's day (1 October) until the appearance of the first leaves of spring or, at the very least, until Saint Andrew's day (30 November). Pannage went by the name of *charnage* in Anjou, *porcage* or *oublage* in Normandy, and *paisson* in Auvergne and Bourbonnais. Then there was pasturage for larger livestock such as cows and oxen as well as horses. Lambs and goats were either limited in number or prohibited, however. Pasturage was not allowed in young brushwood and was prohibited from Easter until Saint John's day, the period during which leaves were growing. Grasslands within groves or in open clearings could be used. Grasses were harvested to feed the animals during winter.

Among the materials gathered in the forest whose usage was regulated were clay, marl, sand, sandstone, pebbles, moss for the caulking of boats, heather for bedding down animals, furze for baskets, dead leaves for smoking, black alder to make charcoal that was used in the manufacture of gunpowder, and medicinal plants.

Rules about the use of fruits governed quince, medlar, apples, pears, plums, strawberries, raspberries, and chestnuts. Rules also applied to honey, wax, and loose swarms of bees.

"Small users," including such "customary" users as workers and other residents of towns and villages, were given authorization to collect deadwood, underbrush, and branches for tentering flax and were allowed to engage in pasturage and pannage. "Large users," including nobles, ecclesiastics, and *bourgeois* "living as nobles," enjoyed further rights to higher-grade wood and other materials. The *seigneurs haut justiciers* had the power to grant hunting rights.

Forest products were essential for forges, glassworks, pottery works, and other manufacturing enterprises that devoured scrub wood in ever increasing quantities owing to mercantilist and militarist policies and the needs of the king's armies. The forest was also indispensable to the navy, which consumed huge amounts of wood for masts and hulls and which saw its needs increase because of the maritime and colonial policies adopted by the government. The sale of wood from the royal domain was essential to the royal finances, as were the taxes levied on the sale of wood by private individuals on the basis of a general right of wardenship over all the forests of the realm. These taxes included dues known as *droit de gruerie* and, in Normandy, *droit de tiers et danger*. The *droit de gruerie* was a fraction of the selling price of the wood ranging from one-twentieth to one-half, depending on the place. To this there was sometimes added what was known as a *grairie* or registration fee. *Gruerie* and *grairie* were collected even on sales of wood grown on cultivated lands. These fees were seldom collected in Champagne and Burgundy and were unknown in provinces south of Berry and Poitou. The

Norman *droit de tiers et danger* was similar. The *tiers* amounted to one-third the selling price of the wood and the *danger*, to one-tenth. Thus the king collected 13/30ths of the sale. During the period under study the *tiers et danger* was becoming more and more common.

Besides the king's powers as monarch and lord of the crown domain, he had general powers of stewardship over the forests of the kingdom stemming from the importance of wood to the national well-being. These general powers established limits to the rights of private individuals, landowners, *tréfonciers* or owners of soil and subsoil rights, and users of forest products. Land ownership carried with it eminent rights over streams and forests, powers of justice, from which derived powers to pursue and to levy fines, and *droit de gruerie*, in this case a police power. A distinction was made between the *tréfoncier* or owner of the soil and subsoil rights and the forest user. The *tréfoncier* owed no common dues but was subject to the police powers of the king or *seigneur*. He paid the landlord a share of what he earned from the sale of wood. As time went by the rights of the *tréfoncier* were curtailed. Increasingly, he was forbidden to uproot trees or to clear forest land. He was obliged to leave the forest in its natural state and forbidden to cut and sell wood without the permission of royal officials. The forest user, on the other hand, was obliged to pay common dues in money or in kind. He was not allowed to alter the land without authorization. In theory, privileged persons could not use their privileges in cases involving streams and forests. Privileged nobles, ecclesiastics, and bourgeois could not have cases in which they had a stake transferred to courts of their own choosing. Royal officials kept an increasingly close watch on all forests. They gradually forced *seigneurs*, landowners, and communities to acknowledge the king's power to regulate exploitation of the forest. In August 1573, for example, an edict inaugurated what was known as the "reserved quarter," requiring bishoprics, abbeys, priories, benefices, commanderies, and religious communities to set aside one-fourth of the forests under their control to be allowed to develop naturally. This measure was announced again in ordinances of 1596 and 1669 and eventually extended to secular communities as well.

When it came to transactions involving the property of the Eaux et Forêts (petitory, possessory, sales, exchanges, subdivisions, sale at auction, *retrait lignager* or *féodal*), jurisdiction belonged to the "*baillis, sénéchaux*, and other ordinary judges." As for cases pertaining specifically to streams and forests, wherever there was no court of attribution, jurisdiction over disputes and in administrative matters belonged to the *parlements* and other ordinary judges. Wherever there were special courts and a separate Eaux et Forêts administration, however, these bodies acted as a court of attribution, which heard cases involving the streams and forests and supervised this administration.

At the beginning of the seventeenth century, the royal court of Eaux et Forêts was governed by a dozen or so ordinances and edicts and a large number of regulations and decrees, which delineated a sphere of competence and range of procedures not very different from those laid down by the ordinance of 1669. All this rather confused legislation was loosely enforced because of unrest due to the Wars of Religion. Officials prevaricated, and landowners and users did as they pleased. The forests were devastated. Virgin forest receded, and the area of scrub brush expanded to take its place. Henri IV reorganized the Eaux et Forêts with the ordinance of May 1597.

The hierarchy was as follows. At the bottom were the *grueries*, which had jurisdiction over a forest or two or three neighboring forests. The *gruyers*, or officials of the *gruerie*, also had cognizance of all seigneurial or royal rights over forest owners in their region. The term *gruyer* was employed in the Ile-de-France, the Orléanais, the *bailliage* of Sens, etc. Synonyms were used elsewhere: *verdier* in Normandy, *maître sergent* in Champagne, *maître garde* or *seyrayers* in Maine and Anjou, *garde-marteau* in the forest of Villers-Cotterêts, as well as castellans, captains, concierges, and foresters. Provided their offices by the king, they were received by the Tables de Marbre [the Tribunal of streams and forests] in some places and by the *parlements* in others. They were forbidden to take part in commerce. They supervised the *gardes* and *sergents*, issued titles to usage rights and determined the locations and limits of applicability of those rights, marked sold wood with the imprint of the royal mallet, and heard cases in various locations involving fines up to 60 sols. They were also supposed to keep records of fines, confiscations, and small sales and report on their activities twice a year to the *maîtres particuliers*.

The Eaux et Forêts employed a large number of *sergents* or "forest guards," royal officials provided offices by the king and received by the Tables de Marbre or, where there were none, by the *parlements*, where they took an oath and therefore had no need of witnesses or records. In Normandy *sergents dangereaux* saw to the collection of the *tiers et dangers*. *Sergents traversiers* or *chevaucheurs* checked on the work of ordinary *sergents*, riding on horseback from one place to another. There were also *garenniers*, who took care of the *garennes* or rabbit warrens, *parquiers*, who supervised royal *parcs* in which seized animals were kept, tenders of fish hatcheries, ponds, and rivers, fishermen and fishmongers assigned to certain ponds, engineers to build dikes, mills, and millponds, *bigres* to look for swarms of bees on the loose, *goupilier* for fox hunts, and *louvetiers* for tracking down wolves.

The district of each *maîtrise particulière* was made up of a certain number of *grueries*. In theory, the district of a *maîtrise particulière* north of the Loire coincided with that of a *bailliage*. In 1604 the *généralité* of Rouen included nine *maîtrises particulières*: Rouen, Pont-de-l'Arche, Pont-Audemer, Caudebec, Neufchâtel, Evreaux, Arques, les Andelys, Gisors.

The size of the staff of a *maîtrise particulière* varied from place to place. The *maîtrises particulières* of Normandy generally included, below the *maître particulier*, or chief, a *lieutenant général*, *lieutenant particulier*, *procureur du roi*, *garde-marteau* or keeper of the hammer with the royal seal for marking sold wood, *gruyers*, *sergents dangereux*, *sergents* responsible for collecting fines, *huissiers*, and *greffiers*. The *maîtrise particulière* at Issoudun in Berry employed only a *maître particulier*, a *lieutenant*, and a *procureur du roi*, however.

The *maîtres particuliers* were provided their offices by the king and received and installed at the Table de Marbre or else at the *parlement* in the district where the *maîtrise particulière* was located. They required the "*attache*" or consent of the *grand maître*. They were supposed to make an annual visit to all the forests in the *maîtrise* and sent a report to the Chambre des Comptes. They saw to it that the royal coat of arms was stamped on the *pieds-corniers* or trees marking the boundaries of a sale, on the *arbres de lisière* or *de paroi* marking the line between corner markers, and on the *baliveaux* or staddle, young trees left to grow naturally within each cut area as a reserve. The *garde-marteau* used his own hammer and initials to mark windfallen wood and illegally cut trees in the forests of the king, clergymen, or private owners. The *maîtres particuliers* decided what wood was to be cut and sold and awarded contracts to merchants who were not supposed to be either members of their family, forestry officials, *gentilshommes*, royal officers, *avocats*, or beneficed clergy. They granted rights to use of the forest. They heard civil and criminal cases pertaining to streams and forests either in first instance or upon appeal from the *grueries* and *verderies*. They were authorized to assume jurisdiction over offenses committed in the forests of individual *seigneurs* who neglected their duty. And they were supposed to audit all accounts in their *maîtrise* and furnish a report to the Chambre des Comptes.

Jurisdiction over cases in dispute was gradually usurped almost everywhere by their lieutenants. The lieutenants continued to hand down judgments in the name of the *maître particulier* even though the decisions were theirs alone. The *maîtres particuliers* kept on issuing their own decisions in Orléans, Bauge, Angers, and Senlis, but cases were prosecuted by their lieutenants.

A certain number of *maîtrises particulières* went to make up a *grande maîtrise*. Under Henri III there were seventeen *grandes maîtrises*. By edict of January 1597 Henri IV did away with them and established in their place a unique *grand maître et général réformateur des eaux-et-forêts*. On 17 June 1598, Clausse de Fleury became *grand maître* with the title *surintendant des forêts*. He was succeeded by his son Nicolas in 1611. Nicolas resigned in 1635. In reality, however, the authority of the *surintendant* was limited to the Ile-de-France and Normandy. Because it was impossible to reimburse all the other *grands maîtres* what they had paid for their offices, eight remained on duty in ill-defined jurisdictions. Each was assisted by a *receveur général des bois* and a *contrôleur général*.

The *grands maîtres* were supposed to check annually on the royal forests, navigable rivers, fish hatcheries, mills, forests held in *gruerie*, and forests in mortmain to see that royal regulations and laws were observed. During his visit the *grand maître* executed royal orders, *mandements*, and letters patent, issued ordinances pertaining to the police of his department, removed officers if need be, determined what wood was to be sold, and selected sections of forest to be placed in reserve. He was entitled to first hearing of any cases brought before him during the course of his visits, subject to subsequent appeal. He could also carry out any reforms he deemed necessary and deal with any abuses or offenses committed by officials or private individuals.

Other superior courts also dealt with cases pertaining to streams and forests, namely, the Tables de Marbre. The Table de Marbre of Paris, the "tribunal of the forests and streams of France," was the first tribunal to be set up in conjunction with the *parlement* of Paris. Following this example, other Tables de Marbre were set up in conjunction with various *parlements*. There were none at Bordeaux, Grenoble, or Aix, however. But in those places a number of *conseillers* from *parlement* and specialist *avocats* formed what was known as a Chambre des Eaux et Forêts, which played the role of a Table de Marbre. In one form or another there was a superior court dealing with cases involving streams and forests attached to each *parlement*.

In principle the Tables de Marbre were neither courts of first instance nor sovereign courts. They were ordinarily supposed to be appeals courts, whose decisions were subject to further appeal to *parlement*. When sitting as an appellate tribunal, each Table de Marbre included the *lieutenants généraux* of the *grands maîtres* of the district, one *lieutenant particulier*, one *avocat* and one *procureur du roi*, and six *conseillers* of the Table de Marbre, which also supplied the *huissiers*. Petitions submitted to a Table de Marbre such as that of Paris, for example, had to bear the following preamble: "To our lords, the *grands maîtres*, investigators and general reformers of the streams and forests of France, at the general court of the Table de Marbre of the Palace, in Paris."

From the mid-sixteenth century, however, the Table de Marbre also begain hearing some cases as a sovereign court and handing down final judgments. It had sovereign jurisdiction over all appeals of judgments handed down in cases involving uses, abuses, offenses, and embezzlements pertaining to streams and forests. In such cases the tribunal was supposed to consist of the *premier président* or a *président à mortier* of the Paris *parlement*, the seven most senior councillors of the Grand-Chambre, and a number of *lieutenants généraux*, *lieutenants particuliers*, and *conseillers* of the Table de Marbre. A petition asking that a case be heard in final judgment was supposed to be headed, "To our lords, ordained as judges by the king to render final judgment in cases pending at the Table de Marbre of the Palace in Paris."

There was constant conflict between the *grands maîtres* and the Tables de Marbre. The *grands maîtres* heard a large number of cases locally in first instance, disposed of them in a day or two, confiscated horses and other animals, and handed out reprimands to the *maîtres particuliers*. The Tables de Marbre would have preferred that all these cases be remanded to them.

Furthermore, the *grands maîtres* claimed the right to hear appeals in all cases. The Tables de Marbre wanted to reserve the hearing of all appeals and the issuance of final judgments to themselves. A precedent was set by a ruling issued on 30 May 1608, in a conflict between the *grand maître* of the Ile-de-France and Normandy and the *lieutenants* and *conseillers* of the Table de Marbre of Paris. The *grands maîtres* lost the power to hear appeals and issue final judgments. These *hommes d'épée* were stripped of their most important judicial powers, which were handed over to their lieutenants, *hommes de robe longue*.

At the top of the hierarchy concerned with streams and forests, above the specialized officials, was the chancellor of France. He received reports and petitions from the *surintendant des bois*, the *grands maîtres des Eaux et Forêts*, the *procureurs du roi* attached to the Tables de Marbre and the *maîtrises*, and the *maîtres des requêtes* who made the circuit of each district. The chancellor saw to it that the major decisions were made by the king's Council, which issued edicts and regulations, decided on the sale of wood and the issuance of usage rights, effected reforms, distributed wood for heating, paid officials their stipends, matched payments with monies received by the *receveurs généraux des bois*, audited accounts, and quashed decrees of *parlement* regarding the forests.

The competence of Eaux et Forêts officials extended to anything that might prove harmful to navigation, to the transport or floating of logs from royal forests on rivers suitable to the purpose, and to fishing rights. They also oversaw questions of passage, bridges, ferries, boats, canal locks, stakes for nets or other moorings installed in rivers by fishermen, fish hatcheries, and mills. They relinquished jurisdiction to the *prévôts des marchands* in cases involving disputes over the possession of merchandise and to dyke and levee officials in matters pertaining to flooding along rivers.

Officials of the Eaux et Forêts had jurisdiction over all disputes involving islands and islets, sand spits, landings, crossings, alluvial deposits, fishponds, marshes, dams, dockyards, and drains. They also dealt with all suits arising out of contracts, sales, promises, leases, or partnerships involving such commodities as wood fuel, building materials, charcoal, and the like, so long as these goods had not been conveyed outside the forest of origin or beyond the rivers and ponds. In addition, they concerned themselves with disputes involving the payment of wages to laborers, lumbermen, and fishermen.

These same officials also had jurisdiction over fights, violent acts, assassinations, and murders committed in connection with the activities of hunting or fishing; they shared this jurisdiction with the captains of the hunt. In cases of theft, murder, kidnapping, piracy, or other violence committed against travelers, however, they had the power only to conduct investigations and issue warrants and then only if the perpetrator was caught in the act. Such cases were turned over to regular judges for trial.

These same officials had jurisdiction over streams and forests on property owned by members of the clergy, both secular and regular, and on property owned by lay *seigneurs* or other individuals, provided they were asked to intervene by one of the parties to the case. In forests where some *seigneur* maintained a special judge for cases pertaining to streams and forests, the royal officials could act only if their participation was requested. Wherever the *seigneur* had no special judge, and only a regular judge was available, however, royal officials of the Eaux et Forêts had priority and could contest jurisdiction over such cases whether requested to do so or not.

From the end of Henri IV's reign until the period of Louis XIV's personal government, the forests suffered severe damage. Civil and foreign wars brought negligence, violation of laws and regulations, and depredation in their wake. Large numbers of officials were appointed for purely fiscal reasons. In December 1635 Louis XIII made the offices of *grands maîtres triennal*, thus tripling their number, and in 1645 Louis XIV made them *quadriennal*. In 1652 the *grande maîtrise* of Orléans was divided into a *grande maîtris* for Orléans and Blois and another for Poitou, Saintonge, Angoumois, and Bordelais. The badly supervised officials of the Eaux et Forêts became increasingly dishonest. *Apanagés*, *engagistes*, and forest users found them easy to corrupt. Forests were cut without method as financial needs dictated. By 1661 scrub brush was everywhere making severe inroads into the virgin forest. The amount of virgin forest land was only one-fifth what it had been in the time of François I, and the scrub itself was of poor quality. The king's income from forest lands had fallen to practically nothing. Wood for building cities and fleets was running out, and there was a shortage of fuel for towns and industries.

Louis XIV took responsibility for the Eaux et Forêts away from the chancellor and therefore the courts and transferred it to the finance ministry. In September 1661 Colbert, *intendant des Finances*, was given yet another seat on the Conseil royal des Finances with the title "*Conseiller ordinaire au* Conseil royal des finances and *intendant des finances* responsible for the department of forests." From this point on, the forests were the responsibility of the Conseil royal des Finances and, from the time Colbert assumed the post, of the *contrôleur général des Finances*. One of the *intendants des Finances* who worked with the *contrôleur général* was also assigned special responsibility for the Eaux et Forêts. The *grands maîtres* addressed their correspondence to this *intendant*. Procedures were still by and large judicial, but executive procedures were taking on an ever increasing prominence. With these changes a new era began for the administration of the forests, an era that lasted until the Revolution.

Between 1661 and 1679 Colbert carried out a thoroughgoing reform of the Eaux et Forêts with the help of *commissaires* chosen among the *maîtres des requêtes* and the *intendants des provinces*. Each *commissaire* was assisted by a *grand maître* or *maître* from the Eaux et Forêts. The *commissaires* had final judgment in cases involving amounts up to 3,000 livres. Beyond this limit appeal could be made to the king's Council. The *commissaires* appointed a tribunal of ten judges chosen from among the judges of the *bailliages, sénéchaussées,* and *présidiaux.* They also appointed a *procureur du roi* to help with the reforms. If this *procureur* asked for the death penalty, penal servitude, or a sentence involving the loss of civil rights, the *commissaires* had final say in the case in their own tribunal. The king could have the case transferred to the *requêtes de l'Hôtel du Roi* in Paris, however.

The reform *commissaires* conducted preliminary investigations preparatory to the reform proper. They took control of the registry of deeds and, using reports of surveys and measurements, traced the former outline of the forest. They had all owners of land bordering the forest bring their deeds to the registry and had all holders of rights to use the forest, gather fuel, or graze animals bring in their titles as well. Then the records of fines, judgments, and reports submitted by wardens and *sergents* were examined, as were all records of sales. A check was made of all forests belonging to the Church and of all forests in which the king enjoyed the *droit de gruerie* or the *droit de tiers et danger* to see that the "high woods" or virgin forest had indeed been cut only after the granting of letters patent authenticated by *parlement* and that, in exploiting scrubland, the proper number of seedlings had been left to guarantee regrowth of the forest. Communal woodlands were reorganized. The *commissaires* assumed jurisdiction in cases brought against *seigneurs* or *gentilshommes* by their subjects on account of encroachments or rabbit warrens. They also gave their advice to the *contrôle général des Finances* and to the king's Council and suggested regulations for inclusion in the ordinance of 1669. Finally, they handed down judgments.

Besides providing Colbert with an inventory of available resources, these activities helped to reestablish order and furnished information useful for preparing the future reforms.

In 1661 the northern half of France as far south as Poitou, Berry, and Burgundy was relatively well staffed by officials of the Eaux et Forêts. There were *maîtrises particulières* or *grueries* in 85 different places, employing 1,200 officials in all. In the southern half of the country there were fewer such offices. There were *maîtrises particulières* in only 17 places, employing 180 officials. There were also two *grandes maîtrises,* one in Toulouse, the other in Bordeaux. In Guyenne and Provence there was not a single *maîtrise particulière.* There were three in the *généralité* of Limoges, one in Forez, two in Auvergne, one in Bourbonnais, six in Languedoc, and two in Dauphiné.

Colbert began a reorganization of the system. The *triennal* and *quadriennal grands maîtres* were eliminated by the edict of April 1667. The kingdom was divided into eight departments administered by *commissaires* appointed by the *grands maîtres* of the Eaux et Forêts. After Colbert, Louis XIV issued an edict in February 1689 creating 16 departments, with a *grand maître* in charge of "investigations and general reform" in each. The edict of March 1703 carved out of the old *grande maîtrise* of Caen a new one centered in Alençon. The annexation of Lorraine increased the number of *grandes maî-*

trises. In 1789 there were 20: (1) Paris (10 *maîtrises particulières*); (2) Soissons (11 *maîtrises*, 2 *grueries*); (3) Picardy, Artois, Flanders (8 *maîtrises*); (4) Hainault (4 *maîtrises*); (5) Champagne (8 *maîtrises*); (6) Trois-Evêchés (6 *maîtrises*, 2 *grueries*); (7) Burgundy, Franche-Comté, Alsace (16 *maîtrises*); (8) Lyonnais, Dauphiné, Provence, Auvergne (9 *maîtrises*); (9) Languedoc, Roussillon (6 *maîtrises*, 2 *grueries*); (10) Guyenne (5 *maîtrises*, 2 *grueries*); (11) Poitou, Aunis, Saintonge, Angoumois, Limousin, Marche, Bourbonnais, Nivernais (14 *maîtrises*, 2 *grueries*); (12) Touraine, Anjou, Maine (9 *maîtrises*, 1 *gruerie*); (13) Brittany (7 *maîtrises*, 2 *grueries*); (14) Rouen (8 *maîtrises*); (15) Caen (5 *maîtrises*); (16) Alençon (5 *maîtrises*, 2 *grueries*); (17) Berry, Blésois, Vendômois (8 *maîtrises*, 2 *grueries*); (18) Lorraine and Barrois (16 *maîtrises*); (19) Orléanais, Gâtinais, and the county of Beaugency (3 *maîtrises*); (20) Clermontois (6 *maîtrises*).

Colbert made forest legislation uniform. "The Edict establishing general regulations for streams and forests" of August 1669 was no doubt less innovative than has been said. It mainly recast earlier regulations and procedures and established an over-all order. Its text is a marvel of order and clarity. It established boundaries of jurisdictions, reduced the number of opportunities for conflict, and gave detailed specifications of procedures to be followed. The most important thing is that the edict was enforced. It remained in effect as the law governing use of the forests of France until 1827.

The Admiralty Courts

In all cases involving the sea the admiralty courts had jurisdiction. At the beginning of the seventeenth century there were fifty admiralty courts in France. Those that were under the authority of the admiral of France came under the jurisdiction of the general court of the admiralty at the Table de Marbre of the Palace in Paris. A *lieutenant général* from the admiralty of Guyenne joined with this court to hear appeals from the admiralty courts of Sables-d'Olonne and La Rochelle (located at Lucon until 1634), these courts being under the jurisdiction of the Table de Marbre of Paris because they were located in Guyenne. A Table de Marbre modeled on the one in Paris was set up at the Palace of Justice in Rouen to serve all of Normandy. Admiralty courts that did not fall under the jurisdiction of a Table de Marbre came within the purview of the *parlement* in the district where they were located. The Tables de Marbre were not sovereign courts, moreover, and judgments they handed down could be appealed to the *parlements* of Paris or Normandy.

The jurisdiction of each admiralty court was demarcated by the paths of rivers and streams and in some cases extended to certain islands. It covered the sea, the shore, rivers and their banks as far upstream as the highest tide of the month of March, ports and docks. On the Garonne, for example, the effects of the March tide were felt as far upstream as Langon, 80 kilometers from the cape of Ambès. It was more common at the time, however, to place the limit of jurisdiction at Castets, 64 kilometers from the cape. The admiralty court of Bordeaux thus had jurisdiction over 80 kilometers of sea coast, from Cazaux point to Grave point, 100 kilometers along the banks of the Garonne, 50 or so kilometers along the Dordogne, and 20 along the Isle, for a total of about 250 kilometers. Thus the judges of the admiralty courts had to contend with the problem of distance and the problem of conflict with officials of the Eaux et Forêts.

Though the number of admiralty courts fluctuated somewhat, there were still around 50 in 1789. The one in Dunkirk was directly responsible to the Paris *parlement*. Seven reported to the Table de Marbre of the Palace in Paris and from there to the Paris *parlement*: among these were Calais, Boulogne, Abbeville, Saint-Valéry-sur-Somme, Eu and Le Tréport, Les Sables-d'Olonne, and La Rochelle. Seventeen reported to the Table de Marbre of the Palace in Rouen and from there to the *parlement* of Rouen: among these were Dieppe, Saint-Valéry-en-Caux, Fécamp, Le Havre, Rouen, Honfleur, Caen, Bayeux,La Hougue, Cherbourg, Coutances, and Granville. Eight admiralty courts established by the edicts of April and June 1691 were responsible to the governor of Brittany. Justice was administered by these courts in the king's name, and appeals went to the *parlement* of Brittany. Among these were the courts at Saint-Malo, Brest, and Vannes, to name three. There was an admiralty court at Guérande; more precisely, the *sénéchaussée* there handled admiralty cases separately between 1632 and 1693. The admiralty court at Brouage, which was transferred to Marennes in about 1649, and the courts at Bordeaux and Bayonne answered to the *parlement* of Bordeaux. The *parlement* of Toulouse heard appeals from the admiralty courts of Aigues-Mortes, Vendres, and Sérignan, which were established in 1630; and from Agde and Frontignan, which were established in 1632. In 1691 the admiralty court of Frontignan was replaced by courts in Sète and Montpellier. In 1692 Agde absorbed the admiralty courts of Vendres and Serignan. The admiralty court of Marseilles was responsible to the *parlement* of Aix, as were the admiralty courts at Martigues, Toulon, Fréjus, and Antibes, which, though established during the sixteenth century, actually commenced operations in 1612. The admiralty court at Arles, established in 1555 but actually in operation only after 1631 was also responsible to the Aix *parlement*. So was the admiralty court of La Ciotat, whose district was carved out of the district of the Toulon court in 1649, and that of Saint-Tropez, which was established in March 1649 at the expense of the Fréjus court. The admiralty court of Collioure was set up in April 1691. It reported to the sovereign council of Perpignan. Its seat was transferred to Perpignan in 1718. The admiralty courts of Bastia and Ajaccio, which were established by royal regulation of 21 August 1768, were responsible to the superior council of Corsica.

Colbert was prejudiced against the judges of the admiralty courts, whom he believed to be negligent and corrupt. He thought of restoring the cases assigned to them to ordinary judges or else of transferring such cases to the *intendants* of the navy. The latter were already overwhelmed with work, however. In addition, Colbert's inquiries revealed many admiralty judges to be competent, diligent, and honest men. He therefore let the admiralty courts continue to hear cases under the watchful eye of navy or provincial *intendants*, in ports where there were any, and elsewhere under the supervision of the *commissaires ordonnateurs des classes*. The naval ordinance promulgated at Fontainebleau in August 1681 capped the regulations governing the operation of the admiralty courts, incorporating many of the practices that had been adopted previously.

Admiralty judges had exclusive jurisdiction over all cases involving the construction, rigging, arming, provisioning, equipping, sale, and allocation of ships; over all contracts involving maritime commerce, charter parties, hiring or chartering of vessels, bills of lading, loading of ships, hiring and pay of sailors, sailors' food on board ship, insurance policies, bonds of bottomry or bonds payable upon completion of a voyage, etc; seizures on the high seas, willful damage, shipwreck, grounding, damages to ships or their cargo, property left on board ship following a death at sea; *droits de congé, tiers, dixième, balise, ancrage* and other dues payable to the admiral; dues levied or claimed by *seigneurs* or other individuals with coastal property on fishing grounds or fish and on cargo and ships entering and leaving port; on fishing on the ocean, in salt ponds, river mouths, beds, fishing grounds, nets, purchases and sales of fish in boats or inlets, ports, and harbors; damage to fishing grounds; paths used for hauling vessels coming in from the ocean; damage to quays, dikes, jetties, and palisades; the depth and cleanliness of harbors and roadsteads; muster and inspection of the harbor watch and jurisdiction over disputes arising in connection with watch duty; offenses committed by the personnel of the coast guard while under arms; piracy, theft, or desertion by crew members and jurisdiction over all offenses committed on the high seas, along the coasts, and in the harbors and ports of France.

Admiralty judges were responsible for receiving the masters of a number of guilds concerned with the construction and fitting of ships, including ships' carpenters, caulkers, ropemakers, mastmakers, and sailmakers. The admiralty judges also had jurisdiction over any malpractice in these various trades.

Officials of the general courts of the admiralty at the Tables de Marbre could assume initial jurisdiction over any civil or criminal case covered by the ordinance if there was no special court in the place where they were located. They could also hear appeals, except in cases resulting in loss of liberty. In these cases, appeals went directly from the special courts to the *parlements* under the provisions of the criminal ordinance of 1670. In cases involving values of more than 3,000 livres, these officials could take jurisdiction away from the special courts when a case was brought before them on appeal of some interim order of the lower court.

The courts of *parlement* were not supposed to deal with such cases at first hearing. Decisions of the special courts involving amounts up to 50 livres and decisions of the general courts involving amounts up to 150 livres could be executed forthwith; no appeal was permitted. Admiralty officials were prohibited from holding a direct or indirect interest in any dues within their cognizance, failing which they were subject to removal from office and to a fine of 1,000 livres. They were forbidden to demand fish or merchandise from fishermen, mariners, or merchants. The ordinance of 15 January 1783 made it illegal for admiralty officials to hold an interest in any privateer. The penalty for violating this law was removal from office and a fine of up to 1,500 livres.

Under the terms of the letters patent of 10 January 1770, admiralty officials were supposed to make a personal inspection of all ships entering, leaving, or putting in to a harbor within twelve hours of arrival or departure. They were to issue an inspection report to the ship's captain and owner, indicating the nature of the cargo, the names of the passengers and the fees paid. They were required to keep copies of all these reports. Inspections were to be carried out by three officials, a number reduced to two by the council decree of 22 June 1771. In their ports of residence they were allowed to use hired inspectors in their stead. In other ports, or *ports obliques* as they were called, they were allowed to appoint sworn *commissaires* to represent them. According to letters patent of 21 February 1772, ships were not subject to inspection when they merely put in to a harbor, that is, when they remained at anchor away from any dock or mooring. They were subject to inspection, however, whenever they ventured inside a harbor breakwater, moored to a jetty, or pulled up alongside a dock in such a way as to be in contact with the mainland.

Police and justice officials, administrators, government agents, and admiralty officials all kept an eye out to make sure that treaties of navigation and commerce were respected. They published declarations of war, truces, and peace treaties in the ports, or instructions from the various ministries. They worked to restrict the privileges of cities and *seigneurs*. They sued to acquire patrimonial rights along the seacoast and river banks. In sum, they aided in the ongoing process of administrative and political centralization and helped enforce mercantilist and protectionist economic policy.

The Connétablie

The *Connétablie* was treated in part 3 above.

The Consular Courts

After the edict of 1569 the king established tribunals, judges, and consuls in many cities for the purpose of hearing cases involving disputes between merchants. At Besançon, for example, a consular court was set up by an edict of August 1700. Letters patent of 20 October introduced the commercial law or *Code Marchand* into Franche-Comté. Every year in late November or early December the merchants gathered to hear a mass of the Holy Ghost at the church of the Franciscans, after which they selected twenty notable merchants by vote. These twenty merchants then chose a judge and two consuls. In 1726 two assessors were added, one a senior consul and the other a senior merchant of the city. They were normally nonvoting members of the court but were allowed to vote when they stood in for a judge who was under suspicion, absent, or unable to carry out his duties. These magistrates had final judgment in cases involving amounts up to 500 livres. In more important cases the parties paid a deposit to the court, and decisions could be appealed to *parlement*. The competence of this court covered disputes between merchants over merchandise, payments due in Besançon, or cases arising out of transactions at the Besançon fairs. A royal declaration of 1715 also assigned it jurisdiction over bankruptcies. Cases involving merchants or wholesalers not residing at Besançon or originating in fairs held at other locations were within the competence of ordinary judges, however, as were cases of fraudulent bankruptcy after the royal declaration of 11 January 1716. The parties to a case were required to plead without the assistance of an *avocat* or *procureur*, but they became accustomed to seeking help or representation from certain merchants of the city, who specialized in this kind of business.

Quicker and less costly than the regular courts, the consular courts were quite active. Hearings were held twice a week. In 1751, 83 hearings were held and 400 cases were heard. Merchants themselves recognized that the courts assured the victory of "good faith over fraud" and avoided "the difficulties [associated with other courts], which distract men from their ordinary occupations with lengthy trials and often consume more in fees than the case is worth."[14]

Notes

1. Edict of December 1770.

2. Cited by Armand Brette, *Atlas des bailliages ou juridictions assimilées ayant forme unité électorale en 1789*. Collection des documents inédits sur l'histoire de France (Imprimerie Nationale, Librairie Ernest Leroux, 1904), p. xvii.

3. Civil ordinance of April 1667, Isambert, vol. 18, pp. 105, 125, 133, 152, and 155.

4. In 1618 a fire destroyed the large black marble table imported from Germany by Philip the Fair and used by certain courts to promulgate their decisions; despite the destruction of the table, these courts continued to be referred to as the Table de Marbre, and the name was eventually extended to similar courts in the provinces.

5. C.B.F. Boscheron des Portes, *Histoire du Parlement de Bordeaux depuis sa création jusqu'à sa suppression: 1451–1790* (Bordeaux: Charles Lefebvre, 1877), p. 17.

6. Cited by Maurice Gresset, *Le monde judiciaire à Besançon: 1674–1789* (1974), p. 59.

7. See the list in E. Laurain, "Essai sur les présidiaux" *Nouvelle revue historique de droit français et étranger* (1895), p. 382.

8. The Châtelet was the fortress that housed the courts of Paris, Orléans, Melun, Montpellier, etc.

9. Cited by Suzanne Pillorget, *Claude-Henri Feydeau de Marville, Lieutenant général de police de Paris, 1740–1747, suivi d'un choix de lettres inédites* (Editions Pedone, 1978), p. 83.

10. The Bureau des Finances was established in 1696 and later combined with the Chambre des Comptes of Dôle. In 1771, when the Chambre des Comptes was abolished, the Bureau regained its independence and established its seat at Besançon.

11. Daniel Jousse, *Traité de la juridiction des Trésoriers de France, tant en matière de domaine et de voirie que de finances* (1777), cited by Jean-Paul Charmeil, *Les Trésoriers de France à l'époque de la Fronde* (A. & J. Picard, 1964), p. 150.

12. The *élection* at Auxerre was abolished in 1665, and those at Briançon, Crest, Die, and Embrun went at about the same time. Those in Bar-sur-Aube and Sainte-Menehould were abolished in September 1654. New *élections* were established at Guise in 1633, Franc-Alleu in 1716, Salers and Thiers, temporarily established in 1653, Issoudun in December 1654, and Mauriac in 1661. The *élections* of Bar-sur-Aube and Sainte-Menehould were reinstated in 1696, and new *élections* were created at Joinville in 1696, Eu in 1695, and Saint-Lô in March 1691.

13. A table of *élections* may be found in Charmeil, *Les Trésoriers de France*, pp. 420–21.

14. Cited by Gresset, *Le monde judiciaire*, pp. 78–79.

17

Professional and Social Status in the Courts and Administration

The Professional Hierarchy

The Courts

The Regular Courts: The Parlements. Although "the learned *Almanach royal* lists the Grand Conseil before *parlement*," little was done to exploit the great possibilities offered by the Grand Conseil, which remained "a simplified version of *parlement*."[1] Thus we may consider the Grand Conseil along with the various *parlements*, all of which were modeled on the *parlement* of Paris. The *parlements* as a group were always viewed as parts of a unified system of justice. As Du Tillet, the chief clerk of the Paris *parlement* put it, "the sovereign justice of the king is unique and vested by him in his *parlements*, which together make up a single court divided into a number of districts."[2] Despite minor differences, all the *parlements* resembled one another, and we may treat them as a group.

The Chambers. All the *parlements* included a Grand-Chambre. This was the primary chamber of *parlement* from which all others originated, and it remained the most important of all the various chambers. In most of the *parlements* procedural necessities required that this chamber be broken down into a number of others. Usually there was a criminal court known as the *Tournelle criminelle* and often a civil court known as the *Tournelle civile*. There were also one or more Chambres des Enquêtes, one or two Chambres des Requêtes, a Chambre des Vacations, and, in some cases, a Chambre de l'Edit for the Protestants.

Directly presiding over the Grand-Chambre was the *premier président*, who received a commission to represent the king. In his absence he could be replaced by a *président à mortier*, the *président de la Tournelle*, or the dean of the lay councillors. In 1685 the Grand-Chambre of the Paris *parlement* included 9 *présidents à mortier*, 33 councillors (21 laymen and 12 clerics, a number increased in 1756 to 37), 2 born honorary councillors, the archbishop of Paris, the abbot of Cluny, 6 other honorary councillors (appointed by letters of commission that could be issued only to gowned officeholders; these honorary councillors had precedence over all other councillors and even over the *maîtres des requêtes*), 4 *maîtres des requêtes* serving quarterly terms (who sat as voting members of *parlement* when not working for the king's Council or traveling on business and who had the right to meet in the chamber of *parlement*, under the chairmanship of the most senior man), 2 *avocats du roi*, 1 *procureur du roi*, or a certain number of *avocats généraux* and a *procureur général*, who were referred to as "the king's men."

After 1653 no one could enter directly into the Grand-Chambre of the Paris *parlement*. Councillors in the Chambres des Enquêtes were promoted in order of seniority to the Grand-Chambre as members of the latter died off. Their rank in the Grand-Chambre depended on their seniority in *parlement*. The Grand-Chambre was thus composed of seasoned men who had generally served more than twenty-five years in *parlement*.

In the *parlement* of Toulouse the Grand-Chambre included the *premier président*, 4 *présidents à mortier*, 32 councillors (2 of whom were clerics), 3 honorary councillors, the archbishop of Toulouse, the bishop of Mirepoix, and the abbot of Saint-Sernin; from the time of Louis XIV on, there were also 2 knights of honor, *gentilshommes* who sat to the right of the *présidents à mortier*, 4 *maîtres des requêtes* serving quarterly terms, and "the king's men."

In the *parlement* of Besançon, the Grand-Chambre, which was established in 1704, does not seem to have had any specific personnel of its own. The magistrates of this *parlement* sat for a year in each of the chambers in turn: the Grand-Chambre, the Tournelle, the Chambre des Enquêtes, the Chambre des Eaux et Forêts et Requêtes du Palais, and during vacations by rotation in the Chambre des Vacations.

The members of the Grand-Chambre were sometimes faced with staggering amounts of work. In Paris the Grand-Chambre heard all cases in which the *procureur général* took part on the king's behalf, that is, all cases bearing on matters of government or administration; all cases involving the appanages or the peers of France; all cases involving the regale; all cases from the Hôtel-Dieu, the Grand Bureau des Pauvres, and the University of Paris as a body; all cases of *lèse-majesté;* all criminal trials of the principal officials of the Crown, the *présidents* and councillors of *parlements*, and the *présidents, maîtres, correcteurs,* and *auditeurs* of the Chambre des Comptes; cases involving offenses committed by ecclesiastics, *gentilshommes,* and court officers, in both first and last instance; appeals of judgments handed down by the Chambres des Enquêtes and Chambres des Requêtes of *parlement;* cases in which the vote of the chambers was tied; and appeals of judgments rendered by the *présidiaux, bailliages,* and *sénéchaussées.*

Ranking below the Grand-Chambre was the Chambre des Enquêtes, of which there might be more than one. The role of this chamber was to hear appeals submitted to *parlement* in writing in cases involving the examination of witnesses, that is, cases in which proof required the interrogation of witnesses whose statements were then recorded in the records of the court. It heard both civil cases and "petty criminal cases," that is, cases in which the only punishment was the payment of a fine or award of damages. The Chambre des Enquêtes also had jurisdiction over cases taken away from other courts and referred to it by Council decree.

The Paris *parlement* had five Chambres des Enquêtes. Each was staffed by 3 *présidents* and 32 councillors, 16 laymen and 16 clerics. Only councillors in the Chambre des Enquêtes could be nominated as *présidents*. The *parlement* of Toulouse had first two and then three Chambres des Enquêtes. Some *parlements* had only one. In 1756 the king began streamlining the Paris *parlement*, aiming to decrease the number of officers working for it and to increase his authority. He reduced the number of Chambres des Enquêtes to three, each of which employed only two *présidents*. The latter no longer held the office of *président* but were merely commissioned to act as *présidents* while holding the office of councillor.

Farther down in the hierarchy came one or two Chambres des Requêtes du Palais, which were barely part of *parlement* at all. The members of these chambers had to purchase not only their offices but also letters of commission "to serve in the Requêtes du Palais." The Requêtes had initial jurisdiction over civil, personal, possessory, and mixed actions involving privileged individuals granted the right of *committimus* under the Great or Small Seal. *Committimus* was a privilege granted by the king to certain individuals to plead in first instance, whether as plaintiffs or defendants, before designated judges and to transfer cases in which they had a stake from other courts for the purpose. Such a privilege was granted to people whom the king took under his protection and safeguard. The *grande chancellerie* issued letters of *committimus* under the Great Seal. When these letters were invoked, the cases were heard either by the *maîtres des requêtes de l'Hôtel* or by the Chambres de Requêtes du Palais in Paris. The chancelleries attached to the provincial *parlements* issued letters of *committimus* under the Small Seal that were valid within the jurisdiction of the *parlement* to which they were attached. These cases were heard by the Chambre des Requêtes of the *parlement* involved.

Beneficiaries of letters of *committimus* issued under the Great Seal included the princes of the blood, other princes, dukes-and-peers, crown officers, knights and officers of the Ordre du Saint-Esprit, members of the king's Council, ambassadors, *maîtres des requêtes*, royal secretaries employed by the *grande chancellerie*, the officers, domestics, and commensals of the royal household and the households of the queen and Children of France and the first prince of the blood, along with the associated household officers, and, in general, all the *fidèles*, clients, and other devoted servants who, because they had served the king in opposition to local authorities, had reason to fear reprisals by provincial corps, companies, colleges, and individuals.

Two Chambres des Requêtes served the Paris *parlement*. Each employed 3 *présidents* and 10 to 12 councillors. The other *parlements* had only one Chambre des Requêtes, and the one attached to the Besançon *parlement* had so little to do that it was necessary to give it jurisdiction over the Eaux et Forêts as well.

A special chamber known as the Tournelle heard appeals and issued final judgments in "major criminal cases," that is to say, cases for which the penalty might involve loss of life or liberty. Its members were therefore all laymen recruited from the other chambers of *parlement* in rotation. In the Paris *parlement* they were replaced every three months to reduce the pressure and to keep them from becoming inured to the job. The Tournelle criminelle was staffed each quarter by 4 *présidents à mortier*, 6 councillors from the Grand-Chambre, and 2 councillors from each Chambre des Enquêtes, or 20 magistrates in all. In the Toulouse *parlement* the magistrates were also rotated every three months, but a single magistrate might be compelled to hear criminal cases every year for three or four years in succession.[3] The Tournelle criminelle of Toulouse employed 3 *présidents à mortier* and 10 councillors. These figures were increased in the eighteenth century to 5 *présidents à mortier* and 18 councillors.

There were also "Tournelles civiles." The one attached to the Paris *parlement* had only a sporadic existence, appearing in 1667, again in 1697, and so on.

All the *parlements* had a Chambre des Vacations, which, during periods when the regular courts were adjourned for vacation, met to deal with urgent matters, mainly criminal cases, and to make temporary registration of royal ordinances, edicts, and letters so that they might be executed. Formalities such as the reception of officeholders were repeated before the Grand-Chambre at its next sitting. In the Paris *parlement* the Chambre des Vacations sat from the Exaltation of the Holy Cross (14 September) to the day after Saint Martin's day (12 November). It was made up of a *président* and twelve councillors chosen in rotation from among the members of the Grand-Chambre and the councillors of the Chambre des Enquêtes.

Parlements often featured special chambers to deal with local affairs or to relieve the Grand-Chambre of the burden of certain types of cases. For example, the Chambre de la Marée of the Paris *parlement* had jurisdiction over all civil and criminal cases involving trade in ocean fish. It employed a *président à mortier*, the dean and assistant dean of the lay councillors of the Grand-Chambre, and a number of other judges in auxiliary capacities. At the Toulouse *parlement* a Chambre du Guet met three times a week to decide minor cases referred to it by the Grand-Chambre or the Tournelle. It was staffed by one *président* and twelve councillors, three from each chamber, who were changed every two weeks.

Some *parlements* included a Chambre de l'Edit to deal with Protestants. Articles 30 to 57 of the edict of pacification issued at Nantes in April 1598 established special chambers and procedures to hear cases and disputes in which "followers of the so-called reformed religion are principal parties or guarantors, whether as plaintiff or defendant, in both civil and criminal cases." The edict gave its sanction to the chamber that had been established at Castres for the district of the Toulouse *parlement*. It instituted a chamber at the Paris *parlement* to cover the districts not only of that *parlement* but also of the *parlements* of Normandy and Brittany, until a Chambre de l'Edit could be set up at each *parlement*. The edict established a Chambre de l'Edit at the *parlement* of Bordeaux to cover the jurisdiction of that *parlement* and another at the parlement of Grenoble to cover the territory of the *parlements* of Dauphiné and Provence. Protestants within the jurisdiction of the *parlement* of Burgundy could choose whether they wished their cases to be heard at the Chambre de l'Edit of the Paris *parlement* or the *parlement* of Dauphiné.

The Chambres de l'Edit were supposed to consist of two *présidents*, one Catholic, the other Protestant; twelve councillors, six Catholic, six of the "other religion"; one substitute for the *procureur général*, a Catholic, and one deputy *avocat général*, a Protestant; two *commis* from the *greffe civil et criminel;* Catholic and Protestant *huissiers;* and a paymaster and fine collector. The *présidents* and councillors had to be chosen from the *corps* of the *parlements*, and new offices had to be created as needed to insure that there would be the required number of Protestants.

The Chambres de l'Edit were supposed to be incorporated into the corresponding *parlements*. Their members were to be regarded as *présidents* and councillors in *parlement*, entitled to vote and take part in the deliberations of all the chambers and to receive the same stipends, powers, and privileges as the other *présidents* and councillors. The Chambres de l'Edit were supposed to follow the procedures and style of the *parlements* with which they were associated. Except for the one in Paris, they were supposed to have an equal number of judges from each religion, and from this fact they came to be known as "halved chambers." The Chambres de l'Edit had the right to examine newly appointed *présidents* and councillors before they took the oath before *parlement*. Otherwise the examination and oath could be administered by the Conseil privé. In the case of the Chambre of Languedoc, the chancellor of France was authorized to administer the oath. The chambers could receive lower-ranking officeholders, royal and otherwise, whom the *parlements* were authorized to receive and who happened to be Protestants, but their oath had to be sworn before the court of *parlement*. These chambers were competent to deal with matters of public tranquillity and police in the cities in which they were located.

The provisions of the edict were indifferently enforced owing to a lack of good will on the part of the *parlements*. The council decree of 7 May 1604, stipulated that, in order to claim the right to have a case heard by the Chambres des l'Edit, the parties had to profess to have been members of the "so-called reformed religion" for at least six months.

The Chambre de l'Edit at the Paris *parlement* had one *président* and sixteen councillors. The king himself chose them from among the magistrates in *parlement*. He was allowed to appoint six Protestant councillors under the provisions of the Edict of Nantes but in fact appointed only one.

A Chambre de l'Edit for Normandy was established in August 1599 at the *parlement* of Rouen.

In the *parlement* of Toulouse the king chose the members of the Chambre de l'Edit from a list of twelve names prepared by the *parlement*. Eight men were named by the king by letters of commission valid for a period of one year, even though article 42 of the Edict of Nantes stipulated that these magistrates were to be appointed for the longest possible term. In 1611 the queen picked eight men of her own choosing. Then a Council decree was issued ordering that four of them be replaced each year. On 6 June 1637, *parlement* decided that the two most senior members of each chamber of *parlement* would go to the Chambre de l'Edit and that the two most senior members of that chamber would serve for a second year. But there were exceptions, either granted by *parlement* or imposed by the king. The edict of March 1639 created two new offices, a deputy *procureur général* and a deputy *avocat général*. The Chambre of Languedoc met at Castres from 1595 to 1621; at Béziers from 1623 to 1629; at Puylaurens in 1629; at Revel in 1630; at Saint-Félix-de-Caraman in 1631 and 1632; at Castres from 1632 to 1670; and at Castelnaudary from 1671 until it was done away with in 1679.

As for the Bordeaux *parlement*, the king established the Chambre de l'Edit at Nérac, a Protestant town and former residence of the kings of Navarre. He appointed its members by letters patent of June 1600. The Bordeaux *parlement* was unwilling to register these letters unless the Protestant *président* and councillors were called "councillors in the Cour and Chambre de l'Edit" and not regarded as members of the *corps* of the Court of Parlement. When the Protestant appointees appeared to take their oath of office in February 1601, *parlement* exempted them from the oath on the grounds that they had already sworn an oath before the chancellor. They were not inscribed in the roster of the Court of Parlement, nor, for that matter, were the Catholic magistrates serving in the Chambre de l'Edit (one *président*, three councillors from the Grand-Chambre and three from the Enquêtes) for a long time to come. On 22 March 1601, the Chambre de l'Edit was installed at Nérac.[4]

Until 1690 the king gave four *maîtres des requêtes* in the Grand Conseil commissions as *présidents*. These men acted in rotation as *premiers présidents* in order of seniority. In February 1690 the king created a number of new offices, one *premier président* and eight *présidents*, four per semester. In January 1738 these were eliminated and replaced by *commissaires*. A *conseiller d'Etat* served as *premier président*, and each semester four *maîtres des requêtes* were commissioned to act as *presidents*. Issued for periods of one year, these commissions were rarely renewed. The edict of January 1768 set a maximum term of three years for the *premier président* and four years for the *présidents*, thus limiting the number of consecutive commissions that could be granted. Until 1768 there were 52 councillors. The edict of January

1768 reduced the number to 44. It was then increased to 54 by the edict of November 1774. There were also honorary councillors, but they had no function.

The number of magistrates. In 1598 the various chambers of the Paris *parlement* employed magistrates of various categories in the following number: 7 *présidents*, 40 clerical councillors, 4 of whom were *présidents* in the Chambre des Enquêtes, 100 lay councillors, 4 of whom were *présidents* in the Chambre des Enquêtes and 1 in the Chambre des Requêtes, and 2 *avocats généraux* and 1 *procureur général*, the "king's men." Some "clerical" councillors were in fact laymen. In all there were 150 magistrates. In 1685 there were 267 magistrates in the Paris *parlement*, 33 of them members of the Grand-Chambre, 165 councillors in the Enquêtes, 66 councillors in the Requêtes, and 3 "king's men."

In 1724 the number of councillors in the *parlement* of Brittany was set at 94, including the *présidents* in the Chambre des Enquêtes and Chambres des Requêtes.

Between 1774 and 1790 the number of magistrates in the Bordeaux *parlement* was 153.

The *parlement* of Burgundy included a *premier président*, 9 *présidents à mortier*, 2 knights of honor, 1 born honorary councillor, the abbot of Cîteaux, 72 councillors, 6 of them clerics, and a prosecutorial staff consisting of 2 *avocats généraux*, 1 *procureur général*, and 8 deputies.

The *parlement* of Toulouse included 116 magistrates.

The auxiliaries of justice. Attached to each court were various auxiliary personnel, a variety of ministerial officials. Thus in 1598 the Paris *parlement* employed 4 *greffiers* with their clerks, 22 tipstaffs, 4 notaries, and a number of collectors and paymasters, *procureurs*, *avocats* who were not officeholders, chancellery staff, and so on. The Burgundy *parlement* had a clerk's office including 1 *greffier des présentations*, 1 *greffier des affirmations*, 5 clerks, 15 tipstaffs for the main court and 6 more for the *requêtes du Palais*. The bar of the *parlement* of Burgundy consisted of about 150 *avocats*, who were not officeholders; 100 *procureurs*, who were; and a chancellery staff, including a keeper of the seals, 25 royal secretaries, a number of referendaries, sealers, collectors, clerks, recorders, wax-melters, and tipstaffs. We find the same kinds of personnel in all the *parlements*, with minor differences. The *parlement* of Toulouse boasted of having 6 chief clerks, all nobles, with 40 assistants. It also had a chancellery employing 25 royal secretaries, who were assisted by various referendaries, sealers, recorders, and wax-melters; 117 *procureurs* with their clerks; and a number of *avocats*.

The professional hierarchy. The professional hierarchy was similar in all the *parlements*. Based on the priority ranking in *lits de justice* and assemblies, the order of precedence, from top to bottom, was approximately as follows at the end of the seventeenth century: the *premier président*, the *présidents à mortier*, the princes of the blood, the six ecclesiastical peers, the lay peers in order of seniority, the members of the Conseil privé (if they had served on the council for twenty years or had been councillors in *parlement* for ten years), the born honorary councillors, the knights of honor, the honorary councillors, the *maîtres des requêtes*, the members of the Grand-Chambre, the councillors in the Chambres des Enquêtes, the councillors in the Chambres des Requêtes, and the emeritus *présidents* and councillors, each in the train of his own chamber. Except for the princes of the blood, the peers, and the born honorary councillors, all were present or former councillors of *parlement*. They were followed by the "king's men," the *avocats généraux* and the *procureur général*.

After the magistrates came the ministerial officials, the auxiliaries of justice: first the clerks, headed by the civil clerk; the royal secretaries and other chancellery officials; and the tipstaffs, led by the premier tipstaff.

All these auxiliaries were lower-ranking members of the court but not of the *corps* of the court, though this point was arguable in the case of the civil clerk, the criminal clerk, and the premier tipstaff.

In Bluche's view, the real internal hierarchy of the Paris *parlement* was as follows: *premier président, présidents, procureur général*, head clerk, *avocats généraux*, councillors, premier tipstaff, and deputies.[5]

Avocats, procureurs, and notaries were attached to the court but not members of it. The *avocats*, who interpreted the law, could on occasion sit as councillors in the lower courts. If the king's men were absent, it was even possible for the *premier président* to commission one of them to act as *avocat général* and possibly even to rank ahead of the ministerial officials. The *procureurs* and notaries, who did the "base" work of taking care of procedural matters but who were royal officials nonetheless, ranked after the royal secretaries, *greffiers*, and premier tipstaffs but ahead of all the other chancellery officials, tipstaffs, and sergeants.

The *premier président* was the "king's man" *par excellence*. He held his post by virtue of royal commission, even though he was required to compensate his predecessor and was given a royal brevet entitling him to compensation from his successor. Strictly speaking, the "king's men" were the *avocats généraux* and *procureur général*, who were responsible for "protecting the king's interests and the rights of the public." Appointed by the king, the *procureur général* prepared written briefs. He corresponded directly with the chancellor and secretaries of state. He might bring orders from the king to sessions of *parlement*. He supervised the "king's men" in lower courts, who were viewed as his deputies. The *avocats généraux* represented the king in oral argument. They presented the briefs prepared by the *procureur général* at hearings. When the court began its deliberations, they left the chamber and returned to hear the reading of the decision.

In the *parlement* of Rennes the hierarchy was modified by the introduction of a distinction between natives and nonnatives of Brittany. The Edict of Union of 14 August 1532 had declared Brittany to be united and joined to France in perpetuity, provided that the rights, liberties, and privileges of the country were kept and observed. These conditions were further clarified by the Edict of Plessis-Macé of September 1532. Accordingly, when the Rennes *parlement* was established by the Edict of Fontainebleau in March 1554 in order to uphold justice in Brittany "in the customary form and manner" while at the same time upholding the king's authority, half the magistrates were Bretons or "natives" and half were from other provinces or "non-natives." The *parlement* at first met for three-month sessions, and at that time the majority of the "nonnatives" were Parisians. The edict of 1600 lengthened the session to six months, however, and the number of Parisians fell off until only a few young men remained, and they eventually obtained posts with the Paris *parlement*. Most of the "nonnatives" came from Maine, Anjou, and Poitou. Some nonnative magistrates settled permanently in Brittany and established dynasties there: among these were the Descartes, the Jacquelots, the Huberts, the Marbeufs, etc. Other dynasties continued to divide their interests between Brittany and their native region: the Boylesves, the Denyaus, the La Forest d'Armaillés, the Le Febvres, the Foquets, and the Du Ponts. In the February semester of 1640 there were 16 nonnative magistrates out of a total of 47, and in the August semester 22 out of 52.

In order to be a nonnative magistrate, one had to have been born outside Brittany into a non-Breton family. The king reserved the right to appoint the *premier président*, who was in theory a nonnative. Two Bretons were named *premiers présidents*, however: Henry de Bourgneuf got the job in 1622, thanks to his connections in the Paris *parlement*, and Merdy de Catuélau was appointed in 1777 as a peace offering. Men from other provinces obtained posts presumably reserved for native Bretons, and Bretons sometimes obtained posts reserved for nonnatives (which carried with them higher stipends) by invoking the services rendered by their ancestors, their birth outside Brittany, their long absence from the province, or their relatives in other provinces.

The regulation of 27 June 1656 stipulated that children of men who settled in Brittany were to be regarded as natives. According to the regulation of 21 July 1683, the distinction between natives and nonnatives was supposed to be made on the basis of the principal residence of the family of the appointee over the past forty years. The holders of posts reserved for nonnatives and their descendants were presumed to be nonnatives with no intention of settling in Brittany. If such a person was appointed to a nonnative office and received a nonnative, however, the office could still shift from nonnative to native status as it was passed on from father to son and son to grandson.

When the *parlement* changed over from semester sittings to annual sittings in 1724, it became difficult to find nonnatives willing to accept these posts, even at low prices. Five officeholders petitioned the king to eliminate their offices while continuing to pay stipend and emoluments to a family member during the officeholder's lifetime. Two others had their offices redeemed, one by the king, the other by *parlement*. In 1735 there were 43 nonnatives in the Rennes *parlement*. By 1788 this number had dropped to 24, out of a total of 80 *présidents* and councillors.

The Special Courts. The professional hierarchy in the Chambres des Comptes was somewhat different. According to Sauval,[6] for example, the Chambre des Comptes of Paris included the following magistrates: 1 *premier président*, 12 *présidents*, 74 *maîtres des comptes*, 34 *correcteurs*, 78 *auditeurs*, 1 *avocat général*, 1 *procureur général*, 4 newly created deputies, and 1 *contrôleur général des restes*. Below them in rank were the auxiliaries: 2 *greffiers en chef*, 1 *greffier au plumitif* (clerk-recorder), 2 assistant clerks, 1 commissioned bookkeeper, 1 premier tipstaff, 32 other tipstaffs, 31 *procureurs*, and 3 collector-paymasters (1 *ancien*, 1 *alternatif*, 1 *triennal*).

The *présidents*, *maîtres*, *auditeurs*, and *correcteurs* were divided into two categories. One category was made up of those who were received as "lawyers," that is, as graduates in law examined on the law; these wore the long gown. The other category wore the short gown. In Paris, however, from the time of the state entry of Queen Marie-Thérèse in 1660, all wore the long gown and the *bonnet*.

In ceremonies the *présidents* had the right to wear black velvet gowns, *maîtres* to wear black satin gowns, *correcteurs*, black damask, and *auditeurs*, black taffeta. The *avocat general* and *procureur général* wore black satin gowns, the *greffiers*, black damask, and the premier tipstaff, black taffeta.

The court had two semesters, one beginning in January, the other in July. The *premier président*, the *procureur général*, and the *avocat général* were always on duty, however.

The *premier président* and three senior *présidents* worked in the *grand bureau*. The three junior *présidents* worked in the *second bureau*. The *maîtres* alternated between the two bureaus on a monthly rotation.

The professional hierarchy of the Cours des Aides was close to that of the *parlements*. The Cour des Aides of Paris, for example, employed 1 *premier président*, 7 *présidents*, 46 councillors, 3 *avocats généraux*, and 1 *procureur général*. Among the auxiliaries were 4 *greffiers en chef*, 4 court secretaries, 1 *greffier criminel*, 1 *greffier des présentations*, 1 *greffier des décrets*, and 2 head clerks to serve at hearings and dispatch decrees issued in response to reports. In ceremonies the *presidents* wore black velvet gowns; the councillors, the "king's men," and the *greffier en chef* wore scarlet gowns.

The Cour de Monnaie of Paris employed the following personnel as magistrates in 1670: 1 *premier président*, 8 *présidents*, 26 councillors, 2 *avocats généraux*, 1 *procureur général*, and 2 deputies. Among the auxiliaries were 1 *greffier en chef*, 1 premier tipstaff, and a number of other tipstaffs. Minor changes were made on occasion, as in 1702, when two posts were set aside for knights of honor, generally *nobles d'épée*. The edict of September 1771 combined the two semesters into one, reduced the number of *présidents* to 5, counting the *premier président*, cut the number of councillors to 20, eliminated the two knights of honor and replaced them with two honorary councillors. The edict of July 1778 reestablished two semesters and ordered that the posts of knight of honor and honorary councillor not be filled when vacated. The court was henceforth composed of 1 *premier président*, 6 other *présidents*, and 30 councillors.

Quite a few magistrates and ministerial officials remained in the post in which they began their professional careers until the end of their lives. For others, however, a court office was either the culmination of a career or a stepping-stone to higher office. The same was true of offices in the lower courts. A man's career was never independent of his social status. A particular status was in many cases a prerequisite for certain kinds of career. Quite often a man's career contributed to his or his family's social mobility. Thus it is preferable to study careers in both the sovereign courts and the lower courts in conjunction with the social hierarchy.

An Ambiguous Level in the Hierarchy: The Trésoriers de France et Généraux des Finances *and the* Grands Maîtres des Eaux et Forêts

In the early part of the sixteenth century, before the reforms introduced by Francis I, the four *trésoriers de France et généraux des Finances* were members of the government and high administration. Close to the king, they went to the provinces every year to carry out some of their duties in the *circonscriptions* for which they were responsible. During the period we are studying, their functions were combined and their numbers increased. They formed a company within each *généralité* known as the *bureau des Finances*, and they were required to reside in the place where this bureau was located. Thus they were no longer members of the government or high administration but rather constituted a level of the hierarchy in their own right as the magistrates of a special set of tribunals. They were still regarded as members of the sovereign courts, however. Indeed, they belonged to the *corps* of the Chambres des Comptes. They were received by a Chambre des Comptes before being received by the *bureau des Finances* that employed them. They were voting members of the Chambre des Comptes that received them, and *trésoriers* working for the *bureau des Finances* in the *généralité* of Paris met almost daily with the Chambre des Comptes of that city. They also had seats in the Cours des Aides, where their rank was equal to that of the *présidents* and above that of the councillors; this was the rank held by the *trésoriers* of Paris at the burial of Louis XIII. When the Paris *parlement* met on 27 April 1620, in an Assembly of Chambers to deliberate on the question of the annual dues, the *trésoriers de France et généraux des Finances* for the *généralité* of Paris were ordered to send representatives. Their company sent its two *présidents*, who were seated among the senior members of the Grand-Chambre. The *trésoriers de France et généraux des Finances* were "councillors of the king." They were empowered to receive edicts and letters patent directly from the king, authenticate them, and give their approval or suggest changes. They could send deputations to the king on public business or to defend their own interests as a *corps* and were entitled to submit remonstrances. Thanks to these powers and privileges they always enjoyed a high social status, even after their offices had been reduced to merely formal posts by the *intendants des provinces*.

All the *bureaux des Finances* employed magistrates and auxiliaries. Accounting officials remained a class apart and were never considered members of either the *corps* or the company. Consider the example of the *généralité* of Paris, which stretched along the rivers from Normandy and Picardy to Champagne and Burgundy. Magistrates employed by the *bureau des Finances* for this *généralité* were known as "councillors of the king, *trésoriers de France et généraux des Finances* and *Grands Voyers* for the *généralité* of Paris." They were assisted by a *procureur du roi* and an *avocat du roi*. Because they did not handle royal funds, they were not required to post a bond when installed in their offices.

During the first half of the seventeenth century, a period marked by frequent wars, their number grew constantly. In 1586 there were 10 of them. The edict of 1621 increased this number to 12, and in 1626 another edict increased it to 14. By 1631 there were 18, and this number rose to 19 in 1633 with the addition of a seal-keeper. An *avocat du roi* and a *procureur du roi* were added to deal with the royal domain. In 1635 four new "titles" were created for each bureau. These were known as *présidents intendants généraux* of the *bureau des Finances*. Another *avocat du roi* and another *procureur du roi* were added. These "titles" were done away with in 1637, but 4 new offices raised the number of *trésoriers de France* to 23.

The number of auxiliaries grew in the same way. At the beginning of the century there were 3 *greffiers* (an *ancien*, an *alternatif*, and a *triennal*), 3 clerks, and 3 tipstaffs. In 1627 they were joined by 1 *premier huissier garde-meubles concierge*, 1 *maître-clerc*, 3 *huissiers* for the domain, 1 *greffier ordinaire*, 1 *greffier des présentations*, and 10 assistant *procureurs*. A whole new chancellery was established in 1636.

Thus in 1637 the *bureau des Finances* of Paris employed the following personnel as magistrates: 2 *présidents trésoriers généraux de France*, 21 *trésoriers généraux de France* including one seal-keeper, 3 *procureurs du roi*, and 3 *avocats du roi*. As auxiliaries there were 3 *greffiers*, 3 *maîtres-clercs*, 1 *greffier* and 1 clerk for hearings, 1 *greffier des présentations*, 1 *premier huissier garde-meubles*, 6 *huissiers*, and 10 assistant *procureurs*. The chancellery employed 1 notary-secretary for hearings, 1 notary-secretary for audits, 1 wax-melter, 1 hearings clerk who collected the seal fee and kept the key to the strongbox in which letters were stored, and 1 sergeant-at-arms. There were also accounting officials who were called upon when the magistrates needed them and who could consult but not vote. In this group were 3 *receveurs généraux* and 3 *contrôleurs généraux des Finances*, 3 *receveurs généraux* and 3 *contrôleurs généraux* of the *taillon*, 3 collector-paymasters, 1 collector of *épices*, 3 payers of rents on the *tailles*, 3 contrô-

leurs des rentes, 3 *trésoriers des Ponts et Chaussées*, and 3 *contrôleurs des Ponts et Chaussées*. Offices were shared by an *ancien*, an *alternatif*, and a *triennal*, serving one-year terms in succession.

Thus the *bureau des Finances* employed 29 magistrates, 23 *trésoriers*, and 6 of the "king's men," as well as 31 auxiliaries and ministerial officials and 28 accounting officials, for a total of 88 officers.

At the beginning of 1693 the hierarchy was as follows: *premiers présidents*, *seconds présidents*, knights of honor, honorary councillors, *présidents trésoriers de France*, *trésoriers de France*, *généraux des Finances et grands voyers*, *procureurs du roi*, *avocats du roi*, their deputies, *greffiers en chef*, and *premiers huissiers*.

The edict of March 1693 eliminated the Chambre du Trésor and split the *bureau des Finances* of Paris into a Chambre des Finances et de la Voirie and a Chambre du Domaine, which entailed the creation of an office of "*second président*," an office of *procureur du roi*, an office of *avocat du roi*, and 7 new *trésoriers de France*. This brought the number of *trésoriers* to 30. Subsequent additions had raised the number to 37 by December 1712, and in August 1716 this figure was reduced to 36.

In June 1771, Maupeou trimmed the bureau to "a single court and judicial *corps*." He eliminated 2 *présidents*, 24 *trésoriers de France*, and 2 members of the prosecutorial staff. All these posts were restored by the edict of June 1782.

The head of the *corps* was subsequently known as the "*président premier*" rather than *premier président*, however, which meant that he was placed on a level with the *présidents présidiaux* rather than the *premiers présidents* of the sovereign courts. The *bureaux des Finances* were thus demoted from the rank of the sovereign courts to that of the lower courts. Humiliated and disheartened, the *corps* virtually ceased to carry out its functions. In 1790, 14 posts of *trésoriers de France* went unfilled.

The *grands maîtres des Eaux et Forêts*, who were first officeholders and then, after 1667, *commissaires*, were generally nobles. When the War of the League of Ausburg broke out in February 1689, the king created 16 offices of *grand maître des Eaux et Forêts*, each with his own department. Two other offices for Orléans had been restored in 1670. In 1703 a *grand maître* was named for Alençon, raising the number of offices and departments to 19. In September 1706 these offices were split in half, raising the number of titularies to 38. During the two wars being fought in this period the king also established 33 *maîtrises particulières*, expanded the number of offices in each *maîtrise*, and in 1704 eliminated the Tables de Marbre, which were replaced by the Chambres des Eaux et Forêts.

This creation of new offices created confusion in the administration of the Eaux et Forêts. Following the War of the Spanish Succession, the declaration of 8 January 1715 and the edicts of July 1715, May 1716, and October 1716 did away with most of the new offices. The council decree of 24 November 1719 eliminated all the *alternatifs* holding titles of *grand maître*, thus reducing the number of *grands maîtres* to 19, increased to 20 by the annexation of Lorraine. Stipends and bonuses were reduced.

The *grands maîtres* constituted a company to which each member paid an entry fee of 300 livres and annual dues of 100 livres. In theory the company met once every two weeks and appointed a secretary, chosen from among the *avocats au Conseil*, to take charge of affairs, keep the books, and correspond with *grands maîtres* residing in the provinces whose opinions were required. The purpose of the company was to defend the competence and privileges of the *grands maîtres* and to arbitrate conflicts among them as to the bounds of their departments. On 1 January the *grands maîtres* as a body paid a visit to the royal court, to the new *contrôleurs généraux* and ministers, and to the *intendant des Finances* in charge of the Eaux et Forêts to submit their petitions and give their advice and consultation.

The control the *grands maîtres* exercised over the forests aroused opposition. They were highly unpopular, particularly as wood became scarce and expensive owing to its use for heating houses, forges, and ovens in glass, salt, and lime works. The *cahiers* of the Estates General of 1789 called for getting rid of the *grands maîtres*. There was also a unanimous outcry against the *maîtrises particulières*, whose officials were accused of charging enormous fees for the delivery of wood, exacting huge fines for minor infractions, and imposing intolerable limitations on forest-use rights. The remedy suggested was to turn supervision of the forests over to the regular judges.

After the appointment of Maynon d'Invault as *contrôleur général* on 27 September 1768, various projects had been considered, in particular one presented to the Assembly of Notables in 1787 and another presented by Lamoignon in 1788. On 7 September 1790, the Constituent Assembly eliminated the *tribunaux des Eaux et Forêts*. Responsibility for punishing and clearing offenses was turned over to the district courts. A number of judicial offices were ordered eliminated, including those of the *grands maîtres*. A decree of 15 September 1791 gave responsibility for forest conversation and administration to a general office of conservation located in Paris, with 35 *conservateurs* and 300 inspectors.

The Ordinary and Extraordinary "Jurisdictions" or Lower Courts

The Ordinary Jurisdictions: Présidiaux, Bailliages, *and* Sénéchaussées. As a first example, consider the leading *bailliage* and presidial court in France, the Châtelet of Paris. The *prévôt* of Paris, who had the rank of *bailli*, was the king. In case of a vacancy in the *prévôté*, it was the *procureur général du roi* in *parlement* who held the seat of *prévôt*. The king entrusted the *prévôté* to a "*garde de la prévôté*," as he was called until 1685. A *noble d'épée*, this *prévôt* was at once *bailli*, *prévôt*, and head of the *présidial*. He was officially recognized as the highest ranking of all the *baillis* and *sénéchaux*. He was further distinguished from the rest by the fact that he was allowed to take part in debate and to vote when he presided over an audience or council meeting.

His judicial and administrative duties were in fact carried out by lieutenants.

The *lieutenant civil* was the real head of the Châtelet. He had jurisdiction over all disputes and matters of distributive justice. He held court every morning at the *parc civil* and two afternoons a week at the Chambre civile. After a long dispute over police powers between the *lieutenant civil* and the *lieutenant criminel*, full powers were given to the former by the decree of *parlement* dated 12 March 1630. Police court was held twice a week until 1667.

The *lieutenant criminel* was also embroiled in conflict with the *lieutenant criminel de robe courte*, who, along with his *archers*, was responsible for making inspections in the city of Paris. The edict of January 1691 declared that in last resort both had concurring jurisdiction over *cas prévôtaux* mentioned in the ordinance of 1670, a jurisdiction they shared concurrently with the *prévôt* of the Ile-de-France. The *présidial* was to settle disputes over jurisdiction. Exclusive jurisdiction over cases of desertion was attributed by the declaration of 5 February 1731 to the *prévôt* of the Ile-de-France. The edict of July 1783 stripped the *lieutenant de robe courte* of all attributions of jurisdiction.

The *lieutenant particulier civil et criminel* was the first-ranking councillor in the Chambres civiles et criminelles. The Council decree of 29 November 1605 combined this office with that of *assesseur criminel*. After the Nouveau Châtelet was combined with the Ancien in May 1684, there were two *lieutenants particuliers*. They replaced the *lieutenants civil*, *criminel*, and *de police* whenever one of them was absent. One of them held hearings at the *présidial*, the other presided over the Chambre du Conseil and, after the hearings at the *parc civil*, held hearings of the Ordinaire on Wednesdays and Saturdays. The two *lieutenants particuliers* switched positions once a month. Both were *rapporteurs* in the Chambre du Conseil and the Chambre criminelle.

Two *auditeurs* took written depositions from witnesses and played a part in judging cases. Cases of minor importance they judged themselves. The edict of April 1685 did away with these two posts and replaced them with the office of *juge-auditeur*.

Some of the councillors at the Châtelet investigated and judged cases. There were 26 of them under Henri IV and 34 at the end of the Mazarin ministry in 1661.

Forty-eight *commissaires* commissioned to act as investigator-examiners were stationed in the sixteen *quartiers* of Paris. They were responsible for "police," that is, for maintaining order and protecting the safety of the public. In criminal matters they conducted investigations and inquiries. In the civil domain they affixed seals after a death, bankruptcy, or judicial interdiction, examined local accounts, and oversaw and managed local affairs. They disposed of property ordered sold by decree or judicial order and distributed the sums obtained. They assessed expenditures, examined manufactured goods and other articles, oversaw the opening of the gates, and so on.

The *lieutenants*, *auditeurs*, and *conseillers* performed their duties in different chambers. The *parc civil*, in which the *lieutenant civil* personally heard cases every morning except Monday, was the most important court in the Châtelet. It published ordinances, edicts, declarations, regulations, wills with entailments, and so forth. It certified auctions and received *requêtes* for the *garde-nobles* and *bourgeoises*. It heard cases involving benefices and ecclesiastics and had jurisdiction over cases involving personal status. When it finished its hearings, either the *lieutenant particulier* or a councillor held what was known as the *"audience de l'ordinaire"* to examine preliminary investigations under way. On Wednesdays and Saturdays this same official held the *"audience des criées"* to consider allocations of property by decree, court auction, or court-ordered trust.

The *auditeurs* alternated every three months in presiding over the Chambre des Auditeurs. Whichever one was not presiding served in an advisory capacity. The name "Chambre des Auditeurs" was kept even after 1685, when hearings began to be held every day at noon by a single *juge-auditeur*. This chamber had initial jurisdiction over all personal cases involving amounts up to 50 livres, increased to 90 livres on 1 September 1785. Its decisions could be appealed to the *présidial*.

The Chambre civile kept written records of its proceedings and handled cases involving amounts in excess of 100 livres and other "major trials" pertaining to certain kinds of affairs, particularly those involving benefices.

The affairs of the company were deliberated in the Chambre du Conseil, which also heard and kept written records of civil and administrative cases reported to it.

The Chambre du procureur du roi was the "primary judge and protector of the merchants, artisans, craftsmen, masters, and sworn journeymen of Paris." Its judgments had to be upheld by the *lieutenant civil*.

The *présidial* kept its records in common with the *parc civil*.

The Chambre de Police was the place where, in 1635, the *lieutenant civil* began hearing cases in two successive sittings. The first was the "ordinary" session, for petty police matters. The second was the "extraordinary" session, for major police matters. Cases were brought before this tribunal upon request of one of the parties or report of the *commissaires*.

Then there were the Chambre criminelle and the Chambre de la commission, which heard extraordinary cases sent to the Châtelet by decree of the king's Council.

Beginning in 1667, steps were taken to improve the division of labor within the Châtelet. The task of the *lieutenant civil* was divided up. Earlier, on 9 November 1637, it had been decided that, because of the importance of the post, it would henceforth be assigned by commission and could not be held by one person for more than three years in a row. In 1643, however, it was again made an office for the sake of Dreux d'Aubray, who died in September

1666. The office was eliminated and replaced by two new offices, one *lieutenant civil* and one *lieutenant de police*, by the edict of 15 March 1667.

There were twenty-seven seigneurial courts in Paris in addition to the jurisdictions of the *prévôt de l'Hôtel* and the *bailliage* of the Palace, privileged places where malefactors could seek refuge. The edict of December 1666 granted free access to these places to the officers of the Châtelet for purposes of *police générale* and (by *concurrence* and *prévention*) *police particulière*. The council decree of 14 April 1667 lifted impediments on the actions of the *lieutenant de police* in these places. Then, in February 1674, an edict was issued by the king, who, "recognizing the inconvenience caused the Residents of Paris by the large number of lower courts, and the conflicts to which the uncertainty as to the limits of their jurisdiction and the *prévention* of the officers of the Châtelet have often given rise . . . combines and incorporates into the Court of the Châtelet of Paris the *Bailliage* of the Palace and all the seigneurial courts in the City and Faubourgs of Paris as far as its suburbs," except those "within the walls and galleries of the Palace." Nineteen courts were thereby eliminated. The king allowed the *bailliages* of Sainte-Geneviève and Saint-Martin-des-Champs to remain. In April 1674 he reestablished the courts of the archbishop of Paris, and on 21 January 1675, those of the abbey of Saint-Germain-des-Prés. On 14 August 1676 he reopened the courts of the Chapter of Paris and on 20 March 1678 those of the Commanderies of the Temple and of Saint-Jean-de-Latran, but "only for the enclosures, courts, and cloisters." These concessions were essentially by way of atonement.[7]

Because of the increasing number of cases it became necessary to establish a Nouveau Châtelet in February 1674. The new Châtelet had the same number of offices as the old. Officeholders were supposed to switch from one to other every year. The declaration of 27 August 1674 divided the territory under the jurisdiction of the Châtelet between the new and the old and also divided cases from the provinces to be assigned to each (on the grounds that they involved the seal of the Châtelet).

The alternating service of the court officers was a system whose disadvantages outweighed its advantages. The decree of 18 April 1674 restored a single *lieutenant de police*. For thirty years the post was held by Gabriel-Nicolas de La Reynie. The edict of 7 September 1684 combined the Nouveau Châtelet with the Ancien. The two offices of *lieutenant particulier* were retained.

The edict of January 1685 established judicial forms and procedures, the main outlines of which persisted down to the Revolution. By council decree of 16 October 1684 the councillors were grouped into four "columns," each with fourteen councillors led by four of the most senior of the group. From January 1685 on, each column served for a month at a time staffing the *parc*, the *présidial*, the Chambre du Conseil, and the Chambre criminelle in rotation. Councillors on duty in these hearings also had to report to the Council. The edict of April 1685 eliminated the *auditeurs* and created the office of *juge-auditeur*. By virtue of the edict of January 1685, the *lieutenant civil* was the sole judge in the Chambre civile, where he was assisted by an *avocat du roi* in hearing all summary and provisional cases whose value did not exceed 1,000 livres: these included evictions, payment of rent due under verbal rental agreements, seizures and sales of furnishings, repair of buildings, wages and salaries when there were no written contracts, and disputes over contracts for merchandise and payments involving sales by itinerant merchants to residents of Paris. The Chambre du Conseil, which was presided over by the *lieutenant civil* or one of the *lieutenants particuliers*, assisted by one of the four columns of councillors, judged cases reported to it after being left in abeyance by the *parc civil* or *présidial*, cases treated as *appointement à mettre* or *appointement en droit* in the other chambers. When sitting as a presidial court (with seven judges handing down final judgment), the Council judged cases not heard by the *présidial* and had final jurisdiction over cases within the competence of the criminal judges. In the Chambre du Conseil, the "assembled Company" deliberated and handed down decisions in certain cases, including registration of royal letters and Company affairs. It examined *conseillers* and *avocats* prior to their reception. It received *commissaires*, *procureurs*, *greffiers*, and notaries. The ordinance of 1685 separated the *parc civil* and the *présidial*, which thereafter kept separate minutes and records. From that date forward a *lieutenant particulier* normally presided over the *présidial*. He was assisted by one column of councillors. Under the terms of the same ordinance, the *lieutenant criminel* had sole judgment in the Chambre criminelle, where he was assisted by an *avocat du roi* in hearing minor criminal cases, that is, cases in which the maximum penalty was payment of damages and court costs. Major criminal cases, that is, cases in which the possible penalty included loss of life or liberty, were judged by special procedure in the "Chambre du conseil du criminel" by the *lieutenant criminel*, who was assisted by a column of councillors.

With these measures the king hoped to parcel out the work load and reduce the number of conflicts of jurisdiction, which remained high.

In the *bailliage* de Besançon there were only 4 magistrates under the *bailli* in 1688: 1 *lieutenant général*, 1 *lieutenant particulier*, 1 *procureur fiscal*, and 1 *avocat fiscal*. A *greffier* was the only auxiliary. He called upon the services of 25 deputy *procureurs*. The *bailliage* shared 37 notaries with the *parlement*. An edict of August 1692 added 1 *lieutenant criminel*, 4 *assesseurs*, and a number of *greffiers* and *huissiers*. The edict of September 1696 joined the newly created *présidial* to the *bailliage* and added 2 *présidents*, 1 *lieutenant assesseur criminel*, 2 honorary councillors, 5 *assesseurs*, 2 *avocats du roi*, and several *greffiers* and *huissiers*.

The *bailliage* of Arbois, a city of 5,050 inhabitants in 1674, included within its jurisdiction only the city and some twenty-odd villages. It employed 9 magistrates: 1 *lieutenant général*, 1 *lieutenant criminel*, 1 *lieutenant particulier*, 3 *assesseurs*, 1 *avocat du roi*, 1 *procureur du roi*, and 1 deputy. Among the auxiliaries were 1 *greffier civil et criminel*, 1 *receveur des consignations*, 1 *commissaire* for the seizure of real property, 18 *avocats*, 7 *procureurs*, 7 notaries (4 of whom were also *procureurs*), 3 country notaries, and 3 *huissiers* (one of whom was an *audiencier*).

The *bailliage* of Quincey (20 kilometers southwest of Besançon) included within its jurisdiction the town of Quincey (whose population was 925 in 1764, according to the *intendant*) and 40 villages. It employed 5 magistrates: 1 *lieutenant général*, 1 *lieutenant criminel*, 1 *assesseur*, 1 *procureur du roi*, and 1 deputy. Among the auxiliaries were 1 *greffier civil et criminel*, 1 clerk, 1 *receveur des consignations*, 1 *commissaire* for the seizure of real property, 1 recorder of seizures, 2 *avocats*, 6 *procureurs* (2 of whom were also notaries), 7 *huissiers* (including 1 *premier huissier audiencier* and 1 *huissier audiencier*).[8]

The Extraordinary Jurisdictions.

Grandes maîtrises des Eaux et Forêts. In 1692, the *grand maîtrise des Eaux et Forêts* of Bensançon employed 1 *grand maître*, 1 *lieutenant général*, 4 councillors, 2 *avocats du roi*, and 1 *procureur du roi*.

Elections, salt warehouses, *maîtrises particulières des Eaux et Forêts*, special admiralty courts. Paris is a good example of the staff employed in a large *élection*. At the end of the seventeenth century the Paris *élection* employed 26 magistrates: 1 *président*, 1 *lieutenant*, 1 *assesseur*, 20 *élus* and councillors, 1 *procureur du roi*, 1 *avocat du roi*, and 1 deputy. In 1703 another *président* was added, and the senior *président* became *président premier*.[16]

The auxiliaries included a *greffier en chef*, a *premier huissier*, and a number of other *greffiers* and *huissiers*. Six specialized *procedures* took care of both the *élection* and the salt warehouse.

Burgundy had no *élections*. In Bresse, however, which fell under the jurisdiction of the Dijon *parlement*, the *élection* of Belley employed 10 magistrates, including a *président* and a number of *élus* and "king's men." The election of Bourg-en-Bresse employed 14 magistrates and 1 *huissier*.[9]

During the eighteenth century the Paris salt warehouse employed 15 magistrates (an *ancien* and an *alternatif* when there were 2 and an *ancien*, *alternatif*, and *triennal* when there were 3): 2 *présidents*, 2 *grenetiers*, 2 *lieutenants*, 3 *contrôleurs*, 2 *contrôleurs*-inspectors of weights and measures, 2 *procureurs du roi*, and 2 *avocats du roi*. Among the ministerial officials were 3 *greffiers en chef*, 1 *premier huissier audiencier*, a number of *huissiers*, and the 5 *procureurs* who also took care of the *élection*, as well as a whole staff of clerks, domainial officials, and day laborers.

The Dijon salt warehouse employed 6 magistrates and 2 *huissiers*, and the warehouse at Dombes employed 3 magistrates.[10]

The edict of April 1667 eliminated most of the officers of the Eaux et Forêts and pruned back the staff of the *maîtrises particulières* to 1 senior *maître particulier*, 1 *procureur du roi*, 1 hammer-keeper, 1 *greffier*, 1 surveyor, and however many sergeants of the guard were needed. In 1678, the *maîtrise particulière* of Avallon actually employed 1 *maître particulier*, 1 *lieutenant*, 1 hammer-keeper, 1 *procureur du roi*, 1 *greffier*, 2 *huissier audienciers*, 1 sworn surveyor, and 6 sergeants of the guard. In 1692 the *maîtrise particulière* of Besançon employed 1 *maître particulier*, 1 *lieutenant*, 1 *procureur du roi*, and a number of *greffiers* and *huissiers*. During the War of the League of Augsburg and the War of the Spanish Succession other offices were created which seem to have found no takers. In many cases the duties of these offices were carried out by the *maîtres particuliers*, who paid for the privilege. Exceptions must be made for the inspectors-conservators of the Eaux et Forêts, whose offices were created by the edict of March 1706. There were 2 of these in the *maîtrise* of Auxerre for the royal forests of Frétoy and Mailly-la-Ville. In 1733 the *maîtrise* of Auxerre employed 1 *maître particulier*, 1 *lieutenant*, 1 hammer-keeper, 1 *procureur du roi*, 1 *greffier*, 2 *huissiers audienciers*, 1 sworn surveyor, 1 general of the guard, and 4 sergeants of the guard. Broadly speaking, the edict of 1667 seems to have been enforced up to 1790, except for a hiatus while Louis XIV was fighting his major wars.[11]

The special admiralty courts, such as the one at Bordeaux in the admiralty of Guyenne, employed 1 *lieutenant général*, 1 *lieutenant particulier*, 1 *procureur du roi*, 3 councillors, 5 *greffiers*, 5 *huissiers*, 6 interpreters, 18 consuls, a number of brokers, 5 inspectors-measurers, 5 coast guardsmen, 1 physician, 2 surgeons-major and 2 apothecaries, and 1 dues collector. The office of *lieutenant général* usually remained within a single family, and the holder of this office could put himself on a par with councillors in *parlement*.

A special admiralty court usually employed 1 *lieutenant général*, 1 *lieutenant particulier* (who heard cases), 1 *procureur du roi*, 1 *greffier*, and a few clerks and *huissiers*.

The Court Auxiliaries. At each level in the judicial hierarchy we find "auxiliaries of justice." At the highest level were the *avocats*, who did not own their offices unless they were *avocats au* Conseil du Roi. After the edict of 1525 they were required to be graduates in law and after 1610 *licenciés* in law. The job of the *avocat* was to set forth his interpretation of the law and the way it should be applied in a given lawsuit or criminal trial. Thus *avocats* acted not merely as counselors of the parties to a case or the accused in a criminal trial but also in a sense as counselors to the judges. If the number of judges was less than required or the *avocat du roi* was missing, moreover, an *avocat* might be called upon to replace the absent official. The position of *avocat* was therefore an honorable one, and it was no derogation for a *gentilhomme* to practice the profession. At a somewhat lower level in the hierarchy were auxiliaries concerned with procedural matters, such as *greffiers*, *procureurs*, notaries, *huissiers*, and *sergents*. The work done by these men was not similar but rather analogous to that done by manual workers in the crafts and trades; in other words, it was, *mutatis mutandis,* mechanical work. Hence these were regarded as "base" occupations, particularly the positions of *procureur* and *sergent*. But they were royal officeholders.[12] Finally, the lowest echelon of auxiliaries included the scribes and clerks working for ministerial officials, who formed corporations or, as they were known, *basoches*, a word that may have been derived from Basilica (i.e., the Palais royal). In Paris there was a *basoche* of legal clerks from the Paris parlement and a *basoche* of legal clerks from the Châtelet, said to have numbered some 6,000 all told. In Toulouse there was a *basoche* of legal clerks from the *parlement* and another from the *sénéchaussée*. There were also *basoches* in Dijon, Grenoble, and Bordeaux, in the *sénéchaussées* of Montauban and Carcassonne, and practically anywhere where there was a *corps* of *procureurs*.

These *corps* enjoyed official status. Frequently the king appointed their officers, who swore an oath into his hands. Disputes between different *basoches* could be taken before the Grand Conseil. Each *basoche* was a world unto itself, with its own constitution and statuses. In Toulouse, the *basoche* of the *sénéchal*, which had been established "in honor of God, Our Lady his glorious mother, and Our Lord Saint John the Baptist, one of the four notaries of God and the Catholic faith," had its own book of statutes, of which the first pages had been taken from the four Gospels. Each *basoche* was a moral person with its own coat of arms. The *basoche* of the *parlement* of Toulouse had for its coat of arms three golden writing desks on a field of azure, capped by a helmet and morion and bordered by two supporting angels. The *basoche* at Paris decked itself out in blue or white ribbons and the one at Toulouse in green ribbons. At hearings of the higher and lower courts, members of the *basoche* wore black caps and gowns.

Every clerk was required to place his name on the books of the *basoche*, to which he paid an entry fee and annual dues. On 1 May the *procureurs* and clerks together elected the "king" and officers of the "kingdom" of the *basoche*. The night before, these dignitaries paid a visit to the *premier président* and the "king's men." They paid morning calls on all the members of *parlement*. On 1 May they set up a maypole wreathed with flowers and decorated with the coat of arms of the *basoche* in the Court of May at the Palace. Each *basoche* had a "king," a chancellor, several *maîtres des requêtes*, a *grand maître*, an admiral, a constable, a number of marshals, peers, a great referendary, an *aumônier*, an *avocat général*, a *procureur général*, a *procureur de communauté*, secretaries, notaries, *greffiers*, *huissiers*, *baillis*, an ordinary barber, a surgeon, a physician, a painter, a goldsmith, a stationer, a glover, and an innkeeper. These merchants marked their establishments with the coat of arms in the *basoche*.

The *basoche* of Paris met twice a week, whereas the one in Toulouse met only for major occasions. *Basoches* were the recipients of decrees, which bore the following salutation: "La Basoche régnant en triomphe et en titre d'honneur, à tous présents et à venir, salut." They held hearings to settle disputes between member clerks and minor cases involving member clerks and merchants. For "police" offenses, the "king" of the *basoche*, assisted by seven *maîtres des requêtes*, could sentence clerks to prison. Any petition to the *basoche* had to be headed by the words, "To our lords of the kingdom of the Basoche." Appeals of decisions by the *basoche* could be taken before a court of appeals made up of former clerks who had become *procureurs* or *avocats*.

When there were no cases to be heard, clerks pleaded fictitious causes before the *basoche* and argued over laws and customs.

The "king" of the *basoche* was treated as a noble. Examples can be found dating from 1605, 1637, 1639, etc. When he came before *parlement* with a personal case, the *président* of the Chambre invited him to cover himself with the words, "Cover yourself, king of the Basoche." His *avocat* was also allowed to wear a hat.

After serving in his post for a year, the "king" of the *basoche* became an "emperor" and obtained membership in the community of *procureurs* without test or examination.

Each *basoche* was paired with a religious confraternity that prayed and did good works in the community.

The various *basoches* fitted into a hierarchy, at least within each region. Thus, in Toulouse, the "king" of the *basoche* of *procureurs* in *parlement* received the oath of fidelity from the *sénéchal* of the *basoche* of *procureurs* in the *sénéchaussée* and heard appeals of judgments handed down by the *basoche* of the *sénéchaussée*.

The members of the *basoches* shared intimately in the lives of their masters. From sunrise to sunset clerks worked alongside *procureurs* at their writing tables. One clerk or another might accompany a *procureur* to the Palace. At night one of the clerks carried a lantern ahead of the *procureur*'s wife, to light her way. *Procureurs* and their clerks shared common habits, feelings, and interests, centered on the Palace. Any happenings in the courts soon affected the auxiliaries and their *basoches* throughout the kingdom, arousing the interest of men who were fascinated by the law, restless, aggressive, and sensitive to the interests of the judiciary, whose organization reflected that of the courts.

The Social Hierarchy

Broadly speaking, the social hierarchy was patterned after the professional hierarchy.

The Courts

The Ordinary Courts: The Parlements.

The nobility of the courts. The *parlements*, along with the sovereign councils or superior councils, constituted sixteen courts of justice, to which we should add the Grand Conseil. Together these employed the services of around 1,100 magistrates—*présidents*, councillors, "king's men." These offices were supposed to be held by nobles. In fact they often were, and in any case the offices tended to confer nobility. Any magistrate in these courts enjoyed the privileges of nobility, including a title: *écuyer* for councillors and *chevalier* for *présidents*. Under certain conditions an office might confer nobility on its holder's family. At the beginning of the century, magistracies in these courts carried with them a "gradual nobility," that is, the family became noble if the post was held by two consecutive generations, father and son, and if both remained in office for at least twenty years or else died in office. Then a distinction was made in favor of the Parisian courts. Magistrates in these courts acquired hereditary nobility (i.e., became nobles of the first degree) if they held their posts for twenty years or died in office. This was done for the Paris *parlement* in July 1644 and for the Grand Conseil in December. In 1669 this privilege was taken away and gradual acquisition of nobility restored. Hereditary nobility was again granted to *parlement* in 1690 and to the Grand Conseil in 1717, however, and members held this privilege from then until 1790.

Some provincial courts more than compensated for this disadvantage by closing membership to commoners. The *parlement* of Rennes was one that did this, refusing to receive nonnobles after the reform of the Breton nobility (1668–71). It was a tradition in Brittany that judicial functions were usually performed by nobles. Up to 1671 all "native" magistrates were nobles and most were knights; half of the "nonnatives" were nobles. After 1671, recipients of *lettres de provision* who were not sons of members of *parlement* were required to attach to their letters a confirmation of nobility or other proof of rank. After an investigation, the Rennes *parlement* in 1682 rejected a *bourgeois* who had obtained *lettres de provision* from the chancellery. In 1708 it won recognition from the king that the *parlement* of Brittany was composed exclusively of *gentilshommes*. In 1729 it persuaded the chancellor to refuse *lettres de provision* to a nominee descended from aldermen of Nantes. On 2 January 1732, it issued a regulation stipulating that, except for nominees "descended from *maîtres* in the male line," it would require "confirmations of nobility obtained at the time of the Reformation [of the nobility] carried out in the kingdom in 1666 and subsequent years . . ." If such confirmation was not available, the nominee had to supply other titles. These were then examined by *commissaires* appointed by *parlement* and a report prepared. This regulation was repealed on 9 August 1756 and 12 March 1788. From 1671 on, in fact, only one bourgeois was able to get past the barrier among the "native" magistrates and only two among the "nonnative" magistrates. Of 538 families of magistrates, 323 had acquired their nobility prior to 1500. Nobility became an official prerequisite for membership in the *parlement* of Grenoble in 1762, Aix-en-Provence in 1769, and Nancy, Toulouse, and Bordeaux by decree of 16 February 1780.

In all the courts, moreover, recruitment was mainly from families that had been noble before any of their members entered *parlement*. Out of 680 new members of the 16 courts in the eighteenth century, we find 19 percent commoners, 12 percent nobles of the second generation, 19 percent nobles of the third generation, 11 percent nobles of the fourth generation, and 39 percent nobles of more than four generations. In other words, half could characterize themselves as *gentilshommes*. Of 164 magistrates in the Paris *parlement* between 1685 and 1690 whose social status is known, only 8 (4.8 percent) were commoners when they entered *parlement*. In 1715, out of 303 individuals who possessed ennobling offices in *parlement*, 247 were nobles before acquiring their offices (82 percent), 28 were sons of privileged persons, and only 28 were entirely common upon taking office. Between 1716 and 1771, of 590 families that gave 951 magistrates to the Paris *parlement*, 477, or 81 percent had been ennobled before any member entered *parlement*. Furthermore, those commoners who did enter *parlement* were all owners of *seigneuries* and members of families close to the nobility. The grandfather and great-grandfather of the abbot René Pucelle were *procureurs*, a "base" position. But his father was a well-known *avocat*, a post that was not a derogation from nobility. In 1684, when the abbot was about to be received into *parlement*, his uncle Pierre was a noble in his capacity as a *secrétaire du roi;* his elder brother had been a councillor in the Paris *parlement* since 1675 and had been ennobled by his office; his brother Omer, who had become a professional soldier, was a knight of Saint-Louis (and destined to become *maréchal de camp* in 1704). Through his mother the abbot was related to 21 magistrates, including members of *parlement*, *maîtres des requêtes*, and *conseillers d'Etat*.

All nine *présidents* of the Bordeaux *parlement* between 1774 and 1790 were nobles, seven of them from families ennobled in the sixteenth century and two from families ennobled in the seventeenth century. Of 127 noble councillor's families, 24 had been ennobled in the sixteenth century, 46 in the seventeenth century, and the rest in the eighteenth century. Only 11 common families were represented: 3 councillors, 4 *maître des requêtes*, 4 *greffiers en chef*.

There was a tendency, moreover, for the courts to become closed. It had never been easy for anyone but sons of *maîtres* to gain access to them. The *parlement* of Toulouse refused to receive a canon of Saint-Etienne convicted of embezzlement and immoral acts, a laymen by the name of Jean Fossé who had just separated from his wife, another by the name of Jean de Puis, who was suspected of practicing usury, and "certain others who had practiced the merchant profession and whom the law called *viles negotiatores*." From 1660 on, it became increasingly difficult for the sons of financiers or merchants to gain entry to the Paris *parlement*. Everywhere offices remained in the hands of a small number of families. By the eve of the Revolution it had even become difficult for *avocats* to obtain court offices, and this was one of the reasons why most *avocats* supported the Revolution only to turn against it later on.

A working nobility. The court nobility was a working nobility. Recruitment for the courts was done mainly among the magistrates and lawyers ennobled by their positions. In the Paris *parlement* between 1685 and 1690, of the 156 magistrates whose background can be determined, 62 were sons of magistrates in the Paris *parlement* (39.7 percent), 16 were sons of magistrates in the Chambre des Comptes (10.2 percent), 7 were sons of a magistrate in the Cour des Aides (4.5 percent), 24 had fathers in the government such as *conseillers d'Etat* or *secrétaires d'Etat* (15.4 percent), 17 were sons of *maîtres des requêtes* or *intendants de province* (10.9 percent), 13 were sons of royal secretaries (8.4 percent), and 17 had fathers in the Châtelet of Paris or a comparable *corps* (10.9 percent). Thus the fathers of magistrates were predominantly magistrates in posts that conferred nobility.

Turning next to the mothers of magistrates, whose ancestry has been established in 129 cases, we find 21 (20 percent) with backgrounds in governmental circles of milieus close to the court (9 daughters of chancellors, *secrétaires d'Etat*, or *conseillers d'Etat*, 7 daughters of *intendants des Finances*, *trésoriers de l'Epargne*, and other treasurers, 5 daughters of officials of the royal household), 38 (36 percent) daughters of magistrates in the sovereign courts (20 from *parlement*, including 5 daughters of *premiers présidents* or *présidents*, 12 of councillors, 3 of "king's men"), 18 daughters of magistrates in the other sovereign courts of Paris (7 of *premiers présidents* or *présidents*, 7 of *maîtres des comptes* and *conseillers*, 3 of *auditeurs des comptes*, 1 of a "king's man"), 12 (11 percent) daughters of magistrates in the lower courts (4 of officials of regular tribunals, the Châtelet of Paris, or *lieutenants généraux de bailliage*, and 8 of officials of special tribunals such as *trésoriers de France*, *élus*, inspectors of salt warehouses, etc.), 6 (5.55 percent) daughters of provincial accounting officials such as *receveurs généraux des Finances*, 16 (14 percent) daughters of royal secretaries, 3 daughters of *avocats*, 2 daughters of *procureurs* of the Châtelet, 7 (6 percent) daughters of plain "seigneurs de" this or that, probably rentiers living as nobles, and 4 who were merely daughters of a merchant, a banker, a secondhand dealer, and a merchant described as a "bourgeois of Paris."

Between 1716 and 1771, out of 477 families ennobled prior to the entry of one of their members into *parlement*, 58 (or almost 12 percent) owed their nobility to letters from the king, and 16 of these already had *robins*, officials of the sovereign courts, officials of *bailliages*, or *trésoriers de France* among their number, 14 had royal financial officials such as *receveurs généraux* and *fermiers généraux*, and 9 had royal physicians.

Two hundred forty-one families (nearly 50 percent) had entered the nobility by purchasing an office as royal secretaries.

One hundred thirty-two families (29 percent) had become noble by holding an office in the judiciary or financial administration that conferred nobility.

Nine percent of the ennobled families had become noble by serving as aldermen.

The same was true of the Bordeaux *parlement*. In the late eighteenth century, 71 (46.4 percent) of the 153 members of *parlement* were sons of magistrates in *parlement*. The rest came from the Cour des Aides of Bordeaux, the ranks of the *trésoriers de France*, the lower courts, the royal secretaries, and the aldermen of Bordeaux. In this great commercial city, only 7 were sons of merchants. Eleven sons of royal secretaries who were actually merchants should perhaps be added, but still this number amounts to barely 12 percent of the members of *parlement*, the highest proportion in France.

In Besançon, a city that lived on its courts of justice, practically all the families with members in *parlement* rose to prominence within the world of the judiciary. Of 319 magistrates whose ancestors are known (from the period between 1614 and 1789), only 9 (2.5 percent) were sons of wealthy merchants. The first known ancestor of 33 magistrates was a merchant or wholesaler, but a century and a half had typically elapsed between the merchant and the descendant who became a member of *parlement*. Of those who entered *parlement* 77 percent were already nobles. As for the commoners, almost all of them were already magistrates and holders of fiefs. Quite a few laid claim to nobility and obtained letters confirming their nobility after their entry into *parlement*, whether upholding their claim, restoring or rehabilitating a lapsed title, or granting relief from derogation.

Most of these nobles continued to render service to the state. Most of the *magistrates* had no careers. They went to work for *parlement* straightaway and held the same office for life, at best moving up from the Chambre des Enquêtes to the Grand-Chambre. Consider the list of magistrates in the Paris *parlement* between 1685 and 1690, taking account of their lives and, when appropriate, their careers. This will take us back into the first half of the seventeenth century and down into the first half of the eighteenth century, because 168 or almost three-quarters of the magistrates entered *parlement* after 1665. The most senior magistrate was received in 1627 and had amassed 58 years of service by 1685. In that year 15 councillors from the time of the Fronde were still serving. Out of a total of 216 magistrates, only 61 (21 percent) had had a previous career, 54 of them having held one office and 7, two offices, half of them as councillors at the Châtelet. Seventy-two percent entered *parlement* directly, some 23 percent between the ages of 21 and 25, 46 percent between the ages of 25 and 38, 1 at age 20, 1 at age 19, and 1 at age 17. This last was Nicolas IV Potier de Novion, who was received in 1637 when his father, André I, was *président à mortier* in the *parlement*.

Of 185 members of *parlement* whose lives we are able to follow, 118 (64 percent) remained councillors throughout their careers. Of these 71 continued to serve in the same chamber of *parlement* in which they were first received, while 47 became members of the Grand-Chambre between 1685 and 1721 (an average of 1 per year, except for the year 1715, when there were 10 nominations to the Grand-Chambre). Some of the latter rose to be *doyens* or *sous-doyens*. Among those who remained councillors were most of those who were the first of their families to enter *parlement*.

For 67 individuals (36 percent) the post of councillor was a stepping-stone to other offices such as *maître des requêtes* and to commissions to act as *intendants* of *généralités*, secretary of state, or member of the Conseil d'Etat.

Most of these came from families that had long belonged to the *noblesse de robe*. Only two individuals who represented the first generation of their family to serve in *parlement* became *conseillers d'Etat ordinaires* after serving as *présidents* of their chamber: these were Henri II de Fourcy and Gabriel Bizet. Of those from old families, 16 became *présidents à mortier* and 6 of them remained in this position. Three became *premiers présidents* of provincial *parlements:* René Le Fevre de La Faluère in Rennes in 1687, Nicolas Camus de Pontcarré in 1703, and Pierre de Brillac in Rennes in 1703. Other councillors who belonged to old families became *présidents* in the Chambre des Comptes of Paris (Hugues Bertaut, Claude Lambert de Thorigny in 1685, François Brunet in 1691, Gui Robert in 1701), *procureur général* in the Chambre des Comptes (Charles Bouvard de Fourqueux, 1701), or *président* of the Chambre des Comptes of Dijon (Antoine Portail).

Of the 19 who became *maîtres des requêtes*, 10 remained in the post. Three others became *conseillers d'Etat ordinaires*. Four became *intendants* before moving on to become *conseillers d'Etat* or to occupy other high posts. One such was Jérôme Bignon, who was *maître des requêtes* in 1689, *intendant* in Rouen in 1692, *intendant* at Amiens in 1694, *conseiller d'Etat* in 1698, and *prévôt des marchands* of Paris in 1706. Another was Jean Armand de La Briffe, who served as *maître des requêtes* (1676), *intendant* of Burgundy (1683), *président* of the Grand Conseil, *intendant* of Rouen (1686), and *procureur général* in *parlement* (1689). At this point there is no need to trace the careers of the *contrôleurs généraux des Finances* such as Michel, Chamillard, or Claude Le Pelletier, nor of the minister and secretary of state for foreign affairs Charles Colbert de Croissy.

All told, then, 64 percent of the councillors in *parlement* remained in their positions throughout their careers, whereas more than a third continued their rise to higher posts. Of the latter group, nearly 17 percent rose within *parlement* itself to become *présidents* of a chamber or *président à mortier* or *premier président*. Slightly more than 13 percent became *présidents* of other sovereign courts, *procureurs généraux*, *maîtres des requêtes*, *intendants* of provinces, or *conseillers d'Etat*, and four obtained ministerial posts in the royal government.

The nobles in *parlement* thus rendered services to the state, whether they remained in the courts or followed their careers into other departments of government. This nobility continued to be distinct from the old nobility (even though some members of *parlement*, did, of course, spring from the old nobility) and from the *noblesse d'épée*, which looked upon the *noblesse de robe* as a different and inferior order (even though some men of the gown moved into the nobility of the sword or married their daughters to *nobles d'épée*).

The distinction between the *noblesse de robe* and the *noblesse d'épée*. The distinction between the *noblesse de robe* and the *noblesse d'épée* was reflected in social behavior in several ways. First, when a family belonging to the former moved into the latter, the change was viewed as a social advancement. Second, the *nobles de robe* usually married women from their own station in life. Third, *nobles d'épée* and/or of old families always looked upon the *noblesse de robe* as an inferior order.

These points merit further discussion. In the first place the transition from gown to sword was considered an advancement not only by the families of *robins* but by the whole of society. This jump was made, for example, by the maréchal de Belle-Isle, a descendant of Fouquet, the maréchal d'Estrées, the grandson of Louvois, and the maréchal de Maillebois, Colbert's grand-nephew. Of these, the first two became dukes, the latter a grandee of Spain.

Second, *robins* usually married women of their own station and only rarely women from the *noblesse d'épée* above or from the world of commerce and finance below. Furthermore, they usually married their daughters to men of their own rank. Consider, for example, a sample of members of the Paris *parlement* who held office between 1685 and 1690. Of 196 wives, 7 (3.6 percent) were daughters of men who probably belonged to the *gentilhommerie d'épée;* 2 were daughters of officers in the king's household guard (one captain of the bodyguard and one captain of the French Guards); and 5 were daughters of men who held fiefs *de dignité* (3 marquis, 1 count, 1 baron). Thirty-one (16 percent) of the wives sprang from government circles. Among these were the daughters of the chancellor Louis Boucherat and of the minister and *contrôleur général des Finances* Le Pelletier, 6 daughters of *conseillers d'Etat*, 2 of ambassadors, 8 of *maîtres des requêtes*, 1 of the *intendant* of Poitou, 1 of an *intendant du commerce*, 1 of a *premier commis* in the war department, 3 of *présidents* of the Grand Conseil, 1 of a *grand audiencier* of France, and 1 of the *directeur du commerce* for the East Indies, an alderman and bourgeois of Paris. Sixty (31 percent) of the wives were daughters of men serving in the sovereign courts: 28 magistrates in the Paris *parlement*, 7 of magistrates in provincial *parlements*, 20 of magistrates in the Chambre des Comptes of Paris, 2 of the *premier président* of the Chambre des Comptes of Rouen, 3 of councillors on the Cour des Aides of Paris. Only 2 of the wives were daughters of officials of the lower courts, 1 of a *lieutenant particulier* of the Châtelet and 1 of a notaire-*greffier en chef* of the Châtelet. Twenty-four (12 percent) of the wives were daughters of financial officials: 8 daughters of royal secretaries, 2 of magistrates (1 *président* of the *élection* of Paris, one *élu* of La Flèche), 14 of miscellaneous accounting officials, treasurers, and collectors (including 2 *trésoriers de l'epargne*, 1 *trésorier des parties casuelles*, 1 *trésorier général du marc d'or*, 1 *trésorier des Guerres*, 2 *trésoriers de l'Extraordinaire des Guerres*, 3 *payeurs des rentes sur l'Hôtel de Ville*, 1 *receveur et trésorier de la bourse des Etats de Languedoc*). Of the wives 19 (9 percent) were daughters of royal household officers (13) and officers of princely households (6), including the households of the dauphin, the duc d'Orléans, and the dukes of Longueville, Guise, and Soissons. Only 5 (2.5 percent) were daughters of financiers, 4 of *fermiers généraux* and 1 of a "partner in state contracts." Only 2 (1 percent) were daughters of merchants, one of a silk merchant, the other of a draper.

In the Paris *parlement*, then, the daughters of magistrates rarely married *nobles d'épée*, financiers, or merchants. The large majority married office-holders, most of them members of the sovereign courts or officials close to the king, like their fathers members of the *noblesse de robe*.

A glance at the brothers of these girls gives further confirmation of the social status of the *noblesse de robe*. Of 51 councillors whose date of birth is known, 18 were younger brothers. The 33 others were elder brothers, but of their 61 known younger brothers, 19 were also councillors in *parlement*. Of 245 brothers of councillors in *parlement*, 62 were in the clergy, 54 served in the army, 121 (49 percent) were men of the gown, 2 were merely "seigneurs de" something or other, and 6 held various posts, including 1 *fermier général*, 3 *contrôleurs des guerres*, and 1 *contrôleur des gardes*. Among those who went into ecclesiastical orders (27 regulars, 35 seculars), none belonged to the lower ranks of the clergy. We find 8 bishops, 1 vicar general of the prince-cardinals of Furstenberg and Rohan, 2 *aumôniers du roi* including François Lechassier, *docteur* of the Sorbonne and superior of the seminary of Saint-Sulpice in 1704, 13 commendatory abbots, and 14 priors. We also find soldiers of virtually every rank.

Of 325 sisters of councillors in *parlement*, around 60 percent were married and 31 percent were nuns. Of 183 marriages, 10 were contracted with men of high nobility or high-ranking army officers (5.5 percent). Marie de Lamoignon married Victor, comte de Broglie; Louise-Françoise Le Bouthillier married Philippe de Clerambault, comte de Paulluau and maréchal de France. Other marriages involved 4 *maréchaux de camp*, 1 captain in the "grey musketeers," 1 captain of the French Guards, and 1 colonel of dragoons. Sixteen sisters of magistrates found husbands among the court nobility (9 percent). Marie-Renée de Longueil married Maximilien de Bellefourière, *grand veneur* of France and lieutenant of the hunt at Fontainebleau. Suzanne de Beringhen married the duc de la Force, peer of France. Marie-Thérèse Rouille married the duc de Richelieu. And Marie Le Bouthillier contracted a second marriage with César-Auguste de Choiseul in order to obtain the *tabouret*.

Thirty-two sisters of councillors did, however, marry *robins* with government positions (17.5 percent). Henriette Le Bouthillier married Henri-Louis de Loménie, comte de Brienne and secretary of state for foreign affairs. There were also 4 marriages to members of the Conseil d'Etat, 3 to ambassadors, 1 to an *intendant des Finances*, 16 to *maîtres des requêtes*, and 3 to members of the Grand Conseil. An even larger number, 70, married magistrates in the sovereign courts (38.5 percent). Among the bridegrooms we find 6 *premiers présidents* of the *parlements* of Paris, Rennes (2), Dijon, Metz, and Grenoble; 4 *procureurs généraux* from Paris, Rouen, Rennes, and Metz; 37 councillors of the Paris *parlement;* 8 magistrates from the Chambres des Comptes, including 1 *premier président* in Nantes and 1 in Dijon, 5 *maîtres des comptes*, and 1 *correcteur* but no *auditeur;* 6 magistrates in the Cour des Aides, 1 of them *premier président* at Rouen, along with 3 *prési-

dents and 2 councillors from Paris; and 1 *président* of the Cour des Monnaies. Only 10 of the bridegrooms worked in the lower courts, both regular and special (5.5 percent): there was 1 councillor in the Châtelet of Paris, 2 *lieutenants généraux de bailliage*, 1 *trésorier de France*, 1 *grand maître des Eaux et Forêts* from Normandy, and so on. Around 24 percent married other officeholders. None of the husbands was involved in commerce.

Thus nearly 65 percent of the sisters of councillors married *nobles de robe* with posts in government, the sovereign courts, and the lower courts. Only 13.5 percent married into the high nobility of the army and court, and some of these women married more than once.

This same description holds good for the Paris *parlement* throughout the eighteenth century.

All signs point to the fact that magistrates in the Paris *parlement* belonged to a *noblesse de robe* that was ranked below the high nobility comprising *gentilshommes* and *nobles d'épée*.

The same was true of the other *parlements*. In the Bordeaux *parlement* between 1774 and 1790 marriages took place for the most part within the narrow circle of families associated with *parlement*. Fifteen magistrates had from one to three sons-in-law serving *parlement*. Fifty-seven had brothers-in-law in *parlement*. Other magistrates married in gown circles outside *parlement* or among *notables*, mostly nobles: *jurats, maréchaux de camp, marquis*. Around 20 percent took wives from the families of royal secretaries or merchants, but most who did so were themselves new to *parlement*. Once a family had had members in *parlement* for some time, it stopped marrying the daughters of merchants. Magistrates in Bordeaux did not marry into the great families with property in the jurisdiction of their *parlement* such as the Richelieu's, the d'Aiguillons, the Lesparres, the Duras, or the La Tour du Pins, who belonged to the Versailles circle.

The situation was the same in the *parlement* of Besançon. Of 366 marriages, 71.86 percent were contracted with families belonging to the world of the judiciary; 48.9 percent were with families associated with the sovereign courts. Eight of these marriages were with families associated with sovereign courts in another province; 22.95 percent were with families associated with the lower courts, with the daughters of *lieutenants généraux, lieutenants particuliers*, or *avocats*, but these were marriages arranged before the husband entered *parlement*. About fifty marriages were arranged with the daughters of *gentilshommes* or bourgeois "living like nobles." Only ten or so marriages involved the daughters of bankers or financial officials, and these concerned the few families that mingled members of the sovereign courts, financial officials, and merchants.

The foregoing examples are probably sufficient to make the point. In all the *parlements* and *conseils superieurs* magistrates tended to marry mainly within the *noblesse de robe*.

The high *noblesse d'épée* mingled with the *noblesse de robe* in *salons* and, in the case of a few very old *robin* families, at court, but displayed its contempt whenever the gown claimed to stand on a footing of equality with the sword. The king encouraged competition, however, between the attributes of service rendered to the state and antiquity of the noble line. The regulation of 1759–60 concerning court honors granted the right to ride in His Majesty's carriages, first, to nobles who could trace their nobility back to 1400 and, second, to descendants of high crown officers, knights of the royal orders, ambassadors, ministers, and secretaries of state, some of whom sprang from the same social group as the magistrates in *parlement*. Despite the king, however, in the eyes of *gentilshommes d'épée* of immemorial nobility, the magistrates of the *parlements* and, more generally, *robins* of any sort were a mere "bourgeoisie."

When Monsieur de Turenne learned that the Conseil d'En-Haut in 1661 was to consist of Fouquet, de Lionne, and Le Tellier, he asked "if it was really possible that the leading role in the government was to be given to three *bourgeois*."[13] When the Paris *parlement* claimed priority over the regent in Louis XIII's votive procession, the duc de Saint-Simon declared the claim to be particularly outrageous in that *parlement* "belonged merely to the Third Estate."[14] In the mid-eighteenth century the senior marquis de Mirabeau wrote that "in a state constituted as France is, the Nobility must pride itself on being haughty, brave, and poor, and the Magistracy on being grave, just, austere, and frugal."[15] For him nobles and magistrates were two different species, whatever their judicial status. We find this opposition between the *noble d'épée* and the *noble de robe* at all levels of society and in all parts of the country. In Besançon, for example, two brothers married, one the daughter of an *avocat*, the other the daughter of a noble who had held various military posts. In rejecting the social advances of the former, her sister-in-law said that "she was a petty *bourgeoise* and nothing but the wife of an *avocat* . . . [and] that it was not appropriate for her to hold a walking stick in the presence [of her sister-in-law], that such a bearing was appropriate only for the wives of dukes-and-peers and of colonels . . . [and] that it was as appropriate for her to hold a walking stick as for a sow to spin wool."[16] At Beauvais, the marquis de Saint-Rémy wrote to the *lieutenant général* of Beauvais that "when people like us say something, it is believed." The knight du Metz d'Hécourt said that "it is quite extraordinary for a judge to take such a disagreeable position . . . against people of quality for whom you should naturally have more consideration."[17] Everywhere there was constant social conflict between the sword and the gown.[18]

The gown hierarchy. The *noblesse de robe* was itself deeply divided owing to its hierarchical organization, though it did on occasion unite in common opposition to the king. Within its ranks were a few persons of very ancient nobility, who looked down on the rest. One family that could trace its nobility back prior to the fifteenth century, indeed to 1223, with no known ennoblement was the d'Argouges family, which enjoyed court honors and which was represented in the royal armies, the episcopate, and the Order of Malta. They were related by marriage to families of the high *noblesse d'épée* such as the Harcourts and Rochefoucaulds and to old *robins* families such as the Barrins, the La Galisonnières, the Mesgrignys, and the Testu de Balincourts. In the eighteenth century they won the right to ride in the king's carriages. Families of such rank accounted for only about 7 percent of the magistrates of the Paris *parlement*, but their peers accounted for only about 5 percent of the kingdom's nobility.

There were many degrees in the value judgments members of *parlement* made of one another and in the behavior they adopted toward their colleagues. The older nobles in the company sometimes showed a great deal of contempt for their more recently ennobled colleagues. The *premier président* was always chosen from a family that enjoyed "birth, vast property, and credit at court." In the Paris *parlement*, de Mesmes, who was appointed in 1712, represented the seventh degree of nobility in his family. The appointment of Portail as *premier président* in 1724 caused a kind of scandal, because he was merely the grandson of a person ennobled by virtue of his office. As Barbier wrote, "Monsieur Portail does not have before him a birth in keeping with the rank of *premier président*." In 1753, J.-B. Bochart de Saron, a member of a family that had enjoyed noble status since 1466, and Claude-Louis Aubert de Tourny, who was *avocat général* in the Grand Conseil and the son of a well-known *intendant* but reputed to be the grandson of Colbert's *valet de chambre*, were candidates for the post of *avocat général* in the Paris *parlement*. Everyone agreed that the nobility of the latter was insufficient and he was rejected. Jacques II Frecot de Lanty was rejected in 1751 for the post of *président aux enquêtes*, because his father had been a banker ennobled by the purchase of a royal secretaryship. In 1751 the *premier président* Mathieu-François Molé, comte de Champlatreux, looked down on his fellow councillors on account of his high birth. More than a quarter of the councillors of *parlement* were kept at arm's length by their colleagues because of their low birth.

Sources of income and range of wealth. There was great disparity in wealth and income among the members of the courts. Their salaries and *épices* were quite insufficient to maintain their rank and to live in a manner appropriate to a magistrate, so that it was necessary to combine several sources of income including a fair proportion derived from landholdings. In every court there were relatively "poor" magistrates. In the estimation of contemporaries, the "poverty" line in the Paris *parlement* in the eighteenth century was 8,000 livres of rent. Thus the *doyen*, Pierre de Paris, who had only 6,000 livres of rent, fell below it. Some set the poverty line even higher. According to a *commissaire* by the name of Dubuisson, the *premier président* Portail "died poor; they say that his widow will have barely 25,000 livres of rent." The *président* René-Charles de Maupeou was not a wealthy man, according to Barbier: "They say he has only 40,000 livres of rent."[19]

Let us once again look at our sample of magistrates serving in the Paris *parlement* between 1685 and 1690. They lived on income from land, *rentes*, shares in farms, and loans to various individuals. For the most part their wealth seems to have been in land, even though most of them owned a *hôtel* and several smaller houses in Paris. One hundred thirty-four councillors owned 260 *seigneuries*, mostly in Beauce and Brie, regions that produced large amounts of wheat. Fifty-one of them owned one *seigneurie*, 48 of them owned two, 22 owned three, 9 owned four, and 4 owned as many as five. The value of these *seigneuries* varied widely, from 10,000 livres for one in Gastines, which belonged to Antoine-René Le Bigot, to 500,000 livres for one in Villeneuve-le-Roi, which was owned by Louis II Le Pelletier. These must have brought in 500 and 25,000 livres per year respectively.

If magistrates were eager to own *seigneuries*, possession of which conferred social rank, they were even more eager to own *fiefs de dignité*. François Le Coq, seigneur de Corbeville, paid 67,000 livres for a marquisate attached to his land at Goupillères. Other titles were bought for various sums by Charles-Leonard Aubry for his land at Castelnau-en-Berry, by Arnauld de La Briffe in 1692 for his land and *seigneurie* at Ferrières, by Henri II de Bullion for Coucy in 1681, and by Louis-Alexandre Croiset for Estiau in 1702. In the same way Thomas Dreux became marquis de Brezé in 1685 and Pierre Doublet de Crouy became marquis de Baudeville in 1704.

As for baronies, François Briçonnet, *seigneur* de Millemont, Rozay, and Garancière, had his land at Autheuil made a barony in 1677, and the same was done at various times by François Fiot at Montpont and François de La Forêt d'Armaillé at Craon.

Jérôme-Joseph Goujon was baron of Chalreranges, comte d'Autray, and marquis de Thuisy.

On the whole this situation did not change between 1715 and 1789. Within *parlement* there was a group of millionaires with fortunes in excess of a million livres and annual *rentes* in excess of 50,000 livres. The *président* Henault had 3 million and the *président* Bernard de Rieux, who married a daughter of Samuel Bernard, around 7 million. The *président* Molé was said to enjoy *rentes* of between 300,000 and 400,000 livres.

Below this level came a second group of magistrates with fortunes in excess of 500,000 livres and annual incomes in excess of 25,000. This group included the *présidents* Charles Amelot and Jean-Baptiste Lambert de Thorigny and dozens of ordinary magistrates.

A third group was composed of men with fortunes ranging from 150,000 to 400,000 livres yielding from 8,000 to 15,000 livres of *rente*. These were commonplace. According to Barbier, one magistrate by the name of Laverdy who was included in this category was reduced in 1763 to living "as a bourgeois." Others in this group were Séguier and Omer-Louis-François Joly de Fleury.

Below this level came the "poor."

The same hierarchy of fortunes existed in all the courts, scaled down according to the grandeur of the institution. In the *parlement* of Bordeaux between 1774 and 1790 only a minority of magistrates had annual incomes of less than 4,000 livres, while the majority of citizens fell below this level, to judge by the 1755 assessment of the *vingtième* on the officers of *parlement*, the "patriotic contribution" of 1789 (of one-fourth of the annual income), and the compulsory graduated loan of the Year II (1795). Nine-tenths of the magistrates had annual incomes between 4,000 and 20,000 livres, putting them in a category to which only 10 percent of the citizens of Bordeaux belonged. The *premier président* Saige had an annual income of 40,000 livres, J.-B.-M. de Verthamon, 36,000. They were not the wealthiest men in this commercial city, however. Eight citizens of Bordeaux earned between 40,000 and 80,000 livres annually.

The social status of a magistrate was generally based on the ownership of land, which represented the bulk of his fortune and his largest source of income. Like their Parisian counterparts, magistrates in Bordeaux were on the lookout for *fiefs de dignité* and *seigneuries*. Among them there were, under Louis XVI, 5 marquis, 4 counts, 4 viscounts, 1 *captal*, and 28 barons. As *seigneurs* they enjoyed social prestige, claimed every last livre that was due them, and in some cases made handsome incomes from their seigneurial rights. The rights attached to the marquisate of Dunes near Valence-d'Agen, which was owned by the councillor Démons de Saint-Pauly, were estimated in 1783 to be worth 6,000 livres per year.

For the most part, however, the *seigneuries* owned by magistrates were devoted to the production of first-quality wine for the wine trade. Most of these were spread out along the left bank of the Garonne from Lesparre to Langon. Owners of these estates did not increase their size but did rationalize their operations. They rearranged their boundaries and enclosed plots, and trade in land was quite lively. Magistrates produced Médocs, Graves, and Sauternes for export to England, Flanders, and Holland. We know a good deal about the activities of *président* Montesquieu, for example. Seventy-five percent of the magistrates' rural income came from wine. Members of *parlement* produced 7 percent of the wine exported through the port of Bordeaux. The *président* Pichard owned 169 *journaux* of Château-Lafitte vineyards in 1790. These yielded 700 to 750 bottles per *journal*, and each bottle sold for around 6 livres. Depending on the year, the *président* made between 30,000 and 40,000 livres minus the cost of cultivation. Prices varied widely, however, depending on the vineyard, the year, the weather, the military situation, and changes in taste. Magistrates also made money on crops, pine forests, and sheep, but their income from such activities amounted to only one-seventh of what they made from wine. They invested in newly built houses in town, in plantations in the Antilles, and in the colonial trade. They also made loans to private individuals.

In comparison with these outside sources of income, they made little money from their offices. After deducting the *capitation* and the *dixième*, the salary of the *premier président* was only 1,191 livres. A *président* made 742 livres, a councillor 67, and a "king's man" 590. These salaries amounted to 2 percent of the price of the office. After deductions, *épices* brought in another 1,000 livres, on the average.

Things were the same in the Besançon *parlement*. Magistrates lived not so much on their salaries and *épices* as on pensions, bonuses, royal commission, loans (sometimes at usurious rates of interest), income from skillfully managed rural properties and forges. In the late seventeenth century the salary of a councillor was 400 livres, besides which he earned *épices*, up to a quarter of the total *épices* in a case for a *rapporteur*, and commissions, which amounted to about 2,000 livres in all. But after 1761 he was required to pay the *capitation*, without *doublement*, and the 4 sols per livre, which amounted to 484 livres 16 sols, plus a *vingtième* of 40 livres or 524 livres 16 sols in all, against a salary of only 400 livres. Even the most active magistrates at this point were earning no more than 1,500 livres all told in Besançon, 2,000 in Toulouse, 500 to 3,000 in Rouen, and 1,500 to 2,000 in Dijon. The *premier président*, who paid a *capitation* of 800 livres in 1716, counting his pensions and special bonuses earned 20,000 livres per year, as did the *procureur général*. A provincial governor such as the maréchal de Duras made 54,000 livres. The most active *avocats* earned several thousand livres per year. Professors of law at the university who pleaded cases earned about 3,000 livres in addition to their professorial salaries. *Procureurs* in *parlement* had incomes between 1,500 and 6,000 livres. Notaries' incomes were 800 livres in 1787 and 1,500 livres in 1788, and *huissiers* made between 300 and 400 livres.

There was extreme disparity of wealth in the *parlement* of Besançon in the eighteenth century. Among the few millionaires was the councillor Jean-Jacques Pourcheresse d'Etrabonne, who owed his vast wealth to the fact that he was also a forgemaster. The *procureur général* Doroz owned three estates in Santo Domingo valued at more than 1,000,000 livres as well as other real estate.

We find only *présidents* in the category of those with fortunes estimated at between 400,000 and 1,000,000 livres. Two of these were forgemasters.

Between 160,000 and 400,000 livres we find the bulk of the magistrates in *parlement*, particularly the most senior of them, along with the *lieutenant général* of the *bailliage*, one noble *avocat*, and a number of other nobles.

Thirty-six percent of the magistrates fell into the category of those with fortunes between 60,000 and 160,000 livres, mostly magistrates from families that had not previously been represented in *parlement*, because the longer a family had had members in *parlement*, the wealthier it became. At this level we also find magistrates of the lower courts, one *avocat*, and two *procureurs* from *parlement*.

Most of the lower-court magistrates and some *avocats* fell into the category of 25,000 to 60,000 livres.

Between 10,000 and 25,000 livres we again find some councillors of the *bailliage*, most of the *avocats*, and, for the first time, ministerial officials, notaries, *greffiers*, and *huissiers*.

Between 4,000 and 10,000 livres we find a single *avocat* and a number of *procureurs*, *greffiers*, and *huissiers*.

Below 4,000 livres the only representatives of the judiciary we find are ministerial officials and legal assistants.

The average fortune for the 34 members of *parlement* was 364,491 livres. For the 24 magistrates of lower courts and *avocats* in the sample, the average was 43,215 livres.

The fortunes of most members of *parlement* grew steadily. The fortune of the Pourcheresse family, for example, grew from 16,000 livres to 1,000,000 livres in two generations thanks to the Fraisans forges. Similar growth was recorded by the Pourcy family at Quingey, the Jobelot family at Montureux, and the Mouret family at Châtillon. The *président* Mouret had 80,000 livres when he married in 1698 and 377,000 livres when he died in 1729. His son had 960,000 livres in 1788. It was also common for the father, uncles, and aunts of a man who had taken the gown to leave him their offices, *seigneuries*, and other property, making him the representative of the family and perpetuating its position of service to the state through the courts. Strategic marriages also contributed to the increase of family fortunes. During the eighteenth century the gulf between members of *parlement* and magistrates and *avocats* in the lower courts widened. The *avocats* of Besançon were on a nearly equal footing with members of *parlement* in 1676, but by 1789 they had fallen far behind and were overtaken by the ministerial officials.

The range of wealth in the Toulouse *parlement* on the eve of the Revolution duplicated the range of wealth at Besançon almost exactly.

The unity of the judiciary and its *esprit de corps*. Despite the diversity of rank and wealth that existed in the world of the judiciary, there was nevertheless unity among those associated in one capacity or another with the courts. "The society surrounding *parlement* is not governed by wealth but by background, privilege, and professional tradition."[20] In other words, all who worked in or around the *parlements* were united by an *esprit de corps*. This was the result of a common education. Future members of *parlement* often had preceptors who prepared them for the duties of office they would eventually assume. At the age of twelve or so they were sent to a *collège*, where they mingled, during the second half of the seventeenth century and throughout the eighteenth, with the scions of France's leading families.

One-fourth of the future members of the Paris *parlement* were sent to study at the Collège de Beauvais and at Juilly with the Oratorians. Half studied with the Jesuits at the Collège Louis-le-Grand. As for the Bordeaux *parlement*, some future members, like the Montesquieus, went to Juilly, others to Louis-le-Grand, but most remained in Bordeaux at the Collège de la Madeleine which was run by Jesuits, or went to the municipal *collège* of Guyenne, whose reputation had fallen badly by the end of the eighteenth century. Similarly, future members of the Besançon *parlement* generally attended *collèges* run by the Jesuits. Every city in Franche-Comté had a Jesuit *collège*. After the Jesuits were expelled in 1764, these *collèges* were run by the secular clergy. At Jesuit schools future members of *parlement* wore swords and were taught to respect the idea of nobility and to revere *parlement.* They received a humanistic education, reading and expounding the texts of ancient authors, mainly Latin, writing Latin compositions, engaging in oratorical contests and public debates, and acting in plays. This practical training was capped by classes in philosophy, where logic, ethics, metaphysics, mathematics, cosmography, and a little physics were studied. The Copernican system was being taught at Louis-le-Grand by 1663. When students finished *collège* they might be accepted along with young *nobles d'épée* into a royal academy for the education of young gentlemen, where they learned dancing, fencing, and horsemanship. Many then completed their education with a grand tour that took them around the Continent, to England and Italy, and sometimes as far as the Levant.

Then they began their study of the law. A majority of magistrates in Bordeaux studied law at the University of Bordeaux, but some went to Toulouse or Paris. A majority of magistrates in Besançon studied at the University of Besançon. More important than the education that future magistrates received in law school, though, was the juridical training they obtained from tutors and from lectures in which a renowned *avocat* would speak to a small group of magistrates' sons. Whether licentiates or doctors, future members of *parlement* were required to do a stint as *avocats* and to attend hearings of *parlement* for a period of two years. Thus all magistrates shared a common fund of experience.

All magistrates in the *parlements* attempted to emulate a certain way of life. As they saw it, they acted as models not only for other court officials but for everyone in society below the rank of prince or duke-and-peer. They enjoyed enormous prestige. Whenever *parlement* as a body passed by a military post, the guards were obliged to take arms and the drummers to beat an attack. In 1745, during the War of the Austrian Succession, the sovereign courts of Paris went to visit the king in Péronne. The militia of the town lined their route, beat the drums, and saluted the magistrates with cannon fire from the town square. In important ceremonies councillors from the various *parlements* wore red gowns and the same lined red hats that *présidents à mortier* normally wore in hearings, which aroused the jealousy of the other sovereign courts and of the *avocats*. Magistrates sat on *fleurs de lis*. The *premier président* was permitted to speak to dukes-and-peers with his cap on and to *présidents à mortier* with his cap off from 1681 on. Dukes-and-peers were obliged to remove their hats before offering their opinions. When received, dukes-and-peers were required to swear to "conduct themselves as magnanimous peers of France and good officers of the sovereign courts." The second part of the phrase was eliminated in 1663, but dukes-and-peers were still required to take note of the honor they received in being seated in so august a tribunal.

The magistrates' awareness of their eminent position in government and society gave rise to a common ideology. To begin with, there was the enduring ideal of the magistrate. As defined by d'Aguesseau, the magistrate had a vocation; he was "chosen by God" to be a "priest of justice." His profession was that of a "minister," analogous to that of a priest. He was dedicated to the love of his country, to justice, and to serving the public. He was therefore bound to "observe traditional mores and follow the example of his forebears, to follow in their footsteps with the utmost respect." "Honor" and "dignity" were to be his motives in everything. Magistrates were entrusted with the preservation of the moral legacy of their forefathers, symbolized by libraries, family portraits, heirlooms, and collections. Most of them were religious and even devout. Almost a quarter of the magistrates in Paris were true Jansenists. The majority of the rest voted with them in crucial cases out of confusion between the austere morality of the magistrate and the morals of Jansenism and out of a desire to defend the liberties of the Gallican church and a belief in the superiority of Council over pope. The vast majority of magistrates were convinced that the *parlements* in general and the *parlement* of Paris in particular were the heirs of the ancient general assemblies of the Franks and the courts of *Grands* consulted by the king when they were the king's real Council. They therefore believed that *parlements* ranked above even the Estates General and that the king was bound to seek their counsel in governing.

The life-style of magistrates. Inspired by this ideal, magistrates in all the *parlements* tried to live up to a common style of life. During the last quarter of the seventeenth century, magistrates in the Paris *parlement*, particularly those belonging to old families, were part of the city's highest society. Their lavishly decorated *hôtels* were used to show off collections of paintings, china, coins, and books. Many gave frequent and splendid receptions. *Présidents* always dined with guests.

Quite a few of the Paris magistrates owned châteaux in the Ile-de-France, including the Longueils, the Le Pelletier family (at Ménilmontant), and François Le Coq, who owned Les Porcherons. Le Coq spent 30,000 livres to restore three main buildings flanked by five massive towers and 25,000 livres to furnish seventeen rooms. Members of *parlement* gave dinners renowned for their gastronomical delights.

The magistrates supported a large number of merchants and domestic servants. They made loans to Parisian merchants and helped to run factories. They gave generously to the poor, often more than they left in their wills. It was fashionable to aid the poor and help with their education.

Some magistrates, particularly those belonging to old families, took part in the intellectual and artistic movements of the time and made names for themselves. Jean-Jacques de Mesmes became a member of l'Académie française in 1676, Nicolas Potier in 1681, and Jean-Antoine de Mesmes in 1710. Chrétien-François de Lamoignon refused membership in l'Académie française but became an honorary member of the Académie royale des Inscriptions et Médailles because he was a numismatist.

Broadly speaking, this description of the life-style of magistrates holds good up to 1789.

The situation in the other *parlements* was similar. In Bordeaux the *premier président* had eight aides and a number of secretaries. Other magistrates had an average of three aides and a number of other assistants. Magistrates dominated the academy that was founded in 1712. They were represented in the administration of the museum, in a society of amateurs founded in 1783 to promote free public instruction in the arts and sciences, and in the Philanthropical Society founded in 1786. Magistrates belonged to the Masonic lodges, mostly the Lodge of France, which was the most aristocratic. But 23 belonged to the Lodge of the Grand-Orient and 4 to the Harmony Lodge, of which 16 *avocats* were also members. The Freemasons staged a feast in honor of exiled members of *parlement* who returned in 1775.

In Besançon a member of *parlement* lived in an apartment with six or seven rooms, besides which there were stables, coachhouses, and a woodshed. It became increasingly common to devote particular rooms to certain uses: we find antechambers, salons, dining rooms, kitchens. Magistrates in the lower courts and *avocats* made do with three or four rooms and a kitchen. *Procureurs* had two or three rooms plus a kitchen, and *huissiers*, one or two rooms and a kitchen. The *procureur*'s serving woman slept in the kitchen and his clerk in the study.

The *intendant* of the province was served by 25 domestics and the governor by 23, while the *premier président* of the *parlement* had 12. The *présidents à mortier* employed an average of 2 serving women, 2 domestics, and a coachman. Councillors on the average employed 2 serving women and 2 lackeys. Magistrates in the lower courts and *avocats* employed an average of 1 or 2 serving women and sometimes a lackey. Ministerial officials and legal assistants had perhaps one serving woman, sometimes none at all.

Everybody owned a country house as a source of both prestige and supplies. In the case of a magistrate this was likely to be a fief or *seigneurie* with a château and seigneurial residence, almost always in the vineyard region. In the late eighteenth century the *présidents à mortier* set the tone of Besançon's high society with their enormous town houses, gracious country châteaux, splendid carriages, and large domestic staffs. The gulf between them and ordinary councillors in *parlement* began to widen. At mid-century the annual expenses of a *président* amounted to 25,000 livres, while those of a councillor amounted to only 7,000 livres. A *président* spent twenty times as much as a notary and a councillor spent eight times as much. Lavishness of style was thus apportioned to the professional hierarchy.

Magistrates in *parlement* were the most important people in the city where they spent their income. They had a monopoly of the places on municipal courts. They supported the charitable institutions, dominated the university, and were members of church councils. Their sons and brothers were parish curates and inmates of the monasteries. *Robins* took part in the foundation and administration of hospitals and in organizing the "general alms."

They were moving forces in the intellectual life of the city. As conscientious scholars, they took an interest in history and law. They kept abreast of developments in literature and philosophy and joined philosophical and literary societies. They were prominent in café life, in the salons, in the Académie des Sciences, Belles-Lettres, et Arts of Besançon, founded in 1752, and in the Masonic lodges, particularly in the last third of the eighteenth century. They were clients of artists and gave balls, feasts, concerts, and theatrical productions.[21]

The *esprit de corps* within the *parlements* eventually grew into a vertical bond uniting all levels of the judiciary. Magistrates took up cudgels in behalf not only of their *huissiers* but also of their *avocats* and *procureurs* against the royal government and administration and the *noblesse d'épée*. Conversely, in the battles among the *parlements* and the provincial *intendants* and the Paris bureaucracy, the *parlements* were supported by their *avocats*, *procureurs*, and the entire *basoche* to the point of strikes and rioting in the streets. This solidarity did not break down until the last quarter of the eighteenth century.

The crisis in the courts: the decline in the price of offices. Nevertheless, these august tribunals, composed of the Fathers of the Country, experienced, as did most of the lesser courts, a crisis revealed by the falling price of offices. Up to the time of Louis XIV's personal government, the price of office was on the rise. In 1665 the king sought to limit this rise by setting a maximum price for each office, because it was thought that offices were becoming so expensive that *gentilshommes* could no longer afford them. The maximum price for an office of councillor in the Paris *parlement*, for example, was set at 90,000 livres. Actually, such offices continued for some time to change hands between private individuals at prices around 100,000 livres. After 1715, however, prices headed sharply downward: 50,000–60,000 livres between 1728 and 1741 and 35,000–40,000 livres between 1741 and 1752. An edict of 1757 set the maximum at 50,000 livres and did nothing to halt the decline.

In Bordeaux the office of *président à mortier* sold for between 114,000 and 135,000 livres during the seventeenth century. By 1730 the price had fallen to 72,000 livres and continued to fall slowly thereafter. An office of councillor in *parlement* sold for about 25,000 livres in 1700, 38,000 in 1730, and 25,000 in 1790. By way of comparison, it should be noted that an office of royal secretary in the chancellery of the Bordeaux *parlement* sold for around 14,000 livres in 1700, 42,000 in 1730, and 116,000 in 1790, no doubt because this office carried with it hereditary nobility and allowed its holder to take a share in the *affaires extraordinaires* of the kingdom. An office of councillor in the Cour des Aides sold for 19,000 in 1700, 22,000 in 1730, and 29,500 in 1790; in nominal terms the price therefore rose, but in real terms it fell. In the same three years, an office of *trésorier de France* sold for 34,000, 45,000, and 35,000 respectively.

At Besançon, an office of councillor in *parlement* from the group of offices created in 1693 was sold by the king for 15,000 livres. While the councillor's salary was modest, his privileges were considerable. From 1720 to 1760 these offices changed hands at prices between 25,000 and 30,000 livres. The peak seems to have come in 1744, when the office sold for 40,000 livres. After 1760 the price fell to 28,000–30,000 livres. An office of *président à mortier* that sold for 36,000 when created in 1692 brought 62,000–65,000 livres between 1711 and 1765 and subsequently rose as high as 80,000, probably because these offices were scarcer than councillors' offices and brought greater consideration. By way of comparison, an office of royal secretary in the chancellery of *parlement* that sold for 33,000 before 1748 rose to 61,000 in 1772 and 72,000 in 1781. An office of councillor in the *bailliage* and *présidial* fell from nearly 6,000 livres in 1726 to less than 2,000 in 1789. By contrast, ministerial offices rose. An office of *procureur* in *parlement* went up from 8,000 livres in 1726 to 18,000–28,000 livres after 1715. An office of *huissier* in the *bailliage* rose from less than 2,000 livres in 1726 to more than 4,000 after 1780. The price trend bore no relation to the professional and social status of the post.

In the *parlement* of Brittany the councillor Peschart sold his office to his grandson in 1645 at the special price of 60,000 livres, five times what he had paid for it in 1598. After negotiating with *parlement*, Louis XIV issued an edict in November 1666, registered on 22 December, which set the maximum price of councillors' offices in Rennes at almost the same level as in Paris. An office of *président à mortier*, however, was pegged at 350,000 livres in Paris but at only 150,000 in Rennes. An office of *avocat general* was 150,000 livres in Paris and 90,000 in Rennes. The edict of October 1689 revoked the maximum and put an end to the exile of the Vannes *parlement*. Prices were already on the decline, however, and never reached the maximum, even though the amount of principal tied up in the office increased after 1675 because of the additional investments required to obtain salary increases and to pay off the annual dues. Prices fell off even more sharply when the *parlement* began meeting on an annual basis in 1724. The offices of "non-native" councillors fell the most.

The office of *président à mortier*, which rose to 130,000–174,000 livres in 1651–52, fell to 123,000–160,000 in 1696–99, to 125,000 in 1738, to 90,000 from 1756 to 1775, and to 87,000 in 1787. An office of "native" councillor sold in 1609 for 40,000 livres, in 1630 for 56,000, and in 1649 for 112,000. In 1661 one sold for as much as 183,000 livres, but generally the price was around 145,000 livres. The edict of 1666 set a maximum price of 100,000 livres. Between 1680 and 1689 they sold for 75,000 to 90,000 livres; from 1701 to 1725 they sold for between 65,000 and 88,000. Between 1730 and 1765 the price did not exceed 55,000 livres, and one office sold for 30,000 in 1759. After 1765 the price fell to 30,000–32,000 livres, although in 1786 the post of Kergariou sold for 41,200 livres, a price that was deemed exorbitant.

An office of "nonnative" councillor was worth 25,000 livres in 1603, 70,000 in 1631, and 98,000 in 1663. The edict of 1666 set the maximum at 70,000 livres. After *parlement* began meeting on annual basis, however, the price fell to 29,000 in 1729, to 20,000 in 1747, to 10,000 in 1759, and to 8,740 in 1783, falling even lower after the post remained unfilled for ten years.

Reasons for the decline. In general, then, the price of a magistrate's office fell during the eighteenth century. As always there is more than one reason for this decline. The salary of a magistrate was low and was eaten up by taxes. In the mid-eighteenth century, a councillor in the Paris *parlement* earned a salary of 416 livres. Of this he had to pay 360 livres for the *capitation* and 41 livres for the *dixième*. This left him 15 livres. Of course this salary was supplemented by a share of the *épices*, half of which went to the *rapporteur* in a trial, while the other half was shared among the rest of the judges. Accordingly, between 1759 and 1766, a post that cost around 50,000 livres might bring in an average of 1,200 livres to a relatively inactive councillor, a return of 2.37 percent on his investment. A councillor who served often as *rapporteur* might earn as much as 2,400–3,000 livres, or a 5 percent return on his investment. The income itself was still low and attracted few people to office. In the *parlement* of Rennes a nonnative councillor might earn a total of 1,000 livres, while a native councillor could make 750. From 1724 on, these amounts increased to 1,200 and 900 livres, respectively. *Présidents à mortier* could make as much as 3,000 livres, counting salary, *épices*, and living allowances. *Présidents* in the Chambre des Enquêtes made a little less before 1724 and 2582 livres per year thereafter. *Présidents* in the Chambres des Requêtes made 1,200 livres until 1724 and 1,700 livres thereafter. The average *procureur général* made more than 5,000 livres. *Avocats généraux* earned 2,600 livres on the average prior to 1724. These incomes were all fairly low, considering the expenditures that magistrates were obliged to make on account of their prestigious position in society.

Allowances must be made for the privileges that went with office. Magistrates were exempted from the *ban* and the *arrière-ban;* from billeting soldiers and members of the royal entourage in their homes or on their lands; from all imposts, subsidies, *tailles* and *gabelles*, duties on salt, and city gate fees; but not from the *capitation, dixième,* and *vingtième*. They were granted dispensation from *tutelle* and *curatelle,* watch and guard duty, etc. They were exempt from *droits seigneuriaux* in both selling and buying and from rendering personal homage on fiefs they held. They enjoyed the indult granted by the popes to all the *parlements* of the realm. They could be judged only by *parlement* as a body. They were exempt from personal arraignment before any judge for the purposes of deposition, interrogation, or pleading, unless permission was expressly granted by a general assembly of their company. They had the right of *committimus* to the *requêtes du Palais.* Anything they claimed to have seen in the course of their official duties carried supreme authority and brooked no challenge, for their words *faciunt per se probationem probatam*. In certain districts their homes were free zones of asylum.

Probably the most important reason for the decline of office prices was the fact that most offices were kept within a small circle of families, which passed them on from one family member to another. From father to son, from father-in-law to son-in-law, from uncle to nephew, and even from cousin to cousin and friend to friend, posts changed hands. In order to become a *président à mortier* it was usually necessary to belong to a dynasty of *présidents à mortier*. Frequently this was true even for a plain councillor's post. The number of buyers was therefore limited, preferential prices were offered to certain purchasers, and prices tended to fall. The decline in the price of office did not make *parlement* any more accessible than it had been, however. By the end of the eighteenth century, for example, *avocats* could no longer hope to become magistrates. There were too many *avocats*, and many of them were needy. On the eve of the Revolution they broke with the *parlements* over the question of doubling the size of the third estate and voting by head.

The low incomes of magistrates were also due in part to the large number of cases removed from the jurisdiction of the courts and transferred to the king's Council, many of these having to do with the activities of the provincial *intendants*, and to the many disputes that were settled by executive order from the ministerial bureaus. This transfer of power away from the *parlements* diminished their prestige and influence and may have tended to discourage people from seeking offices, thereby causing prices to fall.

For this reason the *parlements* felt bound to regain their lost prestige and influence by mounting a political opposition. As Cardinal de Bernis put it,

> a meritorious councillor in *parlement* who is aware of his merit cannot expect anything from fortune: his fate is forever determined . . . His post subjects him to a hard, laborious, and withdrawn existence . . . His work brings him no distinction. He must therefore seek to make up by reputation for what he cannot expect from fortune. And his reputation is never brighter than when he persuades his Company to stand up to the Court at times when either the cause of religion or the well-being of the people is threatened. Every wise magistrate should therefore belong to the party of opposition.[22]

Because of their political opposition, however, the *parlements* were constantly threatened with exile or the elimination of posts. Hence, over time, *parlements* came to be shrouded in insecurity, and this no doubt helped to discourage prospective buyers and lower the price of offices.

The Special Courts: The Chambres des Comptes, Cours des Aides, *and* Cours des Monnaies. The other sovereign and superior courts were similar to the *parlements*, though in some measure inferior to them. As with *parlement*, holding office on one of these courts was consistent with nobility and conferred a "gradual nobility" (except for the Cour des Monnaies of Paris, which conferred gradual nobility only after 1719). In 1644 and 1645 the Parisian courts acquired the right of hereditary nobility, but in 1669 they were returned to the system of gradual nobility. Later on they again obtained hereditary nobility, in 1691 for the Cour des Aides and in 1704 for the Chambre des Comptes.

Taking into account the points that mattered to contemporaries, we find that the ranking of the courts according to prestige remained virtually unchanged between 1690 and 1791. In Paris, *parlement* ranked first, followed by the Chambre des Comptes, the Cour des Aides, the Grand Conseil, and the Cour des Monnaies. The younger the entry age (i.e., the more entry was determined by family seniority rather than by career achievement), the more prestigious the court. The average entry age in *parlement* was 22 years 7 months; in the Chambre des Comptes, 24; in the Grand Conseil, 27 years; and in the Cour des Monnaies, 36 years 11 months. The larger the number of nobles in the narrow sense (i.e., men who were noble prior to their assumption of office), the higher the prestige. On 1 January 1787, *parlement* was 87 percent noble in this sense; the Chambre des Comptes, 61 percent; the Cour des Aides, 50 percent; the Grand Conseil, 25 percent; and the Cour des Monnaies, 5 percent. The same order obtains if we consider how ancient the nobility of court members was and count the number of dynasties in each court. If, however, we look instead at how easy it was to move from a court into a post in the government or senior administration as a *premier président*, ambassador, *maître des requêtes, conseiller d'Etat, intendant des Finances*, secretary of state, or minister, then the Grand Conseil, the breeding ground of *maîtres des requêtes*, ranks immediately after *parlement*. The Chambre des Comptes, where posts were held by an unchanging roster of families, follows behind the Cour des Aides. If we consider the factors of family seniority, services rendered, posts held, marriages contracted, property and total fortune, proportion of fiefs and *seigneuries*, life-style, and intellectual role, we come back to the original hierarchy: *parlement*, Chambre des Comptes, Cour des Aides, Cour des Monnaies. The prestige enjoyed by members of each of these courts was similar in kind but smaller in degree as we descend the hierarchy. All in all there was a considerable distance between the *premier président* of the Paris *parlement* and a councillor on the Cour des Monnaies, especially if the councillor was a commoner who came to the court at the age of sixty or seventy after having been a *procureur du roi* in a *bailliage* or a *président* in an *élection* or a *grenetier* in a salt warehouse. Socially, the Cour des Monnaies of Paris ranked below the Châtelet and the *bureau des Finances* of Paris. From 1719 on, however, when a magistrate on this court died, his son, usually in his forties, succeeded him and became a noble and councillor in turn. And his grandson was in a position to attend the Collège Louis-le-Grand and be educated as a young *gentilhomme*.

Mutatis mutandis, the position of provincial courts relative to their *parlement* was analogous.

Offices in the special courts offered more opportunity to make money than did offices in *parlement*, and the technical nature of a magistrate's duty in these courts made them appear more substantial, so that the price of offices in the special courts generally did not decline.

In the last quarter of the seventeenth century the prices of the various offices on the whole corresponded to the scale of social values. In Paris an office of *président* on the Grand Conseil changed hands privately for 170,000 livres; an office of *maître des requêtes* went for 118,000; the office of lay councillor in *parlement* sold for 100,000; and a post of councillor on the Grand Conseil went for 70,000. To become a *trésorier de France* in Paris, one had to pay 70,000 livres; a royal secretaryship in the Grande Chancellerie cost 45,000; *auditeur des Comptes* in Paris, 45,000; *lieutenant général* in the *bailliage du Palais*, 15,000. A sworn port overseer in charge of unloading wood paid 14,000 for his post, and a tipstaff at the Châtelet paid 458 livres for his.

The offices of councillor on the Grand Conseil and councillor in *parlement* lost half their nominal value between 1700 and 1750, as did the post of councillor in the *parlements* of Dauphiné and Brittany. The value of the office of *maître des requêtes* dropped less, about 33 percent: "The truth is that these *maîtres des requêtes* earn almost nothing . . . [but] on the other hand, these positions are much sought after by those who want to be at court, approach ministers, have offices, become provincial *intendants*, and be in a position to rise to great heights such as a place as *conseiller d'Etat* or even higher."[23] The price of an office as *auditeur des Comptes* in Paris held its own. The cost of becoming a royal secretary in the Grand Chancellerie increased. The value of an office depended on the opportunity it offered to make money and, even more important, to rise socially.

The Trésoriers de France *and* Généraux des Finances, *and the* Grands Maîtres des Eaux et Forêts

Trésoriers de France. The *trésoriers de France* and *généraux des Finances* were in a position to make more money than members of ordinary courts, but the profits of office were still mediocre. In 1627 *trésoriers généraux de France* were entitled to 3,287 livres in salary and dues. In that year the king sold the office for 76,340 livres. The salary thus represented a return on the investment of 4.4 percent, and to this amount would have been added *épices* on judgments rendered. Thus the over-all return on investment would have been in excess of 5 percent, the normal rate of return on real property. In 1637 the salary and dues were ostensibly increased to 4,074 livres, not counting *épices*. Owing to the demands of war on the king's treasury, however, the salary and dues were subsequently cut on several occasions: by one-quarter in 1640 and 1641; three-eighths from 1642 to 1645; half in 1646; 100 percent of the salary and 75 percent of the dues in 1647; and 100 percent of both salary and dues in 1648. What is more, every time the treasurer's salary was increased, he was obliged to make a loan to the king, that is, to increase the principal of his investment, on which the salary increase was supposed to be interest (but was not paid). In addition, the number of offices was increased. Even if the officeholder's jurisdiction was expanded, the expansion never matched the multiplication of officeholders, so that the share of each in the *épices* was reduced. Thus it was hard to sell newly created offices, and the price the king could ask for new offices tended to decline.

Trésoriers généraux de France continued to enjoy a high social status, however, thanks to the prestige they owed to the memory of their grandeur in times past and to the privileges of office. Their post conferred gradual nobility, by custom (but not stature) from January 1552 on and by law from March 1600 until 1705. They obtained the title of *chevalier* and thus a place in the high nobility. From 1705 on they enjoyed hereditary nobility of the first degree. By edict of August 1715 the Paris bureau was restored to the system of gradual nobility, but the edict of September 1720 nullified this clause retroactively, so that hereditary nobility may be taken to have been in effect without interruption since 1705. This nobility conferred on treasurers all the privileges of the sovereign courts.

The *capitation* schedule of 1695 classed the *présidents*, *trésoriers de France*, *avocats* and *procureurs du roi*, and *greffier en chef* of the *bureau des Finances* of Paris in the eighth category along with the *maréchaux de camp* and councillors in the Paris courts. Those from the provinces were classed in the tenth category along with the colonels. The *premier huissier* of the Paris bureau was classed in the fifteenth category.

The average age of those assuming the office of treasurer in Paris was 31. Of the officeholders in the *bureau des Finances* 96 percent remained permanently in their posts, and the average tenure was 26 years 4 months. In 1791, of 19 *trésoriers de France* "on duty," 3 were in their forties, 8 were in their fifties, 4 in their sixties, and 4 in their seventies. The holders of these offices usually did not rise to higher positions but grew old in their posts, which they held for the rank. Promotion was possible, however: some *trésoriers de France* bought offices as *maîtres des comptes*, and a few born commoners even became magistrates in the Chambre des Comptes either after twenty years' service, which entitled them to nobility, or before that much time had elapsed.

Of 164 magistrates in the eighteenth century, 46 were noble when they took office, i.e., about 28 percent. Most of these had been ennobled by office, and some were the sons and successors of men ennobled by office.

In Normandy during the first half of the seventeenth century, the *trésoriers de France* either intermarried or married into families associated with the Chambre des Comptes or the Cour des Aides and occasionally into families associated with *parlement*. Marriages with the daughters of bourgeois "living as nobles" had become rare. Occasionally treasurers married their daughters to a knight, a *seigneur* and patron, or a baron. They apparently stood on a footing of equality with magistrates in the provincial Chambres des Comptes and Cours des Aides.

Treasurers were sometimes as wealthy as magistrates. Richard Grisel, sieur de Franqueville and *trésorier général de France* at Rouen, had in 1612 a fortune valued at 187,929 livres, not counting the value of the land he owned at Franqueville, which is not known. Of this amount, 124,329 livres (66 percent) consisted of *rentes* and farms on taxes; 12,700 livres (6.8 percent) was in houses in the city of Rouen; 5,900 livres (2.3 percent) was in farms; and his office was worth about 45,000 livres (24 percent). His annual income must have been about 17,000 livres, including 11,804 livres (68 percent) in *rentes* and farms on indirect taxes; 404 livres (2.3 percent) for the houses he owned; 366 livres (2 percent) for his land, excluding Franqueville; and of course 4,500 livres (27 percent) for the office (2,500 livres in salary, 500 in bonuses, 225 livres in *droits de bûche*, 156 livres in *droits de présence*, plus a number of other dues and miscellaneous stipends).

Pierre de Pagalde, *trésorier général de France* at Rouen, died in 1617 and left a fortune valued at 80,000 livres: 20,870 livres (24 percent) in *rentes* on the king, at least 6,000 livres (8 percent) in land, and an office valued at 55,000 livres (68 percent). His annual income was 7,640 livres: 1,900 livres in *rentes* (25 percent), 240 livres from his land (3 percent), and 5,500 livres from his office (72 percent).

Trésoriers de France enjoyed a considerable amount of leisure. Hence they sometimes acquired other posts in other jurisdictions and held them concurrently with their treasurerships: among the posts they sought were those of *avocat du roi*, *procureur du roi*, *correcteur* or *auditeur des Comptes*, councillor in *parlement*, *président* or councillor in a *bailliage* or *sénéchaussée*, or an office in the king's household. They sometimes held more than one treasurership in various *bureaux des Finances*. They also accepted royal commissions. The only posts they were forbidden to hold were accounting offices.

Because treasurers had plenty of leisure time, they could indulge in literary or scientific activities. A list of all the illustrious names among the treasurers would be long indeed. We shall confine ourselves to citing a few examples. The scholar Charles du Fresne du Cange (1610–88) was a *trésorier de France* at Amiens. Among the *trésoriers de France* in Paris were Jean-François Regnard, the author of *Le joueur* and *Le légataire universel;* Mignot de Montigny, a member of the Academy of Berlin and the Académie des Sciences de Paris, who collaborated with Cassini on the *Carte de France;* Le Febvre de La Planche et Lorry, an *avocat du roi* and author of the *Traité du domaine*. La Bruyère was a *trésorier de France* at Caen, and Jean Racine held the post at Moulins.

Grands Maîtres. The price of an office of *grand maître des Eaux et Forêts* rose steadily from 1689 to the Revolution. The older posts sold for an average of 122,000 livres under Louis XIV and 350,000 livres in 1785. Of course the price varied widely depending on the profit that could be expected in each department. In 1771 the prices ranged from 230,000 livres for the office of *grand maître* of the Languedoc department to 508,000 for the Ile-de-France department. The reason for this variation in price was that these offices produced a good deal of revenue, in the form of salary, indemnity for heating and secretarial costs, "days" of work owed by monestaries and churches, and royal bonuses. In addition, between 1745 and 1770, there was a special bonus of five deniers per livre, which returned about 8.33 percent on the investment required to obtain it. In 1770 this was converted to a 5 percent *rente*. The *grand maître* had the authority to sell wood and award contracts for the exploitation of forest land, which gave him considerable power and many occasions to turn a profit. In 1760, each *grand maître* in the departments of Alençon, Caen, Paris, and Rouen earned a total of 25,000 livres annually, and in Berry, Languedoc, Metz, and Poitou, each *grand maître* a total of 16,000 livres annually.

Along with profit came prestige. The *grands maîtres* bore the title of *chevalier*. They were known as members of the *corps* of *parlement*. They could take part in debate and vote in the Chambres du Conseil and hearings before sovereign judges. They were seated on the left after the *doyen* of the Chambre. They dressed in black for hearings and wore a sword at their side. When the Chambres des Eaux et Forêts were created in February of 1704, the king granted the *grands maîtres* and the magistrates in these Chambres the right of *committimus* to the *petit sceau*. When the Paris *parlement* was granted the right of *committimus* to the *grand sceau* in 1724, the *grands maîtres* also reaped the benefits.

The post of *grand maître* was therefore much sought after. Between 1689 and 1790 there were 128 *grands maîtres*. A *grand maître* was supposed to be at least twenty-six years of age, but after 1715 the king granted age exemptions to one-quarter of them. Seven assumed office after the age of fifty. The average age upon assuming office was thirty-three. Fourteen of them sprang from twelve Parisian families, while seventy-nine issued from sixty-four provincial families. They came mainly from the provinces of the north of France. But the provincial families in question had spent a generation or two in Paris prior to the birth of the member who became a *grand maître*, so that they too might be viewed as Parisian. Thirty-five were given posts in their native departments.

In a sample of 128 *grands maîtres*, 45 had held no other post previously. Eighty-three held a wide variety of other posts. Twelve had been *avocats*. Most had held offices, either in royal and princely households, as magistrates (16 came from the courts), in the army, as financial accountants (15), or in a chancellery (4). None had been a *maître particulier*, however. No official of any *maîtrise* rose to become a *grand maître*. It was impossible to make a career in the Eaux et Forêts.

Tenure of office ranged from 5 to 28 years, 15 years being the average tenure. A third held office for more than 20 years. They did not hold other offices concurrently. Most went into retirement upon leaving office. It therefore seems that their purpose in seeking the office was to obtain rank and in some cases to come by opportunities for making a profit from speculation.

In general the fathers of *grands maîtres* had the same professional and social status as their sons prior to taking office.

Out of 135 *grands maîtres*, 103 were nobles before taking office. Of these 103, 85 had been ennobled, 8 of them on their own account and the rest through their fathers or grandfathers. Families had been ennobled in 62 cases by holding a royal secretaryship; 7 were descendants of *trésoriers de France*, 5 were descendants of members of *parlement*, and 9 were descendants of municipal officeholders. Social ascendancy thus began mainly with financial offices. Among the progeny, however, we find neither financiers nor financial officeholders. Most of the sons and sons-in-law took the gown in the courts or entered the army. A majority of the *grands maîtres* mingled with Parisian high society. They lived in comfortable *hôtels* and had substantial fortunes.

Although they had to go into debt to purchase their offices, probably because they lacked liquid funds, they were wealthy men. When Pierre Savary died in 1694, he left a fortune of 344,000 livres, including the fiefs of Boutervilliers and La Grimbardière (67,000 livres), *rentes* and bills payable worth 91,000 livres, and his office of *grand maître* at Rouen, valued at 186,000 livres. Alexandre-Claude Le Febvre de La Faluère, *grand maître* of the Ile-de-France from 1703 to 1745, died in 1747, leaving a fortune estimated at 807,000 livres. His office had been sold in 1746 for 440,000 livres. Raffy, *grand maître* of Poitou from 1734 to 1754, sold his post in 1754 for 342,000 livres. When he died in 1760, he left 721,000 livres, 200,000 of which was still due on the price of the office.

Thus *grands maîtres* were not as wealthy as *fermiers généraux* and approximately the equals in wealth of the average member of *parlement*. Their fortunes were roughly comparable to those of the wealthiest *premiers commis* in the ministry of foreign affairs.

The Lower Courts—Ordinary and Special

A Typical Example: The Châtelet of Paris. Among the lower courts, the most prestigious was the Châtelet of Paris, which contemporaries even regarded as being superior in status to one of the sovereign courts, the Cour des Monnaies of Paris. Even though the edict of December 1665 stipulated that a man must be 27 years of age to enter a presidial office, the average age of those taking office in the Châtelet between 1660 and 1700 was, thanks to letters of exemption, only 22 years and 10 months.

The Châtelet offered great opportunities for further advancement. Forty-one percent of the councillors received between 1661 and 1700 held other offices subsequently. They remained in the Châtelet for fewer than ten years. Most moved up to the Paris courts, half to *parlement*. Those who went into the Cour des Monnaies became *présidents*. One became *lieutenant criminel* and another *lieutenant particulier* in the Châtelet. Of those who became councillors in *parlement*, some rose to the Grand-Chambre or became *présidents à mortier*. A few became *maîtres des requêtes* and from there moved on to accept commissions as *intendants* and *conseillers d'Etat*. As Delamare recorded, the Châtelet of Paris was "a veritable seminary for magistrates."[24] Nine out of ten magistrates who left the Châtelet to enter *parlement* were nobles. Half of the councillors who moved from the Châtelet to the sovereign courts had an ancestor who was a member of one of these courts or a *conseiller d'Etat*.

Of the 59 percent who spent their entire careers in the Châtelet, two-thirds held office for more than twenty years, and 15 percent held office for more than forty years. The members of this group were of diverse social origin. Rubbing elbows in the same tribunal and dispensing justice together were knights who were grandsons and great-grandsons of members of *parlement* and the sons of notaries, *procureurs*, *avocats*, and wealthy merchants. Some members of illustrious families spent their entire careers as councillors in the Châtelet.

Châtelet offices did not confer nobility until 1768. The edict of August 1768 laid it down that the office of *lieutenant* would carry nobility with it. Councillors and king's men obtained personal nobility after ten years in office. This nobility became transmissible after forty years in office or in case of death in office after twenty years of service.

Between 1661 and 1700 nobles and men in the process of becoming nobles came to constitute a majority of the councillors in the Châtelet. Of 195 families about which we have information for 1661, 37 percent were noble, 9 percent were represented by councillors in the process of becoming nobles, and 30 percent were commoners. Twenty-four percent were of undetermined status. By 1700, 46 percent were noble, 12 percent were in the process of becoming noble, 40 percent were commoners, and 2 percent were of undetermined status. The noble families were generally of recent nobility. Half the nobles in the Châtelet were sons of ennobled men, and another quarter were grandsons of ennobled men. Of 64 families 30 were ennobled by holding a royal secretaryship, 26 by holding a judicial or financial office, 5 by royal letters, and 3 by holding the post of aldermen.

Most of the councillors in the Châtelet were Parisians. In a sample of 145, 42 (28 percent) had fathers in the high *noblesse de robe*, including magistrates of the sovereign courts, *maîtres des requêtes*, *intendants des provinces*, and *conseillers d'Etat*. Forty had fathers in the chancellery, including 37 royal secretaries (26.5 percent). Fourteen were sons of *trésoriers* or *receveurs de France*. Twelve were sons of magistrates in the Châtelet or one of the other lower courts (8 percent). Sixteen were sons of ministerial officials. Seven were sons of merchants (4.6 percent). Two were sons of a *seigneur* (1.3 percent). The profession of the father cannot be determined in 12 cases (8 percent). The route to the Châtelet was through the legal profession and legal office.

When traced back to the sixteenth century, many of these families are found to have descended from *avocats*, *procureurs*, *greffiers*, notaries, and officials of *élections*, *bailliages*, and *sénéchaussées*. Many also descended from merchants, artisans, and small shopkeepers, but, "on the whole, families paused for a time on an intermediate level in their rise from mercantile activity to the Châtelet."²⁵ A few were descendants of peasants, vine growers, or husbandmen from the vicinity of Paris. Since most of the genealogies date back no farther than to an *avocat* or *procureur*, however, it is possible that many of the families rose from the peasantry.

Councillors in the Châtelet were often younger brothers whose eldest brothers were members of one of the sovereign courts. Then, too, there were many sons waiting to take over their father's office as a *maître des comptes*, *maître des requêtes* or what have you. Many men held a post as councillor in the Châtelet between a chancellery office and an office in one of the sovereign courts. A typical model of family ascension over a period of four generations was as follows. Beginning in the world of commerce, the family would move to occupy a post in finance or an office as notary or *procureur*, then to a chancellery office, frequently that of royal secretary. Then the son of the royal secretary would do a stint as a councillor in the Châtelet before obtaining office in one of the sovereign courts. Some families continued their ascent, moving from the gown to the sword. An eldest son or only child might become a captain in the cavalry or dragoons. One Belin was the father of a captain in the regiment of Vermandois and of a canon of Notre-Dame.

The Châtelet participated as a body in all public ceremonies, in which "it ranked below the superior courts and above all the other companies."

Councillors in the Châtelet had fortunes ranging from 300,000 to 650,000 livres. They gave their daughters dowries ranging from 50,000 to 66,000 livres. Typical of the composition of these fortunes, it seems, was that of René-Joseph de La Vaigne, which in 1693 was 30 percent Parisian real estate, 34 percent *rentes*, and 35 percent the value of the office, an ideal balance. During the last quarter of the seventeenth century, the price of the office varied between 20,000 and 30,000 livres, which was comparable to the price of an office of *lieutenant général* in the provincial *bailliages* and higher than the average price of the office of presidial councillor in the provinces. The salary was 400 livres. The *épices* were limited by the edict of March 1673. In 1702 the office of councillor at the Châtelet belonging to Jean Parent was sold for 30,000 livres. It yielded 1,838 livres per year, a 6 percent return on the investment, no worse than a *rente* or the return on a house.

The councillors of the Châtelet lived in luxurious and opulent residences, decorated with tapestries and embellished with silver service, candlesticks, and the like, clocks, Venetian glass, pier glass on the fireplace, and tables that stood on gilt wooden legs. They employed three or four domestic servants—a chambermaid, a cook, a lackey, and a coachman—compared with eight for a councillor in *parlement*. They owned at least two horses and used carriages, berlins, barouches, and sedan chairs. They lived like councillors in *parlement* of low rank.

Many of them seem to have taken an interest in the humanities, mathematics, and philosophy. Their libraries have not been catalogued but contained 280 volumes on the average; three had fewer than 100 volumes, and three had between 1,000 and 2,000 volumes. The libraries of Claude Hardy and J.-B. Hautin contained 18,000 volumes apiece, making them comparable to the libraries owned by members of the sovereign courts. Among the books were many religious works: Bibles, lives of saints, prayer books, Jansenist works such as *Le catéchisme* of Montpellier and Nicole's *Essais de morale*. There were of course many law books as well: books on French customary law, the customs of Paris and its surrounding area, the new ordinances of Louis XIV, and the usual practical manuals such as Louet's *Les arrêts* and the *Journal du Palais*. There were also many ancient classics, with Greek works generally in Latin translation. There was a good deal of history, including works by Scipio, Dupleix, Mézéray, and Bossuet, as well as an abundance of maps and travel accounts. Furetière's dictionary was common, those of Moreri and Bayle less so. Literary works were limited to memoirs such as those of Sully and Retz and to collections of letters such as that of Guez de Balzac. Works in the exact sciences were rare.

Councillors owned anywhere from five to forty paintings, 72 percent of which were concerned with the "joyous mysteries" of the Rosary: the Virgin, the Child Jesus, the childhood of Christ. The "dolorous mysteries" were represented by numerous ivory Christs. The "glorious mysteries" were for the most part unrepresented. After 1700, the proportion of paintings on religious subjects drops to 26 percent, as religious paintings give way to landscapes, still lifes, and portraits.

Councillors in the Châtelet were obsessed with the idea of acceding to the high magistracy. The Châtelet was the anteroom of the sovereign courts of Paris, a "sovereign court of the second rank."[26]

The Châtelet was affected by the crisis that beset the sovereign and lower courts. The price of offices rose until the beginning of Louis XIV's personal government, then fell right up to the time of the Revolution. Between 1640 and 1660 an office of councillor in the Châtelet sold for 40,000 livres. Between 1666 and 1668 the price rose to between 58,000 and 68,000 livres. By 1670 it had fallen back to 45,000 livres and by 1674 to 30,000. In 1693 the price was 22,000 livres. It rose to 30,000 in 1702 and between 1740 and 1760 fluctuated between 3,000 and 5,000 livres. According to Barbier, who was writing in 1751, one had to wait one's turn to buy one of these offices in 1700, but now, i.e., in 1751, "there is more than one up for grabs. . . . Such is the change that has overtaken offices that yield no income." By contrast, "positions as *fermier général*, which can be bequeathed and promised in advance . . . and offices in the Chambre des Comptes have held up well and even gone up in price."[27]

What had happened was this. The salary of the councillor's post, which had been 500 livres in 1646, had fallen to 300 livres by 1726. As for *épices*, between July 1767 and June 1768 one councillor earned only 82 livres 10 sols 9 deniers. Beyond this, the hope of further professional and social and advancement was not as bright as it had been, because the sovereign courts were becoming more and more difficult to penetrate. Between 1661 and 1700, 45 judges from the Châtelet were accepted as councillors by the Paris *parlement*. Only 10 were so honored between 1715 and 1740, and none thereafter. Of these 55, only 4 did not have an ancestor who was a member of a sovereign court. Between 1715 and 1740 the Grand Conseil took in only 6 councillors from the Châtelet, and 3 of these were accepted prior to 1720. The office of councillor in the Châtelet therefore ceased to be attractive.

This statement obviously does not apply to the various lieutenancies, especially the post of *lieutenant général de police*, which became a veritable ministry under La Reynie, the d'Argensons, Feydeau de Marville, Sartine, and Lenoir. The *lieutenant général* met with the king weekly, either in the presence of his superior, the secretary of state for the royal household, or alone in *tête-à-tête* with the king. The holder of this office was thus in a position to rise to the highest posts in the kingdom. Claude-Henry Feydeau de Marville, *lieutenant général de police* in Paris from 1740 to 1747, was merely a "faithful and energetic executant," but when he resigned he went on to become a *conseiller d'Etat semestre*, *premier président* of the Grand Conseil, *conseiller d'Etat ordinaire* in 1756, and member of the Conseil royal des Finances in 1766—quite a handsome promotion—and ended his career as *doyen* of the Council and *directeur général des Economats*. Others went even further to become secretaries of state and ministers.

The Lower Courts in the Provinces. Excepting the office of *lieutenant général de police*, the Châtelet was typical of the lower courts in general even though it was the premier *juridiction* in the kingdom. For this reason we can allow ourselves to treat the other lower courts more briefly, as they differed from the Châtelet only in degree. We can also treat the regular and special lower courts together, since, in the provinces and particularly in small cities, they were often controlled by the same families. An exception should probably be made for the salt warehouses, which were staffed by persons of slightly lower social status.

The *lieutenants généraux* of the *bailliages* and *sénéchaussées* were generally *fidèles* of the king who were noble before coming to hold office and who stood above other local officeholders. During the seventeenth century, the other *lieutenants*, councillors, and king's men in the *présidiaux*, *bailliages*, *sénéchaussées*, and *élections* were recruited from among their own sons as well as from the sons of *avocats*, *procureurs*, *huissiers*, bourgeois rentiers, and merchants. It was not uncommon for these offices to be held by a family for several generations. But a lower court office could also serve as a stepping-stone to the acquisition of letters of nobility, a post in the sovereign courts, or a career in the army.

These offices conferred a social rank corresponding to their place in the hierarchy. The children of councillors in *bailliages* and *présidiaux* married one another. If there were not enough daughters to go around, magistrates in the *bailliage* would look to the daughters of *élus* and vice versa. Marriages with daughters of wealthy merchants were rare, and the daughters of magistrates were seldom married off to impoverished *gentilshommes*. In 1692, the *lieutenant particulier civil* and *assesseur criminel* of the *bailliage* and *siège présidial* of Beauvais was the son of a rentier, "an officer of the late queen," a post that required him to work only one quarter out of the year and that carried with it honors and privileges. In a region noted for manufacturing and commerce, the uncles of this *lieutenant particulier* were three extremely wealthy merchants. The *lieutenant particulier* married the daughter of a councillor in the *présidial*. The bride's grandfather was also a councillor in the *présidial*. One of her uncles was a councillor in the *présidial*, another a *président* in the *élection*. Of four cousins, one was a councillor in the *élection*, another an *avocat*, another a Sorbonne doctor and chancellor of the cathedral chapter, and yet another a councillor on the Cour des Monnaies of Paris. All were commoners, "bourgeois."

Socially, the lower-court magistrates normally ranked below sovereign-court magistrates, but they could rank above a magistrate who had only recently entered one of the sovereign courts and always ranked above ministerial officials employed by the sovereign courts, except the *greffier en chef* and *premier huissier*. A lower-court magistrate outranked a so-called *honorable homme* of the first half of the seventeenth century, this being a term used to describe merchants and rentiers. Magistrates sometimes referred to themselves as *écuyers* and more commonly as *nobles hommes*. *Ecuyer* became an increasingly common term in the eighteenth century.

Lower-court magistrates lived in plush interiors decorated with Flemish tapestries and oil paintings depicting religious subjects. They were often more cultivated than the merchants, in whose homes it was common to find only a few pious books and some aids to calculation. Of course there were some who owned no more than a few practical manuals of law. But quite a few possessed collections of works on jurisprudence, Latin and Greek classics that seem to have been read for pleasure, and books of theology and the works of the Church Fathers. The presence of the *Augustinus*, not uncommon, would seem to testify against Jansenist tendencies.

The magistrates constitued a reasonably cultivated elite with an austere way of life.

They were looked down upon by the magistrates of the sovereign courts. Perrot de Fercourt, *président* on the Grand Conseil, addressed scathing criticisms to the *lieutenant général* of Beauvais in a note that dispensed with formulas of politeness. Lower-court magistrates were held in even greater contempt by the high provincial *noblesse d'épée* and by ordinary *gentilshommes*.[28]

Lower-court magistrates possessed fortunes that ranked below those of sovereign-court magistrates and royal secretaries. Their wealth varied widely from individual to individual. In 1620, Georges de Foix, a councillor in the *présidial* at Rouen, owned an office worth 9,500 livres and 4,018 livres' worth of land and *rentes* that yielded 236 livres per year in income. His total fortune amounted to 13,518 livres and his income was between 1,100 and 1,200 livres annually. He was one of the poorest magistrates. In 1633, Jean Le Terrier, *écuyer* and sieur de Pierreficques, who was *lieutenant* for the *bailli* of Caux at Montivilliers, possessed a fortune of 159,000 livres: 140,000 livres (88.1 percent) in land; 5,152 livres (3.2 percent) in *rentes*; and an office worth 14,000 livres (8.8 percent). His total income came to 7,449 livres: 5,665 livres from *property* in land (76 percent), 384 livres from *rentes* (5.2 percent), and 1,400 livres from his office (18.8 percent).

For nearly all the lower-court magistrates, land made up half of their wealth. Land was the most dependable form of property, for officeholders were obliged to buy expensive salary increases or bonuses and offices could become too dear to be sold. The renewal of the annual dues, or Paulette, could not be relied upon, and there were constant threats that offices would be eliminated. *Rentes* were more reliable. But it was land that offered the greatest security of all; what is more, land was an even better way of acquiring social status than an office, particularly if the land in question was a *seigneurie* or fief. Land yielded wine, garden vegetables, and domanial or seigneurial dues in kind, including grains, bread, butter, lard, eggs, a Christmas capon, an Easter lamb, firewood, hemp and flax, cloth, and linen. Landowners could lease livestock at half price. The office therefore usually accounted for a limited part of the magistrate's fortune, usually no more than a third. Still, offices were sought after because they enhanced the officeholder's social standing and brought exemptions, together with awareness of which properties were encumbered by debt and which owners were in difficulty and hence might need to borrow money. The magistrate could then advance a loan to the needy landowner, thereby opening the way to future acquisition of the property. Finally, it was possible in practice both to serve as a magistrate and to own a seigneurial office and collect seigneurial receipts.

The families of lower-court magistrates had a near monopoly of seigneurial offices, places as aldermen, and churchwardenships.

These officeholders and their families dominated the small cities and rural parishes in which they lived.

In Paris during the eighteenth century, the importance of the lower-court magistrates seems to have declined somewhat, perhaps because of the importance of the sovereign courts in the capital. In the *élection* of Paris, the average age of those assuming office was thirty-two, with a range of from twenty-five to fifty years of age. These officeholders were generally not graduates. Most remained in office until they died, and those who resigned did not hold other offices but went into retirement. There was no way to rise to higher positions. Only 7 percent were noble. Most were commoners. Two-thirds married daughters of officeholders, particularly *élection* officials. The remaining third married lawyers, doctors, merchants, and domanial officials. The *élection* officials were apparently on a footing of equality with the notaries of the Châtelet, the *payeurs des rentes de l'Hôtel de Ville*, and successful *avocats*. They seem to have been slightly superior in social status to officials of salt warehouses and well above legal assistants and minor ministerial officials such as *huissiers* and *sergents*.

Officials in the Paris salt warehouse took office, on the average, at the age of 38 years 7 months. The youngest was 18 years 10 months old when he took office, and the oldest 66 years 1 month. The majority were the sons of merchant notables. The majority of those who took office past the age of 40 were themselves merchants, and two-thirds of them belonged to the Six-Corps. The majority of those who took office before they reached the age of 40 were *avocats*. Fifty-nine percent kept their positions in the salt warehouse until they died. A few went on to other positions. Among these, the *président* Firmin-François Gissey became *président premier* of the *élection* in 1755, and the *contrôleur* Claude de Visigny became a royal secretary. Fathers were succeeded by their sons. We find brothers, uncles, and nephews all serving together in the warehouse. In the Desnaux family, the office of *grenetier ancien* was passed on from father to son for five generations from 1595 to 1747.

Since salt-warehouse officials served only one year out of every two or three, they often held their posts concurrently with other positions, such as *quartinier*, Paris city councillor, or occasionally alderman, consul, *juge-consul*, or, most commonly, merchant. Salt-warehouse officials paid dearly for their posts. In 1748–50, an office of *lieutenant* in a salt warehouse was worth 47,000 livres and an office of *contrôleur des mesures* was worth 47,000 to 56,000 livres. In the same period, an office of *correcteur* in the Chambre des Comptes of Paris was worth 50,000 livres; an *auditeur des Comptes*, 45,000 livres; a councillor on the Cour des Aides, 39,500 to 44,000 livres; a councillor on the Cour des Monnaies, 30,000 to 34,000 livres; a councillor in *parlement*, 35,000 to 40,000 livres; an office of *commissaire* in the Châtelet, 40,000 to 43,000 livres; a notary in the Châtelet, 40,000 livres; a councillor in the Châtelet, 7,000 to 9,000 livres; a councillor in the *élection* of Paris, 28,000 livres; a city councillor, 16,000 to 20,000 livres; a *quartinier*, 16,500 to 21,000 livres. Despite the rather high price of salt-warehouse offices, the holders of these offices ranked socially somewhat below officials in the *élections*, halfway between the magistrates of the *présidial* and the members of the consular court of Paris.

The Decline of the Judicial Order. All the offices in the *présidiaux*, *bailliages*, and *sénéchaussées* were affected by the crisis in the judicial order revealed by the falling price of offices. The crisis was less severe in the *élections* and salt warehouses, which seem not to have been hit by the extreme depression of 1751. In the *élection* of Paris the office of *élu* sold for around 30,000 livres from 1740 to 1787. The crisis was severe in the regular lower courts, however. The progress of the crisis and the principal reasons for it have been well studied in the case of the *présidiaux*. The number of cases handled by these courts dwindled steadily throughout the eighteenth century, profits declined,

offices became impossible to sell, and the price of a vacant office consequently fell precipitously.

Because the lower courts were energetic agents of royal authority in the
provinces, the king established *présidiaux* in cities where different seigneurial courts, such as Beauvais and Pamiers, quarreled as to jurisdiction. Hence
the number of *présidiaux* almost doubled from 1580 to 1710. This proliferation
was occasioned by the needs of war. "A *présidial* is always an ornament to
a city, and sometimes its very life's blood."[29] Cities like Senlis, in which
trade was of little or no importance, lived on their courts. Louis XIII established *présidiaux* in Lectoure (1622–34), Nérac (1629), Montauban (1630),
Gueret, Millau, Rodez, Brioude, Le Puy-en-Velay (1635), Valence (1636),
and eighteen other places in ten years. Establishments recommenced in 1696,
when *présidiaux* were set up in Burgundy and Franche-Comté and later in
Ypres and Valenciennes (1704). In order to establish new courts, the old
ones had to give up parts of their jurisdictions. In 1703 a *bailliage en chef*
was established at Villers-Cotterêts. It was granted jurisdiction over 220
villages formerly in the *bailliage* of Crépy-en-Valois, which thereafter retained jurisdiction over only 66 villages. This meant a reduction in *épices*
and other legal fees. By 1714 the value of the office of *lieutenant particulier*
at Crépy had dropped by two-thirds.

The companies of presidial officeholders frequently had to pay considerable sums in order to keep their jurisdiction from being dismembered or
to buy up competing offices. Companies thus became overburdened with
debt, and prospective office buyers shied away from places in which this
debt was excessive. The *présidial* of Carcassonne was down to six officeholders in 1710. Twenty offices lay unclaimed at the *parties casuelles* because
the company owed more than 100,000 livres. In May 1715, the company of
officeholders in the *présidial* of Blois owed a principal of 103,620 livres and
25,000 livres in back interest. Its jurisdiction had been pared back to "three
parishes with about 280 fires, in view of the erection of Leuroux, Saint-
Aignan, and Ménars as duchies and marquisates." It was customary to make
a prospective officeholder sign an obligation to pay off the debts of the
company he was about to enter prior to his installation in office.

Like the cutoff point for presidial cases, the salaries of presidial officials
did not change between 1552 and the end of the eighteenth century. In Provins
in 1717, the *premier président* earned 317 livres; the *second président*, 300;
the *lieutenant général*, 148; councillors, 50 livres apiece; the *avocat du roi*,
75 livres; and the *procureur du roi*, 97 livres. The amount paid in salary
depended on the importance of the court. Salary payments were subject to
withholding and delays. Salary increases were granted in exchange for compulsory loans. The Paulette or annual dues further reduced salaries. In 1742
the *lieutenant général* received 270 livres of his salary of 300 after deduction
of the *dixième*. He was obliged to pay 222 livres 4 sols 5 deniers in annual
dues equal to one-sixtieth of the official value of his office.

Epices were meager. In Beauvais at the beginning of the seventeenth century, councillors seldom collected more than 200 livres per year in *épices*. The *lieutenant général* collected one-third more. What is more, these amounts were declining steadily. For the two years 1707 and 1708, councillors received only from 27 to 37 livres in *épices*, and the *lieutenant particulier* 38 livres 4 sols 8 deniers, an average of 17 livres per year.

Officeholders had to give more to the king in "finance" than they took in. No one had any further interest in buying such ruinous offices. In Provins eight offices were left unpurchased in March 1718 "because of the excessive *capitation*, which is greater than the salary." No officer "paid or redeemed the loans and annual dues." Men already in office were forced to live in the country, and months went by during which it was impossible to find enough officers to hold a hearing in a *présidial*.

Ordinary *bailliages* met with the same difficulties. At Mehun-sur-Yèvre, where the *bailliage* was supposed to employ a *lieutenant général*, a *lieutenant particulier*, an *assesseur criminel*, and a *procureur du roi*, the only office that was actually filled in January 1718 was that of *procureur du roi*. On 4 September 1726, the Bordeaux *parlement* was forced to issue a decree ordering that all pending trials before *bailliages* and *sénéchaussées* were to be heard by a minimum of three judges, "and if three judges were not available in any court, this number was to be made up by the addition of an appropriate number" of graduates.[30]

The officers of *bailliages* and *sénéchaussées* were in effect forced to attend to the vineyards and estates or else to acquire offices in other *corps* such as the *élections* or the *maréchaussée*, in which offices were less expensive and yielded higher salaries and associated profits.

To cope with this situation, the king sought to eliminate such lower royal courts as *prévôtés*, castellanies, *vicomtés*, and *vigueries* in cities where there were *bailliages* and *sénéchaussées*, while allowing them to remain elsewhere. The *présidiaux*, *bailliages*, and *sénéchaussées* were to have initial jurisdiction over cases that would have been heard by these lower courts. In 1712 a decree of the Conseil d'Etat joined the three *vigueries* of Carcassonne, Cabardès, and Minervois to the *présidial* of Carcassonne, as the first step in a long process. Under Chancellor d'Aguesseau, lower courts were closed every month. Proof is provided by the edict of 1734 eliminating the *prévôté* of Le Mans. Between 1733 and 1745 at least twenty-four lower courts were closed. The edict of June 1749 closed the lower courts in any city where there was a *présidial*, *bailliage*, or *sénéchaussée* and subsumed the jurisdiction of the defunct court within one of the latter. Subsequently other courts outside these cities were also closed, as the edict had anticipated. The king made one court of several *prévôtés*, castellanies, *victomés*, or *vigueries* that covered the same territory, and cases were to be heard by this new court without possibility of appeal. Beginning around 1740 the king issued letters patent combining seigneurial courts with the nearest *bailliage* or *sénéchaussée* when the *seigneur* could not or would not discharge his duties satisfactorily.

A few *présidiaux* survived after 1750. Riom was prospering. Beauvais, Senlis, and Orléans (thanks to Pothier, who became a professor at the university in 1750) had an adequate number of magistrates. Elsewhere, however, prospective buyers continued to shun offices despite the reforms. There was a danger that the only officers left would be the *lieutenants*.

As has already been noted, the only remedy for the situation in the *présidiaux* was to raise the threshold beyond which cases were sent to a higher court.

The Place of Lower-Court Magistrates in Local Urban Elites. Despite the crisis in the lower courts, court officers occupied an important position in local urban elites on the eve of the Revolution. Extensive studies of this question have been carried out for Orléans, Troyes, and Reims. We shall examine Troyes and Reims.

Troyes and Reims were among the thirty largest cities in France. Troyes had a population of 28,000 and Reims, 32,000. Located at the junction of several major highways, these cities were noted for manufacturing and commerce, Troyes for cotton and Reims for wine and wool. Each city had a *bailliage*, an *élection*, a *maîtrise des Eaux et Forêts*, a *maréchaussée*, and, from 1699 on, a *lieutenant général de police*.

In both cities social prominence was shared by merchants and officeholders. Merchant families formed dynasties comparable to the dynasties of magistrates. Merchants rarely purchased local offices. In Troyes only one magistrate was the son of a merchant. Merchants wealthy enough to do so bought ennobling offices such as royal secretaryships in Paris or Lyon. The *bailliage* was the near monopoly of a group of families. In Troyes the same commoner families owned most of the offices for generation after generation. The Paillot, Comparot, Corrard, Huez, and Sourdat families also ruled the *élection* and kept merchants out. But the councillors of the *bailliage* and the *élection* were in turn stymied at their place in the hierarchy. They could not rise to a position on one of the sovereign courts, not even in cities where a sovereign court sat. In Montpellier during this period only one councillor in the *sénéchaussée* rose to the Cour des Comptes, Aides et Finances. By contrast, nine younger sons of families represented on the Cour des Comptes became councillors in the *sénéchaussée*. This impediment to social ascent no doubt played a role in setting off the Revolution.

A third of the magistrates in the Reims *bailliage* and an eighth of those in the *bailliage* of Troyes were nobles. In Reims there was a university with a law school. Four magistrates in the *bailliage* had studied there and two were professors. In Reims between 1750 and 1789 there were seven buyers of an office of magistrate in the *bailliage*, of whom one was a professor of law, one a *lieutenant* in the *maréchaussée*, one a *procureur du roi* in the *élection*, and one a *président* in the salt warehouse. These men were relatively old when they became magistrates: the average age was forty-six. We must therefore conclude that the *bailliage* in Reims was, in spite of every-thing, still esteemed more highly than the special lower courts. The new magistrates were not succeeding relatives and had no relatives sitting on the *bailliage*. In Troyes during the same period fifteen new officers entered the *bailliage:* two councillors succeeded their fathers, and two others had uncles sitting on the *bailliage*. The median age was twenty-nine. Thus the situation of the courts was quite different in these two cities, even though both were commercial centers.

The mayor of Reims was a *noble d'epée*. The *procureur syndic* of the city was the *procureur du roi* in the *élection* and in 1785 became a councillor in the *bailliage*. The city council included four nobles and two royal secretaries. There were also seven merchants, one of whom, a wine merchant, purchased a royal secretaryship in 1777. Through patronage and clientele relationships, the nobles, royal officeholders, and merchants monopolized all the offices in the municipality from 1639 on.

In Troyes commoner officeholders and merchants were in the majority on the city council. The mayor, Claude Huez, was a councillor in the *bailliage*. He was still in office when he was torn to shreds by the mob in a riot in September 1789. He had an uncle and a cousin sitting on the *bailliage*. There were three other magistrates from the *bailliage* and two from the *élection* on the city council, whose membership also included eight merchants, of whom the two wealthiest were textile manufacturers.

The social position of a lower-court officer therefore varied from city to city in the years just prior to the Revolution. Despite the decline of the lower courts, these officers still played a large role in municipal government.

Offices and Social Mobility

In order to gain a better idea of the place of royal officeholders in French society, we shall next take an over-all view of the role played by offices in social mobility at all levels of society, from top to bottom.

Factors Involved in Social Mobility. To judge by the complaints of the no-bility in the Estates General of 1614–15 and in assemblies held at the time of the Fronde, the selling of offices made officeholding the primary avenue of social ascension. *Gentilshommes* complained constantly about the steady increase in the price of offices. Their grievance was that money was making it possible for offices to be snapped up by base individuals, by the de-scendants of cobblers, drapers, and lackeys who had become wealthy thanks to ignoble, mechanical trades engaged in for profit and always vile and shameful. Commerce in particular, and above all "finance," the manipulation of royal monies, the farming of taxes, and participation in *"affaires extraor-dinaires"* and loans to the king, were singled out as especially worthy of blame. As these nobles saw it, a whole host of parvenus moved from office to office until they arrived at the sovereign courts, where they were permitted to sit on *fleurs de lis*. From there they insinuated themselves into the royal councils and even into the nobility itself, at the expense of the old warrior families, *gentilshommes* who for generations since time immemorial had indulged in man's noblest pursuit, the profession of the soldier.

The *gentilshommes* attacked even the Paulette, or annual dues. The Paulette, they charged, had the effect of making offices heritable; at the same time it promoted social mobility by raising the price of the few posts that did come up for sale, thereby restricting access to commoners who had become rich. Kept out were the *gentilshommes*, who had been impoverished by war, the need to pay ransoms, the fixity of seigneurial dues in a time of rising prices, and the demands of being noble, which required never-ending displays of largesse.

There is no doubt that venal offices did play an important role in promoting social mobility, though the way in which this happened varied sharply from the myth created by contemporaries. Consider the question of access to the nobility, for example. A great change begins to occur during the first third of the sixteenth century, at about the time of François I. The new pattern of social promotion gradually assumed more and more importance. By the time of, say, Louis XIII, it had become established, and it persisted until the middle of the eighteenth century. The old pattern was this: a family acquired nobility by having its members go into the military, then the principal avenue to a noble station. A family might also acquire nobility by purchasing a *seigneurie*, fief, or noble estate and living on its rents, "without engaging in trade or commerce." After three or four generations, other noble families and *gentilshommes* would recognize it as noble. This peer recognition was the means of conferring nobility. Thus nobility was the result of a social consensus. The body social itself generated nobility.

The new pattern was quite different. The number of families reaching nobility in the old way steadily diminished. By the time of Richelieu, the old pattern was almost entirely a thing of the past. The new pattern was to acquire nobility by holding an office that conferred nobility. Gradually, the number of families acquiring nobility in this manner increased. Most held ennobling offices such as royal secretaryships, magistracies in the sovereign courts, and so on. A smaller number obtained letters of nobility from the king. In other words, ennoblement by society itself gave way to ennoblement by the state. The state, too, changed in nature, from arbiter and coordinator to absolute, centralizing monarchy. There was a simultaneous transition from an organic society made up of *corps*, which reacted spontaneously to events, to a mechanical society organized and mobilized by the sovereign. By the beginning of the seventeenth century, officeholding had become the principal avenue to nobility. In a broader sense, officeholding also became the major form of social advancement. The turning point for a family came when one of its members managed to purchase a minor royal office in finance or the judiciary. The family then underwent a social mutation.

The new state, meanwhile, had needs of its own and to meet them constantly increased the number of officeholders, *commissaires*, *commis*, tax farmers, and other officials that it employed, mainly for the purpose of collecting taxes. The state was constantly turning *commis* and *commissaires* into officeholders and making offices of posts that it sold or authorized to be sold. The number of venal offices and hence the number of opportunities for social ascension therefore increased.

In order to study the role of venal offices in social mobility, the phenomenon must be studied in its entirety, from the lowest to the highest ranks in society. In a country as diverse as France was in the seventeenth and eighteenth centuries, however, it is important to distinguish between different modes of social ascension in different provinces and regions. We must at least consider several examples.

Let us look first at the province of Franche-Comté, which returned to French possession in 1674. Louis XIV made Besançon the provincial capital. In that city we find nearly all levels in the judicial hierarchy, including both regular and special courts. The sale of offices was introduced in the province by the edict of August 1692.

Cities that Lived on Their Courts and Administrative Offices. Besançon lived primarily on its courts of justice. It was the presence of these courts that attracted people with cases to plead and, along with them, a whole host of people who earned their living by ministering to the needs of plaintiffs, defendants, lawyers, and magistrates. It was because Besançon was a court town that its population increased from 14,000 at the time of the conquest to 30,000 on the eve of the Revolution. Of this number, several hundred people actually belonged to the world of the judiciary, including magistrates, *avocats*, ministerial officials, and legal assistants. The presence of the *parlement* of Franche-Comté assured the gown of preeminence in the city of Besançon.

Let us look concretely, then, at how a person might rise socially in Franche-Comté. Consider a well-to-do peasant who manages to get hold of a little extra money. He might send one of his sons to a *collège*, for there were Jesuit *collèges* in every city. After the Jesuits were expelled in 1764, these *collèges* were run by the secular clergy. Our peasant's son would not have finished his full course of study. He would have left school after a few years. It would have been pointless for him to finish the full course, since the university was closed to him. The professors would have been glad to accept him, but the students did not wish to study alongside the son of a man of no account. A case of this sort actually occurred.[31]

After three or four years in a *collège*, our peasant's son would go to work as a clerk in the office of a notary or assistant *procureur*. He would live with his employer and eat with his employer's family. After seven or eight years he would become a legal assistant or adviser, helping his clients with procedural questions. Unless he was lucky enough to marry the daughter of a *procureur* or notary, however, he could not aspire to such a position himself. In most cases he would remain a legal assistant all his life. He might never even rise above the level of notarial clerk. On the other hand he might become the clerk or secretary of an *avocat* or magistrate. He could also become a *commis* in the *bureau des Finances*, a business agent for a magistrate or *gentilhomme*, a trial solicitor, or, if he could obtain a commission, a clerk responsible for affixing seals, drawing up inventories, carrying out investigations, or taking oaths.

A relatively successful legal assistant might be able to gain a little more ground for his own son. First he would send his son to *collège* for a few years and then find him a position as clerk with a notary, where he would remain for at least seven years. Next, after the son had reached the age of twenty-five, and if his father's or family's savings allowed, the young legal assistant might, if the occasion arose, purchase a royal office of notary, assistant *procureur*, or *huissier*, either at Besançon or elsewhere in the province. With a little luck, the new *procureur* or notary might be able to become a judge in a seigneurial court. Some might go into the army and become lieutenants or captains in the infantry or artillery but not in the cavalry, the noble branch of the service. A few might hit upon the right combination for a lightning rise through the financial administration. This was the case with Antoine Girod, who was born in 1700, became a *procureur*'s clerk in 1730, an employee of the Recette des Finances of Salins, and then in 1743 *trésorier de l'armée* for Maillebois. After that he rose to become *trésorier principal* for the troops at Besançon and in 1761 was granted permission to take possession of the fief of Noisy. In 1764 he purchased an ennobling office as royal secretary in the chancellery of the Besançon *parlement*. He died a noble in 1783. Such cases were exceptional, however. Most men on the rise remained ministerial officials all their lives. Some families remained stuck at this level for several generations, as son succeeded father in the post of notary or *procureur*. An example was the Tavenier clan, which yielded four successive generations of *procureurs* to the *parlement* between 1676 and 1768.

If a ministerial official was successful and ambitious, however, he might be in a position by the third generation to send one of his sons through a full course of study, starting with *collège* courses in philosophy and then moving on to the University of Besançon, where now the other students might still treat him with condescension but would not oppose his presence. The great-grandson of our peasant would be able to finish three years of legal studies and take his degree as a *licencié*. A fourth year would entitle him to the degree of "doctor of law." Even as a *licencié* he was eligible to take an oath on the Bible as an *avocat*. After two years of practical training, he was ready to be inscribed on the office roll of *avocats*. This was a crucial step for the individual and for his family. For all that the ministerial offices were offices, they remained ignoble offices, and no noble could hold one without derogation. The title of *avocat*, on the other hand, was a prestigious one. Lower-ranking magistrates listed their title as *avocat* in *parlement* before their other title. Former magistrates in a *présidial* or *parlement* would have themselves listed on the roll of *avocats* after stepping down as magistrates. *Avocats* were privileged individuals who enjoyed exemption from collections and militia duty. Their privilege of *committimus* to the *requêtes du palais* entitled them to have cases in which they were defendants heard initially by *parlement*. *Avocats* lived as nobles, and if the successful ones among them grew wealthy, they did so without harming their social status, because their profits were seen as honoraria rather than mercenary gain.

Our new *avocat* might practice for twenty years as a pleading *avocat* and then become a consulting *avocat*. If he was successful, he might hold other posts concurrently, such as the office of seigneurial judge, *directeur et trésorier au bureau de l'hôpital Saint-Jacques*, or secretary of the university. Some avocats became forgemasters, heads of factories, *maîtres de pension*, or *secrétaires de l'intendance*. Others went into the army, where they might rise to the rank of captain of cavalry or become military engineers or musketeers. After leaving the army, some went back to being *avocats*. Most remained *avocats*, however. In trials it was not unusual for a party to have the father for *procureur* and the son for *avocat*. Of 311 individuals who remained *avocats*, 104 were the sons of *procureurs*, notaries, *huissiers*, or *greffiers*.

Our family would continue its rise in the fourth generation. One son might buy an office as an accountant in the financial administration: a *receveur particulier de bailliage*, a *trésorier de la maréchaussée*, a *payeur des gages*, or a *receveur des consignations*. Then, in the fifth generation, would come magistracies in finance or, still more highly esteemed, in the judiciary: *élu* or *trésorier de France* in finance or *conseiller de bailliage* or *lieutenant particulier* in the judiciary. Finally, in the sixth generation, *parlement* would become accessible to our family, which would thereby acquire gradual nobility if it had not already been ennobled by holding an office as *trésorier de France* or *secrétaire du roi*. After *parlement*, a particularly fortunate member of the family might rise to a post as *maître des requêtes de l'Hôtel du Roi*, become an *intendant de province*, and receive the rank of *conseiller d'Etat*.

Of course this model of social ascension was rarely followed through to the end. Few families climbed all the rungs of this ladder. We know nothing about the early stages of the ascent of many families who made it to *parlement*. There were also other ways to rise. A few sons of ministerial officials entered *parlement*. Between 1676 and 1789, 6 out of 306 (or 1.96 percent) magistrates in *parlement* were the sons of ministerial officials: one of these became a *président* in the Chambre des Requêtes, one became an *avocat général*, and four became councillors. The *président* was Claude Bonaventure Alviset, who was the son of a notary who was also civil clerk at the ecclesiastical court known as the Officialité. At the age of twenty-two, Claude Bonaventure Alviset bought the post of *lieutenant particulier* in the *bailliage* of Besançon and then in 1716 at the age of sixty-one became *président* in the Chambres des Requêtes. He founded a dynasty of councillors in *parlement*. Such cases were exceptional. They should be viewed in light of the fact that no son of a legal assistant ever entered *parlement*.

There are cases on record of families that rose steadily over a period of four generations, from a great-grandfather who was a legal assistant to a grandfather who was a *procureur* or notary to a father who was a magistrate in a lower court to a son who became a councillor in *parlement*.

Other families remained at the same level for several generations, however. Some even descended to a lower echelon in the hierarchy for a time. But none ever descended below the level of *avocat*. The son of a councillor in *parlement* or a *lieutenant général* in a *bailliage* who failed to become a magistrate never sank to the level of *procureur* or notary. Instead he became an *avocat*.

In our example we assumed that it was the son of a peasant who became a legal assistant. But many legal assistants had fathers who were master bakers, pastry makers, painters, cabinet makers, saddlers, weavers, goldsmiths, surgeons, or postmasters (around 45 percent, in fact).

Ministerial officials were often the sons of legal assistants but might also be sons of husbandmen, merchants, master artisans, or vine growers. The merchants included tanners, tailers, clothiers, and grocers.

Avocats were frequently the sons of ministerial officials as well as goldsmiths, surgeons, apothecaries, watchmakers, or entrepreneurs. We know of a vine grower by the name of Nodier whose son became a master in the construction trade. In turn, his son, Antoine Melchior Nodier, became an *avocat* and later *président* of the criminal tribunal at Doubs during the Revolution. The great-grandson of the vine grower was Charles Nodier, the writer.

Avocats were never sons of husbandmen or vine growers. Twenty-four percent were sons of merchants. Some were sons of doctors, and most were sons of men of law. Thirty-nine percent of the magistrates in the lower courts were sons of merchants. Others were sons of physicians, apothecaries, or surgeons (28 percent). Thirty-three percent were sons of men of law.

Nine-tenths of the magistrates in *parlement* belonged to the family of a magistrate when they entered *parlement*, and most belonged to families in which there had been magistrates for several generations. Those who were not descended from office-holders in the judiciary came from families in which there were financial officeholders, usually magistrates rather than accounting officers. It generally took three or four generations to go from a ministerial official to a councillor in *parlement*, and sometimes it took as many as six to eight generations. Out of 319 members of *parlement* 33 had a merchant or wholesaler as their earliest known ancestor. In the other cases at least a century and a half had elapsed between the merchant and the first councillor in *parlement*. Magistrates in *parlement* usually had the gown to thank for their social advancement rather than trade or finance.

Of the magistrates in *parlement* 77 percent were noble before entering office. Twenty-three percent were commoners who were ennobled by their offices as councillors, *procureurs généraux*, deputies, *maîtres de requêtes*, or *greffiers en chef*. But these commoners held fiefs before entering *parlement*, and some called themselves nobles. Ennobling offices helped to buttress dubious claims to nobility.

Commercial Cities. The pattern we have described for the city of Besançon is typical of cities whose activities were mainly judicial and administrative. Although this pattern also applies to a large extent to commercial cities and their surrounding regions, some modifications are required. Consider the example of Nantes, a major center of maritime trade. In Nantes was located the Chambre des Comptes for the province of Brittany, whose *parlement* was located at Rennes. Ennobling offices in the Chambre des Comptes and royal secretaryships in the Petite Chancellerie of Brittany were purchased mainly by wholesale and retail merchants and *"financiers."* There were two main reasons for this. First, these offices secured certain privileges, particularly the *franc-fief*, which was important because almost all wholesalers and *financiers* acquired fiefs. Second, every merchant hoped to secure high judicial office for his son so as to consolidate the acquisition of nobility and social consideration. A 1787 memorandum from Nantes concerning the price of French ships said that

> in France, nobility is the sole source of honor and consideration. The merchant whose work has been favored by fortune hastens to quit his estate or at least to join a title to it, something made necessary by our laws and customs. Before long his children forget their father's profession and his grandchildren look with disdain upon the obscure, if useful, source of the honors they enjoy. We are unable to cite the name of a single commercial house in this city that has remained in commerce for as many as four generations; hardly any have made it through three generations.[32]

Now, from 1672 on, one had to be noble to enter the Rennes *parlement*. This meant that, even though the sons of councillors and other officers in the *sénéchaussées* and presidial courts did buy offices in the Chambre des Comptes of Nantes, most of the higher positions in this body, the offices of *président* and *maître des comptes*, were purchased by the sons of important merchants who were then obliged to abandon their commercial activities and live as nobles, since the edicts that declared maritime commerce not to be a derogation from nobility explicitly excluded magistrates of the superior courts. *Maîtres des comptes* married the daughters of important merchants, and *présidents* married into the nobility. In the lower reaches of the Chambre des Comptes hierarchy, *correcteurs* and *auditeurs* were generally the sons of ministerial officials such as notaries and *procureurs*, of members of the liberal professions such as physicians, of minor officials in the judiciary, and of merchants of medium importance. There was some social tension between the two groups. Both had the privilege of "gradual nobility" once they entered the Chambre des Comptes, however. In other words, a man whose father and grandfather had each held an office in the Chambre des Comptes for twenty years or had died in office before twenty years had elapsed was entitled to full nobility and could pass that nobility on to his descendants. This rule was known as *"patre et avo consulibus."* It applied to the *trésoriers de France et généraux des Finances*, who in Brittany were included in the Chambre des Comptes.

Merchants clamored for royal secretaryships attached to the Breton chancellery, which not only brought exemption from *francs-fiefs* and *lods et ventes* but also conferred a higher sort of nobility than did the sovereign courts, a nobility that was transmissible in the first degree, provided the father had served twenty years or had died in office. The edict of 1724 eliminated the grant of nobility transmissible in the first degree and retained only personal nobility. The edicts of October and December 1727 reestablished the grant of nobility in the first degree, however, and reaffirmed the traditional privileges of the post in return for a payment to the royal treasury. By virtue of the edict of December 1701, these offices could be held by individuals in wholesale trade, which explains their attractiveness to merchants. Thirty percent of these offices were bought by wholesale merchants from Nantes or St. Malo. The rest were bought by officers of the *présidiaux*, rentiers living as nobles, notaries, physicians, and *avocats*. A few were acquired by nobles who lacked written proof of their nobility. Commoners who bought these offices thereby acquired legal nobility. Actual social assimilation into the true nobility required several more generations, however.

As soon as they were able, Bretons who owned a royal secretaryship in the Breton chancellery would acquire a royal secretaryship in the Grande Chancellerie of France and get rid of the other office. Of 44 such cases, 17 were *financiers*, suppliers to the royal farms or financial officials, accountants, or *receveurs généraux* or *trésoriers généraux des Finances* (38 percent), and 14 were wholesale merchants or shipfitters (32 percent). A few were noble soldiers from old families who needed confirmation of their nobility.

Descendants of men who obtained nobility in this way could attempt to enter *parlement*. Magistrates in the Breton *parlement* were nobles who held offices in *parlement*. This social group was not an economic unit. Immensely wealthy magistrates rubbed elbows with others whose fortunes were quite modest. But all were nobles and "Fathers of the Country."

Commercial Agricultural Regions. Next, we shall give further modifications of the previous two patterns in order to describe the social hierarchy in our third example, the important grain-growing area known as the Beauce. Much of the grain grown in the Beauce was sold elsewhere, in neighboring areas such as Orléans and above all in the markets of Paris. The *gentilshommes* who owned and the peasants who worked the land of the region were agricultural entrepreneurs who produced for the market. *Gentilshommes* in the Beauce were well off, and quite a few made enough money to acquire additional land and expand their *seigneuries*. Seigneurial dues played a small part in the economy of the region, and property in the Beauce assumed quite modern, almost capitalist forms. Although there were *bailliages* and *présidiaux* like that of Chartres in the Beauce, its *parlement* was the *parlement* of Paris and its sovereign courts, the courts of Paris. Social advancement thus had to take the form of geographical mobility and migration to Paris.

It was possible for a family in the Beauce to raise itself, in most cases over a period of eight or more generations (requiring one hundred fifty to two hundred years), from the lowest to the highest levels of the social hierarchy. There was a bottleneck to negotiate, however, between the level of an agricultural worker or artisan and that of a wealthy peasant or merchant. In other words, the primary difficulty was to move from the world of the simple manual laborer to that of the entrepreneur who organizes and distributes work even if he continues to shoulder a part of the burden of manual labor himself. What was required for this transition, as the economy was then organized, was the ability to do varied kinds of work. An artisan or agricultural worker had to be able not only to perform his own basic tasks but also to collect seigneurial dues or tithes, to hire transportation, to sell wheat as a small merchant on the market. In other words, he had to begin to work his way into the power structure and the system of enterprise.

If he succeeded in doing this, one of his sons might be able to become a merchant selling various wares. In this region, crisscrossed by roads and highways leading to Paris, the best way to accumulate cash at this level was to operate a hotel. Our new merchant might aspire to become a collector for a *seigneurie* or a postmaster at the same time he ran his hotel.

By the third generation, a grandson might become a legal assistant or even rise to the position of *procureur* or notary while carrying on other activities at the same time. Some notaries were also farmers and collectors of seigneurial dues, for example.

By the fourth generation, a great-grandson might be able to finish his studies, attend the University of Orléans, acquire a degree as "*licenciés ès-loix*," and have his name inscribed on the roll of *avocats*. The family was then well placed for further social advancement. Seigneurial and royal offices came within its reach. Among the accessible royal offices were those attached to the salt warehouses and *élections* and the positions of *lieutenant particulier* and *lieutenant criminel* in a *bailliage* or *présidial*.

At this point the family was in a position to acquire ennobling offices such as royal secretaryships in the Grande Chancellerie at Paris, *trésoriers généraux* de France, or magistracies in the Chambre des Comptes or *parlement* in Paris. Between 1560 and 1600, 48 percent of residents of the Beauce who obtained nobility did so by acquiring ennobling offices, 17 percent did so via the military profession, 17 percent by living nobly on *seigneuries*, and 8 percent by letters of nobility. During the seventeenth century, 61 percent rose by acquiring ennobling office, 3 percent via the military profession, 22 percent by living nobly on fiefs and *seigneuries*, and 11 percent by letters of nobility.

Among the families represented in the *parlement* between 1685 and 1690, about ten came from the Beauce, Ile-de-France, and Beauvaisis.

Commerce and finance played a much less important role in creating access to offices than historians have believed. Most *financiers*, *partisans*, and *traitants* came not from banking or commercial circles nor from the lower reaches of society but rather from the families of officeholders and even nobles. In seventeenth- and eighteenth-century France, social advancement was accomplished mainly through the legal profession and the office of magistrate, except in important commercial seaports.

Thus it was possible to rise in French society, and it was possible even to rise from quite humble origins to the very highest ranks. But how often was this possibility realized? Statistical information is lacking. Because social mobility was very slow it was often incomplete. A family might die out or leave only daughters who married into other families before it had had a chance to rise very high. An agricultural worker by the name of Jehan Peigne was living at Tancrainville in the Beauce in 1544. His descendants began to rise thanks to commerce, in which they engaged while also working as legal assistants and trial solicitors for the princes of Condé during the seventeenth century. Late in that century they first acquired seigneurial offices. After that they managed to purchase various *seigneuries* and became the *seigneurs* of Tancrainville. But the last Jehan Peigne, seigneur de Tancrainville, died on the threshold of nobility sometime after 1760, leaving three daughters and no sons. It often took more than two centuries for a family to rise from humble origins to the nobility.

According to Necker's treatise on *L'administration des finances de France*, there were many, too many, opportunities for ennoblement through office in 1788. In all of France, Necker estimated, there were 4,000 ennobling offices: 80 offices of *maître des requêtes*, 1,000 offices in the various *parlements*, 900 in the Chambres des Comptes and Cours des Aides, 70 on the Grand Conseil, 30 in the Cours des Monnaies, 20 on the Provincial Council of Artois, 80 in the Châtelet of Paris, 740 in the *bureaux des Finances*, 50 *grands baillis*, *sénéchaux*, and governors, 900 royal secretaryships, and 200 commissioned offices in the *parlement* of Nancy and the sovereign court of Alsace.

As Professor Meyer has rightly pointed out,[33] however, many of these ennobling offices were actually held by nobles, including the vast majority of offices in *parlement*, some posts in the Chambres des Comptes, and all the offices of *grands baillis*, *sénéchaux*, and governors, to name a few. According to Professor Bluche, the percentage of commoners admitted to the Paris *parlement* was only 9.3 percent in 1715 and 11.25 percent in 1771.

Furthermore, Necker failed to take account of the clause requiring nobility in the second degree in the provincial Chambres des Comptes and *bureaux des Finances*, which covered more than 1,200 ennobling offices.

Nor does Necker allow for the requirement that ennobling offices had to be held for a period of twenty years. One-fifth of all ennobling offices were resold before this period of time had elapsed and thus did not produce nobility. Many owners of ennobling offices were satisfied simply to enjoy their privileges and their personal nobility.

In all, the 4,000 ennobling offices probably created slightly more than 2,000 actual nobles between 1700 and 1788, which is a far cry from the fantastic accounts given by Necker and the third estate in 1789. Professor Meyer estimates that, in the Chambre des Comptes at Nantes, allowing for posts virtually monopolized by the local nobility and for those sold during the twenty years prior to the Revolution, which had no time to produce their ennobling effect, we still find 280 posts conferring gradual nobility offered between 1780 and 1789 and therefore 140 families ennobled by these posts in Brittany, Poitou, and Anjou. Over the course of the century in Brittany, 773 families were ennobled by these posts, we are told, and, after allowing for the elimination of some offices and the failure of certain families to perform the necessary formalities, 300 ennobled families were left. To this number should be added a hundred or so families from neighboring provinces who were ennobled by holding offices in Brittany.[34]

Thus, although the phenomenon of ennoblement and social advancement by means of officeholding cannot be neglected, it can hardly be said to have undermined the foundations of French society. Why was social mobility so limited?

The fault does not lie with the Paulette or annual dues of 1604, which some have blamed for making offices more hereditary. In spite of the Paulette new families continued to enter the Paris *parlement*, and there is little difference between the period prior to the Paulette and the subsequent period.

	Period 1550–99	*Period 1600–1649*
First family to serve in *parlement*	54.4%	47.2%
Councillors of the second generation	27.7%	28.7%
Councillors of the third generation	12.1%	15.0%
Councillors of the fourth generation	5.8%	19.2%

Nor did the Paulette seem to make much difference in the number of offices held by a single family.

	Period 1588–1605	*Period 1605–22*
	17.5%	19.4%

Between 1550 and 1604, we find 51 instances of two brothers serving together in *parlement* and 8 instances of three brothers serving together. Between 1605 and 1650 we find 69 instances of two brothers serving and 10 instances of three brothers serving.

Thus neither heritability nor nepotism noticeably increased after the Paulette.

We can say the same thing about the price of offices. The dizzying rise in prices that lasted until 1660 or so did not prevent men of law and lower-court officers from gaining access to the sovereign courts. Afterward prices remained steady or fell.

In the second half of the seventeenth century access to the superior courts and the other major *corps* of officeholders became more difficult, as the families already in place reserved the available offices for themselves. Following the Hundred Years' War the upper strata of French society had been renewed, and this process of renewal continued right through the first third of the seventeenth century. Families that had emerged in the time of Charles VIII, Louis XII, and François I were now in the superior courts and had at least three generations of nobility, equivalent in the eyes of the world to ancient nobility. They were bent on closing all further access to magistracies.

The existence of this circle of families, which passed offices on from generation to generation, reduced the chances of new men gaining a foothold. Over the course of the eighteenth century opportunities for advancement became rarer and rarer.

At the same time the state had evolved in such a way that offices became a less attractive means of social advancement as other avenues gradually opened up: there were commissions to be had, jobs as *commis*, and positions in the bureaucracy for new functionaries. This reduced the prestige of the *corps* of officeholders and diminished the profits of office. It also gave rise to a battle between the superior courts and the king that lasted throughout the eighteenth century. This intestine war helped to turn prospective buyers away from whatever offices did become available.

One question has not yet been raised. I have thus far treated venal offices without distinguishing between venality and the office, since they were inseparable in fact. But we also need to ask what effects officeholding would have had on social mobility if venality had not existed. Our answer can only be hypothetical. But it seems likely that social mobility would have been reduced, because the monarchy increased the number of offices precisely because it was selling them and because it also profited when offices were resigned or bequeathed and therefore stood to benefit indirectly from the private trade in offices. Apart from this important consideration, however, the consequences for social mobility may not have been very different in the absence of venality. The fact is that a candidate for office had to make sure in advance that he had a chance of not being rejected when it came first to asking for *lettres de provision* and later for installation in office by his corps. Thus it is quite likely that even if offices had not been sold, they would have been sought perhaps by a smaller number of men but largely by the same men, from the same social background, over the same number of generations, because no one else could gain access. Social mobility depended first and foremost on the hierarchical principle according to which society was organized. A man's rank in that hierarchy depended on his quality, on the length of time he had occupied a particular status, on the services he had rendered the king, the embodiment of the state, on the posts he had managed to obtain, on the marriages he had managed to contract, and on the property in land he had managed to acquire under the hierarchical feudal and seigneurial system. Social mobility was also tremendously dependent on favor, friendship, fidelity, and patronage. All these factors were important and probably counted for more than the sale of public offices in determining the degree of social mobility.

Notes

1. François Bluche, *Les magistrats du Grand Conseil au XVIIIe siècle* (Les Belles Lettres, 1966), p. 41.

2. *Recueil des rois de France*, 1607 ed.: Du Conseil privé du Roy, cited by A. Floquet, *Histoire du Parlement de Normandie*, vol. 6 (Rouen, 1842), p. 479.

3. M. Dubédat, *Histoire du Parlement de Toulouse*, vol. 1 (Arthur Rousseau, 1885), p. 272.

4. Concerning the Chambres de l'Edit, see vol. 1, p. 388.

5. François Bluche, "Les magistrats des cours parisiennes au XVIIIe siècle," *Revue historique de droit français et étranger* 1 (1974): 87–106.

6. Henri Sauval, *Histoire et recherches des antiquités de la ville de Paris*, vol. 2, book 8 (1724), pp. 395–96, based on documents dated prior to 1670.

7. Delamare, *Traité de la police*, book 1, title 10, chap. 1.

8. Information provided by Mr. Maurice Gresset.

9. Information provided by Mr. Maurice Gresset.

10. The edict establishing a salt warehouse at Gannat provided for 8 magistrates to serve the associated court, along with 12 auxiliaries of justice, and to staff the sales division, 2 keepers of the measures, 3 *receveurs particuliers*, 3 *greffiers*, 3 *maîtres-clercs*, 2 measurers, and 2 carriers (May 1627).

11. Information provided by Mrs. Andrée Corvol.

12. Concerning the corps of auxiliaries of justice, see vol. 1, pp. 436–46.

13. François Bluche, *Les magistrats du Parlement de Paris au XVIIIe siècle, 1715–1771* (Besançon: Imprimerie Jacques & Demontrond, 1960), p. 304, based on Hermant's *Mémoires*.

14. Cited by Glasson, *Parlement de Paris*, vol. 2, p. 16.

15. Mirabeau, *L'ami des hommes*, vol. 1, pp. 99–100.

16. Cited by Maurice Gresset, "Monde judiciaire à Besançon," typescript, Archives Départementale de Doubs, E 3942, T. F. Merceret, part 2, p. 245.

17. Cited in Pierre Goubert, "Les officiers royaux des Présidiaux, bailliages et Elections," *XVIIe siècle* 42 (1959): 62.

18. See other examples above, pp. 221–23.

19. Cited in Bluche, *Les magistrats du Parlement*, pp. 143–51.

20. Ibid., p. 238.

21. For a full study of the world of the judiciary, see the masterpiece of Maurice Gresset cited in note 16 above.

22. Cited in William Doyle, *The Parlement of Bordeaux and the End of the Old Regime: 1771–1790* (London and Townbridge: Ernest Benn, n.d.).

23. See examples and figures cited in Roland Mousnier, *La vénalité des offices sous Henri IV et Louis XII* (2d ed., Paris: 1970).

24. Cited by Philippe Rosset, "Les conseillers au Châtelet de Paris à la fin du XVIIᵉ siècle," *Paris et Ile-de-France* 21 (1970): 173–292, and 23–24 (1972–73): 144–97.

25. Ibid., p. 264.

26. Ibid., p. 196–97.

27. Barbier, *Journal*, vol. 3, pp. 276–79, cited ibid., p. 257.

28. See above, pp. 331–34.

29. E. Laurain, "Essai sur les présidiaux," *Nouvelle revue historique de droit français et étranger*, 1895, p. 525.

30. Ibid., p. 537.

31. In 1772, for the son of a master wigmaker from Besançon.

32. Cited by Jean Meyer, *La noblesse bretonne au XVIIIᵉ siècle* (S.E.V.P.E.N., 1966), p. 431.

33. Ibid., p. 428.

34. Ibid., pp. 186, 427.

18

Procedures in the Sovereign and Lower Courts

Calendar and Agenda

Broadly speaking, the sovereign and lower courts followed the same schedule as the *parlements*. The year opened on the day after Saint Martin's winter festival, 12 November. The Toulouse *parlement* took a two-week vacation at Christmas time, from the day before Christmas Eve (23 December) until the day after Kings (6 January), a thirteen-day vacation at Easter, from Holy Tuesday until Quasimodo, and eighteen days for Pentecost, from the Thursday before the holiday until the Sunday of Trinity. Its summer vacation ran from the Assumption in August (15 August) until Saint Martin's day (11 November). But defaults were judged until the eve of the festival of the Holy Cross (13 September), and the Chambre des Vacations sat from 14 September until 10 November. The Bordeaux *parlement* also ended its vacation on 12 November, but until the end of the eighteenth century the judicial year really got seriously under way only after Epiphany (6 January). The *parlement* of Besançon took a four-day vacation at Christmas, a week at Shrove Sunday, two weeks for Easter, a month from Ascension until the Monday after Corpus-Christi, three days at Assumption, and, finally, the period from 7 September until Saint Martin's day. The Chambre des Vacations met from 9 September until 27 October. Its magistrates worked no more than two hundred days per year.

In Paris, Bordeaux, and Toulouse, there were hearings from seven o'clock in the morning until eleven o'clock. In Toulouse the Grand-Chambre held hearings on Mondays, Tuesdays, and Thursdays. From 1663 on, it added an afternoon hearing on Tuesdays and Fridays from 1 December to 30 May. At the Besançon *parlement* the Grand-Chambre held hearings on Mondays, Tuesdays, and Thursdays. These were preceded by investigative hearings. The Grand-Chambre disposed of 250 cases annually in hearings and issued 71 written decrees. The Tournelle held its major hearings on Saturdays and its investigative hearings on Wednesdays and Fridays. In 1751 its civil section issued 55 written decrees and its civil section, 35 decrees. The Chambre des

Enquêtes met on Wednesdays and Fridays to hear cases in which written records were kept. It issued 38 decrees in 1751. The Chambre souveraine des Eaux et Forêts et Requêtes du Palais held hearings for the Eaux et Forêts on Wednesdays and Fridays and for the Requêtes on Saturdays. In 1751 it held 72 hearings for the Eaux et Forêts and heard 257 cases; for the Requêtes, it handed down 13 written judgments. The Chambre des Vacations held 19 hearings in 1751 and heard 64 cases.

The *parlement* of Bordeaux held its regular hearings in the morning and afternoon hearings on certain days of the week. Hearings known as the "*quinzaines*" were held at regular intervals to dispose of relatively minor cases and cases involving the poor. Meetings of "*grands commissaires*" were held for the purpose of issuing definitive judgments on certain urgent matters. Meetings of "*petits commissaires*" were held to make findings in questions of fact and to verify titles produced in connection with litigation. Assemblies of the chambers were held to register edicts and to discuss decrees. Conferences were called by the *présidents*.

The *parlements* swore an oath each time there was a change of reign. At the Toulouse *parlement*, however, an oath was taken annually. At the first session after vacation each year, following the mass, the *premier président* delivered a speech behind closed doors in the Grand-Chambre. The *greffier* then read out the royal ordinances laying down the duties of magistrates. The *premier président* would then kneel before the most senior of the *présidents à mortier*, who held in his hand an object known as the "*juratoire*," which might be either an old painting depicting Christ on the Cross, or the Gospels, or a missal opened to *Te igitur*. The *président* then stretched out his hands and swore to observe the ordinances and see to it that they were observed by others. Then he took the *juratoire* himself and received oaths in succession from the governor and *lieutenants généraux* of the province, the prelates, the *présidents à mortier*, the *maîtres des requêtes*, and the councillors, all of whom swore on their knees. The rules that magistrates swore to obey were as follows. They were not to break off their judicial work in order to attend to private affairs. They must not hear the arguments of any party to a case outside the official hearing. They were to suffer no interruption by the *procureurs*. They must never interrupt the *président* while asking questions in council and never speak out of turn. All deliberations were to be kept secret. Insults to *avocats*, *procureurs*, or parties to a case were not to be tolerated. They were not to confer with magistrates from other chambers during hearings. They were to write their own decrees and reports. Disobedience to the king was forbidden. They were to carry out their duties faithfully and to show respect for one another. Silence was to be maintained during arguments. Magistrates were to be modest in their clothing, furniture, valets, horses, carriages, and gold rings. They were to avoid public dances and farces involving actors and mountebanks. They were not to laugh immoderately or to use perfume or musk. They had to make themselves available to litigants and show themselves to be kind and humane. They were to dispense justice fearlessly, placing honor and the welfare of the public above all else.

After the magistrates had finished, the *huissiers* took their oath and then opened the doors to admit the lower-ranking officers and the public. The *premier président* would then deliver a second speech for the benefit of the public. The *greffier* read out the ordinances pertaining to *avocats*. *Avocats* were required to make accurate statements in hearings and loyally to execute the duties of their office. They were not to leave the city without handing over memoranda to the *procureurs* and without designating other *avocats* to replace them. At hearings they were to wear their broad gowns and round *bonnets*. They must not represent both parties in the same case. They must not engage in unwarranted proceedings. They should give alms to the poor. They must notify the court if cases touched on the king's interests. They must correctly apply the laws and customs of the kingdom. They must not hinder the disposition of cases. They were to take no more than their just due in salary. They must not leave the Palais during hearings. They were to be clear, concise, and brief.

Then the "king's men" took their oath, followed by the *juge mage*, the criminal judge, the *lieutenant général*, the *lieutenant particulier*, the "king's men" of the *sénéchaussée*, and the *avocats* in the order they were inscribed on the rolls.

The *greffier* then read out the ordinances pertaining to the *procureurs*. They were to be diligent and loyal, to refuse unjust causes, and to indicate cases that touched on the king's interests. They were to prepare written documents in a suitable style and take only moderate salaries. They were not to purchase dues in litigation. They must not infringe upon the rights of the *avocats* during argument. They must not canvass the judges or delay the progress of a case. They were to appear on time for morning sessions and maintain decorum and silence.

The *procureurs* then took their oath.

At the sound of the great bell of the Palais, everyone withdrew.

On the next day, the *avocat général* gave the opening speech behind closed doors before the assembled chamber. The king's men gave a list of cases involving the royal domain and requested that these be disposed of quickly. Then the *premier huissier* assembled the *procureurs* and read out loud a list of cases, which he later had posted in the *procureurs'* room. When this was done, the hearing began. The *huissiers* opened the doors and read the list of cases. The *greffier* reread the ordinances to recall the oath and instruct the populace. The hearing was then adjourned.

Hearings could begin in the various chambers as early as the following day.

According to article 144 of the ordinance of Blois, all the courts were supposed to hold a general assembly of all chambers known as the "*Mercuriale*," once every six months on the first Wednesday after Saint Martin's day and Easter. The king's men were supposed to see to it that this meeting was held and report to the king if it was delayed or cancelled. This assembly was held behind closed doors. A speech was supposed to be given by either the *avocat général* or the *procureur général*. In theory this speech was supposed to contain criticisms and warnings directed at the magistrates, *avocats*, and *procureurs* concerning their private life, morals, performance in office, and infractions of ordinances governing the Palais style. These criticisms were supposed to be followed up by a series of graduated sanctions issued in the name of *parlement*: remonstrances, notification of the king, suspension, expulsion from office, elimination of the office. In reality, this speech had become, at least as early as the beginning of the eighteenth century, a mere set piece on a subject chosen by the *premier président*, such as "*amour-propre*," "the choice of amusements," or "correcting one's own faults." In Paris the number of those attending the *mercuriales* had fallen to 66 by 1770 and to 26 by 1786.

The last opening address in the Paris *parlement* was delivered by the *avocat général* Dambray on 24 November 1788, and the last *mercuriale* by the *procureur général* Armand Joly de Fleury on 22 April 1789.

Initiation and Conclusion of Proceedings

Court proceedings of all kinds, whether legislative, administrative, civil, or criminal, were initiated either by petition of a party, on the initiative of the sovereign or lower court, or by the *procureur du roi*.

The "King's Men"

The king's men were the main driving force in all the sovereign and lower courts. In particular, the *procureur du roi* was "the eye of *parlement* and the vigilant sentinel of the magistrates."[1] In theory, if no subject filed a petition, the *corps* of magistrates was supposed to take action to enforce the law itself in any criminal case and whenever the public welfare was at stake. In fact, it was difficult to do so on the basis of public outcry alone. Accordingly, the king, the supreme judge and the man responsible for protecting the welfare of the public, maintained a representative with each court, who acted in his behalf, namely, the *procureur*. The civil ordinance of 1667 issued a reminder that the *procureur général* was to be heard in all "affairs involving the king, the church, the public, or moral questions." The criminal ordinance of 1670 upheld his right to take the initiative in prosecution, investigation, pleas, and arrests.

The *lettres de provision* of the *procureur du roi* gave him "the proxy to represent the king and stipulate in the king's name in any question involving public order."[2] The *procureur du roi* was therefore obliged to intervene whenever the interests of the king, as the embodiment of the realm, were at stake. When royal ordinances, edicts, and declarations were issued, they were supposed to be addressed to him alone; he would then petition *parlement* for their registration, and *parlement* would immediately set aside all other business to consider the petition. The *procureur* was required to make sure his deputies in all the various lower courts received copies of these texts. The *procureur général* was required to review all proposed ordinances, edicts, and regulations called to his attention and to note his observations and amendments in the margins. The *procureur* was supposed to introduce the sovereign's envoys and representatives of other courts to his own bench. He was also responsible for submitting the king's orders sent in the form of, say, a *lettre de cachet*. It was his task to request an audience with the king on behalf of his sovereign or lower court and to accompany the deputation. When ordered to do so by his court, he was supposed to go to the king to receive his orders and report to the court on his visit and on the results of any investigations he was assigned to undertake. He was supposed to ensure that laws and regulations were enforced and see to it that judges punished all infractions and thereby secured law and order by judicial means. He was responsible also for the proper administration and conservation of crown property. He was charged with petitioning for nullification of alienations of the royal domain and with punishing officers and administrators of the domain who were guilty of misrepresentation. It was his responsibility to exercise tutelage and protection over various moral or civil persons, including the Church, civil or religious communities, prisons, hospitals, the poor, minors, and absentees.[3]

The *procureur du roi* was assisted by one or more *avocats du roi*.

The *procureurs généraux* performed other duties as needed beyond their ordinary duties. The *procureur général* of the Paris *parlement*, for example, was "*trésorier garde des Chartes et Papiers de la Couronne*." He was also overseer of the *prévôté de Paris* whenever the seat was vacant and until a permanent overseer was appointed by the king. The *procureur général* performed this duty for some period of time after 19 May 1721, and again after 21 December 1752. The *procureur du roi* at the Châtelet sent orders from the *procureur général* to the syndic of the community of notaries and to the *greffiers* of the Châtelet instructing them to head all acts and judgments issued within the Châtelet's jurisdiction with the name of the *procureur général* as long as the post remained unfilled.

The *procureur général* always submitted written briefs and final arguments. Petitions, requisitions, and briefs bore his signature. Briefs had to be agreed upon and issued in common by the *procureur du roi* and *avocat du roi* or the *procureur général* and *avocats généraux*. In theory, the *avocats du roi* were the spokesman for the king and were bound to support the brief of the *procureur général*. "The *procureur du roi* wields the pen, and the *avocats du roi* hold the floor." There were exceptions to this rule. When the Grand-Chambre assumed jurisdiction in civil or administrative cases, the *procureur du roi* prepared a brief, submitted it, and sometimes made his own oral argument. When the *procureur général* was ordered by the chancellor or keeper of the seals to take a certain position in a case, he was bound to comply. But the *avocats généraux* remained free to form their own opinions and could give oral arguments at variance with the written brief. "The pen is a slave but speech is free." The *procureur du roi* and *avocats du roi* held daily conferences with the *avocats* for the parties. These conferences often led to agreement among the *avocats* and hence among the parties, obviating the need to continue the trial. If the *avocats du roi* were unable to discharge their duties, the court might commission an *avocat* to take their place. In Paris, the *procureur général* could appoint one of his deputies to replace an *avocat général*.

The *procureur du roi* was assisted by deputies, even within the court to which he was attached. The *procureur général* personally discharged his duties in the Grand-Chambre or the Assembly of Chambers. In Paris he left it up to his twelve deputies to represent him in the Chambres des Enquêtes, the Chambre des Requêtes, and the Tournelle criminelle, where the deputies filed briefs and final arguments in his name. The *procureurs du roi* in the lower courts were regarded as deputies of the *procureur général*. He submitted the names of prospective appointees to the chancellor or keeper of the seals, who issued the *lettres de provision* to deputies. The *procureur général* sent the texts of registered laws to his deputies. He kept up an unending correspondence with them, gave them advice, and supervised their work.

The *procureur général* had his offices in a rented house. The *procureur général* in Paris had space not only for his own offices but also for his first secretary, his library, and his archives. He worked in his offices from eight in the morning until noon. During the morning he held a "prosecutor's hearing" with his three *avocats généraux* and disposed of conflicts among the various chambers of *parlement* and declinatory pleas challenging the competence of the court. The *procureur général* also assigned cases to the twelve deputy *procureurs*, who then prepared briefs in his name. The *procureur général* hired and paid his own staff. At the end of the eighteenth century this consisted of a first and second secretary, three *commis*, and additional *commis* when there was pressing work to be done. A document that had to be sent to all the lower courts could require 451 copies. An office boy tended the fire, fetched wood, and provided light, paper, ink, and quills. In 1775 Guillaume-François-Louis Joly de Fleury needed 16,000 livres to pay his staff and 4,000 livres to pay the rent and other expenses. Until 1774 he had received 6,000 livres for office expenses, raised in that year to 9,000 livres. The rest came out of his emoluments, which he estimated at 52,400 livres per year including salary, bonuses, and royal pension. Until 12 August 1787, he was exempt from postage fees on letters and packages sent under his seal.

The *procureur général* exchanged voluminous correspondence not only with his deputies in the lower courts but also with many other individuals and agencies, including bishops, archbishops, curates, churchwardens, chapters, hospitals, notaries, *procureurs*, *bailliages*, *sénéchaussées*, lower courts, *maréchaussées*, consular courts, and prison wardens. He did this because he was their protector and adviser, marvelously well informed by the count-less letters he received and the investigations he had carried out. He gave interpretations of edicts and regulations and advice on the wisdom of en-forcing them at any particular time. He counseled moderation when officials showed excessive zeal. He avoided scandal and encouraged diligence and courage.

For example, in 1760, the *procureur du roi* at Mâcon consulted the *procureur général* concerning the wisdom of enforcing the declaration of 24 January 1713, forbidding the manufacture of spirits from grains, lees, beers, and grape marc. The *procureur général* reviewed the text of the declaration and then inquired of the celebrated apothecary and chemist Rouelle, a mem-ber of the Royal Academies of Science of Paris and Stockholm, as to the advantages and disadvantages of spirits in regard to both health and com-merce. Rouelle replied that spirits could be manufactured from grape marc so as not to be noxious to health, and he explained how this was to be done. The *procureur général*, Guillaume-François-Louis Joly de Fleury, then re-plied to the *procureur du roi* at Mâcon on 14 August telling him not to enforce in all its rigor the declaration of 24 January 1713.

The main duty of the *procureur général* was to call the court's attention to certain points by means of briefs and final arguments. In final argument, the *procureur général* gave a detailed account of the needs to which he thought the court ought to respond and of the reasons for his intervention, e.g., in order to respond to any act threatening the maintenance of law and order. The court was supposed to respond by issuing a decree, "Making law upon requisition of the *procureur général*." In principle the court always complied with the wishes of the *procureur général* in the registration of royal acts, approval of regulations, investigations of future judicial officeholders, oaths of judges and consuls, maintenance of law and order, and procedural questions.

The *procureur général* filed a written brief stating his opinion, based on the evidence brought forward in the case under examination and his advice as to the enforcement of the law. Whenever the public interest was involved, the *procureur général* asked to see the documents concerning the case in question. He therefore filed briefs concerning the registration of letters pat-ent, seditious works, the award of contracts, the erection of a parish, trans-actions involving Church property, transfer of jurisdiction over cases to the king's Council, etc. The court was not bound to accept the arguments of the *procureur général*.

The *procureur général* could file both a brief and a final argument in the same case. On 11 December 1788, he submitted a brief reserving judgment on the question of the ownership of a house claimed by the Carmelites of Reims. In his final argument he asked for the appointment of *commissaires* to conduct a more thorough investigation into the facts.

In civil matters the *procureur du roi* employed formulas that had legal effect, such as, "On the king's behalf I do not object to hearing the intervention of this party," or "On the king's behalf I wish to state that I persist in the argument made by me in the brief."

There was a series of such formulas to enable the *procureur général* to express a position ranging from complete agreement to hesitant acceptance to categorical rejection. In political and legal matters, for example, his complete agreement with the king's wishes was expressed by the word "*requiert*." On 11 January 1612, the *procureur général* argued in favor of the registration of the letters patent of 16 December 1611, prohibiting the carrying of firearms. He expressed his hesitancy, however, by using the word "consent" rather than "require." On the same day the *procureur général* "consented" to the authentication of the letters patent of 23 December 1611, ordering the court to register the treaty signed on 12 December 1610 by the king's deputies and the ambassador of the archdukes of Flanders for the purpose of renewing the neutrality pact between the duchy of Burgundy, the *vicomté* of Auxonne, and the *pays* of Bassigny together with their dependencies on one side and the "franche-comté" of Burgundy, the city of Besançon, and their dependencies on the other side. When the *procureur du roi* deemed royal letters to be contrary to the public interest, he "opposed" their registration. On 12 March 1612, for example, the *procureur général* "opposed" authentication of the letters patent of 28 May 1610, concerning the widening of the highways and crossroads in the Ile-de-France by two rods on either side.[4]

During the latter part of the eighteenth century the *procureur général* increasingly confined himself to work in the courts and took less and less interest in general administrative matters. The separation of justice from administration, which was completed by the Constituent Assembly, had already begun to be realized in day-to-day behavior.

During times of crisis the king's men manifested their esprit de corps and their solidarity in opposition to the king. This happened during the Fronde and again at the time of the Maupeou and Lamoignon reforms. Even though the *avocats* and *procureurs* were representatives of the sovereign legislator and judge and indispensable to the operation of the courts, they were not treated as the equals of the other magistrates. When *parlement* was received as a body for an audience with the king, the *procureur général* and *avocats généraux* entered last and were not introduced to the king by name. Instead, the words spoken were merely, "Sire, these are your men." When Guillaume-François-Louis Joly de Fleury died, the *parlement* of Paris did not come to a halt or suspend even a single session. No mention of his death appears in its minutes, and no speech was made to welcome his successor. Many magistrates attended his funeral, but as individuals rather than as official representatives. By contrast, when the *premier président* d'Ormesson died on 26 January 1789, the *président à mortier* Bochart de Saron and the eighteen councillors present immediately suspended the first hearing of the court on the following day in his honor. Hearings did not resume until the 29th, and the entire *corps* went to anoint d'Ormesson's body with holy water.

Judgments

Only the sovereign courts could issue decrees (*arrêts*), "fixed and unalterable judgments of a sovereign power."[5] The lower courts only handed down *sentences*, judgments subject to appeal. A sovereign court could issue an *interlocution*, or provisional judgment, before handing down a final decree. Any company could issue an *arrêté*, or "resolution taken by a company on the basis of some deliberation" and not a definitive judgment.

There were several kinds of decrees, depending on the nature of the decision: general decrees, decrees of regulation, decrees "issued in red gown" establishing jurisprudence or doctrine, prohibitory decrees to prevent hasty execution, *arrêts d'appointement* in cases examined in writing, preliminary decrees, and final decrees rendering judgment on the main issue of a case.

In Paris and Dijon ten judges, including a *président*, were required to issue a decree. At Grenoble and in all the other *parlements* as well as almost all the sovereign courts, seven judges were required. The *parlement* of Bordeaux used so-called presidential decrees, which were issued by *présidents* alone. These were extensive dissertations on the points at issue in which the court justified its decisions by reference to legal principles. The presidential decrees were therefore an exception to the rule that judgments were usually rendered without giving the grounds on which they were based.

Registration Procedures

Registration and Remonstrances

Ordinances, edicts, royal declarations, and letters patent of all sorts were submitted by the *procureur général* to the *premier président*. The *premier président* was then obliged to assemble all the chambers of *parlement* for the purpose of authentication. The general assembly was often preceded by deliberations held by the *premier président* in conjunction with the *présidents à mortier*, some of the senior councillors and *présidents*, and the king's men. In Paris during the reign of Henri IV, the *premier président* frequently held a preliminary meeting of the "Three Chambers," the Grand-Chambre, the Tournelle, and the Chambre de l'Edit, which tended to usurp the political role of *parlement*. If registration promised to be difficult, the *premier président* would go with certain *présidents à mortier* to remonstrate with the king's Council, with individual Council members, with the prime minister or other ministers, the chancellor, *surintendant*, or secretaries of state and try to have the offending edicts withdrawn or amended.

If the king persisted, the assembly of all the chambers had to be convoked. For if the king attempted to use the "*procédure de la déclaration*" to raise taxes, with publication in the Audience de France at the Chancellery, he would have to cope with prohibitory decrees from the courts and with the *procédure d'opposition.*[6]

Registration worked this way. Once the edict was sent to the *procureur général*, he called a meeting of the *avocats généraux* and together the king's men then prepared a brief in the matter. The *premier président* then called an assembly of the chambers. In this assembly the first *avocat général* summarized the edict together with the brief. The king's men then withdrew. The member of the Grand-Chambre who acted as *rapporteur* for the court in governmental matters or, if he was unavailable, a magistrate designated by the *premier président* then read the edict and the brief. If there were no problems, as was the case nine times out of ten, the *premier président* took the votes in order of seniority, starting with the *présidents à mortier*, followed by the members of the Grand-Chambre, the Chambre des Enquêtes, and the Chambre des Requêtes. The *premier président* then indicated the results, and the *greffier* read the registration decree. This decree sometimes included amendments, which the king generally accepted.

If there were problems, however, the most senior *président à mortier* would ask the *rapporteur* to study the edict and prepare a report. The *rapporteur* would then ask for *commissaires* to be chosen in each chamber of *parlement* to help him examine the matter. The *premier président* and the *présidents à mortier* were *commissaires ex officio*. The *premier président* appointed the *commissaires* from the Grand-Chambre. He persistently attempted to arrogate the right to appoint the *commissaires* from the Enquêtes and Requêtes as well. Except for a few occasions, however, these chambers succeeded in retaining the right to elect their own *commissaires*, usually three per chamber. The general assembly then met again to consider the opinion of the *commissaires*, presented by the *rapporteur*. This done, the *premier président* counted the votes. He first asked for the opinion of the *rapporteur*, then of the *présidents à mortier*, the *commissaires nés*, the *commissaires* from the Grand-Chambre, and, finally, of the *commissaires* from each of the seven Chambres des Enquêtes and Chambres des Requêtes in their numerical order. He then canvassed the other members of the Grand-Chambre and the Chambres des Enquêtes and Chambres des Requêtes, as above. Most of the members simply stated that they accepted one of the previously stated opinions. Each time a new opinion was put forward, the *greffier* recorded it. On 3 December 1751, seventeen different opinions were heard. Sixty-eight votes went to the one with the most support. The rest claimed fewer than twenty votes apiece. Several got only one vote. The various opinions had to be boiled down to two. Those who had supported opinions garnering the fewest votes chose one of the others and gave up their own. Little by little unpopular opinions were eliminated and the candidates narrowed down. When the choice came down to three candidates, the supporters of the one with the least votes chose between the other two, one of which emerged the winner. This long winnowing process was conducted without discussion, because each member of the court was entitled to offer his opinion only once. Magistrates could not augument or amend their opinions as they heard others, nor could they propose amendments to opinions stated by their colleagues.

The general assembly might decide to make remonstrances to the king. Making remonstrances was one of the duties of the *corps* of officeholders whose members bore the title of "councillors to the king," such as the companies connected with the *bailliages*, *sénéchaussées*, and *présidiaux*, the companies of the *trésoriers de France et généraux des Finances*, and so on. This duty and power had been granted to the courts by the royal declaration of 1563, by article 1 of the Moulins ordinance of February 1565, and by the Blois ordinance of May 1579. But constant repetition of the same remonstrances had paralyzed the king's legislative power and led to attempts to impose limits with the edict of 1641 and article 1 of the civil ordinance of April 1667, which was supplemented by letters patent of 24 February 1673. The courts showed scant respect for the edict of 1641, which was nullified by the Fronde. They were forced to yield to the regulations of 1667–73. But the power to remonstrate prior to registration was restored by the declaration of 15 September 1715.

Once the assembly of chambers decided on a remonstrance, a committee of members of *parlement* determined what points were to be included. The text was then usually drawn up by the *premier président*. Occasionally there might be another writer. The remonstrances of April 1753 were drawn up by *commissaires*, because the *premier président*, the senior Maupeou, removed himself from responsibility. It was customary for the writer to take account of all the opinions expressed. The art was to conceal the incoherency and contradictions. During the eighteenth century remonstrances were ostensibly to be prepared within a week after the king's men submitted their brief. In fact the king sometimes ordered the *premier président* to have them ready the next day. When this happened, the committee was dispensed with, and the *premier président* wrote out the remonstrance along the lines set by the discussion. This document was then hastily read to the company, which approved it without debate. In most cases the *premier président* took his time. In order to avoid a resumption of debate, he had the document read to *parlement* on the day before the day set by the king for its delivery. Sometimes he even delayed until the morning of the delivery date and had the remonstrances read to *parlement* just before he climbed into his carriage to go to the king.

In principle, remonstrances were presented to the king and members of the Conseil d'Etat by the *premier président*, who headed a delegation of members of *parlement*. In exceptional cases remonstrances might also be presented by the king's men. Prior to June 1652, for example, at the time of Louis XIV's final operations against the rebel princes and their Spanish allies, the *parlement* of Paris asked that the royal troops be removed from the city. Its request was not granted. It then issued a decree ordering that remonstrances be drawn up, and this was done by the *procureur général*,

Nicolas Fouquet, because the *premier président*, Mathieu Molé, was also the keeper of the seals and at the king's side. *Parlement* dispatched the king's men to Saint-Germain-en-Laye where Louis XIV was staying to ask specifically that the troops be removed to a distance of at least ten leagues from Paris. Nicolas Fouquet and the *avocat général*, Bignon, left on Friday and arrived late in the evening. They saw Mathieu Molé at eleven o'clock at night on his way home after a meeting of the Council and informed him of the *parlement*'s request. The next day, Saturday, they were granted an audience between three and four o'clock in the afternoon. From the chambers of sieur Duplessis-Guénégaud, secretary of state, they were taken to the king's offices by sieur Sainctot, *maître des cérémonies*, and introduced by Duplessis. They found the king seated in the midst of his Council. At his side were the queen mother, Anne of Austria, the king's brother the duc d'Anjou (later duc d'Orléans), the keeper of the seals, Prince Thomas, the duc de Bouillon, Villeroy, du Plessis-Parslin, Servien, *surintendant* La Vieuville, and four secretaries of state, Michel Le Tellier, Loménie de Brienne, Duplessis-Guénégaud, and Phélypeaux de La Vrillière. They laid out *parlement*'s request. The king answered, as was customary, that the keeper of the seals would make his wishes known. Mathieu Molé explained that first the maréchal de l'Hospital and the duc d'Orléans would have to be consulted. The king's men remained at Saint-Germain through Saturday and Sunday. "We were visited by a great many persons of quality and by most of those we have named as composing the king's Council, who wished to offer their respects and civilities to *parlement* in our persons." On Sunday the king's men dined with the keeper of the seals. Then, at three in the afternoon, they met with representatives of the king's Council: Molé, Bouillon, Villeroy, Le Tellier, and Duplessis-Guénégaud, assisted by the maréchal de l'Hospital and the comte de Béthune who had been sent by the duc d'Orléans. On Tuesday the king's men had their last audience after the king's dinner at around three o'clock. In the king's offices, the king, surrounded by his Council, answered them in writing. He would remove his troops if the prince de Condé and the duc d'Orléans would do the same. He then gave them leave to return to *parlement*.[7]

If, after hearing the remonstrances of *parlement*, the king persisted and sent a *jussion* or order to register the edict immediately in its present form and terms, *parlement* might carry out the registration using the formula, "On the express orders of the king." This was a disavowal of responsibility on the company's behalf. Such a registration did not preclude later amendments.

Lit de Justice

On the other hand, *parlement* might persist in refusing to register an edict in the face of repeated *jussions*. The king would then decide to hold a *lit de justice*.

In that event, the king would go to *parlement*. Notified in advance, the members of *parlement* would be dressed in red gowns with scarlet hoods. The officers of the king's bodyguard would take command of the palace gates. Normally, the chancellor or keeper of the seals, as the chief judicial officer, would also come to *parlement* to await the king in the company of a number of *conseillers d'Etat* and *maîtres des requêtes*. Or he might go with these *robins* to accompany the king. The king arrived flanked by the *premier gentilhomme de la Chambre* and the captain of the bodyguard designated for the post, followed by the other captains of the bodyguard. He then took his seat on the throne in the corner of the Grand-Chambre. On his right sat the princes of the blood and dukes-and-peers, and on his left the cardinals, ecclesiastical peers, and marshals of France. The chancellor or keeper of the seals sat at his feet. Everyone took his habitual place. The king removed his hat and then replaced it, after which he announced that, according to custom, the chancellor would state his wishes. The chancellor then climbed up to the royal seat, knelt on one knee, asked the king's permission to speak, and returned to his place. He then donned his hat and explained the situation and the king's intentions and wishes. At this point, the *premier président* and each of the *présidents* and councillors knelt on one knee. The chancellor had them rise by order of the king. With all standing and uncovered, the *premier président* replied in the name of *parlement*. The chancellor then had the doors opened and ordered the *greffier en chef* to read the edicts at issue. He then ordered the king's men to state their conclusions on behalf of the king's service. With the king's men kneeling, the first *avocat général* began to say a few words, at which point the chancellor had them all rise. The *avocat général* then went on with his speech, stating that the king's men required execution and publication of the edicts. The chancellor again climbed to the king's side, received his orders while kneeling, and then heard the opinions of the princes of the blood and the lay peers seated on the high benches at the king's right. The chancellor then passed in front of the king, did a deep bow, and went to the left to receive the opinion of the ecclesiastical peers and marshals of France. He then descended to the *parquet* and canvassed the *présidents*, members of the Grand-Chambre, and councillors in the Enquêtes and Requêtes. This done, he climbed back up to the king and reported to him on the opinion of the court. He then resumed his own place and, with his hat on, uttered a royal declaration concerning each edict or declaration:

> The king, sitting in his *lit de justice*, has ordered and does order that the declaration that has just been read shall be registered in the registry of his *parlement*, and that on the fold of said declaration it shall be noted that it has been read and registration ordered upon requisition of the *procureur général* so that it may be executed in its form and content, and authentic copies sent to the *bailliages* and *sénéchaussées* of the jurisdiction, there to be read, published, and registered; the deputies of the *pro-*

cureur général are hereby ordered to aid in this and to certify to the court that it has been done within the month.[8]

The king's wishes could be at variance with the wishes of the court and the majority of votes cast in a *lit de justice*, which duplicated the Curia Regis of old. According to royalist theory, however, this fact did no violence to the consciences of members of *parlement*, because, so the theory went, *parlement* does not exist without the king. According to the theory of the mystical body of the monarchy, moreover, the king is the head and his subjects the limbs of the mystical body of which the kingdom is composed. It was the job of the head to decide on what was good for the body as a whole and to speak its innermost wishes, which could well differ from its expressed wishes. In contrast, the *parlement* claimed to be the descendant of the General Assembly, or *Parlamentum*, of the Frankish nation and the true council of the king and constantly demanded the right to deliberate and to vote freely in the king's absence.

The king might send a prince of the blood accompanied by the governor of the province or a high crown officer to deliver his orders to proceed with registration.

Once the king's wishes had been unequivocally expressed, everyone had to accede to them. At times of crisis, however, *parlement* often assembled after a *lit de justice* to record its protest and declared that the enforced registration was null and void because it violated the customary constitution of the state. This became commonplace during the second half of the eighteenth century. The king and his Council viewed this procedure on the part of *parlement* as itself a violation of the kingdom's customary constitution, however.

Civil and Criminal Procedures

In the language of the courts, civil procedures, Furetière tells us, were the procedures regularly used in cases involving commerce and pecuniary interest, meaning not only trade in commodities and money but also relations between families and individuals such as engagements, kinships, and bequests as well as a whole range of conventions and contracts whose nature was such as to alter a person's status or fortune. A crime was an action committed in violation of the law, either civil or natural. State crimes included murder, theft, and fraud and deserved to be punished with loss of life or liberty. Common offenses included fornication and the breaking of a promise or vow. A criminal case might be treated as a civil case (*civilisée*) if it was of minor importance. In a case involving an exchange of insults between persons of low status, for example, the judge could choose not to announce the indictment but rather to subpoena the accused and determine the appropriate reparations on the basis of the story he told on the witness stand. A civil case could become a criminal case if one party accused the other of fraud in the documents submitted. Furetière speaks of "regular procedures for civil trials." In criminal cases the law distinguished between regular and extraordinary procedures. Under the regular procedure the trial was public, the accused had the right to avail himself of the advice of a lawyer, who offered "counsel" both to the accused and to the judge, and torture was not used. "Extraordinary procedure" meant a secret trial in which the accused did not have the benefit of counsel and in which torture could be used to obtain a confession if there were strong indications of guilt.

In all the sovereign courts and in many lower courts, magistrates were bound to enforce a number of different laws and *coutumes*. A magistrate in the Bordeaux *parlement*, for example, had to enforce not only the written law, which was not Roman law pure and simple, but also the modifications of that law owing to local *coutumes* and increasingly to the *coutumes* of localities stretching all the way from Provence to Guyenne: Bordeaux, Bayonne, Dax, Saintes, Saint-Jean-d'Angely, and Saint-Sever; there were also the *Usances* of Marsan, Cursan, Gabardan, and other regions. The magistrates of the sovereign court of Lorraine and Barrois, which became the *parlement* of Nancy, had to enforce not only canon law but also fifteen codes of law, since 1,404 localities out of 1,951 were subject to the "*coutume du duché*," 348 to the *coutume de Saint-Michel*, 34 to the *coutume du Bassigny*, 34 to written law, 20 to both written law and *usages*, and 1 to *usages*.

Proof

Criminal cases raised the problem of proof of guilt. The problem of proof also came up in civil cases, since the plaintiff had to prove that the facts he alleged were true and the judge had to distinguish between truth and falsehood in the contradictory allegations made by both parties and their counsel in regard to questions of fact.

The problem was to eliminate the danger that judges could err or be deceived. Magistrates in the seventeenth and eighteenth centuries were professionals who were no longer satisfied with supernatural or religious proofs by ordeal, the judgment of God, judicial duel, or oaths. Although they still had the accused swear an oath to tell the truth before interrogating him, this was a secondary consideration. Magistrates were not satisfied with intuitive proof through inner conviction according to their consciences, which was the standard of proof used by a jury but which the church fathers deemed arbitrary, a method that was a "respecter of persons" and therefore condemned by divine law. Magistrates accepted only a rational and legal proof. Belief in this mode of proof rested on belief in the reality of the external world outside human consciousness and on the possibility of arriving at the truth about this world by reasoning founded on data perceived either directly through the senses or indirectly through witnesses. Reasoning created conviction. Judges were thus following Aristotle and Saint Thomas Aquinas. In many cases it would have taken too long to reach the absolute truth, for the judge could not delay the disposition of a case indefinitely. In such cases he had to rely on probabilities.

Rational and legal proof resulted from the application of a rigid system of precise rules. The admissibility and authority of each kind of evidence were governed by a rigorous order of preference.

Notoriety was not proof but made proof unnecessary and carried conviction by itself. Carrying conviction equal to notoriety were confession in due legal form before a judge, *res adjudicata*, and legal presumption.

Next came "full proofs," which were proofs of which the judge was entirely convinced and which left him no choice in his judgment. An avowal or confession by the accused in a hearing or during interrogation was one such proof. The testimony of two trustworthy witnesses was another. The production of a notarized document or a recognized private deed was a third. The production of the books of a merchant kept in due form and supported by the merchant's oath and good reputation was a fourth.

Next came the "semiproofs," insufficient by themselves to form the basis of a judgment but sufficient to require further investigation and, in criminal cases, to submit the accused to torture. These included the deposition of a single witness, an irregular or extrajudicial confession by the accused given under a private seal or before a notary, similarity of handwriting, and so on.

Lastly, there were the imperfect or slight proofs, which were good only as a basis for further investigation, for the issuance of a warrant, or for the imposition of a bond. A "grave indication" slightly less credible than a semiproof was considered an imperfect proof. Two such indications constituted an *indice violent*, i.e., an indication of sufficient gravity to warrant torture. The conjunction of several "slight indices," such as an imperfect confession, the deposition of a witness concerning a fact merely related to the case in question, and so on, could be taken as equivalent to a "grave indication."

A proof deemed "full" in civil law was only a semiproof in criminal law. In a criminal case, a confession in court had to be backed up by the testimony of witnesses; witnesses had to be heard a second time to see if they maintained their testimony when confronted by the accused. Judgments that could not be appealed and capital sentences had to be supported by irrefutable proofs. Temporary measures, light sentences, and damage awards in civil cases required less substantial proof. Judges did, however, recognize fractions of proof, quarters and eighths, which could be added together to arrive at a full proof. On 3 May 1763, Voltaire wrote to Damilaville concerning *l'affaire Calas*: "I have learned one of the reasons for the judgment handed down in Toulouse, which will certainly dumbfound you: these Visigoths go by the maxim that four quarter-proofs and eight eighth-proofs make two full proofs, and they call hearsay testimony by the name of a quarter-proof or an eighth-proof."[9] No matter how refined the system, its application requires common sense.

Oral testimony had long been preferred to written depositions. Loisel repeated the old adage, "Witnesses before letters," in paragraph 763 of his *Institutes coutumières*. In the early seventeenth century, moreover, many contracts were still oral, in spite of the ordinances. Writing, it seemed, was dead testimony and as such inferior to the living testimony of men of faith. It seemed contrary to natural law to place one's trust in a piece of parchment, which was nothing but the skin of a dead animal, or in a scrap of paper, whereas it seemed quite natural and in keeping with the law, human and divine, to trust in the testimony of witnesses. Nevertheless, the use of written proofs made steady progress from the sixteenth century on. The adage, "Letters before witnesses" took on increasing importance.

An *acte authentique*, i.e., a document sealed by the public authorities, by a judicial official, or by a notary, constituted a full proof. The cogency of a notarized document came from the fact that the notary had ascertained the will of the parties through his own senses. Article 17 of the ordinance of April 1453 made it possible to attack a judgment through a criminal proceeding against "false inscription," however. Other notarized documents could be attacked in criminal proceedings by producing two witnesses. The criminal ordinance of 1670 and the ordinance on counterfeits of July 1737 extended the criminal proceedings against "false inscriptions" to all *actes authentiques*.

Private documents, notes of hand, and chirographs could be used in court. A note of hand (*cédule*) was a small piece of paper on which was written a promise, an obligation, an acknowledgment of debt, a order for payment, or a letter of exchange under private seal. A chirograph was a signed, un-sealed private note by which a debtor acknowledged his indebtedness. Since the chirograph was a private document, the creditor who held a note of this kind had no lien against the real property of the debtor and had a claim only on a share of his movable property.

Notes of hand and chirographs were only semiproofs and had to be sup-plemented by an adminicle, commencement of proof, or imperfect proof. If they were acknowledged by the signer before a judge and transformed into a sort of written avowal, however, they could be treated in the same way as *actes authentiques* and used as full proof. Article 92 of the ordinance of Villers-Cotterêts (1539) established a way of proceeding if the document was not spontaneously acknowledged. The signer was subpoenaed and had either to appear in person or be represented by a proxy specially accredited before the secular judge, where he must either acknowledge the note of hand or deny that it was his. If he failed to appear, the note of hand was considered to be avowed, thereby establishing a lien as of the day judgment was rendered.

In order to facilitate the use of written documents in the courts, article 111 of this same ordinance laid it down that all decrees, investigative reports, contracts, commissions, and other procedural documents be written in French, registered, and delivered to the parties.

Article 54 of the Moulins ordinance of 1566 tried to deal with the disadvantages associated with the testimony of witnesses and possible challenges to such testimony by providing that henceforth any agreement exceeding 100 livres in value should be accompanied by a contract between the notary and the witnesses and that this contract should in itself constitute sufficient proof, exclusive of any other witnesses and allegations. Only if the written document was lost would the evidence of witnesses be taken. Signed and sealed private agreements were usable as proof as before. The civil ordinance of 1687 (title XX, art. 2) gave preference to written documents over oral testimony even in cases involving sums of less than 100 livres.

The decree of *parlement* of 28 June 1599 made voluntary depositions subordinate to the preparation of a written document. Title XXX, article 3 of the ordinance of 1667 distinguished between the voluntary deposition, for which a written document was required, and the "necessary deposition," the proof of which could be administered by witnesses.

If the handwriting of a note of hand or chirograph was not challenged, the document constituted proof without an adminicle, just as a notarized document did. If the handwriting was challenged but confirmed by the prescribed verification procedure, the document was treated as a notarized document.

If a written document was invoked which had not been written expressly for the purpose of substantiating the contract in litigation but which lent probability to the agreement, further oral testimony was required during the first third of the seventeenth century. In 1630, however, a precedent was set allowing such a text to be admitted as a "commencement of proof by written document." Witnesses were used only to impugn the document. Title XX, article 3, of the ordinance of 1667 admitted the possibility of proof by witnesses, "when commencement of proof by written document has been made."

The declarations of 30 July 1730 and 29 September 1733 introduced a formality known as the "*bon pour*." All privately signed notes, promises, and receipts would have no effect if the body of the text had not been written by the same hand supposed to have signed the note or if it did not at least bear a mark of approval of the amount of money or quantity of foodstuff, merchandise, or other goods. The declaration of 1733 made an exception for documents essential to commerce and for agreements between men involved in a craft or trade or in the tilling of the soil. Little attention was paid to the Moulins ordinance in commercial trials.

When witnesses were heard, the value of their testimony had to be weighed. According to Roman and canon law, the judge had to take account of seven factors: the witness's social status, age, sex, discrimination (*discretio*), reputation, fortune (*fortuna*), and good faith.

Assessing the relative weights of statements made by the accused and by other witnesses took on vital importance in criminal trials. Lengthy experience in these matters from the thirteenth century on had made it possible to establish rules, which were ably summarized by Daniel Jousse, a councillor of the *présidial* in Orléans, in his *Nouveau commentaire sur l'ordon-*

nance criminelle du mois d'août 1670, which was published in 1753.[10] Judges were bound first to consider the "quality of the accused," "whether he was a common man or a respectable person by virtue of his rank and birth." "Those who have some rank that raises them above others should be interrogated with greater consideration and circumspection." "If the accused appears to be firm and intrepid . . . the judge must be severe." With a witness "who is timid and trembling . . . he should use gentle and ingratiating words." "If the accused is a man of spirit and learning, the judge should examine him very carefully, using cogent arguments drawn from the indictment itself." If he was a stubborn rogue, "the judge should wear him down by asking a great many questions, catching him up with his own answers, turning him this way and that, asking even about seemingly unimportant details of the crime that might help to make clear whether or not the accused is speaking in good faith." If the accused was a man who was "simple and rough . . . without dissimulation . . . the judge should question him in a straightforward manner about all the facts, one after another."

The judge "is appointed equally for the conviction and for the defense of the accused," who is presumed innocent until proven guilty. The judge was therefore bound to maintain his dignity, to avoid displays of unwarranted anger or familiarity, and to refrain from using the familiar form of the second-person pronoun with the accused. Judges were to ask questions in an assured manner and a firm tone of voice, but always with the same inflection and with moderation and prudence. They must not manifest either weakness or compassion.

The judge was supposed to begin his questioning of the accused not with questions about the substance of the crime or offense but rather with questions about the circumstances and the evidence, beginning with the most general matters, the most remote from the crime itself, and gradually working toward greater and greater detail. Where was the defendant on the day of the crime, and with whom? Had he any knowledge that such a crime had been committed, and if so, by whom? How had he come by that knowledge? Who else was present? Did he converse with anyone? Was it not a fact that, on the day the crime was committed, he was in the very place where it had occurred? And so on.

The judge should not ask his questions in accordance with the order of events and in the light of each item of evidence, because to do so would give the accused the opportunity to invent a false but consistent story. Judges were therefore advised to reverse the order of questions frequently, to go back to earlier parts of the story by asking fresh questions, and to follow a roundabout path. If the accused was lying, he would come to a point where he no longer remembered all his lies and fell into contradicting himself. He would assent to apparently insignificant facts which, when added up, might compel him to confess. It was therefore advisable for the judge to write out his questions in advance and arrange them in a cunning order.

Judges were not supposed to resort to subterfuges or to misleading questions. They were not to alarm the accused with false fears or threats, nor were they to try to gain his confidence by holding out false hopes or promises of immunity. They must refrain from attempting to compel his testimony with threats of mistreatment, solitary confinement, or confinement in irons. Judges were allowed to be clever but not to use misrepresentation or lies. They must use only just and legitimate means of interrogation and were warned "to be on their guard lest they become ministers of calumny and oppression" or fall into "unjust and tyrannical" methods.

The judges should allow the accused to say all he wished to day. If he began to confess his crime, the judge should allow him to speak and have everything he said written down. When he was done, the judge should resume the examination and press him further for as long as was necessary to obtain a full confession, "taking advantage of the favorable moment when the accused appeared to be ready to admit everything."

Judges were advised to question the accused about all the circumstances of the crime: the time, place, occasion, weapon used, manner in which the crime was committed, and accomplices. They should go into minute detail and bring out contradictions between the defendant's story and the facts, inferences from the evidence, or previous statements. Improbable statements should be pointed out. Judges should "keep their eyes fixed on the accused while interrogating and should observe every movement. If he trembles, cries, or sighs, the judge should ask why. If he wavers or hesitates, if he answers slowly and meditates over his responses, the judge should press him with repeated questions. All this should be noted in the report of the interrogation."

Once the accused had confessed, the same questions should not be repeated in subsequent interrogations, "because this would place the defendant in the position of denying in a second or third interrogation what he has already admitted in the first." If the accused did deny what he had previously admitted, the judge was instructed to ask him the grounds for his denial and to ask him "a large number of detailed questions" aimed at shedding light on the contradiction.

Judges were free to interrogate the defendant as often as they deemed useful. It was customary to conduct three interrogations. During the first interrogation, the judge questioned the accused about matters bearing a distant relation to the crime itself, about evidence based on the testimony of witnesses or the arrest warrant, and perhaps about two or three matters related to the main body of the case, to sound the defendant out. During the second interrogation the judge would proceed to detailed questioning about the heart of the matter, indicating the salient points of evidence and any contradictions that may have turned up after the first session. By the third interrogation the judge would have gathered all the evidence, testimony, documents, and other items and "combined them into a coherent case to present to the accused and thereby overcome his stubborn persistence in denying his guilt."

This procedure was based on the assumption that judges were benevolent, broad-minded, well balanced, discriminating, and blessed with common sense and plenty of time, not petty, sly, crafty, hasty, or quick to judge.

In criminal cases, in order to obtain full proof (the only proof really considered perfect, namely, confession), it was permissible in cases in which there was a strong presumption of guilt in a capital crime to submit the accused to what was called the *question préparatoire*, that is, torture intended to extract from him a confession of his crime. After sentencing and before execution, the condemned prisoner might be subjected to the *question préalable*, torture intended to force him to denounce his accomplices. Each of these forms of torture could be administered in two degrees of intensity: the *question ordinaire* and the *question extraordinaire*. The criminal ordinance of August 1670 expressly provided for the continuation of these tortures. The *question préparatoire* was to be used, according to title XIX, article 1, "if there is considerable and unshaken proof against the accused for a crime that deserves the death penalty," in which case "any judge may order that [the defendant] be submitted to torture if the proof is insufficient" to convict him. As for the *question préalable*, title XIX, article 3, provided that "the death sentence may order that the condemned prisoner be tortured before being put to death in order to make him reveal his accomplices."

Torture was administered in a so-called *chambre de la question*. In Toulouse this was known as the *chambre de la géhenne* and was located in the *Capitole*. Two magistrates were assigned by the Toulouse *parlement* to attend, and they were assisted by two *capitouls* (the name given to city magistrates in Toulouse), one of the king's men, a *greffier*, and two *sergents*. The *patient*, as the person undergoing torture was called, was made to swear on the Holy Gospel to tell the truth. If he persisted in denying his crime, the torturer entered and examined the *patient*'s mouth with his fingers to see if any magic "charms" had been hidden there as proof against pain. If all was well, the torture began.

In the Paris *parlement*, the *question ordinaire* was administered by forcing the *patient* to swallow four tankards of water of two and a half pints (Paris measure) each, a total of about nine liters. The *patient* was stretched out with his arms extended, his midsection raised by a trestle under his kidneys. The torturer opened his mouth with iron tongs and an assistant poured the water into a funnel inserted into the *patient*'s mouth. This caused him to swell up. He was then struck on the stomach, causing him to vomit blood and water. In the Toulouse *parlement*, the punishment used was strappado. The *patient* hung by his hands from an iron spike known as the *bouton de géhenne* attached to a long rope passing over a pulley. He was lifted off the ground and then drawn either by attaching a heavy weight to his feet or by attaching chains which were then pulled by the torturer. In Toulouse the water torture was reserved for the *question extraordinaire* and carried to such lengths that some victims died on the spot. Each *parlement* had its share of tortures and atrocities, which it is not necessary to describe or even to list.

During torture the magistrates delegated by *parlement* exhorted the condemned man to speak. If he persisted in his denials, the torture was renewed a second or third time. The reports document the victim's cries, tears, and supplications, mention the appearance of foam around the mouth, frenzy in the eyes, tongues hanging out of mouths, and pleas on the part of victims to be allowed to die. In the end the victim might pass out for anywhere from one hour to four hours. The attending physician then did his utmost to revive the *patient* so that he could sign the report of his torture. A report from Rouen dated 28 September 1788 indicates that the *patient* was unable to sign "inasmuch as his fingers were crushed" by the *grésillons*, or clamps made of pieces of wood or iron place between the fingers and then squeezed by ropes.[11] Daniel Jousse urges judges to continue their work "coolly" in these circumstances.[12] After torture the *patient* was dumped onto a mattress in front of a fire to rest and revive his exhausted body. His signature on the report was necessary if it were to have effect.

It was customary not to renew the *question* once the accused had been unbound from the instrument of torture and not to condemn him to the *chambre de la question* a second time for the same piece of evidence.

Many magistrates and other professionals continued to have confidence in torture in the eighteenth century. Daniel Jousse indicates that the *question préparatoire* is just and equitable and the *question préalable* a "very useful thing, yielding much good for civil society."[13] The drawbacks were evident, however. The procedure was inhuman. It led to errors: sturdy, hardened men admitted nothing and could not be convicted of any crime, even if they really were guilty, while weaker and less robust defendants admitted whatever the judge wanted them to, even if they were innocent. The "Philosophes" launched a movement of protest against torture. Their efforts were aided in the second half of the eighteenth century by a deluge of judicial errors: the notorious *affaire Calas* at Toulouse, the La Ferrière case at Mantes, the Langlade, Lebrun, Montbailli, Martin, and Cahuzac affairs in various cities around the country, the case of the Fourré family (1760–65) at Rouen, which was also the site of the condemnation of the serving woman Victoire Salmon for the poisoning of her master in 1782, and, last but not least, the Verdure case. The Verdure family was finally saved after ten years in the courts (1780–90). The Salmon girl was declared innocent by a decree of 23 May 1786. Magistrates in the Paris *parlement* began to prescribe torture more sparingly. The *procureurs généraux* in the reign of Louis XVI, the Joly de Fleury, never asked for the administration of the *question préparatoire* after 1774. After that date it was used in the Paris *parlement* only three times in 1774, once in 1777, and three times in 1778. Louis XVI abolished the *question préparatoire* on 24 August 1780. His declaration of 1 May 1788 was intended to do away with the *question préalable*. On 8 May he forced *parlement* to accept it in a *lit de justice*.

Civil Procedure

We cannot hope to do more than give a brief sketch of the broad outlines of a civil trial in a region using customary law, our purpose being merely to indicate the spirit of the proceedings. Oral proceedings had been in use since the ordinance of 1273, and later written proceedings were also used.

From the outset of a case, the *procureurs* and *avocats* kept written records, of course. But these were used mainly by the attorneys themselves and by their clients. At first, judges refused to give official recognition to any facts other than those developed in oral arguments and during hearings. Only in petitory suits involving a question of property could the defendant obtain a written copy of the plaintiff's suit before responding to its substance. All other arguments had to be oral, however.

Civil suits were initiated by a petition filed by the plaintiff with a competent judge. A date was then assigned for the plaintiff to appear before the judge. He would appear at the hearing with his counsel or advocate and state his complaint. The advocate would then argue the case. The judges would then issue a subpoena summoning the defendant to court.

The summoned defendant would appear with his counsel and be officially apprised of the suit against him. He would then ask for a continuance in order to obtain his own *procureur*. The *procureurs* for both parties were made known to the *greffe des présentations* where there was one. In subsequent hearings the defendant could make declinatory and dilatory pleas. A declinatory plea was made when the defendant felt he had been haled before a judge lacking competence to hear the case. A dilatory plea was filed to obtain a postponement of proceedings. The defendant could challenge judges on the grounds that they were relatives or allies of the plaintiff or related or allied among themselves, up to the fourth degree in either the direct line (father and son, grandfather and grandson, etc., for the great-grandson or great-great-grandson) or the collateral line (two brothers, uncle and nephew, cousins-german, second cousins or cousins once removed). The defendant could attack the form of the action and attempt to have it dismissed. The judges heard all the motions and arguments, generally in a series of hearings, and decided on all these points.

Once all the defendant's complaints had been disposed of, the substance of the action could be heard. The defendant would orally lay out his defense, contradict the plaintiff's allegations of fact, and challenge him on points of law. The judges would listen to the arguments and, if they felt the facts warranted, could issue their judgment at the conclusion of the hearing.

If the judges found the case to be a complicated one, however, they could issue a judgment known as the *appointement*, which defined the limits of each party's case. Their qualities and arguments would then be written down. The parties thereafter had to make their case on the basis of these arguments.

The *appointement* fixed the matters in dispute, and no declinatory plea or evocation was allowed thereafter. The judges could pronounce judgment only on what was contained in the *appointement*. An *appointement à mettre* was a judgment calling for the submission of further written arguments by both parties. In simple cases this might be enough for judgment to be handed down. In more complicated cases the judges might issue an *appointement en droit* asking the parties to "give their reasons in the form of memoranda," which might be either simple written arguments or written arguments together with challenges to the argument of the other side to be submitted weekly over a certain period of time. The *appointement au conseil* was issued either to allow the parties an interval to polish and correct their arguments before resubmitting the case to the council or to allow the appellant who had made verbal appeal to draft a written argument stating his reasons and grounds for appeal.

After the issuance of an *appointement*, the parties listed facts and arguments in detail in a written document. This did not yet constitute the beginning of the written proceedings in the narrow sense, however. The only purpose of using written documents at this stage was to pin down precisely the words that had been spoken in the hearings. This allowed the advocates to polish their arguments and to make their points more clearly and precisely. But they were not allowed to insert points not made in oral argument. Accordingly, there was a procedure known as "checking the articles," which had fallen into disuse in the lower courts but which persisted in the sovereign courts until the ordinance of 1667. This was a procedure carried on in the presence of the judges who had heard oral arguments in a case, in which each advocate checked to see that his adversary's articles matched his oral arguments. The Paris *parlement* did not allow replies or rejoinders. But the Châtelet of Paris and the other lower courts in the jurisdiction did allow up to four exchanges of this sort.

After written documents had been submitted, the judges could hand down a decision if they felt they had sufficient information. They could either deliberate immediately after the hearing while the documents were still on the table or they could deliberate on another day in the council chamber, if need be after hearing a commentator report on the case but without examining new documents or hearing further petitions.

If the judges remained in doubt as to the facts or grounds of the case, however, they could issue an *appointement en faits contraires* to the two parties. It was only then that the investigative procedure, the written proceedings in the narrow sense, actually began. The advocates would then draft their clients' claims, followed by articles containing the facts that the clients intended to prove with the aid of witnesses. After this, the witnesses would be heard by the judge, assisted by a scribe who recorded the questions and answers. Then the *juge rapporteur* would report on the investigation to the other judges, who would deliberate and issue their judgment in the case. In actuality, the proceedings began anew in writing.

Oral proceedings persisted because oral argument was the quickest and cheapest way to dispose of a case, and oral proceedings allowed counsel the greatest scope to assist and protect their clients. Thus oral proceedings were preferred when the nature of the case allowed. But if we look at daily practice in the courts, we find that cases disposed of after the first few hearings by oral argument were not always the most numerous, nor were they the most important. The problem was that oral proceedings tied up an entire chamber in hearing arguments in a single case. Only a very few cases could be heard each day. Proceedings tended to drag on at great length. It was difficult to schedule a hearing, and public hearings tended to be lengthy owing to the need to hear the arguments of the advocates. Parties could obtain long postponements, and their advocates constantly had to recall what had already been said. Postponement after postponement meant that years might elapse before written proceedings could begin. And in many cases written proceedings were indeed necessary. This only meant that all the arguments had to be recast in writing, however. Thus there was much procedural duplication. It would have been wiser to begin with written proceedings immediately. A single statement of the case would then have sufficed. A single judge could have conducted the investigation and reported on the results to the council. Oral arguments could have been eliminated, the advocates could have submitted only written documents, and the parties could have dictated statements to the notary assisting the judge.

In view of all these drawbacks of oral proceedings, magistrates and lawyers naturally tended to avoid them as much as possible. Before 1667 one way of doing this was known as "investigation at the bar." Upon request of one of the *procureurs*, the chamber would commission a councillor to investigate the case "at the bar." The *procureurs* would then be responsible for making arguments in the case before this councillor. Once the defense had been filed, the plaintiff immediately offered the defendant an *appointement en droit*. If, after five notifications, the defendant had not responded, the councillor commissioned to hear arguments in the case would sign the judgment. Many hearings were thus rendered unnecessary.

Another way of avoiding oral proceedings was for the *procureurs* representing the two parties to agree between themselves to proceed to the *appointement en droit* and have it registered with the court clerk without even being heard by a councillor at the bar.

At times the courts were so crowded that judges were forced to resort to what was known as an *appointement général* at the end of the session. This meant that all cases remaining to be pleaded, meaning a majority of all cases, were *ipso jure* assigned to the council according to their place on the calendar, and written arguments were to be filed with the council.

Thus magistrates tended to accord precedence to written argument over oral argument. But when the civil ordinance of 1667 was drawn up, Pussort, Colbert's uncle, reestablished oral proceedings in all their pristine purity against the advice of the *premier président*, Lamoignon. Investigations at the bar were eliminated (title XI, art. 11). *Appointements à mettre, en droit,* or *au conseil* were prohibited unless announced publicly by the judge during the hearing, thus eliminating private agreements between *procureurs.* Article 17 defined "summary cases" that had to be pleaded without the assistance of an advocate or *procureur* and had to be judged in open hearing after a required interval had elapsed and "on the basis of the act of coming to plead alone, without other procedure or formality." This rule applied to all the lower courts except the *présidiaux,* but not to the sovereign courts. If the facts were disputed and proof by witnesses was allowed, the witnesses could be heard at the next session of the court. If the dispute could not be settled on the spot, the documents were left on the table for immediate deliberation, and judgment was handed down in the following session of the court, without *épices* or *vacations.* Summary cases were defined as purely personal cases involving values of up to 200 livres and falling within the competence of the lower courts, including police matters, payments, rents, salaries, affixing and removal of seals, compilation and closing out of inventories, oppositions to seizures and executions, etc.

At the same time a serious effort was made to speed up the preparation of preliminary documents and get down more quickly to the investigation proper. The ordinance eliminated replies, rejoinders, counterrejoinders, etc., as well as first and second additions and similar byways of written procedure (title XIV, art. 3). It abolished the practice of investigating the interpretation of a customary law or usage by interviewing what was known as a *turbe,* or group of ten witnesses (title XIII). On appeal, summary cases that were purely personal had to be judged as written cases by the sovereign courts. The *appointement en droit* or *appointement* ordering the parties to furnish written memoranda stating their grounds came to be almost the only ones in use. The ordinance in effect transformed the *appointement en faits contraires.* The documents that used to be produced as consequences of this *appointement* now preceded it. When one party wished to make use of the investigative procedure and proof by witnesses, it submitted a list of the points it wished to see investigated to the tribunal. Similarly, the opposing party responded in writing. The facts alleged by both sides were then discussed in a hearing, at the conclusion of which the judge either granted the request for an investigation or rejected it. If he granted the request, he issued an interlocutory judgment known as an *appointement à verifier* listing the points to be investigated.

The *appointement général* was retained.

The civil ordinance of 1667 and its supplements of August 1669 and 1673 remained in effect until the Revolution. Despite the efforts made to simplify and speed up procedure, the restoration of oral argument and the combined use of oral and written procedures meant that trials continued to be slow. In 1735 the abbé de Saint-Pierre repeated the same criticisms and made the same proposals for reform in his *Mémoire sur la manière de rendre les procès moins nombreux* as Thomas Basin, the bishop of Lisieux, had suggested in

1455 in his proposal for procedural reform, which was based on the written proceedings according to canon law in use at the Sacra Romana Rota, an ecclesiastical court at Rome.

Criminal Procedure

Criminal procedure in the early seventeenth century was still governed by the Villers-Cotterêts ordinance of April 1539. The system enunciated in this document was supplemented by the more detailed provisions of the ordinance of 1670, which laid down more stringent requirements.

Criminal proceedings could be initiated in three ways. First, charges could be brought by a civil party. Second, a royal or seigneurial *procureur* could bring charges after receiving a complaint or other word that a crime had been committed. Finally, judges had the power to investigate criminal acts.

The preliminary investigation was secret. A single criminal judge, the *lieutenant criminel* or seigneurial judge, was in charge. Witnesses were heard one at a time in chambers by either the judge himself, special investigative officers, or a *sergent* assisted by a royal notary. Depositions were written out in full. If witnesses were scarce, monitory letters could be issued upon request of the *procureur du roi*. A monitory letter was an order issued by an ecclesiastical judge to be posted on the doors of the church and read before the sermon. It instructed the faithful to tell the curate whatever they knew about a particular crime. The curate gathered all the depositions and sent them under seal to the criminal judge.

The judge then transmitted the results of the investigation to the *procureur du roi*, who noted his conclusions at the end of the document. Depending on what the *procureur* had to say, the judge would then either shelve the case or issue a warrant for the accused. This warrant could either be a subpoena to appear in court or an arrest warrant. It was executed by a *sergent* assisted by two witnesses or bailiff's assistants during the daytime. Forcible entry was authorized if necessary.

The accused, whether he appeared voluntarily or was arrested and haled into court, was supposed to be immediately interrogated by the judge. He was required to answer questions without benefit of counsel and without knowledge of the charges against him. Tradition required that he swear an oath to tell the truth. All his answers were taken down by a clerk.

If the accused confessed, his confession was transmitted to the *procureur du roi* to see if the *procureur* wished to ask for sentencing. If so, the statement of the interrogation was sent to the civil party. The *procureur du roi* and the civil party both submitted arguments in writing. These arguments were made known to the accused, and he had the right to reply. He was then brought into court to hear the judgment. If the accused denied guilt or if the parties deemed the confession inadequate and did not wish to ask for sentencing, however, the judge would issue an interlocutory judgment deciding whether the case was to be tried according to ordinary or extraordinary rules. Under the ordinary procedure the accused was apprised of the charges against him as well as of the results of the investigation, and he had the right to an attorney. This procedure was used only in cases of minor importance.

Usually, the judge decided in favor of extraordinary proceedings. He then notified the parties of the date set for hearing witnesses, who were again subpoenaed.

At the hearing the judge had the witnesses swear an oath to tell the truth. He then asked them what they knew about the case. If the testimony of a witness agreed with what he had stated in his original deposition, the judge had the deposition read by the clerk and asked the witness if it contained the truth. He then had the clerk write down what points of the deposition were to be left standing and what points needed correction.

Next, the judge had the witness confront the accused. The oath was administered to both. The judge asked if they knew each other and asked the witness if the defendant was indeed the person of whom he had spoken in his original deposition and later testimony. The accused then had to formulate his "reproaches," i.e., his grounds for impugning the integrity of the witness. Only after this was the deposition read. The judge then asked first the witness and then the defendant if it contained the truth. What they said was taken down. The accused could make observations aimed at causing the witness to retract his testimony or to contradict himself.

The accused could make statements in his own defense and attempt to prove them by means of witnesses. He could use both indirect proofs—such as establishing an alibi, showing that the person believed dead was in fact living, or establishing that another person was guilty of the crime—and direct proofs—such as that the alleged crime was in fact committed in self-defense or was committed in a moment of insanity.

The records of the proceedings were then transmitted to the *procureur du roi*, who stated his conclusions. The judge took these into account in issuing his ruling. If the *question préparatoire* was called for, the torture was administered.

Then the judges deliberated in chambers in the presence of the king's men. The accused was interrogated in the presence of the entire court. At no time did he enjoy the benefit of counsel. The members of the court then stated their opinions, either by voice vote or by secret ballot. A simple majority decided the case. No grounds for the decision had to be given. The sentence was sent to the clerk who read it to the prisoner in the warden's office. The accused was held in prison throughout the trial.

When a sentence involved loss of life or liberty, appeal to a sovereign court was compulsory. Appeal brought an automatic stay of execution of the sentence.

No complaints were lodged against this manner of proceeding by the Estates General of 1614–15 or by the Assembly of Notables of 1617–18 and 1626–27. Far from regarding the secret proceedings, the absence of an attorney for the accused, and the arbitrary power of the judge as barbarous, these bodies admired the social utility of such practices.

Gradually, however, the procedure was weighed down by the introduction of countless useless formalities and documents. These developments were interpreted in a variety of ways. Auzanet, one of the drafters of the criminal ordinance of 1670, wrote to a friend that "the evil has reached the point where a number of rules of one *parlement* have changed two or three times in thirty years and cases are still judged according to different rules within the chambers of the same *parlement*."[14]

Pussort, Colbert's uncle, began work on a codification of ordinances on 6 September 1661. Colbert submitted the plan to the king in 1664 and 1665. The king accepted it. According to Colbert's *Mémoire* of 15 May 1665, the aim was to "reduce to a single body of ordinances all that is necessary to establish jurisprudence on firm and secure foundations and also to reduce the number of judges." A Council of Justice composed of *conseillers d'Etats* and *avocats* began meeting at the Louvre on 25 September 1665. On 26 January 1667, it began meeting with a delegation from the Paris *parlement* headed by the *premier président*, Lamoignon. On the recommendation of this body the king's Council adopted first the civil ordinance, which was registered by the Paris *parlement* on 20 April 1667, and, later, the criminal ordinance, which was registered by the Paris *parlement* on 26 August 1670. Pussort was largely responsible for the preparation of both texts.

The ordinance of 1670 updated and supplemented the ordinance of 1539. It was designed to afford additional guarantees to the accused while at the same time providing for stringent measures to punish criminals.

The new ordinance declared that charges must be brought either by the *procureur du roi* or the seigneurial *procureur*. Private parties could only sue for damages. For offenses not subject to penalties involving loss of life or liberty, a private transaction between the injured party and the offender put an end to the public proceedings.

In order to make the filing of charges easier, complainants were no longer required to become civil parties to the case, which required the payment of certain court fees. Henceforth, "complainants shall not be viewed as civil parties . . . if they do not expressly declare themselves such in their complaint" (title III, art. 5). A civil party could withdraw his complaint with twenty-four hours of filing but not thereafter. If he withdrew he was not held responsible for fees incurred subsequently.

To prevent alteration, depositions had to be written by a court clerk in the presence of a judge. The taking of depositions through a *sergent* or notary was prohibited. Interlinear additions were not allowed, and erasures or cross-references had to be approved and signed by the witness and by the judge (title VI, art. 12).

As before, the investigation resulted in the issuance of a warrant, which was done only after the *procureur du roi* had presented his conclusions. The ordinance made legal a new form of warrant: a subpoena requiring a witness to appear in court but not requiring him to cease to perform any duties (title X, arts. 10 and 12).

If the accused did not appear, the judge then issued a bench warrant, which did require cessation of all duties.

If the accused still did not appear and furnished no excuse (excuses were known as the "*essoines des accusés*"), the judge then issued a warrant for his arrest. If the accused had a fixed abode, however, an arrest warrant was issued only in cases involving possible loss of life, liberty, or civil rights (title X, arts. 3 and 4).

No preliminary investigation was required in cases of flagrant crime, public dueling, or complaints filed by the *procureur du roi* against vagrants or by masters against their servants (title X, arts. 5, 6, 8).

In cases set for disposition by extraordinary procedure, bail was not allowed.

On the other hand, protection against indefinite confinement of accused individuals was provided by requiring *procureurs du roi* to submit a list of all persons under indictment confined to prison during the previous six months. This list, submitted twice a year to the *procureurs généraux*, indicated the disposition of each case that had come up for judgment, together with information about the condition of the accused and the state of the proceedings against him (title X, art. 20).

The administering of an oath to the accused during interrogation was made legal by title XIV, article 7.

Witnesses who retracted or changed essential elements of their depositions after being examined were to be prosecuted and punished for perjury (title XV, art. 11). This was an unfortunate provision, which was to have the effect of assuring the obstinacy of uncertain or vindictive witnesses.

The ordinance confirmed the practice of having the accused appear for a final interrogation before judgment. When the *procureur du roi* called for a penalty involving loss of life or liberty, the ordinance made legal the customary practice of requiring the accused to sit during this interrogation on a small wooden bench known as the *sellette*. This had the advantage of allowing him to be interrogated without chains but the disadvantage of stigmatizing him as guilty. Otherwise the accused stood uncovered behind the bar enclosing the *parquet* of the chamber. In several courts the defendant was not interrogated when the *procureur* did not call for a penalty involving loss of life or liberty. The declaration of 13 April 1703 reaffirmed the requirement that the accused always be examined on the *sellette* or behind the bar.

In courts whose judgments were subject to appeal, decisions had to be handed down by at least three judges or graduate assessors. In sovereign courts seven judges were required for both investigative decisions and final decrees. When there were not enough judges, the required complement could be made up by graduates. A tie vote always decided in favor of the accused. In the sovereign courts the most severe judgments had to pass by a majority of at least two votes (title XXV, art. 12).

Judges in the lower courts had to give their reasons for passing sentence or freeing the defendant. The sovereign courts were not bound to give reasons for their decisions.

If the charges appeared to be baseless, the judges could do one of three things. First, they could find the defendant innocent and thereby open the way to an action for damages against the civil party. Second, they could dismiss the case. This could be done only by the sovereign courts when sufficient evidence was lacking. A suspicion remained, however, and the accused was not entitled to sue for damages. Finally, they could postpone hearing the case pending further investigation. Postponements could be for a definite period if the crime was not a brutal one and if evidence pointing to the accused was slight, or for an indefinite period if the crime was serious and if considerable evidence had been gathered against the defendant. Proceedings could be reopened at any time if new facts came to light.

The execution of warrants, the conduct of investigations, and the return of judgments could not be hindered or delayed by any form of appeal.

The ordinance established a series of penalties for persons convicted of committing a crime, ranging from death, torture, a life sentence in the galleys, exile for life, a term in the galleys, whipping, and public amends to exile for a fixed period.

To exile a man from the jurisdiction of a *parlement, bailliage,* or *sénéchaussée* was in reality a harsh penalty. If the exile was for life, it entailed confiscation of all property owned by the convicted man. If it was for a fixed period, exile was always accompanied by fines, the amount of which was left up to the discretion of the judges. These fines took priority over all other claims against the property of the accused and remained as a lien against that property. Exile made it difficult for a man to communicate with members of his family or with his servants, clients, and friends. It cut him off from his *corps* or community and left him isolated and without resources.

If a man was charged in absentia and the warrant for his arrest could not be executed, the ordinance specified what was to be done, simplifying the procedure that had been used earlier in such cases. The property of the fugitive was seized. He was then tried in absentia. Sentence could be passed. If the death penalty was imposed, the fugitive was executed in effigy in a public place. Execution of penalties against his property was carried out in accordance with the terms of the sentence. If the convicted man then appeared, the judgment in absentia was dropped *ipso jure*, but certain of its effects remained. After one year, the fruits accruing to his property and the amounts obtained from sale of his chattels were permanently lost to him. After five years all pecuniary awards, fines, and confiscations were deemed to be the same as if they had been established in adversary proceedings and to have the same value as if ordered by decree.

Were the provisions of the criminal ordinance respected? To answer this question we would need accurate statistics on criminal justice. It seems that, in the criminal domain, jurisprudence remained diverse, particularly where local customs were respected. Although the king reserved the right to interpret ordinances, edicts, declarations, and letters patent as he saw fit (ordinance of 1667, title II, art. 7), the courts retained their freedom to make their own interpretations.

The court clerks only took notes during the proceedings and later prepared full texts of the interrogations outside the courtroom. It often happened that witnesses and defendants failed to understand the questions put to them. The transcriptions made by the clerks frequently bore only a remote resemblance to the words uttered by the witnesses. Documents submitted to the courts were frequently erroneous or bogus.

The secrecy of proceedings was sometimes violated because of favorites or bribery. Either the civil party or the accused or their friends might obtain copies of documents, suborn witnesses, and agree beforehand upon the answers they would give to questions put before the judges. Before the Revolution the transmission of documents had become commonplace in the districts of the Rouen and Toulouse *parlements*. With the connivance of their jailers, prisoners could obtain the services of counsel. There was, incidentally, a legal right to counsel for appeals asking for a judgment to be overturned or revised.

The ordinances elicited learned commentary. Previously, lawyers had access only to practical manuals explaining the usages of which the laws were a part. Occasionally, an interpretation of one aspect or another of the law would be given when it was needed in support of a complex of current practices. Practice ceased to rule the interpretation of texts, however. Texts began to shape practice and govern the behavior of lawyers in minute detail. Jurists gave strict interpretations of the ordinances and worked hard to uncover all their consequences. This intellectual movement may be compared to the one that swept theologians during the Reformation, changing their attitude to the Word of God compared with that of traditional Catholicism.

The works of the jurists Jousse and Muyart de Vouglans (for the ordinance of 1670) were respected by judges as much as the ordinances themselves.

The secret, inquisitional procedure was for a long while accepted by the public as a necessary, if stringent, measure.

The protest against this form of procedure began with the works of La Bruyère (*Les caractères, De quelques usages, De l'homme*). Among the magistrates, the first criticism came from Augustin Nicolas, *président* in the Dijon *parlement*, who asked, in his *Mémoire*, "whether torture is a sure way of uncovering hidden crimes." This book was published in 1682 in Amsterdam and included arguments that were to be taken up later by others. Torture was not mentioned in Mosaic law, Christ's teachings, or canon law. An invention of the devil, it was an affront to common sense and natural reason. A man who, though good, is neither stoic nor athletic may succumb to the unbearable pain of a half-hour of torture and confess his guilt, whereas a strong, vigorous man may well resist and admit nothing. An innocent man

who is subjected to torture might be maimed for life, only to be declared
innocent later on. It was better to let a few criminals go unpunished because
evidence was lacking and no confession could be obtained.

Secret, inquisitorial proceedings were attacked and contrasted unfavorably
with English methods in numerous works, including Montesquieu's *Lettres
Persanes* (letter 78) of 1721 and his *Esprit des Lois* (books VI and XII) of
1748; the marquis of Beccaria's *Traité des délits et des peines*, whose French
translation, published in February 1766, met with huge popular success and
was approved by Buffon, Diderot, Helvétius, and d'Alembert; and many of
Voltaire's writings, such as the *Mémoires pour les Calas*, *La relation de la
vie et de la mort du chevalier de La Barre*, and the *Commentaire sur le
traité des délits et des peines*, to name a few. These authors called for the
rights of the defense to be respected and for this to be insured by making
discussions public, providing the defendant with counsel, abolishing torture,
and relying on inward conviction and trial by jury, the members of the jury
deciding in their own minds whether the deed had been proven. If the jury
found the defendant guilty, the judge would then pronounce the sentence
prescribed by law for that particular crime.

The *avocats généraux* Servan and Hérault de Sechelles attacked torture
and the system of legal proofs in their invocations of 1766 and 1786, respectively. In 1780 the Academy of Chalôns-sur-Marne held a competition
on the following theme: "Means to moderate the stringency of the penal
laws in France without harming the public safety." Prizes were awarded to
the *Mémoires* of the future revolutionary Brissot de Warville and to the entry
of an *avocat* in the Aix *parlement* by the name of Bernardi. Their demands
were incorporated into the *Cahiers* of 1789.

But the *avocat général* Séguier applied to the Paris *parlement* on 7, 8,
and 10 August 1786 for the suppression of the "Memoir for three men
condemned to be broken on the wheel," written by a *président* in the Bordeaux *parlement* by the name of Dupaty as an attack on criminal procedure,
because Séguier regarded the 1670 ordinance as being as close to perfection
as possible.

The royal declaration of 24 August 1780, did away with the *question
préparatoire*. The edict of 8 May 1788 revised the ordinance of 1670. It
replaced the *sellette* by a wooden chair. Henceforth, grounds had to be given
for all judgments, and the crimes and offenses committed had to be expressly
stated. The edict reaffirmed the abolition of the *question préparatoire* and
abolished the *question préalable*. These were replaced by a "supreme interrogation" on the very day scheduled for execution. A majority of three
votes was required to condemn a man to death. A full month must expire
between the passing of a death sentence and the execution, except in cases
of sedition or riot. Capital sentences had to be transmitted along with the
necessary information to the keeper of the seals, who could order a new
trial or grant a commutation of sentence on the king's behalf. These were,
as the "king's men" said, "acts of humanity."[15] But the edict succumbed

to the opposition of the Paris *parlement*, which nullified the registration of all legislative acts imposed by the king during the session of 8 May 1788.

The Constituent Assembly would later adopt a system similar to the English system.

Control over Proceedings by the King's Council

The king's Council exerted control over the procedures used by the sovereign and lower courts by exercising its power to quash decisions handed down by these courts. This power had been granted by the ordinance of 18 May 1529, the Blois ordinance of May 1579, and the Rouen edict of 15 January 1597. The procedural rules applicable to appeals to the king's Council had been laid down by the regulations of 27 January 1660, 3 January 1673, 14 October 1684, and 17 June 1687, and by the regulation governing council procedure of 28 June 1738 (d'Aguesseau).

"It has always been taken by the Council as a principle that the power to quash was introduced more for the maintenance of the ordinances than for the benefit of the justiciables." Appeals presented the king with an opportunity to exert control over the way in which justice was administered. The quashing of a decision was "an act of supervision, or, if you will, of high police" (Joly de Fleury, 1762).[16]

An appeal to the Council to quash a decision could be made only when all other appeals had been exhausted. Appeal could therefore be taken only from decisions of the sovereign courts and from those of the lower courts granted the power to judge in last resort: the Tables de Marbre for the Eaux et Forêts, the *présidiaux* in cases falling under the first article of the edict, the mercantile courts in cases up to 500 livres, the extraordinary commissions, and so on.

The basis for the appeal to the Council was that the prince was the source of all justice and all public authority and that, as sovereign, he had the right to establish order in the courts. A decree from a sovereign court exhausted the normal avenues of justice. The quashing of such a decree was an extraordinary exercise of the prince's sovereign power, a step that was taken either by the prince on his own or in response to a civil petition filed by his subjects.

The king exercised his power to quash decisions in his Council, even though the Council was neither a regular court nor a tribunal for hearing disputes. But the Council did consist of "the king accompanied by those who assist him in the administration that is his," so that it was legitimate for the Council to quash the decrees of sovereign courts, even though it was, in the opinion of the Paris *parlement*, "not even a *corps*, much less a tribunal having permanent authority in the state."[17] Despite constant opposition from the sovereign courts, the Council continued to quash their decrees. The king himself asked the Conseil des Dépêches or Conseil des Finances to quash certain decisions of the courts, whereas appeals brought by civil petition filed by one of the parties were taken up by the Conseil privé or Conseil des parties.

A decision could be quashed by the Council on the following grounds:

1. Procedural irregularities: an insufficient number of judges, lack of jurisdiction or power, amendment to a judgment not approved by all the judges, a decision handed down in a tie vote, etc.

2. Abuse of power by the courts: opposition to the views of the royal government; infringement of legislation, affront to public order, or disrespect of grants of royal favor and privilege; enroachment on the jurisdiiction of other judges.

3. Violation of royal ordinances, and, from 1667 on, attempts to interpret the ordinances, interpretation having been reserved as an exclusive right of the king.

4. Infringement of custom, the sovereign law, which gave force to all other laws, even the most fundamental and sacred.

5. Issuance of a dubious judgment, one held in disrepute by the public on account of the notoriety of the deed, committed in circumstances of public knowledge.

Broadly speaking, the following procedure was followed in appealing a decision to the Council in the eighteenth century. One had to have been a party in the case to have standing to make an appeal. The petition asking that the decision be quashed had to be signed by the party and by two *avocats* on the Council. The chancellor turned the petition over to a *maître des requêtes*, who would prepare a report for a committee of the Appeals Office of the Conseil privé. If the members of the committee and the person preparing the report were unanimous in disapproving the petition, it was rejected. The committee members signed a dismissal order, which was then authorized by the chancellor. Most petitions were rejected.

If a single vote was cast in favor of the petition, however, it was then submitted to the Council. The Council would then issue a decree ordering the appellant's petition to be transmitted to the party benefitting from the original judgment, notifying that party that he must appear as defendant in the hearings on the appeal. The petition was also transmitted to the *procureur du roi* at the tribunal that had handed down the original decision, so that he might furnish the Council with the grounds for the decision, in view of the fact that no grounds had to be given in the text (despite the demands of the Estates General of 1560 and 1614). From 1738 on, the *procureur* had to submit a written justification stamped with his mark. He need not prepare this text himself; it might be done by the *rapporteur* for the trial. These texts were of many varieties. Some gave a complete exposition of the case and of all proceedings. Others sought merely to refute the grounds on which appeal had been filed. The texts explained why the court had respected some custom, applied a particular ordinance or rule of written law, or felt itself bound by some precedent, "the public law of its jurisdiction." When the decision under appeal had been handed down by one of the sovereign courts of Paris, the *maître des requêtes* preparing the report on the appeal always communicated with the magistrate who had acted as *rapporteur* in the case to learn about the circumstances surrounding the affair and the reasons for the decision. Even the Grand Conseil, which was viewed as part of the royal entourage, stated grounds for its decisions when they were appealed. Only the Paris *parlement* did not explain its decisions.

With this information in hand, the Council deliberated on the report submitted by the *maître des requêtes* and handed down its decision in the appeal, known as an *arrêt de cassation*. This decision concerned the decision under appeal but not the substance of the case in question. If the Council decided to quash the decision under appeal, that decision was overturned and the case was returned to the courts for a new trial. The case could be submitted either to the court that had rendered the overturned decision or to another tribunal upon issuance of letters patent. The Council also had the power to assume jurisdiction over the case itself, however.

The decision to quash a decision of the courts was not subject to further appeal via the procedures of civil petition or opposition. But if the Council assumed jurisdiction over the case and handed down a decision on its substance, that decision was subject to appeal by petition. Decisions quashed by the Conseil des Dépêches or Conseil des Finances at the king's behest were subject to further appeal only through the representation procedure.

The Influence of the Social Status of Magistrates on Procedures

Did the social status of magistrates have an influence on the procedures they followed? Were magistrates induced by their rank in the social hierarchy, their concern for rank and prestige, and their position, in most cases, as *seigneurs* to favor their own interests and the interests of others like them in court proceedings and decisions? It is difficult to answer these questions. For one thing, not enough research has yet been done on the procedures actually followed by the courts and on the question of whether the judgments handed down were actually in keeping with the law and the evidence. For another, it is possible to interpret the behavior of judges in various ways in view of the fact that they were obliged to enforce the law. In a case involving a magistrate who was a *seigneur* on one side and a village within his *seigneurie* on the other in a dispute over usage rights, historians are inclined to see injustice if the court finds in favor of the magistrate who is also a *seigneur*. But to have a reasonable opinion in the matter, we would have to know exactly what the law was, what the customs were, what rights were at issue, whether the decision handed down complied with the law, and what the customary and reciprocal rights of the various parties were. How commonly was the law violated, and in what ways? It is another question entirely to ask whether seigneurial property was just or unjust in itself and whether or not another form of ownership might have been preferable under the circumstances.

No clear answers can be given, I think, to the questions raised. But the problem can be made more precise and the nature of the difficulty clarified.

Did magistrates sometimes yield to their feelings and passions at the expense of strict justice? It is pointless to answer that, human nature being what it is, this must have happened, since even the most self-possessed of men are sometimes carried away by passion. This is not the answer of a historian. The historian must not make assumptions about human nature. Rather, he must seek to determine what, if any, effects of the passions can be discerned at a particular time in a particular place.

Consider religious passions, for example. The Catholic magistrates in the Rouen *parlement* undoubtedly violated the law in their efforts to close down the Protestant temple at Quevilly near Rouen during the period of Louis XIV's personal government. The magistrates set a prisoner free on the condition that he go spy on Protestant services and help the authorities catch the worshippers in a violation of the law. He accused Protestants of taking children whose fathers had died Huguenots but whose mothers had abjured and returned to the Catholic faith and of leading these children to Protestant services. He also accused Calvinist ministers of having welcomed relapsed apostates into their services.

Neither charge warranted prosecution. In the case of the children, article 39 of the declaration of 1 February 1669 stated that "the children of a Protestant father who had died a Protestant shall remain in the hands of their relatives of the would-be reformed religion." The council decree of May 1683 for Normandy decided that the children of fathers who had died Protestant whose mothers had embraced the Catholic religion would be entrusted to the care of Protestant relatives of the father. And the declaration of 17 June 1683 ordered that only children "whose father had abjured the reformed religion" should be raised as Catholics. In the case of the allegedly relapsed apostates, the required formalities had not been performed. Their putative abjuration had not been reported to the consistory. Accordingly, the ministers were not guilty of any crime for allowing these individuals to attend services. Neither case justified the closing of the temple.

The Rouen *parlement* further violated the criminal ordinance of 1670 with its decree of 3 January 1685. The ministers were served, not with a simple "subpoena to appear and be heard," which would have allowed them to continue preaching and keep the temple open, but rather with a personal subpoena that was supposed to be used only in very grave cases in which evidence of guilt abounded. The personal subpoena prohibited the ministers from carrying on with their preaching and thus made it possible to close down the temple.

By decree of 6 June 1685, which violated the terms of the declarations of 1669 and 1683 and the council decree of 1683, the *parlement* fined the uncles, aunts, grandfathers, and grandmothers of the children in question and had the children seized by bailiffs and guards and transported to the Collège des Jésuites, the Nouvelles Catholiques, and the Bureau des Valides. The relapsed apostates were sentenced to banishment in perpetuity and forced to make public apology for their alleged crimes. After being found innocent, the ministers were arrested upon leaving the Grand-Chambre on the pretext of not having submitted full lists of all worshippers to the *parlement*.

The *parlement* had heeded the wishes of certain of its members, who were inflamed against the Protestants: the *président* Poërier d'Amfreville, the councillor Fauvel de Touvents, who acted as *rapporteur* in the trial, and the *procureur général* Le Guerchois.[18]

In this instance the effects of passion are obvious.

On the other hand, we find the magistrates of the Paris *parlement* fighting to overcome their religious passion in the matter of witches. Witches were assumed to be under the thumb of Satan. For Christians, the existence of the Devil was an article of faith, and he was believed to work pernicious effects in the world. Inspired and aided by the Devil, witches were supposed to commit unnatural and supernatural acts. The possibility of such acts could not be denied, because Holy Scripture was full of miracles, particularly in the Gospels, and these miracles were also unnatural or supernatural acts. Magistrates were therefore inclined to believe in the existence of witches, to try those accused of witchcraft, and to condemn them if they confessed. During the first half of the seventeenth century, many witches were tried.

Physicians and theologians from the Sorbonne did not deny the possibility of witchcraft. They merely stated that, in each individual case, it was necessary to proceed carefully in order to determine whether one was dealing with a witch or a diseased mind, a depraved imagination, a melancholic, or a liar. On 19 July 1615, the Paris Faculty of Theology consulted in one such case and, in an opinion signed by André du Val, Philippe de Gamaches, and Nicolas Ysambert, declared that the "possessed" individuals on trial were in fact melancholics and lunatics who needed medical cures more than exorcism. Besides, Satan was the father of the lie. He was not to be believed when he or one of his demons caused people to accuse themselves of witchcraft.

The magistrates of the Paris *parlement* were gradually won over by the opinions of the physicians and theologians. They may also have been influenced by the Christ-centered movement in religion, which attempted to purge Christianity by restoring its essence, tender love for the true God and true Man, Jesus Christ, and for all human beings.

In 1624 the Paris *parlement* instituted an automatic appeals procedure in cases of witchcraft. In 1640 it imposed sanctions on lower-court magistrates who attempted to circumvent this procedure. In the 1640s it ceased to recognize witches and refused to convict anyone of the crime of witchcraft, trying them instead for any harm they may have done. *Parlement* took the position that possession and pacts with the Devil were rare and unusual phenomena.

Magistrates in the lower courts under the jurisdiction of the Paris *parlement* looked upon possession as an everyday occurrence, however. Between

1640 and 1660 they continued to condemn witches and to carry out sentences against them in defiance of the regulation of 1624. On 10 August 1641, the Paris *parlement* condemned the *lieutenant de justice*, the *procureur fiscal*, and the *greffier* of a seignurial court to be hanged in the place de Grève for the murder of a woman accused of witchcraft. Slowly but surely, the lower-court magistrates were won over to the view of *parlement*.

The Paris *parlement* was completely at odds with the other *parlements* and the lower courts under them, whose magistrates shared the passions and superstitions of the people over whom they sat in judgment. There were still epidemics of witchcraft trials, as in Normandy and Béarn in 1670, in Guyenne in 1680, in the Toulousain and Bigorre. Gradually, however, the provincial *parlements* were won over to the view of the Paris *parlement*, though not before contradictory judgments had been handed down and a bewildering series of inconsistent precedents set. An index of the change can be seen in the decree issued by the Dijon *parlement* on 4 August 1662, in connection with the possession of the nuns of Sainte-Ursule in the city of Auxonne. The government intervened in the case. A council decree of 25 April 1672, issued at the behest of *premier président* Claude Pellot, nullified the proceedings of the Rouen *parlement*. In 1671 the Bordeaux *parlement* applied the new case law. The other *parlements* did the same between 1670 and 1680. The decisions of the courts were transformed by the king into the law of the land. The edict of July 1682 concerning soothsayers, magicians, sorcerers, and poisoners speaks only of "alleged magic" and provides for punishment only of acts of sacrilege and assault on persons.[19]

Thus in this instance, magistrates were able to overcome both their passions and their precedents in order to effect an improvement in the law.

Hence there are two contradictory answers to the question raised earlier. Examination of other cases yields ambiguous results. Consider, for instance, the Commission des Grands Jours of Auvergne (1665–66), which was made up of magistrates from the Paris *parlement*. This body imposed a sentence of three years at hard labor on Gilbert de Trintry, a *gentilhomme* who had shot one peasant sleeping in a meadow, cut off the hand of another who refused to pay an unenforceable debt of fourteen livres, and killed the guinea hens of yet another. The *greffier* of the court, one Dongois, found it "rather extraordinary that a *gentilhomme* should be condemned to hard labor." Flechier, preceptor to the children of Louis-François de Caumartin, a *maître des requêtes* delegated as sealkeeper to the court in question, was positively outraged that a *gentilhomme*, a "nobleman," should be "chained like a slave" for the journey to Toulon, even if he was guilty.[20] The court itself commuted his his sentence to nine years' banishment and reduced his fine from 200 to 100 livres. This case poses the following question: Was the court relatively indulgent out of respect for aristocratic prejudices, or was it relatively harsh because the *robins* had it in for a *noble d'épée*?

Procureur général Guillaume-François Joly de Fleury refused to allow the comte de Clermont to determine the disposition of a criminal case in July

1733. Joly ordered the *procureur du roi* in the Châtelet to prosecute the case "for the public good," so that the country need not endure the impertinences of well-born young men on the pretext that they were protecting a prince of the blood—this in spite of the fact that the complainant had dropped the charges. "M. le comte de Clermont took a haughty attitude and said that he [the *procureur général*] ought to know that the wishes of a man like himself should be obeyed as if they were orders. M. *le procureur général* . . . answered that he had plenty of respect for Messieurs the princes of the blood, but that he took his orders only from the king."[21] The actions of the *procureur général* seem to have been at odds with the ordinance of 1670, which provided that proceedings could be ended by an agreement between the civil party and the defendant in a case. This suggests that passion may have prejudiced this *robin* against a courtier and *noble d'épée*. But the public order was at stake.

On 9 April 1782, the young comte de Moreton-Chabrillant, captain of the guard of the comte de Provence, entered the Comédie Française, "wearing a pink habit, a sword, and a feathered hat." The count attempted to have Pernot-Duplessis, a *procureur* in *parlement*, removed from his seat in the balcony. Duplessis, who was "clad in the attire of his estate, a black habit, and wearing a long-haired wig," refused, saying, "Monsieur, I have *paid* for the right to sit here like anyone else." To this the count replied, "What! A bloody *robin* has the gall to challenge me!" He then struck the *procureur* with his fist and called him a "thief, a crook, and a swindler." The guard arrested Duplessis as a thief. The *procureur* brought charges at the Châtelet. They were dismissed. On what grounds? He appealed to *parlement*. His advocate, Blondel, "stressed the general interest of the Public in defending an individual who, by virtue of his merely being a *citizen*, should have been protected against any insult in a place in which *money alone placed noble and commoner on an equal footing by according equal rights to both*." On 7 August 1782, the Tournelle sentenced the count to pay 6,000 livres in damages and to declare in open court that the man he had insulted was a "man of honor and probity."[22] This seems clear enough. But was the sentence more or less harsh than the sentence that would have been meted out in a similar case if another *robin* or a merchant or an artisan had insulted a *robin*? Did the sentence conform to statute and case law in all respects? Can we be sure that the court had been influenced solely by the merits of the case and had not been swayed by feelings of hostility against a courtier and *noble d'épée*? Or was it perhaps swayed by fear?

Thus we find contradictory cases, dubious cases, ambiguous cases, for which there are always at least two possible interpretations. It is to be hoped that future statistical studies will help to give more definite answers to the questions that have been raised.

Notes

1. M. Dubédat, *Histoire du Parlement de Toulouse*, vol. 1 (Arthur Rousseau, 1885), p. 264.

2. Paul Bisson, *L'activité d'un procureur général au Parlement de Paris à la fin de l'Ancien Régime: Les Joly de Fleury* (S.E.D.E.S., 1964), p. 130.

3. See the list of duties of the *procureur du roi* in Emile Chenon, *Histoire générale du droit français*, vol. 1 (Sirey, 1929), pp. 558–64.

4. M. Dillay, "Conclusions du procureur général au Parlement de Paris relatives à la vérification et à l'enregistrement des lettres patentes," *Revue historique de droit français et étranger* 33 (1955): 255–56.

5. Furetière, *Dictionnaire*.

6. See vol. 1, pp. 374–80.

7. Relations of Nicolas Fouquet, Bibliothèque Nationale, Manuscrits Gaignières, no. 2799, fol. 289–301, *Journal d'Olivier Lefèvre d'Ormesson*, vol. 2, introduction, pp. xvi–xix.

8. Flammermont, *Remontrances*, vol. 2, p. 312.

9. Cited by Philippe Lévy, *Preuve*, p. 39, n. 1. Voltaire, in chap. 23 of his *Commentaire du traité des délits et des peines*, goes even further: "Elsewhere, half-proofs are admitted that at bottom are no more than doubts, because there is of course no such thing as a half-truth; but in Toulouse quarter-proofs and eighth-proofs are also admitted. For example, hearsay testimony may be regarded as a quarter-proof, and even weaker hearsay testimony as an eighth-proof, so that eight rumors that are merely an echo of groundless rumblings may become a full proof. It was more or less in accordance with this principle that Jean Calas was condemned to the wheel."

10. Daniel Jousse, *Nouveau commentaire sur l'ordonnance criminelle du mois d'août 1670* (1753; 3d ed., Delure L'Aîné, 1756), pp. 257–68.

11. Cited by A. Floquet, *Histoire du Parlement de Normandie*, vol. 7 (Rouen, 1842), pp. 376–79.

12. Ibid.

13. Ibid., p. 370.

14. P. Clément, *Lettres . . . de Colbert*, vol. 6, appendix, p. 397.

15. Flammermont, *Remontrances*, vol. 3, p. 774.

16. Cited by Tony Sauvel, "Les demandes de motifs adressés par le roi aux Cours souveraines," *Revue historique de droit français et étranger* 35 (1957): 539.

17. Cited by Michel Antoine, "Le mémoire de Gilbert de Voisins sur les cassations (1767)," *Revue historique de droit français et étranger* 36 (1958): 6, 25.

18. A. Floquet, *Histoire du Parlement de Normandie*, vol. 6, pp. 107–29.

19. According to Robert Mandrou, *Magistrates et sorciers* (Paris: Plon, 1968).

20. Arlette Lebigre, *Les Grands Jours d'Auvergne* (Hachette, 1976), p. 107.

21. Cited by Bisson, *L'activité d'un procureur général*, pp. 93–95.

22. Bailey Stone, "Robe Against Sword: The Parlement of Paris and the French Aristocracy, 1774–1789," *French Historical Studies* 9 (1975–76): 282–84.

Guide to Further Reading

Antoine, Michel. "Le mémoire de Gilbert de Voisins sur les cassations (1767)." *Revue historique de droit français et étranger* 36 (1958): 1–33.

———— et al. *Guide des recherches dans les fonds judiciaires de l'Ancien Régime*. Imprimerie Nationale, 1958.

Antonetti, G. "Le partage des forêts usagères ou communales entre seigneurs et communautés d'habitants." *Revue historique de droit français et étranger* 41 (1963): 238–86, 418–42.

Aubert, Felix. *Recherches sur l'organisation du Parlement de Paris au XVIe siècle (1515–1589)*. 1912.

Aubry, Gerard. *La jurisprudence criminelle du Châtelet de Paris sous le règne de Louis XVI*. Librairie générale de Droit et Jurisprudence, 1971.

Berlanstein, L. R. *Barristers of Toulouse in the Eighteenth Century (1740–1793)*. Baltimore: Johns Hopkins University Press, 1975.

Bisson, Paul. *L'activité d'un procureur général au Parlement de Paris à la fin de l'Ancien Régime: Les Joly de Fleury*. S.E.D.E.S., 1964.

Bitton, David. *The French Nobility in Crisis (1540–1640)*. Palo Alto, Calif.: Stanford University Press, 1969.

Bluche, François. *Les magistrats du Parlement de Paris au XVIIIe siècle, 1715–1771*. Besançon: Imprimerie Jacques & Demontrond, 1960.

———. "Les magistrats des cours souveraines au XVIIIe siècle. Hiérarchie et situation sociale." *Revue historique de droit français et étranger*, 1974, pp. 87–106.

———. "Les officiers du grenier à sel de Paris au XVIIIe siècle." *Paris et Ile-de-France* 21 (1970): 293–336.

———. "Le personnel de l'Election de Paris, 1715–1791." *Paris et Ile-de-France* 26–27 (1975–76): 321–73.

———. "Les officiers du Bureau des Finances de Paris au XVIIIe siècle (1693–1791)." *Bulletin de la Société Historique de Paris et de l'Ile-de-France* 97 (1970): 1–69.

———. *Les magistrats de la Cour des Monnaies de Paris au XVIIIe siècle (1715–1790)*. Les Belles-Lettres, 1966.

———. *Les magistrats du Grand Conseil au XVIIIe siècle*. Les Belles-Lettres, 1966.

———. "La connétablie de France (1715–1790)." *Bulletin de la Société Historique de Paris et de l'Ile de France* 103–4 (1976–77): 115–50.

Cambon de Lavalette, Jules. *La chambre de l'Edit de Languedoc*. Sandoz & Fishbacher, 1872.

Carré, Henri. *Le Parlement de Bretagne après la Ligue*. 1888.

Charmeil, Jean-Paul. *Les Trésoriers de France à l'époque de la Fronde*. A. & J. Picard, 1964.

Cheruel, A. *Journal d'Olivier Lefèvre d'Ormesson*. 1652.

Church, W. F. "The Decline of the French Jurists as Political Theorists (1660–1789)." *French Historical Studies* 5 (1967–68): 1–16.

Cocard, Monique. "Le Bureau des Finances de la généralité de Paris, 1625–1645." Mimeographed, Centre de Recherches sur la Civilisation de l'Europe moderne, 1962.

Constant, Jean-Marie. *Nobles et paysans en Beauce aux XVIe et XVIIe siècles*. Université de Paris-Sorbonne, 1978.

Coumoul, Jules. "Précis historique sur le Ministère public." *Nouvelle revue historique de droit français et étranger* 5 (1881): 299–314.

Cremer, Albert. *Der Adel in der Verfassung des Ancien Régime, die châttelenie d'Epernay und die souveraineté de Charleville im 17. Jahrhundert*. Bonn: Ludwig Röhrscheid, 1981.

———. "Bürger am Hof, Versuch und Scheitern am Beispiel der Richter am pariser parlement, 1560–1610," in *Mentalität und Lebensverhältnisse, Rudolf Vierhaus zum 60 Geburtstag*. Göttingen: Vandenhoeck & Ruprecht, 1982.

Crépillon, P. "Un 'gibier des prévôts.' Mendiants et vagabonds au XVIIIe siècle entre la Vire et la Dives, 1720–1789." *Annales de Normandie* 17 (1967): 223–52.

Croquez, Albert. *La Flandre wallonne*. H. Champion, 1912.

Cummings, Mark. "The Paulette Reconsidered: Its Impact on Venality of Office in Seventeenth Century France." Department of History, Brandeis University, Waltham, Mass. 02154.

Dalat, Jean. "Montesquieu magistrat." Part. 1: "Au Parlement de Bordeaux." *Archives des lettres modernes* 13 (1971).

Dawson, Philip. "Sur le prix des offices judiciaires à la fin de l'Ancien Régime." *Revue d'histoire économique* 42 (1964): 390–92.

Decorde. *Les avocats au Parlement de Normandie*. Académie des Sciences, Belles-Lettres et Arts de Rouen. Vol. 73, pp. 99–207.

Desmaze, Charles. *Le Châtelet de Paris*. 2d ed., Librairie académique Didier & Cie., 1870.

Devèze, Michel. *La vie de la forêt française au XVIIe siècle.* 2 vols. S.E.V.P.E.N., 1961.

———. *La grande réformation des forêts sous Colbert.* Nancy, 1962.

Deyon, Pierre. *Etude sur la société urbaine au XVIIe siècle. Amiens capitale provinciale.* Mouton, 1967.

Dillay, Madeleine. "Conclusions du Procureur général au Parlement de Paris relatives à la vérification et à l'enregistrement des lettres patentes." *Revue historique de droit français et étranger* 33 (1955): 255–66.

Doyle, William. *The Parlement of Bordeaux and the End of the Old Regime (1771–1790).* London and Townbridge: Ernest Benn.

Dubédat, M. *Histoire du Parlement de Toulouse.* 2 vols. Arthur Rousseau, 1885.

Durand, Yves. *Les fermiers généraux au XVIIIe siècle.* Paris: PUF, 1971.

Egret, Jean. *Louis XV et l'opposition parlementaire, 1715–1774.* Paris: Armand Colin, 1970.

Esmein, Adhémar. *Histoire de la procédure criminelle en France.* L. Larose & Forcel, 1882.

Esmonin, Edmond. *La taille en Normandie au temps de Colbert (1661–1683).* Paris: Hachette, 1913.

Floquet, A. *Histoire du Parlement de Normandie.* Vols. 4–7. Rouen, 1842.

Fourmont, H. de. *Histoire de la Chambre des Comptes de Bretagne.* 1854.

"Forêt en Ile-de-France (La)." *Paris et Ile-de-France* 28 (1977).

Girard, E., and J. Joly. *Trois livres des offices de France.* Etienne Bicher, 1638.

Gosselin, M. *Les procureurs près le Parlement de Normandie.* Vol. 68. Académie des Sciences, Belles-Lettres et Arts de Rouen, 1866, pp. 350 ff.

Goubert, Pierre. *Beauvais et le Beauvaisis de 1600 à 1730.* Imprimerie Nationale, 1960.

Goulard, Dr. Henri. *Une lignée d'exécuteurs des jugements criminels. Les Samson (1688–1847).* Melun: Librairie Archambault, 1968.

Gouron, Marcel. *L'amirauté de Guyenne.* Librairie du Recueil Sirey, 1938.

Gresset, Maurice. *Le monde judiciaire à Besançon, 1674–1789.* 1974.

Guérout, Jean. "La question des territoires des bailliages royaux. L'exemple de la 'prévôté et vicomté' de Paris (XIIIe–XVIIIe siècle)," in *Actes du C^e Congrès national des Sociétés savantes*: Section de Philologie et d'Histoire jusqu'à 1610. Vol. 2, pp. 7–18. Paris, 1975 (vol. 2 published in 1978).

———. "La taille dans la région parisienne au XVIIIe siècle." *Paris et Ile-de-France* 13 (1962): 145–358.

Guilhiermoz, P. "La persistance du caractère oral dans la procédure civile française." *Nouvelle revue historique de droit français et étranger* 13 (1889): 21–65.

Guyot, *Repertoire universel et raisonné de jurisprudence.* 17 vols. Visse, 1784–85.

——— and Merlin. *Traité des droits . . . annexés en France à chaque dignité, à chaque office, à chaque état.* 3 vols. Visse, 1786–88.

Hamscher, A. *Parlement of Paris after the Fronde (1653–1673).* Pittsburgh: University of Pittsburgh Press, 1976.

Hunt, Lynn A. "Local Elites at the End of the Old Regime: Troyes and Reims, 1750–1789." *French Historical Studies* 9 (1975–76): 379–99.

Jousse, Daniel. *Nouveau commentaire sur l'ordonnance criminelle du mois d'août 1670.* 3d ed., Delure L'Aîné, 1756.

Koenig, Laure. *La communauté des procureurs au Parlement de Paris aux XVIIe et XVIIIe siècles.* Cahors: A. Coueslant, 1937.

La Roche-Flavin. *Trèze livres des Parlements de France.* Bordeaux: Simon Millanges, 1617.

La Cuisine. *Le Parlement de Bourgogne, Dijon, Loireau-Feuchot.* 3 vols. Paris: A. Durand, 1857.

Laurain, E. "Essai sur les présidiaux." *Nouvelle revue historique de droit français et étranger,* 1895, pp. 355, 522, 738.

Lebigre, Arlette. *Les Grands Jours d'Auvergne.* Paris: Hachette, 1976.

Mahuet, Hubert de. *La Cour souveraine de Lorraine et Barrois (1641–1790).* Nancy: Société d'impression typographique, 1959.

Mandrou, Robert. *Magistrats et sorciers en France au XVIIe siècle.* Paris: Plon, 1968.

Marquis Marie de Roux. *Louis XIV et les provinces conquises*. 1938.

Maugis. *Histoire du Parlement de Paris*. Vol. 2. Auguste Picard, 1914.

Meyer, Jean. *La noblesse bretonne au XVIIIᵉ siècle*. 2 vols. S.E.V.P.E.N., 1966.

———. *La noblesse parlementaire bretonne face à la prérévolution et aux débuts de la Révolution: Du témoignage à la statistique*. Offprint from Ernst Hinrichs (ed.), *Vom Ancien Regime zur französischen Revolution*. Göttingen: Vandenhoeck & Ruprecht, 1978, pp. 279–317.

———. "Noblesse et racisme." In *Ni Juif, ni Grec*.

Monplot, Françoise. "Les conseillers au Parlement de Paris (1685–1690)." Mimeographed, Centre de Recherches sur la civilisation de l'Europe moderne, 1970.

Mousnier, Roland. *La vénalité des offices sous Henri IV et Louis XIII*. 2d ed., Paris: PUF, 1970.

———. ed. "Serviteurs du roi. Quelques aspects de la fonction publique dans la Société française du XVIIᵉ siècle." *XVIIIᵉ siècle*, 1955.

———. *La stratification sociale à Paris aux XVIIᵉ et XVIIIᵉ siècles. I. L'échantillon de 1634, 1635, 1636*. Paris: Editions A. Pedone, 1976.

——— et al. "La mobilité sociale au XVIIᵉ siècle." *XVIIᵉ siècle* 31 (1979): 1–77.

Paquin, Pierre. *Essai sur la profession d'avocat dans les duchés de Lorraine et de Bar au XVIIIᵉ siècle*. Verdun: Imprimerie Frémont, 1976.

Paulhet, Jean-Claude. "Les parlementaires toulousains à la fin du XVIIᵉ siècle." *Annales du Midi* 76 (1964): 189–204.

Pillorget, Suzanne. *Claude-Henri Feydeau de Marville, Lieutenant général de police de Paris, 1740–1747, suivi d'un choix de lettres inédites*. Editions Pedone, 1978.

Pocquet. B. *Histoire de Bretagne*. Vol. 5. Rennes: Librairie générale I. Plihon & L. Hommey, 1913.

"La Preuve." *Recueils de la Société Jean-Bodin pour l'histoire comparative des institutions*. Vol 17, part 2: "Moyen Age et Temps modernes." Brussels: Editions de la Librairie Encyclopédique, 1965.

Richet, Denis. "La formation des grands serviteurs de l'Etat (fin XVIᵉ siècle–début XVIIᵉ siècle): Parlement de Paris, Chambre des Comptes, Cour des Aides." *L'Arc* 65 (1976).

Rogister, J.-M. J. "Procédures de vote au Parlement de Paris au XVIIIᵉ siècle." Congrès de la Commission internationale pour l'histoire des Assemblées d'Etat et des régimes parlementaires. Strasbourg, September 1977.

———. "The State of Research on French Parlements in the XVIIIth Century" in *Anciens pays et assemblées d'Etat*, LXXᵉ Colloque, 26–29 November 1975, ed. H.G.A. Kortrisk-Heule. 1977. Pp. 463–72.

———. "The Crisis of 1753–1754 in France and the Debate on the Nature of the Monarchy and of the Fundamental Laws" in Rudolf Vierhaus, ed. *Herrschafts Verträge, Wahlkapitulationen, Fundamentalgesetze*. Göttingen: Vandenhoeck & Ruprecht, 1977.

Rosset, Philippe. "Les conseillers au Châtelet de Paris à la fin du XVIIᵉ siècle." *Paris et Ile-de-France* 21 (1970): 173–292; 23–24 (1972–73): 144–97.

Saint-Leger, A. de. *La Flandre maritime et Dunkerque sous la domination française (1659–1789)*. Charles Tallandier, 1900.

Salmon, J.H.M. "Storm over the Noblesse." *Journal of Modern History* 53 (1981): 242–57.

Saulnier, Frederic. *Le Parlement de Bretagne (1554–1790)*. 2 vols. Rennes: J. Plihon & L. Hommey, 1909.

Sauval, Henri. *Histoire et recherches des Antiquités de la ville de Paris*. 3 vols. 1724.

Sauvel, Tony. "Les demandes de motifs adressés par le roi aux Cours souveraines." *Revue historique de droit français et étranger* 35 (1957): 529–48.

Shennan, J.H. *The Parlement of Paris*. London: Eyre & Spottiswoode, 1968.

Stone, Bailey. "Robe Against Sword: The Parlement of Paris and the French Aristocracy, 1774–1789." *French Historical Studies* 9 (1975–76): 278–303.

Sturdy, D.J. "Tax Evasion, the Faux Nobles and State Fiscalism. The Example of the Généralité de Caen, 1634–35." *French Historical Studies* 9 (1975–76): 549–72.

Trévédy. *Organisation judiciaire de Bretagne avant 1790.* 1893.

Viguerie, Jean de. *L'institution des enfants. L'éducation en France (XVIe–XVIIIe siècle).* Paris: Calmann-Lévy, 1978.

Villain, Jean. *Le recouvrement des impôts directs sous l'Ancien Régime.* Marcel Rivière, 1952.

Waquet, Jean-Claude. *Les grands maîtres des Eaux et Forêts de France, de 1689 à la Révolution.* Geneva-Paris: Droz, 1978.

Wood, James B. *The Nobility of the Election of Bayeux, 1463–1666.* Princeton, N.J.: Princeton University Press, 1980.

5   The United General Farms of the King's Domains and Rights

The king collected indirect taxes and income from his domains through farmers. In exchange for a lump-sum payment, he would concede his right to collect these revenues to the farmers. Their profit consisted of the difference between the amount they paid the king and the amount they actually collected, less the costs of collection. Besides the right to collect certain taxes, the king also gave the farmers help in collecting the sums due in the form of space, storehouses, officers, and clerks. All these reverted to the king upon expiration of the contract for the farm, and they might be passed on to the next farmer.

From the king's standpoint, the system of farming presented a number of advantages. It yielded a regular income that could be reckoned years in advance. The farmer acted as a local disbursing agent for the royal treasury, paying out salaries, *rentes*, and so on, on the spot, thereby reducing the costs associated with the transport of funds. In addition, the system lent itself to the floating of short-term loans either by assignment of debt or through the issuance of negotiable notes by the farmers, giving rise to a sort of fiduciary currency.

In theory, the king farmed each local tax to a different farmer. The contract for the farm was awarded by local *élus* at a public auction. The proliferation of farms to which this system gave rise proved inconvenient. In 1559 the king began efforts to combine all taxes of a given type in a particular province or even throughout the country into a single farm known as the *ferme générale*. De jure the farmer was still an individual, but the *ferme générale* was actually administered by a partnership of financiers. In 1598 Sully combined the *traités* for the provinces around Paris into a general farm known as the *cinq grosses fermes*. In the same year he set up a *ferme générale des grandes gabelles*, which combined the levy of taxes on salt with the sale of the product. And in 1604 he set up a *ferme générale des droits d'aide*. Still, at the time of Henri IV's death, there were besides these three farms forty-five other farms each covering one province, together with a host of smaller organizations. A large number of contracts were divided among a great many companies of farmers. There were still ten farms on the *gabelles*. Nearly half of the *aides* were still being collected by different farmers. An effort was made to increase concentration still further by a noble official, Antoyne Feyda, a onetime *receveur général des Finances*, who served as *fermier général des aides de France* from 1611 to 1625 and as *fermier général des gabelles de France* from 1622 to 1625. But he loaned so much money to the king that he was forced to relinquish his farms in 1625 and ended in bankruptcy in 1626. All the *fermiers généraux* in turn farmed out one or more *généralités* to *sous-fermiers* chosen by themselves or by the *élus*, and these *sous-fermiers* in turn farmed out a portion of their rights to *arrière-fermiers*. It was the latter who actually had funds collected by royal clerks. We find certain common traits shared by all the *fermiers*, the Largentiers, the Moissets, the Paulets: all were men of standing, officeholders, titled, and on the way up in the hierarchy. All were able to make their initial advance thanks to an inheritance, a windfall of some kind, or less frequently thanks to profits earned in commerce. Most important, all acquired one or more protectors at court and became the creature, the client, sometimes the *fidèle*, and always the *domestique* of one of the grands, of the king's favorite, Sully, or occasionally of the king himself.

After 1625, the large farms gradually fell apart owing to the financial distress brought on by the great wars. Not until Colbert did the trend toward concentration resume.

19 Tax Farming

Four kinds of "collections" or "receipts" were farmed out: the *gabelles*, the *traites*, the *aides*, and the *domaines*. Before the Fronde and for a few years after 1643, the *tailles* were also farmed.

The *Gabelles*

In the minds of contemporaries, salt was one of France's three most important products, along with wheat and wine. Large amounts of salt were used in cooking, preserves, and the raising of livestock. Control over the salt supply even enabled the king of France to exert diplomatic pressure on other countries, such as Switzerland, for example. Because salt is heavy and difficult to conceal, it was relatively easy for the royal government to tax its use and establish a royal monopoly over its supply. But the manner in which this was done varied widely from place to place in a kingdom whose provinces had been incorporated at different times and continued to press federalist claims.

The Pays de Grandes Gabelles

The *pays de grandes gabelles* covered twelve *généralités* in 1661: Paris, Soissons, Amiens, Châlons (Troyes), Orléans, Tours (Touraine and Maine), Bourges, Moulins, Dijon, Rouen, Caen, and Alençon. In these areas the tax on salt was a direct tax. It was paid by all individuals who were liable to payment of the *tailles*. Every such taxpayer was obliged to consume a certain amount of salt each year and to pay the taxes due on that amount. This was referred to as the *devoir de gabelle*. This "tax salt" was supposed to be used exclusively for "kitchen and table," that is, for domestic consumption. The consumer could also make further purchases of salt under the "voluntary sale" for large-scale uses such as the feeding of livestock, the preservation of meat, or manufacturing applications. The compulsory consumption amounted to one minot (39 liters) for 14 persons. The *droits de gabelles* were augmented by *crues locales*, taxes collected by municipalities and provinces, and by the *droits manuels*, which went to pay the salaries of officeholders. Finally, beginning in the last period of Louis XIV's reign, there was an additional assessment of from several centimes to one sous per livre. In Paris in 1713 the market price would have been 4 livres 10 sous per minot, but with the various taxes the actual cost came to 45 livres per minot. The price varied from province to province and was 60 livres 7 sous in Ile-de-France and 54 livres 15 sous in Normandy. Salt was sold either in *chambres à sel*, to which no court was attached, or in *greniers* (salt warehouses) which had a court in addition to sales personnel. In 1661 there were 229 salt warehouses. In 1674 the 37 *chambres à sel* were transformed into salt warehouses. Thus in 1700 the *pays de grandes gabelles* probably contained 266 salt warehouses, 16,859 parishes, and 8,588,500 inhabitants.

The Pays de Petites Gabelles

The *pays de petites gabelles*, we are told, included the Lyonnais, the Mâconnais, Bresse, Bugey, Forez, Beaujolais, Velay, Vivarais, Languedoc, Dauphiné, Provence, Roussillon, a portion of Auvergne (the *prévôtés* of Brioude, Langeac, Saint-Flour, and Livradois), and a portion of Gévaudan (the *élections* of Rodez and Millau), for a total of 5 *généralités*, 52 salt warehouses, 5,122 parishes, and 3,508,733 inhabitants in 1700. In 1763 the number of salt warehouses is said to have been 135. Inhabitants of these areas were not required to take a fixed quantity of salt each year. The tax was lower than in the *pays de grandes gabelles*. In 1780 a minot sold in Provence for between 22 livres 8 sous and 27 livres 6 sous.

The Pays de Salines (*Regions with Salt Mines*)

In 1654 there were salt mines in the Trois-Evêchés, Clermontois, and Alsace. The salt works at Moyenvic were added with the Treaty of Vincennes in 1661. Those at Marsal were annexed with the Treaty of Nomeny in 1663. Lorraine, which was occupied from 1670 to 1697, had salt works. And in 1678 Franche-Comté was annexed, with salt works at Chaux (from 1714 on), Salins, and Montmorot. The salt trade was carried on by merchants who were licensed by the farmer. To the price of salt was added a "works duty" levied by the farmer's agents. The price of a minot was 36 livres in the Trois-Evêchés (Metz, Toul, Verdun) and 12 livres 10 sous in Alsace.

The Pays de Quart-bouillon

The *pays de quart-bouillon* consisted essentially of a portion of the Norman coast within the *généralité* of Caen, including the *élections* of Avranches, Coutances, Carentan, Valognes, Bayeux, and Pont-l'Evêque. Property owners collected sand saturated with sea water and boiled it to obtain salt, one-quarter of which had to be turned over to the salt warehouses.

Exempt Provinces and Territories

Among the exempt areas were Artois, the city of Ardre, Hainault, Cambrésis, Flanders, Boulonnais, Calaisis, the principality of Sedan, Brittany, Béarn, Soule, Labourd, Gex, Arles, the Comtat Venaissin, and newly denominated *pays* in Alsace. Different regulations governed the sale of salt in each of these places. But salt was not taxed in any of them, nor was it included in the *ferme générale*.

Areas That Had Bought Exemption from the Gabelle

Exemption from the *gabelles* had been bought by Poitou, Aunis, Angoumois, Périgord, Agenais, Bazadois, Saintonge, Limousin, Auvergne as far as Alagnon and Jordanne, la Marche, Combraille, Guyenne, Bordelais, Condomois, Bigorre, Quercy, Landes, Armagnac, Nebouzan, the Quatre-Vallées, Comminges, Saint-Gironnais, the Vigueries, and the Viguerie de Rivière-Verdun.

In an earlier period these areas had been subject to payment of a tax on salt to the kings of England amounting to one-fifth or one-quarter of the price of salt purchased at the marsh. This tax was subsequently collected by the king of France. In 1549 these areas purchased an exemption from payment of the tax. They continued to be subject to royal domain dues levied on salt and to various import duties such as the *comptablie* of Bordeaux, the *convoi et traite* of Charente, and so on. In 1780 a minot sold for 7 livres in Périgord and 11 *livres* in Auvergne.

The *Traites*

The *traites* (from the Latin *trahere*, to extract) were customs duties. Since they were exclusively intended to raise revenue, however, they were levied on goods both entering and leaving certain areas and at the borders of internal provinces as well as at the borders of the kingdom. They also included tolls for the use of certain transport routes. As far as the *traites* are concerned, the provinces of France may be divided into three categories.

The Etendue *or the* Cinq Grosses Fermes

In this area the duties included the *rêve* or *domaine forain*, which was an exit duty, as well as the *haut passage*, the *imposition foraine* or *traite domaniale*, the *trépas de Loire*, and the *traite d'Anjou*, to name a few. These duties were collected at the border of a region comprising twelve contiguous provinces, known as the *Etendue*. Inside this area trade was free, except for tolls and local duties, and the duties mentioned above were collected only at the frontier. Included within the *Etendue* were Ile-de-France, Normandy, Picardy, Champagne, Burgundy, Bourbonnais, Nivernais, Berry, Orléanais, Touraine, Poitou, Aunis, Anjou, and Maine. Beaujolais, Bresse, Dombes, and Boulonnais were added in the seventeenth century.

"Provinces Said to be Foreign"

Provinces that were said to be "foreign" constituted twenty-one distinct tariff regions. They were subject to export and import duties in their trade with the Etendue as well as with their trade among themselves and with "actual foreign countries." So-called foreign provinces included Artois, Flanders, Hainault, Cambrésis, Franche-Comté, Brittany, Saintonge, Angoumois, Limousin, Auvergne, Marche, Lyonnais, Forez, Bordelais, Guyenne, Périgord, Quercy, Rouergue, Velay, Vivarais, Dauphiné, Landes, Chalosse, Armagnac, Languedoc, Provence, Soule and Navarre, Béarn, Bigorre, Astarac, Comminges, Couserans, the pays de Foix, and Roussillon.

No line of customs offices separated the Etendue from the so-called foreign provinces. All merchandise entering or leaving had duties assessed at certain specified points.

The most important duties were the following: the duty assessed by the *prévôté* of Nantes, port and harbor duties in Brittany, the *traite* of Charente, the *traite foraine* of Arzac, the *convoi* and *comptablie* of Bordeaux, the *coutume* of Bayonne, the *patente* of Languedoc, the *foraine* and *traite domaniale* of Provence and Languedoc, the *denier de Saint-André* on the Rhône, the 2 percent of Arles and the *liard* of Albaron, the customs duties of Lyon and Valence, the *table de mer* of Marseille, and the royal toll at Aix, among others.

To take one example, the customs duty of Lyon, first assessed in 1540, was a privilege accorded to the city, allowing it to assess a duty of 2.5 percent ad valorem on merchandise passing through Lyon. In order to prevent transporters from avoiding payment of the duty, customs offices (referred to as *oblique* offices to distinguish them from the central office in Lyon) were placed on all routes by which merchandise that normally would have passed through Lyon might be carried. Ultimately, the Lyon duty came in this way to be assessed throughout Lyonnais, Forez, Beaujolais, Dauphiné, Languedoc, and Provence. The duty was increased to 5 percent on all non-French merchandise.

Originally a simple toll, the Valence customs duty eventually came to be assessed by *oblique* offices throughout Dauphiné. When the farmer discovered that wagoners were avoiding Dauphiné, he obtained the right to collect the duty on all merchandise that could have or should have been carried through Dauphiné, and his *oblique* offices ultimately enclosed a perimeter comparable to that of the Lyon duty. The duties applied to nineteen categories of merchandise and depended on the weight and estimated value of the cargo.

Provinces Said to be "like Actual Foreign Countries"

These were the provinces that had most recently been incorporated into the kingdom: Alsace, Franche-Comté, the Trois-Evêchés, Lorraine, and the pays de Gex. They could trade freely with foreign countries but merchandise passing between them and France in either direction was dutiable.

Tolls

Apart from royal tolls, hundreds of other tolls were collected by nobles, *seigneurs*, convents, and cities. These tolls were often collected by farmers. Royal tolls were legally part of the royal domain, but the king had them collected along with the *traites*. It was sometimes difficult to distinguish between a toll and a *traite*. The *denier de Saint-André*, for example, was a duty levied on all merchandise passing up, down, or across the Rhône from Roquemaurette-en-Vivarais to Caussande, that is, along the branch of the Rhône known as the Brassière de Fourques. The duty amounted to 1 denier per livre of value or to 1 sol per livre on foreign goods. It was actually levied on all goods traveling down the Rhône from Lyon to Marseille, the Dauphiné, or the Comtat. It was not levied on merchandise from Lyon that was destined for Languedoc, nor was it levied on shipments from one locale to another within Languedoc or on shipments from Arles to Tarascon. It did have to be paid, however, on shipments from Tarascon to Beaucaire, except during periods when fairs were being held.

In 1724 a royal commission looked into the rights of landowners and found that, even though some tolls had been done away with, 3,120 remained. Between Arles and Lyon there were thirty or so tolls on the river and the neighboring highway, almost all on cargo passing up and down the river. All these tolls included a charge per load of cargo. In most cases there were additional charges on certain objects: oil, coal, fabric, and so on. There were also charges on the boat hauling the cargo. There were eleven tolls on the Rhône between Lyon and the Savoy frontier. The Ain had seven tolls. The Saône had eighteen between Auxonne and Pont-Saint-Vincent where the river entered Lyon. There a chain was stretched across the river, and a duty of three deniers per load had to be paid.

Tolls were frequently doubled, the amount paid to the private toll collector being matched by an equal amount paid to the king. Tolls were doubled on the Rhône in 1659.

The Disadvantages of the Traites and Tolls, and Attempts to Simplify Them

The *traites* and tolls hindered traffic, raised the cost of goods, diminished production and consumption, and afforded inadequate tariff protection. According to Colbert, merchandise shipped from the Etendue to Spain was subject to duties paid to the *cinq grosses fermes* upon leaving Poitou, to *convoi* and *comptablie* in Bordeaux, to the duties of Arzac in Landes, to the *coutume* in Bayonne, and to innumerable tolls.

Within a single customs zone, duty might have to be paid two or three times on a single object. At the Valence customs station, a cargo coming from Provence and headed for Bresse via the Rhône highway was subject to the Valence duty. Beyond Lyon duty had to be paid again at the port of Authon. If the cargo left the Rhône at Lyon, a duty was levied at the Montluel bureau. If the shipper wished to avoid multiple payment by choosing a route through the Dauphiné, the cargo could not be left for more than four days in any one place.

Raw silk from Languedoc, Provence, Dauphiné, the Levant (via the port of Marseille), and Italy arrived at Lyon after payment of a duty at Valence. If it was sent to Nantua, Gex, or Bugey for preparation, spooling, and throwing, a second duty had to be paid at the Bresse or Bugey bureaus. A third duty had to be paid at the same bureaus if the silk was shipped back to Lyon. There the silk was woven into fabric for shipment to Avignon, Toulouse, Geneva, Switzerland, Franche-Comté, Lorraine, and Savoy, and a fourth duty was levied.

The payment of duties invariably gave rise to disputes and added to the length of journeys. The lists of items subject to duty were confused. The old ad valorem tariffs were no longer correct. The custom was to pay duties on the cartload, the case, the bale, or the piece, a confusing set of denominations. Customs agents constantly engaged in fraud and extorted bribes. Merchants were well advised to accompany important shipments personally, because an ordinary wagoner was unlikely to surmount all these difficulties.

Colbert and his successors attempted to raise customs barriers against foreign competition, to simplify and reduce internal duties, and to increase the economic unity of France.

The edict of September 1664 converted all duties on exports from the Etendue into a single export duty, payable at the customs office located nearest the point of loading of cargo and foodstuffs. All import duties were combined in a single duty payable at the first customs office on the route. A number of minor local duties were eliminated, and exemptions were abolished. Application of the edict was not complete. The *traite d'Ingrande* on the Loire continued to be collected.

As for tolls, the declaration of 31 January 1663 ordered that edicts promulgated since the time of Charles VIII commanding that all tolls be handed over to the king should be enforced, in particular the edicts of Louis XIII (1633 and 1635) eliminating tolls on the Seine, the Loire, and their tributaries. The declaration prohibited the establishment of new tolls or the reinstitution of old tolls that were no longer being collected. Unverified royal letters pertaining to the establishment of tolls were to be submitted to *parlement*. The edict of 1669 enunciated the principle that all navigable rivers belonged to the royal domain and ordered that legitimate duties be displayed on a sign posted in the access way to bridges and passageways. Landowners could seize cargos only up to the amount that was due them. The edict of April 1683 confirmed the right of those authorized to collect tolls and duties to go on doing so, but required that one-twentieth of the revenue be paid to the king. The government attempted to establish precise lists of dutiable items and to set tariffs. The doubling of the Rhône tolls was revoked. On 19

December 1708, however, tolls throughout the kingdom had to be doubled for a period of seven years, although in fact the ensuing poverty made it necessary to grant partial and temporary exemptions until peace was restored. In 1779 a commission was given the responsibility of eliminating all remaining tolls, but 1,600 of them remained in existence in 1789.

As for *traites* on foreign trade, Colbert attempted to establish a sort of customs cordon on certain products. The moderate tariff of 1664 renewed or inaugurated import duties on wax, tin, copper, oil, soap, certain fabrics, and certain items of hosiery. The tariff of 1667 was more protectionist. The duty on wool stockings was raised from 3 livres 10 sous to 8 livres per dozen, that on a piece of English or Dutch cloth from 40 to 80 livres, and that on a hundred wool caps from 8 to 20 livres. Marseille was declared a free port in 1669 because of its use as an entrepôt, but customs duties were levied all around the city. In 1674, the city of Marseille was obliged, in spite of its exemption, to levy the tin duty of 2 livres 6 sols per pound of metal. The Treaty of Nijmegen obliged Louis XIV to remove the tariff of 1667, even though he was the victor. The king subsequently reinstated his protectionist policies as circumstances permitted. In 1687 he established duties on English and Dutch merchandise even higher than those of 1667. The 1699 tariff was similar in intent. In 1701 the cargo duty of 50 sous per barrel was raised to 3 livres 10 sous.

Between 1716 and 1723, the *prévôt des marchands* of Lyon, one Cholier, expressed the wishes of all French merchants when he asked that "all local duties and internal customs stations be eliminated and that a unique import and export duty be levied at the limits of French soil, in order to restore to commerce the liberty that it enjoyed in the past and that can alone revive it."[1] Vauban added that internal barriers to trade "make Frenchmen alien to Frenchmen, violating the principles of sound policy, which should always aim to maintain a certain uniformity among the subjects of the prince, in order to bind them more firmly to him."[2] The men who farmed these duties felt, however, that by signing a contract with them, the king had undertaken not to change any part of the tariff structure for the duration of the contract, and since one contract succeeded another, the system perpetuated itself.

Throughout the eighteenth century, 5 percent ad valorem duties inspired by the tariffs of 1667 and 1699 were collected on the borders, except for the so-called foreign provinces. There were duties on oil, soap, iron, tin, calico, and other such products; on fish from foreign fisheries; a so-called *droit d'indult* or *droit d'indulgence* on products imported from the Far East; and a freight duty, or tax on all vessels of foreign registry. In addition to these duties, there were the *domaines d'Occident*, a duty of 3.5 percent ad valorem on all colonial products destined for consumption in France; colonial products that were to be reexported could be stored in entrepôt duty-free. Internally, the government had granted exemptions from the payment of duties and tolls to certain categories of merchandise and by the eve of the Revolution had thereby succeeded in creating a free, unified internal market for steel, textiles, paper, soap, sugar, and coffee. Under oath, the merchant or his agent declared each item of merchandise, indicating its point of origin, its destination, its weight, its size, and its value. Customs officers inspected cargo and issued certificates of verification; collectors then calculated the duties. The merchant could pay on the spot and obtain a receipt, or he could ask for a "bonding receipt," which allowed him to pay his duty at another customs office, whereupon his bond would be refunded. If he had to continue his route into territory governed by another customs system, he could obtain a *passe-avant*, which allowed him to proceed along a specified itinerary and pay the various duties at his destination, or a *passe-debout*, which allowed him to be reimbursed if he left the territory without having disposed of his merchandise. When disputes arose, they were heard by *juges des traites*, and appeal could be taken to the Cour des Aides.

The *Aides*

Aide, a term used during the fourteenth century to denote any kind of tax, eventually came to mean taxes on food and drink. Often collected at the gates of cities and towns, the *aides* were commonly confused with *entrées* and *octrois* by the people who paid them.

In 1598 there were many kinds of *aides*, highly unequal but quite modest; collection was spotty, and there was a tendency for these taxes to increase. Among the *aides* levied on incoming food and drink was the *nouveaux cinq sols* per *muid* of wine (a *muid* was equal to 268 litres and was divided into 288 pints). On wholesale sales, there was a tax known as the *gros*, which amounted to 5 percent of the selling price, collected on each sale, exchange, or transfer on wine and such drinks as beer, cider, and perry as well as on fresh and salted ocean fish, livestock with cloven hooves, and wood. The *gros* on wood tended to be converted into an *octroi*. On retail sales, there was the *quatrième* (25 percent), which in certain places was reduced to a *huitième* (12.5 percent). There was also a measuring fee paid to domanial officials at the time of each sale for calculating the capacity of a vessel in *muids de Paris* when the vessel in question was marked according to another system of measurement. This came to five sous per *muid* of wine, fifteen sous per *muid* of *eau-de-vie*, and six sous per *muid* of beer, cider, or perry. These fees were doubled to arrive at the brokerage fee due the broker involved in the sale. Then there was the *pancarte*, or sous per livre due on all foodstuffs and merchandise passing through the walls of a fortified city, as provided by the declaration of March 1597. By this date there was probably also the *trop bu* or *gros manquent*, a tax levied on each peasant who harvested his own crop. The peasant had to pay this tax on the amount of wine that had been drained from his barrels beyond his own normal consumption on which no *gros* had been paid.

These taxes affected different persons unequally. Ecclesiastics were exempt from payment of the *nouveaux cinq sols* on wines produced from their benefices. They were exempt from payment of the *gros* on wines produced from their sacerdotal title or benefice. Nobles were exempt from payment of the *gros* on wine from their domain. The commensals of the king, the royal secretaries, and the officers of the Cours des Aides of Paris and Rouen were exempt under the same conditions. The *bourgeois* of certain cities were also exempt.

Some people residing in certain provinces and cities also enjoyed at least partial exemptions. The *pays d'aides* were the *généralités* of Paris, Soissons, Amiens, Châlons, Orléans, Bourges, Moulins (except for the *élections* of Gueret and Combrailles), Lyon, Poitiers, La Rochelle (except for the *élection* of Marennes), Rouen, Caen, Alençon (which was carved out of Rouen and Caen in 1635), plus Angoulême, Bourganeuf, Mâcon, Bar-sur-Seine, and Auxerre, which belonged to other *généralités*. The other provinces were known as *pays exempts* even though they in fact had to pay various *aides*. Within the *pays d'aides* diversity was the rule. Certain parishes were exempt from payment of one levy but had to pay others. The *gros* was not paid in Normandy except for Rouen and its suburbs. But the *quatrième* was paid there as well as in the *généralité* of Amiens and the *élections* of Pontoise and Bar-sur-Seine, whereas other areas paid the *huitième*. The countryside around certain cities was exempt from payment of the *gros* while the city had to pay: this was the case in Auxerre, Bar-sur-Seine, Chartres, Issoudun, Orléans, Lyon, Tours, and Poitiers.

In Brittany, the *devoirs* or taxes on drinks yielded a good deal of revenue, but it went to the province. The provincial Estates farmed this income out for two years. There were two kinds of *devoirs*. The *grand devoir*, which had to be paid on *vins hors*, or imported wines, was 20 livres per hogshead. The *petit devoir* was a *gros* of 5 livres 10 sols. Wine produced within the province but transported out of the bishopric where it had been produced was liable to a *grand devoir* of 13 livres 6 sols 3 deniers and a *petit devoir* of 2 livres 15 sols. Wine that was not transported out of its bishopric of origin was subject to lower taxes. The king collected the *impôt* of 22 sols 10 deniers per hogshead of *vin hors* and 11 sols 5 deniers on Breton wine, as well as the *billot* of 6 *pots* per hogshead of 120 *pots* (5 percent). *Seigneurs*, religious communities, and ancient inns were exempt from payment of the *impôt* and the *billot*.

In Languedoc, the tax known as the *équivalent* was collected by the province. The provincial Estates farmed out the revenue from this tax for six years. It amounted basically to 2 deniers per livre on meat and fish and a sixth of the price of wine sold at retail.

After Alsace was occupied, the *aides* there were replaced by a tax on drinks of 16 sols 8 deniers per measure of wine sold at retail by tavern keepers and 8 sols 4 deniers per measure of beer. The revenue from this tax was used by the province.

The *pancarte* was eliminated in 1602. Because this tax was contrary to custom, it had provoked revolts. The other levies continued to rise until

1661 to pay the costs of war. Paris was particularly affected. In 1610, the *cinq sols des pauvres* was included in the contract for the farms of 1610 and legalized by the declarations of 31 January 1613, and 28 December 1625. The *cinq sous des batardeaux* was included in the contract of 20 September 1630. Inaugurated on 15 January 1629, the *dix sous du canal* (of Briare) was eliminated in 1632 everywhere but in Paris, where this tax continued to be collected.

Between 1632 and 1641 there was a deluge of new taxes, of which we shall mention only a few. In 1632 came the *annuel*. The edict of March 1577 and the declaration of 30 December 1581 had made it compulsory for whole-sale and retail beverage merchants to buy licenses. In 1632 this was changed and merchants were required to pay an "annual licensing fee" of 8 livres in the cities, 6 livres 10 sols in villages and towns. This fee was cut in half for merchants who had obtained letters of heredity. This annual fee had to be paid for each separate cellar or point of sale. Separate licenses, each requiring payment of the fee, had to be obtained for wholesale sales, retail sales, sales of wine, beer, cider, or perry. The fee was doubled if the average sale was greater than three *muids*.

In the same year retail merchants had to pay a *huitième* on each *muid*, innkeepers who served drinks with meals had to pay 5 livres, and tavern keepers who served drinks by the tankard had to pay 4 livres. A duty of 10 sous per *muid* was levied on drink entering the city of Paris.

In 1633 a tax known as the 45 *sous des rivières* was instituted to reimburse toll keepers along the Seine whose tolls had been done away with by the declaration of 12 January 1633. These sums were used for the armies.

The declaration of 31 December 1636 imposed a tax of 3 livres per *muid* on wine entering Paris in order to pay the salary of 2,000 *fantassins*.

In November 1640 the "general subsidy" imposed a tax of 5 percent on the sale, resale, and exchange of all merchandise. It was converted into an entry duty by the declaration of 8 January 1641 and then changed to a tax of 40 sous per *muid* of wine by the declaration of 19 April 1642, limited to the jurisdiction of the Cours des Aides of Paris and Rouen, with the following exceptions: the cities and *élections* of Lyon, Montbrison, Saint-Etienne, Mâcon, Bar-sur-Seine, Auxerre, Tonnerre, Vézelay, and Joigny. The decree of 1 February 1640 established a tax known as the *barrage*, which was originally intended to pay for upkeep of the streets of Paris and its suburbs. This amounted to 2 sous on wine and 1 sou on cider and perry, 10 sous on *eau-de-vie*. On 13 July 1641, the 20 *sous de Sedan* was assessed in order to pay for the upkeep of 8,000 men. In October 1646, a council decree verified on 15 December by the Cour des Aides imposed a tax on all merchandise entering Paris, with no allowance for rank or privilege. The Fronde inter-rupted the increase in taxes. But when the Fronde was over the rise con-tinued, now taking the form of hikes in existing taxes rather than creation of new ones. In 1654 the *barrage* was raised to 8 sous on wine, 5 sous on cider and perry, and 6 livres on *eau-de-vie*. In 1657 and 1658 the general subsidy was increased by one-fourth and the *cinq sols anciens et nouveaux* were raised to 14 sous per *muid* of wine except in the *généralités* of Tours, Orléans, and Lyon. The declaration of 16 April 1663 raised the *gros* by 25 percent. Normandy, which did not pay the *gros*, had to pay this increase.

Colbert had the idea of equalizing the tax burden by assessing less in the form of direct taxes and more in the form of indirect taxes, which fell more heavily on the wealthy, the well-to-do, and the privileged. He also wished to discourage wine growing and to encourage the planting of wheat. He tried to achieve these goals first by offering better terms to tax farmers and later by coordinating and simplifying the existing tax structure in lieu of a complete overhaul of the system, which was impossible.

Two ordinances were issued in June 1680 "concerning entry duties, *aides*, and other levies," one covering the jurisdiction of the Cour des Aides of Paris, the other the jurisdiction of the Cour des Aides of Rouen. These two ordinances laid down the basic structure of *aides* that lasted until the Revolution.

In the first place, the bewildering maze of duties was simplified. All the various levies on goods entering Paris were combined in a single "entry duty": 18 livres per *muid* of wine, 15 livres per *muid* of liqueur (Muscat, Cioutat, Condrieu, Arbois, Spain, etc.), 2 sols per *muid* of verjuice, 45 livres per *muid* of *eau-de-vie*. A levy of 2 *muids* of wine on every 3 *muids* of grapes harvested was assessed on the vineyards of Passy, Suresnes, Issy, etc. Officials could make inspections without warrants in the presence of two witnesses. A deduction of one *muid* in twenty-one was allowed for lees, leakage, and filling. Thirty-five sols per *muid* had to be paid on cider, 17 *sols* 6 *deniers* on perry. The levy on apples and pears was calculated by taking 3 *muids* of fruit as equivalent to 1 *muid* of liquid. The duties on beer had been set by the edicts of December 1625 and March 1646 at 37 sols 7 deniers for Paris, 30 sols elsewhere. Assessment of the duty was made at the brewery.

In the provinces, the *anciens et nouveaux cinq sols* were set at 14 sols per *muid* of wine sold and consumed in cities, suburbs, towns, parishes, hamlets, and isolated villages. This tax was due each time the wine was transported from one province in which it was in force to another, and each time the wine was taken out of the *pays d'aides*. An "entry subvention" was collected wherever the *quatrième* was in force. A *subvention par doublement* was collected on all beverages entering the kingdom, and within the borders of France, on wine transported from one province where *aides* were assessed to another. The *gros* known as the *vingtième* and *augmentation* were maintained on wholesale sales. On retail sales a so-called *droit réglé* was assessed, combining the *huitième* and the *augmentation*. There was a tax of 5 livres 8 sols on wine sold by the tankard and 6 livres 15 sols per *muid* on wine served with meals. In regions where the *aides* were not assessed, a similar *subvention* had to be paid. Cider and perry were also taxed. The annual license fee was increased.

Combining all the various duties simplified the task of officials charged with collecting taxes and keeping records. Inspections were stepped up and rules for carrying them out were codified. Whenever goods were transported, a declaration had to be made. Wine being shipped to Paris had to be accompanied by a "wagon letter" stating the point of origin and the intended recipient. This letter had to be stamped at every *bureau des aides* along the way. Wine being shipped to destinations other than Paris had to be accompanied by a "removal permit" issued by the farmer or one of his agents, stating the name and address of the buyer and the price of the wine. Wagoners were required to show this permit on demand. These rules were based on regulations issued by the Cour des Aides of Paris on 4 June 1613 and 9 April 1651 for the *généralité* of Tours and on 13 September 1651 for the *élection* of Troyes.

Wagoners were allowed to store the wine for six months if a declaration was made at the nearest bureau.

Bonding receipts, *passe-avant* (or transire), and *passe-debout* (a 24-hour transit permit granted by a town) could all be used.

An inventory of the grape harvest was instituted by the declaration of 15 June 1534 and carried out according to strict regulations. One month after the harvest, officials of the *bureaux des aides* were allowed to inspect storerooms, presses, and wine cellars without obtaining a warrant, except in the city. A second inspection, known as the *récolement*, allowed the agent to determine how much wine was gone and to collect taxes on that amount, which was presumed to have been sold. Every landowner was entitled to three *muids* personal consumption, and ploughmen were entitled to consume three *muids* per plow. If more than the allowable amount was missing, a sale was suspected. In principle inspections should have been rare, taking place only when fraud was suspected. In fact, however, they were carried out systematically.

Thorough searches were also carried out on the premises of retail merchants. Sellers were required to declare all beverages before commencing sales operations. Officials marked all casks and blocked secondary routes to prevent illegal entry of beverages. They were allowed to summon a locksmith to open a wine cellar without obtaining a warrant from a judge, provided there were two witnesses. Retailers could elect to pay off their duties in one lump-sum payment.

Exemptions were limited. The exemption accorded to ecclesiastics from payment of the *nouveaux cinq sols* on grapes and wines produced from their benefices was extended by council decrees of 30 June 1670 and 18 June 1671, and by a decree of the Cour des Aides issued on 16 September 1673, but the exemption on grapes and wines from their sacerdotal titles was eliminated. In addition, ecclesiastics were required to pay the *anciens cinq sols* as an entry duty on all wines. They were not required to pay the *gros* or the *augmentation* on wine from their benefices but did have to pay all retail duties on wines, even those produced from their benefices.

Nobles, officers of the sovereign courts, royal secretaries, and the king's commensals had to pay the *anciens* and *nouveaux cinq sols*. They were exempt from payment of the *gros* when selling wine from their estates. Not being subject to the *récolement*, they abused the privilege by selling wine produced by others. Retail duties had to be paid by all except royal secretaries, "archers of our good city of Paris," members of the Swiss Guard serving the king and princes of the blood, and the "twelve" and "twenty-five" privileged merchants who followed the court and were allowed to sell a fixed quantity of wine in Paris, duty-free. Royal secretaries enjoyed this privilege in the city in which they carried out their duties. The *bourgeois* of certain cities were allowed to sell wine "*à huis coupé et pot renversé*." In other words, they could set up shop behind a door arranged so that the upper portion could be opened while the lower portion was kept closed, and pour the contents of a pot of wine into a vessel supplied by the buyer.

Collection of the *aides* was improved considerably when the United Farms were securely established in 1691.

The Domains

In 1598 the royal domain was divided into two parts, corporeal and incorporeal. The corporeal domain consisted of all real property actually possessed by the king, including lands, *seigneuries*, forests, and buildings, together with the associated feudal and seigneurial dues such as *cens*, *lods et ventes*, *relief et rachat*, *quints et requints*, and so on. The incorporeal domain consisted of all rights belonging to the king by virtue of his position as suzerain lord or sovereign. Among these was the "*amortissement et nouvel-acquêt*," an indemnity paid the king by men entitled to mortmain when they acquired real property that would thereafter be exempt from *droits de mutation* unless the acquisitor designated a "man living and dying" to the king. This indemnity amounted to one-fifth of the value of noble property and one-sixth of the value of common property. Another such right was the "*franc-fief et nouvel acquêt*," an indemnity owed by commoners who acquired noble property. This indemnity was seen as compensation for the damage inflicted on the feudal hierarchy when noble property fell into the hands of a commoner. It was set at one year of income from the property out of every twenty years (5 percent), plus one year of income on the occasion of each transfer. There were also rights associated with the administration of justice, such as *greffes*, *petits sceaux*, and *droits de contrôle* for notarized documents authenticated by royal seals, instituted in 1588. Other rights attached to domanial offices or offices whose titularies exercised supervisory functions and issued royal guarantees conferring authenticity in court, either directly or through agents: these included notaries, *tabellions*, *greffiers*, seal keepers, and such administrative offices as wine brokers, sworn fabric measurers, sworn woodcutters, sworn hay binders and weighers, etc. These offices were regarded as belonging to the royal domain and were farmed out. From 1580 on, however, they were often, in virtue of the ordinance of 1566, sold as hereditary property, though the king retained the option to buy them back at any time. Sale of the office made the acquisitor surrogate to the king as *seigneur*, and hence the acquisitor or his heir could be a woman or child, could hold the office concurrently with other offices, could have its duties carried out by an agent, and could transmit the office to his or her heirs. The *marc d'or* for offices (1578) and the Paulette or annual dues might perhaps be classified as part of the royal domain, but the *états royaux* listed them separately as *revenus casuels*.

The corporeal domain brought in a relatively small proportion of the king's income. Royal governments were inclined to increase the *droits de contrôle*. Increasing numbers of contracts, engagements, and obligations were authenticated by royal mark, and such authenticated documents carried legal weight in the courts. The king thus offered his guarantee to private parties and was paid for his services.

In 1598 almost all of the domain had been alienated, though the king retained the option to buy back what he had sold at any time. The king could recover any alienated portion of the domain by reimbursing the owner, and he could then resell it to someone else. He could gain by the exchange, because he reimbursed the owner the amount of the purchase price and resold at a price corresponding to the new value of money. But the extent of the royal domain was unknown. There was no general register of property belonging to it, and the king's lands and castles were dispersed throughout the kingdom. The royal domain brought in little income. Many *engagistes* paid no dues, the conditions under which the portion of the domain engaged by them had been alienated having been forgotten. Parts of the domain were farmed out at ridiculously low prices. In fact the king's property was being pillaged. One question-and-answer manual for people wishing to enter the Chambre des Comptes contained the question, "How can a royal castle be recognized?" and answered, "By the fact that it is in ruins."

Sully attempted to liberate the royal domain by entering into contracts with financiers. The financier agreed to buy back some alienated portion of the domain and then reimbursed himself and reaped a profit by exploiting it for sixteen years, at the end of which he turned the property over to the king net of all encumbrance. In 1607 Sully contracted for the redemption of 30 million livres worth of royal lands, and in 1609 he contracted for the redemption of domanial offices. But the contractor was forced by the resistance of the *sergents* to ask for release from his agreement to redeem the offices. And the murder of the king and the resumption of civil war interrupted the repurchase of royal lands.

Following the rebellion of the princes and *parlement* in 1615, Louis XIII revoked the contracts negotiated by Sully and undertook to resell a number of domains and *greffes* and to sell newly created domanial offices, actions that were very badly received.[3] At the Assembly of Notables in 1626, Richelieu asked on 2 December for 20 million livres to redeem parts of the royal domain. He expected to reap 6 million livres per year in this way. But the notables refused to supply the money and advised him to put the domain out to farm as before and to require the farmers to pay the dispossessed owners 6.25 percent on their principal until they were fully reimbursed. Nothing could be done.

From 1627 until the Treaty of the Pyrenees in 1659, and especially between 1643 and 1648, there was a spate of creations of domanial offices, and portions of the royal domain were sold and resold. These actions, it has been said, played a large part in the popular uprising of 1648 and in the Fronde, because such offices as charcoal weighers and brokers, woodcutters, corders, counters, and inspectors, wine inspectors, weights and measures inspectors, and hay sellers are supposed to have caused prices in Paris to rise.

The king attempted to raise the *droits de contrôle*. The edict of 1627 extended the need for royal approval to a larger number of notarized documents. In 1654 bailiff's writs were required to obtain approval. The edict of March 1655 created a "stamp tax," but it could not be enforced.

By 1661 the situation was one of complete disorder. The bulk of the domain had been alienated and the rest usurped. Dues were not paid. The royal domain was bringing in 80,000 livres annually, not counting the income from wood.

Colbert inaugurated efforts to buy back all of the corporeal domain beginning in 1666. This put him in a position to lease the domain to farmers. By 1682 the lease was bringing in 5,540,000 livres. Colbert also announced plans to compile a general register of all lands belonging to the royal domain. But the register for Champagne was not begun until 1678 and was completed only in 1681. In the other provinces the work was never carried through to completion. In Flanders the king made do with land registers dating from the time of Spanish domination. Apart from the farm, Colbert also took steps to improve production in the forests. In 1669 an ordinance governing the organization of the Eaux et Forêts was issued and a thorough reform of the forest administration was undertaken. As late as 1682, however, the king still did not know for sure which forest lands in Provence were his, and in Auvergne *intendants* "discovered" forests that belonged to the king. Nevertheless, proceeds from the sale of wood rose from 168,788 livres 16 sous 9 deniers in 1661 to 1,028,786 livres 8 sols in 1683. The territory of the domain was expanded. The declarations of 1668 and 1683 asserted the king's right to act as *seigneur* over islands and *créments*,[5] or alluvial deposits in rivers.

As for the incorporeal domain, Colbert tried to increase the royal income not only by farming out the king's rights but also by introducing the stamp tax and tax on official forms. An edict of April 1674 revoked the declarations of 19 March and 2 July 1673 concerning official forms and imposed a tax on parchment and paper manufactured in the kingdom. The use of stamped paper for all court documents and notarized documents was made compulsory throughout the country. This raised the cost of going to court to obtain a favor or to settle a dispute and played a part in triggering rebellions in

Brittany and Bordeaux. The ordinance of 1680 and the declaration of 19 June 1681 made the use of stamped paper compulsory for all court documents, notarized deeds, receipts for payment of royal dues, passports, permits, writs, diplomas, and public records. Stamped paper was not required for private contracts. Flanders, Hainault, Cambrésis, Artois, Alsace, and Franche-Comté were exempt from the use of official forms.

During the period when France was obliged to fight major wars against foreign allies (the War of the League of Augsburg, the War of the Spanish Succession) and when exchange rates worsened as a result of the outflow of money necessary to maintain armies on foreign soil, every possible source of revenue had to be exploited. In December 1691 efforts to compile a general register of lands belonging to the Crown were begun. The edict of August 1692 reaffirmed the doctrine of the *directe royale universelle:* any property not held of a lord was presumed to be held of the king as suzerain lord. The edict of December 1693 began a systematic accounting of islands and alluvial deposits in rivers, harking back to the declarations of 1668 and 1683. Men in possession of such property who were able to produce titles were allowed to retain possession provided they paid a *cens* equal to one year's income from the property. If they could not produce a title, the *cens* was increased to two years' revenue. Despite these efforts, the yield of the corporeal domain apparently fell from 4,500,000 livres in 1699 to 3,800,000 livres in 1705. The forests, which were exploited separately from the *ferme générale* on the domain, brought in about 2,000,000 livres annually.

In times of difficulty, the incorporeal domain was the great resource of the *contrôleurs généraux.* The edict of March 1693 made it compulsory to obtain a royal stamp for all notarized documents within two weeks of notarization. It was also made compulsory that excerpts from all such documents be recorded in public registers kept by the *greffiers* of sovereign and lower courts, for which a fee was charged. Documents that were not recorded could not be used in court. An exception was made for contracts drawn up before the notaries of Paris, in consideration of a loan of one million livres made by these notaries as a group to the king in 1694; in addition, documents notarized in Paris had to be drawn up on stamped paper that was more expensive than stamped paper elsewhere in the kingdom. It was still cheaper to have documents prepared in Paris, however. Clients seem to have flocked to Paris from all parts of the kingdom, and almost all important sales of real estate were concluded by Parisian notaries.

In 1705 private contracts were also made subject to royal approval, except for commercial contracts, letters of exchange, and promissory notes. Approval on writs was still required.

Entry of excerpts from documents in public registers, which had always been done when the parties to a contract wished to insure that their wishes could not later be put in doubt and which had been a power within the jurisdiction of the *lieutenants civils*, was made compulsory by the edict of December 1703 and the declaration of 19 July 1704 in cases of donations *inter vivos*, donations occasioned by death (except in direct line or by marriage contract), substitutions, separations of property, emancipations, interdictions, and letters of *surcéance* (postponement), ennoblement, and *naturalité*.

In 1703 all transfers of real property (except in direct line or by marriage contract) were made subject to a tax known as the *centième denier* (1 percent), or, when only the usufruct was transferred, the *demi-centième* (0.5 percent). Real property included property in land and associated rents and usufructs, such as the income from seigneurial courts, seigneurial dues, and feudal dues.

Royal approval of legal documents, registration of their contents, and the *centième denier* were not required in Alsace. Flanders, Hainault, Cambrésis, and Artois paid an annual lump sum in lieu of enforcing these regulations.

In addition to fees for approval of legal documents, there were fees charged for mortgages, for affixing the *petit scel* or royal seal, and for filing documents with a court clerk.

Taxes were levied to pay the salary of the *contrôleurs des comptes* in the sovereign and lower courts. These offices were eliminated in 1716. But the taxes continued to be levied. In 1727 they were incorporated into the contract for the *ferme générale* under the name *droits réservés*.

Taxes on tobacco were also part of the royal domain. These were often farmed out along with the *traites*. From 1629 to 1674 the king collected an import duty on tobacco. The declaration of 27 September 1674 gave the king a monopoly over sales of tobacco, which he immediately farmed out. In 1718 the king conceded the import duty on tobacco to John Law's Compagnie des Indes. The declaration of 1 August 1721 stated that the king reserved the exclusive right to import tobacco and to sell it wholesale or retail. Growing tobacco was prohibited within the kingdom, except in Flanders, Artois, Hainault, Cambrésis, Alsace, and Franche-Comté, where it could be grown and sold freely. In 1723 the monopoly was given once more to the Compagnie des Indes. The company then transferred the concession to the farmers general in 1730. The king recovered the monopoly in 1747 and thereupon leased it to the farmers general.

Notes

1. Cited by Sebastien Charléty, "Le régime douanier à Lyon au XVIIᵉ siècle," *Revue d'histoire de Lyon* 2 (1903): 138.

2. Cited by E. Lavisse, *Histoire de France*, vol. 7, part 1, p. 204.

3. *Batardeaux* were made of stone and moorings arranged on either bank of a river perpendicular to the flow in such a way as to force the bulk of the current to flow in the center of the river bed, thus deepening the channel.

4. Mousnier, *Vénalité*, pp. 196–97.

5. According to Trevoux's *Dictionnaire*, *crément* was "an administrative term denoting an augmentation or increase of land area as a result of the formation of new land in rivers or along their banks, from the Latin verb *crescere*."

20 The Concentration of the Farms before 1726

After the Fronde, in 1653 and 1654, the king took steps to establish an administration for the collection of indirect taxes, perhaps because of abuses committed by the tax farmers. This administration employed salaried *commissaires* to collect taxes and to supervise a host of officials and agents. Sometimes these *commissaires* received a percentage of the taxes they collected, in which case it was common to speak of an "interested administration." Early efforts in this direction had been made in 1594, but the results were not good.

The administration slowed the rate of tax receipts. *Commissaires* could not advance money to the king. Since they made no profit, it was hard to attract lenders. Thus the "service of the treasury" was in difficulty. Furthermore, it was now up to the government to bear the costs of tax collection, so that rather than receive advances from the tax farmers, the government had to lay out funds to aid with collections.

In twelve *généralités* there were supposed to be twelve *commis généraux de l'Epargne* in charge of the administration of indirect taxes or of the *gabelles* at the very least.

Whatever the reasons may have been, there is no doubt that the government very quickly returned to the tax farming system. Colbert took steps to consolidate the farms and to set up *fermes générales*. These were entrusted to associations of *financiers* enjoying good credit, the so-called *fermiers généraux* or farmers general. In 1663 Colbert established a general farm on the *aides* on wine "together with other associated duties." In 1664 a general farm was established to collect the *grandes gabelles* and *traites* outside the *cinq grosses fermes*. In April 1668 the *financier* François Legendre took the general farm on the *petites gabelles*. Legendre was the last to sign a lease for a farm in his own name, the custom of having the lease signed by a dummy partner having taken hold. On 1 September 1668, Legendre took a six-year lease on a whole group of farms: the general farm on the *grandes gabelles* and *traites*, the general farm on the *cinq grosses fermes*, and the general farm on the *aides* and associated duties. Soon thereafter he added his farm on the *petites gabelles* to this group. The whole package was known as the Fermes-Unies (United Farms). It yielded 43,700,000 livres annually to the royal treasury and enabled Colbert to reduce the *taille* to 33,832,000 livres.

The Dutch War, which began in 1672, reduced the amount of receipts from indirect taxes. Colbert was forced to divide collection of these taxes among three farms: one for the *grandes gabelles* and *cinq grosses fermes*, another for *aides* and other duties, and a third for *petites gabelles*. All told, these yielded 50,450,000 livres.

After the Peace of Nijmegen Colbert reestablished the United Farms in June of 1680. In December he combined all the domains of France and Flanders in one general farm on the domain. On 26 June 1681, a contract was signed with Fauconnet, combining a number of general farms: the general farm on the *grandes gabelles*, another on the *cinq grosses fermes*, another on the *aides* and associated duties, and still another on the domains. In 1685, following the death of Colbert, the general farm on the *petites gabelles* and the farm on the "domanial rights from the West and Canada" were added to this contract. In practical terms this amounted to a monopoly. The only items not included were tobacco and a few lesser farms. Meanwhile, Colbert had issued a series of regulations governing the operation of the general farms: these included the "common title for all the farms" of July 1681, the ordinance on the *gabelles* of May 1680, and the ordinances on entry duties, *aides*, and other duties of June 1680, one for the jurisdiction of the Cour des Aides of Paris and another for the jurisdiction of the Cour des Aides of Rouen. In 1683 the leases on farms yielded 65,892,000 livres, of which 64,124,000 livres came from the general farms alone.

In 1687 Colbert's successor Le Pelletier went back to having two "general farms," one for the *gabelles* and *traites* and another for the *aides* and domains, which all told yielded only 63,000,000 livres annually.

During the War of the League of Augsburg, the *contrôleur général*, Pontchartrain, returned to the system of the United Farms in the contract signed with Pointeau in 1691. Not included in this contract were the general farm on documents and writs, established in 1693, the farm on tobacco, and certain small farms. The war hampered trade, however, and thus spelled ruin for the farmers general. Collection of the *traites* had to be taken over by a government administration in 1703. In 1709 the *aides*, *gabelles*, and domanial revenues were also taken over by the administration. The king chose some of the farmers general as his *commissaires*. When peace came, the king attempted to reinstate the general farms with the Nerville contract in September 1714 and the Bonne contract in 1715.

After the great wars between France and the European allies, France was left, at the time of Louis XIV's death, with debts of 2 billion livres *tournois*, 600 million of which were in paper due immediately and already depreciated. Each year 165 million livres had to be found to service the interest on this debt. All the state's revenue up to 1722 had been spent in advance. Certification of bonds held by creditors reduced the amount of outstanding short-term paper to 250 million livres, at 4 percent interest. A chambre de justice set to work in order to force real or alleged profiteers to cough up their ill-gotten gains.

This financial distress provoked conflict between the *financiers* and the bankers. The Company of Farmers General signed the Manis contract in 1715 promising the state 48,500,000 livres the first year and 50,000,000 livres each year thereafter in exchange for the right to collect all the traditional taxes. But a Scottish banker by the name of John Law proposed to liquidate the state's debt and secure new sources of income by establishing a bank to deal in money and a company to deal in commodities. This was the "System" of Law, as it was known. Its adoption inagurated a struggle with the farmers general and the *receveurs généraux des Finances*.

In May 1716, Law was authorized to establish a bank, a private joint-stock company. As payment for shares in his bank, Law accepted the government's depreciated paper, a fair portion of which he thereby succeeded in withdrawing from circulation. He issued bank notes which the government forced the *receveurs généraux* to accept at face value, without discount.

In August 1717 Law founded the Compagnie d'Occident, which was granted the right to exploit the Louisiana territory and a monopoly on furs from Canada. Law issued 200,000 shares at 500 livres each (100 million in all), for which he accepted depreciated government paper. From this paper Law was supposed to receive 4 million in annual interest, which was the company's only operating capital.

The *financiers*, led by the commissary Joseph Pâris-Duverney, then launched a counteroffensive. Using the name Aymard Lambert, they signed a contract for general farms at 48,500,000 livres. But they transferred their rights to a joint-stock company with 100 million livres capital, consisting of 100,000 shares at 1,000 livres each. They promised a dividend of 12 to 16 percent to be earned from the collection of indirect taxes. This "Anti-System" enjoyed some success, since these shares were obviously a better investment than Law's and the source of this company's profits more certain. The Pâris brothers were backed by tax farmers, speculators, court bankers, *receveurs généraux*, and "businessmen."

This group launched an attack on Law's bank by demanding payment in gold for all the bank notes they had been forced to accept. Law responded by having the value of the bank note fixed by edict and having the *louis d'or* devalued by reducing the amount of gold it contained. He shored up his System by obtaining from the king the right to use royal monies for his bank's profit and by adding the general farm on tobacco and the trading companies for Africa and the East to the Compagnie d'Occident. In 1718 Law's bank became a royal credit bank, and in May 1719 the Compagnie d'Occident became the Compagnie des Indes.

The Compagnie des Indes contracted for the general farms at a price of 52 million livres and immediately made a loan to the king of 1,200,000 livres at 3 percent interest (the Pillavoine contract). In September and October 1719 it also acquired the general farm on the *droits de contrôle*, the general farm on the *gabelles* for Franche-Comté, and other farms. The duties of the *receveurs généraux des Finances* were confided to the company, the collection of the *tailles* in particular. Thus the company was in a position to supplant all the farmers and all financial officeholders, or at any rate to supervise their activities.

The company sold shares up to the amount of the principal of existing *rentes*. It accepted certificates of *rente* and all sorts of state paper in payment for its shares. Dividends were supposed to replace the interest on the state paper. But the king gave 48 million *livres* out of the Pillavoine contract for these dividends. In other words, Law was planning to imitate the "Anti-System" and the Pâris brothers, at least until his trading company had successfully established itself. In January 1720 Law was named *contrôleur général des Finances*. In February the bank and the company were combined. Law appointed the thirty members of the board of directors. He hired farmers general and their assistants. Twenty special offices were established to amalgamate the *fermes générales* and the *recettes générales*. Law attempted to simplify the tax structure. He envisioned a complete overhaul of the fiscal system. But for the time being he decided to give up the idea of liquidating the state debt through the profits on commercial and banking activities and settled for making improvements in the traditional system of tax collection.

Meanwhile, the price of shares in Law's concerns was continuing to rise. Speculation reached a fever pitch in February 1720. It became clear that profits could not begin to match the prices for which shares were selling. Prices began to fall in March. By the end of 1720 Law's System was in ruins and Law himself in exile.

The *contrôleur général des Finances*, Le Pelletier de La Houssaye, reestablished the *recettes générales*. Indirect taxes were collected by the so-called Cordier administration as of 5 January 1721. Forty *financiers* were named royal *commissaires* in exchange for a contribution of 140,000 livres each, on which the government paid 5 percent annual interest. Each *commissaire* received a salary of 18,000 livres per year. The government paid all collection costs: employees' salaries, rent on office space, supply of salt and stamped paper. Joseph Pâris-Duverney was appointed head of the administration for one year and reappointed subsequently until 1725. In 1723 the administration was given an "interest" in its collections (i.e., officials received a percentage of the taxes they collected). If less than 57 million livres was collected, the *commissaires* were to be charged a penalty of two sous for each missing livre. If more than 57 million was collected, however, they collected one sou for each additional livre. Joseph Pâris-Duverney introduced double-entry bookkeeping and supervised the operation of the administration as best he could, but there was nothing he could do about deceit and negligence. Furthermore, there was a tendency for the administration to break down into subadministrations, each with an interest in collecting its own quota. This made over-all supervision more difficult.

In 1725, the new prime minister, the bishop of Fréjus, soon to be named Cardinal Fleury, had the idea of creating an "aristocracy of finance," the so-called forty pillars of the state, which was supposed to serve as a counterweight to the aristocracies of sword and gown. On 9 July 1726, a royal declaration did away with the Cordier administration. On 19 August 1726, the general farms were reinstated with the Carlier contract. Forty farmers general promised to advance 80 million livres each year for six years. They were to collect the four categories of indirect taxes: *gabelles*, *aides*, *traites*, and domanial dues. The general farms were subsequently perpetuated by twelve successive contracts, although their scope was progressively reduced from 1780 onward.

21   The *Fermes Générales* from 1726 to 1791

The Importance of the *Fermes Générales* for the Revenues of the Monarchy

A large part of the royal revenues derived from the *fermes royales unies* or the *fermes royales et générales unies* or, as they were more commonly known, the *fermes générales du roi*, the king's general farms. The income from the farms accounted for 24.2 percent of royal revenues in 1643 and for 46.7 percent in 1662. In 1726 the Carlier contract yielded 80 million livres, compared with total royal revenues for 1725 estimated at 204 million, so that the general farms yielded about 40 percent of the total. In 1725 the indirect taxes yielded a total of 99 million livres, or more than 48 percent of the total revenue. The *recettes générales* yielded 87,500,000 livres in direct taxes in 1725, or less than half the total taxes collected in that year and only 7,500,000 more than the sum advanced under the Carlier contract of 1726. In 1786 the contract for the general farms, which by then had been pared down to include only the *gabelles*, tobacco, and Paris entry duties, was still yielding 144 million. The total revenue for 1788 can be estimated at 459,919,500 livres. In other words, the general farms of 1786 yielded about 33 percent of the total. To get an idea of the total revenue from indirect taxes, however, we would have to add 49 million coming from the *Commission générale des aides* and 43,715,000 livres from the *Administration générale des domaines*, administrations rather than farms. Thus indirect taxes accounted for 236 million livres or 52 percent of the monarchy's total revenue, as against 179,373 livres in direct taxes. Thus even at this late date the lease on the general farms still accounted for a considerable and indispensable portion of royal revenues. The cost of the lease on the general farms rose continuously from 1726 to 1774 (in nominal terms): in 1726 it went for 80 million, in 1744 for 92 million, in 1750 for 102 million, in 1768 for 132 million, and in 1774 for 152 million. After 1780, when a portion of the indirect taxes began to be collected by administrations rather than farms, the cost of the lease fell: in 1780 the contract on the *gabelles*, *traites*, tobacco, and Paris entry duties went for 127 million, and in 1786 in cost 144 million. The sums collected in the form of indirect taxes rose because the tax rate increased (an additional 4 sous per livre was added between 1705 and 1715, 5 sous per livre in 1763, and 10 sous per livre in 1781), because production and consumption increased, and because tax collection methods were improved.

The Influence of the Farmers General

The farmers general took in associates known as *croupiers* in their transactions. A farmer general could divide his investment into from four to eight *croupes*. Each *croupier* subscribed for one of these shares and took a corresponding share of the profits. *Croupiers* had no voice in how business was done, no administrative responsibilities, and no official existence. Families as well as individuals could act as *croupiers*. In 1774 thirty-eight out of sixty farmers general divided their investments into *croupes*.

In addition, the king sometimes forced farmers general to accept *croupiers* as partners who received their share of the profits even though they put up none of the initial investment. Madame du Barry was a partner of the farmer general Bouret d'Erigny. Louis XV had a one-quarter share in the investments of farmer general de La Haye, another quarter share in the investments of farmer general Saleur, and a half share in the investments of farmer general Poujaud.

The king also taxed the profits of the farmers general to provide money for pensions. In 1774 fifty-five out of sixty farmers general were required to pay pensions. The beneficiaries of these payments were courtiers, protégés of the *contrôleur général*, and agents of the government.

The farmer did not always have enough cash to put up his share of the advance. Before 1756, 622,000 livres was required, and after 1767 this increased to 1,560,000. If the farmer did not have the cash, he borrowed from various individuals by issuing notes bearing an interest of 6.5 percent. Spinsters and others of modest means thus became creditors of the farmers general with an interest in the prosperity of the *fermes générales*.

In addition, the farmers general exerted influence through the various posts they had the power to fill. In 1774, according to Lavoisier, the general farms employed 29,500 permanent agents and 5,000 to 6,000 temporary collectors, including an army of guards said to have employed 23,000 men in 1784. Agents were issued royal commissions granting them authority to collect taxes. The farmers general then contracted for the services of these royal *commis* and thereby acquired their authority.

Agents of the general farms had various ranks. To begin with, there were two major categories. The higher category consisted of *préposés*: *directeurs*, *contrôleurs*, *receveurs*, and their employees, secretaries, copyists, etc. The lower category consisted of *commis simples* such as tax collectors and guards.

It was possible to make a career as a *préposé*. After 1774, a young man wishing to make a career of this sort spent at least a year after finishing his studies working for a *procureur* of in the Hôtel des Fermes in Paris. He could then be nominated as a deputy controller general in training, attached to a provincial director general or controller general or to one of the correspondence bureaus in Paris. After a year those who performed poorly were dismissed. The rest were allowed to compete with the *sous-chefs* of the Hôtel des Fermes for places as provincial controllers general. After rising through four echelons of the hierarchy, a lucky man might become a provincial director, and after climbing through another four echelons he might become director of a correspondence bureau in Paris or a *receveur général de la ferme*.

Promotion depended on job performance. Supervisors periodically evaluated and graded their employees, indicating their rank, salary, age, height, place of birth, family composition, profession prior to coming to work for the farms, educational level, income, problems, and capabilities. The regulations of 1781 made it obligatory for employees in Paris to work from nine in the morning until one in the afternoon and from three in the afternoon until seven in the evening.

The salary offered for these posts could be attractive. In 1781 provincial directors earned from 12,000 to 15,000 livres annually. They frequented the higher strata of bourgeois society in the provinces. *Contrôleurs généraux*, *contrôleurs*, and *receveurs* were also well paid.

Below these ranks, salaries fell off very rapidly. *Inspecteurs des domaines* earned 2,000 to 2,400 livres, and the bulk of the collectors earned less—600 to 1,200 for a *captaine général* of the guard and 300 livres for an ordinary guard. But all were exempt from the *taille*, the *vingtièmes*, and the salt taxes, and their *capitation* was light. There were also bonuses offered by the company for the capture of smugglers, and percentages of funds collected were available to some. Guards, who were hired without qualifications or knowledge of life and customs and who knew how to write in only one out of five or six cases, also found their posts attractive because the average wage earner at the time was getting fifteen to twenty sous a day in the provinces and thirty to forty sous in Paris.

From 1773 on, the *préposés* were entitled to a paid retirement in the form of certain posts specially reserved for the purpose. *Commis simples* received retirement benefits, half of which consisted of the proceeds of compulsory contributions, the other half of funds from the general farms. These employees could claim their retirement benefits after twenty years of service in the collection of *gabelles*, *traites*, tobacco duties, and Paris entry duties. This system was not extended to cover the *aides* and *domaines*.

Thus by the second half of the eighteenth century the *commis* had taken on some of the characteristics of functionaries. Careers in the general farms were much sought after. The Company of Farmers General recruited the *préposés* itself. *Commis simples* were recruited by provincial and local department heads with the approval of the company. The farmers general were thus a power to be reckoned with. As *préposés* they recruited "well-born" and educated young men from the families of farmers general, financiers, lawyers, royal officeholders, *préposés*, and even impoverished *gentils-hommes* who were also clients or *fidèles* of ladies at court, government personnel, or high administrative officials. Beginning their careers as copyists and slowly climbing through the ranks of the hierarchy over the years, these young men became imbued with an esprit de corps that tied them to the general farms.

A good many Frenchmen of all orders had an interest in the careers of these men. *Commis* were increasingly required to post bonds. Those who handled funds were at first required to post real property as a bond. Later, after 1756 and the Seven Years' War, money bonds were also required. In 1756 a provincial *contrôleur général* had to post a bond of 10,000 livres; a provincial director, 30,000 livres in real estate and 30,000 livres in cash; a *receveur général du tabac*, 120,000 livres; and a simple *commis*, 2,000 to 3,000 livres. Cash bonds were treated as loans by the government and earned 5 percent interest. The government gradually increased the amount of bond required. The decree of 17 February 1779 required the posting of real property as bonds by all employees, whether they handled funds or not, and of cash bonds by all employees who handled funds. Thus all *commis* were required to post bonds, and the bonds required of *préposés* were increased considerably.

In order to come up with the necessary security, a protector or patron was essential. Backers were sought in all orders of society. The *généralités* of Caen and Rouen had 200 employees, among whose backers we find 24 *écuyers* or *chevaliers*, 2 *seigneurs*, 33 wholesalers and merchants, 30 "*bourgeois de*" one city or another, 16 "*sieurs*," 15 *avocats* and *procureurs*, 10 *laboureurs*, 6 *marchands-laboureurs*, 7 physicians, surgeons, and apothecaries, 11 judicial officeholders of the lower ranks, 3 financial officeholders of the lower ranks, 3 officers of the sovereign courts, 4 financiers, 2 employees of the farms, 4 farmers general of the domains, 3 notaries, 2 army officers, 5 artisans, 2 industrial entrepreneurs, 6 priests, 2 teachers, 2 municipal magistrates, 10 widows, 6 people of miscellaneous professions, and 5 individuals whose professions are unknown.

In November 1750, Marie-Victoire de Noailles, widow of the count of Toulouse, put up a 200,000 livre bond for a Parisian *receveur de sel*. Jean-Baptiste de Suffren, marquis de Saint-Tropez, posted a 12,000 livre bond for a *receveur directeur* in Soissons. Louis Potier, marquis de Novion, put up 6,000 livres for a saltpeter *receveur*. And Jean-Baptiste Oudry, ordinary painter to the king and professor at the Académie royale de Peinture et Sculpture, put up 30,000 livres for a *receveuse de la formule* with offices on the *pont Notre-Dame* in Paris.

Princes of the blood, great nobles of the sword and gown, commensals of the king, ecclesiastics, officeholders, lawyers, merchants, artisans, college regents, widows, and countless thousands of property owners all across France had an interest in the general farms through such bonds. These links between the general farms and a whole host of people dispersed throughout the various ranks of society gave the farms additional influence.

The Gradual Extension of Centralized, Hierarchical Administration by the General Farms

The Company

The farmers general were in charge of the general farms and formed a company, as did the *receveurs généraux des Finances*, the *régisseurs généraux des Aides*, and the *administrateurs généraux du Domaine*. Unlike these last three companies, whose members were united only by the similarity of their duties, the farmers general formed a *corps* that had the status of a moral person with a will of its own. A *doyen* represented the company's interests to the *contrôleur général*. An *intendant des Finances* was assigned to deal with the company, and the company called as a body on various ministers, visiting Necker, for example, on 14 July 1777.

After negotiations with the *intendant des Finances* and the *contrôleur général*, the contract for the general farms, which ran for six years, was prepared in the company's offices by its Comité des Caisses. The agreement between the king and the farmers general was formalized by the official minutes of the Conseil royal des Finances granting the lease. On 5 October 1755, for example, the minutes recorded approval of the contract with Pierre Henriet. The minutes listed the various taxes and duties to be collected, the amount of the lease (in this case 110 million per year), the assignment of products to the various Chambres des Comptes, and instructions authorizing the signers of the lease to take possession of buildings, equipment, personnel, and commodities that had been used by the previous farmers.

On 21 October Pierre Henriet submitted the signed contract to the council clerk and agreed to abide by all its clauses. On the same day he signed a counterletter in favor of his backers, the farmers general, at the Hôtel des Fermes in the presence of two notaries. In this letter he acknowledged that he was not a member of the corporation and claimed no part of the lease. On 23 October the farmers general themselves filed documents with the council clerk, in which they agreed with Henriet "one for all and all for one another" to abide by the minutes of 5 October.

On 24 October the sixty farmers general and their six adjoints signed the incorporation papers. Among the stipulations was that a mass be said each day at the Hôtel des Fermes.

On 31 August 1756, a council decree declared that the rights of Henriet and his backers were now in effect. The new lease was registered by the sovereign courts and on 1 October 1756 it came into force.

In public law, then, there was but a single farmer general for each lease, the so-called *adjudicataire général*, the man who actually signed the lease. The other farmers general were officially listed only as his backers. With each new lease there were a new *adjudicataire général* and a new set of backers. Between 1726 and 1786 there were twelve leases, hence by law twelve distinct companies of farmers general. Each time a new lease was issued, the company was dissolved and its books closed out. A new series of books was begun for the new lease, thereby making it easier for the royal government to keep an eye on the company's dealings.

The leases were the result of secret negotiations between the government and the *financiers*. Up to 1780, however, the legal fiction that the lease was awarded by competitive bidding was maintained. When the government and *financiers* reached an agreement, notices were posted in the chambers of all councils, sovereign courts, and lower courts. These notices announced the date of the next auction for the lease. The lease was awarded, and new notices were posted indicating the date of a second auction. Bids were once again taken, and the final award was made.

In private law, the farmers general jointly signed an "act of incorporation." One such was the "act of incorporation by the parties interested in the David lease of 29 January 1774," in which Lavoisier took part. Responsibility of the members of this corporation was unlimited. The company was collectively responsible for the financial obligations of each member. The partners were all equal. Each contributed the same share, and each was entitled to the same share of the profits, salaries, and other emoluments of operation. Each had to bear an equal share of any losses.

The king set the number of farmers general. He issued "royal notes" awarding the first available vacancy to a specific individual. The king could grant the farmers general permission to trade places among themselves. Each one was nominated by council decree upon report of the *contrôleur général des Finances*. The king issued a brevet awarding the title and dignity of farmer general, which carried with it exemption from the *taille*, the *ving-tièmes*, and the salt tax. The Company of Farmers General then deliberated before registering the sovereign's nomination decree. Between 1726 and 1756 there were 40 farmers general. The number increased to 60 between 1756 and 1780, was reduced to 40 in 1780, and rose again to 42 in 1786 and 44 in 1787.

The king could issue council decrees appointing "adjoints" or partners of each individual farmer general. Adjoints were generally relatives, usually sons or nephews, who learned the trade as deputy controllers in provincial offices or as scribes at the Hôtel des Fermes. They replaced the officially designated farmer general during his absence, received a share of the profits, and inherited the office if its holder died.

The Social Status of the Farmers General

Powerful protectors were needed if one wished to become a farmer general, adjoint, or subfarmer (the Company of Farmers General was quite willing to deal with subfarmers and between 1726 and 1756 subcontracted for the collection of *aides*, Paris entry duties, and *domaines* with twenty-seven companies of subfarmers). Awards were almost always made on the recommendation of individuals with influence at court, such as members of the royal family, royal favorites, and ministers. The duchesse de Châteauroux obtained a royal note promising the first vacancy for farmer general to her protégé Camuset, who finally received his post in 1749, five years after the death of his protectress. Jeanne-Antoinette Poisson, marquise de Pompadour, married the farmer general Le Normant d'Etiolles in 1751. She played a leading role in the choice of a number of farmers general. Ministers and *contrôleurs généraux des Finances* always had individuals beholden to them in the general farms. Choiseul, for example, had Jean-Joseph de Laborde as farmer general and court banker.

The farmers general came from all the provinces of France. A third were natives of Paris and the Ile-de-France. Of the families of provincial origin, forty-three placed one of their members as farmer general after a generation had resided in the capital, while seventy-two had no prior residence in Paris.

Of 134 farmers general whose fathers are known, we find that 24 had fathers who were wholesale or retail merchants, 21 magistrates (5 in the sovereign courts, 12 in the lower courts of justice, and 4 in the lower financial tribunals), 18 accounting officers (2 *receveurs généraux des Finances* and 16 *receveurs des tailles, trésoriers de l'extraordinaire des guerres, payeurs des rentes de l'Hôtel de Ville*, and other treasurers), 8 ministerial officials (notaries, *procureurs, huissiers*, and *greffiers*), 3 *avocats* in *parlement*, for a total of 47 royal officeholders, and, with the *avocats*, 32 men of law; there were 18 whose fathers were employed by the farms (6 farmers general, 3 subfarmers, 6 *commis*, and 3 commissaires), 9 whose fathers were physicians or surgeons, and 2 whose fathers were army officers.

Contrary to a prevalent social myth, then, the farmers general did not emerge from the lower strata of the populace. They were not lackeys. Contrary to a myth prevalent among historians, only a small number came from the world of commerce.

The social status of farmers general may be inferred from their quality and from the marriages they made. For the most part they were ennobled men. In 1726, 14 of them (35 percent) were commoners, 19 *écuyers* (48 percent), and 7 royal secretaries (17.5 percent). By 1762 there were only 9 commoners (14 percent), 1 knight and 28 *écuyers* (47 percent), and 23 royal secretaries (37 percent). It should be noted, however, that this was a time when titles were devalued, and the quality of *écuyer* was often taken by notables in the process of ennoblement. In 1774, 15 of the farmers general were commoners (17 percent), 56 *écuyers* (64 percent), and 16 royal secretaries (18 percent). In 1786 there were 6 commoners (11 percent), 32 *écuyers* (67 percent), and 11 royal secretaries (20 percent).

We have information about first marriages in 184 cases, and it should be noted that these men usually married before they became farmers general. Six married the daughters of merchants (3.5 percent), and 2 married the daughters of "*bourgeois de*" one city or another (1.01 percent). Eight married daughters of rank (4.3 percent) and 7, daughters bearing noble titles (4.1 percent). Three married daughters of army officers (1.75 percent). Seventeen married daughters of magistrates (5 from the sovereign courts, 4 from the lower courts, 1 *maître des requetes*, 1 provincial *intendant*, 6 magistrates in finance), or 10.5 percent of the total. Seventeen married the daughters of accounting officials (6 *receveurs généraux des Finances* and miscellaneous *receveurs* and *trésoriers*), or 10.5 percent again. Forty-two married daughters of farm employees (27 percent general, 10 subfarmers or partners, 5 *commis*), or 22.5 percent of the total. Eight (4.3 percent) married the daughters of physicians or surgeons. These marriages led to a higher social status for the individual even before his promotion to farmer general.

A man who became a farmer general could expect to see his sons become farmers general, councillors in the *parlements* of Paris and Metz, *maîtres de requêtes* and intendants, marquis and masters of ceremony at court, thus primarily *nobles de robe*. His sons and daughters could be expected to marry mainly into the *noblesse de robe*. A few daughters did marry into the high *noblesse d'épée*. This was an exception which contemporaries took to be the rule. The post of farmer general thus led to upward social mobility. Distinguished as "Farmers General of His Majesty," these men were admitted to the salons of high society. Some gave sumptuous receptions in their Parisian *hôtels* and suburban *châteaux*. Others were amateurs of art, music, and science, patrons and philantropists or even scholars in their own right. In a society which, during the second half of the eighteenth century, witnessed the rise of a new ideal of happiness associated with pleasure, luxury, and money, finance acquired a distinctive individuality as a social order. The French regarded finance as inferior to the sword and slightly inferior to the gown. Men of finance constituted the lowest division of the second legal order, the nobility, and mingled in society with the higher divisions of that order.

As the abbé Expilly wrote in 1772, "At bottom, what is truly distinguished in the nation? Is it not correct to say that in Paris, he who has the best horses occupies the first rank? And that in the provinces, he who is the most well-off holds that place? Hence the distinction between estates is merely illusory, and the real distinction, which ought to be based on personal merit, is actually based on the relative degree of wealth or poverty. Still, the prejudice remains."[1] Indeed, prejudice remained to such an extent that farmers general did their best to establish their descent from illustrious ancestors belonging to the *noblesse d'épée*.

The Central Administration of the General Farms

The administration of the general farms grew more and more centralized over the course of the century. Prior to the Henriet contract (1756–62), each farmer general had offices in his private *hôtel*. He paid his own *commis* and secretaries. The Company of Farmers General maintained limited offices in the Hôtel des Fermes on the rue de Grenelle-Saint-Honoré near the Saint-

Eustache church, premises acquired by the company at the end of the seventeenth century. In 1756 the company's offices were consolidated in the Hôtel des Fermes and the hôtels de Longueville (the tobacco monopoly) and de Bretonvilliers (Paris entry duties) as well as the salt warehouse. Employees were recruited by the company. Their number was increased, and they were henceforth paid out of the funds of the general farms. In that same year the company assumed direct responsibility for *aides* and *domaines* rather than subcontracting for their collection. A truly centralized administration was constantly being perfected.

By 1763 the central administration was able to describe itself as such.

In principle, decisions were taken by the company as a whole. The company did not delegate its authority to a board of directors. It had no president, secretary, or treasurer, either elected or appointed. No farmer general could assume sole responsibility for any part of the general farms. Each farmer general was supposed to have an equal voice in all financial and administrative decisions. Decisions taken by the company in regard to important issues were preceded by deliberations, the minutes of which were signed by the majority of farmers general, countersigned by the *contrôleur général des Finances*, and registered by the Cour des Aides.

The farmers general made their decisions known in various ways. "Orders" were interpretations of a law and had to be signed by the *contrôleur général* and published. "Circulars" were similarly interpretations of a law but were intended for the personnel of the farms only, not for the general public. "Memoirs" and "instructions" contained directives in regard to administrative matters and had to be signed by at least six farmers general. They were issued by commissions that were known first as "assemblies" and later, after 1780, as "committees." There were seventeen such commissions in all. A new chairman was elected each year. Seven of these commissions were concerned with issues of interest to all the farms. The *assemblées des caisses* was composed of ten farmers general. The administrative committee had nineteen members. The personnel committee had nine. The committee on bonds, six. The committees on retirement, litigation, and archives each had four members. Ten other assemblies were concerned with the administration of particular farms. The committee on the *grandes gabelles* was made up of twenty-one farmers general. The committee on the *petites gabelles* had eleven members. The committee on the tobacco monopoly had twenty-five members, that on *traites*, twenty-six members. The committee on Paris entry duties had twelve members. Three committees dealt with *aides*, each with ten members. Three other committees were concerned with *domaines*, each with twenty members.

Each farmer general sat on four or five different committees. The membership rotated every two years, so that during the course of a six-year lease each farmer general would have the opportunity to sit on a majority of the committees. The Company appointed members to the committees and to all administrative posts, but these appointments had to be approved by the *contrôleur général des Finances*. Each year the *contrôleur général* had a decree listing the appointments registered by the Cour des Aides and published in the *Almanach royal*.

The *assemblée des caisses* was the most important of all the committees and acted as a management committee for the entire company. It served as an intermediary between the Company and the *contrôleur général des Finances*. It was this committee that negotiated contracts. In 1780 its name was changed to the "administrative committee." Its membership did not rotate. Only the wealthiest and most experienced farmers general were admitted to membership. They were appointed for life. After becoming a farmer general in 1768, Lavoisier was named to the administrative committee in 1783.

Each committee elected some of its members to act as "correspondents" for one-year terms. They were responsible for preparing reports to be read to the full committee and for relaying the committee's decisions and instructions to the "provincial directors." Each correspondent took charge of one of the "correspondence bureaus" at the central office and in effect supervised a certain number of provincial directors.

Thus each committee maintained relations with a specific bureau in the central administration. In 1774 the administration employed 591 *commis* in two sections, one section for general business pertaining to the general farms, the other section supervising the various individual farms. The general business section was divided into five subsections, which in turn were divided into bureaus. The subsection known as Recettes Générales was under the control of the administrative committee. It was in contact with the Caisse de Paris and its two bureaus, one for receipts, the other for expenditures, as well as with the 181 Recettes Provinciales or provincial collection offices. Another subsection, the Comptes Généraux or general accounting department, was under the control of the *assemblée des Caisses*. Its general offices and office of true accounts were in contact with twelve accounting offices. The personnel subsection, which was under the control of the committees on personnel, retirement, and bonds, was divided into an office for bonds and an office for retirement. The legal-affairs subsection, which was supervised by the litigation committee, included a Farm Council consisting of six *avocats*, five *procureurs*, and several legal assistants. The subsection known as the General Secretariat was supervised by the archives committee.

The general management section was divided into "correspondence bureaus." Each was under the control of a farmer general, who represented a committee and acted as correspondent. Each bureau had a managing director and corresponded with several provincial directorates, but there was no specialization in one particular form of tax. It was not unheard of for a provincial directorate to have to correspond with two correspondence bureaus.

In addition, contact with the provincial directorates was maintained by "touring farmers general," who acted as representatives of the central administration. Each year the Company elected six to eight farmers general to represent it on tour. Each was assigned to undertake a designated inspection tour and granted unlimited authority to act in the Company's name. The touring inspector traveled in the company of assistants and *écuyers*, fifteen to eighteen men in all wearing the uniforms of the general farms. Such an inspection tour was made by the philosopher Claude-Adrien Helvétius, who was a farmer general from 1728 to 1751. In 1737 and 1738 he conducted inspections in the directorates of Châlons-sur-Marne, Charleville, and Langres. Farmers general began their careers by making an inspection tour during which they learned how the system worked.

Each provincial directorate covered a territory corresponding to a *généralité*, except for the *aides*, whose districts frequently corresponded to *élections*. Ostensibly, there should have been one provincial directorate for each category of receipt: one for salt, one for tobacco, one for *traites*, and one for *aides*. In fact, however, two or three categories of receipts were often combined in a single directorate. Thus the *gabelles*, *traites*, and tobacco duties might be combined under the same provincial director and the same *contrôleur général*, and the same guards might be used to collect all three. The *aides* and *domaines* were always separate, however. In 1763 there were 123 provincial directorates for 33 *généralités*.

The provincial director had his offices in the same city as the king's intendant. He had the same powers as an *avocat* and played the same role. His duties were strictly set forth in a minutely detailed commission. He was required to send a huge volume of reports and statistics to the correspondence bureau over him. These were used by the farmer general acting as correspondent and relayed by him to the appropriate committee. The provincial director paid his own office workers, who did their work at his home. Provincial directors were valued above all for their ability to audit accounts and for their detailed knowledge of laws, regulations, and local customs. The provincial director was supposed to confine himself to carrying out the strict letter of the law. All improvements and initiatives for change were supposed to come from the correspondent and his committee. This system of administration worked efficiently. For an example of how collections were made, let us consider the *grandes gabelles*. For each salt storehouse, the provincial director would have "sixth books" prepared, so called because, from 1710 on, an extract from these remarkable registers was published every six months in each parish, advising the residents to come pick up their salt. The sixth book recorded the name of every resident of the district, whether exempt or not, including beggars and paupers. There was a place in the book for each "hearth." The records included the first and last names, ranks, and level of *taille* or head tax for each person associated with each hearth, except for children under eight years of age. The number of livestock of each species was also recorded. When the head of the family came to pick up his salt, the officers of the salt warehouse marked him down for the amount sold in the register. Names were collected for the sixth book from the collectors of the *tailles* or, in cities where no *taille* was collected, from the municipal magistrates, who were required to submit copies of their rolls and census every year or risk being fined.

In 1788 the *grandes gabelles* produced 39,500,000 livres for the king. The *petites gabelles* yielded 14,000,000 livres, and other taxes on salt yielded 5,060,000 livres. The cost of collection was 7.5 percent for the *grandes gabelles* and 8.5 percent for the *petites*.

In the tobacco administration, the provincial director supervised a main warehouse, which employed a general manager and an office staff consisting of scribes, warehousemen, and guards, as well as secondary warehouses, with similar staffs, and retail sales personnel known as *buralistes*, licensed tobacconists. In 1774 there were 453 secondary warehouses. According to Necker, in 1785 there were 10,000 *buralistes*. Collection costs amounted to more than 10 percent of the revenue collected.

For the *traites*, the general farms maintained 1,400 customs posts, 1,000 of them for the Etendue and the "foreign" provinces. In each *généralité* the provincial director supervised a central customs station, which employed a large staff, including a collector, a comptroller, inspectors, scribes, customs agents, and guards. Attached to the central customs station were a number of substations, each employing a collector, an inspector, and guards. Each substation controlled a number of minor customs posts staffed by an inspector and one or two guards. The Etendue was protected by two concentric circles of customs stations, one near the border, the other three or four leagues in from the border.

For the *aides*, the provincial director maintained a *bureau des aides* in each city, staffed by a comptroller, a collector, and a number of agents. In the countryside each group of two or three parishes was assigned a comptroller and a number of agents on horseback. There were also clerks to receive declarations from producers, wholesalers, and retail merchants and to collect duties. Agents of the *bureaux des aides* wore uniforms and were armed. Like guards working in the collection of the *gabelles*, *traites*, and tobacco duties, these agents had the right to conduct searches without a warrant.

As for the *droits de contrôle*, or fees collected for the stamping of certain documents, the registers were initially given to special officers known as *contrôleurs des actes*. In 1713–14, however, these offices were eliminated. Notaries were assigned to collect these fees. Then, in 1719, a general farm for stamps, deeds, and writs was created, and in 1726 all receipts from the royal domains were assigned to the general farms. But still the farmers continued for a time to use notaries to collect these taxes. Little by little, however, this job was taken away from the notaries and turned over to agents of the general farms under the control of the provincial directors. By 1774 the transition was complete.

There was a considerable amount of smuggling and fraud, affecting salt, tobacco, *traites*, and *aides*. The farmers general, who enjoyed regalian rights, maintained a veritable private army. There were 19,500 such guards in 1768 and 23,000 in 1784. They staffed 352 divisions of 24 to 200 men each, commanded by a captain general. Divisions were subdivided into brigades of 2 to 8 men commanded by a brigadier. Fixed brigades assigned to the salt warehouses never ranged farther than a day's march from their headquarters. They were commanded by a brigadier and a deputy brigadier. A third of the brigades were mobile brigades. Members of these brigades rode on horseback and ranged over an entire fiscal district. Each consisted of a captain, a lieutenant, and at least four men.

Guards were generally involved with salt, tobacco, and, until 1778, *aides*, all at the same time. They oversaw the shipment of wine, spirits, and cider. They kept an eye on tobacco smugglers, clandestine manufacturers, and resellers who evaded payment of taxes. The Company actually bought tobacco in Virginia and Maryland and had it processed in Arles, Cette, Le Havre, Marseille, Morlaix, Paris, Toulouse, Nancy, and Valenciennes. Tobacco was sold in plugs known as "carrots" or in rolled leaves. The buyer could either chop it for chewing, smoke it, or grind it for snuff. The latter was the preferred method, and consumers demanded "ground tobacco." The Company at first licensed retailers to manufacture ground tobacco. In 1758, however, it began manufacturing ground tobacco itself in ever increasing amounts. This caused retailers to lose money. They were also the losers when the Company took steps to reduce their profit margins as a way of keeping the price of tobacco down. The Company refused to pay any surtax on tobacco, but in 1781 it was forced to accept a surtax of two sous per livre. The Company paid a portion of this surtax itself and forced retailers to pay the rest without increasing the price of tobacco. From 1781 on, the law allowed the Company to sell snuff for 9 livres 16 sous. But the Company actually sold tobacco wholesale at 3 livres 12 sous and allowed retailers to sell it at 4 livres, with only 8 sous profit. Retailers found it advantageous to buy tobacco at a low price from sailors or smugglers (who got it from provinces where tobacco could be grown freely) and then to grind it themselves clandestinely and mix it in with what they sold to their customers. Above all, the guards fought against evasion of the salt tax. They checked the sixth books, inspected houses, patrolled rivers and highways to combat smuggling of both salt and tobacco, and watched salt merchants to see that they delivered no more than the allowed quantities of salt and deposited the correct sums of money at the salt warehouses. The fixed brigades kept an eye on subsidiary sellers to guard against a black market in salt.

These guards were not organized until after 1680 and enjoyed their heyday under Louis XIV. Soldiers in winter quarters easily became involved in smuggling and illegal dealing in salt. In years when the harvest was poor, many peasants sought additional income from smuggling. Troops on the move carried with them from camp to camp hundreds of horses loaded with salt from regions where the price was low to regions where it was high. Led by their officers, these troops lined up in battle formation to drive off the employees of the farms. In March 1695, several brigades of guards armed with muskets, pistols, and bayonets fought a battle with twenty to twenty-five dragoons near the village of Allemande and emerged victorious. Between 1690 and 1715 the guards took part in a number of pitched battles. In 1707 bands of anywhere from fifty to eighty dragoons took part in illegal dealings in salt. These bands were too much for the guard detachments, which consisted of fifteen to twenty men. In the same year peasants in lower Normandy and along the coast of Brittany also organized in groups. In July 1707, Foucault, the *intendant* of Caen, was forced to order the *maréchaussée* to "impress" men into the brigades in order to bring them up to strength adequate to combat the smugglers. In January 1710 M. de Mazarin, *directeur des Aides* in Caen, mustered the brigades of Caen and Laval to attack the cavalry regiment of Saint-Aignoy, which was smuggling salt in Brittany. On 15 January the guards fought 150 horsemen from the regiment, capturing 49 of them together with 124 loads of salt. Several officers of the brigades were killed in the fighting. Other battles were also fought, one near Mortain with 180 horsemen, another in June 1710 near Laval with 200 to 250 horsemen. At Falaise in February of 1711, 100 to 120 soldiers with 50 loads of salt attempted to break the blockade around the *grande gabelle* region by outflanking the brigades of the guard. But the guards hired peasants as "bounty hunters" and, after a fierce battle, stopped the soldiers in their tracks.

After 1715 a relative calm was restored. But smuggling continued. Illegal dealing in salt was endemic in the areas of *grande* and *petite gabelle*, smugglers moving from Brittany toward Maine and Anjou. Between 1780 and 1783, 2,342 men, 896 women, and 201 children were found guilty of illegal dealing in the area of Laval and Angers. Horses and wagons were confiscated.

There were few army veterans among the guards. Of 429 officers and men belonging to the guard on 1 January 1789, we find that 46.8 percent were agricultural laborers, 9.8 percent merchants, 14.2 percent sons of general farm employees, 7.2 percent soldiers and sailors, and 11 percent servants. Eighty-four percent of the officers and noncommissioned officers could read and write and prepare reports. But only 4 percent of the men had these abilities, and 61 percent could do no more than sign their name. Most officers and noncoms had either been *commis simples* or served in the army. The average term of service in the brigade was six years for an ordinary guard and sixteen years for officers and noncoms. Guards were recruited from the local populace. Ninety-one percent of them had been born within 100 kilometers of where they were stationed. They married local women. Seventy-five percent of the officers and noncoms and more than 50 percent of the guards were married. Each couple had an average of 2.18 children. According to their superiors, 85 percent of the members of the guard brigades deserved to be rated either good or excellent, energetic and zealous.

The Decline of the General Farms

By 1780 a crisis had hit the general farms. According to a widespread myth, the farmers general were allies of the highest nobility and identified with those who were accused of living in pleasure and corruption. Beginning in 1780 Necker refused to accept anyone but sons of farmers general as adjoints, and this gave rise to the belief that the aristocracy of finance had closed its ranks to new members. In the same period *préposés* were asked to increase the amount of the bonds they posted, forcing some of them to withdraw from their positions and closing access to all but the wealthiest men with the most powerful patronage. The gap between *commis simples* and *préposés* grew wider, in the same way as the analogous gap between *commis* and *premiers commis* in ministerial bureaus and between *avocats* and office-holders in the courts, which also widened during this period. The possibility of rising in the social hierarchy seemed to diminish everywhere in the kingdom. A relatively small group of families had apparently gained an exclusive hold on power and on the wealth and influence deriving from it, putting an end to outsiders' hopes of upward mobility. The higher echelons of society seemed to be closed to newcomers.

The general farms were accused of having spread their tentacles into every corner of society. In 1730 the Company had acquired the lease on the tobacco monopoly from the Compagnie des Indes. In 1732 it acquired the domanial rights for Canada and the western colonies. In 1738 it purchased the farms on taxes from the duchies of Lorraine and Bar. These were included in the lease for 1762 and distributed among the five major sources of revenue in 1780.

The farmers general were readily accused of poor administration. To take one example, the company monopolized the manufacture of ground tobacco from 1781 on, as we have seen. Retailers sought protection from the *parlements* and the Cours des Aides. In the years following 1782, the courts said that the farmers general did not have the right to monopolize the manufacture of ground tobacco and allowed retailers to produce their own on the grounds that the quality of tobacco was poor and the product excessively moist. The farmers general answered this charge by saying that it was necessary to have water in tobacco in the amount of one-seventeenth the gross weight, and that retailers were charged for only sixteen-seventeenths of the weight sold to them. With this additional information in hand, most of the courts rescinded their original judgment and ordered the retailers to obey the orders of the farmers general. Two courts remained obstinate, however: the *parlement* of Rouen, even though in practice the farmers general had free rein in Normandy, and the *parlement* of Rennes, which refused to acknowledge that even the Conseil d'Etat had authority in this area. The farmers general acceded to the Rennes court and settled for selling only plugs of tobacco in Brittany, where in any case they did little to combat tobacco smuggling.

The Paris entry duties were widely evaded, even though the city had special gates for the entry of goods, each watched over by an inspector and a number of guards, and even though it was divided into twenty-nine zones for the administration of markets and stores, each zone being assigned a duty collector. Despite these precautions, Paris consumed one-fifth more goods than taxes were paid on. This represented a loss for the general farms of six million livres annually. On the recommendation of Lavoisier construction of a wall was begun in 1783. By 1789 it was nearly complete. Fifty-eight of sixty-six planned gates had been built. But *"le mur murant Paris rend Paris murmurant"*: the wall around Paris set Paris murmuring. It became the symbol of the "tyranny" of the farmers general and led to their being identified with the ministerial "despotism" of the absolute monarchy.

One criticism that was commonly leveled at the general farms was that there were too many farmers general. In 1753 the marquis d'Argenson claimed that only six or seven of the forty farmers general actually did any work. Around 1780 the general farms were in fact run by an active minority of the farmers general, including Delahante, Paulze, Lavoisier, de La Borde, and Parseval. In 1774 Turgot asserted that ten *commissaires* could have run the general farms more efficiently than sixty farmers general. Another criticism that was heard was that the farmers general had stood in the way of any improvement of the tax system. The farmers general took the view that the king should not alter the tax system while the contract with them was in force, and one contract followed hard upon another. What the farmers general had in fact done was to perfect the techniques for collecting taxes levied under an obsolete system.

By the 1770s the farmers general were no longer seen as an indispensable adjunct to the treasury, which had been their great strength. In 1774 the state borrowed money for the first time on the international money market. The bankers took their revenge against the fiscal system. In 1780 the monopoly of the farmers general over the royal debt was broken. It was obvious that the public debt was going to fall into the hands of international banking houses and joint-stock companies, both commercial and industrial. This was John Law's posthumous revenge against the Pâris brothers.

Necker began dismantling the general farms with the regulation of 9 January 1780. He established "interested" administrations for the *aides* and *domaines*, the latter embracing the Eaux et Forêts as well. In 1783 an administration was established for the *traites* also, but the farmers general were named *commissaires*. Necker altered the membership of the committees that governed the farms, chose the leading correspondents himself, and played an active role in the administration. An *intendant des Finances* regularly attended meetings of the *comité des caisses*. In 1780 broad powers of inspection were granted to four *premiers commis* assigned to investigate the four "collections" still within the purview of the general farms: *gabelles*, tobacco duties, *traites*, and Paris entry duties. The authority of the *contrôleur général* over the general farms was increased, and the farms were increasingly integrated into the royal tax administration.

The farmers general were detested. In 1778 the remonstrances of the Cour des Aides of Paris were published. The Grand Remonstrances of 1775 attacked the greed and tyranny of the farmers general. In 1782, Louis-Sébastien Mercier wrote in his *Tableau de Paris* (III, 119) that he could not pass by the Hôtel des Fermes without being gripped by a desire to "destroy this immense infernal machine, which grabs every citizen by the throat and sucks his blood." The *cahiers de doléances* for the Estates General of 1789 demanded that the general farms be completely eliminated.

On 12 July 1789, the offices of the collectors of Paris entry duties were attacked and several of them were sacked and set afire. The collection of entry duties came to a halt. This was a prelude to the taking of the Bastille. During the course of the year customs offices were burned and salt warehouses destroyed. The collection of indirect taxes ceased. In August 1789 the Constituent Assembly ordered the Company to close out its books. The *gabelles* were abrogated on 14 March 1790, the *traites* were converted into a single tariff on 20 October 1790, and procedures for the stamping and registration of documents were reformed by the edict registered on 5 December 1790. Entry duties were eliminated on 19 February 1791, and *aides* were eliminated on 2 March. The tobacco monopoly was done away with on 20 March 1791. On the same day, the Mager lease of 1786 was declared null and void. The general farms went out of existence.

The Constitutent Assembly named five *commissaires* to liquidate the company. This work took a long time, because it could only be done as provincial collectors turned in their receipts and account books. On 5 June 1793, the Convention lost its patience and sacked the *commissaires*. It ordered the transfer of farm funds to the central treasury and had the offices and papers of the Hôtel des Fermes placed under seal. A decree of 29 September authorized the farmers general to refer to their papers and archives so that they might render accounts on 1 April 1794.

But the farmers general had become one of the symbols of the old society and the old order. They also faced the bitter opposition of their former employees, who were determined to wreak vengeance. One such was Dupin, a former deputy comptroller general of the farms, who had since become deuputy for Aisne. Another was Gaudot, a former collector of entry duties at the Port Saint-Paul, who had been prosecuted for forging financial documents and for having stolen from two to three hundred thousand francs from the general farms. When he was released from prison after 10 August, he sought access to the trial records in order to destroy them. On 26 September 1793, Dupin obtained passage of a decree ordering the farmers general to render accounts to a commission of five auditors, all former employees of the farms. This commission was chaired by Dupin himself, and Gaudot was a member.

On 24 November 1793 (4 *Frimaire, an* II), the farmers general were placed under arrest and obliged to wind up their bookkeeping within the month. On the same day nineteen of them were incarcerated in the former Port-Royal convent. Before long thirteen more were in prison. On 4 December they were transferred to the Hôtel des Fermes. On 27 January 1794, they submitted their accounts to the commission of auditors.

The accounts showed a surplus of 10 million. However, a law of 23 *Nivôse* and a decree of 29 *Nivôse, an* II, adopted at the instigation of Dupin and Gaudot, had already "placed under national protection" the chattels, real estate, and income of the farmers general. Once the decree of 10 March 1793, had been adopted, ordering the confiscation of the property of men condemned to death by the Republic, a death sentence for the farmers general became a necessity for a Convention with its back to the wall. On 5 May 1794 (16 *Floréal, an* II), Dupin read a report to the Convention. He accused the farmers general of various peculations and asserted that they owed the state 130,345,262 livres 12 sols 1 denier. He asked that the farmers general be sent before the revolutionary tribunal, and his request was granted.

On the night of 16 *Floréal*, 34 farmers general were transferred to the Conciergerie. Interrogation took place on the 18th (7 May) before the *procureur de la République*, Fouquier-Tinville. The indictment returned by Fouquier-Tinville repeated the charges made by Dupin and added that the farmers general had betrayed their trust out of hatred for the Republic and a desire to aid the enemies of the state. The jury was unanimous in finding the farmers general guilty of a conspiracy against the people of France, and the president of the court read the decision condemning them to death and ordering the confiscation of their property. After being brought back to the Conciergerie, they mounted the tumbrels that were to convey them to the place de la Révolution. The first heads fell at about five in the afternoon. Twenty-eight farmers general were guillotined. Ten others were executed along with members of their families. Ten escaped death. Those who died were victims of the enmity of dishonest employees and of a political and social myth. They died as "aristocrats."

Audit commissions continued to examine the archives of the general farms after Thermidor. On 8 May 1806, the farmers general associated with the last four leases (Alaterre, David, Salzard, and Mager) were granted final discharge, and the general farm was declared to have amassed a surplus of 8,037,062 livres 10 sols 6 deniers, which amount was due the farmers from the state. The farmers general were rehabilitated.

Notes

1. Cited by Yves Durand, *Les fermiers généraux au XVIIIe siècle* (Paris: PUF, 1971), p. 648.

Guide to Further Reading

Baulieu, E. P. *Les gabelles sous Louis XIV*. Paris-Nancy, 1903. Reprinted in 1974 by Slatkine Reprints, Geneva.

Benoist, Charles. "La hiérarchie des professions dans l'ancienne société française." *Séances et travaux de l'Académie des Sciences morales et politiques*, 71st year, vol. 75, first half of 1911, 98–110.

Boislisle, A.M. de. *Correspondance des contrôleurs généraux des finances avec les intendants des provinces.* 3 vols. Imprimerie Nationale, 1874–97.

Bosher, J. F. *The Single Duty Project.* London, 1964.

———. *French Finances, 1770–1795. From Business to Bureaucracy.* Cambridge, Eng.: Cambridge University Press, 1970.

Bouchary, Jean. *Les manieurs d'argent à Paris à la fin du XVIIIᵉ siècle.* 3 vols. 1939–43.

Bouloiseau, Marc. "Une source peu connue de l'histoire économique et sociale: Les rapports des directeurs de la régie des aides et droits réunis. L'exemple du Saumurois (1783)." *Bulletin d'histoire économique et sociale de la Révolution française*, 1969, pp. 131–63.

Bouteil, J. *Le rachat des péages au XVIIIᵉ siècle.* 1925.

Bouvier, Jean, and Henry Germain-Martin. *Finances et financiers de l'Ancien Régime.* 1964.

Callery, Alphonse. "Les douanes avant Colbert et l'ordonnance de 1664." *Revue historique* 18 (1882): 49–91.

Chardon, M. E. *La direction de l'enregistrement, des domaines et du timbre dans les généralités de Tours et de Rouen.* Rouen, 1900.

Charléty, Sébastien. "Le régime douanier à Lyon au XVIIᵉ siècle." *Revue d'histoire de Lyon* 1 (1902), fasc. 6; 2 (1903), fasc. 2: 126–37.

Chaussinand-Nogaret, Guy. *Les financiers de Languedoc au XVIIIᵉ siècle.* S.E.V.P.E.N., 1970.

Cochin, G. *L'impôt sur le sel en France.* 1902.

Dent, Julian. *Crisis in Finance: Crown, Financiers and Society in Seventeenth Century France.* New York: St. Martin's Press, 1973.

Desné, Roland. "La tournée du fermier général Helvétius dans les Ardennes (1738)." *XVIIIᵉ siècle* 3 (1971): 3–40.

Durand, Yves. *Les fermiers généraux au XVIIIᵉ siècle.* Paris: PUF, 1971.

Encyclopédie méthodique. Article "Finances." Panckouke, 1784–87.

Faure, Edgar. *Law.* Collection "Trente journées qui ont fait la France." Paris: Gallimard, 1977.

Flour de Saint-Genis. *Histoire documentaire et philosophique de l'Administration des Domaines.* 2 vols. Le Havre, 1903.

Gandolf, E. *Le tabac sous l'Ancien Régime: La ferme royale (1629–1791).* Vesoul, 1914.

Gayot, Gérard. "La ferme générale dans les Ardennes in 1738." *XVIIIᵉ siècle* 3 (1971): 75 ff.

Germain-Martin and M. Benzançon. *Histoire du crédit en France sous le règne de Louis XIV.* Vol. 1: *Crédit public.* Sirey, 1913.

Goubert, Pierre. *Les Danse et les Motte de Beauvais.* S.E.V.P.E.N., 1959.

Heumann, Pierre. "Un traitant sous Louis XIII: Antoine Feydeau." *Revue d'histoire moderne* 13 (1938): 5–45.

Jannet, Claudio. "Le monde de la finance au XVIIᵉ siècle." *Journal des Economistes* 10 (1892): 68–86.

Lévy-Bruhl, Henri. "Les différentes espèces de sociétés de commerce en France aux XVIIᵉ et XVIIIᵉ siècles." *Revue historique de droit français et étranger* 16 (1937), 294–332.

Llorca, E. "Analyse des mécanismes commerciaux en économie urbaine sous l'Ancien Régime: Grasse dans la première moitié du XVIIIᵉ siècle (octrois)." *Provence historique* 21 (1971): 444–73.

Malzieu, M. de. *Histoire des Fermes du roi.* 1746.

Marion, Marcel. *Histoire financière de la France depuis 1715.* Vol. 1: *1715–1789.* 1914.

Matthews, George T. *The Royal General Farms in Eighteenth-Century France.* New York: Columbia University Press, 1958.

Meyer, Jean. "Impôts provinciaux et fermes d'impôts au début du XVIIIᵉ siècle." *Actes du 93ᵉ Congrès national des Sociétés savantes.* Tours, 1968, pp. 47–57.

Moreau de Beaumont, Jean-Louis. *Mémoire concernant les impositions et droits.* 5 vols. New edition, Paris: 1787–95.

Morineau, Michel. "Budgets de l'Etat et gestion des finances royales en France au XVIIIᵉ siècle." *Revue historique* 536 (1980): 289–336.

Mouton, Léo. "Deux financiers au temps de Sully: Largentier et Moisset." *Bulletin de la Société de l'Histoire de Paris et de l'Ile-de-France* 64 (1937): 65–105.

Pasquier, Jean. *L'impôt des gabelles en France aux XVIIᵉ et XVIIIᵉ siècles.* 1905.

Puisieux, R. *L'impôt du tabac sous l'Ancien Régime.* 1906.

Robisheaux, Earl. "The Private Army of the Tax Farms: The Men and Their Origins." *Histoire sociale, Social History* 6 (1973): 256–69.

Roux, P. *Les fermes d'impôts sous l'Ancien Régime.* 1916.

Véron de Forbonnais. *Recherches et considérations sur les Finances de France depuis l'année 1595 jusqu'à l'année 1721.* 2 vols. Basel, 1758.

Vidal, Jacques. "L'impôt de l'équivalent des aides à Narbonne." Actes du 93ᵉ Congrès national des Sociétés savantes. Tours, 1968, pp. 9–25.

Vührer, A. *Histoire de la dette publique en France.* 1886.

6 The King's *Commissaires*

Every year the king made use of a large number of *commissaires* to execute new edicts (which were always followed by council decrees), to remedy the evil effects of the great many abuses that were committed, and to settle disputes that were beyond the capability of local officials to deal with and that demanded government intervention. To accomplish these ends, the king sent either individual *commissaires* or commissions consisting of several persons to represent him in the provinces. *Commissaires* were sometimes selected from the *maîtres des requêtes* who were making inspection tours as a part of their regular duties. Other *commissaires* were chosen from among local officials.

Commissions awarded by the king often carried with them the power to "commission and delegate" authority to persons chosen by the *commissaires* themselves to carry out a portion of the duties assigned to them. Regular officeholders and the *corps* never had the power to delegate the authority vested in them for the performance of their ordinary duties. If an officeholder received a commission, however, the commission could grant him the power to delegate his authority. A *commissaire* could delegate his authority only if he was expressly authorized to do so by his letters of commission. Such authorization always specified that persons to whom authority was delegated could prosecute cases only "up to but not including issuance of final judgment." In other words, the designated individual was authorized only to investigate and prosecute, not to decide or judge.

The circumstances that led to the appointment of *commissaires* and commissions recurred time and again. Commissions that were repeatedly pressed into service first became permanent and then were transformed into bureaucratic departments. As for individual *commissaires*, temporary appointments were transformed first into permanent appointments and then into bureaucratic positions. These positions tended to develop into offices that could be put up for sale. Then, because of the ''financing'' of such offices, their legal status tended to become akin to that of patrimonial property that could be passed on to the heirs of the officeholder.

22   Governors

The evolution traced above was well advanced by the late sixteenth and early seventeenth centuries in the case of governors of provinces, cities, and fortresses, even though publicists such as Du Haillan, Du Tillet, and Charles Loyseau were still arguing that governors should be viewed as *commissaires*. Broadly speaking, the nature of the office of governor remained unchanged down to the time of the Revolution. What did change was that the king increasingly insisted that governors obey his orders, thus leaving them their honors while depriving them of their functions.

Authority was vested in a governor by means of letters patent signed by the king, countersigned by a secretary of state, and sealed in the Grande Chancellerie with the royal seal. In these letters the king made mention of the "post" and reminded the nominee that this post had been "provided" his predecessor, just as in *lettres de provision*. The letters declared that the offices were "governments." However, Charles Loyseau, writing in 1606, states in chapter IV of book IV of his *Traité des offices* that governorships were in fact commissions, not offices. His argument is that no edict was issued appointing a governor to an established office. Furthermore, the ordinances that mentioned governorships never spoke of offices but only of "estates," a general term indicating a quality. Governorships were not officially a part of the *parties casuelles*. Furthermore, governors were not allowed to resign, according to article 272 of the Blois ordinance of 1579. Unlike officeholders, governors were not paid by the king's *receveurs* out of accounts assigned to a regular source of royal revenue. Instead, Loyseau tells us, they were paid either a salary, like army captains, or a pension, like *commissaires*, disbursed either by the *trésoriers de l'extraordinaire des guerres* or the *trésoriers de l'Epargne* on the basis of statements of account that could be changed from one year to the next. Commissions were legally revocable, and according to Loyseau at least one had in fact been revoked in the reign of every king on record. For all these reasons, Loyseau came to the conclusion that governorships were not offices but commissions.

There was an even better proof of this assertion, as far as Loyseau was concerned. This was the fact that the authority of a governor relied on "the use of force and the bearing of arms." Now, such authority could not be vested in anyone merely because he owned an office. Rather, it could only be delegated by special commission from the king, who as sovereign lord had the exclusive right to use force in a manner other than that prescribed by regular laws and judicial forms. Only the king had the power to delegate the extraordinary extrajudicial powers vested in the governor, who was authorized to use them only when necessary and then only in the king's name, not in his own name. By contrast, an officeholder used his own name in carrying out the duties of his office. Governors, like *commissaires*, were appointed to carry out special missions.

Loyseau goes on to cite a whole series of ordinances to show that the duties of governors were no broader than those of *commissaires*. Among the ordinances he cites are those of Louis XII (1498) and Henri II and the Blois ordinance of May 1579 (arts. 271 through 278). Governors were not allowed to take over the regular duties of judicial officers or "to insinuate themselves in any way into the administration of justice." They could not assume jurisdiction over cases pending before regular judges or overrule their competence to hear ordinary cases. Governors were forbidden to interfere with the tax system and in particular were admonished not to "levy or have levied any taxes . . . or to allow others to levy taxes." Governors were not allowed to exercise seigneurial rights, particularly rights belonging to the sovereign lord. Hence they were not allowed to issue letters of grace, remission, or pardon or to authorize fairs and markets or legitimize children, and so forth.

Governors were not to exceed the authority explicitly vested in them by their letters patent. They had full power and authority to enforce royal edicts and ordinances and to require the obedience of subjects, villagers, and residents of their governments. They were urged to "make people live together in union and harmony" and to settle any disputes that might arise. Accordingly, they frequently intervened in all sorts of cases as negotiators and arbitrators. They were told to "take notice of and measures to deal with all affairs in the aforementioned region," that is, to attend to conditions likely to pose a threat to the welfare of the public, such as famine, plague, migration, and conspiracy, to say nothing of riots, uprisings, and foreign aggression. Governors were required to lend their assistance to judges and royal officials for the enforcement of judicial decisions and ordinances and for the levying of taxes. They were bound to assemble the three orders to hear the king's will and to take notice of the wishes of his subjects. Governors were responsible for roads, bridges, and crossings. It was their duty to bring thieves, vagabonds, wrongdoers, and criminals of all sorts to justice for trial by the appropriate judges. Governors were supposed to guard against the levying of troops without the king's permission as well as rebellions and other forms of disobedience. They were in charge of guarding cities to pre-

vent the king's enemies from carrying out any attacks and had the duty to
recapture any city that was occupied. They had command over troops in
garrison and had the power to levy troops, to call the *ban* and *arrière-ban*,
to obtain the assistance of the nobility and the bourgeois militia, and to make
use of the *prévôts des maréchaux*. The governors supervised the conduct
of troops passing through their territory, particularly in regard to the provision of supply points or other sources of supply. "And generally [governors
were responsible for] doing whatever we ourselves would do, and giving
whatever orders we ourselves would give, for the good of our service in the
aforementioned territory, were we present in said territory ourselves."[1]

Broadly speaking, then, what emerges from these letters is that the governors stood above the various hierarchies at work within their territories.
They supervised their work, set them tasks, gave them help if needed, and
intervened in both exceptional and recurrent affairs that posed a threat to
the political unity, social order, or general welfare of the region or to the
king's important interests and to the laws of the kingdom, affairs distinct
from those involving the satisfaction of the public's current regular and
specific needs. These royal lieutenants were supposed to act like the king
and therefore to concern themselves with government rather than administration. They were agents of government, not administrators. There is no
doubt that the nature of a governorship was different from that of an ordinary
office.

As late as 1718, the *Etat de la France* looked upon governors as *commissaires*. "Their commissions are verified in the *parlement* of their provinces. . . . Their letters of provision are mere commissions whose continuation
depends solely on the king's will."[2]

The number of governors was deemed excessive, and the ordinance of
Blois (art. 271) reduced that number to twelve. In the Estates General of
1614–15 provincial envoys were assigned to twelve large "governments"
for voting purposes. These divisions did not correspond to those indicated
in the Blois ordinance, however. The governments of Paris, Rouen, and
Dijon took in the provinces of which these cities were the capitals. But that
of Lyon included the Lyonnais, Bourbonnais, Auvergne, Marche, and Beaujolais. The government of Orléans included Orléanais, Touraine, Anjou,
Maine, Berry, Nivernais, Poitou, and Angoumois. In reality there were always more than twelve governments. When Richelieu joined the Council in
1624, there were nineteen.[3] In the middle of the seventeenth century, there
were twenty-five or twenty-six. In 1718 the number was thirty-five and in
1774, thirty-nine. Governors were assigned to some newly conquered provinces, such as Alsace, Franche-Comté, Corsica, etc. Other governments had
had their boundaries redrawn. The government of Metz, Toul, and Verdun
was divided into two governments in 1774, one consisting of Toul and Toulois,
the other of Metz and the surrounding region, Verdun and Verdunois. The
government of Haut and Bas-Limousin was split off from the government
of Saintonge and Angoumois. And so on.

If, as Loyseau maintained, provincial governorships as well as governorships of cities and fortresses were not established offices in the full sense of the word, they had nevertheless by his day taken on some of the characteristics of offices. They were in fact sold. The king allowed governors to resign their offices in favor of a designated successor after agreeing with him upon a mutually satisfactory price. The new titulary frequently obtained a royal brevet of possession guaranteeing him a specific sum of money should the office be lost or relinquished. In order to replace a governor, the king was required to reimburse him or allow him to find a buyer. In addition, dignities, favors, and bonuses had to be offered. The king granted *survivances* to governors, and the designated heir was usually a son or other relative. Thanks to resignations and *survivances* and to the custom of not taking a government away from a family, governorships tended to remain in the hands of the same families. This custom persisted into the eighteenth century. The ducs de Duras of the house of Durfort perpetuated their power in Franche-Comté. On 26 June 1674, the maréchal-duc Jacques-Henri I de Duras was given the governorship of the newly conquered province and of the *gouvernement particulier* of Besançon, an imperial city. He was succeeded in 1704 by the maréchal de Tallard. But the grandson of Jacques-Henri I, Jean-Baptiste de Duras, served as commander-in-chief of Franche-Comté under Tallard from 1734 until 1741, when he became governor. His son Emmanuel-Felicité became his designated heir in 1767 and upon the death of his father in 1770 became governor of the province, a post he held until the Revolution. During this period, cousins of the Duras, the Lorges and Randans, were *lieutenants généraux* and commanders-in-chief of the province. These families belonged to the high *noblesse d'épée*. The governors were princes of the blood, princes, dukes-and-peers, dukes, and *maréchaux de France*. The king preferred to appoint governors who had fiefs, *seigneuries*, friends, and relations in a province, who were not "strangers" to the local nobility, the members of *parlement*, and other officeholders in the region. It was hoped that this would give them credit and make it possible for them to command obedience and win respect. Governors tried to enhance their credit in the region by using whatever influence they had at court for the benefit of their province and by obtaining offices and other posts in command of fortifications and cities for nobles of the region. In this way they won the loyalty of their clients. This benefited the king if the governor himself remained loyal but threatened the monarchy if the governor plotted with foreign powers or entered into alliance with them. There is no dearth of celebrated instances of such treachery. One was Biron, a duke, peer, and marshal of France and governor of Burgundy, the conqueror of Bresse, who was executed in 1602 for treason on account of his alliance with Spain and Savoy for the purpose of assassinating Henri IV and carving up the territory of France. Another traitor was Montmorency, the governor of Languedoc. Some governors also had the power to act as viceroys. Jacques-Nompar de Caumont, marquis de La Force and baron de Castelnau, a captain of 100 men-at-arms and governor and *lieutenant général* representing the king in Navarre and Béarn, was named viceroy in these possessions (which were not part of the kingdom of France) in 1593. In Béarn the governor was afforded the same powers as the king according to custom. The governor could name whomever he pleased to hold any post except those of *premier président, conseiller,* or *procureur général* on the sovereign council, and *sénéchal* or vice-chancellor of Navarre. He was served by six corps of militia under the command of *gentilshommes* of the region. It was the governor who convoked the local Estates, which met annually, and who went each year together with an embassy from the Estates to be received by the king at the Louvre. The same was true for Navarre, whose capital was Saint-Jean-Pied-de-Port. But La Force ordinarily resided in the château of Pau and went each year to the king's court to serve for a quarter as captain of the guard. This situation lasted until 1620, when Louis XIII joined Navarre and Béarn to the French crown, making a single province of the kingdom. He combined the two sovereign councils of Saint-Palais and Pau in a single *parlement* of Navarre, located in Pau, reestablished the Catholic religion, and returned to the Catholic church its property and privileges. La Force rebelled in 1621 and took command of a Protestant army. On 15 November 1621, he was sentenced to death and decapitated in effigy at Bordeaux. He finally surrendered in 1622, received a pardon, and lost the government of Béarn and his post as captain of the guard, but was named marshal of France, took the oath of office, and served the king loyally ever after. The governor of Dauphiné, a sort of vice-dauphin, was until 1632 allowed to fill the old provincial offices, except those attached to *parlement* and the Chambre des Comptes and the posts of *trésoriers généraux de France.* Decisions of the sovereign and lower courts were issued in the governor's name. He enjoyed precedence in *parlement.* His authority was almost as great as the king's. A prince of the blood, the comte de Soissons, who was governor of Dauphiné when Richelieu joined the Council, did just as he pleased and was wont to speak derisively about Louis XIII's anger over his actions.

The dangers of this system were obvious. The history of the period is marked by rebellions, lapses, and acts of treason committed by the governors of provinces, cities, and fortresses, which persisted until Louis XIV took personal charge of the government.

In his treatise on *La maladie de la France,* which was presented to the king in 1602, Jacques Leschassier proposed as a remedy the idea of changing provincial governors every three years. Richelieu seriously urged this idea as a solution to the problem in 1625. But it was impossible to put into practice. Men capable of acting as provincial governors were hard to find. One needed the prestige of a very old and very high nobility, the influence that came from owning land and having allies in the region, and the wealth that made it possible to discharge the duties of the office. In 1626 d'Ornano advanced 148,000 livres for the repair of ramparts in a city of which he was governor. When the duc de Randan, a Durfort, asked for the governorship of Franche-

Comté upon the death of the duc de Tallard in 1755, he wrote to the secretary of state for war that he had been commander-in-chief in the province for fifteen years and that he spent 150,000 livres there annually, compared with his annual compensation of 30,000 livres. Governors could increase the amount of their compensation by holding more than one office. In 1773 the duc de Lorge received 13,522 livres per year in emoluments as *maréchal de France*, 20,000 livres as *lieutenant général* for Franche-Comté, 40,000 livres as commander-in-chief of that province, and 12,000 livres as governor of Château-Trompette at Bordeaux, for a total of 85,522 livres. These sums were probably inadequate. Under Richelieu governors received 6,000 livres per year. The provincial estates and other provincial authorities added their gifts to this amount. In Provence the comte d'Alais was allocated a sum for his ordnance company and his guards and 36,000 livres for his personal expenses. In Picardy the duc de Chaulnes received an additional 8,000 livres annually. In Auvergne the maréchal de Toiras received 24,000 livres. Montmorency had 60,000 in Languedoc, and Chevreuse 18,000 in Normandy. The communes also sent the governor and his lieutenants and secretaries bonuses and gifts. When they took up their duties, governors and *lieutenants généraux* made a splendid official entry into their capital city, which made them a gift of 2,000 to 5,000 livres. Still, their compensation was inadequate. But governors and lieutenants owned important fiefs and *seigneuries*. Thus it proved impossible to rotate governors every few years. Another solution had to be found.

Beginning in the time of Henri IV, different remedies were tried, and these continued after that king's death with varying degrees of success, depending on the relative strength or weakness of the royal government. After Louis XIV took personal charge of the government, systematic and continuous efforts were made to deal with the problem.

The king negotiated with existing governors to try to persuade them to accept another governorship or to relinquish the one they had in exchange for gifts, pensions, other posts, and dignities. The king's purpose was to replace these men with creatures of his own. Of the nineteen governors in office when Richelieu joined the Council in 1624, only four remained when the cardinal died in 1642. The fifteen others had been replaced by men devoted either to him or to the king. In 1626, for example, the duc de Vendôme, who was governor of Britanny and who had been compromised in the Châlais conspiracy, was replaced by Thémines, a *maréchal de France*, who had arrested the prince de Condé in 1616. The duc de Guise was removed from the governorship of Provence in 1631 and replaced by the maréchal de Vitry, who had gotten rid of Concini for Louis XIII. The duc de Bellegarde, who had fled in the wake of the plot involving the duc d'Orléans, was replaced in Burgundy by the prince de Condé. The comte de Soissons was transferred from Dauphiné to Champagne and the duc d'Epernon from Limousin to Guyenne. After being taken away from d'Elbeuf, Picardy was given to the duc de Chevreuse. And so on.

Governors were in theory bound to reside in their provinces for six months out of the year, but most preferred to be at court or with the army. The king at first overlooked their absences. Later, he worked actively to keep them away from their posts. It became a custom that governors needed special letters from the king authorizing them to discharge their duties. This custom was made law by the ordinances of 1750 and 1768. Kept far from their provinces, governors ceased to take an interest in their governments, lost their authority, and became ignorant of provincial affairs. Duc Jean-Baptiste de Duras, the governor of Franche-Comté, was called to the court in 1741. On 25 February 1759, in the midst of the conflict that pitted the *parlement* of Besançon against the royal government, he wrote his cousin the duc de Randan, then commander-in-chief of Franche-Comté: "You know better than anyone else that, since the time the king first wished that I should cease to have the honor of command in Franche-Comté, I have had little more knowledge of what was happening there than what I learned from the gazette."[4]

The king was careful never to give the governorship of a city to the governor of the province in which it was located. He took steps to reserve to himself the choice of governors of cities and fortresses. One of Biron's pretexts for revolting was Henri IV's refusal to make him governor of Bourg-en-Bresse, which he had just conquered. This royal policy proved successful. Before long, a governor who rebelled against the king was forced to contend with hostile governors of cities and fortresses and could not take advantage of convenient fortifications to shelter, rest, and feed his troops. In fortified cities the king was careful to name different governors for the city proper and for its attached château. The king was perfectly willing to allow provincial governors to serve as governors of cities as well, but outside their provinces. He made such appointments as a mark of honor or an award of pension as well as to cause difficulties for the governor of the province in which the city was located, should he conceive any evil designs. Under Louis XIII, for example, d'Ornano was governor of Honfleur and Pont-de-l'Arche in Normandy and of Tarascon and Aubenas in Provence.

The king sought to divide authority in the provincial governments as much as he could. The "governor and *lieutenant général*" was usually aided by a "*lieutenant général*" who was responsible for governing in the absence of the governor. Governments were often divided into two or three *lieutenances générals*, each with its own *lieutenant général*. In addition, each government was divided into a number of *circonscriptions*, each commanded by a *lieutenant du roi*. Finally, from the time of Louis XIV's personal government, the king had placed between the governor and the *lieutenants généraux* a "commander-in-chief" who actually exercised the powers of the governor. In 1718 in Languedoc, for example, the governor was the duc du Maine, prince de Dombes. The commander-in-chief was the duc de Rouqelaure, lieutenant general of the royal armies. There were three *lieutenants généraux*, one for Haut-Languedoc, one for Bas-Languedoc, and one for Cévennes and Vivarais. Below them in rank were nine royal lieutenants, each responsible for from two to four dioceses. In the government of the Ile-de-France, the governor was the duc d'Estrées, peer of France. The *lieutenant général* was the marquis de Pomponne, a brigadier in the army. For "l'Isle de France particulière," two marquis served as royal lieutenants. But there were four other royal lieutenants besides these two. For the French Vexin, of which Mantes was the capital, there was the duc de Sully, peer of France. In Beauvaisis it was the comte des Marais, the grand falconer of France. The lieutenant for Noyonnais, Valois, Soissonais, Laonais, and the area from the Marne and Seine to Champagne was J.-F. de Vins, baron de Bruis and captain in the Régiment de Royal Etranger. For the rest of the Ile-de-France, "lying to the left of the Seine," the lieutenant was M. Charles de Tilly, marquis de Blaru.

In 1774 each of the thirty-nine governments had one governor and one or more *lieutenants généraux*. In nineteen cases the governor also served as a *lieutenant général*. Seven of the governors were assisted by a designated heir, a son or other family member. There were sixty-six *lieutenants généraux*, four of whom had appointed designated heirs. In Burgundy the prince de Condé was governor and *lieutenant général;* seven marquis and counts also served as *lieutenants généraux*, each responsible for a specific territory, such as Châlonnais, Charolais, Dijonnais (including the *bailliage* of la Montagne, the county of Auxonne and Bar-sur-Seine), and so on.

In some cases the governor, commander-in-chief, and *lieutenants généraux* all belonged to the same family. In Franche-Comté at one point there were three members of the Dufort family serving in high office. Jean-Baptiste de Duras, who served first as commander-in-chief and then as governor, gave up the post of commander-in-chief in 1741 to his cousin, the duc de Randan, who in 1730 had purchased the post of *lieutenant général* of the province. Randan held both offices simultaneously. His nephew, the duc de Lorge, became his associate in 1765. When Randan died in June 1773, Lorge replaced him as *lieutenant général* of Franche-Comté and commander-in-chief of the province, of which Duras was governor.

These family allegiances did not always have noxious political consequences, however, because the individuals involved might belong to different parties. When the *parlement* of Besançon rebelled in February 1757, the duc de Randan sent information and advice to Versailles, counseling firmness and recommending that jussive letters be sent to *parlement*. He also recommended that *lettres de cachet* be issued ordering the exile or imprisonment of the most actively hostile councillors and that blank *lettres de cachet* be issued for use against possible future opponents of the king. Seditious officeholders should be removed from office and reimbursed. By contrast, his cousin the governor, duc Jean-Baptiste de Duras, who was detained at court, counseled moderation and recommended that an agreement be reached with *parlement*.

Some historians have argued that governors were generally on bad terms with the *intendants des provinces* and even that Richelieu relied increasingly on the *intendants* in order to curtail the power of the governors. This is incorrect. There were more general reasons for the use of *intendants*. Governors and *intendants* were not as a rule locked in conflict, even though all orders from the governor had to be countersigned by the *intendant*. The duties of governor and *intendant* were not opposed but rather complementary. The governor was an agent of government, the *intendant* a magistrate with administrative and judicial responsibilities. Thus we find governors with no *intendant* in their district asking that one be sent. At the time of the very serious insurrection at Moulins in 1640, the governor of Bourbonnais, the comte de Saint-Geran, had the rebels arrested and sent to prison and pressed the magistrates of the local courts to try them. Unable to persuade them to do so, he asked that *commissaires* be sent and breathed a sigh of relief when the government decided shortly thereafter to send an *intendant*. In 1637, the duc de Ventadour, governor of Limousin, asked that a *maître des requêtes* be sent for the *intendance de la justice* and even indicated the name of the man he wanted, M. Le Tonnelier.[5]

The royal government generally sent either the *intendant* requested by the governor or one who could get along with him. In 1767 the king capitulated in the Brittany affair, recalled the duc d'Aiguillon, and in September sent a new commander-in-chief, Emmanuel-Félicité de Duras, son-in-law of the marquis de Coétquen, governor of Saint-Malo, and consequently *seigneur* de Combourg, who was known to be favorable to the Breton nobility and *parlement*. At the same time, the royal government sent a new *intendant*, d'Agay, an intimate of the duc de Duras and also quite well-disposed toward the nobility. Both opposed the policies of the duc d'Aiguillon.[6]

Occasionally, the government did have reasons to dispatch an *intendant* to a province in order to check the governor there. Sometimes, too, a governor and an *intendant* failed to get along for personal reasons. Such cases were rare, however.

An edict of August 1696 created a new category of governors of cities. These governors were distinguished from those previously named by the king via *lettres de provision* or brevets. They were paid compensation and allowances budgeted against tax receipts. These governors generally had charge of walled cities in border provinces.

Elsewhere, however, certain walled cities had governors or "*capitaines chastelains*" who were either without *lettres de provision* or brevets or, if they had them, received no compensation or allowances. Such posts were merely marks of dignity that enhanced a person's status.

Many walled cities had no governor at all.

The edict eliminated governorships without compensation or formal appointment. It established hereditary offices of royal governor in every walled city in the kingdom as well as in regions, territories, and *seigneuries* that owed obedience to the king, except in places where regular letters, brevets, compensations, and allowances were already in effect.

The newly created governorships carried with them the same honors, ranks and seatings, preeminences, prerogatives, and rights as the others. Holders of these posts could reside in the *château* when it was not occupied by the *seigneur* or *engagiste*. Within their city they were supposed to have precedence over the governor and lieutenants of the province or "*département*" in which the city was located as well as precedence over the *seigneur*. They were entitled to a place in all public and private assemblies at the head of either the judicial officeholders or the *corps de ville*, as they wished. Where there was a superior court, however, they had to choose the *corps de ville*. They commanded the bourgeois militia and gave orders to its officers as well as to the commanders of officers and troops passing through the city. They received the oath of officers in the bourgeois militia, lighted the victory fires with the *corps de ville*, reviewed troops along with the mayor and other reviewers, and were authorized to advise the secretary of state for war concerning the status of passing troops.

Those who held these governorships enjoyed the privileges of nobility, including exemption from personal service, contribution to the *arrière-ban*, *tailles*, *tutelle*, and *curatelle* and all other exemptions, prerogatives, honors, and privileges open to *gentilshommes*. They were entitled to compensation of 4 percent of what they had paid for the office.

Among those eligible to obtain these offices were mayors who owned their offices and who were allowed to exercise the duties of mayor and governor at the same time in their city; hereditary nobles; officers of the royal army; and other capable persons who did not hold incompatible offices.

Governors provided with *lettres de provision* were supposed to swear an oath into the hands of the chancellor of France or, at his behest, into the hands of *intendants* or *commissaires* dispatched for the purpose.

Governors were supposed to possess their offices as hereditary property. The widow, heir, or executor of a deceased governor was allowed to dispose of the office by contract and to name a successor who would then be provided by the king.

Subsequent declarations and decrees stipulated that governors were entitled to the enjoyment of the château, to the fruits and grasses of its moats, ramparts, and embankments, to hunting rights, and so forth, and could associate their lieutenants in these rights.

Abolished after the death of Louis XIV, these governorships were reestablished by an edict of November 1733, which ordered execution of the edict of August 1696. The council decree of 1 June 1766 exempted the governorships from the abolition of offices ordered by the edict of August 1764, on the grounds that governorships and lieutenancies were "precious positions to be preserved in a monarchy based on the principle of honor and could be used to compensate the nobility of the kingdom and especially its soldiers . . . [as a] useful and honorable form of retirement." These offices were compensated out of the funds held by the *trésoriers de l'ordinaire des guerres*, who were done away with by the edict of November 1778. The governors of cities and their lieutenants with life tenure thereupon "entered naturally into the class of *rentes viagères*," or life annuities. The king issued a council decree on 8 December 1779, ordering that their compensation be paid out of the *rentes sur l'Hôtel de Ville de Paris*, and one of the thirty paymasters was assigned to this task.[7]

The reforms of the comte de Saint-Germain also made a retirement or annuity of the posts of provincial governor, commander-in-chief, and *lieutenant général*. Up to this time, if governors had been spending most of their time away from their provinces and had thereby been reduced to the status of mere dignitaries, commanders-in-chief and *lieutenants généraux* had remained active agents of the government. The ordinance of 18 March 1776 finally converted all the governorships and lieutenancies into "military favors, which, by proving the confidence of the Prince, add to a man's fortune and make him more considerable . . . [while] compensating his talent, long service, and distinguished actions."[8] As a result, the thirty-nine *gouverneurs généraux* were divided into two groups. Eighteen governorships were reserved for princes of the blood and *maréchaux de France*. These posts brought emoluments of from 18,000 to 60,000 livres.[9] Twenty-one other governorships were set aside for lieutenants general of the army and earned compensation of from 21,000 to 30,000 livres.[10]

There were 114 *gouvernements particuliers*, 25 of them first class with 12,000 livres compensation, 25 second class with 10,000 livres compensation, and 64 third class with 8,000 livres compensation.

Governors who had bought *brevets de retenue* received annual interest of 4 percent from the king. The king henceforth issued new *brevets de retenue* only after making a deduction of one-fourth their value. After the office had been transferred four times, the *brevets de retenue* therefore became worthless.

The governors general were assisted by *lieutenants généraux*, who were paid for their services as second in command. These positions were reserved for military officers who were distinguished by virtue of either service or birth or who deserved special recognition. Only men who had attained the rank of lieutenant general of the army could be authorized to command troops in the provinces.

The number of *lieutenants du roi* in command of cities or castles where there was no governor was cut down to 176. Thirty-five were first-class positions, reserved for *maréchaux de camp* and *brigadiers*. These were paid from 6,000 to 16,600 livres. One hundred forty-one were second class, reserved for lieutenant colonels, majors, and captains of grenadiers, who were paid from 2,000 to 6,000 livres.

There were 478 posts of major, aide-major, and deputy aide-major, reserved for lower-ranking officers.

As a result of the reforms, then, the number of posts associated with governorships of cities and castles and their staffs was reduced from 2,207 to 876 and the payroll from 5,165,485 livres to 3,100,000 livres.

The king withheld *survivances* in connection with these posts, and he did not allow the same man to hold more than one such post at a time, particularly when it came to the positions of governor, lieutenant, and major in a particular city.

The regulation of October 1776 divided France into sixteen military divisions.

The posts of governor and subsidiary posts became purely honorific. They bestowed an annuity but carried with them no duties.

Notes

1. Roland Mousnier, "Les rapports entre les gouverneurs de province et les intendants dans la première moitié du XVIIIᵉ siècle," *Revue historique* 228 (1962), reprinted in *La plume, la faucille et le marteau* (Paris: PUF, 1970), pp. 208, 210–11.

2. In Charles Osmont, chap. 3, p. 260.

3. Ile-de-France, Orléanais, Berry, Brittany, Normandy, Picardy, Champagne, Metz-Toul-Verdun, Burgundy, Auvergne, Maine, Anjou, Dauphiné, Provence, Languedoc, Guyenne, Limousin-Saintonge-Angoumois, Poitou, Béarn.

4. Cited by Yves Durand, *La maison de Durfort à l'époque moderne* (Fontenay-le-Comte: Imprimerie Lussaud, 1975), p. 237.

5. Mousnier, "Les rapports," pp. 206–7.

6. The governor of the province was the duc de Penthièvre. But he was only twice authorized to go to Brittany.

7. Guyot, *Répertoire universel et raisonné de jurisprudence*, vol. 8 (Visse, 1784). See the article entitled "Gouverneurs."

8. Article 1 of the ordinance, cited by L. Mention, *Le comte de Saint-Germain et ses réformes d'après les Archives du Dépôt de la Guerre. Etude sur l'armée française à la fin du XVIIIᵉ siècle* (Librairie militaire L. Baudouin & Cie., 1884), p. 80.

9. The 18 *gouvernements* were as follows: Ile-de-France, Picardy, Flanders and Hainault, Champagne and Brie, Les Trois-Evêchés, Lorraine, Alsace, County of Burgundy, Duchy of Burgundy, Lyonnais, Dauphiné, Provence, Languedoc, Roussillon, Navarre and Béarn, Guyenne, Brittany, and Normandy.

10. The 21 *gouvernements* were as follows: Artois, Le Havre, Boulonnais, Sedan, Toul, Nivernais, Bourbonnais, Berry, Auvergne, Foix-Donezan-Andorra, Limousin, Haute and Basse Marche, Saintonge and Angoumois, Aunis, Poitou, Saumurois, Anjou, Touraine, Maine and Perche, Orléanais, and Corsica.

23 *Commissaires*

We can get a good idea of the various purposes for which *commissaires* were used by looking at the years 1599 and 1600.

During the course of these two years, the Conseil d'Etat et des Finances sent *commissaires* to the provinces on various missions. Among the projects involved were a reform of the system of hospitals and leper houses, a reform of the system of assessment and collection of the *tailles*, a reform of the statutes of *corps* and communities, establishment of regulations for fairs and markets, sale of newly created offices, judgment of acts of violence or piracy committed against vessels flying the English flag, and execution of the Edict of Nantes.

At the same time, a royal chamber established on 8 May 1597 was hearing cases involving various financial misdeeds, for which purpose it sent a number of delegates to the provinces. *Intendants* had already been sent to assist army commanders and provincial governors in reestablishing law and order in areas recently brought back under royal domination, including Lyonnais, Normandy, Brittany, Languedoc, etc.

Commissaires were often chosen from the members of the Conseil d'Etat et des Finances or from among the *maîtres des requêtes*. The same *commissaire* might be assigned to perform two or three different commissions, and the same men were frequently assigned to carry out one mission after another. Méri de Vic, a former *président* in the Toulouse *parlement*, *conseiller d'Etat*, *intendant in Languedoc*, and from 1597 on *intendant* at the fortress of Bellièvre in Lyonnais, was in 1599 named *commissaire* for the execution of the Edict of Nantes in Dauphiné. In July 1600 he was named ambassador to the Swiss Cantons. A *maître des requêtes*, Eustache de Refuge, was named *commissaire* for the execution of the Edict of Nantes in Guyenne and then *intendant* of Lyonnais in 1600, replacing Méri de Vic. After that he served as *commissaire* in Bresse, Bugey, Valromey, and Gex, annexed from Savoy, in 1602 and 1603. Camus de Jambeville, *intendant* for Normandy, became *président* in the Paris *parlement* in 1600 and then in 1601 was sent as *commissaire* to reorganize the tax system in Limousin. The duc

481

de La Force, governor of Béarn, was named *commissaire* for the enforcement of the Edict of Nantes in Guyenne. In October 1600 he rejoined the royal army. Bellièvre resigned as *intendant* of Lyon to undertake preliminary negotiations for the Peace of Vervins. The *conseiller d'Etat* Jeannin was named *commissaire* for the enforcement of the Edict of Nantes in a portion of the jurisdiction of the Paris *parlement*. Later he was sent to negotiate with the United Provinces, then in revolt against Spain.

Letters patent established commissions to enforce the Edict of Nantes on which Catholics and Huguenots would be equally represented. On 6 August 1599, for example, letters patent addressed personally to Lesdiguières, a *conseiller d'Etat* and *lieutenant général* for Dauphiné, Maître Enemond Rabot, seigneur d'Yllins, *premier président* in the Grenoble *parlement*, and Maître Méri de Vic, *conseiller d'Etat*, commissioned these three men to convoke assemblies in the cities and wherever else they might deem it useful to do so for the purpose of reading the contents of the edict, which had already been sent to the *parlement* of Dauphiné for verification. They were enjoined to have all those in attendance swear to abide by the will of the king. They were further ordered to enforce the edict "duly and to the full . . . according to special instructions to be sent" and to do "whatever you may deem appropriate to put the present orders into effect." Similar commissions were sent on 20 March to *commissaires* in Champagne, Ile-de-France, and Picardy, on 29 March to *commissaires* in Poitou, and so on.

The accompanying instructions stipulated that "their ordinances and judgments shall be executed provisionally, notwithstanding any oppositions, appeals, or objections by the parties." These could be taken up only by the king in his Council. Thus decisions of the commissions were to be executed quickly.

The instructions wisely focused the activities of the *commissaires* on the essential point—restoring toleration, that is, the coexistence of the different religions—and on reestablishing relations between the different religious communities. To deal with the private affairs of the Huguenots there were the *chambres de l'Edit* or *mi-parties*, as they were known. The other articles of the edict were to be enforced by the regular magistrates.

The instructions given to the commissions established the geographical boundaries within which they were supposed to act. Generally speaking, each commission concerned itself with the jurisdiction of one of the *parlements*. The jurisdiction of the Toulouse *parlement* was enormous, however, and had two commissions assigned to it. The even larger jurisdiction of the Paris *parlement* had four.

The Catholic *commissaire* was generally a man of the gown. If there was a local *intendant*, he was assigned to oversee the verification of the edict by *parlement* and to take part in its enforcement (this was the case with Charles Turcan in Brittany, Antoine Le Camus in Normandy, and Méri de Vic in Dauphiné). If there was no *intendant*, the king dispatched one of his *conseillers d'Etat*, such as Jeannin, or a magistrate of the sovereign courts, such as Viart de Volay, *président* on the Grand Conseil, or a *maître des requêtes*, such as Eustache de Refuge, Jean-Jacques de Mesmes, Faucon de Ris, Martin Langois, or Palamède de Fondriat.

The Huguenot *commissaire* was chosen to be a figure with connections and influence in the province. Some were *lieutenants généraux*, such as Lesdiguières in Dauphiné, La Force in Guyenne, or Parabères in Poitou. Others were governors of important fortresses, such as Chandieu or Du Bourg de Clermont. Still others were magistrates, such as Du Faur de Pujols or Le Roy d'Heudreville.

In May 1599 the provincial governors were sent commissions ordering them to assist the *commissaires*. Only Lesdiguières, Fervaque, and d'Ornano obeyed, however. Elsewhere the *commissaires* acted alone.

The *commissaires* were supposed to witness the swearing of the oaths as provided under the terms of article 92 of the Edict of Nantes. They then prepared reports on the swearing in two copies, one of which was sent to the chancellor of France, while the other was registered along with the text of the edict and enforcement orders by the competent royal court.

In regard to the coexistence of the two religions, as set forth in article 11 of the edict, the *commissaires* assigned places for religious worship in the *bailliages* and *sénéchaussées* to the Protestant minority and supervised the assignment of land for cemeteries. Articles 7 and 8 of the edict allowed *seigneurs justiciers* to practice *cultes de fief*. The *commissaires* checked the claims of beneficiaries to these rights of private worship. Under articles 9 and 10 they validated Protestant claims of possession. Under article 3 they enforced the reestablishment of masses wherever Catholics were in the minority, established the calendar of compulsory religious holidays and the schedule of bells, and ordered the restitution of Church property. Ordinances issued by the *commissaires* were registered by the *bailliages* and *sénéchaussées* of the district in which they were issued.

In Dauphiné the *commissaires* found that they needed to appoint delegates. The *vice-bailli* of Briançon was commissioned to represent them in the valley of Queyras, along with a Huguenot *gentilhomme* by the name of Bonne de Largentière. They were charged with reestablishing Catholic services in the villages. For the *bailliage* of Les Montagnes, Pierre de La Baume, a councillor in the Grenoble *parlement* and marquis de Gouvernet, and Louis de Grammond, seigneur de Vachères, were commissioned to the same end. Jean d'Alanson and Captain Isaac Bard worked in Nyons, Buis, and the Baronies. These delegates also issued ordinances to accomplish their ends.

The *commissaires* worked in all haste to eliminate the most immediate forms of intolerance. They made use of article 11 in favor of the Huguenots in areas where they were scattered and weak and of article 3 in favor of Catholics in areas where they were oppressed by the Protestants. The rest of the task of enforcement consisted of routine matters of justice and administration, which fell to local officers, judges in the *bailliages* and *sénéchaussées*, and municipal magistrates, who were assisted in their work by the provincial governors. The magistrates did not perform their duties well, however, and were prejudiced against the Protestants. Most of the governors were also prejudiced. Thus it was necessary, down to the time of Louis XIII, for the king to send *commissaires* to enforce the edict over the opposition of local officeholders and municipalities. This gave rise to the idea of converting the temporary powers of the *commissaires* into lasting powers and thus to the idea of using *intendants*.

24   The "*Chambres de Justice*"

In use since the fourteenth century, the *chambres de justice* were commissions assigned the task of hearing cases involving financial wrongdoing. During the period we are considering *chambres de justice* were employed in the years 1497, 1601–2, 1605–7, and 1607. The Estates General of 1614 asked that they be held every ten years. In fact they were held after that demand was made in 1624, 1635, 1643, 1645, 1648, 1656–57, and 1661–65. The last one was held after the death of Louis XIV, in 1716.

Chambres de justice were held to satisfy public opinion, which had been stirred up against the *financiers* by a pamphlet campaign. Some of these pamphlets may have emanated from a group of financiers eager to replace another group in possession of lucrative contracts. The king established a *chambre de justice* by issuing letters patent together with an edict and a declaration. Members of the sovereign courts were commissioned by the king to come to Paris to investigate charges of wrongdoing against public officials. Such commissions were issued in 1585, 1601, 1661–65, and 1635. Among the *commissaires* we frequently find the chancellor and always from three to five *maîtres des requêtes*. The *premier président* of the Paris *parlement* was invariably chosen, along with from one to four councillors and one or two king's men from this *parlement*. One of the king's men played the role of *procureur général*. The *premier président* of the Chambre des Comptes of Paris was always chosen as well, along with two to four *maîtres des comptes*. In 1601 the *premier président* of the Cour des Aides of Paris was named, and two councillors from this court were always included. From 1624 on we always find from five to seven councillors from provincial *parlements*. In 1624, for example, the *parlements* of Grenoble, Bordeaux, Dijon, Aix, and Rennes were represented. Except for Rennes, the same *parlements* were represented in 1661–65, along with those of Toulouse, Pau, and Metz. A royal secretary acted as clerk. *Chambres de justice* had anywhere from eighteen members (1601) to thirty members (1661–65). Obviously, the members were men loyal to the king.

A good idea of the powers of a *chambre de justice* may be had from an examination of the commission that was read at the opening session of one of them, on 3 December 1661, "in the chamber known as the council chamber near the *chambre des comptes*."[1] Following a speech by the chancellor and a response by the *premier président* of the Paris *parlement*, the *avocat général* Talon, *procureur du roi* for the Chambre, rose to announce that, on behalf of the king, letters patent had been delivered ordering the establishment of a *chambre de justice*. An edict and declaration had also been issued, on which he had given his opinion in writing, and he now requested that these be read. He then gave two unsealed "packets" to the men sitting nearest to him, and they passed it down the line to M. Pussort, a councillor on the Grand Conseil, who read the commission, dated Fontainebleau, 15 November 1661: "Louis, by the grace of God, king of France and Navarre, to our very dear and faithful sieur Séguier, *chevalier* and chancellor of France, and to our beloved liegemen [the names of the *commissaires* followed], greetings."

The commission continued as follows:

> By our letters patent in the form of an edict dated the present month of November, we have erected and established a *chambre de justice*, which is to serve in the chamber known as the council chamber, near our *chambre des comptes* of Paris, for the investigation and punishment of abuses and misdeeds having regard to our finances and all crimes and misdemeanors committed in relation thereto. . . . On account of your noteworthy loyalty and affection in our service . . . we hereby commission you and ordain you and appoint you our deputies . . . with *maistre* Denys Talon for our *procureur général* in said chamber and *maistre* Joseph Foucault, our councillor and secretary, to act as clerk.

Upon request of the *procureur général* or deputies to be named by him, the Chambre de Justice was to investigate and judge according to either civil or criminal procedure all cases involving abuses, misdeeds, crimes, and misdemeanors related to finance. Seven judges were required for indictments and interim judgments and ten judges for final judgments and for the infliction of torture or penalties. Judgments of the court were final and were to be executed "notwithstanding oppositions or appeals of any sort whatsoever." The Chambre de Justice could prosecute any wrongdoer, no matter what his "estate, quality, or condition." Any one of the magistrates was authorized to travel by way of "any of the provinces and *généralités* of our kingdoms or other territories, lands, or *seigneuries* obedient to us," for the purpose of investigating and prosecuting any such case from its inception through final judgment. They had the power to commission solvent individuals as accounting officers while awaiting the king's advice and could commission judges to hear cases. Judges delegated by the *commissaires* were empowered to imprison individuals and seize property. With the cooperation of six officeholders and graduates, they were authorized to render final judgment and proceed to execution of that judgment in cases up to 1,500 livres in value. Alone, they could proceed to provisional execution of judgments in cases up to 600 livres in value, pending appeal. For cases that exceeded 1,500 livres in value, investigative records were to be sent under seal to the Chambre de Justice. The members of the Chambre were exempted from service in the sovereign courts and companies. All other courts and judges were prohibited from taking cognizance of cases reserved for the *chambres de justice*. All officers and magistrates were ordered to obey the *chambres*, and all *prévôts des maréchaux*, their lieutenants and *archers*, and all royal *huissiers* and *sergents* were ordered to execute warrants, ordinances, judgments, and decrees issued by the *commissaires*. To obtain execution there was no need to apply to local judges for leave, permission, placet, visa, or *pareatis* [authorization to execute a foreign judgment or arbitrator's award—trans.].

When the commission had been read, M. Pussort proceeded to read the written brief prepared by the *procureur général*, requesting registration of the commission by the Chambre. The chancellor canvassed the members for their opinions on this brief. The *commissaires* approved it unanimously. Then the clerk read the edict and declaration, and they were registered. The Chambre de Justice could then set to work.

The king apprised his subjects that a *chambre de justice* had been established by trumpet blast and public cry at every crossroad and by announcement at Sunday sermon in all churches. He asked for monitory letters from officials. *Financiers* were notified not to leave their residences or else to gather their papers and return within a week. Notaries were ordered to look into their records for evidence of contracts for the purchase of property in the name or for the profit of men of finance over the past twenty years. The king asked the public to denounce wrongdoers, and informers were promised one-sixth of the property recovered. Embezzlers, dummy partners, and accessories were promised absolution if they made a clean breast of their crimes.

When charges came in, the judges began the immense task of subpoenaing papers, examining them, making an inventory of all the documents, hearing witnesses, and collecting other pertinent information. During the period 1661–65 they were forced to hold sessions from 7:30 A.M. until noon and from 2 P.M. until 5:30. The Chambre de Justice of 1624 remained in session for six months and twenty-six days (from 21 October 1624, until 17 May 1625), that of 1661–65 for four years and twenty days (from 3 December 1661, until 23 December 1665). The average session was more than twenty months.

The work of the judges was monitored by the king and his Council. The king and his agents encouraged judges who were inclined to show indulgence to exhibit more rigor. They replaced judges who turned out to lack ability or to be overly enamored of the forms of justice. They directly commissioned delegates by means of letters patent, thereby exercising some control over the men chosen by the *chambres* (a good many delegates were used by all the *chambres*—152 were used in 1661–65, for example). They monitored procedures so as to direct suspicion to a certain *financier* or divert it from another. They sometimes modified the sentences handed down by the judges. And they published and circulated the decisions of the chambers.

The *financiers* tried to avoid the sanctions in a number of ways. Some fled abroad with a part of their fortune and their financial records when they heard that a *chambre de justice* was to be established. For the most part these were *financiers* who worked closely with the royal court, such as *trésoriers de l'extraordinaire des guerres, trésoriers de l'artillerie, trésoriers de l'Epargne*, and some of the major *traitants*. Others formed assemblies, as in 1607, to prevent execution of the edict and refute the evidence against them. Still others, in the provinces, went after the individuals delegated by the Chambre de Justice and their property in order to obstruct the course of justice. Others "redeemed" themselves after the Chambre de Justice was established by paying a sum of money to the king, in exchange for which they were granted immunity from investigation and prosecution for the duration of the Chambre.

Some fugitives were caught. The Chambre de Justice then heard the prisoners, judged those it held, and tried the others in absentia. The Chambre de Justice of 1601 issued fifty-eight sentences. Seventeen of them required that restitution be made to the king. Sixteen imposed fines, contributions to charity, or prison terms. Seven men were temporarily suspended from office. One was temporarily banished from the province. The property of one of the guilty was confiscated, and one man was condemned to death. The Chambre de Justice of 1661–65 handed down 164 sentences. Twenty-eight imposed fines, contributions to charity, and prison terms. Twenty-two required that restitution be made to the king. The property of eighteen men was confiscated. Twelve men were sentenced to death, three to the galleys. Five were banished from the kingdom permanently and one temporarily. Nine others were permanently banished from the province, and six were temporarily banished. Eight offices were eliminated permanently, while ten men were suspended temporarily from their posts. Nine were required to make public amends for their crimes. All sentences were to be executed immediately. The most severe penalties, such as banishment from the kingdom, condemnation to the galleys, and the death sentence, were rarely meted out. But sentences became increasingly severe as time went by.

The king decided how long a *chambre de justice* would remain in session. If he decided on termination while many cases were still under investigation, he would register an edict of abolition granting amnesty to all *financiers* remaining under suspicion and even to some who had already been sentenced. As grounds for his amnesty the king might cite the supplications of friends and relatives of the accused or of a large number of royal officials as well as the harm that would be done to innocent family members. He might well have mentioned, too, how difficult it became to find credit whenever he took action against any of the *financiers*. The edict of abolition was issued in exchange for financial compensation. For this purpose, the Council drew up tax rolls listing either the financial officeholders (rated at a percentage of the value of their office, as in 1608 and 1624) or the *financiers*. The Chambre de Justice of 1661–65 assessed all who were judged guilty in proportion to the amount of their offense. Some of those assessed obtained deferment of their payments, while others obtained abatements. Those who paid on time received a 10 percent discount on the tax. Payment was accepted in the form of treasury receipts and bills, annuity contracts, interest-bearing paper, and other securities.

Those who managed to flee in time could subsequently reinstate themselves and continue with their careers. Warned by Le Tellier and Colbert in 1661, Jean Hérault de Gourville was able to take refuge in the Low Countries, the United Provinces, and London, even though he was hanged in effigy in the Court of the Palace in Paris. Having made friends among the Dutch, he was named to represent the king of France on a mission in Holland in 1667, returned to Paris in 1668, and received letters of amnesty in 1671.

The *chambres de justice* made it possible to appease public opinion, at least temporarily, and allowed the king to raise money and eliminate part of the outstanding public debt. Beyond that, they allowed the king to change personnel, to choose which of two groups of *financiers* would supply his *surintendant*, his *contrôleur général*, and his *intendants des Finances*, his leading tax farmers, and his *partisans* and *traitants* for *affaires extraordinaires*. The Chambre de Justice of 1624–25, for example, allowed Louis XIII to get rid of his *surintendant*, La Vieuville, who harbored dangerous political ambitions, along with his group of *partisans* and *traitants*. The Chambre of 1661–65, which was called after Fouquet, the *surintendant*, had been arrested at Nantes in September 1661, made it possible to try Fouquet and his group of backers for abuse of the public trust and crimes against the state, thus leaving the coast clear for Colbert and his group. The Chambre hit Fouquet's men hard and went easy on Colbert's. Therein lies the reason why the king commuted Fouquet's sentence from banishment to life in prison, in fact a heavier penalty. The king thereby remained master of the situation, demonstrating that the winning group of *financiers* owed its victory to his favor alone. The *chambres de justice* helped the king escape from the grip of the *financiers* and enabled him to dominate them. They ceased to be necessary when more efficient means of managing the economy were introduced: the king himself became *surintendant*, the bureaus of the *contrôle général* were established, the general farms were used to collect taxes, and the *intendants des provinces* were appointed to head up the administration in the provinces. By these means the monarch remained the master.

Note

1. A Chéruel, *Journal d'Olivier Lefèvre d'Ormesson*, vol. 2 (Paris: Imprimerie Impériale, 1861), pp. lxx-lxxx.

25   The *"Grands Jours"*

The *"Grands Jours"* were commissions of royal judges whose purpose was to restore order after a period of disturbances. The *président* of the Grands Jours d'Auvergne, de Novion, defined them rather well in a letter he wrote to Colbert on 24 November 1665: "In your last letter you do me the honor of instructing me that the Grands Jours have three essential duties: the punishment of persons guilty of crimes in general, the punishment of wicked judges within their jurisdiction, and, finally, the task of restoring vigor to good officers and reestablishing the authority of the courts."[1]

Between 1454 and 1481 we find six Grands Jours in action. Under François I there were twelve, and between 1547 and 1596, six. At the behest of the Estates General of 1576, it had been decided that Grands Jours would be held "every year in the provinces most remote from our *parlements*," in the words of the Blois ordinance of 1579, which was never put into effect. Later on, the Estates General of 1614–15 and the Assembly of Notables of 1626–27 asked that Grands Jours be held in the remotest provinces every two or three years. Richelieu proposed a permanent circuit court. Louis XIII is said to have decided on holding Grands Jours every year in the district of every *parlement* in the kingdom. But Grands Jours were actually held only once under Louis XIII, in 1634, owing to the distraction of constant civil and foreign war.

The Grands Jours of Poitiers were established by letters patent issued at Fontainebleau on 2 June 1634. Nineteen *commissaires* were named to the panel. Presiding was the *conseiller d'Etat* Tanneguy Séguier, *président* in the Paris *parlement*. Seventeen councillors from the Paris *parlement* were members. The *avocat général* Talon acted as *procureur général*. The commission had jurisdiction over Poitou, Touraine, Anjou, Maine, Angoumois, and the Haute and Basse Marche. It had cognizance of cases of murder, assault, abuse of authority, rebellion, offenses committed by soldiers, counterfeiting, blasphemy, and sodomy. The commission arrived in Poitiers on 5 September 1634. It ordered the *baillis* and *sénéchaux* "to investigate with all due haste murders, assassinations, thefts, kidnappings, abductions, rapes of women and girls, embezzlement of public funds," and so on.² But the commission encountered a wall of silence. The most important of those accused of crimes were warned in time to make their escape. This was an achievement of a sort. As Richelieu put it, 233 *gentilshommes* and other powerful personages had "found it expedient to sample other climes" and were thereby cut off from their families and friends and rendered powerless. For those who stayed behind, the commission remained at work for four months, tried cases, heard appeals, and took cases away from other courts by evocation. It tried mainly small fry but caused fear nonetheless. The king's power was demonstrated in the provinces on the eve of France's declaration of war against Spain.

The Grands Jours d'Auvergne, held at the beginning of Louis XIV's personal government, were of greater importance. Like the Chambre de Justice, this session of the Grands Jours was one of the steps Louis XIV took to restore order after the death of Mazarin, using Colbert as his principal agent. Foquet was sentenced by the Chambre de Justice at the end of December 1664. Louis XIV's letters concerning the Grands Jours d'Auvergne were ready in January 1665. The declaration of 31 August 1665 explained the place of the Grands Jours in the government's plan of action: "The first and most important objective that we have set ourselves and to which we have dedicated all our care, after the consolidation of our conquests, the securing of public tranquillity, the repair of our system of finance, and the reestablishment of commerce, has been to bring about the reign of justice and, through it, to reign in our state." The king set the following objectives for the commission: to hear civil and criminal cases, dispose of cases had been clogging the court calendar for years, restore some semblance of order, and undertake a "general reform." The commission was granted the powers of a sovereign court and characterized itself as a court. It was supposed to be in session from 15 September until 30 November 1665, but on 6 November the king extended its session until 31 January 1666. Its jurisdiction covered a large part of the territory under the jurisdiction of the Paris *parlement* in central France: upper and lower Auvergne, Bourbonnais, Nivernais, Forez, Beaujolais, and some *bailliages* from Lyonnais, Saint-Pierre-le-Moûtier, Montferrand, Combrailles, Montagnes d'Auvergne, Haute- and Basse-Marche, and Berry. Amended letters patent added Mâconnais to this jurisdiction.

Louis XIV chose members of the Paris *parlement* to serve as *commissaires* for the Grands Jours: 1 *président*, 16 councillors from the 5 Chambres des Enquêtes, 1 *procureur général*, 1 *greffier civil*, 1 *greffier criminel*, and 1 keeper of the seals.

The *président* of the Grands Jours was the *président à mortier* Nicolas Potier de Novion. The 16 councillors were all sons, sons-in-law, brothers, or brother-in-law of councillors on the *parlement* of Paris and the Grand Conseil, *maîtres des requêtes*, *conseillers d'Etat*, or ambassadors. All were wealthy, important men of honor, and all were impartial. The *procureur général* was the *avocat général* Denis Talon. The keeper of the seals was the *maître des requêtes* Louis-François de Caumartin, the son of a *conseiller d'Etat* and a believer in equity and in following the rules of procedure. The *greffier criminel* was Jean Drouet. The *greffier civil*, Nicolas Dongois, succeeded his father and came from an old Parisian bourgeois family that was closely related to the family of Boileau, the famous man of letters.

The *président* had connections in Auvergne with the Ribeyre and Canillac families. One of his daughters had married a Ribeyre, the son of the *premier président* of the Cour des Aides of Clermont, whose sister was married to a Canillac. The *procureur général* also had family ties in the Clermont area. They were chosen partly for this reason, so that they would not be looked upon as "strangers" in the province.

These men were united by a similar social background and choice of political allegiance; all were loyal to the king. They disagreed, however, on a question of professional priority. The king had stipulated that if the *président* de Novion should be indisposed, the commission would be presided over by the keeper of the seals, Caumartin. The councillors from the Paris *parlement* refused to accept a *maître des requêtes* in the chair. Caumartin had to give in, as did the king.

The commission members left Paris with their families, secretaries, servants, and tutors, including one Fléchier, tutor to the Caumartin children. The king paid them a bonus of 900 livres, which covered the costs of travel and lodging. They accordingly agreed to forgo their *épices*, whereupon they were deluged with a flood of unimportant cases. On orders from the king, contained in *lettres de cachet* dated 6 September 1665 and addressed to the aldermen and citizens of Clermont, they were given lodgings, treated to courtesy calls, and entertained with meals, balls, and various other distractions. They were received, acknowledged, and feted by the official *corps* and authorities in all the cities they visited. On 26 September 1665, they held their opening session in the chambers of the Cour des Aides after celebrating a mass in red gowns at the cathedral.

The commission ran into a great deal of trouble in trying to gather information and testimony. It therefore sought to undertake a procedural reform. The king had sent orders to the local judges instructing them to transmit to the clerk of the Grands Jours all documents pertaining to criminal cases disposed of by trial. On 1 October 1665, the commission ordered royal judges, particularly the *prévôts des maréchaux*, to launch investigations into all crimes committed within the purview of the Grands Jours. On 7, 14, and 16 November it asked the clerks of the lower courts for copies of all letters of remission registered with them, so that they could be examined one at a time. But the court records had been neglected, and important documents had disappeared. Curates, vicars, and chaplains avoided publishing monitory letters.

Nothing happened. In one month's time the commission had disposed of only two cases, both unimportant.

It was therefore decided to take the offensive. On 3 October a decree was issued concerning the suppression of evidence, making it a crime to remove a document from the files as a favor to someone or in exchange for money. The decree of 30 January 1666 condemned "frauds" in documents purportedly written by the *sergents*, many of whom did not know how to write or sign their names. Fines of up to 2,000 livres were imposed on royal judges who delayed sending documents and information.

Beyond these measures, the commission delegated some of its members to undertake special missions. On 8 October, two councillors who were clergymen were sent to visit benefices in the possession of ecclesiastics within the jurisdiction of the court. They were charged to hear local complaints, launch investigations, arrest those against whom charges had been brought, examine witnesses, check their testimony, and confront the accused. On 26 October the court gave a *commission de transport* to three of its councillors: Le Pelletier was assigned to Haute-Auvergne, Lefèvre de La Falluère to Bourbonnais, and Joly de Fleury to the Marche. On 7 November, Rochart, the son of the *intendant* of Lyon, was assigned Lyonnais, Forez, and Beaujolais.

The investigations carried out on the spot by these men revealed that quite a few judges lacked professional scruples and were of questionable moral character. Officers in the *bailliages* and *sénéchaussées* were aware of crimes but did nothing to prosecute them. The guilty were acquitted. Letters of remission issued by the Grande or Petite Chancellerie were rubber-stamped by judges without investigation. Criminals were thus absolved of responsibility even before being punished. At the *présidial* for the Marche in Guéret, registration of letters of remission could be bought "with ease." Officers extorted money from countless victims. The officers of the *bailliage* of Montferrand took large sums of money in connection with contracts for the sale of real estate. At the *présidial* of Moulins the Roy and Dubuisson families had increased the amounts charged for certain legal procedures to a scandalous degree. At the *bailliage* of La Tour in Auvergne, officers made arbitrary seizures of oxen belonging to peasants, placed the property of deceased individuals under seal in the absence of any petition from the parties involved, seized property for "salaries and vacations," forced minor girls to pay a price for marriage authorizations, and so on. Since all the officers in each of the lower courts were related to one another, "they all upheld one another so that it was impossible to obtain justice."

The clergy had fallen into disarray. Certain curates had allowed themselves to be contaminated by the environment. The abbé Boyer had murdered a young woman and the child he had fathered. Other members of the clergy had committed kidnappings and assaults and lent their names to laymen so that they might enjoy an ecclesiastical benefice. And this is to say nothing of such "peccadilloes" as frequenting taverns, taking the name of the Lord in vain, keeping mistresses, and fathering children. Monasteries and even convents were rife with "libertinage." Their income was being squandered on banquets for visitors.

Gentilshommes had been using violent means to maintain their tyranny over the peasants. Forcible extortion of money was "the common offense of the *gentilshommes* of Auvergne," according to Dongois, clerk of the Grands Jours. The king's lieutenant in Bourbonnais, the marquis de Levis, was a counterfeiter who manufactured pistoles that were then circulated by his *maître d'hôtel*. Many *gentilshommes* exacted seigneurial dues beyond what they were entitled to, for watch, wine, oxen, supply and transport, and the use of seigneurial mills. They usurped such communal property as meadows, woods, and rights to gather firewood, collected money on every pretext, raised the *cens* without justification, and collected new dues. *Seigneurs* extorted money from some peasants and loaned it to others at rates of interest ranging from 8.3 percent to 25 percent. In addition, the principal indicated on the note for the debt was greater than the sum actually loaned, and the *seigneur* included his "fees and dues" in the total amount. Some *seigneurs* abused their judicial powers to impose arbitrary fines: fines were levied for "being involved in a dispute, 460 livres," for "having separated men who were fighting, 120 livres," and for "having made a girl pregnant," from 30 to 200 livres.

The Canillac family led a reign of terror. Jacques-Timoléon, marquis de Canillac, age seventy-two, accompanied by a bodyguard of valets known as his "twelve Apostles," terrorized his fiefs and *seigneuries* from Clermont to Rouergue. All his close relatives were guilty of serious crimes or misdemeanors. His eldest son stole his neighbors' animals, besieged their homes, and murdered them. His next eldest son murdered a curate. Guillaume de Beaufort-Canillac had not only extorted money but also abducted and held captive a notary who had drawn up a document against him. Gabriel de Beaufort-Canillac, vicomte de La Mothe, had attempted to murder another *gentilhomme*.

The cruelty of Gaspard d'Espinchal, seigneur de Massiac, was that of a sadist.

Charges had been mounting against the Canillacs, and especially against the old marquis, for decades without any effect.

Many other crimes had been committed by commoners who held no offices, by agricultural laborers, by merchants, by "bourgeois de" one city or another, by valets and maids, by artisans and laborers, and by soldiers. There had been thefts of a couple of sacks of wheat, two or three sheep, and the like. Insults had been traded in taverns. Blasphemies had been uttered in church. There had been riots and assaults, bludgeonings and stabbings, battles between men armed with vine props, and crimes of blood.

Everyone in this society, no matter what his social level, "reacted with the same hostility against the decisions of the courts and the men responsible for carrying them out. The peasant is no more willing than his lord to be haled into court and, like his lord, takes physical vengeance against his adversary or against the bailiff sent by his adversary to serve him with a subpoena."[3] The members of this rural society looked upon urban judges and their agents as strangers to their world and viewed their interference as an intolerable form of aggression and coercion. They preferred to settle their affairs by themselves, in their own way. The man who took his case to the courts of the state was violating at least a tacit social pact and infringing certain traditional liberties. Among the *gentilshommes* these sentiments were reinforced by the pride of belonging to a superior race. To bring even a minor case against a *gentilhomme* was to attack his honor. Disputes between *gentilshommes* were supposed to be settled sword in hand; disputes between a *gentilhomme* and one of his inferiors were supposed to be settled by beatings or thrashings, or occasionally with pistol or musket.

The commission was charged first with punishing these abuses and second with preventing their recurrence. It accomplished both goals at the same time, handing down sentences for the one and issuing regulations for the other.

The court expedited its procedures by declaring that it would operate outside the common law. Ordinary delays were reduced by its decision on 1 October 1665 to hear all defense pleas in a single hearing. Sanctions were established for anyone who might try to dissuade witnesses from testifying or to prevent their presence in court. Parties were prohibited from rejecting so many judges that fewer than ten remained. On 30 September it was decided that all charges against the same individual would be judged together. The *prévôts des maréchaux* were, however, allowed to continue making arrests and to seek judicial rulings from the Grand Conseil. The declaration of 31 August announced that fugitives had fifteen days to surrender themselves to the commission, failing which soldiers would be placed in their homes, fortresses, and *châteaux* and maintained at their expense. If their family and friends resisted, the buildings would be razed and the remains sold as scrap for the king's profit. Those under indictment but not yet convicted were required to surrender themselves with all due haste, failing which their property would be seized as if they had been convicted, placed under the king's administration, and operated for the benefit of the king's treasury with no hope of recovery by the owner. Anyone who gave shelter to fugitives, convicted or not, even on the pretext of merely offering hospitality, would be subject, depending on the gravity of the case, to fine, imprisonment, demolition of their *châteaux*, and loss of nobility.

The commission even allowed itself to go beyond the declaration of 31 August and the Moulins ordinance of 1566. Accused of a number of murders, the marquis du Palais had fled in September 1656 along with his son and six of their valets and servants. They had not been convicted of the crimes. Nor had they resisted the authorities, since they had fled before the judges of the Grands Jours arrived. Nevertheless, on 23 November 1665, they were sentenced to death in absentia, fines were imposed, and the du Palais castle was ordered leveled at once, without allowing time for the filing of an objection as provided by the ordinance of Moulins. The forests surrounding the *château* were ordered cut to a height of three feet as a mark of dishonor. Dongois, the clerk, justified this violation of the law as necessary as an "example and terror."

By contrast, the court was relatively indulgent toward lesser folk. Torture (the *question ordinaire* of the Paris *parlement*) was used only twice. Records were reviewed to make sure that all the required formalities had been observed. For example, in the case of Toinette Farge, who had been sentenced to death for infanticide, the court overturned the death sentence on 16 November 1665, on the grounds that the original judges had violated the edict of 1556. This edict had set forth three conditions that had to be met before a woman could be sentenced to death for infanticide: concealment of pregnancy and birth, the duly attested presence of the corpse of a child, and absence of a record of baptism or Christian burial. The trial judges had failed to prepare an affidavit when the infant's body was discovered. It was therefore impossible to produce "duly attested" evidence of the presence of the body of a child that had been born living. When trial records exhibited the least procedural error, it was unusual for the judges of the Paris *parlement* to pass sentence of death.

The court heard 1,360 criminal cases, only 202 of which had not been heard before. Charges against many of the accused were dismissed, and only 692 sentences were actually carried out. Eighty-seven nobles were condemned, along with 26 court officials, 4 ecclesiastics (10 others were sent before the "official principal" for "peccadilloes"), 574 commoners who held no office, including 11 agricultural laborers, 5 "bourgeois de," 9 merchants, 51 valets, lackeys, and maids, 12 soldiers, and 26 artisans or workmen. The sentences were usually "for facts emerging from the trial." In 283 cases the reason for the judgment was indicated: there were 107 murders, including 19 committed by *gentilshommes* and 1 by the abbé Boyer; 14 duels; 34 serious assaults; 2 armed rebellions; 37 thefts; 24 cases of extortion; 8 cases of counterfeiting; 14 rapes; 9 abductions; 8 infanticides; 3 cases of adultery; 13 cases of slander; and 3 cases of blasphemy.

On 30 January 1666, the court issued a summary of its work. Three hundred forty-seven death sentences had been handed down in absentia, and 23 people had been executed. Twelve men had been banished in absentia for life, and 15 other sentences of banishment for life had actually been carried out. As for temporary banishments, there had been 70 in absentia, 66 actually executed. Three people had been sentenced in absentia to life in the galleys, and 2 others had been present to receive their sentences. There had been 18 people sentenced in absentia to a term in the galleys, and 20 others had been present to receive their sentences.

Of the 347 people sentenced to death in absentia, the court had ordered that 94 be executed in effigy, which allowed their property to be confiscated immediately, before expiration of the period allowed for them to turn themselves in.

Nineteen *gentilshommes* had been "stripped of the privilege of nobility" and sentenced to death for dueling, rape, or murder; eight were to be broken on the wheel and eleven hanged. Of the 23 death sentences that were carried out, 6 were *gentilshommes* and 1 an ecclesiastic. The marquis de Levis was sentenced to nine years' banishment and required to pay damages of 15,000 livres to the widow of the *prévôt* killed by his *maître d'hôtel*. Gabriel de Beaufort-Canillac, vicomte de La Mothe, was beheaded on 23 October 1665. The marquis de Canillac was sentenced to death in absentia on 26 January 1666. His property was confiscated, 40,000 livres in fines were imposed, and he was required to pay 60,000 livres in restitutions. His three *châteaux* were ordered destroyed immediately and he lost all his rights of seigniory and justice.

Six court officials were sentenced to death in absentia, 4 were sentenced to temporary banishment, 3 were admonished and 1 reprimanded, 8 were permanently removed from office, 5 were suspended for periods from six months to one year, and all were required to pay heavy fines.

For the future, the court issued a grand decree concerning judicial regulations on 10 December 1665. This was nothing less than a code of penal procedure, the provisions of which were inspired by the behavior and mentality to which the *commissaires* had been witness.

As for the clergy, in consideration of the fact that poverty was the principal cause of misbehavior by the curates of Auvergne, the commission stipulated in its regulatory decree of 30 October 1665 that curates on limited allowance (*portion congrue*) should receive 300 livres annually, free and clear of all charges, and that all who were receiving ecclesiastical tithes, including laymen, should contribute to the payment of this sum. The commission ran into opposition from the Assembly of the Clergy, where the bishop of Amiens proclaimed that the court had "overnight changed the face of Christianity and overturned the economy of the law of grace," because the Grand Conseil had set the limited allowance at a bare 200 livres.

The commission reestablished discipline in ecclesiastical communities and reformed the Ursulines, the nuns of the Hôtel-Dieu of Clermont. It verified letters patent issued over the previous thirty years, authorizing the creation of new religious establishments. It looked into the acquisition of ecclesiastical property over the previous ten years and the amortization of such property. And it heard appeals stemming from cases pitting one religious community against another.

In regard to the nobility, the commission issued a number of regulatory decrees concerning seigneurial dues. On 15 October 1665, it prohibited the collection of dues for which no title was held. It forbade preparation of new land registers without authorization and declared it illegal to force tenants to make "spontaneous" declarations that they were liable to the payment of fictitious dues. On 27 November 1665, the court forbade *seigneurs* to exact fines without legal judgment and to seize chattels and livestock on their own authority. On 9 January 1666, it established quality standards for payments in kind: *seigneurs* could not demand a "better" grade of product, such as white wheat instead of red wheat, white oats instead of gray oats, white wine instead of claret. *Seigneurs* were prohibited from demanding notes of indebtedness from their peasants when they deemed the quality of the product unsatisfactory. As for *corvées*, *seigneurs* were ordered not to require two or three brace of oxen instead of one. They were further ordered to distribute periods of *corvée* over the course of the year and to feed laborers while they were working on *corvée*. The court also made rulings in regard to taxes. *Seigneurs* were ordered not to levy the *aide* four times a year and the *taille* several times. They were also prohibited from charging tolls and *banalités* above the customary amount. *Seigneurs* were enjoined to do their duty and repair bridges, roads, ovens, and mills. For the Haute- and Basse-Marche, it was decided that serfs should not be liable to *corvée* beyond the limits of the castellany, that they should be allowed to return home at night, and that they should not be chained together.

The regulatory decree of 9 January 1666 recommended the establishment of a single class of measures in place of a variety of measures in each category. These were to be known as the "measures of Clermont." The unit of weight was to be sixteen ounces of "the king's weight of the city of Paris." For fabrics, it was to be the ell, three feet eight inches. An exception was allowed for Moulins and the Bourbonnais, where the measures of Moulins were the standard.

The decree of 14 December 1665 prohibited "*fêtes baladoires*," popular celebrations in the villages on certain Sundays and on the principal religious holidays. It was made illegal to hold games and meetings at the same time as mass and vespers. Public lewdness, drunkenness, blasphemy, fighting, and profanity were prohibited.

The commission devoted particular attention to the poor. Between 6 October 1665, and 30 January 1666, it considered the general hospitals and Hôtels-Dieu in its district on eleven separate occasions: it examined hospital accounts, ordered the repair of buildings, studied finances, and looked into disputes among hospital administrators and nuns. The court ordered the nuns of the Hôtel-Dieu of Clermont to tend to the sick and to prepare medication, dismissing the claim of the nuns that these duties should fall to the administrators.

Two regulatory decrees concerning the poor were issued on 30 January 1666. These were in the spirit of the general hospital act for Paris of 1656, which provided for the "general confinement" of the poor but which was not applied in the provinces until 1676. The poor and the sick were to be treated justly and protected from harm. But for their part they had the responsibility to behave as "good paupers" and "good patients," since it was a "privilege" to be admitted to a general hospital. Begging was prohibited, and repeat offenders were punished in the case of men by whipping or the galleys, in the case of women by banishment. Any person who gave shelter to a beggar could be fined, and their bedding burned to prevent epidemics. The truly poor were all to be housed in the general hospital of Clermont, including the disabled, the aged who had no family or resources, orphans between six and thirteen years of age, and those with incurable diseases. Other invalids were to be sent to the Hôtel-Dieu. These establishments were to be financed by collections, by one-third of administrative fines and confiscations, by gifts, legacies, and endowments, by contributions from *compagnons* who obtained their brevet of apprenticeship and from master craftsmen when they completed their masterpiece, and by contributions from officeholders upon taking office. Those receiving public assistance were to be taught a trade in the hospital, where they would work on "manufactures of all sorts." Three-quarters of the proceeds from the sale of what they produced would go to the institution for the upkeep of its inmates, and one-quarter to the inmates themselves as their earnings, to be handed over upon discharge. The working day was set at ten and a half hours in winter, eleven and a half hours in summer. The trade guilds were to send workers to train apprentices. After six years they would be awarded a diploma and could set themselves up in a trade. The internal life of a general hospital was strictly regulated. Contacts with the outside were forbidden. Economy was carried to the point of miserliness in everything: uneaten bits of bread were reused. Religious observance was strict: the day began with a mass, there was common prayer three times a day, devotional readings at mealtimes, and catechism classes. But while there was firm insistence on Christian practice, on observing rites and prescriptions, on obedience, not a word was said about the love of God. What was lacking was the essence of Christianity, charity, the tender love of God and of all men, corresponding to God's tender love for each of his creatures.

When the work of the *commissaires* was complete, a *lettre de cachet* called them back to their regular duties in *parlement* and assured them of the king's "satisfaction" with what they had done.

Grands Jours were also held at Le Puy for Velay at the same time as the Grands Jours d'Auvergne. The Velay region was initially included in the list of areas under the jurisdiction of the Grands Jours d'Auvergne. But it fell within the purview of the *parlement* of Toulouse. The Estates of Languedoc protested through their deputies. The king therefore commissioned certain magistrates from the Toulouse *parlement* to hold Grands Jours at Le Puy from 2 October to 28 November 1666, and at Nîmes from 26 December 1666, until the end of February 1667. The Grands Jours of Le Puy resulted in the beheading of some fifteen *gentilshommes* and in the issuance of thirty regulatory decrees pertaining to Protestants.

The Grands Jours d'Auvergne had far-reaching consequences. The regulatory decree of 10 December 1665 inspired a number of articles included in the criminal ordinance of 1670. Four of the *commissaires* who had served on the commission for the Grands Jours sat on the commission responsible for the final draft of the ordinance: the *président* de Novion, the *avocat général* Talon, and the councillors Malo and Le Boultz. Their regulatory decree of 30 October 1665 lay behind the royal declaration of 30 March 1666 and the edict of June 1671, which upheld the decision to set the limited allowance for curates at 300 livres. The regulatory decree of 14 December 1665 was one reason for the issuance of decrees by the Paris *parlement* on 3 September 1667 and 28 March 1675, and for the royal declaration of 16 December 1698, ordering the postponement of fairs and markets until the day after Sundays and holidays.

Thus it was the empirical determination of facts and positive experience that inspired the ordinances and edicts of Louis XIV.

The Grands Jours demonstrated once more that commissions could succeed where officeholders were impotent. But by delegating representatives to remote provinces under their jurisdiction, they also demonstrated that an individual *commissaire* could often be more effective and economical than a whole commission, a point underscored at about the same time by the commissions responsible for checking community debts in the *pays d'Etat*. And this discovery certainly played a large part in the decision to keep using the *intendants des provinces* and later to increase their authority.

Notes

1. Cited by A. Lebigre, *Les Grands Jours d'Auvergne* (Paris: Hachette, 1976), p. 16.

2. Cited by Georges d'Avenel, *Richelieu et la monarchie absolue*, vol. 4, pp. 24–25.

3. Lebigre, *Les Grands Jours*, pp. 141–42. No violence against tax collectors is revealed by the documents, however.

26

The *Intendants des Provinces*

From the Origins to 1661

The Origins
Intendants des provinces, or provincial intendants as we shall call them here, were usually chosen among the *conseillers d'Etat* and *maîtres des requêtes*. Later, the intendancies became a near-monopoly of the *maîtres des requêtes*. The intendancies probably originated with the inspection tours made by the *maîtres des requêtes*.

The Inspection Tours of the Maîtres des Requêtes. *Maîtres des requêtes* used to serve quarterly terms in either the *requêtes de l'Hôtel*, the king's Council, or inspection tours (*chevauchées*) in the provinces, undertaken as part of their regular official duties. Henri II's edict of August 1553, issued during a period of war and internal unrest, specified the powers of a *maître des requêtes* on an inspection tour. In the judicial sphere, he was empowered to look into the zeal with which court officers were enforcing the law, to hear complaints against them, and to administer reprimands. He was authorized to investigate the behavior of soldiers with regard to the civilian population, to examine cases brought by the *prévôts de maréchaux* and presidial judges, and to prepare a report for the constable of France concerning the punishment of the accused. In the administrative sphere, he was empowered to look into the administration of municipal funds and *octrois*, to examine receipts and expenditures and statements of account, and to investigate heresies and the zeal of judges in punishing them. In the area of finance, he was empowered to assist those who had been commissioned to collect monies due the king, to look into how the people were being treated by the various tax collectors and farmers, and to check to see whether the latter were speculating with royal funds. He was authorized to consult with the people's syndics regarding the assessment of levies for supplies, fortifications, munitions, and military preparations, in order to ensure that the burden would be "equally" distributed, without injustice or excess. In general, he was supposed to prepare an official report on all wrongdoings, abuses, misappropriations, acts of oppression, and harassment. This edict was still in force after the Fronde in the seventeenth century. Some of the most important powers of the intendants are contained in it, and it lay at the root of a number of others.

The *maîtres des requêtes* on inspection tours had no decision-making power, however. They could only gather information. It was the king's Council and the tribunal of the Connétablie that rendered judgment, imposed sanctions, ameliorated conditions, and undertook reforms. The *maîtres des requêtes* remained on tour for only a limited period of time. Theoretically, they toured a different province on each occasion. They were in principle no more than inspectors.

The most important sixteenth-century ordinances insist on this inspector's role. Article 33 of the Orléans ordinance of 1560 laid it down that *maîtres des requêtes* should be scrupulous in making their inspections and taking down "the complaints of all individuals and inserting them in their reports," which were to be submitted to the chancellor. These clauses were reiterated in article 7 of the Moulins ordinance of 1566. Article 209 of the Blois ordinance of 1579 specified that the reports should include not only complaints from the king's subjects but also mention of any violations of the ordinances and any other cases warranting punishment or correction.

A *maître des requêtes* making an inspection tour might be charged with a special commission by the king's Council, however, asking him to undertake some extraordinary task in the place to which he was being dispatched. The Council sometimes sent *maîtres des requêtes* on extraordinary missions outside their normal inspection tours, assigning them to some specified place, as it did also with *conseillers d'Etat* and *présidents* in the sovereign courts. Thus the *maîtres des requêtes* were sometimes assigned limited and temporary missions as *commissaires*. These missions included such tasks as having edicts and letters patent registered, executing council edicts and decrees, and thus establishing, say, a presidial court or a farm office, selling an office, ordering a *trésorier de France* or an *élu* to collect some tax, recovering funds from the *recettes générales,* trying rebels and executing those found guilty, and so on.

By way of example, consider the commission given to one *maître des requêtes,* the sieur de Gourgues, as he embarked on an inspection tour in 1616.[1] The commission reads as follows:

Louis by the grace of God King of France and Navarre, to our beloved and loyal councillor and *maistre des requestes ordinaires* of our *hostel,* the sieur de Gourgues, greetings. . . . Fully confident of your affection and fidelity for the good of our service, of your prudence, of your experience in your position, and having made you our deputy and sent you to our provinces of Poitou and Guyenne, we have also commissioned you and made you our deputy, and do hereby commisssion you and make you our deputy, to receive any and all complaints such as may be made to you by our officers and subjects in the provinces of Poitou and Guyenne and in the cities and localities thereabout, of violations of our edicts and ordinances by our subjects in these provinces of whatever quality and condition, even including wrongdoing by our officers, both in our courts and in our finances. And we further commission you to prepare reports of such disputes and disturbances and to investigate them thoroughly and to send these reports and the information thus obtained to our very dear and loyal knight, the Chancellor of France, sieur de Sillery, for further action by us according to the case. If need be, however, and until it is otherwise ordered by us, you may attend to these disturbances, disputes, violations, and wrongs temporarily as you see fit for the benefit of our service and justice and to secure peace, union, and tranquillity for our subjects. For this purpose and for all that is necessary to accomplish it we have granted and do hereby grant full power and special mandate to you. We further order our courts of *parlement*, governors and *lieutenants généraux* of our provinces, *baillis*, *sénéchaux*, *vissénéchaux*, and all other officers and justiciars to whom it may fall to lend you aid, favor, and assistance should you so request; and we further order all our *huissiers* and *sergents* to serve such writs and other court orders as may be necessary for the execution of the present mandate.[2]

This clear statement calls for three remarks. First, the *maître des requêtes* has already been "made a deputy" at the time he receives his commission. Second, his duties went beyond those set forth by the edict of 1553, for he was empowered to judge cases and make decisions on a temporary basis (it should be borne in mind, however, that the edict of 1553 dealt only with regular duties, not with special missions). Third, he was authorized to call upon the aid of the *parlements* of Paris and Bordeaux, doubtless because it was the normal thing to commission a *maître des requêtes* to deal with unrest in Poitou, even if the courts generally looked askance upon the granting of special commissions.

Maîtres des requêtes continued to make inspection tours, with or without additional commissions, throughout the seventeenth century, at least at times and in places where there were no intendants. We still find them in Brittany in an interval during which there was no intendant, prior to the intendancy of Pomereu, which began in 1689. After that date there was always an intendant in the province.

The Intendants. The first time the word "intendant" was used to describe a special *commissaire* seems to have been in 1555, in a commission issued to Pierre Panisse, *président* of the Cour des Aides of Montpellier, making him responsible for "the intendancy of justice in the isle of Corsica." During the period of unrest that lasted from 1580 until 1600, the number of *commissaires* increased and some assumed titles such as "superintendant of justice," "intendant of justice," or "intendant of finances" (not to be confused with the *intendants des Finances* who worked with the *surintendant des Finances* and *contrôleur général des Finances*). The term "intendant" connoted superiority. Loyseau explains that the chancellor had been granted the "intendancy" as the "overseer and auditor of all the affairs of France."[3] The intendants of princes had for that reason formerly been called chancellors. Furetière tells us that "intendant, in the household of a Prince or a Great Lord, means his First Officer, the person entrusted with supervising his lord's household, revenue, and affairs," or, in other words, the superior officer of the household.[4] Thus in the late sixteenth century, when *commissaires* took upon themselves the title "intendant," their intention was to indicate that they were superior *commissaires* and furthermore that they had been granted certain decision-making powers in virtue of which they were not merely inspectors but also judges and reformers.

After 1600 the title of intendant disappeared. Although the number of *commissaires* remained large, their field of action was drastically curtailed, being limited, for example, to certain financial matters or to the application of the Edict of Nantes. When the princes and the Protestants began stirring up trouble after 1614, the number of *commissaires* again increased, however. Between 1621 and 1628, during the civil wars with the queen mother and the Protestants, this number rose prodigiously. Some *commissaires* again began taking the title of intendant. Between 1624 and 1631, fourteen out of seventeen *généralités* had intendants. Usually one intendant served from two to four *généralités*. Each royal army had one or more army intendants. The titles were various: *intendant de justice*, *intendant de justice et police*, *intendant de justice, police, et finances*. Given the uncertainty of the administrative nomenclature in this period, it is not at all clear that these different titles corresponded to different duties.

These intendants (who were all *conseillers d'Etat*, *maîtres des requêtes*, and in a few cases magistrates of provincial courts) held commissions granting them absolute powers within specified limits, further delineated by various edicts and ordinances. Consider, for example, the commission granted to Séguier in 1621, naming him intendant of justice for Auvergne. Under its provisions, his wishes in regard to procedures, warrants, ordinances, and judgments were to be executed in spite of any opposition or appeal. All governors, *lieutenants généraux* and *lieutenants particuliers*, captains, *baillis*, *sénéchaux*, judges, and *prévôts des maréchaux* were bound to obey him and to provide him with aid, assistance, and armed force. Appeals from his decisions could be taken up only by the king's Council.

These full powers could only be exercised within narrow limits, however. Séguier's mission in 1621 was above all one of surveillance and inspection. He was to preside in court and monitor the actions of the judges. He was to hear complaints from the king's subjects. He was to bring indictments and try the accused. He was also supposed to investigate the administration of community affairs and settle disputes between officers and mayors and so on. Broadly speaking, his mission was to impose standards on the behavior of the courts, which were responsible for local administration.

The intendants of the army and of such border provinces as Picardy, Champagne, Aunis, and Saintonge had jurisdiction over crimes committed by soldiers and later over crimes committed by civilians as well. They pursued spies and traitors. They monitored the provisioning of troops with food and munitions, supervised the stocking of storehouses, the drafting of forced labor, and the improvement of navigation on rivers and streams. They were also responsible for arming vessels, signing on seamen, and loading cannons on board ship.

Typical of the commissions granted to such men is the council decree entitled "Instruction to sieur de Vertamont, counselor to the king in his Conseil d'Etat and *Maître des Requêtes ordinaire* of the king's *hôtel*, ordained by His Majesty for the post of intendant of justice in Guyenne, concerning the matters he will have to treat in said province in regard to finances," dated 12 April 1630.[5] At Bordeaux, Vertamont was to summon the agents of the tax farmer collecting imposts on the rivers of Bordeaux, Charente, and elsewhere, in order to inform them that he had orders from the king to establish an office at La Teste-de-Buch. He was then to go there and open an office. He would take with him letters from the governor of Guyenne, the duc d'Epernon, addressed to the officers serving on his estates at La Teste-de-Buch, Lesparre, and Castelnau, ordering them to lend a hand in the establishment of the new office. He was further to inform the duke that the king would grant him an annuity of 2,000 livres as indemnity for the losses he would suffer as a result of the establishment of the new office.

Vertamont was then to go to Bayonne to establish an office at Hourgane, south of Dax. This belonged to the comte de Grammont. To secure the count's aid in the establishment of the office, Vertamont was to promise him reimbursement within two or three years of 34,000 livres that the count had advanced to the king for the purpose of recruiting, arming, feeding, and supplying soldiers in Béarn in 1628 to fight against the rebel prince de Rohan. He was further to promise the count a payment of 6,000 livres toward his pension of 1628.

Vertamont was also charged with overseeing the registration of a number of edicts by the Bordeaux *parlement*. On his way through Paris he was supposed to make inquiries of the sieur de Laubardemont, *premier président* of the Cour des Aides of Agen (then being created), and of the sieur Dalibard, who had contracted for the offices of this court, concerning the number of officeholders to be installed.

Vertamont was instructed to look into the losses suffered by the tax farmer collecting imposts on the rivers of Bordeaux, Charente, and elsewhere, so that the Council might judge the merits of the discount being requested by the farmer.

Vertamont was further instructed to visit the *bureau des Trésoriers de France* at Bordeaux. He was to tell them that the king took a very dim view of their refusal to assess the full amounts indicated in the commissions for the regular *taille* and the *crue des garnisons*. He was to order them to send commissions immediately to the *élections* for the collection of all levies, even though the edicts had not yet been presented to their bureaus for registration. An *arrêt de surcéance* (postponement) had been issued by the Bordeaux *parlement*, but the king had quashed it. Vertamont was ordered to do the same for the *élus* of Bordeaux, etc. "And other affairs concerning the king's service in the province of Guyenne His Majesty entrusts to him to conduct as he in his prudence may deem fit."

Thus the intendants exercised the king's own power, but until 1633 they exercised it only in specific and limited areas. Nowhere do we find intendants exercising the full range of powers of the intendant of a later period.

The Expansion of the Intendant's Powers

The Reasons behind the Expansion. No edict was issued to establish the position of provincial intendant. Had any such edict been issued, the sovereign courts would at once have taken a dim view of the matter. Richelieu himself was opposed to the idea, of which he says nothing in his *Mémoires*. In a "Political Testament" probably written by his secretaries around 1638, Richelieu envisioned a reduction in the number of *commissaires* after peace had been restored, as he hoped it soon would be, and proposed stripping them of the title of intendant, which may have pleased their vanity but which was an aberration and an insult to the king's officeholders. Chancellor de Marillac made a timid effort to include the intendants in the text of his ordinance of January 1629. This so-called Code Michaut was never put into effect, however.

The problem was that once the king made his "great choice" in 1631, war, the most important cause of social and political transformations, was destined not only to continue but to expand in scope. In 1632 the move toward the Rhine began to pick up speed. Richelieu increased the number of costly alliances with the Swedes, the United Provinces, and the German Protestants. Finally, on 19 May 1635, the undeclared war with Spain gave way to open warfare. According to Mallet, treasury receipts, which had stood at around 40 million livres tournois, rose to 57 million in 1632, to 32 million in 1633, to 120 million in 1634, and to 208 million in 1635, with the disbursement of funds for open war with Spain. Thereafter receipts oscillated around 100 million livres annually. This growth in expenditure, implying an increased need of tax revenue, was one reason why intendants not only continued to be used but grew into a new institution, thereby changing the very nature of the position of intendant.

In effect, the regular finance officials, the *trésoriers de France*, *élus*, *receveurs généraux*, and *particuliers*, moved too slowly to meet the needs of war. As magistrates, the *trésoriers de France* were intent on respecting due legal forms. They did not like to levy taxes before the relevant edicts had been verified. Because of the emergency, however, the king did not care to brook any opposition or amendments to his will and wished to use his full powers to determine the content of important edicts.

Tax returns were slow and incomplete and rife with bad debts, and these failings were blamed on the practices of financial officials. In the government's view all (and in reality probably a good many) of the *trésoriers de France* and *élus* distributed the tax burden so poorly that some parishes and individual taxpayers were crushed by it. Tax collectors were not very effective in collecting the sums due. Many financial magistrates made no effort to adjust the assessment of the *taille* to the actual resources of the taxpayers. The *trésoriers de France* at Bordeaux had made no changes in the assessment of the *taille* in the sixty years prior to 1634. Others gave tax relief to parishes in which they had relatives, friends, or farmers and increased the burden on other parishes. In the parishes tax assessor-collectors gave breaks to wealthy and influential taxpayers, rich "plowmen" and "parish cocks," and farmers in the employ of *gentilshommes* and *seigneurs*, shifting the burden onto the poorest taxpayers who could no longer afford to pay. Too many collectors and agents were used in collecting taxes. Some of them abused their positions. All made too much use of coercive methods and used bailiffs and *archers* to seize property in payment of tax debts. The costs of collection were too high and taxpayers were ruined. The tax base shrank. Rebellions grew more numerous and more serious, with uprisings by the Croquants and Nu-Pieds, to name two.

In these troubled times the provincial governors asked for intendants to help them. This was the second reason for the institutionalization of the use of intendants. The governors, who were primarily men of the sword, felt the need of a commissioned magistrate to work alongside them, to secure the benefit of judicial assistance from the courts. This need was felt, for example, by the duc de Ventadour in 1637 when unrest swept through Limousin, and by the comte de Saint-Géran in 1640 during the Moulins insurrection.

The Process of Institutionalization. The use of intendants came to be institutionalized in the following way. The first phase was begun by the royal government in December 1633, when it attempted to increase its tax receipts and at the same time to give relief to its "weakest and most helpless" subjects in the hope of forestalling rebellion, by sending *commissaires* to the provinces to "equalize" the *taille* and other direct taxes, that is, to adjust the assessment on parishes and individuals to their actual capacity to pay. This mission was frequently entrusted to *maîtres des requêtes* and especially to *intendants de justice* in the provinces. On 16 May 1634, instructions were issued to these *commissaires*. They were supposed to consult the *trésoriers de France* about the causes of existing inequities but were not obliged to follow the advice they received. Once discovered, inequities were to be remedied on the spot by peremptory action. The distribution of the *taille* among parishes as laid down by the *élus* was to be corrected. Accurate information about the ability of the different parishes and individual tax-payers to pay their taxes was to be collected. The *élus* were to be ordered to make inspection tours to gather information that could be used in the future as the basis of a further "equalization" of the distribution of the *tailles* as between *généralités* and *élections*, to be undertaken by the king's Council. Suits brought against parishes by individual taxpayers who felt they had been overassessed were to be left by the *commissaires* to the regular judges, the *élus* initially, with appeals to be taken to the Cours des Aides. In other words, the *commissaires* were now being made responsible not merely for inspecting the work of the officeholders and reporting their mistakes but for redoing all that had been done. There is evidence that these instructions were actually carried out in the *généralités* of Lyon, Amiens, Bordeaux, Moulins, and Rouen, and it therefore seems likely that they were carried out in all the *pays d'élection*. The instructions were sometimes followed with a vengeance, for we learn that in Péronne the upshot was "sale of the furniture of the leading men in town" and that in Rouen there were trials for misappropriation of public funds that were still going on in November 1636. It may have been this commission to which Chancellor Séguier was referring when, in a conference held on 8 July 1648, and attended by the duc d'Orléans, Mazarin, and the deputies of the sovereign courts, he said "that the decree issued for the recall of the intendants was just; that it is an evil that cannot be imputed to the queen, who had found the intendants established by the late king in 1635." It may also have been alluded to by the *avocat général* Omer Talon in his speech to the Paris *parlement* on 6 July 1648: "It is not only since the Regency that intendants have been sent to the provinces. Intendants were ordered dispatched on occasion fifteen years ago, and for the past eleven years they have been dispatched to and may be found in all the provinces." This would place the beginning of in-stitutionalization in 1633 and an expansion of the process in 1637.[6]

This commission was still fundamentally a temporary measure, however. The royal government had not yet conceived the intention of replacing reg-ular officeholders. Thus in May 1635 it issued an edict creating *intendants*, *présidents*, and *généraux* in the *bureaux des Finances*, an edict that Caillet mistook some years ago for an edict of creation formally institutionalizing the intendants.

The king wished to place direct representatives in the *bureaux des Fi-nances* in order to force the *trésoriers de France* to discharge their duties properly. He therefore appointed four *intendants généraux* and *présidents* in each *bureau des Finances*. They were to preside over the Chambres des Comptes, enforce edicts, ordinances, regulations, and commissions, and, if the opposition of the *trésoriers de France* made it necessary, register and enforce such orders on their own so that there would be no delay in the collection of taxes. The king left the *trésoriers de France* all their previous duties, but he issued orders that half of them were to undertake inspection tours of the *élections* each year, a duty they had previously neglected.

This measure did not yield the expected results, perhaps because authority was divided among four individuals rather than concentrated in the hands of one and because the officers appointed were still members of regional companies rather than representatives of the king's Council. A year after the edict was issued, abuses by financial officials were still being blamed as much as violence by soldiers for the persistent discontent.

Thus it proved necessary to move on to a second phase. In 1637 the cities of France were obliged to contribute to a compulsory loan. The king's Council divided the total among the *généralités* and within each *généralité* among the cities and sent the assessments to the *trésoriers de France*, along with orders that these be passed on to the *élus*. But the Council feared that these so-called loan *tailles* would run into opposition and decided to assign *maîtres des requêtes* and intendants to supervise their collection. Commissions were issued in July to the intendants Le Prévost at Lyon, Le Maistre de Bellejambe in Picardy, Luillier d'Orgeval for the *généralité* of Soissons and the Ile-de-France, de Villemontée at La Rochelle, Dupré for the *généralité* of Montauban and perhaps also that of Toulouse, Harouys in Champagne, and de Sève at Abbeville, as well as to two individuals who may not have been intendants, the *maître des requêtes* Pinon at Bourges and M. Gobelins in the *généralité* of Orléans, ordering them to "attend to the collection of the loan." The intendants may also have been assigned to attend to the assessment of the *tailles* at the same time, because de Villemontée, intendant of Poitou, Angoumois, Saintonge, and Aunis, carried out this task as well in July 1637, using troops from the regiment of La Meilleraye and the carabineer company of sieur de Courbisan.

The number of intendants seems to have been increased in order to facilitate the task of collecting these funds. Previously, intendants had had to cover very large districts, comprising several *généralités*, and their number must have been small. De Laubardemont was *intendant de justice* "in the provinces of Touraine, Anjou, Le Mayne, and Loudunois." Villemontée supervised the west of France from the Loire to the Gironde. These districts had no fixed borders. Later on, in 1644, Angoumois seems to have been combined in a single intendancy with Limousin and Basse-Marche. In 1637 the trend was toward breaking up these huge districts. Laonnois and Thiérarche, which had been under the authority of Le Maistre de Bellejambe, intendant for Picardy, were transferred to Luillier d'Orgeval, intendant for the *généralité* of Soissons and the Ile-de-France, at the time of the compulsory loan. Bellejambe protested this new enroachment on his territory: he had previously been deprived of the Abbeville region and Boulonnais, which were given to de Sève. D'Orgeval advised him to calm down, adding that "in any case there was the same battle to fight with M. de Thou and M. Lasnier," which suggests that Bellejambe's enormous district had been curtailed in other ways. The carving up of an intendancy was indeed what was happening, for d'Orgeval was concerned not only with the compulsory loan but with all the other duties of an intendant in Laonnais and Guise.

These facts tend to confirm the assertions of Omer Talon. It may be that between 1637 and 1641 the intendants carried out the duties of *trésoriers de France*, *élus*, or local tax assessor-collectors only sporadically, as required by pressing need. Indeed, the royal regulation of 27 November 1642 repeats the same old complaints about inequities and includes an ultimatum to the *élus*: if they did not follow the strict letter of the present regulation and establish an equitable assessment for 1642, the king would send *commissaires* to replace his officeholders.

At this point a third phase became necessary. The intendant Charreton had completed the assessment of taxes for the *élection* of Comminges in February 1642, suggesting that intendants were already carrying out the duties of finance officials. In any case, the regulation of 22 August 1642 concerning the collection of *tailles* and *subsistances* for 1643 accomplished a revolution of sorts. The Council assigned the intendants the brunt of the task of assessing and supervising the collection of *tailles*, *taillons*, *crues*, and *subsistances*. Commissions concerning these taxes were sent to both the intendants and the *trésoriers de France*. The role of the latter was reduced to one of attending to legal formalities and serving as technical advisers. The intendants, on the other hand, were made responsible for overseeing the work of the *bureaux des Finances* and for obtaining from the *trésoriers* the approvals and orders needed for the execution of their commissions. If the *trésoriers de France* refused to go along with the wishes of the intendant or adopted delaying tactics, the orders of the intendant alone were enough to have royal commissions carried out. It was the intendant who was ordered to visit the *élections*. The *trésoriers de France* were supposed to elect one of their number for each *élection* or group of *élections* to accompany the intendant. In each *élection* the intendant was supposed to choose three trusted *élus* and, with them, as well as the *trésorier de France* chosen to represent his peers, the *procureur du roi*, the *receveur des tailles*, and the *greffier* of the *élection*, carry out the task of distributing the *tailles* among cities, towns, and parishes. If the *élus* raised any difficulties, the intendant could call upon other officeholders and notables to carry out a valid assessment. Intendants were instructed to assess officeholders, privileged individuals, wealthy peasants, and farmers in the employ of *gentilshommes* and *seigneurs*. Intendants were further authorized to try anyone—*gentilhomme*, *seigneur*, or whatnot—who impeded the collection of *tailles*. Appeals were not allowed. Tax collectors were issued receipts only after their accounts had been verified, and the intendants were authorized to remove any suspect collector and replace him with a designated agent.

In summary, intendants either replaced finance officials and regular judges in collecting taxes or assumed charge of their activities. The "companies" of officeholders were effectively nullified, along with their power to make remonstrances and to resist the king's will. Officeholders were reduced to individuals as against the intendant. Regular officeholders were, moreover, stripped of the duties that had been theirs by virtue of their position. Henceforth, they would have duties only when chosen by the intendants to act as *commissaires* on a temporary basis, after having been judged individually to be loyal and capable men. This was a revolution of sorts, the result of which was to make the intendant, the direct and responsible representative of the central government, the administrator of the tax system in the provinces. In the minds of the members of the Council this quasi-revolution was definitive. Louis XIII intended his royal declaration and regulations of 16 April 1643 to give the full force of law to the regulations of 22 August 1642: the first twenty articles of the declaration reproduced the earlier regulations word for word.

After the death of Louis XIII on 14 May 1643, the Cour des Aides attempted to take advantage of the situation and limit the effects of the royal revolution by issuing its verification decree of 21 July 1643. But the regulation of 22 August 1642 had already been put into effect by the intendants, and the declaration and regulations of 16 April 1643 were immediately executed, without waiting for the verification of the Cour des Aides, which seems to have had no effect. Not only did the intendants take full responsibility for collecting the taxes, they went even farther than the declaration of 16 April 1643 required: several of the intendants personally selected the *trésoriers de France* who were to accompany them to the *élections* instead of leaving the choice up to their colleagues. Everywhere, moreover, *trésoriers de France* and *élus* competed with one another for commissions from the intendants and were of the greatest help to them in carrying out their duties.

The Nature of the New Institution

Thus an institution that was, in legal and practical terms, new was born under the already old name of "intendant." A financial administration composed of intendants and tax farmers took the place of the old financial administration composed of financial officeholders, the *trésoriers de France* and the *élus*. No longer was the intendant merely an inspector, auditor, and righter of wrongs; he was now an administrator and reformer. This was an innovation: never before had *commissaires* been dispatched to virtually every corner of the kingdom and assigned permanent responsibility for financial administration along with their other duties, thereby supplanting regular officeholders in their principal functions. The term "intendant" was kept, but now it came to designate a *commissaire* of quite a new sort. A new institution was born.

The Range of Powers of an Intendant. At the same time, the royal government moved away from the old system of granting limited, piecemeal powers to the intendants, aimed at a specific object and within one particular area, such as the army, justice, or finance, or perhaps within two of these areas but with separate commissions for each. Instead, intendants were granted a whole range of powers, including powers in the three areas of justice, administration, and finance, all combined in a single commission. The change

in the institution was reflected in the commissions. Some intendants had
their powers expanded in this way at a quite early date. In 1633 the *maître
des requêtes* Isaac de Laffemas could already claim the title of "intendant
of justice, administration, and finance for the provinces and armies of Champagne, Toul, Metz, Verdun, and the Pays Messin."[7] The available evidence
shows that he did indeed exercise his powers in all three of these areas. The
intendant of Champagne, Vignier, described only as "intendant of justice
and administration," was given a commission in 1636, the terms of which
imply that he was to have regular duties in a long-term assignment, "so long
as he shall please us," as the document reads. These duties seem to have
included, perhaps for the first time, almost the full range of powers of the
classic intendant: oversight of the courts and the power to sit as sovereign
judge in criminal cases; tutelage over cities and communities; supervision
of the *élus* and thus of the regular financial administration; and powers to
rectify abuses implying general administrative authority. In addition, Vignier
had power over extraordinary finances and the military, connected with the
dispatching of troops.

The commission given to Mesgrigny in 1638 for Champagne indicates a
reverse, however, for he had no power in the area of finance. He was granted
political power and general administrative authority. He had control of the
state police and sovereign judgment in criminal cases. He was empowered
to oversee the courts and make summary judgments, even in civil cases.
And he had tutelage over cities and communities. By contrast, the commission given to Jeannin de Castille for Champagne in 1642 awarded him no
power over the cities and communities but did grant him almost all the other
powers: political, military, and general administrative authority and authority
over the courts and over military and civilian finances as well as the military
police. Thus, over a period of years the institution remained in transition,
moving forward with hesitation and occasionally moving in reverse. But the
clear tendency was to group powers that had previously been kept separate.

The commission by which the *maître des requêtes* de Ris was made intendant for the Lyonnais on 15 May 1643 was the first to combine all the
powers that subsequently came to be identified with the intendant, a range
of powers that remained substantially unchanged down to the time of the
Revolution, with minor variations from time to time and place to place.[8]
First, there was a general prescription to enforce all ordinances in the areas
of justice, administration, and finance and to prevent abuses. This was followed by more specific instructions. The intendant was to attend the governor's councils, give his advice, and confer with the governor. He was to
investigate rebellions, which it was up to the governor to put down, and sit
in sovereign judgment over those responsible. In the absence of the governor
he was responsible for the quartering, feeding, and discipline of troops. He
was to maintain tutelage over cities and communities by presiding over their
assemblies, supervising their elections, and auditing their accounts and debts.
The intendant was also responsible for presiding over the assessment of

taxes. He had the preponderant vote and was in fact authorized to go so far as to impose his will over the majority. He also had responsibility for the collection of taxes and the supervision of all accounting officials. He was also supposed to inspect the work of officeholders in justice and finance. Broadly speaking, the intendant was "generally responsible for doing whatever is necessary for the good of our service" in the areas of justice, administration, and finance. He had the power to issue orders that were binding without further formality and that could be appealed by moral and physical persons only to the king's Council. The intendant was authorized to requisition armed forces from governors, troop commanders, and *seigneurs* and to call upon the authority of royal and municipal magistrates.

Thus the intendant became not only a judge delegate and reform inspector but also, in the broadest possible sense, an administrator in the areas of justice, "police," and finance. His powers as judge and administrator complemented the governmental powers of the provincial governor. They were not in conflict. The intendant was not the rival but the collaborator of the governor. On occasion, of course, governors and intendants did come into conflict by force of circumstance or as a result of personal antipathies.

Subdelegation. Normally intendants did not have the power to "subdelegate" their authority. To do so they required a special authorization from the king. Prior to 1642 such authorization was never granted to intendants. The commission given to Pomereu for the *généralité* of Amiens on 15 November 1627 did give him the power to subdelegate, but Pomereu was not an intendant. He was rather a *commissaire* responsible solely for the sale of offices, and it was for this purpose that he was authorized to subdelegate. Intendants were authorized to subdelegate for the purpose of executing any special commission they might receive. For example, the intendant for Provence and Dauphiné was commissioned in 1628 to sell offices in Auvergne and Bourbonnais, for which purpose he was authorized to subdelegate. The *commissaires* of 1633–34, some of whom were intendants, appointed a large number of subdelegates for the purpose of assessing the *tailles*. But Isaac de Laffemas, in his commission of intendancy of 3 August 1635, was not expressly authorized to subdelegate. Rather, he was authorized merely to commission certain local officeholders to attend to certain affairs. Not even this right was included in the commissions of other intendants.

When the intendants were permanently assigned the task of assessing the *tailles*, however, they were granted the power to subdelegate by council decree of 22 August 1642. This power was reiterated in article 19 of the declaration of 16 April 1643 and thereafter mentioned from time to time in council decrees such as that of 6 November 1647. Since this power was now included in the text of various laws, it was no longer necessary to mention it in the commissions given to the intendants. Commissions issued up to the time of the Fronde do not in fact make any mention of the power to subdelegate.[9] There is reason to believe that intendants, overwhelmed by the volume of work to be done, made use of the power to appoint subdelegates. For example, Jean Le Camus

> *conseiller du roi* in his *Conseils d'Estat et privé, maître des requêtes ordinaire de son hostel, intendant de justice, police, finances et armées* for Champagne, commissions and subdelegates, this sixteenth day of March, 1645, the sieur Boucherat de la Rocatelle in virtue of the power vested in us by His Majesty . . . to render justice, in our absence and during the period of our commission . . . to the subjects of His Majesty in all civil and criminal cases that may be pleaded before you, for both the *ordinaire* and the *extraordinaire*, billeting, disputes between soldiers, revenues, supplies, munitions, contracts, *taille, taillon, subsistances, gabelles*, salt duties, *aides*, and other manner of taxes,

etc., for the city and *élection* of Troyes.[10] This commission is all the more remarkable in that it empowers the subdelegate not only to investigate but also to sit in judgment on his own and to make provisional execution of sentence without waiting for the outcome of any possible appeal. Appeals were to be taken to the intendant.

The disappearance of the Intendants during the Fronde and Their Subsequent Reestablishment

The companies of officeholders looked askance at the intendants and their subdelegates. Their feelings on this score played a large part in triggering the "*Fronde parlementaire.*" On 30 June 1648, the Chambre Saint-Louis, sitting at the Palais de Justice in Paris and composed of deputies from the sovereign courts of that city, submitted a proposal for the recall of all intendants and other *commissaires* holding unverified commissions. The Paris *parlement* then recast this proposal in the form of a decree on 4 July. The royal government was forced to give in. A series of royal declarations (dated 1 July, 13 July, and 18 July 1648) transformed the petitions of the Chambre Saint-Louis into edicts. Intendants were to be kept on only in the border provinces, Languedoc, Burgundy, Provence, Lyonnais, Picardy, and Champagne. They were not to take any part in the assessment or collection of taxes or participate in any other activities exept those related to the armies. These terms were confirmed by the declaration of 22 October 1648. In fact, even the intendants in the border provinces had to give up trying to carry out duties that had become impossible to fulfill. Some of them were attacked, and Fouquet was nearly killed. The subdelegates disappeared with the intendants.

The royal government never stopped trying to restore the *commissaires* in the provinces, at least until the exile of Mazarin in February 1651. In June 1649 a rumor started that the king's Council was preparing to send *maîtres des requêtes* to the provinces on inspection tours, which aroused considerable emotion. In fact, *lettres de cachet* were sent to each *bureau des Finances* announcing which *maître des requêtes* had been named to tour the *généralité*. These *maîtres des requêtes* were not supposed to interfere in any way with the duties of officeholders. Their sole responsibility was to investigate unrest, violence, extortion, and violations of council ordinances and decrees and to report on their findings to Chancellor Séguier, who would decide what was to be done. But the *trésoriers de France* were required "to render accounts to the *maîtres des requêtes* who will make these visits in regard to any matters affecting our service and the acceleration of our tax receipts."[11] It was recognized that this might lead to action being taken by the *maîtres des requêtes*. The companies of officeholders reacted against the royal decision, and in November 1649 the government announced that it had decided not to send the *maîtres des requêtes* after all.

We do find *maîtres des requêtes* in the provinces after this date, however. Pinon was in Bourges in December 1649, for example, and Gaulmin in Moulins in 1649 and 1650. The latter claimed the title of "royal envoy" for Bourbonnais and acted as an intendant. Other *maîtres des requêtes* were at this time acting as intendants for justice, administration, and finance attached to the royal armies on maneuvers in a particular province; one such was La Margrie in Normandy. On 3 May 1650, the *maître des requêtes* Moran arrived in Montauban. The *trésoriers de France* refused to receive him because the terms of the *lettre de cachet* suggested "a kind of intendant." Everywhere *trésoriers de France* maintained that for the *maîtres des requêtes* to require them to account for the discharge of their duties far exceeded the authority allowed them by ordinance. The government, moreover, was constantly trying to expand the powers of the *maîtres des requêtes* on inspection tours. The Council sent Gaulmin all matters concerning the administration and discipline of troops, "from which it cannot but be inferred that *Messieurs les maîtres des requêtes* are now tantamount to intendants in the *généralités*, who without assuming the title usurp the authority."[12] A regulation of 8 October 1650 assigned the *maîtres des requêtes* an important role in collecting financing for provisions and garrisons, a role that had once again been assumed by the *trésoriers de France* following the recall of the intendants.

During the course of the year 1650 the government also made use in several places of *conseillers d'Etat* and *intendants des Finances*, the latter of course being the direct superiors of the *trésoriers de France*. In August and September of 1650, the *conseiller d'Etat* de Bezon was sent to the *généralité* of Bourges for the purpose of seeing to military discipline and of providing provisions for troops in the place of the *bureau des Finances*. In January 1650, the *maître des requêtes* Foullé arrived at Limoges for the purpose of inspecting the *généralité*; he was also assigned to serve as *intendant des Finances* in charge of the same district. He claimed charge over the *bureau des Finances* for the purpose of assessing the *tailles*, just as the intendants had done. In the end he closed down the bureau and with the help of a cavalry regiment took over the administration of the royal finances.

The government also sent treasury agents to serve as *contrôleurs généraux des Finances* in the *généralités*. Agents were sent to all the *généralités* to check the statements and accounts of the tax collectors, replacing the *trésoriers généraux* de France. The agents retrieved funds from the local coffers and transported the cash to the central treasury.

On occasion the government exploited dissension among the Cours des Aides and the *trésoriers de France*. For example, the *premier président* of the Cour des Aides of Cahors was named *commissaire* for the *généralité* of Montauban in July 1649, and councillors from the Cour des Aides of Paris were named to carry out the functions of the *bureaux des Finances*.

In the border provinces the government tried to increase the powers of the army intendants to the point where they were practically indistinguishable from those of provincial intendants. In Champagne in 1650, Pages was at once intendant for justice, administration, and finance attached to the army in Champagne, *maître des requêtes* on inspection tour, which gave him the right to oversee the work of all officeholders, and *commissaire général* for troop subsistence, which gave him the right to replace the *trésoriers de France* in dealing with the *étapes*. To this end he was authorized to review troops, place contracts for supplies, authorize disbursements, and issue payment orders. In Picardy, Garin, "playing the role of intendant, confiscated provender on *lettre de cachet* in violation of the royal declaration abolishing the post of intendant."[13]

For a number of reasons, including the general war that had been raging since February 1651, the absence of Mazarin, and the need for the queen to negotiate with the Frondeurs, come to some accommodation with them, and uphold the banishment of Mazarin, the government was obliged to give ground in 1651 and 1652. At the end of 1651 a council decree prohibited anyone from assuming the duties of a provincial intendant without a commission verified by the *parlements*. After trying to dictate orders to the *trésoriers de France* in Limoges, the *maître de requêtes* Baltazard received a sharp warning from the *surintendant* de La Vieuville dated 4 February 1652 and addressed to M. Baltazard, intendant for the *généralité* of Poitiers": "Remember what you have been told; do not perform any of the duties of an *intendant des finances*, only see to it that the regular officeholders execute the decrees of the Council and the orders of the king. Try to remain on good terms with the officeholders."[14] On the other hand, treasury agents again seem to have been sent as commissaires to the *généralités* in 1651.

But changed circumstances, including the general exhaustion, the king's return to Paris on 21 October 1652, Mazarin's return in February of 1653, and the gradual waning of unrest that became noticeable everywhere after the fall of Bordeaux on 3 August 1653, restored to the government some freedom of action. Early in August 1653 there was again talk of sending *maîtres des requêtes* out to the *généralités*. Of course officials of the government claimed that they would be sent simply to make their regular inspection tours as set forth in the declaration of July 1648 and without any sealed commission. The officeholders were not deceived, however. They repeatedly approached the ministers of the government, who spoke only of the necessity to make "prompt recovery [of funds owed the king] and to accelerate the collection of the *taille*." On 27 August it was announced that the *conseiller d'Etat* Miromesnil would be sent to Rouen as a *commissaire*, to work, like the old intendants, in the subsistence department. On 5 September 1653, the *bureau des Finances* of Tours announced that "within a few days" M. de Heere, "intendant for this *généralité*," would arrive with orders from the Council. To all intents and purposes these orders harked back to the regulation of 22 August 1642 and the declaration of 16 April 1643, mandating the replacement of the companies of officeholders by the intendant in the area of finance and assigning the intendant to act as administrator of finance in the provinces. During the last quarter of 1653, intendants were in the process of regaining their former powers in a good many *généralités*.

Still, prudence was necessary for several years to come. The draft of the instructions issued to the *conseiller d'Etat* Le Febvre when he was sent to Dauphiné as intendant on 19 November 1654 is revealing. The words "intendant for justice, administration, and finance in the province" were struck out and replaced by "intendant for justice, administration, and finance for such troops as may be in this province." The Council had empowered him to contract for supplies and make disbursements in the place of the *trésoriers de France*. These clauses were struck out and replaced by language instructing the new intendant to assist in negotiating such contracts and to audit statements of expenditure. The intendant was granted extensive powers to deal with conspiracies and rebellions and to enforce all orders from the Council, however. It was expressly stated that the intendant "shall go as often as he deems necessary for His Majesty's service to the *bureau des Finances* of Grenoble to carry out the duties of his commission along with the officers of said bureau. . . . And in general sieur Le Febvre shall do whatever he may deem necessary for the benefit of His Majesty's service."[15] These were very broad powers, and in all likelihood they were extended, as was customary, by special commissions and decrees attributing specific authorization.

Thus little by little the commissions issued to provincial intendants returned to the standard form described above. They usually now included the "power to subdelegate and commission others to undertake such affairs and in such places as you may deem fit to assign to them." Typical of these commissions was that issued to Garibal for the intendancy of Auvergne on 15 January 1656.[16]

From 1661 to 1715

The Colbert Era

The Increase in the Number of Commissaires. The long war was ended in 1659 by the Peace of the Pyrenees, and it may be said that until the outbreak of the Dutch War in 1672 the kingdom experienced a period of comparative calm, for the War of Devolution in 1667 was brief and cost relatively little. Louis XIV used Colbert to attempt a reorganization of the kingdom in a way that might satisfy some of the desires of the Frondeurs. In particular, he attempted to place limits on the number and power of the intendants. Forceful steps were taken between 1661 and 1672. But these efforts were undone by the Dutch War. The goal remained as the government's ideal, however. Colbert took many steps toward it both during and after the Dutch War up to the time of his death in 1683.

After the Fronde the government once again began sending intendants to the provinces. They were used widely after 1656, and by 1659 there were intendants almost everywhere. The king chose them from among his *fidèles*, *conseillers d'Etat*, and *maîtres des requêtes*, especially the latter, who gradually moved toward a monopoly of the appointments. Thus intendants were generally from Parisian families, though families that may have been Parisian for only a few generations. All were nobles and owed their nobility to their birth, not just to their offices, which gave them high nobility and the title of *chevalier*. They owned *seigneuries* and assumed the name that went with them. Some even held *fiefs de dignité*; there were marquis and counts among their number. They owed their appointment as intendants to the influence of such creatures of the king as the secretary of state for war, first Le Tellier and later his successor Louvois, and the *contrôleur général des Finances*, Colbert, as well as to the influence on these men of provincial governors and army generals. The intendants were royal creatures or favorites.

The government avoided the use of the term intendant as much as possible. Least offensive to the officeholders, according to Fouquet, was the title "*commissaires* dispatched to execute the king's orders."

The Rotating Inspectors. The government would have liked to reduce the number of intendants and have them make tours like ordinary inspectors. In 1659 Mazarin and Colbert came up with a plan: they proposed pairing the *généralités* in order to reduce the number of intendants, combining those of Poitiers with those of Limoges and those of Lyon with those of the Dauphiné and linking up *généralités* traversed by common highways. Only in the newly acquired border provinces would there be one intendant per *généralité*. The two *généralités* of Languedoc, a border province but an old one and even a *pays d'Etats*, were to remain an exception, combined in a single intendancy. Colbert may even have intended for a time to entrust several *généralités* to a single *commissaire*.

For related reasons the government would have liked to reduce the amount of time each intendant spent in any one *généralité* to a very short period. In 1663 there was some talk of moving them about from *généralité* to *généralité* so that after a few years they would have served everywhere in the kingdom and thereby acquired a better knowledge of the whole.

Above all the government wanted to prevent the intendants from supplanting the officeholders. The role of *commissaires* was supposed to be to make inspections and report to the king's Council, to transmit the Council's orders to *corps*, companies, and communities, and on rare occasions, but only on special commission from the king, to undertake independent activities of their own. For Colbert as for Louvois the role of the *commissaires* was to look into everything and to familiarize themselves with all that was going on in order to report to the king. Evidence that this was the role envisioned for the *commissaires* may be found in the commission issued to sieur de Ménars in February 1674 for the *généralité* of Orléans. Ménars was commissioned solely to eliminate abuses in the army, the courts, and finance. He was to advise the governors and *lieutenants généraux* of Orléans and sit in sovereign judgment over soldiers and rebels. In the area of finance he had jurisdiction over community debts pending appeal to the king's Council. He was to look into the collection of taxes and refer pertinent matters to the Council. He was to audit public accounts, review the assessment of the *tailles* and contracts for exploitation of the royal domain, and undertake any necessary reforms. He was to reform the Eaux et Forêts. As for the courts, he was to preside over the *présidiaux* and the *bailliages* and look into any abuses of their authority. If abuses were found, they were to be referred to the Council, which would attend to them by referring them back to *parlement* or to some other body. He was authorized to subdelegate his authority. Appeals from his orders could be taken to the Council only. He had the power to requisition assistance from military and civilian officials. The commission, which was addressed to him personally, was supplemented by letters of accreditation to the governor, the main sovereign and lower courts, and the cities.[17]

The investigative role of the *commissaire* and the need to refer findings to the Council were thus repeatedly underscored. Stringent limits were placed on the ability of the *commissaire* to take direct action. It is striking to note that in both administrative and judicial matters provision was made for the Council to refer cases back to the Paris *parlement*.

Numerous letters from Colbert and Louvois to the *commissaires* emphasize that their duties are above all investigative, final decision being left up to the king. Colbert took steps to prevent the intendants from overstepping their authority with regard to the sovereign and lower courts and to keep them from taking action of their own accord, without special authorization from the Council, which might infringe on the competence of local companies of officeholders. He also endeavored to instill in the intendants a respect for royal ordinances, edicts, and decrees.

To take one example, in December 1670 the intendant Voysin de La Noiraye used his authority to assess a tax on persons subject to the *taille* in the *généralité* of Tours. The Cour des Aides nullified this tax in a number of decrees. Colbert wrote to the intendant on 12 December, asking him to send all the decrees issued by the Cour des Aides so that the king could pass a resolution without depriving a sovereign company "of its natural and ordinary competence."

Another example concerns the intendant for Rouen, de Creil, who became involved in a conflict with the Cour des Aides of Normandy. On 27 January 1673, Colbert sent him the following message:

> His Majesty, as always unwilling to allow any impediment to his authority, a portion of which he has vested in you, has quashed the decree of the Cour des Aides and forbidden the court and the *avocat général* to promulgate its like in the future. However, His Majesty has further ordered me to write you that, in the light of the explanations that you yourself have provided for each article, he deems you to have been wrong on nearly every count; he has determined that you had set up your own court before which *avocats* and *procureurs* appeared along with the parties and that either you yourself or your subdelegates had assumed jurisdiction over cases normally lying within the jurisdiction of the *élus* and the Cour des Aides. To which he has ordered me to add that, if you do not change your conduct in this regard and adopt a diametrically opposite course of action, he will be unable to retain you in your position.[18]

Colbert then advised the intendant to study carefully the regulations concerning the *tailles* and the farms and the ordinances concerning the duties of *commissaires* dispatched to the provinces, and follow them to the letter. He also reminded his correspondent that, while the regulations gave him the power to set the *tailles* on his own, he could only increase them, never the opposite, and then only when it was clear that the collectors had not dared to set the tax as high as they should have done. In other words, the intendant was not to invoke any powers other than those expressly authorized by the appropriate ordinances and regulations, and then only when the regular officeholders failed to do their duty. If they failed to do their duty in some area not covered by the ordinances and regulations pertaining to the powers of the intendant, he was to inform the Council and await further orders. Letter no. 232 continues: "Your job is merely to see to it that the *élus* and the Cour des Aides enforce the regulations on the *tailles* in a timely manner, and if they fail to do so, you are to inform the Council, which will supply you with the appropriate remedies and give you such powers as His Majesty may deem necessary for the good of his service and the prosecution of his affairs."

The circular letter of 24 April 1676 advised all the intendants to give free rein to the judges who were supposed to assume jurisdiction over existing taxes, *gabelles*, *aides*, and the *cinq grosses fermes*. The intendants were to involve themselves only in cases of exceptional gravity when requested to do so by the agents of the farms themselves; such cases were to be referred to the Council for final decision.

Impelled by necessity to exceed the limits of their authority, the intendants had to be reprimanded constantly. To take one example, consider the letter sent by Colbert to Le Vayer, intendant of Soissons, on 22 November 1682. A declaration of 23 February 1677 had ordered that writs served on taxpayers by bailiffs, *sergents*, and *archers* be sent for inspection within four days to the *bureaux des Finances* or *élections*. In order to speed up the collection of tax revenues, Le Vayer invoked a council decree of 27 January 1670 as grounds for interfering in this inspection. Whereupon Colbert wrote him the following letter:

> The declaration of 1677 contains the express law established by the king in regard to the inspection of writs. It was sent to *parlement*, registered, and notified to all the courts, and there is therefore no question that it abrogates all previous laws on this subject. *Jurisdiction in the matter belongs to the regular judges*, and you were not authorized and should not have *interfered without express authorization issued subsequent to the date of this declaration*. This is the invariable rule of the kingdom's universal justice, particularly as it applies at present in the area of finance, which is intended to leave to the regular judges jurisdiction over matters normally within their purview until such time as they may abuse their authority. The function of the intendants and *commissaires* in the provinces is only to see to it that the judges do their duty and execute the laws and ordinances established by the Prince, and if they should fail to do so, to advise the Council of such failure. They are not to assume direct jurisdiction over any affairs other than those for which they have been granted specific power by the King.[19]

The intendants were more than ready to act for reasons of state. For example, Morant, the intendant at Aix, invoked the "greater good of the public" in issuing an ordinance concerning the waters of Aubagne. On 1 July 1682, Colbert wrote him that on such grounds "it would be easy to overturn all the established orders in the kingdom. . . . The master is the only one who may take such resolutions. . . . It is never allowed to individuals like us to judge what may or may not be for the greater good of the public, when we do not have the power to do so."[20]

According to this doctrine, under the intendant's judicial powers and powers incident thereto the intendant was authorized to conduct investigations and report to the king's Council, which could then choose among four different courses of action. The first course was to refer the case to regular judges with orders to the intendant to see to it that the judges did their duty. This was the most common choice in this period. The second possible course of action was for the king's Council to reach a decision in the case itself and issue a decree. The third course of action was for the king to set up a special court consisting of *commissaires*, such as the Chambre de Justice that sat in judgment over the *financiers* after the arrest of Fouquet and the Grands Jours d'Auvergne, to name two striking examples. The fourth possible response was for the king to issue a special commission to the intendant authorizing him to judge the specific case in question. This could be done either by *lettre de cachet* or by a decree of attribution. In the latter case, the intendant was required to have the decree registered by the sovereign or lower court that normally would have had jurisdiction in the matter. The intendant then had several options. He could judge the case himself in a royal tribunal such as a *bailliage*, *présidial*, *bureau des Finances*, or *élection* over which he would preside. This was the option preferred by the government as representing the least possible enroachment upon the prerogatives of the officeholders. Or he could judge the case in conjunction with a number of officeholders chosen to act as assessors. Or he could judge the case in conjunction with law graduates chosen as *commissaires* rather than assessors. All three options were quick, summary proceedings that cost little, avoided complicated procedures, and dispensed with the services of *procureurs* and *avocats*.

The royal policy that Colbert carried out with regard to the intendants is reflected in the number of letters sent by the *contrôleur général*. In 1670 Colbert sent 103 letters concerning commerce and industry. Of these only 29 were addressed to intendants, 22 were addressed to ambassadors, 7 to consuls, 12 to various officeholders, 12 to aldermen and mayors, 13 to manufacturers, traders, and directors of trading companies, and 9 to *inspecteurs généraux des manufactures*, engineers, and tax farmers concerned with the *aides*.

Casual subdelegates. The policy with regard to the intendants also affected the government's attitude to subdelegates. The king in no way wished to set up a nationwide network of subdelegates that would have performed various duties in the place of existing officeholders. The position of the royal government as set forth in Colbert's letter to Monsieur de Sève, intendant at Bordeaux, dated 18 May 1674, is quite clear:

> I cannot refrain from pointing out to you that what most pains the King in the conduct of the *commissaires* he has dispatched to the provinces is their establishment of large numbers of subdelegates in all the localities of their departments. They then attribute to these subdelegates, on their own authority, the authority to assume jurisdiction over all sorts of affairs, quite often abusing their own authority in the process and extending that authority as their fantasies, passions, and interests may dictate.
>
> On this point I must tell you that the subdelegates that you have introduced are a very great abuse, established by the *commissaires* without reason, ground, or necessity. In all the provinces they are a universal

source of complaint, complaint that frequently reaches the eyes and ears
of His Majesty. It is true that your commission gives you the power to
name subdelegates. But the king's intention and the primary use of this
power were never for affairs or brief duration to which you were unable
to attend because a number of affairs claiming your attention happened
to arise at the same time. I therefore think it my duty to advise you that
nothing you could do would be more agreeable to His Majesty than to
reduce the number of subdelegates and only to make use of them in the
manner I have just explained.[21]

Colbert's circular letter to the intendants on 15 Jun1 682 forbade them to
appoint any permanent subdelegate with general competence over a broad
range of cases. They were allowed only to name temporary subdelegates to
deal with specific cases. Once these cases were disposed of, the subdelegates'
commissions were to expire.[22]

This policy did not yield the desired results owing to the effects of war
and of preparations for combat.

The intendants were not rotated from place to place as planned. Up to
1661 they remained for an average of three years in their departments. Between 1661 and 1688, the average tour of duty in twenty-two *généralités* of
the *pays d'élections* was four years six months. For newly annexed or occupied provinces, such as Alsace, Walloon Flanders, Cambrésis, maritime
Flanders, Hainault, the region of the Sambre-et-Meuse and beyond the Meuse,
Franche-Comté, and Lorraine (which was returned to its duke in 1698), the
average tour of duty was six years nine months. For the *pays d'Etats*, including Languedoc, Provence, Dauphiné, Burgundy, Bourbonnais, Artois,
the county of Foix, Nébouzan, Couserans, Comminges, and Bigorre, the
average tour was nine years five months.

The intendants were increasingly limited to a single *généralité* apiece. In
1679 Colbert officially ended the pairing of *généralités* because of the increase
in the number of financial cases owing to the Dutch War. Intendancy and
généralité became synonymous.

The intendants saw their sphere of responsibility enlarged and little by
little began once more to supplant the officeholders. The changes were slow
but steady. In October 1662 the intendants were given responsibility for
checking on community debts. In 1666 and 1667, in preparation for and
during the War of Devolution, it became necessary to allow them to carry
out some of the duties of the *trésoriers de France*. When the Dutch War
came everything had to be left to the intendants. They assumed ever greater
control over the officeholders, setting them tasks and supervising their work.
In many cases the intendants simply took over, selecting one or two loyal,
energetic, and capable officeholders to act as assistants or subdelegates.
Judgments were handed down by subdelegates.[23] Colbert urged them to take
initiatives. In 1674, when new taxes were imposed, Colbert wrote to the
intendant of Bordeaux that he ought not to wait for the tax farmers' requests
but rather make up for their negligence and press them to do what had to

be done to get on with the collection of taxes. "This is where it becomes necessary to go beyond the action of the regular judges, who schedule hearings in a case only when everything is in order."[24] Implicit in such action was the need to gather information about how collections were proceeding, and it was but a short step from there to actually taking control of the process in a time of emergency. As an institution, the system of intendancies again became what it had been before the Fronde, under the pressure of similar needs.

The War of the League of Augsburg and the War of the Spanish Succession

After the death of Colbert, the *contrôleur général des Finances* and the secretary of state for war continued efforts to keep the provincial intendants in check. But gradually the limitations on their authority were whittled away. It became necessary to make increasing use of *commissaires* and particularly provincial intendants and their subdelegates for a number of reasons. Among these were the liquidation of debts from the Dutch War, the policy of peacetime annexations, which required the maintenance of a standing army on a war footing, the desire to find work for the nobility, a brief war against Spain in 1684 which was ended by the Truce of Regensburg, the outbreak of 1688 of a war against a coalition of European powers that lasted until the Treaty of Ryswick in 1697, and finally the affair of the Spanish succession which led in 1701 to the outbreak of a new European war that ended with the Treaties of Utrecht with England and the United Provinces in 1713 and the Treaty of Rastadt with the emperor in 1714. Though the principles on which the system of intendancies was based did not change, the intendants assumed all-embracing responsibilities and powers in the years 1688–90.

The Increased Duration of Commissions. The duration for which commissions were issued increased considerably. The average tenure in the twenty-two *généralités* of the *pays d'élection* rose to five years two months. In the *pays d'Etats*, which from 1688 on included Brittany, the average rose to thirteen years three months. Allowance must be made, to be sure, for the exceptionally long tenure of Nicolas de Lamoignon, sieur de Basville, who served as intendant of Languedoc from August 1685 until June 1718. The average tenure in newly annexed territories rose to eight years three months. In Alsace Jacques de La Grange served as intendant from 1673 until 1698 and Félix Le Pelletier de La Houssaye from 1700 until 1715.

The Social Status of the Intendants. The *maîtres des requêtes* consolidated their monopoly over the intendancies. One notable exception to the rule was Jacques de La Grange, intendant for Alsace, who was not a *maître des requêtes* but a *commis* of the secretary of state for war and later *commissaire des guerres* for the northern frontier region. All the other intendants were members of the nobility of office consisting of high government officials and officers of the sovereign courts. The celebrated Basville belonged to the Lamoignon family, whose members were among the king's *fidèles*. Basville was the second son of Guillaume de Lamoignon, *premier président* of the Paris *parlement*, and Madeleine Potier, daughter of the secretary of state Potier d'Ocquerre. The intendant's elder brother was a *président* in the Paris *parlement* when he died in 1709. The future intendant Nicolas de Basville was born in 1648 and successively became an *avocat* in the Paris *parlement* in 1666, a councillor in 1670, and a *maître des requêtes* in 1673. He was a creature of Colbert, with whom his father had worked. He then served successively as intendant at Montauban, Pau, and Poitiers, where he led the first dragonnades. After Colbert's death Basville courted Louvois and in August 1685 was named *conseiller d'Etat semestre* and intendant of Languedoc. From then until 1718 he did not leave the province, not even for the death of his mother in 1705 or his brother in 1709.

His son Urbain-Guillaume de Lamoignon, seigneur de Courson, was born in 1674, became avocat and then councillor in the Paris *parlement* in 1692, *maître des requêtes* in 1698, and intendant of Rouen from 1704 to 1709. His father's friend, the *contrôleur général* Desmaretz, had him appointed intendant for Guyenne. On his way to Bordeaux he went to spend three days with his father in October 1709, with the permission of the *contrôleur général*. Basville had not seen his son for twelve years. But during the three days they spent together they conferred about ways of executing jointly orders common to both Guyenne and Languedoc. Thereafter they never saw each other without official permission. At the age of seventy-one, blind and worn, Basville returned to Paris in 1719. He died on 17 May 1724 at age seventy-six. The explanation of his devotion to his duty is suggested by a letter from Father de La Rue, a missionary in Languedoc, to the *contrôleur général* Chamillart in 1703: "The *honor of service* is more important to him than health or relaxation, as long as his services shall be wanted."[25] He even commanded the esteem of Saint-Simon: "Basville was a handsome spirit, a superior mind, very enlightened, very energetic, and very hard-working."[26] The "honor of service" was the leading motive of all the intendants.

The provincial intendants frequently worked under former intendants or relatives of former intendants. The career of Michel Le Peletier, seigneur de Souzy, is noteworthy in this regard. His father, Louis Le Peletier, a councillor in the Paris *parlement*, was a cousin and friend of Michel Le Tellier, who first served as secretary of state for war and then in 1672 became chancellor of France. Louis Le Peletier's three sons were *fidèles* and creatures first of Le Tellier and then of Louvois. The eldest, Claude, was born in 1631, served as councillor in the Paris *parlement*, *président* in the Enquêtes, *prévôt des Marchands* in 1668, and *conseiller d'Etat* in 1676. In 1683 he succeeded Colbert as *contrôleur général des Finances*, resigned in 1688, became *surintendant des Postes*, and stayed on as minister with access to the king's councils. He retired in 1697. In 1711 he died, leaving among his ten children a number of *présidents* and one *premier président* in *parlement*. The second of Louis Le Peletier's sons, Jérôme, was born in 1633, took holy orders, became a clerical councillor in *parlement*, and later served as *conseiller d'Etat* and managed the affairs of his two brothers until his death in 1696.

The third son, Michel, who was destined to become an intendant, was born in 1640, became an *avocat du roi* at the Châtelet in 1660 and a councillor in *parlement* and *commissaire* assigned to the Grands Jours d'Auvergne in 1665, a *maître des requêtes*, and then, at the behest of Louvois, intendant for Franche-Comté in February 1668 and for Lille in June 1668. To Louvois he wrote, "I profess to be your man, and I wish to hold all that I possess by your grace and to be beholden to no one else." He served in Flanders for fifteen years. He pressed for a nomination as *conseiller d'Etat* and was rewarded in 1683, thanks to Le Tellier, despite Louvois's distaste for "getting him bogged down in the futilities of the Council at his age," then forty-two.[27] He was in fact recalled from the intendancy of Lille, recall being the fate of all intendants named *conseillers d'Etat* over the previous ten years, and left that city on 26 December 1683. But he was a granted a commission as *intendant des Finances* on the staff of his brother Claude. He kept this commission even after Claude had ceased to be *contrôleur général des Finances*. He had his commission turned into an office in December 1700, purchased the *survivance* for his son of twenty-five, and in 1701 resigned in his son's favor and became a councillor on the Conseil royal des Finances. In another connection, after Louvois died on 16 July 1691, the king detached the administration in charge of fortresses and the corps of engineers from the secretariat for war. He appointed Michel Le Peletier to head this administration, giving him the title of director general of inland and costal fortifications, because as intendant he had built the citadels of Lille, Tournay, Cambrai, Douai, Condé, and Valenciennes. He worked in tête-à-tête with the king every Monday after dinner. He was required to appear before His Majesty at all times as the ministers did, cane in hand and wearing no cloak. "The gown reigns everywhere," Saint-Simon observed.

When Louis XIV died in 1715, Michel Le Peletier lost his post as director general. But he remained a member of the Conseil royal des Finances until 1720. Louis XIV had appointed him to the Regency Council. At first the regent allowed him access only when financial affairs were being discussed, but later he relented and allowed him to attend all meetings. As vice-doyen of the Conseil d'Etat, he presided over two bureaus: one in charge of the *gabelles*, *tailles*, and *cinq grosses fermes*, the other in charge of petitions of appeal. In 1720, at the age of eighty, he retired to the abbey of Saint Victor. He died on 10 December 1725, leaving a son and a daughter. Michel Robert Le Peletier des Forts, later comte de Saint-Fargeau, became councillor in the Metz *parlement* in 1695, and in the Paris *parlement* in 1696, *maître des requêtes* in 1698, and *intendant des Finances* in 1701. He married Marie-Madeleine de Lamoignon de Basville, the intendant's granddaughter, in 1706. In 1720 he became *commissaire général des Finances* following Law's downfall. In 1721 he became *conseiller d'Etat ordinaire* and in 1723 a member of the Conseil royal des Finances. From 1726 to 1730 he was *contrôleur général des Finances*. The daughter, Marie-Claude Le Peletier, married Jacques-Etienne Turgot in 1688. He was then *avocat général des Requêtes de l'Hôtel* and in 1708 became intendant for Moulins. Their son, the *prévôt des marchands* of Paris, was the father of the illustrious Turgot, intendant of Limousin and *contrôleur général des Finances*.

The foregoing should give some idea of the families, loyalties, careers, marriages, and offspring of the men who served as intendants during Louis XIV's personal government.

The Organization of the Intendancies. Intendants in this period frequently regarded their official papers as personal and took all documents with them when they left office. Thus the new intendant arriving in the *généralité* not infrequently found himself without information concerning affairs in the region. His secretary might be able to obtain some official papers from the secretary of his predecessor. But this was not always the case. In 1700 Pinon, appointed intendant of Alençon, complained that he had received from his predecessor, M. de Pomereu, "neither memoirs nor instructions concerning the affairs of his *généralité*." The *contrôleur général* intervened and on 17 February 1700 received an answer from M. de Pomereu: "My surprise at this groundless complaint was all the greater because in all honesty I was unaware that it was customary hitherto for intendants to provide their successors any fuller memoir. . . . Hitherto, I say, because when I arrived in Alençon eleven years ago I received no instructions from M. de Basville other than a few words upon my arrival, and from M. Larcher[28] I got nothing but a few minutes' conversation at an inn somewhere in the country, with no memoir and very few documents."[29] When Bercy, the intendant of Moulins, desperately wanted to lay hands on the papers of his predecessor d'Ormesson in 1684, he was refused by the trustee who held them on the grounds that a council decree and a subpoena were necessary.[30] In 1697 a *procureur du roi* in each intendancy was appointed *garde des anciennes minutes du Conseil et des Commissions extraordinaires*, responsible for preparing briefs in the king's name and for stating the government position in court in matters entrusted to *commissaires* or pertaining to ecclesiastic or secular communities or to minors. Was he also responsible for preserving the intendancy's archives?

The intendants established offices of their own. In 1661 they had quite small staffs, including a private secretary, one or two scribes whom they chose personally, and two guards from the *prévôté de l'Hôtel*, who wore a haqueton in the king's colors, rose, white, and blue, and were made available by the chancellor. Some intendants preferred to use guards from the Connétablie. Besides their subdelegates, the intendants were supposed to have "secret inspectors" to give them "loyal and disinterested advice" concerning "both general administration and the collection of royal taxes."[31]

Little by little the intendants' staffs grew larger. In 1710 the intendant of Alsace employed a private secretary for correspondence with the court, a general secretary for *subsistances*, a *commis* for petitions, another for correspondence with the *baillis*, and a third for correspondence with the cities of the district. During the six winter months fifty-five *commis* were employed in gathering and distributing provender, collecting exercises, and leading convoys from certain storage sites to points of consumption. All these employees were paid by the intendant. The secretaries also received court allowances, bonuses from the cities, towns, and *bailliages*, and fees in connection with leases, contracts, and public procurement.

The Subdelegates. The number of subdelegates also increased, particularly after 1688. In 1687 Lebret, the intendant of Provence, prided himself on using very few of them. He had only one in his employ in 1688 and used him only for investigations. But special commissions for the verification of city and community debts had already made it necessary to use subdelegates and, from 1665 on, to increase their number. After 1688 we find subdelegates of three kinds. First, there were temporary subdelegates commissioned by the intendant to look into a specific matter and, if the case were one of minor importance, to render judgment on it themselves. If the matter was one of preparing an indictment in a civil or criminal case, an officer of the *bailliage* or a law graduate would be chosen. If it was a question of repairing a bridge or a church, the choice would fall on an architect or contractor. Their commission was terminated when the matter was disposed of. Second, there were the so-called general subdelegates, who were assigned to a specific place for an indefinite period of time and authorized to investigate and in some cases to judge a wide variety of affairs. The men appointed to these positions were either magistrates, including lieutenants in the *bailliage* or *présidial*, councillors in the *bailliage*, *prévôts*, *élus*, and councillors in the salt warehouses; or accounting officials, such as collectors of the *tailles*; or ministerial officials such as royal notaries or *procureurs*; or *avocats*. "Permanent" appointees, the general subdelegates were assigned a specific seat and had jurisdiction over a specified area. Their number varied widely. Around 1700 there were thirty or so in the *généralité* of Moulins, about fifteen in the *généralités* of Châlons and Besançon, and about sixty in the *généralité* of Brittany. Simon de Coustures, *premier avocat du roi* at the *présidial* of Limoges, served as a subdelegate for twenty-five years.

There was also a group of *commissaires* referred to as "subdelegates in this part." They were qualified temporary appointees who served alongside the general subdelegates until after the edict of 1704 and probably after 1715, perhaps throughout the eighteenth century. Both general and temporary subdelegates in this part both received commissions from the intendant. Around 1680 the commission issued for a criminal case had the following form:

> N——, *chevalier*, intendant of justice, administration, and finance in the *généralité* of . . . , to sieur . . . . His Majesty having commissioned us by council decree of . . . to investigate . . . , to prosecute the case by extraordinary procedure, and to judge it in last resort, we have commissioned and subdelegated you, and do hereby commission and subdelegate you, to investigate the statements contained in the petition of . . . against . . . and their accomplices and to prosecute the case by extraordinary procedure up to but not including final judgment, for which purpose all documents pertaining to the case are to be sent to you in a pouch closed and sealed by the clerk of the intendancy. And so that you may do this, we do hereby grant you power in virtue of the power vested in us by His Majesty.

And so on. The commission for a civil case read as follows:

> N——, *chevalier*, intendant of . . . , to sieur . . . . Having by our judgment of . . . granted permission to authenticate the contract of . . . concluded without private signatures between . . . , we have commissioned and do hereby commission you to have authentication of the aforesaid contract undertaken in your presence by experts and on the basis of such documents of comparison as to which the parties may agree, or, failing such agreement, such documents as you may stipulate. And so that you may do this, we grant you power in virtue of the power vested in us by His Majesty.[32]

During the Wars of the League of Augsburg and the Spanish Succession, intendants in the border provinces also served as army intendants and were therefore forced to be absent for long periods of time, and so a third category of subdelegates came into being: the "general subdelegate in the absence of the intendant." In other words, the intendant commissioned a general subdelegate to coordinate the actions of the other subdelegates and to supervise the intendance during his absence. Beginning in 1702, some of these general subdelegates were issued royal letters patent sealed with the Great Seal and appointing them general subdelegate for the intendancy. These letters were a commission from the king to carry out all the duties of the intendant during his absence. A portion of the general subdelegates were commissioned by the king right up to the time of the Revolution. Among the general subdelegates granted these broad powers to act in the absence of the intendant were Ulrich Obrecht, a professor of law at the University of Strasbourg and royal praetor, Denis Baudouin, *commissaire des guerres* at Landau in 1693, and Pierre d'Andrezel, *commissaire aux fortifications* at Neuf-Brisach in 1701, all of whom served in Alsace.

Permanent local general subdelegates were found less frequently in the border provinces because there the intendant, as army intendant, employed other agents to gather information and execute his decisions. These men took care of hospitals and storehouses, supplies of food and meat for the troops and of provender for the horses, review of troops, conduct of convoys, and pay and discipline of the soldiers. They had the power to arrest soldiers who misbehaved and turn them over to the *prévôts des maréchaux*. During the winter and in peacetime, these officials assumed the title of *commissaires ordonnateurs* and served as subdelegates in the cities of, say, Alsace. In this province, the intendant could also make use of the royal praetor who was found in most of the major cities. In theory the royal praetor belonged to the corps of city magistrates, attended all assemblies and councils, where he assumed the first rank as the king's representative, and was the first to state his opinion and cast his vote, which outweighed all others. The royal praetor became an agent of the intendant and played the role of subdelegate after 1685 in Strasbourg, Haguenau, and Colmar, and after 1695 in Obernai, Rosheim, Turckheim, Wissembourg, and Landau. In Alsace the intendant was also able to make use of the *baillis* of *seigneurs*. The king allowed the *seigneurs* to maintain their "regencies," which in the large *seigneuries* were true state institutions, with judicial corps, *chambres des comptes*, etc. Granted absolute power, their *baillis* became agents of the intendant and corresponded directly with the intendant without going through the regency. They participated in the collection of the subvention that replaced the *taille* and of various others taxes and drafted *corvée* laborers. In 1701 there were fifty-nine seigneurial *bailliages*, in addition to which the edict of April 1694 established five royal *bailliages* (royal prefectures at Haguenau, Mundat and Wissembourg, Landeck, Germersheim, and Saint-Hippolyte).

No funds were provided for the remuneration of subdelegates. After a while the permanent local general subdelegates tired of performing time-consuming duties solely for the honor, particularly since such subdelegates were generally "continued in their functions" by one intendant after another. The abbé de Breagelongne served as subdelegate at Brioude under five different intendants: de Marle, d'Albeige, de Vaubourg, de Bérulle, and d'Ormesson. D'Esparbier, a judge at Moissac, was used as subdelegate for the first time in 1680 and kept on until 1708 by seven successive intendants for the *généralité* of Montauban. The intendants feared that the enthusiasm of their subdelegates might flag. They wished to enhance the authority of the subdelegates and grant them the power to make final disposition of minor cases of all sorts in order to speed up the solution of various problems. For these reasons the intendants were favorable to the proposal submitted to the *contrôleur général* on 15 April 1702 by sieur Caquez, *contrôleur* of the *tailles* and *gabelles*, suggesting that the position of subdelegate be turned into an office. The sale of these offices was done under the name of a *traitant*, Antoine Dagincourt, "*bourgeois de Paris*." The edict of April 1704 established a hereditary office of subdelegate in each *chef-lieu* of each *élection* in the regions subject to the *taille* and in each bishopric or *bailliage* in the *pays d'Etats*, as well as in other important cities in which a subdelegate was already established or seemed to be needed. Subdelegates were to enjoy rank, seating, and the right to express an opinion and to vote in all jurisdictions in both hearings and in council chambers, with priority just below the dean of councillors. They were to receive compensation at the rate of ten percent of what they paid for their offices but were not allowed to share in the *épices* unless they already held court offices. They were exempt from the *taille*, *ustensile*, billeting of soldiers, and all other taxes, from *collecte*, *tutelle*, *curatelle*, and other public charges, and they were entitled to a minot of free salt each. Cases in which they were involved were to be judged by the royal court nearest the city in which they served. Their duties were to keep the intendant informed, to offer their opinion on what ought to be done, to transmit orders from the intendant to the appropriate destination, and to see to it that these orders were carried out.

Generally speaking, these offices were acquired by men who were already acting as subdelegates. None of the offices was sold without the approval of the intendant. The purchasers were received and installed and carried out their duties despite the opposition of the officeholders' *corps*, mayors, and aldermen, encouraged by the *parlements* and Cours des Aides, which looked upon the subdelegates as monsters. But the intendants and council decrees invariably came down in favor of the subdelegates.

Because of the edict the office of subdelegate became a hereditary life tenure. Each was assigned a precise seat and territorial jurisdiction, frequently coinciding with a previously established district such as an *élection*, a *viguerie*, or a *bailliage*. The intendants interpreted the terms of the edict so as to allow their subdelegates to retain powers to hand down judgments and make decisions. The subdelegates became "subintendants," and by creating the new office of clerk of the subdelegate, the edict of January 1707 bestowed its sanction on their activities. Since the intendants were now supposed to rely exclusively on subdelegates who owned their offices, these men were overwhelmed with work and unable to leave their posts even for a short period. Thus the intendants were forced to continue to turn to temporary subdelegates to deal with specific cases. The number of subdelegates decreased, however, from sixteen to fourteen in the *généralité* of Tours and from thirty-one to seven in the *généralité* of Moulins.

The Orders of the Intendants. Intendants took action by issuing orders, of which there were many different kinds. The term was applied, first of all, to simple orders for the supply of food, provender, wagons, and so forth. It also applied to more complex procurement orders, contracts for work on fortifications, for the collection of dues and *octrois*, etc. There were proclamations fixing the price of such products as bread, wine, and meat, prohibiting the distribution of salt, trade in grains, cultivation of grazing land, or the cutting of wood, and setting forth lists of public projects. Orders were countersigned by the secretary of the intendancy, published, and provisionally put into effect pending appeal, which could be taken only to the king's Council. Some were issued in the form of administrative regulations after consultation with a minister.

The Responsibilities of the Intendants. The duties of intendants were astonishingly similar in the different provinces. There were some differences, however, and we must therefore treat three cases separately, albeit briefly: an intendancy in a *pays d'élections*, an intendancy in a *pays d'Etats*, and an intendancy in a conquered territory. We shall be looking at both the powers of the intendant and the areas in which these powers were exercised.

The Powers of Intendants in the Pays d'Élections. Consider the *généralité* of Soissons. In theory the intendant was to leave all ordinary judicial and financial matters to the magistrates. He was supposed to keep an eye on them and see to it that they carried out their duties and abided by royal edicts and decrees. If not, he was supposed to submit a report and wait for a decision to be issued in the form of a council decree granting him the power to act. But if the magistrates failed to live up to their obligations, the intendant was authorized to issue provisional orders.

Take the affair of 1697. According to the ordinance of 1680, *aide* duties had to be paid on cider and perry, for cider half the duty on wine and for perry half the duty on cider. There were also duties on apples and pears to be used for making these liquors, assessed at the rate of three *muids* of fruit to one *muid* of liquor. Landowners were therefore in the habit of declaring mash apples and pears to be eating fruit, which exonerated them from the payment of all duties. The *élus* came down in favor of the landowners and against the tax farmer with the concession to collect *aides*. These were the circumstances when, at the behest of the tax farmer, the intendant, de La Houssaye, issued his order of 28 October 1697. The order began with the following preamble: "In view of the petition submitted by sieur Maulgue, *fermier des Aides* for the *généralité* of Soissons." This was followed by the words, "We order," which indicated that a decision had been taken by the intendant and that obedience was compulsory. The intendant referred the farmer's appeal to the regular judges, the *élus*, "who should have jurisdiction over it." Meanwhile, however, "on a provisional basis, in order to preserve the king's rights," the schedule of duties promulgated by the Council on 27 January 1687 would be enforced. Those subject to payment of the tax were required to declare their fruit purchases to the *bureau des Aides* before pressing or fermentation. They were to place the fruit in "measuring vessels" and pay the duty as specified in the schedule before taking the fruit away. The order specified penalties to be applied in case of violation, including confiscation of fruit, cider, and perry and payment of a fine of one hundred livres. Appeal of the order was allowed, but in the meantime it could be carried out. The *élus* of Noyon did not give way, however, and on 14 November 1697 ordered suspension of all writs against taxpayers. The intendant then referred the matter to the king's Council, which on 4 January 1698 issued a decree ordering execution of the intendant's order, which it found to be in compliance with the ordinance issued by the Conseil royal des Finances of 27 January 1687.

The intendant intervened in ordinary cases only if the magistrates failed or seemed about to fail to do their duty. Thus in 1699, when the comte de L——, seigneur de Pinon, had his sergeant and valets seize and beat one Dauphin, an agricultural laborer, who filed charges with the royal judges, the intendant Sanson wrote to the *lieutenant criminel* of Laon to say that "since this case falls within the purview of the regular judges, His Majesty has ordered me to see to it that justice is duly done to this individual. I think that it will be done and that you will act with your usual integrity."[33]

If an "extraordinary affair" such as the imposition of a new tax, the enforcement of the Edict of Fontainebleau (which revoked the Edict of Nantes and led to a number of arrests), the encouragement of new manufacturing projects, or something of the sort was involved, however, then responsibility fell to the intendant alone. When the capitation was established in 1695, it was the intendants who were given the responsibility of classifying taxpayers into twenty-two categories, and this procedure was maintained subsequently. In 1706 in Clermont-en-Beauvaisis, the intendant d'Ormesson assessed sieur Cuvillier, a councillor in the *bailliage*, at seventy livres. Sieur Fourcroy, councillor in the *bailliage* and *prévôt forain*, was assessed at fifteen livres. Sieur Thouret, councillor in the *prévôté foraine*, was assessed at twenty livres. And sieur Grelier, councillor in the *bailliage* and mayor, was assessed at fifty livres. Cuvillier complained to the *contrôleur général* Chamillard, who referred the petition back to the intendant. On 15 March 1706, the intendant replied by pointing out that Cuvillier was well-off, had no family to support, and enjoyed more than 3,000 livres in *rentes*. Fourcroy, on the other hand, was poor and had children to support. Thouret was merely a councillor in the *prévôté foraine*, a lower court connected with a suburb of the town, and had little property. And Grelier had to bear the burden of taxes on his two posts. Cuvillier could easily afford the tax and was wrong to have filed a complaint.

In regard to the Protestants, the intendants were at first made personally responsible for the execution of decrees and the surveillance of new Catholics, because the issue was still only one of economics and management rather than of distributive justice. After the Peace of Ryswick, however, it became necessary for the royal courts to resume the prosecution and punishment of heresy. The intendants were nevertheless obliged to keep Protestants under permanent surveillance. The circular letter of 2 June 1699 issued the following orders: "Although you are not yet required to punish violators, you should nonetheless be diligent in identifying and prosecuting them and in seeing to it that the judges do their duty."[34] In cases that called for quick action, where the only competent judges were suspect, intendants were supposed to apply to the minister and await orders on how to proceed.

In all extraordinary cases the intendants took action either by issuing orders or by issuing letters that had the effect of orders and carried with them coercive power. In other words, they acted by executive rather than judicial means.

Finally, in such extraordinary circumstances as a rebellion, a refusal to pay taxes, a famine, or an epidemic the intendants were empowered to take direct action, provided they reported on what they were doing to the king's Council and were ready to execute the Council's orders. In cases of unlawful assembly and violent acts, for example, the intendant could have those caught in the act arrested on the spot. But when an interval had elapsed and the charges merited a possible death sentence, scrupulous intendants felt that the legal forms ought to be respected and asked to be commissioned by council decree to sit in final judgment on the case, which they heard with a *présidial*. If the popular uprising had been provoked by a suspected violation of the law, as was the case with the unrest at Noyon, La Fère, Marle, and Chauny in 1697, which was caused by the removal from military storehouses of wheat that had been purchased for the army, leading to the fear that it would be sold illegally, the intendant might show indulgence. In this particular case de La Houssaye condemned only three of the accused, one to nine years' banishment, one to three years', and the third to a reprimand. He was himself hauled over the coals by the *contrôleur général* for this indulgence.

When a devastating epidemic struck Soissons, Noyon, Laon, and La Fère in 1668, Dorien, the intendant, ordered the neighboring communes to supply food to the infected cities or face a fine of 500 livres.

The Areas in Which the Powers of the Intendants Were Exercised in the Pays d'Élection. The intendant played a role in all the king's affairs, comprising justice, finance, and administration. His principal role was in finance. The warrant for the *taille* was fixed by the Council, and the *contrôleur général* then informed the intendant how much his *généralité* was to contribute. A proposed distribution of this amount among the *élections* was to be submitted. The intendant then made personal visits to all the *élections*, and his proposal reflected his estimate of their ability to pay. The Council then established the amount that each election was to be taxed. Commissions were then sent to the intendants authorizing them to collect this amount, along with a *lettre de cachet* to the *trésoriers de France*. The commissions ordered the intendants to proceed with the assessment. The *trésoriers de France*, together with the *élus*, then prepared the parish-by-parish distribution, and the intendant gave his approval. He further supervised the collectors in each parish who assessed each individual subject to the *taille*. He checked to see whether there were any individuals who were underassessed. Abatements were sometimes granted to wealthy but influential taxpayers. The intendant kept an eye on the collection of taxes. He checked armorial bearings, letters of ennoblement, letters of confirmation, and letters of exemption issued to communities. He prosecuted tax collectors who used the king's funds for their own affairs. He checked over the contracts between the *receveurs généraux* and *receveurs particuliers* concerning the recovery of *tailles*. If need be the intendant obtained writs and distraints or placed a bailiff's man in the residence of a recalcitrant taxpayer in order to collect what was due.

As for the capitation, which was established on 18 January 1695, the intendant approved the tax roles in accordance with the schedule established by the Council and his own estimate of the means of each taxpayer. When the capitation was reestablished on 12 March 1701, it was the intendant who divided the total to be collected in the *généralité* among the taxpayers in proportion to their wealth. The capitation remained in effect until 1789.

For the *dixième*, an income tax instituted by the declaration of 14 October 1710, the intendant collected declarations, prepared tax rolls, tried tax evaders, and appointed auditors.

In regard to the farms, the intendant prevented encroachments on the royal domain, punished abuses, and supervised the employees of the farmers general. The Council established the amount of salt to be taxed each year. It then sent a commission to the intendant instructing him to order assessment of this tax. Along with the officers of the salt warehouses, the intendant divided the total amount among the various parishes after being informed by the officers of the variations in population from one district to the next. Collectors in each parish divided the total amount of salt to be purchased among the various residents. In order to prevent misappropriation, the intendant required officers of the salt warehouses to inspect the agents of the farms. He also prepared reports concerning the activities of individuals dealing illegally in salt and applied to the king for orders to have them arrested.

For the farm on tobacco the intendant looked for individuals who might be growing tobacco illegally. If any were found, he submitted a report and enforced the ban on growing this crop.

The intendant submitted reports on subfarmers holding the monopoly on powder and saltpeter.

The intendant determined postal rates. If need be he could obtain a council decree granting him jurisdiction over disputes between the farmer having the monopoly of coaches and carriages on the one hand and municipalities on the other.

As for *aides* and *traites*, the intendant enforced the government's decrees and ordinances. He inspected weights and measures. And he confiscated prohibited merchandise pending further orders or a decision of the courts.

In regard to the royal domain, domanial dues, and streams and forests, the intendant was responsible for establishing accurate lists of royal possessions, land registration, receipt of oaths and homages, authorizations, declarations, and consents. This work was done by the *trésoriers de France* under his supervision. The intendant pressed the *trésoriers de France* to prosecute *engagistes* whose situation was irregular. After judgment was handed down by the *trésoriers*, the intendants reported the results to the *contrôleur général*. The intendant had jurisdiction over all matters relating to the farm on fees for the Small Seal and stamps for notarized documents.

The intendant had charge of all extraordinary affairs. He advised the *contrôleur général* concerning the creation of offices. He kept an eye on the activities of the *traitants* who contracted for the sale of offices, gave them assistance, and pressed them to be more active or to use coercion. He supervised salary increases and augmentations of dues and urged companies of officeholders to purchase increases.

During this period, which was one of prolonged warfare, the intendant played an important role in the administration of the army. He supervised recruitment and on 20 January 1692 prohibited forced recruitment, nullified promises extracted by violence, and ordered officers and recruiters not to mistreat the rural populace.

The intendant was in charge of troops and their supplies. He inspected the troops to make sure that no dummies were being passed off as real by their officers and to insure that their equipment was in good condition. The intendant acted as an intermediary between commissaries and the secretary of state for war in negotiating contracts for the supply of troops. He supervised purchases of wheat for the army, paying particular attention to see to it that wheat buyers employed by military commissaries did not use their passports to trade with civilians or even with the enemy, a practice that was liable to trigger uprisings by artisans and ferrymen. The intendant also contracted for horses and wagons to transport wheat. If need be he commissioned the collectors of the *tailles* to levy special taxes to pay for this transportation. He also requisitioned labor but always applied for compensation of the laborers whom he drafted. Intendants were careful to keep purchases as secret as possible and in amounts not so large as to cause the price of wheat or other commodities to rise.

Intendants were also in charge of accommodations for troops passing through their district. Soldiers in transit were provided with food for themselves and their horses, bedding, cooking utensils, fuel for fires, and candles. These supplies were provided by local residents. Municipalities were reimbursed by the government (from 21 November 1665 on). Intendants were responsible for prosecuting municipalities that held on to this money rather than reimburse their residents. Camp suppliers were reestablished at the end of the reign and made responsible for keeping camps well stocked, under terms set forth in contracts that they negotiated with the intendants. The intendants enforced the terms of these contracts, for otherwise suppliers were likely to flee if prices rose. Subcontractors to these suppliers were watched by the intendants and prosecuted if they gave short weight or reported a larger number of troops and horses than there actually were.

Intendants were in charge of winter quarters. Soldiers were lodged with local residents from 1 November until 31 March. The intendants determined the amount of wood and the number of candles to be supplied to each soldier. They heard complaints on the subject of billeting. They upheld the exemptions granted to royal officeholders and members of the clergy. They assessed a special tax, the *ustensile*, and a similar tax for provender. They negotiated contracts with suppliers of bread and provender. And they took action against officers who taxed too heavily.

The intendant had charge of assembling the *ban* and *arrière-ban*, as was done every year from 1689 to 1695. For this, he listed all members of the nobility and designated which of them would be required to serve personally in the military and which would be allowed to contribute money in lieu of personal service. The intendant was also responsible for equipping, arming, and maintaining the militia and, as of 29 November 1688, fortress guards, for which purpose he collected special taxes.

The intendant was in charge of the military police and the maintenance of discipline in the army, including its officers. He sat in judgment over soldiers charged with extortion or insubordination by the *prévôts des maréchaux*. He saw to it that the victims were compensated.

The intendant was also responsible for the administration of justice. He had charge of the recruitment of personnel by the courts. He urged selected individuals to present themselves as candidates for vacant seats and looked into the moral background and capability of the applicants.

The intendant monitored the diligence of officeholders and worked to prevent them from acquiring too many offices at once as well as to root out favoritism.

The intendant settled jurisdictional disputes and conflicts over priority between various *corps* of officeholders on a provisional basis in emergencies. But he always referred such cases ultimately to *parlement*, which had sole power to rule in this regard.

The intendant paid particular attention to the activities of the king's men: the *avocats*, notaries, *procureurs*, and *huissiers*. He ordered the *procureurs* to enforce decrees and instructed *avocats*, *procureurs*, and *greffiers* not to take exorbitant honoraria.

The intendant tried lawsuits that involved the state or the public order, for which purpose he employed two law graduates for administrative cases and six for criminal cases.

The intendant sat in judgment over disputes of cities, communities, and corporations with one another or with private individuals. He also heard disputes between communities and their *seigneurs*, officeholders, or creditors, and conflicts between villages and their *seigneurs* over dues, *banalités*, etc., and between villages and private individuals over water rights, etc. He judged conflicts between the clergy and villagers concerning tithes, religious establishments, chapels, etc. And he decided on disputes between corporations over questions of privilege or precedence.

The intendant personally prosecuted criminal cases: thefts, acts of violence, fraud, salt smuggling, disorderly conduct, rebellion, extortion, violations of ordinances. When the charges merited the death sentence, he received a special commission to undertake the prosecution.

The intendant was also responsible for "police" or general administration. He established codes of regulations and settled disputes in all areas in which the state intervened. He kept an eye on the political and religious opinions and activities of all the king's subjects. He was consulted concerning candidates for the clerical assemblies. He took part in the election of abbots and priors of monasteries. On the king's orders he eliminated stubborn candidates and electors and arranged for the election of a candidate acceptable to the king. He rid the monasteries of monks of dubious morals, heretics, and so forth. With regard to Protestantism he played a very active role, seeing to it that all council decrees concerning Protestants were enforced. He attempted to keep Protestants from leaving the kingdom, supervised the education of their children and the care of orphans, saw to the baptism of the newborn, established schools for young girls, and so on.

As part of his general administrative responsibilities, the intendant worked to insure the security and salubriousness of public streets and squares. He kept a watch on women of ill repute, vagrants, soldiers, beggars, and vagabonds. He fined or banished prostitutes and other disreputable characters. He dispatched *prévôts des maréchaux* to arrest and judge beggars and bohemians. In destitute municipalities he took charge of the cleaning of streets and sewers. He made sure that cities continued to receive food supplies during epidemics. In time of famine, the intendants were ordered by the declaration of 5 September 1693 to appoint *commissaires* in each election to check on grain stocks and force those holding such stocks to transport at least half of what they held to the markets at specified times. He established and oversaw the operation of general hospitals and *dépôts de mendicité* in which able-bodied beggars were put to work. The declaration of 1680 and the council decree of 1697 instructed him to inspect prisons twice a year and receive the prisoners' complaints. The intendant supervised the enforcement of regulations established by municipalities in regard to holidays, amusements, prices charged by butchers, fishmongers, and innkeepers, the sale of butter, wood, and charcoal, precautions against fires, the flushing of ditches, and the repair of roads; he punished violations with fines, prison terms, or confiscation of property.

Also included within the intendant's general administrative responsibilities were agriculture and trade in foodstuffs, manufacturing, and public works. To begin with, the intendant kept an eye on the level of supply and on prices. He prepared reports on the price of wheat and gave reasons and suggested remedies for price increases. He fought against hoarding and other forms of "monopoly." In 1698 the intendant de La Houssaye issued an ordinance to force peasants to bring their harvests to market. He ordered that from ten in the morning until two in the afternoon purchases could be made only by individuals and bakers, not by grain dealers. A certificate was needed for the transport of wheat in order to keep it from falling into enemy hands. In 1709 the intendant sent escorts to protect convoys against pillagers.

In 1715 the intendant was instructed to carry out an investigation and report on the nature and quality of land, the amount of each crop being grown, the market value, the state of commerce, etc.

For the purpose of broadening the tax base and improving the standard of living, intendants were asked to keep an eye on manufactures and encourage mayors, aldermen, and leading citizens to hire more workers and raise the quality of the output. The intendants enforced council decrees regulating factory conditions, spinning, weaving, and dying. They encouraged certain types of production and prohibited others, such as the weaving of stockings. Since the intensification of commerce that could stimulate production depended on transportation, intendants reported on the condition of roads, bridges, and canals and noted where work was needed. Repairs were proposed to the Council. If the plans were approved, the intendant would draw up detailed specifications and send them to the Council. If these were approved, the intendant solicited bids and awarded the contract to the lowest bidder. Intendants were always consulted about work to be undertaken. They gradually supplanted the *trésoriers de France* in responsibility for road maintenance.

In the Pays d'Etats. In the *pays d'Etats* the intendants concentrated most of their efforts on extraordinary circumstances such as protests, conflicts, and litigation. Ordinary cases were left to the officeholders, and there was a tendency to turn extraordinary new cases over to the officeholders and the Estates. Thus in Brittany in 1694, the intendant Nointel made assessments for the capitation but had the tax collected by the *trésorier des Etats*, who was appointed *commissaire* and reported to the Chambre des Comptes at Nantes. He did not have the capitation approved by the Estates, and it yielded little.

In November 1695 the Estates of Brittany asked for a subscription of 1,400,000 livres. The king agreed on 21 January 1696, and the capitation was levied by the *trésorier des Etats* acting as an officer of the Estates. Thus the intendant lost control over the capitation.

In 1701 the subscription was renewed, this time at two million livres. The council decrees of 21 January 1702 and 3 October 1703 set up a bureau for the revision of the capitation at Rennes. Its staff consisted of two representatives of each order, who were suggested by the Estates and approved by the king. The intendant presided. The bureau had final authority over all abatements of the capitation requested by individuals and communities. On 14 January 1706, however, the Estates adopted a regulation stripping the bureau of this power and laying it down that the capitation would be assessed for the nobility, by nobles, for the cities, by the deputies of third estate, and for the countryside, by appointed *commissaires*. Many did not pay as a result. In 1713 the authority of the capitation bureau was restored, and by 1714 receipts were running ahead of expectations.

By contrast, the intendant took charge of establishing the *dixième*, an income tax, in 1710. The royal declaration of 14 October 1710 was registered by the *parlement* of Brittany on 14 November. In orders issued on 17 November Ferrand, the intendant, issued instructions on the assessments to his subdelegates and on collection to the hearth-tax collectors and auditors. The subdelegates examined the declarations made by the taxpayers and supervised the collection process. But the Estates were hostile to the new tax, and until 1715 it had to be collected by subscription.

Although the intendant in Brittany was a permanent appointee, his status remained that of a *commissaire extraordinaire*. The only *commissaire ordinaire* and true representative of the king was the governor, and in his absence the commander-in-chief.

In the Conquered Provinces. Consider the example of Alsace, which suggests that in the conquered provinces the intendant allowed the courts to function as normally as possible. In 1698 Daniel Burbelack, *bourgeois de Haguenau*, purchased a site near the city from its magistrate. On this site he wished to build a tile factory and most likely encountered opposition on the part of the magistrate. In any case he submitted a petition to the intendant asking for authorization to build his factory. The intendant heard arguments in the case and, against the magistrate's wishes, refused to assume jurisdiction, referring it instead to the regular judge, whose decision could be appealed to the sovereign council of Colmar. He has left us with a clear statement of his thoughts in the matter: since the case involved the execution of a contract in favor of an individual, it was strictly within the purview of the regular judge, even though the municipality and therefore the public had an interest in its outcome. Where the common law came into conflict with the necessities of administration, it was thus the regular judge who had jurisdiction. Hence administration should continue to use judicial means, in the view of the intendant, whereas in this case the municipality of Haguenau would have preferred to rely on more rapid executive means of enforcement.

The intendant limited his role to one of expediting this judicial form of administration. In 1681 the magistrate of Colmar asked the intendant to require the *bailli* of Kientheim to complete work that he was supposed to do along the course of the Ill River and, furthermore, to order the nearby villages to repair certain ditches. The intendant merely sent the request to the *bailli* with orders to respond within a week. This he thought was sufficient.

Nevertheless, where the public interest was at stake the intendant was forced to develop a system of administration for dealing with matters in areas similar to those with which intendants in the *pays d'élections* had to deal: the royal domain, assessment and collection of royal taxes, community debts, common and patrimonial funds of cities and communities, the postal and coach system, streams and forests, horse breeding, trade in grains, smuggling, regulation of manufacturing, factory regulations, discipline of workers, regulation of religion. Parties with grievances turned to *procureurs* and *avocats* who filed petitions and prepared briefs. The intendant then sent a sergeant to the defendant's residence to notify him of the plaintiff's complaint. After seeing the reports of both parties, the intendant handed down an executory sentence and a judgment in the case. The procedure was written, convenient, rapid, and entailed no court costs.

The situation in the conquered provinces was quite similar to that in the *pays d'élections*. The only difference was that the intendant had to be careful to abide by the terms of the treaty of capitulation, which guaranteed the residents of conquered territories that their traditional customs and institutions would be respected. His task was complicated by fragmentation and particularism.

From the Death of Louis XIV to the Seven Years' War

During the first half of the eighteenth century the institution of intendancies was extended and consolidated without considerable change in either the extent of its responsibilities or the procedures by which it operated. The tradition of Colbert lived on, particularly in Orry, who was *contrôleur général* from 1730 to December 1745. The guiding principle was still to prevent the intendants from encroaching on the duties of officeholders but to give them full support and encouragement to take initiatives within their own sphere of responsibility. Following in the wake of Colbert's influence was that of Delamare and his *Traité de la police*, which appeared sometime after 1707. As Delamare used the term, "police"' included religion, morals, health, food supplies, roads, public tranquillity, the sciences and liberal arts, commerce, manufacturing and the mechanical arts, domestic servants and manual laborers, and poverty—in short, every department of government administration. The tendency that emerged clearly even before 1715 was for the intendants to concern themselves with all these things. The institution was vital enough for a former intendant, François Richer d'Aube to write, in 1738, a *Mémoire concernant Messieurs les intendants départis dans les différentes provinces et généralités du Royaume* of 637 pages, a treatise on the ideal intendant and his training.

Recruitment and Training

Recruitment and training remained unchanged. Intendants were selected from the ranks of the nobility of office. They owed their professional ascendancy to the favor of a grand or a minister and became the *fidèle* and creature of their patron. Richer d'Aube belonged to a Norman family ennobled in the sixteenth century and attached to the house of Gaston d'Orléans. They "belonged to the Orléans." The family rose through the ranks of the magistracy during the seventeenth century. The first of them, François, became a financial magistrate as *trésorier de France* at Alençon when the number of offices was increased in 1635. The second, his son Alexandre-François, rose to the post of councillor in the Rouen *parlement*. In 1719 he gave up his post to his son, François II, seigneur d'Aube, a resident of Paris who was named *commissaire* on the Conseil de Commerce in 1720 on the recommendation of the regent, the duc d'Orléans. In 1720 François II Richer became intendant of Caen. In 1722 he became a *maître des requêtes* and served as intendant of Soissons from 1727 to 1731. But he never became a *conseiller d'Etat*, probably because he "belonged" to Orléans. Tourny was the grandson of one Chrysostome Aubert, a native of Berry, seigneur de la Panne and d'Egrignon, the youngest son of Léon-Urbain Aubert who, after coming to Paris to work as clerk to an *avocat*, offered his loyalty to Chancellor de Pontchartrain, a Phélypeaux, who became his patron. Léon Aubert agreed to farm the income from his minister's property, became a *traitant*, and in 1682 purchased an ennobling office as a royal secretary. Then, in 1704 he was made *receveur des Finances* at Caen and in 1708 *président* of the Chambre des Comptes, Cour des Aides et Finances of Rouen. He became first seigneur de Tourny and then in 1702 marquis de Tourny. His fourth son, Louis-Urbain, the future intendant, was born in 1695 and continued to enjoy the protection of the Pontchartrains. His godmother was the great and powerful lady Mme Marie de Maupeou, the wife of the great and powerful lord, Monseigneur Louis Phélypeaux, *chevalier* and comte de Pontchartrain, minister-secretary of state and *contrôleur général des Finances*. His godfather was the messire Louis-Urbain Le Febvre de Caumartin, *conseiller d'Etat ordinaire* and *intendant des Finances*. After the death of Pontchartrain in 1727, Louis-Urbain Aubert, marquis de Tourny from 1721 on and intendant-to-be, continued to enjoy the protection of the chancellor's grandson, the comte de Maurepas, secretary of state, of the marquis de La Vrillière, minister and secretary of state, and of all the Phélypeaux.

Installed as a *maître des requêtes* in March 1720, Tourny received excellent practical training in the Conseil privé and made useful contacts. In 1722 he began working for the Eighth Bureau, which was concerned with food supplies, supplies for troops in transit, provender, hospital beds, and billeting for His Majesty's troops, and for the Twelfth Bureau, which was concerned with *économats*, the accounts of *commis*, and the administration of property belonging to fugitive Protestants. In 1724 he went to work for the bureau that dealt with the liquidation of guild debts. In 1725 he started working for the Fourth Bureau, which was looking into the privileges of the city of Paris. All these jobs were taken up on commission from the king. Some of Tourny's colleagues on the Conseil privé made brilliant careers: Orry, d'Argenson, Rouillé, Amelot de Séchelles, Maupeou, and Machault all became ministers; Hérault, Bertin, de Bernage, and Lescalopier became intendants; and Verthamon and de Gourgues became *présidents* of sovereign courts. Among the personal friends he made at this time were Trudaine, de Courteille, and d'Ormesson, all *maîtres des requêtes*.

In 1730, the prime minister, Cardinal Fleury, named Philibert Orry *contrôleur général des Finances*. Orry appointed Tourny intendant for Limoges, a post of the second rank suitable for an inexperienced intendant. He did a good job and was then named by Orry to be intendant for Bordeaux on 15 July 1743. Tourny held this post until 18 July 1757. Intendants were normally promoted from Limoges or Riom to Bordeaux or Lyon. Thanks to the patronage of the comtesse de Toulouse, Tourny was named *conseiller d'Etat* by brevet on 22 April 1755. He never rose higher than *conseiller d'Etat semestre*, holding seats on the first "*bureau de parties et de cassation*," the third "*bureau de parties et pour l'examen des requêtes en vue d'arrêt*," and on various special commissions. He died on 29 November 1760. His son, Claude-Louis Aubert de Tourny, *maître des requêtes*, received an "anticipated appointment" to the intendancy of Bordeaux, a sort of *survivance*, at the time his father was awarded his brevet as *conseiller d'Etat*. He often stood in for his father and actually succeeded him in September 1757. But he died a bachelor on 14 September 1760. The second son was an ecclesiastic. The marquisate of Tourny thus fell to the third son, Louis-Gallyot, *maître de camp* of the queen's cavalry, who later became *maréchal de camp*.

The salary, emoluments, and bonuses that the king paid to his intendants were insufficient, we are told, to cover their professional expenses and costs of representation. All were landowners, however, with *seigneuries* and *fiefs de dignité* whose incomes helped to cover their living expenses. For his marriage Tourny had been given the land, *seigneurie*, and marquisate of Tourny, which brought in 7,000 livres annual income. His wife, the daughter of a royal secretary, brought him 250,000 livres plus the *seigneurie* and barony of Nully and various other *seigneuries* in Champagne. In 1740 Tourny bought the barony of Selonge in Burgundy, including vineyards and the Vernois forge, which yielded 7,000 livres paid each year by the forgemaster. Generally speaking, however, intendants found themselves less wealthy upon leaving office than they were upon entering.

The Work of an Intendant

John Law said that France was governed by thirty intendants. The Venetian ambassador to the French court said in 1746 that each intendant was a "subdelegate of the minister."[36] Intendants took a hand in any matter in which either the king's interest or the public interest was at stake. Thus the work load was overwhelming, inspired by the example of Colbert, whom Tourny emulated to perfection in Bordeaux, driven not only by an ideal of service but also by an ardent personal will to dominate and create and by a passion to bend the entire administration to his will. Tourny invariably rose two or three hours before dawn. Even before the offices of the intendancy had opened their doors, he had gone through his employees' hoppers and distributed files and documents to be worked on during the day. Always on the job, he sometimes interrupted his labors to receive visitors, inspect work sites, preside over banquets and ceremonies, see artists, or attend meetings of the Academy. Except on official occasions, he ate a quick and meager meal at his desk while continuing to work on his documents. At the end of the day he returned to his study, sat down again with his pen, and continued his meditations well into the night.

On Tuesday and Saturday mornings he looked over the mail. On Wednesdays and Fridays at eleven o'clock he held audience. The other mornings of the week were reserved for work with his secretaries. Wednesday afternoons were devoted to finance, and Thursday afternoons to auditing accounts and planning works of beautification. He worked alone four afternoons a week and all day Sunday. Thousands upon thousands of reports were drafted in his fine, quick hand.

In spring and autumn Tourny conducted inspection tours in his *généralité*. He also had to make trips to Versailles and Paris, to the court and to ministerial offices.

He modeled his methods on those of Colbert, as reflected in the latter's instructions to his son Seignelay.[37] He wanted all decisions to be based on solid information. He demanded reports, made personal inspections, and consulted the most competent advisers. He prepared accounts in columnar form and made them highly legible so that the facts could speak for themselves and the conclusions leap to the eye. He had records kept up to date so that a reader could follow the progress of a debate day by day. He thought constantly about what decision he ought to make and tried to reach a decision as quickly as possible. He badgered his associates, writing them daily and on occasion several times each day. The aldermen of Bordeaux complained of having received as many as seven letters from him on a single day. Friendship and consideration played no part in his decisions. "The administrator is a judge," he wrote. As a *commissaire* of the Council or the king, he was concerned not to make friends but to enforce the authority of the king, which was vested in him. He was notified that Montesquieu, seigneur de La Brède, was forcing some taxpayers to work against their will: "If something of this sort has begun," he wrote on 7 September 1754, "I beg you, let it cease at once." Earlier, on 5 December 1750, Montesquieu had complained that Tourny "does not know how to give the smallest pleasure or render any service."[38]

Though particularly accentuated by the powerful personality of Tourny, these traits were shared by all the intendants.

The Extent of an Intendancy and Its Associated Bureaucracy

Efforts were made during this period to reduce the extent of certain intendancies that were thought to be too large. Prior to the death of Louis XIV, four intendancies covered the whole of southern France: the intendancy of Pau (Lower Navarre and Béarn), the intendancy of Languedoc, the intendancy of Montauban (Quercy, Rouergue, the *élections* of Armagnac, Astarac, Lomagne, Rivière-Verdun, Comminges, and the *pays* of Nébouzan and Quatre-Vallées), and the intendancy of Bourdeaux (*élections* of Bordeaux, Agen, Condom, Périgeaux, Sarlat, la Soule, la Bigorre, and le Marsan, the *élections* of Lannes and Bayonne, and the *pays* of Labourd). The latter three were obviously too large. There had long been two intendants in Languedoc, perhaps since as far back as the time of Basville. Because of the unity of this large *pays d'Etats* it was impossible to divide it up into two intendancies. This was not the case with the intendancies of Bordeaux and Montauban. Thus in April 1716, the intendancy of Auch was created out of territories taken from these two intendancies: Bayonne, the *pays* of Labourd and Soule, the *élection* of Lannes, and Bigorre, all detached from the intendancy of Bordeaux; Quatre-Vallées, Nébouzan, and the *élections* of Astarac, Comminges, Rivière-Verdun, and Lomagne, detached from the intendancy of Montauban. The king added Lower Navarre and Béarn. The *commissaire* assigned to the new district assumed the title of "intendant for Navarre, Béarn, and the *généralité* of Auch."

The bureaucracy associated with the intendancies remained modest in size but showed a tendency to grow. In Bordeaux, Tourny employed a first secretary, Dupin des Lèzes, whom he had brought with him from Limoges. Dupin headed a department of his own, besides which he countersigned orders, frequently prepared reports, and was delegated to carry out special missions requiring contact with important figures. When the intendant was absent, the first secretary sent him reports about everything that was going on and offered his own recommendations.

In the intendancy of Bordeaux there was in fact a general subdelegate, though he bore no such title. The post was filled by Thomas de Sorlus, chevalier de Saint-Louis, *avocat* in the *parlement*, and subdelegate for Bordeaux. When the intendant was absent, Sorlus signed orders in his stead. He was authorized to sign abatements of the capitation and taxes on industry. He was delegated by the intendant to redo the assessment of the *tailles* in parishes where the original assessment had been done poorly. On occasion he represented the intendant with official bodies, such as the Aldermen of Bordeaux.

The offices of the intendancy employed nine secretaries. Restais, who had been Tourny's secretary on the Conseil privé, followed him to Limoges and Bordeaux. His department had responsibility for municipal offices, tolls, the paper trade, nurseries, *économats*, prohibited merchandise, the *maréchaussée*, manufacturing, criminal affairs, Protestantism, and so forth, some twenty different categories in all.

Dasvin was responsible for military affairs, the accounts of the *extraordinaire des guerres* and the *étapes*, royal roads, petitions for tax abatements owing to losses of livestock or other losses due to hail, fire, etc., indemnities for expropriation, and so on.

Lacombe was responsible for community accounts, restoration of churches for which the cost was to be borne by communities, court costs to be borne by certain individuals, etc.

Five copyists prepared correspondence and recorded orders and correspondence with the court. Two of them, Fabre and Mouton, prepared fair copies of letters to the court and subdelegates. The "other three" recorded incoming and outgoing letters, kept logs, prepared orders on dictation from the intendant or on the basis of drafts approved by him. The work was too much for this small staff, and in 1747 the intendant secured the appointment of two additional secretaries, bringing the total staff to eleven.

To pay these employees the king gave the intendant 5,000 livres to be divided among the staff. In 1747 this sum was reduced to 2,500 livres. If divided equally this payroll would have provided a salary of 600 livres for each employee, at a time when room and board at the *collège* of Bordeaux came to 450 livres. The intendant secured royal bonuses for his secretaries, who might also receive additional bonuses from the communities. Thus Dupin, who received 1,080 livres from the king, earned an over-all compensation of 5,000 livres. The secretaries of the first rank earned in excess of 1,000 livres: Restais made 2,400 and Dasvin 1,200. Secretaries of the second rank made from 700 to 800 livres. And those of the lowest rank made from 500 to 600 livres.

Subdelegates

Subdelegate officers were eliminated in 1715. Subdelegates once again became *commissaires* of the intendants.

Between 1747 and 1756 the intendant of Bordeaux employed seventeen subdelegates in Bordeaux, Lesparre, Blaye, Libourne, Sainte-Foye, Bergerac, Sarlat, Périgeaux, Nontron, Agen, Villeneuve, Montflanquin, Marmande, Condom, Nérac, Casteljaloux, and Bazas. Five of them had assistants. Seven were judges, councillors in a *présidial* or *élection*, or *trésoriers de France*. Six were *avocats*. One was a *gentilhomme* who was not a law graduate, Basterot de Saint-Vincent, subdelegate as Lesparre. Eight had served the previous intendant as subdelegates and were kept on by Tourny. Son succeeded father in the position of subdelegate, and son-in-law succeeded father-in-law. Subdelegates often chose their sons or sons-in-law as assistants. At Bazas, for example, the Bourriol family filled the position of subdelegate for several generations. This sort of thing occurred in all the intendancies. In the *généralité* of Riom, comprising seven *élections* and more than a thousand parishes, the intendant, Rossignol, employed twenty subdelegates between 1734 and 1750; the same remarks could be made about them as about the subdelegates in the *généralité* of Bordeaux.

Subdelegates received no salary as such but rather compensation at established rates for their work in certain regular activities, such as the drawing of lots for militia service, along with bonuses for extra work, such as the reestablishment of the *dixième*, depending on how much work they actually did. In the *généralité* of Riom, we are told, they earned about 2,000 livres per year each. Besides this income, however, they enjoyed a thousand small benefits. They were exempt, for example, from *lods et ventes* and from billeting troops. They also benefitted from the "*moins imposé*," a kind of tax abatement. For instance, Faget, subdelegate at Marmande, was given an abatement when his daughter married, a *moins imposé* amounting to 200 livres on one of his properties. The ostensible reason for granting this abatement was as an indemnity for damages allegedly caused by flood waters that actually had not come within a league of his land. Since the property in question was assessed for a tax of only forty livres, the community was forced to pay the subdelegate the difference.

The Procedures Used by the Intendants

The procedures used by the intendants and the areas with which they were concerned were basically the same in this period as in the period 1690–1715, and the reader may refer to our treatment of this earlier period for details. Intendants maintained constant correspondence with the *contrôleur général des Finances*, the *intendants des Finances*, and the secretary of state in charge of their *généralité*. If the *généralité* happened to lie in a border province, they also corresponded with the secretary of state for war, whose authority took precedence even over the authority of the *contrôleur général*. When important personages were involved, the intendants also corresponded with the chancellor and, when there was one, with the prime minister. Intendants were innovators and reformers. Consider the matter of the *taille tarifée*, for example. Many writers had protested the arbitrariness in the assessment of the *taille*. La Bruyère, Fénelon, Vauban, and Boisguillebert had all expressed the wish that the amount of the tax be adjusted more equitably to the size of a man's income. The abbé de Saint-Pierre included a proposal to this end in his *Mémoire sur la taille tarifée*. Taxpayers subject to the *taille* were to declare their income. Income was to be classified according to its source and taxed at a specific rate for each category under this classification. For example, rental income to the owner of a house was to be taxed at four sous per livre, income from land held as a farm was to be taxed at three sous per livre, and so on. The total amount raised in this way was then to be compared with the sum required by the king. The assessment would then be increased or decreased proportionally as required to meet this sum.

Orry ordered that this procedure be applied in a circular letter sent to the intendants in February 1732. Tourny then issued orders in 1733 asking all those who were subject to the *taille* in the *généralité* of Limoges to make a declaration including the following items: the amount of various sorts of domanial land held; the quantity of seed used each year; the number of persons living on the land; the number of livestock maintained; the amount of *rentes* encumbering the income from the land; the terms of the lease regarding the payment of taxes and, for land farmed out on lease, the cost of the lease. A separate account was to be prepared for each domain, for mills, forgers, and tile works, for the various professions, and for the wages of day workers (indicating the number of days worked). False declarations were to be punished by fines. Those who failed to file a declaration would be assessed double. The *taille* of 1740 was based on these declarations in 635 parishes out of 976.

When there were disputes, Trudaine recommended that surveys be made and sent instructions and sample forms on 3 November 1740. The surveyor called upon the *syndic*, collectors, and prominent residents of the area to witness his work. He assigned numbers to each plot of land and each house, indicated the surface area of the plots, and left a blank space on his report form for an income estimate. An estimator or *abonnateur* then estimated the income of the surveyed lands. For this reasons the *taille tarifée* was also referred to as the *taille abonnée*. Tourny first tried this system out in a small number of parishes. The men appointed to serve as expert *abonnateurs* were merchants from Limoges.

In a circular letter dated 15 July 1741, Tourny published the tax schedule and indicated the distribution of taxes for 1742. The fundamental tax rate was set at two sous per livre on income. One-third was to be paid by the landowner subject to the *taille* and two-thirds by the farmer, sharecropper, or tenant. If the income was in the form of *cens*, seigneurial rents, tithes, or *agrières*, the tax rate was fixed at one sou per livre, two-thirds to be paid by the landowner and one-third by the farmer, who was to collect the dues. The basic tax on commerce was two sous per livre on profit. An investor in the business had to buy one-third of the tax and the merchant two-thirds. Day workers owed three deniers per livre on 140 days' wages. Members of guilds paid four and a half deniers per livre on their income for 170 days' work. Deductions were provided for the elderly, the handicapped, and heads of families. Those subject to the *taille* owed three livres for a pair of oxen, fifteen sous for a cow, ten for a sow, six for a hog, four for a goat, one for a sheep. The *taille tarifée* was a success in both Limousin and Champagne. The king therefore mandated that it be retained in Limousin by his declaration of 30 December 1761. Turgot, who was responsible for collecting it, was highly critical of the work of his predecessors, but his own surveys yielded almost identical results.

The intendants were responsible for all new taxes on income, such as the restored *dixième*, the *cinquantième*, and the *vingtièmes*.

Intendants were more concerned in this period than in the previous one with building roads and canals, establishing factories, and beautifying the cities by knocking down their walls and ramparts, laying out new boulevards, streets, and vistas in order to facilitate the flow of traffic, setting up gardens, and building monuments. Their efforts were aided by the fact that there were now fewer wars than there had been earlier, and what wars there were, were being fought outside the kingdom.

"Centralized Regionalism?"

Mr. Lhéritier has raised an important problem in regard to Tourny. He argues that between 1745 and 1748 Tourny began making a distinction between the king's interest and the public interest. When the two were in conflict, he says, Tourny gave preference to the public interest over the king's interest. He was, we are told, devoted to the public. Presumably he went over to the side of the people. To serve the people he is supposed to have used the power vested in him by the king in order to escape the tutelage of the ministries in running the province. Tourny, according to this view, was the exponent of a form of government that has been described as "centralized regionalism." The initiatives that he took in behalf of the public interest are supposed to have been reflected in an expansion of commerce and a proliferation of public works.[39]

Is Lhéritier's argument convincing? It is hard to separate the interests of the king from those of the public, because improvements in transportation, expansion of commerce, and creation of jobs through public works increased the tax base and contributed to the maintenance of law and order. Lhéritier has been struck by something Trudaine said in regard to the roads built by Tourny in the *généralité* of Bordeaux: "What does the king care about all that?" But what in fact was the object of this bizarre statement? Whatever it may have been, we know that Tourny had already made tremendous efforts to build roads in Limousin (from which Turgot benefitted in spite of his injustice to his predecessors), and his road-building activities in the *généralité* of Bordeaux do not seem to reflect any new ideal or outlook. The same holds true in regard to manufacturing, commerce, and public works. Tourny's efforts in Bordeaux were certainly on a larger scale, but this was a much wealthier *généralité* than that of Limousin, and he was a much more seasoned intendant, more secure in his authority, at least until his later years.

Lhéritier also finds it noteworthy that, in his view, Tourny relied on the assistance of hitherto decrepit authorities such as the Chamber of Commerce, the *corps* of the city, the *présidiaux*, the admiralty courts, and the *trésoriers de France*, whose vitality was somehow restored. We are told that he met in his office with merchants, harbor pilots, and representatives of guilds and communities and reported on their views to the *contrôleur général*. This is presumably meant to suggest that his aim was to involve those whose activities he administered in his work in behalf of the public interest. But in so acting he was doing no more than encouraging others to act and gathering information about what they were doing, part of his normal role as intendant. Had he not behaved in the same way when he was at Limoges, making due allowance for the limited resources of Limousin as compared with those of Bordeaux? And did not the other intendants do the same?

Lhéritier points out that on one occasion Tourny held wheat belonging to the king in Bordeaux, and that Machault wrote to him on 10 February 1749 to say that "it seems that you prefer the interests of Bordeaux and Guyenne to those of His Majesty." But was there anything new in this? Not only in the eighteenth but already in the seventeenth century the king's local agents, closer to the populace and more aware of their difficulties, sought to make the lives of the king's subjects easier and to lighten their burden. One would be tempted to say they always did this. They always interceded on behalf of the local population to request reductions of taxes and exemptions from prohibitions and interdictions. What local agent of the king did not withhold wheat at one time or another, out of fear of rising prices and famine? We should be careful not to place too much weight on Machault's words. The king's interests, moreover, were the interests of a broader public than that of the intendant, the interests of the kingdom as a whole, for which the king bore the responsibility.

Thus Lhéritier's thesis, that Tourny's thinking and behavior show a change from dedication primarily to the king's interests to dedication primarily to the public's interests between 1745 and 1748, does not appear to be adequately supported by the facts. It would be worthwhile to see if such a change is indicated at this time by the statements and above all the behavior of other intendants.

From the Seven Years' War until 1789

As far as the study of the intendants is concerned, the unity of this period lies in the gradual weakening of the power of the central government, which was looked upon, rightly or wrongly, as consisting entirely of royal creatures and favorites. The series of capitulations by the government in the face of opposition from the *parlements*, temporarily halted by the interlude of the Maupeou reforms, weakened the authority of the king and, little by little, that of the intendants.

The Intendancies

By 1787 a series of additions and deletions had brought the number of intendancies to thirty-two for continental France plus one for the island of Corsica and a number of others for the colonies of the East Indies, Africa, and America. The intendancies of continental France were as follows: Paris, Amiens, Soissons, Orléans, Bourges, Lyon, Dombes, La Rochelle, Moulins, Riom, Poitiers, Alençon, Caen, Brittany, Provence, Languedoc, Roussillon, Burgundy, Franche-Comté, Dauphiné, Metz, Alsace, Flanders and Artois, Hainaut and Cambrésis (with the district of Saint-Amand and the *pays* d'Entre-Sambre-et-Meuse and outre-Meuse), plus the duchies of Lorraine and Barrios.

Intendancies were added and deleted, and their boundaries fixed, by edicts addressed to the Chambre des Comptes for registration. Thus, while the intendants continued to be regarded officially as *commissaires*, the post of intendant was indeed looked upon as permanently established. One man might succeed another in the job, but the post remained, independent of the man who occupied it.

The edict of July 1787 eliminated the intendancy of Pau and Bayonne and divided its district between the two intendancies of Bordeaux and Auch. In 1767 a ''department'' of Pau and Bayonne had been split off from the intendancy of Auch and entrusted to a *commissaire*. In 1775 it was divided between the intendancies of Bordeaux and Auch. In 1784 an intendancy of Pau and Bayonne was instituted. But in July 1787 the king said that ''the general plan of administration that we desire requires that we reestablish the division that we laid down upon our accession to the throne.''[40] As a result the fortresses of Marsan, Tursan, and Gabardan, the *élection* of Lannes, the city of Bayonne, and the *pays* of Labourd were returned to the *géneralité* of Bordeaux. The *pays* of Foix, Nébouzan, and Quatre-Vallées—Bigorre, Soule, Navarre, and Béarn—were restored to the *généralité* of Auch.

Titles and Duties of the Intendants

The intendants took on some majestic titles. For example, one intendant headed his commission to a subdelegate, issued on 7 October 1784, with the following words: "We, Antoine-François-Alexandre Boula de Nanteuil, Chevalier, Seigneur de Mareuil, Saint-Clair, Lignères, Saint-Denis, La Grange-Dumont, Nanteuil-lès-Meaux, Truet, Clermont, and other places, councillor to the king in his councils, *maître des requêtes ordinaire* of the king's *Hôtel*, honorary councillor in his court of *parlement* at Paris, intendant of justice, police, and finance, and *commissaire* charged with the execution of His Majesty's orders in the *généralité* of Poitiers . . ."[41]

According to the jurists Guyot and Merlin, writing in 1787, the duties of the intendant combined administration and law enforcement. Their regular duties concerned such matters as religion and public instruction, agriculture, streams and forests, commerce, manufacturing, navigation, arts and crafts, war, police, communities of inhabitants, colonies, domains, finance, and routine justice. Consider the category of religion and public instruction in detail. We find that the intendants were concerned with Protestant sects, the Jews of Alsace, fabrics of parochial churches, repair and maintenance of churches, lodging of curates, livings for curates, *économats*, administration and conservation of property in mortmain, room and board of oblates, *décimes* (extraordinary tithes levied on the clergy), universities, *collèges*, public libraries, etc. A similarly lengthy list of responsibilities could be provided for each of the other categories. In addition to these regular duties, intendants also had extraordinary, temporary duties: taking possession of a newly acquired province, city, or canton in the name of the king, setting up a new superior court, closing down a sovereign company or temporarily suspending its functions, reestablishing such a company, hearing the testimony of the litigants and preparing a report on it for the council in a case being tried before a court subsidiary to the king's Council, determining the boundaries of provinces and *généralités*. In cases whose nature placed them within the purview of the *parlements*, Cours des Aides, or Chambres des Comptes, the intendants could be commissioned to prosecute and sit in sovereign judgment, sometimes alone, sometimes along with officeholders and law graduates. Such cases included embezzlement, rebellion, or inability of accounting officials to pay funds due the royal treasury, even in Hainault and Flanders, whose inhabitants had the privilege of not being liable to have cases in which they were involved removed from the jurisdiction of their regular judges, because cases involving royal funds were considered to be above the ordinary rules (examples of this occur in 1761, 1769, 1774, 1779, and 1780). Finally, intendants might be asked to publish the texts of legislation for which registration was refused.[42]

The intendants exercised their powers on their own. An exception to this rule occurred in Franche-Comté, where the edict of October 1771 establishing the *bureau des Finances* of Besançon specified that this bureau would have joint jurisdiction over cases in litigation previously falling within the purview of the intendant alone. Litigation was to be heard by two judges, a *trésorier de France* acting as *rapporteur* and the intendant acting as *président*. If they split, the decision was up to the king's Council. The intendant was to be *premier président* of the bureau and was obliged to have the bureau register his commission and install him in his post.

The Intendants as Provincial Representatives?

Paul Ardascheff has written a book about the provincial intendants under Louis XVI which is actually a study of intendants during the second half of the eighteenth century. He takes the position that the intendants had become the representatives of their provinces vis-à-vis the central government, instead of being, as they had been under Louis XIV, the agents of the central government in the provinces. He places much weight on a sentence uttered by the archbishop of Aix: "The king's man is becoming the province's man."[43]

But this sentence was uttered on 31 December 1787 at the opening session of the reinstated Estates of Provence, at a time when the authority of the intendants was being undermined everywhere by the idea of administration through elected notables. It says nothing about the thirty years from 1757 to 1787.

Ardascheff adduces as further proof for his contention the fact that intendants requested reductions of taxes for their intendancies, showed circumspection with regard to provincial privileges, prohibited the export of grain from their province, or did the reverse, as in 1776 when free export of grain from Marseilles was continued in spite of orders from the *contrôleur général* that it be halted. But none of this was new. Intendants had always acted this way.

It does seem correct to say that between 1757 and 1787 intendants built more roads, devoted more attention to the encouragement of manufacturing and to the beautification of cities, spent more time on hospitals and the poor than they had done during the War of the League of Augsburg and the War of the Spanish Succession, at a time when "the fatherland was in danger" and "terror was on the rampage." But this was only natural, now that wars were being fought in far-off places and the kingdom was growing wealthier, to the advantage of the central government as well as the provinces.

What is beyond dispute is that the vocabulary of the intendants underwent a change, as did the vocabulary of society as a whole and, for that matter, of the king and his ministers themselves. The king's edicts, letters from the ministries, intendants' reports, orders, and official speeches all celebrated the "century of Enlightenment," heaped scorn upon the "centuries of barbarism and ignorance," and cited Montesquieu, Voltaire, and Rousseau. The official phraseology was "philosophical." There was constant talk of reason, nature, humanity and its inalienable rights, sensibility, the love of mankind and the public good, the love of liberty, of citizens, patriots, natural rights, sensitive souls, the love of peoples, and the cult of mankind.

The use of fashionable phraseology does not necessarily indicate a change in behavior, however. The intendants do not seem to have used different procedures or shouldered new responsibilities under Louis XVI by comparison with what had been the case during the second half of Louis XIV's reign, from 1690 to 1715.

Merely because that prolific writer, Sénac de Meilhan, asserted that the intendants, "guided by public opinion, increasingly sought to make a name for themselves by going easy on the people and undertaking useful projects rather than by toadying to the wishes of the ministries,"[44] we need not follow him by extending his assertion to cover the entire second half of the eighteenth century and by seeing the phenomenon as something really new. What is needed is a comparative study of official correspondence during the reign of Louis XVI and official correspondence during the second half of the reign of Louis XIV, based on an analysis of the laws, a compilation of statistics, and a knowledge of the surrounding circumstances.

Heritability and Stability of the Office of Intendant

The reason such a study is needed is that a problem concerning the role of the intendants does indeed crop up. Officially the intendant remained a *commissaire*. But his position gradually took on the characteristics of an office. To begin with, there were severe restrictions on the king's choice. The sovereign had to choose thirty-three intendants, counting only the intendants of continental France, from among eighty *maîtres des requêtes*. Only five intendants were not *maîtres des requêtes*: La Guillaumye, *conseiller d'Etat*, intendant for Corsica; Taboureau des Réaux, honorary councillor in *parlement*, intendant for Valenciennes; Cochet de Garnerans, *premier président* in the *parlement* of Dombes, intendant for Dombes; de Clugny, intendant general for the navy and colonies and intendant for Perpignan; and Le Camus, director of the Librairie, intendant for Pau-Bayonne. Intendants were frequently chosen from among the *maîtres des requêtes* by seniority. When favor played a part in the choice, it fell upon those who had distinguished themselves in the world of the gown. The posts of *maîtres des requêtes* and intendant were monopolized by a small number of families, 200, perhaps 300 at most. The same names crop up time and time again. Furthermore, these families were tied together in numerous ways. *Maîtres des requêtes* and intendants were frequently related to one another by blood or marriage. Whole groups of intendants belonged to a single large family. The Maussions, the family that provided the last intendant of Rouen from 1787 to 1790, were related to the Aubert de Tournys, who provided Bordeaux with two intendants. The intendant from the Maussion clan was respectively son-in-law and father-in-law to the two members of the Perrin de Cypierre family who served as intendants of Orléans after 1760. He was also the brother-in-law of Chaumont de La Galaizière senior, who served as intendant of Montauban (1756–58), Lorraine (1758–77), and Alsace (1777–90), with his son as assistant in 1789 and 1790. Royal favor fell only on men within this small circle of families. Auget de Montyon was a relative of *contrôleur général* Maynon d'Invault and a protégé of Trudaine, intendant des Finances and director of the Ponts et Chaussées; Chaumont de La Galaizière was a creature of Choiseul; De Flesselles was "devoted body and soul" to the duc d'Aiguillon; and de Maussion became intendant of Rouen in 1787 through the influence of his father-in-law, the intendant of Orléans, a creature of de Noailles.

Intendants tended to remain in their posts for long periods. There were sixty-eight intendants under Louis XVI. Twenty-nine held their post for more than ten years; twenty-four, more than twenty years; thirteen, more than twenty-five years; seven, more than thirty years; and two, more than forty years. Once a man had held a post for twenty years or more it was almost impossible to remove him. Becoming an intendant assured a man of a brilliant career. The commissions of intendants were never revoked. An intendant who fell into disgrace was simply sent to a more modest intendancy. This happened to Montyon, who went from Aix to La Rochelle, and to d'Agay, who went from Rennes to Amiens. Or else he became a *conseiller d'Etat*.

Furthermore, many intendancies acquired a kind of heritability. Fifteen intendants were sons of intendants. Thirteen were sons or relatives of men who had occupied high administrative posts. The intendant Gravier de Vergennes was the son of an ambassador and nephew of the secretary of state for foreign affairs. Turgot was the son of a *maître des requêtes, conseiller d'Etat*, and *prévôt des marchands* of Paris. The intendant Terray was a nephew of the abbé Terray, *contrôleur général des Finances*. Rouillé d'Orfeuil was the son of a *maître des requêtes*, the grandson of an intendant, and a relative of a secretary of state for foreign affairs. The Feydeau family counted among its number *maîtres des requêtes, conseillers d'Etat*, a *lieutenant général de police*, a keeper of the seals, and six intendants. The intendancy remained within the family without interruption for 114 years, from 1673 until 1787. Son succeeded father in a number of intendancies: the Bertier de Sauvignys in Paris, the d'Agays in Amiens, the Rouillé d'Orfeuils in Châlons, the La Bourdonnaye de Blossacs in Poitiers, the Guignard de Saint-Priests in Montpellier, and the Amelot de Chaillous in Dijon. Dynasties of intendants seemed to be in the process of forming.

Some intendants were inclined to put down roots where they were stationed. Du Cluzel, intendant for Tours, refused a more highly rated intendancy because he had property within his *généralité*. Ballainvilliers, intendant for Auvergne, turned down the intendancy of Bordeaux. Turgot, intendant for Limousin, refused the intendancy of Lyon. The king was not, moreover, averse to naming a man from the province or *généralité* as intendant. Chazerat, who administered Auvergne from Riom for eighteen years from 1772 to 1790, came from an old family of magistrates of the province. He was the son of the *premier président* of the Cour des Aides of Clermont-Ferrand and had succeeded his father in this post. His wife was the daughter of a *président* in the local *bureau des Finances*. They had connections with a large number of people in the area and owned land there. Chazerat died in Riom in 1824. The case of Cochet de Garnerans in Dombes was similar. Des Gallois de La Tour, the last intendant of Aix, belonged to one of the oldest families in Provence. He succeeded his father as intendant for Aix and *premier président* in the *parlement* of Provence. There are many similar cases.

The Intendants as Noble Magistrates

Long terms of office, heritability, and local recruitment or local roots all contributed to giving the intendants some independence with regard to the ministers. Other circumstances might further enhance this independence. The intendants were magistrates. Almost all came from families whose members had served in *parlement*. All had been councillors in the *parlement* or the Grand Conseil, because the edict of 1683 required candidates for the position of *maître des requêtes* to have served for six years as councillor on a sovereign court, a period shortened in practice by the special waivers of the age requirement that were sometimes granted. The *maîtres des requêtes* were magistrates and belonged to a company. Some intendants retained the intependent spirit of the magistracy.

Intendants could also gain independence by virtue of their nobility. All intendants were nobles. Of sixty-eight intendants under Louis XVI, five were taken to possess immemorial nobility dating back to before the earliest ennoblements in the thirteenth century; these included Turgot and Feydau de Brou. The nobility of five others may have been equally ancient. Five came from families ennobled by holding posts in the magistracy during the fourteenth and fifteenth centuries, such as the Amelot and d'Agay families. Ten belonged to the old judicial nobility, that is, to families that had been ennobled during the sixteenth and first half of the seventeenth centuries and that maintained an unbroken noble line for a hundred years or at least four generations, such as the Lefèvre de Caumartin and Dupré de Saint-Maur families, which had been noble since 1501, and the De Flesselles family. Twenty-six came from families that had been ennobled two or three generations earlier, during the second half of the seventeenth or the first part of the eighteenth century. These included the families of Sénac de Meilhan, d'Aine, Auget de Montyon, Bertier, Calonne, Vergennes, and Terray. Issued from a family of Burgundian peasants, Thomas Bertier became a protégé of the treasurer of the Burgundian Estates and in 1668 a royal secretary. His son served as councillor on the Dijon *parlement*. His grandson, the marquis de Sauvigny, was intendant of Moulins (1734–40), Grenoble (1740–43), and Paris (1774–76). And his great-grandson served first as assistant intendant of Paris (1768–78) and later as intendant in his own right (1778–89). Most held titles attached to *fiefs de dignité* and were barons, viscounts, counts, and marquis. Bear in mind, however, that these titles had lost some of their value in the second half of the eighteenth century. Many ennobled individuals had acquired them. The son of a wealthy bourgeois could buy a post as royal secretary and call himself baron de Ballainvilliers. The son of one ennobled gentleman graced his name with the title of marquis de Reverseaux.

The Intendants as Men of Wealth

The intendants gained further independence from the fact that they were wealthy men. One had to be wealthy to bear the expense of being an intendant, which required staging balls and banquets. The salary, pension, and bonuses that went with the job were at best a supplement and rarely sufficed to cover expenses. Caze de La Bove, intendant of Brittany from 1774 to 1783, could not get by on the 40,600 livres he received each year from the king. When Ballainvilliers was suggested for the intendancy of Languedoc on 31 March 1786, the *contrôleur général*, Calonne, took into consideration not only the fact that Ballainvilliers had married his niece but also that he had 80,000 livres of *rente*. In fact, repairs to his *hôtel* cost the new intendant 200,000 livres and his representation at the first session of the Estates cost him 24,000 livres. When Amelot was nominated intendant for Dijon, his fortune amounted to 650,000 livres. After serving in the post for several years it had been reduced to 540,000 livres. Most intendants were large landowners and derived huge incomes from their property in land. Guéau de Reverseaux, intendant of Moulins (1777–81) and of La Rochelle (1781–89), had an annual income of 40,000 livres from his various properties, particularly his huge estates around the château de Reverseaux near Chartres. Etienne-Louis Journet, intendant of Auch from 1768 to 1775, had an annual income of 50,000 livres. Another intendant, Joly de Fleury, the future *contrôleur général*, was judged to be "not very wealthy" because his annual income was only 10,000–12,000 livres.

Another source of independence for the intendants was that they often held their posts longer than the ministers under whom they served. Between 1774 and 1789 there were twelve different *contrôleurs généraux des Finances*. Half the intendants held their posts for a period longer than these fifteen years and saw these ministers and many others come and go. Disgrace was a serious matter but not necessarily a catastrophe for an intendant, particularly if he had a protector. One councillor in *parlement*, Le Camus de Neville, was exiled by Maupeou but became an intendant after Maupeou himself had fallen into disgrace. Montyon became a *conseiller d'Etat* even though he had fallen into disgrace while intendant, thanks to the protection of the comte d'Artois. The only intendant to be found guilty of misappropriation of funds, Orceau de Fontette, was dismissed in disgrace by Turgot but nevertheless became a *conseiller d'Etat* thanks to the protection of the comte de Provence.

The Intendants as Members of the "Robe du Conseil"

While all these factors may have helped the intendants to stand up to the ministers and to act as representatives of their *généralités* and provinces, we cannot be sure that this was the case. Many of the factors mentioned were nothing new: nobility, wealth, membership of a small circle of families that had traditionally served in high governmental and administrative posts were all familiar characteristics. Although intendants were magistrates, they belonged to an inner circle within the magistracy, the so-called *robe du Conseil*, consisting of secretaries of state, *conseillers d'Etat*, and *maîtres des requêtes*. While similar to the *robe du Parlement*, the *robe du Conseil* was nevertheless a distinct and antagonistic group, owing to the fact that it consisted of men who had rallied to the side of the king and his government and who owed their importance and power entirely to the king's having singled them out from among those devoted to him. This was a fundamental reason for their obedience and loyalty. Members of the *robe du Conseil* were appointed; they were individualistic, personally accountable, and used to following the orders of their superiors in the bureaucracy. The *robe du Parlement*, on the other hand, was recruited by cooptation. Its strength lay in corporate solidarity, which assured its independence as a corporate body. Members of both groups may have belonged to the same social world, but they moved in different and antagonistic professional and political milieus. Furthermore, the influence of Paris on the intendants weakened the influence of the provinces. All were Parisians by education, family background, career connections, and taste. Some intendants spent several consecutive months each year in Paris. Some were glad to exchange a good intendancy for one less good but closer to Paris. If, in all likelihood, they found it increasingly difficult to hold out against public opinion and pressure groups in their *généralités* and provinces, this was certainly due more than anything else to the increasing incoherence of the central government as well as to its series of surrenders to the sovereign courts and provincial Estates. Consider, for instance, the situation of one intendant, Calonne, who was forced in 1775 to reinstate the *parlement* he had closed down in 1771. His consternation is readily understandable. Public opinion, moreover, held the intendant to be the king's man and reproached him for exercising a paternal, despotic, and arbitrary power.

Much work is needed before the question raised by Ardascheff can be answered.

Official Correspondence

All the ministers, *conseillers d'Etat*, and intendants moved in the same circles and knew one another. Thus official correspondence had the tone of conversation among men of the world. Ministers and intendants were addressed simply as "Monsieur." In letters from ministers the "Monsieur" followed two or three words of introduction, while in letters from intendants it appeared on top. Ministers never prescribed, ordered, or prohibited. They recommended, advised, or urged: "I should be obliged if you would . . ." Both ministers and intendants ended their letters with the formula, "Your very humble and very obedient servant." Ministers, however, expressed their "sincere attachment" to the intendant, while intendants stated that they were "honored" to be servants of the minister and indicated their "profound respect." The *contrôleur général* and minister of finance, Lambert, wrote to the intendant of Languedoc on 21 February 1788 as follows: "I have received, Monsieur, along with the letter that you did me the honor of sending on the 29th of last month, the copy of the deliberations on each article. I thank you for this new token of your affection." *Intendants des Finances* and *intendants des provinces* addressed one another as "Monsieur and dear colleague." The same tone appears in correspondence between intendants and their subdelegates, who were recruited among the magistrates and men of law.

When the intermediate commissions began their work on 5 January 1788, they were sent a "protocol for the intermediate commissions of the provincial assemblies," which for the first time indicated the formulas by which letters sent or received by the commissions should open and close. The dehumanization of the administration was under way.

Speed and Efficiency

The intendants showed constant concern for speed and efficiency. They always demanded speed, attention to detail, accuracy, and honesty of their subdelegates, secretaries, and *commis*. They were hampered by the slowness of communications and the formality of the hierarchy. To give some idea of the speed of communications, a few figures will suffice: an official letter sent from the *contrôle général* on 4 September arrived in Orléans and Metz on 7 September, in Tours and Caen on 8 September, in Dijon and Besançon on 9 September, in Poitiers on 10 September, in Saintes on 11 September, in Bayonne on 15 September, and in Aix on 18 September. As for bureaucratic formalities, on 21 February 1787, the *intendant des Finances*, Blondel, asked the opinion of the intendant of Amiens regarding the petition of one Sorel, a tile manufacturer at Vitremont in Picardy, who had applied for authorization to take clay wherever he could find it and pay compensation to the owner of the land. On 3 March the intendant asked for the opinion of his subdelegate in Péronne, who had jurisdiction over Vitremont. On 12 May the subdelegate responded: to grant Sorel's request would raise many problems, and it was preferable to encourage the tile industry by means of subsidies. On 19 May the intendant relayed this answer to the *intendant des Finances*, indicating that he concurred with his subdelegate. On 15 July Blondel's successor as *intendant des Finances*, Tolozan, asked the intendant of Amiens how large a subsidy it would be appropriate to give Sorel. On 22 July the intendant passed this question along to his subdelegate. On 30 July the intendant of Amiens relayed his subdelegate's reply together with his approval to Tolozan. On 17 November Tolozan informed the intendant of Amiens of the *contrôleur général*'s decision, approving the recommendation of the intendant and his subdelegate. On 3 December the intendant notified his subdelegate of the decision that had been taken and asked him to inform the tile manufacturer.

In spite of these difficult conditions, ministers and intendants sometimes worked with miraculous dispatch. On 5 January 1783, the *contrôleur général* answered a letter that had been sent from Pau on 23 December 1782 and that had reached him on 2 January. The intendant for Dijon answered a letter from a minister dated 10 May on 15 May. On 9 May 1783, the intendant for Bordeaux sent Vergennes a request for authorization to establish a literary society. The letter arrived at Versailles on the 19th and Vergennes issued the authorization on the 20th. On 22 June the minister Villedeuil asked the intendant of Bordeaux for his opinion concerning the installation of a school for deaf-mutes founded in 1786 by the abbé Sicard. On 6 June the intendant responded with his opinion. Such achievements were truly prodigious feats.

The Intendants' Archives and Bureaus

The intendants acquired better and better instruments for carrying out their mission. Intendancies were by now equipped with archives to which each new intendant added additional material, so that cases could be decided on the basis of precedents and recommendations based on information of high quality. The duties of the intendants' secretaries were of such importance that the post of secretary came to be regarded as offering the opportunity of a promising career. It was often filled by an *avocat* or a law graduate intent on being called to the bar. But the profession of *avocat* was incompatible with a job that was time-consuming and that made a man dependent on others, and the orders of *avocats* refused to accept intendants' secretaries for membership or to take back a former member who had left to work for an intendant. Secretaries and *commis* working for the intendancy were thus stuck in their situation, but there was ample scope to pursue a full career where they were. In Brittany the position of *commis* in the intendancy was much sought after. Department heads were allowed to wear swords by special dispensation of *parlement*. When one *commis* died suddenly in 1781, forty young men applied for his position. The intendant Caze de La Bove raised the salaries of his assistants. The head of the war department, subdelegated to the bureaus, was raised to 4,200 livres from 2,400 livres. The first secretary in the *bureau de Finance* went from 1,800 to 2,000. The staff secretary went from 1,500 to 2,000. And so on. Furthermore, all bonuses were deposited in a common fund: 3,000 livres from the director of *domaines et contrôles*, 1,000 livres from the farmer of the *devoirs*, 1,000 livres from the general farm, etc. On 24 April 1784, the minister awarded a retirement pension of 500 livres to each of his two assistant department heads, who had worked for him since 1760. Bertrand de Molleville, who was then an intendant, hired them as "writers" with a salary of 400 livres. In Rennes it was widely believed that former employees of the intendancy would obtain pensions automatically. Thus clerks and secretaries working for the intendancy came to have many of the characteristics of the modern bureaucrat.

Subdelegates

The subdelegates consolidated their power. In Provence between 1770 and 1790 there were sixty-five subdelegations that varied widely in size and population. Generally speaking, subdelegations coincided with *vigueries*, districts that had once marked the boundaries of judicial and administrative jurisdictions and that had come to be used for tax and survey purposes. But the boundaries of many subdelegations cut through the boundaries of *vigueries* and *sénéchaussées*. The same subdelegation might contain both communities belonging to the *pays de Provence* and communities belonging to adjacent lands. In the subdelegation of Marseilles there were two subdelegates, one for administration and the other for commerce and maritime affairs. The responsibilities of subdelegates sometimes overlapped. The subdelegate of Salon was responsible for militia operations in Eyguières, a town in which another subdelegate resided. The subdelegate of Aubagne was responsible for the coast guard in his subdelegation and in all the suburbs of Marseilles in Allauch as far out as Pierrefeu and Simiane. In Brittany Caze de La Bove proposed reducing the number of subdelegations from sixty-five to twenty. In fact a scant five were done away with. Subdelegates still received no salary but were paid bonuses. In Brittany Bertrand de Molleville regularly assigned them the responsibility of representing him in ceremonies, contract negotiations, and other appearances of all sorts. The subdelegates gradually came to occupy a special place in public opinion. The *Etrennes bretonnes*, the Rennes annual directory, began in 1762 giving the addresses of subdelegates in such major commercial centers as Nantes and Saint-Malo. In 1786 Dinan, Josselin, and Lamballe were added to this list. By 1787 the directory included a full list of subdelegates, classified by bishopric.

The Last Days of the Intendants

The council decree of 30 January 1785 turned over to the Estates of Brittany authority to administer all major highways with full powers of the intendants. During the 1784–85 session of the Estates the king granted them the power to award *octrois* and monitor municipal finances. He also relinquished the authority to administer stud farms. The intermediate commission of the Estates acquired its own means to act, independent of the royal government, through "diocesan bureaus" and correspondents. The intendant, Bertrand de Molleville, fought against the king's decision to relinquish his authority. He wrote the *contrôleur général* that there was nothing left for him to do in the province. This was an exaggeration, since he retained jurisdiction over cases involving the *domaines, contrôles, centième denier*, and amortization; over the *maréchaussée* and the militia; over duties on paper and playing cards; over gunpowder and saltpeter; over smuggling and prohibited merchandise; over exploitation of mines and forges; over the sale of paper and postal service; over epidemics and contagions; over public welfare, *dépôts de mendicité*, and *économats*; over public works in the cities, city streets, and community administration. But there is no question that the key functions, the functions that profoundly influenced the life of the people, had been turned over to the Estates.

Fréville has rightly concluded that in Brittany the *commissaire* dispatched by the central government gradually lost his role as an executant and manager, a head of administrative services, and became instead more of a political operative, responsible for keeping an eye on the province and for keeping the government informed. If need be, he could provide government ministers with detailed accounts of the various matters within his purview. This conclusion might perhaps be applicable to intendancies throughout the kingdom after 1787.

The National Constituent Assembly set up new administrative institutions. A decree of 14 December 1789 declared that all concentrations of population were to be regarded as municipalities. On 22 December the *départements* were established. On 25 June 1790, a circular letter from the secretary of state Saint-Priest to the intendants instructed them to file their papers with the new local assemblies. Some intendants enjoyed brilliant careers under the Revolution and Empire. Claude Petiot, head of the war department in the intendancy of Brittany, became *procureur général syndic* in the *département* of Ille-et-Vilaine, *commissaire aux armées*, member of the Conseil des Anciens under the Directory, administrator of the Cisalpine Republic, and then, on 8 February 1796, minister of war, crowning his career finally as senator of the Empire. He died on 25 May 1806. His eldest son, Pierre-François, became an auditor for the Conseil d'Etat, crown intendant for Tuscany, and in 1811 was made a baron.

If the monarchy had lasted, it is not beyond the realm of possibility that the intendants would have become officeholders in the full sense, or else bureaucrats.

Notes

1. Published in Gabriel Hanotaux, *Origines de l'institution des intendants des provinces* (Champion, 1884), pp. 234–36. Hanotaux mistakenly thought this to be an intendant's commission.

2. Minute, Archives de la Guerre, 13, document 75.

3. Charles Loyseau, "Cinq livres du droit des offices," in *Oeuvres*, new ed. (Pierre Lamy, 1640), p. 401.

4. Furetière, *Dictionnaire* (The Hague, 1609).

5. Arch. Nat., K 891, document no. 1.

6. Texts cited by Roland Mousnier, *La plume, la faucille, et le marteau* (Paris: PUF, 1970), pp. 181–82.

7. Cited by d'Arbois de Jubainville, *L'administration des intendants d'après les Archives de l'Aube*, p. 198.

8. Roland Mousnier, *Lettres et mémoires adressés au chancelier Séguier*, vol. 2: *Commissions d'intendants* (Paris: PUF, 1964), pp. 1043–89.

9. See the commissions published ibid., pp. 1043–89.

10. Cited by d'Arbois de Jubainville, *L'administration*, p. 211.

11. Cited by Mousnier, *La plume*, p. 315.

12. Cited ibid., p. 316.

13. Ibid., p. 318.

14. Ibid.

15. Arch. nat., K 891, *minute d'arrêt du Conseil du Roi*.

16. Published by Mousnier, *La plume*, pp. 212–13.

17. The commission has been published by Charles Godard, *Les pouvoirs des intendants sous Louis XIV, particulièrement dans les pays d'Elections: 1661–1715* (Société du Recueil Sirey, 1901), pp. 458–59.

18. Pierre Clément, *Lettres, instructions et mémoires de Colbert* (Imprimerie Impériale, later Imprimerie Nationale, 1861–82), vol. 2, part 1, no. 232, p. 266.

19. Cited by Pierre Dubuc, *L'intendance de Soissons sous Louis XIV: 1643–1715* (Albert Fontemoing, 1902), p. 299, based on Depping, *Correspondance administrative*, vol. 3, p. 306, and Bibliothèque nationale, Fonds Clairambault, 431–32.

20. Clément, *Lettres*, vol. 4, p. 157.

21. Ibid., no. 98, p. 108.

22. Ibid., no. 155.

23. Circular of 15 June 1682, Clément, *Lettres*, vol. 4, no. 155.

24. Cited by Godard, *Les pouvoirs*, p. 65.

25. The *généralités* of Alençon, Amiens, La Rochelle (Aunis before 1694), Bordeaux, Bourges, Caen, Champagne, Flanders (split off from Picardy), Grenoble, Limoges, Lyon, Metz, Montauban, Moulins, Orléans, Paris, Poitiers, Riom, Rouen, Roussillon, Soissons, Tours.

26. Cited by H. Monin, *Essai sur l'histoire administrative du Languedoc*, pp. 3 and 32.

27. Cited by Albert Croquez, *La Flandre wallonne et les pays de l'intendance de Lille sous Louis XIV* (H. Champion, 1912), p. 47.

28. His predecessor in Châlons.

29. A. M. de Boislisle, *Correspondance des contrôleurs généraux des finances avec les intendants des provinces* (Imprimerie Nationale, 1897), vol. 2, no. 80, p. 24.

30. Godard, *Les pouvoirs*, pp. 35–36.

31. Ibid., p. 36, n. 3: 1685 text.

32. Ibid., pp. 26–27, n. 1, based on Gauret, *Stile du Conseil du roi*, p. 463.

33. Dubuc, *L'intendance de Soissons*, pp. 110–11, based on the archives of the *greffe* of Laon, *procédures criminelles, liasse* 32.

34. Ibid., p. 186.

35. Bibliothèque nationale, ms. français 21 812, unpublished.

36. Michel Lhéritier, *Tourny: 1695–1760* (Paris: Félix Alcan, 1920), p. 243, n. 2.

37. Clément, *Lettres*, vol. 3, part 2.

38. Lhéritier, *Tourny*, p. 240 and n. 3.

39. Ibid., vol. 2, pp. 7–12.

40. Guyot and Merlin, *Traité des droits* (Visse, 1787), vol. 3, pp. 131–33.

41. Paul Ardascheff, *Les intendants de province sous Louis XVI*, trans. Jousserandot (Paris: Félix Alcan, 1909), vol. 2, p. 116.

42. Ibid., p. 181.

Guide to Further Reading

Antoine, Michel. "Le gouvernement et l'administration sous Louis XV." *Dictionnaire bio-graphique*. Editions du Centre national de recherche scientifique, 1978.

———. "La notion de subdélégation dans la monarchie d'Ancien Régime." *Bibliothèque de l'Ecole des Chartes* 132 (1974): 267–87.

Ardascheff, Paul. *Les intendants de province sous Louis XVI*. Vol. 2. Translated by Jousse-randot. Paris: Felix Alcan, 1909.

Avenel, Vicomte Georges d'. *Richelieu et la monarchie absolue*. Vol. 4.

Barbiche, B. "Les commissaires du régalement des tailles en 1598–1599." *Bibliothèque de l'Ecole des Chartes* 108 (1960): 58–96.

Bayard, F. "Les Chambres de Justice de la première moitié du XVIIᵉ siècle." *Cahiers d'histoire* 19 (1974): 121–40.

Boislisle, A. M. de. *Correspondance des contrôleurs généraux des finances avec les intendants des provinces*. 3 vols. Imprimerie Nationale, 1897.

Bonney, Richard. *Political Change in France under Richelieu and Mazarin (1624–1661)*. New York: Oxford University Press.

Bordès, Maurice. *D'Etigny et l'administration de l'intendance d'Auch (1751–1767)*. 2 vols. Auch: Frédéric Cocharaux, 1957.

Busquet, Raoul. *Etudes sur l'ancienne Provence*. Librairie ancienne Honoré-Champion, 1930.

Clément, Pierre. *Lettres, instructions et mémoires de Colbert*. 10 vols. Imprimerie Impériale, later Imprimerie Nationale, 1861–82.

Croquez, Albert. *La Flandre wallonne et les pays de l'intendance de Lille sous Louis XIV*. H. Champion, 1912.

Dubuc, Pierre. *L'intendance de Soissons sous Louis XIV (1643–1715)*. Albert Fontemoing, 1902.

Dumas, F. *La généralité de Tours au XVIIIᵉ siècle: Administration de l'intendant du Cluzel (1766–1783)*. Paris: Hachette, 1894.

Durand, Yves. *La maison de Durfort à l'époque moderne*. Fontenay-le-Comte: Imprimerie Lussaud, 1975.

Esmonin, Edmond. "Les intendants du Dauphiné." *Annales de l'Université de Grenoble* 34 (1923).

———. "Origines des subdélégués des intendants." *Bulletin de la Société d'histoire moderne*, 1 December 1946.

Fréville, Henri. *L'intendance de Bretagne (1689–1790)*. 3 vols. Rennes: Plihon, 1953.

Garrisson, F. "Essai sur les commissions d'application de l'Edit de Nantes. Part I: Règne de Henri IV." Thesis, Faculté de Droit, Université de Paris, 1950.

Godard, Charles. *Les pouvoirs des intendants sous Louis XIV, particulièrement dans les pays d'Elections (1661–1715)*. Société du Recueil Sirey, 1901.

Guérin. L. *L'intendant de Cypierre et la vie économique de l'Orléanais (1760–1787)*.

Guyot. *Répertoire universel et raisonné de jurisprudence*. Vol. 8: "Gouverneurs." 1784.

——— and Merlin. *Traité des droits*. Vol. 3: *Les intendants des provinces*. Visse, 1787.

Gruder, Vivian R. *The Royal Provincial Intendants*. Ithaca, N.Y.: Cornell University Press, 1968.

Hanotaux, Gabriel. *Origines de l'institution des intendants des provinces*. Champion, 1884.

Hughes, Gustave d'. "Essai sur l'administration de Turgot dans la généralité de Limoges." Thesis in letters, Paris, 1859.

La Force, Duc de. *Le maréchal de la Force: Un serviteur de sept rois (1558–1652)*. Paris: Plon, 1950.

Le Bigre, Arlette. *Les Grands Jours d'Auvergne*. Paris: Hachette, 1976.

Lhéritier, Michel. *Tourny (1695–1760)*. 2 vols. Paris: Félix Alcan, 1920.

Livet, Georges. *L'intendance d'Alsace sous Louis XIV (1648–1715)*. Strasbourg: Publications de la Faculté des Lettres de l'Université de Strasbourg, 1956.

————. *Le duc Mazarin, gouverneur d'Alsace (1661–1713)*. *Lettres et documents inédits*. Publication 10 of the Institut des hautes études Alsaciennes. Strasbourg: Edition F. X. Le Roux, 1954.

Loyseau, Charles. "Cinq livres du droit des offices." In *Oeuvres*. New ed., Pierre Lamy, 1640.

Maletke, Klaus. " 'Trésoriers généraux de France' und Intendanten unter Ludwig XIV. Studien zur Frage der Beziehungen zwischen 'Officiers' und 'Commissaires' im 17. Jahrhundert." *Historische Zeitschrift* 220 (1975): 298–323.

Mention, Léon. *Le comte de Saint-Germain et ses réformes d'après les Archives du Dépôt de la Guerre. Etude sur l'armée française à la fin du XVIIIe siècle*. Librairie militaire L. Baudouin, 1884.

Moreau, Henri. "Les subdélégués dans la généralité de Bourgogne sous l'intendant Bouchu et ses premiers successeurs." *Annales de Bourgogne* 20 (1948): 165–89.

Mousnier, Roland. "Etat et commissaire. Recherches sur la création des intendants des provinces." *Forschungen zur Staat und Verfassung, Festgabe für Fritz Hartung*. 1958. Reprinted in *La Plume, la faucille et le marteau*. Paris: PUF, 1970, pp. 181–99.

————. "Les rapports entre les gouverneurs de province et les intendants dans la première moitié du XVIIIe siècle." *Revue historique* 228 (1962). Reprinted in *La plume, la faucille et le marteau*, pp. 210–13.

————. "Recherches sur les syndicats d'officiers pendant la Fronde: Trésoriers généraux de France et Elus dans la révolution." *XVIIe siècle* 42–43 (1959). Reprinted in *La plume, la faucille et le marteau*, pp. 301–33.

————. *Lettres et mémoires adressés au chancelier Séguier (1633–1649)*. 2 vols. Paris: PUF, 1970.

Necker, Jacques. "Sur la nomination aux intendances de province." In *De l'administration des finances de la France*. Vol. 3, pp. 379–86. 1784.

Richou, J. "Histoire des commissions extraordinaires sous l'Ancien Régime." Thesis in law, Paris, 1905.

Ricommard, J. "Les subdélégués des intendants jusqu'à leur création en titre d'office." *Revue d'histoire moderne*, September-December 1937.

————. "L'édit d'avril 1704 et l'érection en titre d'office des subdélégués des intendants." *Revue historique* 195 (1945).

————. "La vente des offices de subdélégués." *Revue historique de droit français et étranger*, 1942–43.

————. "La suppression et la liquidation des offices des subdélégués," *Revue historique de droit français et étranger* 26 (1948).

Vialatte, Louis. *Rossignol, intendant de la généralité de Riom et province d'Auvergne (1734–1750)*. Aurillac: Imprimerie J. Brousse, 1924.

Zeller, Gaston. "L'administration monarchique avant les intendants. Parlements et gouverneurs." *Revue historique* 197 (1947): 180–215.

7 The Emergence of a Bureaucracy

The ministries and intendancies employed in their bureaus clerks of various ranks, ranging from first and second secretary, bureau chief, *commis* first class, and *commis* second class down to scribe and copyist. These clerks gradually assumed more and more of the characteristics of the modern bureaucrat but never really became bureaucrats in the full sense. The members of the *corps des Ponts et Chaussées* came even closer in practice to being bureaucrats, so close, in fact, that the historian may consider them to have been such despite the absence of legal recognition of their status. Doubt remains in regard to certain other public servants, such as royal engineers, naval *commissaires*, and the like. Thus it will behoove us first to look at the *corps des Ponts et Chaussées* before turning to a more doubtful case.

27   The *Corps des Ponts et Chaussées*

The inspectors general and engineers working for the *corps des Ponts et Chaussées* (Department of Bridges and Highways) were at first *commissaires*. Their commissions were issued in the form of council decrees based on reports filed by the *contrôleur général des Finances*. One *commissaire* served as director general of Ponts et Chaussées, a post he held jointly with an *intendant des Finances*. In 1736 the *Almanach royal* began listing the *contrôleur général des Finances* as director general of Ponts et Chaussées. An *intendant des Finances* was assigned "detailed responsibility" for Ponts et Chaussées. The council decree of 1 April 1743 assigned this task to Daniel Trudaine, *intendant des Finances*. Commissions had been given since 1716 to one inspector general and "architect-engineer," one "engineer and first architect," three inspectors, and twenty-one engineers assigned to the *généralités*. This number soon had to be increased. All these *commissaires* received fixed compensation. Though there was no legal entitlement, practically all received a retirement pension after long years of service, when they could no longer carry out their duties owing to age or ill health. In practice, then, they held their posts for long periods. But recruitment was not competitive. The king readily allowed the son of an engineer or the apprentice who had worked with him to have the master's *survivance* and eventually to succeed him in office.

These permanent *commissaires* formed the basic staff of the department. They were reinforced by temporary *commissaires* used to carry out large projects such as the construction of bridges on the Loire. Among the temporary appointees were deputy inspectors, deputy engineers, and project supervisors, who worked under the supervision of the permanent staff. This is where the mettle of sons and apprentices could be tested. The engineer for the *généralité* of Lyon, Deville, supervised his son's work as deputy inspector on the Guillotière bridge project in 1719. The younger Deville became a deputy engineer in 1732 and then succeeded his father as engineer for the *généralité* of Lyon in 1741.

As this corps of *commissaires* came into its own, offices with similar responsibilities gradually died out. The intendant for dikes and levees, for example, was replaced by an engineer of similar title in 1718. Formally speaking, the *trésoriers de France* no longer had the power to inspect the work of the Ponts et Chaussées except in conjunction with the intendant and upon the issuance of a specific commission (the *trésoriers* in the *généralité* of Paris were exempted from this requirement). In 1719, however, a council decree commissioned four *trésoriers de France* to inspect the maintenance of roads.

Interpretive instructions attached to the council decree of 3 May 1720 made the intendants responsible for deciding which roads would be designated major royal roads and highways, destined to be widened to a width of seventy-two feet, lined with ditches, straightened, repaired, and edged with trees. Other roads were to be thirty-six feet wide. The intendants were also supposed to prepare a general road plan, together with maps, and suggest routes for each individual road.

Carrying out this project meant finding workers to do the job. The intendants recruited compulsory labor from communities along the way, generally imposing *corvées* of six days' labor per year, gradually increased after 1726. By 1736 *corvées* had been established in all *généralités* in the *pays d'élections*. General rules were laid down on 13 June 1738.

The project also required the assistance of skilled experts: inspectors, engineers, and deputy engineers. This need eventually led to the creation of the Ecole des Ponts et Chaussées. On 10 February 1744, a drafting office was set up in Paris. Following a proposal submitted by Trudaine, the council decree of 14 February 1747 appointed Perronet, the engineer for the *généralité* of Alençon, project director for the entire kingdom and also made him head of the drafting office with responsibility for training draftsmen in the art of drawing, in science, and in other practical skills required by the Ponts et Chaussées. The school soon grew into an entity distinct from the drafting office and was dubbed the Ecole des Ponts et Chaussées. This became its official name in 1775. Regulations governing the operation of the school were issued by the *contrôleur général des Finances* on 11 December 1747, supplemented by the regulations of 19 February 1775, and reiterated by the regulations of 20 April 1784, signed by Calonne.

After some initial groping, recruitment settled down into a regular pattern. Candidates for admission to the school had to be of good family. The sons of guild craftsmen were rejected, because the manual trades were considered to be base occupations. Candidates were required to be well-bred and of good moral character and to have completed a third-year class in a *collège*, good grammar being essential because of the need to engage in extensive correspondence, draft clear plans, and defend them against criticism. They also had to be unmarried.

Prospective students began their training by working as draftsmen, surveyors, or project supervisors in the office of a chief engineer. When the engineer thought the student was ready, he submitted a letter of recommendation to the admissions board. This letter was an absolute necessity. It carried greater weight if the candidate was the son of an engineer.

Candidates with the necessary recommendations then did six months' training as *aspirants* or *surnuméraires*. In 1748 *aspirants* began studying at Blondel's school of architecture. They took compulsory courses in mathematics and drafting. Grades were issued quarterly. Those with the best grades in basic mathematics and drafting were then admitted to the Ecole, provided they had the size and stamina to withstand the rigors of working for the Ponts et Chaussées.

The school was divided into three classes of twenty students each. Courses began in November. They met every day except Sundays and holidays, in winter from eight in the morning until two in the afternoon and from four in the afternoon until nine in the evening, and in summer from six in the morning until two in the afternoon. Written examinations were given each winter and graded by a jury composed of inspectors general, architects, members of the Academy of Sciences, and royal painters. Prizes were awarded to the best students. During the summer students worked on projects under the supervision of a chief engineer, acting as maintenance inspectors. Graduates were rated according to the courses they had taken, the work they had done in instructing other students, their test results, and their practical work. Beginning in 1773, each of these items counted for a specified number of "points" in the rating. Students were ranked on the basis of the total number of points they amassed.

In the first class, students continued their studies in theoretical and practical geometry, mechanics, hydraulics, and computation and measurement of surfaces and solids. If they had not qualified for admission to the second class after two years of study, they were dismissed.

In the second class, students began studying the use of surveying equipment and architecture, continued advanced studies in theoretical and practical geometry, and began drawing up plans for bridges of wood and stone and other public works.

In the third class, they prepared to assume the duties of a deputy inspector or engineer.

Students with the best grades were admitted to the next-higher class as vacancies appeared. Thus the length of a student's schooling varied with the quality of the student and the need for deputy engineers. In 1767 the minimum duration of the program was two years eight months and the maximum nine and a half years. The corresponding figures in 1776 were four years five months and twelve years. In that year one deputy engineer graduated at age twenty-four, while another graduated at age thirty-seven.

Many students became discouraged by this slow advancement. Between 1769 and 1788, 387 students were admitted but only 141 graduated as deputy engineers. Two hundred forty-six students dropped out. Those who failed to graduate became architects, entrepreneurs, project supervisors, or engineers in the *pays d'Etats*.

Thus students for the school were recruited partly on the basis of competitive examination, partly on the basis of attainments. Deputy engineers were then graduated after a winnowing process involving a series of competitive examinations.

Graduates were strictly rank-ordered, and their career opportunities and salaries were based on this ranking. It was customary for the *intendant des Finances* in charge of the Ponts et Chaussées to meet on Sundays for an exchange of views with the first engineer and inspectors general, chief engineers who happened to be in Paris, the engineer in charge of dykes and levies, and sometimes also the *trésoriers de France* commissioned to look after the Ponts et Chaussées in the *généralité* of Paris, together with one or two members of the Academy of Sciences. The council decree of 7 July 1750 reorganized the corps: it was henceforth to be headed by an architect–first-engineer, who supervised four inspectors general, a director of the office of surveyors and draftsmen, and twenty-five chief engineers who served in all the provinces as needed, supervising and inspecting work and issuing certificates of acceptance.

Below this group in rank came a second group of employees divided into three categories by the instructions of 16 December 1754: the deputy inspectors, later known as the inspectors of Ponts et Chaussées, who reported directly to the inspectors general and the first engineer; the deputy engineers, who reported to the engineers; and the students from the Ecole des Ponts et Chaussées assigned to various work sites. The edict of January 1772 did away with the office of intendant general of dykes and levies.

Thanks to the code of regulations issued by Trudaine and Perronet and to custom, the engineers of the Ponts et Chaussees acquired a status akin to that of a modern bureaucrat. Each was obliged to obey the orders of his superior in the hierarchy. The intendant in each *généralité* was the ranking representative of the Ponts et Chaussées and gave orders to the chief engineer. All officials had to make do with their official salary; collusion with contractors was strictly forbidden. Engineers were required to maintain secrecy about their activities. They were not allowed to publish anything without the approval of their superiors. They were supposed to avoid public discussion of their work and refrain from answering attacks by journalists or writers. The engineer was supposed to work for the good of the state and keep his mouth shut.

Engineers were obliged to reside in the district to which they were assigned. Unauthorized absences were not allowed. Their private lives were subject to strict rules. Marriages had to be approved by Trudaine and Perronet. They were supposed to marry into good society, choosing women who were pleasing to the eye and provided with sufficient dowry. Engineers were required to seek admission into the highest society and to frequent the nobility and high clergy. They were to maintain a level of existence commensurate with their station and avoid contact with people from lower walks of life.

Promotion was handled in such a way as to take account only of merit and leave recommendations aside. Perronet kept a table listing engineers and inspectors in order of seniority, and this ranking governed all promotions, which came slowly. Exceptions were made only for the most able. One story has it that Louis XV once pointed out to Trudaine a man whom the marquise de Pompadour wished to recommend for the post of chief engineer. Trudaine is said to have answered, "That is not allowed, Sire." "Why?" asked the king. "Because such an appointment would require Your Majesty to have the goodness to name two chief engineers, one to receive the salary of the post and the other to carry out the duties that the gentleman proposed is not capable of fulfilling." The king did not press the matter any further.

Salaries were modest. Students at the school were paid 1,000 livres. Deputy engineers started at 1,200 per year. The pay was too low. Beginning in 1782, the family of a deputy engineer had to agree to pay 600 livres for his upkeep. A few years later the salary was raised to 1,500 livres. Deputy inspectors (later called inspectors) received 1,800 livres per year, but they needed nearly 2,000 to live, not counting the capitation or costs of correspondence. The position required keeping a valet and two horses. Chief engineers were paid 2,400 livres per year. After taxes this left 2,022 livres. Inspectors general were paid 6,000 livres, the first engineer, 8,000. But Perronet received the exceptional salary of 16,000 livres.

The salary was supplemented by payments to cover travel costs, office expenses, and sometimes housing. Functionaries almost always received bonuses for the work they did. These amounted to an average of 200 to 300 livres annually for a deputy engineer and could run as high as 2,400 livres for a chief engineer, thus doubling his salary. *Généralités* and cities paid additional sums for work done by the engineers on the side. Some engineers managed to triple their basic salary in this way.

There was no fixed retirement age. Some engineers stayed on the job until they were past eighty, others worked until they died. Those who were forced to quit for reasons of age or ill health were never refused a pension. If in need, engineers' widows also received pensions. The instructions of 20 April 1784 provided a pension of 500 livres and an inspector's brevet or 800 livres and an engineer's brevet to deputy inspectors and engineers, respectively, if they were judged worthy after twenty-five years of service.

Engineers looked upon one another as old schoolmates and displayed a lively *esprit de corps*. Some founded dynasties of engineers, son following in the footsteps of father. Highly skilled and devoted to duty and country, French engineers were the envy of all Europe. Foreign governments asked for graduates of the Ecole des Ponts et Chaussées to be sent to their countries to build roads or to organize similar corps of experts. The king of Denmark made such a request in 1763, and three French engineers were working in the service of the king of Spain in 1783. Perronet, the head of the corps, received letters of nobility in March 1763. He had thirteen bridges built according to his plans. In 1778 the Court of Russia asked him to plan a bridge on the Neva. By 1792 he had become a member of the Royal Academies of Science, Architecture, and Agriculture in Paris, of the Royal Society of London, of the academies of Stockholm and Berlin, and so on. He died in office on 8 February 1794 at the age of eighty-six.

It should be noted, however, that while the engineers of the Ponts et Chaussées were, according to custom, modern bureaucrats in most respects, by law they remained commissioned servants of the state.

28   The Engineers of the *Corps des Fortifications*

As superintendent of fortifications, Sully in 1604 issued a code of regulations known as the Grand Règlement, which set forth the duties of engineers working for the *Corps des Fortifications*. These rules were still in force at the end of the seventeenth century, and some at the end of the eighteenth. Each of the engineers in question was assigned responsibility for a certain district within a province. All were under the orders of the governor of the province in which they were stationed. The engineers proposed projects for the coming year and drew up plans including design drawings, reports, surveys, and cost estimates. They hired contractors to do the work and kept an eye on their progress. When the work was complete, the engineers inspected the finished product before accepting delivery.

The engineers were themselves subject to scrutiny by a number of office-holders: the *contrôleurs des Fortifications*, the *trésoriers des Fortifications*, and the *surintendant des Finances*. But the engineers were *commissaires*. In Sully's time there were only a few of them, from four to six in number, usually chosen from among the architects by the *surintendant des Finances*.

During the wars fought by Louis XIII and Louis XIV down to the time of the Peace of the Pyrenees in 1659, the number of engineers increased. In 1643 they were placed under the authority of the secretary of state for war, Michel Le Tellier, represented in the provinces by the intendants for justice, administration, and finance. Names that were destined to become famous came to the fore: the chevalier de Clerville, d'Aspremont, Mesgrigny, and Vauban. The engineer's status did not change, however: he remained a *commissaire* and belonged to no *corps*.

After 1661, administrative control over the engineers was divided between the war department and the navy department, between Le Tellier and Louvois on the one hand and Colbert and Seignelay on the other. The technical aspects of the engineers' work were overseen by a single authority, however: the *commissaire général des Fortifications*, a post held by the chevalier de Clerville until 1668, when he was replaced by Vauban, who was named *commissaire général* officially in 1677 when de Clerville died. In 1691 there were 267 active engineers. A formal organization began to take shape. Under Louvois's wartime administration, all the engineers in a particular place were grouped under an engineer brigadier, who commanded a deputy brigadier, a brigade captain, and a number of ordinary engineers. During peacetime the intendant for justice, administration, and finance in each *généralité* supervised the work of the engineers and regulated bidding on projects and final acceptance of completed work. For each site or group of sites there was a senior engineer who gave orders to the other engineers. All of them were *commissaires*. Under Colbert's administration, there were three major sections: coastal fortifications, land fortifications, and coastal fortifications in Provence. Each was headed by an *intendant des Fortifications*, who owned his office. Within each section, projects in one particular region might be placed under the command of an engineer general, a *commissaire*. Within each fortified city or group of smaller cities, a senior engineer had responsibility for the work of his subordinates: engineers second class, deputy engineers, and project inspectors. All were *commissaires*.

Following the death of Louvois, the king established a "department of land and coastal fortifications" on 22 July 1691 and appointed an *intendant des Finances*, Michel Le Peletier de Souzy, to serve as director general. Vauban remained *commissaire général des Fortifications*. Around these two leaders a "bureau of fortifications" was organized.

Until this point there had been two categories of engineers: combat engineers, who built trenches, and *bâtisseurs*, who built fortresses. Combat engineers were officers in the royal army who had acquired battlefield experience in trench building. Their engineer's brevet did not raise their rank but did allow them to be promoted to higher ranks within the army. Fortress engineers were recruited among the master masons and architects. Quite a few of them had worked on royal projects in Paris, Versailles, etc. They were assisted by experts in hydraulics and map makers. Those who worked under Colbert and the navy department were civilians, who figured on the payroll of the Corps des Fortifications and received a royal brevet as engineers. Those who worked under Louvois and the war department were classed with the retired army officers and received the equivalent of a retirement pension. They figured on the rolls of the regiments as lieutenants or company commanders but rarely rose higher than the rank of captain.

Beginning in 1698, the director general of fortifications attempted to bring all the engineers together under the umbrella of a single organization. Fortified cities were grouped together in twenty-three directorates, each under the command of a director supervised by the intendant of the appropriate *généralité*. The position of *intendant des Fortifications* was eliminated in 1692. Each directorate was divided into a number of districts known as *chefferies*, consisting of a fortress or group of fortresses. Each *chefferie* was assigned to a chief engineer, who had command over one or more ordinary engineers.

From 1697 on, prospective engineers were required to pass an entrance examination administered by either Vauban or Sauveur, a mathematician and member of the Academy of Sciences. Those who passed this examination were then sent for training to a chief engineer, who reported on their progress to the director general. If a candidate's progress was unsatisfactory, he was sent to the infantry. If he was judged worthy of promotion, he had to wait for a place to become available. During the War of the Spanish Succession, this waiting period was short, because many engineers were killed or wounded. Between 1699 and 1715, 334 engineers were taken into the service. Twenty-eight of these were killed, and 95 others died of wounds or illness or else retired prior to 1714. A man had to serve two years before he became eligible to be inscribed on the engineers' payroll. He could then be promoted within the engineering hierarchy by brevet. But he had to wait to be assigned a place as a retired military officer. Each year the king granted only a very few such places to the corps of engineers. In 1714 three-quarters of the ordinary engineers had not yet been made lieutenants. It took years to become a captain. A few ordinary engineers held this rank, and most chief engineers did, but even of the chief engineers thirty had not as yet been assigned regular military rank. Civilian engineers were thus at a disadvantage by comparison with army officers who obtained an engineer's brevet in the field, for the latter enjoyed more rapid advancement. In any case, the civilian engineers were *commissaires* who had to wait to be appointed regular officers. They were not bureaucrats or civil servants in the modern sense.

The director general now and then revoked the commission of an engineer found to be misappropriating public funds. He made sure that engineers lived in a manner commensurate with their position and threatened to "strike from the engineers' payroll," i.e., revoke the commissions of, any engineers who continued "to live a libertine existence." The corps of engineers enjoyed prestige and had an *esprit de corps* of its own. Quite a few nobles (some recently ennobled) joined its ranks.

After the death of Louis XIV, Michel Le Peletier was dismissed. The position of *commissaire général des Fortifications* was eliminated. The marquis d'Asfeld, *lieutenant général*, was appointed by the regent to the post of "First Engineer to His Majesty," at the head of a bureau of fortifications staffed by civilians. D'Asfeld continued to head this bureau until his death on 7 March 1743.

Recruitment of engineers resumed in 1719. The number of engineers increased in 1726 and during the War of the Polish Succession. Thirty engineers were added in 1723 and 33 more in 1726, some replacing engineers who had died or retired, others filling new posts. In all, 297 new engineers were added between 1719 and 1743. D'Asfeld looked upon the corps he commanded as a family. Examination of prospective engineers was done by François Chevallier, a member of the Academy of Sciences and professor of mathematics to the king and the pages of the Petite Ecurie, the nephew of the previous examiner. After field training candidates were admitted to the corps thanks to the backing of such important figures as the comte de Toulouse or the dowager princesse de Conti or upon the recommendation of a relative who was an officer in the royal army. The best recommendation was to be a "child of the corps," that is, a son, grandson, nephew, or brother of one of the royal engineers. Of 309 new engineers who joined the corps between 1716 and 1747, 132 were sons of engineers. Two out of three engineers' sons who applied were accepted. The corps recruited from within.

Engineers remained simply royal brevet holders, commissioned to perform certain specific duties by the king. They might come to hold office. But they were not civil servants or bureaucrats in the modern sense.

After the death of d'Asfeld at the height of the War of the Austrian Succession, the bureau of fortifications was transferred by the regulation of 10 March 1743 to the authority of the secretary of state for war, except for coastal fortifications within the purview of the navy department. The trench engineers had always been under the authority of the secretary of state for war during wartime, moreover.

The new minister of war, Marc-René de Voyer, comte d'Argenson, proposed integrating the engineers into the army. The ordinance of 7 February 1744 fixed "the engineer's term of service and rank," which had previously been fixed by custom. All young combat engineers were named reserve lieutenants but did not receive the corresponding salary. Twenty-five positions with the rank of reserve lieutenant-colonel and ten with the rank of reserve colonel were made available to make room for promotion of engineers, because previously many directors had been forced to end their careers at the rank of reserve captain.

At about the same time as the Ecole des Ponts et Chaussées, the Engineering School of Mézières was established between 1748 and 1751, the first code of regulations being issued on 10 May 1748. The founder of the school was Antoine de Chastillon, chevalier, baron d'Oger, and chief engineer at Mézières. The school taught the basics of arithmetic, geometry, trigonometry, mechanics, hydraulics, drafting, map making, architectural drawing, land layout and measurement, and cost estimating (taking account of the price, weight, and distance of materials). Each week students were required to do four days of theoretical training in the classroom and two days of practical training in the field. Classes were held from eight until eleven in the morning and from two to five in the afternoon. Every student listened to the lecture and then recited in turn on its contents during the same session of the class. A review followed each section of the course, and each student went over what he had learned one more time. Candidates had to undergo a preliminary examination in Paris. The course lasted two years, after which students were sent to work with fortress directors for practical training and a final examination. The Engineering School remained in existence from 1748 until 1793. Five hundred forty-two engineers were graduated.

In order to take the entrance examination candidates had to obtain a letter from the secretary of state for war. They had to submit a baptismal certificate and detailed information about their family countersigned by four *gentils-hommes* from their province. Preference was given to *gentilshommes*, persons "living as nobles," and sons or relatives of army officers. The children of manual workers and retail merchants were strictly forbidden to take the examination. The regulation of May 1777 required that candidates be either nobles or sons of officers of high rank, such as colonel, lieutenant-colonel, major, or captain chevalier de Saint-Louis.

After the necessary credentials were examined the candidate proceeded to the entrance examination proper. Since only the most able were admitted, this was a truly competitive examination. Candidates had to demonstrate thorough knowledge of five treatises on technical subjects: Camus's elements of arithmetic, geometry, and mechanics, and two treatises on hydraulics by Varignon and Mariotte. The latter two works were replaced in 1768 by works of Bossut. One candidate in six was admitted. The effect of the competitive examination was to reduce the proportion of sons of engineers and military officers from two-thirds to thirty-six percent and to increase the proportion of sons of judicial and financial officers and royal secretaries from one-third to two-thirds. Despite the regulation of 1777, one-quarter of the students were still sons of commoners, including old captains chevaliers de Saint-Louis, subdelegates, and *avocats*, some of them in the process of acquiring nobility.

The ordinance of 8 December 1755 combined the artillery and the engineers in an organization known as the Royal Corps of Artillery and Engineering. This was not a happy decision. The ordinance of 5 May 1758 disbanded this unit and created a separate Corps of Military Engineers. The ordinance of 10 March 1759 established a complement of 300 men for this corps, all to be known as ordinary royal engineers. Attached to the new unit were the companies of sappers and mine-layers hitherto attached to the Royal Artillery. The number of royal engineers was increased to 400 on 4 December 1762. Legally, the engineers were still *commissaires*. The ordinance of 31 December 1776 changed the name of the Corps of Military Engineers to the Royal Engineering Corps and set its complement at 329. The engineers were made military offices, henceforth to be referred to by rank and by the title "officer in the Royal Engineering Corps."

Thus little by little all the brevet-holding *commissaires* were made military officers and completely assimilated to the military. The king moved from reliance on the *commissaire* to reliance on the officer. Is it correct to view military officers as civil servants prior to 1789? Although military engineers were recruited by competitive examination, enjoyed stability of tenure, had a precise rank in a hierarchy, were paid a salary supplemented by bonuses or pensions, enjoyed a clear sequence of promotion, and could look forward to paid retirement, it does not seem possible to regard them as civil servants in the modern sense. They had some of the characteristics of the modern bureaucrat, it would seem, but not all of them.

The same question could be asked about other categories of public employee: Were they *commissaires, commis,* officeholders, or bureaucrats? We might raise this question about shipbuilding engineers from 1765 on, or about the personnel in the veterinary schools, or even about navy commissaries during the time of Colbert, from 1670 on. Until further information has been gathered we subscribe to the conclusion reached by Gaxotte: in France it was around 1750 that the celebrated Mr. Bureaucrat first appeared. He was destined for a bright future in the nineteenth and twentieth centuries. The bureaucrat emerged and flourished precisely in the most technical areas of government, in the departments that most required accurate technical knowledge and steady perseverance.

Guide to Further Reading

Blanchard, Anne. *Les ingénieurs du "Roy" de Louis XIV à Louis XVI.* Montpellier, 1979. No. 9 in the Military History Collection of the Montpellier National Defense Studies, this document can be obtained by writing to Université Paul-Valéry (Montpellier III), route de Mende, B.P. 5043, 34032 Montpellier.
Petot, Jean. *Histoire de l'administration des Ponts et Chaussées* (1599–1815). Paris: Librairie Marcel Rivière, 1958.
Taillemite. *Colbert, secrétaire d'Etat de la Marine, et les réformes de 1669.* Paris: Académie de Marine, 1970.

8 The Battle between the Officeholders and the *Commissaires*

A Dispute That Lasted Three Hundred Years

Chancellor Maupeou, the conqueror of the *parlements*, is supposed to have said when they were recalled in November 1774: "In a case that has dragged on for three hundred years, I managed to win a decision in the king's favor. . . . Now he is going to lose it again. . . . He is finished!"[1]

This three-hundred year dispute (the beginning of which the chancellor thus situated in the reign of Louis XI) was the conflict between the sovereign courts and the king's Council and *commissaires*. To the Council, which was composed of *commis*, the courts refused all authority unless the king was present. And they were inevitably drawn into conflict with the *commissaires*, through whom the king attempted to impose his will over them and to regain some of the power that had been lost to the officeholders once offices came to be sold and viewed by their owners as something akin to their own property.

29   Henri IV, Victor

Following the Treaty of Vervins and the Edict of Nantes (1598), the conflict between the sovereign courts and the king's Council abated somewhat owing to the prestige of the newly victorious king, but it was nonetheless real. Henri IV tried to centralize power in his Council, and particularly in the Conseil d'Etat et des Finances. For this purpose he employed Rosny (who became duc de Sully in 1606) in the role of a *surintendant des Finances* without the name, probably as early as 1599. Sully attempted, somewhat prematurely, to accomplish what Antoine has so aptly called the "revolution of 1661": the creation of a ministerial department under the head of finance and having general responsibility for the administration of the entire kingdom, which would use *commissaires* to carry out its decisions in the provinces, thereby relegating the chief judicial officer, the chancellor, who had hitherto controlled the government and administration, to the second rank. "The spirit of justice, which had until then inspired the kingdom and breathed life into its institutions, was replaced by the spirit of finance, by a concern for efficiency and tangible results."[1] Had Ravaillac been prevented from wielding his knife, this revolution would probably have been accomplished in 1605.

Bellièvre and the "Fourth Estate"

Bellièvre, who became chancellor in 1599, always favored the concept of a monarchy tempered by the "fourth estate," the men of the gown. It would have pleased him if the king had never made any decision that was not consistent with previous ordinances, judicial forms, the customs and traditions of the monarchy, and the "fundamental laws of the kingdom." Knowledge of these things, and the responsibility to protect them, belonged to the king's officeholders, particularly the members of the sovereign courts, a number of whom were among the most active members of the king's councils. Accordingly, the king should never make any decision without their advice, which he must always take fully into account. He should pay attention to the remonstrances of his officeholders and never issue a decree without the agreement of his councillors. All royal actions should be taken in council, and the reasons for all decisions should be fully laid out. No seal should be affixed except in public and in due form. If it were necessary to affix the seal to some letter outside the regular forms, this should be done only on express orders from the king in cases on which action could not, in the judgment of his chancellor and council, be delayed until the regular day set aside for affixing the seal. It should be done in the sight of all officers of the chancellery and with the approval of the *maîtres des requêtes* who were present, so that, even in extraordinary circumstances, publicity might serve as a check to royal caprice.

Above all else, the chancellor would have liked to see the *parlements* graced with power and honor. Members of these bodies, in his view, should have been recruited from a few families that owed their nobility to the service of the king. The *parlements* should have been the "emanation" of a respected "estate," influential thanks to the wealth and connections of the men who sat in them. The king, by renouncing the power of evocation, should have ended competition between the courts and the Council in matters of justice. The *parlements* should not only have exercised high powers of justice and administration but should not have been subject to having their decisions overruled by the Council. Beyond all this, the *parlements* should have been asked regularly by the king for their advice in matters of policy, and they should have had the power to take up affairs of state on their own, to act as a true Council of State. Had they been protected from competition with the king's *commissaires* and invested with great authority, the *parlements* would have used all their power in behalf of a king attentive to their remonstrances, serving him but also guiding him.

The chancellor understood that such participation in the government and administration needed to be justified by service and by the demonstrable virtue of the *parlements*. Officeholders were supposed to form an elite. Posts should have gone only to able members of old families, loyal to the king, or to members of new families who distinguished themselves in some way. The chancellor concerned himself with the character of *robins*, with the spotlessness of their morals, and with their professional scruples. He was incensed by the role of money in the recruitment of officers. He was opposed to the sale of offices, but this had become second nature among the French. The king should at least have made use of *survivances* and the forty days clause, of rebates on resignation dues, and of offices vacated by death in order to awaken awareness of the character of a good magistrate, in order to compensate the loyalest and ablest of his subjects and to facilitate their access to office and their rise in the hierarchy.

The chancellor was inspired by the spirit of justice. This, together with the loyalty and hence the obedience due the king, dictated that the dignity of judicial office be respected. Accordingly, procedural forms must be followed to the letter. The king and his subjects must stand in correct relation to one another, and the king's subjects must stand in proper relation to themselves; the courts must see to it that this was the case. The courts must also see to it that both conscience and *raison d'état* were given due weight in providing for the needs of the people. The people's burden must be lightened so that they did not collapse under its weight. The chancellor therefore wished to see taxes reduced and offices eliminated. This would not only increase the importance of the more senior officers who would remain but would reduce the amounts to be paid by the king in salaries and by the taxpayers in *épices* and other dues. A large number of men would be freed for commerce and farming, thereby increasing the number of tax-payers and their capacity to pay. The chancellor dreamed of administering a nation in peace, peace being favorable to both labor and gain.

But the king was turned away from this policy by internal rebellions such as the Biron conspiracy, by the constant threat of sedition, and by the growing need to prepare for intervention in the conflicts between the Habsburgs and the Protestants. In Henri IV's view, the salvation of the kingdom lay in the reinforcement of his authority, in a full treasury and well-stocked arsenals, and in the ability to raise and supply a large army on short notice. What he wanted, beyond all doubt, was a council that would offer its advice if the king asked for it but that stood ready to approve and enforce the king's decisions without discussion, even if those decisions had been reached in private by the king and a secretary of state or favorite, a council that was willing to follow the royal line in reaching decisions on its own, a royal line laid down by a trusted adviser. The king wanted a chancellor willing to sign and seal any letters the king wished to have signed and sealed, without delay and without protest. And he wanted sovereign courts that would register his letters and edicts quickly and quietly. In short, the king wanted absolute monarchy.

Sully, a man of the sword, approved the king's plans and worked for their accomplishment. He thereby increased his influence at the expense of Bel-lièvre, initially the more influential of the two men. At first Sully's activities were confined to questions of finance, but in 1599 he broadened his horizons to include matters of general policy. Between 1602 and 1604 he waged an intense battle against Bellièvre, the climax of which was the creation of the annual dues or Paulette. With Villeroy's help Sully triumphed. When he submitted the proposal for the forty days clause and the farm on the *parties casuelles* to the Conseil d'Etat et des Finances in September 1602, Sully ran into violent opposition from Chancellor Bellièvre. As *président* of the Con-seil, Bellièvre several times objected to the inclusion of the question in the agenda. Henri IV forced him to open debate on the issue. After a stormy session it was adopted by a bare majority, seven councillors voting with Sully and five with Bellièvre. The chancellor did not give up, however. He refused to sign the decree, which therefore remained unenforceable, and he sent the king a memoir detailing his objections. Since the issue was an affair of state rather than a judgment, the minority could prevail if the king chose to take its side.

Bellièvre's objections were first of all political. The king's authority would suffer damage if the proposal were adopted. He would no longer be able to choose his own officers and would be forced to accept whatever candidate was nominated by any officeholder who paid his annual dues. Corrupt men or men of small ability could gain office solely because of their wealth. They might even become *présidents* in the Chambre des Enquêtes where the younger members of *parlement* were trained, thereby leading to a breakdown of discipline. In the provinces, if money were allowed to create *lieutenants généraux* in the *bailliages* and *présidiaux*, "dangerous monopolies" might be born. The king would thus be ill served and his subjects ill treated and highly discontent. Complaints about the large number of offices would only heighten this discontent, and it would be impossible to reduce this number: how could the king even speak of eliminating the office of someone who had paid the annual dues for twenty years? The example of the good officer would have only limited effect. The king would no longer be able to give offices to his loyal supporters, nor would he be able to compensate a magistrate for excellent service by absolving him of the resignation tax, because it would be impossible to deprive the farm of any revenues already used to cover specific expenditures. Officers would therefore not be so zealous in the performance of their duties.

The chancellor next turned to objections of a social order. He was afraid that the price of offices would rise. Prices might in fact go so high that it would become impossible for *gentilshommes* to place their sons in the sovereign courts and for councillors in *parlement* to find seats for their children. The *parlements* would fill their ranks with the sons of speculators, and scorn would be heaped upon a system of justice fallen into corruption.

Finally, there was reason to fear the possible economic and financial consequences of such action. Since elimination of offices would become impossible, a large number of them would remain permanently. As a result, "trade would be abandoned" and France would grow poor, hurting the ability of the nation to pay taxes. And yet the offices brought the king little money; half of what was collected in *tailles* had to be used to pay their salaries.

The king studied Bellièvre's memoir. But he was influenced by a desire to increase his income. Perhaps he also thought that the sale of offices had already produced all the evil effects that Bellièvre feared and that the magistracy was already sadly degraded. In graver circumstances, particularly in 1597 when the fall of Amiens had left a breach in the kingdom's defenses and seemed to deliver Paris and all of France into the hands of the Spaniards, had not the sovereign courts used all their power to oppose the creation of badly needed offices, despite the supplications of the king and his councillors? Did it not appear that what was uppermost in the minds of the officeholders was the need to maintain the importance of their positions, their only source of honor and profit? And that the general interest and ideas of policy had been subordinated to the special interests of a corps and an estate?

It was already too late to adopt a policy predicated on the interests of the "fourth estate." Henri IV answered the chancellor's objections by saying that "the state of his affairs forced him to overlook these considerations," and he ordered Bellièvre to sign the decree and enforce the edict. The chancellor had to give in. The king had made an important choice. By refusing to eliminate the sale of offices and to do away with a large number of those already in existence, and by enabling a small group of families to monopolize most of them and pass them on from one generation to the next, the king condemned himself and his successors to rely increasingly on *commissaires* to enforce their will and to run the government and administration for the good of all. Thus he had chosen, no doubt without being aware of what he had done, a course that implied constant conflict and intestine struggle between officeholders and *commissaires*. Chancellor Bellièvre's defeat was decisive. In December 1604 the king forced Bellièvre to accept a coadjutor, Sillery. In October 1605 he stripped Bellièvre of the seals. Along with a docile chancellor, the king's instrument Sully controlled the Council. Sully gained a victory for the *gentilshommes*, the *nobles d'épée*, over the *robins*. In government and administration Sully behaved as a soldier, heading straight for his objective. The power of the executive, an executive form of administration, had won out.

Sully and the "Revolution of 1661" in 1605

Sully took a seat on the Conseil des Finances in 1596 and was regarded as the head of finance from June 1598 on. He began using the title of *surintendant des Finances*, probably sometime in 1599, and was subsequently named Grand Voyer of France (1599), *grand maître de l'artillerie* (1599), *surintendant des Fortifications* (1599), *capitaine du château* of the Bastille (1602), and duke-and-peer of France (1606). From 1605 on Sully acted as the real head of the king's Council, over which the chancellor or keeper of the seals ostensibly presided. He exercised the powers of a "principal minister" without having the title.

The administration of France was unified at the top in the person of Sully. He appointed his creatures to all the key posts. Loyal and trusted associates served him as secretaries and on special missions. Sully saw to it that their careers prospered, and he obtained offices for them. As head of the royal finances he supervised the *contrôleur général des Finances* and the *intendants des Finances*. Through them his authority extended to the whole hierarchy of financial officials, including magistrates such as the *trésoriers de France* and the *élus* and accounting officials like the *trésoriers de l'Epargne*, the *receveurs généraux* and *particuliers*, the *trésorier des parties casuelles*, the *trésoriers de l'ordinaire* and *de l'extraordinaire des guerres*, the *trésoriers de la Marine*, and the *trésoriers des Ponts et Chaussées*. As *grand maître de l'Artillerie* he had a lieutenant general serving under him and was represented in each arsenal by a lieutenant, who commanded the local artillery commissars and inspectors. As *Grand Voyer* of France he appointed one or more lieutenants in each *généralité* to oversee bridges and roads; these were usually chosen from among the *trésoriers de France*. As *surintendant des bâtiments royaux* he gave orders to the *intendant* Jean de Fourcy and the *contrôleur général* Jean de Donon. Sully held the sovereign courts in low esteem. In his *Mémoire des entreprises des Cours sur les finances où il faut remédier*, which he wrote in his own hand in 1599 or 1600, he wrote:

> In Provence . . . the Chambre des Comptes issues payment orders and charges travel, private bills, gifts, and other expenditures to the king's account. In Languedoc the *parlement* orders payment in full of *rentes* notwithstanding the reduction of one-half ordered by the king. . . . The Cour des Aides has freed accounting officials imprisoned by the *trésoriers* and suspended by them for failure to post security. . . . In Limoges . . . the Chambre des Comptes [of Paris] in one year and in a single account issued orders causing the expenditure of ten thousand *écus* not allocated in the king's accounts. . . . In Brittany . . . the *parlement* has issued orders for payments not authorized by the king. . . . In Paris . . . the Cour des Aides has quashed all judgments and ordinances of the *commissaires du régalement*."[2]

Sully's principal tools were the king's Council and the royal *commissaires*. As the center of royal power, the king's Council constantly intervened through a multitude of decrees in the government and administration of the kingdom. According to one royal secretary, Jules Gassot, Sully "was by himself the Conseil des Finances," the section of the king's Council that developed resources and ordered expenditures, "and the rest of the Conseil served merely to authorize actions he took on his own."[3] It was through the Council that the countless detailed regulations governing administrative procedures were transformed into decrees, declarations, and edicts and couched in the form of letters patent. One hundred forty such regulations are known.

Sully used a large number of *commissaires* to carry out his decisions once they had been authorized by the Council. *Commissaires* were sent to take charge of local finance offices, to investigate cases of embezzlement, to reform the *gabelles*, to oversee the assessment of taxes and the equalization of the *tailles*, etc. At the same time Sully increased the number of long-term and even permanent *commissaires*, who were in effect nothing less than intendants of justice, administration, and finance, though at this early date they went under a variety of different titles. Among these *commissaires* were Raymond de Bissouze in Guyenne from 1594 to 1611; Miles Marion in Languedoc; and Antoine Le Camus, sieur de Jambeville, in Normandy. In Lyon there was no break between intendants: Méri de Vic served from 1597 to 1600, Eustache de Refuge from 1601 to 1607, and Guillaume de Montholon from 1607 to 1617. A series of *"chambres de justice"* or *"chambres royales"* looked into abuses by financial officeholders, *traitants*, and *partisans:* *chambres* held sessions in May and June of 1597, from November 1601 to October 1607, and from 20 January 1605 to September 1607.

The centralization of power and the use of *commissaires* curtailed the power of the sovereign courts. Sully "was much feared by all those companies, which he was always belittling in some way."[4]

Although the opposition of the courts to Sully's rule did not reach the point of open rebellion, it was nonetheless real. The letters establishing the *chambres de justice* prohibited the sovereign courts from hearing cases of embezzlement committed in connection with the royal finances as long as the *chambres* remained in session. In spite of this ruling, the *parlement* of Brittany heard appeals of judgments handed down by *commissaires* sent to the provinces by the *chambres*. The *chambres des comptes* were normally responsible for detecting and punishing infractions committed by financial officeholders in the course of their official duties. The Chambre des Comptes of Brittany opposed the collection of taxes assessed on the officeholders of the province in 1604 by the Chambre de Justice. A number of council decrees were issued to remind the sovereign and lower courts that they were not to hear cases reserved to the *chambres de justice*.

To deal with the Chambre des Comptes of Paris, Henri IV made use on several occasions of jussive letters issued to Sully. In connection with modifications demanded in 1598 by the Chambre des Comptes to "secret articles" in an agreement between Henri IV and a Ligueur, the duc de Mercoeur, governor of Brittany, the king pointed out that "in such affairs, I transmit my power to no one, and in my kingdom it falls to me alone to wage war or to grant or sue for peace at my pleasure."[5] In 1599 he in fact ordered the Chambre des Comptes to cease examining his accounts and to include only those items approved by the Council, which thus gained control over the king's accounts and superseded the Chambre des Comptes in certain of its powers. Sully was the first person not a member of the company to be granted access to the archives of the Chambres des Comptes, when he was assigned in 1598 to establish a list of all gifts awarded by the king since his accession to the throne. In 1604, the Chambre des Comptes, which had never before allowed documents to leave its archives, was forced to transmit the accounts of payment of *rentes* assigned to the clergy to Sully's offices in the Arsenal under the surveillance of a *maître des comptes*. The Chambre raised its protest at each new demand but had to give in to the king's will. It resented this high-handedness as a form of tyranny.

The declaration of 23 August 1598 announced that *commissaires* would be dispatched to all provinces of the kingdom to "equalize" the *tailles*. In fact, three-man commissions were dispatched only to the *pays d'élections*. These consisted of a *conseiller d'Etat* or *maître des requêtes*, who acted as *président*, a *trésorier de France*, and a councillor in the Cour des Aides. Little by little their power was extended to include "reform of abuses com-

590	The Battle between the Officeholders and the *Commissaires*

mitted in connection with finance, *aides*, and *gabelles*." The *commissaires* were authorized to constitute a court to hear litigation, and appeals of their judgments could be taken only to the king's Council. The Council intervened constantly to supplement or amplify the instructions given to the *commissaires* or to lend them support. This greatly irritated the Cours des Aides of Rouen and Paris, because appeals of financial litigation legally belonged to them. Despite the decisions of the Council they continued to hear appeals of judgments handed down by the *commissaires*. A small war had broken out within the nation's institutions.

The creation of the office of Grand Voyer of France and the extent of the competence and powers granted both to him and to his lieutenants encountered opposition from the companies, hostile to the centralization of power and to the concomitant curtailment of their own authority that this implied. The sovereign courts raised difficulties in connection with the registration of letters patent pertaining to the new institution. The Paris *parlement* did not verify the edict of May 1599 until the month of September. The Bordeaux *parlement* registered the declaration of 7 June 1604 in August, but only on condition that the Grand Voyer's lieutenants not enroach on the jurisdiction of *voyers particuliers* and other officers with responsibility for roadways. Sully got around these objections. The *trésoriers de France*, having lost the power over roadways that they had held for a century, rebelled against the lieutenant of the Grand Voyer. This happened at Caen, for example, in 1608. Sully was obliged to take steps to consolidate his authority and that of his lieutenants.

The edict of December 1601 was a reminder of the royal monopoly on the casting of cannon and cannon balls and prohibited the export of copper, cannon, and munitions. The right to sell gunpowder to private individuals was restricted to the *commissaires*. The sovereign courts declared their opposition to this measure. The Paris *parlement* registered the edict with restrictions on 8 May 1602. Jussive letters were required to force it to lift its restrictions, which it did on 19 June. The Chambre des Comptes registered the edict of 24 July 1602, with amendments. Among other things it authorized the import of gunpowder, provided the amount imported was declared.

None of this opposition got very far against a king who was ready to leap into the saddle at a moment's notice. It is symptomatic, however, of the discontent prevalent in the sovereign courts, which represented the officeholders against the king's Council and other *commissaires*.

Notes

1. M. Antoine, *Le Conseil du Roi sous le règne de Louis XV*, pp. 630–31.
2. Cited in B. Barbiche, *Sully* (Paris: Albin Michel, 1978), pp. 70–71.
3. Jules Gassot, *Sommaire mémorial* (Champion, 1934), p. 245.
4. Ibid.
5. Barbiche, *Sully*, p. 72.

30 From the Accession of Louis XIII to the Fronde

Like all regencies, that of Marie de Médicis, which followed the assassination of Henri IV and lasted from 15 May 1610 to 2 October 1614, experienced difficulties. With the king dead and a child on the throne, the body politic seemed to fall apart. Many, particularly the *gentilshommes*, seemed to feel that they had given their pledge only to a man, not to an institution, and felt free not to honor that pledge when the man died and was replaced by his infant son, as though the law had died with the king; these men no longer felt bound by any obligation: only the limitations of their forces hampered their actions. When the king died, nobles fortified their castles. Bands of robbers took to the field and attacked homes and castles, pillaging, marauding, holding captives for ransom, and carrying off funds from the royal treasury. The cities were breeding places of disorder and sedition. The princes and grandees enlisted the support of lesser nobles. Soldiers and armies roamed the countryside, hurling challenges at one another and sometimes coming to blows.

The Sale of Offices and the Opposition of the Sovereign Courts

It was not long before festering grievances made themselves known. Sully, unable to get the Council to ratify his decisions without dissent, resigned on 26 January 1611.

From this point on, the interests of the officeholders and their battle against the *commissaires* played an important role in French internal politics, underlying the claims and counterclaims of princes, grandees, and Protestants. In order to satisfy the wishes of the *gentilshommes* and officeholders, the new government began eliminating certain offices, suspended execution of a great many edicts creating new offices, and on 22 July 1610 revoked an even larger number of edicts. A new contract for collection of the annual dues was signed on 27 September 1611, reflecting the spirit of Bellièvre's counsel. The terms of this contract would, it was hoped, mollify the officeholders by holding out the benefit of the annual dues to heads of companies, *premiers présidents* in the Chambres des Comptes and Cours des Aides, and *lieutenants généraux civils* in the *présidiaux*, and by granting exemption from the forty days' clause when the officeholder resigned in favor of his son or son-in-law. Steps were taken to provide offices at moderate prices to needy but deserving *gentilshommes* and to keep the price down for offices resigned in favor of more distant relatives or strangers or offices left vacant by death.

Thus, in these cases, the advantage of paying the annual dues was lessened. The sovereign courts took it upon themselves to interpret the complaints of the officeholders. On 29 March 1612, the new government reinstated Henri IV's conditions on the annual dues and included new beneficiaries. Accordingly, the sovereign courts did not follow the prince de Condé when he wrote to them, left the court with the other princes, and issued his manifesto of 19 February 1614 against the annual dues, the price of offices, the Council, and other royal *commissaires:* "The prices of all judicial and financial offices have risen to excessive heights. There is no longer any recompense for virtue, since all power now belongs to favor, alliances, kinship, and money. . . . The nobility . . . is now . . . banished from judicial and financial offices for want of money." He also echoed the complaint that "the *parlements* have been prevented from carrying out their duties unimpeded." He joined with the officeholders in asking that the government "see to it that the sovereign courts are allowed to carry out all their duties unhindered, and not tolerate any reduction or curtailment of their dignity and authority in the future."[1]

We have seen how, in the Estates General that opened on 27 October 1614, the issue of the sale of offices and the annual dues as well as the question of the pope's power over the king and the sovereignty of France divided the *noblesse d'épée* and the *noblesse de robe*, the *gentilshommes* and the third estate, thereby allowing the king to mediate and thus to dominate.[2]

When he dismissed the deputies, however, the king promised to end the sale of offices and hence also the annual dues. This aroused the sovereign courts. The prince de Condé stirred up the young councillors in the Chambres des Enquêtes of the Paris *parlement*, who at first thought of remonstrating with the king on the issue of the annual dues. Upon reflection, however, they thought it more proper to deal with major issues of state. On 28 March 1615, all the chambers of *parlement* assembled and issued a decree inviting the princes, dukes, peers, and officers of the Crown to a meeting to deliberate on "the service of the king, the relief of his subjects, and the welfare of his state."[3] *Parlement* claimed the right to examine the *cahiers* of the Estates General. The king immediately forbade princes and peers to attend the meeting. On Sunday, 29 March, he notified *parlement* that he alone had the power to issue such an invitation and prohibited execution of its decree. On 31 March *parlement* capitulated, asserting that it had issued its decree only "subject to the king's good pleasure" and that it would obey.

But Condé continued to stir up trouble. In the Chambres des Enquêtes "almost all the members are devoted to him and will do as he desires." On 1 April the Enquêtes asked for an Assembly of Chambers to demand an answer from the king in regard to certain affairs of state. The king forbade *parlement* to concern itself with such matters and to make remonstrances to him concerning them. On 10 April *parlement* decided to ignore this prohibition, which the king renewed on the following day. A truce was declared for the Easter holiday. On 29 April *parlement* resolved to prepare remonstrances for submission to the king.

The other sovereign courts complained more and more frequently that their officers were facing ruin. The unrest spread to officers of the lower courts and accounting officials as well. Some openly rallied to the side of the princes. On 13 May 1615, the king decided to suspend the abolition of venality until 1 January 1618 and to grant the officeholders the favor of the annual dues until that date.

The Paris *parlement* thereby received satisfaction. It could not withdraw its remonstrances, however, for that would have made it only too clear that it had acted solely in the interest of the officeholders, who wished to perpetuate the sale of offices and the annual dues. In order to save face it submitted its remonstrances on 22 May 1615.

The Remonstrances of 1615: The *Parlement* and the King's Council

The remonstrances of 22 May amounted to a program for a general reorganization of the kingdom, a "reform" based on the *cahiers* of the Estates General of 1614–15 and traditional customs. They were also a treatise on the claims of the sovereign courts and other royal officeholders who bore the title of "councillor to the king." The *parlement* stated that it had the duty, dating back to the time when Philip the Fair and Louis X had assigned it a permanent seat in Paris, to preserve the Constitution of the State, to verify laws, ordinances, and edicts, to approve the creation of new offices, to ratify treaties (including both peace treaties and treaties of alliance, as well as contracts between the Crown and private individuals), and participate in other important affairs of state (as established by letters patent addressed to it). Even what was approved by the Estates General had to be verified in *parlement*, the seat of the royal throne and of the sovereign *lit du justice*. The *parlement* based its case on tradition, on sacrosanct customs, and on the "fundamental laws of the kingdom." It cited as precedents the example of King John the Good, the declaration of war on England with the advice of *parlement* under Charles V, the agreement of 1405 between the Houses of Orleans and Burgundy, the remonstrances made to Louis XI by the *président* de La Vacquerie and the benevolent response of that thing, so jealous of his authority, as well as the remonstrances to the same prince concerning the abuses of the Court of Rome. It continued with the example of Louis XII, who did not stand up to the encroachments of Pope Julius II and who awarded his daughter's hand only on advice of the *parlement*, called to Tours for the purpose. Under Francis I, *parlement* sent memoranda concerning the reform of the government. *Parlement* deliberated on the Treaty of Madrid and other treaties, as well as on important interpretations of the Salic Law in behalf of Philippe de Valois and Henri IV. In May 1588 at Chartres Henri III thanked *parlement* for its remonstrances. While kings did not always welcome these remonstrances (witness Francis I in regard to the Concordat and Charles IX), they always repented later and dismissed their ministers in disgrace. The greater and more absolute the power, *parlement* reasoned, the more wise statecraft demanded that it be used prudently in order to make it last. It therefore advised the king to use his "absolute" power infrequently, absolute here meaning unconditional and unlimited, a power to give orders that the king's subjects must obey without argument. In other words, the king should govern France, *parlement* maintained, through the Grand Conseil and above all with the advice of the *parlement* of Paris.

In regard to the crucial questions of recruitment for the king's Council and the use of *commissaires*, *parlement* took a clear stand. The king must not choose for his Council *commis* selected among his favorites and the creatures of his favorites. Rather, he should choose dignitaries qualified for the position by birth and status.

> Your Majesty is most humbly supplicated to choose for your Council, along with the princes of your blood, other princes, and crown officers, senior councillors of state who have benefitted from the experience of high office and who are sprung from great houses and ancient families, who, by dint of natural affection and particular interest, are compelled to uphold your state, and to eliminate from consideration persons who have gained prominence in recent years, not by their own merit and for services rendered to Your Majesty, but rather by the favor of those who wish to make creatures for themselves.[4]

Parlement further asked that the Council not be allowed to overrule its decisions and that anyone who wished to appeal a decision of *parlement* should be allowed to do so only as provided by law and royal ordinance. It wished to see a reduction in the number of evocations of cases away from its jurisdiction under those ordinances.

As for the use of *commissaires*, *parlement* did not ask that this be eliminated entirely, since government and administration required assistance of this sort. But it did ask "that no commission be issued, either to render sovereign judgment or to try any accused, unless it has been verified in your *parlement*."[5] In this way *parlement* hoped to gain control over the choice and activities of all *commissaires* who might be required to pronounce on the law, and thereby to secure some control over a large part of the work of the government and the administration.

Royal Doctrine

The king, on the advice of his mother, the queen, princes, crown officers, dukes, peers, and other lords and notables on his Council, on 23 May 1615, reiterated the royal doctrine, which was also based on tradition, custom, and the fundamental laws, because it was held that constancy of behavior revealed the nature of the bonds that tied together the various members of society, respect for which was crucial to the very existence of that society. The king pointed out to the *présidents* and councillors of *parlement* "that they had exceeded the power attributed to them by the laws of their institution, which was established only to render justice to his subjects and not to take jurisdiction over affairs of state unless commanded to do so."[6]

As proof that this interpretation of the fundamental law was correct, the king first of all cited the answer that had been given by sieur de La Vacquerie, *premier président* or *parlement*, speaking for that court, to the duc d'Orléans, first prince of the blood (and later Louis XII), who was involved in a dispute with Anne de Beaujeu, the sister of King Charles VIII, who had charge of the kingdom's affairs: "That *parlement* was instituted only to render justice to the king's subjects and not to interfere in his affairs unless commanded to do so by the chief ordained by God, to whom alone they owed obedience." The king next cited the example of Francis I, who had quashed and declared null and void a decree of *parlement* that would have restricted the power of his mother, the regent, Louise de Savoie. The king ordered that this decree be brought to him for cancellation within a fortnight and prohibited any such unwarranted encroachments on his power in the future. Finally, Louis XIII pointed out that Charles IX, shortly after attaining his majority, had quashed a decree by which *parlement* attempted to assume jurisdiction over an affair of state on its own authority and without orders from the king; Charles IX had ordered this decree destroyed and stricken from the records. On these grounds, Louis XIII quashed, revoked, and declared null and void the decree of 28 March 1615 and prohibited *parlement* from concerning itself in the future with affairs of state unless ordered to do so. The king further ordered that the decree of 28 March and the remonstrances of 22 May should be stricken from the record and removed from the registers of *parlement*.

Once again both sides had taken a clear stand. The king's wish was to be an absolute sovereign with the power to appoint officers (especially in his courts) and *commissaires* (particularly in his Council) of his own choosing and to issue as he deemed fit laws, regulations, and orders necessary to the common good, after receiving the enlightenment of such counsel as he might request. *Parlement*, while asserting the king's sovereignty against the pope and the emperor, claimed to be the supreme judge, responsible for establishing the regulations governing the king's Council, the Estates General, the courts, the *commissaires*, the government, and the administration; in short, *parlement* claimed to be the true council of the kingdom, in which the king's will was formed. Subsequently, both king and *parlement* detailed and specified their respective doctrines and searched for additional precedents and arguments in support of their respective positions. On the king's side, for example, many works were published by the *conseillers d'Etat* of 1632–33, in particular Cardin Le Bret (*De la souveraineté du roi*, 1632), and during the Fronde the government instigated the publication of numerous satirical pamphlets. On *parlement*'s side, a spate of *Mazarinades* (lampoons against Cardinal Mazarin) flowed forth during the Fronde, and during the eighteenth century the *avocat* Le Paige published the *Lettres historiques sur les fonctions essentielles du Parlement, sur le droit des pairs et sur les loix fondamentales du Royaume* (Amsterdam, 1735–54). There were of course also royal edicts and council decrees arguing for the king's position, and remonstrances from *parlement* arguing its position. Nothing essential in either position was changed, however: two opposing concepts of monarchy were pitted against one another.

To return to the case in question, for the time being the Paris *parlement* was interested mainly in preserving its prestige. The decision to retain the sale of offices and the annual dues, even on a temporary basis, produced desirable political effects. When, on 10 September 1615, the government declared Condé and his accomplices guilty of *lèse-majesté*, the provincial *parlements* quickly registered the declaration. The *parlement* of Rouen contributed to the defense of its province and the army of the princes wrote Normandy off as lost. The Paris *parlement* decided to delay registration for one month, but it prohibited any levy of troops and enjoined the princes to return to the king's court and the *gentilshommes* to withdraw to their homes, failing which they would be liable to prosecution for *lèse-majesté*, which was tantamount to registration of the decree. Condé and the other princes were forced to negotiate at Loudun on 3 May 1616. The king was able to have Condé arrested on 1 September without any protests on the part of *parlement* or the officeholders.

After the execution of the queen's favorite and principal minister Concini during the Assemblée des Notables at Rouen (1617–18), Louis XIII revoked the annual dues by council decree of 15 January 1618 but delayed ending the sale of offices until such time as he had found a source of funds to replace the *parties casuelles*. But the sovereign courts increasingly resorted to assemblies, complaints, oppositions to edicts, supplications, and remonstrances. The rebellions of the queen mother, the princes, and the Protestants cost the king a great deal, and the suppression of the annual dues decreased the amount flowing into his treasury. Some councillors in *parlement* and *lieutenants généraux* of *bailliages* and *sénéchaussées* were won over by the rebels. The king reestablished the annual dues on 31 July 1620, in exchange for a rather heavy loan from the officeholders.

When Richelieu took over as prime minister, he had great plans for general reform of the kingdom. In 1625 he proposed eliminating the annual dues and, later, the sale of offices itself. His object was to establish the king's authority and therefore the authority of the king's *commissaires*. As late as 1629 Richelieu was urging the king to "reduce and moderate the companies, which, by claiming sovereignty, were every day standing in opposition to the good of the kingdom."[7]

For various reasons, however, including the conspiracies and rebellions of the grandees, the undeclared war against the Spanish and Austrian Habsburgs, the subsidies paid to foreign Protestants and the civil war against domestic Protestants, the "great choice" of April 1630 reaffirmed on the Day of Dupes [10 November when Richelieu was reappointed—trans.], Richelieu's victory over the queen mother and Marillac, and the war policy, the king was forced to lay out larger and larger sums of money, and this outlay finally became overwhelming when France at last declared war in 1635. Money had to be sought in every way available: increase in the *tailles*, supplementary centimes for the army, increase in indirect taxes, creation of new indirect taxes, recourse to the so-called *affaires extraordinaires*, creation of offices, splitting of offices on a semestrial basis in the courts, increase of salaries in exchange for an advance which was in fact a disguised loan, recourse to compulsory loans, increase in the annual dues, tightening of the conditions under which the annual dues could be enjoyed, and demand of a loan as a prerequisite to permission to pay the annual dues. The courts were deluged with "bursal edicts," and since it was necessary to have these verified and registered, the king could not push the courts too far. As a result, reforms first had to be postponed from 1626 to 1629 and then abandoned altogether.

The Courts against the Council and the *Commissaires*

All these policies dismayed the sovereign courts and officeholders. Quite a few *présidents* and councillors agreed with the queen mother and Chancellor de Marillac that the Habsburgs were sincere, that they were truly the champions of the Catholic faith and had no hegemonic designs, and that the king had been deceived on this crucial point by Richelieu and his creatures. Others, though "good Frenchmen," felt, first during the time of Richelieu and later under Mazarin, that it was possible to secure a peace that would offer France full security, and that the king's favorites and their *fidèles* sought to prolong the war solely to make themselves indispensable and to justify their honors, their positions, their pensions, and their bonuses. The courts were in no haste to register the bursal edicts or to see them enforced.

Some of the new measures hit the courts and officeholders directly: the *affaires extraordinaires*, the new offices they were forced to buy, the "loans" they had to make to the king in order to avoid creation of new offices or to secure the elimination of old ones, and the requirement to purchase wage increases. In cases where it proved impossible to avoid the creation of new offices (on a wholesale basis with the creation of semestrial offices, for example), the existing officeholders suffered a loss of prestige as well as of *épices* in the case of court officers and *droits et taxations* in the case of financial officers.

In addition, officeholders, most of whom owned estates and *seigneuries*, were affected indirectly by any change in the tax structure: any increase in indirect taxes, for example, threatened to force them to diminish the rent they charged farmers of their land and threatened to deprive farmers and *censitaires* of the means to pay the various dues and rents they owed.

Last, and perhaps most important of all, the officeholders, particularly in the courts, were affected by the king's increasing use of his Council and *commissaires*. The regulation of October 1622 established that the date of rank of members of the sovereign courts who received brevets as *conseillers d'Etat* would henceforth be not the date the brevet was issued but rather the date they actually arrived to serve on the Council. This resulted in the demotion of several officers and stirred considerable sentiment. The position of all officeholders was diminished relative to that of *conseillers d'Etat* who made their careers working for the Council.

The sovereign courts complained that a growing number of cases were being removed to the Council, thereby diminishing their jurisdiction. They particularly complained of being ordered by council decree to register edicts, which limited their power to make remonstrances. In the minds of the court officers, the cruelest blow was that these orders were issued by a principal minister who was a mere creature, a favorite of the king, not entitled to his post by birth or by possession of a high crown office. In their view the orders came merely from a *commis* of the king, a private secretary, a "domestic," and not from a "company." The Council, they felt, was not a *corps*, not a company. The officers acknowledged the superior authority of the king, in whom "alone was vested the supreme power" along with the "right to absolute command" (limited by God's commandments, by the fundamental laws of the kingdom, and by previous ordinances); hence they acknowledged also that the Council had authority when the king was present, when he surrounded himself with private individuals whose advice he wished to consult. But alone, without the presence of the king, the Council had no authority as a *corps*.

The officeholders scorned the *commissaires* employed by the Council, especially when they assumed the title of intendant and attempted to prevent the officeholders from carrying out their duties. A decree issued on 8 May 1627, by the Paris *parlement* forbade M. de Turquant, *maître des requêtes*, to assume the title of *surintendant* of justice and administration of Lyon and forbade officeholders to recognize him as such until his commission had been registered by the court.

In 1628, Servien, a *maître des requêtes* and "intendant for justice and administration in Guyenne," tried a number of residents of La Rochelle for *lèse-majesté*, piracy, rebellion, and collaboration with the English. On 5 May the Bordeaux *parlement* forbade him or anyone else to assume the title of intendant for justice and administration in Guyenne and to execute any commission within the court's jurisdiction without its prior approval. Servien nevertheless tried the accused in the admiralty court. On 17 May *parlement* subpoenaed the *commissaire* to appear in person. On 9 June *parlement* decreed that the ordinance issued by Servien in execution of his judgment should be torn to bits and burned by the *exécuteur de la haute justice* and that he himself should be arrested and his property seized and recorded. The Council was obliged to issue a decree on 29 June quashing these three decrees and declaring them "null and void, in contempt of the king's authority, and incompetent." In 1636 the king commissioned the *conseiller d'Etat* Rigault to act in justice and administration in Metz and the surrounding countryside. The *parlement* of Metz asserted in its decree of 13 November 1638 that Rigault had exceeded the authority vested in him by his commission, which was limited to jurisdiction over the bearing of arms, monopolies, illegal assemblies, actions inimical to the king's service and the tranquillity of the public, minor cases involving disputes between bourgeois of Metz and soldiers garrisoned there (which Rigault heard without regard to the rank of the person involved or the type of case, whether civil or criminal, real, personal, or mixed property), violations of the edict of pacification pertaining to religion, enforcement of decrees issued by *parlement*, and execution of all writs, distraints, orders to auction, warrants, judgments as between creditors, divisions of property, inheritances, trusts, examination of trustees' accounts, donations, *appels comme d'abus*, and so on. *Parlement* prohibited Rigault from exercising any powers other than those specified in his commission and formulated remonstrances to be submitted to the king.[8]

During the Assemblée des Notables of 1626–27, the *premiers présidents* and *procureurs généraux* of the *parlements* of France met separately and prepared a list of complaints with twenty-three articles. They complained in particular of the "intendants of justice . . . who continue to be the source of various difficulties, to wit, among others, diminishing the jurisdiction, censorship, and vigilance of your *parlements*, officeholders in *sénéchaussées*, *bailliages*, and other jurisdictions, and judges subordinate to them." They agreed that *maîtres des requêtes* could, as in the past, be sent on inspection tours to supervise the performance of the courts, gather information about abuses, and if need be bring charges against those guilty of wrongdoing; but the cases should then be turned over to *parlement* for judgment. They further asked that the position of intendant be done away with. If, however, this was impossible owing to "the needs of war or other accidents," then the king should choose his intendants from among the members of *parlement*, which should be asked to vote their approval. This would have made the intendants representatives of the sovereign courts.[9]

The Weapons Used by the Sovereign Courts in Their Battle with the King

To defend the interests of the officeholders, the *parlements* could draw on any of a number of weapons. When the princes of the blood and other princes and grandees rose up in opposition to the king, the *parlements* refused to register royal declarations against the rebels and refused to aid in the fight against them. When, for example, Monsieur broke with Richelieu and the heir apparent fled first to Orléans and then to Lorraine and the entire kingdom was plunged into turmoil, the Paris *parlement* refused on 26 April 1631 to register the royal declaration of 30 March charging Gaston d'Orléans's accomplices with *lèse-majesté*. This was tantamount to authorizing the rebellion. The king was forced to return to Paris immediately. On 13 May he held a *lit de justice* and forbade *parlement* to interfere in affairs of state. On the same day he exiled some of the *présidents* and councillors outside Paris. *Parlement* gave in. The king did not then push matters to the limit. On 30 May he acceded to Richelieu's request to recall the exiled officers. After the queen mother fled to the Netherlands in July, the king returned to Paris on 22 August "in order to go to *parlement* and force it to register his declaration against those who had followed his mother, together with his edict increasing the number of officeholders, whereby the king restored to the *parlement* its regular Paulette, by which it set such great store that it had balked at abiding by the king's will."[10] As time went by the other sovereign courts were granted the same favor. In exchange they agreed not to join the rebels and registered the edicts creating new offices; in 1632 the Toulouse *parlement* declared its opposition to the rebel Montmorency.

The attitude of the sovereign courts toward the so-called popular uprisings was often ambiguous. They had frequently warned the king that to refuse their demands was to damage their honor and prestige and lower their esteem in the eyes of the public. Thus slighted, they risked losing the respect of the crowd and sacrificing their authority. They would then become "incapable of securing the obedience of the populace." In fact, criticism of the government and its policies by the courts often incited the populace to rebellion. When artisans, workers, and peasants attacked the offices of the tax farmers and the homes of *partisans* and *traitants*, the *parlements* often stood idly by and by their inaction allowed the rebellion to spread. In some case they opposed the measures taken against the rebels. The *Va-nu-pieds* and *Croquants* would not have gotten far if the *parlements* and officeholders had done their duty.

In some cases the sovereign courts themselves rebelled. This happened, for example, in 1629 and 1630, when revolts were breaking out all over the kingdom. On the pretext that the king had not paid their salaries, the Chambre des Comptes of Montpellier in February 1629 deputized three of its members to seize money collected from the *gabelle* in Montpellier, Beaucaire, and Pont-Saint-Esprit: the deputies smashed the chests in which the money was kept and carried it away. The *parlement* of Dauphiné had warehouses in which grain for the army was being stored broken open, thus encouraging the populace to rise up and seize wheat from other storage places. When the rumor seized Dijon that *élus* would be established there, the people, spurred on by some members of *parlement*, took arms on 12 March 1630 and burned the homes of those who they believed were in favor of this move. In August the *parlement* of Provence tolerated popular demonstrations, organized the nobility, and instigated an attack on the intendant to drive him out of the area. The king's ministers and officers were burned in effigy on the public square. Only rarely were officeholders directly involved in rebellion, however.

The sovereign courts' favorite weapon was legislative obstruction. Before preparing briefs and including controversial edicts in the agenda of an Assembly of Chambers, the *premiers présidents* and *procureurs généraux* would wait for a *lettre de cachet* from the king. The Assembly of Chambers would decide that it could not register the edicts and that remonstrances to the king were required. The king would then send a jussive letter. The Assembly would maintain its opposition. Six or seven jussive letters might be issued in succession, without effect. Months would pass. The king would then hold a *lit de justice* to have the edicts registered. The courts would then continue not to enforce them and would submit various demands to the king. The government would have to negotiate an accommodation, frequently requiring major modifications in the edicts and the withdrawal of some of them.

The King's Weapons against the Sovereign Courts

But the government was not without weapons of its own. To begin with, it could always threaten to end the sale of offices and the annual dues. Then, too, it could bargain over the terms for renewal of the annual dues at the expiration of each nine-year term. The government would delay granting the renewal as long as it could in order to force *parlement* to verify all pending bursal edicts. *Parlement* would simulate strenuous opposition in order to obtain the annual dues on the best possible terms. The government would offer very bad terms, and the officeholders would protest and redouble their opposition. The government would then eliminate the annual dues, these being a favor it was not obliged to grant. If the officers refused to accept this favor on the government's terms, the government refused to grant it. Finally, after lengthy negotiations and further bluffs and threats of this sort, the government and officeholders would reach an understanding under which the government would grant the annual dues and the courts would verify the bursal edicts. This was the pattern in 1621 and 1630 and to some extent also in 1639, at which time the burden of the loan and the annual dues became too great for the officeholders to bear.

The annual dues also served the king as a wedge with which to split the ranks of his officeholders. On 22 February 1621, he granted the favor of the annual dues to the sovereign courts on the same terms as in 1604. By way of compensation, however, he charged the other officeholders more, requiring more of officers in the lower courts than of those in the sovereign courts, and still more of accounting officials. At each subsequent renewal of the annual dues the same pattern was repeated. In this way the king could cause trouble between the *lieutenants généraux civils* in the *présidaux* and the *parlements*, because the former were obliged to pay the loan from which members of *parlement* were exempt. But the *lieutenants généraux* were distinguished from the run-of-the-mill officeholders of the lower courts by being taxed less, at a rate equal to that applied to the *trésoriers généraux de France*, who were regarded as members of the *corps* of the Chambres des Comptes. In 1622 the *lieutenants généraux* were granted priority over the *trésoriers généraux de France*, and they were often issued brevets as *conseillers d'Etat* and promised a seat on the Council, which placed them on a level with the *présidents* of the sovereign courts and above councillors in *parlement*.

Now, it was with the *présidiaux* that the intendants worked. Instead of submitting their commissions to the *parlements* for registration, the intendants would apply to the *lieutenants généraux civils*, who would then have the commission registered by the presidial court. Intendants would also send their orders to the *lieutenants généraux*, who would convey them to the officeholders under them for enforcement. Cases sent to the intendants by the king's Council for judgment would be heard in conjunction with officers of the *présidiaux*. When a *parlement* wished to challenge an intendant, it would order the *présidiaux* not to carry out his orders, decrees, or judgments and to send all cases in which he was involved to the company for judgment. It was thus a fact of some importance that the annual dues made it possible to sow discord between the *présidiaux* and the *parlements*. Broadly speaking, the annual dues to a large extent enabled the government to secure the obedience of the officeholders until April 1648.

As the sovereign lawgiver, the king could also use repressive legislation against the *parlements*. This was one of the purposes of the important ordinance drafted by de Marillac, the keeper of the seals, which later came to be known, pejoratively, as the Code Michaud. It was submitted to the Paris *parlement* in January 1629. The ordinance attempted to guarantee the authority of the Council by reducing the power of the *parlements* to make remonstrances. Under its provisions, the *parlements* would be allowed to delay enforcement of an edict for at most two months. During this time they were required to submit their remonstrances. Subsequently, however, the king having expressed his will, they would be required to publish and enforce the edict. They could then make further remonstrances. In a roundabout way, moreover, the ordinance legalized the intendants as an institution. Article 58, which was devoted to the *maîtres des requêtes* on inspection tours, repeated prescriptions contained in old ordinances concerning their authority for surveillance and control but also extended their powers. *Maîtres des requêtes* could still send information they had gathered to *parlement* for judgment, but now they could also choose another course and send it instead to the *requêtes de l'Hôtel* or the king's Council. They could also judge abuses and violations in summary fashion on their own. Their judgments were to be executory "notwithstanding any possible objections or appeals." Finally, they were authorized to supervise the collection of direct and indirect taxes.

These powers were almost the same as those listed in the commissions of intendants; even the terms were the same. Furthermore, in article 81, the keeper of the seals inserted the word "intendant" in a royal ordinance for the first time, defining the function of that official as one of taking precautions against possible abuses: "No one shall be employed as an intendant of justice or finance to represent us in our armies or provinces who is a domestic of the generals of said armies or the governors of said provinces, or employed in the affairs of such a person, or a close relative thereof."[11] The existence of the intendants was thereby legalized in a roundabout way.

On 26 December 1629, a decision was made to hold a *lit de justice*. The compulsory registration took place on 15 January 1629. The king allowed *parlement* only two months to submit its remonstrances prior to dispatch of the edict to the *bailliages*. He then left for Italy on 16 January. De Marillac's ordinance made the *parlements* furious. The *premier président* of the Paris *parlement* threatened to try the keeper of the seals for violating the fundamental laws of the kingdom. *Parlement* refused to issue copies of the registration and verification to the keeper of the seals and demanded that execution be stayed. The king's intervention was required to secure issuance of the registration decree of 5 September 1629. The ordinance was registered, over protests, by the Bordeaux *parlement* on 6 March, by the Toulouse *parlement* on 5 July and by the Dijon *parlement* on 19 September. The whole affair created a revolutionary situation in the kingdom. On 15 July 1630, Marillac told Richelieu that "France is full of sedition; the *parlements* are not punishing anyone. The king has sent judges to hear these cases. [But] *parlement* stops execution of their judgments and so sedition is authorized."[12] The government was forced to forgo its attempts to enforce the ordinance.

The opposition of the sovereign courts obliged Louis XIII to have further recourse to repressive legislation with the Edict of Saint-Germain-en-Laye (February 1641), which prohibited the *parlements* and other courts of justice from taking cognizance of affairs of state and administration in the future and which also established regulations governing the use of remonstrances.[13] The preamble of this edict contained a theory of government that was more monocratic than monarchical in nature. The power of the sovereign, recognized by all his subjects, was supposed to rally all the parties of the state, thereby assuring its greatness and happiness. Government by a single individual is the soul that inspirits monarchies with force and vigor. If there is any weakening in the absolute authority of the ruler, the dignity of the state suffers and the government splits into factions. Proof of this assertion was provided by the Ligue, as well as by the history of Louis XIII's minority and youth following the attack on the fundamental laws of the kingdom by the Paris *parlement* in May 1615. By contrast, since the king had reclaimed his full authority and restored the strength and majesty of the monarchy,

France had become a powerful state and by its exploits won the admiration of all Europe.

Louis XIII, wishing to strengthen the state as embodied in his successors as well as to familiarize his *parlements* with the legitimate limits of the authority vested in them by the kings of France, declared that the Paris *parlement* and the other royal courts had been established only to render justice to his subjects. He therefore forbade the courts to take any cognizance of affairs that might concern the state or its administration or government, such affairs being reserved to the king alone, unless the king granted the courts special powers by means of letters patent. The king reserved the right to ask the *parlements* for advice on public affairs if he saw fit to do so.

Since the Paris *parlement* had frequently impeded execution of edicts and declarations verified in the presence of the king sitting in a *lit de justice*, the king ordered that these be carried out immediately according to both letter and spirit. Officeholders were allowed to make remonstrances concerning the execution of edicts and declarations one time only. They were then obliged to carry them out according to the verification made on the king's authority.

As for edicts and declarations concerning the government and administration of the state, officeholders in the courts to which they were sent were required to publish and register them without taking any cognizance of their contents or deliberating over them in any way. Remonstrances were therefore eliminated in matters of this kind.

The courts were, however, allowed to make remonstrances in connection with edicts and declarations pertaining to finance. After receipt of the king's orders, they were obliged to suspend all other business and proceed at once to the verification and registration of the edicts in question, unless the king allowed a second and final set of remonstrances. In no case were the officers of the courts supposed to amend the edicts or declarations; nor were they to use the words "we must not and cannot," which were deemed injurious to the prince's authority.

As a clear sign that the creation and elimination of offices depended solely on the king's will, Louis XIII eliminated the post of *conseiller président* in the Chambre des Enquêtes, which was occupied by Barillon, and the councillors' posts occupied by P. Scarron, L. Bitot, Sain, and Salo, whom he ordered to withdraw from the company.

As a way of tightening discipline, the king ordered that *mercuriales* (Wednesday sessions of the courts) be held every three months according to procedures laid down in the ordinances.

A third weapon that the king could use in his battle with the officeholders was his power to increase the authority of his Council over the courts and officeholders in general. To combat the aristocracy of officeholders the king depicted himself as an absolute and popular sovereign. In the words of Cardin Le Bret, "the earliest men, who saw that they were exposed to harm from their enemies, that the wealthiest men abused their authority, and that the laws were scorned and trampled underfoot by the most powerful, decided to remedy these evils by establishing kings and granting them sovereign authority.''[14] Now, the king could not do everything by himself and in any case required the advice of others, so that it was his will that the authority of his Council be acknowledged by all. The *conseillers d'Etat* considered themselves to be a "company" of officers. They held a "perpetual" commission granting them "rank and dignity" forever. They possessed "all the marks of the highest officers of the kingdom; their *provisions* are notified in the form of royal orders sealed with the Great Seal; they take the same oath as other officeholders; the king's choice of these individuals is tantamount to certification of their moral quality and competence. And finally, there is no time limit on their appointment." Hence they were supposed to enjoy rank and title outside the Council and to enjoy priority in the sovereign courts, whereas mere *commis* had no rank in their own right apart from their commission.[15] The king gave official recognition to this theory. In 1616 he granted his keeper of the seals, a mere *commis*, the right to preside over *parlement* as if he were the chancellor, that is to say, as if he were a crown officer.

The position of head of the *conseillers d'Etat* therefore conferred upon its occupant priority and authority over the members of the sovereign courts outside the chambers of the Council itself. The king, particularly after 1632, issued letters to his most loyal and senior *conseillers d'Etat* appointing them honorary *conseillers d'Etat*, which allowed them to be seated and to express their opinion in any of the chambers and assemblies of *parlement*, including the Conseil Secret, with the same rank they held in the Council itself, thus showing that the position of *conseiller d'Etat* carried with it a preeminence that was maintained outside the council precincts. The regulation of May 1643 forced *avocats* in *parlement* who wished to practice before the Council to swear a new oath into the hands of the chancellor or keeper of the seals, even though they had already sworn an oath to *parlement*, on the grounds that the Council was a "tribunal superior to *parlement*." *Parlement* fought back and managed to avoid allowing the keeper of the seals to preside over its meetings. In 1632, after registering the letters of Bouthillier and La Ville-aux-Clercs, it decided not to receive any more honorary *conseillers d'Etat* who were neither gown nor sword. On 15 June 1654, after registering the letters of Jean d'Estampes de Valençay and Jacques de Mesgrigny, it decided not to receive more than six honorary *conseillers d'Etat* belonging to the gown and six belonging to the sword, and not to allow more than four members of any one order to sit at one time. In this way *parlement* cut its losses. It had not been able, however, to prevent the king's will from making itself felt, nor had it been able to keep the king from proclaiming "how much the dignity of the *conseiller d'Etat* has been heightened."

The members of the Council constituted the first "company" of the kingdom, and "the authority of said Councils is determined by the pleasure of the kings, who have always wanted council decrees to carry the same authority as if they had been issued in their presence, as they have shown on every occasion,"[16] words that indicate clearly that it was the full Council as a body that enjoyed the king's full authority. The sovereign courts were forced to acknowledge that the Council had full authority over their decrees. In 1632 the Council took the position that, armed with the king's authority as sovereign judge, it could nullify and quash any decree issued in violation of the ordinances or in opposition to the royal authority, any decree detrimental to public utility or inimical to the rights of the Crown. With so broad and flexible a definition, it was hard not to find quite a few decrees that fell under its sanction.

All sections of the Council quashed decrees from the sovereign courts. In affairs of state, the Conseil d'En-Haut, for example, issued decrees on 23 May 1615 and 23 September 1648, quashing the decree of *parlement* dated 28 March 1615, explained in its remonstrances of 22 May, the decree of Union of 13 May 1648, and the decree of 22 September 1648, by which *parlement*, acting on its own authority, convoked the princes of the blood, dukes-and-peers, crown officers, and officers of the other courts to deliberate on governmental reforms.

Similarly, in the area of finance, the Conseil d'En-Haut quashed decrees of the sovereign courts concerning the bursal edicts and struck down amendments made to these edicts by the *parlements* when it could do so without too great a risk of rebellion.

Finally, the question of the authority of the Conseil d'En-Haut might also come up in litigation between private individuals that became an affair of state, such as a suit involving a grandee and a loyal creature of the king or a suit between a private individual and a tax farmer, the outcome of which might affect the king's rights, to give two examples. The Council was hesitant on this score. Some, like du Vair, the keeper of the seals, thought that the Council ought to "use the ordinary channels of justice" in such cases and therefore that the Council should merely issue leters patent referring the cases back to the *parlement* and allowing it to quash its own decrees. Others, such as Barbin, Mangot, and Concini, thought that the Council should act with *absolute authority*, since such cases were "affairs of the king," and therefore that it should quash the decrees of *parlement* on its own. Thus one party thought that *parlement* should not be stripped of its functions but merely regulated, while the other party held that the Council itself had the power to judge, like a superior court. Under Richelieu the second party prevailed. But in 1648 there were again *conseillers d'Etat* ready to support the claims of *parlement* in this matter.

Thus the authority of the Conseil d'En-Haut was fully and completely established. It could quash any decree of *parlement* and *a fortiori* any decree of the other sovereign courts.

The other sections of the Council also claimed full authority over judicial and "administrative" decisions of the sovereign courts. The courts did not contest the powers of the Conseil privé and the Conseil d'Etat et des Finances in certain specific cases mentioned in the ordinances (ordinance of Orléans, January 1560, art. 45, and ordinance of Blois, May 1579, art. 92). The councils were allowed to suspend judgments of the courts upon petition by one of the parties charging factual error or upon civil petition on the grounds of misrepresentation by one of the litigants. The *maîtres des requêtes* would then examine the record. If they found that the petition had merit, they would report their findings to the Council. If the Council accepted the report, it did not then judge the case but rather sent it back to the court that had issued the suspect judgment for a rehearing. The Conseil privé could also assume jurisdiction over a case upon request of one of the parties if that party's adversary had relatives or allies in the court in question (such as a father, child, son-in-law, brother-in-law, uncle, nephew, or cousin german) or if the *présidents* or councillors had a stake in the case or if they had been consulted by the litigants, had prepared briefs for them, or had been asked to participate in the case. In any of these cases the Council could refer the case to another court or judge it itself. When there was a question as to which sovereign court was supposed to hear a particular case, the Conseil privé decided according to the procedure known as *règlement de juges*. Finally, the Conseil privé had jurisdiction over objections to the affixing of the seal to letters appointing officers, since the king had the sole power to choose and install his own officers.

The councils had the power to receive civil petitions and petitions charging procedural errors; they did not have to refer the case back to the original court for a new hearing but could overturn the judgment of the court on their own authority and then proceed to a hearing of the case on its merits. They suspended execution of judgments or quashed them upon simple petition to the Council. The Conseil privé judged some of the cases sent to it for *règlement de juges* itself. The king issued general evocations to tax farmers; courtiers; rebels, nobles, Protestants, cities, or individuals who surrendered; magistrates; and *commissaires*, so that any cases in which they became involved could be submitted to sovereign judgment by the Council, which thus became responsible for a considerable part of the administration of the kingdom. The councils became the true sovereign courts and stripped the courts of the bulk of their jurisdiction, leaving them only the worthless honor of their title. The courts did not resign themselves to this state of affairs.

In 1615, 1630, and 1644, the Council attempted to quell the agitation in the sovereign courts by issuing regulations that referred all litigation between private individuals to them and the lower courts. The astute Séguier even attempted in 1644 to secure registration of edicts by referring to the courts all cases involving the enforcement of edicts verified by the company in question, unless the company had made amendments to the edicts later stricken out by judgment of the Council. Regulations, decrees, and declarations frequently stated that "judgments thus granted to the sovereign courts shall not be quashed or stayed except as legally allowed by the Ordinances," that is to say, upon civil petition or charge of error and not upon ordinary petition to the Council, which would have made it possible to preserve the administrative authority of the *parlement*.

But the attempt was made in vain. All these practices spread. As early as 1632, any judgment handed down by any of the sovereign courts except the *parlement* of Paris could be quashed "in the Conseil d'Etat or Conseil privé, even though the king is not present." The Paris *parlement* still enjoyed the privilege that its decrees could be quashed only by the Conseil d'En-Haut after a hearing of its *premier président* and king's men. But in 1645 even the Conseil des Finances quashed a decree of *parlement* prohibiting the establishment of a *présidial* at Saint-Quentin upon petition of its residents, and *parlement* was unable to persuade the Conseil d'En-Haut to quash the decision of the Conseil des Finances. *Parlement*, supported by the other sovereign courts, pressed its objection. But the Council as a body declared that it held supreme authority over all of their decisions, an authority that was general and all-embracing.

The victory of the Council paved the way for the establishment of the authority of individuals and groups commissioned by the king, the intendants in particular. The sovereign courts maintained that cognizance of all cases that "lay in litigious jurisdiction" or involved respect for edicts and ordinances belonged in the first instance to the lower courts and on appeal to themselves, and that no commission, whether special or general, collective or individual, could deprive them of such jurisdiction. But Le Bret had earlier explained that by article 98 of the ordinance of Blois the king had expressed his intention to refer all cases involving private individuals and affairs to the officers who ought to have jurisdiction over them, but not cases "involving public affairs and affecting the state." For such cases, the king "may commission whomever he deems fit to assume jurisdiction." Individuals thus commissioned were superior to the officeholders as long as they were performing their duties, because "it is a maxim of canon law that *Omnis delegatus major est ordinario in re delegata.*"[17] One of Colbert's secretaries later added that the ordinance of Blois and the subsequent ordinance of 24 October 1648 "had been extorted from the kings by popular violence and were therefore null and void."[18]

The king had a fourth weapon in his battle against the courts: his intendants could resort to armed force, the *ultima ratio regum*. Once the king reached a decision and stated his judgment in the form of an order, his armies could carry it out. This was done at the time of the Nu-Pieds rebellion and other revolts in Normandy in 1639. Prior to the outbreak of violence in Rouen, the *premier président* of the *parlement* there had refused to take any preventive measures. During the riots *parlement* did not immediately impose the severe sanctions that might have put an end to the trouble but contented itself with going as a body to the site of the insurrection, a *pro forma* appearance that was totally without effect. It did almost nothing to protect the tax farmer Le Tellier de Tourneville and his offices. After the insurrection it was lax in prosecuting the leaders and showed no haste to reestablish the tax offices. The *parlement* did nothing at all about the other revolts in Normandy. Hence on 10 November 1639, the king sent General Gassion, who had served in the Thirty Years' War, to Normandy with 1,200 horses and 4,000 foot soldiers. The general attacked the Nu-Pieds in Lower Normandy and defeated them. On 15 November 1639, the king ordered Chancellor Séguier to go to Normandy on a mission that lasted from 19 December 1639 to 27 March 1640. Séguier took with him a whole commission of *conseillers d'Etat*, *maîtres des requêtes*, and officers from the Grande Chancellerie. He arrived in Rouen on 2 January 1640 and remained there until 11 February, after which he visited Lisieux, Caen, Bayeux, and Coutances. The chancellor had full command of the armies under Gassion. Acting on his own authority, without investigation or assessor and on verbal orders, he condemned several rebels to death, "by military judgment," as he put it, and had them broken on the wheel or hanged. Among these was Gorin, the ringleader of the August riots in Rouen, who died on 7 January 1640. "This wartime order was deemed the best way to enhance the king's authority. What is more, it was thought that in an affair of this kind, when a man is caught *in flagranti* in insurrection, it is best to try him after he is dead," according to the *maître des requêtes* François de Verthamont.[19] The chancellor violated the rule according to which the accused in a criminal case had the right to be heard. The rioters were outlaws and were thus made to serve as an example.

Finally, the chancellor proscribed officeholders wherever he stayed: officers of the sovereign courts, judicial officeholders, financial officeholders, and municipal *corps*. The *parlement* of Rouen was hit with an interdiction. Since 1637 it had been stubbornly refusing to register fiscal edicts. It had fought against tax farmers and intendants. Its failure to take action against the rioters when it had command of the Rouen city militia was regarded by the king as a dereliction of duty. As of 17 December 1639, the king forbade the officers of *parlement* to perform any judicial duties. Chancellor Séguier banished the members of *parlement* from the city on 8 January 1640. The king had the *parlement* of Normandy replaced by a commission of magistrates from the Paris *parlement* from 28 January 1640 until 26 October 1641. On that date the Rouen *parlement* was reinstated, but only sixteen of its members were restored to duty. The others remained proscribed until March 1643. In addition, the *parlement* was punished by the inauguration of two semestrial sessions, accompanied by the creation of a large number of new posts. In October 1643, after the death of Louis XIII and during the regency of Anne of Austria, the government, weakened by the fact that Louis XIV was still a minor, did away with the semestrial sessions and eliminated forty of the offices created in 1641. But the edict of September 1645 reestablished the semestrial sessions, and this was the primary reason why the Rouen *parlement* joined the Fronde and welcomed the rebel duc de Longueville on 6 January 1649.

Until August 1648 the king subjected the *corps* of officeholders to the tutelage of the intendants and the king's Council, royal *commissaires* who represented him and reported to him and who often carried out the most important duties of the officeholders, thereby enabling the sovereign to regain control over the companies, drained and weakened by the sale of offices and the annual dues.

Notes

1. Cited in Roland Mousnier, *La vénalité des offices sous Henri IV et Louis XIII* (2d ed., Paris: PUF, 1971), p. 607.

2. See above, chap. 13, pp. 221–26.

3. Mousnier, *Vénalité*, p. 628.

4. Isambert, vol. 16, p. 65.

5. Ibid., p. 69.

6. Ibid., p. 62.

7. Mousnier, *Vénalité*, p. 292.

8. Guyot and Merlin, *Traité des droits* (Visse, 1787), vol. 3, pp. 122–25.

9. Mousnier, *Vénalité*, p. 648.

10. Robert Arnauld d'Andilly, "Journal de la Cour sous Louis XIII," Bibl. Institut, Godefroy, 285, fol. 36. Cited in Mousnier, *Vénalité*, p. 659.

11. Cited in Mousnier, *Vénalité*, p. 650.

12. Ibid., p. 654.

13. Isambert, vol. 16, pp. 529–35.

14. Book I, chap. 1, p. 3, cited in Roland Mousnier, *La plume, la faucille et le marteau* (Paris: PUF, 1970), p. 174.

15. Le Bret, book II, chap. 2, p. 149, 159–60.

16. *Traité* attributed to Marillac, second quarter of seventeenth century, Cinq cents Colbert 194, fol. 55 r.

17. Le Bret, book IV, chap. 13, pp. 493–500 and 149–50.

18. Pierre Clément, *Lettres, instructions et mémoires de Colbert* (Imprimerie Impériale, later Imprimerie Nationale, 1861–82), vol. 1, pp. 253–57.

19. Cited in Madeleine Foisil, *La révolte des Nu-Pieds et les révoltes normandes de 1639* (Paris: PUF, 1970).

31

The Fronde and Its Failure

Parlement against the Council, Intendants, and Tax Farmers

Early in 1648 the Paris *parlement* became infuriated with the Council, the intendants, and the tax farmers: more precisely, with the council that negotiated the contracts with the tax farmers and assigned intendants to do their bidding. Besides the reasons already mentioned for *parlement*'s outrage, there was the fact that it was difficult for magistrates in *parlement* to participate in these contracts, even with the concealment afforded by notaries and dummy partnerships. Some magistrates had managed to take part in the contract for the *aides* in the Ile-de-France and Normandy. Among them were five *présidents à mortier:* Nesmond, Longueil, de Novion, de Mesmes, and de Bailleul.

De Novion had invested 57,000 livres. After him, investments were made by a councillor on the Grand Conseil, Portail (500 livres), a *président* in the Chambre des Enquêtes, Blancmesnil (3,000 livres), and six councillors in the Enquêtes (who invested from 150 to 700 livres). According to statements made by *président* de Mesmes on 23 July 1648, two-thirds of the families in *parlement* had lent money to the contractors for the *cinq grosses fermes* at either 5 percent or 5.55 percent. But the members of *parlement* resented the fact that the *traitants* were monopolizing contracts for the collection of royal taxes. On 24 July 1648, Pithon, a councillor in the Chambre des Enquêtes, complained during deliberations over the lease on the farms that the *traitants* were "offering so much that no one can outbid them."

The members of *parlement* were beginning to worry that the *partisans* and *traitants* might compete with them for offices in *parlement*. They feared for their brothers, sons, and nephews. It was generally believed that the *financiers* had purchased offices under assumed names. *Parlement* wanted to keep the sons of *partisans* and *traitants* out of the courts. Already there was one son of a former *traitant* serving as a *président* in the Third Chambre des Enquêtes: Thoré, the son of *surintendant* Particelli d'Emery. The councillor Bonneau was the son and nephew of a *partisan*. Several councillors had either a father or an uncle involved in the farms: Ribère, Le Vasseur, de Malo, and Gillot, all in the Chambres des Enquêtes.

Parlement took a dim view of marriages between magistrates of the company and the daughters of *financiers*. A nephew of the *président* de Mesmes had married a daughter of La Bazinière. *Président* de Bailleul had married the sister of Le Ragois de Bretonvilliers, a former *payeur des rentes* who had, to be sure, become a *président* in the Chambre des Comptes. Hervé, a councillor in the notorious Troisième des Enquêtes, had married a daughter of Le Ragois Bourgneuf. The *président* Le Cogneux was the brother-in-law of the *président* de Thoré. His son was the brother-in-law of Galand, a council secretary with a stake in the *partis*.

Of course the newcomers quickly absorbed the *esprit de corps* of *parlement*. The former *financier* Daurat, who had been involved in business and tax collection, nevertheless attacked the profession of *traitant* when he became a member of the Troisième des Enquêtes. Still, the *financiers* posed a threat to families in *parlement* and magistrates in the lower courts with designs on seats in *parlement*.

Support for *Parlement* and Justification of Its Actions

Parlement believed that it had good reason for its opposition. On 30 May 1645, the *président* Barillon pointed out that France was governed by two kinds of laws. Some laws were merely temporary administrative regulations, while others established the very foundations of the monarchy. Not even the sovereign could claim to be exempt from obedience to the latter. On this point the members of *parlement* were unanimous. They were divided on the extent of their opposition, however. Some, like the *avocat général* Omer Talon (who was admittedly one of the "king's men"), held that the king alone had the power to judge his actions, because the royal power, which came to him from on high, was embodied in his person and could not be divided. The king was obliged to account for his actions only to God and to his conscience. The sign that the royal power issued from heaven and that God's omnipotent right hand assisted the king, God's reflection on earth, was none other than the fact that the sovereign allowed the magistrates to express their innermost feelings, scrutinize his wishes, and speak against them in his presence (*lit de justice* of 15 January 1648). In consequence, *parlement*'s only recourse against the express will of the king was the remonstrance.

Others, however, maintained that *parlement* could go against the king's express will and make decisions in its own right. In effect, officeholders received their power from the prince. Thus, the royal power, the unique foundation of all government, was transmitted to them, and they might therefore have occasion to rise up against errors committed, not by the king as sovereign, but by the person occupying the throne, who was after all only a man. This theory was put forward by the *président* Le Coigneux and councillors Broussel, Le Cocq de Corbeville, and Menardeau of the Grand-Chambre. The majority supported them.

Parlement knew that the people would follow it because its cause was a popular one: opposition to royal taxation. The people of Paris felt a kind of sentimental attachment to the Paris *parlement*, and even a kind of veneration for it. They paid close attention to its deliberations. For debates on edicts some 220 or so persons from the eight chambers of *parlement* plus the king's men would meet, dressed in fine red cloth and ermine. The *premier président* would open the session by intoning the words: "What is to be done for the public interest?" Debate was quite lively. The opinions expressed were often caustic, speakers playing to an audience that listened from loges. Notes and messages were sometimes sent from the loges to the halls and galleries. Accounts of the proceedings were carried down the stairways into the court-yard and the jumble of nearby streets, where heavy crowds gathered on the days of important sessions. When the *présidents* and councillors left the chamber they were greeted as "fathers of their country."

The people of Paris were firm allies of the peasants in the surrounding countryside, who came to the city to market their produce and frequently came into contact with urban artisans, even marrying into the same families. Some Parisians owned fiefs and *censives* in the suburbs, and ties of patronage and service grew up between them and the peasants. Thus the peasantry was affected when *parlement* became aroused.

Declarations made by the Paris *parlement* were echoed in the countryside, and the example of Paris was often followed. *Parlements* in the provinces, city dwellers, and peasants in the countryside all became agitated. Everyone had some complaint of his own against the king's Council and against the "Parisian" *traitants* and *commissaires* it sent, who trampled on local liberties, privileges, and customs. Peasants in many areas such as Saintonge, Quercy, and Périgord each wanted a piece of some "Parisian." As *parlement* pressed forward with its agitation, the kingdom fell into anarchy and came apart at the seams. If the battle of Lens had been lost, who knows what might have happened.

The Paris *parlement* believed it could count on the support of the provincial *parlements*. It was sure of the support of officeholders in the ordinary lower courts, as well as those in the extraordinary lower courts who had been stripped of their functions by the intendants as a way of helping the *traitants*, such as the *trésoriers de France* and the *élus*. The Syndicat des Elus, which was established on 26 October 1641 and the Association des Trésoriers de France, created in 1599, were ready to follow *parlement* and lend it their support.

The Renewal of the Paulette and the Crystallization of Discontent

It was the question of renewing the annual dues or Paulette, which expired on 31 December 1647 that crystallized all the various discontents. At first the principal minister and the officeholders engaged in the usual negotiations. When Omer Talon, *premier avocat du roi* in the Paris *parlement*, advised Mazarin to grant the annual dues to *parlement* on 5 January 1648, Mazarin, who was irritated by the issue, answered in this way: "It was appropriate that the hope of obtaining [the annual dues] served some purpose, until all the king's business had been settled."[1] On 17 January 1648, Mathieu Molé, *premier président* of the Paris *parlement*, pointed out, in connection with the refusal to verify the edicts, that "since the annual dues were not granted, the Company maintained its customary firmness in these encounters." When *parlement* appeared to weaken, the Council issued a declaration on 30 April 1648, granting the annual dues in return for the elimination of four years' salary payments. Only officeholders in *parlement* would receive the annual dues for nothing. But the company was well aware that since 1621 the king had maintained the upper hand by granting unequal concessions to different groups of officeholders, thereby dividing their ranks. *Parlement* therefore maintained an unbroken front with the other officeholders, and the consequence of the declaration of 30 April was the decree of 13 May, the so-called arrêt d'Union, which, in contempt of the royal interdictions of 1615 and 1641, created the Assemblée de la Chambre Saint-Louis.

According to the arrêt d'Union, the four sovereign companies of Paris, *parlement*, the Chambre des Comptes, the Cour des Aides, and the Grand Conseil, were to elect deputies who would gather in the Chambre Saint-Louis to consider ways to reform the state. On 18 May the king's Council did away with the annual dues. The queen declared that to establish "an assembly and to make of the four sovereign companies a fifth without orders from the king . . . was a sort of republic within the monarchy." In order to get the annual dues reinstated, *parlement* disregarded the verbal interdictions of the chancellor and the queen and the decrees issued by the Conseil d'En-Haut on 7 and 10 June, which quashed the arrêt d'Union.

The Assemblée de la Chambre Saint-Louis and the New Constitution

The Assemblée de la Chambre Saint-Louis met from 30 June until 9 July 1648 and came to three decisions, which were submitted to *parlement* and transformed by it into decrees. These decisions pertained to three main issues: the authority of the sovereign courts as against the king's Council and other royal *commissaires*, the defense of taxpayers against imposts and other financial expedients, and the protection of wholesalers, retailers, and artisans, particularly in Paris. In what follows we shall concentrate mainly on the first of these three issues.

In regard to the authority of the sovereign courts, the assembly came to a decision in its first meeting on 30 June and in its first article stated the following: "The commissions of the intendants of justice, and all other extraordinary commissions not verified in the sovereign courts, shall be revoked effective immediately."[2] On 1 July, in article 6, the assembly prohibited holding any subject of the king prisoner for more than twenty-four hours without interrogating him as laid down in the ordinances and turning him over to his natural judge; it further prohibited the use of *lettres de cachet* to prevent any royal officeholder from carrying out his duties or to banish or imprison any such official. Finally, on 7 July the assembly demanded in article 17 that all litigation be referred to the sovereign courts, that all evocations be eliminated, particularly those accorded to tax farmers and *traitants*, that individuals be prohibited from appealing to the king's Council and that the Council be prohibited from quashing decrees of the sovereign courts, and, finally, that the *maîtres des requêtes*, from whose ranks most of the intendants were drawn, be prohibited from judging cases in last resort.

Article 3, which was adopted during the second session on 1 July, launched a counterrevolution within the government against the royal revolution effected by the use of *commissaires*, the instruments of the modern state and its *raison d'état*. On the surface the article was concerned solely with the creation of imposts: "No impositions and taxes shall be made except by virtue of edicts and declarations duly verified in the sovereign courts, to which jurisdiction belongs, with *free suffrage*, and furthermore, *execution* of said edicts and declarations shall be the exclusive province of said courts . . ." The mention of "free suffrage" referred to the verification of edicts in the presence of the king, sitting in *lit de justice*. The gentlemen of *parlement* were willing to allow the *lit de justice* only as an occasion for the king to come to them to hear their advice on a question of general policy. When it was a question of making law, they held that the presence of the king violated the freedom of suffrage; in other words, they claimed the right to deliberate upon edicts and ordinances and to cast their votes on their own, without interference by the king.

Their action was therefore in essence revolutionary because according to the fundamental laws of the kingdom, the king and his kingdom were an indissoluble whole. The king was the head of the mystical body of the monarchy. When the king came to *parlement* in the company of the peers, princes, high crown officers, and *conseillers d'Etat*, he was reconstituting the "Cour le Roi," the Curia Regis. The presence of the king did not infringe the court's freedom of opinion, because the court, as epitome of the kingdom, did not exist without the king. The king collected the opinions of the court through the chancellor, but he then determined its profound wishes by himself, and these were necessarily identical with his own profound wishes. By law, the profound wishes of the kingdom could differ from the opinions expressed by the members of *parlement*, and in matters of state the king could decide against the majority. This was the "mystery of the monarchy." By its actions, therefore, *parlement* was overthrowing the customary constitution of France. It was making a distinction between two elements that in reality were united, inseparable, and indispensable: the king and the kingdom, a single entity.

If *parlement* had succeeded, and assuming that it limited itself to deciding fiscal laws, the result would have been a monarchy in which all taxes would have been voted by *parlement* and levied under its authority. A judicial power, *parlement* would also have wielded a portion of the legislative and executive power as well. Its influence would have extended far beyond the area of finance, for it could have forced the king to accept the foreign and internal policies it preferred by refusing to provide the means of carrying out these with which it disagreed. *Parlement* would thus have changed France from an absolute monarchy to a monarchy in which the king merely executed the will of the "fourth estate," composed of men of the gown, men who owned the revenue of their office and to all intents and purposes owned the office itself—a fourth estate that was in principle an aristocracy, composed of nobles or men in the process of acquiring nobility, but in fact an oligarchy of magistrates, in control of a judicial government and administration.

The assembly sought further to consolidate the material and moral position of this oligarchy. In addition to the articles reestablishing the salaries and dues, article 19, adopted on 8 July, demanded that no offices be created "in either judiciary or finance" except by edicts verified in the sovereign courts. Furthermore, the status of the sovereign companies, the *trésoriers de France*, the presidial judges, and other judges was not to be altered in any way, whether by increasing the number of officeholders, establishing semestrial offices, or breaking up existing jurisdictions to create new companies.

The Paris *parlement* issued all these proposals in the form of decrees. In doing this it felt that it had solid support. The Rouen *parlement* had sent deputies to the Assembly and to the Paris *parlement* to secure the recession of the order that it meet on a semestrial basis. The Association des Trésoriers de France and the Syndicat des Elus joined with the Assembly and *parlement*. On 23 May the Association sent a circular letter to the *bureaux des Finances* asking for proof of the bad conduct of intendants in the area of finance and for evidence of pressure applied by them and by the *traitants*. Seventeen bureaus replied to this letter during June and July of 1648. The circular letter stirred up considerable emotion. Some provincial intendants, along with *traitants* and *partisans*, denounced the *trésoriers de France* to the Council. The Council sent six of them to the Bastille. The *trésoriers de France* appealed to *parlement*. On 13 June 1648, delegates from *parlement* were received at the Palais-Royal by the queen and the king's Council. The chancellor blamed the circular letter sent by the *trésoriers de France* for the actions of France's enemies, who were now menacing the country's borders "in order to test the affections of the populace and to see whether the reports they have received that opinion is divided are true."[3] But *parlement* persisted in its opposition, aided by the *trésoriers de France*. Conferences were held on 8 and 10 July at the Palais d'Orléans, and when the chancellor told the deputies of the four companies that it was impossible to do without the services of the intendants and *traitants*, the *trésoriers de France* offered to collect the *tailles* so scrupulously that the king would have four million livres in his coffers every month. *Parlement* therefore remained steadfast in its opposition.

The king's Council gave way. The edict of 18 July revoked all extraordinary commissions, in particular those of the intendants, except in the border provinces. The edict of 31 July made law of almost all the proposals of the Chambre Saint-Louis pertaining to justice and administration, except for article 6 which would have guaranteed officeholders the right to carry out their duties freely and to raise objections to governmental interference without limits of any kind. The same edict forbade the officeholders to continue their assembly. Furthermore, the government granted the annual dues on the same terms as in 1604, which were most advantageous. But this time *parlement* had gone too far to turn back. It was afraid of losing its popularity by striking an agreement that would have suggested it had been out only for itself. It therefore pressed on.

The next step was for *parlement* itself to interfere in the fiscal administration in the place of the king's Council. It demanded that its *commissaires*, the most active of whom was Broussel, a councillor in the Grand-Chambre, be allowed to prepare a list of duties on merchandise being brought into the city of Paris and, further, that they be allowed to revise the contracts with the farmers of the tax on salt and other taxes. Finally, on 22 August, at the behest of Broussel, *parlement* decided to prosecute some of the leading partisans: Catelan, Tabouret, and Le Fèvre.

The first consequence of *parlement*'s interference in policy was a frightful deficit in the treasury. No one paid any taxes. The peasants were convinced that the king was going to do away with taxation altogether. The *traitants* were increasingly reluctant to advance any money to the royal treasury. Badly paid, the king's armies began to fall apart. *Parlement* was making it difficult to wage war by drying up the king's sources of cash. It fanned the flames of rebellion by convincing people that their taxes were too heavy, unjust, and unnecessary, destined only to win glory for the king and to maintain the court in luxury, at a time when the Habsburg's ambitious designs threatened the very existence of the kingdom and the court was so poor that it had scarcely enough money to live. The queen had to borrow from private lenders and pawn the crown jewels. Mazarin was forced to pawn his diamonds to pay the Swiss Guards and had to borrow from friends. The sovereign courts showed no more civic spirit than they had in 1597 when the Spanish made their surprise attack on Amiens, or in 1636, the "year of Corbie," when the strategic border along the Somme was twice penetrated and the kingdom's capital threatened.

The Barricades and the Civil War to the Peace of Rueil

Fortunately, on 20 August the prince de Condé defeated the Spanish at Lens. On 25 August the king's Council decided to have arrested the members of the Paris *parlement* who had been most vehement toward the court: Broussel, the councillor in the Grand-Chambre, Blancmesnil, *président* in the Chambre des Enquêtes, and *président* Charton. The arrests were successfully carried out on Wednesday, 26 August, but triggered an insurrection in Paris on that same day. Barricades went up on Thursday, 27 August and Friday, 28 August. The court was forced to capitulate and free Broussel, who left prison in triumph.

Embittered, the queen had but one thought: to punish those who had "given the king Broussel for a partner." The court therefore departed for Rueil to await the prince de Condé and the troops from Flanders. Paris prepared for a siege. But the inhabitants of the city deplored the fact that the king's absence cut into business. At Rueil the court was afraid that the provinces would rebel and refuse to pay taxes. Condé, "Monsieur le Prince," the victorious general whose support was essential, despised *parlement*, but he also despised the cardinal. Neither side wished for war. On 22 October a royal declaration upheld the broad outlines of the constitution set forth by the Chambre Saint-Louis, the new Constitution of France. It was registered on 24 October 1648. On that day the Treaty of Westphalia was signed in Münster, sealing the victory of the king of France over the emperor, giving France the bishoprics of Metz, Toul, and Verdun and the rights of the Austrian Habsburgs in Alsace, as well as scotching the emperor's designs on European hegemony. The 350 states that made up the Holy Roman Empire were granted quasi-sovereignty. But the event, so important for France and for the life of every French man and woman, went almost unnoticed: Westphalia is a long way from the Pont-Neuf.

The court returned to Paris. The violation of the customary constitution remained, as did the insult to royal sovereignty and the injury to the government's prestige. The war with Spain was still raging, and the Constitution of 22 October was going to make it impossible to fight. *Parlement* continued to hold assemblies and wanted to carry through its reforms, and it was still dead set against the cardinal. The court resigned itself to civil war. During the night of 5 January 1649, the queen, after eating the *gâteau des Rois*, left for Saint-Germain with the boy king. Monsieur and Monsieur le Prince followed. Condé blockaded the city. Though his forces were invincible in the open country, he lacked the means to take Paris. *Parlement* sent the king word that its quarrel was not with him but with Mazarin, a favorite, a creature who had usurped the king's power. Hence *parlement* was not in a state of rebellion but rather carrying out its duty. Some princes rallied to the Fronde, however: the duchesse de Longueville and her brother Conti, who split with their brother Condé, and the duc de Longueville, the governor of Normandy, carried the *parlement* of Rouen and the province of Normandy with them. The duc de Bouillon, a member of the La Tour d'Auvergne clan and prince of the sovereign principality of Sedan, and his brother, the vicomte de Turenne, both nephews of the princes of Orange, also joined, as did d'Elboeuf, the Lorraine prince. By remaining loyal to his family Turenne betrayed the king. He attempted to lead his army from Germany to Paris to come to the aid of *parlement*, but failed and had to flee to Holland. The princes negotiated with Spain. A Spanish envoy was received by *parlement*. France seemed to have gone back to the time of the Second League.

Owing to disgust and fear on the part of the Parisians, the *premier président* Molé was able to negotiate a peace treaty in the early days of March 1649 at Rueil. The king confirmed his declaration of 23 October 1649, with some modifications. The *"Fronde parlementaire"* was over. But the basic problem remained. The peace was no more than a truce.

The Fronde of the Princes and the Participation of *Parlement*

By forcing the queen to call upon the help of the prince de Condé, by accepting the help of certain princes, and by refusing to reject the idea of an accord with the enemy, *parlement* had helped lay the groundwork for the introduction of the army, i.e., the high nobility and the *gentilhommerie*, into politics. Condé, for himself and his friends, laid claim to governorships, honors, money—in short, to all of France. The Fronde of the princes was under way. The princes of the blood, other princes, and dukes, the Condés, Contis, Longuevilles, and Bouillons, involved their *fidèles*, great nobles and ordinary *gentilshommes*, and even *fidèles* of the king such as the vicomte de Turenne, the La Trimoilles, and the Durfort de Lorges in the conflict. The Frondeurs were constantly trying to work out some kind of union with *parlement* and the city of Paris. In the midst of this imbroglio, with its interplay of vanity, ambition, and intrigue, its shifting alliances and dramatic gestures, important constitutional questions were raised. The pen waged war alongside the sword, as journalists wrote in weeklies and writers of all sorts unleashed a torrent of pamphlets and songs for and against Mazarin. These were known as *"Mazarinades,"* from the title of a satirical poem attributed to Scarron that appeared in 1651 under the title *La Mazarinade*. The king, *parlement*, and the princes all extended their political theories between 1649 and 1652.

The Doctrine of *Parlement*

The Frondeurs found their scapegoat in Mazarin. They accused him of usurping power and of being a thief who was stealing France blind, for he was head of the Council and chief of the intendants in the provinces and armies, that small group of "favorites" and "creatures" for whose benefit the repressive government worked in disregard of all traditional rights, liberties, exemptions, and privileges. Mazarin was therefore a tyrant twice over, by usurpation and by practice. His presence in the government and his activities as its head violated the customary constitution of the kingdom, "the fundamental laws," to which all parties made reference.

Parlement was agreed that Mazarin was violating the customary constitution by being, in their eyes, a foreigner. Mazarin had, in April 1639, received "letters of naturality" that had been registered and verified by the Chambre des Comptes in June 1639. Such letters merely exempted their beneficiary from certain disabilities to which foreigners were liable, however: he could bequeath his property in the kingdom and possess an ecclesiastical benefice, for example. Nominated for a cardinalate by the king, he had received the "crown hat," a cardinal's hat that the king of France could obtain from the pope for a person of his choosing. Louis XIII had named him godfather to the future Louis XIV and superintendent of his education. In the eyes of *parlement* and the other Frondeurs, however, none of these favors did anything to alter the fact of foreign birth. The king's favorite was still an Italian, a Roman, a foreigner. As the Frondeurs saw it, while the king could elect to employ foreigners in his service, only Frenchmen were entitled to participate in government decision-making.

According to *parlement* and the Frondeurs, Mazarin also violated the customary constitution because he was a cardinal. As they saw it, a cardinal could be neither principal minister nor minister of state nor a member of the royal councils. The presence of a cardinal in one of these positions violated, in the first place, the organic constitution of the state and the social division of labor. It was up to the nobility to command and to the clergy to pray and secure heaven's favors for the nation. Hence ecclesiastics ought not to be in the government. Furthermore, canon law prohibited them from taking part in secular affairs. More than that, they were forbidden to condemn any criminal to the loss of life or liberty. When Mazarin made the decision to go to war, which was viewed as tantamount to a royal judgment, when he ordered the levy of troops, appointed officers, caused the blood of thousands of men to be spilled on the field of battle, and obliged millions of others to die in poverty to finance the war, it was an intolerable scandal. Mazarin's friends might have rejoined that he was not a priest. All his life he remained a mere tonsured cleric, who never got beyond thinking in the last years of his life that he might become a priest. But he was a cleric, a cardinal. *Parlement* and the Frondeurs held that no cardinal should ever be a minister, because a cardinal's rank as a prince of the Church gave him sufficient authority to usurp the king's sovereign power.

Parlement and the Frondeurs further held that Mazarin was violating the customary constitution by infringing the rights of the Paris *parlement*. This great court of magistrates attempted to justify its claims by concocting a vast historical myth, in which legendary figures were not lacking. The *présidents* and councillors of the Paris *parlement* held that the *parlement* of Paris was the *parlement* of France. It was, they argued, the heir of the General Assembly of the Franks, which had chosen Clovis's father Pharamond as king because of his prowess. Under the first dynasty, the Merovingians, the Franks had gathered annually and in this assembly made laws, concluded peace treaties, declared war, forged alliances, and dealt with all important matters. All decisions were made by "free suffrage," a detail included as a criticism of the *lits de justice*.

Under the second dynasty, the Carolingians, France grew much larger thanks to the conquests of Charlemagne and his children. It became "impossible to assemble the whole monarchy as in the past." The kings contented themselves with assembling the most important people in the kingdom every year in one place or another. This form of government was continued for three hundred years under the third dynasty, the Capetians. It was in the time of Philip Augustus that people began referring to this assembly as *parlement*. Philip the Fair established a fixed location for its meetings. It was not required to hear cases every day and so began to assume appellate jurisdiction over important cases involving private individuals. But it was still the representative of the General Assembly of the Franks, an epitome, as it were, of the three estates: nobility, clergy, and common people. As such it retained jurisdiction over public affairs. It verified peace treaties. The king justified his decision to wage war before *parlement*. It decided on taxes, the nomination of magistrates, and new titles. The consent of *parlement* was tantamount to the consent of the people. The fundamental law of the monarchy remained what it had been: *parlement* must always grant its consent on behalf of the people.

The king was always a participant in *parlement*'s deliberations and resolutions. Since *parlement* had been fixed in one location, however, the king had elected to receive the counsel of a few notable individuals. By doing so he resolved no issues, because these advisers always acted in the capacity of individuals, not as a *corps;* their function was to make proposals to *parlement*, which was the king's true Council. *Parlement* was not subject to the jurisdiction of the so-called king's Council, which was not a state *corps*. "The Council has no public character." "Conseil d'En-Haut" was a new and prestigious title intended to provide support for ministerial tyranny. This title did not in fact come into use until 1643.

The king was present in the Council not to destroy laws but to preserve them. Therein lay his true sovereignty, the result of a contract between the king and his people sealed by the king's oath. The king was supposed to uphold the established order. Together with his Council he could decide on such compensations, honors, and dignities as depended upon his grace alone. He could decide to wage war or to lay siege to one city rather than another. All this was by his grace; it was his prerogative to decide and to execute his decisions. But as soon as the question at issue was one in which the people had an interest, *parlement* must be brought into the matter. It was in his *parlement* that the king contracted with his people, and there all questions must be submitted to consideration by "free suffrage." As *parlement* saw it, the decree of the Conseil d'Etat of 18 January 1652 did not have the power to overturn the decree of *parlement* of 29 December 1651, directed against Mazarin, because ancient law prescribed that government was never to be entrusted to a foreigner. To go against this law the king would have had to come to *parlement* with a declaration abolishing this law, for verification by "free suffrage" in *parlement*.

Parlement and its supporters held that there was a difference between the king's person and the kingship. The king did indeed embody the kingship, so that in his person he was the body of the kingdom. But the kingdom also had a soul: law, justice, ancient custom, the public orders, the governmental order, Salic Law. The would-be king's Council did indeed possess the person of a minor king (who officially attained his majority in September 1651), a child who had been spirited away from the princes of the blood, from *parlement*, and from the capital city of the kingdom. The Council did not possess the body of kingship, however, but only its shadow. The soul was elsewhere: in *parlement*. The king was sovereign only in his *parlement*.

And what if Mazarin and his henchmen killed the king to make sure of their plunder? *Parlement*, representing the Assembly of the Franks, would recognize the duc d'Anjou, the king's brother, and would grant sovereign authority to the duc d'Orléans during the minority of the young prince. If in turn the duc d'Anjou was assassinated by the royal favorite and his creatures, *parlement* would dispose of the crown as it saw fit. There was no need of convoking the Estates General.

Indeed, there was never any need of convoking the Estates General. *Parlement* could "render sovereign decisions in all matters." It could propose to the king the names of men to serve as *conseillers d'Etat* and ministers, it could remove them from office, and it could receive their oath to the king. It was "the repository and as it were the perpetual tutor of the sovereign authority." It was further stated that "a decree issued by the *parlement* of Paris with the participation of the princes of the blood and the dukes-and-peers of the Crown in an affair of state is above all sovereign authority, or rather, it is itself sovereign authority."[4]

Parlement was in principle a supporter of all customary rights of birth or status. Accordingly, the king was to govern his Estates himself, in every detail, as God governs all parts of the universe. The king was to act as his own prime minister and was not to include in his Council a person designated to act as prime minister, particularly not a favorite like Mazarin, who had never wanted peace because peace would have ruined his opportunity to rob the king's treasury. While acting as his own governor the king had the duty to consult on all important matters with the princes of his blood, men born to act as his advisers, whose rights were inviolable.

If, owing to youth or weakness, the king allowed the government to be run by a favorite who then usurped the king's power at the expense of the princes of the blood, thereby behaving as a tyrant, then it was up to the princes of the blood, the high crown officers, and the members of *parlement* to reestablish order. The princes recognized to be of royal blood were in fact members of a family that the state had chosen to rule it and protect it from harm. Their quality and dignity were sacred. All recognized descendants of Hugh Capet belonged to the kingdom. They were not private individuals. They could not renounce their natural rights in the face of the "Mazarin cabal," which was abusing the king's sovereign authority. Beyond that, Mazarin and his henchmen were holding the young king and his Spanish mother prisoner.

It was up to the princes of the blood to restore the state to its original form and to establish, under the sovereign authority of the king, a legitimate Council, composed of princes of the blood, other princes, high crown officers, senior *conseillers d'Etat* who had held high office, and members of great houses and ancient families, all of whom sat in *parlement*. All of these men were entitled by nature and by blood to take part in the government and in the management of public affairs, by virtue of the ancient and fundamental laws of the kingdom, which excluded women and foreigners. And they were entitled to play this role during the king's youth, not merely until he had attained his official majority at the beginning of his fourteenth year but until he reached his actual majority at age twenty-one. They were further entitled to play this role if the king was indisposed in mind or body or if he was held prisoner, as he now was. In such cases Monseigneur le duc d'Orléans was the legitimate regent and guardian of the kingdom as first prince of the blood. He was to govern in conjunction with the above-mentioned Council and was not to allow anyone to participate in the regency in violation of the laws of the state, not even the mother of the king.

Parlement was also ostensibly a supporter of the rights of the nobility, though its support was conditional on its being understood to belong to the nobility itself. *Parlement* agreed that all the usual exemptions, honors, rights, and immunities, the full luster of the nobility, should be restored, and that nobles should control the government in peace as well as war.

In principle *parlement* also supported the Estates General, provided they were held intermittently and all articles and edicts there drawn up were submitted to *parlement* for scrutiny and verification.

The doctrine summarized above was that of the most extreme members, who for a long time carried *parlement* in their wake. Among the *présidents* and councillors many shades of opinion were to be found, however.

The "Union of Classes"

Broadly speaking, the provincial *parlements* shared the opinions of the Parisian magistrates. There were, however, various shades of opinion in the *parlements* and other sovereign courts. Moreover, the Paris *parlement* attempted to take the lead and coordinate the efforts of all the other courts. In January 1649 it urged all the *parlements* to follow its lead. The Rouen *parlement* sent one of its councillors, François Myron, to act as accredited representative to the *premier président* of the Paris *parlement*. Furthermore, the various *parlements* maintained that, taken together, they all constituted one *parlement*, the *parlement* of France, each of them being a "class" within this larger body. Any action taken against any one of them was considered to be an action against them all. In support of this "theory of classes" the *parlements* adduced, to begin with, Charles VII's ordinance of 12 November

1454 pertaining to the reestablishment of the *parlement* of Toulouse. The *parlements* of Toulouse and Paris, said the ordinance, had the same power and authority and "were to be viewed as united and as constituting a single *parlement*. And the *présidents* and councillors of the aforementioned *parlements* and of each one of them are to be regarded as all being one." *Présidents* and councillors from any *parlement* had always been allowed to sit in all the others. Henri II, in his declaration of 24 November 1549, granted the magistrates of the *parlements* of Piedmont and Savoy "access and the right to vote and take part in deliberations in the other *parlements* of the kingdom." In the same year the king chose magistrates from all the *parlements* to render justice in Bordeaux in place of the *parlement* of that city, which had been shut down for laxity in dealing with the unrest in Guyenne. Under Charles IX, Chancellor de l'Hospital told the Paris *parlement* in a speech delivered on 7 September 1560 that "the various *parlements* are merely different classes of the king's *parlement*." On 10 September 1586, the *avocat général* Thomas de Verdun, writing on the County of Eu in a report on the preparation of a compilation of "Local Customs of Normandy," made the following statement: "All the *parlements* are but a single court, instituted and ordained for the distribution of justice and dispatched to various regions for the convenience of the king's subjects, with equal and identical authority and sovereignty." This was the opinion of the *premier président* of the Rouen *parlement*, Claude Groulard. The *président* of the Toulouse *parlement*, writing at the beginning of the seventeenth century in his "thirteen books on the *parlements* of France," asserted that "all the *parlements* of France are, properly speaking, only one *parlement*, dispersed in the various provinces so as to render justice more conveniently to the king's subjects."[5] Du Tillet, the *greffier en chef* of the Paris *parlement*, took a similar view: "The king has but one sovereign justice, committed by him to his *parlements*, which together constitute but one court with various districts."[6]

All the essential claims made by the *parlements* during the eighteenth century had already been formulated in the seventeenth.

Divisions among the Rebels Lead to Failure

The Fronde failed to achieve its aims. Louis XIV returned in triumph to Paris on 21 October 1652. The last of the Frondeurs surrendered at Bordeaux on 3 August 1653. The king had won a military victory. He might have been beaten. That he won owed largely to a few hundred military officers of all ranks, who chose to honor the oath they had sworn to the sovereign and who fought and won the civil war. The prestige of the monarchy and its sacred character also played a large part in the victory. Was it an accident, a mere coincidence, that the greatest generals of the time, Condé and Turenne, were defeated when they fought against the king and victorious when they fought for him?

Divisions among the rebels also contributed to the king's victory. Despite their common hatred of the Council and the intendants, royal officeholders never managed to forge a thorough and lasting alliance. The actions of the various *parlements* were scattered and uncoordinated. The *parlement* of Rouen followed its governor, the duc de Longueville, and joined the Fronde against the king in 1649. By contrast, the parlements of Bordeaux and Provence joined the Fronde in opposition to their governors, the duc d'Epernon and the comte d'Alais, respectively (the governors were a kind of *commissaire*). Other *parlements* did very little, like that of Toulouse. The Paris *parlement* subscribed to the theory of classes, but, proud of its seniority, it claimed to be the only Court of Peers, which the other *parlements* disputed. The Paris *parlement* sometimes invited the other *parlements* to join it in opposition to the government but sometimes humiliated and scorned them, as though it were a body of a quite different kind.

The *trésoriers de France* came into conflict with the *élus*. The *trésoriers de France* claimed to be the successors and heirs of the four *trésoriers de France* and the four *généraux de Finances* who had worked closely with the king in the administration of royal finances prior to the reforms carried out by Francis I. Thus they considered themselves to be of higher status than the *élus*. They held that the *élus* owed them respect and obedience "for their salary and dues and for everything involving the king's finances and their administration." The *élus*, they claimed, must execute orders issued by the *trésoriers de France* "to hasten collection of the king's taxes." The *trésoriers de France* were supposed to preside over "the assessment and distribution of the *tailles* and *subsistances* in all the *élections* and *généralités* of the kingdom."

Since 1552 the *élus* had been unable to resign themselves to the installation of *trésoriers de France* and *généraux des Finances* in the *généralités*, which, by creating an intermediate echelon of regional financial administrators between themselves and the king's Council, had reduced their importance. They denied that the *trésoriers de France* were part of the same institution as the *généraux* of earlier times, who had been sovereign administrators. The function of the *trésoriers*, on the other hand, was specific and merely provincial. The *élus* denied any superiority to the *trésoriers*, arguing that they, the *élus*, were judges and therefore superior in the hierarchy of public servants to the *trésoriers de France*, who were merely financial officeholders. Socially, they were also superior, being the sons of *gentilshommes*, officeholders in the sovereign courts, and the better families in the towns, while the *trésoriers de France* were the sons of tax farmers' agents and *procureurs*. The *élus* also claimed superiority by virtue of their general culture and professional training.

The Syndicat des Elus tried to organize the opposition by sending out circular letters to its members beginning in November 1648. Throughout France *élus* refused to allow *trésoriers de France* access to their offices, refused to carry out their orders, and appealed their ordinances to the Cour des Aides. Consultations between the Syndicat des Elus and the Association des Trésoriers de France in May or June of 1649 were inconclusive. The *trésoriers de France* had no choice but to ask the king's Council for a general regulation, which would have granted the *bureaux des Finances* almost all the powers of the provincial intendants. The king's Council was careful not to take sides in the conflict, however. The dispute continued unabated until 1653.

The Cour des Aides of Paris could not forgive the *trésoriers généraux de France*, who were regional officials, for having held on to the rank of members of the sovereign courts, much less for claiming that as such they were subject to the orders of the king's Council alone and did not recognize the jurisdiction of the Cour des Aides, setting themselves up between the Cour and the *élus* in principle as a different authority but in fact as a rival one. The *élus* condemned by the *trésoriers généraux de France* to pay fines appealed their sentences to the Cour des Aides, which frequently set these sentences aside, even when they had been issued in connection with "hastening the collection of the king's taxes." When necessary, the Cour des Aides even subpoenaed *trésoriers de France* to appear before it in person. The Cour des Aides betrayed the cause of the officeholders by accepting royal commissions for its members in the *généralités*. By verifying these commissions the Cour increased the powers granted to the *commissaires*, allowing them to preside over the assessment of the *tailles* and salt taxes.

The Chambres des Comptes of Paris and Rouen tried to subject the *trésoriers généraux de France* to their authority and to curtail their jurisdiction. The Chambre des Comptes of Paris took it upon itself to convey the royal declarations of October 1648 and March 1649 concerning the pacification of unrest to the *trésoriers généraux de France* within its jurisdiction, as *parlement* did for the *baillis* and *sénéchaux*. Furthermore, in order to indicate the subordinate status of the *trésoriers généraux* even more clearly, the Chambre des Comptes characterized the *procureurs du roi* assigned to the treasurers' companies as deputy *procureurs* in the Chambre des Comptes. The *trésoriers généraux de France* refused to countenance the setting of a precedent that would have reduced them below the status of a sovereign company. Following the advice of their association's council, they refused to register the declarations sent by the Chambre des Comptes and would not enforce their execution. They waited to receive letters patent from the king's Council before proceeding to enforcement. The Chambre des Comptes subsequently made further inroads into the responsibilities of the treasurers. It set aside, for example, the certification of receipt of homage from a *gentilhomme* from Anjou that had been drawn up by the *bureau des Finances* in Tours and ordered that homages should henceforth be received in the *sénéchaussée* of Maine by the *procureur du roi* in the presidial court of Le Mans, acting as subdelegate for the Chambre des Comptes. The *trésoriers généraux de France* held this action to be illegal on three counts: the Chambre had no right to set aside ordinances issued by the *trésoriers généraux;* it had no right to subdelegate its authority; finally, it had no right to receive homages in places other than its own seat, and each *bureau des Finances* was entitled to receive homages in its own district to the exclusion of the Chambre des Comptes. The Chambre des Comptes of Rouen allowed *receveurs* and *commis* to submit their accounts without verification by the *bureau des Finances* of Rouen, as though that bureau did not exist. The *trésoriers généraux de France* in Rouen resigned themselves to submit this dispute to the Council in 1650, and once again the Council was given the opportunity to arbitrate in a dispute between officeholders.

In 1649 the Paris *parlement* issued a decree in favor of the *lieutenants généraux* of the *bailliages* and *sénéchaussées*, who were attempting to receive the faith and homage of the king's vassals in place of the *trésoriers généraux de France*. The *parlement* of Toulouse treated the *trésoriers généraux de France* in Montauban as subordinates, and they complained that this had compromised their public image. The Toulouse *parlement* issued a decree ordering the *bureau des Finances* in Montauban to reverse the king's commissions for the *tailles* of 1649 and reduce their amount by 900,000 livres, because the king had agreed to collect only 40,000,000 livres for the entire kingdom and the *généralité* of Montauban should not be required to bear more than one-seventeenth of the total. The *trésoriers généraux de France* opposed *parlement* on this. But in a number of *élections* in their district, the *élus* carried out *parlement*'s orders.

All the *corps* of officeholders had but one goal: to expand their own jurisdiction at someone else's expense. It was impossible for them to maintain a common front against the king's Council and the other *commissaires*. Because their desires conflicted with one another, they were forced to turn to the king's Council, thereby enabling it to secure recognition of its superior authority and to use its role as arbitrator to stall for time so that it might come out on top in the end.

Parlement and the *nobles d'épée* were also unable to maintain a common front. Both the princes of the blood and *parlement* were bent on standing up for their reciprocal rights, but each group was determined to gain control and to use its absolute power to its own advantage. By "nobility" the *gentilshommes* meant themselves. They met in Paris in an assembly that lasted from 25 February until 5 March 1651 at the Convent of the Cordeliers. This was followed by meetings in the provinces as late as July 1652. The *gentilshommes* who attended these meetings expressed their views in a *Journal de l'Assemblée de la Noblesse* and in various *cahiers* kept for the Estates General, which were convoked but never met. The *gentilshommes* acknowledged that the state had indeed been created by the kings but argued that it was supported and held together by the blood of *gentilshommes*, the true bedrock of the monarchy. Without a monarchy there was no nobility, but without nobles there was no monarchy. They demanded the reestablishement of their exemptions, honors, immunities, and rights, foremost among them the right to participate in the formulation of government policy. The third estate was supposed to execute the orders of the nobility in its behalf, and the third estate included the officeholders, even the members of *parlement,* who were merely "bourgeois." Hatmakers and chandlers had usurped the posts in *parlement* through the "tyranny of favoritism."

Parlement, princes of the blood, and *gentilshommes* also differed over the convocation of the Estates General. Everyone except the princes and the *parlement* wished to see the Estates General held. People of all sorts, *gentilshommes* to the fore, asked that the Estates be called to embody the customary constitution. A body of doctrine concerning the Estates General was worked out in detail in a number of "Mazarinades." This doctrine was fairly well summed up by Claude Joly, the canon of Notre-Dame, in 1652.[7] It posed a threat to the claims of the *parlements* and the other sovereign courts.

Kings, it was held, were established by the people to secure justice. The people had the right to check the king's actions by remonstrating with him through the Estates General, an assembly of the three orders of the kingdom. Once the Estates General had presented their remonstrances and requests, along with their prayers, the king was bound to be generous in granting them all that they wished, provided it was just. The Estates General were above the fundamental laws of the kingdom, above the law.

The Estates General had the power to reestablish ancient customs, laws, and ordinances, firmly and with vigor. This right was irrevocable. The power of the Estates was a public right.

The Estates General should meet regularly. They should be allowed to elect *commissaires* and deputies to enforce customs, laws, and ordinances. Between sessions these elected officials were supposed to see to it that decisions of the Estates were enforced.

It was further argued that the Estates General should be allowed to establish a special Chambre de Justice to enforce their decisions. This was to consist of councillors from *parlement* and other sovereign courts, who would have the power to judge infractions between sessions of the Estates.

The Estates General should be allowed to ask the king to get rid of bad ministers and should have the power to propose others. They should further be allowed to propose officers, i.e., magistrates, treasurers, and *receveurs,* or else force a return to the old system, under which three candidates would be elected for each office and the king would choose among them.

In sum, then, the ideal was that of a state of orders, a *Ständestaat,* which Claude Joly had seen in operation in Germany when he accompanied the duc de Longueville there to participate in the negotiations at Münster.

Parlement against the Estates General: The Victory of the Council and the *Commissaires*

Under the system proposed by Joly, the *parlements* and the other sovereign courts would have become instruments of the Estates General. Behind Joly's doctrine lurked the idea of abolishing the sale of offices.

Parlement proclaimed its faith in the Estates General but did all it could to prevent the meeting, as did the government. On 23 January 1649, the government convoked a meeting of the Estates for 15 March 1649. Elections were held in several provinces and *cahiers* were prepared. On 29 March royal letters postponing the meeting until 1 October were issued, ostensibly on account of the campaign against the Spanish. On 18 September new royal letters adjourned the electoral assembly until further orders. During the summer of 1650, the nobility, i.e., the *gentilshommes*, irritated by these delays, held meetings in many places to attempt to convince the king that the Estates General should be convoked. The assembly of the nobility in Paris in February and March of 1651 reiterated this demand. *Parlement* was irritated. Some members of the gown quarreled with men of the sword, and there was talk among the *gentilshommes* of throwing the *premier président* into the Seine. In the face of orders from the Council, the Assembly of the Nobility refused to disperse. The nobles moved toward open rebellion. But Condé and the princes returned to Paris and advised the queen to convoke the Estates General at Tours in order to secure dissolution of the assembly. The meeting was set for October 1651. The princes' aim was to hold the Estates before the king's majority was proclaimed and to establish a government under the Estates General, which they would control, for a period of five years (until the king attained his real, as distinct from his official, majority). *Parlement* opposed this innovation, which would have ended its influence. Nevertheless, assemblies were held in the *bailliages* between July and September 1651 for the purpose of preparing the *cahiers* of the three orders and choosing deputies. But the Estates General were again postponed until 1 November 1652. Nothing more was heard of it.

The princes were united against Mazarin. But once they believed victory was in hand, they fell to bickering. Coalitions formed against the man who emerged from the chaos apparently on his way to power.

The disunity in the orders, *corps*, and companies made the king's final victory much easier.

It took a long time to restore order and the king's authority. Several years were needed to obliterate all traces of the constitution of the Chambre Saint-Louis. More Assemblies of the Nobility were held in the provinces. The aftereffects of the Fronde were felt until the Spanish were defeated at Dunes on 14 June 1658, and the Peace of the Pyrenees was signed in November 1659, ending the hopes of the opposition.

In the meantime, however, a series of crucial acts proclaimed the victory of the king's Council and the other *commissaires*. The Council issued regulations in 1654 and between 1 April 1655 and 4 May 1657, which took the decisive step, naming the king's Council the "first company in the kingdom," divided into three sections: the Conseil d'Etat et des Finances, the Conseil privé, and the Conseil des Finances. The Council quashed decrees of *parlement* and had increasing recourse to evocations, even though the declaration of 11 January 1657 attempted to reign it in somewhat.

The declaration of 23 October 1653 forbade magistrates in *parlement* to go to work for great lords as intendants of their political or private affairs or to receive pensions from them. It further prohibited *parlement* from taking cognizance of general affairs of state and of financial matters. *Parlement* was not to infringe upon the rights of those in charge of the administration of such affairs in any way. *Parlement* again tried to rally its forces. The king returned from Vincennes, where he had been hunting, to hold a *lit de justice* on 10 April 1655. There he ordered *parlement* to hold its peace and forbade it to hold further assemblies. *Parlement* gave in.

Beginning in 1656 intendants were reinstated everywhere.

The officeholders had been defeated by the *commissaires*.

Notes

1. Roland Mousnier, "Journées révolutionnaires," in *La Plume*, p. 286, n. 1.

2. Isambert, vol. 17, pp. 72–84.

3. Mousnier, *La Plume*, p. 308.

4. Cited by Mousnier, *Mazarin et le problème constitutionnel*, pp. 13–14.

5. La Roche-Flavin, *Trèze livres des Parlements de France*, book I, last paragraph; book II, chap. 2, secs. 25 and 35.

6. *Recueil des Roys de France, Du Conseil privé du Roy*, 1607 ed.

7. *Recueil de Maximes véritables et importantes pour l'institution d'un Roy, Formulaire d'Etat*.

32

The Personal Government
of Louis XIV, 1661–1715

On 8 March 1661, Mazarin died and Louis XIV assumed control of the government. He took steps to satisfy the Frondeurs in ways that would leave his monocratic absolutism intact. He governed himself, going so far as to assume the post of *surintendant des Finances* personally. He had no prime minister. He eliminated cardinals, bishops, and foreigners from the councils of government. But he also removed the queen mother, the queen, and the princes of the blood, for even though the royal family had rights under the customary constitution, the king remained free to consult or not to consult the princes of the blood, and to entrust them with governmental missions or not, just as he saw fit. The king governed with the aid of a few "creatures." This, too, was customary: kings had always governed with the help of favorites. At the same time the king ignored the Council's claim to be a *corps*, a company, because he intended to hold on to the power to select its members at will, and because he wanted it clearly understood that it was the king who was running the government, with advice from the Conseil d'En-Haut.

The king rejected the arguments put forward by the supporters of the Estates General and repudiated the *Ständestaat*, because the only states to survive as powers during the Thirty Years' War were those in which the prince had been able to overcome the *Stände* and govern absolutely, at least for a while. States that had remained pure *Ständestaaten* had fallen to the second rank. Absolutism was made necessary by the wars that raged in Europe. Necessity ruled in the fight against the hegemonic designs of the Habsburgs, in the affair of the Spanish Succession which the government had foreseen and which revealed the ambitions of the maritime and colonial powers, and more generally in all the wars that threatened the very existence of France and involved the nation's forces in combat on all its borders and before long on the seas as well. *Raison d'état* and the salvation of the state became the ultimate arbiters, justifying whatever actions the government took to further successful prosecution of the war, even if those actions were dictatorial.

Louis XIV continued the process of subduing the officeholders and reducing their status. He made scant use of the annual dues, which had shown themselves almost as likely to generate opposition as to secure the obedience of the officeholders. Besides, over the years renewal of the annual dues had come to be accepted as customary and almost as a right. The king did, however, resort to the weapon of setting a maximum price on offices, and he held the threat of future reductions in that maximum over the head of the officeholders. The importance of offices began to decline as a result.

Even more important, the king methodically diminished the political role of the courts and expanded that of the king's Council. The courts ceased to be sovereign. In October 1665 the king changed their designation from "sovereign courts" to "superior courts."

By decree of the Conseil d'En-Haut of 8 July 1661, the king enjoined all the *parlements*, the Grand Conseil, the Chambres des Comptes, and the Cours des Aides to defer to and accept the decrees of his Council. But he again acknowledged the right of the courts to address themselves to him by way of supplication and remonstrance. The *parlement* availed itself of this right in August 1661 in connection with a declaration that prohibited the wearing of clothing or ornaments made of gold or silver fabric or foreign cloth.

None of this concerned *parlement*'s role in affairs of state. With an eye to future conflicts with foreign countries and to the financial legislation that would then be required, however, the king wished to establish laws governing the use of the right of remonstrance more strictly than had hitherto been the case. He did this in a rather roundabout way, through the Civil Ordinance of April 1667 (title I, arts. 2 and 4 through 7). *Parlement* and the other courts were required to register and publish all ordinances, edicts, declarations, and other letters immediately upon receipt and to the exclusion of all other business. Ordinances, edicts, declarations, and letters patent published in the king's presence or on his express orders, conveyed by *commissaires*, were to go into effect as of the day of publication. Ordinances, edicts, declarations, and letters patent that were merely sent to the courts could be taken up with the king after deliberation within one week for courts located near where the king was staying and within six weeks for other courts. After that period had elapsed the texts would be treated as though they had been published and were to be enforced and sent via the *procureurs généraux* to the *bailliages*, *sénéchaussées*, *élections*, and other courts within their district. The sovereign and lower courts were not allowed to exempt themselves from respect for the laws in question and could not modify them on the grounds of "equity," "public interest," or "acceleration of justice." The courts were forbidden to interpret the texts. They were ordered to apply to the king in case of difficulty.

During the Dutch War, the king issued letters patent on 24 February 1673, intended to avoid any delay in the execution of his orders. These letters ordered the *procureurs généraux*, upon receipt of ordinances, edicts, declarations, or letters patent concerning public affairs (in both justice and finance) issued on the sole authority of the king and of his own free will and accompanied by *lettres de cachet* ordering registration, to notify the *premier président* (or in his absence the *président*) immediately and to request an assembly of the chambers. The *président* was required to convoke an assembly within three days. The *procureur général* would then present the legislation in question and the *lettres de cachet*, and the councillor acting as *rapporteur* would mark the text as having been "shown to the court" during this session. The *procureur général* would then turn the text over to the councillor acting as *rapporteur* twenty-four hours later. The latter would deliver his report three days later to the assembly of chambers, which would then deliberate on the matter to the exclusion of all other business. The courts were not allowed to hear any objections to registration. They were required to register legislation without restriction or modification of any kind. After issuing the registration decree, they were allowed to prepare remonstrances as to the content of the text of the legislation in question. Remonstrances had to be submitted to the king within a week for the Paris courts and within six weeks for the provincial courts.

The occasion in question was the last on which the Paris *parlement* made remonstrances during the reign of Louis XIV. For forty-two years thereafter registration became merely *pro forma*.

The king made extensive use of *commissaires* for such purposes as the Chambre de Justice of 1661, the Grands Jours of 1665, and of course as provincial intendants. Their competence and powers were constantly being expanded, while the decline of the officeholders continued at an ever increasing pace.

33

The Eighteenth Century: Officeholders versus *Commissaires* under Louis XV and Louis XVI

Reestablishment of the Role of the Council through Remonstrances

Louis XIV's will specified how the kingdom was to be governed during the minority of his great-grandson, the future Louis XV. The precise contents of this will were never made known, however. The first prince of the blood, the duc d'Orléans, had the right to act as regent, since the future king had lost his mother. The duke was afraid that the terms of the will might not be favorable to him. On 2 September 1715, he went to *parlement* to request that it be opened. He brought with him a *lettre de cachet* from the new king ordering the magistrates to "continue the meeting of our *parlement* and the administration of justice to our subjects with the *sincerity that the duty of your position and the integrity of your consciences make incumbent upon you.*" These were virtually the same terms as those used by the companies prior to the Fronde to characterize their duties. Thus obedience to the king was to be guided by respect for the dignity of office and for the forms of justice as well as by concern for the protection of the king's subjects. The duc d'Orléans announced in his speech that Louis XIV, speaking of his will prior to his death, had told the duke that "since it is impossible to foresee every eventuality, if there is something there that is not right, it will be changed." The duke added that, during his regency, he would be fortunate "to be aided by your advice and by your wise remonstrances." This was tantamount to promising *parlement* that it would be allowed to play the role of king's Council to which it laid claim. *Parlement* had the will opened. It gave the duc d'Orléans the title of head of the Regency Council, nothing more. The duc du Maine, Louis XIV's legitimized bastard, was made responsible for the king's education and for the command of the household militia. *Parlement* issued a decree. Basing its decision on the words of Louis XIV as reported by the duc d'Orléans, it declared the duke regent and made him responsible for administration of the kingdom's affairs during the minority of the king and for command of the household militia. In return the regent submitted the declaration of 15 September 1715 to *parlement*. This document provided that, when ordinances, edicts, declarations, and letters patent were submitted to *parlement* for registration, *parlement* would be allowed first to indicate to the king what it deemed best for the welfare of the public. Remonstrances had to be submitted within a week of the deliberations during which they were decided upon. This declaration undid all the efforts of Louis XIII and Louis XIV. It also restored the right of remonstrance to the Chambres des Comptes and Cours des Aides. In May of 1716 *parlement* again began presenting remonstrances.

The regent did not keep his word for long, however. By 1718 he had reestablished absolutism for his own benefit. *Parlement* moved increasingly toward what became systematic opposition to the king's Council and its ordinances, edicts, letters patent, and decrees as well as to other royal *commissaires*, both ordinary and extraordinary. This opposition arose in connection with affairs that in many cases served only as pretexts. The first half of the century was dominated by enforcement of the papal bull *Unigenitus* and by measures against the Jansenists, including the refusal of sacraments to these heretics. Religious affairs were still important during the second half of the century, as the expulsion of the Jesuits attests, but opposition to the royal tax system took precedence. The Paris *parlement* opposed all the Council's reform efforts. Its opposition stiffened after 1750, and other *parlements* were won over. The courts also attacked the *commissaires*, even such ordinary ones as the governors, *lieutenants généraux*, and provincial commanders-in-chief. Brittany, Languedoc, Dauphiné, and Franche-Comté all saw continual incidents. We need only consider a few of the high points of this confused combat between the officeholders and the *commissaires*, whose many vicissitudes were bound up with the whole range of internal politics and the century's whole tendency of thought.

The "Tax War"

It was in the interval between the War of the Austrian Succession and the Seven Years' War, between 1748 and 1756, that a crisis born of the conjunction of financial with religious crisis first made its effects felt. It was necessary to liquidate debts incurred in connection with the Austrian War and to defray the cost of preparing for the next war, which included establishing such technical schools as the Ecole des Ponts et Chaussées and the Engineering School at Mézières as well as chairs in hydrography at the *collèges* of Rouen, La Rochelle, Toulouse, and Marseilles, and, in 1752, the Naval Academy, which brought together seventy-five squadron leaders, captains, engineers, and members of the Academy of Sciences for weekly meetings. In 1750 the Ruelle Arsenal began turning out naval cannon and freed France from the need to buy such armaments from England and Sweden. Between 1749 and 1754 Rouillé, the secretary of state for the navy, had thirty-eight ships either built or repaired, and by 1754 the king had at his disposal 57 warships, 24 frigates, and corvettes, armed galliots, and store-ships—some 110–115 naval vessels in all. When Machault became secretary of state for the navy in 1755, the number of line vessels had reached 63.

The war had laid bare the inadequacies of a tax system that imposed proportionally smaller assessments on those who were wealthiest and who stood highest in the social hierarchy. Machault d'Arnouville, who had been intendant for Hainault and was named *contrôleur général des Finances* in 1745, had sought to meet the expenses of the war by means of the usual expedients. When peace was restored and he had to cope with a deficit, uncollected back taxes, and new needs all at once, he attempted to establish a general, uniform tax, in which all citizens would be assessed equally. In May 1749 he instituted a 5 percent income tax, the *vingtième*. Assessments were to be made on the basis of declarations by the taxpayers, which were to be verified by a *directeur du vingtième*, one for each *généralité*, assisted by inspectors, one per department. Badly paid and yet often zealous, intelligent, and devoted, these officials were soon among the most unpopular of men.

At this point a "tax war" was launched by persons of privilege. The Paris *parlement* was naturally opposed to the *vingtième*. It was forced to register the edict proclaiming the tax by a *lit de justice* on 19 May 1749. The provincial *parlements* were also opposed. But the provincial Estates of Burgundy, Provence, Artois, and Brittany, in which the nobility dominated, resisted in the name of traditional provincial liberties and invoked the terms of the contracts by which they had joined the kingdom. They were supported by their respective *parlements*. Since the *pays d'Etats* paid much lower taxes than the rest of the kingdom, and since the *vingtième* would make them pay just as much as anyone else, the entire population rallied in support of the resistance. The *parlement* of Aix proclaimed Provence "a separate and distinct state" in 1756. During debates on the *vingtième* in the Estates of Brittany in 1752, one deputy expressed his regret that England was a Protestant country and that good Catholics like the Bretons could not join with Britain in opposition to the king of France.

The French clergy declared that its tax immunities were "inextricably intertwined with the form and the constitution of the government . . . for all the *corps* of the state enjoy privileges whereby they are distinguished from one another." The immunity of the clergy had to be assigned "the rank of a primitive and unalterable law on which the law of nations is based." The Assembly of the Clergy refused to pay the new tax in 1750.

The opposition of the sovereign courts revived, and the *parlements* then resumed their Jansenist opposition, which for eighteen years had lain dormant.

The major crisis came in 1753. *Parlement* condemned priests who refused the sacraments to worshippers suspected of Jansenist leanings who could not produce a "confession ticket" showing that they had confessed to a priest approved by the hierarchy and to those who openly declared their opposition to the bull *Unigenitus* of 8 September 1713, which condemned the Jansenist doctrine. The king's Council quashed *parlement*'s decrees and declared the bull to be the "law of Church and State." *Parlement* then prepared the great remonstrances of 9 April 1753. Louis XV refused to receive them. *Parlement* suspended its service as of 5 May. It was exiled. But the suppression of justice caused such embarrassment that the king recalled *parlement*, which on 5 September 1754 registered a declaration ordering that "silence" be maintained concerning *Unigenitus* and all related matters.

The Affair of the Grand Conseil
and the Conflicting Positions of the Participants

The conflict between the Council and *parlement* triggered a verbal war in which each side reaffirmed its own position. Writing in favor of *parlement*, the *avocat* Adrien Le Paige published his *Lettres historiques sur les fonctions essentielles du Parlement, sur le droit des pairs et sur les lois fondamentales du royaume* (published in two parts in Amsterdam in 1753–54), which became one of the major sources of *parlement*'s remonstrances. On the other hand, François de Paule Lagarde harked back to the traditional doctrine of the king's Council in his *Traité historique de la souveraineté du roi et des droits en dépendant* (Paris, 1754). He distinguished between the *parlements* associated with the second dynasty, which were national assemblies, and the *parlements* established by the kings of the third dynasty in Paris and the provinces. The latter were mere courts of justice that had no right to intervene in affairs of state. He based his contentions on council decrees dating from the reign of Louis XIII: the decrees of 28 March and 23 May 1615 and the declaration of March 1641.

Obstruction by the *parlements* became such a hindrance that the king's Council decided to take advantage of the opportunities offered by the Grand Conseil. Accordingly, it installed some fifty obedient councillors in the Louvre during 1755–56, with a number of *maîtres des requêtes* to keep them all in line and a *conseiller d'Etat* presiding. The declaration of 10 October 1755 concerned the execution of decrees, ordinances, and orders issued by the Grand Conseil. In cases assigned to it (and quite a few could be so assigned by evocation) the Grand Conseil's decisions were to be executed throughout the kingdom in the same way as decisions of the courts were executed within their jurisdiction, and, furthermore, bailiffs, sergeants, and other executors were not required to apply to the regular courts or to any other judges for permission to enforce orders of the Grand Conseil. In addition, the king ordered the *procureur général* of the Grand Conseil to have this declaration verified not only in the Grand Conseil but also in all the courts, *bailliages*, and *sénéchaussées* of the realm. The Grand Conseil registered the declaration on 14 October, and the *procureur général* had certified copies sent to all the regular lower courts for registration, along with orders to his deputies to see that this was done within the month and to send certification back to Paris. Thus the Grand Conseil assumed the rank and functions that had belonged to *parlement*, as the supreme court among the regular tribunals with the right to transmit edicts and declarations to all lower tribunals with the requirement that they be registered. This scotched the political pretensions of the sovereign courts.

Parlement responded with its grand remonstrance of 27 November 1755. Earlier, the remonstrances of 9 April 1753 had contended that there was a contract between the sovereign and his people, a solemn commitment of both parties to aid one another which constituted a fundamental law of the state and an eternal tie of reciprocity. In the grand remonstrance of 27 November 1755, in large part inspired by Le Paige, *parlement* maintained that the monarchy had existed for 1300 years and that for 1300 years *parlement* had been the same tribunal, exercising the same functions within the state. It was the true court of France, born with the Empire of the French. Until 1302 it had gone by the names *placite général*, *Cour du roi*, *Placite du roi*, and *Conseil du roi*, and its members had been the king's key ministers. In *parlement* the sovereign dispensed justice. In his absence the members of *parlement* dispensed justice for him. *Parlement* was the council on which the king relied to assume part of the burden of administration, consulting with it on all affairs of any importance. Since the establishment of *parlement* in a fixed location in 1302, kings had been in the habit of taking a few individuals, chosen from the ranks of *parlement*, into their entourage to act as advisers, but *parlement* as a whole nonetheless remained the only true council of the sovereign, and the corps of *parlement* ought to fill all the functions of the king's Council.

The constitution of the monarchy comprised the following: a sovereign, the prime mover and soul of his estates, who alone acted throughout the kingdom, and a tribunal, or rather an august sanctuary, in which the sovereign normally resided, in which the state was concentrated, and in which, to the exclusion of all other places, the law was prepared, determined, consummated, deposited, and executed. *Parlement* also reiterated the idea that all the *parlements* constituted a single body and that the various *parlements* of the realm were merely the "classes" of a unique and indivisible *parlement*, dispersed throughout the kingdom for the convenience of justice. The theory of classes was taken over and developed by the provincial *parlements*. Thanks to the "union of classes," the *parlements* were frequently able to impose their views on the king, as, for example, in 1764, when they obtained the expulsion of the Jesuits. They were also able to take advantage of the financial difficulties caused by the Seven Years' War to win a role in the government.

The king responded to these theories by reviewing the royal theory on 3 March 1766, in a royal sitting known as "the Flagellation," which was concerned with the question of interference in the affairs of Brittany by the Paris *parlement* and with that *parlement*'s protests against the royal *commissaires* sent to the province. The king condemned the "union of classes" as constituting a confederation of resistance, an imaginary corps. Magistrates, the king argued, were in fact mere royal officeholders, responsible for performing what was in fact a royal duty, that of dispensing justice: they constituted neither a corps nor a fourth order. The king condemned the whole political doctrine of the courts. He pointed out that sovereign power resided in his person alone and that legislative power was his exclusively, independent and indivisible. The courts were not involved in the formulation of law but merely in its registration, publication, and execution. Good and worthy councillors were allowed to make remonstrances as part of their duty. All public order emanated from the king. The rights and interests of the nation were necessarily bound up with the rights and interests of the monarch. Indeed, the former were identical with the latter and lay entirely in the king's hands.

The declaration of 10 October 1755 provoked similar reactions in all the provincial *parlements* except for those in Rennes, Besançon, Pau, and Douai and the sovereign councils of Colmar and Perpignan. In Besançon the declaration was withdrawn by the chancellor after the *premier président* of the *parlement* observed that it violated the liberties of Franche-Comté. As for the other courts that remained silent, it is not certain that the declaration was sent to them. In February 1756 the Paris *parlement* invited the princes and peers to join it in considering the attacks on the fundamental laws of the monarchy and on the authority of the king as sovereign in his Court of Peers. The duc d'Orléans submitted to the king a list of claims on behalf of the princes and peers. The Fronde began afresh.

The king prohibited the meeting of *parlement* with the princes and peers but gave up the idea of using the Grand Conseil as a superior commission to register laws and dispense political justice.

The Declaration of Discipline, Damiens's Assassination Attempt, and the Victory of the Sovereign Courts

The king next attempted to discipline the Paris *parlement*. Machault, who had become keeper of the seals, prepared legislation that was brought to a *lit de justice* on 13 December 1756 by Chancellor de Lamoignon. One edict did away with two of the five Chambres des Enquêtes and proposed replacing the *présidents* of the remaining three with *présidents à mortier*. A "declaration of discipline" dated 10 December provided that only officers who had held office for ten years would be admitted to the Assembly of Chambers, a move that excluded the aroused younger officers in the Enquêtes. Furthermore, the Assembly of Chambers would be convoked for general administrative matters only if the *présidents à mortier* deemed it necessary to do so. Otherwise, the Grand-Chambre would decide on its own. Remonstrances could be formulated within two weeks after presentation of the law, but the law was to take effect the day after the sovereign had delivered his response. The magistrates were forbidden to interrupt the operations of justice in any way.

The majority of the members of *parlement* resigned. Robert François Damiens, a servant who had worked for a number of councillors in *parlement*, went to Versailles and during the evening of 5 January 1757 stabbed Louis XV for the sake of the public and the state. Machault, who was held responsible for the attack, was disgraced on 1 February. The members of *parlement* retracted their resignations on the condition that the declaration of discipline not be applied.

The Shortage of Money and the Uprising of the Courts

The sovereign courts continued the "tax war" against the king's Council and the intendants, with whom they were involved in unending jurisdictional conflicts. Because of the Seven Years' War (1756–63), the *vingtième* instituted by Machault was retained and another was instituted by the declaration of 7 July 1756. Because of opposition from the sovereign courts, the Council was forced in the *pays d'Etats* and in other provinces such as Franche-Comté and Dauphiné to agree to a subscription that reduced the amount of the tax, allowed the *commis* installed by the *contrôle général* to be removed, and restored to the Estates the power to assess and collect the tax. Elsewhere, declarations by taxpayers were increasingly allowed to go unchecked, and tax rolls were prepared in such a way as to lessen the burden on privileged individuals and shift the brunt of the tax onto the shoulders of commoners and the poor. In 1759 total receipts came to 285 million and expenditures to 503 million. *Contrôleur Général* Silhouette considered a "general subsidy." The Council did not dare to take this step, however, and Silhouette was forced to propose a third *vingtième*, luxury taxes, and new customs duties and indirect taxes. The privileged protested as though no war was raging. Silhouette was forced to declare bankruptcy and was dismissed in November 1759.

The new *contrôleur général*, Bertin, was also forced to propose a third *vingtième* and a doubling of the *capitation* in February 1760. The sovereign courts protested. What they feared, after the *vingtième*, was the imposition of a proportional territorial tax and elimination of the privileges accorded to certain orders and provinces. The courts attacked the royal power to tax and asserted a national right against the arbitrary authority of the king, a right they employed to their own advantage. The Rouen *parlement* declared that fiscal laws had force only if they were registered by all the *parlements* in the kingdom as constituents of the *parlement* of France and issued a decree prohibiting the collection of taxes. These remonstrances convinced the public that the problems of both taxpayers and treasury could be solved if the *parlements* were left in control, and their criticisms of the government dissuaded Dutch, Swiss, and German capitalists from lending to France. Instead they sent their money to England, at a time when the king of France could no longer pay his troops or fit out his warships. The sovereign courts bear much of the responsibility for the defeats suffered in the Seven Years' War and for the loss of the colonial empire.

The Courts as Masters of Finance and Their Attack on the *Commissaires*

Because of the financial crisis, the courts eventually had to be allowed to share the responsibilities of government with the king and to supplant the king's Council, as they wished. By the end of the war the annual deficit had reached 50 million livres, arrears were enormous, future income had already been pledged, and it proved necessary to eliminate the third *vingtième* and the additional *capitation*. In an edict of February 1763 Bertin preserved the first two *vingtièmes* and announced a revision of privileges. The *parlements* protested, demanded to see his accounts, denied that registration by *lit de justice* had any validity whatsoever (because it violated the freedom of suffrage), and prohibited enforcement of the edicts. They were obeyed. The taxes could not be collected. The king capitulated and appointed l'Averdy, a councillor in the Paris *parlement*, notorious Jansenist, and agent of *parlement* more than agent of the king, to be *contrôleur général*. In November 1763 an edict was issued supplanting Bertin's edict. In December the king affirmed his will to reign "by observing the rules and forms wisely established in his kingdom." He invited the *parlements*, Cours des Aides, and Chambres des Comptes to submit "their views concerning ways of improving and simplifying the establishment of taxes, their distribution, collection, use, and methods of accounting." Letters patent of 28 November established a commission composed of members of the sovereign courts to prepare a plan of reform. This commission was nothing less than a department of the Conseil d'Etat, and the sovereign courts in fact became, as they had wished, the true Conseil d'Etat. The courts everywhere attempted to inspect the tax rolls, collection registers, and accounts so as to assume control over the royal finances. These efforts continued at least as late as 1768.

In 1764 a sort of secret council consisting of twenty or so magistrates began meeting at the home of a councillor in the Paris *parlement*, Michau de Montblin. These men contended that the original constitution had been violated by the kings and that the proper thing was to return to it. They refined Le Paige's theory.

The sovereign courts launched an all-out attack against the *commissaires*. They denied the authority of the *vingtième* inspectors and reproached them for using spies and informers and for not arriving at a high enough estimate of real income. The Cours des Aides claimed jurisdiction over disputes arising out of this tax and denied the comparable claim of the intendants, who they insisted must deposit the tax rolls in the *greffes* of the *élections*. The Cour des Aides of Paris in 1767 and 1768 denounced the increasingly arbitrary authority exerted by the intendants over the assessment of the *tailles*. On 29 June 1767, the two separate brevets for the *taille* were issued. The first was for a fixed amount, which the intendant divided among the various communities in the presence of the *trésoriers de France* and office-holders in the *élection*, whose role was purely consultative. The second was for a variable amount and was divided among the communities by the intendant alone. In each parish, where assessors and collectors were supposed to be free to divide the *taille* among individual taxpayers as they saw fit, the intendant had the authority to fix certain assessments as he saw fit, using a *commissaire* he assigned to the task. The declaration of 7 February 1768 made the use of these *commissaires au rôle*, as they were called, official and increased their number. The Cour des Aides declared that it saw no difference between this method of assessment and collection of the *tailles* by soldiers.

The sovereign courts increasingly complained about abuses committed by the intendants in the use of *corvées*. Among the complaints were the following: too many days of *corvée* labor were being demanded (as many as eighty-six), coercion in the form of fines and occupation by troops was being used, and exemption from the *corvée* was being sold for cash at prices that varied inequitably.

The sovereign courts attacked the intendants for undertaking projects for the sake of prestige or beautification of the cities that were too costly. They also complained that tax surpluses were being held by the intendants for use as they saw fit. They pointed out that what went by the name of the system of intendants was in fact a despotism of *commis*, and that this despotism was protected by a special court, the Intendant's Tribunal, whose judgments could be appealed to the king's Council. Actually, judgment was entrusted to a single magistrate who first consulted with the intendant involved and then issued the intendant's opinion in the form of a judgment of the court.

The sovereign courts of course condemned the general farms, which they accused of incurring excessive costs; the intendants, those "despotic administrators" who judged cases involving the domanial rights (*contrôle*, *insinuation*, *centième denier*); and the king's Council, which intervened in cases involving the other indirect taxes whenever the *élections* and the Cours des Aides found against the farmers general. The king's Council quashed decrees of the other courts at once. In such cases the Council was actually represented by a single *intendant des Finances*, "the sole arbiter of the fate of your subjects."

The sovereign courts complained about the commissions the Council appointed to judge cases of smuggling in the place of the Cours des Aides (in 1733 at Valence and in 1742 at Saumur). On 23 August 1764, they won a concession according to which the Saumur commission would be composed of three officers of the Cour des Aides and a deputy of its *procureur général*, and that similar commissions would be set up at Reims (21 November 1765), Caen (8 January 1767), and Paris (29 August 1775). Only the Valence commission endured with its single judge and six adjoints appointed by him and removable at his discretion. Its decrees could not be appealed and were immediately enforceable.

The sovereign courts constantly claimed the freedom to register or not to register all fiscal laws as well as the right to judge disputes concerning taxes of any sort. For the latter, they demanded that all tax rolls be deposited in "duly regulated and accessible registries." They claimed the right to inspect the accounts of any of the king's *commissaires*, to check their compliance with the laws, and to take action against them if they abused the authority vested in them by the king. In 1768 and 1775 the Cour des Aides of Paris suggested that first the *taille* and later all taxes be assessed by deputies elected by the owners of land, who would work together with the *trésoriers de France* and the *élus* under the supervision of the intendant. This amounted to a plan for provincial assemblies, the first of which was established by Necker in 1778.

To sum up, then, the sovereign courts condemned the executive form of administration that was then being created by extension of the administration's jurisdiction. The courts were in favor of a return to a judicial form of administration through decrees and judgments handed down by regular judges, commanding and supervising the officials who actually enforced the decisions of the courts. In their efforts to establish the superiority of the magistrates, the officeholders, over the *commissaires* and *commis*, the courts made use of a number of affairs of note. Among these were the case of the intendant Bourgeois de Boynes, whom the king had imposed on the *parlement* of Besançon as *premier président* in 1758 and who was forced by that body's opposition to resign in 1761, and the case of the duc de Fitz-James, *lieutenant général* of Toulouse, who was forced by the opposition of the *parlement* of Toulouse to resign his command in 1764. But above all the courts sought to make use of the conflict between the *parlement* of Rennes and the commander-in-chief of Brittany, the duc d'Aiguillon.

The Affair d'Aiguillon as a Weapon against the *Commissaires*

The duc d'Aiguillon had served as commander-in-chief of Brittany in the absence of the governor since 1753. He had performed well in the post, saving Brittany from an English invasion in 1758, building important highways, and considerably improving the situation with regard to *corvées*. But when the *parlement* of Rennes registered the edict of royal capitulation of 21 November 1763, the *procureur général* La Chalotais, furious because d'Aiguillon had tried to prevent him from passing his post on to his son, an incompetent, and jealous of the commander-in-chief, saw to it that remonstrances were adopted reproaching the duke for his "despotism," in other words for abusing the *corvées* and undertaking major projects of public works and beautification, on the grounds that these things fell within the exclusive jurisdiction of the Provincial Estates of Brittany, which had done absolutely nothing.

At the end of 1764, L'Averdy was forced by necessity to order that a surtax be collected in Brittany on the farmed duties. He did so without consulting the Estates of Brittany, which had nothing to do with such duties. Invoking the Act of Union of 1532, however, the Estates nevertheless lodged an objection with *parlement*, which prohibited the levying of the surtax. The king's Council quashed *parlement*'s decree and forbade the Estates to appeal to *parlement* again. The *parlement* first went on strike and then, in May 1765, resigned. There were rumblings of riot in Rennes. Anonymous letters, slanderous and threatening to the king, were sent to the secretary of state at the royal household. La Chalotais's handwriting was recognized. Through various machinations La Chalotais obtained a judgment against the subdelegate of the intendant of Rennes, one Audouard, who had had some demonstrators arrested. The king thereupon had La Chalotais incarcerated and installed a commission composed of *conseillers d'Etat* and *maîtres des requêtes* to take the place of *parlement*. This was mockingly referred to as the "*bailliage d'Aiguillon*." The other *parlements* protested against this "phantom *parlement*."

On 11 February 1766, the Paris *parlement* protested the sending of *commissaires* to Brittany for the purpose of replacing *parlement* and hearing criminal charges against several of its magistrates. It laid stress on its contention that the activities of these *commissaires* were illegal, increasingly presumptuous with each passing day, and based on an improper jurisdiction. The Paris *parlement* was incensed by the fact that the *commissaires* had changed the name and form of their commission and established a special tribunal, whose procedures were illegitimate, at Saint-Malo to prosecute La Chalotais and several other members of the *parlement* of Brittany. On 13 February the Paris *parlement* submitted remonstrances to the king. They were not favorably received. On 3 March 1766, the king went to the Paris *parlement* and what he said earned the session the name "the Flagellation." The king ordered the Paris *parlement* not to concern itself with affairs in Brittany.

Opinion was divided, however. La Chalotais had been an enthusiastic opponent of the Jesuits. His friends tried to paint him as a martyr and victim of the *dévots*. On 15 July 1769, the king recalled the duc d'Aiguillon from Brittany and reinstated the former Rennes *parlement*. La Chalotais demanded justice from the reinstated court. *Parlement* thereupon launched an investigation of d'Aiguillon and the way he had executed the decree against the Jesuits. D'Aiguillon was indicted for abuse of authority and, furthermore, accused of having suborned witnesses against La Chalotais and of having plotted to poison him. On 12 August 1769, the king halted all the proceedings and imposed silence as to the facts. But La Chalotais, supported by the *parlements*, then protested in the name of the natural right of every man accused of a crime to prove his innocence and prosecute his accusers. The duc d'Aiguillon also asked to be judged, but, since he was a peer, by the Court of Peers. His request was approved by council decree on 24 March 1770. From 4 April to 7 April the Paris *parlement*, sitting as a Court of Peers, met to reconsider the charges.

The size of the stakes explains the obstinacy of the courts. The issue was whether the *commissaire* d'Aiguillon had betrayed his sovereign's confidence. What was called for was a detailed inquiry into the administration of the king's affairs by the accused, to see whether or not he had followed the king's orders faithfully and whether or not he had committed any abuses on his own. The Paris *parlement* thereby hoped to gain the power to supervise the most secret acts of the royal administration, to subpoena the king's agents, and to sit in sovereign judgment over the conduct of a *commissaire* and favorite of the king who had served for fourteen years as the chief official in a province. If it gained such power in this case, there would subsequently be no grounds on which to object if it wished to assert a similar power in regard to lesser personages, namely, the intendants, the king's most effective instruments, and other *commissaires* of all sorts. As in England, all these officials would thereby become accountable before the courts for actions carried out in their official capacity. The *parlements* and the other sovereign courts would thus become the real masters of the government and administration.

At the same time the *parlements* were paralyzing the collection of taxes. L'Averdy, their man, had also been forced to attempt reforms such as the *vingtième* and the *taille tarifée* but then, faced with the obstruction of the sovereign courts, had had to resign himself to partial bankruptcies and to costly and difficult borrowing. Maynon d'Invau, who succeeded him in October 1768, found 500,000 livres in the coffers of the *contrôle général* for the balance of the year when he took office. He, too, thought in vain of imposing a genuine *vingtième*. The abbé Terray, who became *contrôleur général* on 21 December 1769, found credit exhausted, tax collections 110 million in arrears, a deficit of 63 million, and the revenues for 1770 and, in part, for 1771 already assigned in advance. Using council decrees he began his surgery on the government's finances, ultimately halting payment of notes from the farms and *rescriptions* from the *receveurs généraux* as of 18 February 1770. One hundred fifty million livres' worth of such notes and *rescriptions* were in circulation. Halting payment resulted in the ruin of large numbers of rentiers and an epidemic of suicides, "the martyrs of the abbé Terray." But once again the *parlements* and the Cour des Aides objected to these desperate measures.

The Maupeou Reforms: The Royal Revolution

It was obvious that the sovereign courts had to be stripped of their political and administrative powers. Chancellor Maupeou attempted to accomplish this feat. His reform is nicely described by the title of a collection of documents published in London in 1775–76: "Historical Journal of the *Revolution* in the Constitution of the French Monarchy Effected by M. de Maupeou, Chancellor of France." A revolution was necessary. The claims put forward by the sovereign courts were leading to an aristocratic revolution favoring the officeholding nobility. Maupeou preferred to see a royal revolution favoring the king, his *commissaires*, and *commis* for the sake of the general good.

The son of a *premier président* of the Paris *parlement*, Maupeou became chancellor in September 1768 at the age of fifty-four. A tough, tyrannical man, he was skillful in affairs, fertile at coming up with expedients, a tireless worker, and feared by everyone.

When Maupeou became chancellor, the Conseil d'Etat included the maréchal prince de Soubise, minister of state, the duc de Choiseul, secretary of state for foreign affairs and war, his cousin the duc de Praslin, secretary of state for the navy, Saint-Florentin, secretary of state for the royal household, Bertin, special minister for the king's income, and L'Averdy, *contrôleur général des Finances*. Choiseul was actually in control of the government and busy making preparations for war against England to avenge the loss of the Seven Years' War. Maupeou did not join this council. In December 1768, L'Averdy, who sowed discord everywhere, was forced to resign. Choiseul replaced him with Maynon d'Invau. Maupeou worked to bring about his downfall, which was accomplished at the 21 December 1769 session of a special council composed of members of the Conseil d'Etat, the Conseil des Finances, and the Conseil des Dépêches. At this meeting the chancellor showed that the means proposed by Maynon d'Invau were inadequate to the task, and Maynon resigned. Maupeou obtained the appointment of the abbé Terray, a clerical councillor in the Paris *parlement* with close ties to Maupeou, as *contrôleur général des Finances*. The chancellor was allied with the duc d'Aiguillon, a friend of Madame du Barry, the king's mistress. Together they formed a "Triumvirate," directed against Choiseul.

Maupeou tried first to halt *parlement*'s efforts to obtain control of the administration. In a *lit de justice* held at his behest on 27 June 1770, the king issued letters patent cancelling the proceedings then under way against the duc d'Aiguillon, proceedings which the king maintained tended "to make the administration's secrets subject to inspection by the courts, and to open to judicial scrutiny the execution of the king's orders and the usage of an authority for which the king is obliged to account to no one but himself." The king must "not allow persons honored by his confidence and made responsible for the execution of his orders to be compromised, investigated, and harassed for executing the aforementioned orders." On 2 July *parlement* declared these letters patent, registered in the king's presence, to be null and void and expelled the duc d'Aiguillon from the peerage until such time as he had cleared his honor before the Court of Peers. The deputies of the *parlement* were acclaimed by the populace when they returned from Versailles. That night, the duc d'Orléans received them at the Palais-Royal. The princes of the blood joined in an alliance with the Paris *parlement*. The provincial *parlements* ratified the decree on 2 July. The Fronde began anew.

Maupeou then tried to push the *parlement* to the limit. He had an edict of regulation registered on 7 December 1770, prohibiting the sovereign courts

from using the terms "unity," "indivisibility," or "class" and from corresponding with one another except as allowed by ordinance. They were forbidden to suspend service or to resign in concert, failing which they faced
loss of their offices. Remonstrances were allowed prior to registration but
were supposed to cease as soon as the king, after hearing them, decided to
enforce registration of the edict. On 10 December *parlement* announced that
it would never recognize this edict as the law of the land and went on strike.
This was the explicit act of rebellion that Maupeou was waiting for.

The use of force required peace with foreign enemies, however, and Choiseul's policy seemed to be making war inevitable. Moreover, Choiseul seemed
to be leaning toward support of the *parlements*. On 24 December 1770, the
king exiled him to his estates at Chantelou. On 6 June 1771, d'Aiguillon
became minister of foreign affairs. The marquis de Monteynard was minister
of war. In order to allow the "revolution" to go forward, the government
worked to maintain peace at all costs and allowed Russia, Prussia, and
Austria to divide Poland for the first time in 1772.

For the first time in living memory, a chancellor, Maupeou, disbanded an
entire *parlement:* this was the next move. Between one and four in the
morning of Sunday, 20 January 1771, each member of *parlement* was awak-
ened by two musketeers and handed a *lettre de cachet*. The magistrates
were summoned to resume their service and answer immediately by "yes"
or "no." Most of them refused. This constituted a duly verified dereliction
of duty, inasmuch as the members were refusing to serve when called, and
on the following night a bailiff bearing a decree of the Council was sent to
each recalcitrant member to notify him that his office had been confiscated
and declared vacant. Two musketeers then handed him a *lettre de cachet*
ordering his immediate exile. The magistrates who had most seriously compromised themselves were sent to the mountains or the coast, some to tiny
fishing villages where they had to sleep on straw.

On 24 January 1771, the chancellor went to the Palace to install the Conseil
privé as an interim *parlement*. The members of the Conseil privé were
commissioned to hold court as *parlement* and to dispense justice in its stead,
both civil and criminal. They were ordered to begin their decrees with the
preamble "decree of *parlement*." The *avocats généraux*, the *procureur général*, and his deputies were assigned to plead cases instead of the *avocats*.
The *procureurs* received positive orders to carry out their procedural service.

There were popular demonstrations against these measures. Litigants stayed
away from court. The *parlements* of Rouen, Dijon, Rennes, Toulouse, Besançon, Aix, and Bordeaux protested in February and the *parlement* of
Grenoble protested in March against the violation of the constitution of the
monarchy and called upon the princes of the blood and peers to support
their demands for convocation of the Estates General. On 18 February the
Cour des Aides of Paris invoked the "nation's rights" in protesting against
"the terrible administration that is being prepared for us" and asked that

the king consult "the nation itself," presumably through a national assembly as recommended by its *premier président*, Malesherbes.

Despite this agitation, the chancellor, accompanied by all his ministers, went to the Palace on 23 February 1771. He took the chair to preside over the members of the Conseil privé acting as *commissaires* who were assembled in the Grand-Chambre and had them register a reform edict. The district of the Paris *parlement*, which comprised half the kingdom, was broken up on the grounds that its great size forced litigants to undertake expensive journeys in connection with their suits and because the very large number of litigants made justice slow and costly. Jurisdiction over the district was divided among *parlement* and six superior councils, one each in Arras, Blois, Châlons, Clermont-Ferrand, Lyon, and Poitiers. These superior councils were courts of justice with sovereign jurisdiction in last resort over all cases, both civil and criminal.

As for the position of magistrate in the superior councils, venality was eliminated with regard to this office but kept for the ministerial officials: *greffiers*, *huissiers*, and *procureurs*. Judges were no longer to receive *épices* or *vacations*. Salaries were increased: 6,000 livres per year for a *premier président*, 4,000 for a *président*, 2,000 for a councillor, 3,000 for the *avocat du roi*, and 4,000 for the *procureur du roi*. In addition, magistrates were awarded personal nobility with all its privileges. This nobility could be transmitted from one generation to the next if father and son held office for twenty years in succession or died in office.

The sale of offices was retained in the other courts, but officeholders were forced to sign blank resignations and the name of their successor was filled in by the chancellor.

The political powers of the Paris *parlement* were curtailed. It retained jurisdiction over affairs involving the peers and peerages. It continued to verify and register ordinances, edicts, declarations, and letters patent, but under the conditions set forth in the disciplinary edict of 7 December. After registration the *procureur général* was required to send the texts of laws to the *procureurs du roi* attached to the superior councils. They in turn were required to read the texts in public hearings without deliberation, and no stay of execution was allowed: the laws were simply promulgated. The *procureurs* of the superior councils were then required to send the texts to the *bailliages* and *sénéchaussées* in their district and to notify the *procureur général* of the Paris *parlement* that this had been done.

Article 14 contained a draft proposal for transforming the seigneurial courts into royal tribunals of first instance. In criminal cases in which seigneurial judges issued warrants before the royal judges, the costs of the trial in first instance were to be borne by the king. If the royal judges acted before the seigneurial judges, the costs of trial in first instance were to be borne by the *seigneur*. According to article 15, in case of appeal all costs of transfer, referral, and enforcement were to be borne by the king.

Two other edicts transformed the provincial council into a superior council and court of last resort. Previously, appeals from this council had been heard by the Paris *parlement*. This superior council heard appeals from the courts of the Eaux et Forêts and the *élections;* in the remainder of the district of the Paris *parlement*, such appeals were heard by the Table de Marbre of the Palace and the Cour des Aides.

The Paris *parlement* thus lost much of its importance and prestige. Its threats to suspend justice were no longer cause for fear. It was easy to reduce the size of the court and obtain a company less likely to be led astray by the great assemblies. It became easier for government ministers to secure a majority among the magistrates in this smaller court.

Each superior council was supposed to consist of a *premier président*, two *présidents*, and twenty councillors, along with a *procureur du roi* and an *avocat du roi* assisted by a number of ministerial officials including a *greffier civil*, a *greffier criminel*, twenty-four *procureurs*, and twelve *huissiers*. All these officials could be removed from office *ad nutum* and were subject to the threat of having their salary withheld, which made it easy for the government to manipulate them.

The chancellor recruited magistrates, with some little difficulty, among the *avocats*, the magistrates of *bailliages* and *présidiaux*, the canons and other members of the clergy, and the magistrates of the Cours des Aides and Cours des Monnaies in the provinces, such as those of Clermont-Ferrand and Lyon. Occasionally, a *gentilhomme* without a law degree was chosen.

The lower courts were unhappy, some because they felt that they should have been elevated to the status of superior councils, others because they had suffered a *diminutio capitis* in that they now fell under the jurisdiction of a superior council rather than that of the Paris *parlement*. The *bailliage* of Le Mans refused to register the edict. On the whole, however, the lower courts went along with the reform.

The provincial *parlements* and the other sovereign courts were outraged and declared that the registration of the edict by *commissaires* from the king's Council was null and void. They ordered officeholders in the regular lower courts under them to pay no attention to decrees issued by the superior councils and ordered litigants not to plead their cases before these bodies. This they did by means of remonstrances and prohibitory decrees that were posted publicly and published in the form of little brochures. The Aix *parlement* concluded with the threat that "sedition overturns the idol in despotic states, and the despot who tramples everything underfoot risks losing his footing and toppling at the first blow." On 23 March the Cour des Aides of Paris joined with the *parlements* by issuing a prohibitory decree forbidding all officeholders under its jurisdiction to enforce the decrees of council *commissaires* and refusing recognition to the superior councils. The Council quashed this decree on 24 March. The Châtelet of Paris had stopped dispensing justice on 10 December of the previous year. The princes of the blood joined the courts and signed a new protest on 4 April 1771: the freedom, property, and security of each citizen could be assured only by magistrates who had tenure in their posts and were not subject to removal and who were responsible for seeing to it that the laws were observed. The fact that they could not be removed from office was one of the main safeguards against the abuse of arbitrary and absolute power and was an integral part of the constitution of the state. The signers of this protest were Louis-Philippe d'Orléans, the duc d'Orléans; Louis-Philippe-Joseph d'Orléans, the duc de Chartres; Louis-Joseph de Bourbon, the prince de Condé; Louis-Joseph de Bourbon, the duc de Bourbon; Louis de Bourbon, the comte de Clermont; and Louis-François de Bourbon, the prince de Conti—many names familiar from the days of the Fronde.

It was necessary to reconstitute the Paris *parlement*. In the hope of finding new magistrates the chancellor issued an edict doing away with the Cour des Aides on 9 April 1771. Cases within its purview were reassigned to the ordinary courts, *parlement*, and the superior councils. This greatly simplified matters. Article 8 of this edict provided that magistrates who lost their positions and who obtained the king's approval to enter another *corps* of magistrates would not have to pay installation dues. The councillors in the Cour des Aides wanted to conduct deliberations after being forced to register the edict dissolving their court. On orders from the maréchal de Richelieu the soldiers of the watch drove them out of their chamber and forced them to retreat from room to room with blows from their rifle butts. The farmers general, the intendants, and the special commissions established to combat smuggling now had a clear field. Terray could undertake his financial reforms unhampered by *parlement* and the Cour des Aides.

On 13 April 1771, the king held a *lit de justice* at Versailles before the council *commissaires* who were replacing the *parlement* and the Grand Conseil. Officeholders were allowed six months to submit their receipts and apply for liquidation and reimbursement. Seventy-five new offices were created: one *premier président*, four *présidents*, fifteen clerical councillors, and fifty-five lay councillors. They were to be divided between a Grand-Chambre and a Chambre des Enquêtes. The Tournelle was to be staffed by councillors drawn in rotation from the Grand-Chambre and the Enquêtes. Salaries were increased and *épices* and *vacations* eliminated. As for recruitment, when a vacancy occurred the court was to name three candidates. If the king refused all of them, the court could propose other names until the king had agreed to one.

The Grand Conseil and its associated offices were also eliminated. Its magistrates, some thirty in number, were thus in a position to acquire offices in the new Paris *parlement*. The competence of the Grand Conseil was assigned to *parlement*. Disputes concerning the indult of the Paris *parlement* and conflicting judgments or decrees issued in last resort by different sovereign or lower courts were transferred by evocation to the king's Council. Enforcement of council decrees and appeals from the *prévôté de l'Hôtel* were transferred to the *maîtres des requêtes de l'Hôtel*.

On the same day, the king received the oath of Bertier de Sauvigny, *conseiller d'Etat* and intendant of Paris, as *premier président* of the new *parlement*. Maupeou installed the new magistrates of *parlement* at the Palace, reminding them that justice was the king's and not their own and that "the duty to notify authority was not the right to combat it." Some twenty former members of the Grand Conseil and eight former members of the Cour des Aides actually took office. They were slowly joined by councillors from provincial *parlements*, lower court judges, and *avocats*. The archbishop of Paris recruited clerical councillors: canons from Notre-Dame, the Sainte-Chapelle, and Meaux and unbeneficed priests from Saint-Sulpice and Saint-Roch.

Procureurs and *avocats* were also needed. An edict issued in May and registered on 10 June 1771 eliminated the offices of 400 *procureurs* and created 100 offices of *avocat-procureur*. Eighty-seven *procureurs* purchased these offices and did preliminary and trial work in the courts. An edict issued in February and registered on 17 May changed the procedural rules laid down by the ordinance of 1667. A June edict doubled court costs and fees. The flow of cases resumed. Quite a few cases were heard in September of 1771.

The lower courts that had refused to recognize the new *parlement* and superior councils and claimed to be tied by oath to the old *parlement* and bound to uphold the laws of the kingdom had to be replaced. An edict of 28 May 1771 eliminated the offices of the Châtelet of Paris. Its fifty-six councillors were replaced by thirty-two new offices, which were filled within a year. The *lieutenant civil* prevailed upon the *procureurs*. By September 1772 the tribunal was functioning.

Some *bailliages* gave in and registered the reform edicts. The king eliminated the offices of those that did not and replaced them with new offices that were filled by men approved by the chancellor. Maupeou took advantage of the opportunity to reduce the number of lower courts. For example, he combined the *sénéchaussée* of Villefranche with that of Lyon. He did the same for the special lower courts, some of whose functions were assigned to the regular courts, as at Mâcon, where the *élection* was combined with the *bailliage*. The general admiralty court in Paris was abolished, and appeals from the admiralty courts in port cities were assigned to the Paris *parlement* or to the superior councils in districts where they operated. The court of the Eaux et Forêts at the Table de Marbre of Paris was abolished. Appeals of judgments handed down by the *maîtrises des Eaux et Forêts* were henceforth heard by the superior councils. An edict of May 1771 abolished the Cour des Aides of Clermont-Ferrand and assigned cases within its purview to the superior council of Clermont. The Cour des Monnaies of Lyon was abolished and its jurisdiction assigned to the Cour des Monnaies of Paris. As for those special courts that were kept, the chancellor greatly reduced the number of officeholders in them, as in the case of the *bureau des Finances* of the *généralité* of Paris and the Cour des Monnaies of Paris.

The edict of 23 May 1771 denied officeholders the right to designate their successor, abolished the right of nomination that had been granted to *apanagés* and *engagistes*, and reversed the king's right to dispose of offices vacated by death or resignation. All offices were once more placed at the king's disposal.

Maupeou would have liked to abolish all the provincial *parlements* and replace them with superior councils. Laws would then have been verified by the Paris *parlement* alone, the only body that would still be allowed to make remonstrances. But Louis XV refused to go along, on the grounds that the provinces must be allowed some means of expressing their rights and needs. Without their *parlements* the provinces would have felt themselves under the thumb of a purely despotic regime.

Maupeou had to limit himself to getting rid of the most active magistrates in the provincial *parlements* and replacing them with men devoted to the king, to dividing up the jurisdictions of the provincial *parlements* by creating superior councils whenever possible, and to abolishing the special sovereign courts and transferring cases under their jurisdiction to other courts. In August 1771 he abolished all the offices in the Besançon *parlement* and reconstituted a new court staffed with loyal officers. The success of this venture persuaded the king to press forward. The Douai *parlement* was abolished on 13 August 1771, and in September an edict established a superior council for Flanders and Hainault. On 2 September the Toulouse *parlement* was abolished and replaced by a new *parlement* the following day. A superior council was created at Nîmes. On 4 September the Bordeaux *parlement* was abolished and on 7 September a new *parlement* installed. On 26 September the turn of the Rouen *parlement* came. On 4 October the Chambre des Comptes of Rouen was eliminated, and cases under its jurisdiction were transferred to the Chambre des Comptes of Paris. A superior council was created at Bayeux. On 1 October the Aix *parlement* and the Chambre des Comptes of Provence were eliminated. Cases under the jurisdiction of the latter were assigned to the new Provence *parlement*. On 21 October the Metz *parlement* got its turn, followed on 31 October by the *parlement* of Dombes, whose jurisdiction was fragmented. Ordinary cases were transferred to the superior council of Lyon, cases pertaining to the royal domain to the Paris *parlement*, cases pertaining to finance to the Chambre des Comptes of Paris, and cases pertaining to roads to the *bureau des Finances* of Lyon. On 25 October the Rennes *parlement* succumbed, and the new *parlement* was installed on the following day. The same happened at Dijon on 5–6 November and at Grenoble on 7–8 November. Also in November the Cour des Comptes, Aides et Finances of Franche-Comté at Dôle was abolished and replaced by a *bureau des Finances* in the charge of the intendant at Besançon.

A thousand magistrates were stripped of their offices, along with an even larger number of *procureurs*, *greffiers*, and *huissiers*. They were reimbursed with royal securities with staggered due dates running well into the future.

These lost three-fourths of their nominal value. Many *avocats* were left without employment. In cities where sovereign courts were located merchants suffered heavy losses when the magistrates were sent into exile. "Patriotic" writers railed against the affront to freedom and the rights of property.

But the king had won the battle. When court resumed session at the festival of Saint Martin in 1771, two-thirds of the Parisian *avocats* rallied to the side of the reforms. In the provinces bishops said mass to inaugurate the opening session of the superior councils, thereby recognizing the legality of the new tribunals. One by one, the princes of the blood capitulated in the autumn of 1772. Even the prince de Condé and the duc de Bourbon went to pay their respects to the new Paris *parlement*. Prosecution of pamphleteers resulted in the almost complete cessation of publication of brochures hostile to the reforms by the end of 1772. A case of corruption, in which a Parisian judge by the name of Goezman was compromised by a war profiteer who was better known as a writer, Beaumarchais, attracted a good deal of attention. But on 26 February 1774 Beaumarchais was publicly censured.

Louis XVI and the End of the Royal Revolution

At the age of sixty-four the king was strong and robust. He had confidence in Maupeou and supported his reforms. The royal revolution seemed complete. But in late April the king came down with smallpox. On 10 May he died. His successor, Louis XVI, age twenty, was imbued with the aristocratic ideology of Fénelon. As a minister of state and mentor he appointed the old comte de Maurepas to the Council. On 2 June 1774, d'Aiguillon was forced to resign. He was replaced by the chevalier de Vergennes, the French ambassador to Sweden. The comte de Muy became minister of war and, on 20 July, Turgot became secretary of state for the navy. Maurepas was a supporter of the *parlements*. "Without a *parlement* there is no monarchy" was his motto. He persuaded the youthful king and his young queen Marie-Antoinette that to retain Chancellor Maupeou and his courts was to risk losing the affection of their subjects. On 24 August 1774, the duc de La Vrillière was sent to ask Maupeou to return the seals of France and to resign his post as chancellor. Maupeou's answer was, "Monsieur, here are the seals, which I return to the king: they were merely entrusted to my safe-keeping. As for the post of chancellor, I shall die with it." He was then handed a letter of exile. The abbé Terray was exiled on the same day.

On 25 August crowds lighted fires of celebration in the streets of Paris and exploded fireworks. On 21 October Louis XVI signed letters recalling the exiled magistrates and ordered all the members of the old *parlement* to return to Paris by 9 November. On 12 November 1774, Louis XVI held a *lit de justice* during which he issued ten edicts restoring to their functions the Paris *parlement*, the Grand Conseil, the Cours des Aides of Paris and Clermont-Ferrand, and the provincial *parlements* and abolishing the superior councils. The king preserved the disciplinary edict of 7 December 1770, established a plenary court composed of princes of the blood, the chancellor, the peers of France, and the *conseillers d'Etat*. This court was empowered to find *parlement* guilty of dereliction of duty in case of suspension of justice or collective resignation. The king further ordered the Grand Conseil to replace *parlement* if *parlement* should cease to perform its duties. These security measures were never applied, however.

It took a year to reestablish the provincial *parlements*. The restoration began at Rouen on 12 November 1774 and ended at Pau on 13 November 1775. Maupeou's magistrates were removed and replaced by the previous magistrates. Everything was restored to what it had been before the royal revolution.

Maupeou is credited with the following jibe: "The king wishes to lose his crown; he is of course its master." In any case, Louis XVI stuck blindly to his philosophy. Maupeou died at home of natural causes on 29 July 1792. On 21 January 1793, Louis XVI was guillotined.

The Uncertainties of Louis XVI and the Blindness of the *Parlements*

Once reestablished, the *parlements* returned to their politics of opposition and remonstrances, with some moderation until 1781. They were driven to resume their obstructionist tactics by the financial crisis stirred up by France's participation in the American War for Independence (1778–83) and by the speculative activities of the Genevan banker and French finance minister Necker, who knew and understood little about French institutions. The *parlements* reverted to an opposition that made them popular with an agitated populace at that time aware of their hostility to the government but unconcerned about their objectives. Now, the *parlements* aimed at taking power themselves in the name of the customary constitution as they saw it, which was a myth. Accordingly, they wished to preserve the existing social structure, a society of orders and *corps*. They took no notice of the fact that the most powerful trend was toward the vesting of administrative power in elected assemblies composed of notables, drawn primarily from the ranks of landowners, the possessors of the most important means of production, and the men of talent, *avocats* and lawyers, who were discontent because access to *parlement* had been shut off.[1] While this current of opinion was hostile to the *commissaires*, particularly the intendants, who were losing prestige and authority, it was no less hostile to the society of orders and *corps*, since it favored assemblies in which nobles, clergy, and commoners would be forced to mingle, distinguished no longer by their quality but rather by the size of their fortunes as indicated by the amount of tax paid (the so-called electoral *cens*).

We might refer to this phenomenon as the transition from a society of orders and *corps* to a society of classes, which in good logic should have harmed the *parlements* and the sovereign courts just as much as the *com-*

missaires. But if the magistrates of the sovereign courts noticed this danger, they do not seem to have been concerned by it. They were convinced of the power of their prestige: witness the *premier président* of the Rouen *parlement*, who, in 1639, when preparations for a popular rebellion were under way, refused to take any precautions on the grounds that when the rebels saw his beautiful gown, they would all fall to their knees (he was quite surprised in the event by the insults and blows that came his way); or, to take another example from the Revolution, the all too notorious Duval d'E-prémesnil, who, as late as 1790, when the National Assembly was busy establishing new political and social structures, remarked, "It will all end with a decree of *parlement*, just wait and see." Blinded by their exclusive concern with external marks of respect, legal formalities, and subtle interpretations of consecrated texts, the magistrates of the sovereign courts had lost contact with the active elements in the country and understood the tendencies of the present as little as they understood the true nature of the social and political institutions of the past.

The *parlements* therefore opposed all fundamental reforms. The government attempted to make the necessary reforms: fiscal reforms based on the principle of equality of taxation as an ultimate goal, economic reforms aimed at freeing industry and stimulating production, and religious reforms based on liberalism and toleration. Following Turgot's relative failure (1774–76), the government abolished *corvées* and mortmain on the royal domain, gradually freed trade in grain, reformed the *vingtième*, and granted civil status to the Protestants. It encountered constant opposition from the *parlements*, speaking in behalf of the society of orders and its concomitant privileges.

At the end of 1786 the annual deficit on receipts of 475 million livres exceeded 100 million *livres*. The third *vingtième*, established for the war by the edict of July 1782, was supposed to end in 1787. The government had borrowed 1,250 million livres since 1776. Repayments continued to be in excess of 50 million livres annually until 1790 and remained very heavy until 1797.

Calonne and the First Assembly of Notables

Calonne, the *contrôleur général*, reverted to earlier projects inspired by Vauban, Turgot, and Necker, with which he hoped to achieve a unification of the various orders and *corps* in the kingdom: among these were a territorial tax in kind on all landed income, without exceptions, a permanent, proportional tax assessed by provincial assemblies of property owners drawn from a hierarchy of elected assemblies representing the taxpayers; transformation of the Caisse d'Escompte into a National Bank to assure credit to the state; replacement of the royal *corvée* by a money tax; freeing trade in grains; reduction of the *gabelle*; abolition of internal *traites* and a uniform customs tariff.

Calonne, a former intendant and *conseiller d'Etat*, had no desire to submit his plans to *parlements* that showed a systematic hostility toward them. He deemed the Estates General useless and dangerous, the right to tax being one of the sovereign's inherent powers. He preferred to resort to an Assembly of Notables. The last one had been held in 1626–7. Once this assembly had adjourned, Calonne planned to have all the edicts registered in *lit de justice* by all the *parlements* of France.

The Assembly of Notables opened on 22 February 1787. It consisted of 144 members chosen by the king: 7 princes of the blood, 14 prelates (7 archbishops and 7 bishops), 36 titled *gentilshommes* (6 of them dukes-and-peers, 6 dukes, 8 maréchaux de France, 16 marquis, counts, and barons), 12 members of the Conseil d'Etat (8 *conseillers d'Etat*, 4 *maîtres des requêtes*), 37 magistrates of the sovereign courts, almost all of them *premiers présidents* and *procureurs généraux*, the *lieutenant civil* of the Châtelet of Paris, 12 deputies from the *pays d'Etats*, and 25 city mayors, 22 of whom were ennobled. These members were distributed among seven *bureaux*, each presided over by a prince of the blood and served by a *conseiller d'Etat* acting as *rapporteur*. The *bureaux* met every morning. *Commissaires* prepared minutes of each day's deliberations during the night. After detailed examination of each project in the *bureaux*, a general assembly was supposed to arrive at a consensus.

Within this expanded version of the king's Council there grew up an opposition led by those who were threatened by the minister's plans: representatives from the *pays d'Etats*, the sovereign courts, and the clergy. As a result, the notables showed an unexpected independence. They generally approved the principle of the reforms, with serious reservations as to the wisdom of provincial assemblies and territorial subventions, but rejected the means for carrying them out. They indignantly rejected the plan of awarding competitive contracts for domanial lands designated as fiefs or *censives* on the grounds that the royal domain was inalienable, "an object of national devotion . . . a sacred tradition," with some maintaining this position pure and simple, and others arguing that only the Estates General had the power to award such contracts. They disapproved the plan of replacing the 20 *grands maîtres* of the Eaux et Forêts and the 175 *maîtrises particulières* by 12 inspectors general and 24 special inspectors under the supervision of a bureau of the king's Council directed by the *contrôleur général des Finances*, because they believed that *commissaires* should not outrank officeholders. On 5 May they asked that royal finances be placed under the control of five "citizens," to be appointed initially by the king and subsequently recruited by cooptation. They refused to approve the necessary taxes that were supposed to be voted by the sovereign courts and Estates General. On 21 May the marquis de La Fayette even called for the convocation of a truly national assembly. The notables were disturbed by contradictions between Necker's 1781 report, which indicated a surplus of 10 million, and the assertions of Calonne, who claimed a deficit of 46 million for that year and 112 million for 1787 and found a deficit of from 145 to 183 million. The notables were exasperated by a notice published by Calonne on 31 March, an attack on privileges and declaration of the king's intention to make those who were not paying enough pay more.

Calonne's enemies besieged the king. On 8 April 1787, Louis dismissed Miromesnil, the keeper of the seals, and Calonne, the *contrôleur général*. He replaced Miromesnil by Lamoignon, a *président* in the Paris *parlement*, and appointed to the post of *contrôleur général* first the *conseiller d'Etat* Bouvard de Fourgueux and then the *maître des requêtes* Laurent de Ville-deuil, who was replaced on 30 August by the *conseiller d'Etat* Lambert. Most important of all, on 30 April 1787, he appointed the archbishop of Toulouse, Loménie de Brienne, to head the Conseil des Finances, and on 26 August 1787 named him principal minister. The king decided to dismiss the notables on 25 May 1787. They had acted more as a representative assembly of the nation than as an enlarged king's Council, even if the nation on this occasion was narrowly defined as the high nobility, the clergy, and the officeholders.

Notables as Ministers: Brienne, Lamoignon, and the Aristocratic Revolution

Louis XVI acceded to the demand that he appoint Loménie de Brienne, even though he did not like him, because he considered the man who was archbishop first of Toulouse and then of Sens to be an atheist. Thus in May 1787 a silent change in the constitution of France took place. The sovereign ceased to govern and gradually disappeared from the scene, taking less and less interest in public affairs. Power was wielded by the principal minister, handpicked by the notables and acting as their representative. Sovereignty had passed to the notables. The Revolution had been made.

The notables wanted economies. Loménie de Brienne obliged them with drastic cuts and, by abolishing jobs, struck at the court nobility, the *gentils-hommes*, the clergy, and the officeholders. But he assured that those men who were retained in their positions would take precedence over the *com-missaires*, the ennobled, and the bourgeois. For sixteen months Loménie de Brienne carried out reforms in the spirit of the Assembly of Notables, a spirit hostile to *commissaires* and *commis*, to men of common blood.

We have already indicated what these reforms were in discussing the various agencies of government individually. It will be worthwhile to pause now to consider them as a whole, so as to appreciate their scope and character.

The regulation of 9 August 1787 cut the number of officers in the king's domestic household in half by making all quarterly offices semestrial. The Grande and Petite Ecurie were combined, to the outrage of the duc de Coigny. All the nobles at court considered themselves to have been injured by this.

As for the staff of the *contrôleur général*, the three *conseillers d'Etat* and sixteen *maîtres des requêtes* who had been acting as department heads were reduced by the regulation of 5 June 1787 to five *maîtres des requêtes*, who were commissioned to act as *intendants des Finances*. Their emoluments were cut in half.

The Conseil royal des Finances et du Commerce was established on 5 June 1787. It had eighteen bureaus working under it. This number was reduced to seven by the regulation of 27 October, largely at the expense of the *conseillers d'Etat*, whose emoluments were reduced to practically nothing.

An edict of August 1787 abolished the office of *directeur général des Postes* (which had belonged to the duc de Polignac) and the post of *intendant des Postes aux chevaux, relais, et messageries*, saving 364,219 livres. The council decree of 12 August limited the use of franking privileges and enabled Loménie to extract an additional 1,200,000 livres annually from his postal administrators.

By council decree of 13 October 1787, all pensions being paid to persons below the age of seventy-five were decreased, by one-tenth for the smallest pensions and four-tenths for the highest. Pensions were henceforth to be paid only by the Royal Treasury in order to avoid payment of more than one pension to a single individual. The total annual cost of new pensions was not to exceed the amount of those eliminated. The court nobility was plunged into despair.

Under the comte de Brienne, who became minister of war on 24 September 1787, a War Council was established on 28 October, consisting of four *lieutenants généraux*, four *maréchaux de camp*, and a brigadier, the comte de Guibert, acting as *rapporteur*. Some of the troops attached to the king's household were eliminated: on 30 September 1787, the gendarmes of the Guard, the Gate Guards, and the Light Horse were disbanded. On 2 March 1788, the 900-man strong gendarmerie de France, which included some wealthy bourgeois, was abolished. But the 1,300-man strong bodyguard, whose members were recruited from the ranks of the *gentilshommes*, were only reduced to four squadrons of 250 men each.

The regulation of 9 October 1787 permanently abolished the Ecole Militaire of Paris, which since the time of the comte de Saint-Germain had been reserved for the best students from twelve provincial *collèges*.

Five posts of colonel general, three of which belonged to princes of the blood, were slated for abolition upon the death or resignation of the incumbent by the ordinance of 17 March 1788.

The eighteen *maréchaux de France*, whose total remuneration came to 2 million livres, were reduced in number to twelve.

A total of 1,261 generals (*lieutenants généraux, maréchaux de camp*, and *brigadiers*) consumed more than 15 million livres. The 359 *brigadiers* were eliminated. The number of *lieutenants généraux* was reduced to 160.

Responsibility for managing logistics and health services for the military was taken away from civilian suppliers and entrusted to the army.

The regulation of 22 May 1781 had stipulated that, in order to become a *sous-lieutenant*, a man had to prove that he had four generations of nobility on his father's side. An exception was made for the sons of knights of the Order of Saint Louis. The ordinance of 17 March 1788 provided that this exception would henceforth apply only to those whose father had served as a captain, which excluded the sons of officers who had risen from the ranks, few of whom rose beyond the rank of lieutenant.

If nobility was "presented," a man would serve a few years as a brevet captain for form's sake and then be promoted to the rank of colonel. The ordinance of 17 March required that the "presented" noble serve as a sub-lieutenant, a captain, and a major before rising to the rank of colonel.

Ordinary *gentilshommes* from the provinces who became *sous-lieutenants* after passing a strenuous examination were assured of rising through the lower ranks until they reached the rank of *capitaine-commandant*. They might then be selected for promotion to major and lieutenant colonel. Every lieutenant-colonel was assured, after twenty years in rank, of becoming a *maréchal de camp*, that is to say, a general.

The total amount saved came to 8 or 9 million livres. But if the court nobles were embittered by the new demands made on them, the *gentils-hommes* were outraged by the privileges the court nobles continued to enjoy.

Economy measures notwithstanding, the deficit remained at 160 million. Additional taxes were needed. In order to make the additional tax burden bearable, Loménie de Brienne issued a declaration on 17 June 1787, estab-lishing free trade in grains. Export could be prohibited only for a one-year period upon demand of the provincial Estates or assemblies. The declaration of 27 June 1787 converted the *corvée* for road work into a money tax to be added to the *taille*. Studies were made of the feasibility of abolishing internal tariffs. The *gabelle* was transformed into a new tax.

Brienne wanted to replace the *vingtièmes*, a scheduled tax on various sources of revenue, by a territorial subvention paid only by landowners. But Calonne had looked to a proportional tax, under which members of all orders would be treated alike and pay according to the size of their income. In keeping with the wishes of the notables, Brienne envisioned a distributed tax of fixed amount apportioned to the needs of the state, at that moment 80 million livres. He decided to retain distinctions between the orders. The clergy would be allowed to follow its customary practice for internally ap-portioning the tithes among the benifices, but it would be required to have its property holdings verified by provincial assemblies to establish the amount of its proportional share.

A declaration of 18 June 1787 extended the obligation to purchase stamped paper to include not only court documents and notarized deeds but also letters of nomination to posts and offices, advertisements, handbills, pro-spectuses, gazettes, almanacs, receipts, letters of exchange, catalogs, reg-isters, and private contracts. The penalty for failure to use stamped paper was not nullification but a heavy fine. This tax was supposed to lighten the burden on landowners and hence on owners of fiefs and *seigneuries*, falling as it did mainly on merchants and financiers.

After the deficit had come to light, the *contrôleur général* could not be retained as the head of the royal finances. Accordingly, the regulation of 5 June 1787 established the Conseil royal des Finances et du Commerce, consisting of the king, the *contrôleur général*, the keeper of the seals, six ministers of state (the duc de Nivernais, the marquis d'Ossun, Bouvard de Fourqueux, Lamoignon de Malesherbes, the baron de Breteuil, and the comte de Montmorin), and two *conseillers d'Etat*. This council was to decide on all major financial operations, especially the scheduling of expenditures. In March 1788 the several *caisses* of the Royal Treasury were abolished and replaced by a single *caisse* managed by five administrators. An honest accounting was to be published each year. The accounting of 28 April 1788 was regarded as a masterpiece, and Necker made use of it in his report to the Estates General on 5 May 1789.

The edict of June 1787 established a hierarchy of assemblies in each *généralité*, which were to be given administrative responsibility: these included municipal assemblies, *arrondissement* assemblies, departmental assemblies, and provincial assemblies. Loménie de Brienne arranged it so that in the municipal assemblies the right to vote would not be limited to property owners but rather extended to all who paid at least ten livres of personal or property tax. In the *élection* of Orléans half the heads of families and single men were able to vote. Only those who paid at least thirty livres in taxes could be elected to the municipal assembly to administer the affairs of the community and elect the *arrondissement* assembly, however. Of the 12,931 electors in the *élection* of Orléans, only 4,450 were eligible for the municipal assemblies. What is more, Loménie de Brienne saw to it that the assemblies reflected the structure of the society of orders, as the notables wished. Alongside three to nine of the wealthiest elected members and the elected *syndic* and *greffier* sat the lord and curate as ex officio members. The provincial *gentilhommerie* and clergy were in a position to play a decisive role in the restricted committee of notables with which Brienne replaced the communal general assemblies. Similarly, of the twenty functioning provincial assemblies, ten were presided over by archbishops or bishops and ten by members of the high nobility, four of whom were dukes-and-peers. Fifteen or twenty of the *procureurs syndics* for the first two orders belonged to the old provincial nobility. All of the *procureurs syndics* for the third estate were magistrates or *avocats*, and half of the ennobled individuals bore the title of *écuyer* or *chevalier*. This reform applied only to the twenty-three *généralités* in the *pays d'élections*. The *généralités* of Bourges and Montauban kept their existing provincial assemblies. Although the committees of notables were theoretically subordinate to the *commissaires* dispatched to represent the king in the provinces, the importance of the *commissaires* was actually much reduced.[2]

Working in tandem with Loménie de Brienne, the keeper of the seals, Lamoignon de Malesherbes, decided, out of a desire to defer to the wishes of the Assembly of Notables, to issue a declaration on 1 May 1788 reforming the criminal ordinance of 1670. Among its other provisions, this declaration specified that judgments involving the death sentence could be executed after a one-month delay to allow time for the king to intervene if he wished. It abolished the _sellette_ [the wooden bench on which witnesses sat to be interrogated—trans.]. It further ordered that all decrees and judgments must enumerate or specify the crimes and misdemeanors of which the accused had been convicted and for which he would be sentenced. A majority of three votes was required to impose the death penalty. The form of torture known as the _question préalable_ was abolished.

Lamoignon also attempted to revive the regular lower courts, which had been overwhelmed by the _parlements_ and stripped of much of their jurisdiction by the profusion of special courts. The edict of May 1788 abolished the twenty-six _bureaux des Finances_, the _élections_, the _juges des Traites_, and the jurisdiction in litigation of the _maîtrises des Eaux et Forêts_ and the salt warehouses. It imposed limits on the activities of seigneurial judges and broke the monopoly of the sovereign courts by restricting their jurisdiction in criminal matters to cases involving the privileged (ecclesiastics, _gentils-hommes_, and officers of the courts) and in civil matters to appeals of cases involving values greater than 20,000 livres along with certain cases pertaining to the regale, the royal domain, and peerages. Candidates for positions in the _parlements_ were required to serve first in the lower courts. In civil cases the presidial courts were to have final judgment up to 4,000 livres. In criminal cases all their judgments were subject to appeal. All the _bailliages_ and _sénéchaussées_ were to be transformed into presidial courts. Above them forty-seven new _grands bailliages_ would be established to sit in final judgment of civil cases up to 20,000 livres in value and criminal cases not involving privileged individuals.

The edict "concerning those who do not profess the Catholic religion," which was presented to the Paris _parlement_ on 19 November 1787, officially acknowledged the existence of non-Catholics and granted them permission to register their marriages, births, and deaths for the purpose of enjoying the attendant civil benefits.

Loménie de Brienne and Lamoignon de Malesherbes, two notables who served as ministers, succeeded in renovating the structure of the society of orders in France: the _taille_ and the tax in lieu of _corvée_ labor remained taxes on commoners; the precedence of the first two orders in the provincial assemblies and in the municipal assemblies, where the provincial nobility was in a position to resurrect itself, was duly recognized; and the officers' ranks in the military were reserved to _gentilshommes_. But _avocats_, lawyers, and merchants' sons could hope to enjoy decent and honorable careers as magistrates in the revamped lower courts, now freed of the oppressive tutelage of the sovereign courts.

As it was, this series of edicts, which amounted to an aristocratic revolution designed to replace Maupeou's royal revolution, did bring certain improvements. It of course ran into opposition from the _parlements_. The interests of the *corps* of *parlement* suffered as a result of the limitation of their jurisdiction attendant upon the creation of the *grands bailliages* and the proliferation of presidial courts, with their new freedom of action. The magistrates were also threatened by the prospect of seeing the power to approve laws pertaining to finance transferred to the provincial assemblies once they had been elected in 1790. In the short run, the king's Council and his *commissaires* would continue to dominate the tame provincial assemblies. Finally, individual members of *parlement* were affected in their capacity as landowners by the imposition of a territorial subvention.

The Opposition of *Parlement* and Its Overshadowing by the Estates General

In order to examine the reforms and the new taxes, the princes of the blood and some peers joined the Paris *parlement* and sat with it as a Court of Peers. The acknowledged leader of the opposition to the government was a councillor in the first Chambre des Enquêtes, Duval d'Eprémesnil. Another councillor in the Enquêtes, Adrien-Jean-François Duport, went even further: he asked for a new constitution to be voted by the national assembly. The leaders of the resistance among the dukes-and-peers were Praslin, Aumont, Montmorency-Luxembourg, and Béthune-Charost. The leader of the princes of the blood was the duc d'Orléans.

These leaders carried in their wake the councillors of the Enquêtes and Requêtes. We know the age of seventy-two of these men: fifty-nine were less than thirty-five years old. *Parlement* was supported by the majority of the 550 *avocats*, 800 *procureurs*, 500 *huissiers*, and the *basoche* of clerks and secretaries in their employ. The livelihood of all these people was bound up with *parlement*'s prestige and competence.

On 22 June 1787, the Court of Peers examined the edict creating the provincial assemblies. This led to a brief against the administration of the intendants as "unconstitutional, tyrannical, and outrageous," but the edict was nevertheless registered without difficulty. On 25 June the declaration of 17 June concerning free trade in grains was also registered, and on 28 June the declaration of 27 June converting the *corvée* into a supplement to the *taille* was approved.

But when the declaration of 28 June extending the use of stamped paper was submitted on Monday 2 July 1787, the majority demanded first to see the statements of receipts and expenditures and a list of cutbacks that had been made. The king refused. On 26 July *parlement* sent its remonstrances. These demanded withdrawal of the stamp declaration and convocation of the Estates General, on the grounds that *parlement* did not have the power to approve a permanent new tax. This may not have been a lawyers' dodge, but in any case it was an abandonment by *parlement* of its most precious prerogative as well as its claim to stand in place of the Estates General, a form of political suicide.

On 30 July Brienne submitted the edict that substituted a territorial subvention for the two *vingtièmes*, but *parlement* stood by its call for the convocation of the Estates General prior to the imposition of any new tax.

On Monday, 6 August 1787, the king held a *lit de justice* at Versailles and had the declaration and edict read and registered. On 7 August the Assembly of Chambers approved a decree declaring that "the transcriptions ordered to be entered into the registers of the court" were "null and illegal." On 13 August the Assembly of Chambers approved another decree declaring that the laws registered on 6 August were "incapable of depriving the Nation of any of its rights and of authorizing a collection of taxes contrary to the principles, maxims, and customs of the kingdom."

On 14 August a council decree quashed these seditious decrees of *parlement* and ordered that the registered laws be enforced. On 15 August the magistrates of *parlement* were exiled to Troyes. All the *présidiaux* and *bailliages* in its jurisdiction supported *parlement* and refused to publish the new laws. In Paris the *basoche* was in a state of insurrection, particularly on 17 August when the king's brothers, the comte de Provence and the comte d'Artois, compelled the Chambre des Comptes and the Cour des Aides to register certain fiscal edicts. The army restored order.

Brienne thought that he would have the situation back in hand within five years. All he had to do was hold on until 1792. He therefore proposed a compromise: he would withdraw the stamp edict and the territorial subvention and continue to collect the *vingtièmes* with scrupulous exactitude and no favoritism, extending the second *vingtième* into 1791 and 1792. *Parlement* agreed and registered the edict of September 1787 ordering collection of an income tax of two *vingtièmes*. A declaration of 20 September granted the court permission to reestablish its seat in Paris.

But this compromise made it necessary for the government to borrow. The king went to *parlement* on 19 November 1787 with the keeper of the seals, the princes of the blood, and a number of ministers and *conseillers d'Etat*, to hold not a *lit de justice* but rather a royal sitting of the court, a sort of expanded version of the king's Council. The king listened to the opinions expressed but did not have the votes counted. He declared that the loans mentioned in the edict were necessary and ordered that the edict be registered. He promised to convoke the Estates General before 1792. The duc d'Orléans protested and maintained that the king's action was illegal because it was contrary to the wishes of a majority of the Court of Peers. After the king had left, the court continued to sit and issued a decree declaring that it had no intention of taking part in the registration of the edict. On 20 November a *lettre de cachet* sent the duc d'Orléans into exile. On 21 November the king had the court registers brought to him and then had the decree of 19 November stricken from the record on the grounds that when he held his council in the midst of *parlement* for the purpose of considering affairs of state, he was not bound by the will of the majority, majority rule being binding only on the courts in the normal course of their duties.

The king proposed a subscription to the *vingtièmes* to the provincial assemblies. These bodies would be given sole discretion to apportion the *vingtième*, without recourse to those hated *commissaires*, the *contrôleurs du vingtième*. But such a plan would have resulted in an increase of taxes on the privileged. It aroused the opposition of the provincial assemblies on the grounds that the nation had a right to approve new taxes. The Court of Peers declared that it had not intended its registration decree of 19 September 1787 to be taken as approving a system that would have required the people to pay the full amount of the territorial subvention. The court thus prevented the king from putting the financial situation in order.

The provincial *parlements* also kept up their opposition. The most active were those in Grenoble, Besançon, and Rennes. The Dijon *parlement* had been engaged in unremitting conflict with the intendant for Burgundy since 1784. The Bordeaux *parlement* had forced the intendant Dupré de Saint-Maur to retire. In several provinces the magistrates proposed alternative plans to the provincial assemblies, suggesting that the provincial Estates be restored. The Estates of Provence were reestablished in October 1787. Other *parlements* placed obstacles in the way of registering the edict on the provincial assemblies. The Bordeaux *parlement* refused on 25 July 1787 to register this edict before it had been given a chance to examine the supplementary regulations. The king exiled the *parlement* to Libourne on the night of 17 August 1787.

The provincial *parlements* did not have to discuss the stamp edict and the territorial subvention, for these had been withdrawn. It was not customary to submit edicts on loans for their approval. They opposed the edict extending the second *vingtième* "without any distinction or exception," when not a single *councillor* in any *parlement* in France paid his *vingtième* on the same footing as other taxpayers. They foresaw the use of a cadastral survey, which frightened them even more than bankruptcy of the state. Even in the major *pays d'Etats* such as Burgundy and Languedoc, it was always the *parlements* that were most uncompromisingly opposed to scrupulous collection of the *vingtièmes* and to the subscription procedure. It was in these circumstances that the "union of classes" reappeared, causing the keeper of the seals to point out once again that each *parlement* was to concern itself only with its own jurisdiction and not with the business of other *parlements*.

The King Is Forced to Take Strong Measures: The Plenary Court

The obstacles raised by the *parlements* forced the government to take strong measures, just as in the time of Maupeou. In May 1788 the king reestablished the Plenary Court, observing as he did that this institution was based on the ancient constitution of his states. The court would make final registration of all laws common to the whole of France. It would merely make provisional registration of laws establishing new taxes, pending approval by the Estates General and the provincial Estates. The existing sovereign courts would continue to register laws peculiar to their individual jurisdictions. The Plenary Court was to consist of the Grand-Chambre of the Paris *parlement*, the princes of the blood, the peers of the realm, the high crown officers, two archbishops, two bishops, two *maréchaux de France*, two governors, two *lieutenants généraux*, six *conseillers d'Etat*, four *maîtres des requêtes*, two magistrates from the Chambres des Comptes and two from the Cour des Aides of Paris, and one *président* or councillor from each provincial *parlement*. It would hold a regular session each year from 1 December until 1 April. Before registering an edict it would be allowed to submit remonstrances. After registration the law would be sent to all the courts of the kingdom for transcription and publication.

Loménie de Brienne thought of combining this "upper chamber" with a "lower chamber" made up of landowners elected to serve as deputies by the provincial assemblies.

In response the Paris *parlement* on 29 April approved one edict prepared by Goislard de Montsabert, which refused to allow the government to tighten up procedures for collecting the *vingtième*, and another, prepared by Duval d'Eprémesnil, which challenged the legality of the Plenary Court by invoking the fundamental laws of the French monarchy. The king attempted to have these two magistrates arrested on the night of 4 May, but they took refuge in the Palais de Justice. On the night of 5 May an officer was sent to arrest them in the Court of Peers, but the officer did not know them by sight and all the members of the court cried out, "We are all Messieurs Duval and Goislard. You will have to arrest us all." In the end, the two magistrates surrendered on 6 May and were incarcerated.

The edict reestablishing the Plenary Court was registered in a *lit de justice* held at Versailles on 8 May 1788 in which the king was assisted by the keeper of the seals. Royal *commissaires* represented the king in *lits de justice* held on 8, 9, and 10 May 1788, at the fourteen other *parlements* and sovereign councils. Along with this edict a number of others were also registered: depending on the *parlement*, these included legislation on judicial reform, civil status for non-Catholics, and fiscal matters. The Besançon *parlement* had to register fifteen laws.

All the *parlements* were forced to adjourn. All except those of Paris and Douai protested the compulsory adjournments and declared registrations obtained by the use of force to be null and void. Some reiterated the demand that the Estates General be convoked. The *parlements* of Rennes and Pau disobeyed the king and continued to meet publicly. The king exiled the *parlements* of Toulouse, Besançon, Dijon, Metz, Rouen, Rennes, and Grenoble. In Rennes and Grenoble the *basoche* stirred up popular unrest during the month of June, and the army was forced to restore order in July of 1788.

The "May edicts" gave the opposition plenty of ammunition for its criticism. The remonstrances submitted on 15 June 1788 by the Assembly of the Clergy demanded absolute freedom to determine how large a gift it would grant to the state. The immunities of the clergy were confirmed by the council decree of 5 July 1788: by way of indication of what was at stake, it is worth noting that the clergy contributed only 1,800,000 livres rather than the 8,000,000 that had been asked. The majority of the high clergy used the traditional constitution of France to challenge the king. The nobility insisted upon the reestablishment of the provincial Estates. In Dauphiné a portion of the third estate launched a battle against the May laws. The royal judge at Grenoble, Jean-Joseph Mounier, allied with some liberal nobles, took the initiative of calling an assembly of notables, 101 of whom met at the Hôtel de Ville in Grenoble on 14 June 1788. Then, on 21 July an assembly of 491 representatives of the three orders met at the château de Vizille. The assembly demanded that for the sake of propriety all the *parlements* be recalled and, even more important, that the provincial Estates be reestablished. All seats in the latter were to be elective, and the third estate was to have a number of seats equal to the first two orders combined. Taxes, such as the tax replacing the *corvée*, were to be apportioned equally among the three orders. The Estates General were to be convoked and would set the amount to be contributed by each province to the total tax bill.[3]

Loménie de Brienne was mainly anxious to gain time. By council decree of 5 July 1788, he invited the French people to make known their opinions concerning the proper forms for holding the Estates General so as to make it "a truly National Assembly, both in its composition and in its effects." Responses to this call were not expected until the early months of 1789. By council decree of 2 August 1788, he met the demands of the Dauphinois and ordered that a preliminary assembly be held at Romans, in which the third estate would enjoy a representation equal to that of the other two orders. This assembly would make proposals to the king concerning the organization of the future provincial Estates of Dauphiné.

The Fiscal Crisis, the Recall of Necker, and the Calling of the Estates General

By August 1788, however, the government found itself paralyzed for lack of money. Advances of 240 million livres were required from the banks and speculators. But the financial community was worried about the opposition to the May edicts and unwilling to stand by its commitments. Empty-handed, Loménie de Brienne was forced to issue a council decree o 8 August setting a date of 1 May 1789 for the meeting of the Estates General and to suspend the reestablishment of the Plenary Court until that date. By council decree on 16 August he issued treasury bills at 5 percent interest to be used by the government to meet its debts in lieu of cash (excepting troop pay, emoluments up to 1,200 livres, and *rentes* up to 500 livres). This touched off a panic. The comte d'Artois and the Polignac faction railed against Loménie de Brienne, who was preventing them and the high court nobility from emptying the public coffers. Driven by this group, Marie-Antoinette and Louis XVI abandoned their minister. On Monday, 25 August, the archbishop of Sens resigned. Necker was recalled, to an enthusiastic welcome by the Bourse, the Palais-Royal, and the Place Dauphine: profitable speculation was about to begin anew.

Necker, who was poorly informed and upset by a few riots on the Pont Neuf and in the Place de Grève, thought that civil war was imminent. He hoped to ward it off by hastening the meeting of the Estates General and by recalling the *parlements* at once. On 14 September the keeper of the seals, Lamoignon, had submitted his resignation at the king's behest. The declaration of 23 September 1788 recalled the sovereign courts and announced that the Estates general would be held in January 1789 and that all plans for judicial reform were to be scrapped. The revolution of the notables and the aristocratic revolution had failed, each in turn. Like the previous royal revolution, they failed because of the blind obstructionism of the sovereign courts, representing the officeholders, and because of the neglect of his duties by a king paralyzed by his scruples, a king who had become a mere plaything tossed about by contradictory influences. One contemporary thought that France had ceased to be a monarchy and had become a republic.

Thanks to advances from the Caisse d'Escompte, Necker was able to reinstate cash payment of state debts as of 14 September. He was of the opinion that new taxes were necessary in order to put an end to the deficit. But he had taken it into his head that the only way to revive the French nation was to consult with the Estates General. He was therefore content to bide his time. Having given up judicial reform, he now gave up administrative reform as well, indicating that he expected nothing from the provincial assemblies and did not seek to establish provincial Estates along the lines proposed by the third estate.

He placed the future in the hands of the "National Party," which consisted of a group of clubs (the most influential of which met at the home of Duport, a councillor in *parlement*), political salons and cafés, and which favored a constitution based not on tradition and history but rather on the nature of things, a party hostile to any sort of *esprit de corps* and to all privileges accorded to provinces, cities, courts, companies, and orders of the state.

The Paris *parlement*, always so far from reality, also gave in to the tide. On 25 September 1788, it asked that "the Estates General indicated for this coming January [be] duly convoked and constituted, following the forms observed in the year one thousand six hundred fourteen."[4] Subsequent explanations notwithstanding, it thereby consummated its political suicide, begun when it first called for a meeting of the Estates General.

But *parlement* thus obliged Necker to issue a council decree on 5 October 1788 calling a second Assembly of Notables "to deliberate solely on the most regular and appropriate manner of moving toward the formation of the Estates General of 1789."[5] The Assembly first met on 6 November 1788. Generally speaking, the notables favored a structure based on the traditional orders.

In its decree of 5 December the Paris *parlement* called for periodic meetings of the Estates General, which it wished to see granted legislative power and the right to charge and try ministers before the courts, ministers who would henceforth be responsible to the Estates General. *Parlement* also called for a continuation of the system under which the orders met and deliberated separately and the clergy and nobility outranked the third estate. It asked for individual liberty for citizens, freedom of the press, and assurances that traditional rights and prerogatives would be respected. These measures would have reduced the king to the position of president of an aristocracy that would have wielded the key powers and enjoyed preeminence in society.

After much hesitation, the government reached a decision that was embodied in the minutes of the council meeting of 27 December 1788. It decided to allow nobles and clerics to represent the third estate and therefore to present themselves as candidates in the elections of the third order. The third estate was granted double representation, but it was made clear that this decision did not imply that the three orders would deliberate in common, since their interests were absolutely equal and identical and should be resolved by free and unanimous decision. Promises of individual liberty and freedom of the press were made, and citizens were promised the right to participate in the administration of the kingdom through expanded provincial Estates and regularly convoked Estates General. This consternated the aristocracy without satisfying the National Party.

From the Estates General to the National Assembly: From a Society of Orders to a Society of Classes

The monarchy having resigned, the electoral modalities prescribed for the Estates General that met on 5 May 1789 paved the way for the transition from a structure based on orders to a structure based on classes. Of the 1,318 deputies seated, the clergy had 326, the nobility 330, and the third estate 661. Unlike the Estates of 1614–15, however, this time curates were not only heavily represented among the clergy but even constituted the majority of the first estate. Their feelings and interests usually coincided with those of the third estate. Among the nobility, the proportion of nobles whose primary occupation was with the king's army, who were soldiers before anything else, had increased: they now accounted for 166 of the 331 nobles, more than half, compared with less than a third in 1614–15. Royal officers of justice no longer made up the majority of the third estate. The largest group consisted of members of the liberal professions: 214 deputies, with jurists heavily in the majority, including 180 *avocats*. The officeholders still formed a considerable group, 207 deputies in all, 173 of whom were judicial officeholders, 27 financial officeholders, and 7 seigneurial officeholders. A major innovation, however, was that now the productive occupations (agriculture, commerce, and industry), whose interests were close to those of the liberal professions, were well represented with 115 deputies.

This change in social composition finally allowed the deputies of the third estate to put over one of their key ideas: the destruction of a social structure based on orders and corps, the reduction of *gentilshommes*, priests, members of *corps* such as companies, *collèges*, corporations, etc., to the status of mere citizens. For them, the "distinction of orders" and the *esprit de corps* were the original sins of the nation. This was the meaning of their battle against ceremonial ritual. This was the point of their efforts to change procedures, to replace the separate deliberation of the orders by common deliberation in a single chamber, thus creating a true Assembly in which deputies of all orders would be merged in a single body, within which natural groups might then form, combining deputies of different orders drawn together by their affinities. "The essence of the Assembly is equality." The third estate was able to capitalize on a flaw in the king's arrangements. No special chamber had been set aside for this order. It therefore met in the great chamber in which the three orders gathered for royal sessions. The third estate referred to this chamber as the "national chamber." It opened its doors to the public. In the eyes of the public the third estate soon came to represent the entire Estates General. This image aided the third estate when it came time to move from a structure based on orders to one based on classes. This happened on 17 June 1789, when the third estate proclaimed itself a National Assembly, when, after the royal session of 23 June the members of the other orders decided to join it, and finally when on 9 July the National Assembly proclaimed itself to be a National Constituent Assembly.

With the transition from the Estates General to the National Assembly the desire to move from a society of orders to a society of classes became apparent—a society of classes dominated by the bourgeois class, the class of wealth and talent, which was able to claim sovereignty on the basis of representativeness of a new kind, "plurality" or, as people at the time were beginning to say, "majority rule," in imitation of the phrase then current in England and America. The law of numbers definitively replaced the *sanior pars*. But the majority was chosen from a new kind of *sanior pars*, a segment of society defined by the amount of tax it paid or, in other words, by a rough index of wealth. Thus the new *sanior pars* was defined in materialistic and quantitative terms.

The End of the "Three-hundred-year Lawsuit": The Abolition of Offices and Commissions

The sovereign National Assembly put an end to a lawsuit that had dragged on for three hundred years, the conflict between the officeholders and the *commissaires*, first by taking charge and making use of them and later by abolishing offices and commissions altogether.

Legislative and executive decisions were made by the National Assembly in the form of decrees. These were then conveyed to the king, who approved and promulgated them. The Council recast them in the form of letters patent, and they were then transmitted to the judicial corps and the *commissaires* for registration and execution.

On 3 November 1789, the National Assembly ordered the *parlements* to adjourn. It then made use, as an interim measure, of their *chambres des vacations* to transcribe, publish, and post its decrees. Most of the *chambres des vacations* registered the decree of 3 November—with recriminations, to be sure, but they did register it. The Rouen and Metz *parlements* protested. The *chambre des vacations* in Rennes refused in the name of the constitution of the Breton nation, associated with France. The National Assembly stuck by its orders, invoking its sovereignty and the fact that Brittany, by electing deputies to the Estates General, had recognized its union with France: the Breton constitution had ceased to exist. The Assembly had the king form another *chambre des vacations*. The other magistrates refused to sit on it. But all the municipalities in the province lashed out at the *chambre des vacations*. The city of Rennes placed its magistrates under house arrest. The National Assembly then established a Provisional Superior Court with judges drawn from the *présidiaux* and the ranks of the *avocats*, on 3 February 1790.

All the *parlements* of France and all the other courts of the monarchy were abolished by the decree of 16–24 August 1790 and the decrees of 6–7 September 1790. "In furtherance of the institution and organization of new tribunals, all those presently in existence—*vigueries, châtellenies, prévôtés, vicomtés, sénéchaussées, bailliages, châtelets, présidiaux*, provincial and superior councils, *parlements*, and in general all tribunals of ancient creation of whatever name or denomination, shall remain abolished." Letters patent of 16 September 1790 established a new judicial order consisting of elected magistrates. Offices were soon abolished. No officeholders were left except for the ministerial officials.

After the creation of municipalities by the decree of 14 December 1789, and of the departments by the decree of 22 December 1789, a circular letter was sent on 25 June 1790 by the secretary of state Saint-Priest to the intendants, instructing them on how they were to transfer power to the new bodies. All commissions, ordinary and extraordinary, of the old monarchy ceased to exist. The work of administration fell to assemblies of notables, which, while not eschewing the occasional use of *commissaires*, normally employed functionaries.

Notes

1. See vol. 1, pp. 598–694, 627–38, and this volume, pp. 251–80.
2. See vol. 1, p. 627.
3. See vol. 1, p. 638.

4. Armand Brette, *Recueil de documents relatifs à la convocation des Etats généraux de 1789* (1894), vol. 1, pp. 28–29.

5. Cited in Jean Egret, *La Pré-Révolution française: 1787–1788* (Paris: PUF, 1962).

Guide to Further Reading

Barbiche, Bernard. *Sully.* Paris: Albin Michel, 1978.

Berce, Yves-Marie. *Histoire des Croquants (Etude des soulèvements populaires au XVIIe siècle dans le sud-ouest de la France).* 2 vols. Paris: Droz, 1974.

Bonney, Richard. *Political Change in France under Richelieu and Mazarin (1624–1661).* New York: Oxford University Press, 1978.

——. *The King's Debts: Finance and Politics in France 1589–1661.* Oxford: Clarendon Press, 1981.

Bosher, J.-F. "The French Crisis of 1770." *History* 57 (1972): 17–30.

Brette, Armand. *Recueil de documents relatifs à la convocation des Etats généraux de 1789.* 4 vols. 1894.

Carré, Albert. "L'Assemblée constituante et la mise en vacances des Parlements (novembre 1789–janvier 1790)." *Revue d'histoire moderne et contemporaine* 9 (1907–8): 241–58, 325–47.

Chauleur, A. "Le rôle des traitants dans l'administration de la France (1643–1652)." *XVIIe siècle* 65 (1964): 16–49.

Cherest, Aimé. *La chute de l'Ancien Régime (1787–1789).* 2 vols. Paris: Hachette, 1884–86.

Collins, J.-B. "Sur l'histoire fiscale du XVIIe siècle: Les impôts directs en Champagne entre 1595 et 1635." *Annales E.S.C.* 34 (1979): 325–47.

Cubells, Madame. "Le Parlement de Paris pendant la Fronde." *XVIIe siècle,* 1957, pp. 171–201.

Doyle, William. "The Parlements of France and the Breakdown of the Old Regime (1771–1788)." *French Historical Studies* 6 (1970): 417–58.

Egret, Jean. *Le Parlement de Dauphiné et les affaires publiques dans la deuxième moitié du XVIIIe siècle.* 2 vols. Grenoble: Imprimerie Allier, 1942.

——. *Les derniers Etats de Dauphiné. Romans (septembre 1788–janvier 1789).* Grenoble: Imprimerie Allier, 1942.

——. *La Pré-Révolution française (1787–1788).* Paris: PUF, 1962.

——. *Louis XV et l'opposition parlementaire.* Paris: Armand Colin, 1970.

——. *Necker, ministre de Louis XVI.* Paris: Champion, 1975.

Flammermont, Jules. *Le chancelier Maupeou et les Parlements.* Picard, 1883.

——. *Remontrances du Parlement de Paris au XVIIIe siècle.* 3 vols. Collection des Documents inédits sur l'histoire de France. Imprimerie Nationale, 1888–98.

Floquet, A. *Histoire du Parlement de Normandie.* Vols. 4–7. 1841–42.

Foisil, Madeleine. *La révolte des Nu-Pieds et les révoltes normandes de 1639.* Paris: PUF, 1970.

——. *Mémoires du président Alexandre Bigot de Monville.* Part I: *Le Parlement de Rouen, 1640–1643.* Editions A. Pedone, 1976.

——. "La Normandie, entre la révolte des Nu-Pieds et la Fronde." *Bulletin de la Société d'histoire moderne* 4, pp. 23–27.

Glasson, E. *Le Parlement de Paris: Son rôle politique depuis le règne de Charles VII jusqu'à la Révolution.* 2 vols. Paris: Hachette, 1901.

Goubert, Pierre. *La vie quotidienne des paysans français au XVIIe siècle.* Paris: Hachette, 1982.

Gresset, Maurice. *Gens de justice à Besançon (1674–1789).* 2 vols. Bibliothèque Nationale, 1978.

Grillon, Pierre. *Les papiers de Richelieu.* 3 vols. published. Editions Pedone.

Guery, A. "Les finances de la monarchie française sous l'Ancien Régime." *Annales E.S.C.*, 33 (1978): 216–39.

Hinrichs, Ernst, Eberhard Schmitt, Rudolf Vierhaus, and Albert Cremer (eds). *Vom Ancien-Régime zur französichen Revolution.* Göttingen: Vandenhoeck & Ruprecht, 1978.

Hudson, David. "The Parlementary Crisis of 1763 in France and Its Consequences." *Canadian Journal of History* 7 (1972): 97–117.

Klaits, J. *Printed Propaganda under Louis XIV: Absolute Monarchy and Public Opinion.* Princeton, N.J.: Princeton University Press, 1977.

Labrousse, Ernest. *La crise de l'économie française à la fin de l'Ancien Régime et au début de la Révolution.* Paris: PUF, 1944.

Lafon, Jacqueline. "La fin du parlement de Paris." *Etudes d'histoire du droit parisien.* Paris: PUF, 1970, pp. 229–46.

Laugier, Lucien. *Un ministère réformateur sous Louis XV: Le Triumvirat (1770–1774).* La Pensée universelle, 1975.

Lefebvre, Georges, and Anne Terroine. *Documents relatifs aux Etats généraux.* 1953.

Le Marchand. "Sur la société française en 1789." *Revue d'histoire moderne* 19 (1972): 73–91.

Le Moy, Albert. *Le Parlement de Bretagne et le pouvoir royal au XVIIIᵉ siècle.* Angers: Imprimerie Bourdin, 1909.

———. *Les remontrances du Parlement de Bretagne au XVIIIᵉ siècle.* Angers: Imprimerie Bourdin, 1909.

Logié, Paul. *La Fronde en Normandie.* 3 vols. Amiens: by the author.

Lublinskaya, A. D. *French Absolutism. The Crucial Phase (1620–1629),* trans. Brian Pearce. Cambridge, Eng.: Cambridge University Press, 1968.

Malettke, Klaus (ed.). *Soziale und politische Konflikte im Frankreich des Ancien-Régime.* Berlin: Colloquium Verlag. Vol. 1, 1981; vol. 2, 1982.

Marion, Marcel. *La Bretagne et le duc d'Aiguillon, 1753–1770.* Fontemoing, 1898.

———. *Histoire financière de la France depuis 1715.* Vol. 1: *1715–1789,* 1914.

Miek, Ilja. *Die Entstehung des modernen Frankreich (1450–1610).* Stuttgart, Berlin, Cologne, and Mainz: W. Kolhammer, 1982.

Moote, A. Lloyd. *The Revolt of the Judges. The Parlement of Paris and the Fronde, 1643–1652.* Princeton, N.J.: Princeton University Press, 1971.

Morineau, Michel. "Budgets de l'Etat et gestion des finances royales en France au XVIIIᵉ siècle." *Revue historique* 536 (1980): 289–336.

Mousnier, Roland. *La vénalité des offices sous Henri IV et Louis XIII.* 1st ed., Rouen: Maugard, 1945. 2d ed., Paris: PUF, 1971.

———. "Quelques raisons de la Fronde: Les causes des journées révolutionnaires parisiennes de 1648." *XVII siècle* 2 (1949): 33–78. Reprinted in *La plume, la faucille et le marteau.* Paris: PUF, 1970. Pp. 265–300.

———. "Recherches sur les syndicats d'officiers pendant la Fronde: Trésoriers généraux de France et Elus dans la Révolution." *XVIIᵉ siècle* 42–43 (1959). Reprinted in *La plume, la faucille et le marteau,* pp. 301–34.

———. *L'assassinat d'Henri IV: Le problème du tyrannicide et l'affermissement de la monarchie absolue.* Collection "Trente journées qui ont fait la France." Paris: Gallimard, 1964.

———. "La participation des gouvernés à l'activité des gouvernants dans la France des XVIIᵉ et XVIIIᵉ siècles." In *Gouvernés et Gouvernants,* part 3, Recueils de la Société Jean-Bodin pour l'histoire comparative des institutions. Vol. 24, pp. 235–97, with bibliography. Brussels: Editions de la Librairie encyclopédique, 1966. Reprinted in *La plume, la faucille et le marteau,* pp. 231–64, without bibliography.

———. *Fureurs paysannes; Les paysans dans les révoltes du XVIIᵉ siècle (France, Chine, Russie).* Paris: Calmann-Lévy, 1967.

———. "The Fronde," in *Preconditions of Revolution in Early Modern Europe.* ed. Robert Forster and Jack P. Greene. Baltimore: Johns Hopkins University Press, 1970.

———. "Mazarin et le problème constitutionnel en France pendant la Fronde." Accademia Nazionale dei Lindei, Colloquio Italo-francese: Il Cardinale Mazzarino in Francia (Rome, 16–17 May 1977). Atti dei Convegui Lincei, 35, pp. 7–16.

——— et al. *Deux Cahiers de la Noblesse pour les Etats généraux de 1649–1651.* Paris: PUF, 1965.

Picot, G. *Histoire des Etats généraux.* 2d ed., 1888. Vol. 5.

Pillorget, René. *Les mouvements insurrectionnels de Provence entre 1596 et 1715.* Editions A. Pedone, 1975.

Pocquet, Barthélemy. *Le pouvoir absolu et l'esprit provincial: Le duc d'Aiguillon et La Chalotais.* Librairie académique Perrin, 1900–1901.

Rogister, J.-M. J. "The Crisis of 1753–4 in France and the Debate on the Nature of the Monarchy and of the Fundamental Laws," In Rudolf Vierhaus (ed.), *Herrschaftvorträge, Wahlkapitulationen, fundamentale Gesetze.* Göttingen: Vandenhoeck & Ruprecht, 1977.

Schulze, Winifried (ed). *Europäische Bauern Revolten der frühen Neuzeit.* Frankfurt am Main: Suhrkamp, 1982.

Villers, Robert. *L'organisation du Parlement de Paris et des Conseils supérieurs d'après la Réforme de Maupeou (1771–1774).* 1937.

Conclusion

We may now attempt to answer the question raised at the outset: Did Loyseau, the duc de Saint-Simon, Domat, and Barnave correctly understand the society in which they were living and its relations to the state? Did they identify the crucial features of that society and the key aspects of its transformation? Do their works mark a change, a transition from one kind of society to another, from one form of state to another?[1] Now that we have examined the behavior of thousands of individuals in the period during which these authors formed their ideas, we can say at once that, broadly speaking, they were right: each of these writers put his finger on certain crucial aspects of reality. This is a finding of some importance, for with some historians it is an article of faith that men are blind to the realities of their own time and unaware of what is really happening. Of course it is true that men never understand more than a part of the society in which they live and that many people are blinded by myth and legend. Myth and legend are of great importance to the historian, moreover. Sometimes they serve to motivate action. On occasion they indicate underlying tendencies and reflect the desire of men to hold beliefs that will enable them to make their actions conform with those tendencies. Myth and legend are always factors in human behavior. But here again we find that there are some men who see clearly, who grasp the essential features of the social and political relations of their time, and who are able to give expression to their insights. No doubt a far larger number of men lived in silence, publishing nothing and uttering no public word but merely acting with rectitude, simplicity, and good sense. It is comforting to think that in every period there are people, perhaps a great many of them, who are less unaware of what is going on than some have claimed, and less guided by blind forces, even if they do commit errors. Do governments and historians take sufficient notice of those who remain silent?

In the society we have been studying, France in the seventeenth and eighteenth centuries, one feature appears to have been crucial. It was clearly identified, I think, only by Loyseau, but exerted a constant influence over men's behavior until the beginning of the Revolution. I am speaking of the

division of French society into two groups: one inferior, consisting of those
who worked mainly with their hands and earned their living by this work,
men referred to as "mercenaries" and of "base" blood; the other superior,
consisting of those who were exempt from manual labor for profit, men
whose principal occupations were mainly cerebral, on which account their
profits were deemed "more honorary than mercenary," men who were called
"honorable" and "worthy." Was this split, which was highlighted in the
eighteenth century by the regulations governing admissions to the Ecole des
Ponts et Chaussées and the Engineering School at Mézières and by other
rules that made it almost impossible for the son of a manual worker to attend
a university, a hard-and-fast one in reality? Work on the seventeenth century[2]
has shown that in the families (or we may say lineages) of manual workers
on the rise in society, family members who rose from the ranks of manual
labor to the status of a ministerial or financial post continued to be conscious
of solidarity with their families and of relations with others who remained
manual workers, at least on the occasion of important family ceremonies
such as marriages, wakes, and the opening of wills. Outside the family,
however, the split was nonetheless real.

Was this society, then, a society divided into two social classes? I think
not. Admittedly, it was a society divided into two main social groups, but
both groups interpreted the social structure in the same way. For this reason
I would argue that this was a society of orders, not classes. For the social
division was quite clearly be based on a judgment as to the *value* of the
social functions and not as to the real social utility or importance of those
functions. It is quite easy to conceive of a society whose members would
agree that manual labor is more useful and honorable than other work, that
manual workers constitute the superior stratum of the society, and that the
political, administrative, and judicial powers that no society of any size can
do without should be entrusted exclusively to manual workers—in particular,
to those manual workers who show an aptitude for planning, making decisions, organizing, leading men, and assembling resources for the completion
of projects of interest to the public, whether public works, public-health
measures, education, justice, defense and police, science and technology,
religion and morals, or production of material wealth or works of art. Such
a society would be a society of orders. Like any society, it would have to
cope with "the wish of all fathers" to pass their own advantages on to their
children. Because of this there is an inherent tendency for social status to
be inherited. Like any society, this one too, would be liable to the risk that
power might be gathered into the hands, not of the most useful members of
society, even though their services are indispensable, but rather of those
with the greatest capacity to do harm, such as the military or the doctors,
for their own benefit and the benefit of their progeny. By the same reasoning,
a society such as French society in the seventeenth and eighteenth century,
based as it was on the inverse principle, that the superior stratum consists

of those not forced to do manual labor, also seems to me to have been a society of orders.

Among those belonging to the broad upper stratum consisting of people who were not obliged to work with their hands, at any rate not for their major occupation and not for profit, a further distinction may be made between upper and lower substrata. The lower substratum included those employed in service occupations, those who laid the groundwork for the decisions of others and carried out the orders of those who wielded power. This category included men responsible for procedural work in the courts, such as *procureurs*, *huissiers*, *sergents*, and notaries, as well as those who drafted, revised, classified, and filed documents, such as secretaries and *commis* working in the bureaus. All these were "base" occupations because they involved service, dependency, execution of the orders of others. But the children of these men could attend university and were not forbidden to rise to higher positions. Above this stratum was another group, consisting of men responsible in the first place to themselves, of men able to live on what they possessed, their property or their *rentes*, or of men who at least pronounced the law, such as *avocats*, or who dispensed judgment and issued orders, such as *seigneurs*, magistrates, and army officers. These were the men who truly held ranks of honor, the men who were regarded as "honorable" and "worthy."

Beyond these major divisions, society was further subdivided into a large number of social levels, or "estates," to use a term current at the time, or, again, "strata," to use a word borrowed from the geologists. But we must be careful lest the use of such static terminology lead us into error. French society was constantly traversed by all of life's crosscurrents. In the first place, there were no clear dividing lines between the various strata. Rather, a whole subtle gradation of social situations, a continuum, lay between one stratum and the next. Because of this, the historian will notice that, at a given moment in time, the people he is studying may move from one estate to another. Their social environment changes completely, and they find themselves living in another stratum. But this transition from one estate to the next is progressive and gradual, a phenomenon bound up with the very diversity of life itself.

Then, too, in every period there are some families that move from one stratum to another, one estate to another, one order to another. There is constant social mobility, both upward and downward, although most families remain at the same social level for an indefinite length of time. The degree of social mobility may vary, but mobility always exists. We are looking at a society whose hierarchy is stable in its broad outlines but in which some families are able to rise or forced to descend. Slowly, by a constant and almost imperceptible motion, the hierarchy changes as a result.

We have described both this hierarchy and the changes that occurred within it.[3] Three points are worth emphasizing. Commerce and industry, trade and manufacture often played a role at some point in a family's rise in society.

They did not play the preponderant role, as Barnave thought, not even in the period when he was writing. Before the middle of the sixteenth century, there were essentially two ways to rise in society: military service and living the life of a noble residing on estates or *seigneuries* leading to recognition as a noble by one's peers. Nobility was therefore generated by the society itself. The importance of these routes to nobility gradually declined, and by the time of Richelieu they played virtually no further role. From the middle of the sixteenth century on, the way to acquire an office was to serve first as a *commis* or lawyer, and little by little the holding of royal office came to be the dominant means of social ascension. This route was essentially the only one by the time of Richelieu. The best way to rise in society was to obtain an office that carried with it letters of nobility. Upward mobility was generated by the state, which created new nobles. Contemporaries decried the role of money. Usually, the money involved in a given individual's rise came from a wide variety of sources. When money did play a dominant role, it should be noted that, except in large commercial cities, it was not money that came from trade and banking but, to a far greater degree, money that came from the farming of royal taxes and from loans of various sorts made to the king in the guise of *affaires extraordinaires*, in short, money from "usurious" activities. As we have seen, moreover, but for a few exceptions it was not the men who dealt in money themselves but rather their descendants who obtained offices and climbed to the nobility. Even in the case of royal secretaries, the legal acquisition of nobility had to be followed by a stage of purification, a period in the social group consisting of the "ennobled."

Beginning in the second part of Louis XIV's reign in the 1690s, it became increasingly easy to get past the bottlenecks, thanks to commissions to serve in such posts as provincial intendant or *commis* in a ministerial bureau or an intendancy, which could eventually lead to acquisition of an office.

Thus in the seventeenth and eighteenth centuries the legal profession and its ancillaries were the best ways to climb in society. Upward mobility began in the *basoche* with a position as clerk and moved from there to ministerial office, to a position as *avocat*, already worthy of a noble, to a magistrate's office and the duties of a royal *commissaire*. The best way to rise was to participate in the exercise of governmental power at one level or another. The steady perfection of state agencies and of the state apparatus exerted greater and greater influence on upward mobility in a society in which important merchant families rarely stayed in trade or banking for more than two or three generations but rather hastened to obtain offices and commissions, sometimes skipping over the lower ranks of the legal profession and jumping instead to the intermediate rank of *financier*, involved with the manipulation of the king's money.

A man at a given level of the social and professional hierarchy could exercise the greatest power consistent with his position by joining the king's service, that is, by working for the state, and so working for the state was a prerequisite for moving up in society.

At the beginning of the seventeenth century the basic principle of social organization was still the hereditary preeminence of the military. Lip service was paid to God and his clergy, legally the first order in the kingdom; but the clerical hierarchy was modeled on the social hierarchy. The soldier was in theory the most important figure in the society. The soldier was noble and the noble was a soldier. The *gentilhomme* had the right to issue orders and to sit in judgment. It was the *gentilhomme* who ought to exercise the powers of the magistrate at every level of the hierarchy. In fact, however, men of ancient nobility, who bore the titles of great *fiefs de dignité* and vast *seigneuries*, by this time had no political power but only a few powers of justice and "police." Within the state they had no power beyond that which the state granted them for its own advantage in making them court nobles and officers of the royal household, ordinary *commissaires*, governors, *lieutenants généraux*, or military officers.

Civilian officeholders began to supplant *gentilshommes* as magistrates. Some of these officeholders were nobles of old families. Most were ennobled, since the principle was that a magistrate must be noble, so that either the candidate had to be ennobled by his post or a man already ennobled had to be chosen. Thus a nobility of office came into being and acquired the right to pass on its nobility to its sons along with an effective right to magistracy, which was consolidated by the sale of offices and by the annual dues, or Paulette. The civilian officeholder was a notable, a dignitary, who combined his rank with a public function. A portion of his income was derived from his estates and *seigneuries* in addition to his *rentes*. Another portion was derived from the emoluments that went with his office. Of these, the salary paid by the king constituted only a small part: Officeholders paid themselves "by their own hands," collecting *épices* and *droits et taxations*. Through the magistrate the courts dominated and controlled the administration. Serving the public in this way helped the officeholder consolidate his position in society. The "finance" he paid for his office established certain property rights, legally subordinate to the king's superior right to create and appoint his officers but nonetheless real and imposing limits on the king's right. The position of the magistracy in the social hierarchy was enhanced to the extent that the royal armies were professionalized and thereby liberated from the feudal hierarchy and its rules. The magistracy was able to claim the highest position in the society, above the *gentilhommerie d'épée*.

But these notables, judges, and administrators already found their situation threatened in the sixteenth century, when their position in society was still on the rise, by the proliferation of special courts whose jurisdictions cut into the jurisdictions of the regular courts. The practice of selling offices encouraged the king to increase their number, which finally reached a peak in the seventeenth century. The regular courts saw their prestige and profits decrease along with the extent of their jurisdiction. The lower courts suffered even more as a result of efforts by the sovereign courts to extend their jurisdiction unduly at the expense of the lower courts.

An even more serious threat was the increase in the number and term of office of the special *commissaires* beginning in the second third of the seventeenth century. Among these were the notorious intendants, who carried out the king's orders and who not only took precedence over many officeholders but also usurped their administrative and frequently their judicial functions as well, as the need to replace a judicial form of administration by an executive form became apparent. This further reduced the importance, prestige, and profits of the courts, to a considerable degree under Louis XIV's personal government and particularly in the 1690s and beyond. These changes were necessitated by war. War was the main driving force behind the transformation of state and society, more powerful and more effective than the economy. Here, it seems, Barnave's ideas need to be modified somewhat.

For a variety of reasons, including improvements in the techniques of administration made necessary by the war, changes in the tax structure, the need to assemble, equip, arm, and feed large armies and powerful fleets, and efforts to stimulate and rationalize the economy in order to increase the tax base and supply the army, the number of *commis* in the ministries, intendancies, and tax farmers' offices was increased as the bureaucratic structure grew in complexity. Even more important, the role of these *commis* began to change. The volume of business and paperwork exceeded the capacities of the king, even so dedicated a bureaucrat as Louis XIV, and overwhelmed even the hardest working *contrôleurs généraux* and the most devoted secretaries of state. The work, moreover, divided itself into categories, as the same set of circumstances repeated itself time after time, so that decisions could be taken on the basis of precedents. The *commis*, who had been mere assistants who prepared and expedited work so that others might make decisions more readily, now began making decisions on their own in large numbers of cases. One man, working alone in an office, made decisions pertaining to a whole category of affairs and had his work signed by his supervisor; some *commis* even had the power to sign decisions on their own. As a result, many *commis* moved up to a higher professional category and perhaps also to a higher social category. An important characteristic of these *commis* is that they did not pay themselves "by their own hands." All their remuneration came from the royal treasury; with all due regard for the caution necessary in making statements about income in a society and economy of this type, it seems possible to assert that they lived mainly by what they earned in the king's service, unlike the officeholders and *commissaires*. In other words, their post was their livelihood, a profession and not just a social rank that happened to be accompanied by a service rendered to the public. In other words, the *commis* were assuming some of the characteristics of the modern civil servant.

The same can be said about certain commissions associated with the technology of construction and destruction: the engineers of the Ponts et Chaussées and the Department of Fortresses and Fortifications. These commissions changed in nature, and by the middle of the eighteenth century those who held them were professionals in many respects comparable to a modern civil servant.

All of these changes helped to diminish the importance, the prestige, and the profits of the officeholders.

This led to disorderly and spasmodic efforts on the part of the courts to assure their survival at the time of the Fronde and later during the second half of the eighteenth century. During the latter period the high nobility returned to the ministries in large numbers. *Gentilshommes* staked exclusive claims to the higher ranks in the army and to some civilian offices. The sovereign courts defended themselves by closing off access and putting forth a historical myth in support of their claims to political and administrative power. Everyone worked to revamp the structure of the society of orders and corps to his own advantage.

This caused great frustration among *avocats* who could no longer hope to gain access to offices in the sovereign courts; the considerable role played by many *avocats* in starting the Revolution is well-known. Much less is known about the role of the *commis*. Further study is warranted in regard to the social situation of the *commis*, their alliances, wealth, and income, what happened to them during and after the Revolution, and what role they played first in the electoral assemblies and later in the revolutionary assemblies. Indications from a few cases are that the *commis* benefitted handsomely from the Revolution, but it remains to be seen whether they reaped these benefits as men who took a hand in making decisions and shared sovereign power or as men who aided other social groups to govern. At some point prior to the actual seizure of power, some of the *commis* allied themselves with men who legally held power already but who had in fact lost most of it, and by fighting against an indecisive government succeeded in demolishing the existing legal structure.

In Barnave's view, it was liquid wealth, the wealth due to commerce, that won out in France over landed wealth. Then society underwent a change. Individuals were classified in the social hierarchy according to their wealth and property, with the "capitalists" on top. The "people" then imposed conditions on the king concerning the assessment of taxes, and they supervised the spending of what was collected. This view was inspired by specialists in English history and theorists of the English revolutions. The historian may wonder whether the application of such a view to France was perhaps premature. It is worth noting that the idea of a social classification based on wealth, independent of "quality," was quite widespread in France on the eve of the Revolution. We find it expressed by the authors of dictionaries, such as Expilly,[4] and by *avocats* like P. L. Lacretelle, who said: "Today property owners and rentiers, whether noble or not, have an equal interest in public prosperity, which now more than ever is based on money and a healthy financial condition." Widespread as it was, was this idea a finding of fact or a wish, a statement of truth or an expression of a desire as though it were a reality? Even before the Fronde people had complained that society was actually based on wealth rather than on birth, quality, orders, and corps. In favor of Barnave's theory is the fact that merchants, manufacturers, and peasants were represented in the Estates General. But the overwhelming majority was composed of jurists, both *avocats* and officeholders, and we cannot be sure that the presence of new classes of representatives was not due primarily to the use of new electoral procedures. Whether or not the same results would have been obtained if these procedures had been used for the Estates General of 1614 is something we shall never know. But at that time the position of the officeholders had not yet been weakened by the rise of *commissaires* and *commis*.

In regard to the *commissaires* of various ranks and their subdelegates and *commis*, as well as the men of law, ministerial officials, and magistrates (who still dominated the Estates General of 1789), the question would seem to be more complex. Leaving aside the case of the *commis*, which remains to be clarified, it in fact appears that, prior to the industrial revolution and economic takeoff, several sources of income and in some cases several professions were necessary if a man wished to live and "maintain his rank" and still more if he wished to enrich himself and move up in society. He had to combine the emoluments, bonuses, and pensions that went with his office or commission together with profits from land, rents, farm leases, and *rentes* of various kinds, income from investments with the farmers general and the notaries, who served as intermediaries between him and the merchants and entrepreneurs, and income from investments with wholesalers and bankers. At least three or four different sources of revenue seem to have been necessary. This finding, applicable to the majority of the deputies in the Estates General, who made the Revolution, does not coincide exactly with Barnave's simplistic views. All this needs to be checked and spelled out precisely. Does it not appear that a change of ideas, a change of social and moral values, far outpaced the real changes in the society and preceded major social and political change?

In international colloquia of historians held this year and last, there was a debate over the question of whether the French Revolution was a necessary or contingent event, whether it could have been avoided or not. Of course it is always risky to say what might or might not have happened, and it is in any case impossible to verify any assertion in this regard. But it can serve the historian as an exciting diversion.

The first cause of the Revolution was the collapse of the supreme organ of state, the king. Had the king been a man of sure judgment, decisive and perseverant (as Louis XVI unfortunately was not), he might have been able to give some direction to the changes. Along with his *conseillers d'Etat*, his *maîtres des requêtes*, and his intendants, recruited from the ranks of the

nobility of office; his farmers general; his subdelegates recruited from the
lower courts; his *commis* working in ministries, intendancies, and tax farmers' offices and drawn mainly from the ranks of the bourgeoisie; his army,
which remained loyal until the end of 1788; and the "state apparatus" with
its connections of the various levels of society, the king might have kept the
initiative and imposed his way of seeing things. But the truth is that there
seems to have been no way for the king to have avoided three basic changes.
First, a proportional tax had to be established, a tax based on income without
regard to its source or its recipient. This reform, which the monarchy had
attempted on numerous occasions, would have had to be extended to provide
for equality of taxation for all the king's subjects. Second, in order to give
coherence and unity to the government, a cabinet council should have been
established, and ministers should have been made jointly responsible to the
king. Its procedures should have been flexible, using simple ministerial orders
or decrees. Third, something had to be done about restoring the representative bodies that had been abolished to meet the needs of the seventeenth-
century wars. Like all wars, these had made a despotic and dictatorial government necessary. But after 1714 a peacetime government should have been
reestablished. The monarchy had been unable to "demobilize." Since this
was a time when war was a frequent occurrence, perhaps provision should
have been made for institutions of two kinds: a monocracy in wartime and
a monarchy in peacetime. Be that as it may, regular, periodic consultation
with the French people was a necessity in time of peace. Since the values
of the French people had changed considerably, and what dominated men's
minds at the time of the Revolution and set the pace of their activity was
the idea of seeking happiness through an improvement in living standards,
through abundance, through material prosperity, as well as the idea that men
were to be distinguished by wealth and talent, the mode of representation
should have been changed from an Estates General to an assembly of some
sort. All these changes would have made for a revolution of sorts. But the
king would have been able to preserve absolute monarchy for the time being,
along with the precedence of the nobility and the clergy over the third estate
and some noble privileges, such as exclusive right to fill the higher ranks of
the army and certain places in chapters and monasteries, together with a
social structure based on orders and corps, albeit much weaker than before.

Thus the king might have accepted the position of the first Assembly of
Notables, which was translated into law by Loménie de Brienne and Lamoignon, and organized a monarchy tempered by an aristocracy based on
a structure of orders and corps. Taken together, the reforms of 1787 and
1788 accomplished a thorough renovation of the hierarchy of orders and
corps associated with the old France, gave the *gentilshommes* and *seigneurs*
and corps of officeholders a new lease on life, so far as it was possible to
do so, and might have promised new life to French society and the French
state. Of course they could not have avoided the problems of reorganizing
the central government and representative institutions any more than the

king could have done. The mad ambitions of the younger councillors in *parlement*, their use of an old way of promulgating laws as an obstructionist device, and the weakness of the king conspired to bring about the failure of these sweeping measures.

The king might have made the plans of the "National Party" his own and taken the lead in carrying out structural reforms. The idea of monarchy and the physiocrats' views concerning the enlightened despot were sufficiently powerful that the king might have been able to keep a system under which judges and administrators were named by him rather than elected by the public or by cooptation, thus preserving an absolute monarchy, though he would have had to accept profound changes in the social structure, official acknowledgment of the transition from a society of orders to a society of classes, separation of the courts and the administration, and organization of a corps of civil servants.

Great changes, a revolution of some sort, were in any case necessary, but not the French Revolution as such. In other words, some kind of revolution was apparently necessary, but the nature of that revolution may have been contingent.

These considerations (and many others) suggest certain hypotheses. In the first place, the state seems to have been as important a factor as the economy in affecting social function, equilibrium, and change. One factor may have been more or less important at a certain time than another. What seems clear is that there is no economic determination of the social and no social determination of the political (contrary to the hypothesis I held when I began my work), but rather a complex and sometimes subtle interaction of mutual influences and reciprocal reactions. Second, there seem to be limits to these mutual influences; in other words, there seems to be some autonomy of the political, the social, the economic, and so on. Consider, for example, a present-day political body of some sort debating the question of the oil crisis or nuclear energy. Its deliberations are governed in part by the same mechanisms and influences that governed the deliberations of the Roman Senate and perhaps, too, the deliberations of a political body of any kind. Thus Roman history can be very enlightening as an instrument of comparison in studying the present-day political body, our contemporary. In other words, men working within a given institution may be forced to act and react in ways dictated by the institution's goals (both apparent and real), its procedures (both as specified in law and as followed in reality), and by the relations that govern the interactions of men assembled under these conditions, as well as the emotions and passions that result from such re-lations. The institution may have a life of its own, independent, to some extent at least, of the political, social, economic, and mental structures of the time and relatively independent of the particular constellation of events. If these hypotheses turn out to be true, we shall perhaps need to make many changes in the questions we ask as historians and in the histories we write, as well as in our social and political theories and even our ideologies, insofar as ideology bears any relation at all to experience.

Notes

1. See vol. 1, pp. 3–47.
2. Roland Mousnier, *La stratification sociale à Paris aux XVIIe et XVIIIe siècles* (Editions A. Pedone, 1976), vol. 1, pp. 41–66.
3. See vol. 1, part I, chaps. 2–6; this volume, pp. 302–74.
4. See p. 441.

Glossary

This glossary is intended as a supplement to the glossary included in vol. 1, pp. 745–64.

Adminicule   In legal proceedings, an item that contributes to proof without constituting a full proof

Apanagé   One who was granted a concession to a portion of the royal domain, generally one of the Children of France, for whom the concession, known as an appanage, constituted his or her share in the late king's patrimony. Cf. *Engagiste*.

Conseiller d'Etat   A member of one of the king's councils. There were three grades of *conseiller*. The *conseiller ordinaire* served the whole year through, the *conseiller semestre* served only six months, and the holder of a *brevet* as *conseiller d'Etat* did not necessarily serve at all—brevets were merely a source of extra income to the Crown and of prestige to their purchasers, who were normally excluded from most council meetings.

Donneurs d'avis   Individuals who suggested possible new sources of tax revenue to the king. They were paid for their advice and sometimes also granted the contract to collect the proposed tax.

Droit d'assise   The right to hold an extraordinary tribunal.

Economats   The revenue from vacant bishoprics, as well as the agency responsible for supervising this revenue.

Edits bursaux   Usually translated as "bursal edicts," these were edicts pertaining to the creation of taxes, particularly extraordinary taxes.

Engagiste   The titulary owner of a portion of the royal domain conditionally sold to be exploited privately.

Extraordinaire des guerres	The financial organization of the army was divided into two parts, the *extraordinaire des guerres* and the *ordinaire des guerres*. The latter included the more permanent elements of *ban and arrière-ban*, *compagnies d'ordonnance*, *francs-archers*, and *prévôté*, while the former included mercenary formations both French and foreign. Both divisions had their own treasurers, who were responsible to the *trésorier de l'Epargne*.
Grand Audiencier de France	An official of the chancellery who reported on every document submitted to receive the royal seal.
Etapes	A tax levied ostensibly for the purpose of acquiring provisions to feed royal troops. See also *Subsistances* and *Ustensiles*.
Etats au vrai	Sometimes translated as "true accounts," these were statements by royal accountants ostensibly reporting actual receipts and expenditures for a specific period of time.
Etats de distribution	To be distinguished from the *états au vrai*. These were statements indicating to royal accountants the amounts they were supposed to collect and disburse during a specified period.
Jurade	The municipal council of Bordeaux.
Litre funèbre	The right to hang armorial bearings in church, which was held by certain *seigneurs haut justiciers* and patron founders.
Mandement	A warrant given to one royal official ordering a second royal official, in charge of some item of the royal revenues, to pay a specified amount of money to the first official.
Marc d'or	A fee paid by the buyer of an office to be allowed to swear an oath of allegiance to the king.
Mortes-payes	Soldiers kept on the royal payroll in peacetime.
Né	Following the title of an office, indicates that the holder is entitled to the office from birth.
Ordinaire des guerres	See *Extraordinaire des guerres*.
Rapporteur	The member of a council responsible for preparing business and presenting it to the other councillors.
Rescription	A payment order, less specific than a *mandement*, and used in some respects like a check against a specified royal *caisse*.
Subsistances and Ustensiles	Assessments to pay for supplies to troops in winter quarters.

Index

687

192–98; and Fouquet, 192; influence of Grands Jours on, 501; influence of Mazarin on, 11; instruction of, in Latin, 11; nurse of, 5; personal government of, 631–33; price of offices under, 348, 353; progeny of, 5; religious attitudes of, 11; response of, to Fronde, 631; and the restoration of order, 492; and sale of offices, 49; style of government of, 17; and the subduing of the office-holders, 632; tutor of, 6; use of *commissaires* by, 633

Louis XV, king of France: character of, 13–14; education of, 13–14; as investor in tax farms, 447; and *philosophes* and *encyclopédistes*, 19; and polysynody, 199–201; stabbing of, 640; style of government of, 19–20; use of *commissaires* by, 634–35

Louis XVI, king of France: character of, 15; contracts smallpox, 653; education of, 14–15; finances under, 201–14; influence of Fénelon on, 653; *intendants* under, 555; judgment of, 681; provincial *intendants* under, 553; and recall of exiled magistrates, 653; and reform efforts, 172; style of government of, 20; and titularization of *premiers commis*, 176

Louis-le-Grand, Collège, 176, 337; and the Copernican system, 338

Louvois, François-Michel Le Tellier, marquis de, 18, 82, 519, 520, 526, 575

Loyseau, Charles, 43, 469, 470, 472, 674

Lyon, Treaty of, xvi

Magistrates: and decline of the judicial order, 357–60; life-style of, 339–41; privileges of, 343; in relation to clergy and nobility, 233; social bias of, 410–14; social status of, 325–40, 360–63

Maille, Armand de, marquis de Brèze, 110

Maine, duc du, 475

Maintenon, Françoise d'Aubigné, marquise de, 18, 82

Maîtres des Requêtes, duties of, 140–43

Mancini, Marie de, 11

Marc d'or, 48; collection of, 207

Marcel, Claude, 42, 43

Maréchaussée, 105

Maréchaux de France, 82, 103–5; and questions of honor, 104

Marguerite, queen of Navarre, 55, 56, 88

Marie-Antoinette, queen of France, 87

Marie-Thérèse, queen of France, 86

Marillac, Michel de, 597; and the Code Michaud, 602

Marillac Ordinance. *See* Code Michaud

Marteau, Jean, 40

Maupeou, René Charles de, 79, 314, 333, 582; disbanding of *parlement* by, 647; and political reform, 382, 551, 645–53

Maurepas, Jean-Frédéric Phélypeaux, comte de, 653

Mayenne, duc de, 55

Mazarin, 10, 71, 509, 519; desperation of, 617; exile of, 515; Frondeurs' complaints against, 620; and Louis XIV, 11; as object of *parlements'* discontent, 618; and renewal of annual dues, 614

Médicis, Catherine de, 9

Médicis, Marie de, 56, 86, 87, 215; dowry of, 55; as regent, 591

Meilhan, Senac de, 554, 556

Ménardeau, Claude, 185

Mercier, Louis-Sébastien, 461

Mesmes, Jean-Jacques de, 339, 483

Metz, Treaty of, 93

Meulan family, 205

Meyer, Prof., 370

Mézeray, F. E. de, 3

Mézières (engineering school), 578, 635

Mirabeau, Victor Riqueti, marquis de, 332

Miromesnil, Armand Thomas de, 657

Moisset, Jean de, 42

Molé, Mathieu-François, 333

Montblin, Michau de, 641

Montescot, Claude de, 190

Montesquieu, Charles de Secondat, baron de La Brède, 335, 407, 553

Montholon, Guillaume de, 588

Montigny, Mignot de, 348

Montmartre, Treaty of, 93

Montmorency, duc de, 109, 472

Moulins ordinance, 392

Nantes, Edict of, xvi

Necker, Jacques, xviii, 201, 202, 211, 213, 370, 371, 450, 654, 655, 660, 667; and conflict for control of finances, 212

Nemours, duc de, 55

Nevers, duc de, 55

Nicolas, Augustin, 406

Nicole, Pierre, 15